# Shooter's Bible ®

## ABOUT OUR COVER

### The Set of Four

The *"Set of Four"* concept came about as a collaborative effort involving Dr. Ugo Gussalli Beretta and Mr. Bob Jepson. Many hundreds of hours of Bulino engraving created by master engraver Angelo Galeazzi reflect not only Mr. Jepson's personal hunting memories but also Dr. Beretta's commitment to the company's 475-year history of creating fine firearms.

Each caliber (.30-06, .375 H&H, 470 N.R., .600 N.E.) is represented by one of the *Big Five*. Each action portrays the lion, cape buffalo, rhino and elephant, with a different leopard portrayed at the bottom to complete the Big Five.

# Shooter's Bible®

## NO. 92
## 2001 EDITION

**ARTICLES EDITOR**
William S. Jarrett

**SPECIFICATIONS EDITOR**
Wayne van Zwoll

**PROJECT MANAGER**
Dominick S. Sorrentino

**PRODUCTION & DESIGN**
Lesley A. Notorangelo/D.S.S.

**ELECTRONIC IMAGING**
Lesley A. Notorangelo/D.S.S.

**FIREARMS CONSULTANTS**
Bill Meade
Frank Zito

**COVER PHOTOGRAPHER**
Ray and Matt Wells

**PUBLISHER**
David C. Perkins

**PRESIDENT**
Brian T. Herrick

## STOEGER PUBLISHING COMPANY

Every effort has been made to record specifications and descriptions of guns, ammunition and accessories accurately, but the Publisher can take no responsibility for errors or omissions. The prices shown for guns, ammunition and accessories are manufacturers' suggested retail prices (unless otherwise noted) and are furnished for information only. These were in effect at press time and are subject to change without notice. Purchasers of this book have complete freedom of choice in pricing for resale.

Published by Stoeger Publishing Company
5 Mansard Court
Wayne, New Jersey 07470

Library of Congress Catalog Card No.: 63-6200
International Standard Book No.: 0-88317-218-6

Manufactured in the United States of America

In the United States:
Distributed to the book trade and to the sporting
goods trade by
Stoeger Industries
5 Mansard Court
Wayne, New Jersey 07470
Tel: 973-872-9500  Fax: 973-872-2230

In Canada:
Distributed to the book trade and to the sporting
goods trade by
Stoeger Canada Ltd.
1801 Wentworth Street, Unit 16
Whitby, Ontario, L1N 8R6, Canada

# Contents

# Foreword

## FEATURE ARTICLES

Our article section leads off with a piece by our knowledgeable and talented Specifications Editor, **Wayne van Zwoll**. His subject this year is "How To Be a Crack Shot on Big Game." Serious hunters are well advised to follow Wayne's advice. **Dave Henderson**, one of several first-timers in Shooter's Bible this year, discusses the hot subject of slug guns and loads. Next in line is an amusing but constructive article on hunting quail by **Dr. Joseph Greenfield, Jr.**, a noted professor of medicine (when he isn't hunting quail and training his obstreperous bird dogs). Still another first-time contributor to these pages is **Richard Grozik**, who tells us about his search for a "perfect" left-handed Model 70. Yes, he found it.

Turning to a few of our old-timers, Shooter's Bible-wise, you'll recognize **Don Lewis**, our reloader *par excellence*, who has chosen the .19 Calhoon wildcat as his subject. Don is followed by our longtime Canadian friend, **Wilf Pyle**, who writes about *Cartridges with Character*. "Some are good, others are bad and ugly," he forewarns. **Gene Gangarosa, Jr.**, a prolific writer on firearms of all kinds, weighs in with his study of the SIG P210 automatic pistol, now celebrating its first half-century. Want more? There's an interesting round-up by **Tom Tabor** of today's scopes, whose performance can mean all the difference when it comes to accuracy. The final segment in this 2001 edition of *Shooter's Bible* is a new and exciting feature about today's *Custom Gunmakers*. Their personal stories and ideas on gun design appear next to photographs illustrating their best works. That wraps up the article section and leads to our annual **Manufacturers' Showcase** starting on page TK. Feel free to browse.

## SPECIFICATIONS

The 2001 *Shooter's Bible* has many new listings – for both items and manufacturers. But perhaps the biggest news is in the back. Our ballistics section has been overhauled to bring you more information in a much more readable form. Instead of adapting manufacturer's catalog pages, we've reorganized the data to supply you with a quick-reference format that shows every (or nearly every) commercial load for any given cartridge. All popular .270 loads, for example, are now in one place, so you can easily compare them as to velocity, energy and flight path. The type is bigger too! No more fumbling for that magnifying glass! It's like having all the ammunition catalogs in print under one cover – and neatly categorized.

This year's specifications section has some names you might not have expected to see in *Shooter's Bible* – Purdey, for example. Why include an English maker whose prices smack of Manhattan real estate? Because Purdey shotguns have long set a standard for excellence. A peek at Purdey gives *Shooter's Bible* readers a look at some of the best double guns available. They're expensive, but mighty interesting.

"Interesting" also describes the Thompson & Campbell rifles from Scotland. Introduced a few years ago at the SHOT show, these unique bolt rifles are still largely unknown Stateside. *We* bring them to you as examples of ingenious engineering. Designed and crafted by a small group of talented young riflemakers, they prove that better bolt rifles *are* indeed possible. And if you want to see something that nobody on your block will believe, turn to Szecri & Fucho's *tour de force:* a bolt-action double rifle produced by another group of fresh young minds. This gun won't be at your neighborhood gun store anytime soon, but it's a noteworthy engineering feat that boasts the highest capacity of any dangerous game rifle.

Of course, most of *Shooter's Bible* is still dedicated to the kinds of rifles, shotguns and handguns that many of us carry on the hunt and to the target range. You'll find all the familiar names here: Beretta, Benelli, Browning, Colt, Dakota, Marlin, Remington, Ruger, Sako, Savage, Thompson/Center, Tikka, Winchester. And in each section you'll find the latest products and retail prices. *Shooter's Bible* is still your one-stop reference for nearly anything that shoots!

This past year, public reactions to tragic and bizarre killings have rocked the firearms industry, which has responded with measured alternatives. Sako has a key lock for its popular Model 75 rifle. This "Key Concept" device is a modification of the cocking piece, which can be instantly rendered either functional or inoperable by the turn of a key. The action is otherwise conventional in form. Sako stresses that this is a sure way to make its rifles safe even when unauthorized people gain access to them. And it does not in any way affect the performance of the rifle when in use. And Remington's new EtronX mechanism in its Model 700 rifle employs a key in the pistol grip that activates an electronic circuit. The circuit replaces the traditional sear and striker; the EtronX trigger is in fact a switch. Remington points out that this system is not just safe; it offers shooters faster lock time and greater accuracy as well.

The optics field has been particularly active of late. You'll find new names (Docter Optik, Sightron and Swift) and products, including Weaver's handsome new "Grand Slam" scopes and practical iron sights from Ashley Outdoors. Finally, there's not room here to describe all the ammunition and components and reloading tools that have been introduced for 2001. You'll just have to read for yourself!

We think you'll find Shooter's Bible 2001 the best edition ever, packed with useful and authoritative information, and chock full of the details that can help make you an expert. We hope you'll enjoy the shopping as much as we've enjoyed putting this big book together!

*William S. Jarrett, Articles Editor*
*Wayne van Zwoll, Specifications Editor*

**Articles**

# How To Be A Crack Shot On Big Game

## By Wayne Van Zwoll

**H**urling a stone into a pond is easy. Boys learn to do that before they're off tricycles. Slingshots and air guns take more attention, not because the launch is that complicated, but because the target is no longer a pond. To earn proficiency with a rifle, you must test yourself on much smaller marks. One of the problems confronting hunters who seek better accuracy is their own vanity. They upgrade to more effective equipment without changing the measure of marksmanship. Bullets replace rocks, but the splash in the pond remains a bullseye. A paper target way out yonder, though, is merciless, with definite margins that shrink alarmingly with distance.

Bullet holes—or lack thereof—form a permanent record of ineptitude. It's much easier to kick dirt near a rock or claim skill by virtue of a few dead animals. "I'm a very good shot with my seven magnum," one hunter told me after missing an elk with another rifle. That's like saying "I'm an excellent driver with a '76 Chevrolet pickup" or "I'm a great tennis player with the racquet I got for my birthday." Equipment we like can help us perform well, but it doesn't make us ace performers. Claiming we'd be deadeyes but for the shortcomings of our gear makes us eligible for membership in the crackpots (a large group not to be confused with the much smaller fraternity of crack shots).

A common measure of marksmanship in the woods is the number of animals killed. But kill tallies have less to do with marksmanship than with shot opportunities. After all, elk are almost as big as ponds, and deer aren't much smaller. You

On the eve of World War I, the .250 Savage (left) was considered adequate for all but the toughest of game. Now hunters use the 30-378 Weatherby for mule deer. Bullet energy is no substitute for shot placement, however, and heavy recoil makes accurate shooting more difficult.

*Weatherby is noted for its powerful cartridges and angular rifle stocks. This new Mark V rifle from the firm's custom shop wears a handsome classic-style stock. Note the trim, low-mounted scope, set well forward. This is a fine big game rifle.*

can shoot poorly and still rack up impressive carcass counts, depending on where you hunt and how much you have to spend. You can also be a crack shot and kill nothing.

Being a technology-driven society, we shouldn't be surprised that rifles and scopes figure so heavily today in discussions at hunting camps. It's a curious fact that the best big game hunters usually carry relatively simple gear—and that includes their shooting irons.

Ken, for example, has hunted for half a century and taken more big mule deer than most modern hunters will ever see in the field. Almost all of them were shot with a Model 99 Savage and a 4x scope. No ear-splitting magnums for Ken. He prefers instead the mild .250 Savage, a cartridge that generates about as much energy at the muzzle as the newest .30 magnums deliver at 500 yards. When Ken shoots, deer wilt. He has even used his little Savage to take several elk, none of which escaped as cripples. Another friend, who happens to be a game warden, has used an early Model 70 Winchester in .270 for all his hunting. It has taken many deer in culling operations, and elk as well. Jim has shot game "about as far as I can see." He can't imagine needing a more potent cartridge.

It's been my experience that elk hunters who travel out West with plans to shoot long distances with cartridges the size of pill bottles don't shoot very well. In fact, sometimes they shoot so poorly that even at modest ranges they miss altogether or make crippling hits. The most deadly marksmen I've hosted in the mountains are those who show up with a .270, .280 or .30-06. The more wear on the rifle, the better. A small scope is a good sign too. If there's no bipod, and if the hunter has installed a shooting sling instead of a padded carrying strap the width of an ironing board, I feel confident there will be some meat to pack.

Some years ago a fellow came to camp with a .300 Weatherby that he claimed was so potent it had merely to scratch a deer to knock it down. He waxed eloquent about his marksmanship too. With his .257 Weatherby, as I recall, he claimed he could shoot pronghorns on the run beyond 500 yards. Because Mama taught me to suffer fools (but not gladly!), I held my counsel. The very next day we had to go looking for a buck this same hunter had crippled with his mighty .300. I hope he learned that high bullet energy is no substitute for precise bullet placement.

There's nothing intrinsically wrong with powerful rifles. They can be as accurate as hunting rifles with less punch. Indeed, the most accurate big game gun I've ever fired was a .300 Weatherby Magnum built by D'Arcy Echols of Providence, Utah. Among the tiny 100-yard groups I've fired

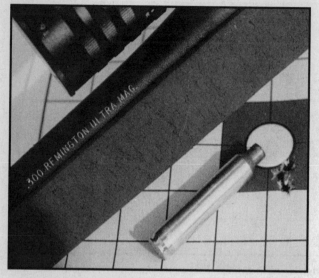

*Powerful cartridges can be very accurate—but shooters must be disciplined to handle the recoil. The author shot this group from the bench with 180-grain Sierra Match bullets from a Remington Ultra Mag built by Texas gunmaker Charlie Sisk.*

with that rifle was one that measured well under two tenths of an inch! Gary, another friend, owns a rifle built by a colorful Carolina riflesmith named Kenny Jarrett, who had chambered the rifle for his own .338 Jarrett (the 8mm Remington Magnum case necked up). This rifle, which shoots half-minute groups at 100 yards, offers far more precision than Gary needs for big game, and far more than most hunters can apply under average hunting conditions. That rifle is, in fact, more accurate than most factory-built sporting rifles regardless of chambering.

Trouble is, those big cartridges generate lots of recoil. Install a muzzle brake to tame the kick and you've got enough blast to rattle the tracks on a D-8 Cat. Even stout shooters quail at the violence of some modern magnums. They like to brag about the awesome power of these rifles, but they don't like to shoot them. A rifle you don't like to shoot is a rifle that will never serve you well, because you won't shoot it often enough to become proficient with it. Furthermore, shooting rifles that rough you up can also lead to bad shooting habits that will carry over to rifles of gentler disposition. Each shot results in a predictable dose of violence. Just as when you hear

the dentist's drill, so do you react as you take up the last ounce on the trigger of a magnum. You flinch, causing your rifle to move involuntarily at the worst possible moment. You may even close your eyes. The shot will go astray.

The solution is simple: Use a rifle you're not afraid of, whether it's a .30-06 or a more modest round. The short .30 magnums with 180-grain bullets are about my own limit for extended shooting. When switching to a .338 Winchester with heavy bullets, I feel the difference and it's not good. While I'm a great fan of the .338 and Weatherby's potent .340, I shoot best with cartridges like the .270. Call me a wimp, but accuracy is what counts. Enthusiasts on the other side of this debate are quick to point out that proper stocking and added rifle weight

*Shooters of slight build are better off using mild cartridges, which they can shoot with precision and comfort.*

reduce recoil without boosting noise. True enough; long barrels tame kick while reducing blast. But I walk and climb a lot when I hunt. It's what I like to do, so I don't carry rifles that feel like post drivers at the end of the day.

I recall one elk hunter who brought along a 14-pound rifle on an elk hunt. I wound up carrying the rifle for him. Recently I met a fellow with a 16-pound rifle who also had the idea that elk had to be shot far away, and that a heavy, powerful rifle was mandatory. Both men were keen shooters who performed well from the bench. In the field, however, they found their rifles ill-suited to the task. Both got their shots at less than 200 yards, where a lightweight .30-06 would have been more than adequate. Indeed, the elk that held the number one spot in the Boone & Crockett book for a whole century was shot with a .30-40 Krag. One of the biggest non-typical elk ever taken fell to a single bullet from a .30-30. I once watched a youngster kill an elk handily with a 95-grain 6mm bullet, and some men I know shoot big animals routinely with .243s. An Inuit hunter I met in the Far North some years ago shot six caribou in one afternoon with a .22 rimfire. And there's that legendary woodsman in British Columbia at the turn of the century who killed 18 big game animals—including two grizzlies—with 20 shots from a .303 Savage.

Recommending modest cartridges is not to advocate stunt shooting with the smallest legal cartridge. There's also good reason, in today's limited seasons, to stack the odds in your favor for one long-range opportunity. You can also train yourself to tolerate recoil. But again, excess power is not an asset. Almost any bullet becomes surprisingly lethal if it's sent to the right place; otherwise a tough animal like an elk can scramble away no matter how much energy has been delivered. In a decade spent guiding elk hunters, I've seen almost instant kills when ordinary softpoint bullets from .270, .280 and .30-06 rifles plowed through the lungs. And I've seen other elk absorb multiple solid hits from magnums before they succumbed. The difference was bullet placement.

If precision is important, high-power scopes must be a top choice among seasoned hunters. Well, some veterans do prefer them—but others, myself included, don't. Why? Because a powerful

*This 1964 vintage Model 70 Winchester has accounted for dozens of deer and elk, as well as moose, caribou, a grizzly bear and a grand slam of North American sheep.*

scope has a small field of view. You can find an animal faster with a low-power scope. And you can stay on target more easily when several animals scatter. It's frustrating to tell a shooter, "The bull on the far right," only to find he can't fit all the elk in his field of view. I've heard of hunters who shot the wrong animals because they couldn't see what was going on around them. Other hunters have taken their eye away from the scope only to lose a shot because they took too long getting back on target. A good friend once missed a chance at one of the biggest elk I've ever seen because he couldn't find the animal in his 8x scope at 60 yards. I suggested to another hunter who was carrying his variable at 8x that he peg it at the lowest setting. He got his shot at 70 steps in thick cover and vowed always to keep the magnification low. You'll usually have time to boost power for long shots. Short ones are often urgent.

Another advantage of low-power scopes is their apparent lack of wobble. When you're breathing hard, a 2.5x or 4x will show plenty of bounce, and a 6x can be hard to control. The higher the magnification, the greater the perceived wobble. Trying to tame the violent reticle gyrations in a powerful glass will cause you to tense up. You'll tire more quickly, and that will introduce even more muscle tremors. Instead of shooting, you hesitate. The reticle movement that wouldn't appear in a low-power scope now approaches eight on the Richter scale. You try to time the shot and yank the trigger, or you wait too long for the reticle to settle down and you lose the shot. From a rest or solid position high magnifica-

*Proper zeroing is essential. For most cartridges, adjust the sights so the bullets hit point of aim at 200 yards.*

tion is more manageable. You may wish for more magnification in order to see the target more clearly. But truly, you don't have to see breeze ruffling the hairs on a deer's shoulder to kill it. If you see a vital area around the intersection of the crosswire, you can shoot. The bullet, after all, is supposed to go to the middle. My longest shots at big game were made with 4x scopes.

As magnification increases, exit pupil diameter —the ability of a scope to transmit light— decreases. To counter this problem, scope makers now install bigger objective (front) lenses. The additional weight and bulk, however, are a high price to pay for extra brightness. Weight translates into more inertia, which on hard-kicking rifles can literally tear a scope from its moorings. Because of the extra bulk, higher mounts are called for. These, in turn, force you to lift your face off the stock, which slows down the aiming process. Big scopes also raise a rifle's center of gravity, adversely affecting its balance and feel. Keep objective diameter to 40mm or less. About all you need for most big game hunting is a 4x32 scope. Pronghorns and other game commonly shot at long range in the open might justify a 6x or even an 8x sight. A 2-7x32 or 2.5-8x36 scope should cover all your needs without encumbering the rifle. Remember, a scope is a *sight*. It's not a binocular, nor a spotting scope.

*Not all new cartridges are giants. The 7mm-08 and .260 Remington, both based on the .308 Winchester case, have plenty of punch for most North American big game and are a pleasure to shoot.*

The next step to better shooting is getting a precise zero. That means adjusting your line of sight to intersect the bullet's trajectory at a specific and practical distance. It should intersect twice—once as the sightline dives into the bullet path up close and once at the true zero range where the bullet's curving track carries it down through the still-straight line of sight. I zero most big game rifles at 200 yards. The first intersection of bullet path and sightline occurs at about 35 yards.

It's important that the vertical crosswire is actually vertical. To check this, I rest my rifle on sandbags or clamp it in a vise, then back away until only a pencil of light is visible through the scope. I can then align the vertical wire with the buttplate. A cockeyed reticle causes you to cant (tip) the rifle. A canted rifle puts the sightline to the side of the boreline; therefore, the sightline must cross the path of the bullet laterally as well as vertically. You can shoot accurately with a cant, but it must be done consistently. Many target shooters who do so are shooting at known yardages, where they can scotch lateral error by zeroing for that distance. Because hunters shoot at varying distances, they're smart to eliminate the cant, first by ensuring that the vertical wire is indeed vertical relative to the rifle, and secondly by refining their positions so the scope is always directly above the rifle.

Before zeroing, check the ring screws (if there are any doubts about the mount's base screws, remove the scope and cinch them before proceeding). While you're at it, check the rifle's guard screws. The front screw should be very tight, the rear screw almost as tight, and the middle screw (if there is one) just snug. Remove the bolt and lay the rifle across a padded chair so that it holds still. In my case, the barrel now points through a window, and across the river to the base of a shed several hundred yards away. Looking down the barrel, I scooch the rifle around until the corner of the shed appears exactly in the middle of the bore. Then, without moving the rifle, I adjust the scope reticle onto that shed corner. The line of sight is now aligned with the line of bore (the same thing can be done with a collimator). This step saves time and ammunition because it ensures that the first bullet will strike within a few inches of point of aim at 100 yards.

At the bench, I place the front sandbag where I'd normally hold my hand on the forend, while the rear bag sits under the toe of the stock. I keep adjusting them until the reticle centers the target naturally—or almost. Fine-tuning aim is easy; I merely squeeze the rear bag with my left hand, taking care not to disturb the rifle's natural point of aim. After shooting and adjusting the scope, I eventually get the bullets to land where I want them—two inches high. The target then goes out to 200 yards. The bullets should now hit exactly

*Synthetic stocks and stainless steel make modern rifles more durable; better optics make them easier to shoot accurately. But the old chamberings still work well. This Browning A-Bolt rifle is bored for the .270 Winchester (introduced in 1925).*

*The author shot this mule deer in central Wyoming with a .300 Dakota. While more powerful than necessary for deer, 180-grain bullets from this big .30 buck the Wyoming wind better than lighter, slower slugs.*

at the intersection of the crosswire. If not, I adjust again. Some hunters, eager to test long-range cartridges and high-power scopes, zero at longer ranges. Except for target shooting at known distances, long zeroes are bad business. A bullet's arc is parabolic, therefore the highest point in a trajectory is slightly beyond halfway to the target. Bullets from most modern big game rounds strike two to three inches high at 100 yards when zeroed at 200. A 300-yard zero places the bullet more than half again as high at the apex of its travel. The result: When a bullet strikes five inches high at 170 yards, you may have to hold low at mid-range to be sure of a killing hit on deer-size game. Cartridges like the .257 Weatherby Magnum, 7mm STW and .300 Rem-ington Ultra Mag reduce the need for hold-under, but they can't eliminate it.

In my view, the best zero range is that range at which a bullet stays just under three inches above line of sight. For a 180-grain .30-06 bullet, 200 yards is a perfect zero range. You can hold center to 250 yards or so because to that distance the bullet will strike within three vertical inches of point of aim. When hunting big game, three-inch displacement seldom matters. From a hunting position, you can't keep wobble much under three inches anyway. If you're zeroing a cartridge with the trajectory of a lightning bolt, you might consider a longer zero. A modest round like the .30-30 requires a shorter zero, say 150 yards; but don't forget that three-inch lid. Not having to hold low on any target is a real advantage. Beyond the point at which a bullet strikes three inches low, the muzzle will have to be elevated.

I once guided a hunter whose rifle was zeroed for 286 yards. At least, that's what he told me. He must have pulled that figure from a ballistics table. I spied a small band of elk on a canyon wall, and we made a successful stalk to a ridge about 250 yards from the animals. He hit one with the first shot, but three more bullets had no effect. When the stricken elk finally died, the hunter remarked with awe: "That's the longest shot I've made in my life." Why did he zero for 286 yards, I wondered, when all the shots he'd taken were under 250? It makes more sense to zero for the range at which you expect to do most of your shooting.

Once you've established a zero, fire three-shot groups at 50-yard intervals out to the farthest range that feels comfortable when shooting at game. For example, I'm now working up loads for the .270 Howell, which has a bit more steam than a .270 Winchester. A 200-yard zero should put 140-grain bullets about six inches low at 300 and 18 inches low at 400. After I've settled on a load, however, I'll shoot groups every 50 yards from 100 to 400 steps. That way, I'll know where the bullets will strike. After checking bullet impacts from the bench, I fire groups from various hunt-

*In the field, use a rest whenever possible, padding it with anything that's soft so the rifle does not bounce from its support.*

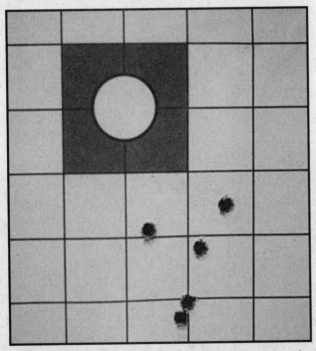

*A two-inch group won't win many benchrest matches, but it may be adequate accuracy for big game hunting. More important than intrinsic accuracy is the shooter's ability to keep the sight on the target as the trigger is squeezed.*

ing positions, with and without a sling. Shooting with a tight sling can depress bullet impact, because the pressure on the forend is just the opposite of what's applied on the bench, where the rifle bounces upward off a solid rest. I have a Ruger Number One in .300 Winchester that once gave me 200-yard groups nine inches lower with a taut sling than from a bench! A bedding job helped, but it's common to see three-inch difference in point of impact between shots fired from the bench and a sling-assisted sit.

Some things to remember: **Changing bullet type** can change bullet path, even if starting velocity is the same. **The height of the scope** mount affects the relationship of sightline to boreline. **Shooting uphill or downhill** extends point-blank range (hold for the horizontal distance to the target). **Elevation** (air density) has little effect on bullet impact except at extreme ranges or elevations. **Range estimation** becomes more critical far away, where it also becomes more difficult. Groups at long range may improve (three inches at 200 yards, say, when a 100-yard group measures two inches). That's because bullets "settle down" as they travel. The off-axis wobbles that cause dispersion close up can all but vanish far away. Resting the barrel against almost anything can cause it to bounce away from the rest and throw the shot wild. Rest only the forend, and pad it with a jacket or your hand. Wood stocks can "walk" over time, changing pressure in the barrel channel, affecting point of impact. Shots from a clean, cold barrel are the shots that matter most in the field; warm-barrel groups may not land in the same place. Save one target for a "cold-barrel group." An annual zero check makes sense—but not in camp, where it can spook game and give hunters nearby reason to crown you with the heaviest frying pan available.

After zeroing, it's important that your body becomes a steady shooting platform. Oddly, few hunters seek the counsel of competitive shooters, who are masters of position. Fewer still read the treatises on shooting position written by U.S. and Soviet coaches. You'll be a better game shot if you become a proficient target shooter, or at least establish shooting positions that hold your rifle reasonably steady. A short time ago, in an effort to "qualify" for elk hunting on a private

*Ken Peterson, a Texas hunter, made two fine shots from the sit with his Remington 700 in .300 Winchester to down this great Utah bull using Nosler Partition bullets.*

*Washington hunter Rich McClure shot this Zimbabwe sable with a .375 H&H, a cartridge renowned for its versatility since its debut in 1912. Recoil is stiff, but African big game includes some animals that are very hard to kill.*

ranch, a young man fired three shots at a sheet of typing paper at 100 yards. He could have used a prone or sitting position, or braced himself, kneeling, against the bench. He could have used a sling. According to the rules, he could have done anything with his rifle to steady it except lay it on sandbags. Instead he chose to stand up, leaning his hip against the bench. His first shot made it into the paper, but his second just nipped the edge. "Better check your ammo," said his companion. The real problem was the youngster's position. Fussing over ammunition was like checking the tire pressure on a car hitting on half its cylinders. From a solid position he probably could have put all three rounds near center, no matter what the load – or loads. Offhand, he simply couldn't hold the rifle still.

The best position in the field is the lowest position: prone. Next best is sitting, then kneeling. Offhand or standing is a last resort, justified only when there's not enough time to drop into a steadier position, or the target can't be seen from any other angle. The best marksmen practice these hunting positions often during the off-season, so their muscles can get used to the stretching. Except in offhand, these shooters use a sling with

*An iron sighted 300 Savage accounted for this beautiful Quebec-Labrador caribou. Even in open country, long shooting is seldom necessary. The proliferation of powerful cartridges causes some hunters to shoot prematurely and farther at the expense of accuracy.*

a shooting loop to transfer the rifle's weight from the forward hand back to the bigger muscles in the shoulder, and to maintain steady tension on the rifle's front end. These expert shooters also give the rifle as much skeletal support as possible. Bones move only at joints, while muscle is elastic. Muscles twitch; bone doesn't. Bone helps you bear the rifle's weight without tiring.

Beyond position, consistent accuracy depends on smart shooting. Each shot must be thought through before firing. Controlling your breath and the trigger is part physical conditioning, part mental effort. Recently I botched two easy shots at an elk because I yanked the trigger. I've been shooting for nearly 40 years and learned early on that yanking triggers is a sin. That didn't stop me. I wanted to kill this elk in a hurry. By hunting season, proper shooting technique should be second nature. Taking time to make deliberate shots helps you hew to that technique.

Sometimes you must think about a shot, because distance, wind or other conditions threaten to pull the bullet off your sightline. On uphill and downhill shots, for example, the secret is to hold low because gravity does not run perpendicular to the bullet's path, thus there's less effect for each yard of bullet travel. Steep angles, however, have little

*Wyoming game outfitter Tim Haberberger demonstrates a good offhand position with a Browning A-Bolt rifle. Even for practiced shooters, offhand is a position of last resort.*

effect on point of impact up close. Not long ago I spied an elk bedded across a broad canyon and figured the hunter I was guiding could get a shot if we dropped to the outside and came up on the rim directly above the animal. Everything worked. This fellow even had a rock rest from prone at the bedded elk 80 yards below. And yet he missed—and missed again. The third shot finally brought the elk down. The shooter excused his poor performance, admitting he'd neglected the angles. I refrained from telling him that he missed because he didn't hold the reticle on the elk. At 80 yards, a 45-degree shot angle would have required a hold for roughly 50 yards. The difference in point of impact between 50 and 80 yards is pretty darn small. This hunter was in other ways quite capable, and had shot some fine groups. He might one day become a crack shot—but only if he can concede his own flaws. Blaming the rifle or the angles, the elevation or the scope, the ammunition, the moon or El Niño won't put antlers on the grass. SB

WAYNE VAN ZWOLL *is a longtime contributor to* Shooter's Bible *and now edits its specifications section. Wayne lives in central Washington state, where he writes columns and feature articles for several magazines, including* **Bugle, Mule Deer, Elk Hunter, Guns & Gear, American Hunter, North American Hunter** *and* **Field & Stream.** *He serves as technical editor for* **Rifle** *and* **Handloader** *and has published four books on firearms and hunting. Competitive shooting, hunting and guiding big game hunters have given Wayne ample field experiences to support his articles. He also teaches marksmanship and runs a Wyoming outdoor skills camp for women.*

*The author demonstrates a practical sitting position for hunters. Note that his elbows are in front of his knees, and that the shooting sling is tight only from the forend to his triceps. The big Burris scope is wonderfully bright, but too bulky and heavy for most large game hunters.*

# Slug Guns And Loads Take A Quantum Leap Forward

### By Dave Henderson

In my youth, which took place shortly after the mid-point of the recently expired century, a shotgun that could put four slugs out of five into a gallon can at 40 paces was considered a tack driver. Fired from smooth-walled barrels designed and choked for shot charges, the slugs were all well under bore size and varied in diameter and weight. Accuracy was problematical at best. Adding any sighting apparatus beyond a front bead was considered an act of conspicuous consumption. "Like putting racing tires on a dump truck," scoffed the elders of my clan when, as an upstart teenager, I showed up one November day with a William's peepsight affixed to the receiver of my shotgun. The truth is, slug shooting has taken a quantum leap forward in the last two decades. Comparing today's slugs to their forebearers is akin to comparing the Space Shuttle with Kitty Hawk.

*The author tests a slug gun at his bench*

The slug gun of my choice today is essentially a 12-gauge bolt-action rifle. Topped with a 2x7 variable scope, it is capable of near minute-of-angle accuracy with saboted bullets that, ballistically, outstrip or challenge such venerable centerfires as the .30-30 Winchester, .45-70 Government, .300 Savage or 30-40 Krag. Where slug hunting for deer was once a "wait-until-you-see-the-whites-of-their-eyes" proposition, today's slug hunter starts pre-heating the oven with some justification as soon as a rack appears on the horizon a furlong away.

Winchester's Supreme Partition Gold, which was introduced in 2000, represents the state of the art. This 12-gauge load develops nearly 3,300 foot pounds of energy at the muzzle, pushing a 385-

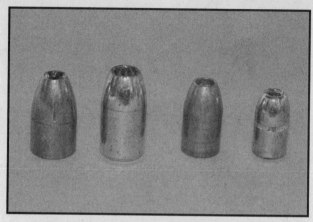

*State-of-the-art copper slugs include (l to r): Remington Copper Solid, Federal Barnes EXpander, Winchester Partition Gold, Hornady H2K Heavy Mag.*

**Today's slug guns and loads are capable of outstanding accuracy compared to those of only 20 years ago.**

grain open-nosed partition bullet at more than 1,900 feet per second with incredible accuracy. Boasting a very un-sluglike ballistic coefficient of .220, the new load retains a full ton of energy at 125 yards and 1,500 foot pounds at 200. Hornady, which entered the sabot slug market in 1997, introduced its H2K Heavy Mag in 1999—a 300-grain, .486-diameter (.200 ballistic coefficient.) expansion bullet that trails only Winchester's innovation in ballistics.

No less an authority than Colonel Townsend Whelen once allowed that it took at least 1,000 foot pounds of energy to turn out the lights on a white-tail. He was referring, of course, to rifles—but the new Winchester and Hornady loads eclipse that figure nearly 250 yards down range. Granted, these numbers wouldn't draw a second glance from a modern rifleman, but they are absolutely cosmic in the short-range world of the shotgun.

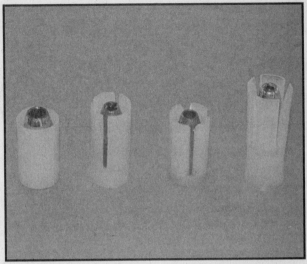

*State-of-the-art in sabots (l to r): Federal Barnes EXpander, Remington Copper Solid, Winchester Partition Gold, Hornady H2K Heavy Mag.*

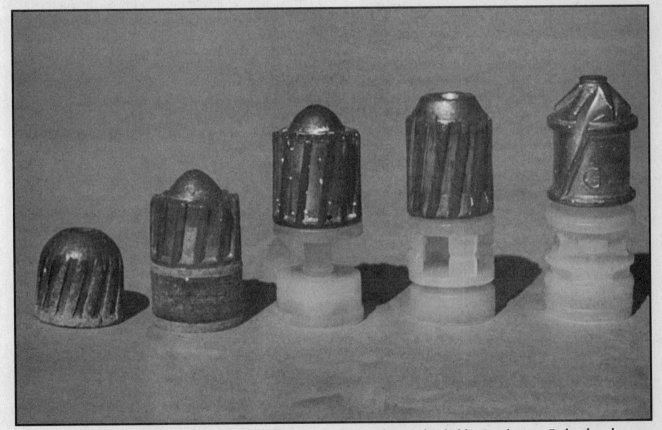

*Fodder for smoothbore slug guns includes (l to r): Foster slug (as loaded by Remington, Federal and Winchester), original Brenneke, Brenneke Magnum, Cervo (formerly loaded by Fiocchi) and the Gualandi (loaded by Challenger, Fiocchi and Nitro).*

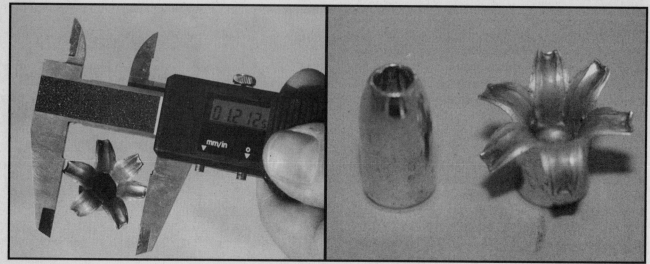

*The Federal Barnes EXpander and Remington's new Copper Solid expand readily on deer-sized game while retaining 100 percent of their mass.*

The new loads are the latest manifestations of a relatively new transition in shotgun slugs. Until the mid-1990s, slugs were universally made of soft lead, using a nose-heavy design for stability. Conventional "rifled" slugs are so named because of the slightly raised ribs swaged into the outside diameter. These may lend the slug a modicum of sales appeal but do nothing for rotation. What keeps the slug pointed head-on is the "rock-in-a-sock" phenomenon of the weight-forward design. Even the finned Brenneke and the later BRI, Winchester and Federal sabots fired from rifled barrels were designed weight-forward to maintain stability when the spinning slowed. But in 1993 that concept went out the window when Remington introduced its Copper Solid sabot slug. Machined out of solid copper bar stock, the new slug featured a notched nose and slight boat tail. It was, essentially, a .50-caliber solid, rear-weighted bullet.

"For years all manufacturers stayed away from any slug design that looked like a bullet," said one prominent executive in the slug industry. "But when the Copper Solid came out and there was no [public or governmental] uproar, the gates were opened for the designers."

The original Copper Solid, while innovative, proved too hard to be consistently effective on deer-sized game, and so Remington redesigned it in 1998 in a softer, readily expandable form. This remodeling by Remington followed the success of the Federal Barnes EXpander—a .50-caliber Barnes Xpander MZ bullet seated in a heavy plastic sabot—that was introduced the previous year. Both are one-ounce, open-nosed, rear-weighted bullets that expand to 1.5 times their original half-inch diameter while retaining virtually 100 percent of their weight. All of the new rear-weighted slug designs use a cup-like plastic sabot rather than the two-piece sleeve type common to early sabot slugs.

The original Copper Solid had a cup-like sabot, but today's designs are more directly related to the original Collet Cup Slug put out in 1990 by a small shop, Gun Servicing of Trenton, NJ. It handloaded 300-grain, .45-caliber Hornady ACP pistol bullets in a unique cuplike sabot, adjusting the powder type and amount for various slug guns. In 1996, prior to the Federal-Barnes introduction, a magnum version was introduced featuring a .50-caliber Barnes Xpander. In fact, the Federal-Barnes design was so similar to Gun Servicing's that some initial concern was expressed over possible patent infringements.

Today, about 3.6 million of the nation's deer hunters go afield armed—either by mandate or personal choice—with slug guns. Their numbers are, moreover, growing annually as whitetails and shooters compete for elbow room, and as more and more municipalities opt for slugs over the potential lethality of the modern rifle. Even such renowned wilderness outposts as Helena, Montana, and Edmonton, Alberta, require slugs for hunting in the suburbs. And so, after being treated like second-class citizens using third-rate equipment for three-quarters of a century, slug shooters now began to see some advances. Their numbers had indeed grown to the point where demand was running ahead of supply. The larger market, in turn, fostered retail competition and spurred technology.

For much of the 20th century, slug-shooting shotguns were essentially modern muskets—like smoothbores shooting "pumpkin balls" that were undersized, relatively round balls of soft lead loosely loaded over cardboard wads, using black-power at first and later primitive forms of smokeless powder. In 1933 the state-of-the-art moved from round ball to the modern Minie Ball. Developed by Winchester-Western ballistician Karl Foster, the slug was essentially a glob of soft lead die-punched into a cup shape, with a heavy nose and thin skirts designed to expand and partially seal the bore.

The Foster slug (improved versions of which are still loaded by Remington, Federal Cartridge and Winchester-Olin) still represents nearly 60 percent of the slug-shooting market—despite having the ballistic coefficient of a Volkswagen Beetle! For most of the century, its only competition was the German-made Brenneke, a bore-filling, finned, attached-wad design which had it origin in 1895 but was not

*The Foster slug's biggest advantage is its molecular cohesiveness. Introduced in 1933, it remains the best seller on the market.*

readily available in the U.S. until the end of World War II. There were no further significant advances until the 1980s, when saboted loads and rifled shotgun barrels came into existence. Slug shooting has been on a fast track ever since. Based on artillery designs, the original sabot featured a .50 caliber one-ounce lead pellet shaped like an hour glass and encased in a two-piece plastic sleeve. The sleeve filled the bore and gripped the rifling to impart spin, then fell off once everything cleared the muzzle. The pellet, stabilized both by the spin and its weight-forward design, had a much better ballistic coefficient than Foster slugs, while retaining its stability and velocity much farther down range.

Originally designed by California-based Ballistics Research Industries (BRI) as a police round capable of shooting through car doors and even engine blocks, the new design was later marketed to sportsmen with a simple change in packaging. Winchester-Olin bought BRI in the early 1990s and Federal Cartridge quickly designed its own version of a previous BRI patent. Accuracy and effective range took a leap forward at that point, but it wasn't until the period between 1996-2000 that major manufacturers were able to come up with saboted loads that proved efficient in the deer woods.

The conventional sabots were accurate but their uncompromising hardness made them unpopular

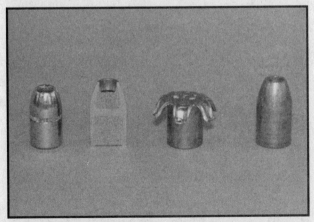

*The new hammers: Hornady's H2K Heavy Mag, a cutaway of Winchester's Partition Gold, and an expanded version of an intact slug.*

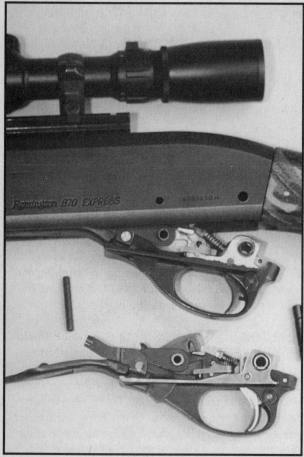

*The market for slug guns is growing. Hastings offers an adjustable trigger assembly for Remington shotguns.*

EXpander, the redesigned Remington Copper Solid, and the Winchester and Hornady innovations in 1999.

## THE GUNS

While the major advances in slug shooting have encompassed the loads, they most likely wouldn't have moved forward if shotgun manufacturers hadn't improved the launching platforms. The advent of the rifled barrel, introduced on commercial guns by Ithaca Gun and Mossberg in 1987, opened the flood gates for slug technology. A rifled barrel improves the accuracy of virtually any slug. But sabots, which are designed for rifling are a waste in a smoothbore. The original Brenneke was a disaster in rifled barrels because the lands and grooves deformed the slug's huge fins. Brenneke remedied the situation by bringing out designs in the early 1990s that were made specially for rifled barrels.

Today, every major manufacturer has at least one model available with a rifled barrel, rifle sights and options for scope mounting. Most 12-gauge barrels have a rifling twist rate of 1-turn-in-34 to 36 inches. The exceptions are Marlin, Browning, Beretta and Benelli, which are 1-in-28 and Ithaca Gun's Fast-Twist model in 1-in-25 (special orders only). Twenty-gauge slug guns now usually sport a slightly faster twist—about 1-in-24. The state of

for deer hunting. One doesn't need a solid bullet, after all, for thin-skinned game like white-tailed deer. Thus, despite the hype over the sabots' extended effective range and accuracy advantage, deer hunters stayed with smoothbores and conventional slugs that were far less expensive.

There was one exception, however. In 1993, a tiny New Jersey company introduced a unique design called the "Lightfield Hybred" sabot. Designed by British artillery expert Tony Kinchen, the Lightfield is essentially an almost full-bore, attached-wad slug (like the Brenneke magnum) encased in a thin-walled, two-piece sabot. The slug's mass and ready expansion made it the only efficient sabot for deer hunting (although caribou, bear, pronghorns and feral hogs, have also been taken with Lightfields). That is until the aforementioned breakthroughs by the Federal Barnes

*The sabot's plastic sleeves grab the rifling to impart spin on the projectile.*

*These bolt action slug guns represent the state of the art (l to r): Savage 210, Mossberg 695, Browning's A-Bolt (discontinued) and Marlin 512.*

Browning, is based on an existing rifle design (the Savage 110 series), with front-locking lugs, 60-degree bolt throw, enclosed bolt face and adjustable trigger. Both the Mossberg and Marlin designs evolved from far more primitive bolt-action shotgun models, which previously existed as inexpensive, entry-level guns. By adding heavy-walled rifled barrels, rifle sights and synthetic stocks to revamped versions of the discontinued Mossberg 595 and Marlin 55 designs, these bargain-basement ($100) bolt guns were converted into affordable, accurate slug guns. Their bolts were locked by dropping the bolt handle into a recess in the receiver. The bolts are ponderous and the triggers are—well—shotgun triggers. But they shoot.

Browning's BPs-12 pump and 12-gauge Gold autoloader are available with optional rifled barrels, while its sister company—U.S. Repeating Arms—offers the Model 1300 series pump with a rifled barrel. In addition to its Model 695 bolt gun, Mossberg offers rifled barrel options on its Model 500 and 835 pumps and Model 9200 autoloader. H&R's unique break-action single shots, which also evolved from inexpensive designs, are available in bull-barreled designs in both 12 and 20 gauge as well as in the entry-level Tracker and dressed-up Topper. Ithaca, which offered the industry's first "slugs-only" smoothbore barrel in 1959, now offers its Model 37 pump in a fixed, rifled barrel version in both 12 and 20

the art, however, is the bolt action slug gun. Mossberg, Marlin and Savage currently produce rifled-barreled bolt actions that offer the accuracy inherent in the turn-bolt design and are priced affordably.

Ironically, the Browning A-Bolt shotgun, which first reached dealer shelves in 1996, was undoubtedly the highest quality commercial slug gun ever made. But with a price tag in excess of $700, it couldn't compete with the Mossberg 695, Marlin 512 or Savage 210 bolts, all of which featured suggested retail prices of $290-$380 but sold for much less. The average shooter may not have discerned a difference in accuracy between the Browning and the cheaper models, but he did note the price tags. As a result, the A-Bolt was discontinued in 1998. The Savage 210, like the

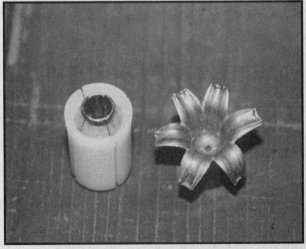

*Expanded and saboted versions of Federal Barnes EXpander.*

gauge and a switch-barrel model in both sizes. Remington has rifled barrel versions of its Model 870 pump and it 1100 and 11-87 autoloaders, while Beretta, Benelli and Franchi—all operating under the same Italian umbrella—offer their rifled barrel autoloaders to the world market. SB

**DAVE HENDERSON** *has been writing steadily for 34 years, the last 14 being devoted solely to writing and editing for outdoor magazines and books. In that time he has produced more than 3,000 newspaper and magazine articles on hunting and shooting. Dave is currently managing editor of* **Whitetail News** *and field editor for* **Buckmasters Whitetail Magazine, Krause's Whitetail Business, Beards & Spurs Magazine** *and* **Outdoor Times.** *He also contributes regularly to* **Gun World, Deer & Deer Hunting, North American Hunter** *and a variety of other publications. In addition, Dave conducts seminars on shotgunning for deer and has authored two books on the subject. This article is his first for Shooter's Bible.*

**The author with the first buck ever taken with Winchester's new Partition Gold sabot. His gun is a Browning Gold Deer Hunter.**

**Slug guns have the same capabilities as some older big bore centerfire rifles, witness this Labrador caribou hunt.**

# A Quail Hunter's Odyssey
## (or Bird Dogs Who Have Owned Me)

### BY JOSEPH C. GREENFIELD, JR., M.D.

I was about ten years old when I first hunted birds. Previously I'd hunted squirrels with a .22 rifle my father had given me, but I'd never seen a bird dog in action. Dad rarely hunted, but when a friend invited him to hunt quail on his plantation in Georgia, he took me along. Our host had owned many fine bird dogs, but on this occasion his kennel contained just two pointers. I don't remember much about the old dog, but the younger one, Lucy, was described as "started" or, in the parlance of the sport, a dog that had no training whatsoever or was too dense to learn. During our quail hunt, Lucy chased covey after covey while our host spent most of his time cursing and yelling at her. It seemed to me then that the appropriate name for a bird dog was "son-of-a-bitch," a phrase I've found useful on many subsequent occasions when identifying obstreperous pointers.

When Lucy finally tired of chasing birds and actually pointed, my father handed me his 20-gauge Parker and said, "Take this shotgun and try to kill this bird." Suddenly, a quail flushed and flew over my left shoulder toward the sun. I still remember watching the bird in flight and squeezing the trigger. The quail crumpled and died, whether from my shot or our host's I will never know. This much I do know: from that time on I was "ruined." I'd found my lifelong pastime.

My father and I went bird hunting on only one other occasion before he was injured in an automobile accident. During this hunt I saw some exceptional dog work: three pointers trailing a covey for approximately 100 yards. At the time, I knew so little about bird dogs that I didn't appreciate what an impressive thing I had just witnessed.

Soon, with money earned from a paper route, I acquired a pack of five or six excellent beagles and was introduced to beagle field trials, an event involving two rabbit dogs chasing a rabbit. The dogs were judged primarily on their ability to stay meticulously on the trail or line. Since speed didn't count as a prized attribute, a winning dog

*The author poses with Hannah (1995).*

*Spot at age 13 was still a bird dog! He is pointing in Bleckly County, Georgia (c. 1961).*

might be so slow the rabbit had time to birth a litter while waiting for the dog to catch up! To win these field trials, I acquired several dogs who possessed the aforementioned characteristics and ended up with a pack that had no interest in jumping and couldn't move a rabbit from one weed patch to another in half a day. The entire experience left a permanent sour taste in my mouth for field trials. So, at age 17, when my Uncle Hal invited me to hunt quail in South Georgia with him, I jumped at the chance.

Uncle Hal had leased bird hunting rights to a 3,000-acre tract of land. He also owned two pointers, Lemon and Mack, both outstanding, well-trained dogs, and two setters. During the season, we hunted on the average of every other week, driving for six hours from Atlanta to Thomasville. For reasons never clear to me, Uncle Hal let the dogs ride inside his station wagon, not in a trailer. He fed them cheese, fresh eggs, and choice meat —a better diet than mine. Soon those dogs were passing volumes of gas so pungent that even breathing became difficult. I vowed: never share a closed vehicle on a long trip with flatulent pointers.

At age 20 I bought my first bird dog, Spot, for $200 from the same man who sold Lemon and Mack to Uncle Hal. That was an enormous sum

of money for a bird dog, but today 25 times that amount wouldn't touch a dog of Spot's abilities. Right from the start, anyone could see that this four-year-old dog knew a lot more about bird hunting than I did. In essence, he trained me. Two years later I purchased Don, a two-year-old dog with minimal training on birds. Don had been allowed to run loose and developed a propensity for rabbit hunting. As a result, he never really overcame his tendency to hunt in swamps and overgrown bottom fields. While he didn't find nearly as many birds as Spot, he still ranked as a solid bird dog with a spectacular style of running—a gentle, rolling, effortless gait that covered a lot of ground. He could run from dawn to dark and never tire.

By contrast, Spot had a driving gait, knocking down weeds, cornstalks, small pine trees, anything that stood in his way. He couldn't keep up with Don on an all-day hunt, though. When he turned five years old, Spot cut his right ankle on some tin cans and severed several tendons. The wound healed soon enough, but his toes splayed out, causing him to limp slightly. Still, Spot was a delight to watch as he circled the borders of fields, crisscrossing them a couple of times, then heading to the woods, hunting 10 or 15 yards from the edge. He could cover a ten-acre field in ten minutes, and when he returned I knew without a doubt there were no birds nearby. And when he didn't come back, you could be just as sure he was on point and would stay that way until sundown, if necessary.

I continued to shoot my grandfather's 20-gauge Parker with good success. Don and Spot had become real meat dogs and—for pointers—excellent retrievers. One time I shot at a covey flushed from the other side of a five-foot-high hog wire fence. I killed two of them and then watched in astonishment as my dogs cleared the fence almost simultaneously, each one returning with a bird in his mouth. I vividly recall seeing Spot, while in the midst of retrieving a dead bird, suddenly point. I'd never seen a dog point with a bird in his mouth, and I still can't understand how any dog could smell another bird with the overwhelming scent of a dead one already filling his nostrils. Indeed, Spot never ceased to amaze me. Once, while jumping a fence, he stiffened in mid-air and landed in a classic point. Apparently he had smelled the birds only after becoming airborne. Spot's sole failing was that he never learned to climb over or crawl under fences. He simply jumped over them. Interestingly, at home I kept him behind a five-foot fence his entire life, and he never jumped out. And yet, when hunting, he would sail over anything in sight without hesitation. This unique approach to fences worked fine until Spot reach the age of eight or nine and began catching his back legs on the barbed wire. I couldn't break him of the habit and numerous times had to literally extract him from fences.

The only drawback with both Spot and Don was their strange propensity for fighting with each other. It's a continuing mystery to me why male pointers can hunt as a team all day without a semblance of discord, and yet when the hunt is over they immediately start tearing each other apart—a canine version of the Hatfields and McCoys, I suppose. Both dogs were always ready to mix it up with the local dogs as well, regardless of their size. Having lost most of these fights, they would customarily return in various stages of disrepair.

Although Spot and Don were wide-ranging dogs who covered large chunks of ground, I could count on them to check back with me on a regu-

lar basis. I learned to walk at a reasonable pace and let the dogs do most of the work. Many of the people I've worked with over the years, however, believed the main purpose in bird hunting was to see how fast they could walk. While skilled as bird hunters, they would speed from one place to the next, wherever they knew a covey was located. The truth is, the only dog they needed was a retriever.

Because Spot and Don were so talented, I didn't learn as much as I should have about the intricacies of bird hunting. I simply followed their lead, enjoying the solitude and the outdoors. As a result, I developed an inflated notion of my prowess as a bird hunter. For example, the deleterious effects of weather conditions—temperature, humidity, direction and wind speed—largely escaped me. Later on, I learned how these factors can dramatically affect a hunter's ability to find birds.

Like most hunters, I became convinced that bird hunting until two hours before sundown was chiefly a waste of time. On several occasions, though, this rule proved incorrect. I remember hunting one morning with Uncle Hal without much success. While he took his regular mid-day siesta, Spot, Don and I worked an area where we had found a few birds in the past. In only 90 minutes we discovered six or seven coveys. Not wanting to make Uncle Hal mad by waking him, I shot sparingly. Mostly, after having observed the

*Spot and Don in 1955. They rode many miles in this dog trailer. The shotgun, a 20-gauge Parker, was the author's first bird gun.*

*Pepper and Tiny back Hannah on a hunt near Asheboro, North Carolina (1985).*

dogs on point, I sat down, watched them for a while, then flushed the birds. Spot, who didn't appreciate this approach, would roll his eyes and give me a look of sheer disgust.

During these years, Georgia was an "open range" state, meaning most livestock didn't have to be fenced. Several times, while driving home at night, I came close to meeting my Maker because so many animals had congregated on the highway after dark. Most of the fallow land in South Georgia was burned each year in winter or early spring. This practice prevented vegetation from growing so thick that it choked out the bird habitat. Predator control constituted a standard part of every farmer's life. Chickens, guineas, turkeys and domestic ducks, all ran loose around the farmhouse. Protecting them from hawks, owls, foxes, snakes, opossums and raccoons was all part of the day's work. The practice of eliminating these predators undoubtedly aided the quail population. Diamondback rattlesnakes populated the hunting grounds in our area, but I encountered surprisingly few. One time I could tell by the way Spot pointed—looking down and drawing back —that he'd found something special. I saw the snake, heard its ominous rattle, and shot it before any harm could be done. A local veterinarian told me one of his clients had lost three dogs in as many days to rattlesnake bites. These imported

dogs had no experience with snakes and, apparently, lacked an innate fear of them.

Like most pointers, Spot never liked to retrieve, but he expected—no, he demanded—that at least one bird would be on the ground after each covey rise. From Spot's vantage point, my sole contribution to the proceedings was killing birds. My erratic marksmanship meant that he frequently became annoyed but usually suffered through the dry spells—but not always. I remember one instance in particular when I couldn't hit the broad side of a barn, even though birds were everywhere. With the first covey rise I scored a neat double miss and repeated my ineptitude, much to Spot's disgust, on the second covey and several singles. Spot's intolerance mounted with each miss. He threw me a look that said in no uncertain terms, "You'd better get on the ball or else," pointing once again on the edge of a peanut field. By now, I had developed a first class case of "buck fever." Spot decided he'd had enough. He went on hunting, but clearly his demeanor had changed radically. Once more he pointed in an open field, but as I was approaching to within 50 yards, Spot jumped into the middle of the covey, flushed the birds, and gave me a withering look. He then trotted arrogantly back to our '39 Chevy and lay down on the back seat. Despite my pleas, he refused to hunt any longer and remained steadfastly aloof all the way home. On our next trip, I did manage to wing a bird down on the first covey rise and Spot appeared satisfied. Despite my all too frequent episodes of poor marksmanship, he never took me to task like that again. I was now convinced that, like many successful bird dogs, Spot could think.

Are pointers truly capable of thinking? Several experiences require me to answer in the affirmative. A number of years ago a friend gave me a superb but ungainly bird dog named Belle. Like many of her kind, she had been forced to learn the art of retrieval, but she didn't like it. I never knew Belle to ruffle a bird's feather she had dutifully retrieved, if not to hand, at least to my vicinity. On one occasion, after I'd hunted her hard for several days, she was ready for a rest. But first she pointed a single quail at the edge of a deep canal. The bird flushed, I fired, and the quail fell on the far side. Belle swam across the canal, picked up the bird, and started to return. I watched from the other side, ready to praise her for being such a peerless retriever. Then much to my dismay, she dipped her paw in the water and stopped. She seemed almost to smile, before backing up and sitting down on the bank. There she proceeded to eat the bird while I, on the opposite bank, turned crimson. After Belle finished her repast, she got up, stretched leisurely, and swam back across the canal and resumed hunting. I'm convinced that dog knew I couldn't cross the canal to reprimand her, so she decided to have a lunch break.

*Tiny, showing off, points (1983) near Yee Haw Junction, Florida*

Another thinking dog I owned was a small lemon and white pointer named Tiny. Nature didn't bless her with a particularly good nose, but with hard work and desire she developed into a pretty good bird dog. We hunted two seasons together before we were joined by Hannah, an outstanding 15-month-old bird-finding machine. Hanna beat Tiny to nearly all the birds, until Tiny grew jealous. Still, like a pro, she accepted the less spectacular jobs of backing and retrieving. One day, Hannah had winded a covey, and although not sure of the precise location, she pointed. Tiny arrived and backed, but no birds could be flushed. I clucked to the dogs to relocate. Tiny started trailing rapidly as if on a hot scent across the field, glancing back to make sure Hannah and I followed. After about 100 yards of this charade, Tiny suddenly wheeled and raced back to our original place and pointed the birds. Hannah and I stood with our mouths agape. I'm convinced that, from the start, Tiny knew where the birds were and decided to lead Hannah and me on a merry chase away from the area so she could return and be first on point.

Hannah developed into a wonderful, wide-ranging dog who, once pointed, was as staunch as a rock. I used her to train the younger dogs, a task that required her to find birds, then hold point while I taught the neophytes to point and back. At times, Hannah had to hold her point even as the younger dogs ran up birds in front of her, a most distasteful experience for Hannah. It could, I suppose, be compared to forcing Einstein to teach Math 101.

*Spot, pounting a covey near the author's home in Atlanta (1951).*

*Belle was not stylish or pretty to look at, but she was a bird-finding machine. Here she was pointing near Albany, Georgia (1960).*

Unknown to me, Hannah was plotting a way out of this onerous training duty. Most young dogs tend to follow their elders, at least until they learn how to hunt on their own. Hannah began enticing the novices to follow her, whereupon she would vacate the area and lose her young companions in some impenetrable palmetto thicket or dense woods, a mile or so from where I was hunting. Hannah would return to me, tail wagging, with a look that seemed to say: "I got rid of them, so now we can do some real hunting." As a result I had to spend half an hour or more searching for lost dogs. Eventually I had to stop forcing her to train young dogs. Can anyone say Hannah was incapable of thinking?

When hunting a fairly large acreage in a vehicle, it's standard practice to run two pointers for an hour or so, then rotate to another brace. Rather than enjoying the break, however, the dogs much prefer hunting to riding in a truck. One dog in particular, named Faith, developed several schemes for being first off the truck. She would start whining in a constant, high-pitched whine that stopped only when she got her way. Another ingenious approach was to hold back her normal bowel movement until the optimal time at which to smell up the dog box. Faith adopted a most damnable strategy. Since she had never quarreled or fought with the other dogs before, this new

plan took me by surprise. Somehow she surmised that if the other dogs were hurt and unable to hunt, I'd have no choice but to let her go. Accordingly, she would wait until I was away from the truck, then macerate the front paw of whichever dog was kenneled with her. In that way, she effectively disabled—for the next week or so—three dogs. Faith would watch her wounded kennel mates hobble around on three legs, unable to hunt, without exhibiting a sign of remorse whatsoever. From then on, she was first on the ground—always.

The most notable example of pointer intelligence I've witnessed involved a partially trained, incredibly stupid dog name Buck and a small setter named Rebel. One afternoon while on a hunt, these two dogs winded a covey of birds, briefly pointed, then flushed the quail. It was hardly a spectacular piece of dog work. My hunting partner, Joey O'Bannon, grabbed Rebel, the nearest at hand, and got his attention in a hurry using a freshly cut stalk from a cabbage tree. Rebel bemoaned his fate loudly, and Buck, perhaps sensing his turn came next, launched a dramatic first strike. He circled Joey, spied a brief opening, then lunged at him, his teeth firmly planted in Joey's backside, and hung on for dear life. The look on Joey's face—a mixture of astonishment and outrage—was priceless.

Whether these episodes demonstrate a dog's ability to think, I cannot prove. I suspect that an animal psychologist would not be convinced; but in my view, having endured a love-hate relationship with pointer bird dogs for more than half a century, I'm absolutely convinced that bird dogs have far more intelligence than we give them credit for. SB

**Joseph Greenfield,** *a James B. Duke Distinguished Professor of Medicine at Duke University, served as Chairman of the Department of Medicine there from 1983 to 1995. For nearly 60 years he has been an avid quail hunter and has become thoroughly familiar with every aspect of the sport. His primary love has been training and hunting with pointer bird dogs. In recent years, Dr. Greenfield has widened his horizons by hunting dangerous game in Africa. These varied experiences, chronicled in voluminous contemporary notes, have formed the basis of a forthcoming book,* **The Odyssey of a Southern Bird Hunter.**

**S682 GOLD E**

# EVOLUTION

**S682 Gold E Trap**

After years of assisting competitive shooters to the victory stand, the Beretta S682 Gold has been re-engineered to create the most sought after competition over-and-under available— the new S682 Gold E.

A true competition gun from end to end, the new S682 Gold E's Optima-Bore® barrel profile reduces felt recoil and improves shot distribution, while the longer, thinner Optima-Choke® tubes (also available in external version) ensure consistent shot distribution year after year. Ventilated top and side ribs dissipate heat as well as improve pointability and target acquisition.

Available in Trap, Skeet and Sporting configurations, the S682 Gold E is as pleasing to the eye as it is to shoot. The low-profile receiver's dual color finish and modern ellipsis graphic give it a truly unique appearance, and a lifetime of precision shooting is ensured by the self-adjusting dual conical locking lugs, replaceable hinge pins and replaceable barrel shoulders. Triggers on all S682 E's adjust to three positions for length of pull (two trigger shoes supplied).

A perfect fit translates to a higher score, so the S682 Gold E stocks are matched to each individual shooting discipline, some fully adjustable and equipped with Beretta's "Memory System," allowing shooters to adjust for comb height and cast. The adjusting mechanisms patented locking system keeps settings secure. A newly designed, double-handled ABS hard case and an assortment of accessories is included.

With one quick, smooth swing serious shooters will recognize the Beretta S682 Gold E as the next stage of serious competition shooting. See it at your Beretta dealer today.

DE PLANO GROUP · NEW YORK MILANO

Beretta U.S.A. Corp., 17601 Beretta Dr., Accokeek, MD 20607, Tel 301.283.2191, Fax 301.283.0435
For a Beretta Worldwide Catalog of firearms & Beretta Sport clothing and accessories, call 1.800.528.7453 ($3 shipping).
Visit the Beretta Gallery in New York and Dallas. For a free firearm lock for your Beretta pistol, semiautomatic shotgun, or bolt-action rifle
send your $4 check or money order for shipping & handling to: Beretta U.S.A Corp., 71 Southgate Blvd., New Castle DE 19720-2000.
www.berettausa.com   www.beretta.com

**Beretta**
A TRADITION OF EXCELLENCE SINCE 1526

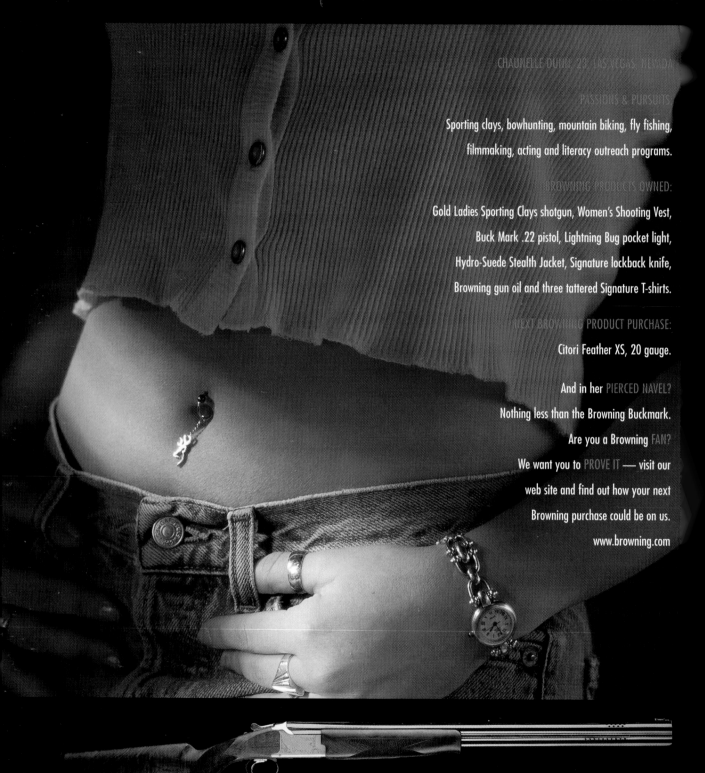

# "A gun is a tool."

*Alan Ladd in "Shane", Paramount Pictures, 1953*

SL8-1 RIFLE
Caliber .223

USC CARBINE
Caliber .45 ACP

# Power tools for a new century.

Man is a tool using being. And for centuries firearms have been one of his most important tools. Whether for hunting, defense, or sport—a truly modern utilitarian firearm gives shooters the power to use and control advanced technology. The highest level of that advanced technology is found in the design and materials used on the HK USC carbine and SL8-1 rifle.

### USC Carbine
Derived from the HK UMP, the USC is a civilian utility carbine that uses the classic hard-hitting .45 ACP cartridge. Matched with the simple and ultra-reliable blowback operating system, the HK USC is a radical departure from traditional firearms designs.

Extensive use of the same durable, reinforced polymers used on HK's new line of military and police arms ensures light weight and durability. And the highest grade of weapons steel is used where it matters—in the cold hammer forged target barrel and the solidly-constructed bolt mechanism.

User ergonomics are not sacrificed. The skeletonized buttstock is topped with a comfortable rubber cheek rest and recoil pad. The web of the pistol grip is open for a comfortable shooting handhold. Hard points located on the top and front of the receiver make attachment of optional Picatinny rails easy, allowing almost any kind of sighting system or accessory to be mounted. If you're looking for a .45 ACP carbine designed and engineered for the tasks of a new age, choose the HK USC.

### SL8-1 Rifle
The caliber .223 companion to the USC—the HK SL8-1 is also constructed almost entirely of reinforced carbon-fiber polymer. Based on the current combat-tested German Army G36 rifle, the SL8-1 uses a proven short stroke, piston-actuated gas operating system, well known for simplicity and reliability.

Designed and engineered to deliver exceptional shooting performance, the SL8-1 is already a favorite among European rifle shooters, due in large part to the many modular sighting systems available. These modular systems include extended and short rail mounts with open sights, a 1.5x scope with an integral carry handle, and a dual optical system that combines a 3x scope with an electronic red dot sight.

The sleek and clean lines of the HK SL8-1 and the USC are functional and modern—they have the look, the feel, and the performance that shooters demand. And like the best kind of tools, they're guaranteed for life. To put a USC or SL8-1 in your hands, see your local authorized HK dealer. In a world of compromise, some don't.

HECKLER & KOCH, INC.
21480 Pacific Boulevard
Sterling, Virginia 20166 U.S.A.
Tel. (703) 450-1900 • Fax (703) 450-8160 • www.hecklerkoch-usa.com

*For more information about HK firearms and the location of your nearest dealer, visit our website at: www.hecklerkoch-usa.com or call (703) 450-1900. Remember, firearms safety begins with you. Read and follow all safety information in the operators manual. Store all firearms in a safe and secure location. Keep firearms away from children. Always be a safe shooter.*

# WHAT'S SO GREAT ABOUT BLOCKING THE FIRING PIN?

## KEY CONCEPT®

*you're in control*

## SAKO 75 OFFERS SOMETHING INNOVATIVE – AGAIN.

The Sako KEY CONCEPT® is a revolutionary step forward in gun safety – the first integral rifle lock in the world. Our invention is astonishingly simple: insert the key, turn and remove it. The firing pin is now blocked. You can relax because only you, the key holder, can use your Sako rifle. Nobody else. To restore full functionality, just insert the key and unlock.

Thanks to the KEY CONCEPT®, your Sako is safe at home, in the car, at the range, during breaks and overnight in the woods. Whenever it's not in active use.

The KEY CONCEPT® has been thoroughly tested with various loads and in all weather conditions. And of course we would never dream of compromising our legendary accuracy. Sako is still the world's most accurate rifle out-of-the-box. Now it is also the safest.

STOEGER INDUSTRIES
5 MANSARD COURT
WAYNE, NJ 07470
TEL (+1) 973 / 872 9500
FAX (+1) 973 / 872 2230
stoegerindustries@msn.com

MORE ON SAKO 75 AND
KEY CONCEPT: www.sako.fi

**sako**
FINLAND

# One Man's Search For The Perfect Left-Handed Model 70

## By Richard S. Grozik

If it hadn't been for the likes of Townsend Whelen, Jack O'Connor, Warren Page and their monthly contributions to the various sporting magazines of my youth, I doubt seriously that I would ever have been motivated to read, let alone graduate, from high school. While the works of these opinionated wordsmiths never appeared in any of my English literature assignments, they were always, for me, required reading both in and out of school. Thanks to their adventurous tales about big game rifles and far-off hunts, I was able to escape to the real world of those self-reliant riflemen. They infused my mind with ballistics, filled my head with hunting lore and opened my heart to the great outdoors.

What kindled my curiosity mostly was the fondness with which these scribes described their favorite big game rifles. What they did with Peter Paul Mauser and Model 70 Winchester bolt-actions lit a fire that eventually led me to haunt cluttered gun shops, noisy shooting ranges and sporting booksellers in search of my own perfect hunting rifle. I read and absorbed every word my mentors wrote about the wood and metal craftsmanship required to transform military actions and factory rifles into compelling, hand-held works of art. These men and their like were the undisputed deans of the American school of classic rifle design, and under their tutelage I was determined to graduate with honors.

Suddenly, as if dropped on my head, a swarm of rifle calibers, bullet weights, sectional densities, ballistic coefficients, terminal velocities, foot

*Master stocker Dan McMillan displays the Exhibition grade English walnut blank destined for the author's left-hand Model 70.*

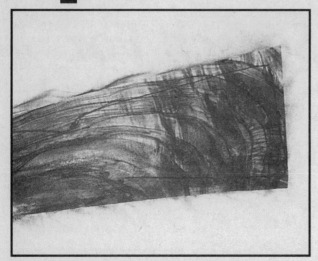

*A close-up view of the extraordinary blank stock selected by the author.*

*The factory Model 70 stock is ready to take center stage on the stock duplicating machine.*

pounds of energy, lands and grooves and rate of twist, all prevented me from carrying on normal conversations with my peers. The truth is, I was born to be a rifleman, and nothing was going to interfere with my sporting destiny. And so, throughout my high school days, I set my sights on duplicating the centerfire feats of my bolt-action heroes and never looked back. Caught in the inescapable claw of controlled-round feeding and hopelessly seduced by the 3-position safety, I knew it had to be a Model 70 Winchester .270

or nothing. As it turned out, the fulfillment of my dream became a long and convoluted process.

The problem was simple: I was a naturally right-handed shooter who was blessed with a left dominant eye. "Bats right, shoots left" should be my epitaph. I could shoot respectably from the right side at the bench, but for quick, instinctive shots it had to be from the left shoulder. There was no getting around my predicament. I would have to spend countless hours practicing from the port side until shouldering the rifle and racking

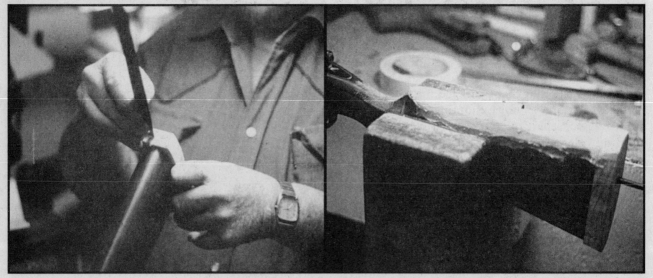

*In preparing the factory stock for duplication, Dan McMillan increases its length of pull, comb height and pistol grip size with wood and plastic putty.*

the bolt became second nature. And if that wasn't enough, Winchester didn't even make a left-handed Model 70!

During my senior year, I inherited a right-handed 1903 Springfield barreled action from my uncle. By working part-time in a macaroni factory, I was able to buy a "semi-inletted" rifle stock from Reinhardt Fajen. It was a simple slab of American black walnut with a rakish Monte Carlo cheekpiece and white line spacers at the plastic fore-end tip, grip cap and buttplate—not exactly what I had in mind. At the time, Fajen didn't have a classic-style 1903 stock in its inventory. I came close to chiseling off a forefinger in a vain attempt to mate barreled action to wood and was saved from any further maiming by going off to college. There I lost the .06 Springfield to my smooth-talking roommate who, without hesitation, sent if off to a gunsmith who knew what he was doing. The rifle came back dressed in a deep-polished blue and a well-inletted and finished stock. As luck would have it, the old centerfire shot like a house afire, placing 3-shot volleys of 180 grain factory ammo in small clusters at 100 yards.

Later, I indulged my left-dominant eye by obtaining a southpaw Savage Model 110 in 30.06. Despite its pedestrian push-feed bolt action, the rifle shot well enough until the bolt fell apart during a late-summer practice session. Savage fixed it with no problem, but I never felt the same about that rifle. Besides, it wasn't a Model 70 Winchester. I had read a few articles about one gunsmith or another who could convert Mauser and Model 70 bolt-actions to lefthandedness, but I lacked the money and the inclination to buy a non-factory rifle, no matter how cleverly it was cobbled together.

After college, I traded my dust-laden Savage 110 for a new Sauer-built .300 Weatherby Magnum with a left-hand bolt. The erotic Mark V was the only port-side action left on the dealer's shelf, and with hunting season just a few weeks away I caved

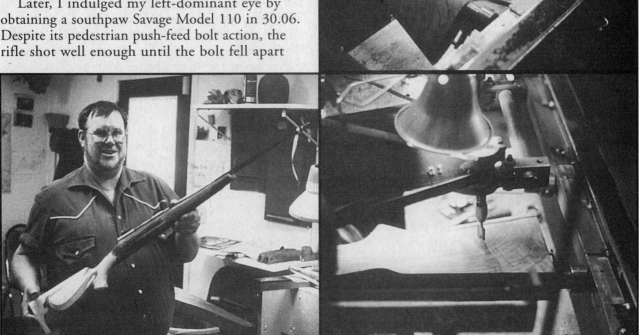

*Using a factory stock as a template, the English walnut blank is shaped and routed by veteran machine operator Ron Smith.*

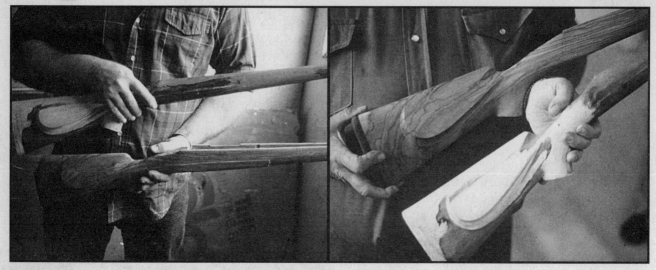

*The factory stock and its offspring are ready for the stocker's bench.*

in to temptation. Its flaming Claro walnut, skip-line checkering, white line spacers and glistening synthetic finish were in keeping with the space age. But its push-feed, nine-locking -lug bolt didn't quash my latent desire to own a claw-extracting, classic hunting rifle. The belted magnum, while ballistically impressive, produced an unmerciful recoil. With the help of RCBS and some reduced handloads, I limited my scope cuts to one, killing a good Wyoming mule deer with a Speer 165 grain bullet. I had finally settled on "the" rifle. Still, those silver-haired patriarchs of the classic rifle school continued to stalk the gun pages, painting pictures of rifles with simple symmetry, uncluttered lines and understated elegance. They also raised their eyebrows at bellowing magnums, extolling instead the virtues of 7x57s, .270s, 30.06s and the like along with precise bullet placement and non-belted cases. I was now more determined than ever to buy a rifle in .270 Winchester. When the "space-age" finish began to check and flake off my Weatherby, I knew it was time to make a change.

The gunshop where I traded the Weatherby told me that a Carl Gustaf left-hand action and a Boots Obermeyer 26-inch medium-tapered barrel—wedded to a custom-fitted Fajen AAA black walnut stock—would finally turn me into a full-fledged rifleman. I was leaning toward a simple, classic stock but succumbed to the shop owner's determination to sell me a racy, California-style

job complete with roll-over Monte Carlo cheek-piece, rosewood fore-end, flared pistol grip and a full complement of white line spacers. "Too soon old, too late smart" was an old adage that some-how came to mind following that purchase.

Six months later, the complete package arrived. I was now the owner of a rifle that weighed over ten pounds, looked like an advertisement for a Weatherby wannabe, and had a length of pull that scoffed at the eye-relief of every scope on the market. The Gustaf action was slick and sure, and the Ober-meyer barrel routinely planted 130-grain Nosler partitions in tight clusters at 100 yards downrange. Amazingly my very first western antelope hit the short-grass prairie with my first shot using the rifle.

As much as I admired its stellar shooting qualities, my new rifle weighed me down afield. The question gnawed at my soul. "When would I own a truly classic bolt-action rifle?" Instead of simply having the rifle restocked, I decided to swap it for a Ruger No. 1 B in .270 Winchester. This rifle with an endearing "1976 Liberty" inscription on its graceful 26-inch barrel, also proved deadly accurate. A classic in its own right, that Ruger single-shot gave me feelings of one-upmanship as I paraded it in front of my fellow riflemen at the shooting range. Alas, it too fell from grace when its salt-cured buttstock began to corrode the receiver around the inletting.

Even after Ruger's nice restocking job, I couldn't shake the still smoldering desire to own a classically stocked left-hand, Mauser-type rifle. As soon as

Dakota Arms unveiled its Model 76 pre-1964 Winchester-style action for lefties, I dug deep in my pocket and laid out a king's ransom for another shoulder-thumping .300 Win. Mag. As the saying goes: "A fool and his money are soon parted." A fellow rifle enthusiast convinced me that a he-man caliber like that would enable me to subdue any creature with hair in all of North America—or anywhere else. Although Dakota's classic stock design helped tame most of the rifle's jolting recoil, I soon developed a nasty flinch that only got worse following numerous shooting sessions at the bench. Once again, instead of having the rifle rebarreled for a milder cartridge, I sold it along with the Ruger, immersing my sorrows in the joys of wingshooting with a classic side-by-side L.C. Smith 16-gauge.

After a ten-year absence from the firing line, I could no longer ignore the empty rifle slot in my gun cabinet. With renewed passion and resolve, I embarked once again on a crusade for that elusive classic rifle prescribed for me by the ever-shrinking cadre of outdoor writers who still lamented the loss of the pre-'64 Model 70. One day, after perusing various shooting publications for the latest bolt-action offerings, I read that Winchester was introducing a Pre-'64 Model 70 in a left-hand action—the "rifleman's rifle"—some 60 years after its first Model 70 left the factory!

Without hesitation, I purchased a left-hand Model 70 Classic Sporter in .270, featuring controlled-

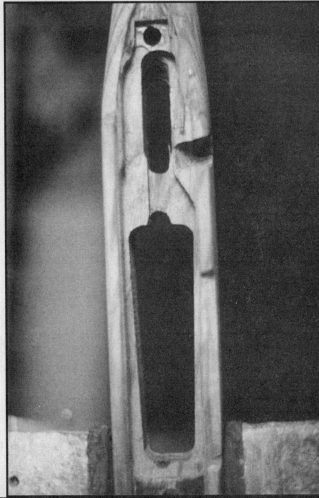

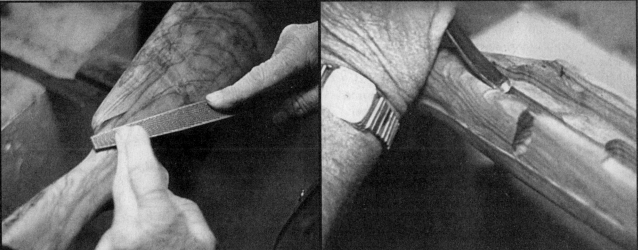

*A master's hands and eyes, plus an assortment of rasps, files and chisels, are required to shape, inlet and mate wood to metal successfully.*

*In its finished form (sans checkering and finishing) the buttstock's sculpted cheekpiece reflects its world-class craftsmanship.*

round feed and a coned breech. Its claw-extracting bolt, with a new anti-bind groove, glided effortlessly on the chromoly steel rails. Its 24-inch, hammer-forged barrel was nicely blued and tapered, and its American black walnut stock, while too short for my long arms, was shaped in the classic mode. Its cast aluminum triggerguard and plastic pistol grip cap, along with the stock, would have to be replaced. Since I planned on restocking the rifle, I had USRAC send me a milled steel triggerguard and grip cap. When all was done, Winchester's Pre-'64 Model 70 proved a first-class piece of engineering.

All I needed now was the right piece of *Juglans Regia* to begin my formal reformation of the sinistral Model 70. It took only one phone call to an old friend (Fred Wenig of Lincoln, Missouri) to end my brief search for good wood. "Better come on down and see for yourself," he advised. When I arrived at Fred's bustling shop, I was transported back to a time when quality craftsmanship was the benchmark for customer satisfaction. As I poked around Fred's private stores of Claro, Bastogne, English and American black walnut rifle blanks, I learned that all of his choice inventory had been carefully seasoned to a moisture content of no less than six percent and no greater than ten percent. With a water-soaked sponge, Fred wetted down a few blanks here and there to reveal the exceptional figure of the wood. Then, as we were leaving the

wood-scented room, he reached behind the door and pulled out a chunk of English walnut that, for once, left me speechless. The blank's tightly contrasting grain flowed uninterrupted from the fore-end through the pistol grip area, spilling into the buttstock in a dazzling marble-cake swirl. When Fred applied the wet sponge to it, I knew fate had finally intervened in my unrelenting quest.

With the blank in one hand and my Model 70 in the other, Fred next led me to Dan McMillan's tool-strewn stocking bench. Dan had been stocking classic rifles for more than 20 years and would take complete charge of the project. Sensing my predilection for a compact, sculpted cheekpiece, straight comb, ebony fore-end tip and a free-floated barrel, Dan decided that I needed a little more length of pull and a longer, more fist-filling pistol grip. Even with the best of inletting, he advised, it would probably be best to glass-bed the rifle. I had visions of hardened bedding goo protruding everywhere, until he showed me a glass-bedded rifle stock that looked as if it were an extension of Dan's meticulous hand inletting. In addition to

*The fore-end of the author's restocked Model 70 is prepared to receive a dense piece of ebony that languished for two decades on Elbert Smith's stocking bench.*

the action, the bedding extended about two inches up the barrel, where the free-floating began. Dan assured me that the rifle would maintain its accuracy from season to season.

Dan then began making the necessary alterations to the factory stock that would serve as a pattern to duplicate and rough inlet the English walnut blank I had selected. Removing the factory pad and adding a piece of wood to the buttstock gave me the 14-inch length of pull I required. Dan  then built up the comb, cheekpiece and pistol grip areas with plastic putty. After letting it cure for half hour or so, he began reshaping the factory stock with rasp and file to fit my physique. To make sure of the dimensions, the rifle was reassembled and my scope mounted. I snapped the rifle to my shoulder several times while Dan and master stocker Elbert Smith (one of three brothers who work at Fred Wenig's shop) checked and rechecked my alignment. After a few minor adjustments to the comb, it was time to take the reworked factory stock, along with my English

*Master checkerer Darrel Smith proudly displays his flawless work and the hand-rubbed warmth of an oil-finished stock.*

*Dan McMillan, the man responsible for its metamorphosis, poses with the author's finished left-handed Model 70 Winchester.*

computerization and CAD-CAM wizardry, it was good to note there remains no real substitute for the precision that only masterful hands and eyes can impart to wood and steel. After attaching a half-inch rifle pad to the buttstock, Dan handed me a classic hunting rifle that fit me like an old pair of hunting boots. All that remained was the checkering and finishing process.

Before I left for home, I discussed my choice of checkering pattern with the third member of the Smith brotherhood, Darrel. His delicate fleur-de-lis' would accent the design nicely, and his flawless, borderless checkering would also enhance the 24 lines-per-inch wrap-around coverage. In keeping with the classic tradition, and to ensure the subtle glow of the well-figured walnut, I selected Fred Wenig's hand-rubbed oil finish. Discarded for all eternity were the Monte Carlo cheekpiece, rosewood accents and white line spacers.

When I returned a few months later to take delivery of the rifle, I was captivated by its functional elegance and world-class fit and finish. My lifelong dream, thanks to Fred Wenig and his master craftsmen, was at last fulfilled. The seed planted deep within me years earlier by those venerable rifle masters of the high plains and lofty peaks had grown at last into a classic rifle. Topped off with a 2.5x-8x Sightron scope, Leupold bases and rings, my sinistral Model 70, with its improved Pre-'64 action and beautiful walnut stock, prints less than minute-of-angle pictures with moly-coated 140-grain Noslers on 100-yard targets. For thousands of dollars less than I might have spent for a customized left-hand Model 70 look-alike, I now possess a classic hunting rifle that will keep company—in my lifetime, at least —with the best of them. SB

walnut blank, to the duplicating room. Using my factory stock as a template, Ron Smith deftly augured it and the blank into their carving cradles. Bathed in a shower of aromatic walnut chips, he demonstrated how two decades of operating hand-controlled stock duplicating machinery could render a perfect clone of the template. Armed with a variety of bits and stylist spacers, he shaped the blank's external contours and routed the inletting to within a few thousandths of the final fit, a virtuoso performance that took less than a long lunch to complete.

Back at the bench with Dan McMillan, I witnessed the hand-inletting process that eventually wedded wood to metal. The barreled action would be brushed with inletting black and pressed to wood time and again before the hand-chiseled fit was consummated. In this age of rampant

**RICH GROZIK**, *author of* **Game Gun** *and* **Birdhunter**, *has written numerous articles for various guns and hunting publications. He began pursuing the hunting sports in the mid-1950s, using a bow and arrow made for him by his father, followed by his first air rifle. From then on, he took careful aim on the shooting sports, eventually turning his lifelong passion for firearms and hunting into a career in wildlife conservation. In addition to freelance writing, Rich continues to provide consulting and marketing services for the outdoors industry. This is his first article to appear in* **Shooter's Bible***.*

# Calhoon's Nineteen Caliber Wildcats

## BY DON LEWIS

The farmer, an old friend of mine, rested his scoped Model 219 Savage 22 Hornet rifle on top of a fence post and fired. Dust spiraled upward from a mound of dirt near a chuck's den, but the hole digger escaped unharmed. "That's my fourth attempt this week on that chuck," my friend complained as he ejected the empty. "I guess my eyes are going bad, or else I'm just a poor shot. That chuck sure is a super hole digger!"

"What kind of a sight picture did you use?" I asked. "That must be about 275 yards across a windy valley. I'm not sure what distance your rifle is sighted in for, but that's a long shot for a 22 Hornet."

"Shucks, he looks as big as a bear standing on top of his mound. I haven't the slightest idea when the rifle was last sighted in, but it has to be five or six years. I've been picking off chucks all around here, so I assume it must be on the money."

The various holes where the farmer had been "picking off chucks" were under 50 yards. A rifle could be off considerably and still connect on 20- to 40-yard shots. Later, I used a 22-250 Varminter wildcat with a 52 grain Match bullet to stop the critter that was causing my old friend so many problems. Then I took his antiquated single shot Hornet home to check it out on the range behind my gunshop. Sure enough, on the 100-yard target it was more than 1_-inches to the right and about an inch high. Not bad for a rifle that hadn't been sighted in for that long, but far from adequate for long range chuck shooting. At 275 yards the old farmer's 45-grain bullet would be around five inches off center and at least a foot low. According

*Since there is no commercial "drop in" stock available for a small BRNO action, it had to be built quite literally from scratch. The inletting job shown is superb.*

*Custom rifle builder Jim Peightal holds the finished 19 Calhoon. The 527 BRNO action requires special scope rings (available from CZ USA). Peightal installed a 4 x 14X x 40mm Springfield Tactical scope incorporating a patented rangefinding reticle and a leveling bubble.*

to Barnes Ballistics computerized program, a 45 grain 22 Hornet bullet at 2650 fps muzzle velocity zeroed at 100 yards is slightly more than 18-inches low at 275 yards. It's easy to see why my friend was not connecting.

This episode took place around 1955, when the 22-250 was still a wildcat (made by necking down 250-3000 Savage brass). The 22 Hornet was a factory cartridge that came to life with the old 22 Winchester Center Fire (WCF) black powder cartridge. Much experimentation was going on back in the 1920s and early 1930s with a variety of wildcat creations, but few ever got past the experimenter's bench. The 22 Hornet made the grade because its case was already a factory round, requiring little more than to replace the black powder with smokeless powder.

I've always been puzzled why Colonel Townsend Whelen, Captain G. L. Wotkyns and their staff at the Springfield Armory chose the black powder Winchester .22 Centerfire back in the late 1920s for their project when the 250-3000 Savage case had already been around since 1915. I've read that .22 caliber experiments were made with 250-3000 brass shortly after Savage put it on the market. During the mid-1930s, a half dozen or more experimenters brought out various versions of what is now the 22-250. J.E. Gebby, for one, named his version "22-250 Varminter" and obtained a copyright on that name. The 22-250 was a winner from the start, but for some unknown reason it remained a wildcat until 1965, when Remington standardized the round to the 22-250 Remington. It's still a winner.

In the heyday of wildcatting—which usually means necking a conventional factory case up or down to accept the desired bullet diameter—it's safe to say that hundreds of these creations were tested and put to death instantly. The 250-3000 case was necked down to the .224 caliber to make the 22-250. On the other side of the coin, the 30-06 case was necked up to make the 35 Whelen.

Admittedly, wildcatting entails much more than simply reducing or enlarging the neck of a case. Transforming a 416 Rigby into a 30-416, for example, requires 10 dies. Many wildcats require shortening the parent brass—or blowing out the shoulder—to a different angle by fire-forming. A good case in point is the new 19 Calhoon wildcat,

whose parent case is the old reliable 22 Hornet with a gentle 5_-degree shoulder angle. To make the 19 Calhoon you must run a lubed Hornet case into a Forster/Bonanza resizing die that reduces the neck to 19 caliber. The case is then primed and loaded with a predetermined powder charge. A 19 caliber Calhoon bullet is seated with the aid of a 19 Calhoon Forster/Bonanza seating die. When fired, the case walls expand against the new chamber and the neck is pushed out to a sharp 30-degree angle. From that point on, the case can be loaded using the same Forster/Bonanza die set. Because the 22 Hornet case has thin walls, it's a good idea to keep a sharp eye out for the beginning stages of case separation. Taking all the taper out of a 22 Hornet case increases the powder capacity of the old case. The sharp 30-degree shoulder angle shortens the neck somewhat, but there is still plenty of neck length for bullet seating.

As for the two new 19 caliber wildcats, one is called the **19-223** (a conventional 223 case necked down to 19 caliber). During fire-forming, neck angle is pushed out from 23 degrees on the factory

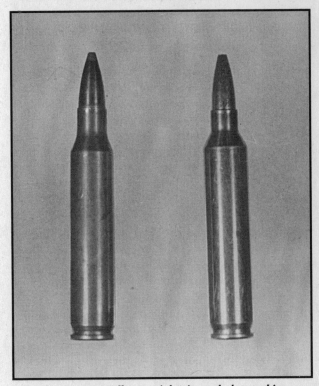

*The 19-223 Calhoon (right) is made by necking down a Remington .223 (left).*

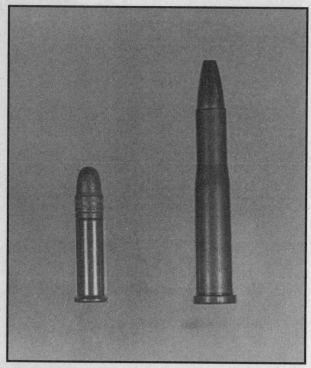

*During the 1920s, the .22 Long Rifle cartridge was popular among varmint hunters. When the 22 Hornet (right) made its debut, the .22LR (left) was quickly abandoned.*

case to a sharper 30 degrees. The case should then be trimmed to an overall length of 1.760 inches, which is the factory case length. The other wildcat is the **19 Calhoon** (see also above).

How did this caliber boring reach fruition? Its inventor, James Calhoon (Havre, Montana 59501) provides this explanation: "In the early 1970s, when the NATO countries were holding field trials for a superior infantry round, of all the calibers that were tested to the 400 meter range—including the 14, 17, 19, 20, 22 and 30— the winning entry was the *4.85mm Experimental.* It lost out to the 223 only because the military preferred a compact, jointed cleaning rod."

Calhoon concludes that the 19 caliber offers high sectional densities, ballistic coefficients comparable to 22 calibers, and velocities similar to the 220 Swift (19-223 only), but with low recoil and longer barrel life. Foremost is the rifling, which is thicker than the 17 caliber and the 20 caliber (5mm Remington Magnum rimfire). Thicker rifling (similar to 224 and 6mm caliber rifling) results in less cleaning and longer barrel life.

The standard question goes like this: "How do I go about getting a custom James Calhoon 19 caliber rifle?" The answer: Simply by ordering a Calhoon Re-Barrel Kit in the desired chambering. The kit consists of a match grade barrel (either stainless or chrome moly) that has been contoured and chambered (threading to be handled by a local gunsmith); two 19 caliber Dewey cleaning brushes; a set of Forster/Bonanza "BR" forming/loading dies; 100 custom 19 caliber Calhoon bullets, gunsmith instructions and loading data.

Calhoon says the 19-223 Re-Barrel kit will fit any 3/8-inch bolt face action, such as the 17 Rem-ington, 221, 222, 223 and 222 Magnum. The 19 Calhoon can be attached to any 22 Hornet action, with the possible exception of the old 23D Savage Hornet with its one-piece barrel and action. The 19 Calhoon can also be rebarreled on some rimfire actions, including the 591 Remington chambered originally for the Remington 5mm Mag-num (20 caliber) rimfire. A Remington 580 rimfire action can be rebarreled with the 19 Calhoon. But how can this be when both actions are designed for rimfire cartridges, while the 22 Hornet is a centerfire cartridge?

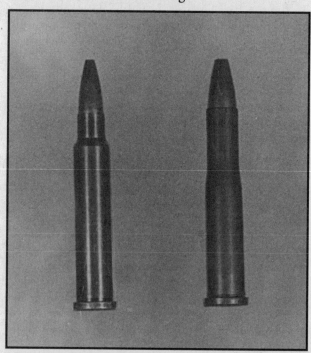

*The 19 Calhoon (left), a necked down Hornet, is shown with its parent case. This new entry offers a much greater muzzle velocity than the .22 Hornet.*

*Writer Don Lewis (right) poses with Jim Peightal, who handled the machine work on the 19 Calhoon held by Lewis.*

There's always someone who can build a better mousetrap and, in this case, it's Dennis Olson (Plains, Montana), who can convert these two Remington rimfire bolts to centerfires. Both the 580 and 591 bolts have six locking lugs with which to guarantee a tight lockup. Thanks to Olson's superb workmanship, the 591 Remington bolt he converted for my 19 Calhoon works flawlessly. Not all rimfire bolts can be converted to centerfire, however (contact Dennis Olson or James Calhoon with regard to other rimfire bolts and actions). Since a 22 rimfire detachable magazine won't accept a Hornet case, the rifle is converted to a single shot.

Whereas the 19 Calhoon in the 591 Remington action is a sleek single shot, I also wanted to build a repeating 19 Calhoon. I began by calling CZ USA about its 22 Hornet 527 BRNO repeating action. They answered by shipping an action complete with magazine and scope rings to the well-known custom rifle builder, Jim Peightal (Ernest, PA). Jim proceeded to thread a 19 caliber

stainless steel Calhoon barrel in the 527 BRNO action. The husky CZ 527 Hornet BRNO action incorporates an adjustable trigger. "The machine work on the bolt and action was super," Peightal comments, "and the two-stage trigger adjusted easily." A clean, crisp trigger is a prime requisite for accuracy, a truism that should be carved in granite.

As for sighting, a 4x14Xx40 Springfield Tactical Rifle scope, complete with integral leveling bubble and the company's Patented Rangefinding reticle, was mounted. This lightweight varmint-hunting scope, with Rangefinding out to 700 meters, is designed primarily for the Government 5.56 (223) cartridge. The Rangefinding reticle offers hands-free automatic bullet drop compensation for Match 223 ammo to 700 meters. If this all sounds confusing, a Rangefinding table will show exactly how to use the exclusive Springfield Mil Dot with the Rangefinding table. Basically, it's a military setup for the 5.56 (223) match cartridge. Knowing the velocity of the bullet in question will work with other calibers. Another afterthought: That bubble

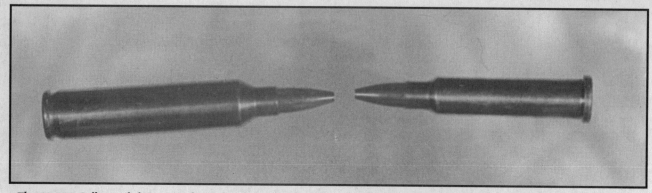

*The 19-223 Calhoon (left) was made on the .223 case, while the 19 Calhoon was built by necking down the .22 Hornet case.*

certainly helps square the reticle when shooting from the offhand position.

As a firm believer in fiberglass thumbhole stocks on varmint rifles, I went to Lone Wolf Adventure Gear (125 N. Hilltop Rd., Columbia Falls, Montana 59912) in search of the stock configuration I wanted, but the 527 BRNO action was not listed in their specification sheet. Lone Wolf didn't have a "drop-in" stock for the 527 action, but they agreed to modify a thumbhole target-type stock that would fit. They even suggested that I send the barreled action to them for the stock fitting, which was quite generous of them considering the amount of work it would take to modify a stock that fit the small 527 BRNO action. It's worth noting that the CZUSA 527 Hornet rifle's stock could have been used by machining the 19 Calhoon heavy barrel to a smaller diameter. The stock chosen for my rifle was a sporting style thumbholer, called the Howler. It was constructed using Lone Wolf's special epoxy and fiberglass/carbon fiber technology. My action was bedded using Lone Wolf's master class bedding system. The epoxy-textured coat is the company's new light granite color. It is temperature neutral and a natural camo.

Where will the two 19 caliber Calhoon wildcats fit in the varmint hunting picture? Are they simply two more possibilities that will fade from the scene, or does either one offer varmint hunters a definite advantage? Predicting the future of a cartridge is risky business. The tide of public opinion is not easy to read. The truth about both 19 wildcats may not be known for several years, but several promising signs indicate growing interest among varmint shooters. Admittedly, the 19-223 Calhoon must fight an uphill battle to win

converts away from such proven cartridges as the 220 Swift and the 22-250 Remington. But note that with 32 grain 19 caliber bullets the 19-223 will produce muzzle velocities slightly over 4000 fps. With a 36 grain Calhoon 19 caliber bullet the fps hits 3840, while the 40 grain bullet is slightly more than 3600 fps. Jim Peightal's 40 grain velocity tests produced an average instrumental velocity of 3575 fps at 15 feet. Without getting involved in higher mathematics, it's safe to say true muzzle velocity is about 3600 fps. According to Jim, some primer cratering could be a sign of excessive pressure. With several other powder weights, though, he averaged just under 3500 fps with no signs of pressure.

Accuracy was acceptable with all Calhoon Dbl HP bullet weights grouping around 5/8-inch at 100 yards. In other words, the 19-223 has the potential for 300-yard varmint-shooting accuracy under ideal weather conditions (Calhoon also offers a 44-grain Dbl HP 19 caliber bullet, but there is no data on it as yet). With the availability of 223 brass and the simplicity involved in making a 19-223 case, this wildcat could appeal to a variety of varmint hunters—especially those with a touch of wildcatting in their blood.

Although I began my centerfire varmint-hunting career with the old Hornet, I've never been a true admirer. In fact, I've been writing the requiem for the 22 Hornet for more than 25 years, but it still hangs on. There may be a change coming, though. The 19 Calhoon may bring new life to the old, near-moribund 22 Hornet case. Every time it seems the Hornet is fading away, some manufacturer revives it as a new chambering. Hornet fans will be displeased with my assessment of their favorite, but ballistics are ballistics. The

22 Hornet was a vast improvement over the 22 Long Rifle cartridge and was welcomed with open arms—but that was back in the mid-1930s.

The advent of the high speed Remington 222 with its inherent accuracy was almost a death blow for the 22 Hornet. Once group shooting became the accepted method for testing a rifle's accuracy, it became apparent that the 22 Hornet lacked accuracy to a considerable degree. Of the dozens that crossed my benchrest during a lifetime of shooting, it was a rare Hornet that could place five shots in less than one inch at 100 yards. I once received an expensive 22 Hornet imported from a manufacturer with a note tied to the trigger guard informing me not to expect superior accuracy results. "Our range tests produced 1.5-inch 10-shot groups at 100 yards with this rifle," the note claimed.

Considering the 22 Hornet shell is not a long range varmint stopper, that disclaimer isn't as bad as it looks. Since the effective accuracy range of the Hornet is under 200 yards, 1.5-inch 100-yard accuracy is sufficient. Bear in mind, too, that the 22 Hornet factory round offered a muzzle velocity around 2700 fps with a 40 grain bullet. And now that Hornady is offering a 35 grain V-Max bullet, muzzle velocities should fall in the 3000 fps range.

As stated earlier, the 19 Calhoon is a 22 Hornet case necked down to 19 caliber and fire-formed to a straight wall case with a 30-degree shoulder angle. This really opens up the Hornet case with its long, tapering 5-degree shoulder angle. Although the extra powder gain is less than 1.5-grains, it represents a distinct advantage for the lighter 19 caliber bullet. According to James Calhoon's ballistic sheet, a maximum charge of 14.5 grains of AA2200 powder from Accurate Arms pushes a 40 grain bullet from the muzzle at 3060 fps. According to Accurate Arms' Loading Guide #1, a maximum load of 14 grains of AA1680 shoves a 40 grain 22 Hornet bullet out of the muzzle at 2785 fps. The 19 Calhoon wildcat is capable of hitting around 3340 fps with a load of 13.5 grains of AA1680 behind a 27 grain bullet. A max load of 14.7 grains of the same powder sends that 27 grain bullet from the muzzle at over 3600 fps. With those velocities, along with 5/8-inch 3-shot group 100-yard accuracy, there's little doubt that the 19 Calhoon offers a significant edge over the 22 Hornet. I believe it will add an additional

100 yards to the effective accuracy range of the 22 Hornet.

It's one thing to suggest going wildcat, but there's also the question of cost. How expensive is it to rebarrel an action to a 19 caliber Calhoon? We've mentioned earlier in this article the Re-Barrel 19 Calhoon kits, plus a need for the services of a local gunsmith in threading the chambered barrel to the action. The Chrome Moly kit costs about $320 and the stainless steel kit is another $366. Gunsmith charges for threading, headspacing and fitting the barreled action in the stock should be a little over $100. For a quick comparison, a match grade stainless steel barrel blank can run well over $200, with chambering and threading adding another $200. If it's a wildcat, case swaging dies can easily exceed $100, with reloading dies costing at least $75. To make a 30-416 Rigby from the 416 Rigby case requires ten dies, which can run up to $400, with loading dies costing another $200 or so.

No one knows what the future holds for either 19 caliber wildcat. Both cartridges have much to offer varmint hunters. The 19-223 wildcat faces some serious competition from such well-established varmint rounds as the 222, 223, 22-250 and 220 Swift. Not only is the case easy to make, but 223 brass is plentiful and inexpensive. Indeed, the 19-223 is close to being a combination of all 224 varmint rounds.

*A custom 19/223 Calhoon is built on a Remington 700 short action and a "Six Hunter/Benchrest fiberglass stock. The scope is a 4x16X Schmidt & Bender. (Helen Lewis photo)*

Dedicated 22 Hornet fans should give the 19 Calhoon some serious attention. They will still have their favorite case, plus top accuracy and a broader range. When weather conditions improve, the 527 BRNO 19 Calhoon outfit will undergo some heavy workouts, including some springtime woodchuck shooting. In fact, It may get a chance to show its stuff in the prairie dog country of South Dakota. SB

**DON LEWIS** *is a retired corporate credit manager who now tests and evaluates firearms shooting gear and reloading equipment. A regular contributor to* **Shooter's Bible**, *Lewis writes on various aspects of ballistics for several publications. He has been the gun writer for the* **Pennsylvania Game News** *for 35 years and has during the past 26 years contributed a weekly outdoor column for the* **Leader Times** *newspaper. He is a contributing editor to the* **Varmint Hunter** *magazine and ballistics writer for* **The Mountain Journal**. *Don also contributes on occasion to* **Precision Shooting** *and* **Fur-Fish-Game**.

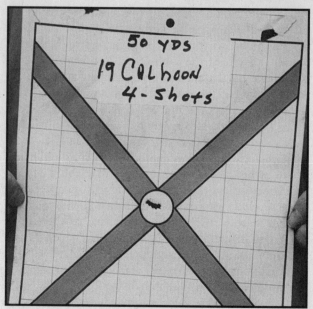

A four-shot, one-hole group at 50 yards is displayed on a specially designed Precise Aim target (from Terry Miller of Beneze, PA).

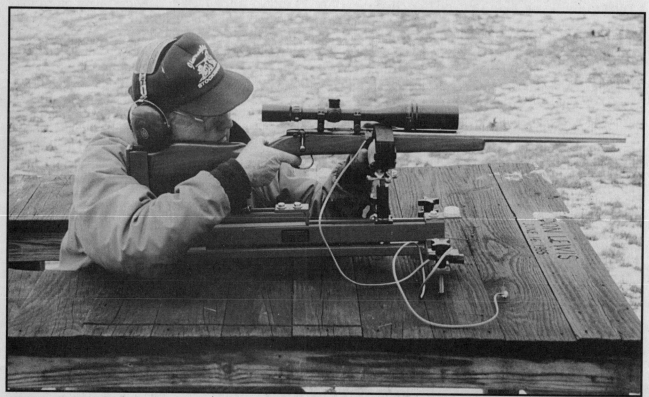

*The author fires a 591 Remington rebarreled for the 19 Calhoon. The scope is a 4x16X Sightron. The wire attached to the rifle is for use with a Model 43 Oshler (Personal Ballistic Laboratory). The rest is a Model 4 National Match Rifle Support. (Helen Lewis photo)*

# Cartridges With Character: The Good, The Bad And The Ugly

## By Wilf E. Pyle

Cartridges, like movie stars, live strange yet interesting lives. They appear and disappear, almost ghost-like, onto the cartridge boards of collectors and shooters, much to our endless fascination. Some cartridge groups have come, gone, returned and gone away again. Like actors, many cartridges are good performers, some are bad, and a few become ugly. All cartridges must strut their stuff before the most critical audience in the world—the hunters and target shooters of North America.

## THE HIGH VELOCITIES

The .22 calibers are not immune to the vagaries of changing markets, fickle shooters and bad luck. The **.225 Winchester** is a good example of a cartridge that went up, then down, and turned ugly in the process. This round came out in 1964 in a redesigned Model 70 bolt action rifle. The shooting public's response to the new rifle is now remembered as a lesson in bad marketing. Everyone hated the way the rifle was finished and designed, the way it felt in the hand and how it looked. In short, the cartridge never stood a chance. Gun writers were quite vocal about it, claiming that the free floating stock on the Model 70 "looked like a canoe route."

The cartridge fared no better. The .225, a derivative of the .30-30 necked down to .22 caliber, was meant to compete with the .22-250—velocity for velocity, bullet weight for bullet weight. Some, including this writer, loved the cartridge, while others feared the pressure signs being developed in tests. Early factory rounds performed well, but some test runs manufactured later indicated vastly inconsistent pressure performance. Cartridge pressure was subsequently reduced by Winchester so that today the .22-250 actually outperforms the .225. The .225 cartridge failed because of a poorly designed rifle and an equally weak cartridge. In both cases, inadequate quality control on the factory floor sent this combo to an early grave, never to haunt or fascinate shooters again.

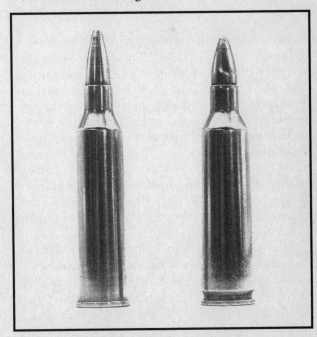

*The .225 Winchester (left) was designed to compete head-to-head with the .22-250 (right). Over time the .225 lost out and is now considered obsolete.*

*For many hunters, the pleasure lies in getting out into the field and using an old-style cartridge.
That's why one cartridge often succeeds over another.*

Remington is not immune to the failed cartridge syndrome. The **.222 Remington** began life in 1952 with the Remington 722 bolt action rifle. The round gained great popularity and earned a reputation as the single most accurate cartridge ever invented. It single-handedly rekindled interest in small caliber, high velocity cartridges capable of great accuracy. The 50 grain bullet traveled 3140 fps with ease, producing half-inch and smaller groups among shooters with even mildly competent skills. The .222 Remington dominated benchrest shooting for years and gained popularity as a 250-yard varmint cartridge.

How could it possibly fail? Some say it didn't really fail, noting that the cartridge experienced a mild resurgence in the early 1970s, with dozens of rifles chambered for the round. These were hardly signs of failure. Others argue that the .222 Remington served its purpose well, and that newer, faster cartridges emerged to replace the early version. There is substance to this argument. The .223 Remington, which became an accepted

military round, resulted from the experimentation and redesign of the .222 Remington. That model may be dying, but hundreds of high quality bolt rifles are still around that need this cartridge. Remington also made the 760 slide action repeater for this cartridge, as did Savage in its long-running over and under Model 24-V. Sako still offers its sweet little Model 75 Hunter in this caliber.

The **.222 Remington Magnum** needs mention as well. It began life as an experimental cartridge designed jointly by the Springfield Arsenal and Remington for military use. Originally, it was made for automatic lightweight rifles and was the inspiration for the .223 Remington. It was introduced in 1958 for the Model 722 and Model 700 bolt action rifles. Sako, for many years, provided an impressive Model 75 in this caliber. It's a fine cartridge, suitable for ranges out to 125 yards on small game like prairie dogs and gophers, or for close-in work of 125 yards or so on larger predators. The cartridge is now overshadowed by the .223 Remington in sales and availability. As an evolutionary improvement in high velocity .22 centerfire cartridges, however, the .222 Remington Magnum's powder capacity is 21 percent greater than the .222 Remington. Its powder capacity is also four percent greater than the .223 Remington. This edge gives it the power needed to produce a fine, long-range number that has maintained sales for more than 25 years. Many older shooters remember the .222 Remington Magnum as one of the easiest magnums to handload. And yet, there is no commercially available rifle chambered for the round in today's market.

The disappearance of the .222 Remington Magnum was not profound. It was simply replaced by a more common military round. Moreover, the kind of varmint shooting represented by the high velocity .22s was disappearing just as those rounds were reaching their pinnacles of success. With less land on which to shoot, especially in the eastern United States, the reduction in the number of varmints to shoot meant there were no longer any reasons to use these cartridges. Many a hunter's closet now contains at least one .22 high velocity that sees little action come springtime.

Just as the .222 Remington made the transition from target to field cartridge, so the **6PPC** has passed through the same evolution from the target range outward to what's left of the gopher fields and ground hog pastures of rural America. Commercial 6PPC cartridges have been available since early 1990, with the only commercial source being Sako-Valmet. This round is loaded with a European-type extruded powder pushing a Sierra hollow point boat-tail bullet weighting 70 grains at around 3200 fps (reloaders can extract even more velocity). The hollow point affords rapid expansion on small game while the boat tail provides an extra measure of long range stability and wind-bucking ability for shooting across open fields and down long draws.

The 6PPC is doubtless held back now by a lack of commercial ammunition and a paucity of commercial rifles chambered for the round. While custom rifles abound in this round, few make it to the field as sporting rifles. For a few years, Sako offered its very sleek, lightweight Sako A1 built on the time-proven Vixen L461 action. This model seems to have slipped away, but the Sako Model

*The 6PPC is a good example of a cartridge that did well on the target ranges but has not yet made the transition to the shooting fields. It offers tremendous small game potential once it matures and makes its move to the field.*

75 Varmint rifle prevails, as does the same model in a stainless steel synthetic version. The jury remains out on this cartridge, however, as a full-fledged sporting round. Ballistically, its performance capability is clearly superior, but the choice of a firearm is holding back further progress. The 6PPC round will prosper as a target number for years ahead, but its movement into the field appears to have slowed.

## DECLINING QUARTER INCHERS

Quarter-inch calibers once did well because they offered the high velocity needed for flat trajectories and improved long range accuracy with hunting weight bullets. Two cartridges have risen to fame in this class, only to falter before making a brief stumbling return to center stage. The first of these is the .250-3000, which has passed through three phases of popularity and then declined. Invented by Charles Newton, it was offered by

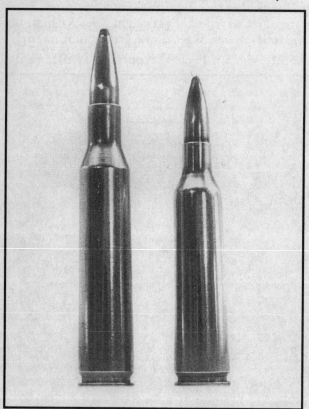

*The .257 Roberts (left), once thought to be the most efficient cartridge of its day, is shown with the .250 Savage (right).*

Savage in what was considered the first cartridge useful for both deer and varmints. The cartridge gained an excellent reputation early on as a hunting round when teamed with the Savage Model 99 rifle. In 1953, it regained popularity when the velocity of the 87-grain bullet was increased slightly to 3030 fps (from 3000 fps) and given a new name: .250 Savage. Savage dropped the Model 99 in .250 Savage but brought the cartridge back in 1971 by popular demand. The Model 99 was also made available for several years in a small carbine with straight grip and plain stock. Currently, the cartridge does not enjoy the popularity it had in the late 1970s, when more .250 Savage rifle models were on the market than at any time previous. The cartridge refuses to die, but it also has difficulty in becoming highly successful. Its 100 grain loading offers mild recoil and less report than more robust big game cartridges, and it remains of small passing interest among youth and women shooters. Yielding 2820 fps at the muzzle, the quarter-incher produces about eight foot pounds of recoil compared to 25 for a standard .30-06 carbine of the same rifle weight. When sighted to three inches high at 100 yards, it can easily take deer out to 300 yards. These features have kept the .250-300 alive in the face of tremendous competition.

The **.257 Roberts** evolved from the lengthy experimentation and testing of various .25 caliber cartridges carried on by several noted gun enthusiasts and firearm writers. While working together, inventors Townsend Whelen and Ned Roberts concluded that the 7 by 57 case necked down to .25 caliber was the most efficient and accurate route to follow. They took their design to Adolph Niedner, the noted riflemaker, and the .257 Roberts was born. The case length of the commercial version, which became available in 1934, is slightly longer (to the point where the abrupt shoulder angle begins) than the experimental cartridge. Loaded originally in bullet weights of 87, 100 and 117 grains, the .257 Roberts covered most of America's shooting needs, becoming known as a dual purpose cartridge.

The round received mixed attention from gun writers, however, and the .257 Roberts did not take off. Few rifles were chambered for it, possibly because the worldwide economic depression was destroying the U.S. manufacturing base. The popular gun writer, Jack O'Connor, did report on the cartridge, though, recommending a load with 39 grains of IMR4064 with a 100 grain bullet, but few other writers bothered to mention the round in their articles. With that, bullet availability for the .257 Roberts slowly declined. The 87 grain was dropped in the 1960s and the 100 grain version followed a few years later. This pattern of cartridge decline is typical, with the varmint weight going first, followed by the intermediate weight, with the heavy bullet hanging on to the end. Today, more rifles are probably chambered for the .257 Roberts than in 1934, whereas only a few commercial cartridge selections are available. Federal offers a Plus P (plus powder) 120 grain loading, while Remington loads the 117 grain soft point and Winchester offers the Plus P in a 118 soft point.

*The Model 100 Winchester never enjoyed the popularity it once promised. Teamed with the .284 Winchester cartridge, there remain no plausible reasons why this combination failed in the marketplace.*

## THE SINGLE SEVEN:

How could a cartridge like the .284 **Winchester** fail in the marketplace? When Winchester introduced this odd-shaped, sharp-shouldered cartridge in 1963, it featured a powder capacity like the .30-06 and a bullet diameter equaling that of the fabled 7 by 57 Mauser. Its design doubtless remains unique among U.S. cartridges, with its rebated rim (a term coined expressly for the .284). The result was a short-necked, fat-bodied and sharp-shouldered number producing muzzle velocities of 3200 fps with 120 grain bullets for varmints, or 2900 fps with 150 grain bullets designed for big game hunting.

Sadly, the .284 Winchester was a good cartridge that arrived before its time. The first rifles offered with this cartridge were Winchester's Model 88 lever action and the Model 100 autoloader. The former became more popular after going out of production than it was when first introduced (records indicate that a total of 284,971 were manufactured). Most hunters were aghast that Winchester would dare to modify the traditional lever action by eliminating the external hammer. And so, despite Winchester's efforts to promote its rifle via television and print advertising programs, the Model 88 failed in the marketplace. The company even enlisted big game "celebrities" to hawk their rifles.

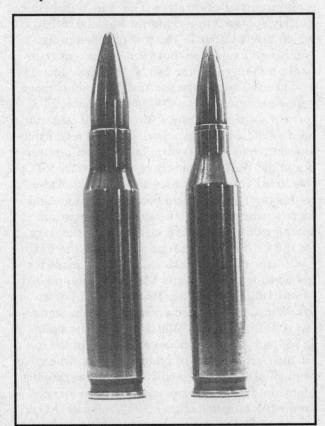

*The .308 (left) and .243 Winchester (right) have become established cartridges, well-received by shooters and hunters.*

Both the Model 88 and Model 100 rifles fired .308 and .243 cartridges, which by the 1970s had become firmly established as top performers appealing to a wide range of shooters. The Model 100 autoloader did not succeed because hunters and shooters saw no need for a powerful autoloader with low clip capacity for big game hunting. Thus it was never very popular, even though 263,170 units were produced up until 1975. As with the Model 88 lever version, the Model 100 is sought out far more seriously today than it ever was during the time (15 years in all) it was available to American shooters. Despite Winchester's efforts, the .284 Winchester cartridge fell off the stage and never returned.

## THE BUSH POPPERS

No single category of cartridges has more variants and hopeful possibilities than those described as *the bush cartridge*, which is a powerful, short range cartridge developed for short, easy-to-handle rifles. Surely, these dynamic cartridges will be an instant hit with hunters. Interestingly, this category includes cartridges that should have been more popular than they actually achieved. Many

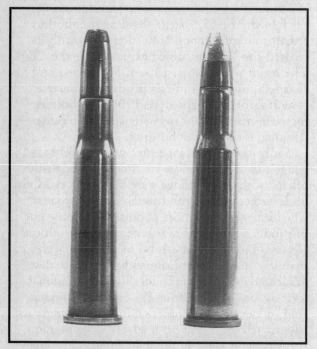

*The .33 Winchester (left) in the old Model 1886 gave rise to the more modern Model 71 in .348 Winchester (right).*

are in the ranks of those that are still hanging on by an economic thread. None have reached star status and have so far been left behind in a wake of possibilities that never translated into realities.

One good example of this type is the .356 Winchester, which ranks among the least understood cartridges of the modern era. It first came to market in 1982 as a vehicle for the Winchester Model '94 Angle eject rifle. Many gun buffs will recall the howls of laughter that greeted Winchester (U.S. Repeating Arms) in its efforts to bolster sagging sales of the lever action rifle. The flat-sided saddle gun that greeted the opening of the new century was by this time in the midst of a collapsing market. In an attempt to bolster sales, the Model '94 was given a new look that included thicker sides and a receiver cut to allow for right-hand ejection and permit rearward mounting of a scope. The design gave rise to an entire series of semi-proprietary cartridges. The .356 Winchester quickly appeared in the Marlin Model 336-ER, which needed little in the way of redesigning. Neither rifle sold well, however, and recent trade books no longer list the Model '94 Angle Eject.

The .356 Winchester cartridge is a short range performer that moves a 200 grain bullet at 2460 fps. For those few hunters who can still claim to need a saddle rifle, this cartridge was a reasonable alternative to the .30-30. Until Browning produced the BLR in a variety of calibers, the .356 was about as powerful a lever as was ever made. In this case, the rifle held back the cartridge and together they died. Again, it was competition among rifle styles and models that set the stage for this cartridge to become a failure in the 1980s.

Perhaps the most beautiful rifle ever made for the hunting fields was the Model '71, an updated Model 1886 Winchester. Toward the end of its life, Winchester correctly noticed that the smokeless version of the .33 Winchester (in the aging 1886) had gained immense popularity in the forest and bush country of North America, where big game hunting at intermediate ranges was thriving. Many outdoor magazines commented positively on the performance of the .33 Winchester on elk, moose and white-tailed deer. At the time, deer populations were rising and small moose and elk populations seemed to be stabilizing. The time was ripe for a rifle that combined power, beauty and utility in one package. And yet it took

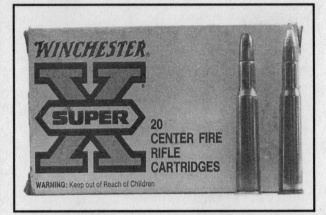

*An old box of .348s along with the 180 grain Remington and 200 grain Winchester cartridges. The lighter load was quickly discontinued, but supplies of the heavier bullet weight can still be found.*

Winchester ten years to finally bring about the transformation of the old 1886 into a modern piece of art. The action was slick and the stock was ample and meticulously finished. The polishing and bluing were excellent, too. It was the kind of rifle that defined quality for years to come, giving rise to the true meaning of the words "rifle nostalgia."

In 1936 the **.348 Winchester** was greeted with much fanfare following its introduction in the Model 71. The cartridge was available in 150, 200 and 250 grain bullets and proved a good performer, offering up to 2890 fps with the lighter bullet. Even the great Jack O'Connor, who had by this time firmly established himself as a .270 fan (and at times a .30-06 advocate), passed favorable comment on the Model 71. Right up until O'Connor's last rifle article, the .348 was the only large bore rifle cartridge to receive his accolades. Other writers, most notably Elmer Keith, commented that the caliber should be larger, leading to some experimental work, opening the .348 up to .450 and naming the wildcat ".450 Alaskan."

What went wrong with this cartridge? Again, the answer was poor timing. The rifle sold reasonably well (47,000 sold between 1935 and 1958), but by 1962 Winchester had discontinued the useful 150 grain and heavy 250 grain bullets. It relied instead on current stocks of 200 grain cartridges with which to supply shooters right up until the 1970s. In the ten years it took for Winchester to move on the design, development

and implementation of the Model 71 and the new .348, things had changed. Scopes were growing in popularity, whereas the Model 71 still wore open (or peep) sights. The powerful Model 71 could not take a scope and Winchester never really dealt fully with this issue until the 1950s with the Models 88 and 100, and again in the 1980s with the angle eject. In some respects, this failure was the beginning of the end for the mighty Winchester rifle firm that had dominated rifle design, cartridge production and outdoor marketing for decades. Shortly after the collapse of the Model 71, Winchester began reorganizing, a process that still has not entirely ended.

The .38-55 was—and remains for some shooters —a highly accurate hunting round. It began life as a target cartridge in the various single-shot Ballards and Winchesters that were so inexplicably popular during the last years of the 19th century. The round, having made the transition from target range to hunting field, became a familiar chambering for various rifles, including the Marlin 1893s, the Savage Model '99 lever rifles, and the Colt Lightning pump. This availability of rifles contributed greatly to the immense popularity of the Model '94 Winchester. The flat-nosed bullet produced excellent kills on deer and moose, and for that reason the cartridge received considerable use across the country by farmers, ranchers, backwoods types and hunters.

As a result, the .38-55 held on well into the 1970s, when cartridge supplies began to dry up.

*The Model 71 Winchester, often considered the ultimate in design and finish, failed in the marketplace, probably because it was too expensive.*

Until then, every backcountry store and outdoorsman had a lifetime supply of .38-55 loads squirreled away for a rainy day. Meanwhile, they continued to use their rifles for practical day-to-day shooting. Some of the wealthier sportsmen noticed, however, that their guides and back-country pals were still using the .38-55 for hunting, a discovery that created an almost cult-like following for the aging .38-55 cartridge. This interest culminated in 1979 when Winchester unveiled its .375 Winchester.

The development of similar digestive systems among different species is considered an example of parallel evolution. This term can also be used appropriately to describe the evolution of the **.375 Winchester**. Without realizing it, Winchester designers were committing a kind of parallel evolution in cartridge design when they evolved a cartridge that copied the ballistics and look of the old .38-55. The .375 was more than a mere copy-cat cartridge, however. It truly was a more modern version of the .38-55, featuring a .375 caliber bullet that weighed 200 or 250 grains. It traveled a nominal 2200 fps in the 200 grain version and

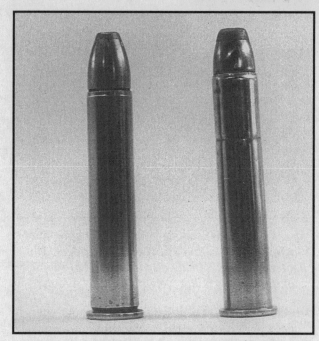

*The .375 Winchester (left) is paired with its older brother, the .38-55 Winchester (right). Who can tell them apart?*

*To be successful, the Model 94 Big Bore in .375 Winchester needed an offset scope mount. Hunters didn't like the idea.*

1900 with the 250 grain bullet. The Model '94 was allegedly strengthened by making the walls of its action thicker in order to handle the increased pressure. The new rifle was given a bright, deep blue finish, and its stock and forend were checkered. The rifle was given a new name too—"Big Bore"—based on the cartridge. The name seemed to suggest that dropping a cartridge on one's foot might break a toe. Despite the look of this rifle, Winchester had to contend with the negative press caused by decades of sloppy Model '94 actions. While safe and efficient, the actions emitted a tinny sound whenever the lever jacked a fresh round into the chamber. The newer Model '94 actions were perceived by shooters as poorly assembled compared to grandpa's older ones.

The Model '94 Big Bore was a legitimate and valiant attempt by Winchester to recapture the old spirit of the Model '94 while creating a modern bush cartridge in the process. This failed for the same reason the regular Model '94 was in decline: its scope had to be mounted in an offset fashion. Also, cartridge supplies were sporadic, with some parts of North America—especially the more remote backwater areas where deer, moose and elk are shot at short range—never having seen these cartridges. The .38-55, meanwhile, refused to die. It remains suitable for short to intermediate range work, but no amount of goodwill can put it back on center stage.

For whatever reason, gaining a degree of popularity is difficult for any caliber larger than .30. There's a kind of bias against large diameter bullets, whereas high velocity .22s, flat shooting .243s and intense shooting .25s continue to dominate. Such is the story of the **.358 Winchester**. No better rifles were ever designed for this round than the Model 88 Winchester lever. Highly accurate and capable of making quick follow-up shots, it seemed the ideal short action, high-powered cartridge/rifle combination had finally arrived. The .358 is described as the best commercial .35 caliber cartridge developed by any U.S. manufacturer. It offered velocity and bullet improvements over the ancient .35 Remington, was slightly more powerful than the old .35 Winchester, and offered far better choices than the .348. With factory loads of 200 and 250 grain producing 2530 and 2250 fps, respectively, the

rifle was more than enough for any game North America had to offer.

The question remains: why did this excellent cartridge fail as a big game round? Rifle selection was, after all, excellent. The Model 88 has been mentioned, and Winchester also marketed its Model 70 bolt action in a special lightweight model for this caliber. Savage offered its Model '99 lever in the early 1960s and continued for several years, but only the Browning BLR is now available with this cartridge. Most pundits can't explain why the .358 never fully developed, but it hangs on. Some rifle researchers claim the Model 88 was advertised as being available in the .358, but none was actually produced. Others claim that American hunters are biased against round or flat-nosed bullets, mostly because these bullet styles shed velocity more rapidly than spire or pointed types, making it difficult to achieve proper range. Part of the problem lies in the fact that, by the mid-1960s, so many cartridges were

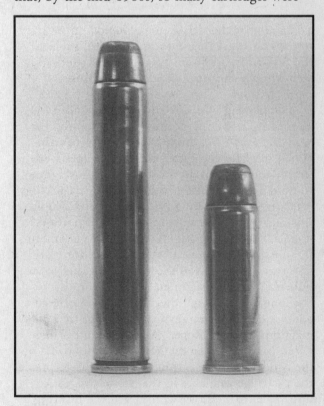

*The .444 Marlin (left) is slowly falling into obsolescence compared to the .44 Magnum (right), which continues to hold its own.*

*Older and less popular cartridges are fun for shooting and hunting in certain situations. Some favorites include (left to right): .222 Remington Magnum, .225 Winchester, 6PPC, .243 Winchester, .284 Winchester, and .32-20.*

available that shooters were confused and reverted to the cartridges their fathers had used, such as the 30-06. In addition, no outdoor writers or well-known shooters were championing the .358 cartridge.

The passing of a rifle cartridge isn't always a bad thing, however. Consider, for example, the case of the .44 **Magnum** and the .444 **Marlin**. When used for big game, these cartridges were simply too weak to do the job. The .44 Magnum showed great promise as a cartridge that could be interchanged between a pistol and a rifle. While this may have been an advantage back in 1860, nobody was paying attention a century later. Still, the possibilities seemed bright indeed for pistol shooters, reloaders and those who cast their own bullets. The enthusiasm and expectations didn't last long, even though the .44 Magnum offered a good selection of top quality rifles. The first .44 magnum rifle was Ruger's Model 44 autoloader. Later, Marlin offered the Model 336, followed by the Model 788 bolt action. And Winchester made the cartridge available in the Model '94 which, until recent times, was considered the hunting rifle against which all others compared (and is still available in several configurations with the .44 magnum). Marlin offered its fine Marlin 336, a

nice carbine-type rifle that found favor among eastern hunters. But all these positives were lost when hunters realized that the .44 Magnum cartridge barely traveled at 1800 fps. That translated into bad trajectories, even at intermediate ranges. Thus, the various rifle models were best used as short range plinkers.

The same observations apply to the .444 Marlin. At first, the cartridge held out some promise, offering more than the traditional .38-55. It also performed better than the .44 Magnum. The Marlin 336 is a fine rifle for short range work, but the performance of the .444 Marlin on big game proved unreliable. In addition, hunting moose and elk at short range became a thing of the past. The ranges at which these big game animals are taken today grow greater each year, with hunters shooting across valleys, along streams and down cutlines.

It really doesn't matter what has happened to the various cartridges, or why some failed as others became more popular. Each cartridge can still be used with a specific rifle or under unique hunting or shooting conditions. Part of the fun lies in finding other cartridges and experimenting with them. For example, the .222 Remington Magnum has long been a favorite of mine, as has the .225 Winchester. The 6PPC has displayed excellent accuracy at distant gophers and promises to become a real working cartridge. Under windy conditions, the .243 can ensure that those pesky field varmints won't be eating the hay crop anymore. The .32-20 is fun, too, especially when larger game is the target. And finally, as summer turns to fall and the deer season opens each year, the .284 Winchester in a Model 100 Winchester carbine will continue to bring home the venison. [SB]

WILF E. PYLE *is an avid outdoorsman who has hunted nearly every species of North American big and small game. He is a well-known authority in the U.S. and Canada on sporting firearms and a frequent contributor to* Shooter's Bible. *He has authored three books on the outdoors, including* **Hunting Predators for Hides and Profits** *and* **Small Game and Varmint Hunting**, *both published by Stoeger Publishing Co. Wilf often writes about cartridges, cartridge history and cartridge performance as well as reloading. He remains fascinated as well by sporting rifles—and wishes he owned more of them.*

# The SIG P210:
# A True Classic Pistol

### By Gene Gangarosa, Jr.

Unquestionably, one of the finest automatic pistols ever placed into mass production is SIG's Model P210 with its superior design features and unsurpassed workmanship. Now celebrating its 50th anniversary, SIG continues to make this amazing gun, one that still outperforms all other automatic pistols in accuracy, reliability and longevity. The P210 put Switzerland's *Schweizerische Industrie Gesellschaft* (Swiss Industrial Company, or SIG) on the map as a preeminent automatic pistol manufacturer. While SIG has since introduced other superb handgun designs, this model remains the classic.

The Browning High Power pistol (right) and the Polish VIS-35 Radom (left) both had a cam located beneath their barrels for unlocking the breech—a significant improvement over the swinging link used in Browning's earlier masterpiece, the Colt Model 1911. SIG took this idea and improved on it by making the fixed cam an enclosed piece completely surrounding the slide stop's shaft.

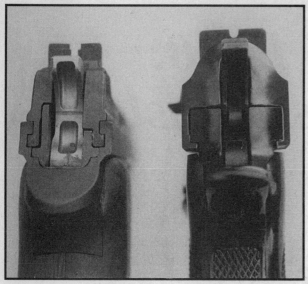

*The P210's low-slung slide (left) compares favorably with the bulkier slide typical of other automatic pistols, such as the Walther P38 (right).*

For all its well-earned reputation, however, the P210's beginnings were modest. Switzerland's search for a new service pistol began in earnest in 1937, when it issued several variants of the Parabellum (Luger) pistol chambered for the 7.65mm (.30 Luger) cartridge. Prior to that, the most recent Luger variant adopted—the Model 06/29—had introduced several cost-cutting measures and was still in production. By the mid-1930s, though, the Swiss had decided the Luger cost too much to manufacture and began their search for a replacement, a process that took more than a decade to bear fruit. As it turned out, the long wait was well worth it.

Meanwhile, in neighboring France, a new service pistol appeared: the Mle 1935A. Credited to a Swiss-born engineer, Charles Petter, this pistol was adopted in 1935 and went into production at the *Société Alsacienne de Construction Mecanique* (SACM) in Cholet, France. By June of 1940, some 9,500 Mle 1935A pistols had been made for the French armed forces. Germany kept the gun in production until 1944, with an estimated total of 23,850 reaching their forces by that year. Following SACM's liberation from Nazi control, the French resumed Mle 1935A production for their own armed forces, keeping it in production until 1950. This model featured Browning's popular

short recoil system combined with a slim, elegant shape and a packaged lockwork mechanism that was removable as a complete unit. This pistol's only real shortcoming was its relatively low-powered .30 caliber cartridge.

SIG purchased the patent rights to this gun in 1937 and spent the war years refining its design. The company also examined several foreign handguns for design improvements and comparative trials. With World War II in full swing by 1939, the Swiss had no problems obtaining various handguns for study. Those models known to have been examined from 1940 to 1944 included Spain's Astra 900, the Walther PP and HP/P38 from Germany, Poland's VIS-35 Radom pistol, the FN Model GP (High Power) and America's Colt M1911A1.

The Swiss also studied the ammunition question closely. By the 1930s the 7.65mm Parabellum (.30 Luger) cartridge, while standard Swiss issue since 1900, had fallen from favor. Always in the shadow of the 9mm Parabellum round, the 7.65mm's chief shortcoming was a bullet that overpenetrated without inflicting significant damage. Because of this lack of "stopping power," the 7.65mm/.30 cartridge had already been rejected in trials in Britain, Germany, the U.S. and elsewhere. By World War II, Switzerland was the only country that still issued handguns chambered for this cartridge to its armed forces. In light of events

*The current P210-6 imported by SIG features a fixed rear sight, matte blue finish, checkered hardwood and a vertically serrated front gripstrap.*

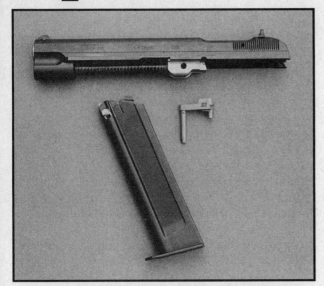

*The P210 .22 Long Rifle cartridge conversion kit features a special slide, barrel, recoil spring and slide stop for converting a P210 in a centerfire caliber to low-cost, low-recoil operation.*

occurring elsewhere, the Swiss decided to experiment with the 9mm Parabellum, which had gained increasing favor throughout the world as an efficient pistol and submachine-gun cartridge. In 1933, Switzerland's factory in Bern converted two of its Model 06/29 Luger pistols for use with the 9mm Parabellum cartridge. Testing with this cartridge confirmed the pistol as a superior choice than the 7.65mm.

By 1944 SIG had developed two advanced pre-production prototypes: the 8-shot SP 44/8 and the 16-shot SP 44/16. The former resembled a Mle 1935A enlarged to fire the 9mm Parabellum cartridge. In contrast, the SP 44/16 broke new ground, most notably by reversing the usual relationship of slide to frame. In most automatic pistols, the slide sits atop and surrounds the frame's upper portion. In this configuration, the slide is by necessity a large, bulky component. But in the SP 44/16 the slide was appreciably slimmer because it lies inside the frame. This relationship of slide to frame also provides the slide with an unusually long bearing surface, thus increasing both accuracy and longevity. Thanks to its low-slung, narrow slide, SIG had to build up the area around the rear sight, allowing more space for shooters to grasp the slide and draw it back for

loading and cocking the pistol. This raised rear portion of the slide remains one of the P210's most recognizable features.

Competition for these SIG entries came mostly from *Waffenfabrik Bern's Ordonnanzpistole 43 W+F*. Based closely on the Belgian-made High Power model developed by Browning and manufactured by FN, the Bern pistol's 40 prototypes appeared in both standard- and high-capacity models. The Swiss military test of 1944 failed to pick a clear winner, although the SP 44/16 won praise for its design features. This favorable reception encouraged SIG to redesign the SP 44/8 so as to include more of the SP 44/16's mechanical features. Once the redesign was completed, the only difference between the two guns was their magazine capacity and the size of the grip. In 1947 SIG announced that its 8-shot SP 47/8 and 16-shot SP 47/16 were ready for further testing and possible military adoption.

Military testing, which began in 1947, pitted the SIG entries in competition with an interesting gas-locked design made at the state weapons factory in Bern. This pistol, known as the *Pistole 47 W+F*, drew on wartime German research by locking the breech with gas pressure until the bullet left the barrel. At that point, the gas escaped from the barrel and an expansion chamber beneath the barrel, allowing the slide to recoil and reload the gun in the usual manner. Both Heckler & Koch

*The P210, when converted to a .22 Long Rifle operation, offers a slightly different silhouette than the standard centerfire model. All controls, however, are located in the same place for easy training.*

in Germany and Steyr GmbH in Austria later borrowed applications of this principle in their P7 and GB models.

In all, Waffenfabrik Bern made a dozen or so prototypes of this pistol. The Swiss government, however, eventually decided on SIG's Browning-system entry, whereupon Bern ceased handgun manufacture. It made its last Model 1929-type Luger in 1947. Interestingly, the Swiss also tested a prototype of a Czech-made pistol later adopted as the vz. 52. This pistol fired a Mauser-derived 7.62mm cartridge with greater energy than the Soviet service round by means of an interesting roller mechanism that restrained its breech from opening prematurely. Though it received high praise for its performance and design features from the Swiss trials commission, the Czech prototype arrived too late. The government had already settled on the latest 8-round SIG entry.

At this juncture in 1948, Sweden entered the picture. Its armed forces were considering both the SP 47/8 and the SP 47/16 for possible adoption. While both pistols earned high marks for their ruggedness, reliability and accuracy, the Swedes found the large grip of the SP 47/16 an encumbrance, opting instead for the handier 8-shot SP 47/8. The Swiss military had arrived at the same conclusion, adopting the SP 47/8 in 1949 as the Model 49 Swiss service pistol. It remained Switzerland's standard service pistol until 1975, at which time the Swiss armed forces continued the tradition by adopting SIG's Model P220, which it called the Model 75. Between 1949 and 1975 SIG produced almost 200,000 Model 49 pistols for the Swiss military.

The Swedes never came through with an official order, but Denmark did. Surplus P210s from the Danish army and police have come into the U.S. in considerable numbers in recent years,

*Note how the SIG P210's unlocking cam (beneath the barrel) encompasses the slide stop shaft. This feature allows more precise function than either the swinging link of an M1911 or the open cam arrangement on the Browning High Power.*

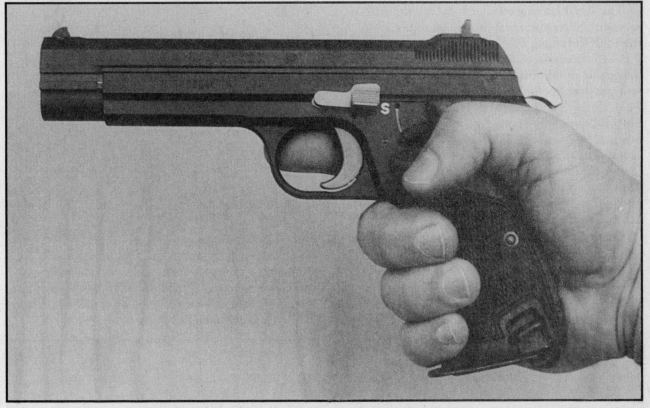

*The P210 sits low in the hand and points naturally. Balance is near perfect and recoil is mild.*

offering would-be P210 owners a less expensive entry into what has become an elite club. With military adoption came an increased interest in garnering commercial sales. In 1957 SIG offered several variants to reach the widest possible audience. For example, the P210-1 has fixed sights, a high-polish blued finish, and wooden grips, either ribbed or checkered. The P210-2 has fixed sights, a matte military blue finish and standard plastic grips (checkered wood grips are, however, an option). SIG never used a P210-3 designation; but there was a Model P210-4, built exclusively for West Germany's border police. It included fixed sights, a matte blue finish and checkered plastic or wooden grips. The P210-5 still has an extended barrel, adjustable rear sight, matte blue finish and special target grips that extend below the metal portion of the grip frame. The P210-6 has a standard-length barrel and, in the beginning, included an adjustable rear sight (but now has a fixed rear sight). The rear sights on current models, incidentally, feature a large square notch that

represents a great improvement over the old-fashioned, U-shaped rear sight notch found on older fixed-sight P210s. The finish on the P210-6 is matte blue, and its grips are made of checkered hardwood. The front gripstrap is serrated vertically for an improved grip. The P210-7 refers to those P210s that have been chambered for the .22 Long Rifle cartridge. It's usually sold as a conversion kit (see below) that originates from an existing centerfire P210, supplying substitute parts rather than creating a complete pistol.

To make the P210 salable to shooters in countries that ban 9mm Parabellum handguns, SIG made its pistol convertible to 7.65mm Parabellum (.30 Luger) simply by substituting the barrel and recoil spring. SIG also developed a .22 Long Rifle conversion kit for the P210, one that contains a special slide, barrel, recoil spring, magazine and slide stop. A small number of P210s feature a lightweight aluminum-alloy receiver for military use, but the vast majority of these pistols feature all-steel construction.

The P210 set new standards for handgun accuracy, durability and reliability. Even today, more than 50 years later, few handguns approach the P210 in these categories. Despite its tipping-barrel design, it outshoots models with fixed and straight-line recoiling barrels. Credit for the P210's superb accuracy lies in its excellent trigger pull and close tolerances. And yet, with all its built-in precision, the P210 is ideally designed for arduous duty, shrugging off the ingress of sand, dirt or mud. As a case in point, SIG P210s have been known to fire well over 100,000 rounds. Few guns of any type, particularly 9mm service pistols, can match that sort of durability.

Despite being designed at a time when military and police forces used only ball ammunition, the P210 feeds modern hollowpoint cartridges with equanimity, thanks in large part to its high standards of fit and finish. And while the P210 is by no means a lightweight pocket model, its slim

*The P210's design eliminates the troublesome muzzle bushing found in John Browning's early automatic pistol designs, notably the Colt Model 1911. Note also the slide rail's long bearing surface.*

*A disassembled P210 displays still another desirable feature: the modular lockwork mechanism.*

profile and smoothness make for comfortable carry. Its relationship of slide to frame (introduced with the experimental 16-shot 1944 model) allows the pistol to sit low in the hand. This "low bore axis" reduces muzzle rise and offers practical accuracy in offhand shooting, even in combat, which is far greater than what shooters experience with lesser pistols.

During its refinement of the short-recoil locked breech designed by Browning, the P210 introduced an enclosed cam located beneath the barrel. Compared to the M1911's swinging link—or even Browning's Model 1935 High Power pistol with its open cam—the SIG's enclosed barrel cam reduced the amount of play noticeably. This enabled the barrel to return to battery in virtually the exact same place from shot to shot. The P210's improved lockup system, while undoubtedly more costly and difficult to manufacture, also contributed greatly to the pistol's accuracy and longevity. Its trigger pull, which is extraordinarily crisp and smooth, further enhances the P210's accuracy.

Other SIG improvements over Browning-inspired designs are its recoil spring and guide

*The P210's bottom-mounted magazine release is less appealing to American shooters than it should be; mostly because it slows down reloading as opposed to a push-button release on the left side of the frame behind the triggerguard. In its favor, the P210's magazine release is ambidextrous and not likely to activate by accident (an especially important consideration for guns equipped with magazine disconnect safeties).*

rod, which act as a connected assembly, hence they cannot work loose from each other. In addition, the P210's lockwork is assembled into a module that combines the sear, hammer, mainspring and disconnector. This module can be removed, if desired, by separating the slide from the frame, decocking the hammer (if cocked), grasping the hammer and pulling straight up. In the latest P210s, a retaining screw must first be removed before the lockwork module can be taken from the frame.

Another improvement in the P210 over the classic Browning designs, such as the Model 1911, concerns the manual safety. When applied in a Browning version, it locks the slide and prevents the reloading process—unless, of course, the manual safety is in the fire position. The possibility of a premature or inadvertent discharge represents a clear safety hazard. In the P210, by contrast, the manual safety merely blocks the sear and has no effect on the movement of the slide. That means a shooter may load the firing chamber of a P210

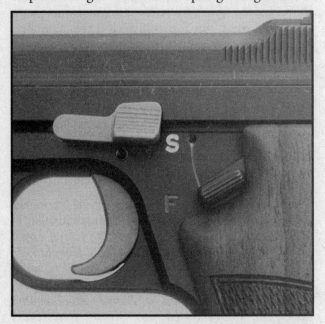

*The manual safety on a P210 is pushed down to fire and up to "safe." When in its safe setting, the slide is free to move, enabling the shooter to load the pistol with the safety on.*

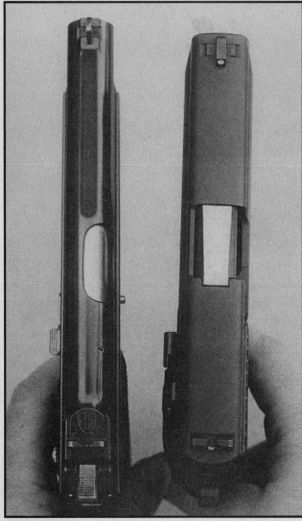

*Thanks to its innovative slide-to-receiver relationship, the left-handed P210 (left) offers a noticeably slimmer slide profile than SIG's later double-action P220 series (right).*

tion. The manual safety's stiffness is legendary, as is the degree of difficulty necessary for right-handed shooters with small hands to reach it. This pistol also features a magazine disconnect safety. Once the magazine is removed from the grip, the firing mechanism is deactivated. Some shooters like magazine safeties while other do not. Shooters with large hands find the protective tang at the rear of the grip undersized, and their hands are often pinched by a recoiling hammer or slide. The low profile of the slide itself can make it difficult for some to grasp for loading and cocking. Being a single-action design, the hammer on the P210 must be cocked before it can fire. From a safety standpoint, once the pistol is cocked there's no safe way to decock the hammer over a loaded firing chamber. Given the pistol's legendary light trigger pull, it would be foolish even to try.

Finally, the cost of a P210 has always been a daunting factor and remains so to this day. It's possible, in fact, to buy three or four excellent service pistols for the price of a single P210. Still, with all its minor weaknesses, the SIG pistol is worth every penny, its excellent features more than compensating for the few shortcomings mentioned above. Indeed, the P210 remains important not only in its own right, but for its historical role as well. Having itself been influenced by earlier designs, the SIG pistol has gone on to inspire later designs. For example, the excellent Czech CZ-75 has copied the P210's slide-to-frame arrangement, while its many copies may look to the P210 as their grandfather, as it were. For those who seek an exceptional automatic pistol, one that can be counted on to perform every mission an automatic pistol is called upon to do, this is the gun for you. [SB]

with the safety still on. The position of the manual safety on a P210 also allows left-handed shooters to attain fire position with the trigger finger; i.e., the index finger of the left hand. With a standard Model 1911 or early Browning High Power pistol equipped with a one-side manual safety, operating the manual safety with the left hand is impossible.

For all its design and manufacturing excellence, the P210 has its shortcomings as well. The magazine release, because of its stiffness and location on the bottom rear portion of the frame, makes reloading a sometimes exasperatingly slow opera-

**GENE GANGAROSA, JR.**, *a teacher and technical writer by trade, has contributed several articles to* **Shooter's Bible**. *His lifelong interest in firearms began during his four-year enlistment in the U.S. Navy (1977-1981). Since 1988 Gene has written several hundred articles for magazines, including* **Combat Handguns, Gun World, Guns, Guns & Ammo** *and* **Petersen's Handguns**. *Gangarosa has also written several books (all published by Stoeger Publishing Co.) on such diverse subjects as the P38, Beretta firearms, compact handguns, service handguns, FN/Browning, Walther handguns, classic rifles and modern rifles.*

# The Modern Scope: It's Come A Long Way

## By Thomas C. Tabor

**M**ost shooters today recognize the inherent advantages provided by telescopic sights. Even those hunters who restrict their shooting to close range are usually better off leaving the iron sights behind and switching to a good scope. Even a scope with low power can offer distinct advantages for almost all shooters. In poor or marginal light situations, a scope enables a shooter to see the target better, while the magnification, even if slight, can often result in placing shots with greater accuracy. The advantages afforded by a scope are not restricted to rifle shooters only, however. In many cases, pistol shooters—and to a somewhat lesser degree shotgun shooters—have discovered they too can benefit by divorcing themselves from the traditional iron sights.

Germany had been making rifle scopes for decades, but not until in the 1930s did America become deeply involved in the business of telescopic scope manufacturing. During that decade, Bill Weaver (founder of Weaver Scopes) and Fred Leupold (of Leupold & Stevens) walked down similar paths that eventually established these companies as world renowned leaders in scope development and production. Many shooters like Bill Weaver felt the German-made sights were far too heavy and cost two to three times that of a good rifle. Moreover, these early German scopes often required complicated mounting systems that made them difficult to install on American-designed rifles. About the same time, Weaver entered the scope manufacturing business with the goal in mind of making rifle scopes strictly for American shooters. And so, as the depression raged, he introduced his compact, 3-power Model 3-30 (later to become known as the Model 330). From there on, the market snowballed.

At about the same time, Fred Leupold's son, Marcus, went hunting one day and missed a perfectly easy shot at a deer. In his disgust, Marcus vowed that he would one day produce a more reliable and superior hunting scope. And that is exactly what he did. Soon a friend enticed him into producing a second prototype for him, and then another. . . and still another. Soon these new Leupold scopes were in big demand and full production had begun in earnest.

*Rifle scopes come in a wide range of sizes, powers and objective diameters. Understanding how the term "exit-pupil" applies to a scope's light gathering ability can help performance in the field.*

A tour of Leupold & Stevens manufacturing plant (located in Beaverton, Oregon) affords a unique insight into the complex workings of a manufacturer engaged in the production of quality telescopic sights. Unlike most companies, Leupold & Stevens' manufacturing approach does not include production by the usual assembly-line method. Each scope is assembled by a single individual sitting at his or her work station. Each scope therefore takes shape as a result of a single employee's abilities and expertise. The company believes that by producing their scopes in this manner it encourages workers to take extra pride in their work, hence better overall quality in its products. This method may take more time and expense, but Leupold & Stevens feels strongly that it results in products of top quality. Every employee must exhibit a complete and thorough understanding of the products they build. First comes the assembly of each eye piece, the windage and elevation adjustments, the lens, and even the microscopic reticles (about one-third the diameter of an average human hair). These tiny wires must first be flattened in order to produce the wider portions of Leupold's "duplex"-style reticles, first developed by Leupold & Stevens over 30 years ago.

Quality control at Leupold & Stevens is assured by inspectors who constantly roam the production area. Parts and fully completed products are pulled from the various lines routinely for testing and intense evaluation. Once the scope assembly has been completed, oxygen is extracted from the inside of the housing and replaced by a pure form of nitrogen (99.999 percent pure, to be exact). The use of nitrogen provides an essentially "bone-dry" atmosphere inside the scope in order

*At Leupold & Stevens all scopes are subjected to the vacuum water test, which simulates the worst possible hunting conditions, whether 10,000 feet above sea level, 50 degrees C. temperature or 100% humidity. All scopes must pass this test.*

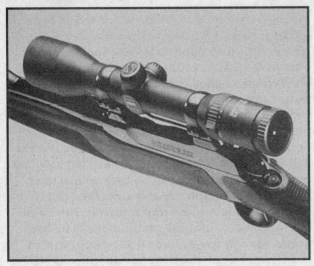

*The Diavari ZM/Z 1.5-6x42 MC variable scope is among the most versatile in the Zeiss line.*

to prevent internal fogging when exposed to wet or humid hunting conditions. Once the oxygen has been replaced, each scope is tested for integrity by submersion in a transparent tank containing water heated to 50 degrees centergrade (122 degrees F.). The lid is then locked down tight and 12 inches of vacuum are pulled on the tank, much like canning beans in a pressure cooker. This warm bath is designed to simulate the worst possible hunting environments, including 10,000 feet above sea level, a temperature of 122 degrees and 100 percent humidity. The goal is to break through the internal seals and cause the scope to leak and fail. All leaks are indicated by a small trail of bubbles trickling to the surface. Once that occurs, the scope is immediately rejected.

Another interesting test of quality and endurance comes by way of a homemade piece of equipment. It's a device made of steel plating and automobile springs simulating the most physical abuse imaginable—a kind of torture chamber designed in-house by company engineers. In this process, a sampling of each scope model is periodically pulled from the production lines—usually four at a time—mounted directly on the steel plating and cinched down tight using normal scope bases and rings. Then the abuse begins. Hydraulics raise the scopes and slam them down. This process is repeated several thousand times, generating a G-force in excess of that produced by

a 375 Holland & Holland Magnum rifle. It stands to reason that recoil—or the inside of a bouncing pickup truck, for that matter—represent more conducive and pleasant environments than Leupold & Stevens' testing equipment. After thousands of drops and jarrings, the scopes are removed and taken to a 100-yard range, where they are mounted onto rifles and test-fired to ensure the integrity of each scope.

Today's scope makers offer an endless array of models and options from which to choose, a luxury which can sometimes become overwhelming. For example, most scope lines come in a wide variety of finishes, including the traditional shiny black, the newer non-glare black matte finish (which appears to be glass-bead blasted), brushed stainless (to match the trendy stainless-colored rifles and pistols), and even a camo pattern. Color and finish may not appear to be a hard choice to make, but other options definitely fall in that category, chief among them the matter of cost. We all want to mount up the best scopes available, but for most of us reality strikes home once we check the hefty price tags accompanying top-of-the-line models. Fortunately, there's a nice selection of scopes available, some guaranteed to fit any family budget and still provide trouble-free performance for many years to come. [For more information about prices check the specifications section

*For the budget-minded sportsmen who wants quality and high performance, the Diavari C 3-9x36 MC makes a strong candidate.*

SIGHTS & SCOPES in this book.] When buying any new scope, be sure to ask about the company's warranty. Most manufacturers will replace or repair defective scopes for a minimal charge (or, in some cases, free of charge).

The decision to buy a fixed power scope or a variable powered unit is obviously an important one. Certainly the quality and dependability of variable-powered units have come a long way in recent decades. Not long ago, variable powered scopes often failed to return to the same point of impact whenever magnification was changed. Now, of course, these problems have been resolved and the versatile variable powered units made totally reliable. On the other hand, there's a cost factor to deal with. When comparing a variable powered model with a fixed powered unit, both made by the same manufacturer, the former is usually priced significantly higher.

The next step is to decide which reticle pattern is best for you. Over the years, a number of new reticle styles have appeared, while some of the old ones have all but vanished from the marketplace. For example, Leupold & Stevens' duplex model features a tapering reticle with a flattened, broader wire construction around the outside and extremely fine crosshairs near the center. Similar styles have been adopted by other companies under different names. For example, one might be called a *4-Plex* or a *Truplex*, depending upon the manufacturer. The crosshair element size also varies from company to company, and sometime a manufacturer will offer a choice within its product line. The basic duplex design has become quite popular with hunters in recent years, surpassing the old-style crosshair. The theory behind the duplex style is its ability to center the target within the scope's view. The heavier element pattern around the perimeter

*Leupold & Stevens tests its scopes on the factory's 100-yard rifle range, which is equipped with a comfortable bench, chronograph and a place to reload.*

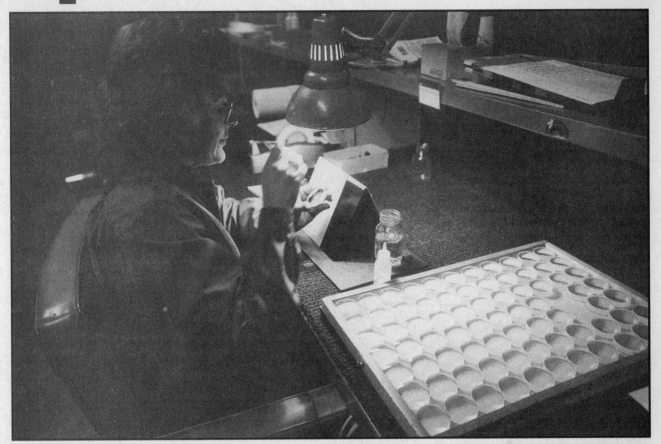

*Hand-inspection plays a big role in the Leupold & Stevens production process. The inspector here is testing a lens to ensure its quality is maintained.*

is also easier to see in poor or marginal light. Bausch & Lomb has carried this basic concept a bit further with a reticle system called the *command post*. It allows shooters the option of changing from a fine crosshair pattern to a heavier, more pronounced pattern simply by turning a selection ring. While not available on all models, the command post is standard with Bausch & Lomb's Elite 3000 3-9x50 scopes.

In 1996, Simmons announced its new reticle, called the *Smart Reticle* or *V-TAC* (for *Varmint* and *Tactical*). This pattern has the ability to calculate target range. A small diamond located at the center of this reticle covers a one-inch area. Marks found on the perimeter of this diamond allow shooters to estimate the distance to the target. The V-TAC was added to the Weaver line in 1999 and is available on a few select models produced by both Simmons and Weaver.

The red dot scopes of the past suffered from inherent problems that severely restricted their usefulness. Often, the dot was so large it obscured much of the target area, making precise shooting difficult at longer ranges or when firing at small targets. The red dots were generally useful only at 70 yards or less, and adverse lighting conditions also presented significant problems. Zeiss has developed a new, improved red dot scope, called the *Varipoint*. Its design includes a dot that shrinks in size as magnification increases. Zeiss has also improved the scope's visibility, particularly when used under adverse conditions.

Another problem shooters have struggled with in the past is *fogging*. Years ago, scope engineers apparently solved the dilemma of internal fogging with an innovative technique: *evacuating the oxygen from inside the scope and replacing it with nitrogen*. Still, the problem of external fogging continued to

# SIMMONS PRODUCT LINE

WTC12 Whitetail Classic

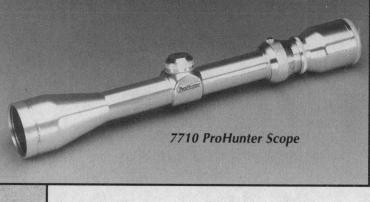

7710 ProHunter Scope

3-9x32mm Rimfire Scope

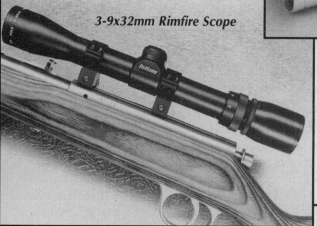

7700 ProHunter Riflescope

1022T Rimfire Target Scope

# WEAVER PRODUCT LINE

*RF 2.5x7 Matte*

*V9/50 and V10/50*

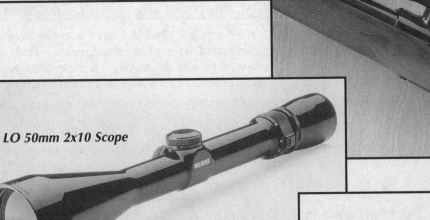

*LO 50mm 2x10 Scope*

*T24 Scope*

*7700 ProHunter Riflescope*

**PHOTOS SUPPLIED BY BLOUNT SPORTING EQUIPMENT DIVISION**

plague shooters. It arose whenever a scope was subjected to fast, severe temperature changes, or when it was exposed to rain, fog or snow. After four years spent looking for an answer to this dilemma, Bausch & Lomb's research and development team came up with a lens-coating system—called the *Rain Guard*—which appears to have solved the problem. This new lens-coating process encourages moisture to form small droplets, leaving the shooter's view clear and unobstructed.

Larger may be better in many cases, but not always when it comes to scopes. A trend has developed over the past few years wherein the objective and ocular lens have grown in size almost to the point of absurdity. As a result, we have lens measuring 50mm, 56mm and, at times, even larger ones. But are they really that much better, or even as good as, the smaller versions. While they may look impressive, they may actually

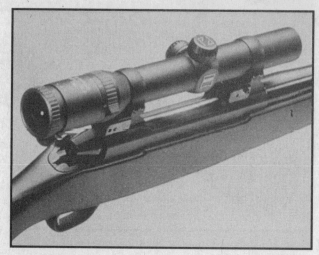

**The Varipoint VM/V 1.1-4x24 made by Zeiss has eliminated many of the problems associated with illuminated red dot sights. It features a 35 percent greater field of view and 30 percent lower weight.**

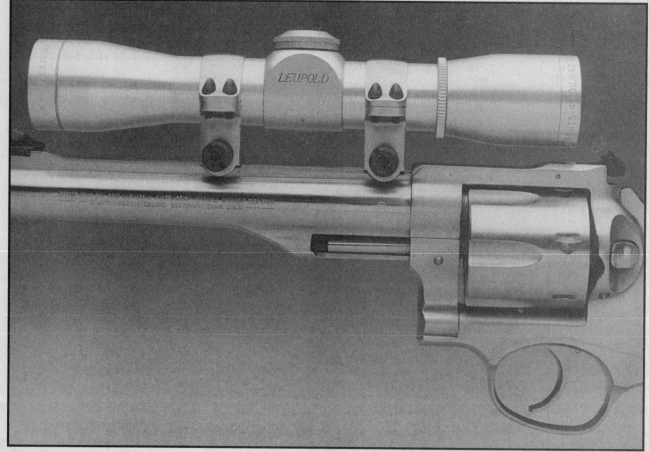

*This 4x pistol scope with silver finish was designed to complement the new stainless hand-guns.*

lack the light gathering ability of a smaller, less impressive-looking scope. After all, its light gathering ability is a main reason why one buys and uses a scope in the first place.

When judging a scope for its performance in low or poor lighting situations, shooters must be knowledgeable about the term *exit-pupil* and how it pertains to the light gathering process (this doesn't pertain to the new generation of night-vision scopes, used by the military for night combat missions or for civilian use). Although many shooters may not be familiar with exit-pupil, it is now common knowledge among those in the optic business that it's a critical element when evaluating a given scope's performance when

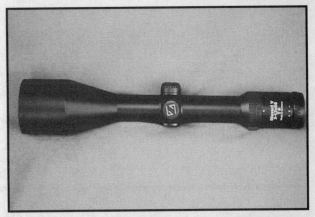

*For all-around hunting purposes, it's difficult to beat the Diavari ZM/Z 2.5-10x48 MC made by Zeiss.*

*Even in brushy, dense forest terrain, telescopic sights offer a real advantage when mounted on any rifle. A scope's light-gathering ability provides a distinct advantage by providing a degree of safety through better identification of the target.*

## BUSHNELL'S PRODUCT LINE

PHOTOS SUPPLIED BY BLOUNT SPORTING
EQUIPMENT DIVISION AND BUSHNELL/
BAUSCH & LOMB

## A SAMPLING OF THE BAUSCH & LOMB PRODUCT LINE

PHOTOS SUPPLIED BY BLOUNT SPORTING EQUIPMENT DIVISION AND BUSHNELL/BAUSCH & LOMB

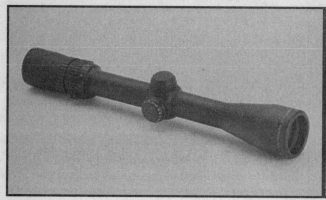

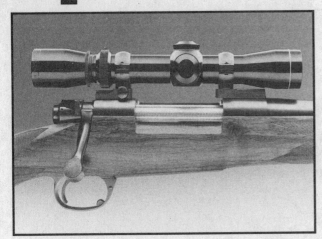

*Leupold & Stevens' line of compact, variable-powered scopes includes a 2x7 compact that is about the same size as a 4x fixed power model.*

dealing with marginal light. By way of explanation, the optimum exit-pupil value for the human eye is 5mm. The closer a scope approaches this value, the better it will perform in poor or marginal light. To determine the exit-pupil value of a scope, it's necessary to know the objective diameter of the scope lens. This information should be available from the manufacturer, dealer, or from brochures and pamphlets that come with each new scope [see also the SCOPES & SIGHTS listings in the specifications section of this book]. Once a scope's objective diameter has been determined, it should be divided (in millimeters) by the magnification. The equation looks like this:

**(Objective Diameter in millimeters) divided by (Magnification) = Exit Pupil**

The closer the exit-pupil value comes to the magic value of 5mm, the better you'll be able to see in poor light conditions. For fixed power scopes, a one-time calculation is all that's needed to check on a scope's effectiveness in poor or low light situations. For variable powered scopes, run the same math using the various power settings. They will indicate which settings are best for early morning or late evening shooting, or at any other times when light is poor.

For example, using the above formula to determine the best setting for optimum visibility for a 3-9x variable scope with an objective lens diameter of 40mm, note the following:

**(Object. Dia. = 40mm) divided by (9 power) = 4.4 exit pupil**

**(Object. Dia. = 40mm) divided by (8 power) = 5.0 exit pupil**

**(Object. Dia. = 40mm) divided by (4 power) = 10.0 exit pupil**

In this case, **8x** is the ultimate setting for this particular scope. When the objectives diameter is increased to 50mm, while maintaining the same power, we find that it doesn't perform as well in poor light as the 40mm scope:

**(Object. Dia. = 50mm) divided by (9 power) = 5.56 exit pupil**

**(Object. Dia. = 50mm) divided by (8 power) = 6.25 exit pupil**

**(Object. Dia. = 50mm) divided by (4 power) = 12.5 exit pupil**

According to this formula, the best option when available light is at a premium is to keep the 50mm scope adjusted to 9 power, even though the exit-pupil value is above 5.0.

Taking another example of a large scope with good magnification, the results are somewhat surprising. Using the example of a 6x20 variable with an objective lens of 50mm, the math below tells the story. Note how, when the scope is adjusted to the higher magnification, performance diminishes

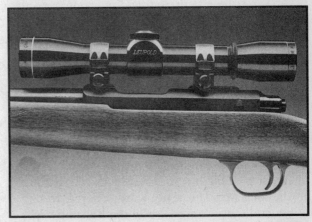

*Leupold's compact 4x is produced with the .22 rifle shooter in mind. The scope is adjusted for parallax-free at 75 yards (most other scopes use 150 yards).*

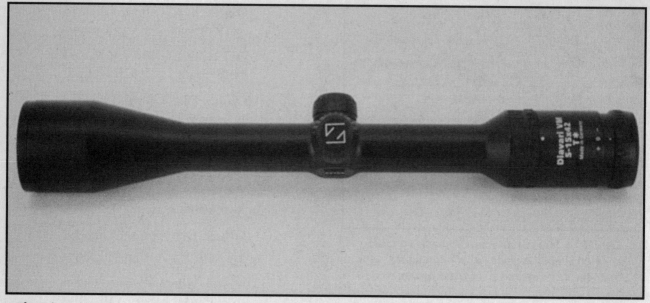

*The Diavari VM/V 5-15x42 rifle scope was developed by Zeiss in response to hunters' requests for a premium performance scope in the higher power range.*

significantly. At full power (20) the scope's exit-pupil rating is only half its optimum value (5.0).

$$\text{(Object. Dia.} = 50mm) \text{ divided by}$$
$$(20 \text{ power}) = 2.5 \text{ exit pupil}$$

$$\text{(Object. Dia.} = 50mm) \text{ divided by}$$
$$(10 \text{ power}) = 5.0 \text{ exit pupil}$$

$$\text{(Object. Dia.} = 50mm) \text{ divided by}$$
$$(6 \text{ power}) = 8.3 \text{ exit pupil}$$

A scope's light gathering ability is not the only factor to consider when making a telescopic sight. Once a shooter understands how to judge, mathematically, how a scope will perform in poor light, it will have a significant bearing on which scope one decides to buy. For those who opt in favor of a variable powered scope, determining the exit-pupil value at the various power settings can definitely enhance one's proficiency in the field. But be forewarned: there are a lot of cheap scopes out there as well as some extremely expensive ones. The cheapest possible buy may not be the "best" buy in the long run. Is it really worth the risk to buy a low-end scope, only to spoil the hunting trip of a lifetime?

No matter how careful you are, a scope takes a lot of abuse. Indeed, it's surprising that any scope can hold up when subjected to the hunting scene. Prospective scope buyers are well-advised to pay heed to the old adage: "You get what you pay for." No one should expect a $40 scope to equal the performance and durability of a top-of-the-line model costing several hundred dollars. But certainly that $40 scope may work out fine for a shooter intent only on plinking. But if your goal is to find a scope for a heavily used—and sometimes abused—big game hunting rifle, one that's often the cause of some shoulder-bruising recoil, it's probably wise to dip deeper into your wallet. The trick is to find a scope model and manufacturer who can also promise *dependability* for a price you can live with. [SB]

**THOMAS C. TABOR** *is a retired air pollution control officer and a major contributor to several publications here and abroad. He lives and works in rurl Western Montana where he can oftern observe deer and elk from his office window. In addition to his frequent appearances in* **Shooter's Bible,** *Tom's articles have been published in* **Handloader's Digest, Varmint Hunter** *and* **Safari.** *Overseas, his work is often found in publications produced by The Sporting Shooter's Association in Australia. He is presently on staff at* **RV Life,** *a Seattle-based magazine, as a widlife columnist.*

# CUSTOM GUNMAKERS

This new section of Shooter's Bible will feature custom guns from the most prestigious of the world's small shops. Mass production of interchangeable parts and the factory manufacture of small arms didn't come about until the 19th century. Until then, all guns were essentially unique unto themselves, though basic mechanisms and styles were shared among many makers. The custom gun survives because connoisseurs of firearms want something better than can be had from factory assembly lines, and they're willing to pay for the hand labor.

In its true sense, "custom" means built to order, with the customer dictating the gun's features and dimensions. There are practical limits to custom orders, of course. Few shops will offer an action to the buyer's specifications. They are constrained by the costs of designing and building actions (as well as by patents and the fact that most of the best actions are already in production) to use what is already available from major arms suppliers. To say that a rifle is not really a custom rifle because it employs a Remington 700 action is being too severe.

# ROGER BIESEN

## RIFLEMAKER

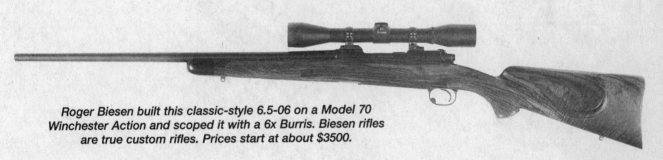

*Roger Biesen built this classic-style 6.5-06 on a Model 70 Winchester Action and scoped it with a 6x Burris. Biesen rifles are true custom rifles. Prices start at about $3500.*

Of all the names in riflemaking, Biesen is among the best known. Al Biesen, a Wisconsin native who moved to Spokane Washington in the 1940s, established his reputation by building rifles for Outdoor Life Shooting Editor, the late Jack O'Connor. Considered the dean of gun writers during the postwar decades that produced a boom in big game hunting, O'Connor was taken not only with Biesen's workmanship, but the lines and feel and function of his rifles. While other able gunmakers have crafted rifles in what has become known as the "classic" style, Al Biesen is among few who can claim to have defined it.

Now Al's son, Roger is carrying on the Biesen tradition. He has been building guns fulltime for more than a decade, in the same Spokane shop used by his father. Roger's guns show the same attention to detail, the same graceful sweep of line that characterizes earlier Biesen rifles. They have the same "gunny" feel, deliver the same fine accuracy. Roger accommodates customer preferences in just about every detail but also offers suggestions. Al is there for a third opinion too, with gunbuilding experience that predates World War II. Like his father, Roger does both the wood and metal work on guns, most of which are bolt-action sporting rifles. Roger points out that he also enjoys the variety of working on shotguns.

Roger Biesen does much of his hand-checkering at home, where his daughter, Paula is establishing a name for herself as a firearms engraver. Paula's floorplates and gripcaps adorn many Biesen rifles, and her work has appeared on guns commissioned for auction by the National Rifle Association, the Rocky Mountain Elk Foundation and Safari Club International. Lately Paula has been asked to engrave rifle barrels and receivers too. Her most challenging project is a rifle Al Biesen is building for himself. "It's a Model 70 Winchester in .30-06," she says. "The wood is a beautiful piece of French walnut that Grandpa squirreled away in 1968. It is really a privilege to work on something like this, but there's also a lot of pressure to come up with a unique design and to execute it very, very well. Grandpa could have gone to the best of engravers."

Paula's modesty belies her talent. Her artistry shows clearly in clean flowing scroll and lifelike animals. She favors animal scenes. "You learn tricks," she says. "Like never setting an animal face-on so you have to make left and right sides exactly the same. But knowing what not to do isn't enough. Achieving fluid forms with a chisel is much tougher than with a paint brush or a pencil. You must breath life into steel by cutting it. You have no colors to help, and three-dimensional effects require lots of astute chisel work. There's no way to brush over or erase a bad mistake."

Paula works at home partly because she's a wife and mom. But partly it's because home has fewer distractions than the shop where Al and Roger work their magic on rifles. "Customers are always stopping in to see Dad or Grandpa, says Paula. "And they talk a lot. Really a lot."

# KENT BOWERLY

## GUNMAKER

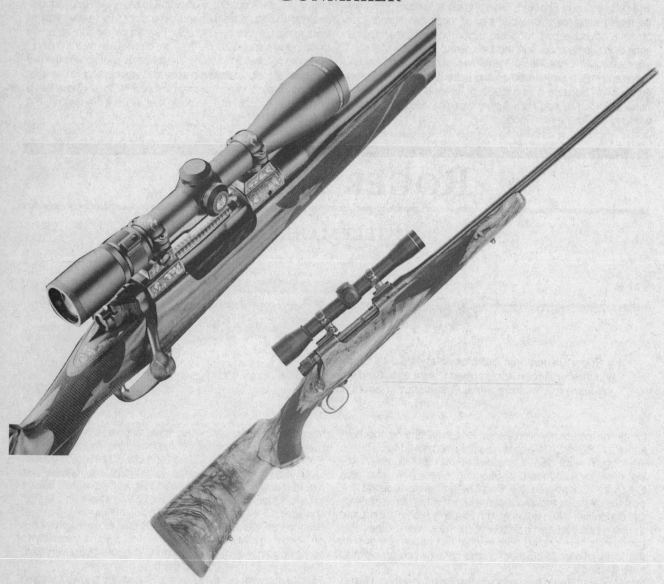

Kent Bowerly began stockmaking in 1958, converting a Springfield 03-A3 with a Roberts semi-inletted stock. His work was admired by friends who offered to pay him to do similar stockwork for them. Thus began a hobby that developed into a legitimate part time avocation.

In the mid 60's, Kent was exposed to the work of master stockmakers, Al Biesen and Earl Milliron. This inspired him to concentrate on classic stock designs. Although basically self taught, Kent credits Earl Milliron with coaching him on tools, techniques, and finishes.

A serious hunter, Kent places a strong emphasis on rifle accuracy and function. He works on the premise that a firearm first must be intrinsically accurate, but also be stocked so its owner can shoot it accurately under field conditions. Kent stocks both rifles and shotguns but says the majority of his work is with the Pre-64 Model 70 Winchester, Dakota 76, and Ruger #1. He also works on a variety of Mausers.

Kent took early retirement as an executive in the boat building industry in 1985 and has since been busy as a full-time stockmaker. He has been a member of the American Custom Gunmakers Guild since 1987 and was Guild treasurer for five years. His work is well respected throughtout the shooting industry. Kent's rifles have appeared on the cover of RIFLE magazine and in Nikon optics catalogs.

# JIM COFFIN

## STOCKMAKER

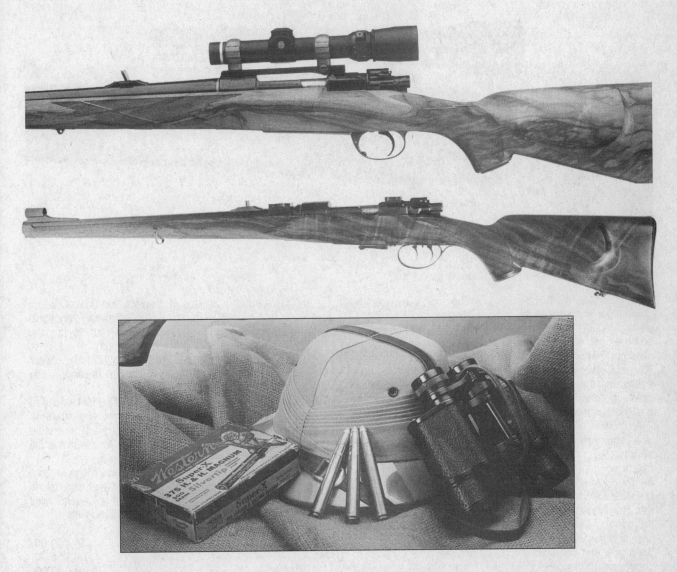

Jim Coffin's interest in guns dates to the second world war. In the late forties he bought surplus 1917 Enfields, and followed up with a Springfield in 1954. That year he also bought his first new rifle, a .30-06 Model 70 Winchester, and a new model 21 Winchester shotgun. During a 22-year career as a Marine pilot, Jim kept his interest in firearms, and was able to hunt near duty stations from Ontario to India. But it wasn't until after retirement that he became intrigued with building his own custom rifles. In 1984 Jim became a member of the American Custom Gunmakers Guild and has since continued to improve and refine his work.

Jim's main interest is in "working guns" - not decorative pieces. He learned to checker and finish a stock long before turning professional, because he reworked many stocks to better their fit. He knows that intrinsic rifle accuracy is of little account if the stock does not help the shooter to aim and execute a shot. He encourages his customers to outline what they want, and to let him serve as an advisor. Jim counts himself fortunate to have attracted some discriminating shooters - and to have made good friends in the process. One rifle job led to a moose hunt down the Copper River in Alaska!

Like many of his colleagues, Jim considers stockmaking an avocation, not a living. His work shows a high level of care because he does care about it. It is his signature. Some of Jim's favorite rifles are built on Mauser and Winchester Model 70 actions. He lives and works in the Willamette River town of Corvallis, Oregon.

# D'ARCY ECHOLS AND CO.

### "LEGEND" DANGEROUS GAME VERSION

D'Arcy Echols, a riflemaker in Utah, is well known in the custom gun fraternity where he has been active for the past 20 years. In 1997 a customer suggested that D'Arcy build a commercial rifle that functioned and shot as well as his custom rifles but that was a bit less expensive. The result is D'Arcy's "Legend" rifle, with the heart of a Winchester Model 70 Classic action and the metalsmithing that has made Echols custom rifles a hallmark of dependability. A McMillan synthetic stock, designed especially for this rifle, adds durability and trims cost. D'Arcy offers three versions of the "Legend."

The standard model comes in 7mm Remington, 300 Winchester, 300 Weatherby, 338 Winchester Magnum chamberings. Cryogenically-treated Krieger chrome-moly barrels complement the M70 action, which D'Arcy modifies to hold four rounds in the magazine instead of the usual three. He also lengthens the loading port for easy access. When fitting the barrel, he remachines then laps the recoil lug seats and lugs, and squares up the receiver face and bolt face. He repins the trigger and bolt stop and grinds sear surfaces for a crisp, consistent 3 1/4-pound trigger pull. The scope base holes are enlarged to accept 8-40 screws, and he installs his own Weaver-style bases.

D'Arcy pillar-beds the actions in the McMillan stocks, which feature a high, straight comb and cheekpiece, functional checkering, an open grip and a cast-off butt to put the shooter's eye right behind the scope. Length of pull is to order. All steel gets a matte blue finish. D'Arcy shoots each rifle a minimum of 40 times to confirm feeding, safety and accuracy.

The Dangerous Game rifle, available in 375 H&H and 416 Remington Magnums, as well as .458 Lott, has a barrel-mounted front swivel and additional action work to ensure flawless feeding with big roundnose bullets. Otherwise it is like the standard model. Iron sights can be ordered.

The Long Range rifle, available in 300 Weatherby Magnum only, has a 26-inch fluted Krieger barrel of slightly heavier dimensions (.750 at the muzzle). Barrel lengths on other Legend rifles depend on chambering and customer special requests.

*Prices:*

| | |
|---|---|
| **LEGEND** | **$4,500.00** |
| **DANGEROUS GAME** (illustrated above) | **4,750.00** |
| **LONG RANGE** | **4,600.00** |

D'Arcy Echols still builds a limited number of walnut-stocked custom rifles (illustrated, below) . . . . . . . . . **Prices on request**

### CUSTOM RIFLE

# DARWIN HENSLEY

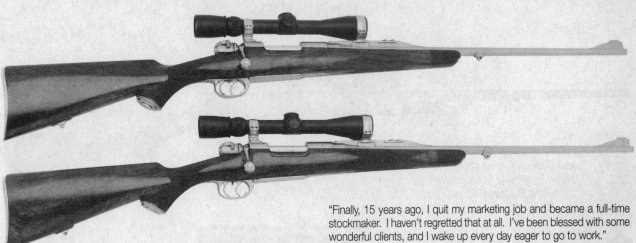

Darwin Hensley was born in 1942 on an Iowa farm. "Life in those times was simple," he says. "if you were bored, you had to fix things or build things to entertain yourself. There was no TV or computer to bombard you with entertainment." Darwin amused himself with a pocket knife, carving and whittling. "We moved to town when I was 10, but I kept that knife busy," he recalls. Darwin spent summers with grandparents on their farm. "Grandpa's 1890 Winchester .22 pump gave me a break from whittling. I still have that rifle."

After graduating from high school, Darwin earned B.A. and B.S. degrees. His favorite field was woodworking, in which he excelled. "I taught art for two years following," Darwin says, "but then I decided there just wasn't enough money in it for my family. I went into marketing and stayed there 25 years. My wife and I raised our two children during that time."

Indulging his fascination with guns, Darwin bought and sold high-grade firearms and did stock work on the side. "But there was never enough time for that," he declares.

"Finally, 15 years ago, I quit my marketing job and became a full-time stockmaker. I haven't regretted that at all. I've been blessed with some wonderful clients, and I wake up every day eager to go to work."

Darwin is a versatile stockmaker, a master of trim profiling as these photos show. "It's important that a rifle shoot and handle well; but beyond that, its design should show a harmony of parts. I mean, the lines, components, engraving, checkering, fit and finish should work together to achieve an overall effect. It's wrong for one of the rifle's parts to draw attention from the whole. I'm very careful to fit a rifle to its owner, physically and in less tangible ways. I like to include subtle details that can only be discovered after careful inspection."

Among the most stunning single-shot rifles displayed at the last Custom Gun Guild show was a Darwin Hensley miniature Gibbs Farquharson (bottom). Chambered in .17 Hornet, it has the slender, classic lines of the two rifles above it – a miniature Jeffery Farquharson in 2R-Lovell (middle) and a miniature Alex Henry in .218 Bee (top). The two bolt rifles above are matched Kurz Mausers, in .22-250 and 7mm-08. Metal work on four of these rifles is by Steve Heilmann. Engraving on the single-shots is by Terry Wallace. The Bee features metalwork by Darwin, who says he sometimes just has to put down that pocket knife to machine a little metal!

# PATRICK HOLEHAN

## GUNMAKER

*Patrick Holehan Classic Hunter and Safari Hunter show the clean, graceful lines of the entire Hunter Series.*

Arizona gunmaker Patrick Holehan is an exuberant young man with a wide smile and a firm handshake. He is also a serious student of classic hunting rifles and a craftsman with an eye for perfection. His tenure in the gunmaking business is not long; but his work reflects the skills of a true professional. Patrick has an artist's sense of proportion. His stocks show grace and elegance in slender contours that stop just short of racy. He is keen to do his best work always, a requisite in what has become a very competitive industry. Patrick Holehan's checkering shows the attention to detail that distinguishes accomplished craftsmen from people who want to become famous building rifles.

While Holehan rifles are custom projects, Patrick offers several basic variations of what he calls the Hunter Series. All are based on Classic Winchester Model 70 actions, and all come with either hand-made walnut or fiberglass stocks that are pillar bedded and reinforced. Patrick trues barrel seating surfaces, laps the locking lugs, hones and polishes the feed ramp and bolt race. He builds up the receiver ring and bridge to a "double square bridge" configuration that accepts quick-release scope rings. Patrick likes cryogenically-treated barrels and uses only those of highest quality. Barrel lengths and contours, like magazine style and capacity, vary with model. Customers can order from a long list of options. The standard Classic Hunter retails for $3350 with a fiberglass stock, $4050 with a wood stock. The Long Range Hunter is in the same price range, as is the Light Weight Hunter with standard magazine. The Light Weight Hunter with blind magazine costs about $300 less. The Safari Hunter retails for $3800 and $4550 with fiberglass and wood stocks. Patrick Holehan also offers both wood and fiberglass stocks as an interchangeable set with all rifle models. Additional cost varies. Holehan rifles are available in any standard chambering and wildcats that will fit the Model 70 action.

# STEVEN DODD HUGHES

## GUNMAKER

After three years of gunsmithing school, Steven Dodd Hughes started working as a full-time professional custom gunmaker in 1978. For more than a decade, his focus was building muzzleloading firearms from patterns of the 18th and 19th century. Hughes now speciaizes in early cartridge guns creating one-of-a-kind single-shot rifles, double-barrel shotguns and a few high-grade lever action rifes. Current projects include a Winchester Model 1873 .44-40 in a Deluxe 1 of 1000 style, sidelock SXS shotguns based on European metalwork and custom Dakota single-shot rifles with a 1920's London flair. Other projects include fancy Marlin lever guns, boxlock "game gun" shotguns and Winchester High Wall and Low Wall custom rifles from .22 to .45-70. Delivery time usuallly runs from 1 1/2 to 2 years and Hughes's base price is about $10,000. He does no bolt-action rifle work of any kind. Hughes has also written numerous magazine articles about the custom gun trade and contributes the *"Fine Gunmaking"* column for Shooting Sportsman Magazine. His book *Fine Gunmaking: Double Shotguns* was published by Krause Pub. in 1998. A new book, Custom rifles in Black & White, was just released by Fandango Press.

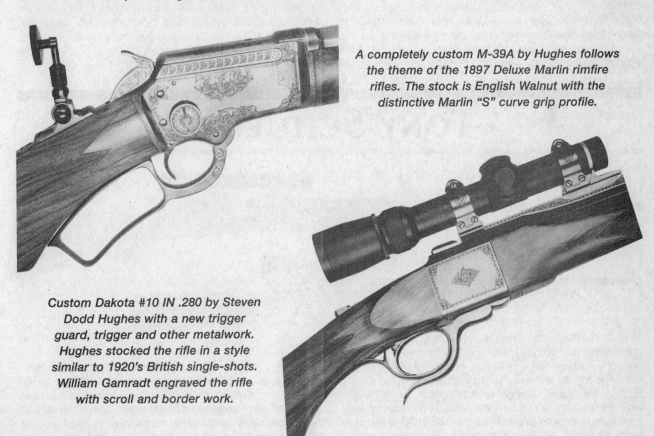

*Hughes designed this custom Winchester High Wall as if it had been created in a London gunshop Circa 1920. It has a 24" octagon barrel with integral quarter-rib and front sight base and weighs 7-1/4 lbs. Stocked in English Walnut, everything is new except the original Winchester action.*

*A completely custom M-39A by Hughes follows the theme of the 1897 Deluxe Marlin rimfire rifles. The stock is English Walnut with the distinctive Marlin "S" curve grip profile.*

*Custom Dakota #10 IN .280 by Steven Dodd Hughes with a new trigger guard, trigger and other metalwork. Hughes stocked the rifle in a style similar to 1920's British single-shots. William Gamradt engraved the rifle with scroll and border work.*

# DAVID MILLER

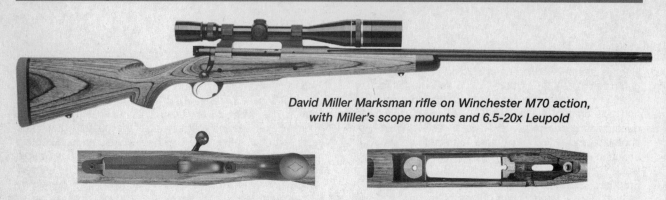

*David Miller Marksman rifle on Winchester M70 action, with Miller's scope mounts and 6.5-20x Leupold*

A fine example of custom rifle building is David Miller's work, shown on this page. David has been making rifles for most of his adult life. Until recently, he was best known for his fine rendering of hand-fashioned classic-style bolt rifles. Several were highlights at annual conventions of Safari Club International. A few years ago he put together a rifle for his own special type of hunting Coues deer at long range in the desert hinterlands south of his Tucson shop. The rifle featured a laminated stock, not the exquisite English walnut his customers were used to seeing. It had a Winchester Model 70 action, pillar bedded for accuracy, and a long fluted barrel chambered in .300 Weatherby Magnum. David used his own scope mounts to attach a 6.5-20x Leupold scope with special range-finding reticle. Fellow hunters saw and shot the rifle and wanted a copy. Now David and partner Curt Crum are busy building both the full-custom Classic rifle and the new Marksman. A

stickler for rifles that shoot well, David puts the best components and workmanship into both rifles. The Marksman lacks only the options, detailing and fine walnut of the custom Classic. David routinely shoots deer at ranges beyond the capability of most hunters. He insists that with practice and the right rifle (a Marksman!), long-distance shooting can put more venison on the table. His collection of records-class Coues deer show that his Marksman gets lots of use. (Base price for this rifle is **$9,000**. For quotes on options and on the Classic rifle, contact David at 3131 E. Greenlee Rd., Tucson AZ 85716.) The gunmakers featured in this section are not the only competent craftsmen in the field. Indeed, there are gunmakers, stockers, metalsmiths and engravers practicing today whose work is the best of its kind ever seen. Quality standards (and prices) continue to climb. In future editions of Shooter's Bible, you'll find the best of the best in custom guns.

# TONY SCHUELKE

Tony Schuelke is a versatile craftsman who came to gunbuilding late, despite his early affinity for firearms.

But Tony is more than a machinist. He's a self-taught craftsman who tackles some of the toughest jobs in custom gun-building. He prefers working on side-by-side shotguns and looks for ways to be creative - especially in checkering. Tony is an accomplished man with a file, checkering not only stocks but bolt handles. He's also proud of the skeleton grip caps he fabricates in his shop. While he doesn't imitate anyone, Tony

takes every opportunity to study the work that he admires.

A good listener when clients approach him with their ideas, he'd rather respond than recommend, pointing out that custom guns - especially side-by-sides - are more like art than implements. Individuality is important to some people, and little details that have no bearing on performance can matter a great deal. Tony keeps shop in Glencoe, MN.

# GENE SIMILLION

## RIFLEMAKER

Coloradan Gene Simillion has been building custom sporting rifles for nearly 20 years. He grew up near renowned stockmaker Keith Stegall and says he got the inspiration to craft rifle stocks from Keith. Later, Gene honed his wood- and metal-working skills in college, graduating with a teaching degree in industrial arts.

"That wasn't too smart," Gene says with a frown. "I should have figured out beforehand that teachers work during hunting season." Gene started building rifles full-time, then spent a year in Kalispell under the tutelage of crack stockmaker Jerry Fisher. Gene also credits Montana Tom Burgess with teaching him a lot about custom metal-smithing. "I'm a student of good workmanship," he says. "So I've paid attention to the likes of Monte Mandarino, D'Arcy Echols and Don Klein."

Gene Simillion notes that little has changed in the stye of his work since the early days. "The clean, classic look is as popular as ever–maybe even more so. I like to think I'm better at the job now." On any project, Gene's aim is to produce a rifle with "accuracy, flawless function, and elegant beauty." He says the main difference between custom rifles and the best factory-built guns is in the detailing.

Two grades of rifles come from Gene's Gunnison, Colorado shop. The Premier Rifle is a true custom effort, built to each customer's exact specifications. Gene prefers to use new Model 70 Winchester Classic actions but will substitute pre-64 Model 70s, Mauser 98s, Remington 700s and others on request. Gene installs his own scope bases. A hand-checkered bolt knob and screwless sling swivel studs are standard. Magnum rifles get a second recoil lug and a crossbolt, a custom magazine box and follower. Extended magazines are an option–so too quarter ribs and iron sights. Stocks are of the finest walnut, hand-checkered in point or fleur-de-lis patterns..

SIMILLION PREMIER RIFLE . . . . . . . . . . . . . . . . . . . . . . $7,500.00
    MAGNUMS . . . . . . . . . . . . . . . . . . . . . . . . . . . . . . . . . 8,000.00

A less costly custom rifle is Gene's Classic Hunter. Built only on the new Winchester 70 Classic action, it also features new bottom metal and a top-quality, cut-rifled barrel hand-bedded in a high-grade checkered walnut stock with screwless swivel bases. The Classic Hunter shows less detailing than the Premier, and the customer has fewer options. Gene came up with this rifle a couple of years ago to bridge the gap between true custom rifles and the semi-custom factory-built rifles like those produced by Dakota.

STANDARD CLASSIC HUNTER . . . . . . . . . . . . . . . . . . . . . $5,400.00
    MAGNUMS . . . . . . . . . . . . . . . . . . . . . . . . . . . . . . . . . 6,000.00
    HEAVY MAGNUMS (.375 H&H and up) . . . . . . . . . . . . 6,500.00

*Gene Simillion Premier Rifle, .270 on a Winchester Model 70 action with Leupold 2-7x scope.*

*Gene Simillion Premier Rifle, 7x57 Mauser on a Mauser 98 action with Zeiss 4x scope.*

*Gene Simillion Premier Rifle, .338 Magnum on a Mauser 98 action with Leupold 1.5-5x scope.*

# CHARLIE SISK

## RIFLEMAKER

About 45 minutes northeast of Houston, in the smaller Texas town of Crosby, 34-year-old gunmaker Charlie Sisk is on the phone talking with customers. It's one of his strengths, this keeping in close touch with the people who order his super-accurate rifles. But it's not the only talent. Charlie built his first gun in high-school machine shop - a .257 Roberts on a 98 Mauser action - and has been working hard ever since to build a reputation in a competitive industry. He specializes in synthetic-stocked bolt rifles that shoot very well. "I'd say they can all shoot half inch, because I've got half-inch groups," he says. "But I'm not a half-inch shooter.'

Such candor endears Charlie to his customers, who are for the most part a pretty critical lot. Charlie's rifle's don't wear handsome wood. They're not engraved. They're meant to be shot. And beauty is only as beauty does. Charlie works almost exclusively on bolt-action rifles. He prefers Model 700 Remingtons but says Winchester 70s come in close behind. He likes Hart barrels becaued he's found them consistently accurate. Still, he takes nothing for granted. "Hart specifies groove-diameter tolerance of .0005-inch," Charlie says. "But mine are air-gauged and don't vary more than .0001. I also inspect each barrel with a bore-scope. And my chambering is done with match-grade live-pilot reamers to ensure concentricity "My rifles have to shoot tight groups."

But bench accuracy isn't enough for hunters who must control lightweight rifles under field conditions. Charlie adds Jewell triggers and takes care that his synthetic stocks fit each client perfectly. They are also meticulously mated to the metal. Rifle balance and weight matter to Charlie, who prides himself in doing all the work on a rifle personally. That includes "blueprinting" actions to square up the bolt with the bore. Charlie makes his own muzzle brakes. He thinks most rifles will shoot about as well as they can shoot if the forend tip puts a little pressure on the barrel. However, he will free-float barrels on request. Charlie Sisk commonly works up loads for his customers. He likes the chance to add service to his product, get to know the customer better - and prove that his hunting rifles are indeed as accurate as any around!

# DALE A. STOREY

## GUNMAKER

"I'm one of those lucky people who knew right away what they want in the way of a career," says Dale Storey. After high school, Dale enrolled in the Colorado School of Trades, perhaps the best-known of American institutions for turning out skilled gunmakers. He started working on guns soon after graduating CST in 1962, but didn't commit to the trade full time until 1981. "Uncle Sam used some of my talents for awhile," he says. After military service and two degrees from Montana State University, Dale taught at a high school and post-secondary schools for 11 years - "to bankroll my gun-shop." Since turning professional, he has worked on a variety of rifles, from the black-powder muzzleloaders that were his early love, to modern bolt guns.

One of Dale's favorite projects is a half-stock plains rifle, true in line and feature to its ancestors. A new interest is Alex Henry rifles. He built one recently, and it is indeed a most elegant black-powder arm. Dale traces his interest in muz-zleloaders to mentor V.M. Starr, who taught him much about their history and how they should be built. Starr was instru-mental in bringing shotgun shooting to the annual black-powder rendezvous at Friendship, Indiana.

Dale Storey now works mainly on modern rifles, emphasizing that the heart of every fine hunting rifle is perfect balance. "No one thing should dominate a rifle, in form or function," he says. "A rifle must point quickly and shoot accurately from hunting positions." He points out that high-quality parts are essential but adds that putting them together is what distinguishes an able craftsman from an assembler. Dale says he can do "almost everything" in building a rifle. He leaves the engraving and inlay work to others, however. Liz Dolbare did that part of the Alex Henry project.

A hunter and shooter, Dale is pleased to call Wyoming home. He works in Casper.

## BENCH ⊕ MASTER® RIFLE REST

The Bench Master Rifle Rest is a rugged, compact and highly adjustable rifle-shooting accessory—one that offers precision line-up and recoil reduction when sighting in a rifle, testing ammunition or shooting varmints. It features three course positions totaling 5.5", with 1.5" fine adjustment in each course position, plus leveling and shoulder height adjustments for maximum control and comfort. Because of its unique design, the Bench Master can easily double as a rifle vise for scope mounting, bore sighting and cleaning. It comes with a LIFETIME Warranty and a list price of only $119.95. For a free brochure, call or write:

**DESERT MOUNTAIN MFG.**
2001 W. Fourth Plain • Vancouver, WA 98660
*Tel:* 360-693-5835  *Fax:* 360-693-7916

# MANUFACTURERS' SHOWCASE

## MODEL G4003
## 12" x 36" GEAR-HEAD,
## CAM LOCK SPINDLE, GAP BED LATHE

**Specifications:**
- Swing over bed: 12"
- Swing over gap: 17"
- Distance between centers: 36"
- Spindle: Cam lock D1-4
- Spindle bore: 1⁷⁄₁₆"
- 9 Speeds: 70-1400 RPM
- Tailstock barrel taper: MT#3
- Tailstock barrel travel: 4"
- Motor: 1½ HP, Single Phase, 220V
- Approx. ship. weight: 1040 lbs.

**Includes:**
- 6" 3-jaw chuck w/ 2 sets of jaws
- 8" 4-jaw chuck w/ revers. jaws
- Steady rest • Follow rest
- 10" Face plate • Tool Box
- Quick change tool post w/ holder
- Two MT#3 dead centers
- One MT#3 live center
- Six change gears
- ½" chuck with MT#3 arbor

The **G4003** is **$1,995.00** and shipped in the lower 48 states for $200.00.

### 3 LOCATIONS
**Bellingham, WA  /  Williamsport, PA  /  Springfield, MO**

**grizzly.com**     Visit our Web site!

**TEL: 1-800-523-4777 • FAX: 1-800-438-5901**

MEDIA CODE
**92C**

272700658

## NEW ENGLAND FIREARMS®
## NRA FOUNDATION
### YOUTH EDUCATION
### ENDOWMENT EDITION SHOTGUNS

The NEW ENGLAND FIREARMS® has a tradition of commitment toward building a brighter future for the shooting sports. By working with nonprofit organizations and state agencies, NEF assists in educating hundreds of thousands of young people throughout the country about the safe and responsible use of firearms. This year, NEF continues a tradition that will provide a completely new level of support for these programs. Through a unique partnership with the National Rifle Association Foundation, NEW ENGLAND FIREARMS® will produce three special new youth shotguns. All sales will provide funding for the Foundation's Youth Education Endowment.

These new NEF youth shotguns are based on our highly successful Pardner® Youth shotguns in 20, 28 and .410 gauge. Each gun is enhanced by a polished blue receiver and real American black walnut stocks and forends. The engraving includes the NRA Foundation's logo and the inscription: "Youth Endowment Edition." This unique youth shotgun provides an excellent beginning for young hunters. At the same time, it helps to build a lasting future for the sports in which you and your family have become involved. See your NEW ENGLAND FIREARMS® stocking, Gold Star Dealer or write:

### H&R 1871®, INC.
60 Industrial Rowe, Gardner, MA 01440

## TRIUS
### *"Setting the Standard for 44 Years"*

The TRIUS 1-STEP is almost effortless to use: (1) Set arm and place target on arm without tension; (2) Step on pedal to put tension on arm and release target in one motion. Adjustable without tools, easy cocking, lay-on loading, singles, doubles, plus piggy-back doubles offer unparalleled variety.

*Birdshooter:* quality at a budget price—now with high-angle retainer. *Model 92:* a bestseller with high-angle clip and can thrower. *TrapMaster:* sit-down comfort plus pivoting action.

**TRIUS PRODUCTS INC.**
P.O. Box 25, Cleves, OH 45002
*Tel:* 513-941-5682
*Fax:* 513-941-7970

Satisfying Shooters Since 1955
TRIUS TRAPS

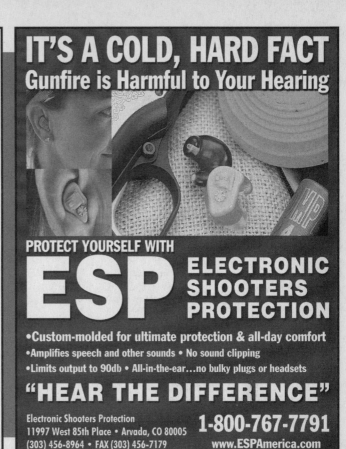
# MANUFACTURERS' SHOWCASE

**Grizzly** Industrial, Inc.

### MODEL G6760 MILLING MACHINE W/ POWER FEED

**Specifications:**
- · Table size: 7⅞" x 35¾"
- · Table travel: 20½" longitudinal, 9½" cross & 13¾" vertical
- · Spindle taper: R-8
- · Spindle travel: 5.4"
- · Max. spindle to column: 15½"
- · Max. spindle to table: 13¾"
- · Number of speeds: 5

- · Range of speeds: 255-1800 RPM
- · Motor: American made, 1½ HP, Single Phase
- · Approx. ship. weight: 1650 lbs.

**Includes:**
- · Way chip protectors
- · Drawbar
- · Tool box
- · Longitudinal table power feed

The **G6760** is **$2,995.00** and shipped in the lower 48 states for FREE!

**3 LOCATIONS**
**Bellingham, WA / Williamsport, PA / Springfield, MO**

**grizzly**.com
*Visit our Web site!*

MEDIA CODE
**92C**

**TEL: 1-800-523-4777 • FAX: 1-800-438-5901**

272700658

### SERIES S MODEL L

**HARRIS** ENGINEERING, INC.

### ULTRALIGHT BIPODS
- • *Versatile*
- • *Sturdy*
- • *Light*
- • *Fast*

**SERIES S BIPODS**
Pivoting Bipod with tension adjustment

Harris Bipods clamp quickly and securely to most stud equipped bolt-action rifles. Folding legs have completely adjustable spring-return telescoping extensions. Time proven design and quality manufacture. Thirteen models available plus adapters for various guns.

**HARRIS ENGINEERING INC.**
999 Broadway • Barlow, Kentucky 42024
*Tel:* 502-334-3633 • *Fax:* 502-334-3000

91

# GLASER SAFETY SLUG, INC.

For over 25 years Glaser has provided a state-of-the-art personal defense ammunition used by the law enforcement and civilian communities Available in two bullet styles, the Glaser Blue is offered in a full range of handgun calibers from 25ACP to 45 Colt (including the 9MM Makarov and 357 Sig) and four rifle calibers; .223, 308, 30-06 and 7.62x39. The Glaser Silver is available in all handgun calibers from 380ACP to 45 Colt. A complete brochure is available on the internet @ www.safetyslug.com or contact:

**GLASER SAFETY SLUG, INC.**
P.O. Box 8223
Foster City, California 94404
*Tel:* 800-221-3489
*Fax:* 510-785-6685

---

## MODEL G4016
## 13½" x 40"
## GEAR-HEAD
## LATHE
## W/ STAND

**Specifications:**
- Swing over bed: 13½"
- Swing over gap: 19"
- Distance between centers: 40"
- Spindle: Cam lock D1-4
- Spindle bore: 1⅜"
- 8 Speeds: 78-2100 RPM
- Tailstock barrel taper: MT#3
- Tailstock barrel travel: 3½"
- Motor: 2 HP, Single Phase, 220V
- Approx. ship. weight: 1410 lbs.

**Includes:**
- 6" 3-jaw chuck
- 8" 4-jaw chuck
- Steady rest • Follow rest
- 12" Face plate • Tool Box
- 4-way turret tool post
- Two MT#3 dead centers
- Live center
- Stand, chip pan & splash guard
- Jog button & emergency stop

The **G4016** is **$2,695.00** and shipped in the lower 48 states for $200.00.

**3 LOCATIONS**
**Bellingham, WA / Williamsport, PA / Springfield, MO**

272700658

**grizzly.com**    Visit our Web site!

**MEDIA CODE**
**92C**

**TEL: 1-800-523-4777 • FAX: 1-800-438-5901**

---

# MANUFACTURERS' SHOWCASE

---

## CHEYENNE PIONEER PRODUCTS *Presents*

**CHEYENNE CARTRIDGE BOXES™**

Authentic antique-looking cartridge boxes styled and constructed like the boxes produces from 1873 to the 1950s–only better. Using the same materials, colors and graphics, Cheyenne Pioneer Products produces a line of cartridge boxes that capture the details of the old-time originals, but are tougher and more durable.

**1880 CLASSICS™** provide Cowboy Action Shooters, Old West enthusiasts and reenactors with an alternative to modern factory ammunition packaging or plastic after market boxes. 45 Colt, 44 WCF, 45 Schofield, 45-70 and 12 gauge boxes are a few examples of offerings available for revolver, rifle and shotgun.

**20TH CENTURY CLASSICS™** satisfies the demands of more modern shooting & reloading aficiandos. This line offers many favorites, such as 44 Magnum and 38 Special. For more information, contact:

**CHEYENNE PIONEER PRODUCTS**
P.O. Box 28425 • Kansas City, MO 64188
*Tel:* 816-413-9196 *Fax:* 816-455-2859
www.cartridgeboxes.com • *e-mail:* cheyennepp@aol.com

---

**NEW ENGLAND FIREARMS®** adds to its top-value lineup of turkey shotguns–a new 10 gauge 3 1/2" shotgun with a 24" barrel, camo stock and forend finish, plus an extra screw-in Turkey full choke tube. The American hardwood stock and forend are finished in green and black camo,with black finish on all metal parts to assure low visibility. Standard features include a ventilated recoil pad, sling swivels and camo sling. In addition the patented NEF Transfer Bay System guarantees a high level of hammer-down safety out in the field. Your shotgun also comes with NEF's "additional barrel" program, which means it can now be factory retrofitted with other 10 gauge shotgun barrels.

For more information, see your New England Firearms stocking, Gold Star dealer, or write:

## H&R 1871, INC.
60 Industrial Rowe Gardner, MA 01440

# MANUFACTURERS' SHOWCASE

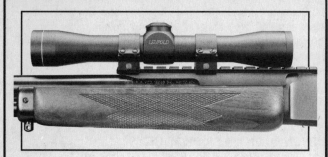

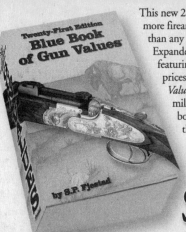

# MANUFACTURERS' SHOWCASE

## FORREST INC. OFFERS RIFLE/PISTOL MAGAZINES

Whether you're looking for a few spare magazines for that obsolete 22 rifle or pistol, or wish to replace a 10-shot with the higher-capacity pre-ban original, all are available from FORREST INC. With one of the largest selections of magazines, they offer competitive pricing especially for dealers who buy in quantity.

FORREST INC. also stocks parts and accessories for the Colt 1911 45 Auto Pistol, the SKS and MAK-90 rifles, and many U.S. military rifles. One of their specialty parts is firing pins for obsolete weapons.

Call or write for more information and a **FREE** brochure, **DEALERS WELCOME!**

### FORREST INC.
P.O. Box 326, Lakeside, CA 92040
*Tel:* 619-561-5800  *Fax:* 1-888-GUNCLIP
*Web:* www.GUNMAGS.com
*E-mail:* SFORR10675@AOL.COM

## STOEGER IGA UPLANDER SIDE-BY-SIDE SHOTGUNS

The UPLANDER SUPREME has all the traditional Uplander features and a lot more. Available in a 12 gauge or 20" gauge, the Uplander Supreme features a high grade American walnut stock and forend with a high gloss finish, single selective trigger, automatic ejectors, and interchangeable choke tubes. Other standard features include a gold trigger, red front and mid-rib bead sights and a soft rubber recoil pad. *Retail price:* $599.00

### STOEGER INDUSTRIES
5 Mansard Court
Wayne, New Jersey 07470
*Tel:* 973-872-9500
*Fax:* 973-872-2230
*E-Mail:* stoegerindustries@msn.com

# MANUFACTURERS' SHOWCASE

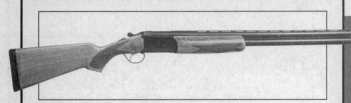

## STOEGER IGA CONDOR SHOTGUNS

Over the years the IGA factory has prided itself on manufacturing rugged, reliable and affordable shotguns. With the introduction of the CONDOR SUPREME DELUXE, IGA has added new dimensions, grace and elegance. The high grade American walnut stock features hand checkering and a soft rubber pad to absorb recoil. The high luster blued barrels feature a stepped-up vent rib with red front and mid-rib beads. They are manufactured from moly-chrome steel for handling steel shot and are fitted with recessed interchangeable choke tubes. Other standard features include single selective trigger, automatic ejectors, automatic safety and 2" chambers. The CONDOR SUPREME DELUXE has an impressive array of features—even for shotguns costing two and three times as much. *Retail price:* $674.00

### STOEGER INDUSTRIES
5 Mansard Court
Wayne, New Jersey 07470
*Tel:* 973-872-9500 • *Fax:* 973-872-2230
*E-Mail:* stoegerindustries@msn.com

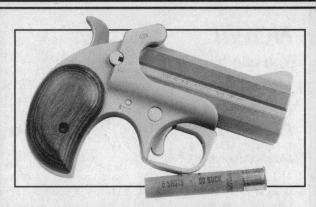

## THE CENTURY 2000 DEFENDER "C2K"
### FROM BOND ARMS, INC.

The Century 200 Defender ("C2K") is the ultimate in self-defense. With its 3.5" double barrel, the C2K chambers the 3" .410 00 Buck Shot with five pellets. It also features a rebounding hammer, retracting firing pins, crossbolt safety, cammed locking lever, spring-loaded extractor and interchangeable barrels. Choice of caliber includes .410 with 3" chambers and .410/45LC with 2.5" chambers.

*For further information, contact:*

**BOND ARMS, INC.**
P.O. Box 1296 • Granbury, TX 76048
*Tel:* (817) 573-4445 • *Fax:* (817) 573-5636

THE

## RUGER
## M77 Mark II

The Ruger M77 Mark II is first and foremost a hunter's rifle. Careful attention to design details and superior craftsmanship in manufacture make it a rifle to be both admired and carried into the back country. Ruger is proud to produce these finely crafted American products which have achieved world leadership in the hands of our discerning customers. There is no finer centerfire bolt-action rifle than the Ruger M77 Mark II.

Sturm, Ruger and Company, Inc.
Southport, CT 06490, U.S.A.
www.ruger-firearms.com

Free instruction manuals for all
Ruger firearms available on request.
Please specify model for which you require a manual.

RUGER M77 Mark II
M77RS MKII

.300 Win. Mag.

Suggested retail price of $706.00.

**RUGER**

Arms Makers for Responsible Citizens

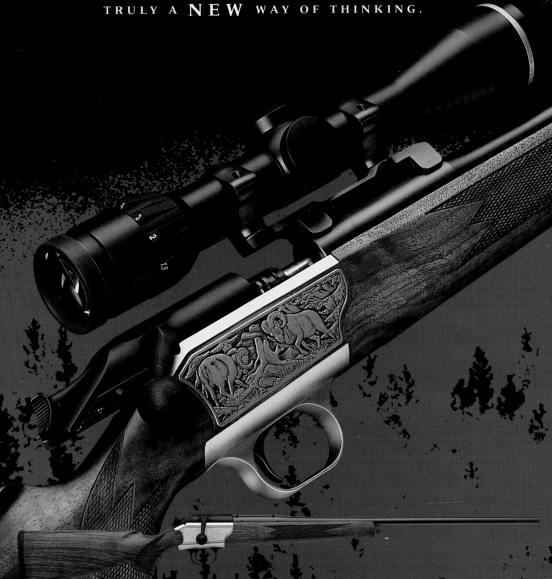

**Handguns**

*Roland Clark – Sundown, 1926*

*For addresses and phone/fax numbers of manufacturers and distributors included in this section, please turn to **DIRECTORY OF MANUFACTURERS AND SUPPLIERS** on page 564.*

# AMERICAN ARMS

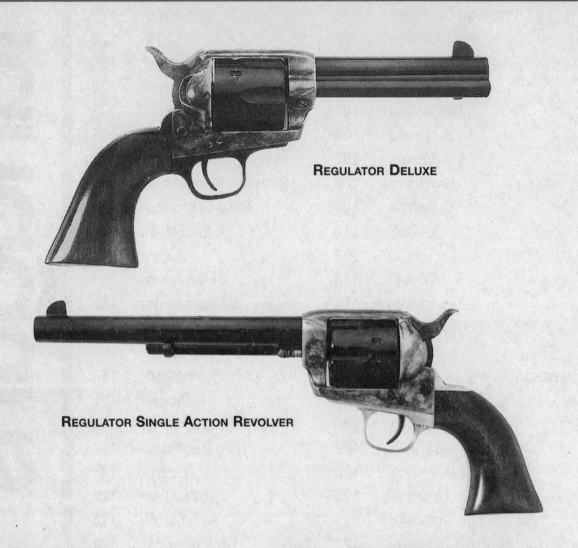

**REGULATOR DELUXE**

**REGULATOR SINGLE ACTION REVOLVER**

## REGULATOR DELUXE

**SPECIFICATIONS**
*Caliber:* 45LC **Barrel Length:** 4.25" or 5.5"
*Features:* Blued steel backstrap and trigger guard; hammer block safety;
*Price:* . . . . . . . . . . . . . . . . . . . . . . . . . . . . . . $365.00

## REGULATOR SINGLE ACTION

**SPECIFICATIONS**
*Calibers:* 45 Long Colt, 357 Mag.
*Barrel Length:* 4.75", 5.5" and 7.5"
*Overall Length:* 8 $^1/_{16}$"
*Weight:* 2 lb. 3 oz. (4.75" barrel)
*Sights:* Fixed
*Safety:* Hammer block
*Features:* Brass trigger guard and backstrap
*Price:* . . . . . . . . . . . . . . . . . . . . . . . . . . . . . . $320.00

## MATEBA AUTO REVOLVER (not shown)

This firearm incorporates the quickness and handling of a semi-auto pistol with the reliability and accuracy of a revolver. May be fired as a single-action or double-action handgun. When fired, the cylinder and slide assembly move back and the recoil causes the cylinder to rotate. The speed of firing is comparable to a semi-auto pistol. The "auto pistol" aspect of this gun aligns the barrel with the bottom chamber of the cylinder. This reduces recoil allowing the shooter to stay "on target" with the least amount of movement.

**SPECIFICATIONS**
*Caliber:* 357 **Capacity:** 6 rounds
*Overall Length:* 8.77" **Barrel Length:** 4"
*Weight:* 2.75 lbs.
*Features:* The mateba has an all blue finish, solid steel alloy frame and walnut grips
*Price:* . . . . . . . . . . . . . . . . . . . . . . . . . . . . . . $1,295.00
6" barrel . . . . . . . . . . . . . . . . . . . . . . . . . . . . . . 1,349.00

# AMERICAN DERRINGER PISTOLS

**MODEL 1**

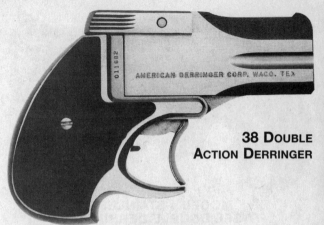

**38 DOUBLE ACTION DERRINGER**

### SPECIFICATIONS

**Calibers:** See below
**Action:** Single action w/automatic barrel selection
**Capacity:** 2 shots **Barrel Length:** 3"
**Overall Length:** 4.82"
**Weight:** 15 oz. (in 45 Auto)
**Calibers:**

| | |
|---|---|
| 22 Long Rifle w/rosewood grips | $285.00 |
| 22 Magnum | 290.00 |
| 10mm Auto | 305.00 |
| 223 | 455.00 |
| 32 Magnum/S&W Long | 290.00 |
| 32-20 | 285.00 |
| 357 Magnum w/rosewood grips | 300.00 |
| 357 Maximum w/rosewood grips | 310.00 |
| 9mm Luger, 38 Special w/rosewood grips | 285.00 |
| 38 Super w/rosewood grips | 300.00 |
| 38 Special +P+ (Police) | 293.00 |
| 38 Special Super Shell | 300.00 |
| 38 Special | 285.00 |
| 380 Auto | 280.00 |
| 40 S&W, 45 Auto, 30 M-1 Carbine | 300.00 |
| 45 Colt | 350.00 |
| 45/.410 | 363.00 |
| 45-70 (single shot) | 352.00 |
| 44-40 Win., 44 Special | 363.00 |
| 45 Win. Mag., 44 Magnum, 41 Magnum | 435.00 |
| 30-30 Win. | 425.00 |
| Comm. Ammo dual calibers | 450.00 |

### MODEL 7 ULTRA LIGHTWEIGHT SINGLE ACTION (7.5 oz.) (not shown)

| | |
|---|---|
| 22 LR, 22 Mag. Rimfire, 32 Mag./32 S&W Long, 38 Special, 380 Auto | $290.00 |
| 44 Special | 530.00 |

### MODEL 8 TARGET (not shown)

| | |
|---|---|
| 45/410 | $475.00 |

### SPECIFICATIONS

**Calibers:** See below **Capacity:** 2 shots **Barrel Length:** 3"
**Overall Length:** 4.85" **Weight:** 14.5 oz. **Height:** 3.3" **Width:** 1.1"
**Finish:** Stainless steel **Safety:** Hammerblock thumb
**Calibers:**

| | |
|---|---|
| 22 LR, 38 Special | $325.00 |
| 9mm Luger | 335.00 |
| 357 Magnum, 40 S&W | 365.00 |

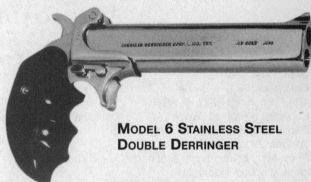

### MODEL 6 STAINLESS STEEL DOUBLE DERRINGER

### SPECIFICATIONS

**Calibers:** See below **Capacity:** 2 shots **Barrel Length:** 6"
**Overall Length:** 8.2" **Weight:** 21 oz.
**Calibers:**

| | |
|---|---|
| 22 Win. Mag. | $405.00 |
| 357 Mag. | 405.00 |
| 45 Auto | 405.00 |
| 45/.410, 45 Colt | 415.00 |

### MODEL 10 STAINLESS STEEL BARREL (10 oz.) (not shown)

| | |
|---|---|
| 38 Special | $270.00 |
| 45 Auto | 295.00 |
| 45 Colt | 350.00 |

### MODEL 11 LIGHTWEIGHT DOUBLE DERRINGER (11 oz.) (not shown)

| | |
|---|---|
| 22 LR, 22 Mag. Rim., 32 Mag./SW, 38 Special, 380 Auto | $275.00 |

# AMERICAN DERRINGER PISTOLS

**MODEL 4**

**MODEL 4 STAINLESS
STEEL DOUBLE DERRINGER**

**SPECIFICATIONS**
*Calibers:* 45 Colt and 3" .410  *Capacity:* 2 shots
*Barrel Length:* 4.1"  *Overall Length:* 6"  *Weight:* 16.5 oz.
*Finish:* Satin or high-polish stainless steel

| | |
|---|---|
| Price: | $390.00 |
| **Also available:** | |
| In 357 Mag. | $375.00 |
| 357 Maximum | 380.00 |
| In 45-70, both barrels | 525.00 |
| In 44 Mag. w/oversized grips | 480.00 |
| 45/410. | 390.00 |
| 45 Automatic | 380.00 |
| **MODEL M-4 ALASKAN SURVIVAL** | |
| in 45-70/45-.410, 45-70/45 Colt | 440.00 |
| **LADY DERRINGER (Stainless Steel Double)** | |
| 38 Special | 325.00 |
| 32 Mag. | 340.00 |
| 357 Mag. | 370.00 |
| 45 Colt, 45/410 | 400.00 |

# AMT/GALENA INDUSTRIES, INC.

## AUTOLOADING PISTOLS

### BACKUP DAO
**SPECIFICATIONS**
*Calibers:* 357 SIG, 380 ACP (9mm Short), 38 Super,
400 Corbon, 40 S&W, 45 ACP .
*Capacity:* 5-shot (40 S&W, 45 ACP); 6-shot (other calibers)
*Barrel length:* 3"  *Overall length:* 5.75"
*Weight:* 23 oz.  *Width:* 1"
*Features:* Locking-barrel action, checkered fiberglass
grips, grooved slide sight
**Prices:**
In 380 ACP, 40 S&W, 45 ACP, 9mm . . . . . . . . . .$319.00
In 38 Super, 357 Sig. 400 Corbon . . . . . . . . . . . . .369.00

**BACKUP**
**(380 OR 9mm
SHORT)**

### HARDBALLER
**SPECIFICATIONS**
*Caliber:* 45 ACP  *Capacity:* 7 shots
*Barrel length:* 5"  *Overall length:* 8.5"
*Weight:* 38 oz.  *Width:* 1.25"
*Sights:* Fixed  *Features:* Long grip safety; rubber wrap-
around Neoprene grips; beveled magazine well; adjustable
trigger, sights; matte rib
**Prices:**
**1911 HARDBALLER** . . . . . . . . . . . . . . . . . . . . . . . .$445.00
**400 ACCELERATOR** (7" 400 Corbon barrel) . . . . . . . .599.00
**COMMANDO** (40 S&W 4" barrel) . . . . . . . . . . . . . . .435.00
**LONGSLIDE 45 ACP** (7" barrel) . . . . . . . . . . . . . . .529.00

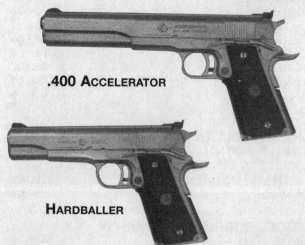

**.400 ACCELERATOR**

**HARDBALLER**

# AMT/Galena Industries, Inc.

## Autoloading Pistols

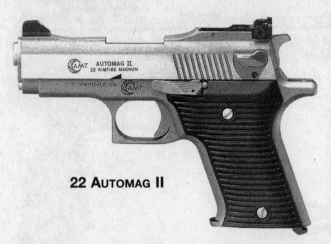

**22 Automag II**

### 22 AUTOMAG II RIMFIRE MAGNUM

The only production semiautomatic handgun in this caliber, the Automag II is ideal for the small-game hunter or shooting enthusiast who wants more power and accuracy in a light, trim handgun. The pistol features a bold open-slide design and employs a unique gas-channeling system for smooth, trouble-free action.

#### SPECIFICATIONS
*Caliber:* 22 Rimfire Magnum
*Barrel lengths:* 3 3/8", 4.5" or 6"
*Magazine capacity:* 9 shots ( 4.5" & 6"), 7 shots (3 3/8")
*Weight:* 32 oz. (6"), 30 oz. (4.5"), 24 oz. (3 3/8")
*Sights:* Adjustable 3-dot  *Finish:* Stainless steel
*Features:* Squared trigger guard; grooved carbon fiber grips; gas channeling system
*Price:* . . . . . . . . . . . . . . . . . . . . . . . . . . . . .$429.00

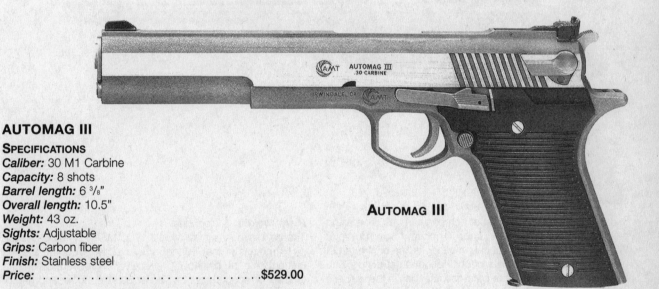

**AUTOMAG III**

### AUTOMAG III

#### SPECIFICATIONS
*Caliber:* 30 M1 Carbine
*Capacity:* 8 shots
*Barrel length:* 6 3/8"
*Overall length:* 10.5"
*Weight:* 43 oz.
*Sights:* Adjustable
*Grips:* Carbon fiber
*Finish:* Stainless steel
*Price:* . . . . . . . . . . . . . . . . . . . . . .$529.00

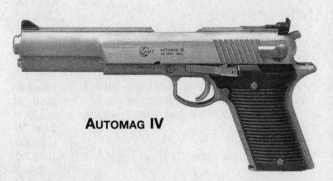

**AUTOMAG IV**

### AUTOMAG IV

#### SPECIFICATIONS
*Caliber:* 45 Win. Mag.
*Capacity:* 7 shots
*Barrel length:* 6.5"
*Overall length:* 10.5"
*Weight:* 46 oz.
*Sights:* Adjustable
*Grips:* Carbon fiber
*Finish:* Stainless steel
*Price:* . . . . . . . . . . . . . . . . . . . . . . . . . . .$599.00

# ANSCHUTZ PISTOLS

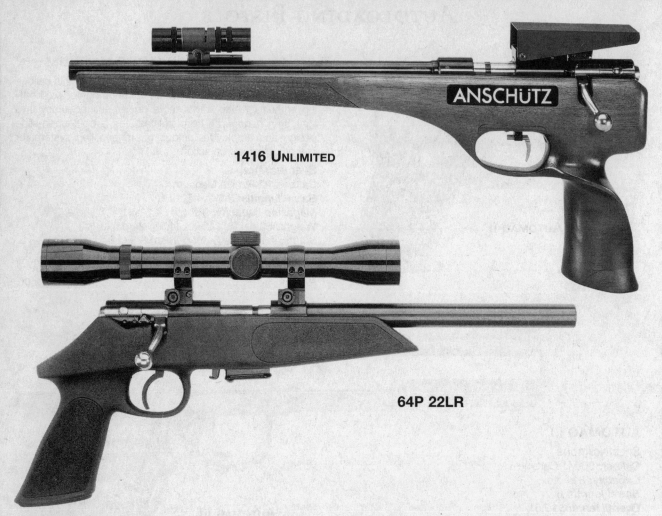

**1416 UNLIMITED**

**64P 22LR**

J.G. Anschutz began as a company in 1856, making pistols, rifles and shotguns. Since its rebirth following World War II, the firm has been best known for its fine rimfire target rifles. But there is also a line of bolt-action target pistols with the same features that have put Anschutz rifles in the winner's circle more often than any other rimfires in recent times.

Anschutz silhouette pistols feature a precisely machined single-shot action with left-side bolt handle and fully adjustable trigger (the blade can be moved longitudinally too). The Model 1416 MSP E "Unlimited" has a 14.1-inch barrel and full stock with wide thumb rest and stippling for a better hold in the Creedmoor position. The available Anschutz rear sight (#6836) has click adjustments of .035mm and a folding sight cover. The available front sight (#6523) has an anti-glare tube and three interchangeable inserts. Pistol weight: 14.1 pounds.

A shorter version of the "Unlimited" is the 1416 MSP E "Production" with 9.8-inch barrel that accelerates match-grade .22 bullets to just under the speed of sound. Avoiding the sound barrier helps ensure the greatest bullet stability and best accuracy.

*Pistol weight:* 3.7 pounds.

The centerfire Anschutz Model 1730 MSP E Field is like the 1416 models in that its trigger is directly below the loading platform, for fine balance. The receiver is grooved, drilled and tapped for scope mounts. The adjustable trigger and grip of this pistol are like those of the 1416s. With its 9.4-inch barrel, the Model 1730 weighs 3.9 pounds.

*Price:* 1416 MSP E Unlimited . . . . . . . . . . . . . . . $975.60
1416 MSP E Production . . . . . . . . . . . . . . . . . 975.60
1730 MSP E Field (not shown) . . . . . . . . . . . 1,730.00
Micrometer rear sight . . . . . . . . . . . . . . . . . . 153.80
Front sight . . . . . . . . . . . . . . . . . . . . . . . . . . . 49.70

Anschutz also offers bolt-action repeating pistols on a 64-type action with a right-hand bolt and 9.8-inch barrels. Both the .22 Long Rifle and .22 Magnum versions are grooved, drilled and tapped for scopes. *Pistol weights:* 3.5 pounds.

*Price:* 64 P .22 LR . . . . . . . . . . . . . . . . . . . . . $490.00
64 P .22 WMR . . . . . . . . . . . . . . . . . . . . . . . 528.00
Micrometer rear sight . . . . . . . . . . . . . . . . . . . 66.00
Front sight . . . . . . . . . . . . . . . . . . . . . . . . . . . 22.00

# BERETTA PISTOLS

## COMPACT FRAME COUGAR PISTOLS

### MODEL 8000 (9mm)  MODEL 8040 (40 CAL.)  MODEL 8045 (45 ACP)

Beretta's 8000/8040/8045 Cougar Series semiautomatics use a proven locked-breech system with a rotating barrel. This design makes the pistol compact and easy to conceal and operate with today's high-powered 9mm, 40 cal. and 45 ACP cal. ammunition. When the pistol is fired, the initial thrust of recoil energy is partially absorbed as it pushes slide and barrel back, with the barrel rotating by cam action against a tooth on the rigid central block. When the barrel has turned about 30 degrees, the locking lugs on the barrel clear the locking recesses, freeing the slide to continue rearward. The recoil spring absorbs the remaining recoil energy as the slide extracts and ejects the spent shell casing, rotates the hammer, and then reverses direction to chamber the next round. By channeling part of the recoil energy into barrel rotation and by partially absorbing the barrel and slide recoil shock through the central block before it is transferred to the frame, the Cougar reduces felt recoil.

**MODEL 8000/8040
COUGAR**

**SPECIFICATIONS**
*Calibers:* 9mm, 40 S&W, 45 ACP
*Capacity:* 10 rounds (8 rounds in 45 ACP)
*Action:* Double/Single or Double Action only
*Barrel length:* 3.6"
*Overall length:* 7"
*Weight:* 32.6 oz.
*Overall height:* 5.5"
*Sight radius:* 5.2"
*Sights:* Front and rear sights dovetailed to slide
*Finish:* Bruniton/Plastic
*Features:* Firing-pin block; chrome-lined barrel; short recoil, rotating barrel; anodized aluminum alloy frame
*Prices:*
Double action only (9mm and 40 cal.) . . . . . . . . .$672.00
Double or Single action (9mm and 40 cal.) . . . . . .695.00
Double action only (45 ACP) . . . . . . . . . . . . . . . .724.00
Double or Single action (45 ACP) . . . . . . . . . . . .748.00

**MODEL 8040
MINI-COUGAR**

### MODEL 8000/8040/8045 MINI-COUGAR

**SPECIFICATIONS**
*Caliber:* 9mm and 40 S&W, 45 ACP
*Capacity:* 8 rounds
*Action:* Double/Single or Double Action only
*Barrel length:* 3.6"
*Weight:* 27.6 oz. (9mm); 27.4 oz. (40 S&W)
*Features:* One inch shorter in the grip than the standard Cougar
*Prices:*
Double action only (9mm & 40 cal.) . . . . . . . . . . .$672.00
Double or Single actions (9mm & 40 cal.) . . . . . . . .695.00
Double action only (45 ACP) . . . . . . . . . . . . . . . .724.00
Double or single action (45 ACP) . . . . . . . . . . . . .748.00

# BERETTA PISTOLS

## SMALL FRAME PISTOLS

### MODEL 3032 TOMCAT

**SPECIFICATIONS**
*Caliber:* 32 Auto
*Capacity:* 7-shot magazine
*Barrel length:* 2.45"
*Overall length:* 4.9"
*Weight:* 14 1/2 oz.
*Sights:* Blade front, drift-adjustable rear
*Features:* Double or single action, thumb safety, tip-up barrel for direct loading/unloading, blued or matte finish
*Prices:*
Matte/Plastic . . . . . . . . . . . . . . . . . . . . . . . . . . .$333.00
Blued/Plastic . . . . . . . . . . . . . . . . . . . . . . . . . . .362.00
Stainless/Plastic . . . . . . . . . . . . . . . . . . . . . . . . .409.00

**MODEL 3032 TOMCAT**

### MODEL 21 BOBCAT DA SEMIAUTOMATIC

A safe, dependable, accurate small-bore pistol in 22 LR or 25 Auto. Easy to load with its unique barrel tip-up system.

**SPECIFICATIONS**
*Caliber:* 22 LR or 25 ACP
*Magazine capacity:* 7 rounds (22 LR); 8 rounds (25 ACP)
*Overall length:* 4.9"
*Barrel length:* 2.4"
*Weight:* 11.5 oz. (25 ACP); 11.8 oz. (22 LR)
*Sights:* Blade front: V-notch rear
*Safety:* Thumb operated
*Grips:* Plastic or Walnut
*Frame:* Forged aluminum
*Prices:*
Matte/Plastic . . . . . . . . . . . . . . . . . . . . . . . . . . .$246.00
Blued/Plastic . . . . . . . . . . . . . . . . . . . . . . . . . . .279.00
Nickel/Plastic . . . . . . . . . . . . . . . . . . . . . . . . . . .322.00
Blued/Engraved/Wood . . . . . . . . . . . . . . . . . . . .356.00
Stainless/Plastic . . . . . . . . . . . . . . . . . . . . . . . . .300.00

**MODEL 21 BOBCAT**

### MODEL 950 JETFIRE
### SINGLE-ACTION SEMIAUTOMATIC

**SPECIFICATIONS**
*Calibers:* 25 ACP
*Barrel length:* 2.4"
*Overall length:* 4.7"
*Overall height:* 3.4"
*Safety:* External, thumb-operated
*Magazine capacity:* 8 rounds
*Sights:* Blade front; V-notch rear
*Weight:* 9.9 oz.
*Frame:* Forged aluminum.
*Prices:*
Matte/Plastic . . . . . . . . . . . . . . . . . . . . . . . . . . .$220.00
Stainless/Plastic . . . . . . . . . . . . . . . . . . . . . . . . .262.00

**MODEL 950 JETFIRE**

# BERETTA PISTOLS

## MEDIUM-FRAME CHEETAH PISTOLS

### MODEL 84 CHEETAH

This pistol is pocket size with a large magazine capacity. The first shot (with hammer down, chamber loaded) can be fired by a double-action pull on the trigger without cocking the hammer manually.

The pistol also features a positive thumb safety (designed for both right- and left-handed operation), quick takedown (by means of special takedown button) and a conveniently located magazine release. Black plastic grips. Wood grips extra.

#### SPECIFICATIONS

*Caliber:* 380 Auto (9mm Short).
*Magazine capacity:* 10 rounds. *Barrel length:* 3.8". (approx.) *Overall length:* 6.8". (approx.) *Weight:* 23.3 oz. (approx.). *Sights:* Fixed front; rear dovetailed to slide. *Height overall:* 4.85" (approx.).
*Prices:* Bruniton/Plastic . . . . . . . . . . . . . . . . . .$565.00
Bruniton/Wood . . . . . . . . . . . . . . . . . . . . . . . .595.00
Nickel/Wood . . . . . . . . . . . . . . . . . . . . . . . . . .639.00

**MODEL 84 CHEETAH**

### MODEL 85 CHEETAH (not shown)

Some basic specifications as the model 84 Cheetah, except has a single line 8-round magazine, ambidextrous safety.
*Prices:* Bruniton/Plastic . . . . . . . . . . . . . . . . . .$533.00
Bruniton/Wood . . . . . . . . . . . . . . . . . . . . . . . .566.00
Nickel/Wood . . . . . . . . . . . . . . . . . . . . . . . . . .596.00
*Also available:*
MODEL 87 in 22 LR. *Capacity:* 7 rounds. Straight blow-back open slide design. *Width:* 1.3". *Barrel length:* 3.8". *Overall length:* 6.8". *Overall height:* 4.7". *Weight:* 20.1 oz. *Finish:* Blued with wood . . . . . . . . . . . . . . . . . . . . . .$565.00
MODEL 87 TARGET in 22 LR. *Capacity:* 10 rounds. *Barrel length:* 5.9". *Overall length:* 8.9". *Weight:* 40.9 oz. *Finish:* Blued with plastic . . . . . . . . . . . . . . . . . . . . . .655.00

### MODEL 86 CHEETAH

#### SPECIFICATIONS

*Caliber:* 380 Auto (9mm Short). *Barrel length:* 4.4". *Overall length:* 7.3". *Capacity:* 8 rounds. *Weight:* 23.3 oz. *Sight radius:* 4.9". *Overall height:* 4.8". *Overall width:* 1.4". *Grip:* Walnut. *Features:* Same as other Medium Frame, straight blow-back models, plus safety and convenience of a tip-up barrel (rounds can be loaded directly into chamber without operating the slide).
*Price:* Bruniton/Wood Grips . . . . . . . . . . . . . . .$566.00

**MODEL 86 CHEETAH**

### MODEL 89 GOLD STANDARD SA

This sophisticated single-action target pistol features an 8-round magazine, adjustable target sights, and target-style contoured walnut grips with thumbrest.

#### SPECIFICATIONS

*Caliber:* 22 LR. *Capacity:* 8 rounds. *Barrel length:* 6". *Overall length:* 9.5". *Height:* 5.3" *Weight:* 41 oz. *Features:* Adjustable target sights, and target style contoured walnut grips with thumbrest
*Price:* . . . . . . . . . . . . . . . . . . . . . . . . . . . . . .$802.00

**MODEL 89 GOLD STANDARD**

# BERETTA PISTOLS

## LARGE FRAME 92/96 SERIES PISTOLS

**MODELS 92FS (9mm) & 96 (40 Cal.)**

**MODEL 92FS COMPACT**

### MODELS 92FS (9MM) & 96 (40 CAL.)
**SPECIFICATIONS**
*Calibers:* 9mm and 40 cal.
*Capacity:* 10 rounds   *Action:* Double/Single
*Barrel length:* 4.9"   *Overall length:* 8.5"
*Weight:* 34.4 oz.   *Overall height:* 5.4"
*Overall width:* 1.5"
*Sights:* Integral front; windage adjustable rear; 3-dot or tritium night sights
*Grips:* Wood or plastic
*Finish:* Bruniton (also available in blued, stainless, silver or gold)
*Features:* Chrome-lined bore; visible firing-pin block; open slide design; safety drop catch (half-cock); combat trigger guard; external hammer; reversible magazine release
**MODEL BRIGADIER** (9mm and 40 cal.). Same as above but with a heavier slide.
*Barrel length:* 4.3". *Overall length:* 7.8". *Weight:* 35.3 oz.
**MODEL 92 COMPACT L TYPE M** (9mm)
*Barrel length:* 4.3" *Overall length:* 7.8" *Weight:* 30.9 oz.

### MODEL 96 COMBAT
**SPECIFICATIONS**
*Calibers:* 40  *Capacity:* 11 rounds
*Action:* Single action only (Combat); single/double (Stock)
*Barrel length:* 5.9"  *Overall length:* 9.5"
*Weight:* 40 oz.  *Sights:* 3 interchageable front sights (Stock)
*Features:* Rubber magazine bumpers; replaceable accurizing barrel bushings; checkered grips; machine-checkered front and backstraps; fitted ABS cases; Brigadier slide; extended frame-mounted safety; competition-tuned trigger and adjustable rear target set and tool set
*Prices:*
MODEL 96 COMBAT (single action only) . . . . . . .$1,700.00
MODEL 96 BRIGADIER (heavy slide and removable
   front sight, 35 oz.) . . . . . . . . . . . . . . . . . . .702.00
MODEL 96 COMPACT (32 oz.) . . . . . . . . . . . . . .655.00

### MODEL 92FS COMPACT AND COMPACT TYPE M
**SPECIFICATIONS**
Same features as the proven 92FS but in a more compact overall size and weight. *Overall length:* 7.8" *Barrel length:* 4.3" *Overall width:* 1.4" *Overall height:* 5.3" *Sight radius:* 5.8" *Weight:* 32.0 oz. Compact, 30.9 oz. Type M (unloaded). Special contoured magazine bottom for improved hand support and control. Compact features a double column magazine, while the Compact Type M features a single column magazine for thinner grip (1.28" instead of 1.39") and reduced weight.
*Prices:* MODEL 92 FS COMPACT
**DA OR SA** . . . . . . . . . . . . . . . . . . . . . . . . . .$655.00
**MODEL 92FS PLASTIC** w/3-Dot sights . . . . . . . . . . .655.00
   For wood grips, **add** . . . . . . . . . . . . . . . . . .37.50
**MODEL 92FS** Stainless w/3-dot sights . . . . . . . . .718.00
**MODEL 96** w/3-dot sights . . . . . . . . . . . . . . . .655.00
**MODEL 92FS BRIGADIER** . . . . . . . . . . . . . . . . .702.00
**MODEL 92FS LIMITED EDITION** . . . . . . . . . . . . . .2,082.00
   (1 of 470, polished stainless, walnut grips, chrome-plated magazine)

**MODEL 96 COMBAT**

# BERNARDELLI PISTOLS

**MODEL P.010**
TARGET

## MODEL P.010 TARGET PISTOL

**SPECIFICATIONS**
*Caliber:* 22 LR *Capacity:* 5 or 10 rounds  *Barrel length:* 5.9" *Weight:* 40 oz.  *Sights:* Interchangeable front sight; rear sight adjustable  for windage and elevation  *Sight radius:* 7.5" *Features:* All steel construction; external hammer with safety notch; external slide catch for hold-open device; inertia safe firing pin; oil-finished walnut grips for right- and left-hand shooters; matte black or chrome finish; pivoted trigger with adjustable weight and take-ups
*Price:* . . . . . . . . . . . . . . . . . . . . . . . . . . . . . . $899.00

# BERSA PISTOLS

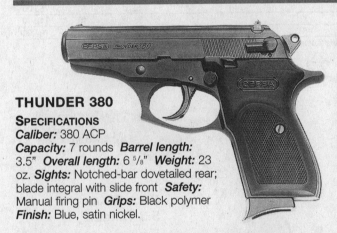

**THUNDER 380**

**SPECIFICATIONS**
*Caliber:* 380 ACP
*Capacity:* 7 rounds  *Barrel length:* 3.5" *Overall length:* 6 ⁵/₈" *Weight:* 23 oz. *Sights:* Notched-bar dovetailed rear; blade integral with slide front  *Safety:* Manual firing pin  *Grips:* Black polymer *Finish:* Blue, satin nickel.

*Prices:* Matte . . . . . . . . . . . . . . . . . . . . . . . . $264.95
Satin Nickel . . . . . . . . . . . . . . . . . . . . . . . . . . . 281.95
9-Shot Deluxe . . . . . . . . . . . . . . . . . . . . . . . . . 274.95

## SERIES 95 (not shown)

**SPECIFICATIONS**
*Caliber:* 32 ACP *Capacity:* 10 rounds  *Action:* Double *Barrel length:* 3.5" *Overall length:* 6 ⁵/₈" *Weight:* 23 oz. *Sights:* Notched-bar dovetailed rear; blade integral with slide front  *Safety:* Manual firing pin  *Grips:* Black polymer *Finish:* Matte blue, satin nickel, Duo-Tone
*Prices:* Matte . . . . . . . . . . . . . . . . . . . . . . . . $248.95
Nickel . . . . . . . . . . . . . . . . . . . . . . . . . . . . . . . 264.95
Duo-Tone . . . . . . . . . . . . . . . . . . . . . . . . . . . . 259.95

# BOND ARMS

## CENTURY 2000 DEFENDER

**SPECIFICATIONS**
*Barrel Length:* 3" *Weight:* 21 oz. *Length:* 5"
*Features:* Custom grip, crossbolt safety, interchangeable barrels, retracting firing pin, rebounding hammer, stainless steel, blade front sight
*Prices:*
CENTURY 2000 DEFENDER . . . . . . . . . . . . . . $369.00
TEXAS DEFENDER. . . . . . . . . . . . . . . . . . . . . . 349.00
COWBOY DEFENDER . . . . . . . . . . . . . . . . . . . 349.00
LEFT-HANDED MODELS (additional) . . . . . . . . . . . 15.00
ADDITIONAL BARRELS . . . . . . . . . . . . . . . 119.00-139.00

# BROWNING PISTOLS

**9MM HI-POWER**
SINGLE ACTION

## HI-POWER SINGLE ACTION AUTOLOADER

Both the 9mm and 40 S&W models come with either a fixed-blade front sight and a windage-adjustable rear sight or a nonglare rear sight, screw adjustable for both windage and elevation. The front sight is an 1/8-inch-wide blade mounted on a ramp. The rear surface of the blade is serrated to prevent glare. All models have an ambidextrous safety. See table below for specifications and prices.

## HI-POWER SPECIFICATIONS 9mm & 40 S&W

| MODEL | SIGHTS | GRIPS | BARREL LENGTH | OVERALL LENGTH | OVERALL WIDTH | OVERALL HEIGHT | WEIGHT* | MAG. CAP. | PRICE |
|---|---|---|---|---|---|---|---|---|---|
| Mark III | Fixed | Molded | 4.75" | 7.75" | 1 3/8" | 5" | 32 oz. | 10 | $608.00 |
| Standard | Fixed | Walnut | 4.75" | 7.75" | 1 3/8" | 5" | 32 oz. | 10 | 646.00 |
| Standard | Adj. | Walnut | 4.75" | 7.75" | 1 3/8" | 5" | 32 oz. | 10 | 701.00 |
| HP-Practical | Fixed | Molded Rubber | 4.75" | 7.75" | 1 3/8" | 5" | 36 oz. | 10 | 695.00 |
| HP-Practical | Adj. | Molded Rubber | 4.75" | 7.75" | 1 3/8" | 5" | 36 oz. | 10 | 753.00 |
| Silver Chrome | Adj. | Molded Rubber | 4.75" | 7.75" | 1 3/8" | 5" | 36 oz. | 10 | 718.00 |
| Capitan (9mm only) | Adj. | Walnut | 4.75" | 7.75" | 1 3/8" | 5" | 32 oz. | 10 | 764.00 |

*\* 9mm weight listed. Overall weight of the 40 S&W Hi-Power is 3 oz. heavier than the 9mm.*

# BUCK MARK 22 LR SERIES

**BUCK MARK STANDARD**
(5.5" BARREL)

**BUCK MARK**
**5.5 TARGET**

## BUCK MARK SPECIFICATIONS

| BUCK MARK MODELS | MAG. CAP. | BARREL LENGTH | OVERALL LENGTH | WEIGHT | OVERALL HEIGHT | SIGHT RADIUS | GRIPS | PRICE |
|---|---|---|---|---|---|---|---|---|
| Standard | 10 | 5.5" | 9.5" | 36 oz. | 5 3/8" | 8" | Molded Composite, Ambidextrous | $278.00 |
| Micro Standard | 10 | 4" | 8" | 32 oz. | 5 3/8" | 9 9/16" | Molded Composite, Ambidextrous | 278.00 |
| Nickel | 10 | 5.5" | 9.5" | 36 oz. | 5 3/8" | 8" | Molded Composite, Ambidextrous | 328.00 |
| Micro Nickel | 10 | 4" | 8" | 32 oz. | 5 3/8" | 9 9/16" | Molded Composite, Ambidextrous | 328.00 |
| Plus Nickel | 10 | 5.5" | 9.5" | 36 oz. | 5 3/8" | 8" | Laminated Hardwood | 372.00 |
| Micro Plus Nickel | 10 | 4" | 8" | 32 oz. | 5 3/8" | 9 9/16" | Laminated Hardwood | 372.00 |
| Plus | 10 | 5.5" | 9.5" | 36 oz. | 5 3/8" | 8" | Laminated Hardwood | 340.00 |
| Micro Plus | 10 | 4" | 8" | 32 oz. | 5 3/8" | 9 9/16" | Laminated Hardwood | 340.00 |
| Camper | 10 | 5.5" | 9.5" | 34 oz. | 5 3/8" | 8" | Composite | 246.00 |
| Challenge | 10 | 5.5" | 9.5" | 25 oz. | 5 3/8" | 8" | Walnut | 311.00 |
| Micro Challenge | 10 | 4" | 8" | 23 oz. | 5 3/8" | 6 1/2" | Walnut | 311.00 |
| Bullseye, Standard | 10 | 7.25" | 11 5/16" | 36 oz. | 5 3/8" | 9 7/8" | Molded Composite, Ambidextrous | 408.00 |
| Bullseye, Target | 10 | 7.25" | 11 5/16" | 36 oz. | 5 3/8" | 9 7/8" | Contoured Rosewood or Wraparound fingergroove | 525.00 |
| 5.5 Field | 10 | 5.5" | 9 5/8" | 35.5 oz. | 5 5/16" | 8.25" | Contoured Walnut or Wraparound fingergroove | 446.00 |
| 5.5 Target | 10 | 5.5" | 9 5/8" | 35.5 oz. | 5 5/16" | 8.25" | Contoured Walnut or Wraparound fingergroove | 446.00 |
| 5.5 Nickel Target | 10 | 5.5" | 9 5/8" | 35.5 oz. | 5 5/16" | 8.25" | Contoured Walnut or Wraparound fingergroove | 500.00 |
| Extra Magazine | | | | | | | | 24.95 |

*Micro 4"-barrel models available for all standard Buck Marks and Challenge. Same price as 5.5".*
*Finishes are matte blue w/polished barrel flats or nickel plated slide and barrel. Pro Target rear sight and 1/8" wide front sight standard.*

# CIMARRON FIREARMS

The Cimarron Firearms Co. has an impressive line of 19th-century replica revolvers and rifles. They are high-quality firearms, faithfully crafted to show the form, fit and function of the originals. They are ideal for Cowboy Action shooting. The single-shot Sharps and Winchester rifles make excellent hunting rifles for shooters who want the feel of another century between their hands.

**1872 OPEN TOP**

**1858 ARMY .44**

## 1872 OPEN TOP

The 1872 Open Top was the first cartridge firing six shooter manufactured by Colt and the forerunner of the famous 1873 Colt Model 'P' or Peacemaker. The Colt 1872 Open Top was manufactured at the same time as the percussion conversion models. The Cimarron Firearms Co. Open Top revolver is manufactured from the ground up, utilizing high quality modern gun steel. It is made much stronger than the original and other Open Top replicas made from percussion parts.

**Barrels:** 5 1/2" & 7 1/2"
**Calibers:** .38 Colt & S&W Special, .44 Colt & Russian, .45 S&W Schofield
**Grips:** Walnut, Early Navy style brass or Later steel Army style.
**Finish:** Blue, charcoal blue, nickel, or original finish
Retail . . . . . . . . . . . . . . . . . . . . . . . . . . . . . . . . . . .**$469.00**
*Also Available:* **1858 ARMY .44** . . . . . . . . . . . . . . .249.00

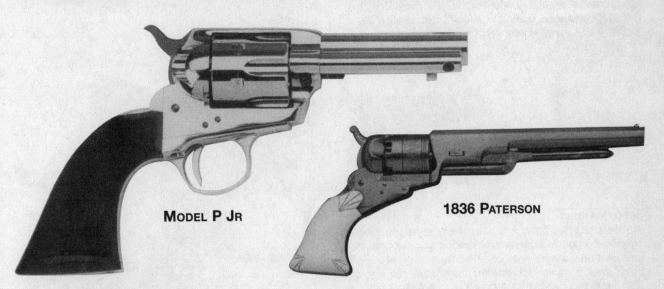

**MODEL P JR**

**1836 PATERSON**

## 1836 PATERSON

The 1836 Paterson in 36-caliber, was produced shortly before the factory shut down in 1942.
**Price:** . . . . . . . . . . . . . . . . . . . . . . . . . . . . . . .$399.00

## MODEL 'P' JR

The Cimarron Model 'P' Jr. (MPJ) is styled after–but 20% smaller than–the famous 1873 Colt Peacemaker. The MPJ features a down-sized traditional style Colt grip instead of the bird's head grip found on the Cimarron Lightning SA model. The MPJ features Cimarron's exclusive Cowboy Comp action and is manufactured to Cimarron's superior level of fit, finish and function. Shoulder rigs and holsters now available for the Lightning SA and Model 'P' Jr.
**Barrels:** 3 1/2" & 4 3/4"
**Calibers:** .38 Special
**Finish:** Blue with case hardened frame
**Price:**
Retail: . . . . . . . . . . . . . . . . . . . . . . . . . . . . . . . . . .$389.00

# COLT M1911 PISTOLS

## MODEL O SERIES 1991 AND XS

**GOVERNMENT 1991 MATTE**

### SPECIFICATIONS

Checkered rubber composite grips • smooth, composite trigger • single action • fixed sights • .45 ACP • 7+1 capacity • beveled mag well • standard thumb safety and service style grip safety

**Price:** Blue . . . . . . . . . . . . . . . . . . . . . . . . . . . . . $573.00
Stainless . . . . . . . . . . . . . . . . . . . . . . . . . . . . 628.00

**Also available:**

**O1991/GOV'T 1991 MATTE**, matte black finish, carbon steel frame & slide, 5" barrel length, 8.5" overall length

**O1091/GOV'T 1991 STAINLESS**, matte stainless finish, stainless frame & slide, 5" barrel length, 8.5" overall length

**O4091U/COMMANDER STAINLESS**, matte stainless finish, stainless frame & slide, 4.25" barrel length, 7.75" overall length

**O4691/COMMANDER**, matte black finish, carbon steel frame & slide, 4.25" barrel length, 7.75" overall length

**COMMANDER**

### SPECIFICATIONS

Stainless brushed finish • front and rear slide serrations • checkered, double diamond, rosewood grips • extended ambidextrous thumb safeties • upswept beavertail with palm swell • three dot dovetail front and rear sights • adjustable 2-cut aluminum trigger • elongated slot hammer • new roll marking and enhanced tolerances • .45 caliber • single action

**Price:** . . . . . . . . . . . . . . . . . . . . . . . . . . . . . . . $750.00

**Also available:**

**O1070XS/GOVERNMENT**, 5" barrel length, 8+1 capacity

**O9850XS/CONCEALED CARRY OFFICERS**, 4.25" barrel length, 7+1 capacity

**O4012XS/COMMANDER**, 4.25" barrel length, 8+1 capacity

**O4860XS/LIGHTWEIGHT COMMANDER**, 4.25" barrel length, 8+1 capacity

# COLT PISTOLS/REVOLVERS

## GOLD CUP
## MODEL O PISTOLS
**SPECIFICATIONS**
Stainless steel frame
- stainless round top slide
- brushed stainless
  finish on both frame and slide
- 5" barrel length and 8.5" overall length
- .45 caliber • 8+1 round capacity
- Enhanced elongated slot hammer
- adjustable aluminum trigger
- dovetail front sight
- bomar-style rear sight • black wrap around grips
- 39 ounce overall weight • single action

**Price:**
GOLD CUP . . . . . . . . . . . . . . . . . . . . . . . . . . $1,116.00

## DEFENDER
## MODEL O PISTOL
**SPECIFICATIONS**
Brushed stainless finish • wrap
around rubber finger groove grips
- skeletonized composite trigger
- single action • three dot dovetail
front and rear sights • .45 caliber • 3" barrel length, 6.75"
overall length • 7+1 capacity • beveled mag well • extended thumb safety and upswept beavertail with palm swell •
lightweight • enhanced tolerances
**Price:** MODEL O7000D . . . . . . . . . . . . . . . . . . . $773.00

## COWBOY SINGLE ACTION REVOLVER
### SPECIFICATIONS
Blue color case finish • first generation grips • .45 Colt caliber • 5.5" barrel length, 11" overall length • 6 round capacity • transfer bar safety • enhanced tolerances
**Price:** MODEL CB1850 . . . . . . . . . . . . . . . . . . . $599.00

**Also available:** TRADITIONAL SINGLE ACTION ARMY REVOLVERS
**P1840,** blue color case finish, .45 Colt, 4.75" barrel length, 10.25" overall length
**P1841,** nickel finish, .45 Colt, 4.75" barrel length, 10.25" overall length
**P1850,** blue color case finish, .45 Colt, 5.5" barrel length, 11" overall length
**P1856,** nickel finish, .45 Colt, 5.5" barrel length, 11" overall length
**P1940,** blue color case finish, .44-.40 caliber, 4.75" barrel length, 10.25" overall length
**P1941,** nickel finish, .44-.40 caliber, 4.75" barrel length, 10.25" overall length
**P1950,** blue color case finish, .44-.40 caliber, 5.5" barrel length, 11" overall length
**P1956,** nickel finish, .44-.40 caliber, 5.5" barrel length, 11" overall length
**Price:** . . . . . . . . . . . . . . . . . . . . . . . . . . . . . . $1,590.00

# CZ PISTOLS

### CZ 75

There are originals which are hard to copy. One of these is the CZ 75 pistol - a product of Ceska Zbrojovka, Uhersky Brod. The CZ 75 B is the basis of the all-steel, semi-automatic, double action pistols of the CZ 75 pistol family.

### CZ 75 B

The pistols of the CZ 75 line are semi-automatic handguns with a locked breech principle. These pistols are manufactured in many versions.

The characteristic features of all versions are the following: large capacity double-column magazine; comfortable grip in either hand; good results at instinctive shooting (without aiming); low trigger pull weight; high accuracy of fire; long service life; high reliability, even with various brands of ammunition; the slide stays open after the last cartridge has been fired; the sights are outfitted with a three-dot illuminating system for better aiming in poor visibility conditions; suitable for COMBAT shooting.

Versions differ in the caliber, size, weight, magazine capacity, trigger mechanism operation, safety elements, surface finish, grip panel types and other specific modifications.

*Caliber:* 9 mm Luger, .40 S&W  *Magazine capacity:* 10 cartridges  *Overall length:* 8.1"  *Barrel length:* 4.7"  *Height:* 5.4"  *Width (acc. to grip panel type):* 1.4"  *Weight with empty magazine:* 2.2 lbs.  *Trigger mechanism:* SA/DA  *Safety elements:* Manual safety, safety stop on the hammer, firing pin safety

*Price:* 9mm . . . . . . . . . . . . . . . . . . . . . . . . . . . . . .$472.00
40 S&W . . . . . . . . . . . . . . . . . . . . . . . . . . . . . . .486.00

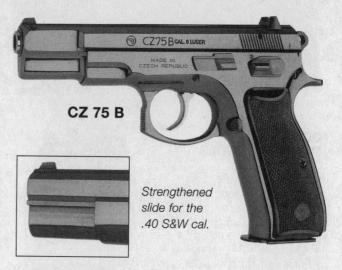

**CZ 75 B**

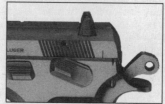

*Strengthened slide for the .40 S&W cal.*

*The pistol with a cocked hammer and with the safety on.*

### CZ 75 STANDARD IPSC

**CZ 97 B**

**CZ 75 CHAMPION**

### CZ 75 CHAMPION

*Caliber/Magazine capacity:* 9 mm Luger / 10, 40 S&W / 10  *Length:* 9.5"  *Barrel Length:* 4.5"
*Height:* 5.6"  *Weight:* 2.2 lbs.  *Mode of operation:* SA
*Safety elements:* Manual safety, safety stop on the hammer
*Price:* . . . . . . . . . . . . . . . . . . . . . . . . . .$1,484.00

### CZ 75 STANDARD IPSC

*Caliber/Magazine capacity:* .40 S&W/10  *Length:* 8.9"
*Barrel Length:* 5.4"  *Height:* 5.9"  *Weight:* 2.8 lbs.  *Mode of operation:* SA  *Safety elements:* Manual safety, safety stop on the hammer
*Price:* . . . . . . . . . . . . . . . . . . . . . . . . . .$1,038.00

### CZ 97 B

*Caliber/Magazine capacity:* .45 Auto / 10  *Length:* 8.3"
*Barrel Length:* 4.8"  *Height:* 5.9"  *Weight:* 2.6 lbs.  *Mode of operation:* SA/DA  *Safety elements:* Manual safety, safety stop on the hammer, firing pin safety, loaded chamber indicator
*Price:* . . . . . . . . . . . . . . . . . . . . . . . . . . . .$621.00

# CZ PISTOLS

## ADAPTER – CZ 75 / 85 KADET

The CZ 75 Kadet conversion kit is a separate accessory for the CZ 75/85 pistol series allowing the firing of .22 LR calibre cartridges. The Kadet adapter features its own sights adjustable for elevation and windage, so the "sighting-in" of the pistol is not affected.

### CZ KADET PISTOL .22 CAL.
**Caliber:** .22 LR  **Barrel length:** 4.9"  **Magazine capacity:** 10 cartridges  **Weight:** 2.4 lbs.

### CZ KADET .22 CAL. CONVERSION KIT
**Caliber:** .22 LR  **Magazine capacity:** 10 cartridges  **Overall length:** 8.1"  **Barrel length:** 4.9"  **Weight:** 1.1 lbs.  **Empty magazine weight:** 0.3 lbs.

The Kadet adapter is supplied in the following variants:
1. An individual adapter assembly, which can be used after the fitting of the appropriate surfaces on the adapter housing to the frame of any CZ 75/85 pistol (in 9mm Luger or .40 S&W calibers)
2. The CZ 75/85 Kadet in .22 LR cal. pistol
**Price:** . . . . . . . . . . . . . . . . . . . . . . . . . . . . . . . .$486.00
   Adapter Kit . . . . . . . . . . . . . . . . . . . . . . . . . . . .489.00

### CZ 75 KADET

The Kadet adapter in its rear (cocked) position

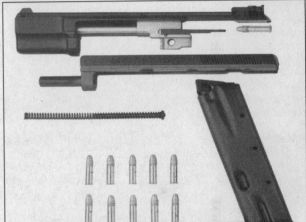

### CZ 83

View of the pistol with cocked hammer and with the safety on

### CZ 83
**Caliber:** 7,65 mm Browning; 9mm Makarov, 9mm Browning  **Magazine Capacity:** 10  **Length:** 6.8"; 6.8"  **Barrel Length:** 3.8"; 3.8"  **Height:** 5.0"; 5.0"  **Weight:** 1.7 lbs.; 1.8 lbs.  **Mode of operation:** SA/DA; SA/DA  **Safety elements:** Manual safety, automatic safety
**Price:** . . . . . . . . . . . . . . . . . . . . . . . . . . . . . .$378.00

### CZ 100

### CZ 100
**Caliber/Magazine capacity:** 9mm Luger/10; .40 S&W/10  **Length:** 180 mm (7.1")  **Barrel Length:** 98 mm (3.9")  **Height:** 130 mm (5.1")  **Weight:** 665 g (1.5 lbs.)  **Mode of operation:** SA/DA  **Safety elements:** firing pin block, loaded chamber indicator, cocking indication button, decocking lever
**Price:** . . . . . . . . . . . . . . . . . . . . . . . . . . . . .$405.00

# DAVIS PISTOLS

**MODEL D-25 DERRINGER**

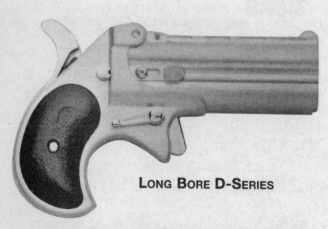

**LONG BORE D-SERIES**

**MODEL P-32**

**MODEL P-380**

## D-SERIES DERRINGERS

**SPECIFICATIONS**
*Calibers:* 22 LR, 22 Mag., 25 Auto, 32 Auto
*Capacity:* 2 shot  *Barrel Length:* 2.4"
*Overall Length:* 4"  *Height:* 2.8"  *Weight:* 9.5 oz.
*Grips:* Laminated wood  *Finish:* Black teflon or chrome
*Price:* . . . . . . . . . . . . . . . . . . . . . . . . . . . . . . . . . $75.00

## LONG BORE D-SERIES

**SPECIFICATIONS**
*Calibers:* 22 Mag., 9mm, 32 H&R Mag., 38 Special
*Capacity:* 2 rounds  *Barrel Length:* 3.5"
*Overall Length:* 5.4"  *Height:* 3.31"  *Weight:* 16 oz.
*Price:* . . . . . . . . . . . . . . . . . . . . . . . . . . . . . . . $104.00
    9mm only. . . . . . . . . . . . . . . . . . . . . . . . . . . 110.00
*Also available:*
BIG BORE D-SERIES.
*Calibers:* 22 WMR, 9mm, 32 H&R Mag., 38 Special.
*Barrel Length:* 2.75"  *Overall Length:* 4.65"
*Weight:* 14 oz.
*Price:* . . . . . . . . . . . . . . . . . . . . . . . . . . . . . . . . $98.00
    9mm only. . . . . . . . . . . . . . . . . . . . . . . . . . . 104.00

## MODEL P-32

**SPECIFICATIONS**
*Caliber:* 32 Auto  *Magazine Capacity:* 6 rounds
*Barrel Length:* 2.8"  *Overall Length:* 5.4"
*Weight:* 22 oz.  *Height:* 4"
*Grips:* Laminated wood  *Finish:* Black teflon or chrome
*Price:* . . . . . . . . . . . . . . . . . . . . . . . . . . . . . . . . $87.50

## MODEL P-380

**SPECIFICATIONS**
*Caliber:* 380 Auto  *Magazine Capacity:* 5 rounds
*Barrel Length:* 2.8"  *Overall Length:* 5.4"
*Height:* 4"  *Weight:* 22 oz.
*Price:* . . . . . . . . . . . . . . . . . . . . . . . . . . . . . . . . $98.00

# DOWNSIZER PISTOLS

## MODEL WSP
## "WORLD'S SMALLEST PISTOL"

"WORLD'S SMALLEST PISTOL"

**SPECIFICATIONS**
*Action:* Single-shot double-action only
*Caliber:* 45 ACP, 357 Mag.
*Barrel length:* 2.1", tip-up barrel
*Overall length:* 3.25"
*Weight:* 11 oz. *Height:* 2.25" *Width:* 0.9"
*Materials:* Stainless steel; CNC machined from solid bar stock
*Price:* . . . . . . . . . . . . . . . . . . . . . . . . $399.00

# EMF/DAKOTA REVOLVERS

## E.M.F. HARTFORD SINGLE-ACTION REVOLVERS

1st and 2nd generations models available. Parts are interchangeable with the original Colts. Forged steel frames, case hardened, steel backstrap & trigger guard. Original blue finish, walnut grips. Barrel lengths: 4.75", 5.5", 7.5", 12" buntline.

### MODEL 1875 REMINGTON SINGLE ACTION REVOLVER
Engraved; case hardened frame
*Price:* Blued . . . . . . . . . . . . . . . . . . $575.00
Nickel . . . . . . . . . . . . . . . . . . . . . . 740.00

### MODEL 1890 REMINGTON POLICE
**SPECIFICATIONS** – *Calibers:* 44-40, 45 Long Colt and 357 Magnum. *Barrel length:* 5.75". *Finish:* Blued or nickel *Features:* Original design (1891-1894) with lanyard ring in buttstock; case hardened frame; walnut grips
*Price:* . . . . . . . . . . . . . . . . . . . . . . $610.00
Nickel . . . . . . . . . . . . . . . . . . . . . 775.00

### 1873 HARTFORD "BUNTLINE"
**SPECIFICATIONS** – *Caliber:* 45 LC *Barrel Length:* 12" *Features:* Steel backstrap & trigger
*Price:* . . . . . . . . . . . . . . . . . . . . . . $670.00

### HARTFORD PINKERTON
**SPECIFICATIONS**
*Caliber:* 45 LC, 357 Magnum
*Barrel length:* 4". Bird's-head grip with ejector tube.
*Price:* . . . . . . . . . . . . . . . . . . . . . . $570.00

### 1873 DAKOTA SINGLE ACTION WITH 5.5" BARREL

### 1873 DAKOTA SINGLE ACTION
**SPECIFICATIONS**
*Calibers:* 357 Mag., 44-40, 45 Long Colt. *Barrel lengths:* 4.75", 5.5" and 7.5". *Finish:* Blued, case hardened frame. *Grips:* One-piece walnut. *Features:* Classic Colt design, set screw for cylinder pin release; black nickel backstrap and trigger design
*Price:* . . . . . . . . . . . . . . . . . . . . . . . . . . $400.00
Engraved . . . . . . . . . . . . . . . . . . . . . . . . 800.00
Buntline (.45 L.C., 12") . . . . . . . . . . . . . . . . 670.00

# ENTRÉPRISE ARMS PISTOLS

## TACTICAL P325 PLUS

### SPECIFICATIONS
*Caliber:* .45 ACP, 10 round magazine.
*Barrel:* 3.25". *Weight:* 37 oz. *Length:* 7.25" overall.
*Stocks:* Black Ergo Ultra Slim, double diamond checkered grip panels.
*Sights:* Tactical2 Ghost Ring sight or Novak Lo-mount sight.
*Features:* Same as the Elite series plus extended ambidextrous thumb safety, front & rear cocking serrations, full length guide rod, barrel throated & frame ramp polished, tuned match extractor, fitted barrel & bushing, stainless steel firing pin, serrated & ramped front sight, slide lapped to frame, dehorned and trigger set at a crisp 4.5 pounds.
*Price:* ...................................$979.00

**TACTICAL P325 PLUS**

## ELITE P425 (and P500, P325)

### SPECIFICATIONS
*Caliber:* .45 ACP, 10 round magazine.
*Barrel:* 4.25" (5" P500, 3.25" P325) *Weight:* 38 oz. (40 oz. P500, 36 oz. P325) *Length:* 7.75" overall
*Stocks:* Black Ergo Ultra Slim, double diamond checkered grip panels.
*Sights:* 3 Dot fixed sights (dovetail cut front sight).
*Features:* Reinforced dustcover, lowered & flared ejection port, squared trigger guard, adjustable match trigger, bolstered front strap, high grip cut, hardened steel magazine release, high ride beavertail grip safety, steel flat mainspring housing (checkered 20 LPI), checkered slide release, extended thumb lock, EDM skeletonized match hammer & sear, match grade disconnector with polished contact points and Wolff springs throughout.
*Price:* ...................................$699.90

**ELITE P425**

## BOXER P500

### SPECIFICATIONS
*Caliber:* .45 ACP, .40 Cal. *Barrel:* 5". *Weight:* 40 oz.
*Length:* 8.5" overall. *Stocks:* Black Ergo Ultra Slim, double diamond checkered grip panels.
*Sights:* Adjustable Competizione "melded" rear sight with dovetail patridge front sight. *Features:* Same as the Elite model plus machined slide parallel rails with polished breech face & barrel channel, front & rear cocking serrations, lowered & flared ejection port, full length stainless steel one piece guide rod with plug, National match barrel 5" Government length, match bushing, stainless steel firing pin, match extractor, oversized firing pin stop, fitted barrel & bushing, slide lapped to frame, barrel throated & frame ramp polished, extractor tuned and trigger set at a crisp 4.5 pounds.
*Price:* 45ACP .........................$1,399.00
40 Cal. ................................1,499.00

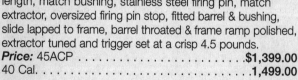

**BOXER P500**

# ENTRÉPRISE ARMS PISTOLS

**MODEL I**

### TOURNAMENT SHOOTERS MODEL I
**SPECIFICATIONS**
**Caliber:** .45 ACP, 40 cal., 38 Super
**Barrel:** 5"  **Weight:** 40 oz.  **Length:** 8.5" overall
**Stocks:** Black ultra-slim double diamond checkered grip panels
**Sights:** Adjustable Competizione "melded" rear sight with dovetail Patridge front sight
**Features:** Same as the Elite model (previous page) plus over-sized magazine release button, ambidextrous thumb lock, flared extended magazine well, fully machined parallel slide rails, polished barrel channel, polished breech face, front & rear cocking serrations, serrated top of slide, stainless steel ramped bull barrel with fully supported chamber, full length stainless steel one piece guide rod with plug, stainless steel firing pin, match extractor, oversized firing pin stop, fitted Bull Barrel, slide lapped to frame, polished ramp, extractor tuned, hard chrome finish and trigger set at a 2 pounds.
**Price:** . . . . . . . . . . . . . . . . . . . . . . . . . . . . .$2,300.00

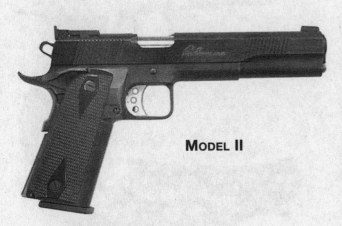

**MODEL II**

### TOURNAMENT SHOOTERS MODEL II
**SPECIFICATIONS**
**Caliber:** .45 ACP, 10 round magazine
**Barrel:** 6"  **Weight:** 44 oz.  **Length:** 9.5" overall
**Stocks:** Black ultra slim double diamond checkered grip panels
**Sights:** Adjustable Competizione "melded" rear sight with dovetail Patridge front sight
**Features:** Same as the Elite model (previous page) plus over-sized magazine release button, ambidextrous thumb lock, front strap checkered (20 LPI), long slide fully machined, parallel slide rails, polished barrel channel, polished breech face, front & Rear Cocking Serrations, lowered & flared ejection port, serrated top of slide, 6" stainless steel national match barrel, national match bushing, full length stainless steel two piece guide rod with plug, stainless steel firing pin, match extractor, oversized firing pin stop, fitted barrel & bushing, slide lapped to frame, barrel throated & frame pamp polished, extractor tuned, black oxide finish and trigger set at 4.5 pounds.
**Price:** . . . . . . . . . . . . . . . . . . . . . . . . . . . . .$2,000.00

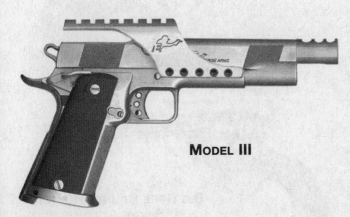

**MODEL III**

### TOURNAMENT SHOOTERS MODEL III
**SPECIFICATIONS**
**Caliber:** .45 ACP, 40 cal., 38 Super
**Barrel:** 6"  **Weight:** 44 oz.  **Length:** 9.5" overall
**Stocks:** Black ultra slim double diamond checkered grip panels
**Features:** Same as the Elite model (previous page) plus fitted barrel and compensator, oversized magazine release button, ambidextrous extended thumb lock, extended slide stop, front strap checkered (20 LPI), trigger guard checkered (20 LPI), frame mounted scope base, flared extended magazine well, slide fully machined, seven port cone-style compensator, full length stainless steel one piece guide rod with plug, stainless steel firing pin, match extractor, oversized firing pin stop, slide lapped to frame, extractor tuned, polished ramp, hard chrome finish and trigger Set at 2 pounds.
**Price:** . . . . . . . . . . . . . . . . . . . . . . . . . . . . .$2,700.00

# EUROPEAN AMERICAN ARMORY

## WITNESS DOUBLE-ACTION PISTOLS

### SPECIFICATIONS
*Calibers:* 9mm, 38 Super, 40 S&W and 45 ACP
*Capacity:* 10 rounds, (45 ACP) *Barrel length:* 4.5"
*Overall length:* 8.1" *Weight:* 33 oz. *Finish:* Blued
or Wonder Finish *Sights:* 3-dot; windage adj. rear
*Grips:* Black rubber
*Prices:* Blue . . . . . . . . . . . . . . . . . . . . . . . . . . . . .$399.00
Wonder Finish . . . . . . . . . . . . . . . . . . . . . . . . . . .419.60
*Also available with decocking feature.*

## WITNESS GOLD TEAM

### SPECIFICATIONS
*Calibers:* 9mm, 40 S&W, 38 Super, 9X21mm, 45 ACP
*Capacity:* 10 rounds; (45 ACP) *Barrel length:* 5.25"
*Overall length:* 10.5" *Weight:* 38 oz. *Finish:* Hard chrome
*Features:* Triple-chamber recoil compensator, single-action
trigger, extended safety competition hammer, checkered
front strap and backstrap, low-profile competition grips,
square trigger guard
*Price:* . . . . . . . . . . . . . . . . . . . . . . . . . . $2,150.00
*Also available:*
**WITNESS SILVER TEAM.** Same calibers as above. Features
double chamber compensator, competition hammer,
extended safety & magazine release, blued finish. *Overall
length:* 9.75" *Weight:* 34 oz.
*Price:* . . . . . . . . . . . . . . . . . . . . . . . . . . . . . . 967.45

## WINDICATOR REVOLVER

### SPECIFICATIONS
*Calibers:* 38 Special, 357 Mag. *Capacity:* 6 rounds
*Action:* Single/Double action *Barrel length:* 2" or 4"
*Sights:* Fixed (No-Snag) or windage adj. *Finish:* Blued only
*Features:* Swing-out cylinder; black rubber grips; hammer
block safety
*Prices:* **38 SPECIAL** w/2" barrel . . . . . . . . . . . . . $198.00
38 SPECIAL w/4" barrel . . . . . . . . . . . . . . . . . . . . 229.00
357 MAGNUM w/2" barrel . . . . . . . . . . . . . . . . . . 229.00
357 MAGNUM w/4" barrel . . . . . . . . . . . . . . . . . . 239.00

## BIG BORE BOUNTY HUNTER
## SINGLE ACTION

### SPECIFICATIONS
*Calibers:* 357 Mag., 45 Long Colt and 44 Mag.
*Capacity:* 6 rounds *Barrel length:* 4.5" or 7.5"
*Sights:* Fixed *Weight:* 37 oz. (4.5") and 42 oz. (7.5")
*Finish:* Blued, color casehardened or nickel
*Features:* Transfer-bar safety, 3 position hammer; hammer-
forged barrel; walnut grips (polymer grips optional)
*Prices:* Blued or color casehardened receiver . . . $339.00
Nickel . . . . . . . . . . . . . . . . . . . . . . . . . . . . . . . . 359.00
*Also available:* In 22 LR/WMR
(4.75" or 6.75" barrel) w/blue finish . . . . . . . . .229.00
Nickel . . . . . . . . . . . . . . . . . . . . . . . . . . . . . . . .259.00

**WINDICATOR REVOLVER**

**BIG BORE BOUNTY HUNTER**
SINGLE ACTION

# FREEDOM ARMS REVOLVERS

**454 CASULL FIELD GRADE**

### MODEL 83 RIMFIRE
SILHOUETTE CLASS 10" BARREL

**SPECIFICATIONS**
**Caliber:** 22 LR (optional 22 Magnum cylinder) **Barrel Lengths:** 5.13", 7.5" (Varmint Class) and 10" (Silhouette Class) **Sights:** Silhouette competition sights (Silhouette Class); adjustable rear express sight; removable front express blade; front sight hood **Grips:** Black micarta (Silhouette Class); black and green laminated hardwood (Varmint Class) **Finish:** Stainless steel **Features:** Dual firing pin; lightened hammer; pre-set trigger stop; accepts all sights and/or scope mounts
**Prices:**
SILHOUETTE CLASS (10" barrel). . . . . . . . . . . . . $1,765.00
VARMINT CLASS (5.13" & 7.5" barrels) . . . . . . . . 1,714.00

### MODEL 83
PREMIER GRADE (50 AE)

### MODEL 97
PREMIER GRADE

## MODEL 97 PREMIER GRADE
FIXED SIGHT . . . . . . . . . . . . . . . . . $1,500.00
ADJUSTABLE SIGHT. . . . . . . . . . . . . . . 1,576.00

**SPECIFICATIONS**
**Caliber:** 357 Magnum, 45 Colt, 41 Magnum
**Capacity:** 6 shots (357) 5 shots (45 and 41)
**Action:** Single Action
**Barrel Lengths:** 4.25", 5.5" and 7.5"
**Sights:** Removable front blade; adjustable or fixed rear
**Grips:** Impregnated hardwood or optional black micanta

## MODEL 83 SILHOUETTE/COMPETITION
### (not shown)
**SPECIFICATIONS**
**Calibers:** 357 Magnum, 41 Rem. Mag. and 44 Rem. Mag.
**Barrel Lengths:** 9" (357 Mag.) and 10" (41 Rem. Mag., 44 Rem. Mag.)
**Sights:** Silhouette competition **Grips:** Pachmayr
**Trigger:** Pre-set stop; trigger over travel screw
**Finish:** Field Grade
**Price:**. . . . . . . . . . . . . . . . . . . . . . . . $1,549.85

## 454 CASULL & MODEL 83
## PREMIER & FIELD GRADES

**SPECIFICATIONS**
**Calibers:** 454 Casull, 41 Rem. Mag., 44 Rem. Mag., .475 Linebaugh, 50 AE, 357 Mag. **Action:** Single action
**Capacity:** 5 rounds **Barrel Lengths:** 4.75", 6", 7.5", 10"
**Overall Length:** 14" (w/7.5" barrel) **Weight:** 3 lbs. 2 oz. (w/7.5" barrel) **Safety:** Patented sliding bar
**Sights:** Notched rear; blade front (optional adjustable rear and replaceable front blade)
**Grips:** Impregnated hardwood (Premier Grade) or rubber Pachmayr (Field Grade)
**Finish:** Brushed stainless (Premier Grade); Matte Finish (Field)
**Features:** ISGW silhouette, Millett competition and express sights are optional; SSK T'SOB 3-ring or 2-ring Leupold scope mount optional; optional cylinder in 454 Casull, 45 ACP, 45 Win. Mag. **($343.00)**
**Prices:** MODEL 83 PREMIER GRADE
W/adjustable sights (50A, 475L, 454C). . . . . . . $1,958.00
W/fixed sights (454C only). . . . . . . . . . . . . . . 1,894.00
357, 41 and 44 Magnums w/adjustable sights . . 1,882.00
W/fixed sights (44 Rem. only). . . . . . . . . . . . . . 1,816.00
MODEL 83 FIELD GRADE
.454C, 475L, 50 AE, adj. sights . . . . . . . . . . . . 1,519.00
.454C fixed sights. . . . . . . . . . . . . . . . . . . . . . 1,484.00
.357, 41, 44 adj. sights . . . . . . . . . . . . . . . . . . 1,442.00
Extra cylinder. . . . . . . . . . . . . . . . . . . . . . . . . 343.00

# GLOCK PISTOLS

**MODEL 17L COMPETITION**

## MODEL 17L COMPETITION

**SPECIFICATIONS**
*Caliber:* 9mm Parabellum
*Magazine capacity:* 10 rounds (17 and 19 rounds optional)*
*Barrel length:* 6.02"
*Overall length:* 8.85"
*Weight:* 23.35 oz. (without magazine)
*Sights:* Fixed (adjustable rear sights **$28.00** add'l)
*Price:* by special order

## MODEL 17 (Not Shown)

**SPECIFICATIONS**
*Caliber:* 9mm Parabellum
*Magazine capacity:* 10 rounds (17 and 19 rounds optional)*
*Barrel length:* 4.5" (hexagonal profile with right-hand twist)
*Overall length:* 7.32"
*Weight:* 22 oz. (without magazine)
*Sights:* Fixed (adjustable rear sights **$28.00** add'l)
*Price:* Fixed Sight . . . . . . . . . . . . . . . . . . . . . . .**$616.00**

**MODEL 19 COMPACT**
**(Fixed Sight)**

## MODEL 19 COMPACT

**SPECIFICATIONS**
*Caliber:* 9mm Parabellum   *Magazine capacity:* 10 rounds (15 and 17 rounds optional)*   *Barrel length:* 4"
*Overall length:* 6.85"   *Weight:* 21 oz.
*Price:* Fixed Sight . . . . . . . . . . . . . . . . . . . . . .**$616.00**
*Also available:*  MODEL 21. *Caliber:* 45 ACP. *Capacity:* 10 rounds (13 rounds optional)*
*Price:* Fixed Sight . . . . . . . . . . . . . . . . . . . . . .**$688.00**

## MODEL 20

**SPECIFICATIONS**
*Caliber:* 10mm  *Magazine capacity:* 10 rounds (15 rounds optional)*  *Action:* Double action  *Barrel length:* 4.6"  *Overall length:* 7.59"  *Height:* 5.47" (w/sights)
*Weight:* 27.68 oz. (empty)  *Sights:* Fixed  (adjustable **$29.00** add'l)  *Features:* 3 safeties, "safe-action" system, polymer frame
*Price:* Fixed Sight . . . . . . . . . . . . . . . . . . . . . .**$668.00**

**MODEL 20**

## MODEL 24 COMPETITION

**SPECIFICATIONS**
*Caliber:* 40 S&W *Capacity:* 10 rounds (15 rounds optional)*
*Barrel length:* 6.02" *Overall length:* 8.85"  *Weight:* 26.7 oz. (empty)  *Safety:* Manual trigger safety; passive firing block and drop safety  *Finish:* Matte (Tenifer process); nonglare
*Price:* . . . . . . . . . . . . . . . . . . . . . . . . .**by special order**
w/Compensated Barrel, Fixed Sights . . .**by special order**
*\*For law enforcement and military use only*

**MODEL 24 COMPETITION**

# GLOCK PISTOLS

## MODEL 23 COMPACT SPORT/SERVICE MODEL

**SPECIFICATIONS**
*Caliber:* 40 S&W  *Capacity:* 10 rounds
*Barrel length:* 4.02"
*Overall length:* 6.85"
*Weight:* 21.16 oz.
*Price:* . . . . . . . . . . . . . . . . . . . . . . . . . . . .$616.00
Also available:
MODEL 22 (Sport and Service models)
*Caliber:* 40 S&W
*Capacity:* 10 rounds (15 rounds optional)*
*Barrel length:* 4.5"  *Overall length:* 7.32"
*Price:* Fixed Sight . . . . . . . . . . . . . . . . . . . . .$616.00

**MODEL 23**

## MODEL 29 SUBCOMPACT

**SPECIFICATIONS**
*Caliber:* 10 mm auto  *Capacity:* 10 rounds
*Barrel length:* 3.78"  *Overall length:* 6.77"
*Weight:* 24.7 oz. (approx.)  *Height:* 4.5"
*Finish:* Matte (Tenifer process); nonglare
*Features:* Safe Action trigger system; two magazines
provided
*Price:* . . . . . . . . . . . . . . . . . . . . . . . . . . . .$668.00

**MODEL 29**

## MODEL 26

**SPECIFICATIONS**
*Caliber:* 9mm  *Action:* DA
*Capacity:* 10 rounds
*Barrel length:* 3.47"  *Overall length:* 6.3"
*Weight:* 19.77 oz.
*Finish:* Matte (Tenifer process); nonglare
*Features:* 3 safeties; Safe Action trigger system;
polymer frame
*Price:* . . . . . . . . . . . . . . . . . . . . . . . . . . . .$616.00
Also available:
MODEL 27. Same specifications as Model 26 but in
.40 S&W
*Capacity:* 9 rounds
*Price:* Fixed Sight . . . . . . . . . . . . . . . . . . . . .$616.00

**MODEL 26**

## MODEL 30 SUBCOMPACT

**SPECIFICATIONS**
*Caliber:* 45 ACP
*Capacity:* 10 rounds (9 round optional)
*Barrel length:* 3.78"
*Overall length:* 6.8"
*Weight:* 24 oz. (approx.)
*Height:* 4.5"
*Finish:* Matte (Tenifer process); nonglare
*Features:* Safe Action trigger system; two magazines
provided; magazine has an extended floorplate that serves
as a finger rest; 6.7-inch slide
*Price:* . . . . . . . . . . . . . . . . . . . . . . . . . . . .$668.00

**MODEL 30**

# HÄMMERLI U.S.A. PISTOLS

## MODEL 160 FREE PISTOL
### $2,189.00 w/electronic trigger $2,410.00

**SPECIFICATIONS**
*Caliber:* 22 LR  *Barrel Length:* 11.3"  *Overall Length:* 17.5"  *Height:* 5.7"  *Weight:* 45 oz.  *Trigger Action:* Infinitely variable set trigger weight; cocking lever located on left of receiver; trigger length variable along weapon axis  *Locking Action:* Martini-type locking action w/side-mounted locking lever  *Barrel:* Free floating, cold swaged precision barrel w/low axis relative to the hand  *Ignition:* Horizontal firing pin (hammerless) in line w/barrel axis; firing pin travel 0.15"  *Grips:* Selected walnut w/adj. hand rest for direct arm to barrel extension

## MODEL FP10 FREE PISTOL
### Price on request

The Hammerli model FP 10 Free Pistol is a completely new development, designed for competitors who must have the best and who know how to take advantage of this advanced pistol's many adjustments and very high level of accuracy. *Features:* Trigger tongue adjustable for length; rotates around its own vertical axis. Adjustable width of rear sight notch; interchangeable front sight posts. Front sight mount with integrated compensator.

## MODEL 208S STANDARD PISTOL
### $2,021.00

**SPECIFICATIONS**
*Caliber:* 22 LR  *Capacity:* 8 rounds  *Action:* Single  *Barrel Length:* 5.9"  *Overall Length:* 10"  *Height:* 5.9"  *Weight:* 36.7 oz.  *Sight Radius:* 8.2"  *Sights:* Micrometer rear sight w/notch width; adj. for windage & elevation; standard front blade  *Trigger:* Adj. for pull weight, travel, slack-weight & creep  *Safety:* Rotating knob on rear of frame

## MODEL 280 TARGET PISTOL
### $1,643.00 ($1,853.00 in 32 S&W)

**SPECIFICATIONS**
*Calibers:* 22 LR and 32 S&W  *Capacity:* 6 rounds (22 LR); 5 rounds (32 S&W)  *Action:* Single  *Barrel Length:* 4.58"  *Overall Length:* 11.8"  *Height:* 5.9"  *Weight:* (excluding counterweights) 34.6 oz. (22 LR); 41.8 oz. (32 S&W)  *Sight Radius:* 8.7"  *Sights:* Micrometer adjustable  *Grips:* Orthopedic type; stippled walnut w/adj. palm shelf  *Features:* 3 steel & 3 carbon fiber barrel weight; combination tool; 4 Allen wrenches; dry fire plug; magazine loading tool; extra magazine
*Also available:*
MODEL 280 TARGET PISTOL COMBO
Conversion Unit (22 LR) . . . . . . . . . . . . . . . . . . $803.00
In 32 S&W . . . . . . . . . . . . . . . . . . . . . . . . . . . **1,013.00**

**MODEL 160**
FREE PISTOL

**MODEL FP10**
FREE PISTOL

**MODEL 208S**
STANDARD PISTOL

**MODEL 280**
TARGET PISTOL

# HECKLER & KOCH PISTOLS

## MODEL HK USP 9 &40 UNIVERSAL SELF-LOADING PISTOL

### SPECIFICATIONS
*Calibers:* 9mm and 40 S&W  *Capacity:* 10 + 1
*Operating System:* Short recoil, modified Browning action
*Barrel Length:* 4.25"  *Overall Length:* 7.64"
*Weight:* 1.74 lbs. (40 S&W); 1.66 lbs. (9mm)
*Height:* 5.35"  *Sights:* Adjustable 3-dot
*Grips:* Polymer receiver and integral grips
*Prices:*
9mm & 40 S&W . . . . . . . . . . . . . . . . . . . . . . . . $689.00
  W/control lever on right . . . . . . . . . . . . . . . . . 707.00
Stainless steel . . . . . . . . . . . . . . . . . . . . . . . . . 749.00
  W/control lever on right . . . . . . . . . . . . . . . . . 767.00
*Also available:*
HK USP45 TACTICAL PISTOL
  w/cleaning kit & case . . . . . . . . . . . . . . . . . . . 999.00

**MODEL HK USP45
TACTICAL PISTOL**

## MODEL USP45 UNIVERSAL SELF-LOADING PISTOL

### SPECIFICATIONS
*Caliber:* 45 ACP  *Capacity:* 10 rounds
*Action:* DA/SA or DAO  *Barrel Length:* 4.41"
*Overall Length:* 7.87"  *Height:* 5.55"
*Weight:* 1.90 lbs.
*Grips:* Polymer frame & integral grips
*Prices:* . . . . . . . . . . . . . . . . . . . . . . . . . . . . . $759.00
Stainless steel . . . . . . . . . . . . . . . . . . . . . . . . . 799.00

**MODEL HK USP45
UNIVERSAL SELF-
LOADING PISTOL**

## HK USP COMPACT UNIVERSAL SELF-LOADING PISTOL

### SPECIFICATIONS
*Calibers:* 9mm, 40 S&W, .357 Sig and 45 ACP
*Capacity:* 10 rounds
*Operating System:* Short recoil, modified Browning action
*Barrel Length:* 3.58"  *Overall Length:* 6.81"
*Weight:* 1.70 lbs. (40 S&W); 1.60 lbs. (9mm)
*Height:* 5"  *Sights:* Adjustable 3-dot
*Grips:* Polymer frame and integral grips
*Prices:*
9mm, and .357 Sig . . . . . . . . . . . . . . . . . . . . . $719.00
*Also available:*
Stainless (9mm and 40 S+W) . . . . . . . . . . . . . . 769.00
45 ACP . . . . . . . . . . . . . . . . . . . . . . . . . . . . . . . 739.00
45 ACP, stainless . . . . . . . . . . . . . . . . . . . . . . . 789.00

**HK USP45 COMPACT
UNIVERSAL SELF-
LOADING PISTOL**

# HECKLER & KOCH PISTOLS

## HK USP45 EXPERT

**SPECIFICATIONS**
*Caliber:* 45 ACP
*Capacity:* 10 rounds
*Operating System:* Short recoil, modified Browning action
*Barrel Length:* 6.02"
*Overall Length:* 9.45"
*Weight:* 2.38 lbs.
*Height:* 5.90"
*Sights:* Adjustable 3-dot
*Grips & Stock:* Polymer frame and integral grips
*Prices:*
Blued . . . . . . . . . . . . . . . . . . . . . . . . . . . . . . $1,369.00

**HK USP EXPERT**

## MARK 23 SPECIAL OPERATIONS PISTOL (SOCOM)

**SPECIFICATIONS**
*Caliber:* 45 ACP
*Capacity:* 10 rounds
*Operating System:* Short recoil, modified Browning action
*Barrel Length:* 5.87"
*Overall Length:* 9.65"
*Height:* 5.9"
*Weight:* 2.66 lbs.
*Sights:* 3-dot
*Grips:* Polymer frame & integral grips
*Price:* . . . . . . . . . . . . . . . . . . . . . . . . . . . . . $2,169.00

**MARK 23 SPECIAL OPERATIONS PISTOL (SOCOM)**

**MODEL P7M8**

## MODEL P7M8

**SPECIFICATIONS**
*Caliber:* 9mmX19 (Luger)
*Capacity:* 8 rounds
*Barrel Length:* 4.13"
*Overall Length:* 6.73"
*Weight:* 1.75 lbs. (empty)
*Sight Radius:* 5.83"
*Sights:* Adjustable rear
*Grips:* Plastic  *Finish:* Blue or nickel
*Operating System:* Recoil-operated; retarded inertia slide
*Price:* . . . . . . . . . . . . . . . . . . . . . . . . . . . . . $1,299.00

# HERITAGE MANUFACTURING

## STEALTH COMPACT PISTOL

**SPECIFICATIONS**
**Caliber:** 9mm and 40 S&W
**Capacity:** 10 rounds
**Barrel Length:** 3.9"
**Overall Length:** 6.3"
**Weight:** 20 oz.  **Height:** 4.2"
**Triggerpull:** 4 lbs.  **Frame:** Black polymer
**Styles:** Model C-1000 17-4 Stainess steel slide; Model C-2000 17-4 Black chrome slide; Model C-1010 17-4 Two-tone stainless steel/black chrome slide
**Features:** Striker-fire trigger; gas-delayed blow back action; frame-mounted ambidextrous trigger safety; drop safety; closed breech safety; magazine disconnect safety
**Prices:**
9mm . . . . . . . . . . . . . . . . . . . . . . . . . . . . . . . . . . **$299.95**
40 S&W . . . . . . . . . . . . . . . . . . . . . . . . . . . . . . . . **329.95**

## ROUGH RIDER SA

**SPECIFICATIONS**
**Caliber:** 22 LR or 22 LR/22 WMR
**Capacity:** 6 rounds  **Weight:** 31 to 38 oz.
**Barrel Lengths:** 4.75", 6.5", 9" (regular grip); 2.75", 3.75", 4.75" (Bird's-Head grip)  **Sights:** Blade front, fixed rear
**Grips:** Exotic hardwood  **Finish:** Blue or nickel  **Features:** Rotating hammer block safety; brass accent screws
**Prices:**
**22 LR** (4.75", 6.5" bbl.) blued, regular grip. . . . . . **$129.95**
**22 LR/22 WMR**
W/blued finish, regular grip: 4.75" & 6.5" barrels . . . . **149.95**
 9" barrel. . . . . . . . . . . . . . . . . . . . . . . . . . . . **149.95**
W/nickel finish, regular grip: 4.75" & 6.5" barrels . . . . **169.95**
 9" barrel. . . . . . . . . . . . . . . . . . . . . . . . . . . . **179.95**
W/blued finish, bird's-head grip:
 3.75" & 4.75" barrels . . . . . . . . . . . . . . . . . . . **149.95**
W/nickel finish: bird's-head grip:
 3.75" & 4.75" barrels . . . . . . . . . . . . . . . . . . . **169.95**
W/steel frame/blue (3.75", 4.75", 6.5" barrels) . . . . **169.95**
W/steel frame/nickel (6.5" barrel). . . . . . . . . . . . . . **189.95**
W/steel frame/blue (9" barrel) . . . . . . . . . . . . . . . . **179.95**

# HIGH STANDARD PISTOLS

## OLYMPIC RAPID FIRE

**SPECIFICATIONS**
**Caliber:** 22 Short  **Capacity:** 5 rounds
**Barrel length:** 4"  **Overall length:** 11.5"  **Weight:** 46 oz.
**Sights:** Click-adjustable for windage and elevations (rear); mounted on vent aluminum rib
**Grips:** Special International  **Finish:** Matte blue
**Features:** Push-button barrel takedown system; trigger adj. for weight of pull and travel; gold-plated trigger, slide stop, safety and magazine release
**Price:** . . . . . . . . . . . . . . . . . . . . . . . . . . . . . .**$1,995.00**

**OLYMPIC
RAPID FIRE**

# HIGH STANDARD PISTOLS

## SUPERMATIC CITATION

### SPECIFICATIONS
**Caliber:** 22 LR  **Capacity:** 10 rounds
**Barrel length:** 5.5"  **Overall length:** 9.5"
**Weight:** 44 oz.  **Finish:** Blued or Parkerized
**Features:** Optional Universal Mount to replace open-sight
rib (deduct $30.00)
**Price:** ....................................$468.00
**Also available:**
SUPERMATIC CITATION MS. Similar to Citation above, except
10" barrel (14" overall), 54 oz. weight, RPM sights click-
adjustable for windage and elevation, checkered right-hand
thumbrest and matte blue finish .............$632.00
TROPHY/CITATION 22 SHORT CONVERSION KIT
(incl. barrel w/sight, slide, 2 magazines) ........$309.00

**SUPERMATIC CITATION**

## OLYMPIC MILITARY

### SPECIFICATIONS
**Caliber:** 22 LR  **Capacity:** 10 rounds
**Barrel length:** 5.5"  **Overall length:** 9.5"
**Weight:** 44 oz.  **Finish:** Matte frame
**Features:** Fully adjustable rear sight; non-adjustable trigger
**Price:** ....................................$562.00

## SUPERMATIC TROPHY

**OLYMPIC**

### SPECIFICATIONS
**Caliber:** 22 LR  **Capacity:** 10 rounds
**Actions:** Recoil-operated semiautomatic
**Barrel length:** 5.5" bull or 7.25" fluted
**Overall length:** 9.5 (w/5.5" bbl.) and 11.25" (w/7.25" bbl.)
**Weight:** 44 oz. (w/5.5" bbl.) and 46 oz. (w/7.25" bbl.)
**Sights:** Click-adjustable rear for windage/elevation;
undercut ramp front  **Grips:** Checkered American walnut
with right-hand thumbrest (left-hand optional)
**Features:** Gold-plated trigger; slide lock lever; push-button
takedown system; magazine release
**Prices: 5.5" BARREL** .....................$542.00
**7.25" BARREL** ..........................587.00

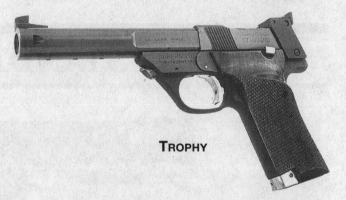

**TROPHY**

## VICTOR 22 LR

### SPECIFICATIONS
**Caliber:** 22 LR  **Capacity:** 10 rounds
**Barrel lengths:** 4.5" and 5.5"
**Overall length:** 8.5" and 9.5"
**Weight:** 45 oz. (w/4.5" bbl.); 46 oz. (w/5.5" bbl.)
**Finish:** Blued or Parkerized frame
**Features:** Optional steel rib; click-adjustable sights for
windage and elevation; optional barrel weights and
Universal Mount (to replace open-sight rib)
**Prices:** ..................................$502.00
   w/5.5" barrel .........................558.00
**Also available:**
22 SHORT CONVERSION KIT 5.5" barrel w/vent rib, slide, two
magazines ...............................$397.00

**VICTOR 22 LR**

# HI-POINT FIREARMS

## SEMI-AUTOMATIC HANDGUNS

Hi-Point Firearms offer reliability and accuracy at an affordable price. Hi-Point handguns are sized to feel good in your hand and provide exceptional recoil control. All models feature sleek lines and a scratch-resistant, non-glare military black finish with high-impact grips. New 3-dot sights.

### 9MM COMPACT POLYMER

**SPECIFICATIONS**
**Caliber:** .9mm parabellum
**Capacity:** 8 shot mag
**Action:** Single action
**Barrel Length:** 3.5" alloy steel barrel
**Sights:** Low-profile 3 dot adj. sights
**Safety:** Quick on-off thumb safety
**Overall Length:** 6.75"  **Frame:** Polymer frame

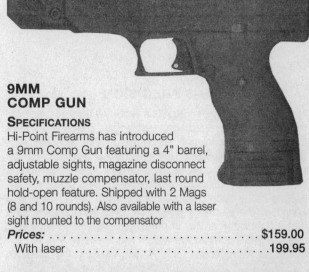

### 9MM COMP GUN

**SPECIFICATIONS**
Hi-Point Firearms has introduced a 9mm Comp Gun featuring a 4" barrel, adjustable sights, magazine disconnect safety, muzzle compensator, last round hold-open feature. Shipped with 2 Mags (8 and 10 rounds). Also available with a laser sight mounted to the compensator
**Prices:** . . . . . . . . . . . . . . . . . . . . . . . . . . . .$159.00
With laser  . . . . . . . . . . . . . . . . . . . . . . . . .199.95

**MODEL 9mm**

### MODEL 9MM

**SPECIFICATIONS**
**Caliber:** 9mm Parabellum
**Capacity:** 9 shots
**Barrel length:** 4.5"
**Overall length:** 7.72"
**Weight:** 39 oz.
**Sights:** 3-dot adjustable
**Features:** Quick on-off thumb safety; nonglare military black finish
**Price:** . . . . . . . . . . . . . . . . . . . . . . . . . . . .$149.00

**380 POLYMER**

### MODEL 380 POLYMER

Model 380 and 380 Polymer similar to 9mm but with 3.5" alloy steel barrel, 29 oz.  **Price:** . . . . . . . . . . . . . .$99.00
**Also available** in 45 ACP. Same specifications as the 9mm except w/7-shot capacity and military black finish.
**Price:** . . . . . . . . . . . . . . . . . . . . . . . . . . . .$159.00
**MODEL 40** in 40 S&W. Same specifications as the 45 ACP w/8-shot capacity . . . . . . . . . . . . . . . . . .159.00
**MODEL 9mm COMPACT** w/3.5" barrel . . . . . . . . . .137.00
Also available w/polymer frame (same price)

# H-S PRECISION PISTOLS

**H-S SILHOUETTE PISTOL**

## H-S PRECISION

H-S Precision single-shot pistols employ a right-handle bolt, with handle engineered so the bolt head is over the well of the grip for good balance. As on the Series 2000 rifles, triggers are fully adjustable and can be set from 2.5 to 3.5 pounds pull. These super-accurate pistols are held to the same accuracy standards as Pro-Series rifles. They're available in many chamberings, in both varmint and silhouette versions. The silhouette pistol has a titanium safety shroud and a lighter barrel that is drilled and tapped for sights. It meets IHMSA competition weight requirements.
***Price:*** (either version) . . . . . . . . . . . . . . . . . . . . **$1,250.00**

## PRO-SERIES 2000 VP, SP (VARMINT, SILHOUETTE PISTOLS)

### SPECIFICATIONS
- ***Pro-Series 2000*** stainless steel pistol action, single shot
- ***Pro-Series 10X*** match grade stainless steel barrel
  - Fluted (except 35 Rem, Silhouette style)
  - Sporter contour, silhouette model
  - Heavy contour, varmint model
- ***Pro-Series*** synthetic stock, center grip with bedding block chassis system
  - Choice of color
  - Metal finish – Teflon® or Pro-Series PFTE Matte Black
  - Weight*
    - 4.5 pounds, silhouette
    - 5.25 - 5.50 pounds, varmint
  - Calibers – 17 Rem, 6mm PPC, 223 Rem, 22-250 Rem, 243 Win, 257 Roberts, 260 Rem, 35 Rem, 308 Winc, 7mm-08 Rem, 7mm BR

# ISRAEL ARMS & FIREARMS INT'L

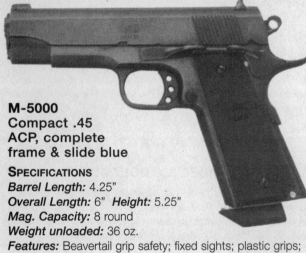

## M-5000
### Compact .45 ACP, complete frame & slide blue

#### SPECIFICATIONS
***Barrel Length:*** 4.25"
***Overall Length:*** 6"  ***Height:*** 5.25"
***Mag. Capacity:*** 8 round
***Weight unloaded:*** 36 oz.
***Features:*** Beavertail grip safety; fixed sights; plastic grips; extended slide stop, safety magazine release; beveled feed ramp barrel; combat style hammer; beveled magazine well; ambi safety
***Price:*** . . . . . . . . . . . . . . . . . . . . . . . . . . . . . . **$475.00**

## M-999
### 1911 Gov. .45 ACP, Stainless Steel Complete, Frame & Slide, Stainless Steel Frame & 4140 Steel, Blue Slide

#### SPECIFICATIONS
***Barrel Length:*** 5"
***Overall Length:*** 8.5"  ***Height:*** 5.25"
***Capacity:*** 7+1 round  ***Weight unloaded:*** 38 oz.
***Features:*** Beveled feed ramp barrel; beavertail grip safety; beveled magazine well; extended slide stop, safety and magazine release; fixed sights; rubber grips; combat style hammer; lightweight steel trigger
***Price:*** . . . . . . . . . . . . . . . . . . . . . . . . . . . . . . **$595.00**

# Smith & Wesson ®

*Jerry Miculek sets world records with Smith & Wesson revolvers * July 24th, 1999*

| 8 Shots on one target in 1.00 seconds | 8 Shots on four targets (2 per target) in 1.06 seconds | 6 shots, reload and 6 shots on one target in 2.99 seconds |
|---|---|---|

# LUGER®

## SHOTGUNS

### AVAILABLE THROUGH STOEGER IND.

A SYMBOL OF QUALITY

# Kahr Arms Pistols

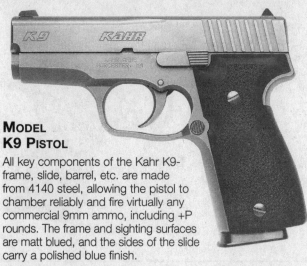

## Model K9 Pistol

All key components of the Kahr K9-frame, slide, barrel, etc. are made from 4140 steel, allowing the pistol to chamber reliably and fire virtually any commercial 9mm ammo, including +P rounds. The frame and sighting surfaces are matt blued, and the sides of the slide carry a polished blue finish.

### Specifications

*Caliber:* 9mm (9x19), 40 S&W *Capacity:* 7 rounds (6 rounds 40 S&W) *Barrel length:* 3.5" *Overall length:* 6" (6.1" 40 S&W) *Height:* 4.5" (4.55" 40 S&W) *Weight (empty):* 25 oz.; 26 oz. (40 S&W) *Grips:* Wraparound soft polymer *Sights:* Drift-adjustable, low-profile white bar-dot combat sights *Finish:* Nonglare matte black finish on slide, frame sighting surfaces, electroless nickel, black titanium, satin hard chrome (matte black, electroless nickel only in 40 S&W) *Features:* Trigger cocking safety; passive firing-pin block; no magazine disconnect; locked breech *Also available:* Model MK9 Micro-Compact 9mm. *Overall length:* 5.5" *Barrel length:* 3" *Weight:* 22 oz.

| | |
|---|---|
| Price: | $605.00 |
| w/night sights | 692.00 |
| In duo-tone | 749.00 |
| w/night sights | 836.00 |

**Prices: K9 Pistol**

| | |
|---|---|
| Matte black | $538.00 |
| Matte black w/night sights | 624.00 |
| Matte electroless nickel | 612.00 |
| Electroless nickel w/night sights | 699.00 |
| Black titanium | 664.00 |
| Black titanium w/night sights | 750.00 |
| Matte stainless | 588.00 |
| w/night sights | 675.00 |

**Prices: Lady K9**

| | |
|---|---|
| Lightened recoil spring, matte black | 545.00 |
| W/night sights | 631.00 |
| Satin electroless nickel | 619.00 |
| Electroless nickel w/night sights | 706.00 |

# KBI Pistols

## FEG SMC AUTO PISTOL

### Specifications

*Calibers:* 380 ACP
*Capacity:* 6 rounds
*Barrel Length:* 3.5"
*Overall Length:* 6 1/8"
*Weight:* 18.5 oz.
*Stock:* Checkered composition w/thumbrest
*Sights:* Blade front; rear adjustable for windage
*Features:* Alloy frame; steel slide; double action; blue finish; two magazines and cleaning rod standard
*Price:* . . . . . . . . . . . . . . . . . . . . . . . . . . . . $224.95

**FEG SMC**

## FEG MODEL PJK-9HP (HI-POWER)

### Specifications

*Caliber:* 9mm Luger Parabellum
*Magazine capacity:* 10 rounds
*Action:* Single *Barrel Length:* 4.75"
*Overall Length:* 8" *Weight:* 21 oz.
*Grips:* Hand-checkered walnut
*Safety:* Thumb safety
*Sights:* 3-dot system *Finish:* Blue
*Features:* One 10-round magazine, cleaning rod
*Price:* . . . . . . . . . . . . . . . . . . . . . . . . . . . . $259.95

**FEG Model PJK-9HP**

# KIMBER PISTOLS

**CUSTOM WALNUT**
**$699.00**

**CUSTOM**
**STAINLESS TARGET**
**$774.00**

## SPECIFICATIONS .45 CLASSIC SERIES

| | BARREL LENGTH | FINISH | SIGHTS | SIGHT RADIUS | APPROX. WEIGHT | OVERALL LENGTH | MAGAZINE CAPACITY | GRIPS |
|---|---|---|---|---|---|---|---|---|
| **CUSTOM** | 5" | Matte Black Oxide | McCormick Low Profile Combat | 6.7" | 38 oz. | 8.7" | 7 | Black Synthetic |
| **CUSTOM STAINLESS** | 5" | Satin Stainless Steel | McCormick Low Profile Combat | 6.7" | 38 oz. | 8.7" | 7 | Black Synthetic |
| **CUSTOM ROYAL** | 5" | Highly Polished Blue | McCormick Low Profile Combat | 6.7" | 38 oz. | 8.7" | 7 | Hand Checkered Rosewood |
| **CUSTOM WALNUT** | 5" | Matte Black Oxide | McCormick Low Profile Combat | 6.7" | 38 oz. | 8.7" | 7 | Hand Checkered Walnut |

**CUSTOM WALNUT** (NOT SHOWN) – **$721.00**

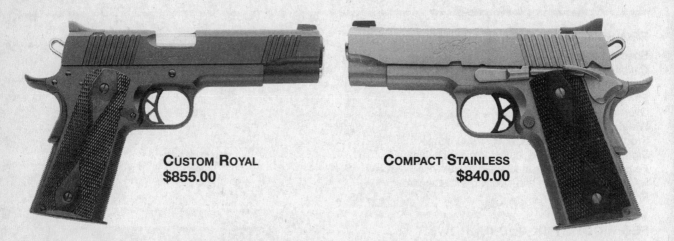

**CUSTOM ROYAL**
**$855.00**

**COMPACT STAINLESS**
**$840.00**

## SPECIFICATIONS .45 COMPACT

| | BARREL LENGTH | FINISH | SIGHTS | SIGHT RADIUS | APPROX. WEIGHT | OVERALL LENGTH | MAGAZINE CAPACITY | GRIPS |
|---|---|---|---|---|---|---|---|---|
| **COMPACT** | 4" | Matte Black Oxide | McCormick Low Profile Combat | 5.7" | 34 oz. | 7.7" | 6 | Black Synthetic |
| **COMPACT STAINLESS** | 4" | Satin Stainless Steel | McCormick Low Profile Combat | 5.7" | 34 oz. | 7.7" | 6 | Black Synthetic |
| **COMPACT ALUMINUM** | 4" | Matte Black | McCormick Low Profile Combat | 5.7" | 28 oz. | 7.7" | 6 | Black Synthetic |

**COMPACT** (NOT SHOWN) – **$734.00**   **COMPACT STAINLESS ALUMINUM** (NOT SHOWN) – **$806.00**

# KIMBER PISTOLS

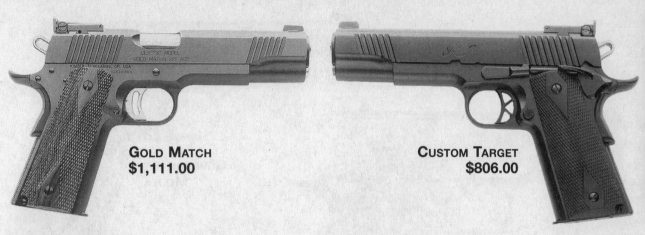

**GOLD MATCH**
**$1,111.00**

**CUSTOM TARGET**
**$806.00**

## SPECIFICATIONS

| | BARREL LENGTH | FINISH | SIGHTS | SIGHT RADIUS | APPROX. WEIGHT | OVERALL LENGTH | MAGAZINE CAPACITY | GRIPS |
|---|---|---|---|---|---|---|---|---|
| **CUSTOM TARGET** | 5" | Matte Black Oxide | Kimber Adjustable | 6.7" | 38 oz. | 8.7" | 7 | Black Synthetic |
| **STAINLESS TARGET** | 5" | Satin Stainless Steel | Kimber Adjustable | 6.7" | 38 oz. | 8.7" | 7 | Black Synthetic |
| **GOLD MATCH** | 5" | Highly Polished Blue | Kimber Adjustable | 6.7" | 38 oz. | 8.7" | 8 | Hand Checkered Rosewood |
| **STAINLESS GOLD MATCH** | 5" | Highly Polished Stainless Steel | Kimber Adjustable | 6.7" | 38 oz. | 8.7" | 8 | Hand Checkered Rosewood |

STAINLESS TARGET (NOT SHOWN) – $912.00  STAINLESS GOLD MATCH (NOT SHOWN) – $1,254.00

**POLYMER**
**$880.00**

**POLYMER GOLD MATCH**
**$1,160.00**

## SPECIFICATIONS .45 POLYMERS

| | BARREL LENGTH | FINISH | SIGHTS | SIGHT RADIUS | APPROX. WEIGHT | OVERALL LENGTH | MAGAZINE CAPACITY | GRIPS |
|---|---|---|---|---|---|---|---|---|
| **POLYMER** | 5" | Matte Black Oxide | Low Profile Combat | 6.7" | 34 oz. | 8.75" | 14 | N/A |
| **POLYMER STAINLESS** | 5" | Satin Stainless Steel Slide | Low Profile Combat | 6.7" | 34 oz. | 8.75" | 14 | N/A |
| **POLYMER GOLD MATCH** | 5" | Matte Black Oxide Slide | Kimber adjustable | 6.7" | 34 oz. | 8.75" | 14 | N/A |
| **POLYMER STAINLESS GOLD MATCH** | 5" | Satin Stainless Steel Slide | Kimber adjustable | 6.7" | 34 oz. | 8.75" | 14 | N/A |

POLYMER STAINLESS (NOT SHOWN) – $950.00  POLYMER PRO CARRY (NOT SHOWN) – $899.00

# LLAMA PISTOLS

GOVERNMENT
MODEL

MINI-MAX 45

## LLAMA CLASSIC AUTOMATIC PISTOL SPECIFICATIONS

| SPECIFICATIONS: | MICRO-MAX | MINI-MAX | GOVERNMENT MODEL |
|---|---|---|---|
| CALIBERS: | .32/.380 ACP | 45 Auto | 45 Auto |
| FRAME: | Precision machined from high-strength steel | Precision machined from high-strength steel | Precision machined from high-strength steel |
| TRIGGER: | Serrated | Serrated | Serrated |
| HAMMER: | External; wide spur, serrated | External; military style | External; military style |
| OPERATION: | Straight blow-back | Locked breech | Locked breech |
| LOADED CHAMBER INDICATOR: | Yes | Yes | Yes |
| SAFETIES: | Extended manual & grip safeties | Extended manual & beavertail grip safeties | Extended manual & beavertail grip safeties |
| GRIPS: | Matte black polymer | Anatomically designed rubber grips | Anatomically designed rubber grips |
| SIGHTS: | Patridge-type front; square-notch rear | 3-dot combat sight | 3-dot combat sights |
| SIGHT RADIUS: | 4 1/4" | 6 1/4" | 6 1/4" |
| MAGAZINE CAPACITY: | 8 shots/7 shots | 10 shots | 10 shots |
| WEIGHT: | 23 oz. | 39 oz. | 41 oz. |
| BARREL LENGTH: | 3 11/16" | 4 1/4" | 5 1/8" |
| OVERALL LENGTH: | 6 1/2" | 7 7/8" | 8 1/2" |
| HEIGHT: | 4 3/8" | 5 7/16" | 5 5/16" |
| FINISH: | Standard; Non-glare combat matte. Deluxe: Satin chrome, Duo-tone | Deluxe Blue | Non-glare combat matte Satin chrome, Duo-tone |
| PRICES: | $264.95 | $291.95 | $298.95 |

# MAGNUM RESEARCH PISTOLS

## MARK XIX COMPONENT SYSTEM

The Mark XIX Component system allows for three caliber changes in two different barrel lengths.

The Desert Eagle Pistol Mark XIX Component System is based on a single platform that transforms into six different pistols–three Magnum calibers, each with a 6-inch or 10-inch barrel. Changing calibers is a simple matter of switching barrels and magazines. (Converting to or from .357 Magnum also involves changing the bolt.)

The barrel design alone sports several improvements. Each barrel is now made of a single piece of steel instead of three. All six barrels, including the optional 10-inch barrels, have a $^7/_8$" dovetailed design with cross slots to accommodate scope rings; no other scope mounts are required. The .50 A.E.'s new 10-inch barrel will fit existing .50s, as well as the new Mark XIX platform.

Hogue soft rubber grips are standard equipment on the new gun. The pistol's gas operation, polygonal rifling, low recoil and safety features remain the same, as do the Mark VII adjustable trigger, slide release and safety levers.

## SPECIFICATIONS
**Calibers:** 357 Magnum, 44 Magnum and 50 A.E.
**Capacity:** 9 rounds (357 Mag.); 8 rounds (44 Mag.);
7 rounds (50 A.E.)  **Barrel Lengths:** 6" and 10"
**Overall Length:** 10.74" (w/6" bbl.); 14.75" (w/10" bbl.)
**Weight:** 4 lbs. 6.5 oz. (w/6" bbl.); 4 lbs. 15 oz. (w/10" bbl.)
(empty)
**Height:** 6.25"  **Width:** 1.25"
**Finish:** Standard black and new Titanium nitride
**Prices:**
357 MAG. w/6" barrel . . . . . . . . . . . . . . . . . . . . $1199.00
357 MAG. w/10" barrel . . . . . . . . . . . . . . . . . . . 1299.00
44 MAG. w/6" barrel . . . . . . . . . . . . . . . . . . . . 1199.00
44 MAG. w/10" barrel . . . . . . . . . . . . . . . . . . . 1299.00
50 A.E. MAG. w/6" barrel . . . . . . . . . . . . . . . . . 1199.00
50 A.E. w/10" barrel. . . . . . . . . . . . . . . . . . . . 1299.00
*(add $500 for Titanium finish, all models)*

**LONE EAGLE**

## LONE EAGLE SINGLE SHOT

This specialty pistol is designed for hunters, silhouette enthusiasts and long-range target shooters. Available w/interchangeable 14-inch barreled actions. Calibers: 22 Hornet, 22-250, 223 Rem., 243 Win., 30-06, 30-30, 308 Win., 35 Rem., 358 Win., 44 Mag., 444 Marlin, 7mm-08, 7mm Bench Rest., 7.62x39, 260 Rem., 440 Cor-Bon. Features ambidextrous grip, new cocking indicator and lever.

**Also available:**
Barreled action w/muzzle brake . . . . . . . . . . . . **$418.00**
Barreled action w/chrome finish . . . . . . . . . . . . **$359.00**
Barreled action w/chrome finish, muzzle brake. . . . **$469.00**
Ambidextrous grip assembly. . . . . . . . . . . . . . . **$119.00**

# MAGNUM RESEARCH REVOLVERS

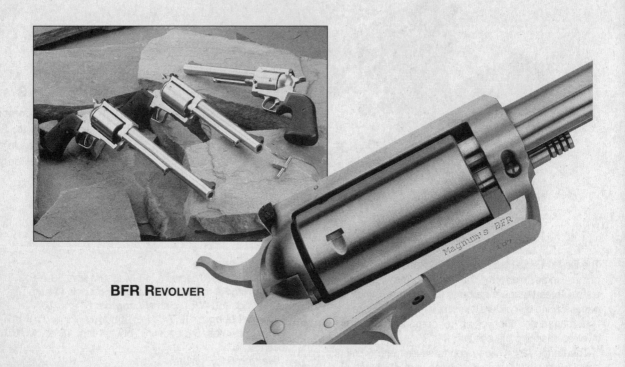

**BFR REVOLVER**

## "SINGLE-ACTION HUNTING REVOLVER"

For the first time, Magnum Research, Inc., creator of the legendary Desert Eagle Pistol, is offering a revolver. Magnum's BFR (Biggest Finest Revolver) is a single-action hunting revolver manufactured in the United States.

Magnum's BFR is available in two models, Maxine and Little Max, both built to close tolerances entirely of stainless steel. The long-cylindered Maxine fires big-bore calibers - .45/70, .444 Marlin, and .45 Long Colt/.410. Little Max is available in .454 Casull, .45 Long Colt + P, .50A.E., and the unique .22 Hornet. Grouse to grizzly,

squirrel to Kodiak bear, there's a BFR for every job.

Barrels lengths vary. The .45 Long Colt + P is available with a 6.5 or 7.5-inch barrel, the .454 Casull is available with a 6.5, 7.5 or 10-inch barrel, the .45/70 is available with a 7.5 or 10-inch barrel and the .22 Hornet is available with a 7.5 or 10-inch barrel. The .50 A.E. and .45 Long Colt/.410 are available only with a 7.5-inch barrel. The .444 Marlin is available only with a 10-inch barrel.

**Price:** . . . . . . . . . . . . . . . . . . . . . . . . . . . . . . . . **$999.00**

## ACCESSORIES

| | | |
|---|---|---|
| BFR821 | Hogue Rubber Finger Groove Grips | $34.95 |
| BFR815 | Hogue Wood Grips Pau Ferro | 74.95 |
| BFR816 | Hogue Wood Grips Goncalo Alves | 74.95 |
| BFR-AAO | Full Choke Tube (0 marks) | 17.00 |
| BFR-AA00 | Modified Choke Tube (2 marks) | 17.00 |
| BFR-AA1 | Scatter Choke Tube (1 mark) | 17.00 |
| BFR-AA2 | Choke Tube Wrench | 5.00 |
| BFR302/W | Millett sights, rear adjustable, white outline | 39.95 |

*Standard equipment sights have fixed orange front ramp and rear sight adjustable for windage and elevation.*

# MAGNUM RESEARCH/ASAI

**ONE PRO 45 PISTOL**

## ONE PRO 45 PISTOL

ASIA (Advanced Small Arms Industries) is a Swiss company founded in 1994 and based in Solothurn, an old Swiss City with long tradition in weapon and watch history. All key components of the **One PRO .45** Series are made to fire any commercially manufactured ammunition, including

**SPECIFICATIONS**
**Caliber:** .45 or 400 COR-BON
**Capacity:** 10
**Barrel Length:** 3.75" (4.52" in IPSC model)
**Overall Length:** 7.04"
**Weight (empty):** 31.1 oz. (23.5 oz. in light alloy frame optional)

+P rounds. The **One PRO .45** and **One PRO 400 Cor-Bon** are available with a patented safety system. A decocking lever allows the hammer to be lowered into the safety intercept notch without risk, and an automatic firing pin lock allows the loaded, decocked gun to be carried safely.

**Operation:** Short recoil, dropping barrel
**Trigger Pull DA:** 8.6 lbs.
**Price:** . . . . . . . . . . . . . . . . . . . . . . . . . . . . $699.00
Conversion kits available (includes recoil spring guide and hard plastic case).
**Price:** . . . . . . . . . . . . . . . . . . . . . . . . . . . . $249.00
   in 400 Cor-Bon Non-Compensated . . . . . . . . . $209.00

**BABY EAGLE FS**

**BABY EAGLE**

The Baby Eagle FS in 9mm offers a frame-mounted safety and a shorter barrel than the standard Baby Eagle Pistol. The FS is available in standard black, matte hard chrome or brushed hard chrome (as shown).

A polymer-frame version is also available. These autoloading pistols are available in 9mm, .40 S+W and .45 ACP.
**Price:**
Baby Eagle . . . . . . . . . . . . . . . . . . . . . . . . . . . $449.00

# MOA MAXIMUM PISTOLS

**MAXIMUM SINGLE SHOT**

## MAXIMUM

This single-shot pistol with its unique falling-block action performs like a finely tuned rifle. The single-piece receiver of stainless steel is mated to a Douglas barrel for optimum accuracy and strength.

**SPECIFICATIONS**
*Calibers:* 22 Hornet to 375 H&H
*Barrel Lengths:* 8.5", 10.5" and 14"
*Weight:* 3 lbs. 8 oz. (8.5" bbl.); 3 lbs. 13 oz. (10.5" bbl.); 4 lbs. 3 oz. (14" bbl.)
*Prices:*
Stainless receiver, blued barrel . . . . . . . . . . . . . $799.00
Stainless receiver and barrel . . . . . . . . . . . . . . . . 883.00
Extra barrels (blue) . . . . . . . . . . . . . . . . . . . . . . 254.00
  Stainless . . . . . . . . . . . . . . . . . . . . . . . . . . . 317.00
Muzzle brake . . . . . . . . . . . . . . . . . . . . . . . . . . 125.00

# NAVY ARMS REPLICAS

**1873 SINGLE ACTION**

**1873 "PINCHED FRAME"
SA REVOLVER**

## 1873 COLT-STYLE SA REVOLVER

This classic Single Action is the best known of all the "six shooters." From its adoption by the U.S. Army in 1873 to the present, it retains its place as America's most famous revolver.

*Calibers:* 44-40 or 45 Long Colt
*Barrel Lengths:* 3", 4.75", 5.5" or 7.5"
*Overall Length:* 10.75" (5.5" barrel) *Weight:* 2.25 lbs.
*Sights:* Blade front; notch rear *Grips:* Walnut
*Price:* . . . . . . . . . . . . . . . . . . . . . . . . . . . . . $385.00

## 1873 U.S. CAVALRY MODEL (not shown)

An exact replica of the original U.S. Government issue Colt Single-Action Army, complete with Arsenal stampings and inspector's cartouche.

*Caliber:* 45 Long Colt *Barrel Length:* 7.5"
*Overall Length:* 13.25" *Weight:* 2 lbs. 7 oz.
*Sights:* Blade front; notch rear *Grips:* Walnut
*Price:* . . . . . . . . . . . . . . . . . . . . . . . . . . . . . $455.00

## 1873 "PINCHED FRAME" SA REVOLVER

A replica of the early "pinched frame" Colt Peacemaker, the first run commercial Single Action manufactured in 1873.

*Caliber:* 45 Long Colt *Barrel Length:* 7.5"
*Overall Length:* 13.75" *Weight:* 2 lbs. 13 oz. *Sights:* German siver blade front, U-shaped "pinched-frame" rear notch
*Price:* . . . . . . . . . . . . . . . . . . . . . . . . . . . . . $415.00

## "FLAT TOP" TARGET MODEL SA REVOLVER (not shown)

A fine replica of Colt's rare "Flat top" Single Action Army revolver that was used for target shooting.

*Caliber:* 45 Long Colt *Barrel Length:* 7.5"
*Overall Length:* 12.75" *Weight:* 2 lbs. 7 oz.
*Sights:* Spring-loaded German silver Patridge front, adjustable notch ear.
*Grips:* Walnut. *Finish:* Blue
*Price:* . . . . . . . . . . . . . . . . . . . . . . . . . . . . . $425.00

# NAVY ARMS REPLICAS

**1875 SCHOFIELD CAVALRY MODEL REVOLVER**

## 1875 SCHOFIELD REVOLVER

A favorite side arm of Jesse James, the hinged-breech 1875 Schofield revolver was one of the legendary handguns of the Old West.

**Caliber:** 44-40, 45 LC **Barrel Lengths:** 3" (Hide Out Model), 5" (Wells Fargo Model) or 7" (U.S. Cavalry Model) **Overall Length:** 8.75", 10.75" or 12.75" **Weight:** 2 lbs. 7 oz. **Sights:** Blade front; notch rear **Features:** Top-break, automatic ejector single action
**Price:** ................................... $695.00

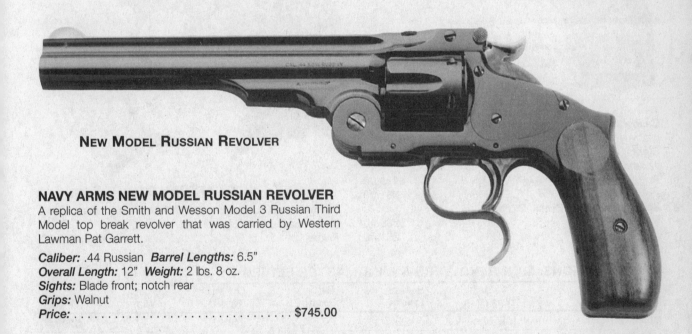

**NEW MODEL RUSSIAN REVOLVER**

## NAVY ARMS NEW MODEL RUSSIAN REVOLVER

A replica of the Smith and Wesson Model 3 Russian Third Model top break revolver that was carried by Western Lawman Pat Garrett.

**Caliber:** .44 Russian **Barrel Lengths:** 6.5" **Overall Length:** 12" **Weight:** 2 lbs. 8 oz. **Sights:** Blade front; notch rear **Grips:** Walnut
**Price:** .............................. $745.00

## BISLEY MODEL SINGLE ACTION REVOLVER (not shown)

Introduced in 1894, Colt's "Bisley Model" was named after the Bisley shooting range in England. Most of these revolvers were sold in the United States and were popular sidearms in the American West at the turn of the century.

This replica features the unique Bisley grip style, low-profile spur hammer, blued barrel and color casehardened frame.

**Calibers:** 44-40 or 45 Long Colt **Barrel Lengths:** 4.75", 5.5" and 7.5" **Sights:** Blade front, notch rear **Grips:** Walnut
**Price:** ................................... $405.00

# NORTH AMERICAN ARMS

**22 LR  MINI-REVOLVER**
w/NAA HOLSTER GRIP

**MINI-MASTER NAA-MMT-M**
(22 MAG. 4" BARREL)

## MINI-MASTER SERIES

**Calibers:** 22 LR and 22 Magnum  **Rifling:** 8 land and grooves, 1:12 R.H. twist  **Grips:** Oversized black rubber **Sights:** Front integral with barrel; rear Millett adjustable white outlined (elelvation only) or low-profile fixed
**Prices:** MINI-MASTER NAA-MMT-M . . . . . . . . . . $299.00
   w/Fixed sight . . . . . . . . . . . . . . . . . . . . . . . . 281.00
MINI-MASTER NAA BLACK WIDOW
   Adjustable sight . . . . . . . . . . . . . . . . . . . . . . $269.00
   Fixed sight . . . . . . . . . . . . . . . . . . . . . . . . 251.00

## MINI-REVOLVERS

**SPECIFICATIONS** (See also table below)
**Calibers:** 22 Short (1 1/8" bbl. only), 22 LR and 22 Magnum
**Capacity:** 5-shot cylinder
**Grips:** Laminated rosewood
**Safety:** Half-cock safety
**Sights:** Blade front (integral w/barrel); fixed, notched rear
**Material:** Stainless steel
**Finish:** Matte with brushed sides

## GUARDIAN 32

Stainless steel autoloading pistol; double action; fixed sights; 6-shot magazine in .32 ACP only
**Price:** . . . . . . . . . . . . . . . . . . . . . . . . . . . . . . . $359.00

## SPECIFICATIONS: MINI-REVOLVERS & MINI-MASTER SERIES

| MODEL | WEIGHT | BARREL LENGTH | OVERALL LENGTH | OVERALL HEIGHT | OVERALL WIDTH | PRICE |
|---|---|---|---|---|---|---|
| NAA-MMT-M | 10.7 oz. | 4" | 7 3/4" | 3 7/8" | 7/8" | $299.00 |
| NAA-MMT-L | 10.7 oz. | 4" | 7 3/4" | 3 7/8" | 7/8" | 299.00 |
| *NAA-BW-M | 8.8 oz. | 2" | 5 7/8" | 3 7/8" | 7/8" | 251.00 |
| *NAA-BW-L | 8.8 oz. | 2" | 5 7/8" | 3 7/8" | 7/8" | 251.00 |
| NAA-22LR** | 4.5 oz. | 1 1/8" | 4 1/4" | 2 3/8" | 13/16" | 176.00 |
| NAA-22LLR** | 4.6 oz. | 1 5/8" | 4 3/4" | 2 3/8" | 13/16" | 176.00 |
| *NAA-22MS | 5.9 oz. | 1 1/8" | 5" | 2 7/8" | 7/8" | 194.00 |
| *NAA-22M | 6.2 oz. | 1 5/8" | 5 3/8" | 2 7/8" | 7/8" | 194.00 |

*Available with Conversion Cylinder chambered for 22 Long Rifle **($288.00)**  **Available with holster grip **($209.00)**

# PARA-ORDNANCE PISTOLS

Built on the proven M1911-A1 single-action autoloading pistol, the Para-Ordnance P-series was developed beginning in 1988. The P14.45 appeared in 1990 as one of the first high-capacity autoloaders of this type. Uninterrupted slide rails, beefier slide stop, contoured feed ramp and ejection port, combat hammer, 3-dot sights, beveled magazine well and polymer magazine are all standard. *Magazine Capacity:* 10+1 in compact models to 18+1 in full-size.

**MODEL P10•45ER**
(BLACK)

**MODEL P12•45 ACP**
(3.5" BARREL, STAINLESS

**MODEL P10•45TR**
(DUOTONE)

**MODEL P10•45SR**
(STAINLESS)

## P-SERIES PISTOL SPECIFICATIONS *(continued on following page)*

| MODEL | CALIBER | BARREL LENGTH | WEIGHT (OZ.) | OVERALL LENGTH) | HEIGHT (W/MAG.) | RECEIVER TYPE | MATTE FINISH | PRICES | LTD. |
|---|---|---|---|---|---|---|---|---|---|
| P10•40ER | 40 S&W, 45ACP | 3" | 31 | 6 5/8" | 4.5" | Steel | Black | $750.00 | $875.00 |
| P10•40RR | 40 S&W, 45ACP | 3" | 24 | 6 5/8" | 4.5" | Alloy | Black | 740.00 | 865.00 |
| P10•40TR | 40 S&W, 45ACP | 3" | 31 | 6 5/8" | 4.5" | Stainless | Duotone | 785.00 | |
| P10•40SR | 40 S&W, 45ACP | 3" | 31 | 6 5/8" | 4.5" | Stainless | Stainless | 799.00 | 899.00 |
| P12•45ER | 45 ACP | 3.5" | 34 | 7 5/8" | 5" | Steel | Black | 750.00 | 875.00 |
| P12•45RR | 45 ACP | 3.5" | 26 | 7 5/8" | 5" | Alloy | Black | 740.00 | 865.00 |
| P12•45TR | 45 ACP | 3.5" | 34 | 7 5/8" | 5" | Stainless | Duotone | 785.00 | |
| P12•45SR | 45 ACP | 3.5" | 34 | 7 5/8" | 5" | Stainless | Stainless | 799.00 | 899.00 |
| P13•45ER | 45 ACP | 4.25" | 36 | 7.75" | 5.25" | Steel | Black | 750.00 | 875.00 |
| P13•45RR | 45 ACP | 4.25" | 28 | 7.75" | 5.25" | Alloy | Black | 740.00 | 865.00 |
| P13•45TR | 45 ACP | 4.25" | 36 | 7.75" | 5.25" | Stainless | Duotone | 785.00 | |
| P13•45SR | 45 ACP | 4.25" | 36 | 7.75" | 5.25" | Stainless | Stainless | 799.00 | 899.00 |

*For recreational purposes, magazine capacities are restricted to 10 rounds.*

# PARA-ORDNANCE PISTOLS

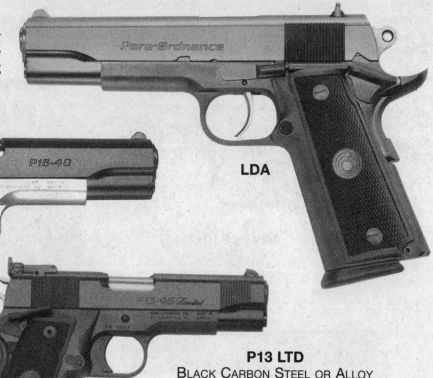

## PARA-ORDNANCE LDA

The Para-Ordnance LDA pistol is a double-action carbon-steel gun in .45ACP, .40 S+W and 9mm. **Capacity:** 14+1, 16+1, and 18+1, respectively **Barrel:** 5" **Weight:** 40 oz.

**LDA**

**P16•40 S&W**
(5" BARREL, DUOTONE)

**P13 LTD**
BLACK CARBON STEEL OR ALLOY

## PARA-ORDNANCE "LIMITED"

Para-Ordnance "Limited" pistols feature adjustable sights, competition hammer, front slide serrations, match-grade barrel, ambidextrous safety, full-length recoil guide.

## P-SERIES PISTOL SPECIFICATIONS *(Cont.)*

| MODEL | CALIBER | BARREL LENGTH | WEIGHT (OZ.) | OVERALL LENGTH) | HEIGHT (W/MAG.) | RECEIVER TYPE | MATTE FINISH | PRICES | LTD. |
|---|---|---|---|---|---|---|---|---|---|
| P14•45ER | 45 ACP | 5" | 40 | 8.5" | 5.75" | Steel | Black | $750.00 | $875.00 |
| P14•45RR | 45 ACP | 5" | 31 | 8.5" | 5.75" | Alloy | Black | 740.00 | |
| P14•45TR | 45 ACP | 5" | 40 | 8.5" | 5.75" | Stainless | Duotone | 785.00 | |
| P14•45SR | 45 ACP | 5" | 40 | 8.5" | 5.75" | Stainless | Stainless | 799.00 | $899.00 |
| P15•40ER | 40 S&W | 4.25" | 36 | 7.75" | 5.25" | Steel | Black | 750.00 | |
| P15•40RR | 40 S&W | 4.25" | 28 | 7.75" | 5.25" | Alloy | Black | 740.00 | |
| P15•40TR | 40 S&W | 4.25" | 36 | 7.75" | 5.25" | Stainless | Duotone | 785.00 | |
| P15•40SR | 40 S&W | 4.25 | 36 | 7.75" | 5.25" | Stainless | Stainless | 799.50 | |
| P16•40ER | 40 S&W | 5" | 40 | 8.5" | 5.75" | Steel | Black | 750.00 | $875.00 |
| P16•40TR | 40 S&W | 5" | 40 | 8.5" | 5.75 | Stainless | Duotone | 785.00 | |
| P16•40SR | 40 S&W | 5" | 40 | 8.5" | 5.75" | Stainless | Stainless | 799.00 | $899.00 |

*For recreational purposes, magazine capacities are restricted to 10 rounds.*

**Also available:** P109RR 3" or 5" barrel in 9mm: **$740.00**

# ROSSI REVOLVERS

**MODEL R462**

All Rossi revolvers feature full-length ejector shrouds, low profile hammers and fixed sights, contoured grips. All will safely fire +P ammunition.

**MODEL R461**

## MODEL R462
### $345.00
**SPECIFICATIONS**
*Caliber:* 357 Magnum  *Capacity:* 6 rounds
*Barrel Length:* 2" heavy  *Overall Length:* 6.5"
*Weight:* 26 oz.  *Height:* 5"
*Grips:* Rubber  *Finish:* Stainless
*Features:* Fully enclosed ejector rod; serrated ramp front sight
*Also available:*
MODEL R461 w/matte blued finish. . . . . . . . . . . $298.00

## MODEL R352
**SPECIFICATIONS**
*Caliber:* 38 Special
*Capacity:* 5 rounds, swing-out cylinder
*Barrel Lengths:* 2"
*Overall Length:* 6.5" (2" barrel)
*Weight:* 24 oz. (2")
*Sights:* Ramp front, square-notched rear adjustable for windage
*Grips:* rubber (2" barrel only)
*Finish:* Stainless steel
*Price:* . . . . . . . . . . . . . . . . . . . . . . . . . . . . . . . $305.00
*Also available:*
MODEL R351 (not shown) w/matte blue finish. . . . . 249.00

**MODEL R352**

# RUGER REVOLVERS

**REDHAWK REVOLVER**

**STAINLESS REDHAWK**
MODEL KRH-44

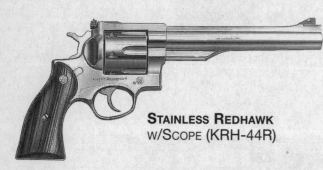

**STAINLESS REDHAWK**
w/SCOPE (KRH-44R)

**SUPER REDHAWK STAINLESS**
MODEL KSRH-9

## BLUED STEEL REDHAWK REVOLVER

The popular Ruger Redhawk® double-action revolver is available in an alloy steel model with blued finish or high-gloss standard steel in 44 Magnum caliber. Constructed of hardened chrome-moly and other alloy steels, this Redhawk is satin polished to a high luster and finished in a rich blue.

### SPECIFICATIONS
*Capacity:* 6 rounds

| CATALOG NUMBER | CALIBER | BARREL LENGTH | OVERALL LENGTH | APPROX. WEIGHT (OUNCES) | PRICE |
|---|---|---|---|---|---|
| **RUGER BLUED REDHAWK REVOLVER** | | | | | |
| RH-445 | 44 Mag. | 5.5" | 11" | 49 | $545.00 |
| RH-44 | 44 Mag. | 7.5" | 13" | 54 | 545.00 |
| RH-44R* | 44 Mag. | 7.5" | 13" | 54 | 578.00 |

*Scope model, with Integral Scope Mounts, 1" Ruger Scope rings.*

## STAINLESS REDHAWK DOUBLE-ACTION REVOLVER

| CATALOG NUMBER | CALIBER | BARREL LENGTH | OVERALL LENGTH | APPROX. WEIGHT (OUNCES) | PRICE |
|---|---|---|---|---|---|
| **RUGER STAINLESS REDHAWK REVOLVER** | | | | | |
| KRH-445 | 44 Mag. | 5.5" | 11" | 49 | $603.00 |
| KRH-44 | 44 Mag. | 7.5" | 13" | 54 | 603.00 |
| KRH-44R* | 44 Mag. | 7.5" | 13" | 54 | 629.00 |
| KRH-455 | 45 LC | 5.5" | 11" | 49 | 603.00 |
| KRH-45 | 45 LC | 7.5" | 13" | 54 | 603.00 |
| KRH-45R* | 45 LC | 7.5" | 13" | 54 | 629.00 |

*Scope model, with Integral Scope Mounts, 1" Stainless Steel Ruger Scope rings.*

## SUPER REDHAWK STAINLESS DOUBLE-ACTION REVOLVER

The Super Redhawk double-action revolver in stainless steel features a heavy extended frame with 7.5" and 9.5" barrels. Cushioned grip panels w/wood inserts provide comfortable, nonslip hold. Comes with case and lock, integral scope mounts and 1" stainless steel Ruger scope rings.

### SPECIFICATIONS
*Caliber:* 44 Magnum, 454 Casull   *Barrel Lengths:* 7.5" and 9.5"
*Overall Length:* 13" w/7.5" bbl.; 15" w/9.5" bbl.
*Weight (empty):* 53 oz. (7.5" bbl.); 58 oz. (9.5" bbl.)
*Sight radius:* 9.5" (7.5" bbl.); 11.25" (9.5" bbl.)
*Finish:* Stainless steell Casull has Target gray finish; satin polished

**KSRH-7** (7.5" barrel) . . . . . . . . . . . . . . . . . . . **$629.00**
**KSRH-9** (9.5" barrel)) . . . . . . . . . . . . . . . . . . . . . **629.00**
**KSRH-7454** (7.5" barrel) .454 Casull. . . . . . . . . . **745.00**

***All Ruger revolvers come with transfer-bar mechanism for safety, plus a lockable box and padlock.***

# RUGER REVOLVERS

**VAQUERO SINGLE ACTION
$498.00 (ALL MODELS)**

**BISLEY-VAQUERO**

The original Bisley single-action design was developed in the 1890s for England's famous target shooting matches held at Bisley Common. Modification and repositioning of the grip to a nearly vertical position reduced a tendency of some standard-frame single-action grips to "ride-up" in the shooter's hand during recoil. Maintaining the same hand positioning on a revolver's grip from shot to shot is crucial to consistent accuracy. The Bisley hammer is lower and has a wide spur. This enables a shooter to cock the hammer with a minimum amount of disturbance to the hand and revolver position. The Ruger Vaquero has become extremely popular since its introduction a few years ago. Its combined the latest Ruger single-action mechanism with the classic appearance of colt revolvers of a century ago. The design of the Bisley-Vaquero has captured renewed interest among serious single-action target shooters and Cowboy Action Shooters alike. As with the Vaquero, the new Ruger Bisley-Vaquero is based on the Ruger New Model Blackhawk, single-action revolver, in production since 1973.

## BISLEY-VAQUERO SINGLE-ACTION REVOLVER

### SPECIFICATIONS

**Calibers:** .44 Magnum and .45 Long Colt
**Capacity:** 6 rounds
**Barrel Length:** 5.5"  **Overall Length:** 11.375"
**Safety:** Transfer bar and loading gate interlock
**Sights:** Blade front; notch rear; fixed
**Sights Radius:** 6.5"
**Weight (Approx.):** 40 oz.
**Grips:** Smooth rosewood with inletted Ruger medallion

**Finish:** Blued: "color case finish" on frame; polished and blued barrel and cylinder
**Features:** Instruction manual, lockable plastic case with lock; heat treated Chrome-moly steel frame, barrel and grip (blued version); 400 stainless steel
**Prices:**
**MODELS RBNV-475 AND RBNV-455** . . . . . . . . . . $428.00
**MODELS KRBNV-475 AND KRBNV-455** . . . . . . . . . 529.00
   (Simulated ivory grips **$36.00** additional)

## SPECIFICATIONS: VAQUERO SINGLE-ACTION REVOLVER

| CATALOG NUMBER | CALIBER | FINISH* | BARREL LENGTH | OVERALL LENGTH | APPROX. WT (OZ.) | CATALOG NUMBER | CALIBER | FINISH* | BARREL LENGTH | OVERALL LENGTH | APPROX. WT (OZ.) |
|---|---|---|---|---|---|---|---|---|---|---|---|
| BNV34 | 357 Mag.+ | CB | 4 5/8" | 10.25" | 39 | BNV475 | 44 Mag. | CB | 5.5" | 11.5" | 40 |
| KBNV34 | 357 Mag.+ | SSG | 4 5/8" | 10.25" | 39 | KBNV475 | 44 Mag. | SSG | 5.5" | 11.5" | 40 |
| BNV35 | 357 Mag.+ | CB | 5.5" | 11.5" | 40 | BNV477 | 44 Mag. | CB | 7.5" | 13 1/8" | 41 |
| KBNV35 | 357 Mag.+ | SSG | 5.5" | 11.5" | 40 | KBNV477 | 44 Mag. | SSG | 7.5" | 13 1/8" | 41 |
| BNV40 | 44-40 | CB | 4 5/8" | 10.25" | 39 | BNV44 | 45 Long Colt | CB | 4 5/8" | 10.25" | 39 |
| KBNV40 | 44-40 | SSG | 4 5/8" | 10.25" | 39 | KBNV44 | 45 Long Colt | SSG | 4 5/8" | 10.25" | 39 |
| BNV405 | 44-40 | CB | 5.5" | 11.5" | 40 | BNV455 | 45 Long Colt | CB | 5.5" | 11.5" | 40 |
| KBNV405 | 44-40 | SSG | 5.5" | 11.5" | 40 | KBNV455 | 45 Long Colt | SSG | 5.5" | 11.5" | 40 |
| BNV407 | 44-40 | CB | 7.5" | 13 1/8" | 41 | BNV45 | 45 Long Colt | CB | 7.5" | 13 1/8" | 41 |
| KBNV407 | 44-40 | SSG | 7.5" | 13 1/8" | 41 | KBNV45 | 45 Long Colt | SSG | 7.5" | 13 1/8" | 41 |

*Finish: high-gloss stainless steel (SSG); "color-cased finish" on steel cylinder frame w/blued steel grip, barrel and cylinder (CB).
**With simulated ivory grips: $565.00.  **All Ruger revolvers come with transfer-bar mechanism for safety, plus a lockable box and padlock.**

# RUGER SINGLE-ACTION REVOLVERS

**NEW MODEL BLACKHAWK REVOLVER**

**NEW MODEL BLACKHAWK REVOLVER MODEL KBN-36 STAINLESS STEEL 6 ¹/₂" barrel**

The Blackhawk has long been the workhorse of Ruger's single-action line. Extremely strong, it easily handles loads that would have jeopardized revolvers a century ago. Adjustable sights make it accurate. *The transfer-bar mechanism prevents slam-fires.*

## SPECIFICATIONS: NEW MODEL BLACKHAWK AND BLACKHAWK CONVERTIBLE

| CAT. NUMBER | CALIBER | FINISH** | BBL. LENGTH | O.A. LENGTH | WEIGHT (Oz.) | PRICE |
|---|---|---|---|---|---|---|
| BN34 | 357 Mag.++ | B | 4 ⁵/₈" | 10 ³/₈" | 40 | $399.00 |
| KBN34 | 357 Mag.++ | SS | 4 ⁵/₈" | 10 ³/₈" | 40 | 489.00 |
| BN36 | 357 Mag.++ | B | 6.5" | 12.25" | 42 | 399.00 |
| KBN36 | 357 Mag.++ | SS | 6.5" | 12.5" | 42 | 489.00 |
| BN34X* | 357 Mag.++ | B | 4 ⁵/₈" | 10 ³/₈" | 40 | 449.00 |
| BN36X* | 357 Mag.++ | B | 6.5" | 12.25" | 42 | 449.00 |
| BN41 | 41 Mag. | B | 4 ⁵/₈" | 10 ³/₈" | 41 | 399.00 |
| BN42 | 41 Mag. | B | 6.5" | 12.25" | 41 | 399.00 |
| BN31 | 30 carbine | B | 7.5" | 13.25" | 43 | 399.00 |
| BN44 | 45 Long Colt | B | 4 ⁵/₈" | 10.25" | 39 | 399.00 |
| KBN44 | 45 Long Colt | SS | 4 ⁵/₈" | 10.25" | 39 | 489.00 |
| BN455 | 45 Long Colt | B | 5.5" | 11 ¹/₈" | 39 | 399.00 |
| BN45 | 45 Long Colt | B | 7.5" | 13 ¹/₈" | 41 | 399.00 |
| KBN45 | 45 Long Colt | SS | 7.5" | 13 ¹/₈" | 41 | 489.00 |

*Convertible: Designated by an X in the Catalog Number, this model comes with an extra interchangeable .38 Special cylinder; price includes extra cylinder. **Finish: blued (B); stainless steel (SS); high-gloss stainless steel (HGSS); color-cased finish on the steel cylinder frame with blued steel grip, barrel, and cylinder (CB). Also available: Models BN44X and BN455X in .45 Convertible (6-shot). Price: **$405.00**

# RUGER REVOLVERS

**NEW SUPER MODEL BLACKHAWK**
SINGLE-ACTION REVOLVER

## NEW MODEL SUPER BLACKHAWK SINGLE-ACTION REVOLVER

**SPECIFICATIONS**
*Caliber:* 44 Magnum; interchangeable with 44 Special
*Barrel Lengths:* 4 ⅝", 5.5", 7.5", 10.5"
*Overall Length:* 13 ⅜" (7.5" barrel)
*Weight:* 45 oz. (4 ⅝" bbl.), 46 oz. (5.5" bbl.), 48 oz. (7.5" bbl.) and 51 oz. (10.5" bbl.)
*Frame:* Chrome molybdenum steel or stainless steel
*Springs:* Music wire springs throughout
*Sights:* Patridge style, ramp front matted blade 18" wide; rear sight click-adjustable for windage and elevation
*Grip Frame:* Chrome molybdenum or stainless steel, enlarged and contoured to minimize recoil effect
*Trigger:* Wide spur, low contour, sharply serrated for convenient cocking with minimum disturbance of grip

*Finish:* Polished and blued or brushed satin stainless steel
*Features:* Case and lock included
*Prices:*
**KS45N**
  5.5" bbl., brushed or high-gloss stainless. . . . . **$499.00**
**KS458N**
  4 ⅝" bbl., brushed or high-gloss stainless . . . . . **499.00**
**KS47N**
  7.5" bbl., brushed or high-gloss stainless. . . . . . **499.00**
**KS411N** 10.5" bull bbl., stainless steel . . . . . . . . **505.00**
**S45N** 5.5" bbl., blued . . . . . . . . . . . . . . . . . **478.00**
**S458N** 4 ⅝" bbl., blued . . . . . . . . . . . . . . . . **478.00**
**S47N** 7.5" bbl., blued . . . . . . . . . . . . . . . . . **478.00**
**S411N** 10.5" bull bbl., blued. . . . . . . . . . . . . . **485.00**

**NEW MODEL SINGLE-SIX**
(W/EXTRA CYLINDER)

## NEW MODEL SINGLE-SIX

**SPECIFICATIONS**
*Caliber:* 22 LR (fitted with 22 WMR cylinder)
*Barrel Lengths:* 4 ⅝", 5.5", 6.5", 9.5"; stainless steel model in 5.5" and 6.5" lengths only *Weight (approx.):* 33 oz. (with 5.5" barrel); 38 oz. (with 9.5" barrel) *Sights:* Patridge-type ramp front sight; rear sight click adjustable for elevation and windage; protected by integral frame ribs. Adjustable sight model available with 5.5", 6.5", or 9.5" barrel.

*Finish:* Blue or stainless steel *Features:* Case and lock incl.
*Prices:*
Blue Fixed sight. . . . . . . . . . . . . . . . . . . . . . . . **$347.00**
  Blue adjustable sight. . . . . . . . . . . . . . . . . . . **352.00**
Stainless steel
  (convertible 5.5" and 6.5" barrels only). . . . . . . **436.00**
*All Ruger revolvers come with transfer-bar mechanism for safety, plus a lockable box and padlock.*

# RUGER REVOLVERS

**MODEL SP101**
**SPURLESS DA**
**$458.00**

**GP-100 357 MAGNUM**
6" HEAVY BARREL

## GP-100 & SP101 DOUBLE-ACTION REVOLVERS

In 1971 Ruger announced the Security Six, Police Service Six and Speed Six double-action revolvers that allowed quick dismantling without tools and handled the most powerful factory loads available. The improved G-P 100 followed in 1985, the SP101 in 1988. Cushioned grips soak up recoil and maintain hand position. Oversize frames bottle high-pressure loads. The cylinder is locked into firing position front and rear to ensure proper alignment.

### SPECIFICATIONS SP101 REVOLVERS

| Catalog Number | Caliber | Cap.* | Sights | Barrel Length | Approx Wt. (Oz.) |
|---|---|---|---|---|---|
| KSP-221 | 22 LR | 6 | A | 2.25" | 32 |
| KSP-240 | 22 LR | 6 | A | 4" | 33 |
| KSP-241 | 22 LR | 6 | A | 4" | 34 |
| KSP-3231 | 32 Mag. | 6 | A | 3 1/16" | 30 |
| KSP-3241 | 32 Mag. | 6 | A | 4" | 33 |
| KSP-921 | 9mmx19 | 5 | F | 2.25" | 25 |
| KSP-931 | 9mmx19 | 5 | F | 3 1/16" | 27 |
| KSP-821 | 38+P | 5 | F | 2.25" | 25 |
| KSP-831 | 38+P | 5 | F | 3 1/16" | 27 |
| KSP-321X** | 357 Mag. | 5 | F | 2.25" | 25 |
| KSP-321XL** | 357 Mag. | 5 | F | 2.25" | 25 |
| KSP-331X** | 357 Mag. | 5 | F | 3 1/16" | 27 |

*Indicates cylinder capacity  **Revolvers chambered for 357 Magnum also accept 38 Special cartridges. Model KSP-240 has short shroud; all others have full.  L = spurless hammer
**All Ruger revolvers come with transfer-bar mechanism for safety, plus a lockable box and padlock.**

### SPECIFICATIONS

| Catalog Number | Finish | Sights+ | Shroud++ | Barrel Length | Wt. (Oz.) | Price |
|---|---|---|---|---|---|---|
| GP-141 | B | A | F | 4" | 41 | $462.00 |
| GP-160 | B | A | S | 6" | 43 | 462.00 |
| GP-161 | B | A | F | 6" | 46 | 462.00 |
| GPF-331 | B | F | F | 3" | 36 | 445.00 |
| GPF-340 | B | F | S | 4" | 37 | 445.00 |
| GPF-341 | B | F | F | 4" | 38 | 445.00 |
| KGP-141 | SS | A | F | 4" | 41 | 498.00 |
| KGP-160 | SS | A | S | 6" | 43 | 498.00 |
| KGP-161 | SS | A | F | 6" | 46 | 498.00 |
| KGPF-330 | SS | F | S | 3" | 35 | 480.00 |
| KGPF-331 | SS | F | F | 3" | 36 | 480.00 |
| KGPF-340 | SS | F | S | 4" | 37 | 480.00 |
| KGPF-341 | SS | F | F | 4" | 38 | 480.00 |
| KGPF-840* | SS | F | S | 4" | 37 | 480.00 |
| GPF-841* | SS | F | F | 4" | 38 | 445.00 |

*38 Special only. B = blued; SS = stainless; A = adjustable; F = fixed. ++ F = full; S = short.

# RUGER REVOLVERS

**BISLEY SINGLE-ACTION TARGET GUN**

## BISLEY SINGLE-ACTION TARGET GUN

The Bisley single-action was originally used at the British National Rifle Association matches held in Bisley, England, in the 1890s. Today's Ruger Bisleys are offered in two frame sizes, chambered from 22 LR to 45 Long Colt. These revolvers are the target-model versions of the Ruger single-action line.

*Special Features:* Unfluted cylinder roll-marked with classic foliate engraving pattern; hammer is low with smoothly curved, deeply checkered wide spur positioned for easy cocking.

*Prices:*
22 LR . . . . . . . . . . . . . . . . . . . . . . . . . . . . . . $402.00
357 Mag., 44 Mag., 45 Long Colt. . . . . . . . . . . . 498.00

## BISLEY SPECIFICATIONS

| Catalog Number | Caliber | Barrel Length | Overall Length | Sights | Approx. Wt. (Oz.) |
|---|---|---|---|---|---|
| RB22AW | 22 LR | 6.5" | 11.5" | Adj. | 41 |
| RB35W | 357 Mag. | 7.5" | 13" | Adj. | 48 |
| RB44W | 44 Mag. | 7.5" | 13" | Adj. | 48 |
| RB45W | 45 LC | 7.5" | 13" | Adj. | 48 |

*Dovetail rear sight adjustable for windage only.*

## OLD ARMY CAP-AND-BALL REVOLVER (not shown)

Reminiscent of pre-cartridge days and faithful to the elegant good look of its predecessors, this Ruger has modern-day strength and can be disassembled without tools. Available in .45 caliber, blued or stainless steel, with fixed or adjustable sights. All Old Armys have 7.5" barrels, rosewood grips, coil springs.

*Price:*
Stainless . . . . . . . . . . . . . . . . . . . . . . . . . . . . $499.00
Blued. . . . . . . . . . . . . . . . . . . . . . . . . . . . . . . 478.00

*(see Black Powder Section)*

**THE NEW BEARCAT**

## THE SBC-4 NEW BEARCAT

Originally manufactured between 1958 and 1973, the 22-rimfire single-action Bearcat features an all-steel precision investment-cast frame and patented transfer-bar mechanism. The New Bearcat also has walnut grips with the Ruger medallion.

**SPECIFICATIONS**
*Caliber:* 22 LR *Capacity:* 6 shots
*Barrel Length:* 4" *Grips:* Walnut
*Finish:* Blued chrome-moly steel
*Price:*
Blued. . . . . . . . . . . . . . . . . . . . . . . . . . . . . . $347.00

*All Ruger revolvers come with transfer-bar mechanism for safety, plus a lockable box and padlock.*

# RUGER P-SERIES PISTOLS

## MODEL P95

Ruger's first centerfire pistols were introduced in 1985. Now available in a wide range of models in 9mm .40 Auto and .45 ACP, the P-series pistols feature 3-dot sights and grips that hug the hand. Polymer-frame models offer a 4-oz. weight savings. Decock-Only pistols can be fired after decocking with a double-action pull of the trigger. Double-Action-Only models feature a spurless hammer. Ambidextrous grip, safety and decocking lever make the P-series pistols suitable for quick firing from either hand. An integral firing pin block prevents discharge unless the trigger is pulled and held rearward. P-series pistols come with a lockable case, spare magazine and magazine loading tool.

**Weight:** 31 to 34 oz., depending on model (95 is 27 oz.)

**MODEL KP95D**

**MODEL KP94 9mm**
(4.5" Barrel)

## SPECIFICATIONS P SERIES PISTOLS

| Cat. Number | Model | Finish | Caliber | Mag. Cap. | Price |
|---|---|---|---|---|---|
| P89 | Manual Safety | Blued | 9mm | 10 | $430.00 |
| KP89 | Manual Safety | Stainless | 9mm | 10 | 475.00 |
| P89D | Decock Only | Blued | 9mm | 10 | 430.00 |
| KP89D | Decock Only | Stainless | 9mm | 10 | 475.00 |
| KP89DAO | Double-Action Only | Stainless | 9mm | 10 | 475.00 |
| P90 | Manual Safety | Blued | 45 ACP | 7 | 476.00 |
| KP90* | Manual Safety | Stainless | 45 ACP | 7 | 513.00 |
| P93D | Decock-Only | Blued | 9mm | 10 | 445.00 |
| KP90D | Decock Only | Stainless | 45 ACP | 7 | 513.00 |
| KP93D** | Decock Only | Stainless | 9mm | 10 | 520.00 |
| KP93DAO | Double-Action Only | Stainless | 9mm | 10 | 520.00 |
| P94 | Manual Safety | Blued | 9mm | 10 | 445.00 |
| KP94*** | Manual Safety | Stainless | 9mm | 10 | 520.00 |
| KP94D | Decock Only | Stainless | 9mm | 10 | 520.00 |
| KP94DAO | Double-Action Only | Stainless | 9mm | 10 | 520.00 |
| P944 | Manual Safety | Blued | 40 Auto | 10 | 445.00 |
| KP944 | Manual Safety | Stainless | 40 Auto | 10 | 520.00 |
| KP944D | Decock Only | Stainless | 40 Auto | 10 | 520.00 |
| KP944DAO | Double-Action Only | Stainless | 40 Auto | 10 | 520.00 |
| KP95D | Decock Only | Stainless | 9mm | 10 | 431.00 |
| KP95DAO | Double-Action Only | Stainless | 9mm | 10 | 431.00 |
| P95D | Decock Only | Blued | 9mm | 10 | 388.00 |
| P95DAO | Double-Action Only | Blued | 9mm | 10 | 388.00 |
| KP97D | Decock-Only | Stainless | .45 ACP | 8 | 460.00 |
| KP97DAO | Double-Action Only | Stainless | .45 ACP | 8 | 460.00 |

*Available w/ambidextrous safety, blued (**$476.00**) Model P90.   **Available w/ambidextrous decocker, blued (**$445.00**) Model P93D.
***Available w/ambidextrous safety, blued (**$445.00**) Model P94.   **All Ruger handguns come with a lockable box and lock.**

# RUGER 22 PISTOLS

**MK-4
STANDARD MODEL**

### MARK II STANDARD MODEL

The Ruger Mark II models represent continuing refinements of the original Ruger Standard and Mark I Target Model pistols. More than two million of this series of autoloading rimfire pistol have been produced since 1949.

The Ruger Mark II pistol, introduced in 1982, uses 22 Long Rifle ammunition in a detachable, 10-shot magazine (standard on all Mark II models except Model 22/45, whose 10-shot magazine is not interchangeable with other Mark II magazines). Designed for easy insertion and removal, the Mark II magazine is equipped with a magazine follower button for convenience in reloading.

The bolts on all Ruger Mark II pistols lock open automatically when the last cartridge is fired, if the magazine is in the pistol. The bolt can be operated manually with the safety in the "on" position for added security while loading and unloading. A boltstop can be activated manually to lock the bolt open.

**MK 678 G GOVERNMENT TARGET MODEL**

**MK 678 TARGET MODEL**
Specifcations and prices for Ruger autoloading .22 pistols are on next page.
***All Ruger handguns come with a lockable box and lock.***

# RUGER PISTOLS

**MODEL P-4 22/45**

**MARK II 22/45**
w/Zytel Frame

**22/45 TARGET MODEL P-512**

## SPECIFICATIONS: RUGER 22 MARK II PISTOLS

| CATALOG NUMBER | MODEL* | FINISH** | BARREL LENGTH | OVERALL LENGTH | APPROX. WT. (OZ.) | PRICE |
|---|---|---|---|---|---|---|
| MK-4 | Std. | B | 4 3/4" | 8 5/16" | 35 | $278.00 |
| KMK-4 | Std. | SS | 4 3/4" | 8 5/16" | 35 | 364.00 |
| KP-4***22/45 | Std. | SS | 4 3/4" | 8 13/16" | 28 | 294.00 |
| P-4***22/45 | Bull | B | 4" | 8" | 31 | 265.00 |
| MK-6 | Std. | B | 6" | 10 5/16" | 37 | 278.00 |
| KMK-6 | Std. | SS | 6" | 10 5/16" | 37 | 364.00 |
| MK-678 | Target | B | 6 7/8" | 11 1/8" | 42 | 326.00 |
| KMK-678 | Target | SS | 6 7/8" | 11 1/8" | 42 | 408.00 |
| P-512***22/45 | Bull | B | 5.5" | 9 3/4" | 35 | 265.00 |
| MK-512 | Bull | B | 5.5" | 9 3/4" | 42 | 326.00 |
| KMK-512 | Bull | SS | 5.5" | 9 3/4" | 42 | 408.00 |
| KP-512***22/45 | Bull | SS | 5.5" | 9 3/4" | 35 | 347.00 |
| MK-10 | Bull | B | 10" | 14 5/16" | 51 | 330.00 |
| KMK-10 | Bull | SS | 10" | 14 5/16" | 51 | 413.00 |
| MK-678G | Bull | B | 6 7/8" | 11 1/8" | 46 | 393.00 |
| KMK-678G | Bull | SS | 6 7/8" | 11 1/8" | 46 | 470.00 |
| KMK-678GC | Bull | SS | 6 7/8" | 11 1/8" | 45 | 486.00 |

*All Ruger handguns come with a lockable box and lock.*

*Model: Std.=standard **Finish: B=blued; SS=stainless steel ***22 cartridge, 45 grip angle and magazine latch*

# SAFARI ARMS PISTOLS

## MATCHMASTER

### SPECIFICATIONS
*Caliber:* 45 ACP
*Capacity:* 7 rounds
*Barrel length:* 5" or 6"
*Overall length:* 8.25"
*Weight:* 40.3 oz.
*Finish:* Stainless steel or black Parkerized carbon steel
*Features:* Extended safety & slide stop; wide beavertail grip safety; LPA fully adjustable rear sight; full-length recoil spring guide; squared trigger guide & finger-groove front strap frame; laser-etched walnut grips
*Prices:*
5" Barrel . . . . . . . . . . . . . . . . . . . . . . . . . . . . $495.00
6" Barrel . . . . . . . . . . . . . . . . . . . . . . . . . . . . 545.00

## ENFORCER

### SPECIFICATIONS
*Caliber:* 45 ACP
*Capacity:* 6 rounds
*Barrel length:* 4" conical
*Overall length:* 7.3"
*Height:* 4 $^7/_8$"
*Weight:* 36 oz.
*Sight radius:* 5.75"
*Finish:* Stainless steel or matte black Parkerized carbon steel
*Features:* Beavertail grip safety; extended thumb safety and slide release; smooth walnut stock w/laser-etched Black Widow logo
*Price:* . . . . . . . . . . . . . . . . . . . . . . . . . . . . . . . $525.00

## COHORT

### SPECIFICATIONS
*Caliber:* 45 ACP
*Capacity:* 7 rounds
*Barrel length:* 4" conical
*Overall length:* 7.3"
*Height:* 5.5"
*Weight:* 37 oz.
*Sights:* Ramped blade front, LPA adjustable rear
*Finish:* Stainless steel or black Parkerized carbon steel
*Features:* Beavertail grip safety; extended thumb safety and slide release; commander-style hammer; smooth walnut stock
*Price:* . . . . . . . . . . . . . . . . . . . . . . . . . . . . . . . $549.00

# SAVAGE ARMS PISTOLS

## BOLT-ACTION HUNTING HANDGUN

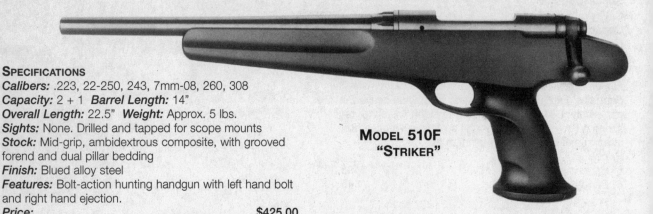

**SPECIFICATIONS**
*Calibers:* .223, 22-250, 243, 7mm-08, 260, 308
*Capacity:* 2 + 1  *Barrel Length:* 14"
*Overall Length:* 22.5"  *Weight:* Approx. 5 lbs.
*Sights:* None. Drilled and tapped for scope mounts
*Stock:* Mid-grip, ambidextrous composite, with grooved
forend and dual pillar bedding
*Finish:* Blued alloy steel
*Features:* Bolt-action hunting handgun with left hand bolt
and right hand ejection.
*Price:* . . . . . . . . . . . . . . . . . . . . . . . . . . . . . . $425.00

**MODEL 510F
"STRIKER"**

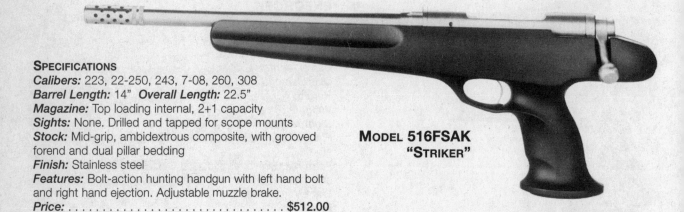

**SPECIFICATIONS**
*Calibers:* 223, 22-250, 243, 7-08, 260, 308
*Barrel Length:* 14"  *Overall Length:* 22.5"
*Magazine:* Top loading internal, 2+1 capacity
*Sights:* None. Drilled and tapped for scope mounts
*Stock:* Mid-grip, ambidextrous composite, with grooved
forend and dual pillar bedding
*Finish:* Stainless steel
*Features:* Bolt-action hunting handgun with left hand bolt
and right hand ejection. Adjustable muzzle brake.
*Price:* . . . . . . . . . . . . . . . . . . . . . . . . . . . . . . $512.00

**MODEL 516FSAK
"STRIKER"**

**SAVAGE ARMS INTRODUCES
"SUPER STRIKER" HUNTING HANDGUNS**

The standard Striker action is the basis for an
exciting new handgun with laminated thumbhole
stock, muzzle brake and stainless construction.
- Custom "dual pillar bedded" laminate thumb-
  hole stock
- Left-hand bollt with right-hand ejection
- Fluted 14" stainless steel barrel with Adjustable
  Muzzle Brake (AMB)
- ESP "Engineered Step Performance" Fully
  Adjustable Two-step Trigger System
- Drilled & Tapped for scope mount
*Price:* . . . . . . . . . . . . . . . . . . . . . . . . . . . . . . $618.00

**MODEL
516BSAK
"SUPER
STRIKER"**

# SIG ARMS PISTOLS

## MODEL P239

**SPECIFICATIONS**
**Calibers:** 357 SIG, 9mm, 40 S&W
**Capacity:** 7 rounds (8 in 9mm)
**Barrel Length:** 3.6"
**Overall Length:** 6.6"
**Height:** 5.2"
**Width:** 1.2"
**Weight (empty):** 27.4 oz.
**Finish:** Nitron Stainless Steel, Two Tone
**Prices:**
Nitron . . . . . . . . . . . . . . . . . . . . . . . . . . . . . . $620.00
  w/"Siglite" night sights . . . . . . . . . . . . . . . . . 720.00
Two Tone . . . . . . . . . . . . . . . . . . . . . . . . . . . . 665.00
  "Siglite" night sights . . . . . . . . . . . . . . . . . . . . 765.00

**MODEL P239**

## MODEL P229S

**SPECIFICATIONS**
**Caliber:** 357 SIG **Capacity:** 10 rounds
**Action:** DA/SA **Barrel Length:** 4.8"
**Overall Length:** 8.6" **Weight (empty):** 40.6 oz.
**Height:** 5.7" **Width:** 1.5" **Finish:** Stainless Steel
**Price:** . . . . . . . . . . . . . . . . . . . . . . . . . . . . . $1,320.00

**MODEL P229S**
**Stainless**
**w/Compensator**

## MODEL P226

**SPECIFICATIONS**
**Calibers:** 357 SIG, 9mm and 40 S&W
**Capacity:** 10 rounds **Action:** DA/SA or DA only
**Barrel Length:** 4.4"
**Overall Length:** 7.7"
**Weight (empty):** 26.5 oz.; 30.1 oz. in 357 SIG
**Height:** 5.5" **Finish:** Blue, K-Kote or Two-tone
**Prices:**
Blackened stainless steel slide . . . . . . . . . . . . . . $830.00
  w/"Siglite" night sight . . . . . . . . . . . . . . . . . . . 930.00
Nickel finish stainless steel slide, DA only
  w/"Siglite" night sights . . . . . . . . . . . . . . . . . . 970.00

**MODEL P226**

# SIG ARMS PISTOLS

## MODEL P232

**SPECIFICATIONS**
*Calibers:* 9mm Short (380 ACP)
*Action:* DA/SA or DAO
*Capacity:* 7 rounds (380 ACP)
*Barrel Length:* 3.6" *Overall
Length:* 6.6" *Weight (empty):*
16.2 oz. *Height:* 4.7" *Width:* 1.2"
*Safety:* Automatic firing-pin lock *Finish:* Blued or stainless steel
*Prices:* Blued finish . . . . . . . . . . . . . . . . . . . . . $505.00
Stainless steel . . . . . . . . . . . . . . . . . . . . . . . . . . 545.00
w/Stainless slide, alloy frame . . . . . . . . . . . . . . . 525.00
w/"Siglite" night sight, Hogue grips, DA only . . . . . 585.00

## MODEL P229

**SPECIFICATIONS**
*Calibers:* 9mm,
357 and 40 S&W
*Capacity:* 10 rounds *Action:* DA/SA
or DA only *Barrel Length:* 3.8"
*Overall Length:* 7.1" *Weight (empty):*
27.5 oz. *Height:* 5.4" *Width:* 1.5"
*Finish:* Blackened stainless steel
*Features:* Stainless steel slide; automatic
firing-pin lock; wood grips (optional);
aluminum alloy frame
*Prices:* Model P229 . . . . . . . . . . . . . . . . . . . . . . $830.00
w/"Siglite" night sight . . . . . . . . . . . . . . . . . . . . . . 930.00
w/Nickel slide . . . . . . . . . . . . . . . . . . . . . . . . . . . 875.00
w/Nickel slide/"Siglite" night sight . . . . . . . . . . . . . 970.00

## TRAILSIDE PL22
.22 LR, with 4.5" Barrel

## TRAILSIDE
## PL22 TARGET
.22 LR, with 6" or 4.5" Barrel
Two-Tone/Laminated Grips
Adjustable Rear Target Sights

## TRAILSIDE
## COMPETITION

## SIG TRAILSIDE PL 22 PISTOL

With an integral frame and barrel, and Hammerli engineering, the new SIG Trailside pistol might be more at home on the target range, punching out the X-ring. But the standard models with 4" and 6" barrels are slim and easy to pack. At 28 and 30 ounces, they're nearly half a pound lighter than the Competition model, which features a hand-filling adjustable grip, modular counterweights and adjustable target sights. All guns feature an adjustable trigger and a top rail for scope mounts. The PL 22 Target model has target sights but a slender profile. Its laminated grips differ from the rubber composite grips of the trail model. The proven blow-back action feeds cartridges from a 10-round magazine.

*Prices:* Standard . . . . . . . . . . . . . . . . . . . . . . . $398.00
Target . . . . . . . . . . . . . . . . . . . . . . . . . . . . . . . . 489.00
Competition . . . . . . . . . . . . . . . . . . . . . . . . . . . . 565.00

## TRAILSIDE PL22
.22 LR, with 6" Barrel

## TRAILSIDE
## PL22 COMPETITION
.22 LR, with 6" Barrel
Two-Tone Competition
Grips Fully Adjustable
Target Sights

# SMITH & WESSON PISTOLS

## FULL-SIZE DOUBLE-ACTION PISTOLS

### MODEL 5900 SERIES

**SPECIFICATIONS**
*Caliber:* 9mm Parabellum  *Capacity:* 15 rounds
*Barrel Length:* 4"  *Overall Length:* 7.5"
*Weight (empty):* 29 oz. (Models 5903, 5943); 38.3 oz.
(Model 5906, 5946); 38 oz. (Model 5906 w/adj. sight)
*Sights:* Front, post w/white dot; fixed rear, adj. for windage only
w/2 white dots. Adjustable sights and night sights available.
*Finish:* satin stainless (Models 5903 and 5943 have stain-
less/alloy construction)
*Prices:* MODEL 5903 . . . . . . . . . . . . . . . . . . . . . $801.00
MODEL 5906 Satin stainless . . . . . . . . . . . . . . . 861.00
  With fixed sights. . . . . . . . . . . . . . . . . . . . . 822.00
  With Tritium night sight . . . . . . . . . . . . . . . . 948.00
MODEL 5946 Double action only . . . . . . . . . . . . . 822.00
MODEL 5943 Double action only . . . . . . . . . . . . . 804.00

**MODEL 5906 DA**
STAINLESS

### MODEL 410, 910, 457

**SPECIFICATIONS**
*Caliber:* 40 S&W, 9mm Parabellum, .45 ACP
*Capacity:* 10 rounds+1 (7+1, .45)
*Barrel Length:* 4" (3.75", .45)  *Overall Length:* 7.5"
*Weight:* 28.5 oz.  *Sights:* 3-dot sights
*Grips:* Straight backstrap  *Features:* Right-hand slide-
mounted manual safety; decocking lever; aluminum alloy
frame; blue carbon steel slide; nonreflective matte blued
finish; beveled edge slide
*Price:* 410, 457 . . . . . . . . . . . . . . . . . . . . . . . . $563.00
910 . . . . . . . . . . . . . . . . . . . . . . . . . . . . . . . . . 509.00

**MODEL 410**

### MODEL 4000, 4500 SERIES

**SPECIFICATIONS**
*Caliber:* 40 S&W, 45 ACP
*Capacity:* 10 rounds, +1 (8 rounds + 1, .45)
*Barrel Length:* 4" (3.75", .45)
*Overall Length:* 7.5"
*Weight:* 28.5 oz. (.40 alloy), 30.5 oz. (.45 alloy), 37.8 oz.
(.40 stainless), 39.1 oz. (.45 stainless)
*Sights:* Post w/white dot front; fixed w/white 2-dot rear,
adjustable and night sights available
*Grips:* Straight backstrap
*Finish:* Stainless steel
*Prices:*
MODEL 4006 w/fixed sights. . . . . . . . . . . . . . . . $864.00
  Same as above w/adj. sights. . . . . . . . . . . . . 899.00
  w/fixed night sight . . . . . . . . . . . . . . . . . . . 991.00
MODEL 4043 DA only (28 oz.) . . . . . . . . . . . 844.00
MODEL 4046 Fixed sights, DA only (39.5 oz.) . . . . . 864.00
  Double action only, fixed Tritium night sight . . . . 991.00
MODEL 4566 w/4.25" bbl., fixed sights . . . . . . . . 897.00
MODEL 4586 DA only, 4.25" bbl., 39.5 oz.,
  fixed 2-dot rear sight, white dot front . . . . . . . . 897.00

**MODEL 4046**

# SMITH & WESSON PISTOLS

## COMPACT AND SIGMA SERIES DOUBLE-ACTION PISTOLS

### MODEL 3900 COMPACT SERIES

**SPECIFICATIONS**
**Caliber:** 9mm Parabellum (traditional double-action)
**Capacity:** 8 rounds  **Barrel Length:** 3.5"
**Overall Length:** 6 ⁷/₈"  **Weight (empty):** 25 oz.
**Sights:** Post w/white dot front; fixed rear adj. for windage
only w/2 white dots. Adjustable sight models include
micrometer click, adj. for windage and elevation w/2 white
dots. Deduct $25 for fixed sights.
**Finish:** Satin stainless
**Prices:** MODEL 3913 LADYSMITH (single side) . . . . $744.00

Smith & Wesson's Polymer-frame Sigma Series pistols
combine traditional craftmanship and the latest technology to allow the guns to be assembled without the usual
"fitting" process required for other handguns.

**MODEL 3913**
LADYSMITH

**SIGMA SERIES SW380**
COMPACT DA

**SIGMA SERIES**
**MODEL SW40F**
FULL SIZE DA

### SIGMA SERIES SW380 COMPACT DA (380 ACP)

**SPECIFICATIONS**
**Calibers:** 38 ACP  **Capacity:** 6 rounds  **Barrel Length:** 3"
**Overall Length:** 5.8"  **Weight:** 14 oz.  **Sights:** Post
w/channel front; fixed channel rear  **Finish:** Blue
**Features:** Lightweight polymer frame with integral thum-
brest; two-piece trigger; corrosion-resistant steel slide
**Price:** . . . . . . . . . . . . . . . . . . . . . . . . . . . . . . . . . $358.00

### SIGMA SERIES SW40E & VE

| MODEL | SW9E | SW9VE | SW40E | SW40VE |
|---|---|---|---|---|
| Caliber | 9mm | 9mm | .40 S&W | .40 S&W |
| Mag. Capacity** | 10 (16)** | 10 (16)** | 10 (14)** | 10 (14)** |
| Barrel Length | 4 inches | 4 inches | 4 inches | 4 inches |
| Sight Radius | 5.9 inches | 5.9 inches | 5.9 inches | 5.9 inches |
| Front Sight | Tritium Dot | White Dot | Tritium Dot | White Dot |
| Rear Sight | Tritium 2-Dot | Fixed 2-Dot | Tritium 2-Dot | Fixed 2-Dot |
| Material, Mechanism | Polymer Frame/Stainless Slide & Barrel, Double Action Only | | | |
| Finish | Melonite Slide & Barrel | Stainless Slide & Barrel | Melonite Slide & Barrel | Stainless Steel & Barrel |
| Weight Empty | 24.7 oz. | 24.7 oz. | 24.4 oz. | 24.4 oz. |
| Length | 7.25" | 7.25" | 7.25" | 7.25" |
| Height | 5.6" | 5.6" | 5.6" | 5.6" |
| Width | 1.3" | 1.3" | 1.3" | 1.3" |
| Rifling | 1:18.75 RH | 1:18.75 RH | 1:16 LH | 1:16 LH |

**Prices:** SW40E, SW9E . . . . . . . . . . . . . . . . . . . . . . . . . . . . . . . . . . . . . . . . . . . . . . . . . . . . . . . $657.00
SW40EV, SW9VE . . . . . . . . . . . . . . . . . . . . . . . . . . . . . . . . . . . . . . . . . . . . . . . . . . . . 447.00

** High Capacity magazines available for law enforcement or export orders only

# SMITH & WESSON PISTOLS

## RIMFIRE SINGLE-ACTION PISTOLS

**MODEL NO. 41**

## MODEL NO. 41

**SPECIFICATIONS**
*Caliber:* 22 LR
*Magazine Capacity:* 12 rounds  *Barrel Lengths:* 5.5" and 7"
*Weight:* 41 oz. (5.5" barrel)  *Overall Length:* 10.5" (7" bbl.)
*Sights:* Front, $^1/_8$" Patridge undercut; rear, S&W micrometer
click sight adjustable for windage and elevation
*Grips:* Hardwood target  *Finish:* S&W Bright blue
*Trigger:* .365" width; S&W grooving, adj. trigger stop
*Features:* Carbon steel slide and frame
*Price:* . . . . . . . . . . . . . . . . . . . . . . . . . . . . . . . $912.00

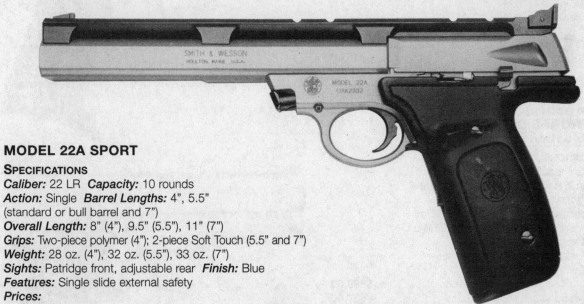

## MODEL 22A SPORT

**SPECIFICATIONS**
*Caliber:* 22 LR  *Capacity:* 10 rounds
*Action:* Single  *Barrel Lengths:* 4", 5.5"
(standard or bull barrel and 7")
*Overall Length:* 8" (4"), 9.5" (5.5"), 11" (7")
*Grips:* Two-piece polymer (4"); 2-piece Soft Touch (5.5" and 7")
*Weight:* 28 oz. (4"), 32 oz. (5.5"), 33 oz. (7")
*Sights:* Patridge front, adjustable rear  *Finish:* Blue
*Features:* Single slide external safety
*Prices:*

| | |
|---|---:|
| 4" | $252.00 |
| 5.5" | 278.00 |
| 5.5" Bull Barrel | 349.00 |
| 5.5" Bull/Synthetic | 323.00 |
| 7" | 316.00 |

*Also available:* in stainless steel (5.5" and 7" only)

*Prices:*

| | |
|---|---:|
| 5.5" Standard | $341.00 |
| 5.5" Bull Barrel | 413.00 |
| 7" Standard | 376.00 |
| 5.5" Bull/Synthetic | 385.00 |

# SMITH & WESSON PISTOLS

## TSW TACTICAL SERIES AUTOLOADERS

### MODEL 3913TSW (double action)
### MODEL 3953TSW (double action only)

**SPECIFICATIONS**
*Frame:* Compact
*Caliber:* 9mm
*Capacity:* 8 Rounds + 1
*Barrel Length:* 3.5"
*Front Sight:* White Dot
*Rear Sight:* Novak Lo Mount Carry 2-Dot
*Grips:* Straight Backstrap
*Weight:* 24.8 oz.
*Overall Length:* 6 ³/₄"
*Material:* Aluminum Alloy/Stainless Steel
*Finish:* Satin Stainless
*Price:* . . . . . . . . . . . . . . . . . . . . . . . . . $724.00

**MODEL 3953TSW**
DOUBLE ACTION

### MODEL 4013TSW (double action)
### MODEL 4053TSW (double action only)

**SPECIFICATIONS**
*Frame:* Compact  *Caliber:* .40 S&W
*Capacity:* 9 rounds + 1  *Barrel Length:* 3.5"
*Front Sight:* White Dot
*Rear Sight:* Novak Lo Mount Carry 2-Dot
*External Safety:* Ambidextrous
*Grips:* Curbed Backstrap
*Weight:* 26.8 oz.  *Overall Length:* 6 ³/₄"
*Material:* Aluminum Alloy/Stainless Steel
*Finish:* Satin Stainless
*Price:* . . . . . . . . . . . . . . . . . . . . . . . . . $844.00

**MODEL 4013TSW**
TRADITIONAL DA

### TRADITIONAL DA MODEL 4513TSW (double action)
### TRADITIONAL DA MODEL 4553TSW (double action only)

**SPECIFICATIONS**
*Frame:* Compact  *Caliber:* .45 ACP
*Capacity:* 7 Rounds + 1  *Barrel Length:* 3.75"
*Front Sight:* White Dot
*Rear Sight:* Novak Lo Mount Carry 2-Dot
*Grips:* Straight Backstrap  *Weight:* 28.6 oz.
*Overall Length:* 7 ³/₄"
*Material:* Aluminum Alloy/Stainless Steel
*Finish:* Satin Stainless
*Price:* . . . . . . . . . . . . . . . . . . . . . . . . . $880.00
   Model 4553 . . . . . . . . . . . . . . . . . . . . . . . 837.00
*Also available:* Full-size TSW pistols with 4" barrels (4.25", .45)
*Capacity:* 10+1 (9mm and .40), 8+1 (.45)
*Length:* 7.5" (9mm and 40), 7 7/8" (.45)
*Weight:* 28.5 oz. (9mm and .40), 30.5 oz. (.45)
*Sights:* Same as compact series, but adjustable and night sights available.

**MODEL 4513TSW**
TRADITIONAL DA

# SMITH & WESSON REVOLVERS

## SMALL FRAME

**MODEL 60LS LADYSMITH**
38 S&W Special

### LADYSMITH HANDGUNS
### MODEL 36-LS AND MODEL 60-LS

**SPECIFICATIONS**
*Calibers:* 38 S&W Special (36-LS and 357 Magnum (60-LS)
*Capacity:* 5 shots  *Barrel Lengths:* 2" (2 $^1/_8$" 357 Magnum)
*Overall Length:* 6 $^5/_{16}$"  *Weight:* 20 oz. (23 oz. 357 Magnum)
*Sights:* Serrated ramp front (black pinned ramp in 357 Mag.); fixed notch rear
*Grips:* Contoured laminated rosewood, round butt
*Finish:* Glossy deep blue (36) or stainless (60)
*Features:* Both models come with soft-side LadySmith carry case
*Prices:*
MODEL 36-LS . . . . . . . . . . . . . . . . . . . . . . . . $478.00
MODEL 60-LS . . . . . . . . . . . . . . . . . . . . . . . . 539.00

**MODEL 37**
**CHIEFS SPECIAL AIRWEIGHT**
38 S&W Special

### MODEL 36
### 38 CHIEFS SPECIAL

**SPECIFICATIONS**
*Caliber:* 38 S&W Special  *Capacity:* 5 shots
*Barrel Length:* 2"  *Overall Length:* 6 $^5/_{16}$"
*Weight:* 20 oz.
*Sights:* Serrated ramp front; fixed, square-notch rear
*Grips:* Uncle Mike's Boot
*Finish:* S&W blued carbon steel; satin stainless Model 637
*Features:* .312" smooth combat-style trigger; .240" service hammer
*Prices:*
MODEL 36 38 CHIEFS SPECIAL . . . . . . . . . . . . . . $394.00
MODEL 37 CHIEFS SPECIAL AIRWEIGHT:
  Same as Model 36, except finish is blue or
  nickel aluminum alloy. . . . . . . . . . . . . . . . . . **483.00**
MODEL 637 CHIEFS SPECIAL AIRWEIGHT:
  With 2" barrel, synthetic round butt, stainless finish.
  *Weight:* 13.5 oz.. . . . . . . . . . . . . . . . . . . . . . **501.00**

**MODEL 60**
**38 CHIEFS SPECIAL**
Stainless

### MODEL 60
### 38 CHIEFS SPECIAL, STAINLESS

**SPECIFICATIONS**
*Calibers:* .357 Mag.  *Capacity:* 5 shots
*Barrel Lengths:* 2 1/8" (357 Mag.); 3" full lug (38 S&W Spec.)
*Overall Length:* 6 $^5/_{16}$" (2 $^1/_8$" bbl.)); 7.5" (3" bbl.)
*Weight:* 23 oz. (2 1/8" barrel); 24.5 oz. (3" full lug barrel)
*Sights:* Micrometer click rear, adj. for windage and elevation; pinned black front (3" full lug model only); standard sights as on Model 36
*Grips:* Uncle Mike's Combat  *Finish:* Satin stainless
*Features:* .312" smooth combat-style trigger
*Prices:*
2 $^1/_8$" Barrel. . . . . . . . . . . . . . . . . . . . . . . . . . . $505.00
3" Barrel. . . . . . . . . . . . . . . . . . . . . . . . . . . . . . 536.00

# SMITH & WESSON REVOLVERS

## SMALL FRAME

**MODEL 317 AIRLITE**

**MODEL 442**
38 SPECIAL

**MODEL 640**

**MODEL 649**
BODYGUARD

### MODEL 317 AIRLITE

**SPECIFICATIONS**
*Caliber:* 22 LR *Action:* Single or double action *Capacity:* 8 rounds *Barrel Length:* 1 ⁷/₈" and 3" *Overall Length:* 6 ³/₁₆" *Weight:* 9.9 oz. (10.5 oz. w/rubber grip) *Finish:* Clear Cote *Sights:* Serrated ramp front; fixed notch rear
*Prices:* 1 ⁷/₈" barrel w/synthetic grips . . . . . . . . . $508.00
3" barrel w/rubber grips . . . . . . . . . . . . . . . . . . . . . 537.00

### MODEL 317 LADYSMITH

**SPECIFICATIONS**
Same as **MODEL 317 AIRLITE** with round butt grip, fixed sights and Dymondwood grip.
*Price:* . . . . . . . . . . . . . . . . . . . . . . . . . . . . . . . . . $568.00

### 38 CENTENNIAL "AIRWEIGHT"
### MODEL 442

**SPECIFICATIONS**
*Caliber:* 38 S&W Special *Capacity:* 5 rounds *Barrel Length:* 2" *Overall Length:* 6 ⁵/₁₆" *Weight:* 15.8 oz.
*Sights:* Serrated ramp front; fixed, square-notch rear
*Finish:* Matte blue
*Price:* . . . . . . . . . . . . . . . . . . . . . . . . . . . . . . . . . $501.00
*Also available:* **MODEL 642 CENTENNIAL AIRWEIGHT**
  Stainless steel w/2" barrel, synthetic round butt grip, double-action only. . . . . . . . . . . . . . . . . . . . . . . $517.00
**LADYSMITH MODEL** (satin stainless). . . . . . . . . . . . . 551.00

### MODEL 640 CENTENNIAL

**SPECIFICATIONS**
*Calibers:* 357 Magnum and 38 S&W Special
*Action:* Double action only *Capacity:* 5 rounds
*Barrel Length:* 2 ¹/₈" *Overall Length:* 6 ³/₄"
*Sights:* Pinned black ramp front; fixed, square-notch rear
*Features:* Fully concealed hammer; smooth hardwood service stock; satin stainless steel finish; round-butt synthetic grips
*Price:* . . . . . . . . . . . . . . . . . . . . . . . . . . . . . . . . . $488.00

### MODEL 649 BODYGUARD

**SPECIFICATIONS**
*Caliber:* 38 S&W Special/357 S&W Mag.
*Capacity:* 5 rounds
*Barrel Length:* 2 ¹/₈"
*Overall Length:* 6 ⁵/₁₆"
*Weight:* 20 oz.
*Sights:* Black pinned ramp front; fixed, square-notch rear
*Grips:* Uncle Mike's Combat
*Finish:* Satin stainless
*Price:* . . . . . . . . . . . . . . . . . . . . . . . . . . . . . . . . . $548.00

# SMITH & WESSON REVOLVERS

## MEDIUM FRAME

**MODEL 617 (6-shot, 6" barrel shown)**

**MODEL 10**
**HEAVY BARREL**

**MODEL 64**

**MODEL 65**

### MODEL 617

**SPECIFICATIONS**
**Caliber:** 22 Long Rifle  **Capacity:** 10 shots
**Barrel Length:** 4", 6" or 8 ³/₈"  **Overall Length:** 9 ¹/₈" (4" barrel); 11 ¹/₈" (6" barrel); 13.5" (8 ³/₈" barrel)
**Weight (loaded):** 42 oz. with 4" barrel; 48 oz. with 6" barrel; 54 oz. with 8 ³/₈" barrel  **Sights:** Front pinned Patridge; rear, S&W micrometer click sight adjustable for windage and elevation  **Grips:** Hogue rubber, square butt
**Finish:** Satin stainless  **Features:** Target hammer and trigger; drilled and tapped for scope
**Prices:** 4" Barrel . . . . . . . . . . . . . . . . . . . . . . . $584.00
    6" Bbl. . . . . . . . . . . . . . . . . . . . . . . . . . . 618.00
    8 3/8" Barrel . . . . . . . . . . . . . . . . . . . . . . . 631.00
**Also available:** 6-shot w/6" barrel . . . . . . . . . . . 572.00

### MODEL 10, 38 MILITARY & POLICE

**SPECIFICATIONS**
**Caliber:** 38 S&W Special  **Capacity:** 6 shots
**Barrel Length:** 4" heavy barrel  **Overall Length:** 9.25"
**Weight:** 33.5 oz.
**Sights:** Front, fixed ¹/₈" serrated ramp; square-notch rear
**Grips:** Uncle Mike's Combat  **Finish:** S&W blue
**Price:** . . . . . . . . . . . . . . . . . . . . . . . . . . . . . $458.00

### MODEL 64, 38 MILITARY & POLICE STAINLESS

**SPECIFICATIONS**
**Caliber:** 38 S&W Special  **Capacity:** 6 shots
**Barrel Length:** 4" heavy barrel, square butt; 3" heavy barrel, round butt; 2" regular barrel, round butt
**Overall Length:** 9.25" w/4" bbl.; 7 ⁷/₈" w/3" bbl.; 6 ⁷/₈" w/2" barrel  **Weight:** 28 oz. w/2" barrel; 30.5 oz. w/3" bbl.; 33.5 oz. w/4" barrel  **Sights:** Fixed, ¹/₈" serrated ramp front; square-notch rear  **Grips:** Uncle Mike's Combat
**Finish:** Satin stainless
**Prices:** 2" Bbl. . . . . . . . . . . . . . . . . . . . . . . . . . $487.00
    3" & 4" Bbl. . . . . . . . . . . . . . . . . . . . . . . . 496.00

### MODEL 65 (HEAVY BARREL) 357 MILITARY & POLICE

**SPECIFICATIONS**
K-frame .357 Magnum or 38 S+W Special with stainless steel frame and 3" or 4" barrel; 6 shots; fixed sights.
**Price:** . . . . . . . . . . . . . . . . . . . . . . . . . . . . . $501.00
**Also available:** MODEL 65 LADYSMITH
Same specifications as MODEL 65 but with 3" barrel only (weights 32 oz.) and rosewood laminate stock; satin stainless finish, smooth combat wood grips.
**Price:** . . . . . . . . . . . . . . . . . . . . . . . . . . . . . $539.00

# SMITH & WESSON REVOLVERS

## MEDIUM FRAME

**MODEL 686**

**MODEL 686 PLUS**

**SPECIFICATIONS**
**Calibers:** 357 Mag, 38 S+W Special  **Capacity:** 6 shots
**Barrel Lengths:** 2.5", 4", 6", 8 3/8"
All models have stainless steel finish, combat or target stock
and/or trigger; adjustable sights optional.
**Prices:** 2.5" Barrel . . . . . . . . . . . . . . . . . . . . . . . $561.00
  4" Barrel . . . . . . . . . . . . . . . . . . . . . . . . . . . 573.00
  6" Barrel . . . . . . . . . . . . . . . . . . . . . . . . . . . 578.00
  8 3/8" Barrel . . . . . . . . . . . . . . . . . . . . . . . . . 601.00

### MODEL 686 PLUS DISTINGUISHED COMBAT MAGNUM

**Capacity:** 7 rounds  **Barrel Lengths:** 2.5", 4" or 6" full lug.
**Overall Length:** 7.5" – 11 15/16"  **Weight:** 34.5 oz. – 45 oz.
**Prices:**
  2.5" bbl. . . . . . . . . . . . . . . . . . . . . . . . . . . . $583.00
  4" Barrel . . . . . . . . . . . . . . . . . . . . . . . . . . . 592.00
  6" Barrel . . . . . . . . . . . . . . . . . . . . . . . . . . . 601.00

**MODEL 66**

**MODEL 696**

### MODEL 66
### 357 COMBAT MAGNUM

**SPECIFICATIONS**
**Caliber:** 357 Magnum, 38 S+W Special  **Capacity:** 6 shots
**Barrel Lengths:** 4" or 6" with square butt; 2.5" with round butt
**Overall Length:** 7.5" w/2.5" bbl.; 9.5" w/4" bbl.; 11 3/8"
w/6" bbl.  **Weight:** 30.5 oz. w/2.5" bbl.; 36 oz. w/4" bbl.; 39
oz. w/6" bbl.  **Sights:** Front, 1/8"; rear, S&W Red Ramp on
ramp base, S&W Micrometer Click, adjustable for windage
and elevation  **Grips:** Uncle Mike's Combat  **Trigger:** .312"
Smooth Combat  **Finish:** Satin stainless
**Prices:** 2.5" Bbl. . . . . . . . . . . . . . . . . . . . . . . . . $545.00
  4" or 6" Bbl. . . . . . . . . . . . . . . . . . . . . . . . . . 551.00

### MODEL 696

**SPECIFICATIONS**
**Caliber:** 44 S&W Special  **Capacity:** 5 rounds  **Action:**
Single or double action  **Barrel Length:** 3"  **Overall
Length:** 8 3/16"  **Weight:** 48 oz.  **Sights:** Red ramp front;
adjustable white outline rear  **Grips:** Hogue rubber  **Finish:**
Satin stainless  **Features:** .500" target hammer; .400"
smooth combat trigger
**Price:** . . . . . . . . . . . . . . . . . . . . . . . . . . . . . . . $573.00

# SMITH & WESSON REVOLVERS

## LARGE FRAME STAINLESS

**MODEL 629**

### MODEL 629
**SPECIFICATIONS**
*Calibers:* 44 Magnum, 44 S&W Special  *Capacity:* 6 shots
*Barrel Lengths:* 4", 6", 8 3/8"  *Overall Length:* 9 5/8", 11 3/8", 13 7/8"
*Weight (empty):* 44 oz. (4" bbl.); 47 oz. (6" bbl.); 54 oz. (8 3/8" bbl.)
*Sights:* S&W Red Ramp front; white outline rear w/S&W
Micrometer Click, adjustable for windage and elevation;
drilled and tapped  *Grips:* Hogue rubber  *Finish:* Satin
stainless steel  *Features:* Combat trigger, target hammer
*Prices:* 4" Bbl. . . . . . . . . . . . . . . . . . . . . . . . . . . . . . $683.00
  6" Bbl. . . . . . . . . . . . . . . . . . . . . . . . . . . . . 689.00
  8 3/8" Bbl. . . . . . . . . . . . . . . . . . . . . . . . . . . . 703.00

### MODEL 629 CLASSIC
**SPECIFICATIONS**
*Calibers:* 44 Magnum, 44 S&W Special  *Capacity:* 6 rounds
*Barrel Lengths:* 5", 6.5", 8 3/8"  (all full lug)  *Overall Length:* 10.5",
12", 13 7/8"  *Weight:* 51 oz. (5" bbl.); 52 oz. (6.5" bbl.); 54 oz. (8
3/8" bbl.)  *Grips:* Hogue rubber
*Prices:* 5" & 6.5" Bbl. . . . . . . . . . . . . . . . . . . . . $731.00
  8 3/8" Bbl. . . . . . . . . . . . . . . . . . . . . . . . . . . 755.00
*Also available:* MODEL 629 CLASSIC DX. Same features
as the MODEL 629 CLASSIC above, plus interchangeable
front sights, wood grips. With 6.5" barrel. . . . . . $939.00
  With 8 3/8" barrel. . . . . . . . . . . . . . . . . . . . . . 970.00
**MODEL 629 POWERPORT** w/6.5" barrel (12" overall
length), weighs 52 oz. Patridge front sight, adjustable black
blade rear sight. *Price:* . . . . . . . . . . . . . . . . . . . . $731.00

**MODEL 610**
**CLASSIC HUNTER**

### MODEL 625
**SPECIFICATIONS**
*Caliber:* 45 ACP  *Capacity:* 6 shots  *Barrel Length:* 5" full
lug barrel  *Overall Length:* 10 3/8"  *Weight (empty):* 45 oz.
*Sights:* Front, Patridge on ramp base; S&W Micrometer
Click rear, adjustable for windage and elevation  *Grips:*
Hogue rubber, round butt  *Finish:* Satin stainless
*Price:* . . . . . . . . . . . . . . . . . . . . . . . . . . . . . . . $695.00
*Also available:* Model 625 Mountain Gun with 4" tapered
barrel; 39.5 oz. and half lug

**MODEL 657**

### MODEL 657
**SPECIFICATIONS**
*Calibers:* 41 Magnum  *Capacity:* 6 shots  *Barrel Length:* 6"
*Overall Length:* 11 3/8"  *Weight (empty):* 48 oz.  *Sights:* Front,
pinned ramp on ramp base; black blade rear, adjustable for
windage and elevation; drilled and tapped  *Grips:* Hogue
rubber  *Finish:* Satin stainless steel
*Price:* . . . . . . . . . . . . . . . . . . . . . . . . . . . . . . . $616.00

### MODEL 610 CLASSIC HUNTER
**SPECIFICATIONS**
*Calibers:* 10mm  *Frame:* N-Large  *Capacity:* 6 rounds
*Barrel Length:* 6.5"  *Overall Length:* 12"  *Weight:* 52 oz.
*Sights:* Interchangeable front; micrometer click adj. black
blade  *Grips:* Hogue rubber  *Finish:* Stainless steel
*Feature:* Unfluted cylinder
*Price:* . . . . . . . . . . . . . . . . . . . . . . . . . . . . . . . $746.00

**MODEL 629**
**CLASSIC DX**

# SPRINGFIELD PISTOLS

## MODEL 1911-A1 PISTOLS

### MODEL 1911-A1 CHAMPION 4-INCH

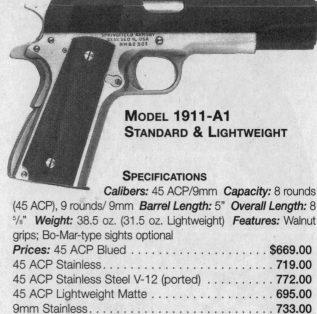

### MODEL 1911-A1 STANDARD & LIGHTWEIGHT

**SPECIFICATIONS**
*Calibers:* 45 ACP/9mm  *Capacity:* 8 rounds (45 ACP), 9 rounds/ 9mm  *Barrel Length:* 5"  *Overall Length:* 8 ⁵/₈"  *Weight:* 38.5 oz. (31.5 oz. Lightweight)  *Features:* Walnut grips; Bo-Mar-type sights optional
*Prices:* 45 ACP Blued . . . . . . . . . . . . . . . . . . $669.00
45 ACP Stainless . . . . . . . . . . . . . . . . . . . . 719.00
45 ACP Stainless Steel V-12 (ported) . . . . . . . . 772.00
45 ACP Lightweight Matte . . . . . . . . . . . . . . . 695.00
9mm Stainless . . . . . . . . . . . . . . . . . . . . . . 733.00
High-capacity (10 rounds, 45 ACP) Parkerized . . . 733.00
Blued . . . . . . . . . . . . . . . . . . . . . . . . . . . 769.00
Stainless . . . . . . . . . . . . . . . . . . . . . . . . . 824.00

**SPECIFICATIONS**
*Calibers:* 45 ACP  *Capacity:* 7 rounds (45 ACP)
*Barrel Length:* 4"  *Overall Length:* 7 ⁵/₈"
*Trigger Pull:* 5-6.5 lbs.  *Sight Radius:* 5.25"
*Weight:* 34 oz.  *Finish:* Parkerized, Blued, Stainless
*Prices:* Parkerized . . . . . . . . . . . . . . . . . . $669.00
Blued . . . . . . . . . . . . . . . . . . . . . . . . . . . 699.00
Stainless . . . . . . . . . . . . . . . . . . . . . . . . . 739.00
Lightweight (26 oz.) matte . . . . . . . . . . . . . . 678.00
Lightweight stainless . . . . . . . . . . . . . . . . . . 748.00

### MODEL 1911-A1 TROPHY MATCH

### 1911-A1 V-10 ULTRA COMPACT BI-TONE

**SPECIFICATIONS**
*Caliber:* 45 ACP and 9mm  *Capacity:* 7 rounds  *Barrel Length:* 3.5"  *Overall Length:* 7.75"  *Weight:* 34.8 oz.
*Sights:* 3-dot fixed combat sights  *Sight Radius:* 5.25"
*Trigger Pull:* 5-6.5 lbs.  *Finish:* Bi-Tone or Parkerized
*Prices:* Parkerized . . . . . . . . . . . . . . . . . . $669.00
Bi-Tone . . . . . . . . . . . . . . . . . . . . . . . . . . 748.00
High-capacity (10 rounds, 45 ACP) . . . . . . . . . . 759.00
Parkerized Stainless . . . . . . . . . . . . . . . . . . 859.00
Stainless . . . . . . . . . . . . . . . . . . . . . . . . . 899.00

**SPECIFICATIONS**
*Calibers:* 45 ACP  *Capacity:* 7 rounds  *Barrel Length:* 5"
*Overall Length:* 8 ⁵/₈"  *Weight:* 40 oz.  *Trigger Pull:* 4-5.5 lbs.
*Sights:* Fully adjustable target sights  *Sight Radius:* 6.75"
*Finish:* Blued, Bi-tone or stainless  *Features:* Match grade barrel; Videcki speed trigger; serrated front strap & top of slide
*Prices:* Blued . . . . . . . . . . . . . . . . . . . . $1,089.00
Stainless . . . . . . . . . . . . . . . . . . . . . . . . 1,149.00

# TAURUS PISTOLS

## SMALL & MEDIUM FRAME

### MODEL PT 22

**SPECIFICATIONS**
*Caliber:* 22 LR  *Action:* Semiautomatic (DA only)
*Capacity:* 8 shots  *Barrel Length:* 2.75"
*Overall Length:* 5.25"  *Weight:* 12.3 oz.  *Sights:* Fixed
*Safety:* Manual  *Grips:* Rosewood grip panels
*Finish:* Blue, nickel, duotone or gold trimmed
*Prices:*
Blue, Nickel or DuoTone . . . . . . . . . . . . . . . . . . $203.00
Gold Trim . . . . . . . . . . . . . . . . . . . . . . . . 219.00

### MODEL PT-25

**SPECIFICATIONS**
*Caliber:* 25 ACP  *Capacity:* 9 rounds
*Action:* Double action semiauto
*Barrel Length:* 2.75"  *Overall Length:* 5.25"
*Weight:* 12.3 oz.
*Finish:* Blue, stainless steel, duotone or gold trimmed
*Sights:* Fixed  *Features:* Rosewood grip panels; tip-up
barrel; push button magazine release
*Prices:*
Blue, Nickel or DuoTone . . . . . . . . . . . . . . . . . . $203.00
Blue w/Gold Trim . . . . . . . . . . . . . . . . . . . . . 219.00

### MODEL PT-938 COMPACT (not shown)

**SPECIFICATIONS**
*Caliber:* 380 ACP  *Capacity:* 10 rounds
*Action:* Double action semiauto
*Barrel Length:* 3"  *Overall Length:* 6.75"
*Weight:* 27 oz.  *Finish:* Blue or stainless steel
*Sights:* Fixed  *Grips:* Checkered rubber grips
*Prices:*
Blue . . . . . . . . . . . . . . . . . . . . . . . . . . . . $453.00
Stainless . . . . . . . . . . . . . . . . . . . . . . . . . . 469.00

### PT 911 COMPACT (not shown)

**SPECIFICATIONS**
*Caliber:* 9mm  *Capacity:* 10 rounds
*Action:* Double action semiauto  *Barrel Length:* 4"
*Overall Length:* 7"  *Weight:* 28.2 oz.
*Safeties:* Manual, ambidextrous hammer drop; intercept
notch; firing pin block; chamber load indicator
*Grips:* Santoprene II  *Sights:* Fixed 3-dot combat
*Finish:* Blue or stainless  *Features:* Floating firing pin
*Prices:*
Blue . . . . . . . . . . . . . . . . . . . . . . . . . . . . $453.00
Stainless . . . . . . . . . . . . . . . . . . . . . . . . . . 469.00
*Also available:*
**PT-111 9MM MILLENNIUM.** *Barrel Length:* 3 1/8" *Sights:* Fixed
3-dot *Capacity:* 10 rounds, polymer frame . . . . . . . $367.00
Stainless . . . . . . . . . . . . . . . . . . . . . . . . . . 383.00

**MODEL PT 22**

**MODEL PT-25**

**MODEL PT 111
MILLENNIUM**

# TAURUS PISTOLS

## LARGE FRAME

### MODEL PT-92

**SPECIFICATIONS**
*Caliber:* 9mm Parabellum **Action:** Semiautomatic double action **Capacity:** 15 + 1 **Hammer:** Exposed
**Barrel Length:** 5" **Overall Length:** 8.5"
**Height:** 5.39" **Width:** 1.45" **Weight:** 34 oz. (empty)
**Rifling:** R.H., 6 grooves **Sights:** Front, fixed; rear, drift adjustable, 3-dot combat **Safeties:** (a) Ambidextrous manual safety locking trigger mechanism and slide in locked position; (b) half-cock position; (c) inertia-operated firing pin; (d) chamber-loaded indicator
**Slide:** Hold open upon firing last cartridge **Finish:** Blue or stainless steel
**Prices:**
Blue . . . . . . . . . . . . . . . . . . . . . . . . . . . . . $508.00
Stainless . . . . . . . . . . . . . . . . . . . . . . . . . . 523.00
*Also available:*
MODEL PT-99 Same specifications as Model PT 92, but has micrometer click-adjustable rear sight.
Blue . . . . . . . . . . . . . . . . . . . . . . . . . . . . . $531.00
Stainless . . . . . . . . . . . . . . . . . . . . . . . . . . 547.00

**MODEL PT-92**

### MODEL PT-945

**SPECIFICATIONS**
*Caliber:* 45 ACP **Capacity:** 8 shots
**Action:** Semiautomatic double **Barrel Length:** 4.25"
**Overall Length:** 7.48" **Weight:** 29.5 oz.
**Sights:** Drift-adjustable front and rear; 3-dot combat
**Grips:** Checkered rubber
**Safety Features:** Manual safety; ambidextrous; chamber load indicator; intercept notch; firing-pin block; floating firing pin
**Finish:** Blue or stainless
**Prices:**
Blue . . . . . . . . . . . . . . . . . . . . . . . . . . . . . $484.00
Stainless . . . . . . . . . . . . . . . . . . . . . . . . . . 500.00
*Also available:*
MODEL 945C w/factory porting (blue) . . . . . . . . . . . $523.00
  w/factory porting (stainless) . . . . . . . . . . . . . . 539.00

**MODEL PT-945**

### MODEL PT-940 (not shown)

**SPECIFICATIONS**
*Caliber:* 40 S&W **Action:** Semiautomatic double
**Capacity:** 10 rounds **Barrel Length:** 4"
**Overall Length:** 7" **Weight:** 28.2 oz.
**Grips:** Santoprene II **Sights:** Low-profile 3-dot combat
**Finish:** Blue or stainless
**Features:** Factory porting standard
**Prices:**
Blue . . . . . . . . . . . . . . . . . . . . . . . . . . . . . $469.00
Stainless . . . . . . . . . . . . . . . . . . . . . . . . . . 484.00

**MODEL PT 99**
**STAINLESS**

# TAURUS REVOLVERS

## MODEL 44

**SPECIFICATIONS**
*Caliber:* 44 Mag. *Capacity:* 6 rounds
*Barrel Lengths:* 4" (solid rib ported); 6.5", and 8 3/8" (vent. rib)
*Weight:* 44 oz. (4"); 52.5 oz. (6.5"); 57.25 oz. (8 3/8")
*Sights:* Serrated ramp front; rear micrometer click, adjustable for windage and elevation
*Grips:* Santoprene I
*Finish:* Blue or stainless steel
*Features:* Transfer bar safety
*Prices:*
4" barrel blue, ported solid rib . . . . . . . . . . . . . . $447.00
   stainless steel, ported solid rib . . . . . . . . . . . 508.00
6.5" and 8 3/8" blue, ported vent. rib . . . . . . . . . 466.00
   stainless steel, ported vent. rib . . . . . . . . . . . 530.00

## MODEL 82

**SPECIFICATIONS**
*Caliber:* 38 Special *Capacity:* 6 shot
*Action:* Double *Barrel Length:* 4" heavy barrel
*Weight:* 34 oz. (4" barrel) *Sights:* Notched rear; serrated ramp front *Grips:* Brazilian hardwood
*Finish:* Blue or stainless
*Prices:*
Blue . . . . . . . . . . . . . . . . . . . . . . . . . . . . . . . . . $297.00
Stainless . . . . . . . . . . . . . . . . . . . . . . . . . . . . . . . 344.00

## MODEL 454 CASULL

## MODEL 85

## MODEL 454 CASULL "RAGING BULL" DA

**SPECIFICATIONS**
*Caliber:* 454 Casull *Capacity:* 5 rounds
*Barrel Length:* 6.5" or 8.375" w/integral vent rib
*Overall Length:* 12" (6.5" barrel); 14" (8.375" barrel)
*Weight:* 53 oz. (6.5" barrel); 62.75 oz. (8.375" barrel)
*Safety:* Transfer bar ignition system
*Sights:* Black Patridge front blade; micrometer click adj. black rear
*Finish:* Polished stainless steel or bright blue steel
*Grips:* Soft black rubber w/recoil-absorbing insert
*Features:* Ported barrel w/internal gas expansion chamber; front and rear cylinder lock
*Prices:*
Blue ported . . . . . . . . . . . . . . . . . . . . . . . . . . . . $750.00
Stainless . . . . . . . . . . . . . . . . . . . . . . . . . . . . . . . 820.00

**SPECIFICATIONS**
*Caliber:* 38 Special *Capacity:* 5 shot
*Action:* Double *Barrel Length:* 2" and 3"
*Weight:* 21 oz. (2" barrel) *Sights:* Fixed sights
*Grips:* Brazilian hardwood *Finish:* Blue or stainless steel
*Prices:*
Blue . . . . . . . . . . . . . . . . . . . . . . . . . . . . . . . . . . $286.00
Stainless Steel . . . . . . . . . . . . . . . . . . . . . . . . . . . 327.00
*Also available:*
MODEL 85CH. Same specifications and prices as Model 85, except has concealed hammer and 2" barrel only.
MODEL 85UL w/2" barrel only and optional porting; weights 17 oz. Features Ultra-Lite Integral Key Lock
Blue . . . . . . . . . . . . . . . . . . . . . . . . . . . . . . . . . . $311.00
Stainless . . . . . . . . . . . . . . . . . . . . . . . . . . . . . . . 342.00
MODELS 85CHB2C/85B2C w/2" barrel, blue finish, ported barrels . . . . . . . . . . . . . . . . . . . . . . . . . . $305.00
Stainless . . . . . . . . . . . . . . . . . . . . . . . . . . . . . . . 345.00

# TAURUS REVOLVERS

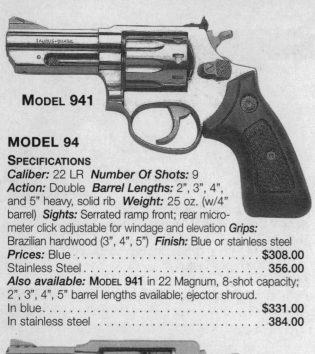

**MODEL 941**

## MODEL 94

### SPECIFICATIONS

*Caliber:* 22 LR  *Number Of Shots:* 9
*Action:* Double  *Barrel Lengths:* 2", 3", 4",
and 5" heavy, solid rib  *Weight:* 25 oz. (w/4"
barrel)  *Sights:* Serrated ramp front; rear micro-
meter click adjustable for windage and elevation  *Grips:*
Brazilian hardwood (3", 4", 5")  *Finish:* Blue or stainless steel
*Prices:* Blue . . . . . . . . . . . . . . . . . . . . . . . . . . . $308.00
Stainless Steel . . . . . . . . . . . . . . . . . . . . . . . . . 356.00
*Also available:* MODEL **941** in 22 Magnum, 8-shot capacity;
2", 3", 4", 5" barrel lengths available; ejector shroud.
In blue. . . . . . . . . . . . . . . . . . . . . . . . . . . . . . . $331.00
In stainless steel . . . . . . . . . . . . . . . . . . . . . . . . 384.00

**MODEL
445SS2**

**MODEL 445**
Bright Blue Steel
2" Barrel, Ported

## MODEL 445
## DOUBLE ACTION

### SPECIFICATIONS

*Caliber:* 44 Special  *Capacity:* 5 shots  *Barrel Length:* 2"
*Weight:* 28.25 oz.  *Grips:* Santoprene I  *Sights:* Serrated
ramp front; notched rear  *Finish:* Blue or stainless
*Features:* Optional porting; heavy solid rib barrel
*Prices:* Blue . . . . . . . . . . . . . . . . . . . . . . . . . . $323.00
Stainless . . . . . . . . . . . . . . . . . . . . . . . . . . . . . 370.00
*Also available:* MODEL **445CH.** Same specifications as Model
445 but features concealed hammer

## MODEL 608
## DOUBLE ACTION

### SPECIFICATIONS

*Caliber:* 357 Magnum  *Capacity:* 8
shots  *Barrel Lengths:* 4" (heavy solid rib);
6.5" and 8 3/8" (ejector shroud)  *Weight:*
51.5 oz. (6.5" barrel)  *Grips:* Santoprene I
*Sights:* Serrated ramp front w/red insert; micrometer
click adjustable  *Finish:* Blue or stainless  *Features:*
Compensated barrel; transfer bar safety; concealed hammer
*Prices:*
4" Blue . . . . . . . . . . . . . . . . . . . . . . . . . . . . $447.00
4" Stainless . . . . . . . . . . . . . . . . . . . . . . . . . . 508.00
6.5", 8 3/8" Blue . . . . . . . . . . . . . . . . . . . . . . . . 466.00
6.5", 8 3/8" Stainless . . . . . . . . . . . . . . . . . . . . . 530.00

**MODEL 605**

### SPECIFICATIONS

*Caliber:* 357 Magnum
*Capacity:* 5 shot
*Barrel Length:* 2.25"
*Weight:* 24.5 oz.
*Sights:* Notched rear; serrated ramp front
*Grips:* Santoprene I
*Safety:* Transfer bar
*Finish:* Blue or stainless
*Features:* Optional porting (**$19.00** add'l.)
*Prices:*
Blue . . . . . . . . . . . . . . . . . . . . . . . . . . . . . . . $303.00
Stainless . . . . . . . . . . . . . . . . . . . . . . . . . . . . . 344.00
*Also available:*
MODEL **605CH** w/concealed hammer and ported barrel
MODELS **605021KL/605029KL** w/Integral Key Lock
(**$20.00** add'l.)

# THOMPSON/CENTER PISTOLS

### ENCORE HUNTER PACKAGE

## ENCORE PISTOL
### SPECIFICATIONS
*Calibers:* 22-250 Rem., 223 Rem., 243 Win., 260 Rem., 45-70 Gov't., 45 Colt/.410 ga., 270 Win., 7mm BR Rem., 7mm-08 Rem., 7.62X39mm, 308 Win., 30-06 Spfd. 44 Rem. Mag., 444 Marlin *Action:* Single break-open *Barrel lengths:* 12" and 15" *Overall length:* 16.5" (12" bbl.); 19.5" (15" bbl.) *Weight:* 4.25, 12"; 4.5 lbs. (15" bbl.) *Trigger:* Adjustable *Safety:* Automatic hammerblock w/bolt interlock *Grips:* Ambidextrous walnut pistol grip w/finger grooves and butt cap; composite grips as accessory. *Sights:* Adjustable rear; ramp front sight blade *Features:* Interchangeable barrels (12"- **$235.96-258.08**; 15"- **$243.27-274.89** Blued, **$272.85** SST); drilled and tapped for T/C scope mounts
*Prices:*

| | |
|---|---|
| 12" Blued | $554.06-577.29 |
| 15" barrel Blued | 561.74-594.94 |
| SST | 620.99 |

*Also available:* ENCORE HUNTER PACKAGE in 22-250 Win., 270 Win., 308 Win. *Barrel length:* 15" *Features:* Weaver-style base and rings, 2.5-7X Recoil Proof pistol scope; blued frame and barrel; black composite grip and forend; soft carry case; no iron sights . . . . . . . . . . . . . **$793.67**
*NEW!* 209x50 black powder magnum, 15" barrel, 1:28 twist, 4 lbs, blued, walnut interchangeable barrel . . . . . . **569.47**

## THOMPSON/CENTER CONTENDER SHOOTER'S PACKAGE
*Calibers:* 7-30 Waters, 223 Rem., 30-30 Win., 22 LR Match *Barrel length:* 14" (10" 22 LR Match) *Overall length:* 16" (10" 22 LR Match) *Weight:* 4 lbs. *Features:* Mounted T/C Recoil Proof 2.5 X 7 scope plus carrying case
*Price:* Blued steel . . . . . . . . . . . . . . . . . . . **$754.39**

## CONTENDER SUPER "16" (Not Shown)
*Calibers:* 223 Rem., 45-70 (bull barrel); 45 Colt/.410 ga.
*Prices:*

| | |
|---|---|
| Blued (223 Rem.) | $525.95 |
| 45-70 Gov't. w/Muzzle Tamer | 531.52 |
| 45 Colt/.410 ga. | 559.70 |

## CONTENDER SUPER "14" BULL BARREL MODELS
*Calibers:* 22 LR Match Grade Chamber, 22 Hornet, 223 Rem., 7-30 Waters, 30-30 Win., and 44 Mag. (Blued version also available in 22 Hornet, 222 Rem., 357 Rem. Max.). *See pg. 13 Catalog* *Barrel length:* 14" bull barrel. *Features:* Fully adjustable target rear sight and Patridge-style ramped front sight with 13.5-inch sight radius. *Overall length:* 18.25" *Weight:* 3.5 lbs.
*Prices:*

| | |
|---|---|
| Blued | $520.24 |
| Match Grade Chamber | 531.50 |
| Stainless | 578.40 |
| Vent Rib Model (14") in 45 Colt/.410, blue | 556.74 |
| Stainless | 613.94 |
| 22 LR Match SST | 590.79 |

## CONTENDER BULL BARREL MODELS
These pistols with 10-inch barrel feature fully adjustable Patridge-style iron sights. All stainless steel models (including the Super "14" and Super "16") are equipped with Rynite finger-groove grip with rubber recoil cushion and matching Rynite forend, plus Cougar etching on the steel frame.
*Standard calibers available:* 22 WMR, 22 Hornet, 22 LR Match, 223 Rem., 30-30 Win., 357 Mag., 44 Mag. and 45 Colt/.410. Custom calibers also available.

*Prices:*

| | |
|---|---|
| Bull Barrel Blue | $509.03-520.29 |
| Bull Barrel Stainless | 578.40-566.59 |
| In 45/.410 - 10 inch SST | 590.44 |
| Vent Rib Model Stainless - 14 inch | 613.94 |
| Match Grade Barrel (22 LR only, stainless) | |
| 10-inch | 578.40 |
| 14-inch | 590.79 |

# TRADITIONS REVOLVERS

### SHERIFF'S REVOLVERS
#### SPECIFICATIONS
*Caliber:* 45 LC
*Action:* Single
*Barrel Length:* 4.75" blued
*Features:* Steel frame and trigger guard
*Price:* . . . . . . . . . . . . . . . . . . . . . . . . . . . . . . . $370.00

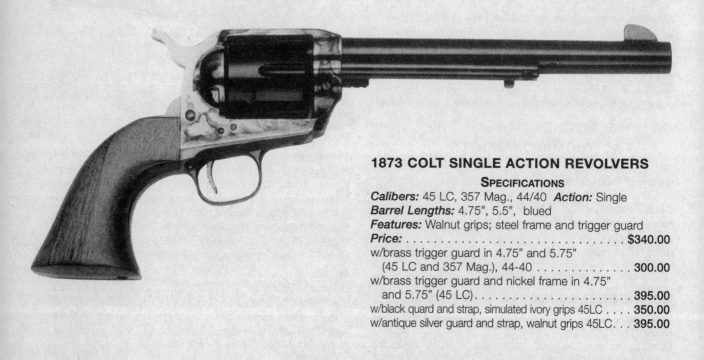

### 1873 COLT SINGLE ACTION REVOLVERS
#### SPECIFICATIONS
*Calibers:* 45 LC, 357 Mag., 44/40  *Action:* Single
*Barrel Lengths:* 4.75", 5.5",  blued
*Features:* Walnut grips; steel frame and trigger guard
*Price:* . . . . . . . . . . . . . . . . . . . . . . . . . . . . . . . **$340.00**
w/brass trigger guard in 4.75" and 5.75"
   (45 LC and 357 Mag.), 44-40 . . . . . . . . . . . . . **300.00**
w/brass trigger guard and nickel frame in 4.75"
   and 5.75" (45 LC) . . . . . . . . . . . . . . . . . . . . . **395.00**
w/black quard and strap, simulated ivory grips 45LC . . . . **350.00**
w/antique silver guard and strap, walnut grips 45LC. . . **395.00**

# UBERTI REPLICAS

## 1871 ROLLING BLOCK TARGET PISTOL

**SPECIFICATIONS**
*Calibers:* 22 LR, 22 Magnum, 22 Hornet and 357 Mag.
*Capacity:* Single shot  *Barrel Length:* 9.5" (half-octagon/half-round or full round Navy Style)
*Overall Length:* 14"  *Weight:* 2.75 lbs.
*Sights:* Fully adjustable rear; ramp front or open sight on Navy Style barrel
*Grip and forend:* Walnut  *Trigger guard:* Brass
*Frame:* Color case hardened steel
*Price:* . . . . . . . . . . . . . . . . . . . . . . . . . . . . . $410.00

**1871 ROLLING BLOCK TARGET PISTOL**

## DRAGOON REVOLVERS (not shown)

*Calibers:* .44 *Capcity:* 6 shots  *Barrel Length:* 7.5"
*Frame:* color-case *Grips:* walnut  *Weight:* 4 lbs.
*Price:* First Model . . . . . . . . . . . . . . . . . . . . $295.00
Second Model . . . . . . . . . . . . . . . . . . . . . . . . 295.00
Third Model . . . . . . . . . . . . . . . . . . . . . . . . . 310.00

## 1873 CATTLEMAN S.A.

**SPECIFICATIONS**
*Calibers:* 357 Magnum, 38/40, 44 Sp., 44-40, 45 L.C.  *Capacity:* 6 shots
*Barrel Lengths:* 4.75", 5.5", 7.5" round, tapered; 18" (Buntline)
*Overall Length:* 10.75" w/5.5" barrel
*Weight:* 2.42 lbs.  *Grip:* One-piece walnut
*Frame:* Color case hardened steel; also available in charcoal blue or nickel
*Price:* . . . . . . . . . . . . . . . . . . . . . . . $410.00-455.00
*Also available:*
45 L.C./45 ACP Convertible . . . . . . . . . . . . . . $485.00

**1873 CATTLEMAN**

## WALKER REVOLVER (not shown)

*Calibers:* .44 *Capcity:* 6 shots  *Barrel Length:* 9" *Frame:* color-case *Grips:* walnut  *Weight:* 4.4 lbs. This is the most massive revolver of the "Old West" era; named after a Texas Ranger who carried it.
*Price:* . . . . . . . . . . . . . . . . . . . . . . . . . . . . . $370.00

## 1875 "OUTLAW"

**SPECIFICATIONS**
*Calibers:* 357 Magnum, 44-40, 45 ACP, 45 Long Colt
*Capacity:* 6 shots  *Barrel Lengths:* 5.5", 7.5" round, tapered
*Overall Length:* 13.75"  *Weight:* 2.75 lbs.
*Grips:* Two-piece walnut  *Finish:* Color case hardened steel
*Price:* . . . . . . . . . . . . . . . . . . . . . . . . . . . . . $435.00
*Also available:* In nickel plate . . . . . . . . . . . . . . $435.00
45 L.C./45 ACP "Outlaw" Convertible . . . . . . . . . 485.00
1890 Police (not shown) . . . . . . . . . . . . . . . . . . 483.00
45 L.C./45 ACP Police Convertible . . . . . . . . . . . 483.00

**1875 "OUTLAW"**

# WALTHER PISTOLS

Models PPK and PPK/S double-action pistols differ only in the overalll length of the barrel and slide. Both models offer the same features, including live round indicator pin to signal a loaded chamber. An automatic internal safety blocks the hammer to prevent accidental striking of the firing pin, except with a deliberate pull of the trigger.

## MODEL PPK & PPK/S

**SPECIFICATIONS**
**Caliber:** 380 ACP and 32 ACP **Capacity:** 6 rounds (PPK), 7 rounds (PPK/S), 8 rounds (PPK/S in 32 ACP only) **Barrel Length:** 3.35" **Overall Length:** 6.25" **Weight:** 21 oz. (PPK); 23 oz. (PPK/S) **Finish:** Walther blue or stainless steel
**Price:** . . . . . . . . . . . . . . . $464.00

## MODEL P 99 COMPACT

**SPECIFICATIONS**
**Caliber:** 9mm Parabellum, 40 S&W, 9x21 **Capacity:** 10 rounds **Barrel Length:** 4" **Overall Length:** 7" **Weight:** 25 oz. **Height:** 5.37" **Width:** 1.2" **Sights:** Windage-adjustable micrometer rear; three interchangeable front blades included; optional modular laser sight and halogen flashlight for installation on front rails **Features:** Polymer frame; blued slide; customized backstrap; three automatic safeties; cocking and loaded chamber indicator; ambidetrous magazine release levers
**Price:** . . . . . . . . . . . . . . . . . . . . . . . . . . . $634.00

## WALTHER PPK/E

The PPK/E has the same dimensions as the USA made PPK/S models but is only available in a high polished blue version. The PPK/E has one round more than the normal PPK due to the longer frame. The PPK/E is available in cal. 9 mmkz (.380 ACP), 7, 65 mm (.32 ACP) and .22 l.r.

**SPECIFICATIONS**

| Caliber | 9mmkz (.380 ACP) | 7,65 mm (.32 ACP) | .22 l.r. |
|---|---|---|---|
| Action | blow back action | blow back action | blow back action |
| Length | 165 mm/6,5" | 165 mm/6,5" | 165 mm/6,5" |
| Width | 28 mm/1,1" | 28 mm/1,1" | 28 mm/1,1" |
| Height | 113 mm/4,4" | 113 mm/4,4" | 113 mm/4,4" |
| Rear sight | 112 mm/4,4" | 112 mm/4,4" | 114 mm/4,5" |
| Barrel length | 86 mm/3,4" | 86 mm/3,4" | 86 mm/3,4" |
| Weight (w/o magaz.) | 715 g/23 ozs. | 720 g/23 ozs. | 670 g/ 21 ozs. |
| Magazine capacity | 7+1 rds | 8+1 rds | 8+1 rds |

## MODEL PP DOUBLE ACTION

**SPECIFICATIONS**
**Calibers:** 380 ACP **Capacity:** 7 rounds **Barrel Length:** 3.85" **Overall Length:** 6.75" **Weight:** 25 oz. **Finish:** Walther blue
**Price:** . . . . . . . . . . . . . . . . . $999.00

**MODEL P 99**

**WALTHER PPK/E**

# WEATHERBY CENTERFIRE PISTOLS

## THE MARK V CFP

The Mark V CFP is built specifically for long-range accuracy on a Weatherby Mark V action. The 15" fluted stainless barrel features a concentrically perfect recessed crown to maintain tack-driving precision.

The Accumark CFP has a molded-in aluminum bedding plate. Crafted of aircraft-grade 6061-T6 aluminum, the two-piece insert is CNC-machined to trim weight, add structural integrity and reduce action torque. The Weatherby CFP is available with either synthetic or wood-laminate stock with removable rear swivel. The grip is suitable for right- or left-handed shooters. **Weight:** 5.3 lbs (wood) or 5.0 lbs (synthetic). **Chamberings:** .223, .22-250, .243, 7mm08, .308.

**Price:**. . . . . . . . . . . . . . . . . . . . . . . . . . . . . . . . **$1,099.00**

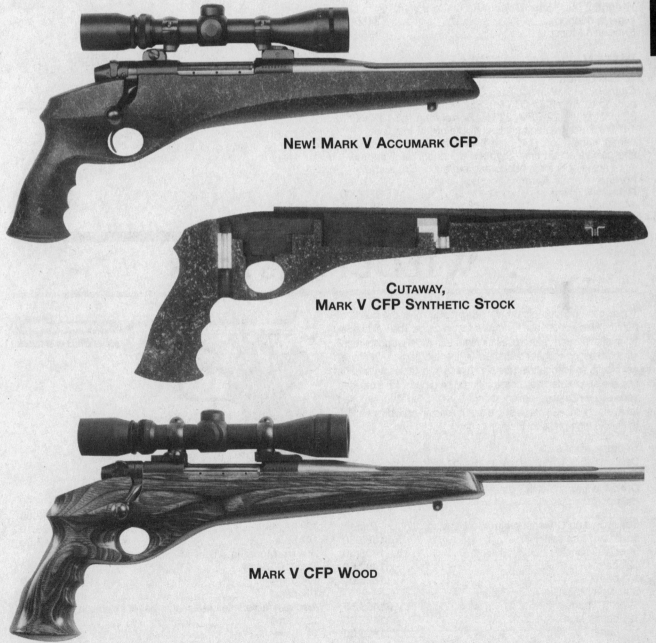

NEW! MARK V ACCUMARK CFP

CUTAWAY, MARK V CFP SYNTHETIC STOCK

MARK V CFP WOOD

# WICHITA ARMS PISTOLS

## SILHOUETTE PISTOL (Right-Hand Rear Grip)

### SPECIFICATIONS
*Calibers:* 308 Win. F.L., 7mm IHMSA and 7mmX308
*Barrel length:* 14 $^{15}$/$_{16}$" *Weight:* 4.5 lbs. *Action:* Single-shot bolt action *Sights:* Wichita Multi-Range Sight System *Grips:* Right-hand center walnut grip or right-hand rear walnut grip *Features:* Glass bedded; bolt ground to precision fit; adjustable Wichita trigger
*Price:*. . . . . . . . . . . . . . . . . . . . . . . . . . . . . . $1,800.00
*Also available:*
WICHITA CLASSIC SILHOUETTE PISTOL. *Barrel:* 11.25".
*Weight:* 3 lbs. 15 oz. *Grips:* AAA grade walnut,
   glass bedded . . . . . . . . . . . . . . . . . . . . . . .$3450.50
ENGRAVED MODEL . . . . . . . . . . . . . . . . . . . . . . .4850.00

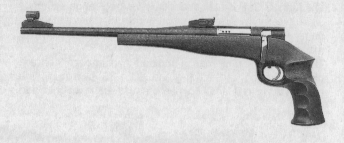

## INTERNATIONAL PISTOL

### SPECIFICATIONS
*Calibers:* 7-30 Waters, 7mm Super Mag., 7R (30-30 Win. necked to 7mm), 30-30 Win., 357 Mag., 357 Super Mag., 32 H&H Mag., 22-RFM, 22 LR *Barrel lengths:* 10" and 14" (10.5" for centerfire calibers) *Weight:* 3 lbs. 2 oz. (10" barrel); 4 lbs. 7 oz. (14" barrel) *Action:* Top-break, single-shot, single action only *Sights:* Partridge front sight; rear sight adjustable for windage and elevation *Grips and Forend:* Walnut *Safety:* Crossbolt
*Price:* 10" Barrel . . . . . . . . . . . . . . . . . . . . . . . . $775.00
14" Barrel . . . . . . . . . . . . . . . . . . . . . . . . . . . . . $875.00

# WILDEY PISTOLS

These gas-operated pistols are designed to meet the needs of hunters who want to use handguns for big game. The Wildey pistol includes such features as: •Ventilated rib •Reduced recoil •Double-action trigger mechanism •Patented hammer and trigger blocks and rebounding fire pin •Sights adjustable for windage and elevation •Stainless construction •Fixed barrel for increased accuracy •Increased action strength (with 3-lug and exposed face rotary bolt) •Selective single or autoloading capability •Ability to handle high-pressure loads

### SPECIFICATIONS
*Calibers:* 45 & 475 Wildey Magnums and 45 Win. Mag.
*Capacity:* 7 shots *Barrel lengths:* 5", 6", 7", 8", 10", 12", 14"
*Overall length:* 11" with 7" barrel *Weight:* 64 oz. with 5" barrel
*Height:* 6"

SURVIVOR AND GUARDSMAN in 45 Win. Mag.    ***Prices***
5", 6" or 7" barrels . . . . . . . . . . . . . . . . . . . . .$1385.60
8" or 10" barrels . . . . . . . . . . . . . . . . . . . . . . . .1408.50
12" barrel  . . . . . . . . . . . . . . . . . . . . . . . . . . .1492.60
14" barrel . . . . . . . . . . . . . . . . . . . . . . . . . . . . .1895.00
SURVIVOR MODEL in Wildey Mags.
8" or 10" barrels . . . . . . . . . . . . . . . . . . . . . . .$1408.50
12" barrel . . . . . . . . . . . . . . . . . . . . . . . . . . . . .1492.60
14" barrel . . . . . . . . . . . . . . . . . . . . . . . . . . . . .1895.00

HUNTER MODEL in 45 Win. Mag.
5", 6" or 7" barrels . . . . . . . . . . . . . . . . . . . . . .$1618.90
8" or 10" barrels . . . . . . . . . . . . . . . . . . . . . . . .1642.50
12" barrel  . . . . . . . . . . . . . . . . . . . . . . . . . . .1728.10
14" barrel . . . . . . . . . . . . . . . . . . . . . . . . . . . . .2115.00
HUNTER MODEL in Wildey Mags.
8" or 10" barrels . . . . . . . . . . . . . . . . . . . . . . . .1642.50
12" barrel . . . . . . . . . . . . . . . . . . . . . . . . . . . . .1728.10
14" barrel . . . . . . . . . . . . . . . . . . . . . . . . . . . . .2115.00
*Also available:* Interchangeable barrel extension assemblies
12" barrel . . . . . . . . . . . . . . . . . . . . . . . . . . . . . .694.40
14" barrel . . . . . . . . . . . . . . . . . . . . . . . . . . . . .1148.00

# Rifles

For addresses and phone/fax numbers of manufacturers and distributors included in this section, please turn to **DIRECTORY OF MANUFACTURERS AND SUPPLIERS** on page 564.

# AMERICAN HUNTING RIFLES

## AHR: A Big Game Rifle From Montana

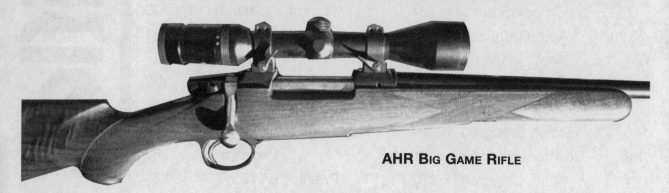

**AHR Big Game Rifle**

The foundation of every AHR rifle is the strong, beautifully finished CZ 550 action. Its smooth and dependable controlled-round CZ 550 complements a rugged adjustable trigger. This classic action wears your choice of a English walnut or all-weather synthetic stock. The classic design in both the walnut and the all-weather stocks is by master stockmaker Jerry Fisher.

The 25-inch American Hunting Rifles barrel - chrome moly or stainless steel - is rifled with the rate of twist best suited to the premium hunting bullets loaded in each specific cartridge. The outstanding accuracy of these barrels often surpasses that of other production rifles that cost much more.

AHR rifles are available in the standard .270 Winchester and .30-06 Springfield, as well as a wide variety of our own proprietary cartridges from a .220 to a .411. All of our cartridges are based on original designs by Ken Howell, noted writer and author of the popular book, Designing and Forming Custom Cartridges.

Hunters will quickly find that the twelve Howell cartridges, designed specifically for hunting varmints and big game, offer more case capacity–and power–than comparable standard rounds.

Howell cartridges are designed for efficiency and long barrel life. These new cartridges confirm experienced hunters' opinion that belted magnum cases aren't necessary for game-killing power.

## A Family of New Cartridges With Roots in Classic Oldies

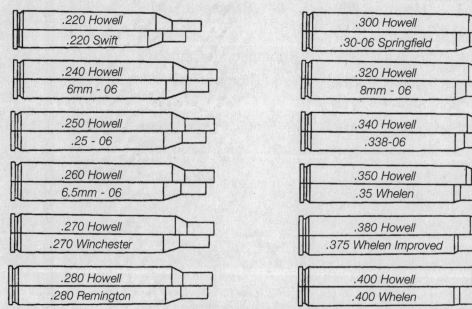

.220 Howell / .220 Swift

.240 Howell / 6mm - 06

.250 Howell / .25 - 06

.260 Howell / 6.5mm - 06

.270 Howell / .270 Winchester

.280 Howell / .280 Remington

.300 Howell / .30-06 Springfield

.320 Howell / 8mm - 06

.340 Howell / .338-06

.350 Howell / .35 Whelen

.380 Howell / .375 Whelen Improved

.400 Howell / .400 Whelen

*Head size is .473 (same as .30-06). Shoulder angle is sharper, at 25 degrees. Case length: 2.60"*

# ANSCHUTZ RIFLES

MODEL 2013
SUPER MATCH

Julius Gottfried Anschutz, son of a German gunsmith, founded J.G. Anschutz in 1856 to build pocket pistols, shotguns and rifles. In 1896 the firm moved out of its small workshop into a factory. Five years later Julius Anschutz died, and his sons, Fritz and Otto, assumed control of the business. By 1911 there were 200 people working at the Anschutz plant. When Otto died shortly after the first world war, Fritz and his sons, Rudolf and Max, continued to build the enterprise.

Growth came to an abrupt halt in 1945, when the factory was shut down pursuant to Germany's surrender in World War II. But five years later J.G. Anschutz GmbH was founded to make air pistols and repair firearms. Soon it turned to target rifles and even resumed manufacture of the Flobert-type guns that had been among the firm's original products. Anschutz target rifles began to build a reputation among the world's elite shooters, and the company grew to 250 employees.

In 1968 Dieter Anschutz, a fourth-generation member of the family, became chief executive, as the Anschutz name became more and more prominent in Olympic competition. In 1992 his son, Jochen, became company president. Jochen and Dieter now manage J.G. Anschutz together. An ultramodern plant in Ulm, Germany produces what have become recognized world-wide as the standard against which all rimfire target rifles and pistols are judged. Anschutz rifles captured all of the gold medals, and all but two of the silver medals in the Barcelona Olympic Games. The company's competition air rifles and pistols have done almost as well as the firearms.

## MODEL 2013 "SUPER MATCH"

Since the 1960s, the Model 54 rimfire action has set the standard in competitive three-position and smallbore prone shooting. The current version, with a heavy, rectangular receiver, attaches to the stock with four action screws. This action is the heart of the Model 2013 Super Match Special — and of the 2013 Benchrest, the 2007, 2012, 1907, 1912, and 1913 rifles. It is also featured in the 1808 D-RT Running Target, 54.18 MS Metallic Silhouette and 1808 MS-R Silhouette rifles. Its fine trigger mechanism, close tolerances and extremely fast lock time make it a logical choice for competitive marksmen. Anschutz .22 rimfire barrels, noted for one-hole accuracy, complement the 54 action.

The 2013 Super Match is the latest and most sophisticated in a long line of Super Match rifles for freestyle shooting events. Available in both right- and left-hand versions, it comes with adjustable two-stage match trigger (with safety). The trigger-piece can be moved longitudinally and tilted up to 15 degrees. There's a forearm accessory rail with hand stop and palm rest fitted to the thumbhole stock. A fully adjustable cheekpiece complements a hook butt assembly adjustable for cant, pitch, length and drop. A host of accessories, including match sights and counter-weights is available.

**Barrel length:** 27.1 inches.
**Rifle weight:** 14.3 pounds.
**Price:** . . . . . . . . . . . . . . . . . . . . . . . . . . . . . . . . . $3,145.00
left-hand . . . . . . . . . . . . . . . . . . . . . . . . . . . 3,299.00

# ANSCHUTZ RIFLES

## MODEL 1907

Match 54 action in an economical rifle, with adjustable cheekpiece and butt assembly.
**Barrel Length:** 25.9 inches
**Rifle Weight:** 10.5 pounds
**Price:**. . . . . . . . . . . . . . . . . . . . . . . . . . . . . . . . $1,639.00
   left-hand . . . . . . . . . . . . . . . . . . . . . . . . . . . . . 1,726.00

## MODEL 1912 "SPORT RIFLE"

Match 54 action in a lightweight international-style rifle engineered to stay under the 6.5kg weight limit. The walnut stock has a forend raiser block, fully adjustable hook buttplate and cheekpiece, and forward hand stop and swivel.
**Barrel Length:** 25.9 inches.
**Rifle Weight:** 11.4 pounds.
**Price:**. . . . . . . . . . . . . . . . . . . . . . . . . . . . . . . . $2,250.00
   left-hand . . . . . . . . . . . . . . . . . . . . . . . . . . . . . 2,356.00

## MODEL 1808 D-RT "RUNNING TARGET"

A fully adjustable trigger, as per the Model 2013 "Super Match" and lightning-quick lock time help competitors excel on the moving-target range. A removable barrel extension improves smoothness of swing. The stock is specially configured for off-hand shooting, with adjustable cheekpiece and butt assembly.
**Barrel Length:** 32.6 inches.
**Rifle Weight:** 9.0 pounds.
**Price:**. . . . . . . . . . . . . . . . . . . . . . . . . . . . . . . . $1,699.00

# ANSCHUTZ RIFLES

### MODEL 54.18 MS R "SILHOUETTE"

Designed expressly for metallic silhouette shooting, this rifle weighs only 8.1 pounds. The adjustable two-stage trigger is set at 4.4 ounces. The Match 54 action has been modified to accept a 5-shot magazine. A rubber buttpad is standard.
**Barrel Length:** 22.4 inches
**Price:**...............................$1,499.00

RIFLES

### MODEL 1827 "FORTNER"

This rifle is built for biathlon competition, an Olympic event that combines skiing and marksmanship. Competitors must shoot twice at the 10-km point, four times at 20 km into the race and twice at a relay point of 7.5 km. Each station requires five shots prone and five standing. The Anschutz 1827 has a straight-pull repeating action to increase speed of fire. It weighs 8.8 pounds and is equipped with magazine holders. The walnut stock features adjustable cheekpiece and butt assembly. A special front sight hood protects the sight and bore from snow.
**Barrel Length:** 21.6 inches.
**Price:**.................................$2,495.00
   left-hand.............................2,745.00

### MODEL 1903

A competitive rifle for riflemen on a budget, the 1903 has a M64-type action with two-stage adjustable trigger. The hardwood stock features a forward accessory rail and an adjustable cheekpiece. The buttplate is vertically adjustable; length of pull can be changed by adding or deleting spacers.
**Price:**.................................$942.00

# ANSCHUTZ RIFLES

## MODEL 1451 (not shown)

An affordable rifle with target-rifle potential, this 5-pound repeater has a trim action, checkered hardwood stock and iron sights on a 21-inch sporter-weight barrel. The receiver is grooved for a scope.

**Price:** . . . . . . . . . . . . . . . . . . . . . . . . . . . . . . . **$370.00**
*(threaded barrel or tangent rear sight $10 extra each)*

## MODEL 1710 REPEATING RIFLE (not shown)

A premium-quality .22 sporter, the 1710 is built on the famous Match 54 action. Adjustable sights and trigger, and a high-grade checkered walnut stock, put this rifle in its own class. There's a choice of "classic," "German," and "Monte Carlo" stocks and single-stage or double-set triggers. The

## MODEL 1743 HUNTING RIFLE (not shown)

This centerfire rifle in .222 Remington has an Anschutz 54-type action with wing safety and claw extractor. The full-length checkered walnut stock has a Monte Carlo comb. Barrel length: 18 inches. This rifle is also available in a half-

## MODEL 1451 R SPORT TARGET

This modestly-priced target rifle has the same action as the 1451 sporter but with a heavier 20-inch barrel adapted to target sights, and a target-style stock with aluminum slide rail and vertically adjustable butt. The two-stage trigger and fast lock time help boost scores. **Weight:** 6.5 pounds.

**Price:** . . . . . . . . . . . . . . . . . . . . . . . . . . . . . . **$486.00**
*(target sights $282 extra)*

sporter barrel is 22 inches, rifle weight 6.6 pounds. A synthetic-stocked version is available.

**Price:** . . . . . . . . . . . . . . . . . . . . . . . . . . . . . **$1,160.00**
  Classic . . . . . . . . . . . . . . . . . . . . . . . . . . . **1,073.00**
  Synthetic . . . . . . . . . . . . . . . . . . . . . . . . . . **1,499.00**

stock version with 22-inch barrel (Model 1740) and in .22 Hornet (both stock styles, Models 1730 and 1733). **Weight:** 6.3 and 6.6 pounds, depending on style.

**Price:** 1743 and 1733 . . . . . . . . . . . . . . . . . . **$1,431.00**
1740 and 1730 . . . . . . . . . . . . . . . . . . . . . . . . **1,297.00**

## MODEL 2013 "BENCHREST"

**Barreled action:** Compact connection between barreled action and stock, heavy rectangular receiver attached with 4 action screws. The accuracy of the barreled action and the

extremely short locktime within a range of milliseconds offer best conditions for success. **Barrel:** Cylindrical match barrel **Stock:** Non-stained stock with wide, flat, forend, especially developed for benchrest shooting **Caliber:** .22 l.r. **Barrel length:** 50 cm/19.6" **Rifling:** 50 cm/16.6" **Total length:** 97 cm/38.1" **Weight appr.:** 4,7 kg/10.3 lbs **Version:** Single loader

**Price:** . . . . . . . . . . . . . . . . . . . **Available upon request**

# ARNOLD ARMS RIFLES

Arnold Arms designed and builds its own Apollo action with a clever extractor that helps ensure positive function. In its center position, the 3-position safety allows the action to be cycled for loading and unloading without fear of discharge. Squaring and truing operations usually reserved for custom rifles are standard on every Apollo. Lugs are lapped and the action glass bedded for accuracy. The Apollo action is optional on some Arnold rifles.

Most Arnold rifles are built on other actions, in a variety of configurations to satisfy every hunter and target shooter. Match-grade barrels and McMillan synthetic stocks are used throughout, though walnut stocks are available by special order. Rifles are available in chamberings from 223 to 458, including Arnold's own line of high-performance cartridges. Some examples of big game rifles:

**ALASKAN TROPHY**

### ALASKAN TROPHY

Each rifle features a fully accurized and trued action in stainless steel with a stainless steel match grade sporting contour barrel and choice of McMillan black or camo stock. Barrel lengths available are 22"-24" for non-magnums and 24"-26" for magnums. Chambering are available in all popular cartridges plus most wildcats and the Arnold line of cartridges.
*Prices:* Remington 700 action rifle start at . . . . **$2,695.00**
Winchester M70 action rifle . . . . . . . . . . . . . . . **2,695.00**

### ALASKAN GUIDE

These rifes come with the same components as the "Alaskan Trophy", but have Express sights and a barrel band for the front sling swivel installed as standard equipment. Available in .338 magnum to .458 magnum.
*Prices:*
Remington 700 SS action built rifle, upgraded with three-. position safety and Ssko style extractor. . . . . **$3,799.00**
Winchester M70 SS action rifle. . . . . . . . . . . . **3,399.00**

**AFRICAN TROPHY**

### AFRICAN TROPHY

Each rifle features a fully trued and accurized action in chrome-moly matte blued steel with sporting contour match grade barrel and synthetic McMillan stock in either black or camo finish. Each rifle is given the Arnold "Accu*Pro" treatment and is availabe in .223 to .338 magnum calibers as well as most wildcats and the Arnold lines of cartridges.

*Prices:*
Remington 700 action rifle start at . . . . . . . . . . **$2,695.00**
Winchester M70 action rifle start at . . . . . . . . . . **2,595.00**
Same as above but with
    walnut stock . . . . . . . . . . . . . . . . . . . . . . . . **P.O.R.**
Same as above but with black teflon coated
    stainless steel barrel . . . . . . . . . . . . . . . . . **Add 229.00**

**GRAND AFRICAN**

### GRAND AFRICAN

This line of custom rifles comes with Express sights and barrel band for front sling swivel, and is available in "A" through "AAA" American dark, English walnut, Bastogne, as well as "Exhibition grade. Available in .338 magnum to .458 magnum. Remington 700 action rifles come equipped with a three-position safety and Sako extractor as a standard upgrade.

*Prices:* With McMillan synthetic stock . . . . . . . **$3,995.00**
With walnut Hunter Classic stock. . . . . . . . . . . **3,895.00**
With "A" English walnut stock, ebony forend
    and steel grip cap. Start at . . . . . . . . . . . . . . **6,595.00**
*Winchester Model 70 action rifles:*
With walnut Hunter Classic stock. . . . . . . . . . . **3,595.00**
With "A" Engllish walnut stock, ebony forend and
    steel grip cap. Start at . . . . . . . . . . . . . . . . . **6,295.00**

# ARNOLD ARMS RIFLES

## MARK II "NEUTRALIZER"

### ARNOLD NEUTRALIZER SERIES RIFLES
#### Mark II "Neutralizer"

Built on the ApolloTM action, stainless steel or chrome-moly with match grade barrel. Choice of calibers .223 to .300 Winchester magnum. Rifle shown shot 3.5" groups at 1,600 yards daily for two weeks in New Mexico, September 1996. Features include Remington 700 action (choice of chrome-moly blued or stainless steel) with detachable box magazine, match grade barrel (chrome-moly or stainless steel) in Palma to heavy varmint contours. McMillan A2 or A3 tactical stocks available in black, woodland, arctic, desert or urban camo. Adjustable cheekpiece standard. Sako extractor, 3-position safety and thicker recoil lug standard on the Neutraizer rifles,

and triggers are set at choice of 2.5 or 3 pounds. Available in .223, .308 and .300 Winchester magnum. Because Match rifles are typically built to order by shooters who know what they want, prices vary with options. Magnum chamberings don't add much to the cost of a match rifle. An adjustable stock or super-accurate barrel, or a sophisticated trigger can boost price substantially.

*Prices:*
Apollo action rifle, includes Jewell trigger . . . . . **$4,599.00**
Remington 700 action with features
   outlined above. . . . . . . . . . . . . . . . . . . . . . **3,499.00**
Remington 700 action with DBM and 2-position
   safety and Remington extractor . . . . . . . . . . **2,999.00**
Winchester Model 70 action . . . . . . . . . . . . . . **2,949.00**
   *Options include Timney, Shilen or Jewell triggers, adjustable buttplate.*

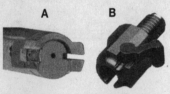
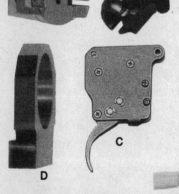

**A. CONE HEAD BOLT AND BREECH** with new combination bolt face provides both drop-in and controlled-round feed capabilities.

**B. 3-POSITION POSITIVE LOCK SAFETY** locks both the bolt and firing pin. Intermediate position allows for easy field stripping and cleaning and ejecting live rounds without accidental discharge.

**C. TRIGGER** is fully adjustable. Each one is hand finished and assembled to precise tolerances and fit.

**D. RECOIL LUG** has 36,500 pounds shear strength. It is designed & surface ground for precise alignment (perpendicular axis to bore centerline) providing perfect mating of receiver and barrel.

### THE APOLLO ACTION

Available for all popular calibers from .222 to .458 including the 6mm, .257, .270, .300, .338 & .458 Arnold Magnums. Finishes include blue, matte black, black teflon or stainless steel.

### VARMINTER II IN 6MM ARNOLD

### VARMINTER II

Fully accurized action with match grade heavy sporter 27" barrel, cryogenically treated, bedded and free-floated in McMillan varminter synthetic stock. Choice of black, woodland, desert or arctic camo. All rifes guaranteed capable of shooting 1/2" groups. Available in all popular varmint cartridges plus many wildcats and the .244, .257 and 6.5 Arnold Magnums.

*Prices:*
Remington 70 CM matte
   blue barreled action . . . . . . . . . . **$2,595.00**
Remington CM blue with
   detachable box magazine. . . . . . . **2,695.00**
   Remington SS barreled action. . . . **2,695.00**
Remington SS with detachable box magazine. . . **2,695.00**
Winchester M70 CM matte blue
   barreled action . . . . . . . . . . . . . . **2,595.00**
Winchester M70 SS matte barreled action . . . . . **2,695.00**
Additional selections include:
Arnold laminated varmint stock . . . . . . . . . . . **Add 199.00**
Teflon coated barreled action . . . . . . . . . . . **Add 229.00**

# ARNOLD ARMS RIFLES

## MATCH RIFLES

ARNOLD AMS COMPANY manufactures a full line of benchrest, 500-yard, Palma and 1,000-yard match rifles, including prone and x-course models. Only the finest components are used in these rifles, which are custom built to customer specifications and requirements. Arnold lists National Match course rifles in the following calibers .223, .243, 6mm Rem., .308 (7.62 NATO) & 7mm-08. All popuar benchrest cartridge chamberings are available, as well as magnums and wildcats for 1,000-yard matches.

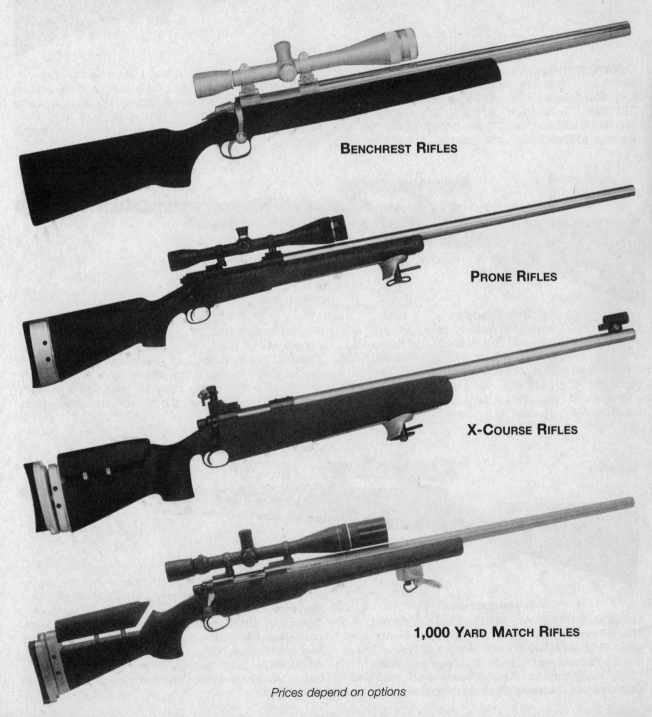

**BENCHREST RIFLES**

**PRONE RIFLES**

**X-COURSE RIFLES**

**1,000 YARD MATCH RIFLES**

*Prices depend on options*

# A-SQUARE RIFLES

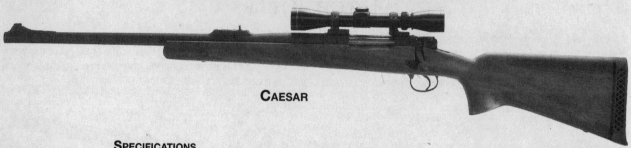

**CAESAR**

### SPECIFICATIONS

**Calibers:** 7mm Rem. Mag., 7mm STW, 300 Win. Mag., 300 Wby. Mag., 8mm Rem. Mag., 338 Win. Mag., 340 Wby. Mag., 338 A-Square Mag., 358 Norma, 358 STA, 9.3x64mm, 375 H&H, 375 Weatherby, 375 JRS, 375 A-Square Mag., 416 Taylor, 416 Hoffman, 416 Rem. Mag., 404 Jeffery, 425 Express, 458 Win. Mag., 458 Lott, 450 Ackley Mag., 460 Short A-Square, 470 Capstick and 495 A-Square Mag.
**Features:** Left-hand Enfield-style action; three-position safety; three-way adjustable target trigger; coil spring ejector; contoured ejection port, dual recoil lugs, Claro walnut stock with flush swivel studs, ventilated pad, leather sling

**HANNIBAL**

### SPECIFICATIONS

**Calibers:** 300 Pegasus, 8mm Rem. Mag., 338 Win., 340 Wby., 338 A-Square Mag., 338 Excalibur, 358 Norma Mag., 358 STA, 9.3x64, 375 A-Square, 375 JRS, 375 H&H, 375 Wby., 378 Wby., 404 Jeffery, 416 Hoffman, 416 Rem., 416 Rigby, 416 Taylor, 416 Wby., 425 Express, 450 Ackley, 458 Lott, 458 Win., 460 Short A-Square, 460 Weatherby, 470 Capstick, 495 A-Square, 500 A-Square, 577 Tyrannosaur

**Barrel Length:** 20" to 26"
**Length of Pull:** 12" to 15.25"   **Weight:** 9.5 lbs.-13.25 lbs.
**Features:** Enfield action with coil spring ejector, contoured ejection port, three-way adjustable target-style trigger, Mauser-style claw extractor and controlled feed, positive safety, dual recoil lugs, flush detachable swivel studs, ventilated pad, leather sling.

**HAMILCAR**

### SPECIFICATIONS

**Calibers:** 25-06, 257 Wby., 6.5x55 Swedish, 264 Win., 270 Win., 270 Wby., 7x57 Mauser, 280 Rem., 7mm Rem., 7mm Wby., 7mm STW, 30-06, 300 Win., 300 Wby., 338-06, 9.3x62 **Barrel Length:** 20" to 26" **Length of Pull:** 12" to 15.25" **Weight:** 8.5 lbs. **Finish:** Deluxe walnut stock; oil finish; matte blue **Features:** Flush detachable swivels, leather sling, on walnut stock with recoil pad; contoured ejection port; target-style adjustable trigger, Mauser-style claw extractor; controlled feed; positive safety, coil spring ejector
**Also available:** GENGHIS KHAN MODEL in 22-250, 243 Win., 6mm Rem., 25-06, 257 Wby., 264 Win. Features benchrest-quality heavy taper barrel and coilchek stock. **Weight:** 11 lbs. (w/scope & iron sights)
**All Prices:** A-square suggests you phone (502-719-3006) for current pricing. Base prices for these semi-custom rifles start at **$3,295.00.**

# AUTO-ORDNANCE

## SEMI-AUTOMATIC RIFLES

This veteran design became famous during the "roaring twenties" and World War II.
These replicas are legal autoloaders, not machine guns.

### THOMPSON MODEL M1 CARBINE

**SPECIFICATIONS**
*Caliber:* 45 ACP  *Barrel Length:* 16.5"
*Overall Length:* 38"  *Weight:* 11.5 lbs.
*Sights:* Blade front; fixed rear

*Stock:* Walnut stock and horizontal foregrip
*Features:* Side cocking lever; frame and receiver milled from solid steel
*Price:* . . . . . . . . . . . . . . . . . . . . . . . . . . . . . . . $960.00

### THOMPSON DELUXE MODEL 1927 A1

**SPECIFICATIONS**
*Caliber:* 45 ACP
*Barrel Length:* 16.5"
*Overall Length:* 41"  *Weight:* 13 lbs.
*Sights:* Blade front; open rear adjustable

*Stock:* Walnut stock; vertical foregrip
*Also available:*
THOMPSON **1927A1C** LIGHTWEIGHT (45 Cal.). Same as the 1927 A1 model, but weighs only 9.5 lbs.
*Price:* . . . . . . . . . . . . . . . . . . . . . . . . . . . . . . . $960.00

### MODEL 1927 A1 COMMANDO

**SPECIFICATIONS**
*Caliber:* 45 ACP
*Barrel Length:* 16.5"
*Overall Length:* 41"
*Weight:* 13 lbs.
*Sights:* Blade front; open rear (adjustable)

*Finish:* Black (stock and forend)
*Price:* . . . . . . . . . . . . . . . . . . . . . . . . . . . . . . $960.00
*Also available:* Auto-Ordnance also offers a 1911A1 autoloading .45 ACP pistol faithful to the original design.
Blued . . . . . . . . . . . . . . . . . . . . . . . . . . . . . . . . 447.00
Parkerized . . . . . . . . . . . . . . . . . . . . . . . . . . . . . 462.00

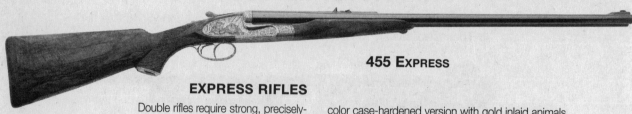

**455 EXPRESS**

### EXPRESS RIFLES

Double rifles require strong, precisely-fitted actions to handle large, high pressure cartridges. Barrels must be joined with absolute precision for optimum convergence. The SS06 and SS06EELL Over-and Under Express Rifles offer rifled barrels of special steel cold-hammered in three calibers: 9.3x74R, .375 H&H Mag. and .458 Win. Mag. An extra set of matching 12 gauge barrels is available. Hand-finished, hand-checkered stocks and forends are made from select walnut or walnut briar. A special trap door compartment for extra cartridges is fitted inside the stock, and a cavity under the pistol-grip cap holds a set of spare front sights. The SS-06 is finished with light engraving on the color case-hardened receiver. The SS06 EELL sports a receiver hand-engraved with game scenes, or a color case-hardened version with gold inlaid animals.

The 455 Side-by-Side Express Rifle action is made of special high-strength steel and forged with an elongated 60mm plate. This increases the distance between the hinge pin and the three-lug locking system to compensate for stress when shooting. To withstand the pressure of high-powered cartridges, the sealed receiver has reinforced sides, and the top tang extends fully up to the stock comb to strengthen attachment of the stock. An articulated front trigger and automatic blocking device eliminate the possibility of simultaneous discharge. The safety (automatic on request) provides for quick, reliable and positive on/off operation. The Boehler steel barrels are joined with a Demibloc chamber system.

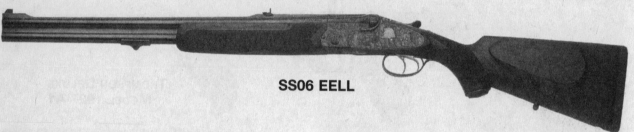

**SS06 EELL**

### SS06 OVER-UNDER EXPRESS RIFLE
**SPECIFICATIONS**
**Calibers:** 375 H&H, 458 Win. Mag., 9.3x94R
**Barrel length:** 24" (12 ga. matching interchangeable barrels available)
**Weight:** 11 lbs.
**Sights:** Blade front sight; V-notch rear sight w/folding leaf (claw mounts for Zeiss scope factory fitted and sighted-in at 100 meters)
**Price:**. . . . . . . . . . . . . . . . . . . . . . . . . . . . . $50,000.00
*Note:* MODEL SS06 EELL is also available in same calibers and features hand-engraved game scenes on the receiver or color case-hardened w/gold inlaid animals. . . . . . . . . $50,000.00

### 455 SIDE-BY-SIDE EXPRESS RIFLE
**SPECIFICATIONS**
**Calibers:** 375 H&H, 416 Rigby, 458 Win. Mag., 470 N.E., 500 N.E.
**Barrel length:** 23" - 25"
**Weight:** 11 lbs.
**Sights:** Fixed front sight w/folding blade; V-notch rear sight
**Price:**. . . . . . . . . . . . . . . . . . . . . . . . . . . $50,000.00
*Note:* MODEL 455 EELL is also available (same price and calibers) featuring Bulino-style game scene engraving or intricate scroll work and walnut briar stock and forend.

### PREMIUM GRADE EXPRESS RIFLE SPECIFICATIONS

| MODEL | 9.3x 74R | .375 H&H MAG. | CALIBER* .416 RIGBY | .458 H&H MAG. | .470 N.E. | .500 N.E. | BARREL LENGTH (CM/IN) | AVERAGE WEIGHT (KG/LBS)** |
|---|---|---|---|---|---|---|---|---|
| SS06 | √ | √ | | √ | | | 62/24 | 5.00/11.0 |
| SS06 EELL | √ | √ | | √ | | | 62/24 | 5.00/11.0 |
| 455 | | √ | √ | √ | √ | √ | 60/23 to 65/25 | 5.00/11.0 |
| 455 EELL | | √ | √ | √ | √ | √ | 60/23 to 65/25 | 5.00/11.0 |

*SS06 EELL Models are available with interchangeable 12 gauge shotgun barrels upon request.
**Weights are approximate, dependent on wood density and barrel length.

# BERETTA RIFLES

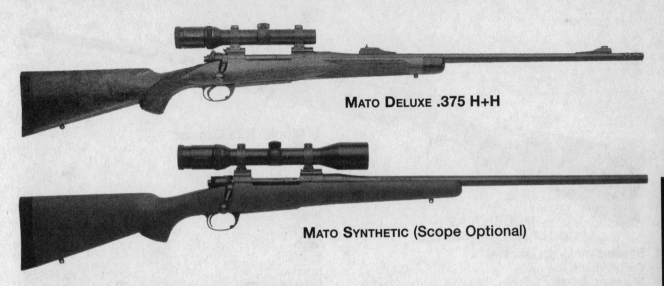

**MATO DELUXE .375 H+H**

**MATO SYNTHETIC (Scope Optional)**

### BERETTA MATO BOLT-ACTION RIFLE

Beretta's Mato was developed with help from Don Allen, whose Dakota rifles have the same clean, appealing lines. ("Mato", incidentally, is the Dakota Indian name for "bear.") This Beretta features controlled-round feed with a Mauser-style extractor that grabs cartridges from a detachable box magazine clipped to a hinged floorplate. The magazine can be top-loaded. A three-position safety allows cycling of the bolt while the striker is locked back. The Mato's sturdy trigger can be adjusted for weight of pull, sear engagement and overtravel. Receivers are machined from bar stock, and the 24-inch barrels are hammer-forged from top-grade chrome-moly steel. Stocks have high, straight combs for quick aim and a classic profile. On the walnut-stocked Deluxe model, wood with exceptional figure is available as an "X-Tra Wood"

option. The Mato is also available with a synthetic stock of Kevlar, fiberglass and graphite. An action-length aluminum bedding block ensures rigidity and perfect fit. All stocks come standard with a solid recoil pad. The Mato in .375 features iron sights and a muzzle brake; its front swivel is on a barrel band. Engraving, fiber-optic sights, a set trigger and other options are available for this rifle, which comes in .270 Win., .280 Rem., 7mm Rem. Mag., .30-06 Sprg., .300 Win. Mag., .338 Win. Mag. and .375 H&H Mag. *Weight:* 8 pounds.

*Price:* Mato Synthetic. . . . . . . . . . . . . . . . . . . . **$1117.00**
  Mato Synthetic .375 . . . . . . . . . . . . . . . . . . . **1474.00**
  Mato Deluxe. . . . . . . . . . . . . . . . . . . . . . . . . **2470.00**
  Mato Deluxe .375 . . . . . . . . . . . . . . . . . . . . . **2795.00**

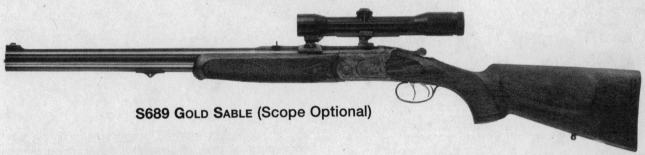

**S689 GOLD SABLE (Scope Optional)**

### BERETTA SILVER SABLE II AND GOLD SABLE OVER/UNDER RIFLES

Built on Beretta's 20-gauge boxlock frame, these over/under rifles are chambered in .30-06, 9.3x74R and .444 Marlin. They feather double mechanical triggers for the utmost in reliability. The front trigger is hinged for greater comfort. The 24" barrels are regulated with iron sights but can also be fitted with hook-type scope rings. Hand-finished walnut stocks fea-

ture a European-style cheekpiece, ventilated recoil pad and initial plate. The Silver Sable has a nickel-colored receiver engraved with game scenes; the Gold Sable has a scroll-engraved case-hardened receiver. *Weight:* 7.7 lbs.

*Price:* Silver Sable II . . . . . . . . . . . . . . . . . . . . . . . . **NA**
  Gold Sable. . . . . . . . . . . . . . . . . . . . . . . . . . . . . **NA**

# BLASER RIFLES

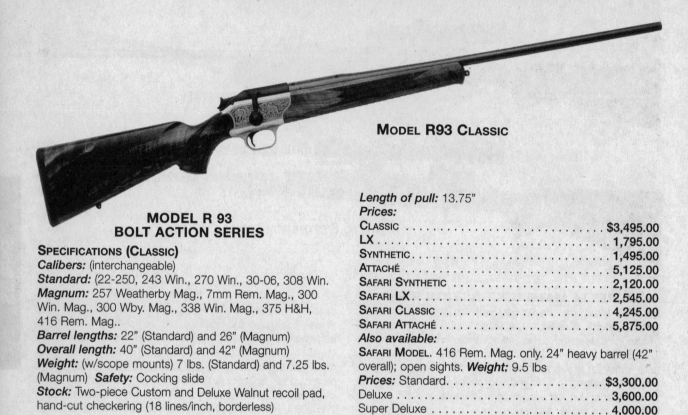

**MODEL R93 CLASSIC**

## MODEL R 93 BOLT ACTION SERIES

### SPECIFICATIONS (CLASSIC)

**Calibers:** (interchangeable)
**Standard:** (22-250, 243 Win., 270 Win., 30-06, 308 Win.
**Magnum:** 257 Weatherby Mag., 7mm Rem. Mag., 300 Win. Mag., 300 Wby. Mag., 338 Win. Mag., 375 H&H, 416 Rem. Mag..
**Barrel lengths:** 22" (Standard) and 26" (Magnum)
**Overall length:** 40" (Standard) and 42" (Magnum)
**Weight:** (w/scope mounts) 7 lbs. (Standard) and 7.25 lbs. (Magnum) **Safety:** Cocking slide
**Stock:** Two-piece Custom and Deluxe Walnut recoil pad, hand-cut checkering (18 lines/inch, borderless)

**Length of pull:** 13.75"
**Prices:**

| | |
|---|---|
| CLASSIC | $3,495.00 |
| LX | 1,795.00 |
| SYNTHETIC | 1,495.00 |
| ATTACHÉ | 5,125.00 |
| SAFARI SYNTHETIC | 2,120.00 |
| SAFARI LX | 2,545.00 |
| SAFARI CLASSIC | 4,245.00 |
| SAFARI ATTACHÉ | 5,875.00 |

*Also available:*
SAFARI MODEL. 416 Rem. Mag. only. 24" heavy barrel (42" overall); open sights. **Weight:** 9.5 lbs

| **Prices:** | |
|---|---|
| Standard | $3,300.00 |
| Deluxe | 3,600.00 |
| Super Deluxe | 4,000.00 |

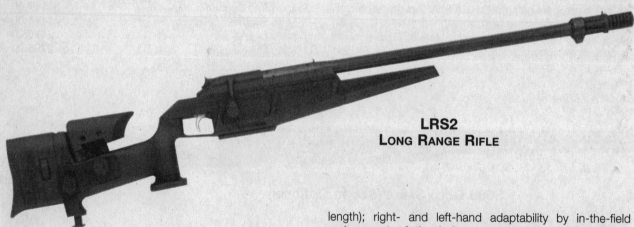

**LRS2 LONG RANGE RIFLE**

## BLASER LRS2 LONG RANGE RIFLE

Superseding the Blaser Long Range Sporter, the LRS2 features many of the same refinements that made the Sporter popular. Among them: straight-line bolt pull with a radial locking system for fast followup shots; a fully adjustable trigger – including fore-and-aft-adjustable trigger blade; a removable, adjustable comb; adjustable buttstock (for length); right- and left-hand adaptability by in-the-field replacement of the bolt assembly; heavy, fluted barrel; ambidextrous magazine release; gas nitrate steel treatment to provide a hard, rust-proof surface. The LRS2 has an improved stock and a new 5-shot in-line magazine. Accessories include a folding bipod, muzzle brake and hand rest. Available in .308 Win., .300 Win. Mag. and .338 Lapua, the LRS2 has also offers quick barrel interchange between the .308 and .300.
**Price:** NA

# BROWNING RIMFIRE RIFLES

**MODEL BL-22 LEVER-ACTION RIFLE**

## RIMFIRE RIFLE SPECIFICATIONS

| MODEL | CALIBER | BARREL LENGTH | SIGHT RADIUS | OVERALL LENGTH | AVERAGE WEIGHT | PRICE |
|---|---|---|---|---|---|---|
| Semi-Auto 22 Grade I | 22 LR | 19.25" | 16.25" | 37" | 4 lbs. 12 oz. | **$465.00** |
| Semi-Auto 22 Grade VI* | 22 LR | 19.25" | 16.25" | 37" | 4 lbs. 12 oz. | **998.00** |
| BL-22 Grade I | 22 LR, Long, Short | 20" | 15.875" | 36.75" | 5 lbs. | **403.00** |
| BL-Grade II | 22 LR, Long, Short | 20" | 15.875" | 36.75" | 5 lbs. | **457.00** |

*Blued or Grayed

## 22 SEMI-AUTOMATIC RIMFIRE RIFLES GRADES I AND VI (See table above for prices)

**SPECIFICATIONS** (See also table above)
**Capacity:** 11 cartridges in magazine, 1 chamber
**Safety:** Cross-bolt type **Trigger:** Grade I is blued; Grade VI is gold colored **Sights:** Gold bead front, adjustable folding leaf ear; drilled and tapped for Browning scope mounts
**Stock & Forearm:** Grade I, select walnut with checkering (18 lines/inch); Grade VI, high-grade walnut with checkering (22 lines/inch).

## STOCK DIMENSIONS

| | SEMI-AUTO | BL-22 |
|---|---|---|
| Length of Pull | 13.75" | 13.5" |
| Drop at Comb | 1 3/8" | .625" |
| Drop at Heel | 2.375" | 2.25" |

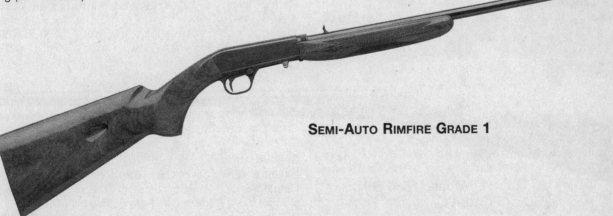

**SEMI-AUTO RIMFIRE GRADE 1**

# BROWNING RIFLES

### MODEL 1885 LOW WALL RIFLE
(HIGH & LOW WALL MODELS)
### $997.00

## SPECIFICATIONS MODEL 1885 LOW WALL OR HIGH WALL

| CALIBERS* | BARREL LENGTH | SIGHT RADIUS | OVERALL LENGTH | APPROXIMATE WEIGHT | RATE OF TWIST (R. HAND) |
|---|---|---|---|---|---|
| **HIGH WALL** | | | | | |
| 22-250 Rem. | 28" | — | 43.5" | 8 lbs. 13 oz. | 1 in 14" |
| 270 Win. | 28" | — | 43.5" | 8 lbs. 12 oz. | 1 in 10" |
| 30-06 Sprg. | 28" | — | 43.5" | 8 lbs. 12 oz. | 1 in 10" |
| 7mm Rem. Mag. | 28" | — | 43.5" | 8 lbs. 11 oz. | 1 in 9.5" |
| 45-70 Govt. | 28" | 21.5" | 43.5" | 8 lbs. 14 oz. | 1 in 20" |
| 454 Casull | 28" | — | 43.5" | 8 lbs. 14 oz. | 1 in 20" |
| **LOW WALL** | | | | | |
| 22 Hornet | 24" | — | 39.5" | 6 lbs. 4 oz. | 1 in 16" |
| 223 Rem. | 24" | — | 39.5" | 6 lbs. 4 oz. | 1 in 12" |
| 243 Win. | 24" | — | 39.5" | 6 lbs. 4 oz. | 1 in 10" |
| 260 Rem. | 24" | — | 39.5" | 6 lbs. 4 oz. | 1 in 10" |

*Also available in 454 Casull*

## LOW WALL TRADITIONAL HUNTER

### SPECIFICATIONS
***Calibers:*** 357 Mag., 44 Mag., 45 Colt ***Barrel Length:*** 24"
***Overall Length:*** 40.25" ***Sight Radius:*** 31" ***Weight:*** 6 lbs. 8 oz. ***Length of Pull:*** 13.5"
***Price:***. . . . . . . . . . . . . . . . . . . . . . . . . . . . . $1,289.00

## MODEL 1885 HIGH WALL TRADITIONAL HUNTER

### SPECIFICATIONS
***Calibers:*** 30-30 Win., 38-55 Win., 45-70 Govt.
***Barrel Length:*** 28" ***Overall Length:*** 44.25" ***Weight:*** 9 lbs.
***Rate of Twist:*** 1 in 12" (30-30 Win.); 1 in 15" (38-55 Win.); 1 in 20" (45-70 Gov't.)
***Price:***. . . . . . . . . . . . . . . . . . . . . . . . . . . . . $1,220.00

### MODEL 1885 BPCR
(BLACK POWDER CARTRIDGE RIFLE)

### SPECIFICATIONS
***Calibers:*** 40-65, 45-70 Govt. ***Barrel Length:*** 30" ***Overall Length:*** 46.125" ***Weight:*** 11 lbs. (45-70 Govt.); 11 lbs. 7 oz. (40-65) ***Sight Radius:*** 34" ***Rate of Twist:*** 1 in 16" (R.H.)
***Price:***. . . . . . . . . . . . . . . . . . . . . . . . . . . . . $1,766.00

# BROWNING A-BOLT RIFLES

## A-BOLT II HUNTER BOLT-ACTION CENTERFIRE RIFLES

BOSS (Ballistic Optimizing Shooting System) is now optional on all A-Bolt II models (except standard and Varmint). BOSS adjusts barrel vibrations to allow a bullet to leave the rifle muzzle at the most advantageous point in the barrel oscillation, thereby fine-tuning accuracy with any brand of ammunition regardless of caliber.

This hard-working rifle features a practical grade of walnut and low-luster bluing. Includes the standard A-Bolt II fast-cycling bolt, crisp trigger, calibrated rear sights and ramp-style front sights. Optional BOSS on a clean, tapered barrel. Receiver is drilled and tapped for a scope mount; HUNTER model has open sights.

*Prices:* No Sights . . . . . . . . . . . . . . . . . . . . . . . . . . . $590.00
**MICRO HUNTER**
  (low-luster blue, shorter barrel and length of pull)
  without sights . . . . . . . . . . . . . . . . . . . . . . . . . . . 585.00

### A-BOLT II STAINLESS STALKER

The barrel, receiver and bolt are machined from solid stainless steel for a high level of corrosion and rust resistance and also to prolong the life of the rifle bore. The advanced graphite-fiber-glass composite stock shrugs off wet weather and rough handling and isn't affected by humidity. A palm swell on both right- and left-hand models offers a better grip. A lower comb directs recoil away from the face. Barrel, receiver and stock have a durable matte finish. The BOSS is optional in all calibers.

## A-BOLT II SPECIFICATIONS (See following page for additional A-Bolt II prices)

| CALIBER | TWIST (R.H.) | MAGAZINE CAPACITY | HUNTER | GOLD MEDAL. | MEDAL. | MICRO MEDAL. | STAINLESS STALKER | COMP STALKER | VARMINT | ECLIPSE |
|---|---|---|---|---|---|---|---|---|---|---|
| **LONG ACTION MAGNUM CALIBERS** | | | | | | | | | | |
| 375 H&H | 1:12" | 3 | — | — | • | — | • | — | — | — |
| 338 Win. Mag. | 1:10" | 3 | • | — | • | — | • | • | — | — |
| 300 Win. Mag. | 1:10" | 3 | • | • | • | — | • | • | — | • |
| 7mm Rem. Mag. | 1:9.5" | 3 | • | • | • | — | • | • | — | • |
| **LONG ACTION STANDARD CALIBERS** | | | | | | | | | | |
| 25-06 Rem. | 1:10" | 4 | • | — | • | — | • | • | — | • |
| 270 Win. | 1:10" | 4 | • | • | • | — | • | • | — | • |
| 280 Rem. | 1:10" | 4 | • | • | • | — | • | • | — | • |
| 30-06 Sprg. | 1:10" | 4 | • | • | • | • | • | • | — | • |
| **SHORT ACTION CALIBERS** | | | | | | | | | | |
| 243 Win. | 1:10" | 4 | • | • | • | • | • | • | — | • |
| 308 Win. | 1:12" | 4 | • | • | • | • | • | • | • | •+ |
| 260 Rem. | 1:10" | 4 | • | — | • | • | • | • | • | •+ |
| 7mm-08 Rem. | 1:9.5" | 4 | • | — | • | • | • | • | — | — |
| 22-250 Rem. | 1:14" | 4 | • | — | • | • | • | • | • | •+ |
| 223 Rem. | 1:12" | 6* | • | — | • | • | • | • | • | + |

• *Magazine capacity of 223 Rem. models is up to 5 rounds on Micro-Medallion (up to 6 on other models).*
+ = *also available in Varmint version of Eclipse*

## A-BOLT II STOCK DIMENSIONS

| | MICRO-MED. | GOLD MEDAL. | HUNTER | VARMINT | STALKER | ECLIPSE | ECLIPSE VARMINT M-1000 |
|---|---|---|---|---|---|---|---|
| Length Of Pull | 13 5/16" | 13 5/8" | 13 5/8" | 13 3/4" | 13 5/8" | 14" | 14" |
| Drop At Comb | 3/4" | 3/4"-1" | 3/4" | 9/16" | 5/8" | 7/16" | 1/2" |
| Drop At Heel | 1 1/8" | 1 3/4" | 1 1/8" | 7/16" | 1/2" | 1 1/16" | 1" |

## A-BOLT II AVERAGE WEIGHTS

| MODEL | LONG ACTION MAGNUM CALIBERS | LONG ACTION STANDARD CALIBERS | SHORT ACTION CALIBERS |
|---|---|---|---|
| Composite/Stainless Steel | 7 lbs. 3 oz. | 6 lbs. 11 oz. | 6 lbs. 4 oz. |
| Micro-Medal. | | | 6 lbs. 1 oz. |
| Gold Medal. | 7 lbs. 11 oz. | 7 lbs. 3 oz. | |
| Medallion & Hunter | 7 lbs. 3 oz. | 6 lbs. 11 oz. | 6 lbs. 7 oz. |
| Varmint | | | 9 lbs. |
| Eclipse | 8 lbs. | 7 lbs. 8 oz. | 7 lbs. 10 oz. |
| Eclipse Varmint | | | 9 lbs. 1 oz. |
| M-1000 | 9 lbs. 13 oz. | | |

## A-BOLT II GENERAL DIMENSIONS

| LENGTH | OVERALL LENGTH | BARREL LENGTH | SIGHT RADIUS* |
|---|---|---|---|
| Long Action Mag. Cal. | 46.75" | 26" | 18" |
| Long Action Std. Cal. | 42.75" | 22" | 18" |
| Short Action Cal. | 41.75" | 22" | 16" |
| Micro-Medallion | 39 9/16" | 20"** | — |
| Varmint Models | 44.5" | 24" | 26" |

*Open sights available on A-Bolt Hunter and all models in 375 H&H.*
**22 Hornet Micro-Medallion has a 22" barrel. BOSS equipped rifles have the same dimensions.*

# BROWNING RIFLES

### A-BOLT II M-1000 ECLIPSE
### 300 WIN. MAG.

### A-BOLT II ECLIPSE MODELS WITH THUMBHOLE STOCK

The proven action and barrel of the A-Bolt II are included in the A-Bolt II Eclipse Series. Each rifle is fitted with a newly designed thumbhole stock configuration. To hold accuracy under changing humidity and precipitation conditions the stock itself is crafted from rugged gray/black, multi-laminated hardwood. This gives the Eclipse a camouflaged look. The custom thumbhole-style stock provides a solid grip and secure feel that adds up to accuracy. The Eclipse is available in two versions: long and short action hunting model with standard A-Bolt II barrel, and a short action varmint version with a heavy barrel. All are BOSS equipped.

### A-BOLT II SERIES

| | Prices |
| --- | --- |
| MEDALLION no sights, BOSS | $771.00 |
| MEDALLION no sights | 695.00 |
| MEDALLION L.H., no sights, BOSS | 798.00 |
| MEDALLION L.H., no sights | 722.00 |
| MEDALLION 375 H&H no sights, BOSS | 863.00 |
| VARMINT, hvy. bbl., BOSS, gloss or satin/matte | 879.00 |

### A-BOLT II SERIES

| | Prices |
| --- | --- |
| STAINLESS STALKER no sights, BOSS | $850.00 |
| STAINLESS STALKER no sights | 774.00 |
| STAINLESS STALKER L.H., no sights, BOSS | 874.00 |
| STAINLESS STALKER L.H., no sights | 798.00 |

| | |
| --- | --- |
| STAINLESS STALKER 375 H&H, BOSS | 957.00 |
| STAINLESS STALKER 375 H&H, L.H., BOSS | 984.00 |
| COMPOSITE STALKER, no sights, BOSS | 682.00 |
| COMPOSITE STALKER, no sights | 609.00 |
| ECLIPSE HUNTER, no sights, BOSS | 969.00 |
| VARMINT no sights, BOSS | 879.00 |
| ECLIPSE M-1000, w/BOSS | 998.00 |

### NEW CARBON FIBER STAINLESS STALKER (not shown)

With steel-lined carbon fiber barrel for lighter weight.
*Chamberings:* 22-250 and .300 Win. Mag.
*Price:* $1,667.00

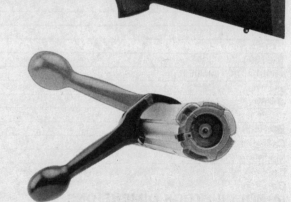

### LEFT-HAND A-BOLT II MEDALLION

Only a few popular bolt-action rifles have traditionally been built in left-hand versions. Browning joins a growing movement to accommodate lefties with its A-Bolt II, Boss is available.

### SAFETY

The top-mounted safety is perfectly positioned for easy operation. This location also allows the shooter to see the status at any angle.

### BOLT

The short 60° bolt throw gives you faster follow-up shots and also permits greater clearance between the bolt handle and scope. The flattened bolt knob itself is canted at a 30° angle to fit your hand more naturally.

# BROWNING RIFLES

## LIGHTNING BLR

### SPECIFICATIONS

*Calibers: Long Action*–223 Rem., 270 Win., 30-06 Springfield (7mm Rem. Mag.) 300 Win. Mag. *Short Action*–22-250 Rem., 243 Win., 7mm-08 Rem., 308 Win. *Capacity:* 4 rounds; 3 in magnum calibers *Barrel Length: Long Action*–22" (24" magnum calibers) *Short Action*–20" *Overall Length: Long*

*Action*–42 ⁷/₈" (44 ⁷/₈" magnum calibers) *Short Action*–39.5" *Approximate Weight: Long Action*–7 lbs. 4 oz. (7 lbs. 12 oz. magnum calibers) *Short Action*–6 lbs. 8 oz. *Sight Radius:* 17.75" (19.75" magnum calibers)

*Prices:* Short Action. . . . . . . . . . . . . . . . . . . . . $630.00
  Long Action . . . . . . . . . . . . . . . . . . . . . . . . . . . 666.00

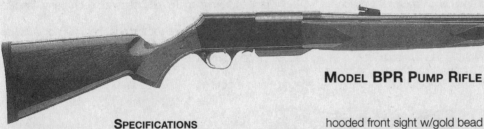

## MODEL BPR PUMP RIFLE

### SPECIFICATIONS

*Calibers:* 243 Win., 308 Win., 270 Win., 30-06 Springfield; 7mm Rem. Mag., 300 Win. Mag. *Capacity:* 4 rounds; 3 in magnum calibers *Action:* Pump action *Barrel Length:* 22" (24" magnum calibers) *Overall Length:* 43"; 45" magnum calibers *Weight:* 7 lbs. 3 oz. (7 lbs. 9 oz. magnum calibers) *Safety:* Crossbolt w/enlarged head *Sight Radius:* 17.5" (19.5" magnum calibers) *Sights:* Adjustable rear sight;

hooded front sight w/gold bead *Stock Dimensions:* Length of pull; 13.75"; Drop at comb: 1 ⁵/₈" (1.75" magnum calibers) Drop at heel: 2" *Features:* Drilled and tapped for scope mounts; multiple lug rotating bolt locks directly into barrel; detachable box magazine w/hinged floorplate; single-stage trigger; recoil pad standard; full pistol grip

*Price:*. . . . . . . . . . . . . . . . . . . . . . . . . . . . . . . . . $725.00
  Magnum. . . . . . . . . . . . . . . . . . . . . . . . . . . . . . . 780.00

## BAR MARK II SAFARI

## BAR MARK II SAFARI & LIGHTWEIGHT SEMIAUTOMATIC RIFLES

The BAR Mark II features an engraved receiver, a redesigned bolt release, new gas and buffeting systems, and a removable trigger assembly. Additional features include: crossbolt safety with enlarged head; hinged floorplate, gold trigger; select walnut stock

and forearm with cut-checkering and swivel studs; 13.75" length of pull; 2" drop at heel; 1 ⁵/₈" drop at comb; and a recoil pad (magnum calibers only). The New Lightweight model features alloy receiver and shortened barrel. Open sights are standard.

### BAR MARK II SPECIFICATONS

*Calibers:* Standard–243 Win., 25-06, 270 Win., 308 Win.; Magnum–7mm Rem. Mag., 300 Win. Mag., 338 Win. Mag.; Lightweight–243 Win., 270 Win., 30-06 Springfield; 308 Win. *Capacity:* 4 rounds; 3 in magnum
*Barrel Length:* Standard–22"; Magnum–24"; Lightweight–20"
*Overall Length:* Standard–43"; Magnum–45"; Lightweight–41"
*Average Weight:* Standard–7 lbs. 6 oz.; Magnum–8 lbs. 6 oz.; Lightweight–7 lbs. 2 oz.
*Sight Radius:* Standard–17.5"; Magnum–19.5"; Lightweight–15.5"

**Prices:**
STANDARD CALIBERS: No sights, BOSS . . . . . . . . . . $849.00
  Open sights, no BOSS . . . . . . . . . . . . . . . . . . . . 793.00
  No sights, no BOSS . . . . . . . . . . . . . . . . . . . . . . 776.00
MAGNUM CALIBERS: No sights, BOSS. . . . . . . . . . $921.00
  Open sights . . . . . . . . . . . . . . . . . . . . . . . . . . . . 866.00
  No sights, no BOSS . . . . . . . . . . . . . . . . . . . . . . 848.00
BAR MARK II LIGHTWEIGHT
  No sights, BOSS, Magnum . . . . . . . . . . . . . . . . . $939.00
  Open sights, no BOSS . . . . . . . . . . . . . . . . . . . . 793.00
  Open sights, no BOSS Magnum . . . . . . . . . . . . . 866.00

# BROWN PRECISION RIFLES

## PRO-HUNTER RIFLE

Designed for the serious game hunter or guide, this custom version of Brown Precision's Pro-Hunter rifle begins as a Winchester Model 700 Super Grade action with controlled feed claw extractor. The trigger is tuned to crisp let-off at each customer's specified weight. A Shilen Match Grade stainless-steel barrel is custom crowned and hand fitted to the action.

The Pro-Hunter Elite features choice of express rear sight or custom Dave Talley removable peep sight and banded front ramp sight with European dovetail and replaceable brass bead. An optional flip-up white night sight is also available, as is a set of Dave Talley detachable T.N.T. scope mount rings and bases installed with Brown's Magnum Duty 8X40 screws.

All metal parts are finished in either matte electroless nickel or black Teflon. The barreled action is glass bedded to a custom Brown Precision Alaskan-configuration fiberglass stock, painted according to customer choice and fitted w/premium 1" buttpad and Dave Talley trapdoor grip cap. Weight ranges from 7 to 15 lbs., depending on barrel length, contour and options.

Optional equipment: drop box magazine, KDF or Answer System muzzle brake, Mag-Na-Port, Zeiss, Swarovski or Leupold scope, Americase aluminum hard case.
**Prices:** . . . . . . . . . . . . . . . . . . . . . . . . . . . . . . . . $2,975.00
Left-hand model . . . . . . . . . . . . . . . . . . . . . . . 3,115.00

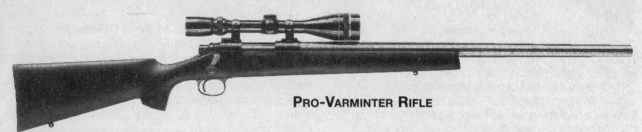

## PRO-VARMINTER RIFLE

The standard Pro-Varminter is buillt on the Remington 700 or Rremington 40X action (right or left hand) and features a hand-fitted Shilen Match Grade Heavy Benchrest stainless-steel barrel in bright or bead-blasted finish. The barreled action is custom-bedded in Brown Precision's Varmint Special Hunter Bench or 40X Benchrest-style custom fiberglass, Kevlar or graphite stock.

Options include metal finishes, muzzle brakes, target or varmint scopes, triggers, barrels, stock dimensions
**Prices:**
Right-hand Model 700 Action . . . . . . . . . . . . . $2,195.00
For Left-hand Model 700. . . . . . . . . . . . . . . . . 2,335.00
Model 40-XB (inc. target trigger) . . . . . . . . . . . 2,625.00

## CUSTOM TEAM CHALLENGER

This custom rifle was designed for use in the Chevy Trucks Sportsman's Team Challenge shooting event. It's also used in metallic silhouette competition as well as in the field for small game and varmints. Custom built on the Ruger 10/22 semi-automatic rimfire action, which features an extended magazine release, a simplified bolt release and finely tuned trigger, this rifle is fitted with either a Brown Precision fiberglass or Kevlar stock with custom length of pull up to 15". The stock can be shortened at the butt and later relengthened and repainted to accommodate growing youth shooters. Stock color is also optional. To facilitate shooting with scopes, the lightweight stock has high-comb classic styling. The absence of a cheekpiece accommodates either right- or left-handed shooters, while the stock's flat-bottom, 1 3/4" forearm ensures maximum comfort in both offhand and rest shooting. Barrels are custom-length Shilen Match Grade .920" diameter straight or lightweight tapered.

**Prices:**
With blued action/barrel. . . . . . . . . . . . . . . . . . $1,135.00
With blued action/stainless barrel . . . . . . . . . . . 1225.00
With silver action/stainless barrel. . . . . . . . . . . 1295.00

# BROWN PRECISION RIFLES

### HIGH COUNTRY RIFLE

High Country Rifle Standard Features: • Remington 700 ADL, BDL or Mountain Rifle standard caliber barreled action • Brown Precision Custom Fiberglass, Kevlar or Graphite stock in Classic configuration with QD sling swivels attached • Custom stock length of pull • Choice of standard recoil pads • Trigger tuned to a crisp pull (customer specifies weight) • Choice of stock finish colors: black, grey, brown or green • Weight: 5 lbs. and up depending on stock, barrel length and contour, caliber, options and customer's intended use.

**Price:** ...........................**starts at $1,355.00**

### HIGH COUNTRY YOUTH RIFLE

This custom rifle has all the same features as the standard High Country rifle, but scaled-down to fit the younger or smaller shooter. Based on the Remington Model 7 or Model 700 barreled action, it is available in calibers 223, 243, 7mm-08, 6mm and 308. The rifle features a shortened fiberglass, Kevlar or graphite stock, which can be lengthened as the shooter grows, a new recoil pad installed and the stock refinished. Custom features/options include choice of actions, custom barrels, chamberings, muzzle brakes, metal finishes, scopes and accessories.

All Youth Rifles include a deluxe package of shooting, reloading and hunting accessories and information to increase a young shooter's interest.

**Price: starts at** ...........................**$1435.00**

### TACTICAL ELITE RIFLE

Brown Precision's Tactical Elite is built on a Remington 700 action and features a bead-blasted Shilen Select Match Grade Heavy Benchrest Stainless Steel barrel custom-chambered for 223 Rem., 308 Win., 300 Win. Mag. (or any standard or wildcat caliber). A nonreflective custom black Teflon metal finish on all metal surfaces ensures smooth bolt operation and 100 percent weatherproofing. The barreled action is bedded in a target-style stock with high rollover comb/cheekpiece, vertical pistol grip and palmswell. The stock is an advanced, custom fiberglass/Kevlar/graphite composite for maximum durability and rigidity, painted in flat black (camouflage patterns are also available). QD sling swivel studs and swivels are standard.

Other standard features include: three-way adjustable buttplate/recoil pad assembly with length of pull, vertical and cant angle adjustments, custom barrel length and contour, and trigger tuned for a crisp pull to customer's specifications. Options include muzzle brakes, Leupold or Kahles police scopes, and others, and are priced accordingly.

**Price:** ...................................**$2695.00**

# CHRISTENSEN ARMS

Christensen Arms pioneered the use of steel-lined carbon-fiber barrels to reduce weight without reducing stiffness. Here are some of the rifles that resulted:

### CARBONCHALLENGER THUMBHOLE

Custom ultra-lightweight graphite barreled precision target and small-game rimfire-class rifle. Up to 20" long match-grade stainless steel barrel liner, semi-auto action, custom trigger, synthetic or wood stock and fitted for scope mounts. Bedded with action free floating. **Weight:** 3 to 5 pounds **Accuracy:** 3 shots .5" or less at 50 yards.
***Price:*** . . . . . . . . . . . . . . . . . . . . . . . . . . . . . . . . **$999.00**

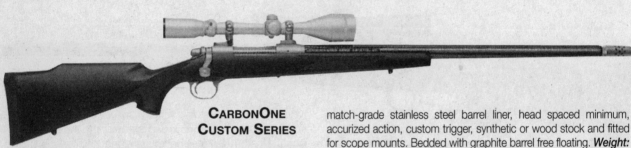

### CARBONONE CUSTOM SERIES

Custom lightweight graphite barreled precision magnum big-game class rifle. All popular Magnum calibers available. Up to 28" long match-grade stainless steel barrel liner, head spaced minimum, accurized action, custom trigger, synthetic or wood stock and fitted for scope mounts. Bedded with graphite barrel free floating. **Weight:** 6 to 7 lbs. **Accuracy:** 3 shots .5" or less at 100 yards.
***Price:*** . . . . . . . . . . . . . . . . . . . . . . . . . . . . . . **$2,750.00**

### CARBONTACTICAL SERIES

Custom lightweight graphite, barreled precision tactical-class rifle. All popular calibers available. Up to 28" long match-grade stainless steel barrel liner, head spaced minimum, muzzle break optional, accurized action, custom trigger, synthetic or wood stock and fitted for scope mounts. Bedded with free-floating graphite barrel. **Weight:** 5 to 8 pounds **Accuracy:** 3 shots .5" or less at 100 yards.
***Price:*** . . . . . . . . . . . . . . . . . . . . . . . . . . . . . . **$2,750.00**

### CARBONRANGER SERIES

Custom lightweight long range precision sniper rifle. Available in 50 caliber. Up to 36" long stainless steel barrel liner, chambered to minimum tolerances. E.D.M. precision machined Omni Wind Runner accurized action (or an action of choice), custom trigger, retractable stock. 5 shots 8" at 1000 yards.
***Prices:*** . . . . . . . . . . . . . . . . . . . . . . . . . . . . . **$10,625.00**

# CIMARRON FIREARMS

## SINGLE-SHOT RIFLES

### BILLY DIXON
### 1874 SHARPS SPORTING RIFLE

It was June 27, 1874 at Adobe Walls on the Canadian River in the Texas panhandle. Young Billy Dixon and 27 buffalo hunters were surrounded by more than 500 Kiowa and Comanche warriors. The Kiowa medicine man told the warriors that his medicine made them invisible to the bullets of the white eyes. When Dixon fired his Sharps sporting rifle and knocked a Kiowa from his horse at 1538 yards (7/8 mile) the Indians departed with haste. The medican man was quirted severly. Billy Dixon was later awarded the Congressional Medal of Honor while acting as scout of the army for Gen. Nelson Miles and lived a long life as a Texas peace officer.
**Barrel:** 32" Octagon **Caliber:** .45-.70
**Prices:**
Retail . . . . . . . . . . . . . . . . . . . . . . . . . . . . . . . **$1,295.00**

### QUIGLEY MODEL
### 1874 SHARPS SPORTING RIFLE

This single shot rifle is capable of the accuracy depicted in the epic film. The Cimarron Quigley model is a faithful reproduction of that long rifle from down under.
**Barrel:** 34" Octagon **Caliber:** .45-70, .45-.120
**Prices:**
Retail: . . . . . . . . . . . . . . . . . . . . . . . . . . . . . . **$1,495.00**

### SILHOUETTE MODEL
### 1874 SHARPS SPORTING RIFLE

The Cimarron Model 1874 Sharps silhouette rifle was created for the shooter who demands a sound, accurate, basic Sharps. The pistol grip stock gives ultimate control for off hand shooting while the shotgun style butt plate provides maximum comfort. The barrel features cut rifling, lapped and polished for maximum accuracy. **Barrel:** 32" Octagon **Caliber:** .45-.70
**Prices:**
Retail . . . . . . . . . . . . . . . . . . . . . . . . . . . . . . . **$1,095.00**

### CIMARRON
### FIREARMS CO. 1885 HIGH WALL

The Winchester single shot hunting rifle was placed on the market in the early 1880's. It is regarded by many as being the most reliable, strongest, most symetrical and altogether best single shot rifle ever produced. It is doubtless stronger than the Sharps rifle, is better designed, made of better materials and is of better appearance than that famous arm. All these rifles proved very accurate and reliable. Regrettably, the Winchester single shot rifle is no longer available. Cimarron's rendition of this John Browning rifle is every bit as strong and accurate as the original. **Barrel:** 30" Octagon **Caliber:** 45-70, 45-90, 40-65, 38-55
**Prices:**
Retail. . . . . . . . . . . . . . . . . . . . . . . . . . . . . . . . **$995.00**

# CIMARRON FIREARMS

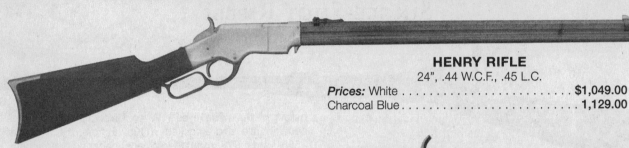

### HENRY RIFLE
24", .44 W.C.F., .45 L.C.
*Prices:* White . . . . . . . . . . . . . . . . . . . . . . . . . $1,049.00
Charcoal Blue . . . . . . . . . . . . . . . . . . . . . . . . 1,129.00

### 1873 WINCHESTER
*"1 of 1,000"*
*Price:* . . . . . . . . special order

**WINCHESTER WHITE**

### WINCHESTER 1873
24", .357, .44 W.C.F
*Prices:* .45 L.C. . . . . . . . . . . . . . . . . . . . . . . . $949.00
White or charcoal blue (shown) . . . . . . . . . . . . . 989.00
with pistol grip . . . . . . . . . . . . . . . . . . . . . . . 1,089.00
White or charcoal blue (shown) . . . . . . . . . . . . 1,129.00

**WINCHESTER CHARCOAL BLUE**

**WINCHESTER 1873 24"**

**WINCHESTER 1873
19" CARBINE**

### WINCHESTER 1873
*Prices:* 24" . . . . . . . . . . . . . . . . . . . . . . . . . . . . $949.00
19" carbine . . . . . . . . . . . . . . . . . . . . . . . . . . . 949.00
*($50 more for charcoal blue)*

# COLT RIFLES

**COLT LIGHTWEIGHT MT6530**

The Colt Match Target Lightweight semiautomatic rifle evolved from the AR-15 and M-16 rifles of the 1970s. This rifle fires from a closed bolt. Buttstock and pistol grip are of tough nylon. A round, ribbed handguard is fiberglass-reinforced to ensure better grip control. Detachable box magazines come in a range of cartridge capacities.

**Calibers:** 223 Rem., 7.62x39
**Barrel Length:** 16"
**Overall Length:** 34.5" (35.5" in 7.62 X 39mm)
**Weight:** 6.7 lbs  **Capacity:** 5 rounds (7.62 X 39mm); 8 rounds (223 Rem. and 9mm)
**Price:**. . . . . . . . . . . . . . . . . . . . . . . . . . . . . . **$1,010.00**

**MATCH TARGET RIFLE**

## MATCH TARGET RIFLES
**Features:** Improved accuracy; suppressed recoil; accepts optics; ideal for competition; 2-position safety
**Price:** . . . . . . . . . . . . . . . . . . . . . . . . . **from $1,194.00**
**Available: MT6601:** .223 or 7.62 x 39 caliber; matte black finish, 1-7 twist; 8 lbs., 20" barrel, 39" overall length
**MT6601C:** Same as above, plus compensator; 8.75 lbs., 20" barrel, 39" overall length
**MT6530:** .223 or 7.62 x 39 caliber; matte black finish, 1-7 twist; 6.7 lbs., 16.1" barrel, 34.5" overall length

**MT6551:** .223 or 7.62 x 39 caliber; matte black finish, 1-7 twist; 8 lbs., 20" barrel, 39" overall length
**MT6700:** .223 or 7.62 x 39 caliber; matte black finish, 1-9 twist; 8.5 lbs., 20" barrel, 39" overall length; heavy barrel with flattop receiver
**MT6700C:** Same as above, plus compensator; 8.75 lbs., 20" barrel, 39" overall length
**MT6731:** .223 or 7.62 x 39 caliber; matte black finish, 1-9 twist; 7.1 lbs., 16.1" barrel, 34.5" overall length; heavy barrel with flattop receiver

# COOPER ARMS RIFLES

## VARMINT EXTREME SERIES

Cooper Arms was founded in 1990 by a small group of ex-Kimber employees whose goal was to produce the world's most accurate and beautiful rifles and make them 100% in America. The company has since gained a reputation for manufacturing some of the world's most accurate rifles. Cooper Arms produces a series of accurate, single shot and repeating, bolt action rifles in three basic stock designs and a variety of calibers ranging from custom cartridges like the .17 Squirrel to the .25-06 Ackley Improved. Produced in either the Custom Classic design or the Western Classic which features Doug Turnbull's case color hardening, hand struck octagon barrels, and AAA select Claro walnut. Cooper produces three action sizes to match each cartridg. The new MODEL 57 is available in .22 Long Rifle and in four configurations.
***Prices:*** .............. from **$1,095.00 to $2,195.00**

**CLASSIC**

### COOPER CLASSIC

Cooper Classic is a value-priced rifle with aluminum bottom metal, 18 lpi checkering but the same high level of performance as more costly Coopers. Varminter and sporter configurations available.
***Price:*** ............................... from **$995.00**

### MODEL 22 REPEATER CUSTOM CLASSIC

Select Claro walnut, 22 lpi checkering, shadow cheekrest, steel grip cap; stock profile by Jerry Fisher, Len Brownell.
***Price:*** .......................... from **$1,050.00**

**MODEL 22 SINGLE SHOT VARMINT EXTREME**

**MODEL 22 VARMINT EXTREME**

### MODEL 22 SINGLE SHOT VARMINT EXTREME

**SPECIFICATIONS**
***Calibers:*** 22-250, 220 Swift, 243, 25-06, 308, 6mm PPC
***Capacity:*** Single shot ***Barrel Length:*** 24" ***Action:*** 3 front locking lugs; glass-bedded ***Trigger:*** Single-stage Match, fully adjustable; Jewell 2-stage (optional) ***Stock:*** AAA Claro walnut, hand checkered, oil finished free-floated barrel channel
***Prices:*** MODEL 38 (mini action) ............ **$1,795.00**
MODEL 21 (short action) ................... **1,795.00**
MODEL 22 (medium action) ............... **1,895.00**

# CZ RIFLES

The rimfire rifles produced by Ceska Zbrojovka Uhersky Brod are ranked among the most sought-after firearms of their kind on the world market. Quality, long service life, accuracy and safe handling are the main virtues of these firearms designed for teenagers, hunters and sports shooters. The CZ 452 - 2E ZKM rimfire rifles offer a compact design with a robustly constructed Mauser-type action. The trigger mechanism has an adjustable trigger pull and a safety located at the rear part of the bolt. The rifles feature a tangent rear sight adjustable for elevation and windage. The receiver is factory milled for telescopic sight mounts. The CZ 452 - 2E ZKM rifles are supplied with a magazine holding 5 or 10 cartridges.

LUX

VARMINT

### CZ 452 - 2E ZMK LUX
*Caliber:* .22 LR (5/10 cartridges)
.22 WMR (5 cartridges)
*Overall length:* 42.6"
*Barrel Length:* 24.8"
*Sight Radius:* 20.0"
*Weight:* 7 lbs.
*Sights tangent rear sight:* 25-200m
*Price:* 22 LR . . . . . . . . . . . . . . . . . . . . . . . . . . . . $351.00
22 mag . . . . . . . . . . . . . . . . . . . . . . . . . . . . . . 378.00

### CZ 452 - 2E ZKM - VARMINT
*Caliber:* .22 LR  *Overall length:* 39"  *Weight:* 7 lbs.
*Price:* . . . . . . . . . . . . . . . . . . . . . . . . . . . . . . . $378.00

AMERICAN

### CZ 452 - 2E ZKM AMERICAN
CZ 452 - ZKM American - This quality rimfire rifle has been adapted to the requirements governing the USA. The barrel is a 22½" long, and is made without open sights. The top of the receiver is fitted with a 9 mm wide dovetail groove for mounting a scope. *Caliber:* .22 LR, .22 WMR  *Overall length:* 40"  *Weight:* 6 lbs.
*Price:* 22 LR . . . . . . . . . . . . . . . . . . . . . . . . . . . . $351.00
22 mag . . . . . . . . . . . . . . . . . . . . . . . . . . . . . . 378.00

RIFLES

# CZ RIFLES

The CZ 550 series rifles represent a new line of elegant, aesthetic and ergonomically designed firearms. The diversified range of CZ 550 models with their characteristics and elegant design solutions meet contemporary requirements for sporting and hunting weapons. The rifles are provided with a compact trigger mechanism featuring a single-set trigger firmly connected to the barrelled action. The trigger can be used as a single stage trigger, the set-trigger can regulate trigger pull and trigger travel before and after discharge. The set-trigger can be easily dismantled without impairing its functional properties or adjustment of the single stage trigger mechanism. The CZ 550 rifles are provided with a two position noiseless safety which is disengaged in a forward direction as standard. Stocks are fitted with sling-swivels as standard, and quick release swivels can be fitted on request. The CZ 550 rifles with open sights are provided with a bead front sight and rear sight located so as not to interfere with even the biggest rifle scopes.

### CZ 550 LUX
*Version:* Fixed magazine; detachable magazine; feeding device *Capacity:* 5 cartridges, 4 cartridges *Caliber:* 5 cartridges

(.243 Win.; .270 Win, .308 Win.; 7x57, 7x64; 6.5x55 SE; 30-06 Sprg.; 9.3 x 62  4 cartridges (.243 Win.; .308 Win.; .22-250) *Overall length:* 44.7"  *Barrel length:* 23.6"
*Weight:* 7.3 lbs.
*Price:* . . . . . . . . . . . . . . . . . . . . . . . . . . . . . . . **$561.00**
with detachable magazine . . . . . . . . . . . . . . . . . . . 582.00

**FS**

*Quick release swivels can be fitted on request*

**AMERICAN**

**PREMIUM**

**VARMINT**

### CZ 550 SAFARI MAGNUM (not shown)
The CZ 550  Safari is a true "Magnum" length action, it has all the features of the CZ 550 line and one standing 2 folding express sights, a Turkish walnut Lux stock is standard. This model is intended for heavy or dangerous game.

*Price:* 7 mm Rem. Mag . . . . . . . . . . . . . . . . . . . . **$717.00**
300 Win. Mag. . . . . . . . . . . . . . . . . . . . . . . . . . . . 717.00
.375 H&H Mag. . . . . . . . . . . . . . . . . . . . . . . . . . . . 756.00
.416 Rigby . . . . . . . . . . . . . . . . . . . . . . . . . . . . . . . 796.00
.458 Win. Mag. . . . . . . . . . . . . . . . . . . . . . . . . . . . 744.00

# CZ RIFLES

## CENTERFIRE RIFLES

The CZ 527 is a precision repeating rifle, designed for sport shooting and hunting. The trigger mechanism is of a single set design with an adjustable set-trigger. It is possible to regulate both trigger pull and trigger travel. The safety is a two-position rotary lever which locks the trigger mechanism, while simultaneously blocking the bolt in a closed position. The top of the receiver has milled grooves to accommodate scope mounts. The stock's surface is finished in a semi-matte polyurethane lacquer.

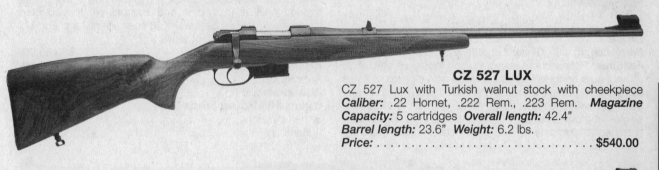

### CZ 527 LUX
CZ 527 Lux with Turkish walnut stock with cheekpiece **Caliber:** .22 Hornet, .222 Rem., .223 Rem. **Magazine Capacity:** 5 cartridges **Overall length:** 42.4" **Barrel length:** 23.6" **Weight:** 6.2 lbs.
**Price:** . . . . . . . . . . . . . . . . . . . . . . . . . . . . . . . . $540.00

### CZ 527 FS
CZ 527 FS - a classic Bavarian style Mannlicher stock of turkish walnut, cheekpiece **Caliber:** .22 Hornet, .222 Rem., .223 Rem. **Magazine Capacity:** 5 cartridges **Overall length:** 38.5" **Barrel length:** 20.5" **Weight:** 6.0 lbs.
**Price:** . . . . . . . . . . . . . . . . . . . . . . . . . . . . . . . . $607.00

### NEW 527 PREMIUM
**Caliber:** .22 Hornet, .223 Rem. **Magazine Capacity:** 5 cartridges **Overall length:** 40.4" **Barrel length:** 21.9" **Weight:** 6.2 lbs.
**Price:** . . . . . . . . . . . . . . . . . . . . . . . . . . . . . . . . $660.00

*The safety in its off position*

# DAKOTA ARMS

### DAKOTA 10 SINGLE SHOT

### SPECIFICATIONS
**Calibers:** Most rimmed/rimless commercially loaded types
**Barrel Length:** 23" **Overall Length:** 39.5" **Weight:** 6 lbs.
**Features:** Receiver and rear of breech block are solid steel without cuts or holes for maximum lug area (approx. 8 times more bearing area than most bolt rifles); crisp, clean trigger pull; removable trigger plate allows action to adapt to single-set triggers; straight-line coil-spring action and short hammer fall combine for fast lock time; smooth, quiet top tang safety blocks the striker forward of the main spring; strong, positive extractor and manual ejector adapted to rimmed/rimless cases. XX grade oil-finished English, Bastogne or Claro walnut stock.

| | |
|---|---|
| **Price:** | **$3,495.00** |
| **BARRELED ACTIONS** | 2,050.00 |
| **ACTIONS ONLY** | 1,675.00 |
| ***Also Available:*** | |
| **DAKOTA 10 MAGNUM SINGLE SHOT** | **$3,595.00** |
| Barreled actions | 2,050.00 |
| Actions only | 1,775.00 |

### DAKOTA 76 AFRICAN GRADE

### DAKOTA 76 RIFLES
### SPECIFICATIONS
**Calibers:**
**SAFARI GRADE:** 338 Win. Mag., 300 Mag., 375 H&H Mag., 458 Win. Mag.
**CLASSIC GRADE:** 22-250, 257 Roberts, 270 Win., 280 Rem., 30-06, 7mm Rem. Mag., 338 Win. Mag., 300 Win. Mag., 375 H&H Mag., 458 Win. Mag.
**AFRICAN GRADE:** 404 Jeffery, 416 Dakota, 416 Rigby, 450 Dakota
**Barrel Lengths:** 21" or 23" (Classic); 23" only (Safari); 24" (African) **Weight:** 7.5 lbs. (Classic); 9.5 lbs. (African); 8.5 lbs. (Safari) **Safety:** Three-position striker-blocking safety allows bolt operation with safety on **Sights:** Ramp front sight; standing-leaf rear **Stock:** Choice of X grade oil-finished English, Bastogne or Claro walnut (Classic); choice of XXX grade oil-finished English or Bastogne walnut w/ebony forent tip (Safari)

| | |
|---|---|
| **Prices: CLASSIC GRADE** | **$3,495.00** |
| **SAFARI GRADE** | 4,495.00 |
| **AFRICAN GRADE** | 4,995.00 |
| **Barreled Actions:** Classic Grade | 2,000.00 |
| Safari Grade | 2,350.00 |
| African Grade | 2,950.00 |
| **Actions:** Classic Grade | 1,750.00 |
| Safari Grade | 1,900.00 |
| African Grade | 2,500.00 |

### DAKOTA ARMS TRAVELER

The Dakota Traveler rifle can be easily broken down and carried in a small case or conventional suitcase, with the largest portion of the disassembled rifle being the barrel. With additional barrels available in a wide range of calibers, it offers great convenience for the traveling hunter.

The Traveler is based on the long-proven Dakota 76 design, and is stocked in checkered walnut. It features threadless disassembly–there are no threads to wear or stretch, no interrupted cuts and no possibility of headspace increasing even after repeated assembly and disassembly. Because of the Traveler's rigid design, it can be quickly taken down without disturbing the scope and mounts, assuring consistent, repeatable accuracy.

Additional barrels/calibers can be fitted on the same action, providing true worldwide hunting capability. Three families of actions are available: standard length, including the .257 Roberts, .25-06, 7x57, .270, .280, .30-06, .338-06 and .35 Whelen; short magnums, including the 7mm Rem. Mag., .300 Win. Mag., .338 Win. Mag., 416 Taylor and .458 Win. Mag.; and Dakota short magnums that include their proprietary 7mm, .300, .330 and .375 Dakota cartridges.

| | |
|---|---|
| **Prices: CLASSIC** | **$4,295.00** |
| **SAFARI** | 5,295.00 |
| **AFRICAN** | 5,995.00 |

# DAKOTA ARMS

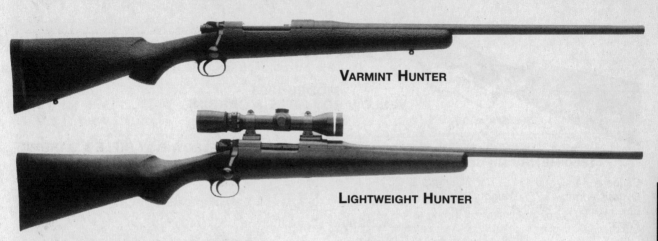

**VARMINT HUNTER**

**LIGHTWEIGHT HUNTER**

## DAKOTA 97 VARMINT, LONG RANGE & LIGHTWEIGHT HUNTER RIFLES

**DAKOTA HUNTER SERIES BOLT ACTION RIFLES (not shown)**
**97 LONG RANGE HUNTER**
Fibergass stock, 2 sling swivel studs, 1" black recoil pad, 13 5/8 length of pull, overall weight 7.7 lbs., overall length 45" to 47", calibers 25-06 through 375 Dakota. RH only.
**Price:**. . . . . . . . . . . . . . . . . . . . . . . . . . . . . . **$1,795.00**
**97 LIGHTWEIGHT HUNTER**
Fibergass stock, 2 sling swivel studs, 1" black recoil pad, 12 5/8 length of pull, overall weight approximately 6-6 1/2 lbs., overall length 43", calibers 22-250 through 330, RH only.
**97 VARMINT HUNTER**
Walnut-stocked round short-action solid-bottom single shot, 24" chrome-moly barrel #4, adjustable trigger, 13 5/8 length of pull, 1/2" black pad, approximate weight 8 lbs, calibers 17 Rem through 22-250, RH only.
**Price:** w/semi-fancy wood stock . . . . . . . . . . . **$2,495.00**
w/semi-fancy wood stock, checkering, floor plate. . . . . **2,995.00**
Barreled action . . . . . . . . . . . . . . . . . . . . . . . . **1,300.00**

## LONG BOW TACTICAL E.R. (ENGAGEMENT RIFLE)

**SPECIFICATIONS**
**Caliber:** 338 Lapua Mag., 300 Dakota Mag., 330 Dakota Mag.
**Action:** Blind magazine
**Barrel Length:** 28" stainless steel
**Overall Length:** 50"-51"
**Length Of Pull:** 12 7/8"-14 3/8"
**Weight:** 13.7 lbs. (w/o scope)
**Stock:** McMillan fiberglass (black or olive drab green); matte finish
**Features:** Adjustable cheekpiece; 3 sling swivel studs; bipod spike in forend; controlled round feeding; claw extraction system; one-piece optical rail; 3-position firing pin block safety; deployment kit; muzzlebrake
**Price:**. . . . . . . . . . . . . . . . . . . . . . . . . . . . . . **$4,250.00**
Action only . . . . . . . . . . . . . . . . . . . . . . . . . . . . **2,500.00**

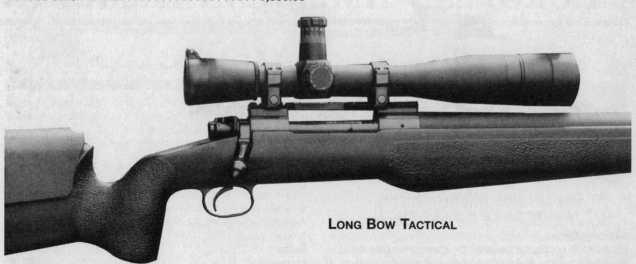

**LONG BOW TACTICAL**

# EMF REPLICA RIFLES

## MODEL 1866
## YELLOW BOY RIFLE & CARBINE

### 1860 HENRY RIFLE (not shown)

**Calibers:** 44-40 and 45 LC  **Barrel length:** 24.25";
**Overall length:** 43.75"  **Weight::** 9.25 lbs.
Blued barrel, walnut stock, brass frame
**Price:** . . . . . . . . . . . . . . . . . . . . . . . . . . . $1,230.00

### MODEL 1866 YELLOW BOY RIFLE & CARBINE

Calibers: 45 Long Colt, 38 Special and 44-40. Blued barrel, walnut stock, brass frame.
**Prices:**
Rifle . . . . . . . . . . . . . . . . . . . . . . . . . . . . . . $920.00
Carbine . . . . . . . . . . . . . . . . . . . . . . . . . . . . 900.00

### MODEL 1873 SPORTING RIFLE

**SPECIFICATIONS**
**Calibers:** 357, 44-40, 45 Long Colt  **Barrel length:** 24.25"
octagonal  **Overall length:** 43.25"  **Weight::** 8.16 lbs.
**Features:** Magazine tube in blued steel; frame is casehard-
ened steel; stock and forend are walnut
**Price** . . . . . . . . . . . . . . . . . . . . . . . . . . $1,150.00

**Also available:**
**MODEL 1873 CARBINE**. Same features as
the 1873 Sporting Rifle, except in 45 Long Colt only
with 19" barrel. **Overall length:** 38.25"  **Weight:** 7.38 lbs.
**Price:** . . . . . . . . . . . . . . . . . . . . . . . . . . $1,150.00

# EUROPEAN AMERICAN ARMORY

### HW 660 WEIHRAUCH RIMFIRE
### TARGET RIFLE (SINGLE SHOT)

**SPECIFICATIONS**
**Caliber:** 22 LR **Barrel length:** 26"  **Overall length:** 45.33"
**Weight:** 10.8 lbs. **Finish:** Blue **Stock:** European walnut

w/adjustable black rubber buttplate and comb
**Features:** Adjustable match trigger; left-handed stock
available; aluminum adjustable sling swivel; adj. vertical
and lateral cheekpiece; rear sight click-adjustable for
windage and elevation; aluminum forend rail; polished
feed ramp; external thumb safety
**Price:** . . . . . . . . . . . . . . . . . . . . . . . . . . . $999.00
Laminated . . . . . . . . . . . . . . . . . . . . . . . . . 1,159.00

# FRANCOTTE RIFLES

August Francotte rifles are available in all calibers for which barrels and chambers are made. All guns are custom made to the customer's specifications; there are no standard models. Most bolt-action rifles use commercial Mauser actions; however, the magnum action is produced by Francotte exclusively for its own production. Side-by-side and mountain rifles use either boxlock or sidelock action. Francotte system sidelocks are back-action type. Options include gold and silver inlay, special engraving and exhibition and museum grade wood. Francotte rifles are distributed in the U.S. by Armes de Chasse (see Directory of Manufacturers and Distributors for details).

**BOLT-ACTION RIFLE**

## SPECIFICATIONS
*Calibers:* 9.3x62, 375 H&H, 416 Rigby, others
*Barrel length:* To customer's specifications
*Weight:* 8 to 12 lbs., or to customer's specifications
*Stock:* A wide selection of wood in all possible styles according to customer preferences; prices listed below do not include engraving or select wood.
*Engraving:* Per customer specifications
*Sights:* All types of sights and scope

| BOLT-ACTION RIFLES | Prices |
|---|---|
| Standard Bolt Action 9.3x62 | $7,000.00 |
| Magnum Action 375 H&H, 416 Rigby | 8,900.00 |

| BOXLOCK SIDE-BY-SIDE DOUBLE RIFLES | Prices |
|---|---|
| Std. boxlock double rifle (9.3X74R, 8X57JRS, 7X65R, etc.) | $12,700.00 |
| Std. boxlock double (Magnum calibers) | 27,500.00 |

| SIDELOCK S/S DOUBLE RIFLES | |
|---|---|
| Std. sidelock double rifle (9.3X74R, 8X57JRS, 7X65R, etc.) | $17,500.00 |
| Std. sidelock double (Magnum calibers) | 27,250.00 |

| MOUNTAIN RIFLES | |
|---|---|
| Standard boxlock | $12,000.00 |
| Std. boxlock (Mag. & rimless calibers) | Price on request |
| Standard sidelock (7RM and .243 WM) | 36,334.00 |

# HARRINGTON & RICHARDSON

**ULTRA VARMINT**

## ULTRA SINGLE-SHOT RIFLES
### SPECIFICATIONS
*Calibers:* 223 Rem. & 243 (Varmint), 25-06, 308 Win.
*Action:* Break-open; side lever release; positive ejection
*Barrel Length:* 22" (308 Win.); 24" bull barrel (223 Rem., Varmint) 26" (25-06) *Weight:* 7 to 8 lbs. *Sights:* None (scope mount included) *Length Of Pull:* 14.25" *Drop At Comb:*
1.25" *Drop At Heel:* 1 1/8" *Forend:* Semibeavertail *Stock:* Monte Carlo; hand-checkered curly maple; Varmint model has light laminate stock *Features:* Sling swivels on stock and forend; patented transfer bar safety; automatic ejection; hammer extension; rebated muzzle; scope base included
*Price:*
Ultra Varmint ........................... $268.95
*Also available:*
ULTRA COMP in 30-06 and 270 Win. *Barrel Length:* 24". *Weight:* 7-8 lbs. Camo laminate stock, muzzle brake scope base included. ................... 303.95

# HECKLER & KOCH RIFLES

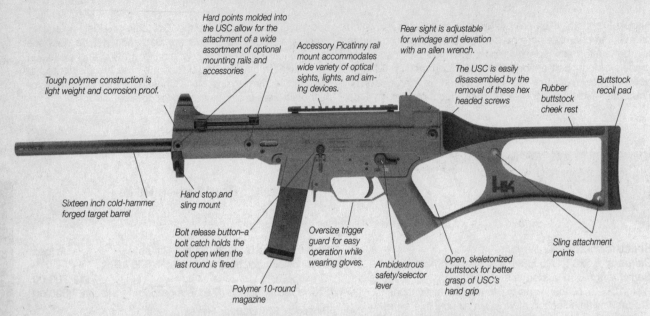

Hard points molded into the USC allow for the attachment of a wide assortment of optional mounting rails and accessories

Accessory Picatinny rail mount accommodates wide variety of optical sights, lights, and aiming devices.

Rear sight is adjustable for windage and elevation with an allen wrench.

The USC is easily disassembled by the removal of these hex headed screws

Rubber buttstock cheek rest

Buttstock recoil pad

Tough polymer construction is light weight and corrosion proof.

Sixteen inch cold-hammer forged target barrel

Hand stop and sling mount

Bolt release button–a bolt catch holds the bolt open when the last round is fired

Oversize trigger guard for easy operation while wearing gloves.

Ambidextrous safety/selector lever

Open, skeletonized buttstock for better grasp of USC's hand grip

Sling attachment points

Polymer 10-round magazine

## HECKLER & KOCH USC .45 ACP AUTOLOADING CARBINE

A combination of advanced polymers, ordnance steel and a simple blow-back action make this a reliable, lightweight autoloading rifle. An optional Picatinny rail mounts easily for attaching a scope or electronic sight. The rear sight is fully adjustable. A bolt catch holds the action open after the last round from the 10-shot polymer magazine. An oversize trigger guard and ambidextrous safety make shooting easier with gloves. The 16-inch hammer-forged barrel and skeleton polymer stock keep weight to only 6 pounds. Sling swivel holes and a rubber cheek rest and recoil pad are standard. ***Price:*** . . . . . . . . . . . . . . . . . . . **$1199.00**

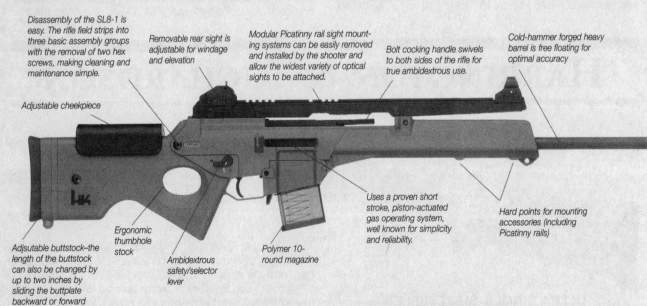

Disassembly of the SL8-1 is easy. The rifle field strips into three basic assembly groups with the removal of two hex screws, making cleaning and maintenance simple.

Removable rear sight is adjustable for windage and elevation

Modular Picatinny rail sight mounting systems can be easily removed and installed by the shooter and allow the widest variety of optical sights to be attached.

Bolt cocking handle swivels to both sides of the rifle for true ambidextrous use.

Cold-hammer forged heavy barrel is free floating for optimal accuracy

Adjustable cheekpiece

Ergonomic thumbhole stock

Adjsutable buttstock–the length of the buttstock can also be changed by up to two inches by sliding the buttplate backward or forward

Ambidextrous safety/selector lever

Polymer 10-round magazine

Uses a proven short stroke, piston-actuated gas operating system, well known for simplicity and reliability.

Hard points for mounting accessories (including Picatinny rails)

## HECKLER & KOCH SL8-1 .223 AUTOLOADING RIFLE

Built largely of polymers around a steel frame, this gas-operated autoloader weighs only 8.5 lbs with a 21" free-floating barrel. The mechanism is based on the proven German G36 design. Field-stripping to three modular components can be done in seconds with the removal of two hex screws. The thumbholes stock includes an adjustable butt and hardpoints for mounting a forend rail. A removable, adjustable rear sight complements a Picatinny scope rail that can also be removed. The safety is ambidextrous; so is the bolt cocking lever. A 10-round detachable box magazine is of clear polymer. ***Price:*** . . . . . . . . . . . . . . . . . **$1599.00**

# HENRY RIMFIRE RIFLES

**HENRY LEVER ACTION .22**

**SPECIFICATIONS**
**Calibers:** 22 S, L, LR  **Capacity:** 15 rounds  (22 LR); 17 rds. (22 L); 21 rds. (22 S) 11 rds (22 mag)  **Barrel Length:** 18"  **Overall Length:** 36.5"  **Weight:** 5.5 lbs. **Stock:** American Walnut  **Sights:** Adjustable rear; hooded front  **Features:** Grooved receiver for scope mount
**Price:** (also carbine and youth model) . . . . . . . . . . . . . . $229.95
.22 Magnum with deluxe checkered stock, 19" barrel . . . . . . . . **299.95**
"Golden Boy" replica of Henry rifle 20" octagon barrel . . . . . . . . **329.95**

**HENRY LEVER-ACTION .22 MAGNUM**

**HENRY GOLDEN BOY**

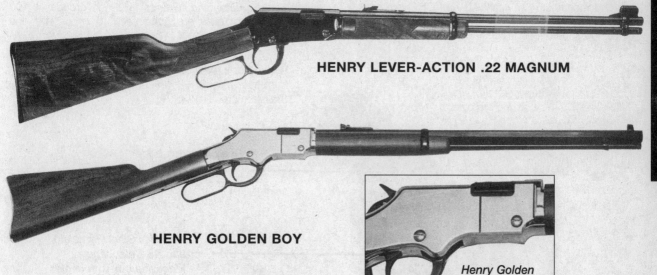

*Henry Golden Boy Detail*

**HENRY PUMP ACTION .22**

Henry Repeating Arms expands its family of .22 rifles with the introduction of the Henry Pump Action .22. Made in America, this rifle features an American walnut stock, grooved receiver for a scope mount and adjustable rear sight.
**Capacity:** 15-rounds .22 long rifle
**Barrel Length:** 18.25"  **Weight:** 5.5 lbs.
**Price:** . . . . . . . . . . . . . . . . . . . . . . . . . . . . . . . . . $249.95

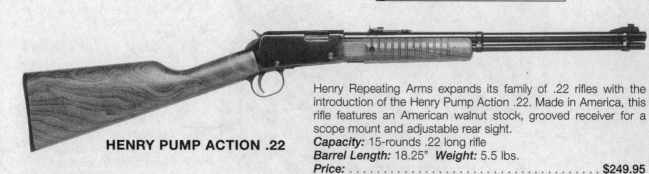

**U.S. SURVIVAL RIFLE .22**

**SPECIFICATIONS**
**Calibers:** 22 long rifle  **Capacity:** 9-shot  **Barrel Length:** 16.25"
**Overall Length:** 35.25"  **Sights:** Adjustable rear sight  **Features:** Barrel and action fit in floating waterproof stock; comes with two 8-round magazines
**Price:** . . . . . . . . . . . . . . . . . . . . . . . . . . . . . . . . . $165.00

# H-S PRECISION RIFLES

In 1978 Tom Houghton bought Atkinson Gun Company and combined it with H-S Engineering to form H-S Precision, Inc., in Prescott, Arizona. Two years later the firm began manufacturing test barrels for Winchester, and two years after that H-S began producing Fiberthane rifle stocks. In 1984 the company came up with an aluminum bedding block, now used on all its Pro-Series stocks, which appeared in 1985. They feature a blend of fiberglass, Kevlar and unidirectional carbon fiber. In 1988 H-S Precision developed a take-down rifle, receiving the patent two years later when the firm moved to Rapid City, South Dakota. There Tom Houghton and his crew updated both engineering and manufacturing with CAD and CNC technology. In 1994 the 15,000-square-foot facility grew with the addition of 10,000 square feet designated for stock production only.

By this time H-S was manufacturing synthetic stocks for both Remington and Winchester. It was also building custom rifles with its own super-accurate cut-rifled barrels. Law enforcement agencies were steady patrons. In 1996 the plant expanded by another 25 percent; the next year the series 2000 single-shot pistol appeared, followed by series 2000 rifles on the company's own actions.

The H-S Precision Pro-Series 2000 action combines many of the best features of the Winchester Model 70 and Remington 700 rifles. Available in two lengths, it is the heart of several H-S Precision semi-custom rifles, including a take-down model. Rifles of 30 caliber and smaller are guaranteed to shoot 1/2-inch groups at 100 yards. Big-bore rifles are guaranteed to shoot into one minute of angle.

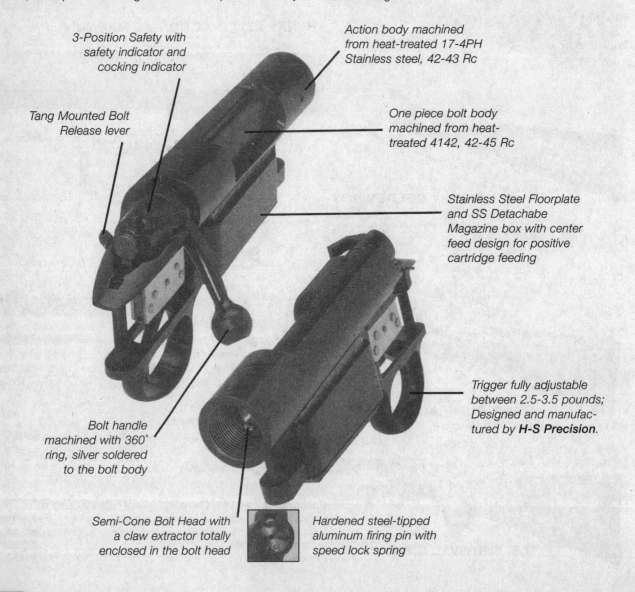

3-Position Safety with safety indicator and cocking indicator

Tang Mounted Bolt Release lever

Action body machined from heat-treated 17-4PH Stainless steel, 42-43 Rc

One piece bolt body machined from heat-treated 4142, 42-45 Rc

Stainless Steel Floorplate and SS Detachabe Magazine box with center feed design for positive cartridge feeding

Bolt handle machined with 360° ring, silver soldered to the bolt body

Trigger fully adjustable between 2.5-3.5 pounds; Designed and manufactured by **H-S Precision**.

Semi-Cone Bolt Head with a claw extractor totally enclosed in the bolt head

Hardened steel-tipped aluminum firing pin with speed lock spring

# H-S PRECISION RIFLES

## PRO-SERIES 2000

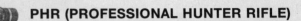

### PHR (PROFESSIONAL HUNTER RIFLE)

The Pro-Series 2000 PHR is a slightly heavier version of the Pro-Series 2000 SPR rifle. Because of the larger magnum calibers, available for the Pro-Series 2000 PHR the increased weight is a necessity. The Pro-Series 2000 PHR is designed to handle the new "super magnums" such as the 300 RemUltra Mag or the 338 Lapua.

#### FEATURES
• *Pro-Series 2000* stainless steel action, magnum only
• *Pro-Series 2000* stainless steel floorplate with detachable magazine • 3 rounds in the magazine box
• *Pro-Series 10X* match grade stainless steel barrel • Fluted (except 416 Rigby) • 24" or 26" magnum contour • Optional muzzle brake • Built in recoil reducer • Choice of color • Metal finish – Teflon® or *Pro-Series* PFTE Matte Black • Weight* – 7.75 - 8.25 pounds • Calibers – 7mm STW, 300 Win Mag, 300 Rem Ulltra Mag, 338 Win Mag, 416 Rem Mag, 375 H&H Mag, 338/300 Ultra Mag, 375/300 Ultra Mag, 338 Lapua, 416 Rigby
• *Pro-Series* synthetic stock with ful length bedding block chassis system, sporter style

### VTD (VARMINT TAKE-DOWN SYSTEM)

Pro Series 2000 Take-Down rifles are covered by the same 1/2 minute of angle accuracy and repeatability guarantee as all other Pro-Series 2000 rifles (3 shots at 100 yards). Pro-Series 2000 Take-down rifle systems are tested for accuracy and repeatability with factory match ammunition.

#### FEATURES
• *Pro-Series 2000* stainless steel action, long or short
• *Pro-Series* stainless steel floorplate with detachable magazine • 4 rounds in the magazine box, standard calibers • 3 rounds in the magazine box, magnum calibers
• *Pro-Series 10X* match grade stainless steel barrel • Fluted • 23.5" varmint contour • Optional muzzle brake • PSV29B - long action • Choice of color • Metal finish – Teflon® or *Pro-Series* PFTE Matte Black • Weight* – 8.50 - 9.00 pounds • Calibers – 308 Win, 300 Win Mag • Options • Additional caliber capabillity by adding a second barrel
• *Pro-Series* synthetic stock with ful length bedding block chassis system, varmint style

### HTR (HEAVY TACTICAL RIFLE)

#### FEATURES
• *Pro-Series 2000* stainless steel action, long or short
• *Pro-Series* stainless steel floorplate with detachable magazine • 4 rounds in the magazine box, standard calibers • 3 rounds in the magazine box, magnum calibers • 3 rounds in the magazine box, 338 Lapua
• *Pro-Series 10X* match grade stainless steel barrel, heavy barrel • Fluted • 24" heavy contour • Optional muzzle brake
• *Pro-Series* synthetic stock with ful length bedding block chassis system, tactical style • PST25 - short action, fully adjustable length of pull and cheek piece • PST26 - long action, fully adjustable length of pull and cheek piece • Choice of color • Metal finish – Teflon® or *Pro-Series* PFTE Matte Black • Weight* – 10.75 - 11.25 pounds • Calibers – 308 Win, 300 Win Mag, 338 Lapua

**Prices:** Sporter, with 2000 action . . . . . . . . . . . . . . . . . **$1,750.00**
Sporter, with customer's M70 or M700 action . . . . . . . **1,150.00**
Pro-Hunter, with 2000 action . . . . . . . . . . . . . . . . . . . . **1,895.00**
Varmint, with 2000 action . . . . . . . . . . . . . . . . . . . . . . . **1,750.00**
Varmint, with customer's M70 or M700 action . . . . . . **1,250.00**
Pro-Hunter Take-Down, with 2000 action and one barrel. **1,995.00**
Varmint Take-Down, with 2000 action and one barrel . . . **1,895.00**

Varmint Take-Down, with 2000 action and two barrels
(same head size) . . . . . . . . . . . . . . . . . . . . . . . . . . . . . **2,895.00**
Varmint Take-Down, with 2000 action and two barrels
(different head sizes) . . . . . . . . . . . . . . . . . . . . . . . . . . **3,095.00**
Additional barrels, same head size . . . . . . . . . . . . . . . . **1,000.00**
Additional barrels, different head sizes . . . . . . . . . . . . . **1,200.00**
*Tactical rifles priced on request only.*

# HOWA LIGHTNING RIFLES

## LIGHTNING BOLT-ACTION RIFLE

The rugged mono-bloc receivers on all Howa rifles are machined from a single billet of high carbon steel. The machined steel bolt boasts dual-opposed locking lugs and triple relief gas ports. Actions are fitted with a button-release hinged floorplate for fast reloading. Premium steel sporter-weight barrels are hammer-forged. A silent sliding thumb safety locks the trigger for safe loading or clearing the chamber. The stock is ultra-tough polymer.

**SPECIFICATIONS**
*Calibers:* 22-250, 223, 243, 270, 308, 30-06, 300 Win. Mag., 338 Win. Mag., 7mm Rem. Mag. *Capacity:* 5 rounds (3 in Magnum) *Barrel length:* 22" (24" in Magnum) *Overall length:* 42.5" *Weight:* 7.5 lbs. (7.7 lbs. in Magnum) *Finish:* Blue
*Price:* STANDARD MODEL . . . . . . . . . . . . . . . . . . . **$464.00**
  In Magnum calibers . . . . . . . . . . . . . . . . . . . . . **486.00**
STAINLESS . . . . . . . . . . . . . . . . . . . . . . . . . . . . . **518.00**
  In Magnum calibers . . . . . . . . . . . . . . . . . . . . . **539.00**
  HUNTER *(hardwood stock, checkered)*
VARMINT (223, 22-250) . . . . . . . . . . . . . . . . . . . . . **496.00**
  Stainless . . . . . . . . . . . . . . . . . . . . . . . . . . . . . **560.00**
  *hardwood stock add $22.00*
  Barreled actions . . . . . . . . . . . . . . . . . **$347.00-443.00**

# JARRETT CUSTOM RIFLES

## STANDARD HUNTING RIFLE

Jarrett's Standard Hunting Rifle incorporates a McMillan stock with Decelerator pad in choice of finishes. #4 match-grade barrel on Remington 700 or Winchester 70 action with Talley scope mounts. Case, sling load data and custom-loaded ammo included. *Finished Weight:* 8.5 lbs.
*Price:*. . . . . . . . . . . . . . . . . . . . . . . . . . . . . **$3,550.00**

**THE "WIND WALKER"**

## WIND WALKER

Same specifications as the Standard model, but with a Kevlar stock and skeletonized Rem. 700 action for lighter weight (finished, with Swarovski 3-10x 42 A1 scope in Talley mounts, the Windwalker weighs 7.25 lbs.). Muzzle brake, case, sling, load data and custom-loaded ammo included.
*Price:* . . . . . . . . . . . . . . . . . . . . . . . . . **Price on request**

# JARRETT CUSTOM RIFLES

## THE WALKABOUT

The WalkAbout is a short, handy rifle built on a Remington 700 short action and chambered for your choice of standard or popular wildcat cartridges. The Jarrett barrel is 20" long; the stock is by McMillan and comes in a variety of finishes.

At 7.5 pounds, finished, the WalkAbout includes Talley mounts and rings with the scope you specify. Case, sling, load data and 20 rounds of ammunition are also furnished.
*Price:* . . . . . . . . . . . . . . . . . . . . . . . . . **Price on request**

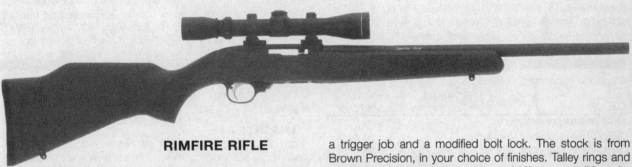

## RIMFIRE RIFLE

The Jarrett Rimfire Rifle is built on a Ruger 10/22 receiver. The 18-inch match-grade barrel is available in Target and hunting contours. Action work includes precise barrel fitting,

a trigger job and a modified bolt lock. The stock is from Brown Precision, in your choice of finishes. Talley rings and bases, and an accuracy guarantee of 1/2 m.o.a. at 50 yards, are part of the package. This is a carefully built rimfire designed for one-hole groups.
*Price:* . . . . . . . . . . . . . . . . . . . . . . . . . **Price on request**

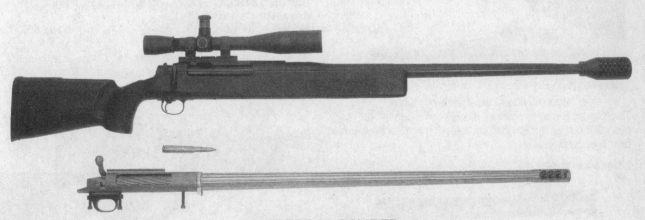

## JARRETT 50 CALIBER

The Jarrett 50 is built on a McMillan receiver in either single-shot or magazine configuration. A match-grade KP barrel with compensator, a McMillan stock and military scope mounts bring rifle weight to 28 to 45 pounds depending on your choice of barrel contour and length (30" to 34"). Jarrett

develops an accurate load and supplies 20 rounds of ammunition. Scope of choice: Leupold Ultra 24X.
*Not shown:* Jarrett special rifles made to order in Tactical, Bench Rest, Youth and Professional Hunter styles.
*Price:* . . . . . . . . . . . . . . . . . . . . . . . . . **Price on request**

# JOHANNSEN EXPRESS RIFLES

Three models are available - the "Classic Safari", the "Safari" and the "Tradition". The first of the three, the "Classic Safari", is the choice of preference for those interested in stalking the Big Five. Equipped with a scope, the "Safari" offers exceptionally reliable accuracy during the day or under poor light conditions. The "Tradition" is ideal for the globe-trotting big-game hunter. All models are available in various calibers with standard and custom features, and each rifle is produced individually. When you buy a Johannsen Express Rifle, you get true custom work.

### TRADITION

### "SAFARI"

Double square bridge action without thumbcut. 4-lb. double-pull trigger. Three-position safety with horizontal lever. Bolt handle close to side of action. Especially suitable for EXPERT scope mount. 2-mm silver bead combined with fold-away 4-mm Holland & Holland-type ivory bead. Express sight with two leaves. Safari-style stock with 1-3/4"/2-1/2" drop. Oil finish.
26" barrel. Length overall 47". Weight from approx. 8 lbs. 6 oz. depending upon caliber. *Standard calibers:* .375 H & H Magnum, 4-shot, or .416 Rigby, 3-shot.
*Price:* . . . . . . . . . . . . . . . . . . . . . . . . . . . . . **$10,250.00**

*Magazine capacities, maximum:*

| CALIBER | NORMAL FLOORPLATE | RIGBY FLOORPLATE |
|---|---|---|
| .300 Weatherby Magnum | 4 | 5 |
| .338-378 Weatherby Magnum | 3 | 4 |
| .375 H & H Magnum | 4 | 5 |
| .416 Rigby | 3 | 4 |
| .450 Dakota | 3 | 4 |
| .500 Jeffery | 3 | 4 |

*Other calibers upon request.*

### "CLASSIC SAFARI"

Single square bridge action with thumbcut. 4-lb. double-pull trigger. Three-position wing safety. Traditional bolt handle. 2-mm silver bead combined with a fold-away 4-mm Holland & Holland-type ivory bead. Express sight with two leaves. Safari-style stock with 1-3/4"/2-1/2" drop. Oil finish. 24" barrel. Length overall 45". Weight from approx. 8 lbs. 3 oz. depending upon caliber. *Standard calibers:* .375 H & H Magnum, 4-shot, or .416 Rigby. 3-shot.
*Price:* . . . . . . . . . . . . . . . . . . . . . . . . . . . . **$9,500.00**

### "TRADITION"

Double square bridge action without thumbcut. Adjustable-pull single-set trigger. Three-position safety with horizontal lever. Low bolt handle. Especially suitable for EXPERT scope mount. "Masterpiece" front sight base with 2.5-mm fluorescent bead. Express sight with two leaves. Stock with straight comb and 1-3/4"/2" drop. Oil finish. 26" barrel. Length overall 47". Weight from approx. 8 lbs. depending upon caliber. *Standard calibers:* .300 Weatherby Magnum, 4-shot, .375 H & H Magnum, 4-shot.
*Price:* . . . . . . . . . . . . . . . . . . . . . . . . . . . . **$10,550.00**

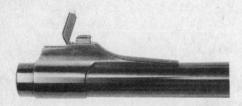

### HOLLAND & HOLLAND-TYPE NIGHT SIGHT
The "Classic Safari" and "Safari" models come with a 4-mm ivory bead that can be flipped up to cover the 2-mm silver bead under poor light conditions.

### EXPRESS SIGHT
The rear sight with its two leaves fits into a special ring base. The rear sight base extends around the barrel and has the second recoil shoulder on the underside, which is important for large-bore rifles.

**WING SAFETY** – The "Classic Safari" features a wing safety with "safe" and "fire" clearly indicated in gold.
**PEEP SIGHT** – For precision sighting with open sights - or to compensate for less than perfect vision - the peep sight mounted on the cocking piece can be raised into position.

# KBI/CHARLES DALY RIFLES

**MODEL CDGA 6345 EMPIRE GRADE
SEMIAUTOMATIC 22LR**

**MODEL CDGA 4103 FIELD GRADE BOLT ACTION**

**STANDARD M-20P SEMIAUTOMATIC**

**MODEL M-12Y YOUTH BOLT ACTION**

## KBI/CHARLES DALY RIFLE SPECIFICATIONS

| ITEM NO. | CAPACITY | CALIBER | BARREL LENGTH | LENGTH | OVERALL PRICE |
|---|---|---|---|---|---|
| **FIELD GRADE** | | | | | |
| CDGA 4103 | 6 | 22LR | 22 5/8" | 41" | $134.95 |
| CDGA 4164 | 10 | 22LR | 20 1/4" | 40 1/2" | 134.95 |
| CDGA 4238 | Single Shot | 22LR | 16 1/4" | 32" | 154.95 |
| CDGA 4279 | 6 | 22LR | 17 1/2" | 34 3/8" | 144.95 |
| **SUPERIOR GRADE** | | | | | |
| CDGA 5047 | 6 | 22LR | 22 5/8" | 41 1/4" | 189.95 |
| CDGA 5159 | 5 | 22 MRF | 22 5/8" | 41 1/4" | 204.95 |
| CDGA 5261 | 5 | 22 Hornet | 22 5/8" | 41 1/4" | 364.95 |
| CDGA 5302 | 10 | 22LR | 20 1/4" | 40 1/2" | 204.95 |
| **EMPIRE GRADE** | | | | | |
| CDGA 6116 | 6 | 22LR | 22 5/8" | 41 1/4" | 339.95 |
| CDGA 6208 | 5 | 22 MRF | 22 5/8" | 41 1/4" | 364.95 |
| CDGA 6270 | 5 | 22 Hornet | 22 5/8" | 41 1/4" | 469.95 |
| CDGA 6345 | 10 | 22LR | 20 1/4" | 40 1/4" | 324.95 |

# KIMBER RIFLES

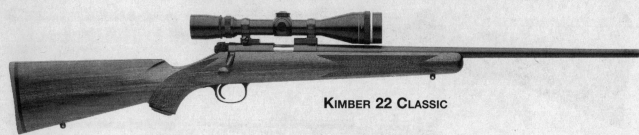

**KIMBER 22 CLASSIC**

### Prices:

CLASSIC . . . . . . . . . . . . . . . . . . . . . . . . . . . . . $950.00

SVT (SHORT/VARMINT/TARGET) . . . . . . . . . . . . . . 950.00

HS (HUNTER SILHOUETTE) . . . . . . . . . . . . . . . . $775.00

SUPERAMERICA . . . . . . . . . . . . . . . . . . . . . . 1,560.00

## MODEL 82C 22 LR SPECIFICATIONS

| MODEL: | CLASSIC | SVT | SUPERAMERICA | HS |
|---|---|---|---|---|
| WEIGHT: | 6.5 lbs. | 7.5 lbs. | 6.5 lbs. | 7 lbs. |
| OVERALL LENGTH: | 40.5" | 36.5" | 40.5" | 42.5" |
| ACTION TYPE: | Rear Locking Repeater, Mauser Claw | Rear Locking Single Shot, Mauser Claw | Rear Locking Repeater, Mauser Claw | Rear Locking Repeater, Mauser Claw |
| CAPACITY: | 5-Shot Clip | | | |
| TRIGGER: PRESSURE | Fully Adjustable Set at 2.0 lbs. | Fully Adjustable Set at 2.0 lbs. | Fully Adjustable Set at 2.0 lbs. | Fully Adjustable Set at 2.0 lbs. |
| BARREL LENGTH: GROOVES TWIST | 22" 8 16" | 18" Fluted 8 16" | 22" 8 16" | 24" 8 16" |
| STOCK: GRADE WALNUT CHECKERING (LPI) COVERAGE | A Claro 18 Side Panel | Gray Laminate None NA | AAA Claro 22 Full Coverage Wrap Around | A Claro 18 Side Panel |
| LENGTH OF PULL | 13 ⅝" | 13 ⅝" | 13 ⅝" | 13 ⅝" |
| METAL FINISH: | Polished & Blued | Stainless steel bbl. Matte blued action | Polished & Blued | Matte "rust" type blue |

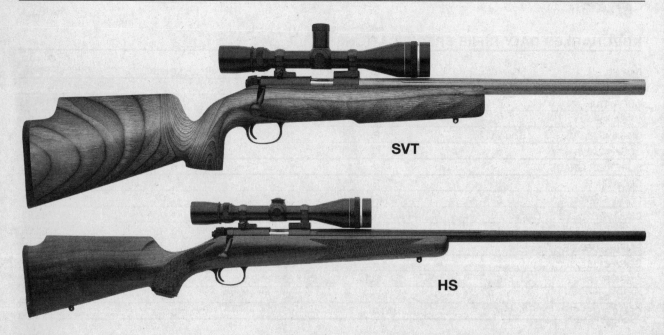

**SVT**

**HS**

# KRIEGHOFF DOUBLE RIFLES

### CLASSIC SIDE-BY-SIDE DOUBLE RIFLE

Krieghoff's Classic Side-by-Side offers many standard features, including: Schnable forearm...classic English-style stock with rounded cheekpiece...UAS anti-doubling device...1" quick-detachable sling swivels... Decelerator recoil pad...short opening angle for fast loading ...compact action with reinforced sidewalls...sliding, self-adjusting wedge for secure bolt...automatic hammer safety...horizontal firing-pins...Purdey-style barrel extension.

### SPECIFICATIONS
*Calibers: Standard*—7x65R, 308 Win., 30-06, 30R Blaser, 8x57 JRS, 8X75 JRS, 9.3X74R; *Magnum*—375 H&H Flanged Mag. N.E., 375 H&H Mag., 416 Rigby, 458 Win. Mag., 470 N.E., 500 N.E.   *Action:* Thumb-cocking break/action *Barrel length:* 23.5 *Trigger:* Double triggers with steel trigger guard *Weight:* 7.5 to 11 lbs. (depending on caliber and wood density)  *Options:* 21.5" barrel; engraved sideplates

*Prices:* STANDARD . . . . . . . . . . . . . . . . . . . . . . $7,850.00
Interchangeable barrels
   (installed, w/extra forearm) . . . . . . . . . . . . . . **4,500.00**
MAGNUM . . . . . . . . . . . . . . . . . . . . . . . . . . . . **9,450.00**
Interchangeable barrels . . . . . . . . . . . . . . . . . . **5,500.00**

---

# L.A.R. GRIZZLY RIFLE

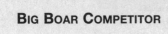

### BIG BOAR COMPETITOR

### BIG BOAR COMPETITOR

### SPECIFICATIONS
*Caliber:* 50 BMG
*Capacity:* Single shot
*Action:* Bolt action, bull pup, breechloading
*Barrel length:* 36"
*Overall length:* 45 1/2" *Weight:* 30.4 lbs.
*Safety:* Thumb safety

*Features:* All-steel construction; receiver made of 4140 alloy steel, heat-treated to 42 R/C; bolt made of 4340 alloy steel; low recoil (like 12 ga. shotgun)
*Prices:* . . . . . . . . . . . . . . . . . . . . . . . . . . . . $2,570.00
PARKERIZED . . . . . . . . . . . . . . . . . . . . . . . . . **2,670.00**
NICKEL FRAME . . . . . . . . . . . . . . . . . . . . . . . **2,820.00**
FULL NICKEL . . . . . . . . . . . . . . . . . . . . . . . . **2,920.00**

# LAZZERONI RIFLES

These state-of-the-art rifles feature 17R stainess steel receivers with two massive locking lugs, a match grade 416R stainless steel barrel, fully adjustable benchrest-style trigger, and a Lazzeroni-designed synthetic stock that is hand-bedded using aluminum pillar blocks. Included is a precision-machined floorplate/triggerguard assembly.

## MODEL L2000ST

### SPECIFICATIONS

**Calibers:** 6.53 (.257) Scramjet®; 7.21 (.284) Firebird™; 7.82 (.308) Warbird®; 8.59 (.338) Titan® **Capacity:** 4 rounds (1 in chamber) **Barrel Length:** 27" **Overall Length:** 47.5"

**Weight:** 8.1 lbs. **Stock:** Lazzeroni fiberglass sporter; right or left hand available
**Prices:** L2000ST . . . . . . . . . . . . . . . . . . . . . . $4,195.00

## MODEL L2000SP
## (Scope not included)

### SPECIFICATIONS

**Calibers:** 6.53 (.257) Scramjet®; 7.21 (.284) Firebird™; 7.82 (.308) Warbird®; 8.59 (.338) Titan® **Capacity:** 4 rounds (1 in chamber) **Barrel Length:** 25" **Overall Length:** 45.5"

**Weight:** 7.8 lbs. **Stock:** Lazzeroni fiberglass thumbhole; right hand only
**Price:** L2000SP . . . . . . . . . . . . . . . . . . . . . . $4,195.00

## MODEL L2000DG

### SPECIFICATIONS

**Calibers:** 10.57 (.416) Meteor® only **Capacity:** 4 rounds (one in chamber) **Barrel Length:** 24" **Overall Length:** 44.5" **Weight:** 9.6 lbs. **Stock:** Lazzeroni fiberglass sporter; right or left hand available.
**Price:** L2000SP . . . . . . . . . . . . . . . . . . . . . . $4,395.00

## MODEL L2000SA

### SPECIFICATIONS

**Calibers:** 6.17 (.253) Spitfire®; 6.71 (.264) Phantom®; 7.21 (.284) Tomahawk®; 7.82 (.308) Patriot®; 8.59 (.338) Galaxy® **Capacity:** 4 rounds, 1 in chamber (Tomahawk, Patriot, Galaxy); 5 rounds, 1 in chamber (Spitfire, Phantom)

**Barrel Length:** 24" (except Galaxy) **Overall Length:** 42.5" **Weight:** 6.8 lbs. **Stock:** Lazzeroni slimline stock; right or left hand avail.
**Price:** L2000SA . . . . . . . . . . . . . . . . . . . . . . $4,195.00

# LONE STAR RIFLE CO., INC.

Lone Star specializes in rolling block rifles, a design popularized by Remington after the Civil War. Some buffalo hunters used rolling blocks because, like the fabled Sharps, they could handle large, powerful cartridges. Now Lone Star is building commercial and custom rifles on these actions. Styles available include:
• Black Powder Silhouette • Creedmoor • Sporting
• Deluxe Sporting • Buffalo Rifle • Custer Commemorative
• Gove Underlever • Cowboy Action

Standard rifles are available in three configurations and come with round barrels, single trigger, case-colored actions and straight-grained American walnut stocks. The match-grade barrels are the same as those used on custom models. Chamberings for the standard rifles include:
• 40-60 and 45-70 in the Silhouette model
• 30-40 Krag in the Sporting model 32-40, 38-55, 40-65, 45-70 and 45 Long Colt in the Cowboy Action model
***Price:*** standard rifles. . . . . . . . . . . . . . . . . . . . **$1,495.00**

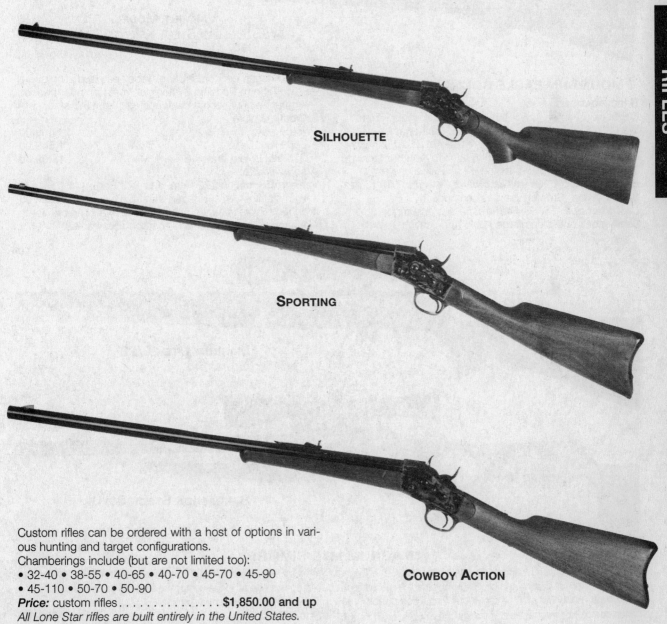

**SILHOUETTE**

**SPORTING**

**COWBOY ACTION**

Custom rifles can be ordered with a host of options in various hunting and target configurations.
Chamberings include (but are not limited too):
• 32-40 • 38-55 • 40-65 • 40-70 • 45-70 • 45-90
• 45-110 • 50-70 • 50-90
***Price:*** custom rifles. . . . . . . . . . . . . . **$1,850.00 and up**
*All Lone Star rifles are built entirely in the United States.*

# MAGNUM RESEARCH

**MOUNTAIN EAGLE**

**VARMINT MODEL**
W/STAINLESS STEEL KRIEGER BARREL

## MOUNTAIN EAGLE BOLT-ACTION RIFLE

**SPECIFICATIONS**
**Calibers:** 270 Win., 280 Rem., 30-06 Springfield, 7mm Mag., 300 Wby. Mag., 300 Win. Mag., 338 Win. Mag., 340 Wby. Mag., 375 H&H Mag., 416 Rem. Mag.
**Capacity:** 5-shot magazine (long action); 4-shot (Magnum action) **Action:** SAKO-built to MRI specifications
**Barrel length:** 24" **Overall length:** 44" **Weight:** 7 lb. 13 oz.
**Sights:** None **Stock:** Fiberglass composite
**Length of pull:** 13 ⁵/₈" **Features:** Adjustable trigger; high comb stock one-piece forged bolt; free-floating, match-

grade, Krieger, benchrest barrel; recoil pad and sling swivel studs; Platform Bedding System for front lug; pillar-bedded rear guard screw; lengthened receiver ring; solid steel hinged floorplate
**Price:**. . . . . . . . . . . . . . . . . . . . . . . . . . . **$1,499.00**
  Left Hand . . . . . . . . . . . . . . . . . . . . . . . **1,549.00**
  375 H&H Mag. and 416 Rem. Mag. . . . . . . . . **1,799.00**
**Also available:**
**VARMINT EDITION.** In 222 Rem. and 223 Rem.
  with stainless steel Krieger barrel (26") . . . . . **$1629.00**
*Mountain Eagle rifles are now available in a left-hand version, and with "Magnum Lite" carbon fiber barrels.*

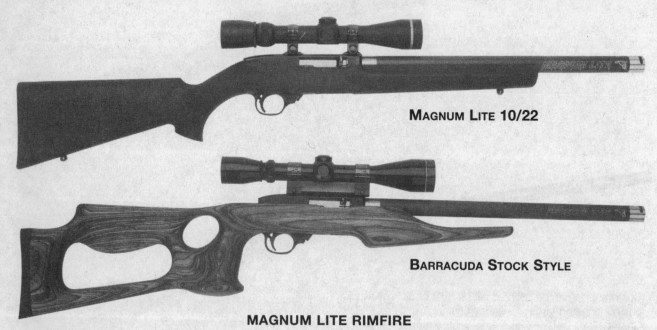

**MAGNUM LITE 10/22**

**BARRACUDA STOCK STYLE**

## MAGNUM LITE RIMFIRE

The Magnum Research Magnum Lite 10/22 rifle is built on a Ruger action with rotary magazine and blowback, autoloading mechanism. The carbon-fiber barrel is 75 percent lighter than a comparable steel barrel but gives match-quality accuracy. An integral muzzle port

reduces whip. Available in .22 Long Rifle and .22 WMR, the Magnum Lite comes with a Hogue composite stock of traditional design, or a Turner laminated "Barracuda" stock.
**Price:** . . . . . . . . . . . . . . . . . . . . . . . . . . . . **$799.00**

# MARLIN .22 RIFLES

## MODEL 60

## MODEL 60C

### SPECIFICATIONS

*Caliber:* 22 Long Rifle *Capacity:* 14-shot tubular magazine *Barrel Length:* 22" *Overall Length:* 40.5" *Weight:* 5.5 lbs. *Sights:* Ramp front sight with brass bead and Wide-Scan hood; adjustable open rear, receiver grooved for scope mount *Action:* Self-loading; side ejection; manual and automatic "last-shot" hold-open devices; receiver top has serrated, nonglare finish; crossbolt safety *Stock:* One-piece Maine birch Monte Carlo stock, press-checkered, with full pistol grip; Mar-Shield® finish

*Price:* . . . . . . . . . . . . . . . . . . . . . . . . . . . . . . $172.00
  Stainess 60SB . . . . . . . . . . . . . . . . . . . . . 219.00
  Stainess, synthetic stock 60SSK . . . . . . . . . . . 236.00
  Stainess, laminated stock 60SS . . . . . . . . . . . 273.00
  New 60C with blued steel, camo stock . . . . . . . 203.00

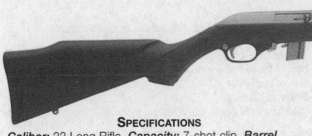

## MODEL 70PSS "PAPOOSE"

### SPECIFICATIONS

*Caliber:* 22 Long Rifle *Capacity:* 7-shot clip *Barrel Length:* 16.25" *Overall Length:* 35.25" *Weight:* 3.25 lbs.

*Action:* Self-loading; side ejection; manual bolt hold-open; crossbolt safety; stainless-steel breech bolt and barrel *Sights:* Screw adjustable open rear; ramp front; receiver grooved for scope mount *Stock:* Black fiberglass-filled synthetic with abbrev. forend, nickel-plated swivel studs

*Price:* . . . . . . . . . . . . . . . . . . . . . . . . . . . . . . $278.00

## MODEL 7000

### SPECIFICATIONS

*Caliber:* 22 LR *Capacity:* 10 shots *Action:* Self-loading; side ejection *Barrel Length:* 18" heavy target; recessed muzzle (16 grooves) *Overall Length:* 37" *Weight:* 5.25 lbs.

*Stock:* Monte Carlo black fiberglass-filled synthetic *Sights:* No sights; receiver grooved for scope mount (1" scope ring mounts standard) *Features:* Manual bolt hold-open; crossbolt safety; steel charging handle

*Price:* . . . . . . . . . . . . . . . . . . . . . . . . . . . . . . $232.00
*Also available:* MODEL 795. Same as Model 7000 but w/screw-adjustable open rear sight w/brass bead; no scope mount *Weight:* 4.5 lbs. . . . . . . . . . . . . . . . . . . . . . $164.00

## MODEL 922M SELF-LOADER

### SPECIFICATIONS

*Caliber:* 22 WMRF *Capacity:* 5-shot nickel-plated magazine *Barrel Length:* 20.5" Micro-Groove *Overall Length:* 39.75" *Weight:* 6.5 lbs. *Sights:* Adjustable folding semi-buckhorn rear sight; ramp front sight w/brass bead and removable Wide-Scan™ hood *Stock:* Monte Carlo walnut finished hardwood, checkered w/rubber rifle butt pad and swivel studs *Features:* Garand type safety; magazine safety; receiver sandblasted to prevent glare; manual bolt hold-open; automatic last-shot bolt hold-open

*Price:* . . . . . . . . . . . . . . . . . . . . . . . . . . . . . . $441.00

# MARLIN .22 RIFLES

### MODEL 25NC (shown) AND 25N

A bolt-action, bottom-fed repeater, the 25N holds 7 .22 Long Rifle cartridges. The 22" Micro-Groove barrel ensures fine accuracy. Fitted with open sights, this rifle readily accepts a scope and can be ordered with one. The hardwood stock has a natural finish. Mossy Oak Break-Up camouflage distinguishes the 25NC stock. **Weight:** 5.5 lbs.

**Price:** 25N . . . . . . . . . . . . . . . . . . . . . . . . . . . . **$195.00**
  with scope . . . . . . . . . . . . . . . . . . . . . . . . . . . . **201.00**
  25NC. . . . . . . . . . . . . . . . . . . . . . . . . . . . . . . . . . . **228.00**

### MODEL 25MN

#### SPECIFICATIONS

**Caliber:** 22 WMR (not interchangeable w/other 22 cartridges) **Capacity:** 7-shot clip magazine **Barrel Length:** 22" with Micro-Groove® rifling **Overall Length:** 41"

**Weight:** 6 lbs. **Sights:** Adjustable open rear; ramp front sight; receiver grooved for scope mount
**Stock:** One-piece walnut finished press-checkered Maine birch Monte Carlo w/full pistol grip; Mar-Shield® finish; swivel studs
**Price:** . . . . . . . . . . . . . . . . . . . . . . . . . . . . . . . . **$223.00**
  Model 25N in .22 Long Rifle . . . . . . . . . . . . . . **195.00**

### MODEL 81TS

#### SPECIFICATIONS

**Caliber:** 22 Short, Long or Long Rifle **Capacity:** Tubular magazine holds 25 Short, 19 Long, 17 Long Rifle cartridges

**Barrel Length:** 22" w/Micro-Groove® rifling (16 grooves) **Overall Length:** 41" **Weight:** 6 lbs. **Sights:** Screw-adjustable open rear; ramp front **Stock:** Monte Carlo black fiberglass-filled synthetic w/swivel studs and molded-in checkering
**Price:** . . . . . . . . . . . . . . . . . . . . . . . . . . . . . . . . **$196.00**
  w/scope . . . . . . . . . . . . . . . . . . . . . . . . . . . . . . . . **203.00**

### MODEL 883

#### SPECIFICATIONS

**Caliber:** 22 WMR (not interchangeable with other 22 cartridges) **Capacity:** 12-shot tubular magazine with patented closure system **Action:** Bolt action; positive thumb safety; red cocking indicator **Barrel Length:** 22" with Micro-Groove® rifling (20 grooves) **Overall Length:** 41" **Weight:** 6 lbs. **Sights:** Adjustable folding semibuckhorn rear; ramp front with Wide-Scan hood™; receiver grooved for scope mount **Stock:** Cut-checkered Monte Carlo American black walnut with full pistol grip; rubber buttpad; swivel studs; tough Mar-Shield® finish

**Price:** . . . . . . . . . . . . . . . . . . . . . . . . . . . . . . . . **$308.00**
**Also available** in stainless steel with laminated stock
  Model 883SS . . . . . . . . . . . . . . . . . . . . . . . . . . **$326.00**
  Clip-fed Model 882 (not shown) . . . . . . . . . . . . **296.00**
  882 SS stainless, synthetic stock . . . . . . . . . . . **314.00**
  882 SV stainless, synthetic, heavy barrel . . . . . . **309.00**
  882L blued, laminated stock . . . . . . . . . . . . . . . **313.00**

# MARLIN .22 RIFLES

## MARLIN 15YN "LITTLE BUCKAROO™"

SINGLE SHOT 22 BEGINNER'S RIFLE

### SPECIFICATIONS

*Caliber:* 22 Short, Long or Long Rifle *Capacity:* Single shot *Action:* Bolt action; easy-load feed throat; thumb safety; red cocking indicator *Barrel Length:* 16.25" (16 grooves) *Overall Length:* 33.25" *Weight:* 4.25 lbs. *Sights:* Adjustable open rear; ramp front sight *Stock:* One-piece walnut-finished press-checkered Maine birch Monte Carlo w/full pistol grip; tough Mar-Shield® finish *Price:* . . . . . . . . . . . . . . . . . . . . . . . . . . . . . . . . . $193.00

## MARLIN 1897 COWBOY

This .22 rimfire with 24" octagon barrel is built on a Model 39 action. The full-length magazine holds 26 short, 21 long and 19 long rifle rounds. A two-level scope adapter lets you add 3/4- or 7/8-inch scopes as well as standard 1" models. Marble open sights and a quick-takedown receiver are standard, as is a checkered, straight-grip walnut stock. *Overall length:* 40", *Weight:* 6-1/2 pounds. *Price:* . . . . . . . . . . . . . . . . . . . . . . . . . . . . . . $687.00

## MARLIN 7000T WITH SCOPE

This accurate, autoloading .22 has a Micro-Groove target barrel 18" long. The nickel-plated box magazine holds 10 rounds. The red, white and blue laminated birch stock accepts forend accessories on an aluminum tail. A rubber buttplate is adjustable for drop, length of pull and cant. *Length:* 37", *Weight:* 7-1/2 pounds. *Price:* . . . . . . . . . . . . . . . . . . . `. . . . . . . . . . . . . $465.00

# MARLIN LEVER-ACTION .22 RIFLE

## MARLIN GOLDEN 39AS

*Introduced in 1891, the Marlin lever-action 22 is the oldest shoulder gun still being manufactured.*

**SOLID RECEIVER TOP.** You can easily mount a scope on your Marlin 39 by screwing on the machined scope adapter base provided. The screw-on base is a neater, more versatile method of mounting a scope on a 22 sporting rifle. The solid top receiver and scope adapter base provide a maximum in eye relief adjustment. If you prefer iron sights, you'll find the 39 receiver clean, flat and sandblasted to prevent glare. Exclusive brass magazine tube

**MICRO-GROOVE® BARREL.** Marlin's famous rifling system of multi-grooving has consistently produced fine accuracy because the system grips the bullet more securely, minimizes distortion, and provides a better gas seal.

And the Model 39 maximizes accuracy with the heaviest barrels available on any lever-action 22.

### SPECIFICATIONS

*Caliber:* 22 Short, Long and Long Rifle *Capacity:* Tubular magazine holds 26 Short, 21 Long and 19 LR cartridges *Action:* Lever; solid top receiver; side ejection; one-step takedown; deeply blued metal surfaces; receiver top sandblasted to prevent glare; hammer block safety; rebounding hammer *Barrel:* 24" with Micro-Groove® rifling (16 grooves) *Overall Length:* 40" *Weight:* 6.5 lbs. *Sights:* Adjustable folding semibuckhorn rear, ramp front sight with Wide-Scan™ hood; solid top receiver tapped for scope mount or receiver sight; scope adapter base; offset hammer spur for scope use—works right or left *Stock:* Two-piece cut-checkered American black walnut w/fluted comb; full pistol grip and forend; blued-steel forend cap; swivel studs; grip cap; Mar-Shield® finish; rubber buttpad *Price:* . . . . . . . . . . . . . . . . . . . . . . . . . . . . $509.00

# MARLIN LEVER-ACTION RIFLES

### NEW MODEL 1894P
### with Ported Barrel

**44 Rem. Magnum/44 Special.** Lever action; 8-shot tubular magazine; squared finger lever; 16.25" ported barrel with deep-cut Ballard-type rifling; hammer block safety; 33.75" o.a. length; approx. wt. 5.75 lbs.; adjustable semi-buckhorn folding rear, ramp front sight with brass bead and Wide-Scan™ hood; solid top receiver tapped for scope mount or receiver sight. Straight-grip genuine American black walnut checkered stock with tough Mar-Shield® finish; deeply blued metal surfaces; receiver top sandblasted to prevent glare; ventilated recoil pad; swivel studs; blued steel fore-end cap; offset hammer spur for scope use – works right or left. Safety lock included.
**Price:** . . . . . . . . . . . . . . . . . . . . . . . . . . . . . . . . . . . . . . . $530.00

**444P OUTFITTER**

### MARLIN 444P AND 1895G

The 444P "Outfitter" and 1895G "Guide Gun" are chambered in .444 Marlin and .45-70 respectively. They feature 2/3-length magazines (5-shot and 4-shot capacity), straight-grip walnut stocks with cut checkering, recoil pads and porting at the muzzle to reduce kick. The Guide Gun received Petersen Publishing's 1998 prestigious "Rifle of the Year" award. **Length:** 37" (barrel 18.5") **Weight:** 6.75 pounds
**Price:** (with sights) . . . . . . . . . . . . . . . . . . . . . . . $595.00

**COWBOY GUN**

### MARLIN 336 COWBOY GUN

Available in 30/30 and 38/55, this rifle has a 24-inch octagon barrel and 6-shot full-length magazine. The checkered, straight-grip walnut stock has a hard-rubber butt. Ballard-type rifling gives fine accuracy with cast bullets. Marble open sights add a traditional touch. **Length:** 42-1/2 inches, **Weight:** 7-1/2 pounds
**Price:** . . . . . . . . . . . . . . . . . . . . . . . . . . . . . . . . . . . . $677.00

### NEW MODEL 336M in
### Stainless Steel with Cut Checkering

**30/30 Win.** Lever action; 6-shot tubular magazine; approx. wt. 7lbs.; 20" stainless steel Micro-Groove® barrel; hammer block safety; 38.5" o.a. length; genuine American black walnut checkered pistol grip stock with fluted comb and tough Mar-Shield® finish; rubber rifle butt pad; nickel-plated swivel studs; adjustable folding semi-buckhorn rear, ramp front sight with brass bead and removable Wide-Scan™ hood; tapped for receiver sight and scope mount; offset hammer spur for scope use – works right or left. Stainless steel receiver, barrel, lever, trigger guard plate, magazine tube and loading gate. Safety lock included.
**Price:** . . . . . . . . . . . . . . . . . . . . . . . . . . . . . . . . . . . . $591.00

# MARLIN LEVER-ACTION CARBINES

## MODEL 1894 COWBOY II

**SPECIFICATIONS**
**Calibers:** 357 Mag./38 Special, 44-40, 44 Mag./44 Special, 45 LC
**Action:** Lever action w/squared finger lever

**Capacity:** 10-shot tubular magazine
**Barrel Length:** 24" tapered octagon (6 grooves)
**Overall Length:** 41.5"  **Weight:** 7.5 lbs.
**Sights:** Adjustable semi-buckhorn rear; carbine front
**Stock:** Straight-grip American black walnut w/cut-checkering and hard rubber buttplate
**Features:** Mar-Shield™ finish; blued steel forend cap; side ejection; blued metal surfaces; hammer block safety
**Price:** .................................. $752.00

## MARLIN 1894S

**SPECIFICATIONS**
**Calibers:** 44 Rem. Mag./44 Special
**Capacity:** 10-shot tubular magazine
**Action:** Lever action w/square finger lever; hammer block safety

**Barrel Length:** 20" w/deep-cut Ballard-type rifling
**Sights:** Ramp front sight w/brass bead; adjustable semi-buckhorn folding rear and Wide-Scan™ hood; solid-top receiver tapped for scope mount or receiver sight
**Overall Length:** 37.5"  **Weight:** 6 lbs.
**Stock:** Checkered American black walnut stock w/Mar-Shield® finish; blued steel forend cap; swivel studs
**Price:** .................................. $510.00
**Also Available:** MODEL 1894CS (not shown) similar to 1894S except .357 Magnum, 18.5" barrel, 9-shot magazine.
**Price:** .................................. $510.00

## NEW MODEL 1895M 450 MARLIN MAGNUM with Ported Barrel

**Chambered for new belted magnum cartridge.** Lever action; 4-shot tubular magazine; 18.5" ported barrel with Ballard-type cut rifling; hammer block safety; 37" o.a. length; approx. wt. 6.75 lbs.; genuine American black walnut straight-grip stock with cut checkering; ventilated recoil pad; tough Mar-Shield® finish; swivel studs; adjustable fold-ing semi-buckhorn rear, ramp front sight with brass bead and Wide-Scan™ hood; receiver tapped for scope mount or receiver sight; offset hammer spur for scope use – works right or left; deeply blued metal surfaces; receiver top sand-blasted to prevent glare. Safety lock included.
**Price:** .................................. $640.00

# MARLIN LEVER-ACTION CARBINES

### MARLIN 1895SS

**SPECIFICATIONS**
*Caliber:* 45-70 Government
*Capacity:* 4-shot tubular magazine
*Action:* Lever action; hammer block safety; receiver top sandblasted to prevent glare
*Barrel:* 22" w/deep-cut Ballard-type rifling
*Sights:* Ramp front sight w/brass bead; adjustable

semibuckhorn folding rear and Wide-Scan™ hood; receiver tapped for scope mount or receiver sight
*Overall Length:* 40.5"  *Weight:* 7.5 lbs.
*Stock:* Checkered American black walnut pistol-grip stock w/rubber rifle buttpad and Mar-Shield® finish; swivel studs
*Price:* . . . . . . . . . . . . . . . . . . . . . . . . . . . . . . . $582.00
*Also available:*
MODEL 1895G "GUIDE GUN" WITH PORTED BARREL. Same caliber, capacity, action, sights. Stock has straight grip, ventilated recoil pad. *Barrel Length:* 18.5" *Overall Length:* 37" *Weight:* 6.75 lbs.
*Price:* . . . . . . . . . . . . . . . . . . . . . . . . . . . . . . . $595.00

### MARLIN 336CS

**SPECIFICATIONS**
*Calibers:* 30-30 Win., and 35 Rem.
*Capacity:* 6-shot tubular magazine
*Action:* Lever action w/hammer block safety; deeply blued metal surfaces; receiver top sandblasted to prevent glare

*Barrel:* 20" Micro-Groove® barrel
*Sights:* Adjustable folding semibuckhorn rear; ramp front sight w/brass bead and Wide-Scan™ hood; tapped for receiver sight and scope mount; offset hammer spur for scope use (works right or left)
*Overall Length:* 38.5"  *Weight:* 7 lbs.
*Stock:* Checkered American black walnut pistol-grip stock w/fluted comb and Mar-Shield® finish; rubber rifle buttpad; swivel studs
*Price:* . . . . . . . . . . . . . . . . . . . . . . . . . . . . . . . $493.00
Model 336 AS 30-30 onlly, birch stock. . . . . . . 418.00

### MODEL 444SS

**SPECIFICATIONS**
*Caliber:* 444 Marlin
*Capacity:* 5-shot tubular magazine
*Barrel:* 22" w/deep-cut Ballard-type rifling
*Overall Length:* 40.5"  *Weight:* 7.5 lbs.
*Stock:* Checkered American black walnut pistol grip stock

with rubber rifle buttpad; swivel studs
*Sights:* Ramp front sight with brass bead and Wide-Scan™ hood; adjustable semibuckhorn folding rear; receiver tapped for scope mount or receiver sight
*Price:* . . . . . . . . . . . . . . . . . . . . . . . . . . . . . . . $582.00

# MARLIN 22 TARGET RIFLE

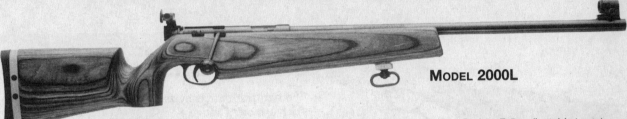

**MODEL 2000L**

### SPECIFICATIONS

*Caliber:* 22 LR only  *Capacity:* Single shot  *Action:* Bolt action; thumb safety; patented two-stage target trigger; red cocking indicator  *Barrel Length:* 22" heavy, selected Micro-Groove w/match chamber and recessed muzzle  *Overall*

*Length:* 41"  *Weight:* 8 lbs.  *Sights:* Fully adjustable target rear peep sight; hooded front sight w/10 aperture inserts  *Stock:* Laminated black/grey w/ambidextrous pistol grip; butt plate adjustable for length of pull, height, angle; aluminum forearm  *Price:* . . . . . . . . . . . . . . . . . . . . . . . . . . . . . . . **$656.00**

# MAUSER RIFLES

**MODEL 96 BOLT ACTION**

**MODEL 96**

### SPECIFICATIONS

*Calibers:* 243 Win., 25-06, 270 Win., 30-06 S'fld, 308 Win., 7mm Rem. Mag., 300 Win. Mag.  *Capacity:* 5 rounds  *Action:* Sliding bolt action  *Barrel length:* 22" (24" magnum)  *Overall length:* 42" (44" magnum)  *Weight:* 6.25 lbs.  *Safety:* Rear tang, 3-position  *Trigger:* Single  *Stock:* Checkered walnut  *Sights:* None; drilled and tapped for Rem. 700 scope mounts and bases  *Features:* Quick-

detachable 1" sling swivels; 16 locking lugs
*Price:* . . . . . . . . . . . . . . . . . . . . . . . . . . . . . **$699.00**
*Also available:* MODEL SR 86 W/28.75" barrel in 308 Win. w/muzzle brake; adjustable black laminated thumbhold stock w/bipod rail. *Weight:* 13.6 lbs. . . . . . . . **$11,795.00**
MODEL M94 w/22" barrel (24" magnum) in 25-06 Rem., 243 Win., 308 Win., 270 Win., 30-06 S'fld, 7mm Rem. Mag., 300 Win. Mag. Features aluminum bedding block, interchangeable barrels ($799.00), combo or single-set trigger, detachable mag., walnut stock.
*Weight:* 7.25 lbs. . . . . . . . . . . . . . . . . . . . . . . **$2,295.00**

# MOSSBERG RIFLES

**SSI-ONE**

### MOSSBERG SSI-ONE SINGLE SHOT INTERCHANGEABLE RIFLE & SHOTGUN

The new Mossberg SSI is a bold step into the competitive centerfire rifle market for the 80-year-old company. This hammerless single-shot with quick-change barrels offers a choice of six chamberings and is easy for left-handed shooters to use.

### SPECIFICATIONS

*Calibers, Gauge:* .223 Rem., .22-250 Rem., .243 Win., .270 Win., .308 Rem., .30-06 Sprg., 12 Gauge Slug  *Finish:* Classic Satin finished stock & forend. Matte blue receiver & barrel  *Length Overall:* 40" Sporter, Varmint, Slug  *Barrel Length:* 24" Sporter, Varmint, Slug  *Action:* Lever-opening, break-action, top tang safety, selective ejector  *Approx. Weight:* 8 lbs. Sporter, Slug 10 lbs. Varmint  *Sights:* Barrel drilled and tapped for scope mounts (scope base included)  *Stock:* Select Walnut

# NAVY ARMS REPLICA RIFLES

## HENRY CARBINE

The arm first utilized by the Kentucky Cavalry, with blued finish and brass frame.

**SPECIFICATIONS**
**Caliber:** 44-40
**Capacity:** 11 rounds
**Barrel Length:** 22"
**Overall Length:** 41"
**Weight:** 8 ³/₄ lbs.
**Price:** . . . . . . . . . . . . . . . . . . . . . . . . . . . . . . . $875.00

This short, lightweight lever-action arm is ideal for close-cover whitetails.

**SPECIFICATIONS**
**Caliber:** 44-40
**Capacity:** 8 rounds
**Barrel Length:** 16 ¹/₂"
**Overall Length:** 34 ¹/₂"
**Weight:** 7 lbs. 7 oz.
**Price:** . . . . . . . . . . . . . . . . . . . . . . . . . . . . $875.00

## HENRY TRAPPER MODEL

## 1866 "YELLOWBOY" RIFLE

The 1866 model was Oliver Winchester's improved version of the Henry rifle. Called the "Yellowboy" because of its polished brass receiver, it was popular with Indians, settlers and cattlemen alike.

**SPECIFICATIONS**
**Caliber:** 38 Special, 44-40, 45 Colt
**Barrel Length:** 24" full octagon **Overall Length:** 42.5"
**Weight:** 8.25 lbs. **Sights:** Blade front; open ladder rear
**Stock:** Walnut
**Price:** . . . . . . . . . . . . . . . . . . . . . . . . . . . . $685.00

## HENRY MILITARY RIFLE

This Civil War replica features a highly polished brass frame and blued barrel; sling swivels to the original specifications are located on the left side.

**SPECIFICATIONS**
**Caliber:** 44-40 or 45 Colt **Capacity:** 13 rounds
**Barrel Length:** 24"
**Overall Length:** 43"
**Weight:** 9.25 lbs. **Stock:** Walnut
**Price:** . . . . . . . . . . . . . . . . . . . . . . . . $895.00

## IRON FRAME HENRY

**SPECIFICATIONS**
**Caliber:** 44-40
**Capacity:** 13 rounds
**Barrel Length:** 24"
**Overall Length:** 43"
**Weight:** 9 lbs.
**Stock:** Walnut
**Finish:** Blued or casehardened **Feature:** Iron frame
**Price:** . . . . . . . . . . . . . . . . . . . . . . . . . . . . $945.00

# NAVY ARMS REPLICA RIFLES

## 1866 "YELLOWBOY" CARBINE

This is the "saddle gun" varient of the Yellowboy rifle.

**SPECIFICATIONS**
*Caliber:* 38 Special, 44-40 or 45 Colt
*Barrel Length:* 19" round  *Overall Length:* 38.25"
*Weight:* 7.25 lbs.  *Sights:* Blade front; open ladder rear
*Stock:* Walnut
*Price:* . . . . . . . . . . . . . . . . . . . . . . . . . . . . . . . . . . . . . . $675.00

## REPLICA 1873 WINCHESTER RIFLE
### (not shown)

Known as "The Gun That Won the West," the 1873 was the most popular lever-action rifle of its time. This fine replica features a casehardened receiver.

**SPECIFICATIONS**
*Caliber:* 357 Mag., 44-40 or 45 Colt
*Barrel Length:* 24"  *Overall Length:* 43"

*Weight:* 8.25 lbs.
*Sights:* Blade front; open ladder rear
*Stock:* Walnut
*Price:* . . . . . . . . . . . . . . . . . . . . . . . . . . . . . . . . . . . $820.00
*Also available:* 1873 CARBINE
  (19" barrel) . . . . . . . . . . . . . . . . . . . . . . . . . . . . $800.00
**1873 "BORDER MODEL" RIFLE**
  (20" Oct. barrel) . . . . . . . . . . . . . . . . . . . . . . . 820.00

## REPLICA 1873 WINCHESTER SPORTING RIFLE

This replica of the elegant Winchester 1873 Sporting Rifle features a checkered pistol grip, buttstock, casehardened receiver and blued octagonal barrel.

**SPECIFICATIONS**
*Caliber:* 357 Mag. (24" bbl. only), 44-40 or 45 Colt
*Barrel Length:* 24" or 30"
*Overall Length:* 48 ³/₄" (w/30" barrel)
*Weight:* 8 lbs. 14 oz.
*Sights:* Blade front; buckhorn rear
*Prices:*
  30" Barrel. . . . . . . . . . . . . . . . . . . . . . . . . . . . . . $960.00
  24" Barrel. . . . . . . . . . . . . . . . . . . . . . . . . . . . . . 930.00

## 1873 SPRINGFIELD CAVALRY CARBINE

A reproduction of the classic U.S. "Trapdoor" Springfield carbine used by the 7th Cavalry at The Battle of Little Big Horn.

**SPECIFICATIONS**
*Caliber:* 45-70 Government  *Barrel Length:* 22"
*Overall Length:* 40.5"  *Weight:* 7 lbs.
*Sights:* Blade front, military ladder rear
*Stock:* Walnut  *Features:* Saddle bar with ring
*Price:* . . . . . . . . . . . . . . . . . . . . . . . . . . . . . . . . . . . $870.00
*Also available:*
**1873 SPRINGFIELD INFANTRY RIFLE** (32.5" bbl.) . . . . $995.00

# NAVY ARMS REPLICA RIFLES

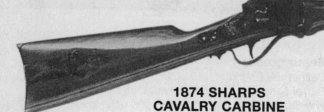

## 1874 SHARPS CAVALRY CARBINE

This cavalry carbine version of the Sharps rifle features a side bar and saddle ring.

**SPECIFICATIONS**
*Caliber:* 45-70 percussion  *Barrel Length:* 22"  *Overall Length:* 39"  *Weight:* 7 ³/₄ lbs.  *Sights:* Blade front; military ladder rear  *Stock:* Walnut
*Price:* . . . . . . . . . . . . . . . . . . . . . . . . . . . . . . $935.00

## 1874 SHARPS SNIPER RIFLE

This replica of the 1874 three-band sharpshooter's rifle was a popular target rifle at the Creedmoor military matches and was the issue longarm of the New York State Militia.

**SPECIFICATIONS**
*Caliber:* 45-70  *Barrel Length:* 30"  *Overall Length:* 46 ³/₄"  *Weight:* 8 lbs. 8 oz.  *Stock:* Walnut  *Features:* Double-set triggers; casehardened receiver; patchbox and furniture
*Price:* . . . . . . . . . . . . . . . . . . . . . . . . . . . . $1,115.00
*Also available:*
SINGLE TRIGGER INFANTRY MODEL . . . . . . . . . . . $1,060.00
PLAINS RIFLE (32" barrel) . . . . . . . . . . . . . . . . 1,055.00

## SHARPS BUFFALO RIFLE

This deluxe version of the rifle that came to be known simply as "buffalo gun" was favored by market hunters on the Great Plains after the Civil War.

**SPECIFICATIONS**
*Caliber:* 45-70 or 45-90  *Barrel Length:* 28" octagonal  *Overall Length:* 46"  *Weight:* 10 lbs. 10 oz.  *Sights:* Blade front, ladder rear (tang sight optional w/set triggers only—$65.00  *Stock:* Walnut  *Features:* Color casehardened receiver and furniture; double-set trigger
*Price:* . . . . . . . . . . . . . . . . . . . . . . . . . . . . $1,090.00

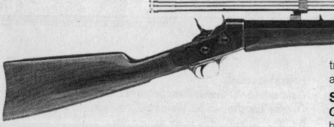

## REMINGTON-STYLE ROLLING BLOCK BUFFALO RIFLE

This replica of the rifle used by buffalo hunters and plainsmen of the 1800s features a case hardened receiver, solid brass trigger guard and walnut stock and forend. The tang is drilled and tapped to accept the optional Creedmoor sight.

**SPECIFICATIONS**
*Caliber:* 45-70  *Barrel Length:* 26" or 30"; full octagon or half-round  *Sights:* Blade front, open notch rear  *Stock:* Walnut stock and forend  *Feature:* Shown with optional 32.5" Model 1860 brass telescopic sight $210.00; Compact Model (18"): $200.00
*Price:* With casehardened steel . . . . . . . . . . . . . 765.00

# NAVY ARMS REPLICA RIFLES

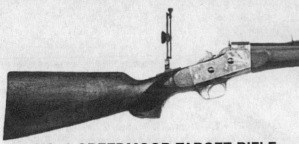

## NO. 2 CREEDMOOR TARGET RIFLE

This reproduction of the Remington No. 2 Creedmoor Rifle features a color case hardened receiver and steel trigger guard, tapered octagon barrel, and walnut forend and buttstock with checkered pistol grip.

**SPECIFICATIONS**
*Caliber:* 45-70 *Barrel Length:* 30", tapered *Overall Length:* 46" *Weight:* 9 lbs. *Sights:* Globe front, adjustable Creedmoor rear *Stock:* Checkered walnut stock and forend *Price:* . . . . . . . . . . . . . . . . . . $930.00

## KODIAK MK IV DOUBLE RIFLE

**SPECIFICATIONS**
*Caliber:* 45-70 *Barrel Length:* 24" *Overall Length:* 39 ³/₄"
*Weight:* 10 lbs. 3 oz. *Sights:* Bead front, folding-leaf express rear *Stock:* Checkered European walnut
*Features:* Color case hardened locks, breech and hammers; semi-regulated barrels
*Price:*. . . . . . . . . . . . . . . . . . . . . . . . . . . . $2,815.00
*Also available:* DELUXE KODIAK MK IV DOUBLE RIFLE (shown) with browned barrels and hand-engraving on satin frame and fittings. *Price:* . . . . . . . . . . . . . . . . $3,690.00

## 1892 BRASS FRAME RIFLE

**SPECIFICATIONS**
*Calibers:* 44-40 or 45 Colt *Barrel Length:* 24.25" octagonal *Weight:* 7.25 lbs. *Sights:* Blade front; semi-buckhorn rear *Stock:* American walnut
*Price:* . . . . . . . . . . . . . . . . . . . . . . . . . . . . . $495.00

## 1892 RIFLE

The Winchester 92 came with several barrel lengths. Two are available from Navy Arms. The "Short Rifle" is a replica of the "Texas Special" 92 Winchester that featured a 20" full octagonal barrel. Color case hardened or blue receiver and furniture.

**SPECIFICATIONS**
*Calibers:* 357 Mag., 44-40 or 45 Colt *Barrel Length:* 20" or 24" octagon *Weight:* 6.25 lbs. or 7 lbs. *Sights:* Blade front; semibuckhorn rear *Stock:* American walnut
*Price:* . . . . . . . . . . . . . . . . . . . . . . . . . . . . . $495.00

### 1892 RIFLE (not shown)
**SPECIFICATIONS**
*Caliber:* 357 Mag., 44-40 or 45 Colt
*Barrel Length:* 24.25" octagon
*Weight:* 7 lbs.

*Sights:* Blade front; semi-buckhorn rear
*Stock:* American walnut
*Price:* . . . . . . . . . . . . . . . . . . . . . . . . . . . . . $495.00

# NEW ENGLAND FIREARMS RIFLES

### SYNTHETIC HANDI-RIFLE

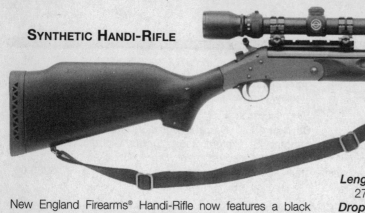

New England Firearms® Handi-Rifle now features a black Monte Carlo synthetic stock and forend. This version includes a factory-mounted scope base and an offset hammer extension to ease cocking when a scope is mounted. The rifles all include the patented NEF Transfer Bar System. Additional rifle barrels are available for factory retrofitting through NEF's Accessory Barrel Program.

**SPECIFICATIONS**
**Calibers:** 22 Hornet, 223 Rem., 243 Win., 270 Win., 280 Rem., 30-30 Win., 30-06 Springfield; 44 Rem. Mag., 45-70 Gov't **Action:** Break-open; side lever release; automatic ejection **Barrel Length:** 22" (26" in 270 Win.) **Overall Length:** 38" (40" in 270 Win.) **Length Of Pull:** 14.25" **Drop At Heel:** 2.25" **Drop At Comb:** 1.5" **Weight:** 7 lbs. **Sights:** Ramp front; fully adjustable rear; tapped for scope mount **Stock:** High density polymer; black matte finish; sling swivels; recoil pad
**Price:** . . . . . . . . . . . . . . . . . . . . . . . . . . . . . . . . $228.95
**Also available:** HANDI-RIFLE with hardwood stock in all chambering plus 308 Win., 7x57, 7x64, .357 Mag. with sights or scope base, depending on chambering and barrel style

### SUPER LIGHT YOUTH HANDI-RIFLE

### HANDI-RIFLE YOUTH, 223 REM AND 243 WIN.

### SURVIVOR 223 AND 308 BULL BARREL

### SUPER LIGHT YOUTH HANDI-RIFLE™

In 1998 New England Firearms introduced a youth version of its Superlight Handi-Rifle with lightweight synthetic stock and new Super Light taper on the barrel. The matte black synthetic stock and forend feature a non-slip finish plus a sling, swivels and recoil pad. Other features include the patented New England Firearms Transfer Bar System, which virtually eliminates the possibility of accidental discharge.

**SPECIFICATIONS**
**Caliber:** 22 Hornet, 223 Rem & 243 Win. **Action:** Single shot; break-open; side lever release; automatic ejection **Barrel Length:** 20" **Overall Length:** 33" **Drop At Heel:** 1 1/8" **Drop At Comb:** 1 1/8" **Length Of Pull:** 11.75" **Weight:** 5 1/3 lbs. **Sights:** Ramp front; fully adjustable rear; tapped for scope mount **Stock:** High density polymer; black matte finish; sling swivels; recoil pad
**Price:** . . . . . . . . . . . . . . . . . . . . . . . . . . . . . . . . $227.95
**Also available:** HANDI-RIFLE YOUTH with hardwood stock, 223 Rem. and 243 Win. . . . . . . . . . . . . . . . . . . . . . . . . . . . 227.95
SURVIVOR available in 223 and 308, the Survivor has hollow synthetic stock, thumbscrew take down. . . . . . . . . . 227.95

# PEDERSOLI REPLICA RIFLES

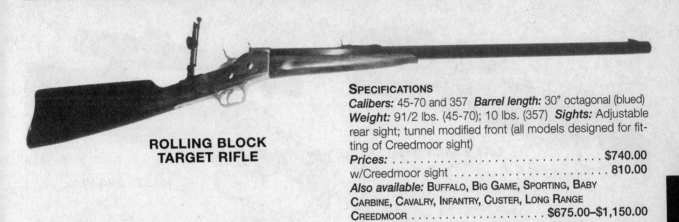

## ROLLING BLOCK
## TARGET RIFLE

**SPECIFICATIONS**
**Calibers:** 45-70 and 357  **Barrel length:** 30" octagonal (blued)
**Weight:** 91/2 lbs. (45-70); 10 lbs. (357)  **Sights:** Adjustable
rear sight; tunnel modified front (all models designed for fitting of Creedmoor sight)
**Prices:** . . . . . . . . . . . . . . . . . . . . . . . . . . . . . . . . . $740.00
w/Creedmoor sight . . . . . . . . . . . . . . . . . . . . . . . 810.00
**Also available:** BUFFALO, BIG GAME, SPORTING, BABY
CARBINE, CAVALRY, INFANTRY, CUSTER, LONG RANGE
CREEDMOOR . . . . . . . . . . . . . . . . . . . . . . $675.00–$1,150.00

## SHARPS CARBINE
## MODEL 766

**SPECIFICATIONS**
**Caliber:** 54  **Barrel length:** 22" round (6 grooves)
**Overall length:** 39"  **Weight:** 7.5 lbs.
**Sights:** Fully adjustable rear; fixed front
**Price:** w/Patchbox. . . . . . . . . . . . . . . . . . . . . . . $925.00
**Also available:**
SHARPS 1859 MILITARY RIFLE (.45/70 set trigger, 30" barrel)
**Price:**. . . . . . . . . . . . . . . . . . . . . . . . . . . . . . 1,095.00
SHARPS SPORTING RIFLE .40/65 set triggers, 32" oct. barrel
**Price:**. . . . . . . . . . . . . . . . . . . . . . . . . . . . . . 1,080.00

SHARPS LONG RANGE TARGET RIFLE (.45/70, .45/90, .45/120,
34" half octagon barrel, target sights)
**Price:**. . . . . . . . . . . . . . . . . . . . . . . . . . . . . . $1,350.00

**SPECIFICATIONS**
**Calibers:** 45-70, 9.3x74R, 8x57JSR  **Barrel length:**
22" (24" 45-70)  **Overall length:** 39" (40.5" 45-70)
**Weight:** 8.24 lbs. (9.7 lbs. 45/70)
**Price:** 45-70. . . . . . . . . . . . . . . . . . . . . . $2,995.00
8x57, 9.3x74. . . . . . . . . . . . . . . . . . . . . . 3,250.00
**Also available:** KODIAK MARK IV w/interchangeable 20-
gauge barrel **Price:**. . . . . . . . . . . . . . . . . . . . $4,250.00

## KODIAK MARK IV
## DOUBLE RIFLE

## MORTIMER
## TARGET RIFLE

**SPECIFICATIONS**
English-style European walnut stock with cheekpiece and
hand checkering; color-case-hardened lock; 54-caliber, 7-
groove barrel (octagon to round) 36" long. **Overall length:**
52"  **Weight:** 8.8 pounds
**Price:**. . . . . . . . . . . . . . . . . . . . . . . . . . . . . . $1,250.00

# PRAIRIE GUN WORKS

**LRT 2 416 PGW**

**M15Ti .284 Wiin.**

**M18Ti left hand 7mm Rem. Mag.**

## LRT-2 SERIES RIFLES

Dangerous game, long range target, and tactical versions are available in this series. The smallest rounds that this action is suitable for is the .378 and Rigby based magnums. These rifles are ideal for large calibers such as the .505 Gibbs (and PGW line of wildcats), and other large rounds like the .585 Nyati. A 4-shot magazine box is available on this rifle. The .408 Cheyenne (.416) is capable of firing a 400-grain bullet at over 3000-fps, making this the flattest shooting and hardest hitting .416 on the market. Stainless pillars and McMillan "Express" or Tactical stocks hold the recoil. These rifles are available with several different scope mount/sight options, plus muzzle brakes. Weights in this series range from 10 to 18 pounds.

## M15 AND M18 SERIES RIFLES

Lightweight rifles based on Ti series of Titanium rifle actions. These rifles feature match grade stainless barrels, kevlar/glass stocks, Titanium scope bases, fully adjustable triggers, and customer supplied specifications such as length of pull, barrel length, and twist. The M15Ti rifle (short) is suitable for cartridges up to the size of the .284 Win. and its wildcats. The M18Ti rifle (long) is suitable for cartridges up to the Remington "Ultramag" and its wildcats. These rifles can be built from 4.25 lbs. to 6.25 lbs.

Some of the unique features found on the Ti series rifles: cone breech, 1/4"-28 base/ring screw attachment, wire EDM lugways, one piece bolt, double plunger ejectors, Sako type extraction, left or right hand bolt/port configurations available, aluminum pillar bedding, removablle muzzle brake with cap, barrel flutes X8.

**Prices:**

| | |
|---|---|
| M15Ti Ultralight | $2,800.00 |
| M18Ti Ultralight | 2,800.00 |
| M15Ti Varmint | 2,400.00 |
| M15Ti Benchrest | 2,400.00 |
| M15 Tactical stainless | 2,900.00 |
| M18 Tactical stainless | 2,900.00 |
| LRT-2 PGW/Gibbs | 3,900.00 |
| LRT-3.50 single shot | 4,200.00 |

## MODEL M-15 ULTRA LITE (not shown)

### SPECIFICATIONS
**Caliber:** Most Short Action calibers
**Action:** Remington 700 Short Action
**Barrel length:** 22" Douglas Match Grade
**Length of pull:** 13.5"
**Weight:** 4.5-5.25 lbs.
**Stock:** Fiberglass-Kevlar composite w/integral recoil lug; recoil pad installed **Finish:** Black or grey textured finish
**Sights:** Custom aircraft-grade aluminum scope mounts
**Features:** Trigger set and polished for 3 lb. pull; bolt fluted, hollowed and tapped w/Ultra Lite custom firing pin and bolt shroud
**Price:** .................................. $2,800.00
*Also available:*
MODEL M-18. Same specifications and price as Model M-15, except chambered for long-action calibers (up to 340 Weatherby)
**Price:** .................................. 2,900.00

# PURDEY

## DOUBLE BARREL RIFLES

### DOUBLE BARREL RIFLE .577 NITRO

The word "Express" was coined by James Purdey the younger to publicize his rifles. He likened their performance to a railway or "Express" train, which was heavy, travelled with great velocity and had a flat trajectory.

The action blocks for all guns are cut from certified forgings, for consistency of grain throughout, and are so fitted to the barrels as to give an absolute joint.

The actioner then fits the fore-part, the locks, the strikers and the safety work before finally detonating the action.

Purdey's double-barrel Express rifles are built to customer specifications on actions sized to each particular cartridge. Standard chamberings include .375 H&H Magnum and .470, .577 and .600 Nitro Express. The Purdey side by side action patented in 1880 is still made now with only very minor changes. The action mechanism, designed by Frederick Beesley, retains a portion of the energy in the mainsprings to facilitate the opening of the gun.

The over-under is derived from the Woodward, patented in 1913.

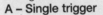

#### A – Single trigger

The Purdey single trigger works both by inertia and mechanically. It is simple, effective and fast. The firing sequence is fixed, therefore no barrel selection is possible.

#### B & C – Double Triggers

The standard double triggers (B) can be augmented with an articulated front trigger (C). This device alleviates damage to the back of the trigger finger on discharge.

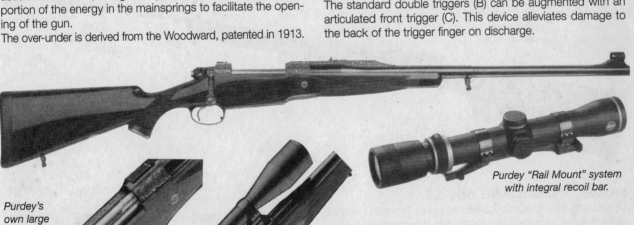

Purdey's own large calibre action

Classic Mauser '98 Action

Purdey "Rail Mount" system with integral recoil bar.

Purdey makes its own dedicated actions for bolt rifles in the following calibers: .375 H&H, .416/450 Rigby or other, .500 and .505 Gibbs.

The action length is suited to cartridge length in each caliber. Mauser Square Bridge and Mauser '98 actions are available.

### RAIL MOUNT SYSTEM

This is Purdey's own system for big bolt rifles. It is very secure and facilitates fast on/off. Rings and mounts are all made with an integral recoil bar from a single piece of steel. This system is recommended for Purdey actions and Mauser Square Bridge actions.

**MODEL 700 BDL DM**

## MODEL 700 BDL DM

The MODEL 700 REMINGTON bolt-action rifle first appeared in 1962. Since then it has become one of the most popular rifles of all time and is now available in myriad configurations and chamberings. MODEL 700 BDL DM rifles feature the standard Remington BDL barrel contour, with 22" barrels on standard-caliber models and 24" barrels on magnum-caliber rifles. The detachable box magazine holds 4 standard rounds, 3 magnums. Chamberings include .270, 30-06, 7mm Rem. Mag., .300 Win. Mag. Stainless version comes in .25-06, .260 Rem., .270, .280, 7mm-08, .30-06, 7mm Rem.

Mag., .300 Win. Mag., 300 Wby. Mag. All barrels have a hooded front sight and adjustable rear sight. Additional features include polished blued-metal finish, high-gloss, Monte Carlo-style walnut stock, white line spacers, 20 lines-per-inch checkering, recoil pad and swivel studs. All models feature fine-line engraving on receiver front rings, rear bridges, non-ejection receiver sides and floorplates.

**Prices:** MODEL 700 BDL DM. . . . . . . . . . . . . . . . $681.00
  Magnum . . . . . . . . . . . . . . . . . . . . . . . . . . . . . . 708.00
  Stainless . . . . . . . . . . . . . . . . . . . . . . . 756.00-783.00

**MODEL 700 BDL SS**

## MODEL 700 BDL AND BDL SS

This Model 700 features the Monte Carlo American walnut stock finished to a high gloss with fine-cut checkering. Also includes a hinged floorplate, sling swivel studs, hooded ramp front sight and adjustable rear sight. Also available in stainless synthetic version (Model 700 BDL SS) with stainless-steel barrel, receiver and bolt plus synthetic stock for maximum weather resistance.

**MODEL 700 BDL**
*Prices:*
In 222 Rem., 22-250 Rem., 223 Rem., 243 Win., .280,
  25-06 Rem., 270 Win., 30-06, 7mm-08. . . . . . . $633.00

In 17 Rem., 7mm Rem. Mag., 300 Win. Mag., .300 Rem
  Ultra Mag, .338 Win. Mag., .338 Rem. Ultra Mag. . . . . . **660.00**
Left Hand in 270 Win., 30-06. . . . . . . . . . . . . . . **660.00**
Left Hand in 7mm Rem. Mag. .300 Rem. Ultra Mag. . . . . . **687.00**
**MODEL BDL SS** (Stainless Synthetic)
In 270 Win. 30-06. . . . . . . . . . . . . . . . . . . . . . . . **681.00**
In 7mm Rem. Mag., 300 Win. Mag., .338 Win. Mag.,
  .300 Rem. Ultra Mag., .338 Rem. Ultra Mag. . . . . . **708.00**

## MODEL 700 BDL SS DM-B
Available in *Calibers:* 7mm STW, 300 Win. Mag., *Barrel length:* 25.5" (magnum contour barrel). Stainless synthetic detachable magazine with muzzle brake.
*Price:* . . . . . . . . . . . . . . . . . . . . . . . . . . . . . . . . **$845.00**

# REMINGTON BOLT-ACTION RIFLES

### MODEL 700 VLS
### (VARMINT LAMINATED STOCK)

The **MODEL 700 VLS** features a blued, heavy-contour varmint barrel, laminated synthetic stock, hinged magazine floorplate and sling swivel studs. ***Barrel length:*** 26" ***Overall Length:*** 45.5" ***Weight:*** 9 lbs. ***Length of pull:*** 13 $^3/_8$" ***Drop at comb:*** .5" ***Drop at heel:*** $^3/_8$" ***Chamberings:*** .223, .22-250, 6mm Rem., .243, .308

***Price:*** ......................................... $675.00
VS with synthetic barrel in .223, .22-250, .308 .... 759.00
Left hand, same calibers .................. 785.00

### MODEL 700 "SENDERO"

Remington's Sendero rifle combines the accuracy features of the Model 700 Varmint Special with long action and magnum calibers for long-range hunting. The 26-inch barrel has a heavy varmint profile and features a spherical concave crown. For additional specifications, see table on the following page.
***Price:*** .25-06, .270 ...................... $759.00
Magnum: 7mm Rem. Mag., .300 Win. Mag..... 785.00

### MODEL 700 SENDERO SF
### (Stainless Fluted)

This version of the Model 700 Sendero features satin-finished stainless steel receiver and bolt and a 26-inch heavy stainless barrel with six longitudinal flutes designed to improve heat dissipation and reduce gun weight (8.5 lbs.). A spherical, concave crown protects the muzzle. Other features include a composite synthetic fiberglass stock, graphite reinforced by du Pont Kevlar, and a full-length aluminum bedding block. ***Chamberings:*** .25-06, 7mm Rem. Mag, 7STW, .300 Win. Mag., .300 Wby. Mag., .300 Ultra Mag., .338 Ultra Mag.
***Price:*** ................................. $916.00
Magnum ............................. 943.00

### MODEL 700 ADL

### MODEL 700 ADL
Synthetic model has a fiberglass-reinforced synthetic stock, positive checkering, straight comb, raised cheekpiece and black rubber recoil pad. Stock and blued metalwork have a non-reflective black matte finish.

***Price:*** ................................. $531.00
Magnum .............................. 557.00
Synthetic ............................. 457.00
Synthetic/Magnum ..................... 484.00
Youth (1" shorter) .................... 484.00

*(See also table on the following page for prices, calibers and additional specifications)*

# REMINGTON BOLT-ACTION RIFLES

### MODEL 700 BDL SS DM
(Stainless/Synthetic)

## MODEL 700/CALIBERS

*Prices:* MOUNTAIN DM 25-06, 260 Rem., 270 Win.,
280 Rem., 7mm-08, 30-06 . . . . . . . . . . . . . $681.00
SENDERO 25-06, 270 Win. . . . . . . . . . . . . . . . . . 759.00
7mm Rem. Mag., 300 Win. Mag. . . . . . . . . . . . 785.00
SENDERO SF 25-06. . . . . . . . . . . . . . . . . . . . . . . . 916.00

7mm Rem. Mag., 7mm STW, 300 Win. Mag.,
300 Wby. Mag., 300 + 338 Rem. Ultra Mags . . . 943.00
BDL SS DM 25-06 Rem., 260 Rem., 270 Win.,
280 Rem., 7mm-08, 30-06. . . . . . . . . . . . . . . 756.00
7mm Rem. Mag., 300 Win. Mag. and
300 Wby. Mag. . . . . . . . . . . . . . . . . . . . . . . . . 783.00

## MODEL 700™ CENTERFIRE RIFLE SPECIFICATIONS

| CALIBERS | MAGAZINE CAPACITY | BARREL LENGTH | ETRON X | MOUNTAIN RIFLE (DM) | SENDERO | SENDERO SF | BDL STAINLESS SYNTHETIC DM | BDL SS | DM-B | BDL LSS |
|---|---|---|---|---|---|---|---|---|---|---|
| 17 Rem. | 5 | 24" | | | | | | | | |
| 220 Swift | 4 | 26" | • | | | | | | | |
| 222 Rem. | 5 | 24" | | | | | | | | |
| 22-250 Rem. | 4 | 24" | • | | | | | | | |
| 223 Rem. | 5 | 24" | | | | | | | | |
| 243 Win. | 4 | 22" | • | | | | | | | |
| | 4 | 24" | | | | | | | | |
| 25-06 Rem. | 4 | 24" | | | • | • | • | | | |
| | 4 | 22" | | • | | | | | | |
| 260 Rem. | 4 | 24" | | • | | | • | | | |
| 270 Win. | 4 | 22" | | • | | | | | | |
| | 4 | 22" | | | | | | | | |
| | 4 | 24" | | | • | | • | • | | •LH |
| 280 Rem. | 4 | 22" | | • | | | | | | |
| | 4 | 24" | | | | | • | | | |
| 7mm-08 Rem. | 4 | 22" | | • | | | • | | | |
| | 4 | 24" | | | | | | | | |
| 7mm Rem. Mag. | 3 | 24" | | | • | • | | • | • | •RH/LH |
| | 3 | 24" | | | | | | | | • |
| 7mm STW | 3 | 24" | | | | • | | | • | |
| 30-06 | 4 | 22" | | • | | | | | | |
| | 4 | 24" | | | | | • | • | | •LH |
| 308 Win. | 4 | 22" | | | | | | | | |
| | 4 | 24" | | | | | • | | | |
| 300 Win. Mag. | 3 | 24" | | | • | • | • | • | | •RH/LH |
| | 3 | 24" | | | | | | | • | |
| 300 Wby. Mag. | 3 | 24" | | | | • | • | | | |
| 300 Rem. Ultra Mag. | 3 | 24" | | | | • | | • | | •RH/LH |
| 338 Win. Mag. | 3 | 24" | | | | | | • | | |
| 338 Rem. Ultra. Mag. | 3 | 24" | | | | • | | • | | •/• |
| 375 H&H Mag. | 3 | 24" | | | | | | • | | |

*All Model 700™ rifles come with sling swivel studs. The BDL, ADL, and Seven™ are furnished with sights. The BDL Stainless Synthetic, LSS, Mountain Rifle, Classic, Sendero and Varmint guns have clean barrels. All Remington CF rifles drilled and tapped for scope mounts.*

# REMINGTON BOLT-ACTION RIFLES

## MODEL 700/CALIBERS
*Prices:*

BDL SS DM-B 7mm STW, 300 Win. Mag. . . . . . . . $845.00
BDL STAINLESS SYNTHETIC 270 Win., 30-06 . . . . . . 681.00
   7mm Rem. Mag., 300 Win. Mag., 300 Ultra Mag.,
   338 Rem Ultra Mag., 338 Win. Mag., 375 H&H Mag. . 708.00
LSS 7mm Rem. Mag., 300 Win. Mag.,
   300 + 338 Rem. Ultra Mag . . . . . . . . . . . . . 771.00
BDL 270 Win. LH, 30-06 LH, . . . . . . . . . . . . . 660.00
   222 Rem., 22-250, 223 Rem., 243 Win.,
   25-06, 270 Win., 30-06, 7mm-08, 280 . . . . . . . 633.00
   7mm Rem. Mag. LH, 300 Rem. Ultra LH . . . . . 687.00
BDL .17 Rem., 7mm Rem. Mag., 300 Win. Mag., 338 Rem,
   Ultra Mag, 300 Rem Ultra Mag., 338 Win. Mag. . . . . 660.00

BDL DM 270 Win., 30-06 . . . . . . . . . . . . . . . 681.00
   7mm Rem. Mag. 300 Win. Mag. . . . . . . . . . . 708.00
ADL 270 Win., 30-06, 308 Win. . . . . . . . . . . . 531.00
   7mm Rem. Mag. . . . . . . . . . . . . . . . . . . 557.00
ADL SYNTHETIC 223 Rem. 22-250, 243 Win., 270 Win.,
   30-06, 308 Win. . . . . . . . . . . . . . . . . . 457.00
   7mm Rem. Mag., 300 Win. Mag. . . . . . . . . . . 484.00
VLS 22-25 Rem., 223 Rem., 243 Win.,
   6mm Rem., 308 Win. . . . . . . . . . . . . . . . . 675.00
VS w/26" Heavy Barrel in 22-250 Rem.,
   223 Rem., 308 Win. RH. . . . . . . . . . . . . . . 759.00
   LH. . . . . . . . . . . . . . . . . . . . . . . . 785.00
w/26" Fluted Barrel in 22-250 Rem., 223 Rem.,
   220 Swift . . . . . . . . . . . . . . . . . . . . 916.00

## MODEL 700™ CENTERFIRE RIFLE SPECIFICATIONS

| Calibers | Magazine Capacity | Barrel Length | Twist (R-H) 1 Turn In | BDL | BDL (DM) | ADL | ADL Synthetic | VLS* 26" Heavy BBL | VS (Varmint Synthetic) 26" Heavy BBL | 26" Stainless Fluted BBL |
|---|---|---|---|---|---|---|---|---|---|---|
| 17 Rem. | 5 | 24" | 9" | ● | | | | | LH only | |
| 220 Swift | 4 | 26" | 14" | | | | | | | |
| 222 Rem. | 5 | 24" | 14" | ● | | | | | | |
| 22-250 Rem. | 4 | 24" | 14" | ● | | | ● | ● | ●/● | ● |
| 223 Rem. | 5 | 24" | 12" | ● | | | NEW | ● | ●/● | ● |
| 243 Win. | 4 | 20" | 9 1/8" | ● | ● | | NEW | | | |
| | 4 | 22" | 9 1/8" | | | | | ● | | |
| 6mm Rem. | 4 | 22" | 9 1/8" | | | | | ● | | |
| 25-06 Rem. | 4 | 24" | 10" | ● | | | | | | |
| | 4 | 22" | 10" | | | | | | | |
| 260 Rem. | 4 | 24" | 9" | ● | | | | NEW | | |
| 270 Win. | 4 | 22" | 10" | ●LH/RH | ● | ● | ● | | | |
| | 4 | 22" | 10" | | | | | | | |
| | 4 | 24" | 10" | | | | | | | |
| 280 Rem. | 4 | 22" | 9 1/4" | | ● | | | | | |
| | 4 | 24" | 9 1/4" | | | | | | | |
| 7mm-08 Rem. | 4 | 22" | 9 1/4" | ● | | | | | | |
| | 4 | 24" | 9 1/4" | | | | | ● | | |
| 7mm Rem. Mag. | 3 | 24" | 9 1/4" | ●LH/RH | ● | ● | ● | | | |
| | 3 | 24" | 9 1/4" | | | | | | | |
| 7mm STW | 3 | 24" | 9 1/2" | | | | | | | |
| 30-06 | 4 | 22" | 10" | ●LH/RH | ● | ● | ● | | | |
| | 4 | 22" | 10" | | | | | | | |
| 308 Win. | 4 | 20" | 10" | | | ● | ● | | | |
| | 4 | 22" | 12" | | | | ● | ● | ●/●** | NEW** |
| 300 Win. Mag. | 3 | 24" | 10" | ● | ● | | NEW | | | |
| | 3 | 24" | 12" | | | | | | | |
| 300 Wby. Mag. | 3 | 24" | 12" | | | | | | | |
| 300 Rem. Ultra Mag. | 3 | 24" | 12" | ●/● | | | | | | |
| 338 Win. Mag. | 3 | 24" | 10" | ● | | | | | | |
| 338 Rem. Ultra Mag. | 3 | 24" | 10" | ● | | | | | | |
| 375 H&H Mag. | 3 | 24" | 12" | | | | | | | |

*Varmint Laminated Stock (also available in 6mm Rem.) **Available w/24" barrel

# REMINGTON BOLT-ACTION RIFLES

## MODEL 700 CLASSIC (.223)

Since Remington's series of Model 700 Classics began in 1981, the company has offered this model in a special chambering each year.

The Model 700 Classic features an American walnut, straight-combed stock without a cheekpiece for rapid mounting, better sight alignment and reduced felt recoil. A hinged magazine flloorplate, sling swivel studs and satin wood finish with cut-checkering are standard, along with 24" barrel. Receiver drilled/tapped for scope mounts.

*Price:* . . . . . . . . . . . . . . . . . . . . . . . . . . . . . . . . **$633.00**

## MODEL 700 MOUNTAIN DM (DETACHABLE MAGAZINE) RIFLE

The Remington Model 700 MTN DM rifle features the traditional mountain rifle-styled stock with a pistol grip pitched lower to position the wrist for a better grip. The cheekpiece is designed to align the eye for quick, accurate sighting. The American walnut stock has a handrubbed oil finish and comes with a brown recoil pad and deep-cut checkering. The Model 700 MTN DM also features a lean contoured 22" barrel that helps reduce total weight to 6.5 pounds (no sights). All metalwork features a glass bead-blasted, blued-metal finish. *Calibers:* 25-06 Rem., 260 Rem., 270 Win., 280 Rem., 7mm-08 Rem., and 30-06 Springfield.

*Price:* . . . . . . . . . . . . . . . . . . . . . . . . . . . . . . . . **$681.00**

## MODEL 700 ALASKAN WILDERNESS RIFLE (AWR)

This custom-built rifle has the same rate of twist and custom magnum barrel contour as the African Plains Rifle below, but features a Kevlar-reinforced composite stock. *Calibers:* 7mm Rem. Mag., 7mm STW, .300 Rem. Ultra Mag., 300 Win. Mag., 300 Wby. Mag., 338 Win. Mag., .338 Rem. Ultra Mag., 375 H&H Mag. *Capacity:* 3 shots *Barrel length:* 24" *Overall Length:* 44.5" *Weight:* 6 lbs. 12 oz.

*Price:* . . . . . . . . . . . . . . . . . . . . . . . . . . . . . . **$1,480.00**

## MODEL 700 AFRICAN PLAINS RIFLE (APR)

The custom-built Model 700 APR rifle has a laminated classic wood stock and the following specifications.

*Calibers:* 7mm Rem. Mag., 300 Win. Mag., 300 Wby. Mag., 300 Rem. Ultra Mag., 338 Win. Mag., 375 H&H Mag. *Capacity:* 3 shots *Barrel length:* 26" *Overall Length:* 46.5" *Weight:* 7.75 lbs. *Rate Of Twist:* R.H. 1 turn in 9.25" (7mm Rem. Mag.); 10" (300 Win. Mag. and 338 Win. Mag., .338 Rem. Ultra Mag.); 12" (30 Wby. Mag. and 375 H&H Mag.)

*Price:* . . . . . . . . . . . . . . . . . . . . . . . . . . . . . . **$1,593.00**

# REMINGTON BOLT-ACTION RIFLES

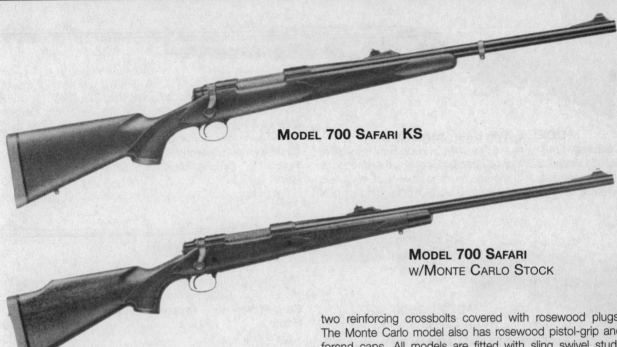

**MODEL 700 SAFARI KS**

**MODEL 700 SAFARI**
w/MONTE CARLO STOCK

**MODEL 700™ SAFARI GRADE** bolt-action rifles provide big-game hunters with a choice of either wood or synthetic stock. Model 700 Safari Monte Carlo (with Monte Carlo comb and cheekpiece) and Model 700 Safari Classic (with straight-line classic comb and no cheekpiece) are the satin-finished wood-stock models. Both are decorated with hand-cut checkering 18 lines to the inch and fitted with two reinforcing crossbolts covered with rosewood plugs. The Monte Carlo model also has rosewood pistol-grip and forend caps. All models are fitted with sling swivel studs and 22" or 24" barrels. Synthetic stock has simulated wood-grain finish, reinforced with Kevlar® (KS).

**Calibers:** 8mm Rem. Mag., 375 H&H Magnum, 416 Rem. Mag. and 458 Win. Mag. **Capacity:** 3 rounds. **Avg. Weight:** 9 lbs. **Overall Length:** 44.5" **Rate of Twist:** 10" (8mm Rem. Mag.); 12" (375 H&H Mag.); 14" (416 Rem. Mag., 458 Win. Mag.)
**Price:** . . . . . . . . . . . . . . . . . . . . . . . . . . . . . . . . . . . **$1,225.00**
   **CUSTOM KS SAFARI.** . . . . . . . . . . . . . . . . . . . . . . **1,410.00**
   **LH CUSTOM KS SAFARI** . . . . . . . . . . . . . . . . . . **1,488.00**

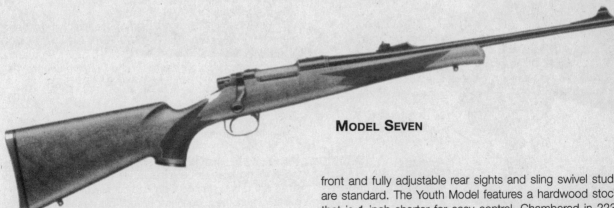

**MODEL SEVEN**

The short-action **MODEL SEVEN** is built to the accuracy standards of the famous Model 700 and is individually test fired to prove it. Its tapered 20" Remington special steel barrel is free floating out to a single pressure point at the forend tip. A fully enclosed bolt and extractor system, ramp front and fully adjustable rear sights and sling swivel studs are standard. The Youth Model features a hardwood stock that is 1 inch shorter for easy control. Chambered in 223, 243, 260, 7mm-08 and 308.

**Prices:**
| | |
|---|---|
| Laminate . . . . . . . . . . . . . . . . . . . . . . . . . . . . . | $633.00 |
| Laminate/Stainless . . . . . . . . . . . . . . . . . . . . . . . | 727.00 |
| Youth (hardwood) . . . . . . . . . . . . . . . . . . . . . . . | 519.00 |
| Stainless Synthetic . . . . . . . . . . . . . . . . . . . . . . | 681.00 |

# REMINGTON RIFLES

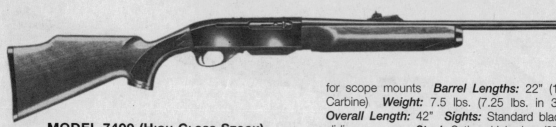

## MODEL 7400 (HIGH GLOSS STOCK)

**Calibers:** 243 Win., 270 Win., 280 Rem., 30-06, 30-06 Carbine, 308 Win. **Capacity:** 5 centerfire cartridges (4 in the magazine, 1 in the chamber); extra 4-shot magazine available **Action:** Gas-operated; receiver drilled and tapped for scope mounts **Barrel Lengths:** 22" (18.5" in 30-06 Carbine) **Weight:** 7.5 lbs. (7.25 lbs. in 30-06 Carbine) **Overall Length:** 42" **Sights:** Standard blade ramp front; sliding ramp rear **Stock:** Satin or high-gloss (270 Win. and 30-06 only) walnut stock and forend; curved pistol grip **Length Of Pull:** 13 ³/₈" **Drop At Heel:** 2.25" **Drop At Comb:** 1 ¹³/₁₆"

**Price:** . . . . . . . . . . . . . . . . . . . . . . . . . . . . . . . . . . **$612.00**
Synthetic . . . . . . . . . . . . . . . . . . . . . . . . . . . . . **509.00**

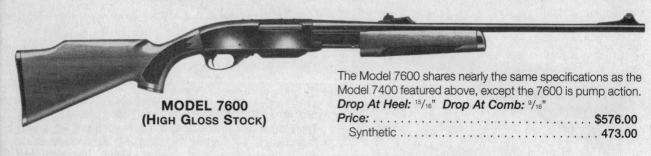

## MODEL 7600
## (HIGH GLOSS STOCK)

The Model 7600 shares nearly the same specifications as the Model 7400 featured above, except the 7600 is pump action. **Drop At Heel:** ¹⁵/₁₆" **Drop At Comb:** ⁹/₁₆"

**Price:** . . . . . . . . . . . . . . . . . . . . . . . . . . . . . . . . . **$576.00**
Synthetic . . . . . . . . . . . . . . . . . . . . . . . . . . . . . **473.00**

## MODEL 700 ETRONX SYSTEM COMPONENTS

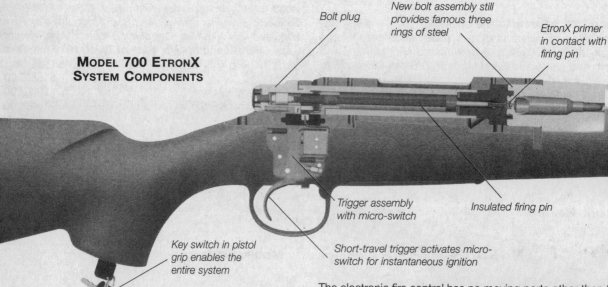

Bolt plug

New bolt assembly still provides famous three rings of steel

EtronX primer in contact with firing pin

Trigger assembly with micro-switch

Insulated firing pin

Key switch in pistol grip enables the entire system

Short-travel trigger activates micro-switch for instantaneous ignition

## REMINGTON 700 ETRONX

Remington's ground-breaking new EtronX System is claimed to be the most significant advance in rifle and ammunition performance since the development of self-contained cartridges. For the first time, cased centerfire cartridges can be fired by a completely non-mechanical system that ignites primers by means of an electric pulse.

The electronic fire control has no moving parts other than the trigger – no sear to be released or firing pin to move and strike the primer. Instead, an internal electric circuit is completed when the trigger is pulled. This sends an electrical charge through the system to our new electrically responsive primer, igniting it instantaneously. The result is the fastest lock time of any rifle ever built. Only Remington could bring you a gun and ammo system this advanced.

In outward appearance, the EtronX resembles a 700 VS SF, with its fluted 26" barrel. The EtronX is chambered in .220 Swift, .22-250 and .243.

# REMINGTON RIMFIRE RIFLES

**MODEL 40-XR BR**

MODEL **40-XR BR** with 22" stainless-steel barrel (heavy contour), 22 LR match chamber and bore dimensions. Receiver and barrel drilled and tapped for scope mounts (mounted on green, duPont Kevlar reinforced fiberglass benchrest stock. Adjustable trigger (2 oz. trigger optional).
*Price:* . . . . . . . . . . . . . . . . . . . . . . . . . . . . . . . . . . **$1,728.00**
*(Additional target rifles are available through Remington's Custom Shop.)*

**MODEL 541-T BOLT ACTION**

This heavy-barreled box-fed .22 has a reputation for accuracy among silhouette shooters. Its checkered walnut stock and a crisp trigger complement a clean barrel contour.
*Price:* . . . . . . . . . . . . . . . . . . . . . . . . . . . . . . . . . $465.00
   HEAVY BARREL . . . . . . . . . . . . . . . . . . . . . . . . . 492.00
   MODEL 581-S . . . . . . . . . . . . . . . . . . . . . . . . . 239.00

### MODEL 552 BDL SPEEDMASTER

The rimfire semiautomatic 552 BDL Deluxe sports Remington custom-impressed. Sights are ramp-style in front and rugged big-game type fully adjustable in rear.
*Price:* . . . . . . . . . . . . . . . . . . . . . . . . . . . . . . . . . **$365.00**

**MODEL 572 BDL FIELDMASTER**

Features of this rifle with big-game feel and appearance are: Du Pont's tough RK-W finish; centerfire-rifle-type rear sight fully adjustable for both vertical and horizontal sight alignment; big-game style ramp front sight; Remington impressed checkering on both stock and forend.
*Price:* . . . . . . . . . . . . . . . . . . . . . . . . . . . . . . . . . **$379.00**

# REMINGTON RIMFIRE RIFLES

## MODEL 597 SERIES

Remington's autoloading rimfire rifles–the Model 597™ Series–are available in 7 versions, offering a choice of carbon or stainless steel barreled actions, synthetic or laminated wood stocks, and chambering for either standard 22 Long Rifle or 22 Magnum ammo. All M597™ rifles feature beavertail-style forends rounded with finger grooves for hand-filling control. The top of the receiver blends into the pistol grip, creating a rimfire autoloader that points like a shotgun but aims like a rifle. Features include a bolt guidance system of twin steel rails for smooth bolt travel and functional reliability. The 20-inch barrels are free-floated for consistent accuracy with all types of rimfire ammunition. A new trigger design creates crisp let-off for autoloading rifles. Bolts on the 22 LR versions are nickel-plated. The magnum-version bolt has a special alloy steel to provide controlled, uniform function with magnum cartridges. All receivers are grooved for standard tip-off mounts and are also drilled and tapped for Weaver-type bases. Adjustable open sights and one-piece scope mount rails are standard, as are spare magazines.

**MODEL 597 (22 LR CARBON STEEL)**

The M597™ is chambered for 22 Long Rifle ammunition and matches Remington's carbon steel barrel with a strong, lightweight, alloy receiver. All metal has a non-reflective, matte black finish. The rifle is housed in a one-piece, dark gray synthetic stock.
*Price:* . . . . . . . . . . . . . . . . . . . . . . . . . . . . . . . . . **$163.00**

**MODEL 597™ LSS**

The M597™ LSS (Laminated Stock Stainless) has a satin-finished stainless steel barrel and matching, gray-tone alloy receiver. Chambered for 22 LR cartridges. Its stock is of laminated wood in light and dark brown tones.
*Price:* . . . . . . . . . . . . . . . . . . . . . . . . . . . . . . . . . **$272.00**

**MODEL 597™ MAGNUM**

Chambered for 22 Win. Mag. rimfire cartridges, the M597™ MAGNUM features a carbon steel barrel, alloy receiver and black synthetic stock.
*Price:* . . . . . . . . . . . . . . . . . . . . . . . . . . . . . . . **$321.00**
W/Laminated Stock . . . . . . . . . . . . . . . . . . . . . **377.00**

**MODEL 597 TARGET**

The Model 597 Target is ideal for the rimfire competition popular today. A heavy 20-inch target barrel and high-comb beavertail stock promise tight groups and high scores. The MODEL 597 SPORTER and STAINLESS SPORTER feature hardwood stocks similar in profile to the 597's.
*Price:* . . . . . . . . . . . . . . . . . . . . . . . . . **Price on request**

# RIFLES, INC.

## CLASSIC MODEL

### SPECIFICATIONS

**Calibers:** Customized for varmint, target or hunter specifications, up to 375 H&H
**Action:** Remington or Winchester stainless steel controlled-round feed with lapped bolt
**Barrel Length:** 24"-26" depending on caliber; stainless-steel match grade, lapped
**Weight:** 6.5 lbs. (approx.)

**Stock:** Pillar glass bedded; laminated fiberglass, finished with textured epoxy
**Features:** Fine-tuned adjustable trigger; hinged floor-plate trigger guard
**Price:**. . . . . . . . . . . . . . . . . . . . . . . . . . . . . . . . **$2,000.00**
    left hand . . . . . . . . . . . . . . . . . . . . . . . . . . . . . **2,100.00**
**Also Available: Signature Series,** a long-range rifle on the stainless Remington 700 action, with 27-inch fluted stainless barrel, McMillan synthetic stock, 300 Rem. Ultra Mag only, 1/2 m.o.a, numbered and signed . . . . . . . . **2,800.00**
    Left-hand . . . . . . . . . . . . . . . . . . . . . . . . . . . **2,950.00**

## SAFARI MODEL

### SPECIFICATIONS

**Action:** Winchester Model 70 controlled-round feed; hand lapped and honed bolt; drilled and tapped for 8X40 base screws
**Barrel Length:** 23"-25" depending on caliber; stainless-steel match grade, lapped

**Weight:** 9 lbs. (approx.)
**Muzzle Break:** Stainless Quiet Slimbrake
**Metal Finish:** Matte stainless or black Teflon
**Stock:** Pillar glass bedded; double reinforced laminated fiberglass/graphite; finished with textured epoxy
**Features:** Fine-tuned adjustable trigger; hinged floor-plate
**Options:** Drop box for additional round; express sights; barrel band; quarter ribs
**Price:**. . . . . . . . . . . . . . . . . . . . . . . . . . . . . . . . **$2,700.00**
    w/Options . . . . . . . . . . . . . . . . . . . . . . . . . . . . . **3,770.00**

## LIGHTWEIGHT STRATA STAINLESS MODEL

### SPECIFICATIONS

**Calibers:** Up to 375 H&H  **Action:** Stainless Remington; fluted, tapped and handle-hollowed bolt; aluminum bolt shroud  **Barrel Length:** 22"-24" depending on caliber; stainless-steel match grade  **Weight:** 4.75 lbs. (approx.)
**Stock:** Pillar glass bedded; laminated Kevlar/Boron/Graphite,

finished with textured epoxy **Features:** Matte stainless metal finish; aluminum blind or hinged floorplate trigger guard; custom Protektor pad
**Price:**. . . . . . . . . . . . . . . . . . . . . . . . . . . . . . . . **$2,600.00**
    left hand . . . . . . . . . . . . . . . . . . . . . . . . . . . . . **2,750.00**
**Also Available: LIGHTWEIGHT 70** in calibers up to 375 H&H.
**Barrel Length:** 22" to 24" (depending on caliber)) stainless steel match grade. **Weight:** 5.75 lbs. **Stock:** Pillar glass bedded; laminated Kevlar/Graphite/Boron finished with textured epoxy. Trigger is fine-tuned.
**Price:**. . . . . . . . . . . . . . . . . . . . . . . . . . . . . . . . **$2,500.00**
    left hand . . . . . . . . . . . . . . . . . . . . . . . . . . . . . **2,650.00**

# RUGER CARBINES

**MODEL 10/22RBM**

## RUGER 10/22 MAGNUM

This .22 Magnum autoloader uses a heavy bolt in a blow-back mechanism that feeds from the proven 10/22 rotary magazine. Integral scope bases augment open sights. The carbine-style walnut stock and 18.5" barrel make this a fast-handling rimfire. *Length:* 37" *Weight:* 6.5 lbs.
*Price:* ................................. $430.00

**MODEL PC9**

After several years of research, Ruger engineers combined 10/22 and P-series technology to create an autoloading rifle that uses popular pistol cartridges and Ruger pistol magazines. This handy carbine meets the needs of personal defense, sporting use, law enforcement and security agencies. Advanced synthetics and precision investment-casting technologies allow for improved performance and substantially reduced costs. The Ruger Carbine has a chrome-moly steel barrel, receiver, slide and recoil springs, and features a checkered Zytell stock with rubber buttplate. Adjustable open sights and patented integral scope mounts are standard. The Ruger Carbine also features a combination firing-pin block and slide lock. Trigger engagement is required for the firing pin to strike the primer. The slide locks to prevent chambering or ejection of a round if the riffle is struck on the buttpad. This safety system is backed up by a manual crossbolt safety located at the rear of the trigger guard. A slide stop locks the slide open for inspection and cleaning.

## MODEL PC9 AUTOLOADING CARBINE

### SPECIFICATIONS

*Caliber:* 9mm or 40 auto  *Capacity:* 10 rounds
*Action:* Mass impulse delayed blowback
*Barrel Length:* 15.25"  *Overall Length:* 34.75"
*Weight:* 6 lbs. 4 oz.  *Trigger Pull:* Approx. 6 lb.
*Rifling:* 6 grooves, 1 turn in 10" RH
*Stock:* du Pont "Zytel" matte black
*Finish:* Matte black oxide
*Sights:* Blade front, open rear plus provision for scope mounts (ghost ring version also available)
*Sight Radius:* 12.65"
*Safety:* Manual push-button crossbolt safety (locks trigger mechanism) and internal firing-pin block safety
*Features:* Bolt lock to prevent accidental unloading or chambering of a cartridge; steel barrel, receiver, slide and recoil spring unit w/black composite stock
*Price:* .................................. $575.00
    w/Ghost Ring Receiver Sight.............. 598.00
*All Ruger long guns come standard with cable lock & keys.*

# RUGER CARBINES

### RUGER MINI-14/5

**Mechanism:** Gas-operated, autoloading. **Materials:** Heat-treated chrome molybdenum and other alloy steels as well as music wire coil springs are used throughout the mechanism to ensure reliability under field-operating conditions. **Safety:** The safety blocks both the hammer and sear. The slide can be cycled when the safety is on. The safety is mounted in the front of the trigger guard so that it may be set to Fire position without removing finger from trigger guard. **Firing pin:** The firing pin is retracted mechanically during the first part of the unlocking of the bolt. The rifle can only be fired when the bolt is safely locked. **Stock:** One-piece American hardwood reinforced with steel liner at stressed areas. Sling swivels standard. Handguard and forearm separated by air space from barrel to promote cooling under rapid-fire conditions. **Field stripping:** The Carbine can be field-stripped to its eight (8) basic sub-assemblies in a matter of seconds and without use of special tools.

## RUGER MINI-14
### SPECIFICATIONS
**Caliber:** 223 (5.56mm)  **Barrel Length:** 18.5"
**Overall Length:** 37 1/4"  **Weight:** 6 lbs. 8 oz.
**Magazine:** 5-round, detachable box magazine
**Sights:** Rear adj.for windage/elevation.
**Prices:** Mini-14/5 Blued . . . . . . . . . . . . . . . . . $606.00
K-Mini-14/5 Stainless . . . . . . . . . . . . . . . . . . . . . . 664.00
K-Mini-14/5P Stainless, synthetic. . . . . . . . . . . . 664.00
(Scope not included)

### MINI-14/5R RANCH RIFLE

### SPECIFICATIONS
**Caliber:** 223 (5.56mm)  **Barrel Length:** 18.5"
**Overall Length:** 37 1/4"  **Weight:** 6 lbs. 8 oz.
**Magazine:** 5-round detachable box magazine.

**Sights:** Fold-down rear sight; 1" scope rings (factory machined scope mount system available on all Ranch models)
**Prices:** Mini-14/5R Blued . . . . . . . . . . . . . . . . . $649.00
K-Mini-14/5R Stainless . . . . . . . . . . . . . . . . . . . . . 710.00
K-Mini-14/5RPS Stainless, Synthetic . . . . . . . . . 710.00

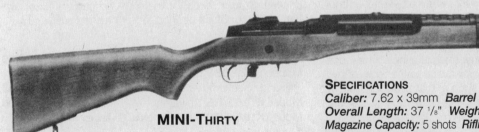

### MINI-THIRTY

This modified version of the Ruger Ranch rifle is chambered for the 7.62 x 39mm Soviet service cartridge. Designed for use with telescopic sights, it features low, compact scope-mounting for greater accuracy and carrying case, and a buffer in the receiver. Sling swivels are standard.

### SPECIFICATIONS
**Caliber:** 7.62 x 39mm  **Barrel Length:** 18.5"
**Overall Length:** 37 1/8"  **Weight:** 6 lbs. 14 oz. (empty)
**Magazine Capacity:** 5 shots  **Rifling:** 6 grooves, R.H. twist, 1:10"
**Finish:** Blued or stainless
**Stock:** One-piece American hardwood w/steel liners in stressed areas
**Sights:** Blade front; peep rear (factory machined scope mount system available on all Ranch models).
**Prices:** Blued . . . . . . . . . . . . . . . . . . . . . . . . . $649.00
Stainless Steel. . . . . . . . . . . . . . . . . . . . . . . . . . 710.00

# RUGER CARBINES

**STANDARD 10/22 CARBINE**

**MODEL K10/22RP "ALL WEATHER"**

**MODEL K10/22RBI INTERNATIONAL CARBINE STAINLESS**

**MODEL 10/22T TARGET**

Introduced in 1964, Ruger's 10/22 is still a best-seller. It follows the Ruger design practice of building a firearm from integrated sub-assemblies. For example, the trigger housing assembly contains the entire ignition system, which employs a high-speed, swinging hammer to ensure the shortest possible lock time. The barrel is assembled to the receiver by a unique dual-screw dovetail system that provides unusual rigidity and strength—and accounts, in part, for the exceptional accuracy of the 10/22.

## SPECIFICATIONS
**Mechanism:** Blow-back, semiautomatic. **Caliber:** 22 LR, high-speed or standard-velocity loads. **Magazine:** 10-shot capacity, exclusive Ruger rotary design; fits flush into stock. **Barrel:** 18.5", assembled to the receiver by dual-screw dovetail mounting for added strength and rigidity. **Overall Length:** 37 1/4". **Weight:** 5 lbs. **Sights:** 1/16" brass bead front; single folding-leaf rear, adjustable for elevation; receiver drilled and tapped for scope blocks or tip-off mount adapter (included). **Trigger:** Curved finger surface, 3/8" wide. **Safety:** Sliding cross-button type; safety locks both sear and hammer and cannot be put in safe position unless gun is cocked. **Stocks:** birch, laminated, American walnut or synthetic. **Finish:** Blued or anodized or brushed satin.

**Prices:**

| | |
|---|---|
| **MODEL 10/22 RB STANDARD** | .$235.00 |
| **MODEL 10/22 DSP DELUXE** (Hand-checkered American walnut) | .279.00 |
| **MODEL K10/22 RB STAINLESS** | .273.00 |
| **MODEL K10/22 RBI INTERNATIONAL CARBINE** w/full-length stock | .267.00 |
| stainless | .287.00 |
| **MODEL 10/22T TARGET** (no sights) Hammer-forged 20" barrel, laminated target-style stock | .397.50 |
| stainless | .445.00 |
| **MODEL K10/22RP** `All Weather" synthetic stock | .230.00 |
| stainless | .273.00 |

# RUGER SINGLE-SHOT RIFLES

Ruger's Farguharson-style single-shot rifle first appeared in 1966. The following illustrations show the variations currently offered in the Ruger No. 1 Single-Shot Rifle Series. Ruger No. 1 rifles have a Farquharson-type falling-block action and select American walnut stocks. Pistol grip and forearm are hand-checkered to a borderless design. Price for any listed model is **$774.00** (except the No. 1 RSI International Model: **$794.00**). Barreled Actions (blued only): **$555.00**

### NO. 1A LIGHT SPORTER
*Calibers:* 243 Win., 270 Win., 30-06, 7x57mm. *Barrel Length:* 22". *Sights:* Adjustable folding-leaf rear sight mounted on quarter rib with ramp front sight base and dovetail-type gold bead front sight; open. *Weight:* 7 1/4 lbs.

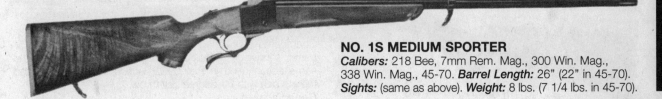

### NO. 1S MEDIUM SPORTER
*Calibers:* 218 Bee, 7mm Rem. Mag., 300 Win. Mag., 338 Win. Mag., 45-70. *Barrel Length:* 26" (22" in 45-70). *Sights:* (same as above). *Weight:* 8 lbs. (7 1/4 lbs. in 45-70).

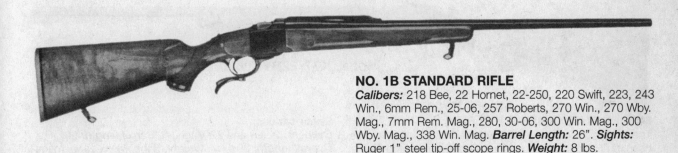

### NO. 1B STANDARD RIFLE
*Calibers:* 218 Bee, 22 Hornet, 22-250, 220 Swift, 223, 243 Win., 6mm Rem., 25-06, 257 Roberts, 270 Win., 270 Wby. Mag., 7mm Rem. Mag., 280, 30-06, 300 Win. Mag., 300 Wby. Mag., 338 Win. Mag. *Barrel Length:* 26". *Sights:* Ruger 1" steel tip-off scope rings. *Weight:* 8 lbs.

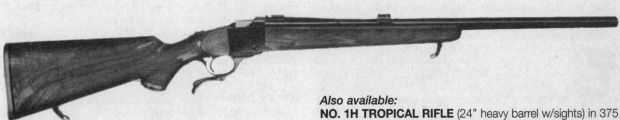

### NO. 1V SPECIAL VARMINTER
*Calibers:* 22-250, 220 Swift, 223, 25-06, 6mm. *Barrel Length:* 24" (26" in 220 Swift). *Sights:* Ruger target scope blocks, heavy barrel and 1" tip-off scope rings. *Weight:* 9 lbs.

**Also available:**
**NO. 1H TROPICAL RIFLE** (24" heavy barrel w/sights) in 375 H&H Mag., 458 Win. Mag., 416 Rigby and 416 Rem. Mag.
**NO 1. RSI INTERNATIONAL** (20" lightweight barrel and full-length stock) in 243 Win., 270 Win., 30-06 and 7x57mm
**NO 1. STAINLESS** (24" standard or 26" heavy barrel) laminated hardwood stock, in .22-250, .25-06, 7mm Rem. Mag., 7mm STW, .300 Wby. Magnum

# RUGER BOLT-ACTION RIFLES

## MODEL 77/22RH HORNET
**$525.00** ($550.00 77/22 RSH w/Sights)

The Model 77/22RH is Ruger's first truly compact centerfire bolt-action rifle. It features a 77/22 action crafted from heat-treated alloy steel. Exterior surfaces are blued to match the hammer-forged barrel. The action features a right-hand turning bolt with a 90-degree bolt throw, cocking on opening. Fast lock time (2.7 milliseconds) adds to accuracy. A three-position swing-back safety locks the bolt; in its center position firing is blocked, but bolt operation and safe loading and unloading are permitted. When fully forward, the rifle is ready to fire. The American walnut stock has recoil pad, grip cap and sling swivels installed. One-inch diameter scope rings fit integral bases.

### SPECIFICATIONS
**Caliber:** 22 Hornet
**Capacity:** 6 rounds (detachable rotary magazine)
**Barrel length:** 20" **Overall length:** 40"
**Weight:** 6 lbs. (unloaded)
**Sights:** Single folding-leaf rear; gold bead front
**Length of pull:** 13 3/4"
**Drop at heel:** 2 3/4" **Drop at comb:** 2"
**Finish:** Polished and blued, matte, nonglare receiver top
**Also available:** MODEL K77/22VHZ Varmint w/stainless-steel heavy barrel, laminated American hardwood stock.
**Price:** (w/o sights) . . . . . . . . . . . . . . . . . . . . . . $575.00

**MODEL 77/44 RS**

Chambered in .44 Magnum, the new 77/44 is a short (18.5" barrel), lightweight (6 lbs.) deluxed grade carbine based on the same action used in the 77/22. Action features right-hand turning bolt with 90-degree bolt throw.
**Capacity:** 4 rounds
**Price:** . . . . . . . . . . . . . . . . . . . . . . . . . . . . . . $580.00

**MODEL K77/22BVZ VARMINT**

## MODEL 77/22 RIMFIRE RIFLE

The Ruger 22-caliber rimfire 77/22 bolt-action rifle has been built especially to function with the patented Ruger 10-Shot Rotary Magazine concept. The magazine throat, retaining lips and ramps that guide the cartridge into the chamber are solid alloy steel that resists bending or deforming.

The 77/22 weighs just under six pounds. Its heavy-duty receiver incorporates the integral scope bases of the patented Ruger Scope Mounting System with 1-inch Ruger scope rings. With the 3-position safety in its "lock" position, a dead bolt is cammed forward, locking the bolt handle down. In this position the action is locked closed and the handle cannot be raised.

All metal surfaces are finished in nonglare deep blue or satin stainless. Stock is select straight-grain American walnut, hand checkered and finished with durable polyurethane.

An All-Weather, all-stainless steel **MODEL K77/22RS** features a stock made of glass-fiber reinforced Zytel.
**Weight:** Approx. 6 lbs.

### SPECIFICATIONS
**Calibers:** 22 LR and 22 Magnum. **Barrel length:** 20".
**Overall length:** 39 1/4". **Weight:** 6 lbs. (w/o scope, magazine empty). **Feed:** Detachable 10-Shot Ruger Rotary Magazine.
**Prices: 77/22R** Blue, w/o sights, 1" Ruger rings . **$498.00**
**77/22RM** Blue, walnut stock, plain barrel,
   no sights, 1" Ruger rings, 22 Mag. . . . . . . . . . . **498.00**
**77/22RS** Blue, sights included, 1" Ruger rings . . . **506.00**
**77/22RSM** Blue, American walnut, iron sights . . . . **506.00**
**K77/22-RP** Synthetic stock, stainless steel, plain
   barrel with 1" Ruger rings . . . . . . . . . . . . . . . . **498.00**
**K77/22-RMP** Synthetic stock, stainless steel,
   plain barrel, 1" Ruger rings . . . . . . . . . . . . . . . **498.00**
**K77/22-RSP** Synthetic stock, stainless steel, gold
   bead front sight, folding-leaf rear, Ruger 1"rings . **506.00**
**K77/22RSMP** Synthetic stock, metal sights,
   stainless. . . . . . . . . . . . . . . . . . . . . . . . . . . . . **506.00**
**K77/22VBZ** Varmint Laminated stock, scope
   rings, heavy barrel, stainless . . . . . . . . . . . . . . **539.00**

# RUGER BOLT-ACTION RIFLES

## MARK II SERIES

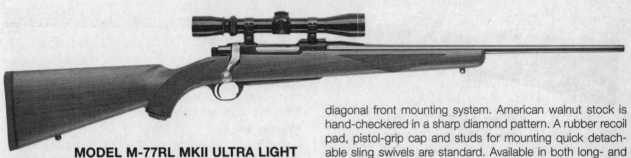

### MODEL M-77RL MKII ULTRA LIGHT

This big-game, bolt-action rifle encompasses the traditional features that have made the Ruger M-77 one of the most popular centerfire rifles in the world. It includes a sliding top tang safety, a one-piece bolt with Mauser-type extractor and diagonal front mounting system. American walnut stock is hand-checkered in a sharp diamond pattern. A rubber recoil pad, pistol-grip cap and studs for mounting quick detachable sling swivels are standard. Available in both long- and short-action versions, with Integral Base Receiver and 1" Ruger scope rings. *Calibers:* 223, 243, 257, 270, 30-06, 308. *Barrel length:* 20". *Weight:* Approx. 6 lbs. *Price:* . . . . . . . . . . . . . . . . . . . . . . . . . . . . . . . . .$677.00

### MODEL M-77R MKII

Integral Base Receiver, 1" scope rings. No sights.
*Calibers:* (Long action) 6mm Rem., 6.5x55mm, 7x57mm, 257 Roberts, 270, 280 Rem., 30-06 (all with 22" barrels); 7mm Rem. Mag., 300 Win. Mag., 338 Win. Mag. (all with 24" barrels); and (Short Stroke action) 223, 243, 308 (22" barrels).
*Weight:* Approx. 7 lbs.
*Price:* . . . . . . . . . . . . . . . . . . . . . . . . . . . . . .$634.00

*Also available:* **M-77LR MKII** (Left Hand).
*Calibers:* 270, 30-06, 7mm Rem. Mag., 300 Win. Mag
*Price:*. . . . . . . . . . . . . . . . . . . . . . . . . . . . . . . .$634.00

### MODEL M-77RS MKII (not shown)

Integral Base Receiver, Ruger steel 1" rings, open sights.
*Calibers:* 243, 25-06, 270, 7mm Rem. Mag., 30-06, 300 Win. Mag., 308, 338 Win. Mag., 458 Win. Mag.
*Weight:* Approx. 7 lbs.
*Price:* . . . . . . . . . . . . . . . . . . . . . . . . . . . . . .$706.00

**MODEL K77RSBZ MKII**

### MODEL K77RBZ MKII

Stainless steel, laminated stock, scope rings
*Calibers:* 223, 22-250, 243, 270, 280, 7mm Mag., 308, 30-06, 300 Win. Mag., 338 Win. Mag.
*Price:* M77RSBZ . . . . . . . . . . . . . . . . . . . . . . $673.00
  With sights & rings (no .223, 22-250, .300 Win. Mag.). . **740.00**

**MODEL M-77RSI MKII**

### MODEL M-77RSI MKII INTERNATIONAL

International full-length stock, Integral Base Receiver, open sights, Ruger 1" steel rings. *Calibers:* 243, 270, 30-06, 308
*Barrel Length:* 18.5" *Weight:* Approx. 6 lbs.
*Price:* . . . . . . . . . . . . . . . . . . . . . . . . . . . . . . $713.00

# RUGER BOLT-ACTION RIFLES

## MARK II SERIES (w/THREE POSITION SAFETY/FIXED EJECTORS)

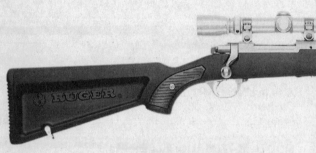

**MODEL M-77VT MK II**
**HEAVY BARREL TARGET**

### MODEL M-77VT MK II
### HEAVY-BARREL TARGET

Features Mark II stainless-steel bolt action Target, gray matte finish, two-stage adjustable trigger. No sights.

**SPECIFICATIONS**
**Calibers:** 22-250, 220 Swift, 223, 243, 25-06 and 308.
**Barrel Length:** 26", hammer-forged, free-floating stainless steel. **Weight:** 9 ³/₄ lbs. Stock: Laminated American hardwood with flat forend.
**Price:** KM-77VT MKII . . . . . . . . . . . . . . . . . . . $759.00

**M-77 MARK II ALL-WEATHER**

### M-77 II MARK II ALL-WEATHER

**KM-77RP MK II ALL-WEATHER** Receiver w/integral dovetails to accommodate Ruger 1" rings, no sights, stainless steel, synthetic stock.
**Calibers:** 223, 22-50, 243, 25-06, 270, 280, 30-06, 7mm Rem. Mag., 300 Win. Mag., 308, 338 Win. Mag. . . . . . . . $604.00
**MODEL K77RSP MKII** Receiver w/integral dovetails to accommodate Ruger 1" rings, metal sights, stainless steel, synthetic stock.
**Calibers:** 243, 270, 7mm Rem. Mag., 30-06, 300 Win. Mag., 338 Win. Mag. *(scope not included)* . . . . . $672.00

**M77RSM MKII**

### RUGER 77 RSM MK II MAGNUM RIFLE

This "Bond Street"-quality African hunting rifle features a quarter rib machined from a single bar of steel; Circassian walnut stock with black forend tip; steel floorplate and latch; a new Ruger Magnum trigger guard with floorplate latch designed flush with the contours of the trigger (to eliminate accidental dumping of cartridges); a three-position safety; Express rear sight and front sight ramp with gold bead sight. Also available in Express Model (long action, no heavy barrel).
**Calibers:** 375 H&H, 416 Rigby. **Capacity:** 4 rounds (375 H&H) and 3 rounds (416 Rigby). **Barrel Length:** 22" **Overall**

**Length:** 42 ¹/₈" **Barrel Thread Diameter:** 1¹/₈" **Weight:** 9 ¹/₄ lbs. (375 H&H); 10 ¹/₄ lbs. (416 Rigby), 7.5 lbs. (others)
**Price:** 375, 416 . . . . . . . . . . . . . . . . . . . . . . . . . . $1,695.00
**Also available:** EXPRESS MODEL, (long action) 270, 7mm, 30-06, 300 Win. Mag., 338 Win. Mag.
**Price:** EXPRESS . . . . . . . . . . . . . . . . . . . . . . . . . . . $1,625.00
**RUGER LARGE ACTION RIFLE.** Standard walnut stock, with or wihtout sights, 24" and 26" barrels in 7 STW, 338 Ultra Mag., .375 H+H, 416 Right, .458 Left.
**Price:** 7 STW and 338 UM (no sights) . . . . . . . . . . $1,195.00
375, 416, 458 (sights) . . . . . . . . . . . . . . . . . . . . . . . 1,375.00

# SAKO RIFLES

## SAKO 75 HUNTER

The **SAKO 75 HUNTER** is the first rifle to offer an action furnished with both a bolt with three locking lugs and a mechanical ejector. This combination results in unprecedented smoothness and reliability. The sturdy receiver helps to zero the rifle with different bullets and loads. The new bolt provides a solid, well-balanced platform for the cartridge. The traditional safety catch is either on or off. Cartridge removal or loading is done by pressing a separate bolt release button in front of the safety. No need to touch the safety to remove a cartridge and then disengage it by mistake under difficult or stressful conditions. The new cold hammer-forged barrel is manufactured in an advanced custom-built robotic cell. The New SAKO features a totally free-floating barrel. Instead of checkering, this all-stainless, all-weather model has soft rubbery grips molded in the stock to provide a firmer, more comfortable hold than with conventional synthetic stocks. The selected moisture stabilized high-grade walnut ensures quality and craftsmanship. Other features include:

• Five bolt siding guides • 70° Bolt Lift • Totally free-floating cold hammer-forged barrel • Positive safety system with separate bolt release button for safe unloading • Detachable staggered 5-round magazine • Five (5) action sizes for perfect cartridge match • All-Stainless metal parts and All-Weather synthetic stock with special grips • Selected moisture stabilized walnut stock with hand-crafted checkering • Integral scope rails

**Prices:**

**SAKO 75 HUNTER**
22"barrel (17 Rem., 222 Rem., 22 PPC, 6PPC, 223 Rem., 22-250 Rem., 243 Win., 7mm-08, 308 Win., 25-06 Rem., 6.5x55 SE, 7x64, 270 Win., 280 Win., 30-06, 9.3x62 . . . . . . . . . . . . . . . . . . . . . . . **$1,184.00**
24" barrel (7mm Rem. Mag., 300 Win. Mag., 338 Win. Mag., 375 H&H Mag., 416 Rem. Mag. . . . . . . **1,219.00**
26" barrel (270 Wby. Mag., 7mm STW, 7mm Wby. Mag., 300 Wby. Mag., 340 Wby. Mag., 300 Rem. Ultra Mag. . . . **1,219.00**

### SAKO 75 STAINLESS SYNTHETIC
22" barrel (22-250 Rem., 243 Win., 308 Win., 7mm-08 22 PPC, 66 PPC, 6.5x55 SE, 25-06 Rem., 270 Win., 30-06, 9.3x62). . . . . . . . . . . . . . . . . . . . . . **$1,284.00**
24" barrel (7mm Rem. Mag., 300 Win. Mag., 338 Win. Mag., 375 H&H Mag.) . . . . . . **1,314.00**
26" barrel (7mm STW, .300 Wby. Mag., 300 Rem Ultra Mag.) Hinged floor plate.

**SAKO 75 VARMINT RIFLE**

**SAKO 75 VARMINT STAINLESS LAMINATED**

## SAKO 75 VARMINT RIFLE

The new SAKO 75 Varmint Rifle uses only the highest grade steel in the construction of the action, bolt, barrel and all internal parts. SAKO cold hammer-forges heavyweight bar stock into one of the truest, most accurate barrels available. The 24" barrel is matched to the appropriate action size to eliminate excessive weight. The barreled action assembly is then cradled into a specially designed stock and is free floating for greater accuracy. The matte lacquered walnut stock features a beavertail forearm for additional stability and support when shooting from sandbags or whenever top accuracy is necessary. The SAKO 75 is the first and only rifle with three locking lugs and a mechanical ejector. Other SAKO features include a one-piece forged bolt with five gliding surfaces, a detachable magazine, and a smooth 70 degree bolt lift.

**Calibers:**
26 calibers from 17 Rem. to 416 Rem. Mag.
**Price:** . . . . . . . . . . . . . . . . . . . . . . . . . . **$1,369.00**
**Also Available:** 75 VARMINT STAINLESS LAMINATED from 223 Rem. to 308 Win. . . . . . . . . . . . . . . . . . . . . . **1459.00**

# SAKO RIFLES

**SAKO 75 HUNTER**

**SAKO ACTIONS**

## SAKO 75 ACTIONS

Sako 75 actions are designed for maximum performance while maintaining graceful lines, strength and reliability. Each of the four action sizes is manufactured for a specific range of calibers. The Sako 75 is the first to offer a bolt with three locking lugs and a mechanical ejector while maintaining a bolt lift of only 70°. Five guiding surfaces prevent the bolt from binding and provide ultra smooth-operation. The two-position safety is located conveniently behind the bolt handle. A separate button in front of the safety allows the bolt to be opened while the safety is on. The detachable magazine can be loaded through the ejection port. When you're building a custom rifle you can't go wrong when you select either our carbon steel or stainless steel actions. The end result will be one of the finest custom rifles in the world.

***Prices:*** White . . . . . . . . . . . . . . . . . . . . . . . . . $609.00
Stainless Steel . . . . . . . . . . . . . . . . . . . . . . . . 639.00

**KEY**

**LOCKED**　　　　**READY**

**THUMB SAFETY, DOVETAILED RECEIVER**

## NEW FOR 2000

The three largest Sako actions now feature "key concept", a mechanism on the cocking piece that locks or unlocks the striker. You can thus render the 75 absolutely safe, disabling it with a turn of the key. Three keys are provided with each rifle, and others can be ordered by rifle serial number from the 7500 patterns. All Sako Model 75 rifles except those built on the smallest actions will soon come standard with the key concept lock.

"The key blends into the rifle contours when the lock is open and the gun is operational," explained Mr. Paul-Erik Toivo, president of Sako Ltd. "When the key is removed, the lock takes effect and the hunting rifle is completely safe and inoperative."

This revolutionary concept puts complete control of the safety and

security of the rifle in the hands of its owner. "When the key is removed, there is no way to operate the gun, even accidentally. Any attempts to pick the lock will render the rifle unusable," said Mr. Tolvo. He also noted that the Sako 75 is considered the very best bolt action rifle in the industry. "The Sako 75 is the best hunting rifle in the world. It is only natural that we wanted to offer it with added security and safety for its owner and society in general. We believe this will become the new standard in gun safety."

# SAKO RIFLES

## FINNFIRE SCOUT

The new scout has a ergonomical competition stock, adjustable cheekpiece and heel plate. The heavy barrel makes it an ideal gun when unerring accuracy is required. (scope and mount not included)

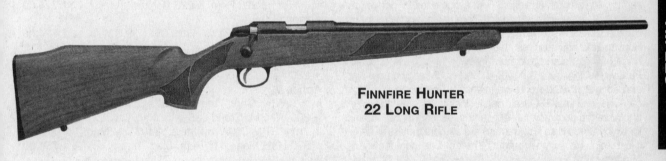

## FINNFIRE HUNTER 22 LONG RIFLE

## FINNFIRE VARMINT HEAVY BARREL

## FINNFIRE 22 LR BOLT-ACTION RIFLE

SAKO of Finland, acclaimed as the premier manufacturer of bolt-action centerfire rifles, presents its 22 Long Rifle Finnfire. Designed by engineers who use only state-of-the-art technology to achieve both form and function and produced by craftsmen to exacting specifications, this premium grade bolt-action rifle exceeds the requirements of even the most demanding firearm enthusiast.

The basic concept in the design of the Finnfire was to make it as similar to its "big brothers" as possible—just scaled down. For example, the single-stage adjustable trigger is a carbon copy of the trigger found on any other big-bore hunting model. The 22-inch barrel is cold-hammered to ensure superior accuracy.

**SPECIFICATIONS**
*Overall length:* 37 1/2" **Weight:** 5 1/4 lbs. (Hunter, Sporter) ; 7 1/2 lbs. (Varmint) *Rate of twist:* 16 1/2"
*Other outstanding features include:*
• European walnut stock
• Luxurious matte lacquer finish
• 50° bolt lift
• Free-floating barrel
• Integral 11mm dovetail for scope mounting
• Two-position safety that locks the bolt
• Cocking indicator
• Five-shot detachable magazine
• Ten-shot magazine available
• Available with open sights
*Price:*
  SCOUT (SPORTER) . . . . . . . . . . . . . . . . . . . . . . $984.00
  HUNTER . . . . . . . . . . . . . . . . . . . . . . . . . . . . . 874.00
  VARMINT . . . . . . . . . . . . . . . . . . . . . . . . . . . . 924.00

# SAKO RIFLES

**DELUXE BOLT-ACTION RIFLE**

## SAKO 75 DELUXE BOLT-ACTION RIFLE

All the fine-touch features you expect of the deluxe grade SAKO are here: **1**-Reliable safety system with a separate bolt release button. **2**-First ever bolt with three locking lugs and a mechanical ejector. Five guiding surfaces prevent bolt binding and provide smooth operation. Four action sizes for perfect cartridge fit. **3**-Totally free-floating cold hammer forged barrel for ultimate accuracy. Test with a slip of paper. **4**-Sako Deluxe 75 Hunting Rifle has stainless steel lined staggered magazine with hinged floorplate and aluminum follower for faultless operation. Positive feeding angle is only 3-5 degrees. **5**-Fancy grade, high-grained walnut. Old-world craftmanship Rosewood pistol grip cap with silver inlay. **6**-Classic detail–Rosewood fore-end tip. And of course the accuracy, reliability and superior field performance for which SAKO is so justly famous are still here too. It's all here—it just weighs less than it used to. Think of it as more for less.

In addition, the scope mounting system on these SAKOs are among the strongest in the world. Instead of using separate bases, a tapered dovetail is milled into the receiver, to which the scope rings are mounted. A beautiful system that's been proven by over 20 years of use. SAKO Original Scope Mounts and SAKO scope rings are available in low, medium and high in one-inch and 30mm.

**Prices: ACTION I**
in 17 Rem., 222 Rem. & 223 Rem. . . . . . . . . . **$1,724.00**
**ACTION III**
In 22-250 Rem., 243 Win., 7mm-08 and 308 Win. . . . **1,724.00**
**ACTION IV**
In 25-06 Rem., 6.5x55 SE, 270 Win., 7x64,
  280 Rem., 30-06, 9.3x62. . . . . . . . . . . . . . . **1,724.00**
**ACTION V**
In 270 Wby. Mag., 7mm Rem. Mag., 7mm Wby. Mag.,
  300 Win. Mag. and 338 Win. Mag. . . . . . . . . . **1,754.00**
In 7mm STW, 300 Wby. Mag., .340 Wby. Mag.,
  375 H&H Mag., 416 Rem. Mag. . . . . . . . . . . . **1,754.00**

**SAKO 75 HUNTER STAINLESS**

**SAKO 75 STAINLESS SYNTHETIC**

**SAKO 75 ACTION**

## SAKO 75 HUNTER STAINLESS

Detachable box magazine, checkered walnut stock, standard and magnum chamberings.
**Price:**
22" 13 calibers, from 222 Rem. to 9.3x62 . . . . **$1,284.00**
24" 7mm Rem. Mag., 300 Win. Mag., 338 Win. Mag.,
  375 H&H Mag. . . . . . . . . . . . . . . . . . . . . . **1,314.00**
26" 7mm STW, 300 Wby. . . . . . . . . . . . . . . . **1,314.00**

# SAKO RIFLES

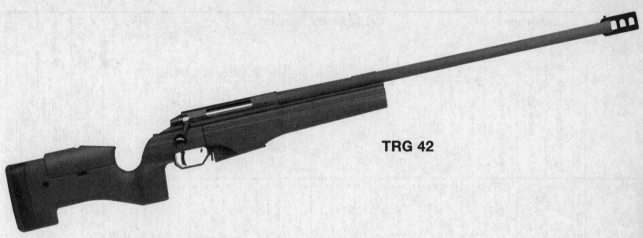

**TRG 42**

## SAKO TRG 22/42

SAKO TRG 22/42 rifles are the ultimate accuracy tools for long-range competition. TRG rifles are manufactured by skilled Sako craftsmen using modern manufacturing methods. The TRG 22 in 308 Win. is a thoroughbred 300 m UIT standard competition rifle, a CISM competition winner and serves the governments of several nations as their primary sniper rifle.

The TRG 42 in 300 Win. Mag and .338 Lapua Mag. is a true long-range competition rifle. It can also be equipped with various implements to fulfill the demanding duties of a tactical sniper.

Both TRG actions and special match grade barrels (chrome-moly or stainless) are cold hammer-forged. The sturdy bolt with three locking lugs feeds rounds reliably from the centerline of a detachable staggered magazine. The high-tech constructed aluminum reinforced composite stock can be completely adjusted to match the individual preferences of all shooters. The target trigger is a fully adjustable 2-stage unit. Optilock quickmount allows any target scope to be positioned properly on the action.

**Prices:** TRG-22 in 308 Win . . . . . . . . . . . . . . $2,699.00
TRG-42 in .338 Lapua or 300 Win Mag . . . . . . . 3,099.00

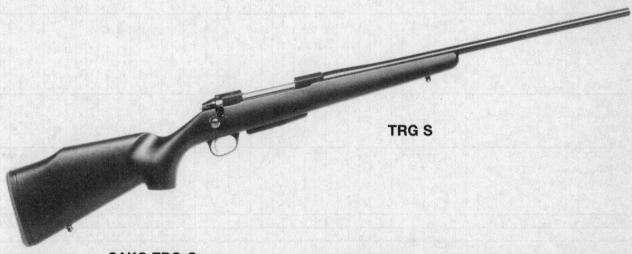

**TRG S**

## SAKO TRG-S

This sophisticated and extremely accurate large-action hunting rifle is designed with same principles as Sako's famed competition TRG rifle. Bolt is massive, with 3 symmetrical locking lugs and thus a short 60 degree bolt lift. Detachable magazine feeds reliably from centerline, straight to chamber. Stock is high-tech composite with integrated fiberglass reinforced skeleton for rigidity and accuracy. Free floating cold hammer-forged barrel, adjustable trigger.

**Calibers** 270 Win, 30-06, 7mm Rem Mag, 300 Win Mag, .338 Lapua Mag, 30-378 Wby. Mag

**Price:** . . . . . . . . . . . . . . . . . . . . . . . . . . . . . . . . $894.00
Magnums . . . . . . . . . . . . . . . . . . . . . . . . . . . . . 929.00

# SAKO RIFLES DATATABLE

Legend: • = as standard   + = as option

Caliber / Rate of Twist columns (with rate of twist): 22 LR (16.5"), 17 Rem (10"), 222 Rem (14"), 223 Rem (12"), 22 PPC USA (14"), 6 PPC USA (12"), 22-250 Rem (14"), 243 Win (10"), 7mm-08 Rem (9.5"), 308 Win (11"), 25-06 Rem (10"), 6.5x55 SE (8"), 270 Win (10"), 7x64 (10"), 280 Rem (10"), 30-06 (11"), 9.3x62 (14"), 270 Wby Mag (10"), 7mm Rem Mag (9.5"), 7mm Wby Mag (9.5"), 7mm STW (9.5"), 300 Win Mag (11"), 300 Wby Mag (11"), 300 Rem Ultra Mag (11"), 338 Win Mag (10"), 340 Wby Mag (10"), 375 H&H Mag (12"), 416 Rem Mag (14"), 30-378 Wby Mag (11"), 338 Lapua Mag (12")

| Model | Action | Total Length Inches | Barrel Length Inches | Weight Lbs (approx.) | Stock Finish (Oiled) | Lacquered | Matte Lacquered | Injection Moulded | Open Sights | Without Sights | Single Stage Trigger | Double Stage Trigger | Detachable | Hinged Floorplate | Magazine Capacity | Stainless Steel Barrel | Stainless Steel Action | Key Concept |
|---|---|---|---|---|---|---|---|---|---|---|---|---|---|---|---|---|---|---|
| 75 HUNTER | I | 41 3/4 | 22 | 6 3/8 | + | | • | • | • | | • | • | | • | 6 | • | • | • |
| | III | 42 7/8 | 22 7/16 | 7 1/4 | + | | • | | | • | • | • | | • | 5 | | | • |
| | IV | 43 3/4 | 22 7/8 | 7 15/16 | + | | • | | | • | • | • | | • | 5 | | | • |
| | V | 45 5/8 | 24 3/8 | 8 5/8 | + | | • | | | • | • | • | | • | 4 | | | • |
| | V | 47 1/4 | 26 | 8 13/16 | + | | • | | | • | • | • | | • | 4 | | | • |
| | V | 47 1/4 | 26 | 8 13/16 | + | | • | | | • | • | • | | • | 4 | | | • |
| | V | 45 5/8 | 24 3/8 | 9 | + | | • | | | • | • | • | | • | 4 | | | • |
| 75 HUNTER STAINLESS | I | 41 3/4 | 22 | 6 3/16 | + | | • | | | • | • | • | | • | 6 | • | • | • |
| | III | 42 7/8 | 22 7/16 | 7 | + | | • | | | • | • | • | | • | 5 | • | • | • |
| | IV | 43 3/4 | 22 7/8 | 7 3/4 | + | | • | | | • | • | • | | • | 5 | • | • | • |
| | V | 45 5/8 | 24 3/8 | 8 3/8 | + | | • | | | • | • | • | | • | 4 | • | • | • |
| | V | 47 1/4 | 26 | 8 5/8 | + | | • | | | • | • | • | | • | 4 | • | • | • |
| 75 DELUXE | I | 45 3/4 | 22 | 6 3/8 | + | + | • | | | • | • | • | | • | 6 | | | • |
| | III | 42 7/8 | 22 7/16 | 7 1/4 | + | + | • | | | • | • | • | | • | 5 | | | • |
| | IV | 43 3/4 | 22 7/8 | 7 15/16 | + | + | • | | | • | • | • | | • | 5 | | | • |
| | V | 45 5/8 | 24 3/8 | 8 5/8 | + | + | • | | | • | • | • | | • | 4 | | | • |
| | V | 47 1/4 | 26 | 8 13/16 | + | + | • | | | • | • | • | | • | 4 | | | • |
| | V | 45 5/8 | 24 3/8 | 9 | + | | • | | | • | • | • | | • | 4 | | | • |
| 75 BATTUE | IV | 40 | 19 1/4 | 7 3/4 | + | | • | | • | | • | • | | • | 5 | | | • |
| | V | 40 1/2 | 19 1/4 | 7 15/16 | + | | • | | • | | • | • | | • | 4 | | | • |
| 75 VARMINT | I | 43 1/4 | 23 5/8 | 8 1/8 | + | | • | | | • | • | • | | • | 6 | | | • |
| | III | 44 | 23 5/8 | 8 5/8 | + | | • | | | • | • | • | | • | 5 | | | • |
| | IV | 44 1/2 | 23 5/8 | 8 13/16 | + | | • | | | • | • | • | | • | 5 | | | • |
| | V | 44 7/8 | 23 5/8 | 9 | + | | • | | | • | • | • | | • | 4 | | | • |
| | V | 44 7/8 | 23 5/8 | 99 | + | | • | | | • | • | • | | • | 4 | | | • |
| | V | 47 1/4 | 26 | 9 1/4 | + | | • | | | • | • | • | | • | 4 | | | • |
| 75 VARMINT LAMINATED STAINLESS | I | 43 1/4 | 23 5/8 | 8 5/8 | | | • | | | • | • | • | | • | 6 | • | • | • |
| | III | 44 | 23 5/8 | 9 | | | • | | | • | • | • | | • | 5 | • | • | • |
| 75 SYNTHETIC STAINLESS | III | 42 7/8 | 22 7/16 | 7 | | | • | | | • | • | • | | • | 5 | • | • | • |
| | IV | 43 3/4 | 22 7/8 | 7 3/4 | | | • | | | • | • | • | | • | 5 | • | • | • |
| | V | 45 3/4 | 24 3/8 | 8 3/8 | | | • | | | • | • | • | | • | 4 | • | • | • |
| | V | 47 1/4 | 26 | 8 5/8 | | | • | | | • | • | • | | • | 4 | • | • | • |
| | V | 47 1/4 | 26 | 8 5/8 | | | • | | | • | • | • | | • | 4 | • | • | • |
| TRG-S (M995) | | 47 1/4 | 26 | 8 1/8 | | | • | | | • | • | • | | • | 3 | | | |
| TRG-22 (TRG-22) | | 45 1/4 | 26 | 10 1/4 | | | • | | | • | • | • | • | | 10 | + | | |
| TRG-S (TRG-42) | | 47 1/4 | 27 1/8 | 11 1/4 | | | • | | | • | • | • | | • | 5 | + | | |
| FINFIRE MODELS | | | | | | | | | | | | | | | | | | |
| HUNTER (P94S) | | 39 1/2 | 22 | 5 3/4 | | | | • | | • | • | • | | • | 5 | | | |
| VARMINT (P94S) | | 40 1/2 | 23 | 7 1/4 | | | | • | | • | • | • | | • | 5 | | | |
| SCOUT (P94S) | | 40 1/2 | 23 | 7 1/2 | | | • | | • | | • | • | | • | 10 | | | |
| SILHOUETTE LIGHT (P94S) | | 39 1/2 | 22 | 6 3/16 | | | | • | | • | • | • | | • | 5 | | | |

• = as standard   + = as option   Rifle weight may varie depending on wood density and caliber. The manufacturer reserves the right to modify specifications.

# SAUER RIFLES

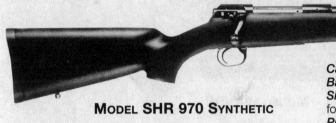

**MODEL SHR 970 SYNTHETIC**

### SIG SHR 970 BOLT ACTION RIFLE

The bolt of this centerfire rifle locks into the barrel, not the receiver, ensuring constant headspace and permitting interchange of barrels. In fact, barrels on the SHR 970 can be switched quickly and easily in the field with no other change if the cartridge head sizes are the same (different-size heads require switching the bolt as well). Hammer-forged barrels conribute to accuracy, as does the bedding block. The 65-degree bolt lift makes followup shots quick and effortless. A three-position safety and detachable box magazine make unloading a snap. Stocks are available in checkered European walnut or synthetic versions, both with quick-

**SPECIFICATIONS**
**Calibers:** 270 Win., 30-06 S'field  **Capacity:** 4 rounds
**Barrel Length:** 22"  **Overall Length:** 41.9"  **Weight:** 7.2 lbs.
**Sights:** Drilled and tapped for scope base  **Stock:** Reinforced synthetic stock, rubber butt pad, QD swivel studs
**Price:** . . . . . . . . . . . . . . . . . . . . . . . . . . . . . . . . . **$499.00**

detach swivel studs. Metal is "Ilaflon"coated to prevent rust and corrosion. The SHR 970 rifle is chambered for the .25-06, .270, .280, 7mm Rem. Mag., .308, .30-06 and .300 Win. Mag. The STR tactical or long range rifle comes only in .308 and .300 Win. Mag. **Barrel lengths:** 22" for standard calibers, 24" for magnums and the fluted STR barrels. **Weight:** 7.2 and 7.4 pounds for the SHR, 11.6 for the STR. **Prices:**

SHR synthetic . . . . . . . . . . . . . . . . . . . . . . . . **$499.00**
SHR walnut . . . . . . . . . . . . . . . . . . . . . . . . . **550.00**
STR. . . . . . . . . . . . . . . . . . . . . . . . . . . . . . . . **899.00**

**SSG 3000 TACTICAL**
Available in .308 Win.

**SAUER 202 SUPREME–SYNTHETIC STOCK**
.243 Win., 25-06 Rem., 6.5x55 Swedish, .270 Win., .308 Win., .30-0 Sprg.

**SAUER 202 SUPREME MAGNUM–WALNUT STOCK**
7mm Rem. Mag., .300 Win. Mag., .300 Wby. Mag., .375 H&H Mag.

### MODEL 202 SUPREME BOLT ACTION
#### SPECIFICATIONS

**Calibers:** 25-06 Rem., 243 Win., 6.5x55, 270 Win., 308, 30-06 S'field; *Supreme Magnum calibers:* 7mm Rem. Mag., 300 Win. Mag., 300 Wby. Mag., 375 Win. Mag. **Action:** Bolt takedown  **Capacity:** 3 rounds  **Barrel Length:** 23.6"; 26" (Supreme Magnum)  **Overall Length:** 44.3"; 46" (Supreme Magnum)  **Weight:** 7.7 lbs.; 8.4 lbs. (Supreme Magnum) **Stock:** Select American claro walnut with high-gloss epoxy finish and rosewood forend and grip caps; Monte Carlo comb with cheekpiece; 22 line-per-inch diamond pattern, hand-cut checking  **Sights:** Drilled and tapped for sights and scope

bases  **Features:** Adjustable two-stage trigger; polished and jeweled bolt; quick-change barrel; tapered bore; QD sling swivel studs; black rubber recoil pad; Wundhammer palm swell; dual release safety; six locking lugs on bolt head; removable box magazine; fully enclosed bolt face; three gas relief holes; firing-pin cocking indicator on bolt rear
**Prices:** Standard . . . . . . . . . . . . . . . . . . . . . . **$985.00**
  Magnum . . . . . . . . . . . . . . . . . . . . . . . . . **1,056.00**
**Also available:** In Left Hand model (270 Win., 30-06 S'field, 7mm Rem. Mag. only). . . . . . . . . . . . . . **$1,056.00**
  Magnum . . . . . . . . . . . . . . . . . . . . . . . . . **1,115.00**
  SSG 3000 Tactical Rifle . . . . . . . . . . . . . . . . **2,150.00**

# SAVAGE ARMS

## CENTERFIRE RIFLES

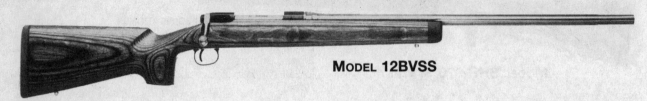

**MODEL 12BVSS**

### MODEL 12BVSS SHORT ACTION VARMINT

**SPECIFICATIONS**
**Calibers:** 223 Rem., 22-250 Rem., and 308 Win.
Single-shot Model 12FVSS available in 223 Rem.
and 22-250 Rem. **Capacity:** 5 + 1 **Barrel Length:** 26"
fluted heavy barrel **Overall Length:** 46.75" **Magazine:**
Top loading internal **Weight:** 9.5 lbs. **Sights:** None. Drilled
and tapped for scope mounts **Stock:** Laminated hard

wood with high comb, ambidextrous grip and ebony tip
**Finish:** Fluted stainless steel with recessed target style
muzzle **Features:** Short Action precision long range rifle
with dual pillar bedding
**Price:** . . . . . . . . . . . . . . . . . . . . . . . . . . . . . . . . . . $560.00
**Also Available:** FVSS with black synthetic
   stock, 9 lbs. . . . . . . . . . . . . . . . . . . . . . . . . . . . . 534.00

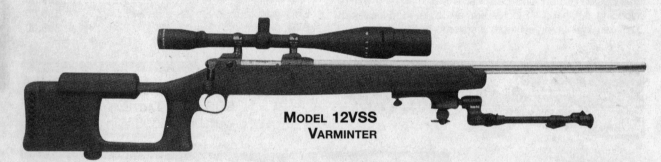

**MODEL 12VSS**
**VARMINTER**

### MODEL 12FVSS-SHORT ACTION
#### SPECIFICATIONS
**Calibers:** .223 Rem., 22-250 Rem. **Overall Length:** 47.5"
**Weight:** 15 lbs. (approx.) **Sights:** Drilled and tapped for
scope mounts **Stock:** Choate™ adjustable black synthetic
stock. **Barrel:** Heavy fluted stainless steel, recessed target

muzzle, button rifled and free floating. **Magazine:** Internal
box with (4) round capacity **Features:** Blue/Stainless steel
bolt action, *Sharp Shooter* trigger, Choate™ stock, and a
fluted stainless barrel. Scopes, rings, bases and bipod not
included.
**Price:** . . . . . . . . . . . . . . . . . . . . . . . . . . . . . . . . . . $550.00

**MODEL 12FV**

### MODEL 12FV SHORT ACTION VARMINT

**SPECIFICATIONS**
**Calibers:** 223 Rem., 22-250 Rem., 308 Win.
**Capacity:** 5
**Barrel Length:** 26"
**Overall Length:** 46.75"
**Magazine:** Top loading internal
**Weight:** 9 lbs.

**Sights:** None. Drilled and tapped for scope mounts
**Stock:** Durable black synthetic with scrolled checkering
and dual pillars
**Finish:** Blued with recessed target-style muzzle
**Features:** Short-action varmint rifle with 26" button rifled
heavy barrel
**Price:** . . . . . . . . . . . . . . . . . . . . . . . . . . . . . . . . . . $429.00

# SAVAGE ARMS

## MODEL 10FP SHORT ACTION TACTICAL RIFLE

### SPECIFICATIONS

**Calibers:** 223, 7mm-08, 260, 308 **Capacity:** 5
**Barrel Length:** 24" heavy barrel **Overall Length:** 43.75"
**Magazine:** Top loading internal **Weight:** 8 lbs.
**Sights:** None. Drilled and tapped for scope mounts

**Stock:** Black synthetic with scrolled checkering and dual pillars
**Finish:** Black non-reflective with recessed target style muzzle
**Features:** Short action heavy barrel rifle with twin pillar bedding
**Price:** . . . . . . . . . . . . . . . . . . . . . . . . . . . . . . . . $450.00

## MODEL 16FSS SHORT ACTION WEATHER WARRIOR

### SPECIFICATIONS

**Calibers:** 223, 243, 7mm-08, 260, 308 **Capacity:** 5
**Barrel Length:** 22" **Overall Length:** 40.75"
**Magazine:** Top loading internal **Weight:** 6 lbs.
**Sights:** None. Drilled and tapped for scope mounts

**Stock:** Durable black synthetic with scrolled checkering and dual pillars **Finish:** Stainless steel
**Features:** Short action satin finished 400 series stainless steel barreled action
**Price:** . . . . . . . . . . . . . . . . . . . . . . . . . . . . $515.00

## MODEL 10FM SIERRA LIGHTWEIGHT

### SPECIFICATIONS

**Calibers:** 243, 7mm-08, 308
**Capacity:** 5 + 1 **Barrel Length:** 20"
**Overall Length:** 41.5" **Magazine:** Top loading internal
**Weight:** 6.25 lbs. **Sights:** None. Drilled and tapped for

scope mount; bases included
**Stock:** Lightweight graphite/fiberglass filled composite stock with positive checkering **Finish:** Blued
**Features:** Blue alloy steel barreled action
**Price:** . . . . . . . . . . . . . . . . . . . . . . . . . . . . $425.00

## MODEL 110FP TACTICAL

### SPECIFICATIONS

**Calibers:** 25-06 Rem., 30-06 Spfd., 7mm Rem. Mag., 300 Win. Mag. **Capacity:** 5 rounds (1 in chamber) **Barrel Length:** 24" (w/recessed target-style muzzle) **Overall Length:** 45.5" **Weight:** 8.5 lbs. **Sights:** None; drilled and tapped for scope mount; bases included **Features:** Black matte nonreflective finish on metal parts; bolt coated with titanium nitride; stock made of black graphite/fiberglass-filled composite with positive checkering; left-hand model available

**Price:** . . . . . . . . . . . . . . . . . . . . . . . . . . . . $429.00
**Also Available:** MODEL 110CY **Calibers:** 223 Rem., 243 Win., 270 Win., 308 Win. **Capacity:** 5 rounds (1 in chamber); top-loading internal magazine. **Barrel Length:** 22" blued. **Overall Length:** 42.5" **Weight:** 6 3/8 lbs. **Sights:** Adjustable; drilled and tapped for scope mounts **Stock:** High comb, walnut-stained hardwood w/cut checkering and short pull.
**Price:** . . . . . . . . . . . . . . . . . . . . . . . . . . . . $450.00

# SAVAGE ARMS RIFLES

**MODEL 11F SHORT ACTION HUNTER**

### SPECIFICATIONS
*Calibers:* 223 Rem., 22-250 Rem., 243 Win., 7mm-08 Rem., 260 Rem., and 308 Win. *Capacity:* 5 *Barrel Length:* 22" standard weight *Overall Length:* 42.75" *Magazine:* Top loading internal *Weight:* 6.75 lbs. *Sights:* Available in right/left hand. Drilled and tapped for scope mounts *Stock:* Durable black synthetic with scrolled checkering and dual pillars *Finish:* Blued
*Features:* Short Action with dual pillar bedded stock
*Price:* . . . . . . . . . . . . . . . . . . . . . . . . . . . . . . . . . $419.00

**MODEL 11G SHORT ACTION CLASSIC AMERICAN STYLE HUNTER**

### SPECIFICATIONS
*Calibers:* 223 Rem., 22-250 Rem., 243 Win., 7mm-08 Rem., 260 Rem., and 308 Win. *Capacity:* 5 *Barrel Length:* 22" *Overall Length:* 42.75" *Magazine:* Top loading internal *Weight:* 6.75 lbs. *Sights:* Available with or without (11GNS) Available in right/left hand. Drilled and tapped for scope mounts *Stock:* American style walnut finished hardwood with fancy scrolled, diamond point checkering and black recoil pad *Finish:* Blued
*Price:* . . . . . . . . . . . . . . . . . . . . . . . . . . . . . . . . . $395.00

**MODEL 10GY SHORT ACTION LADIES/YOUTH RIFLE**

### SPECIFICATIONS
*Calibers:* 223 Rem., 243 Win. and 308 Win.
*Capacity:* 5
*Barrel Length:* 22" standard weight
*Overall Length:* 39.25"
*Magazine:* Top loading internal
*Weight:* 6.25 lbs.
*Sights:* None. Drilled and tapped for scope mounts
*Stock:* American style walnut finished hardwood with cut checkering
*Finish:* Blued
*Price:* . . . . . . . . . . . . . . . . . . . . . . . . . . . . . . . . . $395.00

# SAVAGE CENTERFIRE RIFLES

## LONG RANGE AND SCOUT RIFLES

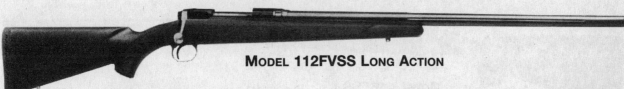

### MODEL 112FVSS LONG ACTION

**SPECIFICATIONS**

*Calibers:* 25-06 Rem., 30-06, 7mm Rem. Mag., 300 Win. Mag. (single-shot model available in 220 Swift, 300 Win. Mag.) *Capacity:* 4 + 1 *Barrel Length:* 26" fluted, stainless steel *Overall Length:* 47.5" *Weight:* 10.3 lbs. *Sights:* Graphite/fiberglass-filled composite w/positive checkering
*Price:* . . . . . . . . . . . . . . . . . . . . . . . . . . . . . . . . $549.00

### MODEL 112BVSS LONG ACTION

**SPECIFICATIONS**

*Calibers:* 25-06, 7mm Rem. Mag., 300 Win Mag., 30-06 Sprgfld., (single-shot model also available in 220 Swift, 300 Win. Mag.) *Capacity:* 4 + 1 *Barrel Length:* 26" fluted heavy barrel, stainless steel *Overall Length:* 47.5" *Weight:* 10 lbs. (approx.) *Sights:* None; drilled and tapped *Stock:* Laminated hardwood w/high comb; ambidextrous grip
*Price:* . . . . . . . . . . . . . . . . . . . . . . . . . . . . . . . . $575.00

### MODEL 112 BT COMPETITION GRADE

**SPECIFICATIONS**

*Calibers:* 223 Rem. and 308 Win. Mag. (single-shot available in 300 Win. Mag.)
*Capacity:* 5 + 1
*Barrel Length:* 26"; blackened stainless steel w/recessed target/style muzzle
*Overall Length:* 47.5"
*Weight:* 10 7/8 lbs.
*Stock:* Laminated brown w/straight comb
*Price:* . . . . . . . . . . . . . . . . . . . . . . . . . . . . . . . . $1,028.00

### SAVAGE "SCOUT" RIFLE-MODEL 10FCM

Ultra-light weight and extremely well balanced, the **NEW 10FCM** SAVAGE "SCOUT" is the ideal rifle for any outdoor situation. Weighing approximately 6 pounds and sporting a 20" barrel, this fast handling carbine is chambered in 7mm-08 and .308. *Features:* DETACHABLE BOX MAGAZINE: Capacity four (4) plus one (1) in the chamber; REMOVABE GHOST RING REAR SIGHT with GOLD BEAD FRONT SIGHT; ONE-PIECE SCOPE MOUNT for long eye relief scope; LARGE BALL BOLT HANDLE; RIFLEMAN'S COMBO SHOOTING SLING/CARRY STRAP WITH Q.D. SWIVEL SET; "Dual Pillar Bedded" synthetic stock
*Price:* . . . . . . . . . . . . . . . . . . . . . . . . . . . . . . . . $528.00

# SAVAGE CENTERFIRE RIFLES

## ALL-WEATHER 116 SERIES

### MODEL 116FSS "WEATHER WARRIOR"

Savage Arms combines the strength of a black graphite fiberglass polymer stock and the durability of a stainless-steel barrel and receiver in this bolt-action rifle. Major components are made from stainless steel, honed to a low refllective satin finish. Drilled and tapped for scope mounts. Left-hand model available (116FLSS).

**SPECIFICATIONS**
**Calibers:** 270 30-06, 7mm Rem. Mag., 300 Win. Mag., 338 Win. Mag. **Capacity:** 4 (7mm Rem. Mag., 300 Win. Mag., 338 Win. Mag.); 5 (270, 30-06) **Barrel Length:** 22" (270, 30-06); 24" (7mm Rem. Mag., 300 Win. Mag., 338 Win. Mag.) **Overall Length:** 43.5"-45.5" **Weight:** 6.5 lbs.
**Price:** . . . . . . . . . . . . . . . . . . . . . . . . . . . . . . **$515.00**
**Also Available:** MODEL 16FSS short action in 243, 7mm-08, 260, 308

### MODEL 116FCSS "WEATHER WARRIOR"

**Calibers:** 270, 30-06, 7mm Rem. Mag., 300 Win. Mag. This bolt-action rifle has the same quality features as the Model 116FSS plus a removable box magazine with recessed push-button release for ease in loading and unloading. Left-hand model available. **Price:** . . . . . . . . . . . . . . . . **$575.00**
**Also Available:** MODEL 16FCSS short action in 243, 7mm-08, 260, 308

### MODEL 116FCSAK WEATHER WARRIOR RIFLE

**SPECIFICATIONS**
**Calibers:** 270 Win. 30-06 Spfld., 7mm Rem. Mag., 300 Win. Mag. **Capacity:** 5 (standard) 4 (magnum) plus one in chamber **Barrel Length:** 22" **Overall Length:** 43.5" **Magazine:** Detachable staggered box type **Weight:** 7.25 lbs. **Sights:** None. Drilled and tapped for scope mount

**Stock:** Lightweight black synthetic with positive checkering
**Finish:** Fluted, satin finished stainless steel
**Features:** Fluted 400 series stainless steel barreled action with Adjustable Muzzle Brake (AMB). Left hand models available.
**Price:** . . . . . . . . . . . . . . . . . . . . . . . . . . . . . . **$668.00**

### MODEL 111FXP3

"Package" rifle with internal-box magazine (C version with detachable box), black synthetic stock, 22" barrel, sling, 3-9x32 scope.

**Calibers:** 223 Rem, 22-250 Rem., 243 Win., 7mm-08 Rem., 260 Rem., 308 Win., 25-06 Rem.,270 Win., 30-06 Sprg., 7mm Rem. Mag., 300 Win. Mag., 338 Win. Mag.
**Capacity:** 5 rounds (4 in Magnum) **Overall Length:** 43.5"
**Weight:** 7.5 lbs.
**Price:** . . . . . . . . . . . . . . . . . . . . . . . . . . . . . . **$460.00**

# SAVAGE ARMS

### MODEL 116SE
### SAFARI EXPRESS

**SPECIFICATIONS**
**Calibers:** 300 Win., 338, .375 H&H, 458 Win. Mag.
**Capacity:** 4 rounds (1 in chamber)
**Barrel Length:** 24" stainless steel w/AMB
**Overall Length:** 45.5" **Weight:** 8.5 lbs. **Sights:** 3-leaf express **Stock:** Classic-style select-grade walnut w/cut checkering; ebony tip; stainless-steel crossbolts; internally vented recoil pad
**Price:** ................................... $925.00

RIFLES

### MODEL 114U

**SPECIFICATIONS**
**Calibers:** 270 Win., 30-06 Spfld (22" bbl.); 7mm STW, 7mm Rem. Mag., 300 Win. Mag. (24" bbl.) **Overall Length:** 43.5" **Weight:** Approx. 7 lbs. **Rifling Twist:** 1 in 10" (270 Win., 30-6 Spfld., 300 Win. Mag.); 1 in 9.5" (7mm Rem. Mag.) **Features:** High gloss American Walnut Stock with ebony tip; Custom checkering on the grip and forend; High luster blued finish on the barrel, receiver, and bolt handle; Precision laser-etched Savage logo on bolt body; Drilled and tapped for scope mounts
**Price:** ................................... $504.00

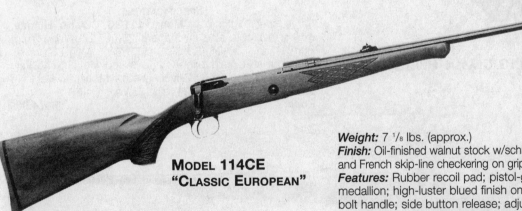

### MODEL 114CE
### "CLASSIC EUROPEAN"

**Weight:** 7 1/8 lbs. (approx.)
**Finish:** Oil-finished walnut stock w/schnabel tip, cheekpiece and French skip-line checkering on grip and forend
**Features:** Rubber recoil pad; pistol-grip cap with gold medallion; high-luster blued finish on receiver barrel and bolt handle; side button release; adjustable metal sights; precision rifled barrel; drilled and tapped
**Price:** ................................... $635.00
**Also available:**
**MODEL 114C "CLASSIC."** Same specifications as above except select grade oil-finished American walnut stock with standard forend profile and checkering.

**SPECIFICATIONS**
**Calibers:** 270 Win., 30-06 Sprgfld., 7mm Rem. Mag., 300 Win. Mag. **Capacity:** 3 rounds (magnum); 4 rounds (standard); plus 1 in each chamber
**Barrel Length:** 22" (standard); 24" (magnum)
**Overall Length:** 43.5" (standard); 45.5" (magnum)

# SAVAGE RIFLES

## HUNTER SERIES 111

### MODEL 111GC CLASSIC HUNTER

**SPECIFICATIONS**
**Calibers:** 270 Win., 30-06 Springfield, 7mm Rem. Mag., 300 Win. Mag. **Capacity:** 5 rounds (4 rounds in Magnum calibers) **Barrel Length:** 22" (standard) 24" (Magnum) **Overall Length:** 43.5" (45.5" Magnum calibers)

**Weight:** 6 ³/₈-7 lbs. **Sights:** Adjustable **Stock:** American-style walnut-finished hardwood; cut checkering **Features:** Detachable staggered box-type magazine; left-hand model available
**Price:** . . . . . . . . . . . . . . . . . . . . . . . . . . . . . . . . $410.00

### MODEL 111FC CLASSIC HUNTER

**SPECIFICATIONS**
Same specifications as **CLASSIC HUNTER** above, except stock is lightweight graphite/fiberglass-filled composite w/positive checkering. Left-hand model available. **Calibers:** 270 Win., 30-06 Splfd., 7mm Rem. Mag. and 300 Win. Mag.
**Price:** . . . . . . . . . . . . . . . . . . . . . . . . . . . . . . . . $420.00

### MODEL 111G CLASSIC HUNTER

**SPECIFICATIONS**
Same specifications as **MODEL 111GC CLASSIC HUNTER**, except available also in **calibers** 25-06, 270 Win., 7mm Rem. Mag., 30-06 Sprgfld., 300 Win. Mag. Stock is American-style walnut-finished hardwood with cut-checkering. Left-hand model available. **YOUTH MODEL** available in 223 Rem., 243 Win., 270 Win., 308 Win.
**Price:** . . . . . . . . . . . . . . . . . . . . . . . . . . . . . . . . $374.00

### MODEL 111F CLASSIC HUNTER

**SPECIFICATIONS**
Same specifications as **MODEL 111G CLASSIC HUNTER**, except stock is black nonglare graphite/fiberglass-filled polymer with positive checkering. Left-hand model available.
**Price:** . . . . . . . . . . . . . . . . . . . . . . . . . . . . . . . . $395.00

# SAVAGE RIFLES

**MODEL 93 FSS STAINLESS**

### SPECIFICATIONS

**Caliber:** 22 WMR **Capacity:** 5 shots **Barrel Length:** 20.75" (1 in 16 twist) **Overall Length:** 39.5" **Weight:** 5.5 lbs. **Sights:** Front bead sight; sporting rear sight w/step elevator. **Stock:** Black graphite/polymer filled stock w/positive checkering on grip and forend. Stainless steel barreled action.
**Price:** . . . . . . . . . . . . . . . . . . . . . . . . . . . . . . . . . $194.00

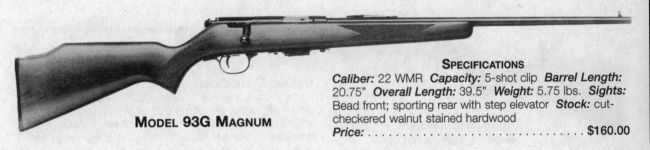

**MODEL 93G MAGNUM**

### SPECIFICATIONS

**Caliber:** 22 WMR **Capacity:** 5-shot clip **Barrel Length:** 20.75" **Overall Length:** 39.5" **Weight:** 5.75 lbs. **Sights:** Bead front; sporting rear with step elevator **Stock:** cut-checkered walnut stained hardwood
**Price:** . . . . . . . . . . . . . . . . . . . . . . . . . . . . . . . . . $160.00

**MODEL 93F MAGNUM**

### SPECIFICATIONS

**Calibers:** 22 WMR **Capacity:** 5 **Barrel Length:** 20.75" free floated **Overall Length:** 39.5" **Magazine:** 5 shot detachable clip **Weight:** 5 lbs. **Sights:** Bead front sight, adjustable rear. Receiver dovetailed for scope mount **Stock:** Black synthetic with positive checkering **Finish:** Blued, button rifled barrel
**Price:** . . . . . . . . . . . . . . . . . . . . . . . . . . . . . . . . . $154.00

**MODEL 93FVSS**

### SPECIFICATIONS

**Caliber:** 22 WMR **Capacity:** 5 rounds **Barrel Length:** 21" heavy weight **Overall Length:** 40" **Weight:** 6 lbs. **Sights:** None. Drilled and tapped for scope mount. Weaver style bases included **Stock:** Black synthetic with positive checkering **Barrel:** Stainless steel, recessed target style muzzle
**Price:** . . . . . . . . . . . . . . . . . . . . . . . . . . . . . . . . . $222.00

# SAVAGE SPORTING RIFLES

### MARK I-G SINGLE SHOT

#### SPECIFICATIONS

**Caliber:** 22 Short, Long or LR  **Capacity:** Single shot
**Action:** Self-cocking bolt action, thumb-operated rotary safety  **Barrel Length:** 20.75"  **Overall Length:** 39.5"

**Weight:** 5.5 lbs.
**Sights:** Open bead front; adjustable rear
**Stock:** One-piece, walnut-finish hardwood, Monte Carlo buttstock w/full pistol grip; checkered pistol grip and forend
**Features:** Receiver grooved for scope mounting
**Price:** . . . . . . . . . . . . . . . . . . . . . . . . . . . . $127.00
**Also available:**
MARK I-G "SMOOTHBORE" (20.75" barrel) . . . . . . . **127.00**
MARK I-G YOUTH (19" barrel) . . . . . . . . . . . . . . . **127.00**

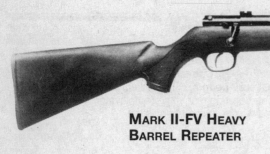

### MARK II-FV HEAVY BARREL REPEATER

#### SPECIFICATIONS

**Caliber:** 22 LR  **Capacity:** 5 shots  **Barrel Length:** 21" heavy weight  **Overall Length:** 39.75"  **Magazine:** 5 shot detachablle clip  **Weight:** 6 lbs.  **Sights:** None. Weaver style bases included  **Stock:** Black synthetic with positive checkering  **Finish:** Blued free floated, button rifled with recessed target style muzzle  **Features:** Heavy barrel with synthetic stock in 22 LR
**Price:** . . . . . . . . . . . . . . . . . . . . . . . . . . . . $194.00

### MARK II-FSS

#### SPECIFICATIONS

**Caliber:** 22 LR  **Capacity:** 10-shot clip  **Barrel Length:** 21" (1 in 16" twist)  **Overall Length:** 39.5"  **Weight:** 5 lbs.
**Stock:** Synthetic  **Sights:** Bead front sight; adjustable open rear  **Features:** Stainless steel barrelled action

**Price:** . . . . . . . . . . . . . . . . . . . . . . . . . . . . $169.00
**Also available:** MARK II-G w/one-piece walnut-finished Monte Carlo-style hardwood stock, blued steel bolt-action receiver, bead front sight . . . . . . . . . . . . . . . . $140.00
MARK II-GY LADIES/YOUTH w/19" barrel (37" overall)
   **Weight:** 5 lbs. . . . . . . . . . . . . . . . . . . . . . . . **140.00**
MARK II-GXP w/4x15mm scope (LH model avail.) . **147.00**
MARK II-F synthetic stock. . . . . . . . . . . . . . . . . . **127.00**

### MARK II-LV

#### SPECIFICATIONS

**Caliber:** 22 LR  **Capacity:** 10-shot  **Barrel Length:** 21" heavy barrel (1 in 16" twist)  **Overall Length:** 39.75"
**Weight:** 6.5 lbs.  **Stock:** Grey laminated hardwood stock; cut-checkered  **Features:** Precision button rifled with recessed target-style muzzle; machined blued steel barreled action; dovetailed for scope mounting
**Price:** . . . . . . . . . . . . . . . . . . . . . . . . . . . . $222.00

# SAVAGE SPORTING RIFLES

### MODEL 64FV
### SEMI-AUTOMATIC HEAVY BARREL

#### SPECIFICATIONS
*Caliber:* 22 LR  *Capacity:* 10 shots  *Barrel Length:* 21" heavy weight  *Overall Length:* 40.75"  *Magazine:* 10 shot detachable clip  *Weight:* 6 lbs.  *Sights:* None. Weaver style bases included  *Stock:* Black synthetic with positive checkering  *Finish:* Blued, button rifled with recessed target style muzzle  *Features:* Semiauto blue alloy steel barreled action
*Price:* . . . . . . . . . . . . . . . . . . . . . . . . . . . . . . . **$164.00**
*Also Available:* MODEL **64F** standard barrel
   with sights 5.5 lbs. . . . . . . . . . . . . . . . . . . . . . . **124.00**
MODEL **64G** standard barrel with sights 5.5 lbs.
   and hardwood stock. . . . . . . . . . . . . . . . . . . **134.00**

### MODEL 900TR
### TARGET REPEATER

#### SPECIFICATIONS
*Caliber:* 22 Long Rifle  *Capacity:* 5-shot clip magazine  *Action:* Self-cocking bolt action, thumb-operated rotary safety  *Overall Length:* 43 $^5/_8$"  *Approx. Weight:* 8 lbs.  *Stock:* One-piece, target-type with walnut finish hardwood; comes with shooting rail and hand stop  *Sights:* Receiver peep sights with 1/4 min. click micrometer adjustments, target front sight with inserts
*Price:* . . . . . . . . . . . . . . . . . . . . . . . . . . . . . . . **$440.00**

### MODEL 24F COMBINATION
### RIFLE/SHOTGUN

## SPECIFICATIONS MODEL 24F COMBINATION RIFLE/SHOTGUN

| MODEL | CALIBER | BARREL LENGTH | OVERALL LENGTH | APPROX. WEIGHT | RIFLING TWIST |
|---|---|---|---|---|---|
| 24F-20 Gauge - $449.00 | 22 LR.† | 24" | 40.5" | 8 lbs. | 1 in 14" |
| 24F-12 Gauge - $476.00 | 22 Hornet | 24" | 40.5" | 8 lbs. | 1 in 14" |
| 24F-12/410 - $504.00 | 223 Rem. | 24" | 40.5" | 8 lbs. | 1 in 14" |
| | 30-30 Win. | 24" | 40.5" | 8 lbs. | 1 in 12" |

*All 20 gauge models come with modified choke barrel. All 12 gauge models come with Full, Modified & IC choke tubes*
*†12 Gauge not available in 22 LR.*

# SPRINGFIELD RIFLES

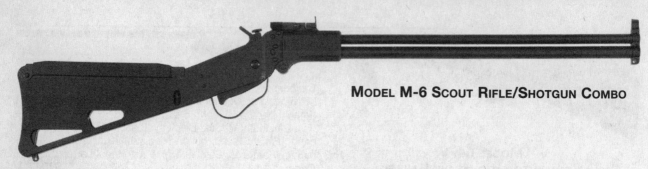

## MODEL M-6 SCOUT RIFLE/SHOTGUN COMBO

**SPECIFICATIONS**
**Calibers:** 22 LR/.410 and 22 Hornet/.410
**Barrel Length:** 18.25" (1:15" R.H. twist in 22 LR; 1:13" R.H. twist in 22 Hornet)
**Overall Length:** 32"
**Weight:** 4 lbs.

**Sight Radius:** 16 ¹/₈" **Finish:** Parkerized or stainless steel
**Features:** .410 shotgun barrel (2.5" or 3" chamber) choked Full; drilled and tapped for scope mount with Weaver base; lockable plastic carry case
**Price:** . . . . . . . . . . . . . . . . . . . . . . . . . . . . . . . . . . . $185.00
Stainless Steel. . . . . . . . . . . . . . . . . . . . . . . . . . . . 219.00

## M1A STANDARD

**SPECIFICATIONS**
**Calibers:** 308 Win./7.62mm NATO (243 or 7mm-08 optional) **Action:** gas-operated, self-loading
**Capacity:** 5- or 10-round box magazine
**Barrel Length:** 22"
**Rifling:** 6 groove, RH twist, 1 turn in 11"
**Overall Length:** 44 ¹/₃"
**Weight:** 9.2 lbs.
**Sights:** Military square post front; military aperture rear, adjustable for windage and elevation
**Sight Radius:** 26.75"

**Prices:**
   Standard w/walnut stock . . . . . . . . . . . . . . . $1,448.00
**Also available:**
**BASIC M1A RIFLE** w/painted black fiberglass stock,
   caliber 308/7.62mm only . . . . . . . . . . . . . . 1,319.00
**M1A SCOUT RIFLE** w/scope mount and handguard, black
fiberglass stock. . . . . . . . . . . . . . . . . . . . . . . . . . 1,529.00
w/walnut stock . . . . . . . . . . . . . . . . . . . . . . . . . . 1,639.00
National Match (match-grade barrel and trigger) . . . 1,995.00
Super Match (heavy match barrel, special rod
   guide, heavy stock) . . . . . . . . . . . . . . . . . . . . 2,449.00

## M1A-A1 SCOUT RIFLE

**SPECIFICATIONS**
**Calibers:** 308 Win./7.62mm
**Action:** gas-operated, self-loading
**Barrel Length:** 18" (w/o flash suppressor) **Overall Length:** 40.5" **Weight:** 8.9 lbs. (9 lbs. w/walnut stock)

**Sights:** Military square post-front, aperture rear with one MOA adjustments **Sight Radius:** 22.75"
**Prices:**
w/walnut stock.. . . . . . . . . . . . . . . . . . . . . . . . . $1,544.00
w/black fiberglass stock. . . . . . . . . . . . . . . . . . . 1,499.00

# STEYR-MANNLICHER RIFLES

## STEYR SSG-PI

The Steyr SSG features a black synthetic Cycolac stock (walnut optional), heavy Parkerized barrel, five-round standard (and optional 10-round) staggered magazine, heavy-duty milled receiver.

**SPECIFICATIONS**
*Calibers:* 243 Win. and 308 Win. *Barrel Length:* 26" *Overall*

*Length:* 44.5" *Weight:* 8.5 lbs. *Sights:* Iron sights; hooded ramp front with blade adjustable for elevation; rear standard V-notch adjustable for windage. *Features:* Sliding safety; 1" swivels.
*Prices:* MODEL SSG-PI Cycolac half-stock (26" bbl. with sights in 308 Win.) . . . . . . . . . . . . . . . . . . . . . **$1,699.00**
MODEL SSG-PII (without sights) . . . . . . . . . . . . . . **1,699.00**
MODEL SSG-P-IV in 308 Win. w/16.75", heavy barrel, no sights. . . . . . . . . . . . . . . . . . . . . **2,659.00**
MODEL SSG-PII McMILLAN 20" or 26" heavy barrel adjustable stock, no sights. . . . . . . . . . . . . . **2,299.00**

## STEYR SCOUT

The Steyr Scout package is equally effective as a sporter, tactical or survival rifle. Among its features are: safe bolt system, roller tang safety and black Zytel stock; integral bipod, flush sling sockets and forward-mounted Leupold 2.5X Scout Scope. Luggage case and two magazines included.

**SPECIFICATIONS**
*Caliber:* 223, 243, 7-08, 308 and 376 Steyr *Capacity:* 5 rounds *Barrel Length:* 19" fluted cold-hammer-forged barrel *Overall Length:* 39.57" w/2 buttstock spacers *Weight:* 7 lbs. (w/scope and mounts) *Sights:* Factory-installed Leupold 2.5 X 28mm IER *Stock:* Zytel w/13.58" length of pull (adjustable, w/spacers)
*Price:* . . . . . . . . . . . . . . . . . . . . . . . . . . . . **$2,699.00**
in .276 Steyre . . . . . . . . . . . . . . . . . . . . . . . . . **2,799.00**

## SBS (SAFE BOLT SYSTEM) MANNLICHER CLASSIC MODEL

**SPECIFICATIONS**
*Calibers:* 243 Win., 25-06, 308 Win., 270 Win., 7mm-08, 30-06 S'fld, 7mm Rem. Mag., 300 Win. Mag. *Capacity:* 4 rounds (3 rounds in Magnum, Prohunter and Forester); detachable staggered box magazine *Barrel Lengths:* 23.6"; 26" (magnum calibers) *Overall Length:* 44.5" *Weight:* 7.5 lbs. *Safety:* 3-position roller safety *Trigger:* Single adjustable trigger *Sights:* Ramp front w/balck adjustment for elevations; rear standard V-notch adjustable for windage; drilled and tapped for mounts

*Finish:* Blued; hand-checkered fancy European oiled walnut stock *Features:* Rotary cold hammer-forged barrel; front locking lug bolt
*Prices:* Standard Calibers (half stock) . . . . . . . **$2,795.00**
Magnum Calibers (half stock) . . . . . . . . . . . . . **2,995.00**
Standard Calibers (half stock carbine) . . . . . . . **2,895.00**
Standard Calibers (full stock) . . . . . . . . . . . . . **2,995.00**
*Also available:* STEYR SBS PROHUNTER in 243 Win., 25-06, 6.5x55, 270 Win., 7mm-08 Rem., 308 Win., 30-06, 260 rem, 280 Rem., w/synthetic half stock; no sights . . . . . **$719.00**
STEYR MAGNUM MODEL in 7mm Rem. Mag. or 300 Win. Mag. w/25.6" barrel . . . . . . . . . . . . **749.00**
STEYR SBS FORESTER in 243 Win, 25-06, 270 Win., 6.5x55, 260 Rem., 280 Rem., 7mm-08 Rem., 308 Win., 30-06 w/23.6" bbl . . . . . . **749.00**
STEYR SBS FORESTER MAGNUM in 7mm Rem. Mag. or 300 Win. Mag.. . . . . . . . . . . . . . . . . . . . . **779.00**

# STEYR-MANNLICHER RIFLES

## STEYR SBS HUNTING RIFLE SERIES

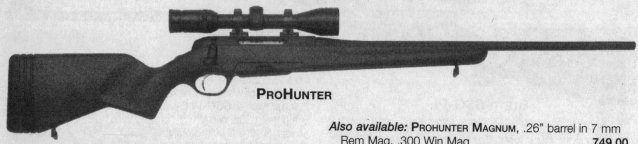

**ProHunter**

### SBS PROHUNTER-SYNTHETIC STOCK
23.6" barrel, no sights, matte blue finish, 2 removable butt spacers, flush mounted QD swivels, 7.4 lbs., .243, .25-06, .260, 6.5 x 55, .270, 7mm-08, .286, .308, .30-06, accepts optional Hi-Capacity magazine kit
**Price:** . . . . . . . . . . . . . . . . . . . . . . . . . . . $719.00

*Also available:* PROHUNTER MAGNUM, .26" barrel in 7 mm
Rem Mag, .300 Win Mag . . . . . . . . . . . . . . **749.00**
PROHUNTER STAINLESS STEEL . . . . . . . . . . . . . . **809.00**
PROHUNTER STAINLESS STEEL MAGNUM . . . . . . . . **839.00**
PROHUNTER CAMO (Mossy Oak, Camo stock,
blued steel) . . . . . . . . . . . . . . . . . . . . . . . **779.00**
PROHUNTER CAMO MAGNUM . . . . . . . . . . . . . . . . **809.00**
PROHUNTER 376 CAMO (in .376 Steyr) . . . . . . . . . **859.00**

**PROHUNTER SS CAMO**

### PROHUNTER MOUNTAIN
20" barrel, no sights, matte blue finish, in .243, 25-06, .260, 6.5x55, .270, 7mm-08, .308, .30-06

**Price:** . . . . . . . . . . . . . . . . . . . . . . . . . . . **$739.00**
PROHUNTER MOUNTAIN STAINLESS STEEL . . . . . . . . **829.00**
PROHUNTER MOUNTAIN CAMO (Mossy Oak, Camo
stock, blued steel) . . . . . . . . . . . . . . . . . . . **799.00**
PROHUNTER MOUNTAIN STAINLESS STEEL CAMO . . . . . **889.00**

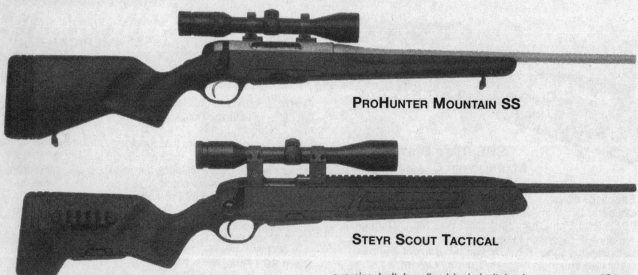

**ProHunter Mountain SS**

**Steyr Scout Tactical**

### STEYR SCOUT TACTICAL
Black synthetic stock with removable spacers, 19.25" fluted barrel, full length optic rail (Weaver style), Integral bipod, oversize bolt handle, black bolt body, emergency "Ghost Ring" sights and two 5 round magazines, .223, .308
**Price:** . . . . . . . . . . . . . . . . . . . . . . . . . . . **$2,069.00**
SCOUT TACTICAL STAINLESS STEEL . . . . . . . . . . **2,259.00**

# STEYR-MANNLICHER RIFLES

## SBS TACTICAL ELITE

### SBS TACTICAL ELITE
### HEAVY BARREL - SYNTHETIC STOCK

**Part#:** 503TE.52.00 *Caliber:* 223 Rem
**Part#:** 516TE.52.00 *Caliber:* 308 Win

26" heavy barrel, two 5 round detachable magazines (w/spare buttstock storage), no sights, matte blue finish, black bolt body with oversize bolt handle, Zytel stock with adj. cheekpiece and fully adj. buttplate, full length Picatinney spec mounting rail, forearm mounting rail, 5 QD swivel receptacals, accepts Hi-Capacity 10 rd magazine with adapter
*Price:* . . . . . . . . . . . . . . . . . . . . . . . . . . . . . . **$2,399.00**

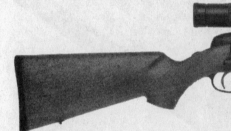

## FORESTER MOUNTAIN

### STEYR SBS FORESTER MOUNTAIN

20" sporter barrel, 5-round detachable magazine, adjustable trigger, no sights, satin-finish classic-style walnut stock, 7.2 lbs., in .243, .25-06, .260, 6.5x55, .270, 7mm-08, .308, .30-06

*Price:* . . . . . . . . . . . . . . . . . . . . . . . . . . . . . **$799.00**
*Also available:* Forester with 24" barrel (in .280 Rem too)
7.4 lbs . . . . . . . . . . . . . . . . . . . . . . . . . . . . **749.00**
Forester Magnum, 26" barrel in 7mm Rem, 300 Win Magnum . . . . . . . . . . . . . . . . . . . . . . . . . . . . **779.00**

### CLASSIC AMERICAN - HALF STOCK

## STEYR SBS CLASSIC AMERICAN

24" sporter barrel, 5-round detachable magazines, adjustable trigger, no sights, satin-finish walnut stock with forend tip, 7.2 lbs, in .243, 25-06, .260, 6.5x55, .270, 7mm-08, .280, .308, .30-06
*Price:* . . . . . . . . . . . . . . . . . . . . . . . . . . . . . **$1,499.00**

### STEYR SBS
### PROHUNTER COMPACT

Synthetic Zytel stock with 2 butt spacers included, special "shock absorbing" recoil pad, 20" barrel with iron sights, flush

## PROHUNTER COMPACT

mounted QD swivels, accepts optional Hi-Capacity magazine kit, matte blue finish, 243, .260, 7mm-08, .308, .376 Steyr
*Price:* . . . . . . . . . . . . . . . . . . . . . . . . . . . . . **$799.00**
*Also available:* PROHUNTER COMPACT STAINLESS STEEL . **889.00**

# SZECSEI & FUCHS RIFLES

The Szecsei & Fuchs double-barrel bolt action rifle may be the only one of its kind. Built with great care and much handwork from the finest materials, it follows a design remarkable for its cleverness. And while the rifle is not light-weight, it can be aimed quickly and offers more large-caliber firepower than any competitor. The six-shot magazine feeds two rounds simultaneously, both of which can then be fired by two quick pulls of the trigger. **Chamberings:** .300 Win, 9.3 x 64, .358 Norma, .375 H&H, .404 Jeff, .416 Rem., .458 Win., .416 Rigby, .450 Rigby, .460 Short A-Square, .470 Capstick, .495 A-Square, .500 Jeff **Weight:** 14 lbs. with round barrels, 16 with octagon barrels. **Price:** . . . . . . . . . . . . . . . . . . . . . . . **Available on request**

# TAYLOR'S RIFLES

Faithful to the original, this "Henry" with its barrel and magazine drawn from one-piece steel, required a good deal of skill to reproduce. Chambered for a cartridge available today, the "Henry" was the first true repeating rifle to be both practical and reliable. Developed from the Volcanic carbines by B. Tyler Henry, inventor of the cartridge, in 1860, this replica would be the pride of its innovator and namesake.

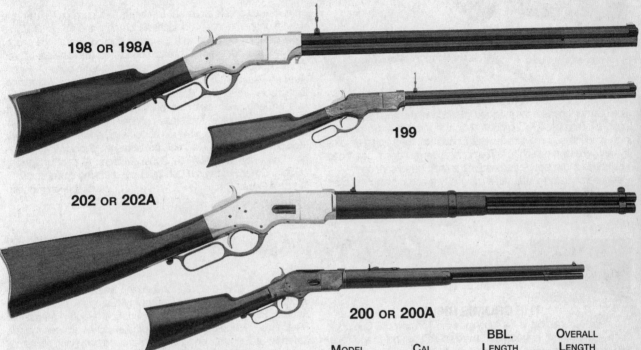

**198 OR 198A**

**199**

**202 OR 202A**

**200 OR 200A**

### 198 - HENRY BRASS FRAME 44/40
### 198A - HENRY BRASS FRAME .45 LC
### 199-HENRY RIFLE STEEL FRAME 44/40

The first real production of Henry Rifle with the Frame and Butt Plate in Steel. Total production was around 400. The first models had no lever latch. Only a few specimens are available now and they are the most valued by collectors around the world.
**Price:** wholesale . . . . . . . . . . . . . . . . . . . . . . . . . . $730.00

| Model | Cal. | BBL. Length | Overall Length | Magazine Capacity |
|-------|------|-------------|----------------|-------------------|
| 198 | 44/40 | 24-1/4" | 43-3/4" | 13-9 shots |
| 198A | 45 LC | 24-1/4" | 43-3/4" | 13-9 shots |
| 199 | 44/40 | 24-1/4" | 43-3/4" | 13-9 shots |

When Nelson King patented his new loading system he could not have known that he was creating a long, successful line of lever action arms. The "66 Yellowboy" lived the fabulous adventure that was the winning of the west. Its fire power, notable even by today's standards, made this an exceptional weapon.
**Price:** wholesale . . . . . . . . . . . . . . . . . $720.00-750.00

### 202 - 1866 YELLOWBOY CARBINE 44/40
### 202A - 1866 YELLOWBOY CARBINE .45 LC
### 1866 YELLOW CARBINE

The first gun to carry the Winchester name, strong and light weight was the perfect saddle companion. This is an exceptional collector's piece and a fine shooting gun.
**Price:** wholesale . . . . . . . . . . . . . . . . . . . . . . $550.00

| Model | Cal. | BBL. Length | Overall Length |
|-------|------|-------------|----------------|
| 202 | 44/40 | 19" | 38 1/4" |
| 202A | 45 LC | 19" | 38 1/4" |

### 200 - 1873 WINCHESTER RIFLE 44/40
### 200A - 1873 WINCHESTER RIFLE 45 LC
### 1873 SPORTING RIFLE

This rifle had a long life from 1873-1927. It is probably the only gun to have given its name to a movie. With its steel frame cartridge loading system it was much more powerful than the .44 Henry, and demand quickly pushed its production into the hundreds of thousands.
**Price:** wholesale . . . . . . . . . . . . . . . . . . . . . . $695.00

| Model | Cal. | BBL. Length | Overall Length |
|-------|------|-------------|----------------|
| 200 | 44/40 | 24 1/4" | 43 1/4" |
| 200A | 45 LC | 24 1/4" | 43 1/4" |

**5505-FRONT SIGHT GLOBE**
Sight has a 3/8" dovetail.

**5508-TANG PEEP SIGHT**
This tang sight is the famous target and hunting sight of the Old West. This sight has the precision adjustment for windage and elevation. Sight is blue finish and will fit original 1873 Winchester Rifles.

# THOMPSON & CAMPBELL RIFLES

*Patented Inver action showing bedding plate.*

## THE INVER RIFLE

The heart of the rifle is the patented Inver action, designed and developed by Thompson & Campbell. Machined from a single block of high-grade steel, it provides flawless functioning, mechanical simplicity and massive strength. The conical triple-lugged bolt head enshrouds and supports the head of the chambered cartridge. Designed primarily for use with a fine quality telescopic sight supplied on quick-detachable mounts, the Inver rifle also incorporates a unique system of open sights. A detachable foresight and flip-up backsight allow precision shooting with the same sighting axis as the scope, thus maintaining the firer's head position on the carefully-tailored stock. A two-stage trigger system is available as an option.
*Action:* Patented front lock-in 3 lug bolt action *Magazine:* Detachable 4 round box *Barrel length:* 22 inches *Safeties:* Stalking safe on tang. wing safety on bolt; Firing pin immobiliser on both *Trigger:* Single stage (two stage optional) *Telescopic Sight:* Best quality optics - owner's preferred choice can be fitted *Open Sights:* Flip up rear aperture; Detachable post foresight *Stock:* Walnut, takedown capacity *Weight:* From 8 lbs *Calibers:* All popular sporting calibers *Other Features:* Flush-fitting pop-out sling swivel studs; fitted case *Price:* . . . . . . . . . . . . . . . . . . . . . . **Available on request**

## THE CROMIE RIFLE

The deluxe Cromie rifle is the flagship of the Thompson & Campbell range. The Cromie is stocked to the owner's personal fit and style with a magnificent stock of exhibition-grade walnut and supplied in a traditional leather carrying case. The action, receiver and detachable scipe mounts are attractively hand-engraved with gold inlays. The action and scope-mount steel are handsomely blued or colour case-hardened. The latter provides a richly marbled finish that is protective and wear resistant. The Cromie model also comes with an octagonal barrel, a distinctive and traditional design feature of many fine old sporting rifles now revived by Thompson & Campbell.
*Action:* Patented front locking 3 lug bolt action *Magazine:* Detachable 4 round box *Barrel length:* 24 inches octagonal profile *Safeties:* Stalking safe on tang. wing safety on bolt; Firing pin immobiliser on both *Trigger:* Single stage (two stage optional) *Telescopic Sight:* Best quality optics - owner's preferred choice can be fitted *Open Sights:* Optional *Stock:* Exhibition grade walnut; takedown capacity *Weight:* 8 lbs *Calibers:* All popular sporting calibers *Other Features:* Flush-fitting pop-out sling swivel studs; fitted case.
*Price:* . . . . . . . . . . . . . . . . . . . . . . . . . . . . . . **Available on request**

## THE JURA RIFLE

Fully stocked, with the walnut running right up to the muzzle, the Jura is true to a long-established Continental tradtion. Owing to its full length stock the Jura is not a takedown rifle, and comes in a full-length carrying case. The 17-inch barrel gives the Jura a significantly shorter overall length than the other Thompson & Campbell models.
The Jura's short overall length makes it both fast-handling and easy to carry even in thick cover. When shooting from the confines of a high seat, and when climbing in and out, the Jura is particularly easy to use. Since much woodland and driven rifle shooting is done from a standing or sitting position, rather than prone as on the open hill, the Jura's stock dimensions, pistol grip contours, scope eye-relief and wide angle lens can be subtly but significantly regulated to provide the most comfortable and accurate fit for this kind of sport.
*Action:* Patented front locking 3 lug bolt action *Magazine:* Detachable 4 round box *Barrel length:* 17 inches *Safeties:* Stalking safe on tang. wing safety on bolt; Firing pin immobiliser on both *Trigger:* Single stage (two stage optional) *Telescopic Sight:* Best quality optics - owner's preferred choice can be fitted *Open Sights:* Optional *Stock:* Walnut; not takedown *Weight:* from 7.5 lbs *Calibers:* All popular sporting calibres *Other Features:* Flush fitting pop out sling swivel studs; fitted case.
*Price:* . . . . . . . . . . . . . . . . . . . . . . . . . . . . . . **Available on request**

# THOMPSON/CENTER RIFLES

### CONTENDER CARBINE

### SPECIFICATIONS
Available in 5 *calibers:* 22 LR Match, 22 Hornet, 223 Rem., 7x30 Waters, 30-30 Win. *Barrels:* 21 inches, interchangeable. Adjustable iron sights; tapped and drilled for scope mounts. *Weight:* 5 lbs. 3 oz.

**Price:**
CONTENDER CARBINE w/standard walnut stock in 22
  Hornet, 223 Rem. 7x30 Waters 30-30 Win. . . . **$571.38**
CONTENDER CARBINE with Match Grade 22
  LR barrel . . . . . . . . . . . . . . . . . . . . . . . . . . . . . . 583.04

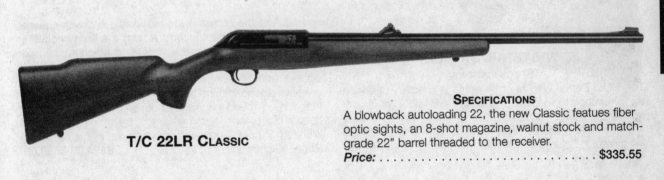

### T/C 22LR CLASSIC

### SPECIFICATIONS
A blowback autoloading 22, the new Classic featues fiber optic sights, an 8-shot magazine, walnut stock and match-grade 22" barrel threaded to the receiver.
**Price:** . . . . . . . . . . . . . . . . . . . . . . . . . . . . . . **$335.55**

### ENCORE RIFLE

### SPECIFICATIONS
*Calibers:* 22-250 Rem., .223 Rem., .243 Win., 25-06 Rem., .260 Rem., .270 Win., .280 Rem., .7mm-08 Rem., 7mm Rem. Mag., .308 Win., .30-06 Spfd., .300 Win. Mag., 45-70 Govt. *Action:* Single-shot, break-open *Barrel lengths:* 24" and 26" heavy barrel (.22-250 Rem., 223 Rem., 25-06 Rem., 7mm Rem. Mag., and 300 Win. Mag. only)

*Overall length:* 38 1/2" (24" barrel); 40 1/2" (26" barrel)
*Weight:* 6 3/4 lbs. (24"); 7 1/2 lbs. (26")
*Trigger:* Adjustable for overtravel
*Safety:* Automatic hammerblock w/bolt interlock
*Stock:* American walnut with Schnabel forend and Monte Carlo buttstock
*Features:* Interchangeable barrels, sling swivel studs
*Price:* . . . . . . . . . . . . . . . . . . . . . . . . . . . . . . . . **$602.44**
  with composite stock . . . . . . . . . . . . . . . . . . . . . 582.29
  45-70 Government . . . . . . . . . . . . . . . . . . . . . . . 597.78
  Composite walnut. . . . . . . . . . . . . . . . . . . . . . . . 618.40

# TIKKA RIFLES

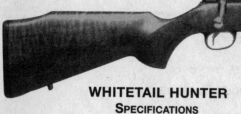

## WHITETAIL HUNTER
### SPECIFICATIONS

**Calibers:** 22-250, 223, 243, 7mm-08, 308 (Medium); 25-06, 270, 30-06 (Long); 7mm Mag., 300 Win. Mag., 338 Win. Mag. **Capacity:** 3 rounds (5 rounds optional); detachable magazine **Barrel Lengths:** 22.5" (24.5" Magnum) **Overall Length:** 42" (Medium); 42.5" (Long); 44.5" (Magnum) **Weight:**

7 lbs. (Medium); 7 1/4 lbs. (Long); 7.5 lbs. (Magnum) **Sights:** No sights; integral scope mount rails; drilled and tapped **Safety:** Locks trigger and bolt handle **Features:** Oversized trigger guard; short bolt throw; customized spacer system; walnut stock with palm swell and matte lacquer finish; cold hammer-forged barrel

**Price:** . . . . . . . . . . . . . . . . . . . . . . . . . . . . . . . . . . . **$624.00**
   Magnum . . . . . . . . . . . . . . . . . . . . . . . . . . . . . . . **659.00**
**Also Available:** Left Hand . . . . . . . . . . . . . . . . **689.00**
   Left Hand Magnum. . . . . . . . . . . . . . . . . . . . . . **719.00**

## WHITETAIL BATTUE
### SPECIFICATIONS

The Tikka Battue with its open sights is specially designed for snapshooting. Wide V-shaped rear sight is height adjustable. Fast, well balanced shots are easy to master with the Tikka Battue. • Walnut stock, oil finished or matte lacquered • Patented buttplate system. The length of pull

and pitch of the buttplate are easily adjusted with optional spacers. • Adjustable trigger pull from 2-4 lbs without first pull • Short and long action, including Magnum, plunger ejector • Special open sights with height adjustable rear sight • Integral scope mount rails, receiver tapped for universal scope mount blocks • Detachable 3-round clip magazine, 5-round magazine as option • Short, free floating, deeply blued, cold hammer-forged barrel • Called, Tikka Whitetail Trapper, if delivered without open sights

**Price:** Magnums . . . . . . . . . . . . . . . . . $624.00-$659.00

## WHITETAIL HUNTER DELUXE

### SPECIFICATIONS
This Whitetail Hunter Deluxe has a select walnut stock plus contrasting grip cap and forend tip and modified cheekrest.
**Price:** Standard Calibers . . . . . . . . . . . . . . . . . . **$759.00**
   Magnums. . . . . . . . . . . . . . . . . . . . . . . . . . . . **789.00**

## WHITETAIL HUNTER SYNTHETIC

### SPECIFICATIONS
Same specifications as the standard Whitetail Hunter, except with All-Weather synthetic stock.
**Price:** . . . . . . . . . . . . . . . . . . . . . . . . . . . . . . . . . . **$624.00**
   Magnum . . . . . . . . . . . . . . . . . . . . . . . . . . . . . **659.00**

**Also available:**
**WHITETAIL HUNTER STAINLESS SYNTHETIC.**
Same specifications as above, except with stainless steel receiver, barrel and bolt. . . . . . . . . . . . . . . . . . . **$689.00**
In Magnum calibers . . . . . . . . . . . . . . . . . . . . . . . **719.00**

# TIKKA RIFLES

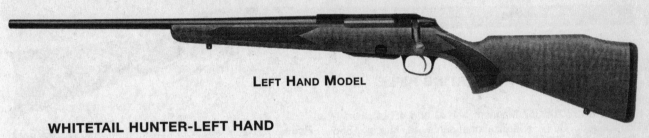

**LEFT HAND MODEL**

## WHITETAIL HUNTER-LEFT HAND

### SPECIFICATIONS
Left-handed shooters will welcome this new Tikka in 223, 22-250 and 308. Same specifications as Whitetail Hunter but with left side bolt handle.

*Price:* . . . . . . . . . . . . . . . . . . . . . . . . . . . . . . . . . . . . **$969.00**

**CONTINENTAL VARMINT**

### SPECIFICATIONS
*Calibers:* 17 Rem., 22-250, 223, 308
*Capacity:* 5 rounds
*Barrel Length:* 26 *Overall Length:* 46"
*Weight:* 8 lbs. 10 oz.

*Finish:* Matte lacquer walnut stock w/palm swell
*Features:* Recoil pad spacer system; quick-release detachable magazine; beavertail forend; cold hammer-forged barrel; integral scope mount rails; adjustable trigger
*Price:* . . . . . . . . . . . . . . . . . . . . . . . . . . . . . . . . . . . . **$734.00**

**CONTINENTAL LONG-RANGE HUNTING RIFLE**

### SPECIFICATIONS
*Calibers:* 25-06 Rem., 270 Win., 7mm Rem. Mag., 300 Win. Mag.
*Capacity:* 5 rounds in standard calibers, 4 rounds in magnum calibers
*Barrel Length:* 26" heavy barrel

*Overall Length:* 46.5"
*Weight:* 8 lbs. 12 oz.
*Finish:* Matte lacquer walnut stock w/palm swell
*Features:* Same as Continental Varmint model
*Price:* . . . . . . . . . . . . . . . . . . . . . . . . . . . . . . . . . . . . **$734.00**
    Magnum Calibers. . . . . . . . . . . . . . . . . . . . . . . . . **764.00**

# UBERTI REPLICAS

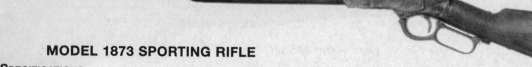

## MODEL 1873 SPORTING RIFLE

### SPECIFICATIONS
**Calibers:** 32/20, 357 Magnum, 44-40 and 45 LC. Hand-checkered. Other specifications same as Model 1866 Sporting Rifle. 20" barrel. Also available with 24.25" or 30" octagonal barrel and pistol-grip stock (extra).

**Price:** . . . . . . . . . . . . . . . . . . . . . . . . . . . . . . . **$973.00**
**Also available:** With pistol grip. . . . . . . . . . . . . . **$999.00**
With pistol grip and 30" barrel.. . . . . . . . . . . . **1,050.00**

## MODEL 1871 ROLLING BLOCK BABY CARBINE

### SPECIFICATIONS
**Calibers:** 22 LR, 22 Hornet, 22 Magnum, 357 Magnum
**Barrel Length:** 22" **Overall Length:** 35.5" **Weight:** 4.85 lbs. **Stock and forend:** Walnut **Trigger guard:** Brass
**Sights:** Fully adjustable rear; ramp front **Frame:** Color-case-hardened steel
**Price:** . . . . . . . . . . . . . . . . . . . . . . . . . . . . . **$490.00**

## HENRY RIFLE

### SPECIFICATIONS
**Calibers:** 44-40, 45 LC **Barrel Length:** 18.5", 22.25", 24.25" (half-octagon, with tubular magazine) **Overall Length:** 38", 41.5", 43.75" **Weight:** 7.9, 9, 9.26 lbs. **Frame:** Brass **Stock:** Varnished American walnut
**Price:** . . . . . . . . . . . . . . . . . . . . . . . . . . . . . **$940.00**
Henry Rifle Steel . . . . . . . . . . . . . . . . . . . . . . . . **990.00**

## MODEL 1866 YELLOWBOY CARBINE
The frist gun to carry the Winchester name, this model was born as the 44-caliber rimfire cartridge Henry and is now chambered for 22 LR, 22 Mag., 38 SP, 44-40, and 45 LC.

### SPECIFICATIONS
**Calibers:** 22 LR, 22 Magnum, 38 Special, 44-40, 45 L.C.
**Barrel Length:** 19", round, tapered **Overall Length:** 38.25"
**Weight:** 7.380 lbs. **Frame:** Brass **Stock and forend:** Walnut
**Sights:** Vertically adjustable rear; horizontally adjustable front
**Price:** . . . . . . . . . . . . . . . . . . . . . . . . . . . . . **$760.00**

# WEATHERBY MARK V RIFLES

## MARK V DELUXE

The Mark V Deluxe stock is made of hand-selected American walnut with skipline checkering, traditional diamond-shaped inlay, rosewood pistol-grip cap and forend tip. Monte Carlo design with raised cheekpiece properly positions the shooter while reducing felt recoil. The action and hammer-forged barrel and hand-bedded for accuracy, then deep blued to a high-luster finish. See also specifications tables below and on the following page.

**Calibers**: 26" Barrel: In 257 Wby. Mag., 270 Wby. Mag., 7mm Wby. Mag., 300 Wby. Mag. and 340 Wby. Mag. . . . . . $1,449.00

In 378 Wby. Mag. . . . . . . . . . . . . . . . . . . . . . . . 1,692.00

**28" Barrel**: In 416 Wby. Mag. . . . . . . . . . . . . . . . 1,875.00

In 460 Wby. Mag. . . . . . . . . . . . . . . . . . . . . . . 2,193.00

## MARK V® MAGNUM RIFLE SPECIFICATIONS

| Caliber | Model | Barrelled Action | Weight* | Overall Length | Magazine Capacity | Barrel Length/ Contour | Rifling | Length Of Pull | Drop At Comb | Monte Carlo | Drop At Heel |
|---|---|---|---|---|---|---|---|---|---|---|---|
| **.257 Wby. Mag.** | Mark V Sporter | RH 26" | 8 1/2 lbs. | 46 5/8" | 3+1 in chamber | 26" #2 | 1-10" twist | 13 5/8" | 1" | 1/2" | 1 5/8" |
| | Eurosport | RH 26" | 8 1/2 lbs. | 46 5/8" | 3+1 in chamber | 26" #2 | 1-10" twist | 13 5/8" | 1" | 1/2" | 1 5/8" |
| | Mark V Deluxe | RH 26" | 8 1/2 lbs. | 46 5/8" | 3+1 in chamber | 26" #2 | 1-10" twist | 13 5/8" | 7/8" | 3/8" | 1 3/8" |
| | Euromark | RH 26" | 8 1/2 lbs. | 46 5/8" | 3+1 in chamber | 26" #2 | 1-10" twist | 13 5/8" | 7/8" | 3/8" | 1 3/8" |
| | Lazermark | RH 26" | 8 1/2 lbs. | 46 5/8" | 3+1 in chamber | 26" #2 | 1-10" twist | 13 5/8" | 7/8" | 3/8" | 1 3/8" |
| | Synthetic | RH 26" | 8 lbs. | 46 5/8" | 3+1 in chamber | 26" #2 | 1-10" twist | 13 5/8" | 7/8" | 1/2" | 1 1/8" |
| | Fluted Synthetic | RH 26" | 7 1/2 lbs. | 46 5/8" | 3+1 in chamber | 26" #2 | 1-10" twist | 13 5/8" | 7/8" | 1/2" | 1 1/8" |
| | Stainless | RH 26" | 8 lbs. | 46 5/8" | 3+1 in chamber | 26" #2 | 1-10" twist | 13 5/8" | 7/8" | 1/2" | 1 1/8" |
| | Fluted Stainless | RH 26" | 7 1/2 lbs. | 46 5/8" | 3+1 in chamber | 26" #2 | 1-10" twist | 13 5/8" | 7/8" | 1/2" | 1 1/8" |
| | Accumark | RH 26" | 8 1/2 lbs. | 46 5/8" | 3+1 in chamber | 26" #3 | 1-10" twist | 13 5/8" | 1" | 9/16" | 1 1/2" |
| | SLS | RH 26" | 8 1/2 lbs. | 46 5/8" | 3+1 in chamber | 26" #2 | 1-10" twist | 13 5/8" | 1" | 1/2" | 1 5/8" |
| **.270 Wby. Mag.** | Mark V Sporter | RH 26" | 8 1/2 lbs. | 46 5/8" | 3+1 in chamber | 26" #2 | 1-10" twist | 13 5/8" | 1" | 1/2" | 1 5/8" |
| | Eurosport | RH 26" | 8 1/2 lbs. | 46 5/8" | 3+1 in chamber | 26" #2 | 1-10" twist | 13 5/8" | 1" | 1/2" | 1 5/8" |
| | Mark V Deluxe | RH 26" | 8 1/2 lbs. | 46 5/8" | 3+1 in chamber | 26" #2 | 1-10" twist | 13 5/8" | 7/8" | 3/8" | 1 3/8" |
| | Euromark | RH 26" | 8 1/2 lbs. | 46 5/8" | 3+1 in chamber | 26" #2 | 1-10" twist | 13 5/8" | 7/8" | 3/8" | 1 3/8" |
| | Lazermark | RH 26" | 8 1/2 lbs. | 46 5/8" | 3+1 in chamber | 26" #2 | 1-10" twist | 13 5/8" | 7/8" | 1/2" | 1 1/8" |
| | Synthetic | RH 26" | 8 lbs. | 46 5/8" | 3+1 in chamber | 26" #2 | 1-10" twist | 13 5/8" | 7/8" | 1/2" | 1 1/8" |
| | Fluted Synthetic | RH 26" | 7 1/2 lbs. | 46 5/8" | 3+1 in chamber | 26" #2 | 1-10" twist | 13 5/8" | 7/8" | 1/2" | 1 1/8" |
| | Stainless | RH 26" | 8 lbs. | 46 5/8" | 3+1 in chamber | 26" #2 | 1-10" twist | 13 5/8" | 7/8" | 1/2" | 1 1/8" |
| | Fluted Stainless | RH 26" | 7 1/2 lbs. | 46 5/8" | 3+1 in chamber | 26" #2 | 1-10" twist | 13 5/8" | 7/8" | 1/2" | 1 1/8" |
| | Accumark | RH 26" | 8 1/2 lbs. | 46 5/8" | 3+1 in chamber | 26" #3 | 1-10" twist | 13 5/8" | 1" | 9/16" | 1 1/2" |
| | SLS | RH 26" | 8 1/2 lbs. | 46 5/8" | 3+1 in chamber | 26" #2 | 1-10" twist | 13 5/8" | 1" | 1/2" | 1 5/8" |
| **7mm Rem. Mag.** | Mark V Sporter | RH 24" | 8 lbs. | 44 5/8" | 3+1 in chamber | 24" #2 | 1-9 1/2" twist | 13 5/8" | 1" | 1/2" | 1 5/8" |
| | Eurosport | RH 24" | 8 lbs. | 44 5/8" | 3+1 in chamber | 24" #2 | 1-9 1/2" twist | 13 5/8" | 1" | 1/2" | 1 5/8" |
| | Synthetic | RH 24" | 8 lbs. | 44 5/8" | 3+1 in chamber | 24" #2 | 1-9 1/2" twist | 13 5/8" | 7/8" | 1/2" | 1 1/8" |
| | Fluted Synthetic | RH 24" | 7 1/2 lbs. | 44 5/8" | 3+1 in chamber | 24" #2 | 1-9 1/2" twist | 13 5/8" | 7/8" | 1/2" | 1 1/8" |
| | Stainless | RH 24" | 8 lbs. | 44 5/8" | 3+1 in chamber | 24" #2 | 1-9 1/2" twist | 13 5/8" | 7/8" | 1/2" | 1 1/8" |
| | Fluted Stainless | RH 24" | 7 1/2 lbs. | 44 5/8" | 3+1 in chamber | 24" #2 | 1-9 1/2" twist | 13 5/8" | 7/8" | 1/2" | 1 1/8" |
| | Accumark | RH 26" | 8 1/2 lbs. | 46 5/8" | 3+1 in chamber | 26" #3 | 1-9 1/2" twist | 13 5/8" | 1" | 9/16" | 1 1/2" |
| | SLS | RH 24" | 8 1/2 lbs. | 44 5/8" | 3+1 in chamber | 24" #2 | 1-9 1/2" twist | 13 5/8" | 1" | 1/2" | 1 5/8" |
| **7mm Wby. Mag.** | Mark V Sporter | RH 26" | 8 1/2 lbs. | 46 5/8" | 3+1 in chamber | 26" #2 | 1-10" twist | 13 5/8" | 1" | 1/2" | 1 5/8" |
| | Eurosport | RH 26" | 8 1/2 lbs. | 46 5/8" | 3+1 in chamber | 26" #2 | 1-10" twist | 13 5/8" | 1" | 1/2" | 1 5/8" |
| | Mark V Deluxe | RH 26" | 8 1/2 lbs. | 46 5/8" | 3+1 in chamber | 26" #2 | 1-10" twist | 13 5/8" | 7/8" | 3/8" | 1 3/8" |
| | Euromark | RH 26" | 8 1/2 lbs. | 46 5/8" | 3+1 in chamber | 26" #2 | 1-10" twist | 13 5/8" | 7/8" | 3/8" | 1 3/8" |
| | Lazermark | RH 26" | 8 1/2 lbs. | 46 5/8" | 3+1 in chamber | 26" #2 | 1-10" twist | 13 5/8" | 7/8" | 3/8" | 1 3/8" |
| | Synthetic | RH 26" | 8 lbs. | 46 5/8" | 3+1 in chamber | 26" #2 | 1-10" twist | 13 5/8" | 7/8" | 1/2" | 1 1/8" |
| | Fluted Synthetic | RH 26" | 7 1/2 lbs. | 46 5/8" | 3+1 in chamber | 26" #2 | 1-10" twist | 13 5/8" | 7/8" | 1/2" | 1 1/8" |
| | Stainless | RH 26" | 8 lbs. | 46 5/8" | 3+1 in chamber | 26" #2 | 1-10" twist | 13 5/8" | 7/8" | 1/2" | 1 1/8" |
| | Fluted Stainless | RH 26" | 7 1/2 lbs. | 46 5/8" | 3+1 in chamber | 26" #2 | 1-10" twist | 13 5/8" | 7/8" | 1/2" | 1 1/8" |
| | Accumark | RH 26" | 8 1/2 lbs. | 46 5/8" | 3+1 in chamber | 26" #3 | 1-10" twist | 13 5/8" | 1" | 9/16" | 1 1/2" |
| | SLS | RH 26" | 8 1/2 lbs. | 46 5/8" | 3+1 in chamber | 26" #3 | 1-10" twist | 13 5/8" | 1" | 1/2" | 1 5/8" |
| **7mm STW** | Accumark | RH 26" | 8 1/2 lbs. | 46 5/8" | 3+1 in chamber | 26" #3 | 1-10" twist | 13 5/8" | 1" | 9/16" | 1 1/2" |
| **.300 Win. Mag.** | Mark V Sporter | RH 24" | 8 lbs. | 44 5/8" | 3+1 in chamber | 24" #2 | 1-10" twist | 13 5/8" | 1" | 1/2" | 1 5/8" |
| | Eurosport | RH 24" | 8 lbs. | 44 5/8" | 3+1 in chamber | 24" #2 | 1-10" twist | 13 5/8" | 1" | 1/2" | 1 5/8" |
| | Synthetic | RH 24" | 8 lbs. | 44 5/8" | 3+1 in chamber | 24" #2 | 1-10" twist | 13 5/8" | 7/8" | 1/2" | 1 1/8" |
| | Fluted Synthetic | RH 24" | 7 1/2 lbs. | 44 5/8" | 3+1 in chamber | 24" #2 | 1-10" twist | 13 5/8" | 7/8" | 1/2" | 1 1/8" |
| | Stainless | RH 24" | 8 lbs. | 44 5/8" | 3+1 in chamber | 24" #2 | 1-10" twist | 13 5/8" | 7/8" | 1/2" | 1 1/8" |
| | Fluted Stainless | RH 24" | 7 1/2 lbs. | 44 5/8" | 3+1 in chamber | 24" #2 | 1-10" twist | 13 5/8" | 7/8" | 1/2" | 1 1/8" |
| | Accumark | RH 26" | 8 1/2 lbs. | 46 5/8" | 3+1 in chamber | 26" #3 | 1-10" twist | 13 5/8" | 1" | 9/16" | 1 1/2" |
| | SLS | RH 24" | 8 1/2 lbs. | 44 5/8" | 3+1 in chamber | 24" #2 | 1-10" twist | 13 5/8" | 1" | 1/2" | 1 5/8" |

# WEATHERBY MARK V RIFLES

**MARK V SPORTER**

## SPECIFICATIONS

**Calibers:** 26" Barrel: 257 Wby. Mag., 270 Wby. Mag., 7mm Wby. Mag., 300 Wby. Mag. and 340 Wby. Mag. . . . . . . . . . . . . . . . . . . . . . . $999.00

24" Barrel: 7mm Rem. Mag., 300 Win. Mag., 338 Win. Mag. and 375 H&H Mag. . . . . . . . . $999.00

*Also available:* EUROSPORT. Same specifications and prices but with hand-rubbed satin oil finish.

## MARK V® MAGNUM RIFLE SPECIFICATIONS (cont.)

| CALIBER | MODEL | BARRELLED ACTION | WEIGHT* | OVERALL LENGTH | MAGAZINE CAPACITY | BARREL LENGTH/ CONTOUR | RIFLING | LENGTH OF PULL | DROP AT COMB | MONTE CARLO | DROP AT HEEL |
|---|---|---|---|---|---|---|---|---|---|---|---|
| **.300 WBY. MAG.** | Mark V Sporter | RH 26" | 8 1/2 lbs. | 46 5/8" | 3+1 in chamber | 26" #2 | 1-10" twist | 13 5/8" | 1" | 1/2" | 1 5/8" |
| | Eurosport | RH 26" | 8 1/2 lbs. | 46 5/8" | 3+1 in chamber | 26" #2 | 1-10" twist | 13 5/8" | 1" | 1/2" | 1 5/8" |
| | Mark V Deluxe | RH 26" | 8 1/2 lbs. | 46 5/8" | 3+1 in chamber | 26" #2 | 1-10" twist | 13 5/8" | 7/8" | 3/8" | 1 3/8" |
| | Euromark | RH 26" | 8 1/2 lbs. | 46 5/8" | 3+1 in chamber | 26" #2 | 1-10" twist | 13 5/8" | 7/8" | 3/8" | 1 3/8" |
| | Lazermark | RH 26" | 8 1/2 lbs. | 46 5/8" | 3+1 in chamber | 26" #2 | 1-10" twist | 13 5/8" | 7/8" | 3/8" | 1 3/8" |
| | Synthetic | RH 26" | 8 lbs. | 46 5/8" | 3+1 in chamber | 26" #2 | 1-10" twist | 13 5/8" | 7/8" | 1/2" | 1 1/8" |
| | Fluted Synthetic | RH 26" | 7 1/2 lbs. | 46 5/8" | 3+1 in chamber | 26" #2 | 1-10" twist | 13 5/8" | 7/8" | 1/2" | 1 1/8" |
| | Stainless | RH 26" | 8 lbs. | 46 5/8" | 3+1 in chamber | 26" #2 | 1-10" twist | 13 5/8" | 7/8" | 1/2" | 1 1/8" |
| | Fluted Stainless | RH 26" | 7 1/2 lbs. | 46 5/8" | 3+1 in chamber | 26" #2 | 1-10" twist | 13 5/8" | 7/8" | 1/2" | 1 1/8" |
| | Accumark | RH 26" | 8 1/2 lbs. | 46 5/8" | 3+1 in chamber | 26" #3 | 1-10" twist | 13 5/8" | 1" | 9/16" | 1 1/2" |
| | SLS | RH 26" | 8 1/2 lbs. | 46 5/8" | 3+1 in chamber | 26" #2 | 1-10" twist | 13 5/8" | 1" | 1/2" | 1 5/8" |
| **.338 WIN. MAG.** | Mark V Sporter | RH 24" | 8 lbs. | 44 5/8" | 3+1 in chamber | 24" #2 | 1-10" twist | 13 5/8" | 1" | 1/2" | 1 5/8" |
| | Eurosport | RH 24" | 8 lbs. | 44 5/8" | 3+1 in chamber | 24" #2 | 1-10" twist | 13 5/8" | 1" | 1/2" | 1 5/8" |
| | Synthetic | RH 24" | 8 lbs. | 44 5/8" | 3+1 in chamber | 24" #2 | 1-10" twist | 13 5/8" | 7/8" | 1/2" | 1 1/8" |
| | Stainless | RH 24" | 8 lbs. | 44 5/8" | 3+1 in chamber | 24" #2 | 1-10" twist | 13 5/8" | 7/8" | 1/2" | 1 1/8" |
| | SLS | RH 24" | 8 1/2 lbs. | 44 5/8" | 3+1 in chamber | 24" #2 | 1-10" twist | 13 5/8" | 1" | 1/2" | 1 5/8" |
| **.340 WBY. MAG.** | Mark V Sporter | RH 26" | 8 1/2 lbs. | 46 5/8" | 3+1 in chamber | 26" #2 | 1-10" twist | 13 5/8" | 1" | 1/2" | 1 5/8" |
| | Eurosport | RH 26" | 8 1/2 lbs. | 46 5/8" | 3+1 in chamber | 26" #2 | 1-10" twist | 13 5/8" | 1" | 1/2" | 1 5/8" |
| | Mark V Deluxe | RH 26" | 8 1/2 lbs. | 46 5/8" | 3+1 in chamber | 26" #2 | 1-10" twist | 13 5/8" | 7/8" | 3/8" | 1 3/8" |
| | Euromark | RH 26" | 8 1/2 lbs. | 46 5/8" | 3+1 in chamber | 26" #2 | 1-10" twist | 13 5/8" | 7/8" | 3/8" | 1 3/8" |
| | Lazermark | RH 26" | 8 1/2 lbs. | 46 5/8" | 3+1 in chamber | 26" #2 | 1-10" twist | 13 5/8" | 7/8" | 3/8" | 1 3/8" |
| | Synthetic | RH 26" | 8 lbs. | 46 5/8" | 3+1 in chamber | 26" #2 | 1-10" twist | 13 5/8" | 7/8" | 1/2" | 1 1/8" |
| | Stainless | RH 26" | 8 lbs. | 46 5/8" | 3+1 in chamber | 26" #2 | 1-10" twist | 13 5/8" | 7/8" | 1/2" | 1 1/8" |
| | Accumark | RH 26" | 8 1/2 lbs. | 46 5/8" | 3+1 in chamber | 26" #3 | 1-10" twist | 13 5/8" | 1" | 9/16" | 1 1/2" |
| | SLS | RH 26" | 8 1/2 lbs. | 46 5/8" | 3+1 in chamber | 26" #2 | 1-10" twist | 13 5/8" | 1" | 1/2" | 1 5/8" |
| **.375 H&H MAG.** | Mark V Sporter | RH 24" | 8 1/2 lbs. | 44 5/8" | 3+1 in chamber | 24" #3 | 1-12" twist | 13 5/8" | 1" | 1/2" | 1 5/8" |
| | Eurosport | RH 24" | 8 1/2 lbs. | 44 5/8" | 3+1 in chamber | 24" #3 | 1-12" twist | 13 5/8" | 1" | 1/2" | 1 5/8" |
| | Euromark | RH 24" | 8 lbs. | 44 5/8" | 3+1 in chamber | 24" #3 | 1-12" twist | 13 5/8" | 1" | 1/2" | 1 5/8" |
| | Synthetic | RH 24" | 8 lbs. | 44 5/8" | 3+1 in chamber | 24" #3 | 1-12" twist | 13 5/8" | 7/8" | 1/2" | 1 1/8" |
| | Stainless | RH 24" | 8 lbs. | 44 5/8" | 3+1 in chamber | 24" #3 | 1-12" twist | 13 5/8" | 7/8" | 1/2" | 1 1/8" |
| **\*\*.30-378 WBY. MAG.** | Accumark | RH 26" | 8 1/2 lbs. | 46 5/8" | 2+1 in chamber | 26" #3 | 1-10" twist | 13 5/8" | 1" | 9/16" | 1 1/2" |
| | Synthetic | RH 26" | 8 lbs. | 46 5/8" | 2+1 in chamber | 26" #2 | 1-10" twist | 13 5/8" | 7/8" | 1/2" | 1 1/8" |
| | Stainless | RH 26" | 8 lbs. | 46 5/8" | 2+1 in chamber | 26" #2 | 1-10" twist | 13 5/8" | 7/8" | 1/2" | 1 1/8" |
| **\*\*.338-378 WBY. MAG.** | Accumark | RH 26" | 8 1/2 lbs. | 46 5/8" | 2+1 in chamber | 26" #3 | 1-10" twist | 13 5/8" | 1" | 9/16" | 1 1/2" |
| **.378 WBY. MAG.** | Mark V Deluxe | RH 26" | 9 1/2 lbs. | 46 5/8" | 2+1 in chamber | 26" #3 | 1-12" twist | 13 7/8" | 7/8" | 3/8" | 1 3/8" |
| | Euromark | RH 26" | 9 1/2 lbs. | 46 5/8" | 2+1 in chamber | 26" #3 | 1-12" twist | 13 7/8" | 7/8" | 3/8" | 1 3/8" |
| | Lazermark | RH 26" | 9 1/2 lbs. | 46 5/8" | 2+1 in chamber | 26" #3 | 1-12" twist | 13 7/8" | 7/8" | 3/8" | 1 3/8" |
| **\*\*.416 WBY. MAG.** | Mark V Deluxe | RH 26" | 9 1/2 lbs. | 46 3/4" | 2+1 in chamber | 26" #3 | 1-14" twist | 13 7/8" | 7/8" | 3/8" | 1 3/8" |
| | Euromark | RH 26" | 9 1/2 lbs. | 46 3/4" | 2+1 in chamber | 26" #3 | 1-14" twist | 13 7/8" | 7/8" | 3/8" | 1 3/8" |
| | Lazermark | RH 26" | 9 1/2 lbs. | 46 3/4" | 2+1 in chamber | 26" #3 | 1-14" twist | 13 7/8" | 7/8" | 3/8" | 1 3/8" |
| **\*\*.460 WBY. MAG.** | Mark V Deluxe | RH 26" | 10 1/2 lbs. | 46 3/4" | 2+1 in chamber | 26" #4 | 1-16" twist | 14" | 7/8" | 3/8" | 1 3/8" |
| | Lazermark | RH 26" | 10 1/2 lbs. | 46 3/4" | 2+1 in chamber | 26" #4 | 1-16" twist | 14" | 7/8" | 3/8" | 1 3/8" |

# WEATHERBY MARK V RIFLES

**SVM**

## WEATHERBY SVM VARMINTMASTER BOLT-ACTION RIFLE

Weatherby's new SVM Varmintmaster has a short Mark V action and a 26" cryogenically stress-relieved Krieger button-rifled barrel of stainless steel. The .823 muzzle of this fluted barrel has an 11-degree target crown. A hand-laminated synthetic stock features an aluminum bedding block and wide, flat forend. The fully adjustable trigger is set for a sear engagement of .012 to .015 and a 4-pound letoff. *Weight:* 8.5 lbs.
*Price:* ................................ **$1,399.00**

**EUROMARK**

## MARK V EUROMARK

The Euromark features a hand-rubbed oil finish and Monte Carlo stock of American walnut, plus custom grade, hand-cut checkering with an ebony pistol-grip cap and forend tip.
*Prices:* **26" Barrel**
In Weatherby Magnum calibers 257, 270, 7mm, 300 and 340 ........................ **$1,699.00**

In 378 Wby. Mag. ........................ **1,986.00**
**28" Barrel**
In 416 Wby. Mag. ........................ **1,986.00**
**24" Barrel**
In 7mm Rem. Mag., 300 Win. Mag., 338 Win. Mag. and 375 H&H Mag. ........................ **1,699.00**

**ACCUMARK**

## MARK V ACCUMARK MAGNUM

Built on the proven performance of the Mark V action, the Accumark is a composite of several field-tested features that help make it the utmost in accuracy, including a hand-laminated raised-comb Monte Carlo synthetic stock by H-S Precison (a combiniation of Kevlar, unidirectional fibers and fiberglass). There's also a molded-in, CNC-machined aluminum bedding plate that stiffens the receiver area of the rifle when the barreled action is secured to the block, providing a solid platform for the action. The Accumark is available in Weatherby Magnum calibers from 257 through 340, 7mm Rem. Mag. and .300 Win. Mag. Please see the specifications on the previous pages for additional information.
*Prices:* **26" Barrel** In 257, 270, 7mm, 7mm STW, 300, 340 Magnum calibers .................... **$1,399.00**
**28" Barrel**
In 30-378 Wby. and 338-378 Magnum calibers. ........................ **1,599.00**
Also available in left hand, additional .......... **50.00**

# WEATHERBY MARK V RIFLES

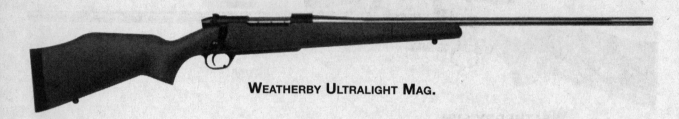

## WEATHERBY ULTRALIGHT MAG.

Weatherby's **MARK VR ACCUMARK ULTRA LIGHTWEIGHT** rifle is based on Weatherby's Mark V lightweight action for standard cartridges. It features a chrome moly receiver, bolt and sleeve. To reduce weight, the bolt handle is skeletonized and the flutes on the boot are deeper and wider than those on other Weatherby Mark V rifles. To reduce weight further without sacrificing strength and structural integrity, the follower, floor plate, trigger housing and other non-critical components are made of lighter alloys. A stainless steel 24-inch barrel with weight-reducing flutes increases portability while maintaining velocity. A recessed target crown on the barrel enhances accuracy. The Ultra Lightweight also features a specially designed Monte Carlo stock with a pillar bedding

system. Hand-laminated of Kevlar and fiberglass materials to provide a sure grip, the stock is teamed with a Pachmayr decelerator pad to dampen recoil. Stock colors are dark gray with black spiderwebbing. Additional specifications include **Calibers:** .243 Winchester, 7mm-08 Remington, .308 Winchester, .25-06 Remington, .270 Winchester, .280 Remington, .30-06 Springfield, and .240 Weatherby Mag. **Overall length:** 44" and 46". **Weight:** about 6 lbs.
**Prices:**
**24" Barrel:** 243, 240 Wby., 25-06, .270, 7mm-08,
.280, .308, .30-06 . . . . . . . . . . . . . . . . . . . . **$1,299.00**
**26" Barrel:** 257 Wby., 270 Wby., 7mm Rem.,
300 Wby., .300 Win. . . . . . . . . . . . . . . . . . . **1,349.00**

## WEATHERBY LIGHTWEIGHT ACCUMARK

Weatherby's **MARK VR ACCUMARK LIGHTWEIGHT** is a standard cartridge rifle designed for hunting varmints, deer and other big-game animals with extended-range accuracy. A lightweight version of Weatherby's legendary Mark V Magnum action, its lightweight action is scaled and designed specifically for standard cartridges, with six locking lugs compared to the Magnum action's nine. Both feature a short 54-degree bolt lift. Action metalwork is black oxide coated with a bead blast matte finish to eliminate glare. Six deep flutes help lighten the overall barrel weight without reducing stiffness while increasing the surface area of the barrel by 40 percent. This helps extend barrel life by reducing heat buildup in the barrel. Muzzle diameter is .722. The barrel, which has a low-lustre brushed finish, is free floated and includes a recessed target crown. Trigger presettings are four pounds of pull with .012-.015 of an inch of sear engagement for

extremely crisp and consistent let-off. The trigger is fully adjustable for sear engagement and let-off weight. The Accumark Lightweight also features a composite stock made of Kevlar and fiberglass. The bedding block is computer-designed and CNC-machined from aircraft quality aluminum. This system stiffens the receiver area of the rifle when the barreled action is secured into the block. The combination of CNC machining and precision molding of the bedding block into the stock helps ensure perfect fit and alignment of the barreled action. The hand-laminated, raised-comb Monte Carlo stock is black with gray spiderwebbing.
**Additional specifications include:**
**Calibers:** .22-250 Remington, .243 Winchester, 240 Wby., 25-06, 270, .280, .308, .30-06, 7mm-08. **Barrel length:** 24". **Overall length:** 44". **Weight:** 7.5 lbs.
**Price:** . . . . . . . . . . . . . . . . . . . . . . . . . . . . .**$1,349.00**

# WEATHERBY MARK V RIFLES

**LAZERMARK**

## LAZERMARK

A custom-carved walnut stock distinguishes this Weatherby. Traditional high-gloss finish.

**Prices: 26" Barrel**
In Weatherby Magnum calibers 257, 270, 7mm,
300 and 340 ........................... **$1,799.00**

378 Wby. Mag. ............................ **2,097.00**
**28" Barrel**
416 Wby. Mag. ............................ **2,097.00**
460 Wby. Mag. ............................ **2,464.00**

**MARK V STAINLESS**

## MARK V MAGNUM STAINLESS

Features 400 Series stainless steel. The action is hand-bedded to a lightweight, injection-molded synthetic stock.

**Prices: MARK V STAINLESS**
**24" Barrel**
.22-250, .243, .240 Wby., 25-06, .270, .280,
7mm-08, .30-06, .308 .................. **$899.00**
7mm Rem. Mag., 300 Win. Mag., 338 Win.
Mag. and 375 H&H Mag. ................. **999.00**

**26" Barrel**
Weatherby Magnum calibers 257, 270, 7mm
Rem. Mag., 300 and 340 ............... **$999.00**
**28" Barrel**
30-378 Wby. Mag. ...................... **1,149.00**
**Also available:**
MODEL **SLS** (Stainless Laminated Sporter) .... **1,299.00**

**MARK V SYNTHETIC**

## MARK V SYNTHETIC

Features an injection-molded synthetic stock with dual-tapered checkered forearm. Comes with custom floorplate release/trigger guard assembly and engraved flying "W" monogram.

**Prices: MARK V SYNTHETIC**
**24" Barrel**
.22-250, .243, .240 Wby, .25-06, .270, 7mm-08,
.280, .30-06, .308 .................... **$699.00**
7mm Rem. Mag., 300 Win. Mag., 338 Win.
Mag. and 375 H&H Mag. ................. **799.00**
**26" Barrel**
Weatherby Magnum calibers 257, 270, 7mm,
300 and 340 .......................... **799.00**
**28" Barrel**
30-378 Wby. Mag. ..................... **949.00**

*For complete specifications on the above rifles, please see the tables on the preceding pages.*

# WEATHERBY MARK V RIFLES

**MARK V SPORTER**

**MARK V CARBINE**

## MARK V RIFLES

Virtually identical in design to the Mark V magnum action, Weatherby's lightweight version is shorter, narrower and lighter than the original. It accommodates up to 30-06 length cartridges, including the 240 Weatherby Magnum. For complete specifications, see table below.

**Prices:** LIGHTWEIGHT SYNTHETIC (24" barrel)
22-250 to 308 Win. Mag. . . . . . . . . . . . . . . . $699.00
CARBINE MODEL (20" in 243 Win., 7mm-08
Rem., 308 Win.) . . . . . . . . . . . . . . . . . . . . . 699.00

## MARK V® RIFLE SPECIFICATIONS

| Caliber | Model | Barrelled Action | Weight* | Overall Length | Magazine Capacity | Barrel Length/ Contour | Rifling | Length Of Pull | Drop At Comb | Monte Carlo | Drop At Heel |
|---|---|---|---|---|---|---|---|---|---|---|---|
| **.240 Wby. Mag.** | Mark V Sporter | RH 24" | 6 3/4 lbs. | 44" | 5+1 in chamber | 24" #1 | 1-10" twist | 13 5/8" | 3/4" | 3/8" | 1 1/8" |
| | Mark V Stainless | RH 24" | 6 1/2 lbs. | 44" | 5+1 in chamber | 24" #1 | 1-10" twist | 13 5/8" | 3/4" | 3/8" | 1 1/8" |
| | Mark V Synthetic | RH 24" | 6 1/2 lbs. | 44" | 5+1 in chamber | 24" #1 | 1-10" twist | 13 5/8" | 3/4" | 3/8" | 1 1/8" |
| | Accumark | RH 24" | 7 lbs. | 44" | 5+1 in chamber | 24" #3 | 1-10" twist | 13 5/8" | 3/4" | 3/8" | 1 1/8" |
| | Accumark Ultra Lightweight | RH 24" | 5 3/4 lbs. | 44" | 5+1 in chamber | 24" #2 | 1-10" twist | 13 5/8" | 3/4" | 3/8" | 1 1/8" |
| **.22-250 Rem.** | Mark V Sporter | RH 24" | 6 3/4 lbs. | 44" | 5+1 in chamber | 24" #1 | 1-14" twist | 13 5/8" | 3/4" | 3/8" | 1 1/8" |
| | Mark V Stainless | RH 24" | 6 1/2 lbs. | 44" | 5+1 in chamber | 24" #1 | 1-14" twist | 13 5/8" | 3/4" | 3/8" | 1 1/8" |
| | Mark V Synthetic | RH 24" | 6 1/2 lbs. | 44" | 5+1 in chamber | 24" #1 | 1-14" twist | 13 5/8" | 3/4" | 3/8" | 1 1/8" |
| | Accumark | RH 24" | 7 lbs. | 44" | 5+1 in chamber | 24" #3 | 1-14" twist | 13 5/8" | 3/4" | 3/8" | 1 1/8" |
| | Mark V Stainless Carbine | RH 20" | 6 lbs. | 40" | 5+1 in chamber | 20" #1 | 1-14" twist | 13 5/8" | 3/4" | 3/8" | 1 1/8" |
| | Mark V Synthetic Carbine | RH 20" | 6 lbs. | 40" | 5+1 in chamber | 20" #1 | 1-14" twist | 13 5/8" | 3/4" | 3/8" | 1 1/8" |
| **.243 Winchester** | Mark V Sporter | RH 24" | 6 3/4 lbs. | 44" | 5+1 in chamber | 24" #1 | 1-10" twist | 13 5/8" | 3/4" | 3/8" | 1 1/8" |
| | Mark V Stainless | RH 24" | 6 1/2 lbs. | 44" | 5+1 in chamber | 24" #1 | 1-10" twist | 13 5/8" | 3/4" | 3/8" | 1 1/8" |
| | Mark V Synthetic | RH 24" | 6 1/2 lbs. | 44" | 5+1 in chamber | 24" #1 | 1-10" twist | 13 5/8" | 3/4" | 3/8" | 1 1/8" |
| | Accumark | RH 24" | 7 lbs. | 44" | 5+1 in chamber | 24" #3 | 1-10" twist | 13 5/8" | 3/4" | 3/8" | 1 1/8" |
| | Accumark Ultra Lightweight | RH 24" | 5 3/4 lbs. | 44" | 5+1 in chamber | 24" #2 | 1-10" twist | 13 5/8" | 3/4" | 3/8" | 1 1/8" |
| | Mark V Stainless Carbine | RH 20" | 6 lbs. | 40" | 5+1 in chamber | 20" #1 | 1-10" twist | 13 5/8" | 3/4" | 3/8" | 1 1/8" |
| | Mark V Synthetic Carbine | RH 20" | 6 lbs. | 40" | 5+1 in chamber | 20" #1 | 1-10" twist | 13 5/8" | 3/4" | 3/8" | 1 1/8" |
| **7mm-08 Rem.** | Mark V Sporter | RH 24" | 6 3/4 lbs. | 44" | 5+1 in chamber | 24" #1 | 1-9 1/2" twist | 13 5/8" | 3/4" | 3/8" | 1 1/8" |
| | Mark V Stainless | RH 24" | 6 1/2 lbs. | 44" | 5+1 in chamber | 24" #1 | 1-9 1/2" twist | 13 5/8" | 3/4" | 3/8" | 1 1/8" |
| | Mark V Synthetic | RH 24" | 6 1/2 lbs. | 44" | 5+1 in chamber | 24" #1 | 1-9 1/2" twist | 13 5/8" | 3/4" | 3/8" | 1 1/8" |
| | Accumark | RH 24" | 7 lbs. | 44" | 5+1 in chamber | 24" #3 | 1-9 1/2" twist | 13 5/8" | 3/4" | 3/8" | 1 1/8" |
| | Accumark Ultra Lightweight | RH 24" | 5 3/4 lbs. | 44" | 5+1 in chamber | 24" #2 | 1-9 1/2" twist | 13 5/8" | 3/4" | 3/8" | 1 1/8" |
| | Mark V Stainless Carbine | RH 20" | 6 lbs. | 40" | 5+1 in chamber | 20" #1 | 1-9 1/2" twist | 13 5/8" | 3/4" | 3/8" | 1 1/8" |
| | Mark V Synthetic Carbine | RH 20" | 6 lbs. | 40" | 5+1 in chamber | 20" #1 | 1-9 1/2" twist | 13 5/8" | 3/4" | 3/8" | 1 1/8" |
| **.308 Winchester** | Mark V Sporter | RH 24" | 6 3/4 lbs. | 44" | 5+1 in chamber | 24" #1 | 1-12" twist | 13 5/8" | 3/4" | 3/8" | 1 1/8" |
| | Mark V Stainless | RH 24" | 6 1/2 lbs. | 44" | 5+1 in chamber | 24" #1 | 1-12" twist | 13 5/8" | 3/4" | 3/8" | 1 1/8" |
| | Mark V Synthetic | RH 24" | 6 1/2 lbs. | 44" | 5+1 in chamber | 24" #1 | 1-12" twist | 13 5/8" | 3/4" | 3/8" | 1 1/8" |
| | Accumark | RH 24" | 7 lbs. | 44" | 5+1 in chamber | 24" #3 | 1-12" twist | 13 5/8" | 3/4" | 3/8" | 1 1/8" |
| | Accumark Ultra Lightweight | RH 24" | 5 3/4 lbs. | 44" | 5+1 in chamber | 24" #2 | 1-12" twist | 13 5/8" | 3/4" | 3/8" | 1 1/8" |
| | Mark V Stainless Carbine | RH 20" | 6 lbs. | 40" | 5+1 in chamber | 20" #1 | 1-12" twist | 13 5/8" | 3/4" | 3/8" | 1 1/8" |
| | Mark V Synthetic Carbine | RH 20" | 6 lbs. | 40" | 5+1 in chamber | 20" #1 | 1-12" twist | 13 5/8" | 3/4" | 3/8" | 1 1/8" |
| **.25-06 Rem.** | Mark V Sporter | RH 24" | 6 3/4 lbs. | 44" | 5+1 in chamber | 24" #1 | 1-10" twist | 13 5/8" | 3/4" | 3/8" | 1 1/8" |
| | Mark V Stainless | RH 24" | 6 1/2 lbs. | 44" | 5+1 in chamber | 24" #1 | 1-10" twist | 13 5/8" | 3/4" | 3/8" | 1 1/8" |
| | Mark V Synthetic | RH 24" | 6 1/2 lbs. | 44" | 5+1 in chamber | 24" #1 | 1-10" twist | 13 5/8" | 3/4" | 3/8" | 1 1/8" |
| | Accumark | RH 24" | 7 lbs. | 44" | 5+1 in chamber | 24" #3 | 1-10" twist | 13 5/8" | 3/4" | 3/8" | 1 1/8" |
| | Accumark Ultra Lightweight | RH 24" | 5 3/4 lbs. | 44" | 5+1 in chamber | 24" #2 | 1-10" twist | 13 5/8" | 3/4" | 3/8" | 1 1/8" |
| **.270 Winchester** | Mark V Sporter | RH 24" | 6 3/4 lbs. | 44" | 5+1 in chamber | 24" #1 | 1-10" twist | 13 5/8" | 3/4" | 3/8" | 1 1/8" |
| | Mark V Stainless | RH 24" | 6 1/2 lbs. | 44" | 5+1 in chamber | 24" #1 | 1-10" twist | 13 5/8" | 3/4" | 3/8" | 1 1/8" |
| | Mark V Synthetic | RH 24" | 6 1/2 lbs. | 44" | 5+1 in chamber | 24" #1 | 1-10" twist | 13 5/8" | 3/4" | 3/8" | 1 1/8" |
| | Accumark | RH 24" | 7 lbs. | 44" | 5+1 in chamber | 24" #3 | 1-10" twist | 13 5/8" | 3/4" | 3/8" | 1 1/8" |
| | Accumark Ultra Lightweight | RH 24" | 5 3/4 lbs. | 44" | 5+1 in chamber | 24" #2 | 1-10" twist | 13 5/8" | 3/4" | 3/8" | 1 1/8" |
| **.280 Rem.** | Mark V Sporter | RH 24" | 6 3/4 lbs. | 44" | 5+1 in chamber | 24" #1 | 1-10" twist | 13 5/8" | 3/4" | 3/8" | 1 1/8" |
| | Mark V Stainless | RH 24" | 6 1/2 lbs. | 44" | 5+1 in chamber | 24" #1 | 1-10" twist | 13 5/8" | 3/4" | 3/8" | 1 1/8" |
| | Mark V Synthetic | RH 24" | 6 1/2 lbs. | 44" | 5+1 in chamber | 24" #1 | 1-10" twist | 13 5/8" | 3/4" | 3/8" | 1 1/8" |
| | Accumark | RH 24" | 7 lbs. | 44" | 5+1 in chamber | 24" #3 | 1-10" twist | 13 5/8" | 3/4" | 3/8" | 1 1/8" |
| | Accumark Ultra Lightweight | RH 24" | 5 3/4 lbs. | 44" | 5+1 in chamber | 24" #2 | 1-10" twist | 13 5/8" | 3/4" | 3/8" | 1 1/8" |
| **.30-06 Springfield** | Mark V Sporter | RH 24" | 6 3/4 lbs. | 44" | 5+1 in chamber | 24" #1 | 1-10" twist | 13 5/8" | 3/4" | 3/8" | 1 1/8" |
| | Mark V Stainless | RH 24" | 6 1/2 lbs. | 44" | 5+1 in chamber | 24" #1 | 1-10" twist | 13 5/8" | 3/4" | 3/8" | 1 1/8" |
| | Mark V Synthetic | RH 24" | 6 1/2 lbs. | 44" | 5+1 in chamber | 24" #1 | 1-10" twist | 13 5/8" | 3/4" | 3/8" | 1 1/8" |
| | Accumark | RH 24" | 7 lbs. | 44" | 5+1 in chamber | 24" #3 | 1-10" twist | 13 5/8" | 3/4" | 3/8" | 1 1/8" |
| | Accumark Ultra Lightweight | RH 24" | 5 3/4 lbs. | 44" | 5+1 in chamber | 24" #2 | 1-10" twist | 13 5/8" | 3/4" | 3/8" | 1 1/8" |

# WINCHESTER BOLT-ACTION RIFLES

Winchester's Model 70, introduced in 1937, has been called "the rifleman's rifle." Its rugged, adjustable trigger, smooth bolt action, Mauser extractor and three-position safety made it an American legend among hunters and target shooters. A "new model 70" in 1964 reduced production costs but dis-mayed shooters who called for a return to the old model. Now Winchester 70s have the clean lines and high-quality fit and finish that sportsmen want. Available in controlled-feed and push-fed versions with many stock variations, they once again have become the archetypal American rifle.

**MODEL 70 CLASSIC FEATHERWEIGHT**

## MODEL 70 CLASSIC MODELS WITH PRE-'64 TYPE ACTION

| Suggested Retail Right Handed | Left Handed | Caliber | Magazine Capacity* | Barrel Length | Nominal Overall Length | Nominal Length of Pull | Nominal Drop at Comb | Nominal Drop at Heel | Nominal Weight (Lbs.) | Rate of Twist I Turn In | Features |
|---|---|---|---|---|---|---|---|---|---|---|---|
| **CLASSIC FEATHERWEIGHT (BLUED)** | | | | | | | | | | | |
| $680 | — | 22-250 Rem. | 5 | 22" | 42" | 13-1/2" | 9/16" | 7/8" | 7 | 14" | Walnut Stock |
| 680 | — | 243 Win. | 5 | 22 | 42 | 13-1/2 | 9/16 | 7/8 | 7 | 10 | Walnut Stock |
| 680 | — | 6.5 x 55mm Swed. | 5 | 22 | 42 | 13-1/2 | 9/16 | 7/8 | 7 | 8 | Walnut Stock |
| 680 | — | 308 Win. | 5 | 22 | 42 | 13-1/2 | 9/16 | 7/8 | 7 | 12 | Walnut Stock |
| 680 | — | 7mm-08 Rem. | 5 | 22 | 42 | 13-1/2 | 9/16 | 7/8 | 7 | 10 | Walnut Stock |
| 680 | — | 270 Win. | 5 | 22 | 42-1/2 | 13-1/2 | 9/16 | 7/8 | 7-1/4 | 10 | Walnut Stock |
| 680 | — | 280 Rem. | 5 | 22 | 42-1/2 | 13-1/2 | 9/16 | 7/8 | 7-1/4 | 10 | Walnut Stock |
| 680 | — | 30-06 Spfld. | 5 | 22 | 42-1/2 | 13-1/2 | 9/16 | 7/8 | 7-1/4 | 10 | Walnut Stock |

*Stainless Models available in 22-250, 243, 308, 270, 30-06.*

*For additional capacity, add one round in chamber when ready to fire. Drops are measured from center line of bore. Rate of twist: RH.

## CUSTOM GUN SHOP RIFLES

| Item No. Right Hand | Item No. Left Hand | Caliber | Magazine Capacity* | Barrel Length | Nominal Length of Pull | Nominal Weight (Lbs.) | U.S. Sugg. Retail |
|---|---|---|---|---|---|---|---|
| **MODEL 70 CLASSIC CUSTOM AFRICAN EXPRESS** | | | | | | | |
| 535-912150 | 535-918150 | 358 STA | 4 | 24" | 14" | 9-3/4 | $3,975 |
| 535-912138 | 535-918138 | 375 H&H Mag. | 4 | 24 | 14 | 9-3/4 | 3,975 |
| 535-912139 | 535-918139 | 416 Rem. Mag. | 4 | 24 | 14 | 9-3/4 | 3,975 |
| 535-912144 | 535-918144 | 458 Win. Mag. | 4 | 22 | 14 | 9-1/2 | 3,975 |
| 535-912154 *NEW* | 535-918154 | 458 Lott | 4 | 22 | 14 | 9-1/2 | 3,975 |
| **MODEL 70 CLASSIC CUSTOM SAFARI EXPRESS** | | | | | | | |
| 535-911150 *NEW* | 535-919150 | 358 STA | 3 | 24" | 13-3/4" | 9-3/4 | $2,695 |
| 535-911138 *NEW* | 535-919138 | 375 H&H Mag. | 3 | 24 | 13-3/4 | 9-3/4 | 2,695 |
| 535-911139 *NEW* | 535-919139 | 416 Rem. Mag. | 3 | 24 | 13-3/4 | 9-3/4 | 2,695 |
| 535-911144 *NEW* | 535-919144 | 458 Win. Mag. | 3 | 22 | 13-3/4 | 9-1/2 | 2,695 |
| 535-911154 *NEW* | 535-919154 | 458 Lott | 3 | 22 | 13-3/4 | 9-1/2 | 2,695 |
| **MODEL 70 CLASSIC CUSTOM SHORT ACTION** | | | | | | | |
| 535-915212 *NEW* | - | 243 Win | 5 | 22" | 13-3/4" | 7-1/2 | $2,068 |
| 535-915211 *NEW* | - | 257 Roberts | 5 | 22 | 13-3/4 | 7-1/2 | 2,068 |
| 535-915249 *NEW* | - | 260 Rem. | 5 | 22 | 13-3/4 | 7-1/2 | 2,068 |
| 535-915218 *NEW* | - | 7mm-08 | 5 | 22 | 13-3/4 | 7-1/2 | 2,068 |
| 535-915220 *NEW* | - | 308 Win. | 5 | 22 | 13-3/4 | 7-1/2 | 2,068 |
| 535-915223 *NEW* | - | 358 Win. | 5 | 22 | 13-3/4 | 7-1/2 | 2,068 |
| **MODEL 70 CLASSIC CUSTOM MANNLICHER** | | | | | | | |
| 535-913249 | - | 260 Rem. | 4 | 19" | 13-3/4" | 6-3/4 | $2,595 |
| 535-913220 | - | 308 Win. | 4 | 19 | 13-3/4 | 6-3/4 | 2,595 |
| 535-913218 | - | 7mm-08 | 4 | 19 | 13-3/4 | 6-3/4 | 2,595 |
| **MODEL 70 CLASSIC CUSTOM ULTIMATE CLASSIC** | | | | | | | |
| 535-900225 | 534-901225 | 25-06 Rem. | 5 | 24" | 13-3/4" | 7-1/2 | $2,617 |
| 535-900226 | 534-901226 | 270 Win. | 5 | 24 | 13-3/4 | 7-1/2 | 2,617 |
| 535-900227 | 534-901227 | 280 Rem. | 5 | 24 | 13-3/4 | 7-1/2 | 2,617 |
| 535-900228 | 534-901228 | 30-06 Spfld. | 5 | 24 | 13-3/4 | 7-1/2 | 2,617 |

# WINCHESTER BOLT-ACTION RIFLES

**MODEL 70 CLASSIC SUPER GRADE**

## CUSTOM GUN SHOP RIFLES (Continued from previous page)

| Item No. Right Hand | Item No. Left Hand | Caliber | Magazine Capacity* | Barrel Length | Nominal Length of Pull | Nominal Weight (Lbs.) | U.S. Sugg. Retail |
|---|---|---|---|---|---|---|---|
| 535-900251 | 534-901251 | 338-06 | 5 | 24 | 13-3/4 | 7-1/2 | 2,617 |
| 535-900247 | 534-901247 | 35 Whelen | 5 | 24 | 13-3/4 | 7-1/2 | 2,617 |
| 535-900229 | 534-901229 | 264 Win. Mag. | 3 | 26 | 13-3/4 | 7-3/4 | 2,617 |
| 535-900230 | 534-901230 | 7mm Rem. Mag. | 3 | 26 | 13-3/4 | 7-3/4 | 2,617 |
| 535-900231 | 534-901231 | 7mm STW | 3 | 26 | 13-3/4 | 7-3/4 | 2,617 |
| 535-900233 | 534-901233 | 300 Win. Mag. | 3 | 26 | 13-3/4 | 7-3/4 | 2,617 |
| 535-900234 | 534-901234 | 300 Weath. Mag. | 3 | 26 | 13-3/4 | 7-3/4 | 2,617 |
| 535-900253 | 534-901253 | 300 Ultra | 3 | 26 | 13-3/4 | 7-3/4 | 2,617 |
| 535-900236 | 534-901236 | 338 Win. Mag. | 3 | 26 | 13-3/4 | 7-3/4 | 2,617 |
| **MODEL 70 CLASSIC CUSTOM EXTREME WEATHER** | | | | | | | |
| 535-916225 | 535-917225 | 25-06 Rem. | 5 | 24" | 3-3/4" | 7-1/4 | $1,960 |
| 535-916226 | 535-917226 | 270 Win. | 5 | 24 | 3-3/4 | 7-1/4 | 1,960 |
| 535-916228 | 535-917228 | 30-06 Spfld. | 5 | 24 | 3-3/4 | 7-1/4 | 1,960 |
| 535-916230 | 535-917230 | 7mm Rem. Mag. | 3 | 26 | 3-3/4 | 7-1/2 | 1,960 |
| 535-916233 | 535-917233 | 300 Win. Mag. | 3 | 26 | 3-3/4 | 7-1/2 | 1,960 |
| 535-916236 | 535-917236 | 338 Win. Mag. | 3 | 26 | 3-3/4 | 7-1/2 | 1,960 |
| **MODEL 94 CUSTOM LIMITED EDITION** | | | | | | | |
| 535-040140 | - | 44-40 | 13 | 24" | 13-1/2" | 7-3/4 | $2,260 |

## SPECIFICATIONS & PRICES: MODEL 70 CLASSIC MODELS

| Suggested Retail Right Handed | Left Handed | Caliber | Magazine Capacity* | Barrel Length | Nominal Overall Length | Nominal Length of Pull | Nominal Drop at Comb | Nominal Drop at Heel | Nominal Weight (Lbs.) | Rate of Twist I Turn In | Features |
|---|---|---|---|---|---|---|---|---|---|---|---|
| **CLASSIC SAFARI EXPRESS** | | | | | | | | | | | |
| $1007 | $1042 | 375 H&H Mag. | 3 | 24" | 44-3/4" | 13-3/4" | 9/16" | 1 5/16" | 8-1/2 | 12" | Sights, Walnut Stock |
| 1007 | — | 416 Rem. Mag. | 3 | 24 | 44-3/4 | 13-3/4 | 9/16 | 1 5/16 | 8-1/2 | 14 | Sights, Walnut Stock |
| 1007 | — | 458 Win. Mag. | 3 | 22 | 42-3/4 | 13-3/4 | 9/16 | 1 5/16 | 8-1/4 | 14 | Sights, Walnut Stock |
| **CLASSIC SUPER GRADE** | | | | | | | | | | | |
| $933 | — | 270 Win. | 5 | 24" | 44-3/4" | 13-3/4" | 9/16" | 13/16" | 7-3/4 | 10" | B&R, Walnut Stock |
| 933 | — | 30-06 Spfld. | 5 | 24 | 44-3/4 | 13-3/4 | 9/16 | 13/16 | 7-3/4 | 10 | B&R, Walnut Stock |
| 933 | — | 264 Win. Mag. | 3 | 26 | 46-3/4 | 13-3/4 | 9/16 | 13/16 | 8 | 9-1/2 | B&R, Walnut Stock |
| 933 | — | 300 Win. Mag. | 3 | 26 | 46-3/4 | 13-3/4 | 9/16 | 13/16 | 8 | 10 | B&R, Walnut Stock |
| 933 | — | 338 Win. Mag. | 3 | 26 | 46-3/4 | 13-3/4 | 9/16 | 13/16 | 8 | 10 | B&R, Walnut Stock |
| **CLASSIC SPORTER LT (BLUED)** | | | | | | | | | | | |
| $669 | — | 25-06 Rem. | 5 | 24" | 44-3/4" | 13-3/4" | 9/16" | 13/16" | 7-3/4 | 10" | Walnut Stock |
| 669 | — | 264 Win. Mag. | 3 | 26 | 46-3/4 | 13-3/4 | 9/16 | 13/16 | 8 | 9 | Walnut Stock |
| 669 | $702 | 270 Win. | 5 | 24 | 44-3/4 | 13-3/4 | 9/16 | 13/16 | 7-3/4 | 10 | Walnut Stock |
| 669 | 702 | 30-06 Spfld. | 5 | 24 | 44-3/4 | 13-3/4 | 9/16 | 13/16 | 7-3/4 | 10 | Walnut Stock |
| 669 | 702 | 7mm STW | 3 | 26 | 46-3/4 | 13-3/4 | 9/16 | 13/16 | 8 | 9-1/2 | Walnut Stock |
| 669 | 702 | 7mm Rem. Mag. | 3 | 26 | 46-3/4 | 13-3/4 | 9/16 | 13/16 | 8 | 9-1/2 | Walnut Stock |
| 669 | 702 | 300 Win. Mag. | 3 | 26 | 46-3/4 | 13-3/4 | 9/16 | 13/16 | 8 | 10 | Walnut Stock |
| 669 | — | 300 Weath. Mag. | 3 | 26 | 46-3/4 | 13-3/4 | 9/16 | 13/16 | 8 | 10 | Walnut Stock |
| 669 | 702 | 338 Win. Mag. | 3 | 26 | 46-3/4 | 13-3/4 | 9/16 | 13/16 | 8 | 10 | Walnut Stock |

# WINCHESTER BOLT-ACTION RIFLES

**MODEL 70 BLACK SHADOW**

**MODEL 70 STEALTH**

## SPECIFICATIONS & PRICES: MODEL 70 CLASSIC MODELS *(Cont.)*

| Suggested Retail Right Handed | Left Handed | Caliber | Magazine Capacity* | Barrel Length | Nominal Overall Length | Nominal Length of Pull | Nominal Drop at Comb | Nominal Drop at Heel | Nominal Weight (Lbs.) | Rate of Twist I Turn In | Features |
|---|---|---|---|---|---|---|---|---|---|---|---|
| **CLASSIC STAINLESS (COMPOSITE)** | | | | | | | | | | | |
| $737 | — | 270 Win. | 5 | 24" | 44-3/4" | 13-3/4" | 9/16" | 13/16" | 7-1/4 | 10" | Composite Stock |
| 737 | — | 30-06 Spfld. | 5 | 24 | 44-3/4 | 13-3/4 | 9/16 | 13/16 | 7-1/4 | 10 | Composite Stock |
| 737 | — | 7mm STW | 3 | 26 | 46-3/4 | 13-3/4 | 9/16 | 13/16 | 7-1/2 | 9-1/2 | Composite Stock |
| 737 | — | 7mm Rem. Mag. | 3 | 26 | 46-3/4 | 13-3/4 | 9/16 | 13/16 | 7-1/2 | 9-1/2 | Composite Stock |
| 737 | — | 300 Win. Mag. | 3 | 26 | 46-3/4 | 13-3/4 | 9/16 | 13/16 | 7-1/2 | 10 | Composite Stock |
| 737 | — | 300 Wby. Mag. | 3 | 26 | 46-3/4 | 13-3/4 | 9/16 | 13/16 | 7-1/2 | 10 | Composite Stock |
| 737 | — | 338 Win. Mag. | 3 | 26 | 46-3/4 | 13-3/4 | 9/16 | 13/16 | 7-1/2 | 10 | Composite Stock |
| 823 | — | 375 H&H Mag. | 3 | 24 | 44-3/4 | 13-3/4 | 9/16 | 13/16 | 7-1/4 | 12 | Sights, Composite Stock |
| **CLASSIC COMPACT** | | | | | | | | | | | |
| $680 | — | 243 Win. | 4 | 20" | 39-1/2" | 13" | 9/16" | 3/4" | 6-1/2 | 10" | Walnut Stock |
| 680 | — | 308 Win. | 4 | 20 | 39-1/2 | 13 | 9/16 | 3/4 | 6-1/2 | 12 | Walnut Stock |
| 680 | — | 7mm-08 Rem. | 4 | 20 | 39-1/2 | 13 | 9/16 | 3/4 | 6-1/2 | 9-1/2 | Walnut Stock |
| **CLASSIC LAREDO** | | | | | | | | | | | |
| $787 | — | 7mm Rem. Mag. | 3 | 26 | 46-3/4 | 13-3/4 | 5/8 | 1/2 | 9-1/2 | 9-1/2 | Composite Stock |
| 787 | — | 300 Win. Mag. | 3 | 26 | 46-3/4 | 13-3/4 | 5/8 | 1/2 | 9-1/2 | 10 | Composite Stock |

## MODEL 70 PUSH FEED MODELS

| Suggested Retail Right Handed | Left Handed | Caliber | Magazine Capacity* | Barrel Length | Nominal Overall Length | Nominal Length of Pull | Nominal Drop at Comb | Nominal Drop at Heel | Nominal Weight (Lbs.) | Rate of Twist I Turn In | Features |
|---|---|---|---|---|---|---|---|---|---|---|---|
| **COYOTE** | | | | | | | | | | | |
| $688 | — | 223 Rem. | 6 | 24 | 44 | 13-1/2 | 5/8 | 3/4 | 9 | 9 | Laminated Stock |
| 688 | — | 22-250 Rem. | 5 | 24 | 44 | 13-1/2 | 5/8 | 3/4 | 9 | 14 | Laminated Stock |
| 688 | — | 243 Win. | 5 | 24 | 44 | 13-1/2 | 5/8 | 3/4 | 9 | 10 | Laminated Stock |
| **STEALTH** | | | | | | | | | | | |
| $737 | — | 223 Rem. | 6 | 26 | 46 | 13-1/2 | 3/4 | 1/2 | 10-3/4 | 9 | Accu Block |
| 737 | — | 22-250 Rem. | 5 | 26 | 46 | 13-1/2 | 3/4 | 1/2 | 10-3/4 | 14 | Accu Block |
| 737 | — | 308 Win. | 5 | 26 | 46 | 13-1/2 | 3/4 | 1/2 | 10-3/4 | 12 | Accu Block |
| **BLACK SHADOW®** | | | | | | | | | | | |
| $491 | — | 270 Win. | 5 | 22" | 42-3/4" | 13-3/4" | 9/16" | 13/16" | 7-1/4 | 10" | Composite Stock |
| 491 | — | 30-06 Spfld. | 5 | 22 | 42-3/4 | 13-3/4 | 9/16 | 13/16 | 7-1/4 | 10 | Composite Stock |
| 491 | — | 7mm Rem. Mag. | 3 | 24 | 42-3/4 | 13-3/4 | 9/16 | 13/16 | 7-1/4 | 9-1/2 | Composite Stock |
| 491 | — | 300 Win. Mag. | 3 | 22 | 42-3/4 | 13-3/4 | 9/16 | 13/16 | 7-1/4 | 10 | Composite Stock |
| **RANGER™ COMPACT** | | | | | | | | | | | |
| $528 | — | 7mm-08 Rem. | 5 | 22" | 41" | 12-1/2" | 3/4" | 1" | 6-1/2 | 12" | Truglo Sights, Hardwood Stock |
| 528 | — | 243 Win. | 5 | 22 | 41 | 12'1/2 | 3/4 | 1 | 6-1/2 | 10 | Truglo Sights, Hardwood Stock |
| 528 | — | 308 Win. | 5 | 22 | 41 | 12'1/2 | 3/4 | 1 | 6-1/2 | 12 | Truglo Sights, Hardwood Stock |

# WINCHESTER LEVER-ACTION CARBINES/RIFLES

## MODEL 94 STANDARD WALNUT RIFLE
The traditional choice for lever-action styling and craftsmanship. Exposed-hammer lever action with angled ejection and crossbolt safety. American walnut stock and forearm have a protective stain finish with precise-cut wraparound checkering. It has a 20-inch barrel with hooded blade front sight and semibuckhorn rear sight. America's favorite deer rifle for half a century!

## MODEL 94 WALNUT TRAPPER CARBINE
With 16-inch short-barrel lever action and straight forward styling. Compact and fast handing in dense cover, it has a 5-shot magazine capacity (9 in 45 Colt or 44 Rem. Mag./44 S&W Special). *Calibers:* 30-30 Win., 357 Mag., 45 Colt, and 44 Rem. Mag./44 S&W Special.

## MODEL 94

| Suggested Retail | Caliber | Magazine Capacity* | Barrel Length | Overall Length | Nominal Length of Pull | Nominal Drop at Comb | Nominal Drop at Heel | Nominal Weight (Lbs.) | Rate of Twist I Turn In | Features |
|---|---|---|---|---|---|---|---|---|---|---|
| **BLACK SHADOW** | | | | | | | | | | |
| $381 | 30-30 Win. | 4 | 24" | 41-3/4" | 13-3/4" | 3/4" | 3/4" | 6-1/2 | 12" | Comp. Hunting Stock, Rifle Sights, SL |
| 381 | 30-30 Win. | 4 | 20 | 38-1/8 | 13-3/4 | 3/4 | 3/4 | 6-1/4 | 12 | Comp. Hunting Stock, Rifle Sights, SL |
| 394 | 44 Rem. Mag. | 5 | 20 | 38-1/8 | 13-3/4 | 3/4 | 3/4 | 6-1/4 | 2 | Comp. Hunting Stock, Rifle Sights, SL |
| **BLACK SHADOW® BIG BORE** | | | | | | | | | | |
| $395 | 444 Marlin | 4 | 20" | 38-1/8" | 13-3/4" | 3/4" | 3/4" | 6-1/2 | 38" | Comp. Hunting Stock, Rifle Sights, SL |
| **RANGER COMPACT** | | | | | | | | | | |
| $347 | 30-30 Win. | 5 | 16" | 33-1/4" | 12-1/2" | 1-1/8" | 1-3/4" | 5-7/8 | 12" | Rifle Sights, SL |
| 368 | 357 Mag. | 9 | 16 | 33-1/4 | 12-1/2 | 1-1/8 | 1-3/4 | 5-7/8 | 16 | Rifle Sights, SL |
| **LEGACY** | | | | | | | | | | |
| $446 | 30-30 Win. | 7 | 24 | 42-1/8 | 13-1/2 | 1-1/8 | 1-7/8 | 6-3/4 | 12 | PG, Rifle Sights, SL |
| 446 | 357 Mag. | 12 | 24 | 42-1/8 | 13-1/2 | 1-1/8 | 1-7/8 | 6-3/4 | 16 | PG, Rifle Sights, SL |
| 446 | 45 Colt | 12 | 24 | 42-1/8 | 13-1/2 | 1-1/8 | 1-7/8 | 6-3/4 | 26 | PG, Rifle Sights, SL |
| 446 | 44 Rem. Mag. | 12 | 24 | 42-1/8 | 13-1/2 | 1-1/8 | 1-7/8 | 6-3/4 | 26 | PG, Rifle Sights, SL |
| **RANGER** | | | | | | | | | | |
| $347 | 30-30 Win. | 6 | 20" | 38-1/8 | 13-1/2" | 1-1/8" | 1-7/8" | 6-1/4 | 12" | Rifle Sights, SL |
| **TRADITIONAL** | | | | | | | | | | |
| $430 | 30-30 Win. checkered | 6 | 20" | 38-1/8" | 13-1/2" | 1-1/8" | 1-7/8" | 6-1/4 | 12" | Rifle Sights |
| 398 | 30-30 Win. not checkered | 6 | 20" | 38-1/8" | 13-1/2" | 1-1/8" | 1-7/8" | 6-1/4 | 12" | Rifle Sights |
| 452 | 44 Mag. checkered | 6 | 20" | 38-1/8" | 13-1/2 | 1-1/8 | 1-7/8 | 6-1/4 | 26" | Rifle Sights. |
| **TRAILS END** | | | | | | | | | | |
| $434 | 357 Mag. | 11 | 20 | 38-1/8 | 13-1/2 | 1-1/8 | 1-7/8 | 6-1/2 | 16 | Rifle Sights, SL |
| 434 | 44 Rem. | 11 | 20 | 38-1/8 | 13-1/2 | 1-1/8 | 1-7/8 | 6-1/2 | 26 | Rifle Sights, SL |
| 434 | 45 Colt | 11 | 20 | 38-1/8 | 13-1/2 | 1-1/8 | 1-7/8 | 6-1/2 | 26 | Rifle Sights, SL |
| **BIG BORE** | | | | | | | | | | |
| $446 | 444 Marlin | 6 | 20" | 38-1/8" | 13-1/2" | 1-1/8" | 1-7/8" | 6-1/2 | 38 | Rifle Sights, LL |
| **TRAPPER** | | | | | | | | | | |
| $337 | 30-30 Win. | 5 | 16" | 34-1/4" | 13-1/2" | 1-1/8" | 1-7/8" | 6 | 12 | Rifle Sights, SL |
| 355 | 44 Rem. | 9 | 16 | 34-1/4 | 13-1/2 | 1-1/8 | 1-7/8 | 6 | 26 | Rifle Sights, SL |
| 355 | 357 Mag. | 9 | 16 | 34-1/4 | 13-1/2 | 1-1/8 | 1-7/8 | 6 | 16 | Rifle Sights, SL |
| 355 | 45 Colt | 9 | 16 | 34-1/4 | 13-1/2 | 1-1/8 | 1-7/8 | 6 | 26 | Rifle Sights, SL |
| **PACK RIFLE** | | | | | | | | | | |
| $484 | 30-30 Win. | 4 | 18" | 36-1/8" | 13-1/2" | 1-1/8" | 1-7/8" | 6-1/4 | 12" | PG, Rifle Sights |
| 495 | 45 Rem. Mag. | 5 | 18 | 36-1/8 | 13-1/2 | 1-1/8 | 1-7/8 | 6-1/4 | 26 | PG, Rifle Sights |
| **TIMBER CARBINE** | | | | | | | | | | |
| $548 | 444 Marlin | 5 | 17-3/4" | 36" | 13-1/2" | 1-1/8" | 1-7/8" | 6 | 12 | Rifle Sights |

*Bushnell 4X32 scope and see-thru mounts available.

# WINCHESTER RIFLES

## LEVER ACTION

### MODEL 94 RANGER

MODEL 94 RANGER is an economical version of the Model 94.
*Also available:* RANGER COMPACT in 30-30 Win. and 357 Mag.
*Price:* . . . . . . . . . . . . . . . . . . . . . . . . . . . . . . . . **$347.00**

### MODEL 94 PACK RIFLE

18" barrel in 30-30 and .44 Maagnum, fuller pistol grip and forend.
*Prices:* 30-30 . . . . . . . . . . . . . . . . . . . . . . . . . **$484.00**
44 . . . . . . . . . . . . . . . . . . . . . . . . . . . . . 495.00

**BLACK SHADOW**

### MODEL 94 BIG-BORE WALNUT

Improved performance. Available in 444 Marlin in walnut and Black Shadow versions.
*Price:* . . . . . . . . . . . . . . . . . . . . . . . . . . . . . **$446.00**

### MODEL 94 TRAILS END

**SPECIFICATIONS**
*Calibers:* 357 Mag., 44 Rem. Mag., 45 Colt. *Capacity:* 11 shot magazine. *Barrel length:* 20". *Overall length:* 38 1/8".
*Weight:* 6.5 lbs. Standard loop or large loop.
*Price:* . . . . . . . . . . . . . . . . . . . . . . . . . . . . . **$434.00**

### MODEL 94 LEGACY
#### Standard Loop Lever

**SPECIFICATIONS**
*Calibers:* 30-30 Win., 357 Mag., 44 Rem. Mag., 45 Colt.
*Capacity:* 6 shots (30-30 Win.); 11 shots (other calibers);
add 1 shot for 24" barrel. *Barrel length:* 20" or 24".
*Overall length:* 42 1/8" w/24" barrel. *Weight:* 6.75 lbs.
*Price:* . . . . . . . . . . . . . . . . . . . . . . . . . . . . . **$446.00**

# WINCHESTER LEVER-ACTION

## .22 RIFLES

The 9422 Series is based on an exposed-hammer, side-ejecting lever action noted for its smoothness and reliability. Checkered American walnut stocks and a rich blue add to the appearance. Open sights augment a receiver grooved for scope mounts.

### MODEL 9422 LEGACY

The Model 9422 Legacy has a semi-pistol grip stock, long forearm nose, and long 22 1/2" barrel. Styled after centerfire levers of a century ago, it features a cut checkered walnut stock and fore-end, adjustable sights. Hammer extension (for use with a scope) included.

### MODEL 9422 TRAPPER

With an overall length of just 33 1/8" the 9422 Trapper won't get in the way when you put it in a scabbard or shove it in a backpack. The short barrel makes it ideal for younger shooters. Cut checkered American walnut stock. Hammer extension included.

### MODEL 9422 TRADITIONAL

The Traditional features a straight grip walnut stock with cut checkering. Modeled after the famous Winchester 94, this rifle has become the standard of comparision for other 22 lever actions. Choose 22 LR or 22 WMR. Hammer extension (for use with a scope) included.

## MODEL 9422 RIMFIRE RIFLES

| Item Number | Caliber | Magazine Capacity | Barrel Length | Nominal Overall Length | Nominal Length of Pull | Nominal Drop at Comb | Nominal Drop at Heel | Nominal Weight (Lbs.) | Rate of Twist 1 Turn In | U.S. Sugg. Retail |
|---|---|---|---|---|---|---|---|---|---|---|
| **LEGACY** | | | | | | | | | | |
| 524-027103 | 22 Rimfire | 15 LR | 22-1/2" | 39-1/8" | 13-1/2" | 1-1-8" | 1-7/8" | 6 | 16" | $467 |
| 524-027104 | 22 WMR | 11 | 22-1/2 | 39-1/8 | 13-1/2 | 1-1/8 | 1-7/8 | 6 | 16 | 488 |
| **TRADITIONAL** | | | | | | | | | | |
| 524-024103 | 22 Rimfire | 15 LR | 20-1/2" | 37-1/8" | 13-1/2" | 1-1/8" | 1-7/8" | 6 | 16" | $437 |
| 524-024104 | 22 WMR | 11 | 20-1/2 | 37-1/8 | 13-1/2 | 1-1/8 | 1-7/8 | 6 | 16 | 457 |
| **TRAPPER** | | | | | | | | | | |
| 524-023103 | 22 Rimfire | 15 LR | 16-1/2" | 33-1/8" | 13-1/2" | 1-1/8" | 1-7/8" | 5-3/4 | 16 | $437 |
| 524-023104 | 22 WMR | 8 | 16-1/2 | 33-1/8 | 13-1/2 | 1-1/8 | 1-7/8 | 5-3/4 | 16 | 457 |

# WINCHESTER RIFLES

## LIMITED EDITION AND HISTORIC

These are modern versions of some of the greatest Winchesters of all time. They are available in either Limited Edition versions (production held to limited quantities) or Classis Tradition versions (small numbers made year to year).

### NEW MODEL 1885 LOW WALL RIMFIRE

The classic Low Wall Winchester in .22 Long Rifle caliber. Its trim stock, half octagon/half round barrel and special chamber dimensions contribute to accuracy. Drilled and tapped for scope mounts or tang-mounted peep (available separately). Limited to 2,400 Grade I and 1,100 High Grade rifles.

### MODEL 1892 SHORT RIFLE

Compact, with 20" barrel and slightly shorter forearm just like the originals over a century ago, this 1892 has dual vertical locking lugs. Chambered in 44 Magnum. Limited quantities still available.

### NEW MODEL 1886 EXTRA LIGHT

This rifle has a 22" round tapered barrel, solid frame, shotgun style steel buttplate and half magazine. Its exceptionally strong action is chambered for powerful 45-70. Two grades in limited numbers: Grade I (3,500) and High Grade (1,000). High Grade features extra fancy checkered walnut stock and engraved game scenes on a blued receiver.

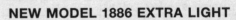

# WINCHESTER RIFLES

## LIMITED EDITION AND HISTORIC

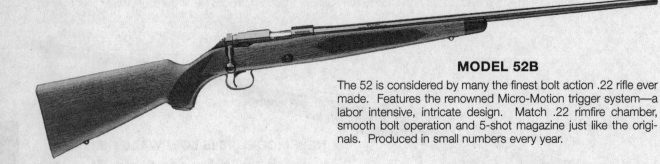

### MODEL 52B

The 52 is considered by many the finest bolt action .22 rifle ever made. Features the renowned Micro-Motion trigger system—a labor intensive, intricate design. Match .22 rimfire chamber, smooth bolt operation and 5-shot magazine just like the originals. Produced in small numbers every year.

### NEW MODEL 1895 .405 WINCHESTER

The most sought-after caliber in the 1895 is the .405 Winchester. This was the gun Teddy Roosevelt described as his "big medicine". He took three of them in .405 caliber on his historic African safari. High grades have engraved elk and whitetail scenes on a polished white receiver. Grade I is blued. (Small quantities available).

## HISTORIC RIFLES

| Item Number | Caliber | Magazine Capacity * | Barrel Length | Nominal Overall Length | Nominal Length of Pull | Nominal Drop at Comb | Nominal Drop at Heel | Nominal Weight (Lbs.) | Rate of Twist 1 Turn in | U.S. Sugg. Retail |
|---|---|---|---|---|---|---|---|---|---|---|
| **LIMITED EDITIONS** | | | | | | | | | | |
| *MODEL 1885 LOW WALL 22 GRADE I* | | | | | | | | | | |
| 527-070102 **NEW** | 22 Long Rifle | n/a | 24-1/2" | 41" | 13-1/2" | 7/8" | 1-1/2" | 8 | 16" | $775 |
| *MODEL 1885 LOW WALL 22 HIGH GRADE* | | | | | | | | | | |
| 527-071102 **NEW** | 22 Long Rifle | n/a | 24-1/2' | 41" | 13-1/2" | 7/8" | 1-1/2" | 8 | 16" | 1,234 |
| *MODEL 1886 EXTRA LIGHT GRADE I* | | | | | | | | | | |
| 534-053142 **NEW** | 45-70 | 4 | 22" | 40-1/2" | 13-1/4" | 1-1/8" | 1-5/8" | 7-1/4 | 22" | 1,156 |
| *MODEL 1886 EXTRA LIGHT HIGH GRADE* | | | | | | | | | | |
| 534-054142 **NEW** | 45-70 | 4 | 22" | 40-1/2" | 13-1/4" | 1-1/8" | 1-5/8" | 7-1/4 | 22" | 1,156 |
| **CLASSIC TRADITIONS - IN LINE CONTINUING MODELS** | | | | | | | | | | |
| *MODEL 1892 SHORT RIFLE LEVER ACTION* | | | | | | | | | | |
| 534-064124 | 44 Magnum | 11 | 20" | 37-3/4" | 13" | 1-1/2" | 2-3/8" | 6-1/4 | 38" | 752 |
| *MODEL 52B BOLT ACTION* | | | | | | | | | | |
| 534-050203 | 22 Long Rifle | 5 | 24" | 41-3/4" | 13-1/2" | 1-3/8" | 2-5/16" | 7 | 16" | 662 |
| *MODEL 1895 GRADE I* | | | | | | | | | | |
| 534-070154 **NEW** | .405 Win. | 4 | 24" | 42" | 13-1/4" | 2-7/8" | 3-5/8" | 8 | 10" | 1,050 |
| *MODEL 1895 HIGH GRADE* | | | | | | | | | | |
| 534-071154 **NEW** | .405 Win. | 4 | 24" | 42" | 13-1/4" | 2-7/8" | 3-5/8" | 8 | 10" | 1,540 |

# Shotguns

*Roland Clark – Pintail Ducks, 1933*

*For addresses and phone/fax numbers of manufacturers and distributors included in this section, please turn to **DIRECTORY OF MANUFACTURERS AND SUPPLIERS** on page 564.*

# AMERICAN ARMS SHOTGUNS

### SPECIALTY SIDE-BY-SIDE
**12 Gauge**

Double-trigger, box-ock 12-gauge doublle with swivels for a carrying strap. Beavertail forend, recoil pad, checkered pistol grip.

### SPECIALTY OVER/UNDER
**12 Gauge**

Boxlock over/under, 10 or 12 gauge, single selective trigger, strap swivels, vent rib, checkered stock.

### SPECIALTY CAMO (SILVER WT/OU)
**SPECIFICATIONS**

Features nonreflective Mossy Oak "Breakup" Camo pattern. Specifications same as WS/OU 12 ga., including auto selective ejectors and AA1 choke tubes (IC-M-F).

## SPECIFICATIONS

| MODEL | GAUGE | BBL. LENGTH | CHAMBER | CHOKES | AVG. WGT. | PRICES |
|---|---|---|---|---|---|---|
| WT/OU | 10 | 26" | 3.5" | CT-2 | 9 lbs. 10 oz. | $995.00 |
| WS/OU | 12 | 28" | 3.5" | CT-3 | 7 lbs. 2 oz. | 799.00 |
| WT/OU Camo | 12 | 26" | 3.5" | CT-3 | 7 lbs. | 885.00 |
| TS/SS | 12 | 26" | 3.5" | CT-3 | 7 lbs. 6 oz. | 799.00 |

*CT-3 Choke Tubes IC/M/F.  CT-2 = Choke tubes F/F.  Drop at Comb = 1 1/8"; Drop at Heel = 2 3/8"*

# AMERICAN ARMS SHOTGUNS

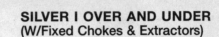

### SILVER I OVER AND UNDER
**(W/Fixed Chokes & Extractors)**

Features polished white frame w/outline engraving; blued trigger guard, top lever and forward latch; radiused rubber recoil pad.

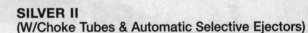

### SILVER II
**(W/Choke Tubes & Automatic Selective Ejectors)**

Same features as Silver I, but with more refined engraving. Models in 16, 20 and .410 gauge have fixed chokes.

### SILVER SPORTING
**(Ported, w/Choke Tubes)**

## SPECIFICATIONS

| MODEL | GAUGE | BBL. LENGTH | CHAMBER | CHOKES | AVG. WEIGHT | PRICES |
|-------|-------|-------------|---------|--------|-------------|--------|
| Silver I | 12 | 26" – 28" | 3" | IC/M-M/F | 6 lbs. 15 oz. | $649.00 |
| | 20 | 26" – 28" | 3" | IC/M-M/F | 6 lbs. 12 oz. | 649.00 |
| | 28 | 26" | 2.75" | IC/M | 5 lbs. 14 oz. | 679.00 |
| | .410 | 26" | 3" | IC/M | 6 lbs. 6 oz. | 679.00 |
| Silver II* | 12 | 26" – 28" | 3" | CT-3 | 6 lbs. 15 oz. | 769.00 |
| | 16 | 26" | 2.75" | IC/M | 6 lbs. 13 oz. | 769.00 |
| | 20 | 26" | 3" | CT-3 | 6 lbs. 12 oz. | 769.00 |
| | 28 | 26" | 2.75" | IC/M | 5 lbs. 14 oz. | 815.00 |
| | .410 | 26" | 3" | IC/M | 6 lbs. 6 oz. | 815.00 |
| Sporting** | 12 | 28" – 30" | 2.75" | CTS | 7 lbs. 6 oz. | 965.00 |

CT-3 Choke Tubes IC/M/F  Cast Off = ³/₈"  CTS = SK/SK/IC/M    Silver I and II: Pull = 14 ¹/₈"; Drop at Comb = 1 ³/₈"; Drop at Heel = 2 ³/₈"
Silver I and II: Pull = 14 ¹/₄"; Drop at Comb = 1 ¹/₂"; Drop at Heel = 2 ¹/₂"    * 2 Barrel Set: **$115.00**  **Silver Upland Lite (12 and 20 ga.) = **$925.00**

# AMERICAN ARMS SHOTGUNS

## BRITTANY SIDE-BY-SIDE

**SPECIFICATIONS**
**Gauges:** 12, 20
**Chamber:** 3"
**Chokes:** CT-3

**Barrel Length:** 26"
**Weight:** 6 lbs. 7 oz. (20 ga.); 6 lbs. 15 oz. (12 ga.)
**Features:** Engraved case-colored frame; single selective trigger with top tang selector; automatic selective ejectors; manual safety; hard chrome-lined barrels; walnut English-style straight stock and semi-beavertail forearm w/cut checkering and oil-rubbed finish; ventilated rubber recoil pal; and choke tubes with key
**Price:** . . . . . . . . . . . . . . . . . . . . . . . . . . . . . . . **$885.00**

## GENTRY SIDE-BY-SIDE

Features boxlocks with engraved English-style scrollwork on side plates; one-piece, steel-forged receiver; chrome barrels; manual thumb safety; independent floating firing pin.

**SPECIFICATIONS**
**Gauges:** 12, 20, 28, .410
**Chamber:** 3" (except 28 gauge, 2.75")

**Barrel Lengths:** 26", choked IC/M (all gauges; 28", choked M/F (12 and 20 gauges)
**Weight:** 6 lbs. 15 oz. (12 ga.); 6 lbs. 7 oz. (20 and .410 ga.); 6 lbs. 5 oz. (28 ga.)
**Drop At Comb:** 1 ³/₈"
**Drop At Heel:** 2 ³/₈"
**Other Features:** Fitted recoil pad; flat matted rib; walnut pistol-grip stock and beavertail forend with hand-checkering; gold front sight bead
**Prices:**
  12 or 20 ga. . . . . . . . . . . . . . . . . . . . . . . . . . . . **$750.00**
  28 or .410 ga. . . . . . . . . . . . . . . . . . . . . . . . . . . 795.00

## PHANTOM SYNTHETIC
**SPECIFICATIONS**
**Gauge:** 12 **Barrel:** 24"/26"/28", cold hammered forged chrome lined with bright blue finish **Choke:** IC-M-F
**Chamber:** 3" **Features:** Gas operated semi-automatic shoots 2 3/4" or 3" shells interchangeably. Approved for steel shot, checkered synthetic forend and stock, screw-in choke tubes (3), magazine cut-off for quick unloading and safety, five round magazine.
**Price:** . . . . . . . . . . . . . . . . . . . . . . . . . . . . . . . **$439.00**

## PHANTOM HOME PROTECTION
**SPECIFICATIONS**
**Gauge:** 12 **Barrel:** 19" threaded barrel for external choketubes (2), and swivel studs **Choke:** SK, M, F
**Chamber:** 3" **Features:** Same as Phantom Synthetic
**Price:** . . . . . . . . . . . . . . . . . . . . . . . . . . . . . . . **$449.00**

## PHANTOM FIELD
**SPECIFICATIONS**
**Gauge:** 12 **Barrel:** 24"/26"/28", cold hammered forged chrome lined with bright blue finish **Choke:** IC-M-F
**Chamber:** 3" **Features:** Same as Phantom Synthetic, except for checkered walnut forend and stock
**Price:** . . . . . . . . . . . . . . . . . . . . . . . . . . . . . . . **$439.00**

# AYA SHOTGUNS

## BOXLOCK SHOTGUNS

### MODEL XXV BOXLOCK

AYA boxlocks use the Anson & Deeley system with double locking lugs, incorporating detachable cross pin and separate plate to allow easy access to the firing mechanism. Barrels are chopper lump, firing pins are bushed, plus automatic safety and ejectors and metal oval for engraving of initials. Other features include disc set strikers, replaceable hinge pin, split bottom plate.
**Barrel lengths:** 26", 27" and 28"

**Weight:** 5 to 7 pounds, depending on gauge.

| MODEL | Price |
| --- | --- |
| MODEL XXV BOXLOCK: 12 and 20 gauge only | $2,635.00 |
| MODEL 4 BOXLOCK: 12, 16, 20, 28, .410 ga. | 1,695.00 |
| MODEL 4 DELUXE BOXLOCK: Same gauges as above | 2,995.00 |

## SIDELOCK SHOTGUNS

AYA sidelock shotguns are fitted with London Holland & Holland system sidelocks, double triggers with articulated front trigger, automatic safety and ejectors, cocking indicators, bushed firing pins, replaceable hinge pins and chopper lump barrels. Stocks are of figured walnut with hand-cut checkering and oil finish, complete with a metal oval on the buttstock for engraving of initials. Exhibition grade wood is available as are many special options, including a true left-hand version and self-opener. Available from Armes de Chasse (see Directory of Manufacturers and Suppliers).
**Barrell lengths:** 26", 27", 28", 29" and 32". **Weight:** 5 to 7 pounds, depending on gauge.

| MODEL | Prices |
| --- | --- |
| MODEL 1: Sidelock in 12 and 20 ga. w/special engraving and exhibition quality wood | $6,895.00 |
| DELUXE | 7,495.00 |
| MODEL 2: Sidelock in 12, 16, 20, 28 ga. and .410 bore | 3,295.00 |
| MODEL 53: Sidelock in 12, 16 and 20 ga. with 3 locking lugs and side clips | 4,602.00 |
| MODEL 56: Sidelock in 12 ga. only with 3 locking lugs and side clips | 7,595.00 |
| MODEL XXV/SL: Sidelock in 12 and 20 ga. only w/Churchill-type rib | 3,892.00 |

### COUNTRYMAN SIDE-BY-SIDE
**SPECIFICATIONS**
**Gauges:** 12 and 10  **Barrel lengths:** 26", 27" or 28"
**Length of pull:** up to 15"  **Features:** Selective ejectors; automatic safety; Cordura covered case; hand-detachable side locks; disc set starters; chopper lump barrels; hand-rubbed select Spanish walnut stock with hand-cut checkering.
**Price:** ........................................... $2,295.00

# BENELLI SHOTGUNS

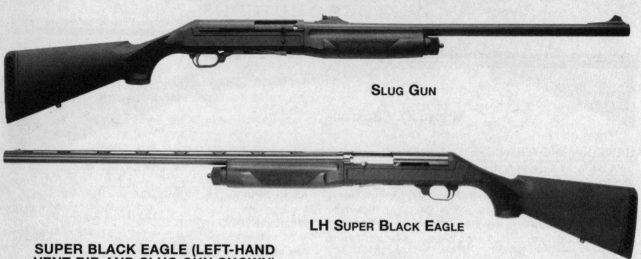

**SLUG GUN**

**LH SUPER BLACK EAGLE**

## SUPER BLACK EAGLE (LEFT-HAND VENT RIB AND SLUG GUN SHOWN)

Benelli's Super Black Eagle shotgun fires every type of 12 gauge shell currently available without adjustment.

The Super Black Eagle also features a specially strengthened steel upper receiver mated to the barrel to endure the toughest shotgunning with magnum loads. The alloy lower receiver keeps the overall weight low.

**Stock:** Satin walnut (28") with drop adjustment kit; high-gloss walnut (26") with drop adjustment kit; or synthetic stock **Finish:** Matte black finish on receiver, barrel and bolt (28"); blued finish on receiver and barrel (26") with bolt mirror polished (camo options available)

**Features:** Montefeltro rotating bolt with dual locking lugs. For additional specifications, see table on folllowing page.
**Prices:** Wood Satin . . . . . . . . . . . . . . . . . . . . . .$1,240.00
Synthetic . . . . . . . . . . . . . . . . . . . . . . . . . . . .1,220.00
Camo . . . . . . . . . . . . . . . . . . . . . . . . . . . . . . .1,330.00
In lefthand, synthetic . . . . . . . . . . . . . . . . . . . .1,250.00
LH Camo . . . . . . . . . . . . . . . . . . . . . . . . . . . .1,340.00
Rifled slug, wood . . . . . . . . . . . . . . . . . . . . . .1,280.00
  Synthetic . . . . . . . . . . . . . . . . . . . . . . . . . . .1,270.00
  Camo . . . . . . . . . . . . . . . . . . . . . . . . . . . . . .1,390.00

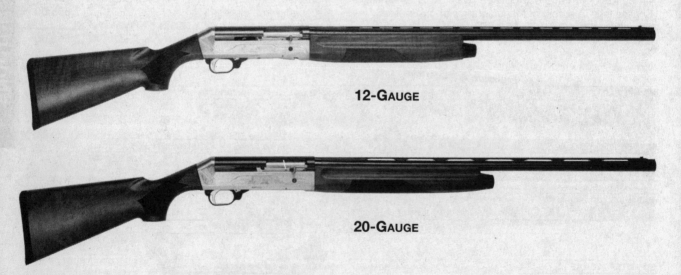

**12-GAUGE**

**20-GAUGE**

## LEGACY (20- AND 12-GAUGE SHOWN)

Features lower alloy receiver and upper steel receiver cover and interchangeable barrel with mid-point bead and red light-gathering bar front sight. Also Benelli's inertia recoil operating system; cartridge drop lever (to indicate "hammer-cocked condition; set of 5 choke tubes for use with lead or steel shot); chambered round removable without emptying the magazine; handles all 2 3/4" and 3" shells within gauge with over 1 1/2 oz. of shot. **Price:** . . . . . . . .$1,350.00

# BENELLI SHOTGUNS

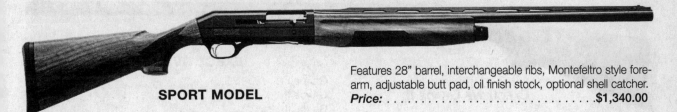

## SPORT MODEL

Features 28" barrel, interchangeable ribs, Montefeltro style fore-arm, adjustable butt pad, oil finish stock, optional shell catcher.
*Price:* . . . . . . . . . . . . . . . . . . . . . . . . . . . . . .**$1,340.00**

## BENELLI SHOTGUN SPECIFICATIONS

| ITEM # | BBL LENGTH | STOCK | RECEIVER | LENGTH | WEIGHT (LBS.) | PULL | DROP: HEEL/COMB | MAG. CAP. |
|---|---|---|---|---|---|---|---|---|
| **SUPER BLACK EAGLE** - 12 Gauge (fires 3 1/2"-3"-2 3/4" shells) - 5 choke tubes - mid & front bead sights - ventilated buttpad | | | | | | | | |
| 10055 | 26" Vent Rib-Ltd. Ed. | Satin Walnut | Upper Steel/Lower Nickel Finish | 47.63 | 7.4 | 14.25 | 2 1/2" / 1 5/8" | 3 |
| 10000 | 28" Vent Rib | Satin Walnut | Upper Steel/Lower Alloy | 49.63 | 7.5 | 14.25 | 2 1/2" / 1 5/8" | 3 |
| 10010 | 26" Vent Rib | Satin Walnut | Upper Steel/Lower Alloy | 47.63 | 7.4 | 14.25 | 2 1/2" / 1 5/8" | 3 |
| 10005 | 26" Vent Rib | Satin Walnut | Upper Steel/Lower Alloy | 47.63 | 7.4 | 14.25 | 2 1/2" / 1 5/8" | 3 |
| 10015 | 28" Vent Rib | Synthetic | Upper Steel/Lower Alloy | 49.63 | 7.5 | 14.25 | 2 1/2" / 1 5/8" | 3 |
| 10020 | 26" Vent Rib | Synthetic | Upper Steel/Lower Alloy | 47.63 | 7.4 | 14.25 | 2 1/2" / 1 5/8" | 3 |
| 10025 | 24" Vent Rib | Synthetic | Upper Steel/Lower Alloy | 45.63 | 7.3 | 14.25 | 2 1/2" / 1 5/8" | 3 |
| 10040 | 28" Vent Rib | Camo | Upper Steel/Lower Alloy | 49.63 | 7.5 | 14.25 | 2 1/2" / 1 5/8" | 3 |
| 10045 | 26" Vent Rib | Camo | Upper Steel/Lower Alloy | 47.63 | 7.4 | 14.25 | 2 1/2" / 1 5/8" | 3 |
| 10050 | 24" Vent Rib | Camo | Upper Steel/Lower Alloy | 45.63 | 7.3 | 14.25 | 2 1/2" / 1 5/8" | 3 |
| 10075 | 28" Vent Rib-LH | Synthetic | Upper Steel/Lower Alloy | 49.63 | 7.5 | 14.25 | 2 1/2" / 1 5/8" | 3 |
| 10070 | 26" Vent Rib-LH | Synthetic | Upper Steel/Lower Alloy | 47.63 | 7.4 | 14.25 | 2 1/2" / 1 5/8" | 3 |
| 10065 | 24" Vent Rib-LH | Synthetic | Upper Steel/Lower Alloy | 45.63 | 7.3 | 14.25 | 2 1/2" / 1 5/8" | 3 |
| 10090 | 28" Vent Rib-LH | Camo | Upper Steel/Lower Alloy | 49.63 | 7.5 | 14.25 | 2 1/2" / 1 5/8" | 3 |
| 10085 | 26" Vent Rib-LH | Camo | Upper Steel/Lower Alloy | 47.63 | 7.4 | 14.25 | 2 1/2" / 1 5/8" | 3 |
| 10080 | 24" Vent Rib-LH | Camo | Upper Steel/Lower Alloy | 45.63 | 7.3 | 14.25 | 2 1/2" / 1 5/8" | 3 |
| **SUPER BLACK EAGLE SLUG** - 12 Gauge (fires 3"-2 3/4" shells) - rifled barre - drilled/tapped receiver, adj. rifle sights - ventilated buttpad | | | | | | | | |
| 10030 | 24" Rifled Bore | Satin Walnut | Upper Steel/Lower Alloy | 45.63 | 7.6 | 14.25 | 2 1/2" / 1 5/8" | 3 |
| 10035 | 24" Rifled Bore | Synthetic | Upper Steel/Lower Alloy | 45.63 | 7.6 | 14.25 | 2 1/2" / 1 5/8" | 3 |
| **MONTEFELTRO** - 12 Gauge (fires 3"-2 3/4" shells) - 5 choke tubes - front sight bead - 4 round magazine capacity - ventilated buttpad | | | | | | | | |
| 10800 | 28" Vent Rib | Satin Walnut | Bued/1 piece alloy | 49.5 | 7.1 | 14.375 | 2 3/8" / 1 1/2" | |
| 10810 | 26" Vent Rib | Satin Walnut | Bued/1 piece alloy | 47.5 | 6.9 | 14.375 | 2 3/8" / 1 1/2" | |
| 10820 | 24" Vent Rib | Satin Walnut | Bued/1 piece alloy | 45.5 | 6.8 | 14.375 | 2 3/8" / 1 1/2" | |
| 10805 | 28" Vent Rib - LH | Satin Walnut | Bued/1 piece alloy | 49.5 | 7.1 | 14.375 | 2 3/8" / 1 1/2" | |
| 10815 | 26" Vent Rib - LH | Satin Walnut | Bued/1 piece alloy | 47.5 | 6.9 | 14.375 | 2 3/8" / 1 1/2" | |
| **MONTEFELTRO** - 20 Gauge (fires 3"-2 3/4" shells) - 5 choke tubes - front sight bead - 4 round magazine capacity - ventilated buttpad | | | | | | | | |
| 10830 | 26" Vent Rib | Satin Walnut | Bued/1 piece alloy | 47.5 | 5.6 | 14.25 | 2 1/4" / 1 1/2" | |
| 10835 | 24" Vent Rib | Satin Walnut | Bued/1 piece alloy | 45.5 | 5.5 | 14.25 | 2 1/4" / 1 1/2" | |
| 10840 | 26" Vent Rib | Camo Wood | Camo/1 piece alloy | 47.5 | 5.6 | 14.25 | 2 1/4" / 1 1/2" | |
| **MONTEFELTRO** - 20 Gauge Short Stocked (fires 3"-2 3/4" shells) - 5 choke tubes - front sight bead - 4 rd. mag. Capacity - ventilated buttpad | | | | | | | | |
| 10831 | 26" Vent Rib | Satin Walnut | Bued/1 piece alloy | 45.7 | 5.4 | 12.5 | 2 1/8" / 1 1/2" | |
| 10836 | 24" Vent Rib | Satin Walnut | Bued/1 piece alloy | 43.7 | 5.3 | 12.5 | 2 1/8" / 1 1/2" | |
| **LEGACY**- 12 Gauge (fires 3"-2 3/4" shells) - 5 choke tubes - mid & front bead sights - 4 round magazine capacity - rubber buttpad | | | | | | | | |
| 10400 | 28" Vent Rib | Select Satin Walnut | Upper Steel/Lower Nickel Finish | 49.63 | 7.5 | 14.25 | 2 1/2" / 1 1/2" | |
| 10405 | 26" Vent Rib | Select Satin Walnut | Upper Steel/Lower Nickel Finish | 47.63 | 7.4 | 14.25 | 2 1/2" / 1 1/2" | |
| **LEGACY**- 20 Gauge (fires 3"-2 3/4" shells) - 5 choke tubes - mid & front bead sights - 4 round magazine capacity - rubber buttpad | | | | | | | | |
| 10420 | 26" Vent Rib | Select Satin Walnut | Upper Steel/Lower Nickel Finish | 47.63 | 6 | 14.25 | 2 1/2" / 1 1/2" | |
| 10425 | 24" Vent Rib | Select Satin Walnut | Upper Steel/Lower Nickel Finish | 45.63 | 5.8 | 14.25 | 2 1/2" / 1 1/2" | |
| **SUPER BLACK EAGLE** - 12 Gauge (fires 3 1/2"-3"-2 3/4" shells) - 5 choke tubes - mid & front bead sights - ventilated buttpad | | | | | | | | |
| 11420 | 28" Vent Rib | Select Satin Walnut | Steel/Lower Nickel Finish | 49.63 | 7.85 | 14.5 | 2 1/4" / 1 3/8" | |
| 11400 | 26" Vent Rib | Select Satin Walnut | Steel/Lower Nickel Finish | 47.63 | 7.75 | 14.5 | 2 1/4" / 1 3/8" | |
| 11430 | 28" Vent Rib | Select Satin Walnut | Steel/Lower Nickel Finish | 49.63 | 7.85 | 14.5 | 2 1/4" / 1 3/8" | |
| 11405 | 26" Vent Rib | Select Satin Walnut | Steel/Lower Nickel Finish | 47.63 | 7.75 | 14.5 | 2 1/4" / 1 3/8" | |
| 11440 | 28" Vent Rib | Select Satin Walnut | Steel/Lower Nickel Finish | 49.63 | 7.85 | 14.5 | 2 1/4" / 1 3/8" | |
| 11410 | 26" Vent Rib | Select Satin Walnut | Steel/Lower Nickel Finish | 47.63 | 7.75 | 14.5 | 2 1/4" / 1 3/8" | |

# BENELLI SHOTGUNS

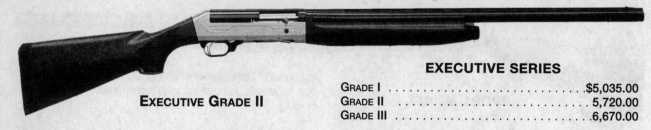

**EXECUTIVE GRADE II**

## EXECUTIVE SERIES

GRADE I . . . . . . . . . . . . . . . . . . . . . . . . . . . . . $5,035.00
GRADE II . . . . . . . . . . . . . . . . . . . . . . . . . . . . 5,720.00
GRADE III . . . . . . . . . . . . . . . . . . . . . . . . . . . . 6,670.00

## BENELLI SHOTGUN SPECIFICATIONS *(Continued from previous page)*

| Item # | BBL Length | Stock | Receiver | Length | Weight (Lbs.) | Pull | Drop: Heel/Comb | Mag. Cap. |
|---|---|---|---|---|---|---|---|---|
| **SPORT** - 12 Gauge (fires 3"-2 3/4" shells) - 5 choke tubes - mid & front bead sights - 4 round magazine capacity | | | | | | | | |
| 10610 | 28" Vent Rib (w/2 ribs) | Select Satin Walnut | Matte/1 piece alloy | 49.63 | 7.1 | 14.375 | 2 1/4" / 1 7/16" | |
| 10615 | 26" Vent Rib (w/2 ribs) | Select Satin Walnut | Matte/1 piece alloy | 47.63 | 6.9 | 14.375 | 2 1/4" / 1 7/16" | |
| **M1 FIELD** - 12 Gauge (fires 3"-2 3/4" shells) - 5 choke tubes - front bead sights - 3 round magazine capacity - ventilated buttpad | | | | | | | | |
| 11000 | 28" Vent Rib | Satin Walnut | Matte/1 Piece Alloy | 49.5 | 7.4 | 14.375 | 2 1/4" / 1 3/8" | |
| 11010 | 26" Vent Rib | Satin Walnut | Matte/1 Piece Alloy | 47.5 | 7.3 | 14.375 | 2 1/4" / 1 3/8" | |
| 11035 | 28" Vent Rib | Camo | Camo/1 piece alloy | 49.5 | 7.4 | 14.375 | 2 1/4" / 1 3/8" | |
| 11040 | 26" Vent Rib | Camo | Camo/1 piece alloy | 47.5 | 7.3 | 14.375 | 2 1/4" / 1 3/8" | |
| 11045 | 24" Vent Rib | Camo | Camo/1 piece alloy | 45.5 | 7.2 | 14.375 | 2 1/4" / 1 3/8" | |
| 11050 | 21" Vent Rib | Camo | Camo/1 piece alloy | 42..5 | 7 | 14.375 | 2 1/4" / 1 3/8" | |
| 11005 | 28" Vent Rib | Synthetic | Matte/1 Piece Alloy | 49.5 | 7.4 | 14.375 | 2 1/4" / 1 3/8" | |
| 11015 | 26" Vent Rib | Synthetic | Matte/1 Piece Alloy | 47.5 | 7.3 | 14.375 | 2 1/4" / 1 3/8" | |
| 11020 | 24" Vent Rib | Synthetic | Matte/1 Piece Alloy | 45.5 | 7.2 | 14.375 | 2 1/4" / 1 3/8" | |
| 11025 | 21" Vent Rib | Synthetic | Matte/1 Piece Alloy | 42.5 | 7 | 14.375 | 2 1/4" / 1 3/8" | |
| **M1 FIELD SLUG** - 12 Gauge (fires 3"-2 3/4" shells) - rifled barrel - drilled/tapped sights - 3 round magazine capacity - ventilated buttpad | | | | | | | | |
| 11060 | 24" Rifled Bore | Synthetic | Matte/1 Piece Alloy | 45.63 | 7.6 | 14.375 | 2 1/4" / 1 3/8" | |
| **NOVA PUMP** - 12 Gauge (fires 3 1/2"-3" - 2 3/4" shells) - 3 choke tubes - mid & front bead sights - 4 round mag. capacity | | | | | | | | |
| 20015 | 28" Vent Rib | Camo Synthetic | Camo | 49.5 | 8 | 14.25 | | |
| 20018 | 26" Vent Rib | Camo Synthetic | Camo | 47.5 | 7.9 | 14.25 | | |
| 20021 | 24" Vent Rib | Camo Synthetic | Camo | 45.5 | 7.8 | 14.25 | | |
| 20000 | 28" Vent Rib | Synthetic | Synthetic | 49.5 | 8 | 14.25 | | |
| 20003 | 26" Vent Rib | Synthetic | Synthetic | 47.5 | 7.9 | 14.25 | | |
| 20006 | 24" Vent Rib | Synthetic | Synthetic | 45.5 | 7.8 | 14.25 | | |
| **NOVA PUMP SLUG** - 12 Gauge (fires 3 1/2"- 3"- 2 3/4" shells) - smooth bore rifle sights | | | | | | | | |
| 20050 | 18.5 | Synthetic | Synthetic | | 7.2 | 14.25 | | |

| Item # | BBL Length | Stock | Choke | Sights | Mag. Cap. | Overall Length | Weight (Lbs.) | Drop: Heel/Comb |
|---|---|---|---|---|---|---|---|---|
| **M1 SPECIAL USE** - 12 Gauge (fires 3"-2 3/4" shells) - matte/1 piece alloy receiver - ventilated buttpad - Pull - 14 3/8" | | | | | | | | |
| 11255 | Practical 26" | Synthetic | F, M, IC•• | Mil. Ghost Ring | 9 | 47.63 | 7.6 | 2 1/4" / 1 3/8" |
| 11215 | Tactical 18.5" | Pistol Grip | F, M, IC•• | Std. Ghost Ring | 5 | 39.75 | 7 | |
| 11216 | Tactical 18.5" | Synthetic | F, M, IC•• | Std. Ghost Ring | 5 | 39.75 | 7 | 2 1/4" / 1 3/8" |
| 11200 | Tactical 18.5" | Synthetic | F, M, IC•• | Rifle | 5 | 39.75 | 6.7 | 2 1/4" / 1 3/8" |
| 11201 | Tactical 18.5" | Pistol Grip | F, M, IC•• | Rifle | 5 | 39.75 | 6.7 | |
| 11260 | Tactical M 18.5" | Pistol Grip | F, M, IC•• | Mil. Ghost Ring | 5 | 39.75 | 7.1 | |
| 11261 | Tactical M 18.5" | Synthetic | F, M, IC•• | Mil. Ghost Ring | 5 | 39.75 | 7.1 | 2 1/4" / 1 3/8" |
| 11600 | M3 Conv. 19.75" | Synthetic | Cyl. Bore | Rifle | 5 | 41 | 7.2 | 2 1/4" / 1 3/8" |
| 11601 | M3 Conv. 19.75" | Pistol Grip | Cyl. Bore | Rifle | 5 | 41 | 7.2 | |
| 11605 | M3 Conv. 19.75" | Synthetic | Cyl. Bore | Std. Ghost Ring | 5 | 41 | 7.4 | 2 1/4" / 1 3/8" |
| 11606 | M3 Conv. 19.75" | Pistol Grip | Cyl. Bore | Std. Ghost Ring | 5 | 41 | 7.4 | |
| 11245 | Entry 14" | Synthetic | Cyl. Bore | Rifle | 5 | 35.5 | 6.6 | 2 1/4" / 1 3/8" |
| 11247 | Entry 14" | Pistol Grip | Cyl. Bore | Rifle | 5 | 35.5 | 6.6 | |
| 11225 | Entry 14" | Pistol Grip | Cyl. Bore | Std. Ghost Ring | 5 | 35.5 | 6.7 | |
| 11227 | Entry 14" | Synthetic | Cyl. Bore | Std. Ghost Ring | 5 | 35.5 | 6.7 | 2 1/4" / 1 3/8" |

| Item # | BBL Length | BBL Rifling | Caliber | Grip | Length of Sight Line | Height/Width | Trigger Action | Weight (Lbs.) | Mag. Cap. |
|---|---|---|---|---|---|---|---|---|---|
| **MP95E/MP90S** - Semi-automatic fixed barrel operation - inertia blow-back system - sequential loading with magazine feed - sq. sectioned sights | | | | | | | | | |
| 30000 | 4.4" | R.H. Pitch 18" | 22 LR | Anatomical, Amb., Fixed | 8.75" | 5.25/2" | single, completely adj. | 2.5 | 6 |
| 30100 | 4.4" | R.H. Pitch 18" | 32 WC | Anatomical, Amb., Fixed | 8.75" | 5.25/2" | single, completely adj. | 2.65 | 5 |
| 30200 | 4.4"/Blue | R.H. Pitch 18" | 22 LR | Anatomical, Amb., Fixed | 8.75" | 5.25/1.75" | single w/release spring | 2.5 | 6,9 |
| 30300 | 4.4"/Chrome | R.H. Pitch 18" | 22 LR | Anatomical, Amb., Fixed | 8.75" | 5.25/1.75" | single w/release spring | 2.5 | 6,9 |
| 30400 | 4.4"/Blue | R.H. Pitch 18" | 32 WC | Anatomical, Amb., Fixed | 8.75" | 5.25/1.75" | single w/release spring | 2.65 | 5 |
| 30500 | 4.4"/Chrome | R.H. Pitch 18" | 32 WC | Anatomical, Amb., Fixed | 8.75" | 5.25/1.75" | single w/release spring | 2.65 | 5 |

# BENELLI SHOTGUNS

## MODEL M1 SERIES

### M1 FIELD W/REALTREE
The M1 Field 12-gauge shotgun combines the M1 Super 90 receiver with a choice of polymer or walnut stocks, including a camouflaged model with an Xtra Brown pattern sealed on the matte finish metal and polymer stock. Available in 21", 24", 26" or 28" barrels with vent rib.

**M1 FIELD W/REALTREE** Camo finish, camo polymer buttstock and forearm .....................**$1,010.00**

### MODEL M1 FIELD
*Also available:*
**MODEL M1 TACTICAL** w/18 1/2" bbl. ...........**$890.00**
   With pistol-grip stock, ghost ring sights .......**970.00**
**M1 PRACTICAL,** 26" barrel, ghost ring sight,
   synthetic stock .......................**1,200.00**
**MODEL M1 FIELD** (polymer stock)
   w/21", 24", 26", 28" bbl. .................**920.00**
**MODEL M3 PUMP/AUTO SERIES**
   Standard stock, 19 3/4" barrel ...........**1,060.00**
   w/Ghost Ring Sight and standard stock .....**1,100.00**

### MONTEFELTRO VENT RIB
*Prices:*
12 Ga.—24", 26", or 28" Barrel
   (20 ga.—24" or 26" barrel only) ...........**$940.00**
Left Hand w/26" or 28" Barrel. ..............**960.00**
20 ga. w/Camo Wood, 26" VR ............**1,040.00**

**SHOTGUNS**

# BERETTA SHOTGUNS

**SERIES 682 GOLD COMPETITION TRAP OVER/UNDER**

**MODEL 682 GOLD TRAP W/ADJUSTABLE STOCK**

These 12 gauge Model 682 Trap guns feature adjustable gold-plated, single-selective sliding trigger; low-profile improved boxlock action; manual safety w/barrel selector; 2.75" chambers; auto ejector; competition recoil pad buttplate; hand-checkered walnut stock.
**Weight:** Approx. 8 lbs. **Barrel Lengths/Chokes:** 30 Imp. Mod./Full (Black); 30" or 32" Mobilchoke® (Black); Top

Single 32" or 34" Mobilchoke®; Combo: 30" or 32" Mobilchoke® (Top), 30" IM/F (Top), 32" Mobilchoke® (Mono), 30" or 32" Mobilchoke® ported
**Prices:** MODEL 682 GOLD TRAP . . . . . . . . . . . . $3,100.00
MODEL 682 GOLD TRAP COMBO. . . . . . . . . . . . . 4,085.00
MODEL 682 GOLD TRAP w/Adjustable Stock. . . . . 3,625.00
   TOP COMBO . . . . . . . . . . . . . . . . . . . . 4,610.00

**MODEL 682 GOLD COMPETITION SKEET O/U**

This 12-gauge skeet gun sports a hand-checkerd premium walnut stock w/silver oval for initials, forged and hardened receiver w/Greyston finish, manual safety with trigger selector, auto ejector, silver inlaid on trigger guard.
**Action:** Low-profile hard chrome-plated boxlock **Trigger:**

Single adjustable sliding trigger **Barrels:** 28" bllued barrels with 2.75" chambers **Stock dimensions:** Length of pull 14.75"; drop at comb 1 3/8"; drop at heel 2.25" **Sights:** fluorescent front and metal middle bead **Weight:** Approx. 7.5 lbs.
**Price:** (incl. fitted case) . . . . . . . . . . . . . . . . . . $3,515.00

**MODEL 682 GOLD SPORTING**

These competition-stye sporting clays feature 28" or 30" barrels with four flush-mounted screw-in choke tubes (Full, Modified, Improved Cylinder and Skeet), pllus hand-checkered stock and forend of fine walnut, 2.75" or 3" chambers and adjustable trigger. MODEL 682 GOLD features Greystone finish–an ultra-durable finish in gunmetal grey w/gold accents. MODEL 686

ONYX SPORTING has black matte receiver and MODEL 686 SILVER PIGEON SPORTING has coin silver receiver with scroll engraving.
**Prices:** 682 GOLD SPORTING . . . . . . . . . . . . . . $3,100.00
   PORTED . . . . . . . . . . . . . . . . . . . . . . . . . . . . 3,230.00
686 ONYX SPORTING . . . . . . . . . . . . . . . . . . . . 1,620.00
686 SILVER PIGEON SPORTING . . . . . . . . . . . . . 1,915.00

# BERETTA SHOTGUNS

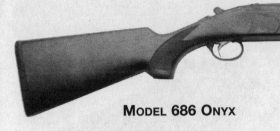

**MODEL 686 ONYX**

### SPECIFICATIONS
*Gauges:* 12, 20 *Chambers:* 3" and 3.5" *Barrel Lengths:* 26"" and 28" *Chokes:* Mobilchoke® screw-in system *Weight:* 6 lbs. 12 oz. (12 ga.); 6.2 lbs. (20 ga.) *Stock:* American walnut with recoil pad (English stock available) *Features:* Auto-matic ejectors; matte black finish on barrels and receiver to reduce glare
*Price:*................................. **$1,565.00**

**MODEL 687 SILVER PIGEON SPORTING**

This boxlock over/under features enhanced engraving pattern, schnabel forend and an electroless nickel finished receiver. *Chamber:* 3". Mobilchoke® screw-in tube system. *Gauges:* 12, 20 and 28 (Field Models)
*Prices:* MODEL 687 SILVER PIGEON SPORTING . . . **$2,340.00**
MODEL 687 SILVER PIGEON SPORTING COMBO . . . . **3,120.00**

## MODEL 687EELL DIAMOND PIGEON (not shown)
## MODEL 687EELL COMBO (20 and 28 ga.)
In 12, 20 or 28 ga., this model features the Mobilchoke® engraved choke system, a special premium walnut stock and silver receiver with engraved sideplate.
*Prices:*
MODEL 687 EELL DIAMOND PIGEON . . . . . . . . . . **$5,540.00**
MODEL 687EELL COMBO (20 and 28 ga.) . . . . . . **6,180.00**
*Also available:*
MODEL 687 EEL DIAMOND PIGEON TRAP O/U. . . . . **$4,815.00**
MODEL 687EELL DIAMOND PIGEON SKEET . . . . . . **4,935.00**
TRAP TOP MONO (Fuil) . . . . . . . . . . . . . . . . . . . **5,055.00**
TRAP TOP MONO FMCT . . . . . . . . . . . . . . . . . . . **5,105.00**
DIAMOND PIGEON SPORTING (12 ga.). . . . . . . . . . **5,680.00**
4-BARREL SET . . . . . . . . . . . . . . . . . . . . . . . . . . **8,405.00**

## MODEL 687EL GOLD PIGEON FIELD (not shown)
Features game-scene engraving on receiver with gold highlights. Available in 12, 20 gauge (28 ga. and .410 in small frame).

### SPECIFICATIONS
*Barrels/Chokes:* 26" and 28" with Mobilchoke®
*Action:* Low-profile improved boxlock
*Weight:* 6.8 lbs. (12 ga.)
*Trigger:* Single selective with manual safety
*Extractors:* Auto ejectors
*Prices:*
MODEL 687EL (12, 20, 26" or 28" bbl.) . . . . . . . . **$4,055.00**
MODEL 687EL SMALL FRAME (28 ga./.410). . . . . . **4,230.00**
MODEL 687EL SPORTING (12 ga. only). . . . . . . . . **4,140.00**

**MODEL ULTRALIGHT OVER/UNDER**

### SPECIFICATIONS
*Stock:* Select walnut *Features:* Nickel finish receiver w/game scene engraving; black rubber recoil pad; single selective trigger
*Price:*................................. **$1,850.00**
*Also available:*
ULTRALIGHT DELUXE w/matte electroless nickel finish receiver w/gold game scene engraving; walnut stock and forend; light aluminum alloy receiver reinforced w/titanium breech plate
*Price:*................................. **$2050.00**

# BERETTA SHOTGUNS

### MODEL 470 SILVER HAWK SIDE-BY-SIDE

**SPECIFICATIONS**
**Gauge:** 12 and 20  **Chamber:** 3"
**Action:** Low profile, improved box lock
**Choke:** IC/IM, M/F  **Barrel Length:** 26" and 28"  **Weight:** 6.5 lbs. (12 ga.); 5.9 lbs. (20 ga.)
**Sights:** Metal front bead  **Stock:** Select walnut, checkered

**Features:** Silver satin chrome finish on receiver, trigger guard, forend iron, top lever, trigger, trigger plate and safety/select lever; hand-chased scroll, engraving on receiver, top lever, forend iron and triggerguard; gold inlaid hawk's head on top lever. **Price:** 12 ga. . . . . . . . . . . . . . . . . . . . . . **$3,630.00**
20 ga. . . . . . . . . . . . . . . . . . . . . . . . . . . **$3,755.00**

### PINTAIL

This 12-gauge semiautomatic shotgun with short-recoil operation is available with 24" or 26" barrels and Mobilchoke®. Finish is nonreflective matte on alll exposed wood and metal surfaces; receiver is aluminum alloy.
**SPECIFICATIONS**
**Barrel Lengths:** 24", 26"; 24" Slug
**Weight:** 7.3 lbs.

**Stock:** Checkered selected hardwood
**Sights:** Bead front
**Price:** . . . . . . . . . . . . . . . . . . . . . . . . . . . . . **$840.00**
**Also Available:**
PINTAIL RIFLED SLUG featuring fully rifed barrel w/1 in 28" twist. Upper receiver and barrel permanently joined as one unit.
**Price:** . . . . . . . . . . . . . . . . . . . . . . . . . . . . . **$1,020.00**

### MODEL 1201 FP RIOT

This all-weather semiautomatic shotgun features an adjustable polymer stock and forend with recoil pad. Lightweight, it sports a unique weather-resistant matte black finish to reduce glare, resist corrosion and aid in heat dispersion; short recoil action for light and heavy loads, tritium sights.

**SPECIFICATIONS**
**Gauge:** 12  **Chamber:** 3"
**Capacity:** 6 rounds
**Choke:** Cylinder (fixed)  **Barrel Length:** 18"
**Weight:** 6.3 lbs.  **Sights:** Blade Front; adjustable rear
**Price:** . . . . . . . . . . . . . . . . . . . . . . . . . . . . . **$890.00**

# BERETTA SHOTGUNS

## FIELD GRADE SEMIAUTOMATICS

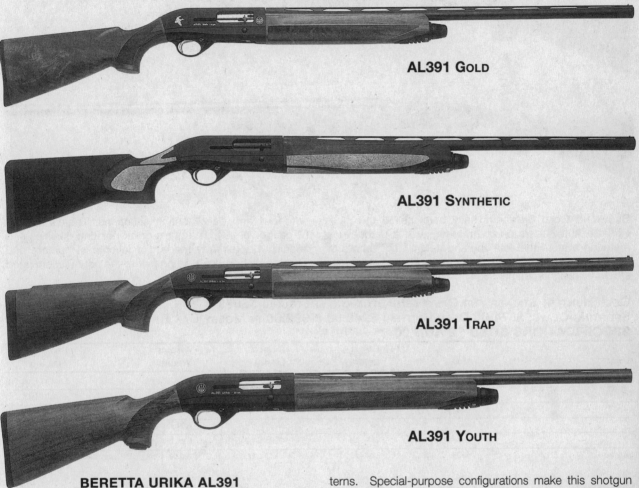

**AL391 GOLD**

**AL391 SYNTHETIC**

**AL391 TRAP**

**AL391 YOUTH**

SHOTGUNS

### BERETTA URIKA AL391 AUTOLOADING SHOTGUN

The new Beretta AL391 features a self-compensating gas valve that ensures reliable functioning with a wide range of factory loads, from skeet to heavy waterfowl charges. The valve is housed in a cylinder that stays with the barrel to permit quick and easy removal of the barrel. A gas valve flange on the front of the forend deflects gas away from the shooter. The gas system is remarkably compact, keeping forend bulk to a minimum. Recoil has been reduced by a small device at the rear of the receiver that cushions bolt thrust, and a spring and polymer ring inside the forend cap. Beretta considered details when designing this new gun, equipping the forend cap with a magnet so the sling swivel does not fall off during disassembly. Both synthetic and walnut stocks adjust for drop and cast via shims. The receiver is of lightweight alloy to limit weight (the lightest 12-bore weighs only 6.6 lbs.) Camouflage versions of the AL391 are available with Advantage, Wetlands and Realtree Hardwoods pat-

terns. Special-purpose configurations make this shotgun suitable for all clay-target games, and there's a youth model with smaller dimensions. All AL 391s, 12- and 20-gauge, are chambered for 2 3/4- and 3-inch shells. The guns come in a molded lockable case with five interchangeable chokes and wrenches, stock shims and two recoil pads, plus gun oil.

*Prices:*

| | |
|---|---:|
| Urika AL391 | $960.00 |
| Synthetic | 960.00 |
| Camouflage | 1,055.00 |
| Gold | 1,150.00 |
| Gold Lightwt. | 1,185.00 |
| Youth | 960.00 |
| Sporting | 1,000.00 |
| Gold Sporting | 1,195.00 |
| Gold Sporting (silver receiver) | 1,230.00 |
| Trap | 1,000.00 |
| Gold Trap | 1,195.00 |
| Parallel Target | 1,000.00 |

# BROWNING SHOTGUNS

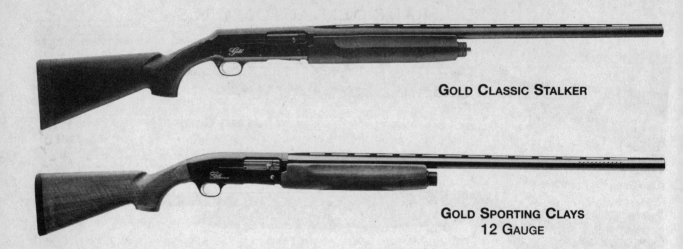

**GOLD CLASSIC STALKER**

**GOLD SPORTING CLAYS 12 GAUGE**

**BROWNING GOLD SHOTGUNS** have been called the most versatile autoloaders on the market, with a unique gas metering system that lets you shoot light 2.75" shells or heavy loads from 3.5" hulls. A huge assortment of barrels, stocks and sights adapts this shotgun to all upland game, waterfowl and deer hunting situations. There's even a 10-gauge version. The gun's quick pointing qualities and reliability has already made it a favorite of hunters and clay target shooters—a fitting heir to the now-discontinued **BROWNING AUTO 5**.

**GOLD HUNTER, STALKER AND CAMO SEMIAUTOMATIC SHOTGUNS: $867.00**
**SPORTING CLAYS: $874.00 DEER HUNTER: $940.00 ($992.00 IN MOSSY OAK BREAK UP CAMO)**
## SPECIFICATIONS GOLD 12 AND 20

| GAUGE | MODEL | BARREL LENGTH | OVERALL LENGTH | AVERAGE WEIGHT | CHOKES AVAILABLE |
|---|---|---|---|---|---|
| 12 | Hunting | 30" | 50.5" | 7 lbs. 9 oz. | Invector-Plus |
| 12 | Hunting | 28" | 48.5" | 7 lbs. 6 oz. | Invector-Plus |
| 12 | Hunting | 26" | 46.5" | 7 lbs. 3 oz. | Invector-Plus |
| 20 | Hunting | 28" | 48.25" | 6 lbs. 14 oz. | Invector |
| 20 | Hunting | 26" | 46.25" | 6 lbs. 12 oz. | Invector |

*Extra barrels: 24, 26, 28, 30" – 12 gauge 3.5": **$393.00**, Mossy Oak Camo: **$418.00** • 24,26,28, 30" – 12 and 20 gauge 3": **$320.00**, Mossy Oak Camo:**$347.00***

**DEER GUN**

## SPECIFICATIONS GOLD 10 HUNTING ($1,136.00) & STALKER ($1,100.00)

| CHAMBER | BARREL LENGTH | OVERALL LENGTH | AVERAGE WEIGHT | CHOKES |
|---|---|---|---|---|
| 3.5 | 30" | 52" | 10 lbs. 13 oz. | Standard Invector |
| 3.5 | 28" | 50" | 10 lbs. 10 oz. | Standard Invector |
| 3.5 | 26" | 48" | 10 lbs. 7 oz. | Standard Invector |

# BROWNING SHOTGUNS

### CITORI GRADE I HUNTING
### 12 GAUGE 3.5" MAGNUM

**Grade I** = Blued steel w/scroll engraving
**Grade III** = Grayed steel w/light relief   **Grade VI** = Blued or grayed w/engraved ringneck pheasants and mallard ducks;
**GL (Gran Lightning)** = High-grade wood w/satin finish

CITORI PRICES (all Invector-Plus chokes unless noted otherwise)
HUNTING MODELS (w/pistol-grip stock, beavertail forearm, high-gloss finish) 12 ga., 3.5" Mag.,28" & 30" barrels . . **$1,563.00**
Same as above in 12 & 20 ga. w/3" chamber 26", 28",
30" barrels . . . . . . . . . . . . . . . . . . . . . . . . . . **1,457.00**
SPORTING HUNTER 12 ga., 3.5" Mag., 28 & 30" barrels . **1,675.00**
Same as above in 12 & 20 ga. 3" chamber, 26", 28",
30" barrels . . . . . . . . . . . . . . . . . . . . . . . . . . **1,575.00**
SATIN HUNTER in 12 ga., 3.5" chamber, 26" & 28" barrel . . **1,490.00**
Same as above w/3" chamber . . . . . . . . . . . . . . . . **1,384.00**
WHITE LIGHTNING 12 & 20 ga., Grade I, 3" chamber . . . **1,552.00**
28 ga., 2.75" chamber . . . . . . . . . . . . . . . . . . . . **1,622.00**
410 ga., 3" chamber . . . . . . . . . . . . . . . . . . . . . **1,622.00**

LIGHTNING MODELS (w/classic rounded pistol grip, Lightning-style forearm) Grade I, 12 & 20 ga., 3" chamber 26"
& 28" barrels . . . . . . . . . . . . . . . . . . . . . . . . . **1,504.00**
Same as above in Grade GL . . . . . . . . . . . . . . . . . **2,080.00**
Grade III . . . . . . . . . . . . . . . . . . . . . . . . . . . . **2,190.00**
Grade VI . . . . . . . . . . . . . . . . . . . . . . . . . . . . **3,343.00**
MICRO LIGHTNING MODEL (20 Ga.) Grade I,
2.75" chamber, 24" barrel . . . . . . . . . . . . . . . . . **1,560.00**
SUPERLIGHT MODELS (w/straight-grip stock, slimmed-down Schnabel forearm; 2.75" chamber, 12 or 20 ga.)
Grade I . . . . . . . . . . . . . . . . . . . . . . . . . . . . . **1,514.00**
Grade III (12 ga. only) . . . . . . . . . . . . . . . . . . . . **2,190.00**
Grade VI . . . . . . . . . . . . . . . . . . . . . . . . . . . . **3,343.00**
LIGHTNING MODELS w/Standard Invector chokes (Lightning models only, 28 and .410 ga., 2.75" chamber, 26" & 28" barrels)
Grade I . . . . . . . . . . . . . . . . . . . . . . . . . . . . . **1,563.00**
Grade GL . . . . . . . . . . . . . . . . . . . . . . . . . . . . **2,192.00**
Grade III . . . . . . . . . . . . . . . . . . . . . . . . . . . . **2,448.00**
Grade VI . . . . . . . . . . . . . . . . . . . . . . . . . . . . **3,600.00**
Grade I Superlight Feather 12 ga. . . . . . . . . . . . . . **1,672.00**
XS 12,20 (28, .410) . . . . . . . . . . . . . . . . **2,132 (2,202.00)**
UPLAND SPECIAL (12 & 20 ga.)
Grade I only, 24" barrel . . . . . . . . . . . . . . . . . . . **1,514.00**

## CITORI FIELD MODEL SPECIFICATIONS

| Gauge | Model | Chamber | Barrel Length | Overall Length | Average Weight | Chokes Available 1 | Grades Available |
|---|---|---|---|---|---|---|---|
| 12 | Hunter | 3.5" Mag. | 30" | 47" | 8 lbs. 10 oz. | Invector-Plus | I |
| 12 | Hunter | 3.5" Mag. | 28" | 45" | 8 lbs. 9 oz. | Invector-Plus | I |
| 12 | Sporting Hunter | 3.5" Mag. | 30" | 47" | 8 lbs. 9 oz. | Invector-Plus | I |
| 12 | Sporting Hunter | 3" | 28" | 45" | 8 lbs. 5 oz. | Invector-Plus | I |
| 12 | Hunter | 3" | 30" | 47" | 8 lbs. 4 oz. | Invector-Plus | I |
| 12 | Hunter | 3" | 28" | 45" | 8 lbs. 1 oz. | Invector-Plus | I |
| 12 | Hunter | 3" | 26" | 43" | 7 lbs. 15 oz. | Invector-Plus | I |
| 12 | Sporting Hunter | 3" | 30" | 47" | 8 lbs. 5 oz. | Invector-Plus | I |
| 12 | Sporting Hunter | 3" | 28" | 45" | 8 lbs. 1 oz. | Invector-Plus | I |
| 12 | Sporting Hunter | 3" | 26" | 43" | 7 lbs. 13 oz. | Invector-Plus | I |
| 12 | Lightning | 3" | 28" | 45" | 8 lbs. 1 oz. | Invector-Plus | I, GL, III, VI |
| 12 | Lightning | 3" | 26" | 43" | 7 lbs. 15 oz. | Invector-Plus | I, GL, III, VI |
| 12 | White Lightning | 3" | 28" | 45" | 8 lbs. 1 oz. | Invector-Plus | I |
| 12 | White Lightning | 3" | 26" | 43" | 7 lbs. 13 oz. | Invector-Plus | I |
| 12 | Superlight | 2.75" | 28" | 45" | 6 lbs. 12 oz. | Invector-Plus | I, III, VI |
| 12 | Superlight | 2.75" | 26" | 43" | 6 lbs. 11 oz. | Invector-Plus | I, III, VI |
| 12 | Upland Special | 2.75" | 24" | 41" | 6 lbs. 9 oz. | Invector-Plus | I |
| 12 | Superlight Feather | 2.75" | 26" | 41" | 6 lbs. 6 oz. | Invector-Plus | I |
| 20 | Hunter | 3" | 28" | 45" | 6 lbs. 12 oz. | Invector-Plus | I |
| 20 | Hunter | 3" | 26" | 43" | 6 lbs. 10 oz. | Invector-Plus | I |
| 20 | Lightning | 3" | 28" | 45" | 6 lbs. 14 oz. | Invector-Plus | I, GL, III, VI |
| 20 | Lightning | 3" | 26" | 43" | 6 lbs. 9 oz. | Invector-Plus | I, GL, III, VI |
| 20 | Lightning | 3" | 24" | 41" | 6 lbs. 6 oz. | Invector-Plus | I |
| 20 | Micro Lightning | 2.75" | 24" | 41" | 6 lbs. 3 oz. | Invector-Plus | I |
| 20 | Superlight | 2.75" | 26" | 43" | 6 lbs. 3 oz. | Invector-Plus | I, III, VI |
| 20 | Upland Special | 2.75" | 24" | 41" | 6 lbs. | Invector-Plus | I |
| 28 | Lightning | 2.75" | 28" | 45" | 6 lbs. 11 oz. | Invector | I |
| 28 | Lightning | 2.75" | 26" | 43" | 6 lbs. 10 oz. | Invector | I, GL, III, VI |
| 28 | Superlight | 2.75" | 26" | 43 | 6 lbs. 10 oz. | Invector | I, III, VI |
| .410 | Lightning | 3" | 28" | 45" | 7 lbs. | Invector | I |
| .410 | Lightning | 3" | 26" | 43" | 6 lbs. 14 oz. | Invector | I, GL, III, VI |
| .410 | Superlight | 3" | 28" | 45" | 6 lbs. 14 oz. | Invector | I |
| .410 | Superlight | 3" | 26" | 43" | 6 lbs. 13 oz. | Invector | I, III, VI |

1. Full & Modified Choke installed; Improved Cylinder and wrench included. GL=Gran Lightning grade. New XS Models available in all 4 gauges, 28" and 30" barrels; weights from 6 lbs. 7 oz. to 8 lbs. 2 oz.

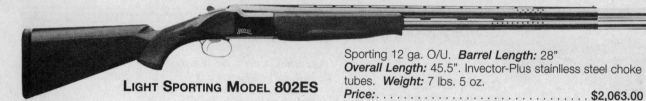

### LIGHT SPORTING MODEL 802ES

Sporting 12 ga. O/U. **Barrel Length:** 28"
**Overall Length:** 45.5". Invector-Plus stainlless steel choke tubes. **Weight:** 7 lbs. 5 oz.
**Price:** . . . . . . . . . . . . . . . . . . . . . . . . . . . . . . . . . . . . . . . . . $2,063.00

### CITORI MODEL 425 SPORTING CLAYS

### MODELS 425 AND ULTRA SPORTER (Not shown) (all Invector-Plus)

MODEL 425 (12 & 20 Ga.)
Grade I, 28", 30", 32" bbls . . . . . . . . . . . . . . $1,948.00
Grade GC (Golden Clays) . . . . . . . . . . . . . . . 3,788.00
For adjustable comb, **add** . . . . . . . . . . . . . . . 231.00

MODEL WSSF 12 Ga. only, 28" barrel, teal wood
    or walnut stock . . . . . . . . . . . . . . . . . . . . . 1,855.00
ULTRA SPORTER (12 Ga. only)
Grade I, Blue or Gray, 28", 30", 32" bbls . . . . . $1,800.00
Grade GC 28", 30", 32" barrels . . . . . . . . . . . . 3,396.00
For adjustable comb, **add** . . . . . . . . . . . . . . . 210.00
*WSSF = Women's Shooting Sports Foundation

## 425 & ULTRA SPORTER SPECIFICATIONS

| MODEL | CHAMBER | BARREL LENGTH | OVERALL LENGTH | AVERAGE WEIGHT | CHOKES AVAILABLE | GRADES AVAILABLE |
|---|---|---|---|---|---|---|
| **425** | | | | | | |
| 12 ga. | 2.75" | 32" | 49.5" | 7 lbs. 15 oz. | Invector-Plus | Gr. I, Golden Clays |
| 12 ga. | 2.75" | 30" | 47.5" | 7 lbs. 14 oz. | Invector-Plus | Gr. I, Golden Clays |
| 12 ga. | 2.75" | 28" | 45.5" | 7 lbs. 13 oz. | Invector-Plus | Gr. I, Golden Clays |
| 20 ga. | 2.75" | 30" | 47.5" | 6 lbs. 13 oz. | Invector-Plus | Gr. I, Golden Clays |
| 20 ga. | 2.75" | 28" | 45.5" | 6 lbs. 12 oz. | Invector-Plus | Gr. I, Golden Clays |
| WSSF 12 ga. Paint | 2.75" | 28" | 45.5" | 7 lbs. 4 oz. | Invector-Plus | Custom WSSF Exclusive |
| WSSF 12 ga. Walnut | 2.75" | 28" | 45.5" | 7 lbs. 4 oz. | Invector-Plus | Gr. I |
| **Ultra Sporter** | | | | | | |
| 12 ga. Sporter | 2.75" | 32" | 49" | 8 lbs. 4 oz. | Invector-Plus | Gr. I, Golden Clays |
| 12 ga. Sporter | 2.75" | 30" | 47" | 8 lbs. 2 oz. | Invector-Plus | Gr. I, Golden Clays |
| 12 ga. Sporter | 2.75" | 28" | 45" | 8 lbs. | Invector-Plus | Gr. I, Golden Clays |
| **Light Sporting 802 ES** | | | | | | |
| 12 ga. Sporter | 2.75" | 28" | 45" | 7 lbs. 5 oz. | Invector-Plus 802 ES Tubes* | Gr. I |

*Sporting Clays models: One modified, one Improved Cylinder and one Skeet tube supplied. Other chokes available as accessories. *Choke tubes included with 802 ES (Six tubes total)*

## SPECIFICATIONS SPECIAL SPORTING CLAYS, TRAP & SKEET & LIGHTNING SPORTING (prices on following page)

| GAUGE | MODEL | CHAMBER | BARREL LENGTH | OVERALL LENGTH | AVERAGE WEIGHT | CHOKES | GRADES AVAILABLE |
|---|---|---|---|---|---|---|---|
| **Special** | | | | | | | |
| 12 | Sporting Clays | 2.75" | 32" | 49" | 8 lbs. 5 oz. | Inv.-Plus | I, Golden Clays |
| 12 | Sporting Clays | 2.75" | 30" | 47" | 8 lbs. 3 oz. | Inv.-Plus | I, Golden Clays |
| 12 | Sporting Clays | 2.75" | 28" | 45" | 8 lbs. 1 oz. | Inv.-Plus | I, Golden Clays |
| 12 | Conventional Trap | 2.75" | 32" | 49" | 8 lbs. 11 oz. | Inv.-Plus | I, III, Golden Clays |
| 12 | Monte Carlo Trap | 2.75" | 32" | 49" | 8 lbs. 10 oz. | Inv.-Plus | I, III, Golden Clays |
| 12 | Skeet | 2.75" | 30" | 47" | 8 lbs. 7 oz. | Inv.-Plus | I, III, Golden Clays |
| 12 | Skeet | 2.75" | 30" | 47" | 8 lbs. 6 oz. | Inv.-Plus | I, III, Golden Clays |
| 12 | Skeet | 2.75" | 28" | 45" | 8 lbs. | Inv.-Plus | I, III, Golden Clays |
| 12 | Skeet | 2.75" | 26" | 43" | 7 lbs. 15 oz. | Inv.-Plus | I |
| 20 | Skeet | 2.75" | 28" | 45" | 7 lbs. 4 oz. | Inv.-Plus | I, III, Golden Clays |
| 20 | Skeet | 2.75" | 26" | 43" | 7 lbs. 1 oz. | Inv.-Plus | I |
| 28 | Skeet | 2.75" | 28" | 45" | 6 lbs. 15 oz. | Invector | I, III, Golden Clays |
| 28 | Skeet | 2.75" | 26" | 43" | 6 lbs. 10 oz. | Invector | I |
| .410 | Skeet | 2.5" | 28" | 45" | 7 lbs. 6 oz. | Invector | I, III, Golden Clays |
| .410 | Skeet | 2.5" | 26" | 43 | 7 lbs. 3 oz. | Invector | I |
| **Lightning Sporting*** | | | | | | | |
| 12 | Sporting Clays | 3" | 30" | 47" | 8 lbs. 8 oz. | Inv.-Pus | I, Golden Clays |
| 12 | Sporting Clays | 3" | 28" | 45" | 8 lbs. 6 oz. | Inv.-Plus | I, Golden Clays |

# BROWNING SHOTGUNS

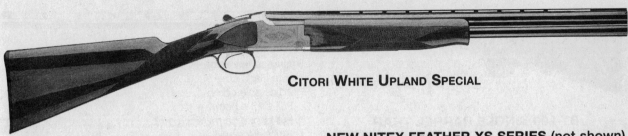

CITORI WHITE UPLAND SPECIAL

## NEW CITORI WHITE UPLAND SPECIAL

has a shorter, straight-grip stock Schnabel forend and 24" barrel, 12 or 20 ga., 2 3/4". Like all Citoris, the White Upland has backbored barrels and automatic ejectors.

*Price:.* . . . . . . . . . . . . . . . . . . . . . . . . . . . . . **1,552.00**

## NEW NITEX FEATHER XS SERIES (not shown)

Sporting clays shotguns with alloy receivers incorporating steel breech face.

*Prices:*

12, 20 ga.. . . . . . . . . . . . . . . . . . . . . . . . . . . . **$2,200.00**
28, .410 ga. . . . . . . . . . . . . . . . . . . . . . . . . . . **2,270.00**

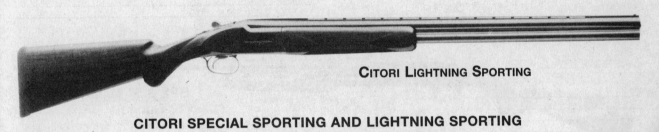

CITORI LIGHTNING SPORTING

## CITORI SPECIAL SPORTING AND LIGHTNING SPORTING

Many of these lively over/under shotguns are available with ported barrels, adjustable combs, the option of high or low ribs. Prices on request to Browning.

*Prices:*
**SPECIAL SPORTING**
Grade I, ported barrels . . . . . . . . . . . . . . . . . **$1,636.00**

**LIGHTNING SPORTING**
Grade I, high rib, ported bbl., 3". . . . . . . . . . . **$1,718.00**
Grade I, high rib, adj. comb . . . . . . . . . . . . . . **1,856.00**
Golden Clays, high rib, adj. comb . . . . . . . . . . **3,507.00**
**SPORTING HUNTER**
Grade I, 3.5" chamber, tapered rib, 12 ga. . . . . **$1,595.00**
Grade I, 3" chamber, 12 & 20 ga., tapered rib. . . **1,500.00**

*(See previous page for specifications)*

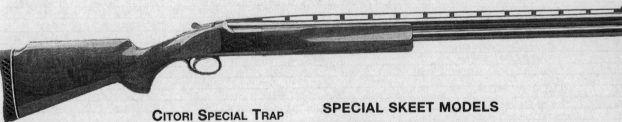

CITORI SPECIAL TRAP

## SPECIAL SKEET MODELS

*Prices:*
**12 & 20 GAUGE, INVECTOR-PLUS, PORTED BARRELS**
Grade I, high post rib . . . . . . . . . . . . . . . . . . . **$1,742.00**
Grade III, high post rib. . . . . . . . . . . . . . . . . . . **2,310.00**
Golden Clays, high post rib . . . . . . . . . . . . . . . **3,434.00**
**28 GA. AND .410 BORE STD. INVECTOR**
Grade I, high post rib . . . . . . . . . . . . . . . . . . . **$1,627.00**
Grade III, high post rib. . . . . . . . . . . . . . . . . . . **2,316.00**
Golden Clays, high post rib . . . . . . . . . . . . . . . **3,356.00**

## SPECIAL TRAP MODELS

*Prices:*
**12 GAUGE, INVECTOR-PLUS, PORTED BARRELS**
Grade I, Monte Carlo stock . . . . . . . . . . . . . . **$1,658.00**
Grade III, Monte Carlo stock . . . . . . . . . . . . . . **2,310.00**
Golden Clays, Monte Carlo stock. . . . . . . . . . . **3,434.00**

# BROWNING SHOTGUNS

**BT-100 TRAP**

## BT-100 SINGLE BARREL TRAP

**GRADE I, INVECTOR-PLUS**

| | |
|---|---|
| Monte Carlo stock. . . . . . . . . . . . . . . . . . . | $2,116.00 |
| Adjustable comb . . . . . . . . . . . . . . . . . . | 2,338.00 |
| Full choke barrel . . . . . . . . . . . . . . . . . . | 2,046.00 |
| Full choke barrel, adj. comb . . . . . . . . . . | 2,266.00 |
| Thumbhole stock . . . . . . . . . . . . . . . . . . | 2,384.00 |
| Full choke barrel . . . . . . . . . . . . . . . . . . | 2,337.00 |

**LOW LUSTER**

Grade I, 12 ga., 32" and 34", adj. trigger pull,
conventional satin stock . . . . . . . . . . . . . . . . . . **1,684.00**

**STAINLESS, INVECTOR-PLUS**

| | |
|---|---|
| Monte Carlo stock. . . . . . . . . . . . . . . . . . . | 2,560.00 |
| Adjustable comb . . . . . . . . . . . . . . . . . . | 2,784.00 |
| Full choke barrel . . . . . . . . . . . . . . . . . . | 2,487.00 |
| Full choke barrel, adj. comb . . . . . . . . . . | 2,707.00 |
| Thumbhole stock . . . . . . . . . . . . . . . . . . | 2,825.00 |
| Full choke barrel . . . . . . . . . . . . . . . . . . | 2,778.00 |
| **TRIGGER ASSEMBLY REPLACEMENT** . . . . . . . . . . . . | 558.00 |

### STOCK DIMENSIONS BT-100

| | ADJUSTABLE CONVENTIONAL | THUMBHOLE | MONTE CARLO |
|---|---|---|---|
| Length of Pull | 14 3/8" | 14 3/8" | 14 3/8" |
| Drop at Comb | Adj.* | 1.75" | 1 9/16" |
| Drop at Monte Carlo | — | 1.25" | 1 7/16" |
| Drop at Heel | Adj.* | 2 1/8" | 2" |

*Adjustable Drop at Comb and Heel.

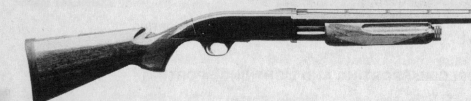

**BPS 3.5" MAGNUM**
(12 Gauge)

## BPS SPECIFICATIONS

| GAUGE | MODEL | CHAMBER | CAPACITY[2] | BARREL LENGTH | OVERALL LENGTH | AVERAGE WEIGHT | CHOKES AVAILABLE[1] |
|---|---|---|---|---|---|---|---|
| 10 Mag | Hunter & Stalker | 3.5" | 4 | 30, 28, 26, 24" | 46-52" | 9.25-9.5 lbs. | Invector |
| 12, 3.5" Mag | Hunter | 3.5" | 4 | 30, 28, 26, 24" | 45-51" | 7.5-8.5 lbs. | Invector-Plus |
| 12, 3.5" Mag | Stalker | 3.5" | 4 | 30, 28, 26, 24" | 45-51" | 7.5-8.5 lbs. | Invector-Plus |
| 12 | Hunter & Stalker | 3" | 4 | 30" | 50.75" | 7 lbs. 12 oz. | Invector-Plus |
| 12 | Hunter & Stalker | 3" | 4 | 28" | 48.75" | 7 lbs. 11 oz. | Invector-Plus |
| 12 | Hunter & Stalker | 3" | 4 | 26" | 46.75" | 7 lbs. 10 oz. | Invector-Plus |
| 12 | Standard Buck Special | 3" | 4 | 24" | 44.75" | 7 lbs. 10 oz. | Slug/Buckshot |
| 12 | Upland Special | 3" | 4 | 22" | 42.5" | 7 lbs. 8 oz. | Invector-Plus |
| 12 | Hunter & Stalker | 3" | 4 | 22" | 42.5" | 7 lbs. 7 oz. | Invector-Plus |
| 12 | Game Gun Turkey Special | 3" | 4 | 20.5" | 40 7/8" | 7 lbs. 7 oz. | Invector |
| 12 | Game Gun Deer Special/Rifled | 3" | 4 | 20.5" | 40 7/8" | 7 lbs. 7 oz. | Fully Rifled Barrel |
| 12 | Game Gun Deer Special/Smooth | 3" | 4 | 20.5" | 40 7/8" | 7 lbs. 7 oz. | Special Inv./Rifled |
| 12 | Game Gun Cantilever Mount | 3" | 4 | 20.5" | 40 7/8" | 7 lbs. 9 oz. | Fully Rifled |
| 20 | Hunter | 3" | 4 | 28" | 48.75" | 7 lbs. 1 oz. | Invector-Plus |
| 20 | Hunter | 3" | 4 | 26" | 46.75" | 7 lbs. | Invector-Plus |
| 20 | Micro | 3" | 4 | 22" | 41.75" | 6 lbs. 11 oz. | Invector-Plus |
| 20 | Upland Special | 3" | 4 | 22" | 42.75" | 6 lbs. 12 oz. | Invector-Plus |
| 28 | Hunter | 2.75" | 4 | 28" | 48.75" | 7 lbs. 1 oz. | Invector |
| 28 | Hunter | 2.75" | 4 | 26" | 46.75" | 7 lbs. | Invector |

## BPS FIELD MODEL PRICES

**SPECIFICATIONS**
*Prices:*

| | |
|---|---|
| HUNTER 3" chamber 26", 28", 30" barrels . . . . . . | $464.00 |
| STALKER, w/synthetic stock. . . . . . . . . . . . . . . | 448.00 |
| Camo . . . . . . . . . . . . . . . . . . . . . . . . | 525.00 |
| GAME GUN Deer Special (20.5" barrel) w/5" rifled slug choke tube . . . . . . . . . . . . . . . . | 500.00 |
| w/barrel for sabot slugs . . . . . . . . . . . . . . . . | 568.00 |
| SMALL GAUGE FIELD (28 gauge, 28" or 26") . . . . . . | 495.00 |
| MAGNUM MODELS Hunting & Stalker Grades (10 ga. and 12 ga.) w/3.5" Mag. chamber (26" and 28" barrels) Hunter . . . . . . . . . . . . . . | 552.00 |
| Stalker . . . . . . . . . . . . . . . . . . . . . . . . . . | 537.00 |
| w/Mossy Oak camo finish . . . . . . . . . . . . . . . | 613.00 |

# CHARLES DALY SHOTGUNS

## IMPORTED BY K.B.I., INC.

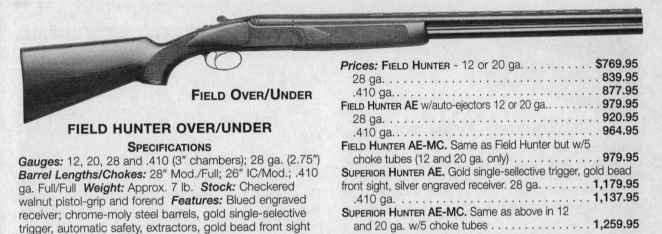

### FIELD OVER/UNDER

### FIELD HUNTER OVER/UNDER

#### SPECIFICATIONS

**Gauges:** 12, 20, 28 and .410 (3" chambers); 28 ga. (2.75")
**Barrel Lengths/Chokes:** 28" Mod./Full; 26" IC/Mod.; .410 ga. Full/Full **Weight:** Approx. 7 lb. **Stock:** Checkered walnut pistol-grip and forend **Features:** Blued engraved receiver; chrome-moly steel barrels, gold single-selective trigger, automatic safety, extractors, gold bead front sight

**Prices:** FIELD HUNTER - 12 or 20 ga. . . . . . . . . . . $769.95
   28 ga. . . . . . . . . . . . . . . . . . . . . . . . . . . . . 839.95
   .410 ga. . . . . . . . . . . . . . . . . . . . . . . . . . . . 877.95
FIELD HUNTER AE w/auto-ejectors 12 or 20 ga. . . . . . . . 979.95
   28 ga. . . . . . . . . . . . . . . . . . . . . . . . . . . . . 920.95
   .410 ga. . . . . . . . . . . . . . . . . . . . . . . . . . . . 964.95
FIELD HUNTER AE-MC. Same as Field Hunter but w/5 choke tubes (12 and 20 ga. only) . . . . . . . . . . . . 979.95
SUPERIOR HUNTER AE. Gold single-sellective trigger, gold bead front sight, silver engraved receiver. 28 ga. . . . . . . 1,179.95
   .410 ga. . . . . . . . . . . . . . . . . . . . . . . . . . 1,137.95
SUPERIOR HUNTER AE-MC. Same as above in 12 and 20 ga. w/5 choke tubes . . . . . . . . . . . . . 1,259.95

### SUPERIOR SPORTING

#### SPECIFICATIONS

**Gauges:** 12 (3" chambers) **Barrel Lengths/Chokes:** 28" & 30" with multi-choke (5 tubes) **Weight:** Approx. 7 lb.

**Stock:** Checkered walnut pistol-grip buttstock w/semi-beavertail forend **Features:** Silver engraved receiver, ported chrome-moly steel barrels, gold single-selective trigger, automatic safety, auto-ejectors, red bead front sight
**Prices:** SUPERIOR SPORTING . . . . . . . . . . . . . . . . . $1,259.95
SUPERIOR TRAP-MC. Same as above (2.75" chamber) 30" bbl. only . . . . . . . . . . . . 1,304.95

### EMPIRE EDL HUNTER

#### SPECIFICATIONS

**Gauges:** 12, 20, .410 ga. (3" chambers); 28 ga. (2.75")
**Barrel Lengths/Chokes:** 26" & 28"–5 multi-choke tubes in 12 & 20 ga.; 26" IC/M in 28 ga.; 26" Full/Full in .410 ga.
**Weight:** Approx. 7 lb. **Sights:** Red bead front; metal bead center **Stock:** Checkered walnut pistol-grip buttstock

w/semibeavertail forend **Features:** Silver engraved receiver, full sideplate, chrome-moly steel barrels, gold single-selective trigger, automatic safety, auto-ejector, recoil pad
**Prices:** EMPIRE EDL HUNTER
   12 or 20 ga. . . . . . . . . . . . . . . . . . . . . . . . $1,595.95
   28 ga. . . . . . . . . . . . . . . . . . . . . . . . . . . . 1,559.95
   .410 ga. . . . . . . . . . . . . . . . . . . . . . . . . . 1,599.95
EMPIRE SPORTING. 12 only, w/30" and 28" ported barrels, no metal bead center sight . . . . . . . . . . . . . . . . 1,499.95
EMPIRE TRAP-MC. 12 ga. w/30" bbl. (unported) metal bead center sight, recoil pad . . . . . . . . 1,539.95

### DIAMOND COMPETITION

**Prices:** DIAMOND SPORTING MC-5
   12 only, 28" or 30" bbl. . . . . . . . . . . . . . . $5,804.95
DIAMOND TRAP AE . . . . . . . . . . . . . . . . . . . . 6,639.95
DIAMOND TRAP MONO AE-MC. . . . . . . . . . . . . 6,539.95

**SHOTGUNS**

# CHARLES DALY SHOTGUNS

## IMPORTED BY K.B.I., INC.

### FIELD HUNTER SIDE BY SIDE

**SPECIFICATIONS**
*Gauges:* 10, 12, 20 and .410 (3" chambers); 28 ga. (2.75")
*Barrel Lengths/Chokes:* 32" Mod./Mod.; 30" Mod./Full;
28" Mod./Full; 26" IC/Mod.; .410 ga. Full/Full **Weight:**
Approx. 6 lbs.-11.4 lbs. **Stock:** Checkered walnut pistol-

grip and forend **Features:** Silver engraved receiver; gold
single-selective trigger in 10, 12 and 20 ga.; double trigger
in 28 and 410 ga.; automatic safety, extractors, gold bead
front sight. Imported from Spain
*Prices:*

| | |
|---|---:|
| 10 ga. | $984.95 |
| 12 or 20 ga. | 809.95 |
| 28 or .410 ga. | 854.95 |
| FIELD HUNTER-MC (5 multi-choke tubes) | |
| 12 or 20 ga. | 939.95 |

### SUPERIOR GRADE (not shown)

**SPECIFICATIONS**
*Gauges:* 12 and 20; 3" chambers
*Barrel Lengths/Chokes:* 28" Mod./Full; 26" IC/Mod.
*Weight:* Approx. 7 lb. **Stock:** Checkered walnut pistol-grip
buttstock and splinter forend
*Features:* Silver engraved receiver, chrome-lined steel
barrels, gold single trigger, automatic safety, extractors,
gold bead front sight
*Prices:*

| | |
|---|---:|
| SUPERIOR HUNTER (12 and 20) | $1,044.95 |
| 28 gauge | 1,084.95 |
| EMPIRE HUNTER | |
| Same as above w/hand-checkered stock auto ejectors, game scene engraved receiver | 1,339.95 |

### DIAMOND DL HUNTER (not shown)

**SPECIFICATIONS**
*Gauges:* 12, 20, .410 ga. (3" chambers; 28 ga. (2.75")
*Barrel Lengths/Chokes:* 28" Mod./Full; 26" IC/Mod.; 26"
Full/Full in .410 ga. **Weight:** Approx. 5-7 lbs.
*Stock:* Select fancy European walnut, English-styled,
beavertail forend, hand-checkered, hand-rubbed oil finish
*Features:* Fine steel drop-forged action with gas escape
valves; fine steel demiblock barrels w/concave rib; selective
auto ejectors, hand-detachable double safety sidelocks
w/hand-engraved rose and scrollwork; front-hinged trigger,
casehardened receiver. Imported from Spain.
*Prices:*

| | |
|---|---:|
| DIAMOND DL 12 or 20 ga. | $6,959.95 |
| 28 or .410 ga. | 7,274.95 |

## RIFLE/SHOTGUN COMBINATION GUNS

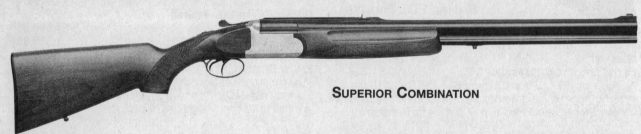

### SUPERIOR COMBINATION

**SPECIFICATIONS**
*Gauge/Calibers:* 12/22 Hornet, 223 Rem.,
30-06 Sprgfld.
*Barrel Length/Choke:* 23.5", shotgun choke IC
*Weight:* Approx. 7.5 lbs.
*Stock:* Checkered walnut pistol-grip buttstock and
semi-beavertail forend

**Features:** Silver engraved receiver forged and milled from
a solid block of high-strength steel; chrome-moly steel barrels, double trigger, extractors, sling swivels, gold bead
front sight
*Prices:*

| | |
|---|---:|
| SUPERIOR COMBINATION | $1,249.95 |
| EMPIRE COMBINATION. Same as above w/deluxe walnut European-style comb/cheekpiece, slim forend | 1,849.95 |

# DAKOTA ARMS INC.

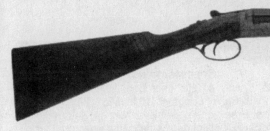

**DAKOTA ARMS AMERICAN LEGEND**
(LIMITED EDITION)

### DAKOTA LEGEND SHOTGUNS

**PREMIER GRADE**

Exhibition Engllish Walnut wood, French Grey Finish, 50% coverage engraving, straight grip, splinter forend, hand rubbed oil finish, double trigger, 27" barrels, game rib with gold bead, selective ejectors, choice of chokes, and Americase.

*Price:* . . . . . . . . . . . . . . . . . . . . . . . . . . . . . . . $12,950.00

**LEGEND GRADE**

Special Selection English Walnut, 27" barrel, game rib, straight grip, splinter forend, double triggers, round aciton, French Grey finish, selective ejectors, checkered butt, stock oval, full coverage scroll engraving, choice of chokes, gold bead, oak and leather case.

*Price:* . . . . . . . . . . . . . . . . . . . . . . . . . . . . . . . $18,000.00

# FOX SHOTGUNS

**DE GRADE ENGRAVED SHOTGUN**

### CUSTOM BOXLOCKS

**SPECIFICATIONS**

*Gauges:* 16, 20, 28 and .410  *Barrel:* Any barrel lengths and chokes; rust blued Chromox or Krupp steel barrels *Weight:* 5 /to 6/lbs.  *Stock:* Custom stock dimensions including cast; hand-checkered Turkish Circassian walnut stock and forend with hand-rubbed oil finish; straight grip, full pistol grip (with cap), or semi-pistol grip; splinter, schnabel or beavertail forend; traditional pad, hard rubber plate, checkered, or skeleton butt *Features:* Boxlock action with automatic ejectors; scalloped, rebated and color casehardened receiver; double or Fox single selective trigger; hand-finished and hand-engraved. This is the same gun that was manufactured between 1905 and 1930 by the A.H. Fox Gun Company of Philadelphia, PA, now manufactured in the U.S. by the Connecticut Shotgun Mfg. Co. (New Britain, CT).

**Prices:***

| | |
|---|---|
| CE GRADE . . . . . . . . . . . . . . . . . . . . . . . . . . . . | $9,500.00 |
| XE GRADE . . . . . . . . . . . . . . . . . . . . . . . . . . . . | 11,000.00 |
| DE GRADE . . . . . . . . . . . . . . . . . . . . . . . . . . . . | 13,500.00 |
| FE GRADE . . . . . . . . . . . . . . . . . . . . . . . . . . . . | 18,500.00 |
| EXHIBITION GRADE . . . . . . . . . . . . . . . . . . . . . | 26,000.00 |

*\*Grades differ in engraving and inlay, grade of wood and amount of hand finishing needed.*

**SHOTGUNS**

# HARRINGTON & RICHARDSON

## SINGLE-BARREL SHOTGUNS

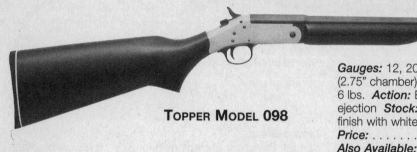

### TOPPER MODEL 098

**SPECIFICATIONS**
**Gauges:** 12, 20 and .410 (3" chamber); 16 and 28 ga. (2.75" chamber) **Barrel Lengths:** 26" and 28" **Weight:** 5 to 6 lbs. **Action:** Break-open; side lever release; automatic ejection **Stock:** Full pistol grip; American hardwood; black finish with white buttplate spacer **Length Of Pull:** 14.5"
**Price:** . . . . . . . . . . . . . . . . . . . . . . . . . . . . . $116.95
**Also Available:** TOPPER DELUXE - MODEL 098 12 ga. 28" mod screw in choke 3.5" . . . . . . . . . . . . . . . . 136.95

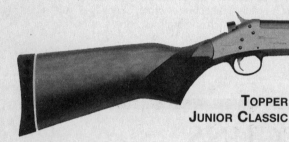

### TOPPER JUNIOR CLASSIC

**SPECIFICATIONS**
Same specifications as the Standard Topper, but with 22" barrel, hand checkered American black walnut stock and 12.5" pull. **Gauges:** 20, 28, and .410.
**Price:** . . . . . . . . . . . . . . . . . . . . . . . . . . . . . . . $150.95

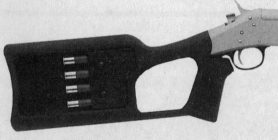

### .410 TAMER SHOTGUN

This barreled .410 snake gun features single-shot action, transfer-bar safety and high-impact synthetic stock and forend. Stock has a thumbhole design that sports a full pistol grip and a recessed open side, containing a holder for storing ammo. Forend is modified beavertail configuration. Other features include a matte, electroless nickel finish.
**Weight:** 5-6 lbs. **Barrel Length:** 20" (3" chamber)
**Choke:** Full
**Price:** . . . . . . . . . . . . . . . . . . . . . . . . . . . . . . . $128.95

### ULTRA SLUG HUNTER

**Features:** 12 or 20 gauge 24" barrel, 3" chamber, fully rifled heavy slug barrel (1:35" twist); Monte Carlo stock and forend of American hardwood w/dark walnut stain; matte black receiver; transfer-bar system; scope rail, swivels and sling; ventilated recoil pad.
**Price:** . . . . . . . . . . . . . . . . . . . . . . . . . . . . . . . $207.95

**Also available:**
ULTRA YOUTH SLUG HUNTER. Features 12-gauge barrel blank underbored to 20 gauge and shortened to 22"; factory-mounted Weaver-style scope base; reduced Monte Carlo stock of American hardwood with dark walnut stain; vent recoil pad, sling swivels and black nylon sling.
**Price:** . . . . . . . . . . . . . . . . . . . . . . . . . . . . . . . $207.95

# HECKLER & KOCH SHOTGUNS

## FABARM SERIES

### HECKLER & KOCH FABARMS SHOTGUNS

Heckler & Koch shotguns have features for top ballistic performance and durability, plus fine handling qualities. Double guns are built on milled steel or alloy monoblocs, with single selective triggers, interchangeable chokes, hand-checkered walnut stocks. They're chambered for 3"shells (turkey and waterfowl models for 3.5-inch magnums). Autoloaders are gas-operated with no parts in the buttstock. They have fixed ejectors and shim-adjustable buttstocks. Camouflage models are available. Pump guns have synthetic stocks, double action bars and Picatinny rails for scopes. Weights vary on all models, depending on gauge and barrel length. Youth and special-purpose shotguns are part of the line.

### FABARM'S TRIBORE BARREL SYSTEM

The ported TriBore Barrel System consists of three distinct internal bore profiles. It offers the advantages of back-boring, but with even less recoil. The first or "overbore" region is just in front of the chamber and forcing cone. Its .7401 diameter reduces pressure and kick. A second bore, or "first choke", is in the middle of the barrel and gradually takes inside diameter to .7244 (cylinder bore), allowing the shot to attain its maximum velocity. The third bore consists of standard choking, followed by a cylinder area at the muzzle so as to let the charge exit with no disruption, to improve downrange pellet distribution.

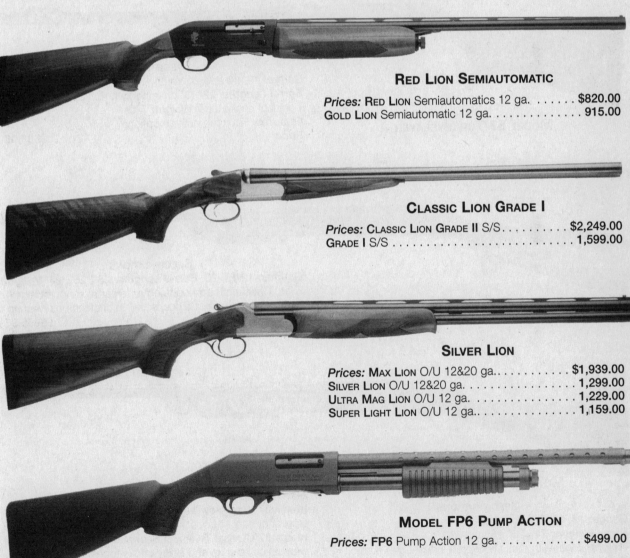

### RED LION SEMIAUTOMATIC

**Prices:** RED LION Semiautomatics 12 ga. . . . . . . $820.00
GOLD LION Semiautomatic 12 ga. . . . . . . . . . . . . 915.00

### CLASSIC LION GRADE I

**Prices:** CLASSIC LION GRADE II S/S . . . . . . . . . $2,249.00
GRADE I S/S . . . . . . . . . . . . . . . . . . . . . . . . . . 1,599.00

### SILVER LION

**Prices:** MAX LION O/U 12&20 ga. . . . . . . . . . . $1,939.00
SILVER LION O/U 12&20 ga. . . . . . . . . . . . . . . 1,299.00
ULTRA MAG LION O/U 12 ga. . . . . . . . . . . . . . 1,229.00
SUPER LIGHT LION O/U 12 ga. . . . . . . . . . . . . 1,159.00

### MODEL FP6 PUMP ACTION

**Prices:** FP6 Pump Action 12 ga. . . . . . . . . . . . $499.00

# ITHACA SHOTGUNS

## MODEL 37 DEERSLAYER II 12 GA.

### SPECIFICATIONS
*Gauges:* 12 or 20 (3" chamber)
*Barrel Lengths:* 20" or 25"
*Choke:* Rifled bore; or smooth bore
*Weight:* 7 lbs.  *Stock:* Monte Carlo cut-checkered walnut stock and forend
*Price:* . . . . . . . . . . . . . . . . . . . . . . . . . . . . . . . . . . $585.95

## MODEL 37 TURKEYSLAYER

### SPECIFICATIONS
*Gauge:* 12, 20 and 20 Youth
*Barrel Lengths:* 22" (3" chamber) withTurkey Tightshot choke tube  *Weight:* 7 lbs.
*Features:* Four camouflage options
*Price:* . . . . . . . . . . . . . . . . . . . . . . . . . . . . . . . . . . $585.95

## CLASSIC 37

### SPECIFICATIONS
*Gauges:* 12,16, 20  *Barrel Lengths:* 28", 26", 24"  *Weight:* 7 lbs. Checkered corncob ringtail forearm, sunburst recoil pad, American walnut stock, screw-in choke tubes, vent rib
*Price:* . . . . . . . . . . . . . . . . . . . . . . . . . . . . . . . . . . $695.95

## MODEL 37 ENGLISH VERSION

### SPECIFICATIONS
*Gauge:* 12, 16, 20 (3" chamber)
*Barrel Lengths:* 24", 26", 28" and 30"
*Weight:* 7 lbs. with slim, checkered straight-grip stock
*Price:* . . . . . . . . . . . . . . . . . . . . . . . . . . $569.95

*Also Available:*
ITHACA 37 WATERFOWLER with extended choke tube for steel shot . . . . . . . . . . . . . . . . . . . . . . . . . $625.95
ITHACA 37 CLASSIC TRAP AND SPORTING CLAYS shotguns with special stocks and Briley choke tubes. Adjustable stocks optional . . . . . . . . . . . . . . . . . . . . . . . . 1,295.00

# KRIEGHOFF SHOTGUNS

**MODEL K-20, 20 GAUGE, 30", SUPER SCROLL NICKEL**

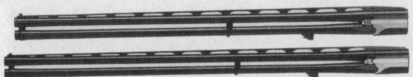

*K-20 Extra barrels, 28 Gauge, 28" and 30". Also available in .410*

## SPECIFICATIONS

**Barrels:** 20 ga/3" (28" Choke Tubes (5) Tapered flat rib, 11-7, 5 mm); 20 ga/3" (30" Choke Tubes (5) Tapered flat rib, 11-7, 5 mm); 28 ga/3" (28" Choke Tubes (5) Tapered flat rib, 10, 5-7 mm); 28 ga/3" (30" Choke Tubes (5) Tapered flat rib, 10, 5-7 mm); .410/3" (28" Choke Tubes (5) Tapered flar rib, 9,5-6mm); .410/3" (30" Choke Tubes (5) Tapered flar rib, 9,5-6mm)

**Chokes:** Choke Tubes (CT) bottom and top, 5 included. Available are Cylinder (C), Skeet (S), Improved Cylinder (IC), Modified (M), Improved Modified (IM), Full (F).

**Sights:** White pearl front bead and metal center bead

**Action:** Case hardened, nickel plated steel with satin grey finish **Trigger:** Single selective mechanical trigger, adjustable for finger length.

**Trigger pull:** Approximately 3-1/2 to 4 lbs.

**Safety:** Top tang push button safety. Can be locked in "off" position.

**Stocks:** Hand-checkered select European walnut with satin epoxy finish.

**Standard stocks are:** # 3 Sporting/International Skeet. #9 Skeet/Field.

**Forearm Standard:** # VII Schnabel.

**Grade:** Standard is classic scroll engraving, similar to the K-80.

**Weight:** Approximately 7 1/4 lbs.

**Case:** All K-20 sporting guns come in a fitted aluminum case holding one, two or three sets of barrels.

**Prices:** . . . . . . . . . . . . . . . . . . . . . . . . . . .**Price on request**

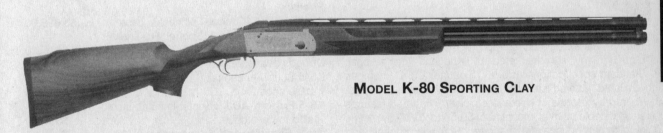

**MODEL K-80 SPORTING CLAY**

## MODEL K-80 TRAP, SKEET, SPORTING CLAY AND LIVE BIRD

**Barrels:** Made of Boehler steel; free-floating bottom barrel with adjustable point of impact; standard Trap and Live Pigeon ribs are tapered step; standard Skeet, Sporting Clay and International ribs are tapered or parallel flat.

**Receivers:** Hard satin-nickel finish; casehardened; blue finish available as special order

**Triggers:** Wide profile, single selective, position adjustable.

**Weight:** 8 1/2" lbs. (Trap); 8 lbs. (Skeet)

**Ejectors:** Selective automatic

**Sights:** White pearl front bead and metal center bead

**Stocks:** Hand-checkered and epoxy-finished Select European walnut stock and forearm; stocks available in seven different styles and dimensions

**Safety:** Push button safety located on top tang.

**Also available:**

**SKEET SPECIAL** 28" and 30" barrel; tapered flat or 8mm rib; 5 choke tubes.

**Price:** Standard . . . . . . . . . . . . . . . . . . . . . .**$7,575.00**

# KRIEGHOFF SHOTGUNS

## SPECIFICATIONS AND PRICES MODEL K-80 *(see also preceding page)*

| MODEL | DESCRIPTION | BBL. LENGTH | CHOKE | STANDARD | BAVARIA | DANUBE | GOLD TARGET | EXTRA BARRELS |
|---|---|---|---|---|---|---|---|---|
| TRAP | Over & Under | 30"/32" | IMI/F | $7,375.00 | $12,525.00 | $23,625.00 | $27,170.00 | $2,900.00 |
| | | 30"/32" | CT/CT | 8,025.00 | 13,175.00 | 24,275.00 | 27,820.00 | 3,550.00 |
| | Unsingle | 32"/34" | Full | 7,950.00 | 13,100.00 | 24,200.00 | 27,745.00 | 3,575.00 |
| | Combo | 30" + 34" | IM/F&F | 10,475.00 | 15,625.00 | 26,725.00 | 30,270.00 | |
| | (Top Single) | 32" + 34" | CT/CT&CT | 11,550.00 | 16,700.00 | 27,800.00 | 31,345.00 | |
| | | 30" + 32" | | | | | | |
| | Combo | 30" + 34" | IM/F&F | 9,975.00 | 15,125.00 | 26,225.00 | 29,770.00 | 2,950.00 |
| | (Unsingle) | | | | | | | |
| | | 32" + 34" | CT/CT&CT | 11,050.00 | 16,200.00 | 27,300.00 | 30,845.00 | 3,375.00 |
| **Optional Features:** | | | | | | | | |
| Screw-in chokes (Top or Unsingle) | | $425.00 | | | | | | |
| Single factory release | | 425.00 | | | | | | |
| Double factory release | | 750.00 | | | | | | |
| SKEET | 4-Barrel Set | 28"/12 ga. | Tula | | | | | $2,990.00 |
| | | 28"/20 ga. | Skeet | | | | | 2,880.00 |
| | | 28"/28 ga. | Skeet | $16,950.00 | $22,100.00 | $33,200.00 | $36,745.00 | 2,990.00 |
| | | 28"/.410 ga. | Skeet | | | | | 2,880.00 |
| | 2-Barrel Set | 28"/12 ga. | Tula | 11,840.00 | 16,990.00 | 28,090.00 | 31,635.00 | 4,150.00 |
| | Lightweight | 28" + 30"/12 ga. | Skeet | 6,900.00 | N/A | N/A | N/A | 2,650.00 |
| | 1-Barrel Set | 28" | Skeet | 8,825.00 | 13,975.00 | 25,075.00 | 28,620.00 | 4,150.00 |
| | International | 28"/12 ga. | Tula | 7,825.00 | 12,975.00 | 24,075.00 | 27,620.00 | 2,990.00 |
| | Skeet Special | | | 7,575.00 | 12,725.00 | 23,825.00 | 27,370.00 | 3,300.00 |
| SPORTING CLAYS | Over/Under w/screw-in tubes (5) | 28" + 30" + 32"/ 12 ga. 30" Semi-Light | Tubes IC/ICTF | $8,150.00 | $13,300.00 | $24,400.00 | $27,945.00 | $2,900.00 |

*Optional engravings:  Super Scroll – $1,995.00:  Gold Super Scroll – $4,450.00:  Parcours – $2,100.00;  Parcours Special – $3,950.00*

## MODEL KS-5

The KS-5 is a single barrel trap gun made by KRIEGHOFF, Ulm/Germany and marketed by Krieghoff International. Standard specifications include: 12 gauge, 2 3/4" chamber, ventilated tapered step rip, and a casehardened receiver (satin gray finished in electroless nickel). The KS-5 features an adjustable point of impact from 50/50 to 70/30 by means of different optional fronthangers. Screw-in chokes and factory adjustable comb stocks are available options. An adjustable rib (AR) and comb stock (ADJ) are standard features.

The KS-5 is available with pull trigger or optional factory release trigger, adjustable externally for poundage. The KS-5 can be converted to release by the installation of the release parts. To assure consistency and proper functioning, release triggers are installed ONLY by Krieghoff International. Release parts are NOT available separately. These shotguns are available in Standard grade only. Engraved models can be special ordered.

**Prices:**
KS-5 32" or 34" barrel, Full choke, case . . . . . .$3,695.00
KS-5 SPECIAL 32" or 34" barrel, Full choke,
   AR ADJ, cased . . . . . . . . . . . . . . . . . . . . . . . .4,695.00

**Options available:**
KS-5 SCREW-IN CHOKES (M, IM, F), add to
   base price . . . . . . . . . . . . . . . . . . . . . . . . . . .$425.00
KS-5 FACTORY ADJ (adjustable comb stock),
   **add** to base price . . . . . . . . . . . . . . . . . . . . . .$395.00

**Other Features and Accessories:**
KS-5 REGULAR BARREL . . . . . . . . . . . . . . . . . .$2,100.00
KS-5 SPECIAL BARREL (F) . . . . . . . . . . . . . .2,750.00
KS-5 SCREW-IN CHOKE BARREL . . . . . . . . . . .2,525.00
KS-5 SPECIAL SCREW-IN CHOKE BARREL . . . . . .3,175.00
KS-5 FACTORY ADJUSTABLE STOCK . . . . . . . . .1,145.00
KS-5 STOCK . . . . . . . . . . . . . . . . . . . . . . . . . . .750.00
KS-5 FOREARM . . . . . . . . . . . . . . . . . . . . . . . . .290.00
KS-5 RELEASE TRIGGER (INSTALLED) . . . . . . . . . . . .295.00
KS-5 FRONTHANGER . . . . . . . . . . . . . . . . . . . . . .70.00
KL-5 ALUMINUM CASE . . . . . . . . . . . . . . . . . . . .425.00
KS-5 INDIVIDUAL CHOKE TUBES . . . . . . . . . . . . . .75.00

# LUGER BY STOEGER SHOTGUNS

**CLASSIC OVER/UNDER**

## LUGER CLASSIC OVER/UNDER SHOTGUN

The new Luger Classic over/under shotgun offers all the features you would expect to find on guns costing twice as much. Standard features include flush-mounted screw-in choke tubes, deeply polished chrome lined barrels, a gold single selective trigger and automatic ejectors. It comes with a hand-checkered select grade European walnut stock and forend. The deeply blued low-profile receiver features classic engraving.

**Price:** . . . . . . . . . . . . . . . . . . . . . . . . . . . . . . .**$919.00**

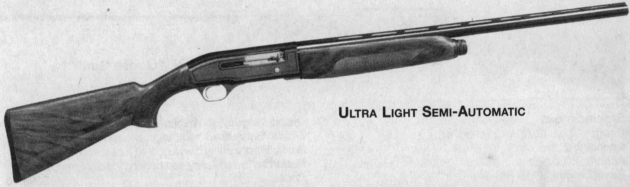

**ULTRA LIGHT SEMI-AUTOMATIC**

## LUGER ULTRA LIGHT SEMI-AUTOMATIC

Quality and craftsmanship immediately come to mind when you see Luger's new semi-automatic shotgun. The classic lines with a richly blued barrel and receiver are complemented by the high-grade glossy finish European walnut stock and forend. This gas-operated semi-auto weighs only 6.5 pounds and handles 2 3/4" light loads as well as 3" magnums. Recessed screw-in choke tubes give flexibility and the chrome lined barrel has been designed to handle steel shot.

**Price:** . . . . . . . . . . . . . . . . . . . . . . . . . . . . . . .**$479.00**

## SPECIFICATIONS

| MODEL | GAUGE 12 | BARREL LENGTH 26" | BARREL LENGTH 28" | BARREL LENGTH 30" | CHOKES CHOKE TUBES | SPECIFICATIONS CHAMBER | SPECIFICATIONS WEIGHT | SPECIFICATIONS TRIGGER | SAFETY MANUAL | BUTT PLATES MOLDED | BUTT PLATES SOFT RUBBER | RIB | LENGTH OF PULL | DROP AT COMB | DROP AT HEEL | OVERALL LENGTH |
|---|---|---|---|---|---|---|---|---|---|---|---|---|---|---|---|---|
| ULTRA-LIGHT | ■ | ■ | | | FM/IC | 3" | 6.5 | S.T. | ■ | ■ | | 1/4" | 14 3/8" | 1.5" | 2.25" | 46" |
| ULTRA-LIGHT | ■ | | ■ | | FM/IC | 3" | 6.5 | S.T. | ■ | ■ | | 1/4" | 14 3/8" | 1.5" | 2.25" | 48" |
| CLASSIC FIELD | ■ | ■ | | | FM/IC | 3.5" | 7.5 | S.S.T. | ■ | | ■ | 1/4" | 14 3/8" | 1.5" | 2 1/8" | 43" |
| CLASSIC FIELD | ■ | | ■ | | FM/IC | 3.5" | 7.5 | S.S.T. | ■ | | ■ | 1/4" | 14 3/8" | 1.5" | 2 1/8" | 45" |
| CLASSIC FIELD | ■ | | | ■ | FM/IC | 3.5" | 7.5 | S.S.T. | ■ | | ■ | 1/4" | 14 3/8" | 1.5" | 2 1/8" | 47" |
| CLASSIC SPORTER | ■ | | | ■ | FM/IC | 3" | 8 | S.S.T. | ■ | | ■ | 7/16" | 14 1/8" | 1 7/8" | 2 3/8" | 47" |

# MARLIN SHOTGUNS

**GARDEN GUN**

## MARLIN GARDEN GUN

The Garden Gun is a mini-shotgun chambered for the .22 Winchester Magnum shotshell. A 22-inch smooth bore barrel, 7-shot box magazine and hardwood stock make this an ideal pest gun for orchard and yard as well as gardens. *Length:* 41", *Weight:* 6 pounds.
*Price:* . . . . . . . . . . . . . . . . . . . . . . . . . . . . . . . . . . . $231.00

## MODEL 55GDL "GOOSE GUN"

**SPECIFICATIONS**
*Gauge:* 12 ga. (2.75" or 3" chamber)
*Capacity:* 2-shot clip
*Action:* Bolt action
*Barrel Length:* 36" full choke

*Overall Length:* 56" *Weight:* 8 lbs.
*Sights:* Brass bead front; U-groove rear
*Stock:* Black synthetic w/ventilated rubber recoil pad
*Features:* Thumb safety; red cocking indicator; swivel studs
*Price:* . . . . . . . . . . . . . . . . . . . . . . . . . . . . . . . . . . . $396.00

## MODEL 512P SLUGMASTER
### WITH PORTED BARREL

**MODEL 512P**

**SPECIFICATIONS**
*Guage:* 12 (up to 3" shells)
*Capacity:* 2-shot box magazine (+1 in chamber)
*Action:* Bolt action; thumb safety; red cocking indicator
*Barrel Length:* 21" rifled (1:28" right-hand twist) and ported
*Overall Length:* 41.75"
*Weight:* 8 lbs. (w/o scope and mount)

*Sights:* Adjustable rear, ramp front fire sights with high-visibility fiber-optic inserts and cutaway Wide-Scan® hood; receiver drilled and tapped for scope mount
*Stock:* Black fiberglass-filled synthetic w/molded-in checkering and padded black nylon sling
*Prices:* . . . . . . . . . . . . . . . . . . . . . . . . . . . . . . . . . . . $377.00

# MAROCCHI SHOTGUNS

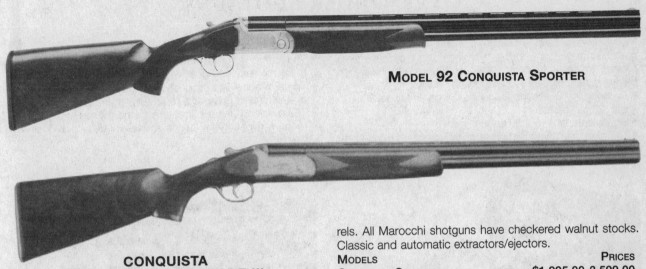

**MODEL 92 CONQUISTA SPORTER**

## CONQUISTA
## SPORTING CLAYS GRADE III

Marocchi shotguns feature concave ventilated ribs. Classic middle rib on barrels fitted with chokes. Boxlock action has replaceable hingepins, adjustable selective trigger and automatic ejectors. Magnum Field model is bored for 3" shells. Classic Doubles are 3" guns with back-bored, ported barrels. All Marocchi shotguns have checkered walnut stocks. Classic and automatic extractors/ejectors.

| MODELS | PRICES |
|---|---|
| CONQUISTA SPORTING | $1,995.00-3,599.00 |
| SPORTING LEFT | 2,120.00-3,995.00 |
| LADY SPORT | 2,120.00-2,300.00 |
| CONQUISTA TRAP | 1,995.00-3,599.00 |
| CONQUISTA SKEET | 1,995.00-3,599.00 |
| CLASSIC DOUBLES | 1,598.00 |

## SPECIFICATIONS CONQUISTA SHOTGUNS (all 12 Gauge)

| | CONQUISTA SPORTING | SPORTING LEFT | LADY SPORT | CONQUISTA TRAP | CONQUISTA SKEET | CLASSIC DOUBLES |
|---|---|---|---|---|---|---|
| **BARRELS** | | | | | | |
| Gauge | 12 | 12 | 12 | 12 | 12 | 12 |
| Chamber | 2 3/4" | 2 3/4" | 2 3/4" | 2 3/4" | 2 3/4" | 2 3/4" |
| Barrel Length | 28",30",32" | 28",30",32" | 28",30" | 29",30" | 28 | 30" |
| Chokes | Contrechokes | Contrechokes | Contrechokes | Full/Full | Skeet/Skeet | Contre Plus |
| **TRIGGER** | | | | | | |
| Trigger type | Instajust Selective | Instajust Selective | Instajust Selective | Instajust | Instajust Selective | Instajust Selective |
| Trigger Pull (Weight) | 3.5 - 4.0 lb.s | 3.5 - 4.0 lb.s | 3.5 - 4.0 lb.s | 3.5 - 4.0 lb.s | 3.5 - 4.0 lb.s | 3.5 - 4.0 lb.s |
| Trigger Pull (Length) | 14 1/2" - 14 7/8" | 14 1/2" - 14 7/8" | 13 7/8" - 14 1/4" | 14 1/2" - 14 7/8" | 14 1/2" - 14 7/8" | 14 1/4" - 14 5/8" |
| **STOCK** | | | | | | |
| Drop at comb | 1 7/16" | 1 7/16" | 1 11/32" | 1 9/32" | 1 1/2" | 1 3/8" |
| Drop at heel | 2 3/16" | 2 3/16" | 2 9/32" | 1 11/16" | 2 3/16" | 2 1/8" |
| Cast at heel | 3/16" Off | 3/16" Off | 3/16" Off | 3/16" Off | 3/16" Off | N/A |
| Cast at toe | 3/8" Off | 3/8" On | 3/8" Off | 5/16" Off | 3/16" Off | N/A |
| Stock | | | Select Walnut | | | |
| Checkering | 20 lines/inch | 20 lines/inch | 20 lines/inch | 20 lines/inch | 20 lines/inch | 18 lines/inch |
| **OVERALL** | | | | | | |
| Length Overall | 45" - 45" | 45" - 49" | 44 3/8"-46 3/8" | 47" - 49" | 45" | 47" |
| Weight Approx.* | 7 7/8 lbs. | 7 7/8 lbs. | 71/2 lbs. | 8 1/4 lbs. | 7 3/4 lbs. | 8 1/8 lbs. |

# MERKEL SHOTGUNS

## OVER/UNDER SHOTGUNS

Merkel over-and-unders were the first hunting guns with barrels arranged one above the other, and they have since proved to be able competitors of the side-by-side gun. Merkel superiority lies in the following details:
- Available in 12, 16 and 20 gauge (28 ga. in Model 201E with 26 ³/₄" barrel)
- Lightweight (6.4 to 7.28 lbs.)
- The high, narrow forend protects the shooter's hand from

the barrel in hot or cold climates
- The forend is narrow and therefore lies snugly in the hand to permit easy and positive swinging
- The slim barrel line provides an unobstructed field of view and thus permits rapid aiming and shooting
- The over-and-under barrel arrangement gives straight-line recoil, eliminating the torque and lateral deflection of side-by-sides

**MODEL 2001EL**

**MODEL 303EL**
**SIDELOCK**

## MERKEL OVER/UNDER SHOTGUN

**SPECIFICATIONS**
**Gauges:** 12, 16, 20, 28
**Barrel Lengths:** 26.75" and 28"
**Weight:** 6.4 to 7.28 lbs.
**Stock:** English or pistol grip in European walnut
**Features:** All models include three-piece forearm, automatic ejectors, Kersten double crossbolt lock, Blitz action and single selective or double triggers.
**Prices:**
**MODEL 2001EL**
12, 20, 28 . . . . . . . . . . . . . . . . . . . . . . . . . . $6,495.00
2001EL Sporter . . . . . . . . . . . . . . . . . . . . . . 6,495.00

**MODEL 2000EL** Kersten double cross-bolt lock; scroll engraved silver-grey receiver; modified Anson & Deeley box action; ejectors; single or double triggers, luxury grade wood; pistol grip or English-style stock.
12 ga., 20 . . . . . . . . . . . . . . . . . . . . . . . . . . . 5,195.00
2000EL Sporter . . . . . . . . . . . . . . . . . . . . . . . 5,195.00
**MODEL 2002EL** Same features as Model 2000EL but with hunting scenes w/arabesque engraving
12 ga. 28"; 20 ga. and 28 ga., 26.75" . . . . . . 9,995.00
**SIDELOCKS**
**MODEL 303** Double trigger, auto ejectors, straight or pistol grip. 12, 20, 28 . . . . . . . . . . . . . . . . 19,995.00

**MODEL 2002EL**

# MERKEL SHOTGUNS

## SIDE-BY-SIDE SHOTGUNS

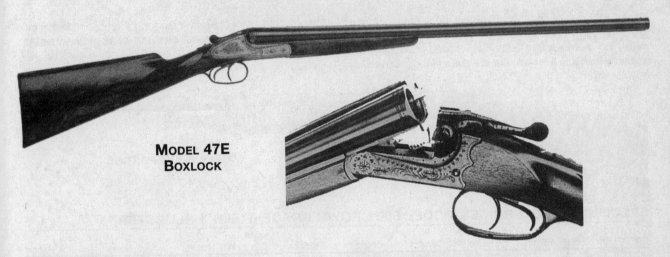

**MODEL 47E**
**BOXLOCK**

### MODEL 47E
Greener cross bolt with double under barrel locking lugs, scroll engraved case hardened receiver, Anson and Deely box-lock action, Holland & Holland ejectors, single selective or double triggers, pistol grip or English style stock., includes fitted luggage case
12 or 16 ga. 28" IC/MOD, MOD/FULL . . . . . . . **$2,795.00**
20 ga. 26 3/4" IC/MOD, MOD/FULL . . . . . . . . .2,795.00

### MODEL 147E
Greener cross bolt with double under barrel locking lugs, fine engraved hunting scenes on silver-grayed receiver, Anson and Deely boxlock grip or English style stock, includes fitted luggage case
12 or 16 ga. 28" IC/MOD, MOD/FULL . . . . . . . **$3,395.00**
20 ga. 26 3/4" or 28" IC/MOD, MOD/FULL . . . . .3,395.00
28 ga. 26 3/4" or 28" IC/MOD, MOD/FULL . . . . .3,595.00

### MODEL 147EL
Greener cross bolt with double under barrel locking lugs, fine engraved hunting scenes on silver-grayed receiver, receiver, Luxury Grade Wood, Anson and Deely boxlock action, Holland & Holland ejectors, single selective or double triggers, pistol grip or English style stock, includes fitted luggage case
12 or 16 ga. 28" IC/MOD, MOD/FULL . . . . . . . **$4,395.00**
20 ga. 26 3/4" or 28" IC/MOD, MOD/FULL . . . . .4,395.00
28 ga. 26 3/4" or 28" IC/MOD, MOD/FULL . . . . .4,595.00

### MODEL 280EL
Greener cross bolt with double under barrel locking lugs, fine hunting scenes on silver-grayed receiver, Anson and Deely boxlock action, Holland & Holland ejectors, double triggers, Luxury Grade Wood, English style stock, includes fitted luggage case.
28 ga. 28" IC/MOD . . . . . . . . . . . . . . . . . . . .**$4,995.00**

### MODEL 360EL
Greener cross bolt with double under barrel locking lugs, fine hunting scenes on silver-grayed receiver, Anson and Deely boxlock action, Holland & Holland ejectors, double triggers, Luxury Grade Wood, English style stock, includes fitted luggage case
410 ga. 28', MOD/FULL . . . . . . . . . . . . . . . . . .**$4,995.00**

### MODEL 280/360EL TWO BBL SET
Greener cross bolt with double under barrel locking lugs, fine hunting scenes on silver-grayed receiver, Anson and Deely boxlock action, Holland & Holland ejectors, double triggers, Luxury Grade Wood, English style stock, includes fitted luggage case
*Price:*
28 ga. 28", IC/MOD; extra barrels - 410 ga. 28"
MOD/FULL7, . . . . . . . . . . . . . . . . . . . . . . . . .**$7,495.00**
*Also Available:*
S models wih Holland & Holland
sidelock actions . . . . . . . . . . . . . . . . . . . . .**from $5,395.00**
147SS model with detachable locks . . . . . . . . . .7,995.00
247 SL and 447 SL models with arabesque engraving
(sidelock)
247SL . . . . . . . . . . . . . . . . . . . . . . . . . . . . . .**$6,995.00**
447SL . . . . . . . . . . . . . . . . . . . . . . . . . . . . . .8,995.00

### FREE HAND STOCKING
(Stock dimensions to customers specs.)
*Price:* . . . . . . . . . . . . . . . . . . . . . . . . . . . . . . .**$1,395.00**

### LEFT HAND STOCKING
(Standard stock dimensions, 4mm cast on)
*Price:* . . . . . . . . . . . . . . . . . . . . . . . . . . . . . . . .**$895.00**

*Note: (12, 20 and 410 ga. supplied with 3-inch chambers; 16 and 28 ga. supplied with 2 3/4 inch chambers)*

# MOSSBERG SHOTGUNS

## MODEL 500 SPORTING

All Mossberg Model 500 pump-action shotguns feature 3" chambers, Milspec tough, lightweight alloy receivers with "top thumb safety." Standard models includes 6-shot capacity with 2 3/4" shells, cut-checkered stock, Quiet Carry forend, gold trigger, blued Woodland Camo or Marinecote metal finish and the largest selection of accessory barrels. Ten-year limited warranty.

**MODEL 500 SPORTING**

## SPECIFICATIONS & PRICES MODEL 500 CROWN GRADE (FIELD & SLUGSTER)

| Ga. | Stock # | Bb;/ Length | Barrel Type | Sights | Chokes | Stock | Length O/A | Wt. | Q.D. Studs | Notes | Prices |
|---|---|---|---|---|---|---|---|---|---|---|---|
| 12 | 54220 | 28" | Vent rib, ported | 2 Beads | Accu-Choke | Walnut Finish | 48" | 7.2 | | IC, Mod. & Full Tubes | $336.00 |
| 20 | Bantam 54132 | 22" | Vent Rib | 2 Beads | Accu-Choke | Walnut Finish | 42" | 6.9 | | Mod. Tube Only, Bantam Stock | 336.00 |
| 20 | 50136 | 26" | Vent Rib | 2 Beads | Accu-Choke | Walnut Finish | 46" | 7.0 | | IC, Mod. & Full Tubes | 336.00 |
| .410 | Bantam 50112 | 24" | Vent Rib | 2 Beads | Full | Synthetic | 43" | 6.8 | | Fixed Choke, Bantam Stock | 336.00 |
| .410 | 50104 | 24" | Vent Rib | 2 Beads | Full | Walnut Finish | 44" | 6.8 | | Fixed Choke | 336.00 |
| 12 | 54232 | 24" | Trophy Slugster™ Ported | Scope Mount | Rifled Bore | Walnut Finish | 44" | 7.3 | Y | Dual-Comb™ Stock | 398.00 |
| 12 | 54244 | 24" | Slugster, ported | Rifle | Rifled Bore | Walnut Finish | 44" | 7.0 | Y | | 367.00 |
| 12 | 54844 | 24" | Slugster, ported | Rifle | Rifled Bore | Walnut Finish | 44" | 7.0 | Y | | 398.00. |
| 20 | 54233 | 24" | Trophy Slugster™ Ported | Scope[e Mount | Rifled Bore | Walnut Finish | 44" | s6.9 | Y | Dual-Comb™ Stock | 398.00 |
| 20 | Bantam 58252 | 24" | Slugster | Rifle | Rifled Bore | Walnut Finish | 44" | s6.9 | Y | Bantam Stock | 367.00 |

## SPECIFICATIONS MODEL 500 COMBOS

| Ga. | Stock # | Bb;/ Length | Barrel Type | Sights | Chokes | Stock | Length O/A | Wt. | Q.D. Studs | Notes | Prices |
|---|---|---|---|---|---|---|---|---|---|---|---|
| 12 | 54243 | 28" 24" | Vent rib, ported Trophy Slugster™ ported | 2 Beads Scope Mount | Accu-Choke Rifled Bore | Walnut Finish | 48" | 7.2 | Y | IC, Mod. & Full Tubes Dual-Comb™ Stock | 457.00 |
| 12 | 54264 | 24" | Vent rib, ported Slugster, ported | 2 Beads Rifle | Accu-Choke Rifled Bore | Walnut Finish | 48" | 7.2 | Y | IC, Mod. & Full Tubes | 440.00 |
| 20 | 54282 | 26" 24" | Vent Rib Slugster, ported | 2 Beads Rifle | Accu-Choke Rifled Bore | Walnut Finish | 46" | 7.0 | Y | IC, Mod. & Full Tubes | 422.00 |
| 12 | 54169 | 28" 18.5" | Vent rib, ported Plain | 2 Beads Bead | Accu-Choke Cyl. Bore | Walnut Finish | 48" | 7.2 | | IC, Mod. & Full Tube Pistol Grip Kit | 386.00 |
| 20 | 54188 | 22" 24" | Vent Rib Slugster, ported | 2 Beads Rifle | Accu-Choke Rifled Bore | Walnut Finish | 42" | 7.0 | | IC, Mod. & Full Tubes Bantam Stock & Forearm | 414.00 |

## SPECIFICATIONS 500/590 MARINER & 500 SPECIAL PURPOSE

| GAUGE | BARREL LENGTH | SIGHT | STOCK # | FINISH | STOCK | CAPACITY | OVERALL LENGTH | WEIGHT | NOTES | PRICE |
|---|---|---|---|---|---|---|---|---|---|---|
| **MODEL 500/590 MARINER™ (CYLINDER BORE BARRELS)** | | | | | | | | | | |
| 12 | 18.5" | Bead | 50273 | Marinecote™ | Synthetic | 6 | 38.5" | 6.8 | Includes Pistol Grip | $445.00 |
| 12 | 20" | Bead | 50299 | Marinecote™ | Synthetic | 9 | 40" | 7.0 | Includes Pistol Grip | 460.00 |
| **MODEL 500 SPECIAL PURPOSE (CYLINDER BORE BARRELS) PERSUADER/CRUISER** | | | | | | | | | | |
| 12 | 18.5" | Bead | 50411 | Blue | Synthetic | 6 | 38.5" | 6.8 | Includes Pistol Grip | 307.00 |
| 12 | 18.5" | Bead | 50440 | Blue | Pistol Grip | 6 | 28" | 5.6 | Includes Heat Shield | 307.00 |
| 20 | 18.5" | Bead | 50452 | Blue | Synthetic | 6 | 38.5" | 6.8 | Includes Pistol Grip | 305.00 |
| 20 | 18.5" | Bead | 50450 | Blue | Pistol Grip | 6 | 28" | 5.6 | | 298.00 |
| .410 | 18.5" | Bead | 50455 | Blue | Pistol Grip | 6 | 28" | 5.3 | | 305.00 |
| 12 | 20" | Bead | 50579 | Blue | Synthetic | 8 | 40" | 7.0 | Includes Pistol Grip | 307.00 |
| 12 | 20" | Bead | 50580 | Blue | Pistol Grip | 8 | 40" | 7.0 | | 307.00 |

# MOSSBERG SHOTGUNS

## 500-SERIES PUMP SHOTGUNS *(cont.)*

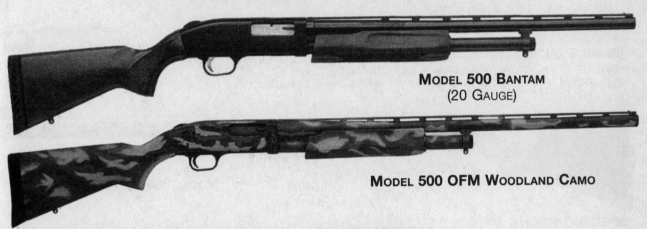

**MODEL 500 BANTAM**
(20 GAUGE)

**MODEL 500 OFM WOODLAND CAMO**

### SPECIFICATIONS MODEL 500 WOODLAND CAMO (6-SHOT)

| | | | | | | | | | | | |
|---|---|---|---|---|---|---|---|---|---|---|---|
| 12 | 52193 | 28" | Vent rib, ported | 2 Beads | Accu-Choke | Synthetic | 48" | 7.2 | Y | IC, Mod. & Full Tubes | $363.00 |
| 12 | Turkey 52195 | 24" | Vent Rib, Ported | Fiber optic sights | XX Full Choke | Synthetic | | | | | 376.00 |
| 20 | Bantam Turkey 58235 | 22" | Vent Rib | | X Full Choke | Synthetic | | | | | 376.00 |

### MODEL 500 SPECIAL HUNTER

| | | | | | | |
|---|---|---|---|---|---|---|
| 12 | 56420 | 28" | Vent Rib, Ported | Accu-Choke | Synthetic | $327.00 |
| 20 | 56436 | 26" | Vent Rib | Accu-Choke | Synthetic | 327.00 |

**590DA™ 6-SHOT**
18.5" Barrel, Ghost Ring® Sights

### SPECIFICATIONS MODELS 590 SPECIAL PURPOSE, 500/590 GHOST RING™, AND HS 410

| GAUGE | BARREL LENGTH | SIGHT | STOCK # | FINISH | STOCK | CAPACITY | OVERALL LENGTH | WEIGHT | NOTES | PRICE |
|---|---|---|---|---|---|---|---|---|---|---|
| **MODEL 590 SPECIAL PURPOSE (CYLINDER BORE BARRELS)** | | | | | | | | | | |
| 12 | 20" | Bead | 50645 | Blue | Synthetic | 9 | 40" | 7.2 | w/Acc. Lug & Heat Shield | 370.00 |
| 12 | 20" | Bead | 50660 | Parkerized | Synthetic | 9 | 40" | 7.2 | w/Acc. Lug & Heat Shield | 425.00 |
| 12 | 20" | Bead | 50665 | Parkerized | Speed Feed | 9 | 40" | 7.2 | w/Acc. Lug & Heat Shield | 462.00 |
| **MODEL 500/590 GHOST RING™ (CYLINDER BORE BARRELS)** | | | | | | | | | | |
| 12 | 18.5" | Ghost Ring™ | 50402 | Blue | Synthetic | 6 | 38.5" | 6.8 | | $360.00 |
| 12 | 18.5" | Ghost Ring™ | 50517 | Parkerized | Synthetic | 6 | 38.5" | 6.8 | | 416.00 |
| 12 | 20" | Ghost Ring™ | 50663 | Parkerized | Synthetic | 9 | 40" | 7.2 | w/Acc. Lug | 482.00 |
| 12 | 20" | Ghost Ring™ | 50668 | Parkerized | Speed Feed | 9 | 40" | 7.2 | w/Acc. Lug | 519.00 |
| **HS 410 HOME SECURITY (SPREADER CHOKE)** | | | | | | | | | | |
| .410 | 18.5" | Bead | 50359 | Blue | Synthetic | 6 | 39.5" | 6.6 | Includes Vertical Foregrip | $319.00 |

**SHOTGUNS**

# MOSSBERG SHOTGUNS

## MODEL 835 ULTI-MAG PUMP SHOTGUNS

Mossberg's Model 835 Ulti-Mag pump action shotgun has a 3 1/2" 12-gauge chamber but can also handle standard 2 3/4" and 3" shells. Field barrels are over-bored and ported for optimum patterns, reduced muzzle-jump and felt recoil reduction. Cut-checkered walnut and walnut-finished stocks, Quiet Carry™ forearms and gold triggers are standard. Camo models are drilled and tapped for scope and feature detachable swivels and sling. All models include a Cablelock™ and 10-year limited warranty.

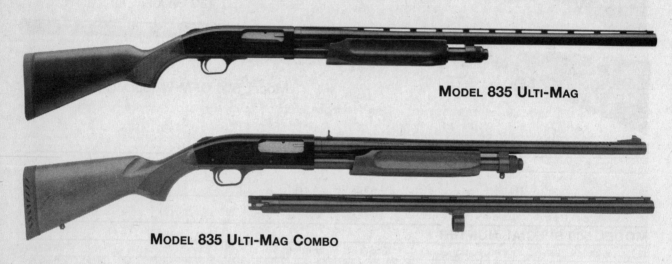

**MODEL 835 ULTI-MAG**

**MODEL 835 ULTI-MAG COMBO**

## SPECIFICATIONS AND PRICES MODEL 835 ULTI-MAG (12 GAUGE, 6 SHOT)

| Ga | Stock No. | Barrel Length | Type | Sights | Choke | Finish | Stock | O.A. Length | W. | Studs | Notes | Price |
|---|---|---|---|---|---|---|---|---|---|---|---|---|
| **ULTI-MAG™ 835 CROWN GRADE** | | | | | | | | | | | | |
| 12 | 68220 | 28" | Vent Rib, Ported | 2 Beads | Accu-Mag | Blue | Walnut Finish | 48.5" | 7.7 | | Mod. Tube Only | $361.00 |
| 12 | 68225 | 24" | Vent Rib, Ported | 2 Beads | Accu-Mag | Matte | Walnut Finish | 44.5" | 7.3 | | X-Full Tube | 378.00 |
| 12 | 68244 | 28" | Vent Rib, Ported | 2 Beads | Accu-Mag | Blue | Walnut | 48.5" | 7.7 | | Mod. Tube only | 482.00 |
| | | 24" | Trophy Slugster™ Ported | Scope Mount | Rifled Bore | | | | | | Dual-Comb™ Stock | |
| 12 | 68223 | 28" | Vent Rib, Ported | 2 Beads | Accu-Mag | Blue | Walnut | 48.5" | 7.7 | | Mod. Tube only | 482.00 |
| | | 24" | Slugster, Ported | Rifle | Rifled Bore | | | | | | | |

| **CAMO** | | | | | | | |
|---|---|---|---|---|---|---|---|
| Ga | Stock No. | Barrel Length | Type | Choke | Finish | Stock | Price |
| 12 | 62040-6 | 24" | Vent Rib, Ported, Fiber Optic Sights | Ulti-Full Only | Rt. X-Tra Brown | Synthetic | $515.00 |
| 12 | 62439-8 | 24" | Vent Rib, Ported, Fiber Optic Sights | Ulti-Full Only | M.O. Shadow Branch | Synthetic | 515.00 |
| 12 | 62234 | 24" | Vent Rib, Ported, Fiber Optic Sights | Ulti-Full Only | R.T. Hardwoods | Synthetic | 515.00 |
| 12 | 68143-8 | 24" | Combo, Vent Rib, Ported | Ulti-Full Only | Woodlands | Dual Comb® | 513.00 |
| | | 24" | Integral Scope Base, Ported | Fully Rifled Bore | Woodlands | | |
| 12 | 62445-9 | 28" | Vent Rib, Ported | Hunter Set | M.O. Shadow Grass | Synthetic | 571.00 |
| 12 | 68231-2 | 24" | Vent Rib, Ported, Fiber Optic Sights | Ulti-Full Only | Woodlands | Synthetic | 414.00 |
| 12 | 68235-0 | 28" | Vent Rib, Ported | Mod Only | Woodlands | Synthetic | 400.00 |
| 12 | 68243-5 | 24" | Combo, VR, Ported, Fiber Optic Sights | Ulti-Full Only | Woodlands | Synthetic | 561.00 |
| 12 | | 24" | Fiber Optic Rifle Sights, Ported | Fully Rifled Bore | Woodlands | | |
| **MODEL 835® SPECIAL HUNTER™** | | | | | | | |
| 12 | 66720-3 | 28" | Vent Rib, Ported | Mod Only | Parkerized | Synthetic (Black) | $363.00 |

# MOSSBERG SHOTGUNS

## MODEL 9200 w/VENT RIB

## SPECIFICATIONS AND PRICES MODEL 9200 (12 Gauge, 5 Shot)

| GA | STOCK NO. | BBL. LENGTH | BARREL TYPE | SIGHTS | CHOKE | FINISH | STOCK | LENGTH O.A. | WT. | Q.D. STUDS | NOTES | PRICES |
|----|-----------|-------------|-------------|--------|-------|--------|-------|-------------|-----|------------|-------|--------|
| **MODEL 9200 CROWN GRADE** | | | | | | | | | | | | $574.00 |
| 12 | 49420 | 28" | Vent Rib, Ported | 2 Beads | Accu-Choke | Blue | Walnut | 48" | 7.7 | | IC, Mod. & Full Tubes | $574.00 |
| 12 | 49435 | 22" | Vent Rib | 2 Beads | Accu-Choke | Blue | Walnut | 42" | 7.2 | | IC/Mod., Full Bantam | 574.00 |
| **MODEL 9200 SPECIAL HUNTER** | | | | | | | | | | | | $491.00 |
| 12 | 46420 | 28" | Vent Rib | | Accu-Choke | Matte | Syn. Black | | | | | |
| **MODEL 9200 JUNGLE GUN AUTOLOADER** | | | | | | | | | | | | $704.00 |
| 12 | 49047 | 18.5" | | Plain, w/ bead sight | Cyc. bore | | Synthetic | | | | | |

## MODEL 695 BOLT ACTION

The 3-inch chambered 12-gauge Model 695 bolt-action shotgun features a 22-inch rifled barrel and rugged synthetic stock. This combination delivers the fast handling and fine balance of a classic sporting rifle. Every Model 695 comes with a two-round detachable magazine and Weaver-style scope bases to give hunters the advantage of today's specialized optics.

Mossberg's fully rifled slug barrels are specially "ported" to help soften the recoil and reduce muzzle jump. Non-rotating dual claw extractors ensure reliable ejection and feeding. Ten-year limited warranty. New fiber-optic sights speed your aim. Also available with Woodland Camo stock.

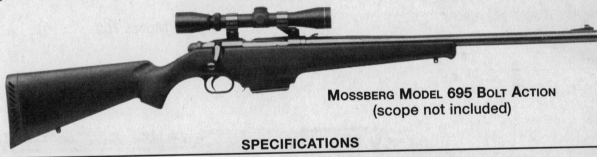

### MOSSBERG MODEL 695 BOLT ACTION
### (scope not included)

## SPECIFICATIONS

| GAUGE | MODEL NO. | BARREL LENGTH | BARREL TYPE | SIGHTS | FINISH | STOCK | CHOKE | PRICE |
|-------|-----------|---------------|-------------|--------|--------|-------|-------|-------|
| 12 | 59001 | 22" | Rifled Ported | Iron | Matte | Black Synthetic | Cyl. Bore | $345.00 |
| 12 | 59802 | 22" | Rifled Ported | Fiber Optic | Matte | Synthetic | Cyl. Bore | 367.00 |
| 12 | 59008 | 22" | Rifled Ported | Fiber Optic | Matte | OFM Camo Synthetic | Cyl. Bore | 397.00 |

## MOSSBERG LINE LAUNCHER

The line Launcher (20" barrel) is the first shotgun devoted to rescue and personal safety. It provides an early self-contained rescue opportunity for boaters, police and fire departments, salvage operations or whenever an extra-long throw of line is the safest alternative. This shotgun used a

12-gauge blank cartridge to propel a convertible projectile with a line attached. With a floating head attached, the projectile will travel 250 to 275 feet. Removing the floating head increases the projectile range to approx. 700 feet.
*Prices:* . . . . . . . . . . . . . . . . . . . . . . . . . . . . . . . . .$963.00
LAUNCHER KIT . . . . . . . . . . . . . . . . . . . . . . . . . . . . .645.00

SHOTGUNS

# New England Arms FAIR

## (Fabrica Armi Di Isidoro Rizzini)

NEW ENGLAND ARMS FAIR *(Fabrica Armi di Isidoro Rizzini)* shotguns: Boxlock, fullly chrome-lined monoblock barrels with vent ribs, choke tubes standard on 12, 16, 20 gauge guns (fixed chokes on 28 and .410), hand-checkered Turkish walnut, single selective triggers, automatic safety and ejectors, straight or semi-pistol grip, custom options available.

*Prices:*
**M500** . . . . . . . . . . . . . . . . . . . . . . . . . . . . . . . $2,250.00
**M600** . . . . . . . . . . . . . . . . . . . . . . . . . . . . . . . 2,995.00
**M702** . . . . . . . . . . . . . . . . . . . . . . . . . . . . . . . 3,995.00
**M900** . . . . . . . . . . . . . . . . . . . . . . . . . . . . . . . 3,995.00

**MODEL 900**

**MODEL 702**

**MODEL 600**

**MODEL 500**

# NEW ENGLAND FIREARMS

**SURVIVOR
20 GAUGE**

**SURVIVOR
.410/45 COLT**

## SURVIVOR SERIES

This series of survival arms is available in 12 and 20 ga. with either a blued or electroless nickel finish. All shotguns feature the New England Firearms action with a patented transfer bar and high-impact, synthetic stock and forend. The stock is a modified thumbhole design with a full and secure pistol grip. The buttplate is attached at one end with a large thumbscrew for access to a large storage compartment holding a wide variety of survival gear or extra ammunition. The forend, which has a hollow cavity for storing three rounds of ammunition, is accessible by removing a thumbscrew (also used for takedown.

**SPECIFICATIONS**
*Action:* Break open, side-lever release, automatic ejection
*Guage:* 12, 20, .41/45 Colt (Combo)  *Barrel Length:* 22"
*Choke:* Modified  *Chamber:* 3" (Combo also available w/2.5" chamber) *Overall Length:* 36"  *Weight:* 6 lbs.
*Sights:* Bead  *Stock:* High-density polymer, black matte finish, sling swivels
*Prices:* Blued finish . . . . . . . . . . . . . . . . . . . . . . $129.95
Nickel finish. . . . . . . . . . . . . . . . . . . . . . . . . . . . 150.95
.41/45 Colt Combo, blued . . . . . . . . . . . . . . . . . 164.95
  Nickel . . . . . . . . . . . . . . . . . . . . . . . . . . . . . . 178.95

**PARDNER YOUTH**

**TURKEY
CAMO YOUTH**

## PARDNER SINGLE-BARREL SHOTGUNS

**SPECIFICATIONS**
*Guages:* 12, 16, 20, 28 and .410  *Barrel Lengths:* 22" (Youth); 26" (20, 28, .410); 28" (12 and 16 ga.), 32" (12 ga.)
*Chokes:* Full (alll gauges, except 28); Modified (12, 20 and

28 ga.)  *Chamber:* 2.75" (16 and 28 ga.); 3" (all others)
*Price:* . . . . . . . . . . . . . . . . . . . . . . . . . . . . . . . $106.95
  w/32" barrel . . . . . . . . . . . . . . . . . . . . . . . . . . 119.95
*Also available:*
**PARDNER YOUTH.** With 22" barrel in gauges 12, 20, 28 and .410 . . . . . . . . . . . . . . . . . . . . . . . . . . . . $114.95
**TURKEY CAMO YOUTH.** 20 gauge, 3", fixed full choke. . . . . . . . . . . . . . . . . . . . . . . . . . . . 128.95

SHOTGUNS

# NEW ENGLAND FIREARMS

**TURKEY GUN W/24" BARREL, TK2 CHOKE TUBE**

## TURKEY GUN

**SPECIFICATIONS**
**Guage:** 12 (3.5" chamber)  **Choke:** Full
**Barrel Length:** 24"  **Overall Length:** 44"
**Weight:** 9.5 lbs.  **Sights:** Bead sights
**Stock:** American hardwood; walnut or camo finish; full
pistol grip; ventilated recoil pad.  **Length Of Pull:** 14.5"

**Price:** with full choke, camo paint,
swivels & sling . . . . . . . . . . . . . . . . . . . . . . . **$128.95**
with screw-in choke, black finish. . . . . . . . . . . . . **142.95**
**Also Available:** TURKEY GUN. With 24" 10 ga., screw in, choke,
black matte finish, swivels and sling. . . . . . . . . . . . . **$199.95**
with camo paint . . . . . . . . . . . . . . . . . . . . . . . . . . . . . **205.95**

## SPECIAL PURPOSE
## WATERFOWL SINGLE SHOT (10 ga.)

This sporting shotgun features a 32" barrel, (48" overall),
Modified choke, camo paint finish, swivels and sling.
**Weight:** 9.5 lbs.
**Price:** . . . . . . . . . . . . . . . . . . . . . . . . . . . . . . . . **$197.95**
**Also Available:** with 28" barrel, walnut finish stock

## TRACKER II RIFLED SLUG GUN

**SPECIFICATIONS**
**Guages:** 12 and 20 (3" chamber)
**Choke:** Rifled bore
**Barrel Length:** 24"  **Overall Length:** 40"
**Weight:** 6 lbs.  **Sights:** Adjustable rifle sights

**Length Of Pull:** 14.5"  **Stock:** American hardwood; walnut
or camo finish; full pistol grip; recoil pad; sling swivel studs
**Price:** . . . . . . . . . . . . . . . . . . . . . . . . . . . . . . . . **$150.95**
**Also available:**
TRACKER SLUG GUN w/Cylinder Bore, both gauges . . . . . **142.95**

# PERAZZI SHOTGUNS

The heart of the Perazzi line is the classic over/under, whose barrels are soldered into a monobloc that holds the shell extractors. At the sides are the two locking lugs that link the barrels to the action, which is machined from a solid block of forged steel. Barrels come with flat, step or raised ventilated rib. The finely checkered walnut forend is available with schnabel, beavertail or English styling, and the walnut stock can be of standard, Monte Carlo, Skeet or English design. Double or single nonselective or selective triggers. Sideplates and receiver are masterfully engraved.

## OVER/UNDER GAME MODELS

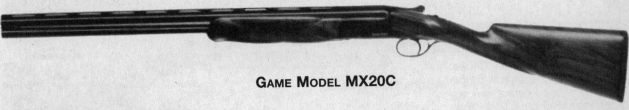

**GAME MODEL MX20C**

### GAME MODELS MX8, MX12, MX16, MX20, MX8/20, MX28 & MX410

**SPECIFICATIONS**
*Gauges:* 12, 20, 28 & .410
*Chambers:* 2.75"; also available in 3"
*Barrel Lengths:* 26" and 27.5"
*Weight:* 6 lbs. 6 oz. to 7 lbs. 4 oz.
*Trigger Group:* Nondetachable with coil springs and selective trigger
*Stock:* Interchangeable and custom; schnabel forend
*Prices:*

| | |
|---|---|
| STANDARD GRADE | $8,840.00 - $17,670.00 |
| SC3 GRADE | 15,000.00 - 23,800.00 |
| SCO GRADE | 25,500.00 - 34,400.00 |
| SCO GOLD GRADES | 28,800.00 - 37,600.00 |

**SCO SIDEPLATE ENGRAVING**
(applicable to MX8 and MX12 models of any version)

## AMERICAN TRAP SINGLE BARREL MODELS

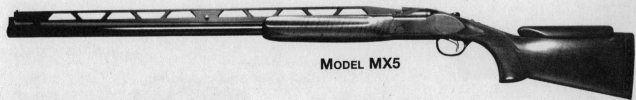

**MODEL MX5**

### AMERICAN TRAP SINGLE-BARREL MODELS MX15, MX15L & MX5

**SPECIFICATIONS**
*Gauge:* 12
*Chamber:* 2.75"
*Barrel Lengths:* 32" and 34"
*Weight:* 8 lbs. 6 oz.
*Choke:* Full

*Trigger Group:* Detachable and interchangeable with coil springs
*Stock:* Interchangeable and custom made
*Forend:* Beavertail

| Prices: | |
|---|---|
| MX5 | $6,600.00 |
| MX15 | 7,520.00 |
| MX15L | 9,090.00 |
| MX2000 | 8,660.00 |

# PERAZZI SHOTGUNS

## COMPETITION OVER/UNDER SHOTGUNS
### *Olympic, Double Trap, Skeet, Pigeon & Electrocibles*

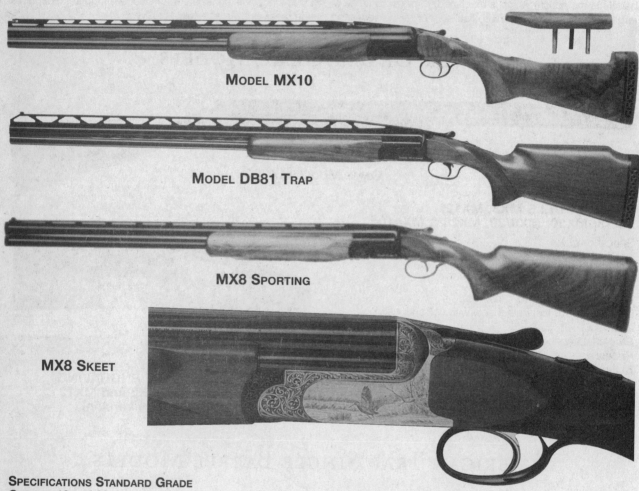

**MODEL MX10**

**MODEL DB81 TRAP**

**MX8 SPORTING**

**MX8 SKEET**

**SPECIFICATIONS STANDARD GRADE**
*Gauges:* 12 and 20
*Barrel Lengths:* 27.5", 28 ³/₈", 29.5", 30.75", 31.5"
*Prices:*
**MX8** 12 ga., removable trigger group 29.5",
   30.75" and 31.5" barrels . . . . . . . . . . . . . . $8,840.00
**MX10** 12 & 20 ga., w/adj. stock and rib 29.5",
   30.75" and 31.5" bbl.. . . . . . . . . . . . . . . . 11,050.00
**MX8/20** 20 ga. removable trigger group
   26.75", 27.5", 28 ³/₈", 29.5", 30.75"
   and 31.5" barrels. . . . . . . . . . . . . . . . . . . 8,840.00
**MX8** 12 ga. w/adj. trigger, 28 ³/₈", 29.5",
   31.5" barrels . . . . . . . . . . . . . . . . . . . . . 9,350.00
**MX8 SPORTING** 12 ga. w/external selector
   and 5 chokes; 27.5", 28 ³/₈", 29.5",
   and 31.5" barrels. . . . . . . . . . . . . . . . . . . 9,790.00
**MX8 CLASSIC** 12 ga. . . . . . . . . . . . . . . . . . 11,160.00
**MX8 SPECIAL** 12 ga. w/adjustable trigger, 29.5",
   and 31.5" barrels. . . . . . . . . . . . . . . . . . . 9,350.00

**DB81 SPECIAL** w/adjustable trigger 29.5",
   30.75"and 31.5" barrels . . . . . . . . . . . . . . . . 9,630.00
*Note:* **PIGEON & ELECTROCIBLE MODELS** available in MX1B,
MX-8, MX-5, MX10 & MX11 only w/27.5", 28.75", 29.5" &
31.5" barrels. . . . . . . . . . . . . . . . . $6,900.00-11,770.00
*Also Available:*
**SC3 GRADE** (Models MX8, MX10,
   MX10/20, MX8/20, MX8 Special,
   DB81 Spec.) . . . . . . . . . . . . . . . . . . . . . . . $15,000.00
**SCO GRADE** (same models as
   SC3 Grade) . . . . . . . . . . . . . . . . . . . . . . . 25,500.00
**SCO GOLD GRADE**
   (same models as above). . . . . . . . . . . . . . 28,800.00
**SCO GRADE SIDEPLATES**
   (same models as above). . . . . . . . . . . . . . 39,100.00
**SCO GOLD GRADE SIDEPLATES**
   (same models above) . . . . . . . . . . . . . . . . 45,450.00

# PURDEY SHOTGUNS

## SIDE BY SIDE GAME GUN

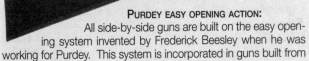

**PURDEY EASY OPENING ACTION:** All side-by-side guns are built on the easy opening system invented by Frederick Beesley when he was working for Purdey. This system is incorporated in guns built from 1880 onwards.

**DEDICATED ACTION SIZES –** Important to the overall weight and proportion of the gun is the action size. Purdey offers dedicated action sizes for each of the bores 10, 12, 20, 28 & .410 in square bar, round bar and ultra bar shapes.

**EXTRA BARRELS –** Purdey's can supply an extra pair of barrels of a different gauge for their guns, such as 28 gauge on a 20 gauge, and .410 on a 28 gauge. These guns are made with a single forend for both bores.

**CHOPPER LUMP BARRELS –** All Purdey barrels, both SxS and O/U, are of chopper lump construction.

Each individual tube is hand filled and then "struck up" using striking files. This gives the tube the correct Purdey profile with wall thickness tollerance of .001". Dependant on the final weight of the

gun wall thicknesses are recommended at, and made to, .032". Once polished the individual tubes are jointed (joined at the breech) using silver solder. The loop iron is similarly fixed. Once together the rough chokes can be cut and the internal bores finished using a traditional lead lapping technique.

**RIBS –** always designed to provide the sighting profile the shooter seeks - are hand-filed to suit the barrel contour exactly, and then soft-soldered (using tin) to the barrels, using pine resin as the fluxing agent. Pine resin provides extra water resistance to the surfaces enclosed by the ribs.

## OVER & UNDER GUN

The Over-Under gun is available in 12, 16, 20, 28 and .410, with each bore made on a dedicated action size. Actions are available in either conventional square bar, round bar or ultra round bar shape. Again, as with Side-by-Side, the shape of the action has an effect on the weight of the gun.

**FIRING SEQUENCE –** Conventionally, the Purdey over-under will shoot the lower barrel first, but can be made to shoot the top barrel first if required. All prices on request.

### THE CHOKE SECTION

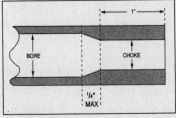

| THE PERCENTAGES OF CHOKE | |
|---|---|
| Cylinder | 45% |
| Improved Cylinder | 50% |
| 1/4 Choke | 55% |
| 1/2 Choke | 60% |
| 3/4 or Modified Choke | 65% |
| Choke | 70% |
| Full Choke | 75% |
| Skeet (2) | 45% |
| Skeet (1) | 40% |

The standard for regulating and patterning the shooting of a gun is the percentage of the shot charge, which is evenly concentrated in a circle of 30" diameter at a range of 40 yards. (Purdey choke restrictions 1/1000 inch.)

| 12 Bore 2.75" 1.25 oz No.6 | |
|---|---|
| FULL CHOKE | .038 - .040 |
| CHOKE | .035 |
| .75 (MOD) | .022 |
| .5 CHOKE | .016-.017 |
| .25 CHOKE | .010-.01 |
| IMP CYL | .007-.008 |
| CYL | .003 |
| SKEET | Open Bore |

| 12 Bore 2.5" 1 oz. No. 6 | |
|---|---|
| FULL CHOKE | .038 - .040 |
| CHOKE | .030 |
| .75 (MOD) | .018-.019 |
| .5 CHOKE | .012-.013 |
| .25 CHOKE | .006-.007 |
| IMP CYL | .003 |
| CYL | .002 |

| 20 Bore 2.75" | |
|---|---|
| FULL CHOKE | .038 - .040 |
| CHOKE | .030 |
| .75 (MOD) | .018-.019 |
| .5 CHOKE | .012-.013 |
| .25 CHOKE | .007-.008 |
| IMP CYL | .006 |
| CYL | .003 |
| SKEET | Open Bore |

| 28 Bore 2.75" | |
|---|---|
| FULL CHOKE | .026 |
| CHOKE | .020 |
| .75 (MOD) | .018 |
| .5 CHOKE | .015 |
| .25 CHOKE | .011 |
| IMP CYL | .007 |
| CYL | .003 |
| SKEET | Open |

# REMINGTON SHOTGUNS

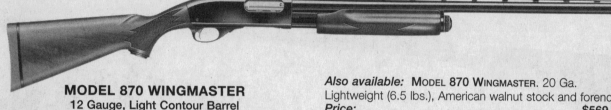

### MODEL 870 WINGMASTER
#### 12 Gauge, Light Contour Barrel

This restyled **870 "WINGMASTER"** pump has cut-checkering on its satin-finished American walnut stock and forend for confident handling, even in wet weather. Also available in Hi-Gloss finish. An ivory bead "Bradley"-type front sight is included. Available with 26", 28" and 30" barrel with REM Choke, it handles 3" and 2 1/2" shells interchangeably.

#### SPECIFICATIONS
**Overall length:** 46.5" (26" barrel), 48.5" (28" barrel), 50.5" (30" barrel). **Weight:** 7.25 lbs. (w/26" barrel).
**Price:** .................................... $569.00

**Also available:** MODEL 870 WINGMASTER. 20 Ga. Lightweight (6.5 lbs.), American walnut stock and forend.
**Price:** .................................... $569.00
   28 ga. .................................... 649.00
   410 ga. .................................... 596.00

MODEL 870 EXPRESS (NOT SHOWN) features the same action as the Wingmaster and is available with 3" chamber and 26" or 28" vent-rib barrel. It has a hardwood stock with low-luster finish and solid buttpad. Choke is Modified REM Choke tube and wrench.
**Overall length:** 48.5" (28" barrel). **Weight:** 7.25" lbs (26" barrel).
**Prices:** 12 & 20 ga. .................... $329.00
Left Hand 12 ga. .......................... 356.00
w/Black Synthetic Stock & Forend
   (Right Hand only) 12 ga. ................ 329.00

### MODEL 870
### EXPRESS TURKEY GUN

The **MODEL 870 EXPRESS TURKEY GUN** boasts all the same features as the Model 870 Express, except has 21" vent-rib barrel and Turkey Extra-Full REM Choke.
**Price:** .................................... $343.00
**Now available:**
   w/stock and forend in Realtree Advantage Camo .... 396.00

### MODEL 870
### EXPRESS DEER GUN

This 12-gauge, pump action deer gun is for hunters who prefer open sights. Features a 20" barrel, quick-reading iron sights, fixed Imp. Cyl. choke and Monte Carlo stock. Also available with fully rifled barrel.
**Price:** With Rifle Sights ................... $300.00
   Fully Rifled ............................ 339.00

### MODEL 870 EXPRESS SUPER MAGNUM
### (not shown)

For those who seek the power and range of 12 gauge 3.5" magnum shotshells, the new MODEL 870 EXPRESS SUPER MAGNUM represents a good value. In addition to having the strength and reliability of the Model 870 Wingmaster, this model has the added versatility of handling 12 ga. 2 3/4" to 3 1/2" loads. The existing breech bolt and receiver have been designed to accommodate the big shells. Also available is a Turkey Camo shotgun with a 23"

vent rib and 3 1/2" chamber with a synthetic stock and forend, plus checkering and vented recoil pad. Fully camouflaged with Real Tree Advantage. Remington also offers Synthetic and Combo models
**Prices:** MODEL 870 EXPRESS SUPER MAGNUM .... $369.00
   TURKEY CAMO .......................... 500.00
   Synthetic Model (26" vent rib) .............. 376.00
Combo (20" fully rifled deer barrel and 26" vent rib
   w/wood stock and forend, vented recoil pad ... 516.00

# REMINGTON SHOTGUNS

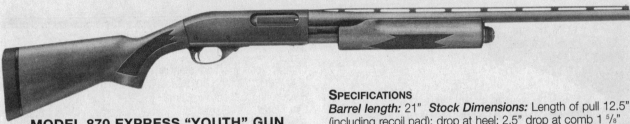

## MODEL 870 EXPRESS "YOUTH" GUN

The MODEL 870 EXPRESS "YOUTH" GUN has been specially designed for youths and smaller-sized adults. It's a 20-gauge lightweight with a 1-inch shorter stock and 21-inch barrel. Complete with REM Choke and ventilated rib barrel, it is also available with a 20" fully rifled, rifle-sighted deer barrel.

**SPECIFICATIONS**
**Barrel length:** 21" **Stock Dimensions:** Length of pull 12.5" (including recoil pad); drop at heel; 2.5" drop at comb 1 5/8"
**Overall length:** 39" (40.5" w/deer barrel) **Average weight:** 6 lbs.
**Choke:** REM Choke-Mod. (vent-rib version).
**Price:** 20-Gauge Lightweight . . . . . . . . . . . . . . $329.00
w/Deer Barrel . . . . . . . . . . . . . . . . . . . . . . . . . . . 363.00
w/Real Tree Advantage camo stock and forend . . . . . . . 396.00

### MODEL 870 SPECIAL PURPOSE

## MODEL 870 SPECIAL PURPOSE MARINE MAGNUM

Remington's MODEL 870 SPECIAL PURPOSE MARINE MAGNUM is a versatile, multipurpose security gun featuring a rugged synthetic stock and extensive, electroless nickel plating on all metal parts. This shotgun utilizes a standard 12-gauge Model 870 receiver with a 7-round magazine extension tube and an 18" cylinder barrel (38.5" overall) with bead front sight. The receiver, magazine extension and barrel are protected (inside and out) with heavy-duty, corrosion-resistant nickel plating. The synthetic stock and forend reduce the effects of moisture. The gun is supplied with a black rubber recoil pad, sling swivel studs, and positive checkering on both pistol grip and forend. **Weight:** 7.5 lbs.
**Price:** . . . . . . . . . . . . . . . . . . . . . . . . . . . . . . . $545.00

### MODEL 870 EXPRESS

## MODEL 870 EXPRESS SYNTHETIC HOME DEFENSE

This 12-gauge pump-action shotgun features an 18" plain barrel with Cylinder choke and front bead sight. The synthetic stock and forend have a textured black, nonreflective finish and positive checkering.
**Price:** . . . . . . . . . . . . . . . . . . . . . . . . . . . . . . . $316.00

## MODEL 870 EXPRESS COMBO

The MODEL 870 EXPRESS in 12 and 20 gauge offers all the features of the standard Model 870, including twin-action bars, quick changing 26" or 28" barrels, REM Choke and vent rib plus low-luster, checkered hardwood stock and no-shine finish on barrel and receiver. The Model 870 Combo is packaged with an extra 20" deer barrel, fitted with rifle sights. The 3-inch chamber handles all 2 3/4" and 3" shells.
**Weight:** 7.5 lbs.
**Price:** . . . . . . . . . . . . . . . . . . . . . . . . . . . . . . . $436.00
with Fully rifled barrel with rifle sights . . . . . . . . . 469.00

# REMINGTON SHOTGUNS

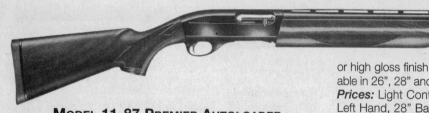

## MODEL 11-87 PREMIER AUTOLOADER

Remington's redesigned 12-gauge MODEL 11-87 PREMIER AUTOLOADER features new, light-contour barrels that reduce both barrel weight and overall weight (more than 8 ounces). The shotgun has a standard 3-inch chamber and handles all 12-gauge shells interchangeably— from 2 3/4" field loads to 3" Magnums. The gun's interchangeable REM choke system includes Improved Cylinder, Modified and Full chokes. Select American walnut stocks with fine-line, cut-checkering in satin

or high gloss finish are standard. Right-hand models are available in 26", 28" and 30" barrels (left-hand models are 28" only).
**Prices:** Light Contour Barrel . . . . . . . . . . . . . . . . $756.00
Left Hand, 28" Barrel . . . . . . . . . . . . . . . . . . . . . . 809.00
**Also available:**
MODEL 11-87 EMBELLISHED RECEIVER . . . . . . . . . . . 756.00

### MODEL 11-87 SPS (not shown)
(Special Purpose Wood or Synthetic)
12 Gauge Autoloader, 3" Chamber/REM/Chokes
26" or 28" Vent-Rib Barrels
**Price:** Wood . . . . . . . . . . . . . . . . . . . . . . . . . . . $705.00
Synthetic . . . . . . . . . . . . . . . . . . . . . . . . . . . . . . 692.00

## MODEL 11-87 PREMIER DEER GUN

## MODEL 11-87 SPS SPECIAL PURPOSE DEER GUN

Features the same finish as other SP models plus a padded, camo-style carrying sling of Cordura nylon with QD sling swivels. Barrel is 21" (41" overall) with rifle sights and rifled and IC choke (handles all 2 3/4" and 3" rifled slug and buckshot

loads as well as high-velocity field and magnum loads; does not function with light 2 3/4" field loads). **Weight:** 8.5 lbs. with black synthetic stock
**Price:** . . . . . . . . . . . . . . . . . . . . . . . . . . . . . . . $725.00
w/fully rifled barrel and cantilevered mount . . . . . 772.00
**Also Available:** PREMIER MODEL with Fully Rifled Barrel and cantilevered mount. . . . . . . . . . . . . . . . . . . . . . . . . $836.00

## MODEL 11-87 SPST TURKEY GUN

12 Gauge Autoloader, 3" Chamber All-Black Synthetic Stock Extra-Full REM Choke Turkey Tube
**Price:** . . . . . . . . . . . . . . . . . . . . . . . . . . . . . . . $705.00
w/Mossy Oak Break-Up Camo Finish . . . . . . . . 805.00

## MODEL 11-87 SPORTING CLAYS NP

MODEL 11-87 PREMIER SPORTING CLAYS NP
Nickel plated receiver, 28" or 30" Ported ligth contour barrel
**Price:** . . . . . . . . . . . . . . . . . . . . . . . . . . . . . . . $948.00

# REMINGTON SHOTGUNS

### SP-10 MAGNUM SHOTGUN

Remington's **SP-10 MAGNUM** is the only gas-operated semi-automatic 10-gauge shotgun made today. Engineered to shoot steel shot, the SP-10 delivers up to 34 percent more pellets to the target than standard 12-gauge shotgun and steel shot combinations. This autoloader features a vented, noncorrosive, stainless-steel gas system, in which the cylinder moves—not the piston. This reduces felt recoil energy by spreading the recoil over a longer time. The receiver is machined from a solid billet of ordnance steel for total integral strength. The SP-10 has a 3/8" vent rib with mid and front sights for a better sight plane. The American walnut stock and forend have a protective, low-gloss satin finish for reduced glare, and positive deep-cut checkering. The receiver and barrel have a matte finish, and the stainless-steel breech bolt features a non-reflective finish. The SP-10 also has a brown vented recoil pad and a padded camo sling of Cordura nylon. **Barrel lengths/choke:** 26" or 30"/REM Choke. **Overall length:** 51.5" (30" barrel) and 47.5" (26" barrel). **Weight:** 11 lbs. (30" barrel) and 10.75 lbs. (26" barrel).
**Price:** . . . . . . . . . . . . . . . . . . . . . . . . . . . . . . . . . **$1,116.00**
**Also available:** SP-10 Magnum in Mossy Oak (Turkey) Camo
**Price:** . . . . . . . . . . . . . . . . . . . . . . . . . . . . . . . . . **1,319.00**
   Synthetic . . . . . . . . . . . . . . . . . . . . . . . . . . . . . **1,199.00**

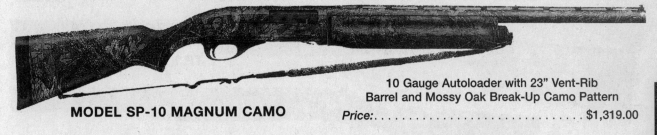

**MODEL SP-10 MAGNUM CAMO**

**10 Gauge Autoloader with 23" Vent-Rib Barrel and Mossy Oak Break-Up Camo Pattern**
**Price:** . . . . . . . . . . . . . . . . . . . . . . . . . . . . . **$1,319.00**

## MODEL 1100 AUTOLOADING SHOTGUNS

The Remington **MODEL 1100** is a 5-shot gas-operated autoloader with a gas-metering system designed to reduce recoil. This design enables the shooter to use 2 3/4-inch standard velocity "Express" and 2 3/4-inch Magnum loads without gun adjustments. Barrels, within gauge and versions, are interchangeable. All 12- and 20-gauge versions include REM™ Choke; interchangeable choke tubes in 26" and 28" (12 gauge only) barrels. American walnut stocks come with design fine-line checkering and a scratch-resistant finish.

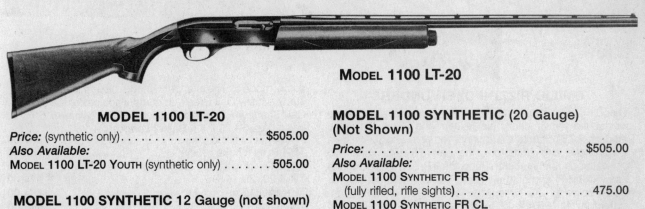

### MODEL 1100 LT-20

**MODEL 1100 LT-20**
**Price:** (synthetic only) . . . . . . . . . . . . . . . . . . . . . $505.00
**Also Available:**
MODEL 1100 LT-20 YOUTH (synthetic only) . . . . . . . 505.00

**MODEL 1100 SYNTHETIC 12 Gauge (not shown)**
**Price:** . . . . . . . . . . . . . . . . . . . . . . . . . . . . . . . . $505.00

**MODEL 1100 SYNTHETIC (20 Gauge)**
**(Not Shown)**
**Price:** . . . . . . . . . . . . . . . . . . . . . . . . . . . . . . . . $505.00
**Also Available:**
MODEL 1100 SYNTHETIC FR RS
   (fully rifled, rifle sights) . . . . . . . . . . . . . . . . . . . 475.00
MODEL 1100 SYNTHETIC FR CL
   (fully rifled, cantilever) . . . . . . . . . . . . . . . . . . . . 585.00

# RIZZINI SHOTGUNS

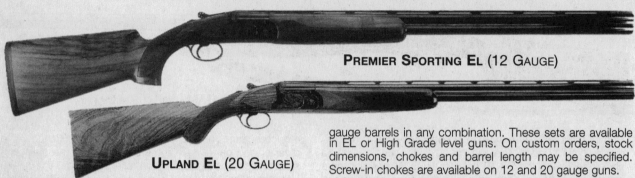

**PREMIER SPORTING EL** (12 GAUGE)

**UPLAND EL** (20 GAUGE)

Rizzini builds a well-finished boxlock ejector over/under that is available in all gauges and in many different configurations.

The **ARTEMIS** and **PREMIER** are production guns built to standard specifications. The EL models, which include the Upland EL, the Sporting EL and the High Grades feature higher grade wood, checkering and hand finishing.

**FIELD** guns are available with case-colored or coin-finish actions with straight grips or round knob semi-pistol grips. Also available are multi-gauge field sets with .410, 28 or 20 gauge barrels in any combination. These sets are available in EL or High Grade level guns. On custom orders, stock dimensions, chokes and barrel length may be specified. Screw-in chokes are available on 12 and 20 gauge guns.

**SPORTING** guns, in 12 and 20 gauge only, feature heavier weight and a target-style rib, stock and forearm. The Sporting models are available in three versions: Premier Sporting, Sporting EL and S790EL.

High Grade models, with or without sideplates, come in four engraving styles, including game scenes and gold inlays.

| *Prices:* | |
|---|---|
| **SPORTING EL** (12 gauge) | **$3,250.00** |
| **UPLAND EL** (20 gauge) | **2,850.00** |
| **S790 EMEL HIGH GRADE** | **8,750.00** |
| **ARTEMIS EL HIGH GRADE** | **12,650.00** |

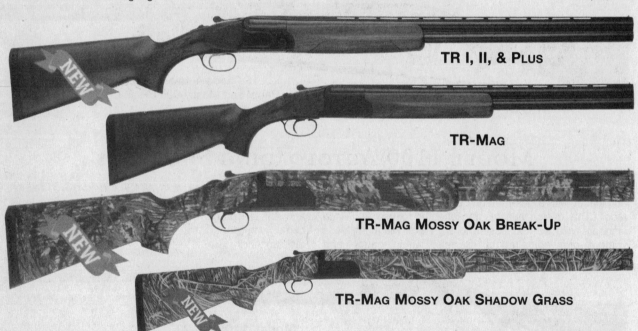

**TR I, II, & PLUS**

**TR-MAG**

**TR-MAG MOSSY OAK BREAK-UP**

**TR-MAG MOSSY OAK SHADOW GRASS**

## EMILIO RIZZINI OVER/UNDERS

The TR-I, TR-I Plus, and TR-II Emilio Rizzini boxlocks have walnut stocks, 3" chambers (except the 28 & 16 gauge models: 2.75" chamber) and ventilated ribs. The TR-1 has a fixed choke and extractors, the new TR-I-Plus has two choke tubes and extractors, and the TR-II has three choke tubes (IC/M/F) and auto ejectors. The TR-MAG series provides powerful 3.5" magnum chambers, choke tubes, extractors (All 10GA, & 12GA.WF) or ejectors (12GA. MOB & 12 GA. MOS) and a ventilated 7mm top rib in three hand-some models: The standard matte blue finish with walnut stock, Mossy Oak Break-up camouflage pattern, and Mossy Oak Shadow Grass camouflage pattern. *Weight:* 6.75-7.5 lbs. (10 ga., 9.75 lbs.) *Barrel Length:* 24-28"

| *Prices:* | |
|---|---|
| **TR-I** (fixed chokes) | **$687.00** |
| **TR-I PLUS** (choke tubes) | **748.00** |
| **TR-II** 12, 16 ga. | **879.00** |
| **TR-II** 20, 28, .410 | **924.00** |
| **TR-MAG** 12 ga. | **764.00** |
| 12 ga. camo | **942.00** |
| 10 ga. camo | **1,132.00** |

# ROSSI SHOTGUNS

**YOUTH MODEL .410**

**FIELD GRADE 12 GAUGE**

## SINGLE BARREL SHOTGUNS

Rossi shotguns have the timeless single-shot break-open breech design updated with modern safety features. These shotguns feature spur hammer, transfer bar action and integral safety that prevents the action from opening or closing when the hammer is cocked. This makes them perfect for beginners. Available in 12, 20 and .410 that accept 2", 2 1/2" Magnum or 3" Magnum shells. Each gauge is offered in a lighter youth model scaled down to fit young shooters. Shotguns feature brass bead front sight, straight stock with pistol grip, oil finished hardwood and sling swivels.

*All Rossi Shotguns Feature:*
*Brass Bead Front Sight*
*Satin, Oil Finished Exotic Hardwoods*
*Straight Stock with Pistol Grip*
*Modified Choke, Suitable for Steel Shot*
*Sling Swivels Installed*
*Ambidextrous Operation*
*Low Profile Serrated Hammer*
*Sure Grip Butt Plate*
*All Models Accept 2 inch, 2 1/2 inch Magnum and 3 inch Magnum Shells*

## MATCHED PAIR

For the year 2000, Rossi is introducing the Matched Pair; a single-shot break-open shotgun in your choice of .410, 20 gauge or 12 gauge, plus a completely interchangeable barrel chambered for .22 Long Rifle. The rifle barrel features fully adjustable sights. This makes the Matched Pair ideal (and economical) for the younger shooter.

| Item # | Barrel Length | Finish | Weight | Length | Stocks/ Grips | Description | Price |
|---|---|---|---|---|---|---|---|
| **FIELD GRADE SHOTGUNS** | | | | | | | |
| S121280S | 28' | blue | 5.25 lbs. | 43 1/4" | wood | S12 12 Gauge 28" Modified Choke | $99.00 |
| S201280S | 28" | blue | 5.25 lbs. | 43 1/4" | wood | S20 20 Gauge 28" Modified Choke | 99.00 |
| S411280S | 28" | blue | 4 lbs. | 43 1/4" | wood | S41 .410 28" Modifiedl Choke | 99.00 |
| **YOUTH MODEL SHOTGUNS** | | | | | | | |
| S201220S | 22" | blue | 5 lbs. | 35 1/2" | wood | S20 20 Gauge 22" Modified Choke Youth Model | $99.00 |
| S411220S | 22" | blue | 3.75 lbs. | 35 1/2" | wood | S41 .410 22" Modified Choke Youth Model | 99.00 |
| **MATCHED PAIR COMBO GUNS** | | | | | | | |
| S12/22R | N/A | blue | TBA | TBA | wood | Matched Pair 12 Gauge/.22LR, Adjustable Sights | $130.00 |
| S20/22R | N/A | blue | TBA | TBA | wood | Matched Pair 20 Gauge/.22LR, Adjustable Sights | 130.00 |
| S410/22R | N/A | blue | TBA | TBA | wood | Matched Pair .410/.22LR, Adjustable Sights | 130.00 |

SHOTGUNS

# RUGER SHOTGUNS

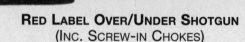

### RED LABEL OVER/UNDER SHOTGUN
#### (INC. SCREW-IN CHOKES)
**Price:** ............................. **$1,369.00**

### SPORTING CLAYS OVER/UNDER
#### MODEL KRL-2036 BR (20 Ga. shown above)
**Price:** w/Screw-in Chokes & 30" Barrels ..... **$1,443.00**

## SPECIFICATIONS RED LABEL AND SPORTING CLAYS OVER/UNDERS

| CATALOG NUMBER | GAUGE | CHAMBER | CHOKE* | BARREL LENGTH | OVERALL LENGTH | LENGTH PULL | DROP COMB | DROP HEEL | SIGHTS** | APPROX. WT. (LBS.) | TYPE STOCK |
|---|---|---|---|---|---|---|---|---|---|---|---|
| KRL-1226 BR | 12 | 3" | F,M,IC,S+ | 26" | 43" | 14 1/8" | 1 1/2" | 2 1/2" | GBF | 7 3/4 | Pistol Grip |
| KRL-1227 BR | 12 | 3" | F,M.IC,S+ | 28" | 45" | 14 1/8" | 1 1/2" | 2 1/2" | GBF | 8 | Pistol Grip |
| KRLS-1226 BR | 12 | 3" | F,M.IC,S+ | 26" | 43" | 14 1/8" | 1 1/2" | 2 1/2" | GBF | 7 1/2 | Straight |
| KRLS-1227 BR | 12 | 3" | F,M.IC,S+ | 28" | 45" | 14 1/8" | 1 1/2" | 2 1/2" | GBF | 7 3/4 | Straight |
| KRL-1236 BR | 12 | 3" | M,IC,S+ | 30" | 47" | 14 1/8" | 1 1/2" | 2 1/2" | GBF/GBM | 7 3/4 | Pistol Grip |
| KRL-2029 BR | 20 | 3" | F,M,IC,S+ | 26" | 43" | 14 1/8" | 1 1/2" | 2 1/2" | GBF | 7 | Pistol Grip |
| KRL-2030 BR | 20 | 3" | F,M,IC,S+ | 28" | 45" | 14 1/8" | 1 1/2" | 2 1/2" | GBF | 7 1/4 | Pistol Grip |
| KRLS-2029 BR | 20 | 3" | F,M,IC,S+ | 26" | 43" | 14 1/8" | 1 1/2" | 2 1/2" | GBF | 6 3/4 | Straight |
| KRLS-2030 BR | 20 | 3" | F,M,IC,S+ | 28" | 45" | 14 1/8" | 1 1/2" | 2 1/2" | GBF | 7 | Straight |
| KRL-2036 BR | 20 | 3" | M,IC,S+ | 30" | 47" | 14 1/8" | 1 1/2" | 2 1/2" | GBF/GBM | 7 | Pistol Grip |
| KRLS-2826 BR | 28 | 2 3/4" | F,M,IC,S+ | 26" | 43" | 14 1/8" | 1 1/2" | 2 1/2" | GBF | 5 7/8 | Straight |
| KRLS-2827 BR | 28 | 2 3/4" | F,M,IC,S+ | 28" | 45" | 14 1/8" | 1 1/2" | 2 1/2" | GBF | 6 | Straight |
| KRL-2826 BR | 28 | 2 3/4" | F,M,IC,S+ | 26" | 43" | 14 1/8" | 1 1/2" | 2 1/2" | GBF | 6 | Pistol Grip |
| KRL-2827 BR | 28 | 2 3/4" | F,M,IC,S+ | 28" | 45" | 14 1/8" | 1 1/2" | 2 1/2" | GBF | 6 1/8 | Pistol Grip |

*F-Full, M-Modified, IC-Improved Cylinder, S-Skeet. +Two skeet chokes standard with each shotgun. **GBF-Gold-Bead Front Sight, GBM-Gold-Bead Middle BR-Briley Ruger choke tube wrench included.*

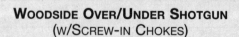

## WOODSIDE SPECIFICATIONS

| CATALOG NUMBER | GAUGE | CHOKE* | BARREL LENGTH | OVERALL LENGTH | APPROX. WT. | STOCK |
|---|---|---|---|---|---|---|
| KWS-1226 BR | 12 | F,M,IC,S | 26" | 43" | 7.75 lbs. | Pistol |
| KWS-1227 BR | 12 | F,M,IC,S | 28" | 45" | 8 lbs. | Pistol |
| KWSS-1226 BR | 12 | F,M,IC,S | 26" | 43" | 7.5 lbs. | Straight |
| KWSS-1227 BR | 12 | F,M,IC,S | 28" | 45" | 7.75 lbs. | Straight |
| KWSS-1236 BR | 12 | F,M,IC,S | 30" | 47" | 7.75 lbs. | Pistol |

### WOODSIDE OVER/UNDER SHOTGUN
#### (W/SCREW-IN CHOKES)
**Price:** ............................. **$1,849.00**

# SAVAGE SHOTGUNS

## MODEL 210FT "MASTER SHOT" SHOTGUN

**SPECIFICATIONS**
*Gauge:* 12  *Choke:* Full choke tube  *Barrel length:* 24"
*Overall length*: 43.5"  *Weight:* 7.5 lbs.

*Finish:* Advantage™ camo pattern
*Features:* Barrel threaded for interchangeable Winchester-style choke tubes; drilled and tapped for scope mounting; positive checkering; ventilated rubber recoil pad and swivel studs; bead front sight with U-notch blade rear; short-lift 60° bolt rotation, controlled round feed; triple front locking lugs
*Price:* . . . . . . . . . . . . . . . . . . . . . . . . . . . . . . . **$466.00**

## MODEL 210F SLUG GUN

*Also available:*
**210F "MASTER SHOT" SLUG GUN** (12 gauge). Features full-length baffle; 24" barrel chambered for 2.75" or 3" shells; three-position, top tang rifle-style safety; no sights; 1 in 35" twist (8-groove precision button rifling).
*Price:* . . . . . . . . . . . . . . . . . . . . . . . . . . . . . . . **$402.00**

# SIG ARMS SHOTGUNS

**TR-40 SILVER**

## SIG APOLLO OVER/UNDER SHOTGUNS

Low-profile receivers and light weight make these five models of Apollo shotguns quick to point. Built in the arms plant of famous Italian maker B. Rizzini, they're available in 12, 20, 28 and .410 gauges. The guns feature boxlock actions machined from solid steel, with automatic ejectors, single selective triggers and a full complement of screw-in choke tubes (28 and .410 barrels have fixed chokes). Embellishments include sideplates with case coloring, gold inlay, nickel finish. Stocks are of Turkish walnut checkered 20 lines per inch. Oil finish and rubber recoil pad are standard. Competition models feature select wood and stock dimensions suited to the game.
*Price:* . . . . . . . . . . . . . . . . . . . . . . . . . . from **$1,335.00**

# SKB SHOTGUNS

## MODEL 385 SIDE-BY-SIDE

Model 385 features silver nitride receiver with engraved scroll and game scene design; solid boxlock action w/double locking lugs; single selective trigger; selective automatic ejectors; automatic safety; sculpted American walnut stock; pistol or English straight grip; semi-beavertail forend; stock and forend finished w/18-line fine checkering; standard series choke tube system; solid rib w/flat matte finish and metal front bead. For additional specifications, see table below.

**Price:**. . . . . . . . . . . . . . . . . . . . . . . . . . . . . . . . . **$1,979.00**
Field Set . . . . . . . . . . . . . . . . . . . . . . . . . . . . . . . 2,839.00
***Also available:***
**MODEL 485 SERIES.** Features engraved upland game scene; semi-fancy American walnut stock and beavertail forend; raised vent rib with flat matte finish.
**Price:**. . . . . . . . . . . . . . . . . . . . . . . . . . . . . . . . . **$2,679.00**
Field Set . . . . . . . . . . . . . . . . . . . . . . . . . . . . . . . 3,829.00

## SPECIFICATIONS MODEL 385 & 485

### FIELD MODELS

| GAUGE | CHAMBER | BARREL LENGTH | OVERALL LENGTH | INTER CHOKE | SIGHTS✓ | RIB WIDTH | STOCK | AVERAGE WEIGHT* 385 | AVERAGE WEIGHT* 485 |
|---|---|---|---|---|---|---|---|---|---|
| 12 | 3" | 28" | 44 1/2" | STND-A | MFB | 5/16" | PISTOL | 7 lb. 3 oz. | 7 lb. 1 oz. |
| 12 | 3" | 28" | 44 1/2" | STND-A | MFB | 5/16" | ENGLISH | 7 lb. 1 oz. | 7 lb. 5 oz. |
| 12 | 3" | 26" | 42 1/2" | STND-A | MFB | 5/16" | PISTOL | 7 lb. 1 oz. | 7 lb. 5 oz. |
| 12 | 3" | 26" | 42 1/2" | STND-A | MFB | 5/16" | ENGLISH | 7 lb. 0 oz. | 7 lb. 4 oz. |
| 20 | 3" | 26" | 42 1/2" | STND-B | MFB | 5/16" | PISTOL | 6 lb. 10 oz. | 6 lb. 14 oz. |
| 20 | 3" | 26" | 42 1/2" | STND-B | MFB | 5/16" | ENGLISH | 6 lb. 10 oz. | 6 lb. 14 oz. |
| 28 | 2 3/4" | 26" | 42 1/2" | STND-B | MFB | 5/16" | PISTOL | 6 lb. 13 oz. | 7 lb. 2 oz. |
| 28 | 2 3/4" | 26" | 42 1/2" | STND-B | MFB | 5/16" | ENGLISH | 6 lb. 13 oz. | 7 lb. 2 oz. |

### 2 BARREL FIELD SETS

| GAUGE | CHAMBER | BARREL LENGTH | OVERALL LENGTH | INTER CHOKE | SIGHTS✓ | RIB WIDTH | STOCK | AVERAGE WEIGHT* 385 | AVERAGE WEIGHT* 485 |
|---|---|---|---|---|---|---|---|---|---|
| 20 | 3" | 26" | 42 1/2" | STND-B | MFB | 5/16" | PISTOL | 6 lb. 10 oz. | |
| 28 | 2 3/4" | 26" | 42 1/2" | STND-B | MFB | 5/16" | PISTOL | 6 lb. 13 oz. | |
| 20 | 3" | 26" | 42 1/2" | STND-B | MFB | 5/16" | ENGLISH | 6 lb. 10 oz. | |
| 28 | 2 3/4" | 26" | 42 1/2" | STND-B | MFB | 5/16" | ENGLISH | 6 lb. 13 oz. | |

*Weights may vary due to wood density. Specifications may vary. *INTER-CHOKE SYSTEMS: COMP - Competition series includes Mod., Full, Imp. Cyl. STND-A - Standard series includes Mod., Full, Imp. Cyl. STND-B- Standard series includes Imp. Cyl., Mod. Skeet STOCK DIMENSIONS: Length of Pull - 14 1/8" Drop at Comb - 1 1/2" Drop at Heel - 2 3/4" ✓MFB-Metal Front Bead

### MODEL 505
### $1,149.00 (Field)
### $1,269.00 (Sporting Clays)

### 505 FIELD OVER AND UNDERS

| GAUGE | CHAMBER | BARREL LENGTH | OVERALL LENGTH | INTER CHOKE | SIGHTS✓ | RIB WIDTH | AVERAGE WEIGHT* |
|---|---|---|---|---|---|---|---|
| 12 | 3" | 28" | 45 3/8" | STND-A | MFB | 3/8" | 7 lb. 12 oz. |
| 12 | 3" | 26" | 45 3/8" | STND-B | MFB | 3/8" | 7 lb. 11 oz. |
| 20 | 3" | 26" | 45 3/8" | STND-B | MFB | 3/8" | 6 lb. 10 oz. |

### 505 SPORTING CLAYS

| GAUGE | CHAMBER | BARREL LENGTH | OVERALL LENGTH | INTER CHOKE | SIGHTS | RIB WIDTH | AVERAGE WEIGHT* 505 |
|---|---|---|---|---|---|---|---|
| 12 | 3" | 30" | 47 3/8" | STND-B | CP/WFB | 15/32" CH/STP | 8 lb. 5 oz. |
| 12 | 3" | 28" | 45 3/8" | STND-B | CP/WFB | 15/32" CH/STP | 8 lb. 1 oz. |

*Weights may vary due to wood density. Specifications may vary. *INTER-CHOKE SYSTEMS: STND-A-Standard series includes Full, Mod, Imp. Cyl. STND-B-Standard series includes Imp. Cyl., Mod, Skeet STOCK DIMENSIONS: Length of Pull-14 1/8" Drop at Comb-1 1/2" Drop at heel-2 3/16" **MFB-Metal Front Bead**

# SKB SHOTGUNS

## MODEL 585 AND 785 SERIES

### MODEL 785 OVER/UNDER

The SKB 785 Series features chrome-lined chambers and bores, lengthened forcing cones, chrome-plated ejectors and competition choke tube system.

**MODEL 785**          *Prices*
FIELD(12 & 20 ga.) . . . . . . . . . . . . . . . . . . . . . . . **$2,049.00**
   28 or .410 ga. . . . . . . . . . . . . . . . . . . . . . . .2,139.00

TWO-BARREL FIELD SET (12 & 20 ga.) . . . . . . . . .2,979.00
   20/28 ga. or 28/.410 ga . . . . . . . . . . . . . .3,079.00
**Skeet** (12 or 20 ga.) . . . . . . . . . . . . . . . . . . .2,139.00
   28 or .410 ga. . . . . . . . . . . . . . . . . . . . . . .2,179.00
   2-Bbl. Set . . . . . . . . . . . . . . . . . . . . . . . . . .4,299.00
**SPORTING CLAYS** (12 or 20 ga.) . . . . . . . . . . . . .2,199.00
   28 gauge . . . . . . . . . . . . . . . . . . . . . . . . . .2,279.00
   2-Barrel Set (12 or 20 ga.) . . . . . . . . . . . . .3,149.00
**TRAP** (Monte Carlo or Std.) . . . . . . . . . . . . . . .2,139.00
   2-Barrel Trap Combo . . . . . . . . . . . . . . . . . .2,979.00

### TRAP MODELS

| GAUGE | STOCK | BARREL√ LENGTH | OVERALL LENGTH | INTER CHOKE | SIGHTS√ | 785 RIB WIDTH | 585 RIB WIDTH | AVERAGE WEIGHT* 785 | AVERAGE WEIGHT* 585 | MANUFACTURERS ID# 785 | MANUFACTURERS ID# 585 |
|---|---|---|---|---|---|---|---|---|---|---|---|
| 12 | STND | 30" | 47 3/8" | COMP-A | CP/WFB | 15/32" CH/STP | 3/8" STP | 8 lb. 15 oz. | 8 lb. 7 oz. | A7820CVTN | A5820CVTN |
| 12 | MONTE | 30" | 47 3/8: | COMP-A | CP/WFB | 15/32" CH/STP | 3/8" STP | 9 lb. 0 oz. | 8 lb. 7 oz. | A7820CVTM | A5420CVTM |
| 12 | STND | 32" | 49 3/8: | COMP-A | CP/WFB | 15/32" CH/STP | 3/8" STP | 9 lb. 1 oz. | 8 lb. 10 oz. | A7822CVTN | A5822CVTN |
| 12 | MONTE | 32" | 49 3/8: | COMP-A | CP/WFB | 15/32" CH/STP | 3/8" STP | 9 lb. 1 oz. | 8 lb. 9 oz. | A7822CVTM | A5822CVTM |

#### TRAP COMBO'S – STANDARD

| GAUGE | STOCK | BARREL√ LENGTH | OVERALL LENGTH | INTER CHOKE | SIGHTS√ | 785 RIB WIDTH | 585 RIB WIDTH | AVERAGE WEIGHT* 785 | AVERAGE WEIGHT* 585 | MANUFACTURERS ID# 785 | MANUFACTURERS ID# 585 |
|---|---|---|---|---|---|---|---|---|---|---|---|
| 12 | STND | O/U-30" | 47 3/8" | COMP. | CP/WFB | 15/32" CH/STP | 3/8" STP | 8 lb. 15 oz. | 8 lb. 6 oz. | A7820TN/7822 | A5820TN/5822 |
| 12 | STND | S/O-32" | 49 3/8" | COMP. | CP/WFB | 15/32" CH/STP | 3/8" STP | 9 lb. 0 oz. | 8 lb. 6 oz. | A7820TN/7822 | A5820TN/5822 |
| 12 | STND | O/U-30" | 47 3/8" | COMP. | CP/WFB | 15/32" CH/STP | 3/8"STP | 9 lb. 0 oz. | 8 lb. 4 oz. | A7820TN/7824 | A5820TN/5824 |
| 12 | STND | S/O-34" | 51 3/8" | COMP. | CP/WFB | 15/32" CH/STP | 3/8"STP | 9 lb. 1 oz. | 8 lb. 6 oz. | A7820TN/7824 | A5820TN/5824 |
| 12 | STND | O/U-32" | 49 3/8" | COMP. | CP/WFB | 15/32" CH/STP | 3/8" STP | 9 lb. 0 oz. | 8 lb. 7 oz. | A7822TN/7824 | A5822TN/5824 |
| 12 | STND | S/O-34" | 51 3/8" | COMP. | CP/WFB | 15/32" CH/STP | 3/8" STP | 9 lb. 1 oz. | 8 lb. 8 oz. | A7822TN/7824 | A5822TN/5824 |

#### TRAP COMBO'S – MONTE CARLO

| GAUGE | STOCK | BARREL√ LENGTH | OVERALL LENGTH | INTER CHOKE | SIGHTS√ | 785 RIB WIDTH | 585 RIB WIDTH | AVERAGE WEIGHT* 785 | AVERAGE WEIGHT* 585 | MANUFACTURERS ID# 785 | MANUFACTURERS ID# 585 |
|---|---|---|---|---|---|---|---|---|---|---|---|
| 12 | MONTE | O/U-30" | 47 3/8" | COMP. | CP/WFB | 15/32" CH/STP | 3/8" STP | 8 lb. 15 oz. | 8 lb. 6 oz. | A7820TM/7822 | A5820TM/5822 |
| 12 | MONTE | S/O-32" | 49 3/8" | COMP. | CP/WFB | 15/32" CH/STP | 3/8" STP | 9 lb. 0 oz. | 8 lb. 6 oz. | A7820TM/7822 | A5820TM/5822 |
| 12 | MONTE | O/U-30" | 47 3/8" | COMP. | CP/WFB | 15/32" CH/STP | 3/8"STP | 8 lb. 15 oz. | 8 lb. 4 oz. | A7820TM/7824 | A5820TM/5824 |
| 12 | MONTE | S/O-34" | 51 3/8" | COMP. | CP/WFB | 15/32" CH/STP | 3/8"STP | 9 lb. 1 oz. | 8 lb. 6 oz. | A7820TM/7824 | A5820TM/5824 |
| 12 | MONTE | O/U-32" | 49 3/8" | COMP. | CP/WFB | 15/32" CH/STP | 3/8" STP | 9 lb. 0 oz. | 8 lb. 7 oz. | A7822TM/7824 | A5822TM/5824 |
| 12 | MONTE | S/O-34" | 51 3/8" | COMP. | CP/WFB | 51/32" CH/STP | 3/8" STP | 9 lb. 1 oz. | 8 lb. 9 oz. | A7822TM/7824 | A5822TM/5824 |

*Weights may vary due to wood density. Specifications may vary. *INTER-CHOKE SYSTEMS COMP. - Competition series includes Full, Mod., Imp. Cyl. STND. B - Standard series includes Imp. Cyl. Mod. and Skeet STOCK DIMENSIONS Length of Pull - 13 1/2" Drop at Comb - 1/1/2" Drop at Heel - 2 1/4" √MFB - Metal Front Bead

### YOUTH & LADIES

| GAUGE | CHAMBER | BARREL LENGTH | OVERALL LENGTH | INTER CHOKE | SIGHTS√ | RIB WIDTH | AVERAGE WEIGHT* 785 | AVERAGE WEIGHT* 585 | MANUFACTURERS ID# 785 | MANUFACTURERS ID# 585 |
|---|---|---|---|---|---|---|---|---|---|---|
| 12 | 3" | 28" | 44 1/2" | COMP. | MFB | 3/8" | | 7 lb. 11 oz. | | A5828CFY |
| 12 | 3" | 26" | 42 1/2" | COMP. | MFB | 3/8" | | 7 lb. 9 oz. | | A5826CFY |
| 20 | 3" | 26" | 42 1/2" | STND-B | MFB | 3/8" | | 6 lb. 7 oz. | | A5806CFY |

#### SKEET MODELS

| GAUGE | CHAMBER | BARREL LENGTH | OVERALL LENGTH | INTER CHOKE | SIGHTS√ | RIB WIDTH | AVERAGE WEIGHT* 785 | AVERAGE WEIGHT* 585 | MANUFACTURERS ID# 785 | MANUFACTURERS ID# 585 |
|---|---|---|---|---|---|---|---|---|---|---|
| 12 | 3" | 30" | 47 1/4" | COMP. | CP/WFB | 3/8" | 8 lb. 9 oz. | 8 lb. 1 oz. | A7820CV | A5820CV |
| 12 | 3" | 28" | 45 1/4" | COMP. | CP/WFB | 3/8" | 8 lb. 6 oz. | 7 lb. 12 oz. | A7828CV | A5828CV |
| 20 | 3" | 28" | 45 1/4" | STND. | CP/WFB | 5/16" | 7 lb. 2 oz. | 6 lb. 15 oz. | A7808CV | A5808CV |
| 28 | 2.75" | 28" | 45 1/4" | STND. | CP/WFB | 5/16" | 7 lb. 5 oz. | 6 lb. 15 oz. | A7888CV | A5888CV |
| 410 | 3" | 28" | 45 1/4" | SK/SK | CP/WFB | 5/16" | 7 lb. 5 oz. | 7 lb. 0 oz. | A7848CV | A5848V |

#### 3 BARREL SKEET SETS

| GAUGE | CHAMBER | BARREL LENGTH | OVERALL LENGTH | INTER CHOKE | SIGHTS√ | RIB WIDTH | AVERAGE WEIGHT* 785 | AVERAGE WEIGHT* 585 | MANUFACTURERS ID# 785 | MANUFACTURERS ID# 585 |
|---|---|---|---|---|---|---|---|---|---|---|
| 20 | 3" | 28" | 45 1/4" | STND. | CP/WFB | 5/16" | 7 lb. 2 oz. | 6 lb. 15 oz. | | |
| 28 | 2.75" | 28" | 45 1/4" | STND. | CP/WFB | 5/16" | 7 lb. 5 oz. | 7 lb. 0 oz. | A78088 | A58088 |
| 410 | 3" | 28" | 45 1/4" | SK/SK | CP/WFB | 5/16" | 7 lb. 5 oz. | 7 lb. 0 oz. | | |

*Weights may vary due to wood density. Specifications may vary. *INTER-CHOKE SYSTEMS: COMP. - Competition series includes 2 -SKI/SCI, 1-Mod/SCIV STND - Standard series includes Skeet, Skeet and Imp. Cyl. NOTE: 785's Are Equipped with Step-Up Style Ribs STOCK DIMENSIONS: Length of Pull - 14 1/8" Drop at Comb - 1 1/2" Drop at Heel - 2 3/16" √CP/WFB - Center Post/White Front Bead

# STOEGER IGA SHOTGUNS

## COACH GUN

## ENGRAVED COACH GUN

The **IGA CLASSIC SIDE-BY-SIDE COACH GUN** sports a 20-inch barrel. Lightning fast, it is the perfect shotgun for hunting upland game in dense brush or close quarters. This endurance-tested workhorse of a gun is designed from the ground up to give you years of trouble-free service. Two massive underlugs provide a super-safe, vise-tight locking system for lasting strength and durability. The mechanical extraction of spent shells and double-trigger mechanism assures reliability. The automatic safety is actuated whenever the action is opened, whether or not the gun has been fired. The polish and blue is deep and rich, and the solid sighting rib is matte-finished for glare-free sighting. Chrome-moly steel barrels with micro-polished bores give dense, consistent patterns. Nickel finish is now available. The classic stock and forend are of durable hardwood...oil finished, hand-rubbed and hand-checkered.

Improved Cylinder/Modified choking and its short barrel make the IGA coach gun the ideal choice for hunting in close quarters, security and police work. Three-inch chambers.

**Prices:** In 12 and 20 Gauge or .410 Bore........ **$415.00**
Nickel, shown . . . . . . . . . . . . . . . . . . . . . . . . . . . **464.00**
***Also available*** with Engraved Stagecoach scene
on the stock: . . . . . . . . . . . . . . . . . . . . . . . . . . . . **479.00**

## UPLANDER LADIES SIDE-BY-SIDE

## UPLANDER LADIES SIDE-BY-SIDE

Crafted specifically with women in mind, IGA's new model features a lightweight 20 gauge with 24" barrel and is equipped with IC/M choke tubes. The durable 13" Brazilian hardwood stock is fitted with a ventilated pad to reduce recoil. Standard features include extractors, double triggers and automatic safety.
**Price:** . . . . . . . . . . . . . . . . . . . . . . . . . . . . . . . . **$489.00**

## UPLANDER YOUTH SIDE-BY-SIDE (not shown)

IGA's lightweight .410 Youth gun has 24" barrels bored modified and full. Both barrels will handle 2 ½'' or 3" shells. The 13" Brazilian hardwood stock includes a recoil pad. Standard features include double triggers, extractors and an automatic safety (activated when the gun is open). New for 2000 is a 20-ga. model with the same dimensions but choked IC and modified.
**Price:** . . . . . . . . . . . . . . . . . . . . . . . . . . . . . . . . **$449.00**

## UPLANDER IGA SIDE-BY-SIDE (not shown)

The **IGA SIDE-BY-SIDE** is a rugged shotgun, endurance-tested and designed to give years of trouble-free service. A vise-tight, super-safe locking system is provided by two massive under-lugs for lasting strength and durability. Two design features that make the IGA a standout for reliability are its positive mechanical extraction of spent shells and its traditional double-trigger mechanism. The safety is automatic in that every time the action is opened, whether or not the gun has been fired, the safety is actuated. The polish and bluing are deep and rich. The solid sighting rib carries a machined-in matte finish for glare-free sighting. Barrels are of chrome-moly steel with micro-polished bores to give dense, consistent patterns. Your choice of traditional stock or the legendary English-style stock. Both are of durable Brazilian hardwood, oil-finished, hand-rubbed and hand-checkered.
**Prices:**
In 12, 20, 28 Gauge or .410 Bore. . . . . . . . . . . **$437.00**
In 12 and 20 Gauge w/Choke Tubes. . . . . . . . . . . **477.00**
***Also available*** with English stock w/choke tubes (IC/M) and fixed (M/M).

*See table on page 349 for additional specifications*

# STOEGER IGA SHOTGUNS

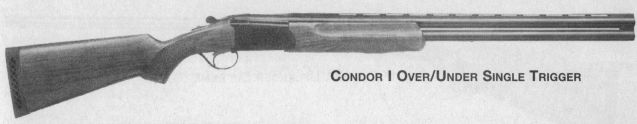

### CONDOR I OVER/UNDER SINGLE TRIGGER

The **IGA CONDOR I O/U SINGLE TRIGGER** is a workhorse of a shotgun, designed for maximum dependability in heavy field use. The super-safe lock-up system makes use of a sliding underlug, the best system for over/under shotguns. A massive monobloc joins the barrel in a solid one-piece assembly at the breech end. Reliability is assured, thanks to the mechanical extraction system. Upon opening the breech, the spent shells are partially lifted from the chamber, allowing easy removal by hand. IGA barrels are of chrome-moly steel with micro-polished bores to give tight, consistent patterns. They are specifically formulated for use with steel shot where Federal migratory bird regulations require. Atop the barrel is a sighting rib with an anti-glare surface. The buttstock and forend are of durable hardwood, hand-checkered and finished with an oil-based formula that takes dents and scratches in stride.

The **IGA CONDOR I** over/under shotgun is available in 12 and 20 gauge with 26- and 28-inch barrels with choke tubes and 3-inch chambers. *Price:* w/Choke Tubes . . . . . . . . . . . . . . . . . . . . . **$559.00**

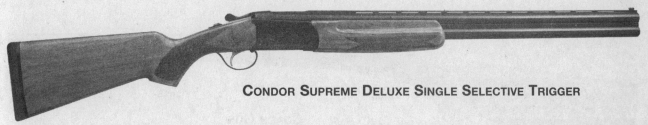

### CONDOR SUPREME DELUXE SINGLE SELECTIVE TRIGGER

The **IGA CONDOR SUPREME** truly compliments its name. The stock is selected from upgraded Brazilian walnut, and the hand-finished checkering is sharp and crisp. A matte-laquered finish provides a soft warm glow, while maintaining a high resistance to dents and scratches. A massive monoblock joins the barrel in a solid one-piece assembly at the breech end. Upon opening the breech, the automatic ejectors cause the spent shells to be thrown clear of the gun. The barrels are of moly-chrome steel with micro-polished bores to give tight, consistent patterns; they are specifically formulated for use with steel shot. Choke tubes are provided. Also, a single, selective trigger and barrel rib with both mid- and front bead. *Price:* . . . . . . . . . . . . . . . . . . . . . . . . . . . . . . . **$674.00**

### SIDE-BY-SIDE TURKEY MODEL
*Price:* . . . . . . . . . . . . . . . . . . . . . . . . . . . . . . . **$559.00**

### OVER/UNDER WATERFOWL MODEL

The 12-gauge **SIDE-BY-SIDE TURKEY MODEL** features IGA's new Advantage™ camouflage finish, plus double triggers, 3" chamber with 24" barrel and wide beavertail forend. The 30" barrel over/under **WATERFOWL MODEL** also features the new Advantage™ camouflage pattern on the barrel, stock and forend, plus single trigger, automatic ejector and Full/Full flush-mounted choke tubes and ventilated recoil pad. *Also available:* **TURKEY MODEL O/U** w/26" barrel in camouflage. *Price:* . . . . . . . . . . . . . . . . . . . . . . . . . . . . . . . **$729.00**

*See table on page 349 for additional specifications*

SHOTGUNS

# STOEGER IGA SHOTGUNS

**IGA UPLANDER SUPREME**

## UPLANDER SUPREME

The Uplander Supreme has all the traditional Uplander features and a lot more. Available in a 12 or 20 gauge, the Uplander Supreme features a high grade American walnut stock and forend with a high gloss finish, single selective trigger, automatic ejectors, and interchangeable choke tubes. Other standard features include a gold trigger, red front and mid-rib bead sights and a soft rubber recoil pad.

**Price:** ................................$599.00
**Also available:**
Youth model, .410 or 20 ga ..................$449.00
Uplander, 12 of 20 ga .......................477.00
Ladies model, 20 ga .........................489.00
Advantage camo, Turkey series in 12 ga .......437.00

**COACH GUN**

## COACH GUN

The Coach Gun with it's 20" barrel is built to the same exacting specifications as the Uplander Field Grade side-by-side. It's an ideal brush gun for close range shooting, home protection and security. The full size stock and wide beavertail forend affords greater comfort while shooting. Each Coach gun is chambered for 2 3/4" and 3" shells.

**Price:**
COACH GUN ................................$415.00

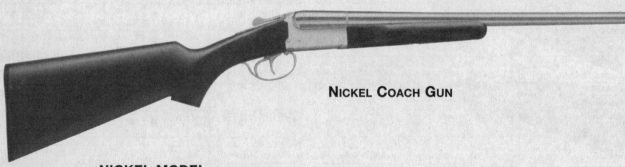

**NICKEL COACH GUN**

## NICKEL MODEL

This highly polished nickel finish model is complemented by a dark Brazilian hardwood stock and forend. Available in 12, 20 or .410 gauge and choked improved cylinder and modified, this little gun will handle 2 3/4" and 3" magnum shells with the best of them.

**Price:**
NICKEL COACH GUN ........................$464.00
**Also available:**
COACH GUN w/ engraved stagecoach scene stock.
**Price:** ................................479.00

# STOEGER IGA SHOTGUNS

| | GAUGE | | | | | BARREL LENGTH | | | | | | CHOKES | | SPECIFICATIONS | | | | | SAFETY | | BUTT-PLATES | | DIMENSIONS | | | |
|---|---|---|---|---|---|---|---|---|---|---|---|---|---|---|---|---|---|---|---|---|---|---|---|---|---|---|
| | 12 | 16 | 20 | 28 | .410 | 20" | 22" | 24" | 26" | 28" | 30" | F | CT | C | W | EX | EJ | T | MA | AU | MO | RV | LOP | DAC | DAH | OL |
| **COACH GUN** Side by Side | ■ | | ■ | | ■ | ■ | | | | | | IC/M | | 3" | 6.75 | ■ | | D.T. | | ■ | ■ | | 14.5" | 1.5" | 2.5" | 36.5" |
| **COACH GUN** Nickel | ■ | | ■ | | ■ | ■ | | | | | | IC/M | | 3" | 6.75 | ■ | | D.T. | | ■ | ■ | | 14.5" | 1.5" | 2.5" | 36.5" |
| **COACH GUN** Engraved | ■ | | ■ | | ■ | ■ | | | | | | IC/M | | 3" | 6.75 | ■ | | D.T. | | ■ | ■ | | 14.5" | 1.5" | 2.5" | 36.5" |
| **UPLANDER** Side by Side | ■ | | ■ | | | | | | ■ | | | | IC/M | 3" | 6.75 | ■ | | D.T. | | ■ | ■ | | 14.5" | 1.5" | 2.5" | 42" |
| **UPLANDER** Side by Side | ■ | | ■ | | | | | | | ■ | | | M/F | 3" | 6.75 | ■ | | D.T. | | ■ | ■ | | 14.5" | 1.5" | 2.5" | 44" |
| **UPLANDER** Side by Side | | ■ | | ■ | | | | | ■ | | | IC/M | | 2.75" | 6.75 | ■ | | D.T. | | ■ | ■ | | 14.5" | 1.5" | 2.5" | 42" |
| **UPLANDER** Side by Side | ■ | | ■ | | | | | | ■ | | | IC/M | | 3" | 6.75 | ■ | | D.T. | | ■ | ■ | | 14.5" | 1.5" | 2.5" | 42" |
| **UPLANDER** Side by Side | ■ | | ■ | | | | | | | ■ | | M/F | | 3" | 6.75 | ■ | | D.T. | | ■ | ■ | | 14.5" | 1.5" | 2.5" | 44" |
| **UPLANDER** Side by Side | | | | | ■ | | | | ■ | | | F/F | | 3" | 6.75 | ■ | | D.T. | | ■ | ■ | | 14.5" | 1.5" | 2.5" | 42" |
| **UPLANDER** English | | | ■ | | | | | ■ | | | | | IC/M | 3" | 6.75 | ■ | | D.T. | | ■ | ■ | | 14.5" | 1.5" | 2.5" | 40" |
| **UPLANDER** English | | | | | ■ | | | ■ | | | | M/M | | 3" | 6.75 | ■ | | D.T. | | ■ | ■ | | 14.5" | 1.5" | 2.5" | 40" |
| **UPLANDER** Ladies | | | ■ | | | | | ■ | | | | | IC/M | 3" | 6.75 | ■ | | D.T. | | ■ | | ■ | 13" | 1.5" | 2.5" | 40" |
| **UPLANDER** Youth | | | ■ | | | | | ■ | | | | | IC/M | 3" | 6.75 | ■ | | D.T. | | ■ | | ■ | 13.5" | 1.5" | 2.5" | 40" |
| **UPLANDER** Youth | | | | | ■ | | | ■ | | | | M/F | | 3" | 6.75 | ■ | | D.T. | | ■ | | ■ | 13" | 1.5" | 2.5" | 40" |
| **UPLANDER** Supreme | ■ | | ■ | | | | | | ■ | | | | IC/M | 3" | 6.75 | | ■ | S.S.T. | | ■ | | ■ | 14.5" | 1.5" | 2.5" | 42" |
| **UPLANDER** Supreme | ■ | | ■ | | | | | | | ■ | | | M/F | 3" | 6.75 | | ■ | S.S.T. | | ■ | | ■ | 14.5" | 1.5" | 2.5" | 44" |
| **UPLANDER** Supreme | | | ■ | | | | | ■ | | | | | IC/M | 3" | 6.75 | | ■ | S.S.T. | | ■ | | ■ | 14.5" | 1.5" | 2.5" | 40" |
| **CONDOR I** Over/Under | ■ | | ■ | | | | | | ■ | | | | IC/M | 3" | 8 | ■ | | S.T. | | ■ | | ■ | 14.5" | 1.5" | 2.5" | 42" |
| **CONDOR I** Over/Under | ■ | | ■ | | | | | | | ■ | | | M/F | 3" | 8 | ■ | | S.T. | | ■ | | ■ | 14.5" | 1.5" | 2.5" | 44" |
| **CONDOR** Supreme Deluxe | ■ | | ■ | | | | | | ■ | | | | IC/M | 3" | 8 | | ■ | S.S.T. | | ■ | | ■ | 14.5" | 1.5" | 2.5" | 42" |
| **CONDOR** Supreme Deluxe | ■ | | ■ | | | | | | | ■ | | | M/F | 3" | 8 | | ■ | S.S.T. | | ■ | | ■ | 14.5" | 1.5" | 2.5" | 44" |
| **CONDOR** Supreme Deluxe | | | ■ | | | | | ■ | | | | | IC/M | 3" | 8 | | ■ | S.S.T. | | ■ | | ■ | 14.5" | 1.5" | 2.5" | 40" |
| **UPLANDER** Camo | ■ | | | | | | | ■ | | | | F/F | | 3" | 6.75 | ■ | | D.T. | | ■ | ■ | | 14.5" | 1.5" | 2.5" | 40" |
| **CONDOR** Supreme Camo | ■ | | | | | | | | ■ | | | F/F | | 3" | 8 | | ■ | S.T. | ■ | | | ■ | 14.5" | 1.5" | 2.5" | 42" |
| **CONDOR** Supreme Camo | ■ | | | | | | | | | | ■ | | IC/M | 3" | 8 | | ■ | S.S.T. | ■ | | | ■ | 14.5" | 1.5" | 2.5" | 46" |

**KEY:** F=Fixed, CT=Choke Tubes, C=Chamber, W=Weight (lbs.), EX=Extractors, EJ=Ejectors, T=Triggers, M=Manual, A=Automatic, MO=Molded, RV=Rubber-Ventilated, LOP=Length Of Pull, DAC=Drop At Comb, DAH=Drop At Heel, OA=Overall Length

*Specifications subject to change without notice.*

SHOTGUNS

# WEATHERBY SHOTGUNS

### ATHENA GRADE V CLASSIC FIELD

The Athena features a boxlock action and sidelock-type plates with fine floral engraving. The hinge pivots are made of high-strength steel alloy. The locking system employs the Greener crossbolt design. The single selective trigger is mechanically operated for a fully automatic switchover, allowing the second barrel to be fired on a subsequent trigger pull, even during a misfire. The selector lever, located in front of the trigger, enables the shooter to fire the lower barrel or upper barrel first.

The breech block is hand-fitted to the receiver. Every Athena is equipped with a matted, ventilated rib and bead front sight. Ejectors are fully automatic. The safety is a slide type located on the upper tang atop the pistol grip. Each stock is carved from Claro walnut, with fine-line hand-checkering and

high-luster finish. Trap model has Monte Carlo stock only. *See* the Athena and Orion table on the following page for additional information and specifications.

### GRADE IV CHOKES
**Fixed Choke**
Field, .410 Gauge
Skeet, 12 or 20 Gauge
**IMC Multi-Choke**
Field, 12, 20 or 28 Gauge
Trap, 12 Gauge
Trap, single barrel, 12 Gauge
Trap Combo, 12 Gauge
*Prices:* ATHENA GRADE III . . . . . . . . . . . . . . . . . $1,999.00
ATHENA GRADE IV . . . . . . . . . . . . . . . . . . . . . . . 2,399.00
ATHENA GRADE V . . . . . . . . . . . . . . . . . . . . . . . . 2,799.00

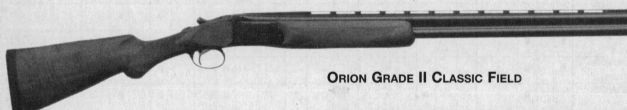

### ORION GRADE II CLASSIC FIELD

### ORION GRADES I, II & III OVER/UNDERS

For greater versatility, the Orion incorporates the integral multichoke (IMC) system. Available in Extra-full, Full, Modified, Improved Modified, Improved Cylinder and Skeet, the choke tubes fit flush with the muzzle without detracting from the beauty of the gun. Three tubes are furnished with each gun. The precision hand-fitted monobloc and receiver are machined from high-strength steel with a highly polished finish. The boxlock design uses the Greener cross-bolt locking system and special sears maintain hammer engagement. Pistol grip stock and forearm are carved of Claro walnut with hand-checkered diamond inlay pattern and high-gloss finish. Chrome-moly steel barrels, and the receiver, are deeply blued. The Orion also features selective automatic

ejectors, single selective trigger, front bead sight and ventilated rib. The trap model boasts a curved trap-style recoil pad and is available with Monte Carlo stock only.
*Weight:* 12 ga. Field, 7 1/2 lbs.; 20 ga. Field, 7 1/2 lbs.; Trap, 8 lbs.
*See following page for prices and additional specifications.*

**UPLAND IMC MULTI-CHOKE**
**Grade I**
IMC Multi-Choke, Field, 12 or 20 Gauge . . . . . . $1,449.00
**Grade II**
Fixed Choke, Field, .410 Gauge . . . . . . . . . . . . . 1,499.00
Fixed Choke, Skeet, 12 or 20 Gauge . . . . . . . . . 1,499.00
IMC Multi-Choke, Field, 12, 20 or 28 Gauge . . . . 1,499.00
IMC Multi-Choke, Trap, 12 Gauge . . . . . . . . . . . 1,499.00
**Sporting Clays (12 ga.)**
Sporting and Field Sporting . . . . . . . . . . . . . . . . 1,649.00
Super Sporting . . . . . . . . . . . . . . . . . . . . . . . . . 1,899.00
**Grade III**
IMC Multi-Choke, Field, 12 or 20 Gauge . . . . . . . 1,799.00

# WEATHERBY SHOTGUNS

**ORION GRADE II CLASSIC FIELD
12 GAUGE OVER/UNDER**

**ORION SUPER SPORTING CLAYS O/U**

*Also available:*
ORION SUPER SPORTING CLAYS (SSC) O/U 12 Ga.
**Barrel Length:** 28", 30", 32". Features include Integral Multi-Choke (IMC) system, including five interchangeable screw-in stainless steel Briley choke tubes; Claro walnut stock w/Sporter style pistol grip. **Weight:** 8 lbs.
**Price:**................................$1,899.00

**Prices:**
ORION I................................$1,449.00
ORION II CLASSIC FIELD................. 1,499.00
ORION II SPORTING CLAYS............... 1,649.00
ORION III FIELD & CLASSIC FIELD........ 1,799.00

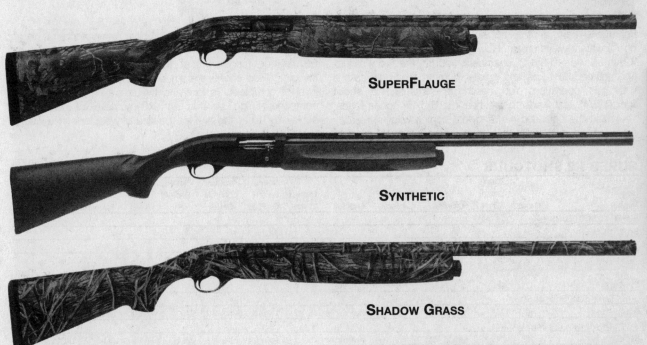

**SUPERFLAUGE**

**SYNTHETIC**

**SHADOW GRASS**

## WEATHERBY SAS
## SEMI-AUTOMATIC SHOTGUN

Weatherby's SAS autoloader is available in 12 gauge with 26- 28- and 30-inch vent rib barrels, and in 20-gauge with 26- and 28-inch barrels. To allow a wide range of shot patterns, it comes with the Weatherby Integral Multi-Choke (IMC) system, including five interchangeable Briley stainless steel screw-in choke tubes: skeet, improved cylinder, modified, improved modified and full. The self-compensating gas mechanism accommodates light and heavy loads, including 3" magnums. A magazine cutoff makes load changes a snap. The Claro walnut stock is carefully checkered and satin-finished. Synthetic stocks come in black, "Superflage" and "Shadow Grass" (12-gauge only). **Weight:** 6.8 to 7.8 lbs.
**Price:** ................................$899.00
 Synthetic .............................929.00
 Camo patterns .......................1,059.00

# WINCHESTER SHOTGUNS

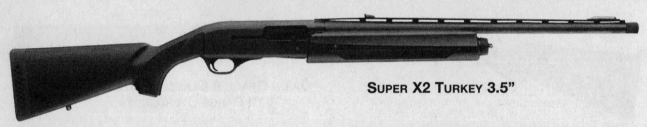

**SUPER X2 TURKEY 3.5"**

Nothing in turkey hunting is more important than shot placement and pattern density. The Super X2 Magnum 3 1/2" Turkey version has all the handling advantages of the Super X2 design. Like a 24" barrel combined with the short receiver. Center balance lets you hold with greater steadiness and less fatigue. The stock, receiver, barrel, bolt, bolt handle, carrier— every exposed part—have a no-luster, no-glare finish that won't give you away. The back-bored barrel fitted with an extra-full extended choke tube offers extreme pattern density. And the standard 3-dot TRUGLO® fiber optic sights give you an instant advantage, with more precise shot placement in early morning low-light conditions. And of course, the gas-operated action reduces the kick of recoil noticeably, something no recoil-operated gun can ever offer.

**SUPER X2 3.5"**

For a long time, a semiauto that handled 3 1/2" shells was only a waterfowler's dream. Now there's the Winchester Super X2. In addition to 3 1/2" chambers, you get the recoil reduction, faster follow-ups and greater comfort that only comes with gas operation. You need the versatility to shoot light 2 3/4" teal loads to the heaviest 3 1/2" goose loads. You need the balanced handling that comes with an all-alloy receiver. The pointability that comes from a shorter receiver length. The weather-resistant durability of a composite stock. And the consistent pattern density when shooting steel, Bismuth or Tungsten shot that you get with the famous Invector® Plus choke system and a back-bored barrel. The level of complexity is low and the operating range of each component high...so that an extreme level of reliability is achieved. This is the gun for the kind of weather only a waterfowler will put up with.

## SUPER X2 SHOTGUNS

| Item Number | Gauge | Barrel Length & Type | Chamber | Shotshell Capacity | Choke(s) | Overall Length | Nominal Length Of Pull | Nominal Drop At Comb | Nominal Drop At Heel | Nominal Weight (Lbs.) | Features | Suggested Retail |
|---|---|---|---|---|---|---|---|---|---|---|---|---|
| **SUPER X2 SHOTGUNS** | | | | | | | | | | | | |
| **3-1/2" MODELS** | | | | | | | | | | | | |
| *3-1/2" Magnum (Black Synthetic Stock)* | | | | | | | | | | | | |
| 511-001252 | 12 | 24" | 3-1/2" Mag. | 5 | Invector(3) | 45" | 14-1/4" | 1-3/4" | 2" | 7-1/2 | Studs, VR | $941 |
| 511-001250 | 12 | 26 | 3-1/2 Mag. | 5 | Invector(3) | 47" | 14-1/4 | 1-3/4 | 2 | 7-3/4 | Studs, VR | 941 |
| 511-001246 | 12 | 28 | 3-1/2 Mag. | 5 | Invector(3) | 49" | 14-1/4 | 1-3/4 | 2 | 8 | Studs, VR | 941 |
| *3-1/2" Turkey (Black Synthetic Stock)* | | | | | | | | | | | | |
| 511-002253 | 12 | 24" | 3-1/2" Mag. | 5 | Invector XF | 45" | 14-1/4" | 1-3/4" | 2" | 7-1/2 | Studs, VR, TRUGLO® | 955 |
| *3-1/2" Turkey (Mossy Oak Break-Up Camo)* | | | | | | | | | | | | |
| 511-005253 | 12 | 24" | 3-1/2" Mag. | 5 | Invector XF | 45" | 14-1/4" | 1-3/4" | 2" | 7-1/2 | Studs, VR, TRUGLO® | 1033 |
| *3-1/2" Camo Waterfowl (Mossy Oak Shadow Grass)* | | | | | | | | | | | | |
| 511-003246 | 12 | 28" | 3-1/2" Mag | 5 | Invector(3) | 49" | 14-1/4" | 1-3/4" | 2" | 8 | Studs, VR | 1033 |
| **3" MODELS** | | | | | | | | | | | | |
| *3" Magnum Field (Walnut Stock)* | | | | | | | | | | | | |
| 511-004350 | 12 | 26" | 3" Mag. | 5 | Invector(3) | 47" | 14-1/4" | 1-3/4" | 2" | 7-1/4 | VR | $799 |
| 511-004346 | 12 | 28 | 3 Mag. | 5 | Invector(3) | 49 | 14-1/4 | 1-3/4 | 2 | 7-3/8 | VR | 799 |
| *3" Magnum (Black Synthetic Stock)* | | | | | | | | | | | | |
| 511-001350 | 12 | 26" | 3" Mag. | 5 | Invector(3) | 47" | 14-1/4" | 1-3/4" | 2" | 7-3/4 | Studs, VR | 799 |
| 511-001346 | 12 | 28 | 3 Mag. | 5 | Invector(3) | 49 | 14-1/4 | 1-3/4 | 2 | 8 | Studs, VR | 799 |

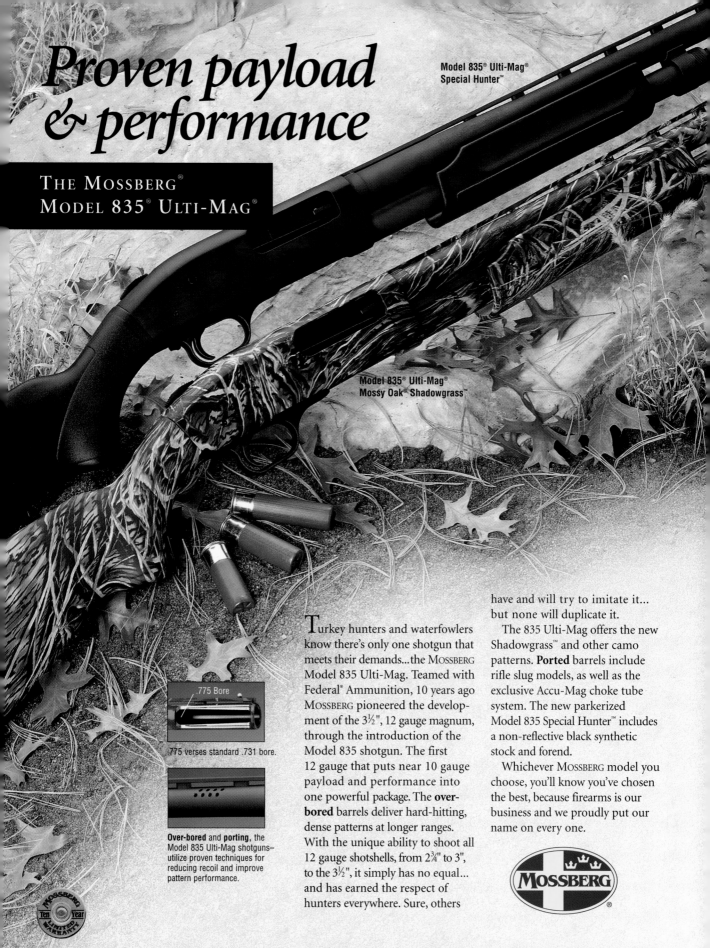

# Proven payload & performance

Model 835® Ulti-Mag®
Special Hunter™

## THE MOSSBERG® MODEL 835® ULTI-MAG®

Model 835® Ulti-Mag®
Mossy Oak™ Shadowgrass™

.775 Bore

.775 verses standard .731 bore.

**Over-bored** and **porting,** the Model 835 Ulti-Mag shotguns—utilize proven techniques for reducing recoil and improve pattern performance.

Turkey hunters and waterfowlers know there's only one shotgun that meets their demands...the MOSSBERG Model 835 Ulti-Mag. Teamed with Federal® Ammunition, 10 years ago MOSSBERG pioneered the development of the 3½", 12 gauge magnum, through the introduction of the Model 835 shotgun. The first 12 gauge that puts near 10 gauge payload and performance into one powerful package. The **over-bored** barrels deliver hard-hitting, dense patterns at longer ranges. With the unique ability to shoot all 12 gauge shotshells, from 2¾" to 3", to the 3½", it simply has no equal... and has earned the respect of hunters everywhere. Sure, others have and will try to imitate it... but none will duplicate it.

The 835 Ulti-Mag offers the new Shadowgrass™ and other camo patterns. **Ported** barrels include rifle slug models, as well as the exclusive Accu-Mag choke tube system. The new parkerized Model 835 Special Hunter™ includes a non-reflective black synthetic stock and forend.

Whichever MOSSBERG model you choose, you'll know you've chosen the best, because firearms is our business and we proudly put our name on every one.

**MOSSBERG**

**O.F. Mossberg & Sons, Inc. • 7 Grasso Avenue • P.O. Box 497 • North Haven, CT 06473-9844**
**Visit our web site at: www.mossberg.com**

# STOEGER IGA SHOTGUNS

**RUGGED, RELIABLE, PERFORMANCE
AT AN AFFORDABLE PRICE**

# WINCHESTER SHOTGUNS

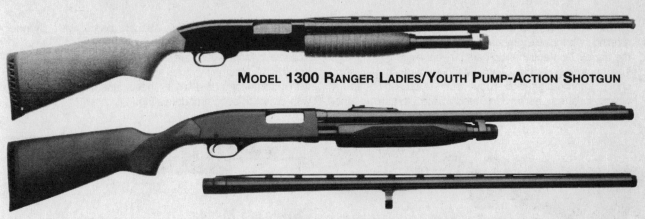

MODEL 1300 RANGER LADIES/YOUTH PUMP-ACTION SHOTGUN

MODEL 1300 RANGER 12 GAUGE DEER COMBO
22" Rifled w/Sights & 28" Vent-Rib Barrels

## MODEL 1300 SHOTGUNS

| Item Number | Ga. | Barrel Length & Type | Chamber | Shotshell Capacity | Chokes | Overall Length | Nominal Length of Pull | Nominal Drop at Comb | Nominal Drop at Heel | Nominal Weight (Lbs) | U.S. Sugg. Retail |
|---|---|---|---|---|---|---|---|---|---|---|---|
| **FIELD MODELS** | | | | | | | | | | | |
| **UPLAND** | | | | | | | | | | | |
| 512-050352 | 12 | 24"VR | 3" Mag. | 5 | W3 | 45" | 14" | 1-1/2" | 2-1/2" | 6-3/4 | $391 |
| 512-050641 *NEW* | 20 | 24"VR | 3" Mag. | 5 | W3 | 45 | 14 | 1-1/2 | 2-1/2 | 6-3/4 | 391 |
| **WALNUT FIELD** | | | | | | | | | | | |
| 512-034329 | 12 | 28 VR | 3 Mag | 5 | W3 | 49 | 14 | 1-1/2 | 2-1/2 | 7-3/8 | 391 |
| 512-034330 | 12 | 26 VR | 3 Mag | 5 | W3 | 47 | 14 | 1-1/2 | 2-1/2 | 7-1/8 | 391 |
| **BLACK SHADOW** | | | | | | | | | | | |
| 512-041303 | 12 | 28 VR | 3"Mag | 5 | W1M | 49 | 14 | 1-1/2 | 2-1/2 | 7-1/4 | 330 |
| 512-041307 | 12 | 26 VR | 3" Mag | 5 | W1M | 47 | 14 | 1-1/2 | 2-1/2 | 7 | 330 |
| 512-041607 | 20 | 26 VR | 3" Mag | 5 | W1M | 47 | 14 | 1-1/2 | 2-1/2 | 6-7/8 | 330 |
| **RANGER MODELS** | | | | | | | | | | | |
| **RANGER** | | | | | | | | | | | |
| 512-035239 | 12 | 28VR | 3"Mag | 5 | W3 | 49" | 14" | 1-1/2" | 2-1/2" | 7-3/8 | 344 |
| 512-035629 | 20 | 28VR | 3"Mag | 5 | W3 | 49 | 14 | 1-1/2 | 2-1/2 | 7-1/8 | 344 |
| **RANGER COMPACT** | | | | | | | | | | | |
| 512-036631 | 20 | 22VR | 3"Mag | 5 | W3 | 42 | 13 | 1-1/2 | 2-3/8 | 6-5/8 | 343 |
| 512-036532 | 12 | 24VR | 3"Mag | 5 | W3 | 44 | 13 | 1-1/2 | 2-3/8 | 7 | 343 |
| **TURKEY MODELS** | | | | | | | | | | | |
| **BLACK SHADOW TURKEY** | | | | | | | | | | | |
| 512-005333 | 12 | 22"VR | 3"Mag | 5 | WXF | 43" | 14" | 1-1/2" | 2-1/2" | 6-3/4 | 329 |
| **MOSSY OAK BREAK-UP TURKEY** | | | | | | | | | | | |
| 512-011344 *NEW* | 12 | 22"VR | 3"Mag | 5 | HDXF | 43 | 14 | 1-1/2 | 2-1/2 | 6-3/4 | 459 |
| **MOSSY OAK BREAK-UP DEER & TURKEY** | | | | | | | | | | | |
| 512-009342 *NEW* | 12 | 22 Smooth | 3"Mag | 5 | RS/HDXF | 43 | 14 | 1-1/2 | 2-1/2 | 6-3/4 | 489 |
| **DEER MODELS** | | | | | | | | | | | |
| **DEER BLACK SHADOW** | | | | | | | | | | | |
| 512-040320 | 12 | 22 Smooth | 3"Mag | 5 | W1C | 43" | 14" | 1-1/2" | 2-1/2" | 6-3/4 | 329 |
| 512-040315 | 12 | 22 Rifled | 3"Mag | 5 | Rifled Barrel | 42-3/4 | 14 | 1-1/2 | 2-1/2 | 6-3/4 | 353 |
| 512-040615 *NEW* | 20 | 22 Rifled | 3"Mag | 5 | Rifled Barrel | 42-3/4 | 14 | 1-1/2 | 2-1/2 | 6-1/2 | 353 |
| **DEER BLACK SHADOW WITH CANTILEVER SCOPE MOUNT** | | | | | | | | | | | |
| 512-040340 *NEW* | 12 | 22 Rifled | 3"Mag | 5 | Rifled Barrel | 42-3/4 | 14 | 1-1/8 | 2-3/4*** | 7 | 395 |
| **DEER BLACK SHADOW COMBO** | | | | | | | | | | | |
| 512-042326 | 12 | 22 Rifled | 3"Mag | 5 | Rifled Barrel | 42-3/4 | 14 | 1-1/2 | 2-1/2 | 6-3/4 | 427 |
| (includes) | 12 | 28 VR | 3"Mag | 5 | W3 | 49 | 14 | 1-1/2 | 2-1/ | 7-3/8 | |
| **DEER RANGER COMPACT** | | | | | | | | | | | |
| 512-036615 *NEW* | 20 | 22 Rifled | 3"Mag | 5 | Rifled Barrel | 42-3/4 | 13 | 1-1/2 | 2-3/8 | 6-5/8 | 366 |

*Includes one shotshell in chamber. For Model 1300 Feature & Choke and Barrel Abbreviations see following page.

# WINCHESTER SHOTGUNS

These tough 12-gauge shotguns feature a front-locking rotating bolt for strength and secure, single-unit lockup into the barrel. Twin-action slide bars prevent binding.

The shotguns handle 3-inch Magnum and shorter shotshells interchangeably. They have a crossbolt safety, walnut-finished hardwood stock and forearm, black rubber buttpad and plain 18-inch barrel with Cylinder Bore choke.

Police and Marine guns are triple-plated: first with copper for adherence, then with nickel for rust protection, and finally with chrome for a hard finish. These guns have a forend cap with swivel to accommodate sling.

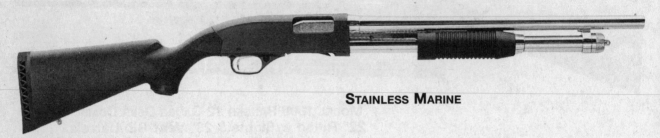

**STAINLESS MARINE**

## SPECIFICATIONS MODEL 1300 DEFENDER

| Suggested Retail | Gauge | Barrel Length & Type | Chamber | Shotshell Capacity* | Choke | Overall Length | Nominal Length of Pull | Nominal Drop at Comb | Nominal Drop at Heel | Nominal Weight (Lbs.) | Features |
|---|---|---|---|---|---|---|---|---|---|---|---|
| **DEFENDER MODELS** | | | | | | | | | | | |
| *SYNTHETIC PISTOL GRIP, 8 SHOT* | | | | | | | | | | | |
| $321 | 12 | 18 | 3" Mag. | 8 | Cyl. | 29-1/8 | — | — | — | 5-1/2 | Studs, MBF |
| *SYNTHETIC STOCK, 8 SHOT* | | | | | | | | | | | |
| $321 | 12 | 18 | 3" MAG. | 8 | Cyl.. | 39-1/2 | 14 | 1-1/2 | 2-1/2 | 6-3/8 | Studs, Truglo |
| 321 | 20 | 18 | 3" MAG. | 8 | Cyl. | 39-1/2 | 14 | 1-1/2 | 2-1/2 | 6-1/4 | Studs, Truglo |
| *STAINLESS MARINE SYNTHETIC STOCK* | | | | | | | | | | | |
| $511 | 12 | 18 | 3" Mag. | 7 | Cyl. | 39-1/2 | 14 | 1-1/2 | 2-1/2 | 6-3/8 | Studs, MBF |
| *CAMP DEFENDER* | | | | | | | | | | | |
| $368 | 12 | 22 | 3" Mag. | 5 | W/C. | 42-3/4 | 14 | 1-1/2 | 2-1/2 | 6-7/8 | Studs, Rifle Sights |

*Model 1300 Feature Abbreviations: MBF=Metal bead front, Rifle=Rifle type front and rear sights. Rifle sights=Adjustable rear sight and ramp style front sight.*

*SB=Scope Bases Included. B&R=Scope, Bases and Rings included. D&T=Drilled and tapped to accept scope bases. Studs=Buttstock and magazine cap sling studs provided*

*(sling loop on pistol grip models).*

*Model 1300 Choke and Barrel Abbreviations: VR=Ventilated rib. W3W=WinChoke, Extra Full, Full and Modified Tubes. W3=WinChoke, Full, Modified and Improved Cylinder Tubes.*

*Cyl.=Non-WinChoke, choked Cylinder Bore. WIM=Modified Tube. WIC=Cylinder Choke Tube. WF=Full Choke Tube. WXF=Extra Full Choke Tube. Smooth=Non-Rifled Bore.*

**SUPREME SPORTING**

## NEW WINCHESTER SUPREME O/U SHOTGUN

Tapered locking lugs between the barrels reduce the bulk of this over/under without sacrificing strength. Back-bored barrels with Invector Plus chokes ensure uniform patterns. Chromed chambers, vent rib, checkered walnut stock are standard. Choose from Field or Sporting Models, both with barrel selector on the safety. Field Model is bored for 3" shells; sporting model has a competition trigger, ported barrels.

*Prices:*
FIELD . . . . . . . . . . . . . . . . . . . . . . . . . . . . . . . .**$1,324.00**
SPORTING . . . . . . . . . . . . . . . . . . . . . . . . . . . . .1,485.00

# Blackpowder

*Roland Clark – The Blind, 1929*

*For addresses and phone/fax numbers of manufacturers and distributors included in this section, please turn to DIRECTORY OF MANUFACTURERS AND SUPPLIERS on page 564.*

# AMERICAN FRONTIER FIREARMS

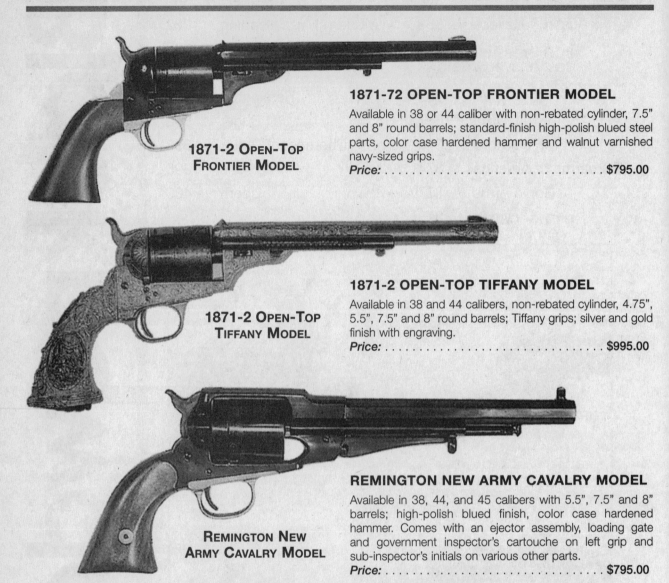

### 1871-72 OPEN-TOP FRONTIER MODEL

**1871-2 OPEN-TOP FRONTIER MODEL**

Available in 38 or 44 caliber with non-rebated cylinder, 7.5" and 8" round barrels; standard-finish high-polish blued steel parts, color case hardened hammer and walnut varnished navy-sized grips.
*Price:* . . . . . . . . . . . . . . . . . . . . . . . . . . . . . . . $795.00

### 1871-2 OPEN-TOP TIFFANY MODEL

**1871-2 OPEN-TOP TIFFANY MODEL**

Available in 38 and 44 calibers, non-rebated cylinder, 4.75", 5.5", 7.5" and 8" round barrels; Tiffany grips; silver and gold finish with engraving.
*Price:* . . . . . . . . . . . . . . . . . . . . . . . . . . . . . . . $995.00

### REMINGTON NEW ARMY CAVALRY MODEL

**REMINGTON NEW ARMY CAVALRY MODEL**

Available in 38, 44, and 45 calibers with 5.5", 7.5" and 8" barrels; high-polish blued finish, color case hardened hammer. Comes with an ejector assembly, loading gate and government inspector's cartouche on left grip and sub-inspector's initials on various other parts.
*Price:* . . . . . . . . . . . . . . . . . . . . . . . . . . . . . . . $795.00

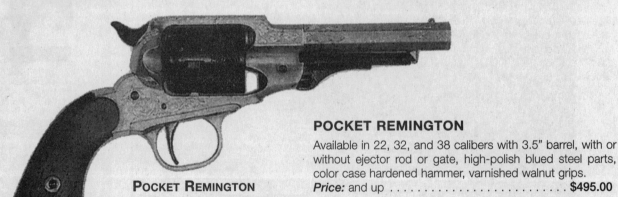

### POCKET REMINGTON

**POCKET REMINGTON**

Available in 22, 32, and 38 calibers with 3.5" barrel, with or without ejector rod or gate, high-polish blued steel parts, color case hardened hammer, varnished walnut grips.
*Price:* and up . . . . . . . . . . . . . . . . . . . . . . . . . . . $495.00

# AMERICAN FRONTIER FIREARMS

### RICHARDS 1851 MODEL NAVY CONVERSION

Available in 38 and 44 calibers with non-rebated cylinder, 4.75", 5.5" & 7.5" octagon barrels, colorcase hardened hammer and trigger, ramrod and plunger, blued steel backstrap and trigger guard; walnut varnished navy-sized grips (Note: No ejector rod assembly on this model)
**Price:** . . . . . . . . . . . . . . . . . . . . . . . . . . . . . . . $795.00

RICHARDS 1851 MODEL NAVY CONVERSION

### RICHARDS 1860 ARMY MODEL CONVERSION

Available in 38 or 44 caliber with rebated cylinder with or without ejector assembly; 4.75", 5.5" and 7.5" round barrels, standard finishes are high-polish blued steel parts (including backstrap); trigger guard is silver-plated brass; colorcase hardened hammer and trigger, walnut varnished army-sized grips.
**Price:** . . . . . . . . . . . . . . . . . . . . . . . . . . . . . $795.00

RICHARDS AND MASON CONVERSION 1851 NAVY MODEL

### RICHARDS AND MASON CONVERSION 1851 NAVY MODEL

Available in 38 and 44 calibers with Mason ejector assembly and non-rebated cylinder, 4.75", 5.5" and 7.5" octagon barrels, high-polish blued steel parts, colorcase hammer and trigger, blued steel backstrap and trigger guard with ejector rod; varnished walnut grips.
**Price:** . . . . . . . . . . . . . . . . . . . . . . . . . . . . . $695.00

POCKET RICHARDS AND MASON NAVY CONVERSION

### POCKET RICHARDS AND MASON NAVY CONVERSION

Available in 32 caliber, non-rebated cylinder, five shot, high-polish blued steel parts, silver-plated brass backstrap and trigger guard with ejector assembly, colorcase hardened hammer and trigger, varnished walnut grips.
**Price:** and up . . . . . . . . . . . . . . . . . . . . . . . . . . $495.00

RICHARDS 1860 ARMY MODEL CONVERSION

### RICHARDS 1861 MODEL NAVY CONVERSION

Same as 1860 Model, except with non-rebated cylinder and navy-sized grips. All blue with silver trigger guard and backstrap.
**Price:** . . . . . . . . . . . . . . . . . . . . . . . . . . . . . $695.00

RICHARDS 1861 MODEL NAVY CONVERSION

# AUSTIN & HALLECK RIFLES

**MODEL 320 LR/SS**

**MODEL 420 LR CLASSIC**

**MODEL 420 LR MONTE CARLO**

## SPECIFICATIONS

**Caliber:** 50 **Action:** In-line percussion (removable weather shroud) **Barrel Length:** 26" (1:28"); 8 lands & grooves; octagon to .75" tapered round **Overall length:** 47.5" **Weight:** 7 7/8 lbs. **Length of pull:** 13.5" **Stock:** Select grade tiger-striped curly maple (Classic model has filled-grain luster finish w/pistol grip cap; Monte Carlo has filled-grain high-gloss finish) **Features:** Match grade target triggers w/trigger block safety; 1" recoil pad; scope not included

**Prices:**

| | |
|---|---|
| MODEL 420 LR MONTE CARLO & CLASSIC STANDARD | $459.00 |
| Stainless Steel Standard | 520.00 |
| Fancy Stainless Steel | 610.00 |
| Hand Select | 737.00 |
| Hand Select Stainless Steel | 800.00 |
| Exhibition Grade | 1,187.00 |
| MODEL 320 LR BLU W/SYNTHETIC STOCK | 380.00 |
| MODEL 320 LR S/S | 446.00 |

**MOUNTAIN RIFLE**

## MOUNTAIN RIFLE

### SPECIFICATIONS

**Caliber:** 50 percussion or flintlock
**Barrel length:** 32" (1:66 roundball or 1:28 bullet twist); 1" octagonal; rust brown finish
**Overall length:** 49"
**Weight:** 7.5 lbs.

**Stock:** Select grade tiger-striped curly maple; filled-grain luster finish
**Sights:** Fixed buckhorn rear; silver blade brass bead front
**Features:** Double throw adjustable set triggers

| Price: | |
|---|---|
| Std. percussion | $578.00 |
| Hand Select percussion | 592.00 |
| Std. flint | 539.00 |
| Hand select flint | 618.00 |

## LIGHTNING FIRE
### SIDE-LOCK MUZZLELOADING RIFLE

The Lightning Fire nipple system uses a musket nipple and musket percussion caps to deliver a huge blast of fire (five times the fire of standard #11 caps) to the powder for instantaneous and complete powder ignition. The fire-slowing right-angle flash channel has been replaced by a natural curving channel that allows the fire to travel unimpeded to the powder so there's less delay between the hammer strike and firing. The Lightning Fire readily shoots two Pyrodex pellets or a wide range of black powder (or black-powder equivalent) charges. The 28 3/4" round barrel features a fast 1-in-32" rifling which provides optimum twist for superior accuracy with bullets and saboted bullets. The windage-and-elevation-adjustable rear sight and ramp front sight both feature bright fiber-optics for rapid, easy target acquisition, even in low-light conditions. Other features: sling swivels, color case-hardened lock, rubber recoil pad and virtually unbreakable ramrod. Wt: 7.85 lbs. .50 Caliber only.
**Price:** . . . . . . . . . . . . . . . . . . . . . . . . . . . . . . . . **$249.99**

## LIGHTNING FIRE RIFLE

Developed by Cabela's, this firearm produces muzzle velocities of over 2,100 fps using Hodgdon Pyrodex Pellets and 250 grain saboted bullets. Ignition is enhanced with a musket nipple and percussion caps that deliver five times the spark of standard #11 caps.

**SPECIFICATIONS INCLUDE:** 24" fluted barrel (blued or stainless), 1 turn in 32" twist rate. Laminated wood stock. **Overall Length:** 43". Fully adjustable rear sight, drilled and tapped for scope mounts. **Weight:** 7.25 lbs. (stainless); 7 lbs. (blue)
**Price:**
Blue . . . . . . . . . . . . . . . . . . . . . . . . . . . . . . **$239.99**
Stainless . . . . . . . . . . . . . . . . . . . . . . . . . . . . . 339.99

## BLUE RIDGE RIFLE

From the era of the American long rifle (1760-1840) comes the design for this faithful reproduction. The so-called "squirrel rifle" was renowned for hitting small, often distant targets and Cabela's Blue Ridge rifles live up to that tradition. Precision-rifled 39" browned octagonal barrels with 1-in-48" twist deliver exceptional precision with patched round balls and will handle conical bullets surprisingly well. 8 lands and grooves. Percussion models have drum and bolster system. Flintlocks have large, sure-spark frizzen and ample priming pan. Locks are color case-hardened. Adjustable double-set, double-phase triggers. Buttplate and trigger guard are polished brass.

| ORDER NO.<br>PERCUSSION | CAL. | OVERALL<br>LENGTH | BARREL<br>LENGTH | WT.<br>LBS. | GROOVE<br>& LANDS | GUN ONLY<br>PRICE | KIT<br>PRICE |
|---|---|---|---|---|---|---|---|
| HJ-21-0007-036 | .36 Cal | 55" | 39" | 7 3/4 | 7 | $379.99 | $419.99 |
| HJ-21-0007-050 | .50 Cal | 55" | 39" | 7 1/4 | 8 | $379.99 | $419.99 |
| FLINTLOCK | | | | | | | |
| HJ-21-0008-036 | .36 Cal | 55" | 39" | 7 3/4 | 7 | $399.99 | $439.99 |
| HJ-21-0008-045 | .45 Cal | 55" | 39" | 7 1/4 | 8 | $399.99 | $439.99 |
| HJ-21-0008-050 | .50 Cal | 55" | 39" | 7 1/4 | 8 | $399.99 | $439.99 |

## KODIAK EXPRESS DOUBLE RIFLE

Early explorers of Africa and Asia often had to rely on large-bore express rifles like this handsome sidelock replica featuring oil-finished, hand-checkered European walnut stock with case hardened steel buttplate. Ramp-mounted, adjustable folding double rear sights, ramp front sight, drilled and tapped for folding tang sight. Color-case hardened lock, blued top tang and trigger guard are all polished and engraved. **Calibers:** 50, 54, 58, 72 **Barrels:** 28" with 1:48" twist (regulated at 75 yards); blued. **Overall Length:** 45.25" **Weight:** 9.3 lbs.
**Price:** . . . . . . . . . . . . . . . . . . . . . . . **$649.99 to 679.99**

# COLT BLACK-POWDER ARMS

## SIGNATURE SERIES

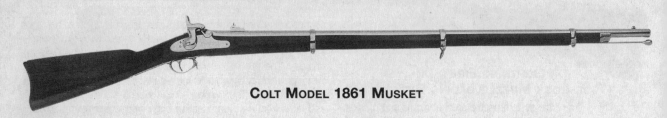

### COLT MODEL 1861 MUSKET

Manufactured to original specifications using modern steels, this re-issue has the authentic Colt markings of its Civil War predecessor. Plus triangular bayonet.

**SPECIFICATIONS**
**Caliber:** .58
**Barrel length:** 40"
**Overall length:** 56"
**Weight:** 9 lbs. 3 oz. (empty)
**Sights:** Folding leaf rear; steel blade front
**Sight Radius:** 36"
**Stock:** One piece
**Finish:** Bright steel lockplate, hammer, buttplate, bands, ramrod and nipple; blued rear sight
**Price:** . . . . . . . . . . . . . . . . . . . . . . . . . . . . . . . . . . $799.95

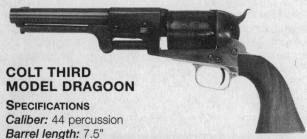

### COLT THIRD MODEL DRAGOON

**SPECIFICATIONS**
**Caliber:** 44 percussion
**Barrel length:** 7.5"
**Overall length:** 13.75"
**Weight:** 66 oz. (empty)
**Sight:** Fixed blade front
**Sight radius:** 10.75"
**Stock:** One-piece walnut
**Finish:** Colt blue with color case hardened frame; hammer, lever and plunger
**Price:** . . . . . . . . . . . . . . . . . . . . . . . . . . . . . . . . . . $499.95

### COLT WALKER 150TH ANNIVERSARY MODEL

**SPECIFICATIONS - Caliber:** 44 **Weight:** 4 lbs. 9 oz. **Barrel length:** 9" **Cylinder length:** 2 7/16" **Finish:** Color case hardened frame and hammer; smooth wooden grips **Features:** Colt's Signature Series 150th anniversary re-issue carries the identical markings as the original 1847 Walker. "U.S. 1847" appears above the barrel wedge, exactly as on the Walkers produced for service in the Mexican War. The cylinder has a battle scene depicting 15 Texas Rangers defeating a Comanche war party using the first revolver invented by Sam Colt. This Limited Edition features original A Company No. 1 markings embellished in gold. Serial numbers begin with #221, a continuation of A Company numbers.
**Price:** . . . . . . . . . . . . . . . . . . . . . . . . . . . . . . . $699.95
    Standard 1847 Walker . . . . . . . . . . . . . . . . . . . . 499.95

### COLT 1849 POCKET REVOLVER

**SPECIFICATIONS**
**Caliber:** 31 **Barrel length:** 4"
**Overall length:** 9.5"
**Weight:** 24 oz. (empty)
**Stock:** One-piece walnut **Finish:** Colt blue and color case hardened frame
**Price:** . . . . . . . . . . . . . . . . . . . . . . . . . . . . . . . . . . $429.95

### COLT 1851 NAVY

**SPECIFICATIONS**
**Caliber:** 36 **Barrel length:** 7.5" **Overall length:** 13 1/8" **Weight:** 40.5 oz. (empty) **Sights:** Fixed blade front **Sight radius:** 10" **Stock:** Oiled American walnut **Finish:** Colt blue and color case hardened frame
**Price:** . . . . . . . . . . . . . . . . . . . . . . . . . . . . . . . . . . $449.95

# COLT BLACK-POWDER ARMS

## SIGNATURE SERIES

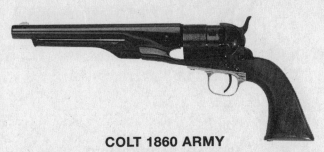

### COLT 1860 ARMY

A continuation in production of the famous cap-and-ball revolver used by the U.S. Cavalry with color case hardened frame, hammer and loading lever. Blued backstrap and brass trigger guard, roll-engraved cylinder and one-piece walnut grips

**SPECIFICATIONS**
*Caliber:* 44 *Barrel length:* 8" *Overall length:* 13.75"
*Weight:* 42 oz. (empty) *Sights:* Fixed blade front
*Sight radius:* 10.5" *Stock:* One-piece walnut
*Finish:* Colt blue with color case hardened frame; hammer, lever and plunger
*Price:* . . . . . . . . . . . . . . . . . . . . . . . . . . . . . . $449.95

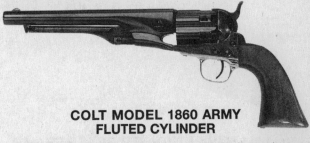

### COLT MODEL 1860 ARMY FLUTED CYLINDER

The first Army revolvers shipped from Hartford were known as the "Cavalry Model"—with fluted cylinder, color case hardened frame, hammer, loading lever and plunger. Features blued barrel, backstrap and cylinder; brass trigger guard, fluted cylinder, one-piece walnut grip and a 4-screw frame (cut for optional shoulder stock)

**SPECIFICATIONS**
*Caliber:* 44 percussion *Barrel length:* 8"
*Overall length:* 13.75" *Weight:* 42 oz. (empty)
*Sight:* Fixed blade front *Sight radius:* 10.5"
*Stock:* One piece walnut *Finish:* Colt blue with color casehardened frame; hammer, lever and plunger
*Price:* . . . . . . . . . . . . . . . . . . . . . . . . . . . . . . $449.95

### COLT 1861 NAVY

A personal favorite of George Armstrong Custer, who carried a pair of them during the Civil War. Loading lever and plunger; blued barrel, cylinder backstrap and trigger guard; roll-engraved cylinder; one-piece walnut grip.

**SPECIFICATIONS**
*Caliber:* 36 percussion *Barrel length:* 7.5"
*Overall length:* 13 1/8" *Weight:* 42 oz. (empty)
*Sight:* Fixed blade front *Sight radius:* 10"
*Stock:* One-piece walnut *Finish:* Colt blue with color case hardened frame; hammer, lever and plunger
*Price:* . . . . . . . . . . . . . . . . . . . . . . . . . . . . . . $449.95

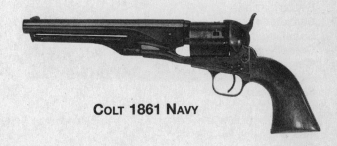

**COLT 1861 NAVY**

**TRAPPER MODEL 1862 POCKET POLICE**

### TRAPPER MODEL 1862 POCKET POLICE

The first re-issue of the rare and highly desirable Pocket Police "Trapper Model." The Trapper's 3.5" barrel without attached loading lever makes it an ideal backup gun, as well as a welcome addition to any gun collection. Color case-hardened frame and hammer; silver-plated backstrap and trigger guard; blued semi-fluted cylinder and barrel; one-piece walnut grip. Separate 4 5/8" brass ramrod.

**SPECIFICATIONS**
*Caliber:* 36 *Barrel length:* 3.5" *Overall length:* 8.5"
*Weight:* 20 oz. (empty) *Sight:* Fixed blade front
*Sight radius:* 6" *Stock:* One-piece walnut
*Finish:* Colt blue with color casehardened frame and hammer
*Price:* . . . . . . . . . . . . . . . . . . . . . . . . . . . . . . $429.95

**BLACK POWDER**

# CVA REVOLVERS/PISTOLS

## 1851 NAVY REVOLVER BRASS FRAME

SPECIFICATIONS
*Caliber:* 44
*Barrel length:* 7.5" octagonal; hinged-style loading lever
*Overall length:* 13"
*Weight:* 44 oz.
*Cylinder:* 6-shot, engraved
*Sights:* Post front; hammer notch rear
*Grip:* One-piece walnut
*Finish:* Solid brass frame, trigger guard and backstrap; blued barrel and cylinder; color case hardened loading lever and hammer
*Price:* . . . . . . . . . . . . . . . . . . . . . . . . . . . . . . . . $129.95

## 1858 ARMY REVOLVER

SPECIFICATIONS
*Caliber:* 44
*Cylinder:* 6-shot, engraved
*Barrel length:* 8" octagonal
*Overall length:* 13"
*Weight:* 38 oz.
*Sights:* Blade front; adjustable target
*Grip:* Two-piece walnut
*Price:*
Brass Frame . . . . . . . . . . . . . . . . . . . . . . . . . . . . $144.95

## KENTUCKY PISTOL

SPECIFICATIONS
*Caliber:* 50 percussion
*Barrel:* 9.75", rifled, octagonal
*Overall length:* 15.5"  *Weight:* 40 oz.
*Finish:* Blued barrel, brass hardware
*Sights:* Brass blade front; fixed open rear
*Stock:* Select hardwood
*Ignition:* Engraved, color case hardened percussion lock, screw adjustable sear engagement
*Accessories:* Brass-tipped, hardwood ramrod; stainless-steel nipple or flash hole liner
*Prices:*
Finished. . . . . . . . . . . . . . . . . . . . . . . . . . . . . . . . $149.95
Percussion Kit . . . . . . . . . . . . . . . . . . . . . . . . . . . 109.95

## HAWKEN PISTOL

SPECIFICATIONS
*Caliber:* 50 percussion
*Barrel length:* 9.75", octagonal
*Overall length:* 16.5"
*Weight:* 50 oz.
*Trigger:* Early-style brass
*Sights:* Beaded steel blade front; fully adjustable rear (click adj. screw settings lock into position)
*Stock:* Select hardwood
*Finish:* Solid brass wedge plate, nose cap, ramrod thimbles, trigger guard and grip cap
*Prices:*
Finished. . . . . . . . . . . . . . . . . . . . . . . . . . . . . . . . $149.95
Kit. . . . . . . . . . . . . . . . . . . . . . . . . . . . . . . . . . . . 119.95

# CVA RIFLES/SHOTGUNS

## YOUTH HUNTER PR4104

The new **YOUTH HUNTER** rifle was custom made for the smaller shooter. It has a 24" octagonal barrel and a shortened hardwood stock. CVA's patented breech plug/bolster system ensures consistent ignition. A 1:48" twist deep-groove rifled barrel, ensures accuracy with round ball or conical bullets. This rifle is also great for the petite lady. Fully equipped with a Williams adjustable rear sight, oversized trigger guard and synthetic ramrod. All Youth Hunter rifles are backed by CVA's lifetime mechanical warranty and include complete shooting instructions.

**SPECIFICATIONS**
**Calibers:** .50 **Barrel:** 24" Blued **Twist:** 1:48
**Stock:** Hardwood **Weight:** 5.5 lbs. **Length:** 38"
**Price:** . . . . . . . . . . . . . . . . . . . . . . . . . . . . . . . **$129.95**

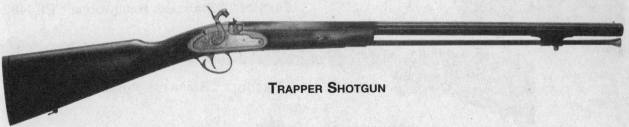

## TRAPPER SHOTGUN

The new chrome lined barrel of the **TRAPPER** gives the shooter the option to shoot either lead or steel shot. The light weight English style hardwood stock allows for quick target pick up and follow through. The engraved color case hardened lock contains an authentic V-type main spring. The barrel has a brass bead front sight, hook style breech and snail type bolster for convenient and easy cleaning. Includes CVA's lifetime mechanical warranty and complete instructions.

**SPECIFICATIONS: MODEL PS419M**
**Gauge:** 12 **Barrel:** 28" Blued **Choke:** Fixed Modified
**Ramrod:** Synthetic **Weight:** 6 lbs.
**Price:** . . . . . . . . . . . . . . . . . . . . . . . . . . . . . . . **$239.95**

## COLORADO MUSKETMAG 100 HARDWOODS™ PR5537

The **COLORADO MUSKETMAG™ 100** (.50 Caliber) and **COLORADO MUSKETMAG™ 120** (.54 Caliber) come with the **MUSKETMAG™** 2-Way Ignition System (#11 or musket caps) and are designed to handle Pyrodex® Pellet loads up to 100 grains in .50 caliber or 120 grains in .54 caliber. The durable Tuff-Lite synthetic stock is available in black or Hardwoods™. The 1:32" twist barrel is great for shooting sabots or conical bullets, has a matte finish to reduce glare, and comes drilled and tapped for easy scope mounting. The Colorado **MUSKETMAG™** series is also equipped with **ILLUMINATOR™ II FIBER OPTIC SIGHTS**, providing the maximum light gathering capability. Includes ramrod, cleaning jag, and complete shooting instructions. The rifle is backed by CVA's lifetime mechanical warranty.

## SPECIFICATIONS

| MODEL | CALIBER | BARREL | TWIST | STOCK | WEIGHT | LENGTH | RETAIL PRICE |
|---|---|---|---|---|---|---|---|
| PR5537 | .50 | 26" Matte | 1:32 | Syn. Hardwoods™ | 7.5 lbs. | 42" | $219.95 |
| PR5530 | .50 | 26" Matte | 1:32 | Synthetic | 7.5 lbs. | 42" | $184.95 |
| PR5531 | .54 | 26" Matte | 1:32 | Synthetic | 7.5 lbs. | 42" | $184.95 |

# CVA RIFLES

## FIREBOLT™ MUSKETMAG™ 150 SERIES – LEGENDARY ACCURACY

The **FIREBOLT™ MUSKETMAG™ 150**, CVA's top of the line magnum In-Line, has a new **MUSKETMAG™** 3-Way Ignition System. The ignition system allows the shooter the choice of using standard #11s, musket caps, or modern 209 primers. Also new for 2001, the FireBolt™ features the **MONO-BLOCK** one piece barrel design and a stainless steel bolt assembly. Choose from stainless steel or blue .50 caliber barrels, both with a non-glare matte finish. Breech plugs are removable for easy cleaning.

Synthetic stocks have CVA's **SUREGRIP RUBBER COATING** in a choice of black, Hardwoods™, or Advantage™ finishes. All feature a checkered forend and pistol grip, raised comb and cheek piece, ventilated recoil pad, sling swivel studs, and oversized trigger guard. FireBolt™ MusketMag™ 150 rifles also feature CVA's new and improved **ILLUMINATOR II™ SIGHT SYSTEM**, providing optimal visibility in low light conditions. The **BULLET GUIDING MUZZLE**, standard on all FireBolts™, makes loading quick and easy.

Standard accessories include breech plug/nipple wrench, synthetic ramrod, cleaning jag, allen wrench and complete instructions. FireBolt™ MusketMag™ 150 rifles are backed by CVA's lifetime mechanical warranty.

**FIREBOLT™ STAINLESS HARDWOODS™ PR4482**

**FIREBOLT™ STAINLESS ADVANTAGE™ PR4481**

**FIREBOLT™ STAINLESS PR4440**

**FIREBOLT™ HARDWOODS™ BLUED PR4483**

**FIREBOLT™ ADVANTAGE PR4447**

**FIREBOLT™ PR4435**

## HUNTERBOLT™ MUSKETMAG™ 150 SERIES

The **HUNTERBOLT™ MUSKETMAG™ 150** series is the basic version of the FireBolt™ with the most important high-end features: **ILLUMINATOR II™** sights, **MUSKETMAG™** 3-Way Ignition System, and **MONO-BLOCK BARREL** design. The 1:32" twist .50 caliber barrels are available in a choice of Weather-Guard nickel or blue with removable breech plugs for easy cleaning.

They also have the same trigger blocking safety as more expensive models.

The all weather synthetic stock features a checkered forend and pistol grip, raised comb and cheek piece, and choice of black, Hardwoods™, or Advantage™ finishes. Prices on following page.

# CVA RIFLES

**STAGHORN PR4500**

### STAG HORN™

The **STAG HORN™**, CVA's most affordable in-line, features a manual notch bolt safety system, CVA's **ILLUMINATOR™ SOLAR SIGHTS,** synthetic stock and ramrod, oversized trigger guard, removable breech plug for easy takedown and cleaning, plus barrels are drilled and tapped for easy scope installation. As with all CVA in-line rifles, breech plug/nipple wrench, cleaning jag, allen wrench and complete instructions are included. CVA's lifetime mechanical warranty applies.

### ECLIPSE MUSKETMAG™ 100 SERIES (not shown)

The CVA 2000 **ECLIPSE MUSKETMAG™ 100** has the **MUSKETMAG™** 3-Way Ignition System, making it the most affordable 209 primer-capable muzzleloader on the market. The stock features **SUREGRIP RUBBER COATING,** for maximum grip and comfort, and CVA's deep groove rifling delivers tack-driving performance in the field or on the range. Other standard features include the new **ILLUMINATOR II™** **SIGHT SYSTEM,** modern trigger with an automatic safety, and tough stainless steel percussion bolt. Breech plugs are removable for easy takedown and cleaning. Stocks are available in black, Hardwoods™, or Advantage™. All barrels are drilled and taped for quick and easy scope installation. Other features include oversized trigger guard, sling swivel studs, checkered grip surfaces, and synthetic ramrod.

## FIREBOLT

| MODEL | CALIBER | BARREL | TWIST | STOCK | WEIGHT | LENGTH | RETAIL PRICE |
|---|---|---|---|---|---|---|---|
| PR4482 | .50 | 24" Matte Stainless | 1:32 | SureGrip Hardwoods™ | 7 lbs. | 42" | $339.95 |
| PR4481 | .50 | 24" Matte Stainless | 1:32 | SureGrip Advantage™ | 7 lbs. | 42" | 339.95 |
| PR4440 | .50 | 24" Matte Stainless | 1:32 | SureGrip Black | 7 lbs. | 42" | 299.95 |
| PR4483 | .50 | 24" Matte Blue | 1:32 | SureGrip Hardwoods™ | 7 lbs. | 42" | 279.95 |
| PR4447 | .50 | 24" Matte Blue | 1:32 | SureGrip Advantage™ | 7 lbs. | 42" | 279.95 |
| PR4435 | .50 | 24" Matte Blue | 1:32 | SureGrip Black | 7 lbs. | 42" | 239.95 |

## HUNTERBOLT

| MODEL | CALIBER | BARREL | TWIST | STOCK | WEIGHT | LENGTH | RETAIL PRICE |
|---|---|---|---|---|---|---|---|
| PR4486N | .50 | 24" Nickel | 1:32 | Syn. Hardwoods™ | 7 lbs. | 42" | $239.95 |
| PR4485N | .50 | 24" Nickel | 1:32 | Syn. Advantage™ | 7 lbs. | 42" | 239.95 |
| PR4453N | .50 | 24" Nickel | 1:32 | Syn. Black | 7 lbs. | 42" | 199.95 |
| PR4486 | .50 | 24" Blue | 1:32 | Syn. Hardwoods™ | 7 lbs. | 42" | 224.95 |
| PR4485 | .50 | 24" Blue | 1:32 | Syn. Advantage™ | 7 lbs. | 42" | 224.95 |
| PR4453 | .50 | 24" Blue | 1:32 | Syn. Black | 7 lbs. | 42" | 184.95 |

## ECLIPSE

| MODEL | CALIBER | BARREL | RIFLING | STOCK | WEIGHT | LENGTH | RETAIL PRICE |
|---|---|---|---|---|---|---|---|
| PR4464 | .50 | 24" Blue | 1:32 | SureGrip Advantage™ | 7 lbs. | 42" | $199.95 |
| PR4421 | .50 | 24" Blue | 1:32 | SureGrip Hardwoods™ | 7 lbs. | 42" | 199.95 |
| PR4419 | .50 | 24" Blue | 1:32 | SureGrip Black | 7 lbs. | 42" | 159.95 |

## STAG HORN

| MODEL | CALIBER | BARREL | RIFLING | STOCK | WEIGHT | LENGTH | RETAIL PRICE |
|---|---|---|---|---|---|---|---|
| PR4500 | .50 | 24" Blue | 1:32 | Syn. Black | 7 lbs. | 42" | $134.95 |

# CVA Rifles

## Caplock Rifles

For many, reliving the past is the essential attraction of muzzleloading, and for these enthusiasts CVA has a selection of sidelock guns to satisfy many tastes and budgets. When choosing a caplock, shooters experience muzzleloading the "way it used to be." From the top of the line Mountain Rifle to the popular Bobcat, CVA offers a broad range of choices. All are covered by CVA's lifetime mechanical warranty and include complete instructions.

### Mountain Rifle PR4200

The **CVA Mountain Rifle** helped launch the rebirth of blackpowder hunting and shooting in the early 1970's. This gun authentically replicates the no-nonsense rifles of the mountain men who first explored the American West. Featuring all browned steel hardware, fine figured American hard maple stock, buckhorn rear sight and German silver wedge plates and blade front sight, this rifle offers custom quality and true traditional appeal. Designed to shoot patched round balls, the 32" browned steel barrel has 1 in 66" rifling and is extremely accurate. Made in the USA and limited to a production run of only 500 guns, the CVA Mountain Rifle is intended for the collector as well as the hunter.

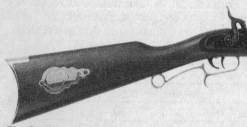

### St. Louis Hawken
### PR454, PR463, PR464

The **St. Louis Hawken** features CVA's patented breech plug/bolster system for reliable ignition. The Hawken style trigger guard gives the shooter a secure grip. Double set triggers allow for sensitive preset trigger pull for greater accuracy. This rifle is accented with brass buttplate, patchbox, trigger guard, wedge plates, nose cap, and thimbles. Left hand model available.

### Bobcat
### PR4102,
### PR4103

### PR4112

The **Bobcat Rifle** is a basic muzzleloader that delivers value without compromising performance, now with a choice of hardwood or synthetic stock. The blued octagonal barrel is the same barrel used on CVA's top of the line hunting rifles. Accuracy with sabots, conical bullets, and round balls is assured by CVA's deep groove rifling. The rifle has fixed sights and a wooden ramrod.

## SPECIFICATIONS

| Model | Caliber | Sights | Barrel | Rifling | Stock | Weight | Length | Retail Price |
|-------|---------|--------|--------|---------|-------|--------|--------|--------------|
| PR4200 | .50 | Fixed | 32" Browned | 1:66 | Am. Maple | 8 lbs. | 48" | $379.95 |
| PR454 | .50 L.H. | Adj. | 28" Blue | 1:48 | Wood | 8 lbs. | 44" | 234.95 |
| PR463 | .50 | Adj. | 28" Blue | 1:48 | Wood | 8 lbs. | 44" | 194.95 |
| PR464 | .54 | Adj. | 28" Blue | 1:48 | Wood | 8 lbs. | 44" | 194.95 |
| PR4102 | .50 | Fixed | 26" Blue | 1:48 | Syn. Black | 6 lbs. | 42" | 94.95 |
| PR4103 | .54 | Fixed | 26" Blue | 1:48 | Syn. Black | 6 lbs. | 42" | 94.95 |
| PR4112 | .50 | Fixed | 26" Blue | 1:48 | Wood | 6 lbs. | 42" | 119.95 |

# DIXIE REVOLVERS

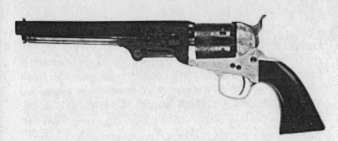

### 1851 NAVY BRASS-FRAME REVOLVER

This 36-caliber revolver was a favorite of the officers of the Civil War. Although called a Navy type, it is somewhat misnamed since many more of the Army personnel used it. Made in Italy; uses .376 mold or ball to fit and number 11 caps. Blued steel barrel and cylinder with brass frame.
*Price:*
Plain Model . . . . . . . . . . . . . . . . . . . . . . . . . . . . . $139.95

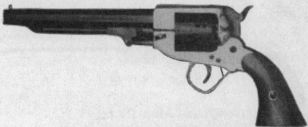

### SPILLER & BURR 36 CALIBER BRASS-FRAME REVOLVER

This revolver has a 7" octagon barrel and six .378 bore chambers. The hammer engages a slot between the nipples on the cylinder as an added safety device. It has a solid brass trigger guard and frame with backstrap cast integral with the frame, two-piece walnut grips and Whitney-type casehardened loading lever.
*Price:* . . . . . . . . . . . . . . . . . . . . . . . . . . . . . . . . $159.95
KIT . . . . . . . . . . . . . . . . . . . . . . . . . . . . . . . . . . . . 149.95

### REMINGTON 44 ARMY REVOLVER

All steel external surfaces finished bright blue, including 8" octagonal barrel (hammer is casehardened). Polished brass guard and two-piece walnut grips are standard.
*Price:* . . . . . . . . . . . . . . . . . . . . . . . . . . . . . . . . $150.00

### 1860 ARMY REVOLVER

The Dixie 1860 Army has a half-fluted cylinder and its chamber diameter is .447. Use .451 round ball mold to fit this 8-inch barrel revolver. Cut for shoulder stock.
*Price:* . . . . . . . . . . . . . . . . . . . . . . . . . . . . . . . . $196.00

### "WYATT EARP" REVOLVER

This 44-caliber revolver has a 12-inch octagon rifled barrel and rebated cylinder. Highly polished brass frame, backstrap and trigger guard. The barrel and cylinder have a deep blue luster finish. Hammer, trigger, and loading lever are casehardened. Walnut grips. Recommended ball size is .451.
*Price:* . . . . . . . . . . . . . . . . . . . . . . . . . . . . . . . . $150.00

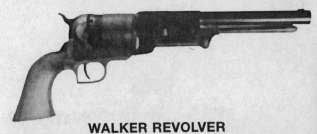

### WALKER REVOLVER

This 4 1/2-pound, 44-caliber pistol is the largest cap and ball revolver commercially built during the 19th century. Steel backstrap; guard is brass with Walker-type rounded-to-frame walnut grips; all other parts are blued. Chambers measure .445 and take a .450 ball slightly smaller than the original.
*Price:* . . . . . . . . . . . . . . . . . . . . . . . . . . . . . . . . $225.00

# DIXIE PISTOLS

**QUEEN ANNE PISTOL**

## QUEEN ANNE PISTOL

Named for the Queen of England (1702-1714), this flintlock pistol has a 7 1/2" barrel that tapers from rear to front with a cannon-shaped muzzle. The brass trigger guard is fluted and the brass butt on the walnut stock features a grotesque mask worked into it. *Overall length:* 13". *Weight:* 2.25 lbs.
Price: . . . . . . . . . . . . . . . . . . . . . . . . . . . . . . . . $225.00
Kit . . . . . . . . . . . . . . . . . . . . . . . . . . . . . . . . . . . 175.00

**CHARLES MOORE
ENGLISH DUELING PISTOL**

## CHARLES MOORE
## ENGLISH DUELING PISTOL

This reproduction of an English percussion dueling pistol, created by Charles Moore of London, features a European walnut halfstock with oil finish and checkered grip. The 45-caliber octagonal barrel is 11" with 12 grooves and a twist of 1 in 15". Nose cap and thimble are silver; barrel is blued; lock and trigger guard are color casehardened.
*Price:* FLINT . . . . . . . . . . . . . . . . . . . . . . . . . . . . . $385.00
PERCUSSION . . . . . . . . . . . . . . . . . . . . . . . . . . . . 323.95

**MANG IN GRAZ
TARGET PISTOL**

## MANG TARGET PISTOL

Designed specifically for the precision target shooter, this 38-caliber pistol has a 10 7/16" octagonal barrel with 7 lands and grooves. Twist is 1 in 15". Sights: Blade front dovetailed into barrel; rear mounted on breechplug tang, adjustable for windage. *Overall length:* 17 1/4". *Weight:* 2 .5 lbs.
*Price:* . . . . . . . . . . . . . . . . . . . . . . . . . . . . . . . . $786.00

**LEPAGE
PERCUSSION DUELING PISTOL**

## LePAGE PERCUSSION DUELING PISTOL

This 45-caliber percussion pistol features a blued 10" octagonal barrel with 12 lands and grooves; a brass-bladed front sight with open rear sight dovetailed into the barrel; polished silver-plated trigger guard and butt cap. Right side of barrel is stamped "LePage á Paris." Double-set riggers are single screw adjustable. *Overall length:* 16". *Weight:* 2.5 lbs.
*Price:* . . . . . . . . . . . . . . . . . . . . . . . . . . . . . . . . $259.95

**SCREW BARREL PISTOL**

## SCREW BARREL
## (FOLDING TRIGGER) PISTOL

This little gun, only 6 1/2" overall, has a unique loading system that eliminates the need for a ramrod. The barrel is loosened with a barrel key, then unscrewed from the frame by hand. A .445 round ball is seated atop 10 grains FFFg and the barrel is then screwed back into place. The .245X32 nipple uses #11 percussion caps. The pistol also features a sheath trigger that folds into the frame, then drops down for firing when the hammer is cocked. Color case hardened frame, trigger and center-mounted hammer.
*Price:* . . . . . . . . . . . . . . . . . . . . . . . . . . . . . . . . $126.95
Kit . . . . . . . . . . . . . . . . . . . . . . . . . . . . . . . . . . . . 95.00

# DIXIE RIFLES

## SHARPS MODEL 1859 CARBINE

About 115,000 Sharps New Model 1859 carbines and its variants were made during the Civil War. Characterized by durability and accuracy, they became a favorite of cavalry-men on both sides. Made in Italy by David Pedersoli & Co.

**SPECIFICATIONS**
**Caliber:** 54 **Barrel length:** 22" (1 in 48" twist); blued, round barrel has 7-groove rifling
**Overall length:** 37 1/2" **Weight:** 7 3/4 lbs.
**Sights:** Blade front; adjustable rear
**Stock:** Oil-finished walnut **Features:** Barrel band, hammer, receiver, saddle bar and ring all color casehardened
**Price:** . . . . . . . . . . . . . . . . . . . . . . . . . . . . . . **$775.00**

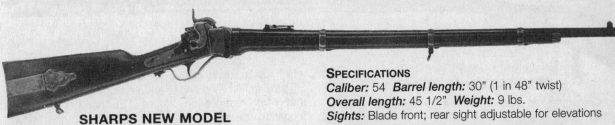

## SHARPS NEW MODEL 1859 MILITARY RIFLE

Initially used by the First Connecticut Volunteers, this rifle is associated mostly with the 1st U.S. (Berdan's) Sharpshooters. There were 6,689 made with most going to the Sharpshooters (2,000) and the U.S. Navy (2,780). Made in Italy by David Pedersoli & Co.

**SPECIFICATIONS**
**Caliber:** 54 **Barrel length:** 30" (1 in 48" twist)
**Overall length:** 45 1/2" **Weight:** 9 lbs.
**Sights:** Blade front; rear sight adjustable for elevations and windage
**Features:** Buttstock and forend of straight-grained oil fin-ished walnut; three barrel bands, receiver, hammer, nose cap, lever, patchbox cover and butt are all color case hard-ened; sling swivels attached to middle band and butt
**Price:** . . . . . . . . . . . . . . . . . . . . . . . . . . . . . . **$895.00**

## 1874 SHARPS LIGHTWEIGHT HUNTER RIFLE

This Sharps rifle in 45-70 Government caliber has a 30" octagon barrel with blued matte finish (1:18" twist). It also features an adjustable ladder rear sight and blade front, making it ideal for blackpowder hunters. The tang is drilled and threaded for tang sights. The oil-finished military-style buttstock has a blued metal buttplate. Double-set triggers. Color case hardened receiver and hammer. **Overall length:** 49 1/2". **Weight:** 10 lbs.
**Price:** . . . . . . . . . . . . . . . . . . . . . . . . . . . . . . **$995.00**

## 1874 SHARPS SILHOUETTE MODEL

This rifle in .40-65 and .45-70 caliber has a shotgun-style buttstock with pistol grip and metal buttplate. The 30-inch tapered octagon barrel is blued and has a 1 in 18" twist. The receiver, hammer, lever and buttplate are color case hardened. Ladder-type hunting rear and blade front sights are standard. Four screw holes are in the tang (two with 10 x 28 threads, two with metric threads) for attaching tang sights. Double set triggers are standard. **Weight** is 10 lbs. 3 oz. without target sights. **Overall length:** 47 1/2". Also available in 45-70
**Price:** . . . . . . . . . . . . . . . . . . . . . . . . . . . . . . **$995.00**

# DIXIE RIFLES

## DIXIE TENNESSEE MOUNTAIN RIFLE

This 50-caliber rifle features double-set triggers with adjustable set screw, bore rifled with 6 lands and grooves, barrel of 15/16 inch across the flats, brown finish and cherry stock.
**Overall length:** 41 1/2 inches. Right- and left-hand versions in flint or percussion.
**Prices:**
PERCUSSION OR FLINTLOCK . . . . . . . . . . . . . . . . . . $575.00
KIT . . . . . . . . . . . . . . . . . . . . . . . . . . . . . . . . . . . . . . 495.00

## PENNSYLVANIA RIFLE

A lightweight at just 8 pounds, the 41 1/2" blued rifle barrel is fitted with an open buckhorn rear sight and front blade. The walnut one-piece stock is stained to contrast with the polished brass buttplate, toe plate, patch-box, sideplate, trigger guard, thimbles and nose cap. Featuring double-set triggers, the rifle can be fired by pulling only the front trigger, which has a normal trigger pull of 4 to 5 pounds; or the rear trigger can first be pulled to set a spring-loaded mechanism that greatly reduces the amount of pull needed for the front trigger to release the lock. Land diameter is .450; recommended ball size is .445.
**Overall length:** 51 1/2".
**Prices:** PERCUSSION OR FLINTLOCK . . . . . . . . . . . $472.00
KIT (Flint or Perc.) . . . . . . . . . . . . . . . . . . . . . . . 415.00

## HAWKEN RIFLE (Not Shown)

Blued barrel is 15/16" across the flats and 30" in length with a twist of 1 in 64". Stock is of walnut with a steel crescent buttplate, halfstock with brass nosecap. Double-set triggers, front-action lock and adjustable rear sight. Ramrod is equipped with jag. **Overall length:** 46 1/2". **Weight:** about 8 lbs., depending on the caliber; shipping weight is 10 lbs. Available in either finished gun or kit. **Calibers:** 45, 50 and 54.
**Price:** . . . . . . . . . . . . . . . . . . . . . . . . . . . . . . . . . . $250.00
KIT . . . . . . . . . . . . . . . . . . . . . . . . . . . . . . . . . . . . . . 205.00

## WAADTLANDER RIFLE (Not Shown)

This authentic re-creation of a Swiss muzzloading target rifle features a heavy octagonal barrel (31") that has 7 lands and grooves. **Caliber:** 45. Rate of twist is 1 turn in 48". Double-set triggers are multi-lever type and are easily removable for adjustment. Sights are fitted post front and tang-mounted Swiss-type diopter rear. Walnut stock, color case hardened hardware, classic buttplate and curved trigger guard complete this reproduction. The original was made between 1839 and 1860 by Marc Bristlen, Morges, Switzerland.
**Price:** . . . . . . . . . . . . . . . . . . . . . . . . . . . . . . . . $1,412.00

## DOUBLE-BARREL MAGNUM MUZZLELOADING SHOTGUN (Not Shown)

A full 10, 12 or 20 gauge, high-quality, double-barreled percussion shotgun with 30-inch browned barrels. Will take the plastic shot cups for better patterns. Bores are choked modified and full. Lock, barrel tang and trigger are case-hardened in a light gray color and engraved.

**Prices:**
12 GAUGE . . . . . . . . . . . . . . . . . . . . . . . . . . . . . . . $449.00
12 GAUGE KIT . . . . . . . . . . . . . . . . . . . . . . . . . . . . . 375.00
10 GAUGE MAGNUM (right-hand = Cyl.,
    left-hand = Mod.) . . . . . . . . . . . . . . . . . . . . . . . . 495.00
10 GAUGE MAGNUM KIT . . . . . . . . . . . . . . . . . . . . 395.00
20 GAUGE . . . . . . . . . . . . . . . . . . . . . . . . . . . . . . . 495.00

# DIXIE RIFLES

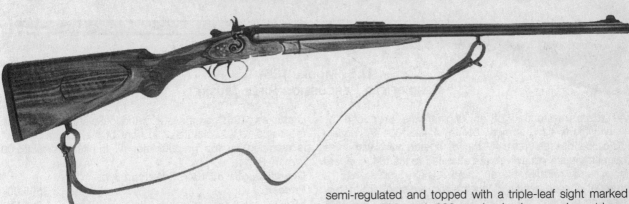

## KODIAK MARK IV .45-70 DOUBLE BARREL RIFLE

Patterned after a classic, limited edition 19th century Colt double rifle, the Kodiak Mark IV has been designed for hunters and collectors. The 24-inch browned barrels are semi-regulated and topped with a triple-leaf sight marked for 100, 200 and 300 yards. Locks, receiver, trigger guard and hammers are case-hardened. The two-piece stock is European walnut; forearm and pistol grip are checkered. The buttstock has a cheekpiece and a solid, red rubber pad. Sling swivels are standard. *Weight:* 10 lbs. *Overall length:* 40"
*Price:*. . . . . . . . . . . . . . . . . . . . . . . . . . . . . . . . $2,495.00

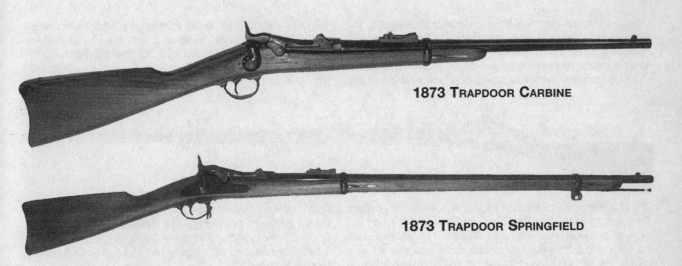

**1873 Trapdoor Carbine**

**1873 Trapdoor Springfield**

## 1873 SPRINGFIELD RIFLE AND CARBINE

Developed from the Allin Conversion of Springfield muskets from the Civil War, 1873 Springfield "Trapdoors" became the firearms that finished the winning of the west. Adopted in 1873 and immediately issued to troops on the frontier, the Trapdoor was the last single-shot, blackpowder rifle of the U.S. military, later supplanted by the adoption of the .30-.40 Krag-Jorgensen bolt rifle.

### RIFLE
*Caliber:* 45-70. *Barrel length:* 32.5" round. 1-22 twist; 3 groove rifling; all furniture blued; sling swivels; open sights; ladder style elevation rear adjustable to 500 yards. *Overall length:* 52" *Weight:* 8.5 lbs. Walnut stock
*Price:*. . . . . . . . . . . . . . . . . . . . . . . . . . . . . . . . $995.00

### CARBINE
*Caliber:* 45-70. *Barrel length:* 22" round. 1-22 twist; 3 groove rifling; all furniture blued; saddle bar and ring; open sights; ladder-style elevation rear adjustable to 400 yards. *Overall length:* 41" *Weight:* 8.5 lbs. Walnut stock.
*Price:*. . . . . . . . . . . . . . . . . . . . . . . . . . . . . . . . $895.00

### OFFICER'S MODEL
*Caliber:* 45-70. *Barrel length:* 26" round. 1-18 twist; 6 groove rifling; pewter ramrod tip and nosecap; case-hardened hammer and lock; walnut stock; checkered wrist and forearm; single set trigger; fully adjustable tang sight. *Overall length:* 45" *Weight:* 8 lbs.
*Price:*. . . . . . . . . . . . . . . . . . . . . . . . . . . . . . . . $1,025.00

# DIXIE RIFLES/MUSKETS

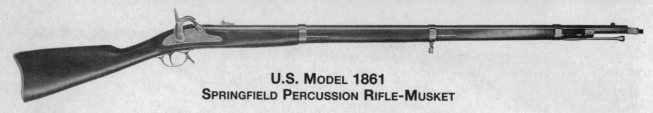

## U.S. MODEL 1861
### SPRINGFIELD PERCUSSION RIFLE-MUSKET

An exact re-creation of an original rifle produced by Springfield National Armory, Dixie's Model 1861 Springfield 58-caliber rifle features a 40" round, tapered barrel with three barrel bands. Sling swivels are attached to the trigger guard bow and middle barrel band. The ramrod has a trumpet-shaped head with swell; sights are standard military rear and bayonet-attachment lug front. The percussion lock is marked "1861" on the rear of the lockplate with an eagle motif and "U.S. Springfield" in front of the hammer. "U.S." is stamped on top of buttplate. All furniture is "National Armory Bright."

*Overall length:* 55 13/16". *Weight:* 8 lbs.
*Prices:* . . . . . . . . . . . . . . . . . . . . . . . . . . . . . . . . . . $595.00
KIT . . . . . . . . . . . . . . . . . . . . . . . . . . . . . . . . . . . . . . 525.00

## 1862 THREE-BAND ENFIELD RIFLED MUSKET

One of the finest reproduction percussion guns available, the 1861 Enfield was widely used during the Civil War in its original version. This rifle follows the lines of the original almost exactly. The 58-caliber musket features a 39-inch barrel and walnut stock. Three steel barrel bands and the barrel itself are blued; the lockplate and hammer are case colored, and the remainder of the furniture is highly polished brass. The lock is marked, "London Armory Co." *Weight:* 10.5 lbs. *Overall length:* 55".
*Prices:* . . . . . . . . . . . . . . . . . . . . . . . . . . . . . . . . . . $495.00
KIT . . . . . . . . . . . . . . . . . . . . . . . . . . . . . . . . . . . . . . 425.00

## U.S. MODEL 1816 FLINTLOCK MUSKET

The U.S. Model 1816 Flintlock Musket was made by Harpers Ferry and Springfield Arsenal from 1816 until 1864. It had the highest production of any U.S. flintlock musket and after conversion to percussion saw service in the Civil War. It has a 69-caliber, 42" smoothbore barrel held by three barrel bands with springs. All metal parts are finished in "National Armory Bright." The lockplate has a brass pan and is marked "Harpers Ferry" vertically behind the hammer, with an American eagle placed in front of the hammer. The bayonet lug is on top of the barrel and the steel ramrod has a button-shaped head. Sling swivels are mounted on trigger guard and middle barrel band.
*Overall length:* 56.5"
*Weight:* 9.75 lbs.
*Price:* . . . . . . . . . . . . . . . . . . . . . . . . . . . . . . . . . . . $725.00

## 1858 TWO-BAND ENFIELD RIFLE

This 33-inch barrel version of the British Enfield is an exact copy of similar rifles used during the Civil War. The 58-caliber rifle sports a European walnut stock, deep blue-black finish on the barrel, bands, breech-plug tang and bayonet mount. The percussion lock is casehardened, and the rest of the furniture is brightly polished brass.
*Price:* . . . . . . . . . . . . . . . . . . . . . . . . . . . . . . . . . . . $475.00

# EMF HARTFORD REVOLVERS

## SHERIFF'S MODEL 1851 REVOLVER

### SPECIFICATIONS
*Caliber:* 44 Percussion *Ball diameter:* .376 round or conical, pure lead *Barrel length:* 5" *Overall length:* 10.5" *Weight:* 39 oz. *Sights:* V-notch groove in hammer (rear); truncated cone in front *Percussion cap size:* #11

*Prices:* Brass . . . . . . . . . . . . . . . . . . . . . . . . . . . . . $150.00
Steel . . . . . . . . . . . . . . . . . . . . . . . . . . . . . . . . . . 200.00

## MODEL 1860 ARMY REVOLVER

### SPECIFICATIONS
*Caliber:* 44 Percussion  *Barrel length:* 8"
*Overall length:* 13 ⁵/₈" *Weight:* 41 oz. *Frame:* Case hardened *Finish:* High-luster blue with walnut grips
*Price:* Brass Frame . . . . . . . . . . . . . . . . . . . . . . . $165.00
*Also available:* CASED SET with steel frame, wood case, flask and mould . . . . . . . . . . . . . . . . . . . . $380.00
Engraved cased set . . . . . . . . . . . . . . . . . . . . . 480.00

## HARTFORD MODEL 1862 POLICE REVOLVER

### SPECIFICATIONS
*Caliber:* 36 Percussion *Capacity:* 5-shot
*Barrel length:* 6.5"
*Prices:* Steel . . . . . . . . . . . . . . . . . . . . . . . . . . . . $250.00
Brass . . . . . . . . . . . . . . . . . . . . . . . . . . . . . . . . . 170.00

## HARTFORD 1863 TEXAS DRAGOON

### SPECIFICATIONS
*Caliber:* 44 *Barrel length:* 7" (round) *Overall length:* 14" *Weight:* 4 lbs. *Finish:* Steel case-hardened frame
*Price:* . . . . . . . . . . . . . . . . . . . . . . . . . . . . . . . . . $330.00

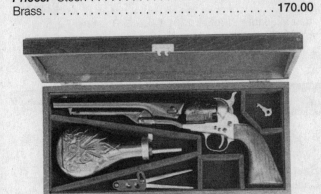

## 1860 ARMY BRASS FRAME CASED SET
*Price:* . . . . . . . . . . . . . . . . . . . . . . . . . . . . . . . . . $315.00

**1851 NAVY**
(36 or 44 Cal.) – $305.00
Brass frame .44 - 150.00

**1847 WALKER**
(44 Cal.)
$330.00

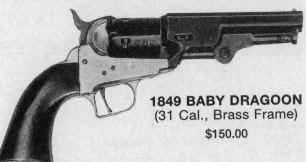

**1849 BABY DRAGOON**
(31 Cal., Brass Frame)
$150.00

**1848 DRAGOON**
(44 Cal.)
$315.00

**BLACK POWDER**

# EUROARMS OF AMERICA

**LONDON ARMORY COMPANY ENFIELD P-1858 2-BAND RIFLE MUSKET MODEL 2270**

**SPECIFICATIONS**
*Caliber:* 58 percussion *Barrel Length:* 33"
*Weight:* 8.5 to 8.75 lbs., depending on wood density
*Stock:* One-piece walnut; polished "bright" brass buttplate, trigger guard and nose cap; blued barrel and bands
*Sights:* Inverted 'V' front sight; Enfield folding ladder rear
*Ramrod:* Steel
*Price:* . . . . . . . . . . . . . . . . . . . . . . . . . . . . . . . . . $470.00

**COOK & BROTHER CONFEDERATE CARBINE MODEL 2300**

Classic re-creation of the rare 1861, New Orleans-made Artillery Carbine.

**SPECIFICATIONS**
*Caliber:* 58 percussion  *Barrel Length:* 24"
*Sights:* Fixed blade front and adjustable dovetailed rear
*Ramrod:* Steel  *Finish:* Barrel is antique brown; buttplate, trigger guard, barrel bands, sling swivels and nose cap are polished brass; stock is walnut  *Recommended ball sizes:* .575 r.b., .577 Minie and .580 maxi; uses musket caps
*Price:* . . . . . . . . . . . . . . . . . . . . . . . . . . . . . . . . $447.00
*Also available:* MODEL 2301 COOK & BROTHER FIELD
with 33" barrel . . . . . . . . . . . . . . . . . . . . . . . . . . . 480.00

**J.P. MURRAY CARBINE MODEL 2315**

Replica of an extremely rare CSA Cavalry Carbine based on an 1841 design of parts and lock.

**SPECIFICATIONS**
*Caliber:* 58 percussion  *Barrel Length:* 23"
*Features:* Brass barrel bands and buttplate; oversized trigger guard; sling swivels
*Price:* . . . . . . . . . . . . . . . . . . . . . . . . . . . . . . . . . $453.00

**C.S. RICHMOND MUSKET MODEL 2370**

**SPECIFICATIONS**
*Caliber:* 58 percussion  *Barrel Length:* 40"
*Price:* . . . . . . . . . . . . . . . . . . . . . . . . . . . . . . . . . $530.00

# EUROARMS OF AMERICA

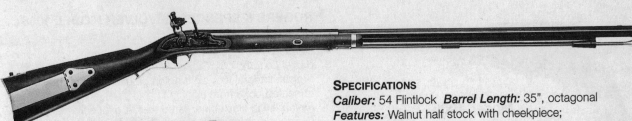

## U.S. 1803 HARPERS FERRY FLINTLOCK RIFLE MODEL 2305

**SPECIFICATIONS**
*Caliber:* 54 Flintlock  *Barrel Length:* 35", octagonal
*Features:* Walnut half stock with cheekpiece; browned barrel
*Price:* . . . . . . . . . . . . . . . . . . . . . . . . . . . . . . . . $640.00

## U.S.1841 MISSISSIPPI RIFLE MODEL 2310

**SPECIFICATIONS**
*Calibers:* 54 and 58 percussion  *Barrel Length:* 33", octagonal
*Features:* Walnut stock; brass barrel bands and buttplate; sling swivels
*Price:* . . . . . . . . . . . . . . . . . . . . . . . . . . . . . . . . $500.00

## U.S. MODEL 1863 REMINGTON ZOUAVE RIFLE (2-BARREL BANDS)

**SPECIFICATIONS**
*Caliber:* 58 percussion  *Barrel Length:* 33", octagonal
*Weight:* 9.5
*Sights:* U.S. Military 3-leaf rear; blade front
*Price:* . . . . . . . . . . . . . . . . . . . . . . . . . . . . . . . . $430.00

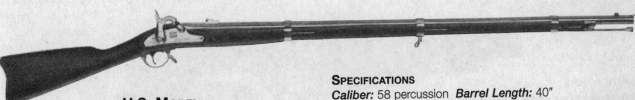

## U.S. MODEL 1861 SPRINGFIELD RIFLE

**SPECIFICATIONS**
*Caliber:* 58 percussion  *Barrel Length:* 40"
*Price:* . . . . . . . . . . . . . . . . . . . . . . . . . . . . . . . . $530.00

## LONDON 3-BAND ENFIELD P-1852 RIFLED MUSKET (not shown)

**SPECIFICATIONS**
*Caliber:* 58 percussion  *Barrel Length:* 54"  *Weight:* 9.5 pounds  *Sights:* ladder rear, blade front
*Price:* . . . . . . . . . . . . . . . . . . . . . . . . $480.00

## LONDON ENFIELD P-1861 (not shown)

**SPECIFICATIONS**
*Caliber:* 58 percussion  *Weight:* 7.5 pounds  *Sights:* military leaf rear, blade front
*Price:* . . . . . . . . . . . . . . . . . . . . . . . . $415.00

# EUROARMS OF AMERICA

**MODEL 1005**

## ROGERS & SPENCER ARMY REVOLVER MODEL 1006 (Target)

**SPECIFICATIONS**
*Caliber:* 44; takes .451 round or conical balls; #11 percussion cap  *Weight:* 47 oz.  *Barrel Length:* 7.5"
*Overall Length:* 13.75"  *Finish:* High gloss blue; flared walnut grip; solid frame design; precision-rifled barrel
*Sights:* Rear fully adjustable for windage and elevation; ramp front sight
*Price:* . . . . . . . . . . . . . . . . . . . . . . . . . . . . . $239.00

## ROGERS & SPENCER REVOLVER LONDON GRAY MODEL 1007 (Not Shown)

Revolver is the same as Model 1005, except for London Gray finish, which is heat treated and buffed for rust resistance; .451 balls, #11 percussion caps

*Price:* . . . . . . . . . . . . . . . . . . . . . . . . . . . . . $245.00
*Also available:* MODEL 1120 COLT 1851 NAVY Steel or brass frame. 36 cal. *Barrel Length:* 7.5" octagonal.
*Overall Length:* 13"  *Weight:* 42 oz.
*Price:* . . . . . . . . . . . . . . . . . . . . . . . . . . . . . 156.00
MODEL 1210 COLT 1860 ARMY Steel frame. 44 percussion
*Overall Length:* 10 ⅝" or 13 ⅝"  *Weight:* 41 oz.
*Price:* . . . . . . . . . . . . . . . . . . . . . . . . . . . . . 177.00

## ROGERS & SPENCER REVOLVER MODEL 1005

**SPECIFICATIONS**
*Caliber:* 44 Percussion; #11 percussion cap
*Barrel Length:* 7.5"  *Overall Length:* 13.75"  *Weight:* 47 oz.
*Sights:* Integral rear sight notch groove in frame; brass truncated cone front sight
*Finish:* High gloss blue; flared walnut grip; solid frame design; precision-rifled barrel  *Recommended ball diameter:* .451 round or conical, pure lead
*Price:* . . . . . . . . . . . . . . . . . . . . . . . . . . . . . $227.00

**MODEL 1006**

## REMINGTON 1858 NEW MODEL ARMY ENGRAVED MODEL 1040 (Not Shown)

Classical 19th-century style scroll engraving on this 1858 Remington New Model revolver.

**SPECIFICATIONS**
*Caliber:* 44 Percussion; #11 cap  *Barrel Length:* 8"
*Overall Length:* 14.75"  *Weight:* 41 oz.  *Sights:* Integral rear sight notch groove in frame; blade front sight
*Recommended ball diameter:* .451 round or conical, pure lead
*Price:* . . . . . . . . . . . . . . . . . . . . . . . . . . . . . $275.00

## REMINGTON 1858 NEW MODEL ARMY REVOLVER MODEL 1020

This model features blued steel frame, brass trigger guard and 8" 44-caliber barrel

**SPECIFICATIONS**
*Weight:* 40 oz.  *Overall Length:* 14.75"
*Finish:* Deep luster blue rifled barrel; polished walnut stock; brass trigger guard.
*Price:* . . . . . . . . . . . . . . . . . . . . . . . . . . . . . $200.00
*Also available:* MODEL 1010 Same as Model 1020, except w/6.5" barrel and in 36 caliber: . . . . . . . . . . . . . $200.00

**MODEL 1010**
**(36 Cal. W/6.5" barrel)**

# GONIC ARMS RIFLES

## MODEL 93 RIFLE SERIES

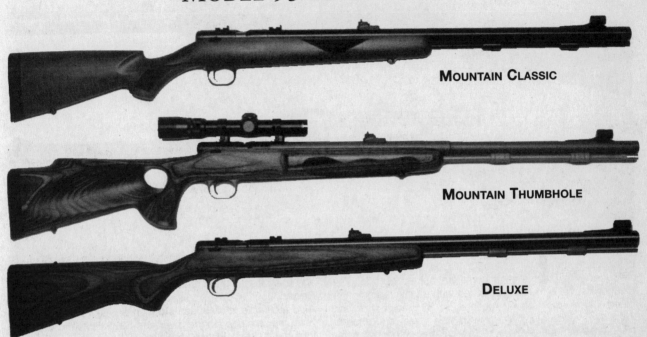

**MOUNTAIN CLASSIC**

**MOUNTAIN THUMBHOLE**

**DELUXE**

### MODEL 93 MOUNTAIN CLASSIC RIFLE

#### SPECIFICATIONS
*Caliber:* 50 Magnum
*Barrel Length:* 26" 4140 chrome-moly blued satin or 416 stainless steel w/matte finish; 1-in-24" twist
*Length Of Pull:* 14"
*Trigger:* Single, adjustable w/side safety
*Weight:* 6.5 to 7 lbs.
*Sights:* Open or peep sights, fully adjustable for windage and elevation; ramp front w/gold bead and protector hood

*Stock:* Walnut or laminated (left or right hand)
*Features:* Unbreakable ram rod; classic cheekpiece; three-point pillar bedding system; 1" decelerator recoil pad; sling swivel studs; E-Z-Load Muzzle System w/muzzle break
*Price:* . . . . . . . . . . . . . . . . . . . . . . . . . . . . . **$2,132.00**
*Also Available:*
**MODEL 93 MOUNTAIN THUMBHOLE RIFLE** w/same specification and features as above, but w/thumbhole Monte Carlo rollover cheekpiece, beavertail forend and palm swell grip.
*Price:* . . . . . . . . . . . . . . . . . . . . . . . . . . . . . **2,132.00**

### MODEL 93 RIFLE

Gonic Arm's blackpowder rifle has a unique loading system that produces better consistency and utilizes the full powder charge of the specially designed penetrator bullet (2,650 foot-pounds at 1,600 fps w/465-grain .500 bullet).

#### SPECIFICATIONS
*Caliber:* 50 Magnum
*Barrel Lengths:* 26"
*Overall Length:* 43"
*Weight:* 6 to 6.5 lbs.
*Sights:* Open hunting sights (adjustable)
*Features:* Walnut-stained hardwood stock; adjustable trigger;

nipple wrench; drilled and tapped for scope bases; ballistics and instruction manual

*Prices:* Open Sights . . . . . . . . . . . . . . . . . . . . . . . **$500.57**
Stainless w/Open Sights . . . . . . . . . . . . . . . . . . . . **603.04**
*Also Available:*
**MODEL 93 SAFARI CLASSIC RIFLE** w/classic walnut
stock, open sights . . . . . . . . . . . . . . . . . . . . . **1,612.00**
**MODEL 93 DELUXE** w/grey laminated stock;
Weaver scope base; open sights; E-Z-Load
Muzzle System . . . . . . . . . . . . . . . . . . . . . . . . **660.24**
Stainless w/open sights . . . . . . . . . . . . . . . . . . . **756.44**

# LYMAN RIFLES

**LYMAN COUGAR-IN-LINE STAINLESS**

**LYMAN COUGAR-IN-LINE RIFLE**

The **LYMAN COUGAR IN-LINE** rifle is designed for the serious blackpowder hunter who wants a rugged and accurate muzzleloader with the feel of a centerfire bolt-action rifle. The Cougar In-Line is traditionally styled with a walnut stock and blued barrel and action. Available in 50 and 54 caliber. Features include a 22" barrel with 1:24" twist and shallow rifling grooves; dual safety system (equipped with a bolt safety notch in receiver and a sliding thumb safety that disables the trigger mechanism); drilled and tapped for Lyman 57 WTR receiver sight; fully adjustable trigger; sling swivel studs installed; unbreakable Delrin ramrod; modern folding-leaf rear and bead front sights; rubber recoil pad.

**Price:** ..................................... **$249.95**
***Also available*** in **stainless steel** on all major parts. Features same as standard version. Stock is semi-Schnabel forend with black Hard Kote finish.

**Price:** ..................................... **$299.95**

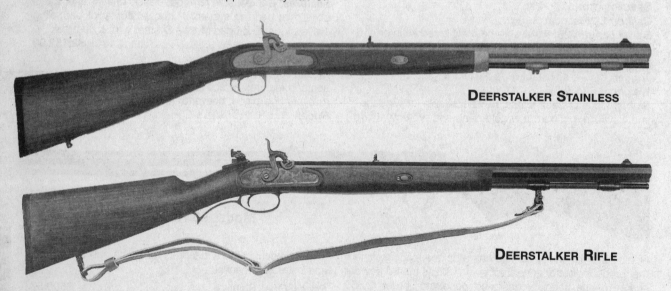

**DEERSTALKER STAINLESS**

**DEERSTALKER RIFLE**

**LYMAN'S DEERSTALKER** rifle incorporates • higher comb for better sighting plane • nonglare hardware • 24" octagonal barrel • case hardened sideplate • Q.D. sling swivels • Lyman sight package (37MA beaded front, fully adjustable fold-down 16A rear) • walnut stock with black recoil pad • single trigger. Left-hand models available (same price). ***Calibers:*** 50 and 54, flintlock or percussion. ***Weight:*** 7.5 lbs.

**Price:** Percussion ......................... **$304.95**
   Left-Hand ............................. **319.95**
   Flintlock .............................. **334.95**
   Left Hand.............................. **349.95**
**DEERSTALKER STAINLESS.** Features all stainless steel parts, plus walnut stock, recoil pad, Delrin ramrod, Lyman front and rear hunting sights.

**Price:** ..................................... **$384.95**

# LYMAN RIFLES

**GREAT PLAINS RIFLE**

**GREAT PLAINS HUNTER**

**Price:**

| | |
|---|---|
| Percussion | **$434.95** |
| Kit | 349.95 |
| Flintlock | 459.95 |
| Kit | 374.95 |
| Left-Hand Model Percussion | 444.95 |
| Left-Hand Model Flintlock | 469.95 |

**Also available:**

**GREAT PLAINS HUNTER.** Same features as standard rifle but with 1 in 32" twist and shallow rifling groove for shooting modern sabots and black powder hunting bullets.

**Price:** Percussion . . . . . . . . . . . . . . . . . . . . . **$434.95**

Flintlock . . . . . . . . . . . . . . . . . . . . . . . . . **$459.95**

The **GREAT PLAINS** has a 32-inch deep-grooved barrel and 1 in 66" twist to shoot patched round balls. Blued steel furniture including the thick steel wedge plates and toe plate; correct lock and hammer styling with coil spring dependability; a walnut stock w/o patchbox. A Hawken-style trigger guard protects double-set triggers. Steel front sight and authentic buckhorn styling in an adjustable rear sight. Fixed primitive rear sight also included. **Calibers:** 50 and 54.

**LYMAN TRADE RIFLE**

The **LYMAN TRADE RIFLE** features a 28-inch octagonal barrel, rifled 1 turn at 48 inches, designed to fire both patched round balls and the popular maxi-style conical bullets. Polished brass furniture with blued finish on steel parts; walnut stock; hook breech; single spring-loaded trigger; coil-spring percussion lock; fixed steel sights; adjustable rear sight for elevation also included. Steel barrel rib and ramrod ferrule.

**Caliber:** 50 and 54 percussion and flint.

**Overall Length:** 45"

**Price:**

| | |
|---|---|
| Percussion | **$299.95** |
| Flintlock | **$324.95** |

# MARKESBERY MUZZLE LOADERS

Markesbery's Black Bear, Grizzly Bear and Brown Bear rifles are made of eight cast, polished molded parts, coupled with an all-cast receiver and trigger guard. Pillow mount system with interchangeable barrels in 36, 45, .50 and 54 calibers. All rifles are constructed with Markesbery's **MAGNUM HAMMER IN-LINE IGNITION SYSTEM**, the 400 SRP (small rifle primer) system or optional No. 11 cap and nipple. This system, along with a 1-26" twist button precision 24" rifle barrel, is available in either 4140 or stainless steel models. All models have a double safety system with half cock and cross bolt hammer safeties. Marble adjustable sights with double adjustment features, hammer thumb rest and rubber recoil pad are standard.

The Black Bear features a two-piece, handcrafted hardwood walnut, black laminate and green laminate pistol grip stock. *Weight:* 6.5 lbs. *Overall Length:* 38.5". The Brown and Grizzly Bear models offer custom-checkered Monte Carlo (Grizzly Bear two-piece or Brown Bear one-piece) thumbhole stocks. *Overall Length:* 38.5" *Weight:* 6.5 lbs. (Brown Bear is 6.75 lbs.). Both models are available in black composite, crotch walnut, Mossy Oak Break-up, XTRA-Grey and Real Tree Advantage camo stock patterns. *Metal finishes:* blued, matte and stainless steel. All models have a solid aluminum ram rod with brass jag and bullet starter.
*Price:* **BLACK BEAR** (two-piece pistol grip stock)
(depending on stock). . . . . . . . . . . . **$536.63-573.73**

**BLACK BEAR**

**BROWN BEAR**

Features one-piece, Monte Carlo thumbhole stock
*Price:* (depending on stock) . . . . . . . . . **$658.83-702.76**
*Also available:* **POLAR BEAR SERIES** w/one-piece Monte Carlo pistol grip stock.
*Price:* (depending on stock) . . . . . . . . . **$539.01-573.94**

**GRIZZLY BEAR**

Features twp-piece, Monte Carlo thumbhole stock
*Price:* (depending on stock) . . . . . . . . . **$642.96-664.20**

# MARKESBERY MUZZLE LOADERS

**POLAR BEAR**

The Polar Bear has Markesbery's standard features plus a one-piece pistol-grip stock of solid hardwood or laminated wood construction in black or green.

## KM POLAR BEAR™ RIFLE SERIES (One piece Monte Carlo pistol grip stock)

| Model | Barrel Length | Twist | Caliber | Suggested Retail |
|---|---|---|---|---|
| KMPB-B-Walnut Finish | 24" | 1-26" | 36, 45, 50, 54 | $539.01 |
| KMPB-B-Black | 24" | 1-26" | 36, 45, 50, 54 | 536.63 |
| KMPB-B-Black Laminate | 24" | 1-26" | 36, 45, 50, 54 | 541.17 |
| KMPB-B-Green Laminate | 24" | 1-26" | 36, 45, 50, 54 | 541.17 |
| KMPB-B-Camo | 24" | 1-26" | 36, 45, 50, 54 | 560.43 |
| KMPB-SS-Walnut | 24" | 1-26" | 36, 45, 50, 54 | 556.27 |
| KMPB-SS-Black | 24" | 1-26" | 36, 45, 50, 54 | 556.04 |
| KMPB-SS-Black Laminate | 24" | 1-26" | 36, 45, 50, 54 | 570.56 |
| KMPB-SS-Green Laminate | 24" | 1-26" | 36, 45, 50, 54 | 570.56 |
| KMPB-SS-Camo | 24" | 1-26" | 36, 45, 50, 54 | 573.94 |

**COLORADO ROCKY MOUNTAIN RIFLE**

New for 2001, this traditional-style muzzleloader features a walnut stock with barrel bands and straight grip. The pronounced hammer spur is reminiscent of the style used by frontiersmen in the 1800s. The same rear-hammer design of other Markesbery rifles has been retained. A No. 11 cap mechanism comes standard, but the company's Magnum Ignition System can be installed.

## KM COLORADO ROCKY MOUNTAIN™ RIFLE SERIES (One piece Straight Grip stock)

| Model | Barrel Length | Twist | Caliber | Suggested Retail |
|---|---|---|---|---|
| KM-CRM-B-Walnut Finish | 24" | 1-26" | 36, 45, 50, 54 | $545.92 |
| KM-CRM-B-Black Laminate | 24" | 1-26" | 36, 45, 50, 54 | 548.30 |
| KM-CRM-B-Green Laminate | 24" | 1-26" | 36, 45, 50, 54 | 548.30 |
| KM-CRM-SS-Walnut Finish | 24" | 1-26" | 36, 45, 50, 54 | 563.17 |
| KM-CRM-SS-Black Laminate | 24" | 1-26" | 36, 45, 50, 54 | 566.34 |
| KM-CRM-SS-Green Laminate | 24" | 1-26" | 36, 45, 50, 54 | 566.34 |

# MODERN MUZZLELOADING

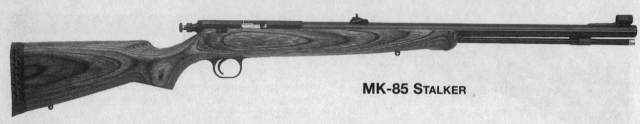

**MK-85 STALKER**

## MK-85 KNIGHT RIFLE

The MK-85 muzzleloading rifles (designed by William A. "Tony" Knight) are lightweight rifles capable of 1 1/2-inch groups at 100 yards. They feature a one-piece, inline bolt assembly, patented double-safety system, Timney feather-weight deluxe trigger system, recoil pad, and Green Mountain barrels (1 in 28" twist in 50 and 54 caliber).

### SPECIFICATIONS
*Calibers:* 50 and 54  *Barrel:* 24", 1:28 twist
*Overall length:* 43"  *Weight:* 7 lbs.

*Sights:* Adjustable high-visibility open sights
*Stock:* Classic walnut, laminated or composite
*Features:* Swivel studs installed; hard anodized aluminum ramrod; combo tool; hex keys.
*Prices:*
MK-85 HUNTER Walnut Stock . . . . . . . . . . . . . . . $549.95
MK-85 KNIGHT HAWK . . . . . . . . . . . . . . . . . . . . . 769.95
MK-85 PREDATOR (Stainless) Laminated Stock. . . . 649.95
MK-85 STALKER Black Composite Stock . . . . . . . . 569.95

**KNIGHT T-BOLT**

### SPECIFICATIONS
*Caliber:* 50  *Barrel Length:* 22" (blued or matte stainless) or 26" (matte stainless only), 1"28 twist  *Overall Length:* 41"  *Weight:* 6 lbs.  *Sights:* Fully adjustable mettalic rear sight; front ramp and bead; drilled and tapped for scope

mounting  *Stock:* Composite (Black Mossy Oak Break Up or Bill Jordan's Advantage)  *Features:* Sling swivel studs installed; patented double safety system; stainless steel breech plug; patented Red Hot nipple; adjustable Knight trigger; In-Line ignition system
*Prices:* Blue Break-Up . . . . . . . . . . . . . . . . . . . . $449.95
Stainless Break-Up . . . . . . . . . . . . . . . . . . . . . . . 519.95
Stainless . . . . . . . . . . . . . . . . . . . . . . . . . . . . . . . 469.95
Blue only . . . . . . . . . . . . . . . . . . . . . . . . . . . . . . . 399.95

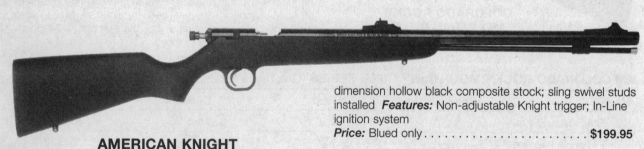

dimension hollow black composite stock; sling swivel studs installed  *Features:* Non-adjustable Knight trigger; In-Line ignition system
*Price:* Blued only . . . . . . . . . . . . . . . . . . . . . . . . $199.95

## AMERICAN KNIGHT
### SPECIFICATIONS
*Caliber:* 50  *Action:* Patented double safety system; one-piece removable hammer assembly; removable stainless steel breech plug w/patented Red Hot nipple  *Barrel:* 22" Green Mountain rifle barrel; blued or matte stainless steel, 1:28 twist  *Overall Length:* 41"  *Weight:* 6 lbs.*Stock:* Full

## BIGHORN (not shown)
### SPECIFICATIONS
50 caliber 22" or 26" blued or stainless, with adjustable fiber-optic sights, checkered stock (black thumbhole available) in a variety of camo patterns; left-hand version available; 7 to 7.3 pounds.

# MODERN MUZZLELOADING

**LK-93 THUMBHOLE WOLVERINE w/MOSSY OAK CAMO**

**MODEL LK-93 WOLVERINE II**

## SPECIFICATIONS
*Calibers:* 50 and 54
*Barrel length:* 22"; blued or stainless (1:28" twist)
*Overall length:* 41"  *Weight:* 6 lbs. 11 oz.
*Sights:* adjustable TRUGLO fiber-optic
*Stock:* Checkered lightweight synthetic molded stock with choice of black or camo finishes
*Features:* Patented double-safety system; adjustable Accu-Lite trigger; removable breechplug; stainless-steel hammer. Also available in youth version.

*Prices:* Blued . . . . . . . . . . . . . . . . . . . . . . . . . . . $269.95
Value Pack . . . . . . . . . . . . . . . . . . . . . . . . . . . . . 299.95
Stainless . . . . . . . . . . . . . . . . . . . . . . . . . . . . . . . 389.95
Blued Advantage or Break-Up . . . . . . . . . . . . . 319.95
Stainless Advantage or Break-up . . . . . . . . . . . . 419.95
*Also Available:* LK-93 THUMBHOLE WOLVERINE
Blued w/Black Stock . . . . . . . . . . . . . . . . . . . . $309.95
Blued w/Camo Stock . . . . . . . . . . . . . . . . . . . . . 359.95
Stainless Steel w/Black Stock . . . . . . . . . . . . . . 379.95
Stainless Steel w/Camo Stock . . . . . . . . . . . . . . 429.95

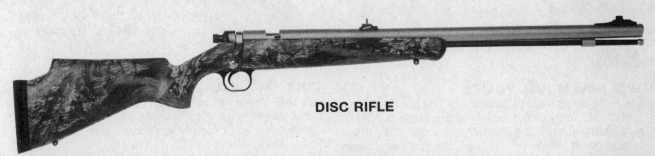

**DISC RIFLE**

## SPECIFICATIONS
*Caliber:* 50  *Action:* Patented double safety system; turn bolt style designed for 209 shotgun primers
*Barrel length:* 24" (Green Mountain barrel; blued or matte stainless rifle grade steel)
*Overall length:* 43"  *Rate of twist:* 1 in 28"
*Length:* 43"  *Weight:* 7 pounds
*Sights:* Metallic rear sight; front ramp and bead
*Stock:* Composite (Black Mossy Oak Break-Up); Bill Jordan's Advantage w/rubber recoil pad; checkered forearm and palm swell pistol grip;
*Features:* Fully adjustable Knight trigger; In-Line ignition system; one-piece removable bolt assembly; removable stainless steel breech plug

*Prices:* Blue . . . . . . . . . . . . . . . . . . . . . . . . . . . $459.95
Stainless . . . . . . . . . . . . . . . . . . . . . . . . . . . . . . 519.95
Mossy Oak Advantage or Break-Up (Blued) . . . . . . 499.95
Mossy Oak Advantage or Break-Up (Stainless) . . . 569.95
*Also Available:* MASTER HUNTER DISC RIFLE with 26" Green Mountain fluted stainless barrel, adjustable trigger deluxe appointments . . . . . . . . . . . . . . . . . . . . . 999.95

### KNIGHT 2000 (not shown)
12 gauge in-line shotgun with back-bored 26" barrel and removable choke; adjustable TRUGLO fiber optic sights; composite stock, adjustable trigger.
*Price.* . . . . . . . . . . . . . . . . . . . . . . . . . . . . . . . . $349.95

**BLACK POWDER**

# Navy Arms Revolvers

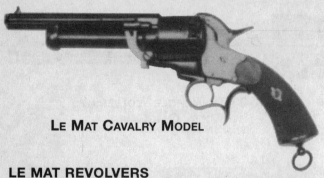

LE MAT CAVALRY MODEL

LE MAT NAVY MODEL

## LE MAT REVOLVERS

Once the official sidearm of many Confederate cavalry officers, this 9-shot .44-caliber revolver with a central single-shot barrel of approx. 65 caliber gave the cavalry man great firepower. *Barrel Length:* 7 ⅝" *Overall Length:* 14" *Weight:* 3 lbs. 7 oz.

| | |
|---|---|
| CAVALRY MODEL | $595.00 |
| NAVY MODEL | 595.00 |
| ARMY MODEL | 595.00 |
| 18TH GEORGIA (engraving on cylinder, display case) | 795.00 |
| BEAUREGARD (hand-engraved cylinder and frame; display case and mold) | 1,000.00 |

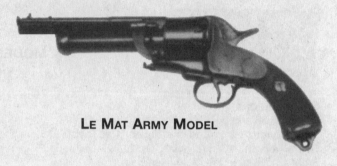

LE MAT ARMY MODEL

1862 NEW MODEL POLICE

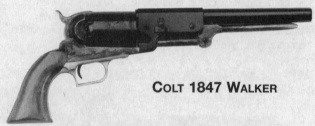

COLT 1847 WALKER

## 1862 NEW MODEL POLICE

This is the last gun manufactured by the Colt plant in the percussion era. It encompassed all the modifications of each gun, starting from the early Paterson to the 1861 Navy. It was favored by the New York Police Dept. for many years. Fluted and rebated cylinder, 36 cal., 5 shot. This replica features brass trigger guard and backstrap. Case hardened frame, loading lever and hammer. *Barrel Length:* 5.5"

| | |
|---|---|
| 1862 POLICE | $290.00 |
| LAW AND ORDER SET | 365.00 |

## ROGERS & SPENCER REVOLVER

This revolver features a six-shot cylinder, octagonal barrel, hinged-type loading lever assembly, two-piece walnut grips, blued finish and case hardened hammer and lever. *Caliber:* 44 *Barrel Length:* 7.5" *Overall Length:* 13.75" *Weight:* 3 lbs.

| | |
|---|---|
| ROGERS & SPENCER | $245.00 |

## COLT 1847 WALKER

The 1847 Walker replica comes in 44 caliber with a 9-inch barrel. Weight: 4 lbs. 8 oz. Features include: rolled cylinder scene; blued and case hardened finish; and brass guard. Proof tested.

| | |
|---|---|
| COLT 1847 WALKER | $275.00 |
| SINGLE CASED SET | 405.00 |
| DELUXE CASED SET | 540.00 |

ROGERS & SPENCER REVOLVER

# NAVY ARMS REVOLVERS

## FIRST MODEL DRAGOON REVOLVER

An improved version of the 1847 Walker, the First Model has a shorter barrel and cylinder as well as a loading lever latch. Used extensively during the Civil War. *Caliber:* 44 *Barrel Length:* 7.5" *Overall Length:* 13.75" *Weight:* 4 lbs. *Sights:* Blade front, notch rear. *Grip:* Walnut

FIRST MODEL DRAGOON . . . . . . . . . . . . . . . . . . . $275.00
*Also available:*
THIRD MODEL DRAGOON w/oval trigger guard
   and cylinder stop . . . . . . . . . . . . . . . . . . . . . . 275.00

**FIRST MODEL
DRAGOON REVOLVER**

**1851 NAVY "YANK"**

A favorite of "Wild Bill" Hickok, the 1851 Navy was originally manufactured by Colt from 1850 through 1876. This model was the most popular of the Union revolvers, mostly because it was lighter and easier to handle than the Dragoon. *Barrel Length:* 7.5" *Overall Length:* 14" *Weight:* 2 lbs. *Rec. Ball Diam.:* .375 R.B. (.451 in 44 cal) *Calibers:* 36 and 44 *Capacity:* 6 shot *Features:* Steel frame, octagonal barrel, cylinder roll-engraved with Naval battle scene, backstrap and trigger guard are polished brass.

1851 NAVY "YANK" . . . . . . . . . . . . . . . . . . . . . . . $155.00
KIT . . . . . . . . . . . . . . . . . . . . . . . . . . . . . . . . . . . 125.00
SINGLE CASED SET . . . . . . . . . . . . . . . . . . . . . . . 290.00
DOUBLE CASED SET . . . . . . . . . . . . . . . . . . . . . . . 470.00

**REB MODEL 1860**

**1860 ARMY**

A modern replica of the confederate Griswold & Gunnison percussion Army revolver. Rendered with a polished brass frame and a rifled steel barrel finished in a high-luster blue with genuine walnut grips. All Army Model 60s are completely proof-tested by the Italian government to the most exacting standards. *Calibers:* 36 and 44. *Barrel Length:* 7.25" *Overall Length:* 13" *Weight:* 2 lbs. 10 oz.-11 oz. *Features:* Brass frame, backstrap and trigger guard, round barrel.

REB MODEL 1860 . . . . . . . . . . . . . . . . . . . . . . . . $115.00
SINGLE CASED SET . . . . . . . . . . . . . . . . . . . . . . . 245.00
DOUBLE CASED SET . . . . . . . . . . . . . . . . . . . . . . . 380.00
KIT . . . . . . . . . . . . . . . . . . . . . . . . . . . . . . . . . . . . 90.00

The 1860 Army satisfied the Union Army's need for a more powerful .44-caliber revolver. The cylinder on this replica is roll engraved with a polished brass trigger guard and steel strap cut for shoulder stock. The frame, loading level and hammer are finished in high-luster color case hardening. Walnut grips. *Weight:* 2 lbs. 9 oz. *Barrel Length:* 8" *Overall Length:* 13 5/8" *Caliber:* 44. *Finish:* Brass trigger guard, steel backstrap, round barrel, creeping lever, rebated cylinder, engraved Navy scene.

1860 ARMY . . . . . . . . . . . . . . . . . . . . . . . . . . . . . $175.00
SINGLE CASED SET . . . . . . . . . . . . . . . . . . . . . . . 310.00
DOUBLE CASED SET . . . . . . . . . . . . . . . . . . . . . . . 505.00
KIT . . . . . . . . . . . . . . . . . . . . . . . . . . . . . . . . . . . 155.00

**BLACK POWDER**

# NAVY ARMS HANDGUNS

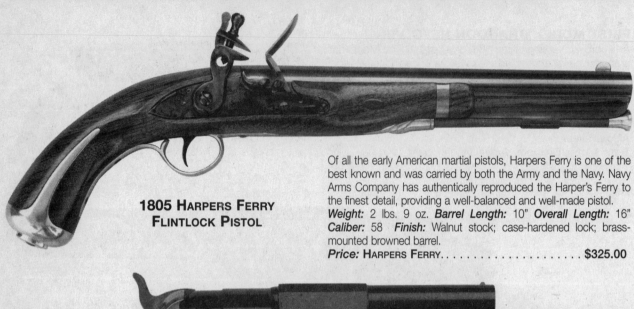

### 1805 HARPERS FERRY FLINTLOCK PISTOL

Of all the early American martial pistols, Harpers Ferry is one of the best known and was carried by both the Army and the Navy. Navy Arms Company has authentically reproduced the Harper's Ferry to the finest detail, providing a well-balanced and well-made pistol. *Weight:* 2 lbs. 9 oz. *Barrel Length:* 10" *Overall Length:* 16" *Caliber:* 58 *Finish:* Walnut stock; case-hardened lock; brass-mounted browned barrel.
*Price:* HARPERS FERRY..................... $325.00

### REB 60 SHERIFF'S MODEL

### 1858 NEW MODEL ARMY REMINGTON-STYLE REVOLVER

### REB 60 SHERIFF'S MODEL

A compact version of the Reb Model 60 Revolver. The Sheriff's model version became popular because the short-ened barrel was fast out of the leather. This is actually the original snub nose, the predecessor of the detective specials or belly guns designed for quick-draw use. *Calibers:* 36 and 44

| | |
|---|---|
| REB 60 SHERIFF'S MODEL | $115.00 |
| KIT | 90.00 |
| SINGLE CASED SET | 245.00 |
| DOUBLE CASED SET | 380.00 |

### DELUXE NEW MODEL 1858 REMINGTON-STYLE 44 CALIBER (not shown)

Built to the exact dimensions and weight of the original Remington 44, this model features an 8" barrel with pro-gressive rifling, adjustable front sight for windage, all-steel construction with walnut stocks and silver-plated trigger guard. Steel is highly polished and finished in rich blue. Barrel Length: 8" Overall Length: 14.25" Weight: 2 lbs. 14 oz.

| | |
|---|---|
| DELUXE NEW MODEL 1858 | $415.00 |

This rugged, dependable, battle-proven veteran with its top strap and rugged frame was considered the Magnum of Civil War revolvers, ideally suited for the heavy 44 charges. Blued finish.
*Caliber:* 44. *Barrel Length:* 8"
*Overall Length:* 14.25" *Weight:* 2 lbs. 8 oz.

| | |
|---|---|
| NEW MODEL ARMY REVOLVER | $170.00 |
| SINGLE CASED SET | 300.00 |
| DOUBLE CASED SET | 495.00 |
| KIT | 150.00 |

*Also available:*

| | |
|---|---|
| BRASS FRAME | $125.00 |
| BRASS FRAME KIT | 115.00 |
| SINGLE CASED SET | 260.00 |
| DOUBLE CASED SET | 410.00 |

# NAVY ARMS RIFLES

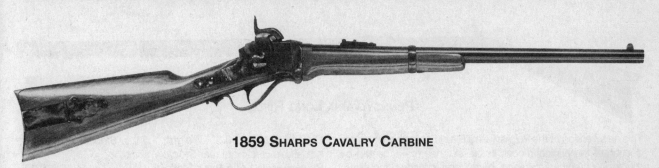

## 1859 SHARPS CAVALRY CARBINE

This percussion version of the Sharps is a copy of the popular breechloading Cavalry Carbine of the Civil War. It features a patchbox and bar and saddle ring on left side of the stock. *Caliber:* 54 *Barrel Length:* 22" *Overall Length:* 39" *Weight:*

7.75 lbs. *Sights:* Blade front; military ladder rear. *Stock:* Walnut
**SHARPS CAVALRY CARBINE** . . . . . . . . . . . . . . . . . **$940.00**
*Also available:*
**1859 SHARPS INFANTRY RIFLE** (54 cal.) . . . . . . . . 1,030.00

## SMITH CARBINE

The Smith Carbine was considered one of the finest breechloading carbines of the Civil War period. The hinged breech action allowed fast reloading for cavalry units. Available in either the Cavalry Model (with saddle ring and bar) or

Artillery Model (with sling swivels). *Caliber:* 50 *Barrel Length:* 21.5" *Overall Length:* 39" *Weight:* 7.75 lbs. *Sights:* Blass blade front; folding ladder rear *Stock:* American walnut
**SMITH CARBINE**. . . . . . . . . . . . . . . . . . . . . . . . . **$600.00**

## 1861 SPRINGFIELD RIFLE

One of the most popular Union rifles of the Civil War, the 1861 model featured the 1855-style hammer. The lockplate on this replica is marked "1861, U.S. Springfield." *Caliber:* 58

*Barrel Length:* 40" *Overall Length:* 56" *Weight:* 10 lbs. *Finish:* Walnut stock with polished metal lock and stock fitting.
**1861 SPRINGFIELD RIFLE** . . . . . . . . . . . . . . . . . . **$550.00**

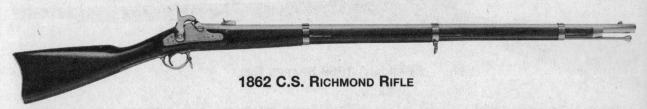

## 1862 C.S. RICHMOND RIFLE

This model was manufactured by the Confederacy at the Richmond Armory utilizing 1855 Rifle Musket parts captured from the Harpers Ferry Arsenal. This replica features the unusual 1855 lockplate, stamped "1862 C.S. Richmond, V.A."

*Caliber:* 58 *Barrel Length:* 40" *Overall Length:* 56" *Weight:* 10 lbs. *Finish:* Walnut stock with polished metal lock and stock fittings.
**1863 C.S. RICHMOND RIFLE** . . . . . . . . . . . . . . . . **$550.00**

**BLACK POWDER**

# NAVY ARMS RIFLES/MUSKETS

## PENNSYLVANIA LONG RIFLE

This new version of the Pennsylvania Rifle is an authentic reproduction of the original model. Its classic lines are accented by the long, browned octagon barrel and polished lockplate. **Caliber:** 32 or 45 (flint or percussion.) **Barrel Length:** 40.5"

**Overall Length:** 56.5" **Weight:** 7.5 lbs. **Sights:** Blade front; adjustable Buckhorn rear **Stock:** Walnut
**PENNSYLVANIA LONG RIFLE** Flintlock . . . . . . . . . . . . . $505.00
  Percussion . . . . . . . . . . . . . . . . . . . . . . . . . . . . 490.00

## BROWN BESS MUSKET

Used extensively in the French and Indian War, the Brown Bess Musket proved itself in the American Revolution as well. This fine replica of the "Second Model" is marked "Grice" on the lockplate. **Caliber:** 75 **Barrel Length:** 42" **Overall Length:** 59" **Weight:** 9.5 lbs. **Sights:** Lug front **Stock:** Walnut

**BROWN BESS MUSKET** . . . . . . . . . . . . . . . . . . . . . . $835.00
**KIT** . . . . . . . . . . . . . . . . . . . . . . . . . . . . . . . . . . . $710.00
*Also available:*
**BROWN BESS CARBINE** **Caliber:** 75 **Barrel Length:** 30"
**Overall Length:** 47" **Weight:** 7.75 lbs. . . . . . . . . . $835.00

## 1803 HARPERS FERRY RIFLE

This 1803 Harpers Ferry rifle was carried by Lewis and Clark on their expedition to explore the Northwest territory. This replica of the first rifled U.S. Martial flintlock features a browned

barrel, case hardened lock and a brass patchbox. **Caliber:** 54 **Barrel Length:** 35" **Overall Length:** 50.5" **Weight:** 8.5 lbs.
**1803 HARPERS FERRY RIFLE** . . . . . . . . . . . . . . . . . $630.00

## "BERDAN" 1859 SHARPS RIFLE

A replica of the Union sniper rifle used by Col. Hiram Berdan's First and Second U.S. Sharpshooters Regiments during the Civil War. **Caliber:** 54 **Barrel Length:** 30" **Overall Length:** 46.75" **Weight:** 8 lbs. 8 oz. **Sights:** Military-style ladder rear; blade front **Stock:** Walnut **Features:**

Double-set trigger, case hardened receiver; patchbox and furniture.
**"BERDAN" 1859 SHARPS RIFLE** . . . . . . . . . . . . . $1,095.00
*Also available:*
**SINGLE TRIGGER INFANTRY MODEL** . . . . . . . . . . . 1,030.00

# NAVY ARMS

### 1858 ENFIELD RIFLE

In the late 1850s the British Admiralty, after extensive experiments, settled on a pattern rifle with a 5-groove barrel of heavy construction, sighted to 1,100 yards, designated the Naval rifle, Pattern 1858. *Caliber:* 58 *Barrel Length:* 33"

*Weight:* 9 lbs. 10 oz. *Overall Length:* 48.5" *Sights:* Fixed front; graduated rear. *Stock:* Seasoned walnut w/solid brass furniture.

1858 ENFIELD RIFLE . . . . . . . . . . . . . . . . . . . . . . $450.00

### 1861 MUSKETOON

The 1861 Enfield Musketoon was the favorite long arm of the Confederate Cavalry. *Caliber:* 58 *Barrel Length:* 24" *Weight:* 7 lbs. 8 oz. *Overall Length:* 40.25" *Sights:* Fixed front; grad-

uated rear. *Stock:* Seasoned walnut with solid brass furniture.

1861 MUSKETOON. . . . . . . . . . . . . . . . . . . . . . . . $405.00
KIT . . . . . . . . . . . . . . . . . . . . . . . . . . . . . . . . . . 365.00

### STEEL SHOT MAGNUM SHOTGUN

This shotgun, designed for the hunter who must use steel shot, features engraved polished lockplates, English-style

checkered walnut stock (with cheekpiece) and chrome-lined barrels.
*Gauge:* 10 *Barrel Length:* 28"
*Overall Length:* 45.5" *Weight:* 7 lbs. 9 oz.
*Choke:* Cylinder/Cylinder

STEEL-SHOT MAGNUM SHOTGUN. . . . . . . . . . . . . $605.00

### T&T SHOTGUN

This Turkey and Trap side-by-side percussion shotgun, choked Full/Full, features a genuine walnut stock with checkered wrist and oil finish, color case hardened locks and blued barrels.

*Gauge:* 12 *Barrel Length:* 28"
*Overall Length:* 44" *Weight:* 7.5 lbs.

T&T SHOTGUN . . . . . . . . . . . . . . . . . . . . . . . . . . $580.00

***Also available:***
UPLAND SHOTGUN (not shown) same basic specifications as T&T Model, but with cylinder bore choking.
     Upland Shotgun . . . . . . . . . . . . . . . . . . . . . . 580.00

**BLACK POWDER**

# PEDERSOLI

**PISTOL LE PAGE**

## PEDERSOLI "PISTOL LE PAGE" .45 INTERNATIONAL FLINTLOCK TARGET PISTOL

**SPECIFICATIONS**
*Caliber:* .45
*Barrel Length:* 10.5"
*Twist:* 1-in-18" twist
*Trigger:* Single set
*Weight:* 2.5 lbs. (also in .44 smoothbore)
*Stock:* Walnut
*Prices:* . . . . . . . . . . . . . . . . . . . . . . . . . . . . . . **$675.00**
    Percussion model in 36, 38 or 44 caliber . . . . . . **465.00**

**TRYON PERCUSSION RIFLE**

## PEDERSOLI TRYON PERCUSSION RIFLE

**SPECIFICATIONS**
*Caliber:* 45, 50 and 54   *Barrel Length:* 32"
*Twist:* 1-in-48" twist (1-in-66" twist for .54 bore)
*Weight:* 9.5 lbs.
*Also available:* Creedmoor version with fast-twist barrel (1-in-21, 451 caliber) and target sights (shown).
*Prices:* Standard . . . . . . . . . . . . . . . . . . . . . . . . . **$595.00**
    Creedmoor. . . . . . . . . . . . . . . . . . . . . . . . . . . **850.00**

**MANG IN GRÄZ**

## PEDERSOLI "MANG IN GRÄZ" PERCUSSION PISTOL

**SPECIFICATIONS**
*Caliber:* 38 or 44
*Barrel Length:* 11"
*Twist:* 1-in-15" (38) or 1-in-18" (44) twist
*Weight:* 2.5 lbs.
*Stock:* Walnut
*Prices:* . . . . . . . . . . . . . . . . . . . . . . . . . . . . . . **$995.00**

# REMINGTON BLACK POWDER RIFLES

**MODEL 700 ML**

**MODEL 700 MLS STAINLESS**

## MODEL 700 ML AND MLS IN-LINE MUZZLELOADING RIFLES

Remington began building flintlock muzzleloaders in 1816. These two in-line muzzleloading rifles have the same cocking action and trigger mechanism as the original versions. The difference comes from a modified bolt and ignition system. The Model 700 ML has a traditionally blued carbon-steel barreled action. On the Model 700 MLS the barrel, receiver and bolt are made of 416 stainless steel with a non-reflective, satin finish. Each is set in a fiberglass-reinforced synthetic stock fitted with a Magnum-style recoil pad. One end of the solid aluminum ramrod is recessed into the forend and the outer end is secured by a barrel band. Instead of an open chamber, the breech is closed by a stainless-steel plug and nipple. In the internal structure of the modified bolt, the firing pin is replaced by a cylindrical rod that is cocked by normal bolt lift. It is released by pulling the trigger to strike a

#11 percussion cap seated on the nipple. Lock time is 3.0 milli-seconds. Barrels are rifled with a 1 in 28" twist. The barrels are fitted with standard adjustable iron sights; receivers are drilled and tapped for short-action scope mount.

**SPECIFICATIONS:**
**Barrel length:** 24"
**Overall Length:** 44.5"
**Weight:** 7.75 lbs.
**Length Of Pull:** 13 3/8"
**Drop At Comb:** .5"
**Drop At Heel:** 3/8"
**Prices:**
MODEL ML. . . . . . . . . . . . . . . . . . . . . . . . . . . . . . $396.00
MODEL MLS STAINLESS . . . . . . . . . . . . . . . . . . . . . . 496.00
**Also available:**
w/Mossy Oak Break-up camo stock . . . . . . . . . $439.00
Stainless Steel. . . . . . . . . . . . . . . . . . . . . . . . . . . 532.00

**MODEL 700 ML YOUTH**

The **MODEL 700 ML YOUTH** rifle offers the same design as the 70 ML, but with a shorter (12 3/8") length of pull. Includes a blued, satin-finished carbon steel 21" barrel (38.5" overall), action and bolt, plus fiberglass-reinforced Model 700 stock

w/rubber recoil pad; drilled and tapped for short-action scope mounts; ram rod stored in forend.
**Price:**. . . . . . . . . . . . . . . . . . . . . . . . . . . . . . . . . $396.00

# RUGER RIFLES/REVOLVERS

**OLD ARMY CAP AND BALL**
**FIXED SIGHT**

## OLD ARMY CAP AND BALL

This Old Army cap-and-ball revolver is reminiscent of the Civil War era martial revolvers and those used by the early frontiersmen in the 1800s. This Ruger model comes in both blued and stainless-steel finishes and features modern materials, technology and design throughout, including steel music-wire coil springs. Fixed or adjustable sights.

**SPECIFICATIONS**
*Caliber:* 45 (.443" bore; .45" groove)
*Barrel Length:* 7.5"
*Weight:* 2 $^7/_8$ lbs.
*Rifling:* 6 grooves, R.H. twist (1:16")
*Sights:* Fixed, ramp front; topstrap channel rear
*Percussion cap nipples:* Stainless steel (#10 or #11)
*Price:* Blued . . . . . . . . . . . . . . . . . . . . . . . . . . . . $478.00
Stainless Steel . . . . . . . . . . . . . . . . . . . . . . . . . 499.00

**MODEL K77/50 RSBBZ**

**MODEL 77/50 RS**

## MODEL K77/50 RSBBZ STAINLESS STEEL BLACK LAMINATED STOCK BLACK POWDER RIFLE

**SPECIFICATIONS**
*Caliber:* .50 *Action:* Bolt action In-line muzzle loader
*Finish:* Non-glare matte stainless steel finish
*Barrel Length:* 22" 400 series stainless steel
*Overall Length:* 41.5"
*Rifling:* 8 grooves, right hand twist (1-turn-in-28")
*Safety:* Three-position wing safety
*Sights:* Single folding leaf rear; gold bead front; rear receiver drilled and tapped for peep sights
*Stock:* Black/gray laminated American hardwood w/rubber buttpad; studs for sling swivels
*Length Of Pull:* 13.75" *Drop At Comb:* 1.78"

*Drop At heel:* 1.94" *Weight (approx.):* 6.5 lbs. (unloaded)
*Features:* Operator's manual, set of 1" stainless steel scope range; standard breech plug wrench; bolt disassemble tool; cleaning tube; right hand 90° turn bolt
*Price:* . . . . . . . . . . . . . . . . . . . . . . . . . . . . . . . . . $601.00
*Also available:*
**MODEL 77/50 RS.** Same specifications as above, except finish is matte blue and stock is birch w/rubber buttpad . . . . . . . . . . . . . . . . . . . . . . . . . . . . . . . . 434.00
**MODEL 77/50 RSO.** Same specifications as above, except for following: *Drop at Comb:* 1 $^{22}/_{32}$" *Drop At Heel:* 1 $^6/_{32}$"
*Stock:* Straight gripped, checkered American black walnut stock, w/curved buttplate . . . . . . . . . . . . . . . . . . 555.00
K77/50 RSP All-weather, stainless, synthetic stock. . . . 580.00

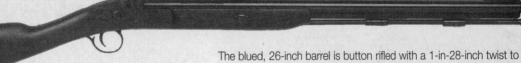

# THOMPSON/CENTER RIFLES

## BLACK MOUNTAIN MAGNUM

The .50 caliber Black Mountain Magnum™ is designed to handle magnum loads of up to 150 grains of FFg black powder or the Pyrodex equivalent volume. It also handles three 50-grain Pyrodex pellets with impressive results. Shooting a Mag Express Sabot with 240-grain XTP bullet, a 150-grain load produces a muzzle velocity of 2203 feed per second. The Black Mountain Magnum™ has a musket cap nipple, the hottest ignition available in a traditional-style muzzleloader. Standard nipples with #11 or #11 Magnum percussion caps can also be used.

The blued, 26-inch barrel is button rifled with a 1-in-28-inch twist to maximize performance with conical projectiles. It is equipped with Thompson/Center's exclusive QLA™ muzzle system for easy loading, even without a short starter. Tru-Glo™ fiber optic sights allow hunters to take advantage of productive dawn and dusk hunting time. Hunters who prefer to use a riflescope will appreciate that the rifle is drilled and tapped for easy scope mounting. The new sidelock rifle is stocked with a tough, durable Rynite® stock.

**Price:** . . . . . . . . . . . . . . . . . . . . . . . . . . . . . . . **$353.52**
***Also Available:*** with walnut stock . . . . . . . . . . . . **387.16**
   .54 with walnut stock . . . . . . . . . . . . . . . . . . . **387.16**
   12-gauge with walnut stock . . . . . . . . . . . . . . **387.16**

## PENNSYLVANIA HUNTER FLINTLOCK RIFLE

The 28" barrel on this model is cut rifled (.010" deep) with 1 turn in 66" twist. Its outer contour is octagonal. Sights are fully adjustable for both windage and elevation. Stocked with select American black walnut; metal hardware is blued steel. Features a hooked breech system and coilspring lock, plus T/C's QLA™ Muzzle System for improved accuracy and easier reloading. ***Caliber:*** 50. ***Overall length:*** 45". ***Weight:*** Approx. 7.50 lbs. ***Price:*** PENNSYLVANIA HUNTER FLINTLOCK . . . . . . . . **$438.00**

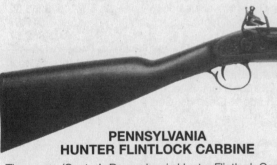

## PENNSYLVANIA HUNTER FLINTLOCK CARBINE

Thompson/Center's Pennsylvania Hunter Flintlock Carbine is 50-caliber with 1:66" twist and cut-rifling. It was designed specifically for the hunter who uses patched round balls only and hunts in thick cover or brush. The 21" barrel is octagonal. Features T/C's QLA™ Muzzle System. ***Overall length:*** 38". ***Weight:*** 6.5 lbs. ***Sights:*** Fully adjustable open hunting-style rear with bead front. ***Stock:*** Select American walnut. ***Trigger:*** Single hunting-style trigger. ***Lock:*** Color cased, coil spring, with floral design.
***Price:*** PENNSYLVANIA HUNTER FLINTLOCK CARBINE . **$438.00**

## FIRE STORM

Designed for Pyrodex pellets, the Fire Storm's removable breech plug is conical, directing flame to the pellet's center for efficient ignition. Available with caplock or flintlock mechanism. ***Caliber:*** 50 ***Barrel Length:*** 26"-with QLA™ Muzzle System built in ***Rifling Twist:*** 1 in 48" for use with Round Balls & Conicals ***Overall Length:*** 41.75" ***Weight:*** 7 lbs. (approximate) ***Rifle Sights:*** Competition click adjustable steel rear sight and ramp style front sights are fitted with Tru-Glo™ Fiber Optics ***Stock:*** Black Composite ***Trigger:*** Single trigger with large trigger guard bow. ***Extra Features:*** Aluminum ramrod is standard ***Loading:*** The Fire Storm™ can accept magnum charges of up to 150 grains of FFG Black Powder or Pyrodex® equivalent (or 3 Pyrodex 50 caliber, 50 grain Pellets). ***Price:*** . . . . . . . . . . . . . . . **$391.00**

# THOMPSON/CENTER RIFLES

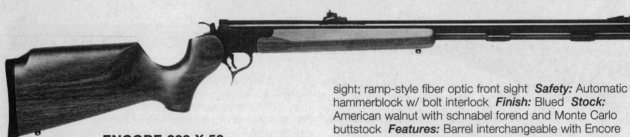

## ENCORE 209 X 50 MAGNUM MUZZLELOADING RIFLE

**SPECIFICATIONS**
*Caliber:* .50 *Action:* Break-open action muzzleloader
*Ignition:* 209 shotgun primer *Barrel Length:* 26" with
QLA Muzzle System *Twist:* 1 in 28" *Overall Length:* 40.5"
*Weight:* 7 lbs. *Sights:* Tru-Glo adjustable rear fiber optic

sight; ramp-style fiber optic front sight *Safety:* Automatic
hammerblock w/ bolt interlock *Finish:* Blued *Stock:*
American walnut with schnabel forend and Monte Carlo
buttstock *Features:* Barrel interchangeable with Encore
rifles; equipped with sling swivel studs; accepts magnum
charges of up to 150 grains of black powder or Pyrodex
equivalent (or three 50-grain Pyrodex Pellets).
*Price:* Blued/Walnut . . . . . . . . . . . . . . . . . . . . . . . $610.18
   ($256.58 accessory muzzleloading barrel only-blued)
Complete Gun-SST/Composite. . . . . . . . . . . . . . 665.91
Accessory barrel only-SST . . . . . . . . . . . . . . . . . 294.97

## BLACK DIAMOND MUZZLELOADING RIFLE

**SPECIFICATIONS**
*Caliber:* .50 *Ignition:* In-line ignition using Flame Thrower
musket cap nipple or No. 11 nipple *Barrel:* Free-floated,
22.5" barrel with QLA *Twist:* 1 in 18" *Overall Length:*
41.5" *Weight:* 6 lbs. 9 oz. *Safety:* Patented sliding thumb
safety *Sights:* Tru-Glo Fiber Optic adjustable rear sight;
Fiber Optic ramp-style front sight *Stock:* Black Rynite
stock with molded-in checkering and pistol grip cap
*Loading:* Accepts magnum charges of up to 150 grains of
black powder or Pyrodex equivalent, or three 50-grain

Pyrodex Pellets *Features:* Removable universal breech
plug; Aluminum ram rod; sling swivel studs; rubber recoil
pad; musket nipple wrench, 5-pack or T/C Mag Express
Sabots, and No. 11 nipple standard
*Prices:* Blued w/walnut stock . . . . . . . . . . . . . . $353.32
Blued w/Rynite Stock. . . . . . . . . . . . . . . . . . . . . . 312.87
Stainless . . . . . . . . . . . . . . . . . . . . . . . . . . . . . . . 362.57
*Also Available:* BLACK DIAMOND PREMIUM PACK (includes T-
Handle Short Starter, 10 Mag Express Sabots, rifle powder
measure, In-line U-View Capper, Super Jag, ball and bullet
puller, 2 Quick Shots, breech plug wrench, Hunter's Field
Pouch, Lube-N-Clean Kit, Gorilla Grease).
*Prices:*
Blued . . . . . . . . . . . . . . . . . . . . . . . . . . . . . . . . . $339.16
Stainless . . . . . . . . . . . . . . . . . . . . . . . . . . . . . . . 397.96

## THE HAWKEN 50 AND 54 CALIBER

Similar to the famous Rocky Mountain rifles made during the
early 1800s, the Hawken is intended for serious shooting.
Button-rifled for ultimate precision, the Hawken is available
in 45-, 50- or 54-caliber percussion or 50- caliber flintlock. It

features a hooked breech, double-set triggers, first-grade
American walnut stock, adjustable hunting sights, solid
brass trim and color casehardened lock. Beautifully deco-
rated; comes equipped with T/C's QLA™ Muzzle System.
*Weight:* Approx. 8.5 lbs.
*Prices:*
HAWKEN CAPLOCK 50 or 54 caliber . . . . . . . . . . . $489.35
HAWKEN FLINTLOCK 50 caliber . . . . . . . . . . . . . . . 501.14

# TRADITIONS PISTOLS

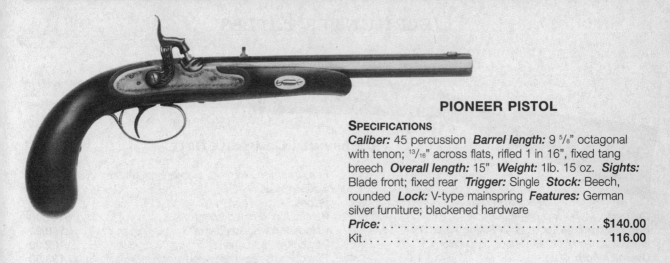

## PIONEER PISTOL

### SPECIFICATIONS
*Caliber:* 45 percussion  *Barrel length:* 9 ⁵/₈" octagonal with tenon; ¹³/₁₆" across flats, rifled 1 in 16", fixed tang breech  *Overall length:* 15"  *Weight:* 1lb. 15 oz.  *Sights:* Blade front; fixed rear  *Trigger:* Single  *Stock:* Beech, rounded  *Lock:* V-type mainspring  *Features:* German silver furniture; blackened hardware
*Price:* . . . . . . . . . . . . . . . . . . . . . . . . . . . . . . . . . $140.00
Kit. . . . . . . . . . . . . . . . . . . . . . . . . . . . . . . . . . . . 116.00

## WILLIAM PARKER PISTOL

### SPECIFICATIONS
*Caliber:* 50 percussion (1:20")  *Barrel length:* 10 ³/₈" octagonal (15/16" across flats)  *Overall length:* 17.5"  *Weight:* 2 lbs. 5 oz.  *Sights:* Brass blade front; fixed rear  *Stock:* Walnut, checkered at wrist  *Triggers:* Double set; will fire set and unset  *Lock:* Adjustable sear engagement with fly and bridle; V-type mainspring  *Features:* Brass percussion cap guard; polished hardware, brass inlays and separate ramrod
*Price:* . . . . . . . . . . . . . . . . . . . . . . . . . . . . . . . . . $262.00

## TRAPPER PISTOL

### SPECIFICATIONS
*Caliber:* 50 percussion or flintlock (1:20")  *Barrel length:* 9 ³/₄"; octagonal (7/8" across flats) with tenon  *Overall length:* 15.5"  *Weight:* 2 lbs. 14 oz.  *Stock:* Beech  *Lock:* Adjustable sear engagement with fly and bridle  *Triggers:* Double set, will fire set and unset  *Sights:* Primitive-style adjustable rear; brass blade front  *Furniture:* Solid brass; blued steel on assembled pistol
*Price:*
Percussion. . . . . . . . . . . . . . . . . . . . . . . . . . . . . $189.00
Percussion Kit . . . . . . . . . . . . . . . . . . . . . . . . . . . 145.00
Flintlock. . . . . . . . . . . . . . . . . . . . . . . . . . . . . . . . 204.00

**BLACK POWDER**

# TRADITIONS

## DEERHUNTER RIFLES

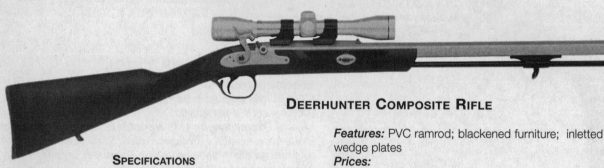

### DEERHUNTER COMPOSITE RIFLE

#### SPECIFICATIONS
**Calibers:** 32, 50 and 54 percussion
**Barrel length:** 24" octagonal **Rifling twist:** 1:48"
(percussion only); 1:66" (flint or percussion)
**Overall length:** 40"
**Weight:** 6 lbs. (6 lbs. 3 oz. in Small Game rifle)
**Trigger:** Single **Sights:** Fixed rear; blade front

**Features:** PVC ramrod; blackened furniture; inletted wedge plates
**Prices:**
Percussion w/blued barrel . . . . . . . . . . . . . . . **$161.00**
Percussion w/nickel barrel . . . . . . . . . . . . . . . **160.00**
Flintlock w/nickel barrel . . . . . . . . . . . . . . . . **182.00**
Flintlock w/select hardwood stock . . . . . . . . . . . **183.00**
**PANTHER** (50 cal.) w/All-Weather composite stock,
  fixed blade sights . . . . . . . . . . . . . . . . . . . **116.00**

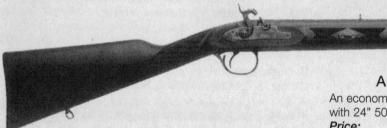

### PANTHER RIFLE
### All-Weather Composite Stock
An economy version of the Deerhunter, the Panther comes with 24" 50-caliber barrel only and fixed blade sights.
**Price:** . . . . . . . . . . . . . . . . . . . . . . . . . . . **$116.00**

### KENTUCKY PISTOL

### BUCKHUNTER PRO
### ALL-WEATHER

## BUCKHUNTER PRO-IN-LINE PISTOLS

#### SPECIFICATIONS
**Calibers:** 50 and 54 Percussion **Barrel length:** 9.5" round
(removable breech plug); 1:20" twist **Overall length:** 14.25"
(also available w/12.5" barrel in wood) **Weight:** 3.2 oz.
(.50); 3.1 oz. (54); 3.4 oz. (wood) **Trigger:** Single **Sights:**
Fold-down adjustable rear; beaded blade front **Stock:**
Walnut or All-Weather **Features:** Blued or C-Nickel furniture; PVC ramrod; drilled and tapped for scop mounting;
coil mainspring; thumb safety
**Price:** . . . . . . . . . . . . . . . . . . . . . . . . . **$226.00**
  w/All-Weather Stock . . . . . . . . . . . . . . . . **240.00**
  fluted nickel w/muzzle brake . . . . . . . . . . . **284.00**

## KENTUCKY PISTOL

#### SPECIFICATIONS
**Caliber:** 50 Percussion (1:20")
**Barrel length:** 10" octagon (7/8" flats); fixed tang
  breech; 1:20" twist
**Overall length:** 15" **Weight:** 2 lbs. 8 oz.
**Trigger:** Single **Sights:** Fixed rear; blade front
**Stock:** Beechwood
**Features:** Brass furniture; wood ramrod; kit available
**Price:** . . . . . . . . . . . . . . . . . . . . . . . . . **$138.00**
  Kit . . . . . . . . . . . . . . . . . . . . . . . . . . . **109.00**

# TRADITIONS RIFLES

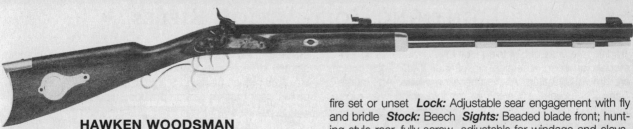

## HAWKEN WOODSMAN

### SPECIFICATIONS
**Calibers:** 50 and 54 percussion or flint (50 caliber only)
**Barrel length:** 28" (octagonal); hooked breech; rifled 1 turn in 48" (1 turn in 66" in 50 caliber also available) **Overall length:** 44.5" **Weight:** 7 lbs. 11 oz. **Triggers:** Double set; will fire set or unset **Lock:** Adjustable sear engagement with fly and bridle **Stock:** Beech **Sights:** Beaded blade front; hunting-style rear, fully screw adjustable for windage and elevation **Furniture:** Solid brass, blued steel or blackened (50 cal. only); unbreakable ramrod

**Prices:** Percussion. . . . . . . . . . . . . . . . . . . . . . . . . $226.00
Flint . . . . . . . . . . . . . . . . . . . . . . . . . . . . . . . . . . 248.00
Percussion, left-hand . . . . . . . . . . . . . . . . . . . . . . 240.00

## PENNSYLVANIA RIFLE

### SPECIFICATIONS
**Caliber:** 50 **Barrel length:** 401/4"; octagonal (7/8" across flats) with 3 pins; rifled 1 turn in 66" **Overall length:** 57" **Weight:** 8 lbs. 8 oz. **Lock:** Adjustable sear engagement with fly and bridle **Stock:** Walnut, beavertail style **Triggers:** Double set; will fire set and unset **Sights:** Primitive-style adjustable rear; brass blade front **Furniture:** Solid brass, blued steel

**Prices:** Percussion. . . . . . . . . . . . . . . . . . . . . . . . $467.00
Flintlock . . . . . . . . . . . . . . . . . . . . . . . . . . . . . . . 474.00

## SHENANDOAH RIFLE

The Shenandoah Rifle captures the frontier styling and steady performance of Tradition's Pennsylvania Rifle in slightly shorter length and more affordable price. Choice of engraved and color case hardened flintlock or percussion V-type mainspring lock with double-set triggers. The full-length stock in walnut finish is accented by a solid brass curved buttplate, inletted patch box, nose cap, thimbles, trigger guard and decorative furniture.

### SPECIFICATIONS
**Caliber:** 50 (1:66") flint or percussion **Barrel length:** 33.5" octagon **Overall length:** 49.5" **Weight:** 7 lbs. 3 oz.
**Sights:** Buckhorn rear, blade front **Stock:** Beech
**Prices:** Percussion. . . . . . . . . . . . . . . . . . . . . . . . $350.00
Flintlock . . . . . . . . . . . . . . . . . . . . . . . . . . . . . . . 365.00

## BUCKSKINNER CARBINE LAMINATED STOCK

## BUCKSKINNER CARBINE

### SPECIFICATIONS
**Caliber:** 50 percussion or flintlock
**Barrel length:** 21": octagonal-to-round with tenon; 15/16" across flats; 1:66" twist (flintlock) and 1:20" (percussion)
**Overall length:** 36.25" Weight: 5 lbs. 15 oz.
**Sights:** Hunting-style fiber optic, click adjustable rear; beaded blade front **Trigger:** Single
**Features:** Blackened furniture: German silver ornamentation; sling swivels; unbreakable ramrod
**Prices:**
Flintlock . . . . . . . . . . . . . . . . . . . . . . . . . . . . . . . $218.00
Laminated Stock, Flintlock. . . . . . . . . . . . . . . . . . 292.00

# TRADITIONS RIFLES

## LIGHTNING BOLT-ACTION RIFLES

Traditions' series of Lightning Bolt rifles includes a variety of models of blued, chemical-nickel, stainless. Stock choices are brown laminated, All-Weather Composite, Advantage™ Camo, or Break-up Camo. All models come with rugged synthetic ramrods, adjustable triggers, adjustable hunting sights, drilled and tapped barrels and field-removable stainless breech plugs. LFS (lightning fire system) allows use of #11 cap, musket cap on provided nipples.

### LIGHTNING W/CHECKERED COMPOSITE STOCK
Fluted Stainless Steel Barrel w/Muzzle Break
**Price:** . . . . . . . . . . . . . . . . . . . . . . . . . . . . . . . . $329.00

### LIGHTNING W/ALL-WEATHER COMPOSITE STOCK
**Price:** Blued . . . . . . . . . . . . . . . . . . . . . . . . . . . . $199.00
Stainless . . . . . . . . . . . . . . . . . . . . . . . . . . . . . . 279.00
w/Brown Laminated stock, stainless steel barrel . . . . . 379.00

### LIGHTNING W/ADVANTAGE™, (OR BREAK UP™ OR SHADOW BRANCH™ OR HARDWOOD™) CAMO COMPOSITE STOCK
**Price:** Blued . . . . . . . . . . . . . . . . . . . . . . . . . . . $229.00
Stainless steel barrel . . . . . . . . . . . . . . . . . . . . . 309.00

## LIGHTNING™ BOLT-ACTION RIFLES WITH LIGHTNING FIRE SYSTEM™ AND FIBER OPTIC SIGHTS

| Model Number | Stock | Caliber | Barrel | Rate of Twist | Sights | Overall Length | Weight | Price |
|---|---|---|---|---|---|---|---|---|
| R61002 | AW Composite | .50p | 24" Blued | 1:32 | Fiber Optic | 43" | 7.1 lb. | $199.00 |
| R61048 | AW Composite | .54p | 24" Blued | 1:48 | Fiber Optic | 43" | 6.8 lb. | 199.00 |
| R61848 | AW Composite | .54p | 24" Stainless | 1:48 | Fiber Optic | 43" | 6.5 lb. | 279.00 |
| R62802 | Brown Laminate | .50p | 24" Stainless | 1:32 | Fiber Optic | 43" | 7.8 lb. | 379.00 |
| R611020 | AW Composite | .50p | 24" Nickel | 1:32 | Fiber Optic | 43" | 7.3 lb. | 209.00 |
| R610022 | AW Comp/Advantage | .50p | 24" Blued | 1:32 | Fiber Optic | 43" | 7.1 lb. | 229.00 |
| R610025 | AW Comp/Break-Up | .50p | 24" Blued | 1:32 | Fiber Optic | 43" | 7.1 lb | 229.00 |
| R61702 | AW Composite | .50p | 24" Fluted Stainless/Muzzle Brake | 1:32 | Fiber Optic | 45" | 7.6 lb. | 328.00 |
| R610020 | AW Composite | .50p | 24" Blued/Muzzle Brake | 1:32 | Fiber Optic | 43" | 7.3 lb. | 228.00 |
| R618025 | AW Comp/Break-Up | .50p | 24" Stainless | 1:32 | Fiber Optic | 43" | 7.6 lb. | 309.00 |
| R61848 | AW Composite | .54p | 24" Stainless | 1:48 | Fiber Optic | 43" | 6.5 lb. | 279.00 |
| R617025 | AW Comp/Break-Up | .50p | 24" Fluted Stainless w/brake | 1:32 | Fiber Optic | 45" | 7.6 lb | 359.00 |
| R630023 | AW SpiderWeb | .50p | 22" Fluted Blued | 1:32 | Fiber Optic | 41" | 6.3 lb. | 239.00 |
| R631023 | AW SpiderWeb | .50p | 22" Fluted C-nickel | 1:32 | Fiber Optic | 41" | 6.3 lb. | 249.00 |
| R637023 | AW SpiderWeb | .50p | 22" Fluted Stainless | 1:32 | Fiber Optic | 41" | 6.3 lb. | 289.00 |

*All composite stocks are checkered*

# TRADITIONS RIFLES

## BUCKHUNTER PRO™ IN-LINE RIFLES

**BUCKHUNTER PRO™ IN-LINE RIFLE**
w/Walnut-Stained Stock

### BUCKHUNTER PRO™ IN-LINE RIFLE
**w/Black Composite Stock, Stainless Barrel, Optional Scope**

Traditions has upgraded its Buckhunter In-line ignition rifles and shotguns with the Buckhunter Pro series. The guns feature an adjustable trigger, thumb safety and a choice of

Ultracoat Teflon, C-Nickel, blued or stainless steel barrels. New slimmed-down matte black composite stocks are available as are two camouflage patterns, laminated, thumbhole or walnut-stained stocks. All Buckhunter Pros have field-removable stainless steel breech plugs and improved adjustable hunting sights. The Buckhunter Pro rifles are available in 50 caliber (1:32") or 54 caliber (1:48") for use with conical and saboted bullets.
*Prices:* . . . . . . . . . . . . . . . . . . . . . . . **$169.00 - $219.00**

### BUCKHUNTER IN-LINE COMPOSITE RIFLE
**SPECIFICATIONS**
*Calibers:* 50 (1:32") and 54 (2:48") percussion *Barrel*

*length:* Blued 24" round *Overall length:* 42" *Weight:* 7 lbs. 6 oz. *Stock:* All-Weather Composite (matte black) *Sights:* Beaded blade front; fully adjustable rear *Features:* Blackened furniture; PVC ramrod; stainless steel removable breech plug; optional Redi-Pak (includes composite powder flask with valve dispenser, powder measure, two universal fast loaders, 5-in-1 loader, cleaning jab and patches, ball puller, 20 conical bullets, in-line nipple wrench
*Price:* . . . . . . . . . . . . . . . . . . . . . . . **$149.00 - $159.00**

## BUCKHUNTER PRO™ IN-LINE RIFLES WITH FIBER OPTIC SIGHTS

| MODEL NUMBER | STOCK | CALIBER | BARREL | RATE OF TWIST | SIGHTS | OVERALL LENGTH | WEIGHT |
|---|---|---|---|---|---|---|---|
| R50102 | AW Composite | .50p | 24" Nickel | 1:32 | Fiber Optic | 43" | 7 lb. 5 |
| R51102 | AW Composite | .50p | 24" Blued | 1:32 | Fiber Optic | 43" | 7 lb. 4 oz. |
| R501025 | AW Comp./Break-Up | .50p | 24" Nickel | 1:32 | Fiber Optic | 43" | 7 lb. 1 oz. |

*Replacement drop-in black and composite stocks available   FCS50101      All composite stocks are checkered*

## BUCKHUNTER™ IN - LINE RIFLES

| MODEL NUMBER | STOCK | CALIBER | BARREL | RATE OF TWIST | SIGHTS | OVERALL LENGTH | WEIGHT |
|---|---|---|---|---|---|---|---|
| R42102 | AW Composite | .50p | 24" Blued | 1:32 | Adj/BB | 43" | 7 lb. |
| R42148 | AW Composite | .54p | 24" Blued | 1:48 | Adj/BB | 43" | 6 lb. 14 oz. |
| R42302 | AW Composite | .50p | 24" Nickel | 1:32 | Adj/BB | 43" | |

# UBERTI REVOLVERS

## PATERSON REVOLVER

Manufactured at Paterson, New Jersey, by the Patent Arms Manufacturing Company from 1836 to 1842, these were the first revolving pistols created by Samuel Colt. All early Patersons featured a five-shot cylinder, roll-engraved with one or two scenes, octagon barrel and folding trigger that extends when the hammer is cocked.

**SPECIFICATIONS**
*Caliber:* 36  *Capacity:* 5 shots (engraved cylinder)
*Barrel Length:* 7.5" octagonal
*Overall Length:* 11.5"
*Weight:* 2.552 lbs.
*Frame:* Color casehardened steel
*Grip:* One-piece walnut
*Price:* . . . . . . . . . . . . . . . . . . . . . . . . . . . . . . . $365.00
w/Lever. . . . . . . . . . . . . . . . . . . . . . . . . . . . . . . 380.00

**PATERSON REVOLVER**

## 1858 REMINGTON NEW ARMY 44 REVOLVER

*Prices:* 8" barrel, open sights . . . . . . . . . . . . . . $256.00
With stainless steel and open sights . . . . . . . . . . 349.00
**TARGET MODEL** w/black finish . . . . . . . . . . . . . . . 295.00
**TARGET MODEL** w/stainless steel . . . . . . . . . . . . . 389.00

**1858 REMINGTON NEW ARMY TARGET MODEL**

## 1860 ARMY REVOLVER

**SPECIFICATIONS**
*Caliber:* 44
*Barrel length:* 8" (round, tapered)
*Overall length:* 13 3/4"
*Weight:* 2.65 lbs.
*Frame:* One-piece, color case hardened steel
*Trigger guard:* Brass
*Cylinder:* 6 shots (engraved)
*Grip:* One-piece walnut
*Price:* . . . . . . . . . . . . . . . . . . . . . . . . . . . . . . . $259.00
*Also available:*
**1860 ARMY FLUTED**. . . . . . . . . . . . . . . . . . . . . . . 270.00

**1860 ARMY REVOLVER**

## 1861 NAVY REVOLVER

**SPECIFICATIONS**
*Caliber:* 36
*Capacity:* 6 shots
*Barrel length:* 7 1/2"
*Overall length:* 13"
*Weight:* 2.75 lbs.
*Grip:* One-piece walnut
*Frame:* Color case hardened steel
*Prices:* **1861 NAVY CIVIC**. . . . . . . . . . . . . . . . . . $270.00
**1861 NAVY FLUTED** . . . . . . . . . . . . . . . . . . . . . . . 295.00
**MODEL 1851** (not shown) . . . . . . . . . . . . . . . . . 249.00

**1861 NAVY REVOLVER**

# Sights & scopes

*Roland Clark – Redheads, 1927*

*For addresses and phone/fax numbers of manufacturers and distributors included in this section, please turn to **DIRECTORY OF MANUFACTURERS AND SUPPLIERS** on page 564.*

# AIMPOINT SIGHTS

## AIMPOINT 5000-XD SIGHT

**SPECIFICATIONS**
**System:** Parallax free
**Optical:** Anti-reflex coated lenses
**Adjustment:** 1 click = 1/4 inch at 100 yards
**Length:** 5.5-6"
**Weight:** 5.8 oz.
**Objective diameter:** 36mm
**Mounting system:** 30mm rings
**Magnification:** 1X
**Material:** Anodized aluminum; black or camo finish
**Diameter of dot:** 3" at 100 yds. or Mag Dot reticle, 10" at 100 yards.
**Price:** . . . . . . . . . . . . . . . . . . . . . . . . . . . . . . . $297.00

## SERIES 3000 UNIVERSAL

**SPECIFICATIONS**
**System:** 100% parallax free
**Weight:** 6 oz.
**Length:** 6.25"
**Magnification:** 1X
**Scope attachment:** 3X
**Eye relief:** Unlimited
**Battery choices:** 2X Mercury SP 675 1X Lithium or DL 1/3N
**Material:** Anodized aluminum, black finish
**Mounting:** 1" Rings (Medium or High)
**Price:** Black . . . . . . . . . . . . . . . . . . . . . . . . . . . $232.00

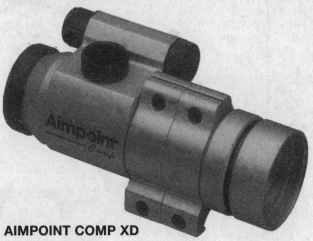

## AIMPOINT 5000 2-POWER XD

**SPECIFICATIONS**
**System:** Parallax free
**Optical:** Anti-reflex coated lens
**Adjustment:** clock = 1/4" at 100 yards
**Length:** 7"
**Weight:** 9 oz.
**Objective diameter:** 47mm
**Diameter of dot:** 1.5" at 100 yards
**Mounting system:** 30mm rings
**Magnification:** 2X
**Material:** Anodized aluminum; black finish
**Price:** . . . . . . . . . . . . . . . . . . . . . . . . . . . . . . . $388.00

## AIMPOINT COMP XD

**SPECIFICATIONS**
**System:** 100% Parallax free
**Optics:** Anti-reflex coated lenses
**Eye relief:** Unlimited  **Batteries:** 3 x 1.5V silver oxide
**Adjustment:** 1 click = 1/4-inch at 100 yards
**Length:** 4 3/8"  **Weight:** 4.75 oz.
**Objective diameter:** 36mm
**Dot diameter:** 7, 10, or 15 MOA
**Mounting system:** 30mm rings
**Magnification:** 1X
**Material:** Black, blue or stainless finish
Also available with 3-minute Dot with Flip Up lens covers and captive metal adjustment covers.
**Price:** . . . . . . . . . . . . . . . . . . . . . . . . . . . . . . . $331.00
Comp MXD 3, 7 or 10 MOA . . . . . . . . . . . . . . 409.00
Comp ML XD 3, 7 or 10 MOA. . . . . . . . . . . . . . 375.00

# ASHLEY OUTDOORS

## SIGHTS AND ACCESSORIES

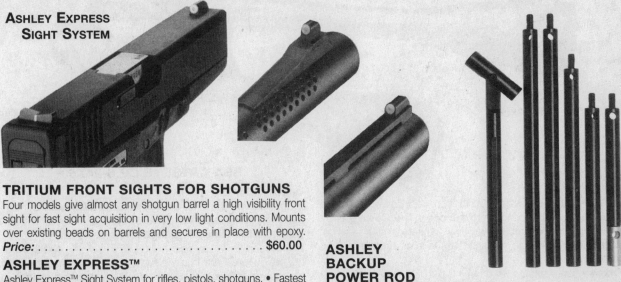

**ASHLEY EXPRESS
SIGHT SYSTEM**

### TRITIUM FRONT SIGHTS FOR SHOTGUNS
Four models give almost any shotgun barrel a high visibility front sight for fast sight acquisition in very low light conditions. Mounts over existing beads on barrels and secures in place with epoxy.
*Price:* . . . . . . . . . . . . . . . . . . . . . . . . . . . . . . . . . $60.00

### ASHLEY EXPRESS™
Ashley Express™ Sight System for rifles, pistols, shotguns. • Fastest acquisition of front sight in poor light • Low profile and snag free
*Price:* Ashley Big Dot Tritium Sight set . . . . . . . . $90.00

### ASHLEY BACKUP POWER ROD FOR MUZZLELOADERS
*Price:* . . . . . . . . . . . . . . . . . . . . . . . . . . . . . . . . . $40.00

### ASHLEY APERTURE™ GHOST RING HUNTING SIGHTS
• Fully adjustable for windage and elevation • Available for most rifles including blackpowder • Minimum gunsmithing for most installations; matches most existing mounting holes • Compact design, CNC machined from steel and heat treated • Perfect for low light conditions and offers minimal target obstruction
*Price:* Ashley Aperture Ghost Ring Hunting Sight Set . . . $90.00
*Available for most rifles including blackpowder*

.191    .230    .150    .218

### GHOST RING SIGHTS FOR RIFLES AND CARBINES
*Price:* rear . . . . . . . . . . . . . . . . . . . . . . . . . . . . . . $60.00
     front . . . . . . . . . . . . . . . . . . . . . . . . . . . . . . . . 30.00

### ASHLEY UTILITY SCOUT RIFLE KIT FOR MAUSER 98 & OTHERS
*Price:* . . . . . . . . . . . . . . . . . . . . . . . . . . . . . . . . . $325.00

# BSA Scopes

**6-24x50**

The BSA name once reserved for superior rifles and motorcycles is now appearing on rifle scopes. The Catseye line, with multi-coated objective and ocular lenses and a European-style reticle for shooting in dim light, includes several models:

- 4x44 • 1.5-4.5x32 • 3-10x44 • 3.5-10x50 • 4-16x50
- 6-24x50 *shown* . . . . . . . . . . . . . . . . . . . . . **$219.95**

A parallax-compensating lens snaps onto the 4x44 to improve target focus at short yardage.

## BSA CATSEYE CE 6-24X50

**SPECIFICATIONS**
*Magnification:* 6x-24x  *Objective Lens Diameter:* 50mm
*Exit Pupil Range:* 8.3-2.1  *Field of View at 100 yd:* 16'-3'
*Optimum Eye Relief:* 3"  *Length/Weight:* 16"/23 oz.
*Price:* . . . . . . . . . . . . . . . . . . . . . . . . . . . . . . . **$219.95**

The Twilight Performance Factor (TPF) is a mathematical expression of a scope's ability to show detailled images in low-light conditions. Normally, the higher the number the better. **BSA's Catseye CE 6-24x50** has a TPF of 17.3 at 6x and a bright 34.7 at 24x.

## BSA PLATINUM PT 8-32 X 44 TS

**SPECIFICATIONS**
*Magnification:* 8x-32x  *Objective Lens Diameter:* 44mm
*Exit Pupil Range:* 5.5-1.4  *Field of View at 100 yd:* 11'-3.5'
*Optimum Eye Relief:* 3"  *Length/Weight:* 17.25"/19.5 oz.
*Price:* . . . . . . . . . . . . . . . . . . . . . . . . . . . . . . . **$239.95**

## BSA PLATINUM 24 X 44 TS

**SPECIFICATIONS**
*Magnification:* 24x  *Objective Lens Diameter:* 44mm
*Exit Pupil Range:* 1.8  *Field of View at 100 yd:* 4.5'
*Optimum Eye Relief:* 3"  *Length/Weight:* 16.25"/17.9 oz.
*Price:* . . . . . . . . . . . . . . . . . . . . . . . . . . . . . . . **$189.95**

BSA Platinum target scopes are fitted with finger-adjustable windage and elevation dials that move point of impact in 1/8-minute clicks. Two sunshades–3-inch and 5-inch–are standard and can be screwed together for shooting in strong backlight. This scope line includes:

- 24x44 . . . . . . . . . . . . . . . . . . . . . . . . . . . . . **$189.95**
- 36x44 • 6-24x44 • 10-50x60
- 8-32x44 . . . . . . . . . . . . . . . . . . . . . . . . . . . . . **239.95**

# BSA SCOPES

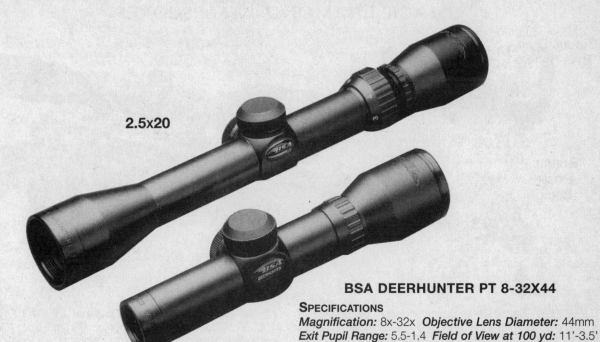

2.5x20

BSA Deer Hunter scopes, from a 2.5x20 (shown) to a 2.5-10x44 offer value for the big game hunter on a budget.
**Prices:** from ............................... $59.95
The Contender series of target scopes offers top-of-the line features like 1/8-minute click adjustments at a moderate price.
6-24x40 ............................... $144.95

## BSA DEERHUNTER PT 8-32X44

**SPECIFICATIONS**
**Magnification:** 8x-32x **Objective Lens Diameter:** 44mm
**Exit Pupil Range:** 5.5-1.4 **Field of View at 100 yd:** 11'-3.5'
**Optimum Eye Relief:** 3" **Length/Weight:** 17.25"/19.5 oz.
**Price:** ............................... $69.95

## BSA DEERHUNTER DH 2.5X20

**SPECIFICATIONS**
**Magnification:** 2.5x **Objective Lens Diameter:** 20mm
**Exit Pupil Range:** 8 **Field of View at 100 yd:** 72'
**Optimum Eye Relief:** 6" **Length/Weight:** 7.5"/7.5 oz.
**Price:** ............................... $59.95

## BSA CONTENDER CT 6-24X40 TS

**SPECIFICATIONS**
**Magnification:** 6x-24x **Objective Lens Diameter:** 40mm
**Exit Pupil Range:** 6.7-1.7 **Field of View at 100 yd:** 16'-4'
**Optimum Eye Relief:** 3" **Length/Weight:** 15.5"/20 oz.
**Price:** ............................... $144.95
The **BSA Contender CT 6-24x40 TS** features TPFs from 15.5 at 6x to 31 at 24x.

# BURRIS SCOPES

## BLACK DIAMOND RIFLESCOPES

**BURRIS DUAL-BIAS SPRING**

**BURRIS POSI-LOCK**

**MODEL 3X-12X-50mm**

Burris's new Black Diamond line includes six models of a 30mm main tube 3-12X50mm with various finishes, reticles, and adjustment knobs. These riflescopes have easy-to-grip rubber-armored parallax-adjust rings, an adjustable and resettable adjustment dial, and an internal focusing eyepiece. Other features include fully multi-coated lens surfaces, 110 inches of internal adjustment, four times magnification range, and 3.5" to 4" of eye relief. Alll models come in a non-reflective matte black finish.

### SPECIFICATIONS
**Models:** 3-12X50mm/6-24x50 **Field of View (feet @ 100yds.):** 34'-12'/18-6 **Optimum eye relief:** 3.5"-4.0"/3.5-4 **Exit Pupil:** 13.7mm-4.2mm/7.6-2.1 **Click adjust value (@ 100 yds.):** .25"/.125 **Max. internal adj. (@ 100 yds.):** 100"/52 **Clear objective diameter:** 50mm/50mm **Ocular end diameter:** 42mm/42mm **Weight:** 25 oz./25 oz. **Length:** 13.8"/16.2" **Reticles available:** Plex, German 3P#1, German 3P#4, Mil-Dot

**Prices: 3-12x/**Plex w/matte finish . . . . . . . . . . . $880.00
  Plex w/matte finish, Posi-Lock. . . . . . . . . . . . . 944.00
  German 3P#4 reticle w/matte finish . . . . . . . . . 908.00
  Plex w/matte finish, Tactical Knobs . . . . . . . . . 917.00
  Mil-Dot reticle w/matte finish, Tactical Knobs . . 1,029.00
**Prices: 6-24x/** Fine Plex. . . . . . . . . . . . . . . . . . $954.00
  Mil Dot . . . . . . . . . . . . . . . . . . . . . . . . . . 1,101.00
  Ballistic MDot . . . . . . . . . . . . . . . . . . . . . . 1,101.00

**1X XER SCOUT**

**2.75X SCOUT**

**BURRIS SPEEDDOT 135**

### SCOUT SCOPES
Made for hunters who need a 7- to 14 inch eye relief to mount just in front of the ejection port opening, allowing hunters to shoot with both eyes open. The 15-foot field of view and 2.75X magnification are ideal for brush guns and handgunners. Also ideal for the handgunner that uses a "two-handed hold." Rugged, reliable and 100% fog proof.

| MODELS | Prices |
|---|---|
| 1X XER Plex (matte) . . . . . . . . . . . . . . . . . . . . . . | $290.00 |
| 2.75X Heavy Plex (matte) . . . . . . . . . . . . . . . . . | 319.00 |

### BURRIS SPEEDDOT 135
1x35mm pistol and shotgun sight. Electronic red dot reticle, 3 moa or 11 moa
**Price:** . . . . . . . . . . . . . . . . . . . . . . . . . . . . . . . $291.00

# BURRIS RIFLESCOPES

**2.5X-10X** TITANIUM GRAY

**2.5X-10X** CARBON BLACK

### T-PLATED LENSES

The toughness of this scope doesn't end with the metal work. The scratch-proof T-Plate coating applied to the objective and eyepiece lenses is remarkable. These lenses do not come with the warning of other "scratch-resistant" coatings about removing all dust before cleaning. T-plated lenses do not require a "soft clean lens cloth". Just knock the mud off the lens and wipe it clean with your dirty shirt tail. Ordinary dirt, dust, and grit won't touch it. This coating technology is prohibitively expensive for ordinary scopes. Mr. T is a premium - quality sight for discriminating hunters.

## BURRIS "MR T"
### • TITANIUM BLACK • DIAMOND SCOPES

Substantially stronger than aluminum, and much lighter than steel, Mr. T is one scope worthy of the description 'tough'. Beyond the whole scope tube and eyepiece being made of solid titanium, each scope is coated with a nitride harder than carbide or hard chrome - - such as titanium nitride, aluminum titanium nitride, or chrome nitride, depending on the color. These nitrides are molecularly bonded to the titanium through high intensity physical vapor deposition for maximum adhesion that will not blister, flake, or chip...The result is an ultra-hard (up to 85 Rockwell C), abrasion resistant surface. *Also available* in Autumn Gold.

**4.5X-14X**

**1.75X-5X**

**3X-9X**

FULLFIELD 3x-9x

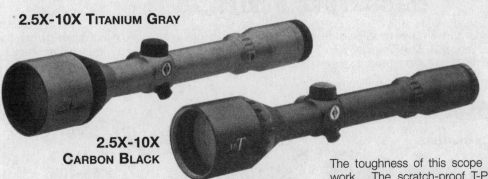

FULLFIELD II 3x-9x

MOST SCOPES

FULLFIELD II 3x-9x

### BURRIS FULLFIELD II VARIABLE SCOPES - A RE-DESIGN OF THE FULLFIELD LINE

The Fullfield II is now much more forgiving for eye positioning both fore and aft, and left and right. New optical design and stray light management contribute to the improvement. Using modern materials, optical systems, and machining techniques, Burris has shaved roughly four ounces of weight on each model without affecting durability or optical performance. In fact, several areas are even stronger and more precisely fitted than before. Overall, the Fullfield is about one inch shorter than its predecessor for a more compact look and feel. Like the Fullfield, and unlike other scopes, Fullfield II eyepieces are sealed with special quad seals rather than old-tech O-rings. And the eyepiece is now part of the power ring. To change magnification, simply turn the entire eyepiece. A European-style adjustable eyepiece is easy to use and requires no locking mechanism. Relocation of the turret on Fullfield II scopes, combined with a shorter eyepiece, allows more room for scope rings. *Also available:* 3.5-10x50

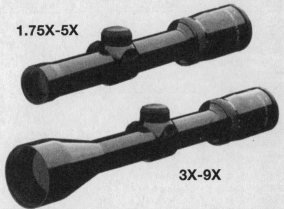

# BURRIS SCOPES

## SIGNATURE SERIES

All models in the Signature Series have HI-LUME (multi-coated) lenses for maximum light transmission. Many models also feature POSI-LOCK to prevent recoil shift and protect against loss of zero from rough hunting use. It allows the shooter to lock the internal optics of the scope in position after the rifle has been sighted in.

**8X-32X SIGNATURE**

**MR. T 2.5X-10X CARBON BLACK**

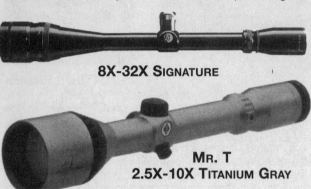

**MR. T 2.5X-10X TITANIUM GRAY**

### SIGNATURE SERIES SCOPES

| Item | Model | Reticle | Finish | Features | List |
|------|-------|---------|--------|----------|------|
| 200510 | 6X | Plex | blk | | $413 |
| 200511 | 6X | Plex | mat | | 431 |
| 200700 | 1.5X-6X | Plex | blk | | 484 |
| 200701 | 1.5X-6X | Plex | mat | | 502 |
| 200706 | 1.5X-6X | Plex | mat | Posi-Lock | 549 |
| 200711 | 1.5X-6X | Electro-Dot | mat | | 604 |
| 200712 | 1.5X-6X | Electro-Dot | mat | Posi-Lock | 651 |
| 200550 | 2X-8X | Plex | blk | | 558 |
| 200551 | 2X-8X | Plex | mat | | 577 |
| 200553 | 2X-8X | Plex | blk | Posi-Lock | 604 |
| 200554 | 2X-8X | Plex | mat | Posi-Lock | 623 |
| 200600 | 3X-9X | Plex | blk | | 571 |
| 200601 | 3X-9X | Plex | mat | | 590 |
| 200597 | 3X-9X | Plex | blk | Posi-Lock | 617 |
| 200598 | 3X-9X | Plexmat | | Posi-Lock | 635 |
| 200580 | 3X-9X | Electro-Dot | blk | | 674 |
| 200581 | 3X-9X | Electro-Dot | mat | | 692 |
| 200590 | 3X-9X | Electro-Dot | blk | Posi-Lock | 720 |
| 200591 | 3X-9X | Electro-Dot | mat | Posi-Lock | 738 |
| 200574 | 3X-9X-50mm | Plex | blk | | 633 |
| 200573 | 3X-9X-50mm | Mil-Dot | mat | Target Knobs | 742 |
| 200571 | 3X-9X-50mm | Plex | mat | Posi-Lock | 671 |
| 200572 | 3X-9X-50mm | Mil-Dot | mat | Posi-Lock | 762 |
| 200607 | 2.5X-10X | Plex | blk | PA | 635 |
| 200608 | 2.5X-10X | Plex | mat | PA | 652 |
| 200630 | 2.5X-10X | Plex | blk | Posi-Lock/PA | 696 |
| 200631 | 2.5X-10X | Plex | mat | Posi-Lock/PA | 714 |
| 200633 | 2.5X-10X | Plex | nic | Posi-Lock/PA | 723 |
| 200610 | 3X-12X | Plex | blk | PA | 691 |
| 200611 | 3X-12X | Plex | mat | PA | 709 |
| 200614 | 3X-12X | Plex | blk | Posi-Lock/PA | 740 |
| 200615 | 3X-12X | Plex | mat | Posi-Lock/PA | 758 |
| 200750 | 4X-16X | Plex | blk | PA | 723 |
| 200751 | 4X-16X | Plex | mat | PA | 742 |
| 200762 | 4X-16X | Fine Plex | blk | Target/PA | 764 |
| 200763 | 4X-16X | Fine Plex | mat | Target/PA | 779 |
| 200767 | 4X-16X | Ballistic MDot | mat | PA | 870 |
| 200756 | 4X-16X | Plex | mat | Posi-Lock/PA | 794 |
| 200765 | 4X-16X | Electro-Dot | mat | PA | 844 |
| 200766 | 4X-16X | Electro-Dot | mat | Posi-Lock/PA | 896 |
| 200800 | 6X-24X | Plex | blk | PA | 742 |
| 200804 | 6X-24X | Plex | mat | PA | 761 |

| Item | Model | Reticle | Finish | Features | List |
|------|-------|---------|--------|----------|------|
| 200803 | 6X-24X | Fine Plex | blk | Target/PA | $779 |
| 200806 | 6X-24X | Fine Plex | mat | Target/PA | 798 |
| 200811 | 6X-24X | Fine Plex | nic | Target/PA | 807 |
| 200814 | 6X-24X | Mil-Dot | mat | Target/PA | 928 |
| 200816 | 6X-24X | Ballistic MDot | mat | Target/PA | 928 |
| 200815 | 6X-24X | 1"-.25" Dot | mat | Target/PA | 835 |
| 200812 | 6X-24X | Plex | blk | Posi-Lock/PA | 796 |
| 200813 | 6X-24X | Plex | mat | Posi-Lock/PA | 815 |
| 200821 | 6X-24X | Electro-Dot | mat | PA | 863 |
| 200850 | 8X-32X | Fine Plex | blk | Target/PA | 798 |
| 200860 | 8X-32X | Fine Plex | mat | Target/PA | 816 |
| 200866 | 8X-32X | Fine Plex | nic | Target/PA | 826 |
| 200853 | 8X-32X | 1"-.25" Dot | mat | Target/PA | 854 |
| 200854 | 8X-32X | Mil-Dot | mat | Target/PA | 946 |
| 200861 | 8X-32X | Ballistic MDot | mat | Target/PA | 946 |
| 200855 | 8X-32X | Fine Plex | blk | Posi-Lock/PA | 854 |
| 200856 | 8X-32X | Fine Plex | mat | Posi-Lock/PA | 872 |

### Mr. T BLACK DIAMOND TITANIUM SCOPES–30mm

| Item | Model | Reticle | Finish | Features | List |
|------|-------|---------|--------|----------|------|
| 200920 | 2.5X-10X-50mm | Plex | titanium gray | | $2129 |
| 200921 | 2.5X-10X-50mm | Plex | carbon black | | 2129 |
| 200922 | 2.5X-10X-50mm | Mil-Dot | carbon black | Target | 2272 |
| 200923 | 2.5X-10X-50mm | Plex | carbon black | Posi-Lock | 2191 |
| 200924 | 2.5X-10X-50mm | Plex | autumn gold | | 2129 |

### BLACK DIAMOND SCOPES -- 30 mm

| Item | Model | Reticle | Finish | Features | List |
|------|-------|---------|--------|----------|------|
| 200906 | 6X-50mm | Plex | mat | | $683 |
| 200900 | 3X-12X-50mm | Plex | mat | PA | 880 |
| 200901 | 3X-12X-50mm | Plex | mat | Posi-Lock/PA | 944 |
| 200903 | 3X-12X-50mm | 3P#4 | mat | PA | 908 |
| 200904 | 3X-12X-50mm | Mil-Dot | mat | Posi-Lock/PA | 1044 |
| 200910 | 3X-12X-50mm | Plex | mat | Target/PA | 917 |
| 200911 | 3X-12X-50mm | Mil-Dot | mat | Target/PA | 1029 |
| 200930 | 6X-24X-50mm | Fine Plex | mat | Target/PA | 954 |
| 200931 | 6X-24X-50mm | Mil-Dot | mat | Target/PA | 1101 |
| 200932 | 6X-24X-50mm | Ballistic MDot | mat | Target/PA | 1101 |
| 200940 | 8X-32X-50mm | Fine Plex | mat | Target/PA | 999 |
| 200941 | 8X-32X-50mm | Ballistic MDot | mat | Target/PA | 1165 |

### ELECTRO-DOT SCOPES

| Item | Model | Reticle | Finish | Features | List |
|------|-------|---------|--------|----------|------|
| 200134 | 3X-9X Fullfield | Electro-Dot | blk | | $487 |
| 200135 | 3X-9X Fullfield | Electro-Dot | mat | | 505 |
| 200711 | 1.5X-6X Signature | Electro-Dot | mat | | 604 |
| 200712 | 1.5X-6X Signature | Electro-Dot | mat | Posi-Lock | 651 |
| 200581 | 3X-9X Signature | Electro-Dot | mat | | 692 |
| 200590 | 3X-9X Signature | Electro-Dot | blk | Posi-Lock | 720 |
| 200591 | 3X-9X Signature | Electro-Dot | mat | Posi-Lock | 738 |
| 200765 | 4X-16X Signature | Electro-Dot | mat | PA | 844 |
| 200766 | 4X-16X Signature | Electro-Dot | mat | Posi-Lock/PA | 896 |
| 200821 | 6X-24X Signature | Electro-Dot | mat | PA | 863 |

# BURRIS SCOPES

## FULLFIELD SCOPES
### FIXED POWER WITH HI-LUME LENSES

**3X-9X GLOSS ELECTRO-DOT**

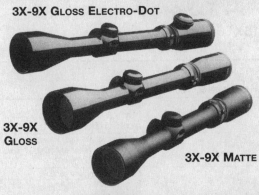

**3X-9X GLOSS**

**3X-9X MATTE**

**2.5X SHOTGUN SCOPE**

## FULLFIELD II SCOPES

| ITEM | MODEL | RETICLE | FINISH | FEATURES | LIST |
|---|---|---|---|---|---|
| 200086 | 1.75-5X | Plex | blk | | 374 |
| 200087 | 1.75-5X | Plex | mat | | 392 |
| 200160 | 3X-9X-40mm | Plex | blk | | 356 |
| 200161 | 3X-9X-40mm | Plex | mat | | 356 |
| 200162 | 3X-9X-40mm | Ballistic Plex | mat | | 356 |
| 200163 | 3X-9X-40mm | Plex | nic | | 383 |
| 200170 | 3.5X-10X-50mm | Plex | blk | | 496 |
| 200171 | 3.5X-10X-50mm | Plex | mat | | 514 |
| 200180 | 4.5X-14X | Plex | blk | PA | 545 |
| 200181 | 4.5X-14X | Plex | mat | PA | 545 |
| 200182 | 4.5X-14X | Fine Plex | mat | PA | 563 |

## FULLFIELD SCOPES

| ITEM | MODEL | RETICLE | FINISH | FEATURES | LIST |
|---|---|---|---|---|---|
| 200413 | 2.5X shotgun | Plex | mat | | 308 |
| 200010 | 4X | Plex | blk | | 314 |
| 200014 | 4X | Plex | mat | | 332 |
| 200050 | 6X | Plex | blk | | 343 |
| 200054 | 6X | Plex | mat | | 361 |
| 200020 | 2X-7X | Plex | blk | | 399 |
| 200024 | 2X-7X | Plex | mat | | 418 |
| 200134 | 3X-9X-40mm | Electro-Dot | blk | | 487 |
| 200135 | 3X-9X-40mm | Electro-Dot | mat | | 505 |
| 200150 | 3X-9X-50mm | Plex | blk | | 427 |
| 200151 | 3X-9X-50mm | Plex | mat | | 445 |
| 200152 | 3X-9X-50mm | Plex | nic | | 454 |
| 200103 | 6X-18X | Fine Plex | blk | PA | 527 |
| 200109 | 6X-18X | Fine Plex | mat | PA | 545 |
| 200104 | 6X-18X | Fine Plex | blk | Target/PA | 563 |
| 200108 | 6X-18X | Peep Plex | mat | PA | 563 |

## COMPACT SCOPES

| ITEM | MODEL | RETICLE | FINISH | FEATURES | LIST |
|---|---|---|---|---|---|
| 200424 | 1X XER | Plex | mat | | 290 |
| 200432 | 1X-4X XER | Plex | mat | | 377 |
| 200310 | 4X | Plex | blk | | 270 |
| 200311 | 4X | Plex | mat | | 289 |
| 200350 | 6X | Plex | blk | | 287 |

| ITEM | MODEL | RETICLE | FINISH | FEATURES | LIST |
|---|---|---|---|---|---|
| 200352 | 6X | Plex | blk | PA | 332 |
| 200356 | 6X Magnum | Plex | mat | PA | 384 |
| 200357 | 6X HBR | Fine Plex | blk | Target/PA | 451 |
| 200358 | 6X HBR | .375" Dot | blk | Target/PA | 488 |
| 200375 | 2X-7X | Plex | blk | | 359 |
| 200376 | 2X-7X | Plex | mat | | 377 |
| 200378 | 2X-7X | Plex | nic | | 386 |
| 200385 | 3X-9X | Plex | blk | | 368 |
| 200387 | 3X-9X | Plex | mat | | 387 |
| 200388 | 3X-9X | Plex | nic | | 396 |
| 200384 | 3X-9X | Plex | mat | PA | 409 |
| 200383 | 3X-9X | Plex | nic | PA | 419 |
| 200390 | 4X-12X | Plex | blk | PA | 500 |
| 200393 | 4X-12X | Fine Plex | blk | Target/PA | 537 |
| 200394 | 4X-12X | Fine Plex | mat | Target/PA | 556 |

## RIMFIRE/AIRGUN SCOPES

| ITEM | MODEL | RETICLE | FINISH | FEATURES | LIST |
|---|---|---|---|---|---|
| 200313 | 4X | Plex | blk | PA | 315 |
| 200352 | 6X | Plex | blk | PA | 332 |
| 200384 | 3X-9X | Plex | mat | PA | 409 |
| 200383 | 3X-9X | Plex | nic | PA | 419 |
| 200390 | 4X-12X | Plex | blk | PA | 500 |
| 200393 | 4X-12X | Fine Plex | blk | Target/PA | 537 |
| 200394 | 4X-12X | Fine Plex | mat | Target/PA | 556 |
| 200858 | 8X-32X | Plex | blk | Target/PA | 818 |
| 200859 | 8X-32X | Fine Plex | mat | Target/PA | 837 |

## HANDGUN SCOPES

| ITEM | MODEL | RETICLE | FINISH | FEATURES | LIST |
|---|---|---|---|---|---|
| 200424 | 1X XER | Plex | mat | | 290 |
| 200220 | 2X | Plex | blk | | 265 |
| 200229 | 2X | Plex | nic | | 284 |
| 200222 | 2X | Plex | blk | Posi-Lock | 302 |
| 200228 | 2X | Plex | mat | Posi-Lock | 311 |
| 200227 | 2X | Plex | nic | Posi-Lock | 320 |
| 200235 | 4X | Plex | blk | | 296 |
| 200237 | 4X | Plex | nic | | 315 |
| 200263 | 10X Target/PA | Plex | blk | Target | 460 |
| 200210 | 1.5X-4X | Plex | blk | | 363 |
| 200214 | 1.5X-4X | Plex | nic | | 381 |
| 200208 | 1.5X-4X | Plex | blk | Posi-Lock | 400 |
| 200213 | 1.5X-4X | Plex | nic | Posi-Lock | 418 |
| 200290 | 2X-7X | Plex | blk | | 401 |
| 200291 | 2X-7X | Plex | mat | | 411 |
| 200293 | 2X-7X | Plex | blk | PA | 444 |
| 200298 | 2X-7X | Plex | nic | | 420 |
| 200294 | 2X-7X | Plex | blk | Posi-Lock | 438 |
| 200297 | 2X-7X | Plex | nic | Posi-Lock | 457 |
| 200281 | 3X-9X | Plex | blk | PA | 453 |
| 200300 | 3X-9X | Plex | nic | PA | 471 |
| 200288 | 3X-9X | Plex | blk | Posi-Lock/PA | 490 |
| 200289 | 3X-9X | Plex | nic | Posi-Lock/PA | 508 |
| 200306 | 3X-12X | Plex | blk | PA | 508 |
| 200307 | 3X-12X | Plex | mat | PA | 517 |
| 200308 | 3X-12X | Plex | blk | PA | 527 |
| 200305 | 3X-12X | Fine Plex | blk | Target/PA | 545 |

## SPEEDDOT 135 SIGHTS

| ITEM | MODEL | RETICLE | FINISH | FEATURES | LIST |
|---|---|---|---|---|---|
| 300200 | 1X-35mm | 3 MOA Dot | mat | | 291 |
| 300201 | 1X-35mm | 11 MOA Dot | mat | | 291 |

## SCOUT SCOPES

| ITEM | MODEL | RETICLE | FINISH | FEATURES | LIST |
|---|---|---|---|---|---|
| 200424 | 1X XER | Plex | mat | | 290 |
| 200269 | 2.75X | Heavy Plex | mat | | 319 |

# BUSHNELL RIFLESCOPES

### ELITE 3200 — 5X-15X

## ELITE™ 3200 RIFLESCOPES

| Model | Special Feature | Actual Magni-fication | Obj. Lens Aperature (mm) | Field of View @ 100yds (ft.) | Weight (oz) | Length | Eye Relief (in.) | Exit Pupil (mm) | Click Value @ 100yds (in.) | Adjust Range @ 100yds (in.) | Selection | Suggested Retail |
|---|---|---|---|---|---|---|---|---|---|---|---|---|
| 32-2632M | Handgun (30-2632S Silver Finish) | 2x-6x | 32 | 10-4 | 10 | 9 | 20 | 16-5.3 | .25 | 50 | Constant 20" eye relief At all powers w/max. recoil resistance | $444.95 |
| 32-2732M | Matte Finish | 2x-7x | 32 | 44.6-12.7 | 12 | 11.6 | 3 | 12.2-4.6 | .25 | 50 | Compact variable for close-in brush ormed. range shooting. Excellent for shotguns | $323.95 |
| 32-3940G | (32-3940M Matte Finish, 32-3940S Silver Finish) | 3x-9x | 40 | 33.8-11.5 | 13 | 12.6 | 3 | 13.3-4.4 | .25 | 50 | For the full range of hunting. From varmint to big game. Tops in versatility. | $351.95 |
| 32-3950G | (32-3950M Matte Finish) | 3x-9x | 50 | 31.5-10-5 | 19 | 15.7 | 3 | 16-5.6 | .25 | 50 | All purpose variable with extra brightness. | $428.95 |
| 32-3955E | European Reticle Matte Finish | 3x-9x | 50 | 31.5-10.5 | 22 | 15.6 | 3 | 16-5.6 | .36 | 70 | Large exit pupil and 30mm tube for max. brightness. | $640.95 |
| 32-4124A | Adjustable Objective | 4x-12x | 40 | 26.9-9 | 15 | 13.2 | 3 | 10-3.33 | .25 | 50 | Medium to long-range variable makes a superb choice for varmint or big game | $469.95 |
| 32-5155M | Adjustable Objective | 5x-15x | 50 | 21-7 | 24 | 15.9 | 3 | 10-3.3 | .25 | 40 | Large objective for brightness | $528.95 |
| 32-3951M | Command Post Reticle | 3x-9x | 50 | 31.5-10.5 | 19 | 15.7 | 3 | 16-5.6 | .25 | 50 | Switch instantly from fine crosshairs to thick 3-pos reticle for low light shooting | $661.95 |

### ELITE 4200 — 2.5-10X40

### ELITE 4200

## ELITE™ 4200 RIFLESCOPES WITH RAINGUARD™

| Model | Special Feature | Actual Magni-fication | Obj. Lens Aperature (mm) | Field of View @ 100yds (ft.) | Weight (oz) | Length | Eye Relief (in.) | Exit Pupil (mm) | Click Value @ 100yds (in.) | Adjust Range @ 100yds (in.) | Selection | Suggested Retail |
|---|---|---|---|---|---|---|---|---|---|---|---|---|
| 42-1636M | Matte Finish | 1.5x-6x | 36 | 61.8-16.1 | 15.4 | 12.8 | 3 | 14.6-6 | .25 | 60 | Compact wide angle for close-in & brush hunting. Max. brightness. Execel. for shotguns | $608.95 |
| 42-2104G | (40-2104M Matte Finish, 40-2104S Silver Finish) | 2.5x-10x | 40 | 41.5-10.8 | 16 | 13.5 | 3 | 15.6-4 | .25 | 50 | All purpose hunting scope w/4x zoom range for close-in brush & long range shooting | $642.95 |
| 42-3640A | Adjustable Objective | 36x | 40 | 3 | 17.6 | 15 | 3.2 | 1.1 | .125 | 30 | Ideal benchrest scope. | $955.95 |
| 42-4165M | Matte Finish | 4x-16x | 50 | 26-7.2 | 22 | 15.6 | 3 | 12.5-3.1 | .25 | 50 | The ultimate varmint, airgun and precision shooting scope. Parallax focus from 10 meter to infinity. | $834.95 |
| 42-6244A | Adjustable Objective, Sunshade (40-6244M Matte Finish) | 6x-24x | 40 | 18-4.5 | 20.2 | 16.9 | 3 | 6.7-1.7 | .125 | 26 | Varmint, target & silhouette long range shooting and airgun. Parallax focus adjust. for pinpoint accuracy. Parallax focus from 10 meter to infinity. | $729.95 |
| 42-6243A | Adjustable Objective and 1/4" MOA dot reticle | 6-24x | 40 | 18-4.5 | 20.2 | 16.9 | 3 | 6.7-1.7 | .125 | 26 | Varmint, target and silhouette long range shooting and airgun. Parallax focus adjust for pinpoint accuracy. Parallax focus from 10 meter to infinity. | $729.95 |

# BUSHNELL RIFLESCOPES

**SPORTVIEW® 3X-9X**

## BUSHNELL SPORTVIEW® RIFLESCOPES

| Model | Special Feature | Actual Magni-fication | Obj. Lens Aperature (mm) | Field of View @ 100yds (ft.) | Weight (oz) | Length | Eye Relief (in.) | Exit Pupil (mm) | Click Value @ 100yds (in.) | Adjust Range @ 100yds (in.) | Selection | Suggested Retail |
|---|---|---|---|---|---|---|---|---|---|---|---|---|
| 79-0412 | Adjustable objective | 4x-12x | 40 | 27-9 | 14.6 | 13.1 | 3.2 | 10-3.3 | .25 | 60 | Long range. | $141.95 |
| 79-1393 | (79-1398 Matte) (79-1393S Matte Silver) | 3x-9x | 32 | 38-14 | 10 | 11.75 | 3.5 | 10.7-3.6 | .25 | 50 | All purpose variable | $68.95 |
| 79-1403 | (79-1403S Silver) | 4x | 32 | 29 | 9.2 | 11.75 | 4 | 8 | .25 | 60 | General purpose. | $57.95 |
| 79-1545 | | 1.5x-4.5x | 21 | 69-24 | 8.6 | 10.7 | 3 | 14-4.7 | .25 | 60 | Low power variable ideal for close-in brush or medium range shooting | $86.95 |
| 79-3940 | Wide angle (79-3940M Matte) | 3x-9x | 40 | 42-15 | 12.5 | 12 | 3 | 4.4 | .25 | 50 | Excellent for use at any range. | $95.95 |
| 79-6184 | Adjustable objective | 6x-18x | 40 | 19.1-6.8 | 15.9 | 14.5 | 3 | 6.7-2.2 | .25 | 50 | Excellent varmint scope. | $170.95 |
| **SPORTVIEW® AIR RIFLE SERIES** | | | | | | | | | | | | |
| 79-0004 | Adjustable objective w/rings | 4x | 32 | 31 | 11.2 | 11.7 | 4 | 8 | .25 | 50 | General purpose for air rifle and rimfire. With range focus & target adjustments | $98.95 |
| 79-0039 | Adjustable objective, with rings | 3x-9x | 32 | 38-13 | 11.2 | 10.75 | 3.5 | 10.6-3.5 | .25 | 60 | Air rifle, rimfire with range focus adjustments and target adjustments | $116.95 |
| **SPORTVIEW® SHOTGUN SCOPES W/CIRCLE-X RETICLE** | | | | | | | | | | | | |
| 79-1548 | Circle-X reticle | 1.5x-4.5x | 32 | 71-25 | 11.8 | 10.4 | 3.5 | 21-7 | .25 | | Turkey hunting, shotgun slugs and muzzeloading | $104.95 |
| 79-2538 | Circle-X reticle | 2.5 | 32 | 45 | 10 | 11 | 3 | 12.8 | .25 | | Short range brush scope, turkey hunting | $76.95 |
| **SPORTVIEW® RIMFIRE SERIES** | | | | | | | | | | | | |
| 79-1416 | 3/4" tube | 4x | 15 | 17 | 3.6 | 10.7 | 3.5 | 3.8 | Friction | 60 | General purpose. | $11.95 |
| 79-3720 | 3/4" tube | 3x-7x | 20 | 23-11 | 5.7 | 11.3 | 2.6 | 6.7-2.9 | Friction | 50 | All purpose variable. | $36.95 |
| **.22 VARMINT™ WITH RINGS** | | | | | | | | | | | | |
| 79-0428 | With rings (79-0428M Matte) | 4x | 28 | 25 | 8.5 | 7.6 | 3 | 7 | .5 | 52 | Compact for .22's | $75.95 |
| 79-3950M | Wide angle (matte) | 3x-9x | 50 | 41-15 | 12.9 | 12.5 | 3 | 17-5.5 | .25 | 50 | Excellent all purpose low light scope | $164.95 |

# BUSHNELL RIFLESCOPES

## 3X-9X (40MM) TROPHY®
## WIDE ANGLE RIFLESCOPE

## BUSHNELL TROPHY® RIFLESCOPES

| Model | Special Feature | Actual Magni-fication | Obj. Lens Aperature (mm) | Field of View @ 100yds (ft.) | Weight (oz) | Length | Eye Relief (in.) | Exit Pupil (mm) | Click Value @ 100yds (in.) | Adjust Range @ 100yds (in.) | Selection | Suggested Retail |
|---|---|---|---|---|---|---|---|---|---|---|---|---|
| 73-1500 | Wide Angle | 1.75x-5x | 32 | 68-23 | 12.3 | 10.8 | 3.5 | 18.3-1.75x | .25 | 120 | Shotgun, black powder or center-fire. Close-in brush hunting. | $262.95 |
| 73-3940 | Wide angle 73-3940S Silver | 3x-9x | 40 | 42/14-14/5 | 13.2 | 11.7 | 3 | 13.3-4.44 | .25 | 60 | All purpose variable, excellent for use from close to long range. Circular view provides a definite advantage over "TV screen" type scopes for running game-uphill or down. | $159.95 |
| 73-3941 | Illuminated reticle with back-up crosshairs | 3x-9x | 40 | 37-12.5 | 16 | 13 | 3 | 13.3-4.4 | .25 | 70 | Variable intensity light control Battery Sony CR 2032 or equivalent | $440.95 |
| 73-3942 | Long mounting length designed for long-action rifles | 3x-9x | 42 | 42-14 | 13.8 | 12 | 3 | 14-4.7 | .25 | 40 | 7" mounting length. | $164.95 |
| 73-3949 | Wide angle with Circle-x™ Reticle | 3x-9x | 40 | 42-14 | 13.2 | 11.7 | 3 | 13.3-4.4 | .25 | 60 | Matte finish, Ideal low light reticle. | $170.95 |
| 73-4124 | Wide angle, adjustable objective (73-4124M Matte) | 4x-12x | 40 | 32-11 | 16.1 | 12.6 | 3 | 10-3.3 | .25 | 60 | Medium to long range variable for varmint and big game. Range focus adjustment. Excellent air riflescope. | $300.95 |
| 73-4154M | Semi-turret target adjustments | 4x-15x | 40 | 26.8-7.7 | 18.7 | 13.7 | 3 | 10-2.6 | .25 | 40 | Medium to long range variable. Focus adjustment from 10mm to infinity. | $337.95 |
| 73-6184 | Semi-turret target adjustments, adjustable objective | 6x-18x | 40 | 17.3-6 | 17.9 | 14.8 | 3 | 6.6-2.2 | .125 | 40 | Long-range varmint centerfire or short range air rifle target precision accuracy. | $378.95 |
| **TROPHY® HANDGUN SCOPES** | | | | | | | | | | | | |
| 73-0232 | (73-0232S Silver) | 2x | 32 | 20 | 7.7 | 8.7 | 9 | 16 | .25 | 90 | Designed for target and short to med. range hunting. Magnum recoil resistant. | $218.95 |
| 73-2632 | (73-2632S Silver) | 2x-6x | 32 | 11-4 | 10.9 | 9.1 | 18 | 16-5.3 | .25 | 50 | 18 inches of eye relief at all powers | $287.95 |
| **TROPHY® SHOTGUN/HANDGUN SCOPES** | | | | | | | | | | | | |
| 73-1420 | Turkey Scope with Circle-x™ Reticle | 1.75x-4x | 32 | 73-30 | 10.9 | 10.8 | 3.5 | 18.8 | .25 | 120 | Ideal for turkey hunting, slug guns or blackpowder guns. Matte finish. | $255.95 |
| 73-1421 | Brush Scope with Circle-x™ Reticle | 1.75x-4x | 32 | 73-30 | 10.9 | 10.8 | 3.5 | 18-8 | .25 | 120 | Ideal for turkey hunting, slug guns or blackpowder guns. Matte finish. | $255.95 |
| **TROPHY® AIR RIFLESCOPES** | | | | | | | | | | | | |
| 73-4124 | Wide angle, adjustable objective (73-4124M Matte) | 4x-12x | 40 | 32-11 | 16.1 | 12.6 | 3 | 10-3.3 | .25 | 60 | Medium to long range variable for varmint and big game. Range focus adjustment. Excellent air riflescope. | $300.95 |
| 73-6184 | Semi-turret target adjustments, adjustable objective | 6x-18x | 40 | 17-6 | 17.9 | 14.8 | 3 | 6.6-2.2 | .125 | 40 | Long-range varmint centerfire or short range air rifle target precision accuracy. | $378.95 |

# BUSHNELL

**BUSHNELL®
HOLOsight®**

## BUSHNELL® HOLOsight®

The BUSHNELL® HOLOsight® delivers instant target acquisition, improved accuracy, and can be tailored to virtually any shooting discipline. How does it work? A hologram of a reticle pattern is recorded on a heads-up display window. When illuminated by laser (coherent) light, a holographic image becomes visible at the target plane - where it remains in focus with the target. Critical eye alignment is not required and multi-plane focusing error is eliminated. With the BUSHNELL® HOLOsight®, you simply look through the window, place the reticle image on the target and shoot. The use of holographic technology allows the creation of virtually any image as a reticle pattern, in either two or three dimensions. Shooters have the flexibility to design reticles in any geometric shape, size and in any dimension to enhance a specific shooting discipline. Since no light is cast on the target, use of the BUSHNELL® HOLOsight® is legal in most hunting, target and competition areas.

## BUSHNELL HOLOsight® SPECIFICATIONS

| Optics | Magni-fication @ 100 yds | Field of View ft @ 100 yds | Weight (oz/g) | Length (in/mm) | Eye Relief (in/mm) | Batteries | Windage Click Value in @100 yds mm@ 100m | Elevation Click Value in @100 yds mm@ 100m | Brightness Adjustment Settings |
|---|---|---|---|---|---|---|---|---|---|
| Holographic | 1x | Unlimited | 6.4/181 | 4.125/104.8 | 1/2" to 10 ft. 13 to 3045 mm | 2 Type N 1.5 Volt | .25 M.O.A./ 7mm @100m | .5 M.O.A./ 14mm@100m | 20 levels |

| Model | Description | | Suggested Retail |
|---|---|---|---|
| 50-0021 | HOLOsight Model 400 | HOLOsight with mounts for Weaver rail and standard reticle. | $567.95 |
| 50-0020 | HOLOsight Model 400 (without reticle) | HOLOsight with mounts for Weaver rail and no reticle. Reticle must be purchased separately. | $478.95 |
| 50-0002 | HOLOsight 2X adapter | Increases effective range of HOLOsight | $248.95 |

| Model | Reticle | Description | Uses | |
|---|---|---|---|---|
| **HOLOsight® RETICLES** | | | | |
| Included w/50-0021 | Standard | 2-Dimensional 65 M.O.A. ring with one M.O.A. dot and tick marks. | General all-purpose handguns, rifles, slug guns, and wing shooting | $111.95 |
| 50-0122 | Dual Rings | 2-Dimensional design with two rings (20 M.O.A. & 90 M.O.A.) | Wing shooting, 20" IPSC targets, slug and turkey guns | $111.95 |
| 50-0123 | Open Crosshairs | 2-Dimensional all-purpose design which does not cover up the target area. Inner circle covers 30" at 100 yards. | General all purpose handguns, short range rifles, slug guns and wing shooting | $111.95 |
| 50-0125 | Dot | 1 M.O.A. Dot | Precision rifle, handgun, and slug gun shooting. | $111.95 |

# BUSHNELL RIFLESCOPES

**70-3940M**

**70-4115A**

**SCOPECHIEF**

**70-6204A**

**70-1563M**

**BANNER**

## BUSHNELL SCOPECHIEF® RIFLESCOPES

| Model | Special Feature | Actual Magni-fication | Obj. Lens Aperature (mm) | Field of View ft @ 100yds/m | Weight (oz/g) | Length (in/mm) | Eye Relief (in/mm) | Exit Pupil (mm) | Click Value in @ 100yds mm @ 100m | Adjust Range in @ 100yds m @ 100m | Selection | Suggested Retail |
|---|---|---|---|---|---|---|---|---|---|---|---|---|
| 70-1563M | Matte Finish | 1.5x-6x | 32 | 74/24.6@1.5x 20/6.7@6x | 14.4/408 | 10.7/272 | 3.5/89 | 14@1.5x 5.3@6x | .25/7 | 100/2.8 | Ideal shotgun, close range scope. | $337.95 |
| 70-3104M | Matte Finish | 3.5x-10x | 40 | 43/14.3@3.5x 15/5.0@10x | 17/482 | 13/330 | 3.5/89 | 12@3.5x 4.2@10x | .25/7 | 50/1.4 | 6 inch mounting length | $294.95 |
| 70-3940M | Matte Finish | 3x-9x | 40 | 42/14.0@3x 14/4.7@9x | 16/454 | 11.5/292 | 3.5/89 | 13.3@3x 4.4@9x | .25/7 | 90/2.5 | Standard, all purpose scope | $255.95 |
| 70-4145A | Matte Finish, Adj. Objective, Sunshade | 4x-14x | 50 | 31/103@4x 9/3.0@14x | 23/652 | 14.1/358 | 3.5/89 | 12.5@4x 3.6@14x | .25/7 | 50/1.4 | Higher magnification with longer objective for enhanced brightness at longer ranges. | $408.95 |
| 70-6204A | Matte Finish, Adj. Objective, Sunshade | 6x-20x | 40 | 21/7.0@6x 6/2.0@20x | 21/595 | 15.75/400 | 3.5/89 | 6.6@6x 2.0@20x | .25/7 | 40/1.1 | High magnification for target shooting and varminting. | $583.95 |

## BUSHNELL BANNER RIFLESCOPES

| Model | Special Feature | Actual Magni-fication | Obj. Lens Aperature (mm) | Field of View ft @ 100yds/m | Weight (oz/g) | Length (in/mm) | Eye Relief (in/mm) | Exit Pupil (mm) | Click Value in @ 100yds mm @ 100m | Adjust Range in @ 100yds m @ 100m | Selection | Suggested Retail |
|---|---|---|---|---|---|---|---|---|---|---|---|---|
| 71-1545 | Wide Angle | 1.5x-4.5x | 32 | 67-23 | 10.5 | 10.5 | 3.5 | 17-7 | .25 | 60 | Ideal Shotgun and median to short range scope. | $116.95 |
| 71-3944 | Black powder scope w/extended eye relief and Circle-x@ reticle | 3x-9x | 40 | 36-13 | 12.5 | 11.5 | 4 | 13-4.4 | .25 | 60 | Specifically designed for black powder and shotguns | $125.95 |
| 71-3948 | Ideal scope for multi purpose guns | 3x-9x | 40 | 40-74 | 13 | 12 | 3 | 13.3-4.4 | .25 | 60 | General purpose. | $120.95 |
| 71-3950 | Large objective for extra brightness in low light | 3x-9x | 50 | 31-10 | 19 | 16 | 3 | 16-5.6 | .25 | 50 | Low light conditions | $186.95 |
| 71-4124 | Adjustable objective | 4x-12x | 40 | 29-11 | 15 | 12 | 3 | 10-3.3 | .25 | 60 | Ideal scope for long-range shooting. | $157.95 |
| 71-6185 | Adjustable objective | 6x-18x | 50 | 17-6 | 18 | 16 | 3 | 8.3-2.8 | .25 | 40 | Long range varmint and target scope. | $209.95 |

# DOCTER OPTIC RIFLE SCOPES

Docter Optic is a well-known name in European optics that has been marketed with varying success in the U.S. This year Outdoor Products of Boulder City, Nevada, is handling Docter Optic's expanded line of rifle scopes and binoculars. It includs these four new models, designed expressly for the American shooter.

| MAGNIFICATION X OBJ. DIA. | FIELD OF VIEW (FT., 100 YDS) | DIA./LENGTH (IN.) | WEIGHT (OZ.) | PRICE |
|---|---|---|---|---|
| 3-9x40 | 31-13 | 1/12.5 | 17 | **$378.00** |
| 3-10x40 | 34-12 | 1/13 | 18.5 | **$626.00** |
| 4.5-14x40 | 23-8 | 1/13.5 | 21.5 | **$652.00** |
| 8-25x50 | 13-4 | 1/16 | 26.5 | **$901.00** |

Some of Docter Optic 30mm scopes feature aspherical lenses, as do the company's binoculars. All Docter scopes offer these advantages:

## RIFLE SCOPE SPECIFICATIONS

• *High strength, one-piece tube construction of aircraft-grade aluminum eliminates weak screw-together joints that can leak or break, won't rust or corrode in adverse weather.*

• *Precise click-stop adjustments of 1/4" at 100 yards for windage and elevation. Wide range of adjustment (50") makes it easier to compensate for mounting errors. Excellent repeatability.*

• *Advanced lens technology and high grade multi-coating provides unparalled light transmission and image resolution for crisp, clear sighting picture - especially advantageous during low light conditions at dawn and dusk when most animal movement occurs.*

• *Every DOCTER scope is subjected to stringent leak and shock testing before it leaves the factory.*

• *Every joint where a leak may possibly occur is sealed with statically and dynamically loaded ring gaskets.*

• *Diopter focusing adapts the focus to your particular needs.*

• *Eye relief of over 3 inches, plus a wide rubber ring on the eye-piece protects the shooter from half-moon cuts, even with heavy calibers.*

A holographic sight is new for Docter Optic this year. Weighing just one ounce, it is not much bulkier than a standard rear sight, yet it offer's the advantage of a single sighting plane. A red dot appears to project itself on the target - there's nothing to line up. You can shoot more quickly than with any other type of sight. Coated, high-quality lenses ensure a clear sight picture. There is no battery switch; batteries last up to five years without rest.

## ONE-INCH TUBE SCOPES

| DESCRIPTION | MAGNI-FICATION | OBJECTIVE LENS DIA. | COLOR | RETICLE |
|---|---|---|---|---|
| 3-9 x 40 Variable | 3x to 9x | 40 mm | Matte Black | Duplex |
| 3-9 x 40 Variable | 3x to 9x | 40 mm | Matte Black | German #4 |
| 3-10 x 40 Variable | 3x to 10x | 40 mm | Matte Black | Duplex |
| 3-10 x 40 Variable | 3x to 10x | 40 mm | Matte Black | German #4 |
| 4.5-14 x 40 Variable | 4.5x to 14x | 40 mm | Matte Black | Duplex |
| 4.5-14 x 40 Variable | 4.5x to 14x | 40 mm | Matte Black | Do |
| 8-25 x 50 Variable | 8x to 25x | 50 mm | Matte Black | Dot |
| 8-25 x 50 Variable | 8x to 25x | 50 mm | Matte Black | Crosshair |

## 30 mm TUBE SCOPES

| DESCRIPTION | MAGNI-FICATION | OBJECTIVE LENS DIA. | COLOR | RETICLE |
|---|---|---|---|---|
| 4 x 32 Fixed | 4x | 32 mm | Matte Black | Duplex |
| 4 x 32 Fixed | 4x | 32 mm | Matte Black | German #4 |
| 6 x 42 Fixed | 6x | 42 mm | Matte Black | Duplex |
| 6 x 42 Fixed | 6x | 42 mm | Matte Black | German #4 |
| 6 x 42 Fixed, Aspherical Lens | 6x | 42 mm | Matte Black | Duplex |
| 6 x 42 Fixed, Aspherical Lens | 6x | 42 mm | Matte Black | German #4 |
| 1.5-6 x 42 Variable | 1.5x to 6x | 42 mm | Matte Black | Duplex |
| 1.5-6 x 42 Variable | 1.5x to 6x | 42 mm | Matte Black | German #4 |
| 1.5-6 x 42 Var., Aspherical Lens | 1.5x to 6x | 42 mm | Matte Black | Duplex |
| 1.5-6 x 42 Var., Aspherical Lens | 1.5x to 6x | 42 mm | Matte Black | German #4 |
| 2.5-10 x 48 Variable | 2.5x to 10x | 48 mm | Matte Black | Duplex |
| 2.5-10 x 48 Variable | 2.5x to 10x | 48 mm | Matte Black | German #4 |
| 2.5-10 x 48 Var., Aspherical Lens | 2.5x to 10x | 48 mm | Matte Black | Duplex |
| 2.5-10 x 48 Var., Aspherical Lens | 2.5x to 10x | 48 mm | Matte Black | German #4 |
| 3-12 x 56 Variable | 3x to 12x | 56 mm | Matte Black | Duplex |
| 3-12 x 56 Variable | 3x to 12x | 56 mm | Matte Black | German #4 |
| 3-12 x 56 Var., Aspherical Lens | 3x to 12x | 56 mm | Matte Black | Duplex |
| 3-12 x 56 Var., Aspherical Lens | 3x to 12x | 56 mm | Matte Black | German #4 |

# LASERAIM TECHNOLOGIES INC.

### LAX LASER SIGHT MODEL LAXB

**LAX**™ (ten times brighter) laser sight has all of the quality features you've come to expect from **LASERAIM**®. The **LAX**™ sight fit allows it to mount quickly and easily to most pistols and revolvers. Producing a 2" dot (at 100 yds), the **LAX**™ has a range of up to 500 yds. Four button cell batteries power the water and shock-resistant sight up to one hour continuous use. Windage and elevation are accomplished with the 3 pin windage and elevation system, giving precise adjustments and yielding 9 ft. of travel at 25 yards. Perfect for hunting, target, or home protection. Adaptable to rifles, shotguns, muzzleloaders, and bows. Available in black. *Universal mount included.* **Length:** 2.75" **Diameter:** 5/8" **Weight (approx.):** 2 oz. Made in U.S.A.
**Price:** . . . . . . . . . . . . . . . . . . . . . . . . . . . . . . . . $79.00

### GI HOT CUSTOM LASERS

The GI HOT (Hotdot® laser) has been custom-designed for Glock models 17 to 30. It allows a two-handed shooting grip by locating the laser close to the bottom of the frame. This patented system internalizes the wires, leaving a clean, easy-to-use laser that conforms to the pistol. A pressure-sensitive pad turns the laser on and off. Four button-cell batteries power it up to one hour continuously. The Easy-lock™ windage & elevation system makes sighting quick and reliable. GI HOT range = 500 yds. **Length:** 1.5". **Weight:** 2 oz.
**Price:** . . . . . . . . . . . . . . . . . . . . . . . . . . . . . . . $229.00

### LA70 SHOTLESS LASER BORE SIGHTER™ (Not shown)

The **LA70** Sʜᴏᴛʟᴇss Lᴀsᴇʀ Bᴏʀᴇ Sɪɢʜᴛᴇʀ™ facilitates sighting to near perfect accuracy without wasting a shot. To check the center of the bore, simply rotate the laser on axis of the gun bore. The LA70 is equipped with a rotational **LASERAIM**™ with constant ON switch and six arbors fitting calibers 22 thru 45, 12-gauge shotguns and muzzleloaders (50 and 54 cal.). **Length:** 8" (w/laser and arbor).
**Price:** . . . . . . . . . . . . . . . . . . . . . . . . . . . . . . . $169.00

**Model LA16**

### MODEL LA16 HOTDOT MIGHTY SIGHT

Ten times brighter than other laser sights, Laseraim's Hotdot Lasersights include a rechargeable NICad battery and in-field charger. Produce a 2" dot at 100 yards with a 500-yard range. **Length:** 2". **Diameter:** .75". Can be used with handguns, rifles, shotguns and bows. Fit all Laseraim mounts. Available in black or satin.
**Price:** . . . . . . . . . . . . . . . . . . . . . . . . . . . . . . . $129.00

# LEICA ULTRAVID RIFLESCOPES

LEICA, the world-renowned maker of high-quality cameras, binoculars and spotting scopes has earned the reputation of producing German-engineered optics with unsurpassed optical performance and mechanical precision. The LEICA ULTRAVID Riflescopes have created a complete hunting product line for the serious outdoor enthusiast. These riflescopes are designed to withstand the most extreme conditions—from frigid Alaskan bays to scorching Kalahari sands. All models provide exceptionally brilliant, high-contrast images, thanks to LEICA's Multi-Coated glass with "ballistic tough" ion-assisted coatings. The lenses are precisely positioned in a durable, one-piece 30mm housing machined from a single block of aircraft-grade aluminum to withstand accidents of all kinds. Waterproofed up to 33 feet and nitrogen-purged to provide a lifetime of fog-proof use, LEICA's ULTRAVID riflescopes are finished in a hard, anodized black matte with titanium accents. In addition, the power selector and diopter adjustment covers feature "soft touch" rubber tactile surfaces for a positive grip even with gloved hands or wet fingers.

**1.75-6x 32mm**

**3.5x-10x 42mm**

**4.5x-14x 42mm "F"**

## SPECIFICATIONS

| Model | Weight | Length | Field of View ft. @ 100 yd. Low | High | Optimum Eye Relief Low | High | Adjustment Range @ 100 Yards` | Prices |
|---|---|---|---|---|---|---|---|---|
| 1.75x-6x by 32 mm | 14 ounces | 11.25 inches | 47 inches | 18 | 4.8 inches | 3.7 | 55 inches | $749.00 |
| 3.5x-10x by 42 mm | 16 ounces | 12.62 inches | 29.5 inches | 10.7 | 4.6 inches | 3.6 | 51 inches | $849.00 |
| 4.5x-14x by 42 mm F | 18 ounces | 12.28 inches | 20.8 inches | 7.4 | 5.0 inches | 3.7 | 67 inches | $949.00 |

# LEUPOLD RIFLESCOPES

## VARI-X III LINE

The Vari-X III scopes feature a power-changing system that is similar to the sophisticated lens systems in today's finest cameras. Improvements include an extremely accurate internal control system and a sharp sight picture. All lenses are coated with Multicoat 4. Reticles are the same apparent size throughout the power range and stay centered during elevation/windage adjustments. Eyepieces are adjustable and fog-free. Reticles are also available in German #1, German #1 European, German #4, Post and Duplex, and Leupold Dot.

**VARI-X III 1.75-6X32mm E (EXTENDED VERSION)**

### VARI-X III 1.5-5X20mm
This selection of hunting powers is for ranges varying from very short to those at which big game is normally taken. The field at 1.5X lets you get on a fast-moving animal quickly. With magnification at 5X, medium and big game can be hunted around the world at all but the longest ranges.
Duplex or Heavy Duplex . . . . . . . . . . . . . . . . . . $635.00
In black matte finish . . . . . . . . . . . . . . . . . . . . . . 660.00
*Also available:*
VARI-X III 1.75-6X32mm. Matte finish . . . . . . . . 683.00

### VARI-X III 2.5-8X36mm
This is an excellent range of powers for almost any kind of game, including varmints. The top magnification provides resolution for practically any situation.
Duplex . . . . . . . . . . . . . . . . . . . . . . . . . . . . . . $678.00
In matte or silver finish . . . . . . . . . . . . . . . . . . . 703.00
Mil Dot (Matte) . . . . . . . . . . . . . . . . . . . . . . . . . 837.00

### VARI-X III 3.5-10X40mm
The extra power range makes these scopes the optimum choice for year-around big game and varmint hunting. The adjustable objective model, with its precise focusing at any range beyond 50 yards, also is an excellent choice for some forms of target shooting.
Duplex . . . . . . . . . . . . . . . . . . . . . . . . . . . . . . $698.00
With matte or silver finish . . . . . . . . . . . . . . . . . 723.00

### VARI-X III 3.5-10X50mm
The hunting scope is designed specifically for low-light situations. The 3.5X10-50mm scope, featuring lenses coated with Multicoat 4, is ideal for twilight hunting because of its efficient light transmission. The new scope delivers maximum available light through its large 50mm objective lens, which translates into an exit pupil that transmits all the light the human eye can handle in typical low-light circumstances, even at the highest magnification
Duplex or Heavy Duplex . . . . . . . . . . . . . . . . . . $796.00
With matte or silver finish . . . . . . . . . . . . . . . . . 821.00

### VARI-X III 6.5-20X50mm Varmint

### VARI-X III 4.5-14X40mm (Adj. Objective)
This model has enough range to double as a hunting scope and as a varmint scope.
Duplex or Heavy Duplex . . . . . . . . . . . . . . . . . . $780.00
With matte finish . . . . . . . . . . . . . . . . . . . . . . . . 805.00
Same as above with 50mm adj. obj., Duplex or Heavy
Duplex; matte finish only . . . . . . . . . . . . . . . . . 903.00

### VARI-X III 6.5-20X40mm (Adj. Objective)
This scope has a wide range of power setting, with magnifications useful to hunters of all types of varmints. Can be used for any kind of big-game hunting where higher magnifications are an aid. Side-focus adjustment allows shooters to eliminate parallax while in shooting position without taking their eyes off the target.
Gloss finish . . . . . . . . . . . . . . . . . . . . . . . . . . . $823.00
With matte or silver finish . . . . . . . . . . . . . . . . . 848.00
*Also available:*
6.5-20X50MM ADJ. OBJ. w/duplex matte finish. . . . 946.00
6.5-20X50MM ADJ. OBJ. w/Mil Dot matte finish . . 1,080.00

### VARI-X III 6.5-20X40MM E.F.R. TARGET
For those situations, such as air rifle or rimfire silhouette, where normal adjustable objective ranges are simply too distant, Leupold offers the EFR (Extended Focus Rifle) model of the 6.5-20. With this model, parallax distances as close as 10 meters can be set.
Fine Duplex (matte) . . . . . . . . . . . . . . . . . . . . . $919.00
Target Dot (matte) . . . . . . . . . . . . . . . . . . . . . . . 963.00

# LEUPOLD SCOPES

## VARI-X II LINE

The Vari-X II line offers magnesium fluoride-coated lenses for improved light transmission, continuous tension adjustment dials with increments as fine as 1/2 minute of angle, a locking eyepiece for reliable ocular adjustment, and a sealed, nitrogen-filled interior for fog-free reliability. Many models are available with Dot, CPC, German #1, German #4, and Post & Duplex reticles in addition to Duplex.

SIGHTS & SCOPES

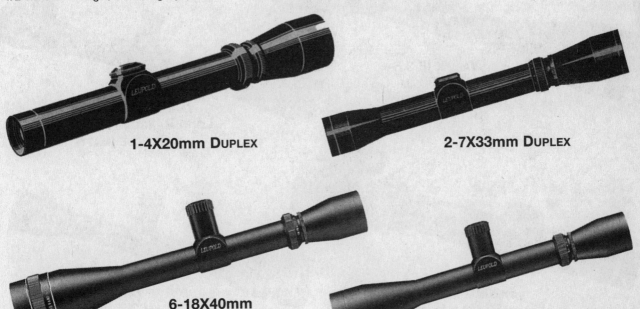

**1-4X20mm DUPLEX**

**2-7X33mm DUPLEX**

**6-18X40mm**

**3-9X40mm DUPLEX**

### VARI-X II 1-4X20mm DUPLEX

This scope, the smallest of Leupold's VARI-X II line, is noted for its large field of view: 70 feet at 100 yards.
Gloss finish only . . . . . . . . . . . . . . . . . . . . . . . . . . $396.00

### VARI-X II 2-7X33mm DUPLEX

A compact scope, no larger than the Leupold M8-4X, offering a wide range of power. It can be set at 2X for close ranges in heavy cover or zoomed to maximum power for shooting or identifying game at longer ranges.
VARI-X II 2-7X 33 SHOTGUN (heavy Duplex) matte . . 428.00

### VARI-X II 3-9X50mm

This LOV scope delivers a 5.5mm exit pupil for low-light visibility: Gloss . . . . . . . . . . . . . . . . . . . . . . . . . . . $510.00
Matte finish . . . . . . . . . . . . . . . . . . . . . . . . . . . . 535.00

### VARI-X II 3-9X40mm DUPLEX

A wide selection of powers offers the right combination of field of view and magnification to fit most hunting conditions. Many hunters use the 3X or 4X setting most of the time, cranking up to 9X for positive identification of game or for extremely long shots. The adjustable objective eliminates parallax and permits precise focusing on any object from less than 50 yards to infinity for extra-sharp definition.
Gloss finish . . . . . . . . . . . . . . . . . . . . . . . . . . . . . $432.00
In matte, silver . . . . . . . . . . . . . . . . . . . . . . . . . . . 457.00
Tactical (Mil Dot, matte) . . . . . . . . . . . . . . . . . . . . 457.00

### VARI-X II 4-12X40mm (Adj. Objective)

The ideal answer for big game and varmint hunters alike. At 12.25 inches, the 4X12 is virtually the same length as Vari-X II 3X9. New fixed objective has same long eye relief and is factory-set to be free of parallax at 150 yds.
Gloss finish . . . . . . . . . . . . . . . . . . . . . . . . . . . . . $594.00
Matte or silver finish . . . . . . . . . . . . . . . . . . . . . . . 619.00
3/4 Mil. Dot (gloss) . . . . . . . . . . . . . . . . . . . . . . . . 728.00
3/4 Mil. Dot (matte) . . . . . . . . . . . . . . . . . . . . . . . . 753.00
AO . . . . . . . . . . . . . . . . . . . . . . . . . . . . . . . . . . . 582.00

### VARI-X II 6-18X40mm Adj. Obj. Target

Features target-style click adjustments, fully coated lenses, adj. objective for parallax-free shooting from 50 yards to infinity.
In matte . . . . . . . . . . . . . . . . . . . . . . . . . . . . . . . $659.00
Target Dot Model . . . . . . . . . . . . . . . . . . . . . . . . . 712.00
Target Dot w/Target knobs . . . . . . . . . . . . . . . . . . 766.00
Duplux w/Target knobs . . . . . . . . . . . . . . . . . . . . . 712.00

# LEUPOLD SCOPES

## ILLUMINATED RETICLE

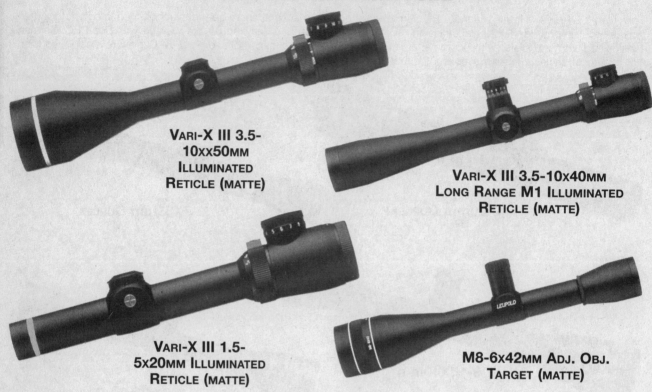

**VARI-X III 3.5-10xx50MM ILLUMINATED RETICLE (MATTE)**

**VARI-X III 3.5-10x40MM LONG RANGE M1 ILLUMINATED RETICLE (MATTE)**

**VARI-X III 1.5-5x20MM ILLUMINATED RETICLE (MATTE)**

**M8-6x42MM ADJ. OBJ. TARGET (MATTE)**

Leupold's Illuminated Reticle Scope helps hunters and target shooters take aim in poor light.

All Leupold Illuminated Reticle Scopes feature the world renowned Vari-X III system with Multicoat 4 lenses, and audible and tactile click adjustments. They are waterproof and fog proof. An eleven-position intensity setting dial allows the brightness of the reticle to be adjusted for any situation. A 3-volt lithium cell supplies the power necessary to keep the reticle evenly and constantly lit.

For big game hunters, the Leupold Vari-X III 1.5-5x20mm Illuminated Reticle Scope, with either an Illuminated Duplex or Illuminated German #4 reticle, makes the aiming point leap right to the eye and offers lightning fast target acquisition. For more general hunting and sporting applications, the Vari-X III 4.5-14x50mm Adjustable Objective and the new Vari-X III 3.5-10x50 models offer extra-big objective lenses for conditions when you must use high magnification in low light. Both models are available in a matte finish with a choice of Illuminated Duplex, Illuminated German #4, or Illuminated Mil. Dot reticles.

Tactical shooters will welcome the Leupold Vari-X III 3.5-10x40mm Long Range M1 Illuminated Reticle and Vari-X III 3.5-10x40mm Long Range M3 Illuminated Reticle models. Both are outstanding choices for military, law enforcement, and other tactical applications.

Both models are available in a matte finish and feature side focus parallax adjusment dials and a 30mm maintube design to enhance long range capability. Each model can be had with either the Illuminated Duplex or Illuminated Mil. Dot reticle.

### LEUPOLD 6 X 42 AO TARGET SCOPE

The Leupold M8 6x42mm Adjustable Objective Target Scope offers all the features needed by hunter benchrest shooters. Both the elevation and windage dials of this scope feature 1/4 minute of angle, target-style click adjustments. An adjustable objective dial offers the ability to correct parallax from a distance of 50 yards to infinity.

The lenses of the M8 6x42mm Adjustable Objective Target Scope are coated with Multicoat 4, the same anti-reflective coating found on the Leupold Vari-X III scopes, for increased light transmission. This combined with superior system design and a very large exit pupil makes the scope one of the brightest Leupold scopes available. The large exit pupil also reduces eye strain. The Leupold M8 6x42mm Adjustable Objective Target Scope is not just for target shooting. Durable and rugged, it offers an ideal scope for low-light hunting conditions. The adjustable objective makes it well suited for long shooting at large game and varmints.

# LEUPOLD SCOPES

## LEUPOLD PREMIER SCOPES (LPS)

The Leupold Premiere Scope (LPS) line features 30mm maintubes, fast-focus eye-pieces, armored power selector dials that can be read from the shooting position, a 4-inch constant eye relief, Diamondcoat lenses for increased light transmission scratch resistance, and finger adjustable, low profile elevation and windage adjustments.

### LPS 1.5-6x42mm
A wide field of view and a generous magnification range make this scope an outstanding choice for all big game hunting. Available in a satin finish.

Duplex (satin) . . . . . . . . . . . . . . . . . . . . $1,476.80
German #1 or German #4 (satin) . . . . . . . . . . . . 1,530.40

### LPS 3.5-14x52mm Adj. Obj.
With a magnification range from 3.5x to 14x, this scope works for all types of hunting. The adjustable objective dial, with increments printed on the slope of the objective bell, can be read without leaving the shooting position. Available in a satin finish.
Duplex (satin) . . . . . . . . . . . . . . . . . . . . . . . $1,569.60
Target Dot, German #1, German #4 (satin) . . . . . 1,623.20
3/4 Min. Mil. Dot (satin) . . . . . . . . . . . . . . . . . 1,703.60

**LPSTM 3.5-14X52mm ADJ. OBJ.**

### SHOTGUN & MUZZLELOADER SCOPES (not shown)

Leupold shotgun scopes are parallax-adjusted to deliver precise focusing at 75 yards. Each scope features a special Heavy Duplex reticle that is more effective against heavy, brushy backgrounds. All scopes have matte finish.

**Prices:**
VARI-X II 1-4x20mm MODEL HEAVY DUPLEX . . . . $421.00
M8-4X33mm HEAVY DUPLEX . . . . . . . . . . . . . . . . 410.00
VARI-X III 2-7X33MM HEAVY DUPLEX . . . . . . . . . . . 463.00

## COMPACT SCOPES

### M8 2.5-20MM COMPACT
This small scope presents the shooter with an enormous field of view for fast target acquisition. It also features generous elevation and windage adjustment. Standard models are parallax adjusted to 100 yards. The Turkey Ranger model, with a special Post & Duplex reticle designed to subtend 9 inches from the post to crosswire at 40 yards, is parallax adjusted to 40 yards. Offered in a matte finish.
Duplex or Heavy Duplex (matte) . . . . . . . . . . . . $316.00
Turkey Ranger (matte) . . . . . . . . . . . . . . . . . . 369.00

M8 4x28MM COMPACT RIMFIRE SPECIAL
  Fine Duplex (gloss) . . . . . . . . . . . . . . . . . 382.00
VARI-X 2-7x28MM COMPACT Duplex (gloss) . . . . . . 467.00
VARI-X 2-7x28MM COMPACT RIMFIRE SPECIAL
  Fine Duplex (gloss) . . . . . . . . . . . . . . . . . 467.00
VARI-X 3-9x33MM COMPACT Duplex (gloss) . . . . . . 519.00
VARI-X 3-9x33MM COMPACT Duplex
  (matte, silver) . . . . . . . . . . . . . . . . . . . . 519.00

### VARI-X 3-9X33MM COMPACT E.F.R.
With an adjustable objective capable of setting parallax as close as 10 meters, this scope is perfectly suited to .22 rimfire silhouette and air rifle shooting.
Duplex (gloss) . . . . . . . . . . . . . . . . . . . . . . $550.00

**M8-2.5x20MM COMPACT**

**4X COMPACT & 4 RF SPECIAL**

**2-7 COMPACT**

**3-9 COMPACT SILVER**

# LEUPOLD SCOPES

## TACTICAL MODELS

**6x42mm AO TACTICAL SCOPE**

The Leupold 6x42mm features 1/4-minute click target-style adjustments for precise corrections in the field. Adjustment travel for windage or elevation is 76 inches. The combination of an exact 6X magnification, adjustable objective and target-style adjustments make it an excellent choice for Hunter Benchrest Competitions as well. Leupold's exclusive Multicoat 4 lens coating is applied to all air-to-glass surfaces to provide the 6X42mm maximum light transmission.
**Length:** 12"  **Weight:** 11.5 ounces
**Two reticles styles:** classic Duplex or a 3/4-minute Military Dot. Black matte finish.
Matte finish . . . . . . . . . . . . . . . . . . . . . . . . . . . . . $628.60
With 3/4-minute Military Dot . . . . . . . . . . . . . . . . . 762.50

**MARK 4 MI 10x40 (MATTE)/MARK 4 MI 16x40 (MATTE)**
**MARK 4 MI 10x40 (MATTE) • M3 10x40 WITH BDC**
  Duplex . . . . . . . . . . . . . . . . . . . . . . . . . . . . . . . . 1,807.00
  Mil Dot . . . . . . . . . . . . . . . . . . . . . . . . . . . . . . . . 1,941.00
**VARI-X II 3-9x40 (MATTE)**
  Duplex . . . . . . . . . . . . . . . . . . . . . . . . . . . . . . . . . 535.00
  Mil Dot . . . . . . . . . . . . . . . . . . . . . . . . . . . . . . . . . 669.00
**VARI-X III 3.5-10x40 (MATTE)**
  Duplex . . . . . . . . . . . . . . . . . . . . . . . . . . . . . . . . . 801.00
  Mil Dot . . . . . . . . . . . . . . . . . . . . . . . . . . . . . . . . . 935.00
**VARI-X III 4.5-14x40 AO (MATTE)**
  Duplex . . . . . . . . . . . . . . . . . . . . . . . . . . . . . . . . . 883.00
  Mil Dot . . . . . . . . . . . . . . . . . . . . . . . . . . . . . . . . 1,017.00

## FIXED POWER SCOPES

### M8-4X

The 4X delivers a widely used magnification and a generous field of view . . . . . . . . . . . . . . . . . . . . . . . . . . . . . $385.00
In black matte finish . . . . . . . . . . . . . . . . . . . . . . . 410.00

**M8-4X33**

### M8-6X

The 6X extends the range for big-game hunting and doubles in some cases as a varmint scope . . . . . . . . . . . $410.00

**M8-6X36**

### M8-6X42mm

Large 42mm objective lens features a 7mm exit pupil for increased light-gathering capability. Recommended for varmint shooting at night.
Duplex or Heavy Duplex . . . . . . . . . . . . . . . . . . . . $510.00
In matte finish . . . . . . . . . . . . . . . . . . . . . . . . . . . 535.00

**M8-6X42mm**

### M8-12X40MM STANDARD (Adj. Obj.)

Outstanding optical qualities, resolution and magnification make the 12X a natural for the varmint shooter. Adjustable objective is standard for parallax-free focusing.
Duplex . . . . . . . . . . . . . . . . . . . . . . . . . . . . . . . . . $571.00
With CPC reticle or Dot . . . . . . . . . . . . . . . . . . . . 625.00

**M8-12X40mm STANDARD**

# LEUPOLD SCOPES

## LONG-RANGE MODELS

*1/4 Minute Click M1 Style Adjustments with Side Focus Parallax*

**VARI-X® III 3.5-10x40MM LONG RANGE M1**

### VARI-X III 3.5-10X40MM LONG RANGE TACTICAL M1

This scope combines the bold 1/4 minute of angle target dial design of the Leupold Mark 4 M1 scopes with the 30 mm maintube and side parallax dial of a long range scope to produce a low profile, close mounted tactical scope of remarkable versatility not only as a tactical scope, but as a sporting scope as well. Available in an all matte (including the Leupold Golden Ring) finish.

Duplex (matte) . . . . . . . . . . . . . . . . . . . . . . . . . **$1,157.00**
Target Dot (matte) . . . . . . . . . . . . . . . . . . . . . . **1,210.00**
3/4 Min. Mil. Dot (matte) . . . . . . . . . . . . . . . . **1,291.00**

### VARI-X III 4.5-14X50MM LONG RANGE

With the increasing popularity of long range shooting, special scopes have been developed to accommodate the additional adjustment necessary to success in this discipline. The 4.5-14x50mm Long Range models with their 30mm maintubes, target style adjustment knobs, and side mounted parallax dials offer the shooter everything necessary to achieve success at great distances.

VARI-X III 4.5-14x50MM LONG RANGE TARGET Fine Duplex (silver) . . . . . . . . . . . . . . . . . . . . . . . . . . . **$1,057.00**
VARI-X III 4.5-14x50MM LONG RANGE TARGET
Target Dot (silver) . . . . . . . . . . . . . . . . . . . . . . **1,110.00**

VARI-X III 4.5-14x50MM LONG RANGE TACTICAL
Fine Duplex (matte) . . . . . . . . . . . . . . . . . . . **1,082.00**
VARI-X III 4.5-14x50MM LONG RANGE TACTICAL
Target Dot (matte) . . . . . . . . . . . . . . . . . . . . **1,135.00**
VARI-X III 4.5-14x50MM LONG RANGE TACTICAL
3/4 Min. Mil. Dot (matte) . . . . . . . . . . . . . . . **1,216.00**

### VARI-X III 6.5-20X50MM LONG RANGE TARGET

Designed with a 30mm maintube to provide additional elevation and windage adjustment, and featuring target style adjustment dials and a side mounted parallax dial, this scope offers the long range shooter impressive magnification and convenient adjustment mechanisms.

Fine Duplex (matte, silver) . . . . . . . . . . . . . . . **$1,166.00**
Target Dot (matte,silver) . . . . . . . . . . . . . . . . . **1,219.00**
3/4 Min. Mil. Dot (matte) . . . . . . . . . . . . . . . . **1,300.00**

### VARI-X III 8.5-25X50MM LONG RANGE TARGET

With a 30mm maintube to provide additional elevation and windage adjustment, target style adjustment dials, and a side mounted parallax dial, this scope offers the long range shooter impressive magnification and convenient adjustment mechanisms.

Fine Duplex (matte) . . . . . . . . . . . . . . . . . . . . . **$1,260.00**
Target Dot (matte) . . . . . . . . . . . . . . . . . . . . . . **1,314.00**

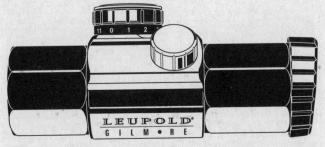

**LG-35, 35MM RED DOT SIGHT**

### LEUPOLD GILMORE RED DOT SIGHTS

The Leupold Gilmore Red Dot Sights feature a compact frame that is easily mounted on any type of firearm, from shotguns and muzzleloaders to rifles and pistols. Eleven dot intensity settings and three different dot sizes available, unlimited eye relief, and 1/3 minute of angle elevation and windage.

### LG-1

2 Minute Dot (matte and silver two tone) . . . . . . **$278.60**

### LG-35

Offered in either solid matte black or a two tone matte and silver finish.

4 Minute Dot (matte, matte and silver two tone) . . . . **$421.40**
8 Minute Dot (matte and silver two tone) . . . . . . . **421.40**

# NIKON MONARCH SCOPES

6.5-20X44 AO

2-7X32

1.5-4x20

5.5-16x44AO

TITANIUM SCOPE
3.3-10x44
5.5-16.5x44

TURKEYPRO

## RIFLESCOPES

MODEL 6500 4x40 Lustre . . . . . . . . . . . . . . . . $330.00
MODEL 6505 4x40 Matte . . . . . . . . . . . . . . . 350.00
MODEL 6510 2-7x32 Lustre . . . . . . . . . . . . . 426.95
MODEL 6515 2-7x32 Matte . . . . . . . . . . . . . . 446.95
MODEL 6520 3-9x40 Lustre . . . . . . . . . . . . . 430.95
MODEL 6525 3-9x40 Matte . . . . . . . . . . . . . . 450.95
MODEL 6528 3-9x40 Silver Matte . . . . . . . . . . 470.95
MODEL 6530 3.5-10x50 Lustre . . . . . . . . . . . . 644.95
MODEL 6535 3.5-10x50 Matte . . . . . . . . . . . . 664.95
MODEL 6540 4-12x40 AO Lustre . . . . . . . . . . . 552.95

MODEL 6545 4-12x40 AO Matte . . . . . . . . . . . . 572.95
MODEL 6550 6.5-20x44 AO Lustre . . . . . . . . . 684.95
MODEL 6555 6.5-20x44 AO Matte . . . . . . . . . . 704.95
MODEL 6570 6.5-20x44 HV . . . . . . . . . . . . . 684.95
MODEL 6575 6.5-20x44 HV . . . . . . . . . . . . . 704.95
MODEL 6630 3.3-10x44 AO . . . . . . . . . . . . . 898.95
MODEL 6680 5.5-16.5x44 AO . . . . . . . . . . . . 938.95

## HANDGUN SCOPES

MODEL 6560 2x20 EER Black Lustre . . . . . . . . . $248.95
MODEL 6565 2x20 EER Silver . . . . . . . . . . . . 268.95

## MONARCH™ UCC RIFLESCOPE SPECIFICATIONS

| Model | 4x40 | 2-7x32 | 3-9x40 | 3.5-10x50 | 4-12x40 AO | 6.5-20x44 AO | 6.5-20x44 AO Hunting | 2x20 EER |
|---|---|---|---|---|---|---|---|---|
| Lustre<br>Matte<br>Silver | #6500<br>#6505<br>- | #6510<br>#6515<br>- | #6520<br>#6525<br>- | #6530<br>#6535<br>- | #6540<br>#6545<br>- | #6550<br>#6555<br>- | #6570<br>#6575<br>- | #6560<br>-<br>#6565 |
| Actual Magnification | 4x | 2x-7x | 3x-9x | 3.5x-10x | 4x-12x | 6.5x-19.46x | 6.5x-19.46x | 1.75x |
| Objective Diameter | 40mm | 32mm | 40mm | 50mm | 40mm | 44mm | 44mm | 20mm |
| Exit Pupil | 10mm | 16-4.6mm | 13.3-4.4mm | 14.3-5mm | 10-3.3mm | 6.7-2.2mm | 6.7-2.2mm | 10mm |
| Eye Relief | 89mm<br>3.5 in. | 101-93mm<br>3.9-3.6 in. | 93-90mm<br>3.6-3.5 in. | 100-98mm<br>3.9-3.8 in. | 92-87mm<br>3.6-3.4 in. | 89-81mm<br>3.5-3.1 in. | 89-81mm<br>3.5-3.1 in. | 670-267mm<br>26.4-10.5 in. |
| Field of View at 100 yards | 26.9 ft. | 44.5-12.7 ft. | 33.8-11.3 ft. | 25.5-8.9 ft. | 25.6-8.5 ft. | 16.1-5.4 ft. | 16.1-5.4 ft. | 22.0 ft. |
| Tube Diameter | 25.4mm<br>1 in. | 25.4mm<br>1 in. | 25.4mm<br>1 in. | 25.4mm<br>1 in. | 25.4mm<br>1 in. | 25.4mm<br>1 in. | 25.4mm<br>1 in. | 25.4mm<br>1 in. |
| Objective Tube Diameter | 47.3mm<br>1.86 in. | 39.3mm<br>1.5 in. | 47.3mm<br>1.86 in. | 57.3mm<br>2.2 in. | 53.1mm<br>2.09 in. | 54mm<br>2.13 in. | 54mm<br>2.13 in. | 25.4mm<br>1 in. |
| Eyepiece O.D. Diameter | 38mm<br>1.5 in. | 38mm<br>1.5 in. | 38mm<br>1.5 in. | 38mm<br>1.5 in. | 38mm<br>1.5 in. | 38mm<br>1.5 in. | 38mm<br>1.5 in. | 35.5mm<br>1.4 in. |
| Length | 297mm<br>11.7 in. | 283mm<br>11.1 in. | 312mm<br>12.3 in. | 350mm<br>13.7 in. | 348.5mm<br>13.7 in. | 373mm<br>14.6 in. | 373mm<br>14.6 in. | 207mm<br>8.1 in. |
| Weight | 315 g.<br>11.2 oz. | 315 g.<br>11.2 oz. | 355 g.<br>12.6 oz. | 435 g.<br>15.5 oz. | 475 g.<br>16.9 oz. | 565 g.<br>20.1 oz. | 565 g.<br>20.1 oz. | 185 g.<br>6.6 oz. |
| Adjustment Graduation | ¼:1 Click<br>½:1 Div. | ¼:1 Click<br>¼:1 Div. | ¼:1 Click<br>¼:1 Div. | ¼:1 Click<br>¼:1 Div. | ¼:1 Click<br>¼:1 Div. | ⅛:1 Click<br>⅛:1 Div. | ⅛:1 Click<br>⅛:1 Div. | ¼:1 Click<br>½:1 Div. |
| Max. Internal Adjustment (moa) | 120 | 70 | 55 | 45 | 45 | 38 | 38 | 120 |
| Parallax Setting (yards) | 100 | 100 | 100 | 100 | 50 to infinity | 50 to infinity | 50 to infinity | 100 |

# NIKON BUCKMASTER SCOPES

**SPECIAL LIMITED EDITION 3-9x40**

4.5-14

Nikon has teamed with Buckmasters to produce a limited edition riflescope line. The first products in this line are a 3-9x40 variable, a large objective 3-9x50 variable and a 4x40 fixed power scope. Built to withstand the toughest hunting conditions, the new scopes integrate shockproof, fogproof and waterproof construction, plus numerous other features seldom found on riflescopes in this price range. Nikon's Brightvue™ anti-reflective system of high-quality, multicoated lenses provides over 93% anti-reflection capability for high levels of light transmission and optical clarity required for dawn-to-dusk big game hunting. These riflescopes are parallax-adjusted at 100 yards and have durable matte finishes that reduce glare while afield. They also feature positive steel-to-brass, quarter-minute-click windage and elevation adjustments for instant, repeatable accuracy and a Nikoplex® reticle for quick target acquisition.

*Prices:* MODEL 6465 1x20 . . . . . . . . . . . . . . . . . . $240.95
MODEL 6405 4x40 . . . . . . . . . . . . . . . . . . . . . . 244.95
MODEL 6425 3-9x40 BLACK MATTE . . . . . . . . . . . . 302.95
MODEL 6415 3-9x40 SILVER . . . . . . . . . . . . . . . . 324.95
MODEL 6435 3-9x50 . . . . . . . . . . . . . . . . . . . . . 452.95
MODEL 6450 4.5-14x40 AO BLCK MATTE . . . . . . . . 400.95
MODEL 6455 4.5-14x40 AO SILVER . . . . . . . . . . . . 420.95

## SPECIFICATIONS

| | 4x40 | 3-9x40 | 3-9x50 | 4.5-14x40 |
|---|---|---|---|---|
| MODEL | #6405 | #6415, #6425 | #6435 | #6450, #6455 |
| Actual Magnification | 4x | 3x-9x | 3x-9x | 4.5-13.5x |
| Objective Diameter | 40mm | 40mm | 50mm | 40mm |
| Exit Pupil | 10mm | 13.3-4.4mm | 16.7-5.5mm | 8.9-2.9mm |
| Eye Relief | 3.5 in. | 3.6-3.5 in. | 3.6-3.5 in. | 3.6-3.4 in. |
| Field of View at 100 yards | 26.9 ft. | 33.8-11.3 ft. | 33.8-11.3 ft. | 22.5-7.5 ft. |
| Tube Diameter | 1 in. | 1 in. | 1 in. | 1 in. |
| Objective Tube Diameter | 1.86 in. | 1.86 in. | 2.2 in. | 2.1 in. |
| Eyepiece O.D. Diameter | 1.5 in. | 1.5 in. | 1.5 in. | 1.5 in. |
| Length | 11.7 in. | 12.3 in. | 12 in. | 14.8 in. |
| Weight | 11.2 oz. | 12.6 oz. | 12.7 oz. | 18.7 oz. |
| Adjustment | 1/4: 1 Click | 1/4: 1 Click | 1/4: 1 Click | 1/4: 1 Click |
| Graduation | 1/2: 1 Div. | 1/4: 1 Div. | 1/4: 1 Div. | 1/4: 1 Div. |
| Max. Internal Adjustment (moa) | 80 | 80 | 70 | 40 |
| Parallax Setting (yards) | 100 | 100 | 100 | 50-∞ |

# PENTAX SCOPES

## LIGHTSEEKER II RIFLESCOPES

**4X-16XAO** LIGHTSEEKER **II**
**$844.00**

**3X-9X** LIGHTSEEKER **II**
**$636.00** (Glossy)  **$660.00** (Matte)

**6X-24XAO** LIGHTSEEKER **II**
**$878.00**

*Features:*
- **Scratch-resistant outer tube.** Under ordinary wear and tear, the outer tube is almost impossible to scratch.
- **High Quality cam zoom tube.** No plastics are used. The tube is made of a bearing-type brass with precision machined cam slots. The zoom control screws are precision-ground to 1/2 of one thousandth tolerance.
- **Leak Prevention.** The power rings are sealed on a separate precision-machined seal tube. The scopes are then filled with nitrogen and double-sealed with heavy-duty "O" rings, making them leak-proof and fog-proof.
- **Excellent eyepieces.** The eyepiece lenses have a greater depth of field than most others. Thus, a more focused target at 100, 200 or 500 yards is attainable. Most Pentax Riflescopes are available in High Gloss, Matte or Satin Chrome finish.

**PENTAX CORPORATION** expands its extensive line of scopes by adding a Mil-Dot reticle option to three of its current models. The Mil-Dot reticle is an extremely accurate device for estimating range up to 1,000 yards, which increases the degree of accuracy for the shooter. First featured on the **PENTAX** 8.5X-32X Lightseeker, Mil-Dot reticles are now also available on the 3X-9X, 4X-16X, and 6X-24X Lightseeker scopes.

The Mil-Dot reticle looks like a standard crosshair, with the addition of four oval dots radiating in each direction from the center. The distance from each dot to the next is one mil, or one yard at one thousand yards. If the shooter knows the height or width of the target or other nearby object, the range to the target can be estimated accurately by making a simple calculation or referring to a Mil-Dot chart.

# PENTAX RIFLESCOPES

## LIGHTSEEKER RIFLESCOPES

**2.5 LIGHTSEEKER SG PLUS
MOSSY OAK® BREAK-UP SCOPE**

**ZERO-X/V SG PLUS
TURKEY STILL-TARGET COMPETITION**

## LIGHTSEEKER RIFLESCOPE SPECIFICATIONS

| MODEL | OBJECTIVE DIAMETER (MM) | EYEPIECE DIAMETER (MM) | EXIT PUPIL (MM) | EYE RELIEF (IN.) | FIELD OF VIEW (FT 100 YD) | ADJUSTMENT GRADUATION (IN 100YD) | MAXIMUM ADJUSTMENT (IN 100 YD) | LENGTH (IN.) | WEIGHT (OZ.) | RETICLE* | RECOMMENDED USE** | PRICES |
|---|---|---|---|---|---|---|---|---|---|---|---|---|
| LIGHTSEEKER 1.75X-6X | 35 | 36 | 15.3-5 | 3.5-4.0 | 71-20 | 1/2 | 110 | 10.75 | 13.0 | P or HP | BG,DG,SG/P | $526.00-546.00 |
| LIGHTSEEKER 2X-8X | 39 | 36 | 11.0-4.0 | 3.5-4.0 | 53-17 | 1/3 | 80 | 11.7 | 14.0 | P | BG,DG,SG/P | 560.00-594.00 |
| LIGHTSEEKER 3X-9X | 43 | 36 | 12.0-5.0 | 3.5-4.0 | 36-14 | 1/4 | 50 | 12.7 | 15.0 | P, HP or MD | BG | 594.00-798.00 |
| LIGHTSEEKER 3.5X-10X | 50 | 36 | 11.0-5.0 | 3.5-4.0 | 29.5-11 | 1/4 | 50 | 14.0 | 19.5 | HP, P | BG,V | 630.00-662.00 |
| LIGHTSEEKER 4X-16X AO | 44 | 36 | 10.4-2.8 | 3.5-4.0 | 33-9 | 1/4 | 35 | 15.4 | 22.7 | MD, HP, P | T,V,BG | 796.00-978.00 |
| LIGHTSEEKER 6X-24X AO | 44 | 36 | 6.9-2.3 | 3.5-4.0 | 18-5.5 | 1/8 | 26 | 16.0 | 23.7 | FP or MD | T,V | 856.00-1018.00 |
| LIGHTSEEKER 8.5X-32X AO | 44 | 36 | 5.0-1.4 | 3.5-4.0 | 13-3.8 | 1/8 | 26 | 17.2 | 24.0 | FP or MD | T,V | 944.00-1098.00 |
| LIGHTSEEKER 2.5X SG PLUS | 25 | 36 | 7.0 | 3.5-4.0 | 55 | 1/2 | 60 | 10.0 | 9.0 | DW | BG,DG,TK | 350.00-364.00 |
| LIGHTSEEKER ZERO-X SG PLUS | 27 | 35 | 19.5 | 4.5-15 | 51 | 1/2 | 196 | 8.9 | 7.9 | DW | BG,DG,TK | 372.00 |
| LIGHTSEEKER ZERO-X/V SG PLUS | 27 | 35 | 19.5-5.5 | 3.5-7 | 53.8-15 | 1/2 | 129 | 8.9 | 10.3 | HP | BG,DG,TK | 454.00 |
| LIGHTSEEKER ZERO-X/V SG PLUS TURKEY STILL-TARGET COMPETITION | 27 | 35 | 19.5-5.5 | 3.5-7 | 53.8-1.5 | 1/2 | 129 | 8.9 | 10.3 | CP | BG,DG,TK | 476.00 |

All scope tubes measure 1 inch in diameter. Scopes are available in high-gloss black, matte black, satin chrome or camouflage, depending on model. *P = Penta-Plex  FP = Fine-Plex  DW = Deepwoods Plex  D = Dot  HP = Heavy Plex  MD = Mil Dot  **BG = Big Game  SG/P = Small Game/Pinking  V= Varmint  DG = Dangerous Game  T = Target  TK = Turkey  CP = Comp-Plex  Add **$20** for matte finish

# Sako Scope Mounts

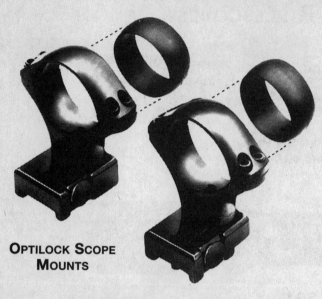

**Optilock Scope Mounts**

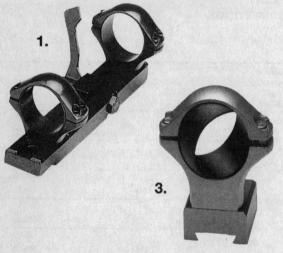

**1.**

**3.**

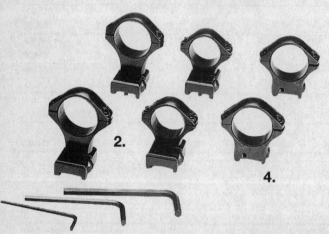

**2.**

**4.**

### OPTILOCK SCOPE MOUNTS

Sako Optilock™ mount keeps the scope centered in all conditions. The scope rests in a tight but gentle grip of the evolutionary ball-bearing type ring. The clasping force is distributed evenly along the scope shaft, not spotlike as in conventional mounts, ensuring your valuable optics won't become twisted or scratched. The mounting of the scope is easier and the point of impact stays intact if the scope and mounts are removed as a unit. Available in 1"/25, 4 mm and 30 mm diameters and 3 heights, also in stainless, to fit any scope.

*Prices:*
1" Low, Medium & High
   (Short, Medium & Long Action) . . . . . . . . . . . . . **$98.00**
30mm Low, Medium & High
   (Short, Medium & Long Action) . . . . . . . . . . . . . **116.00**
1" Medium & High Extended Base
   Scope Mounts . . . . . . . . . . . . . . . . . . . . . . . . . **154.00**

| Scope tube diameter ø | Mount height | mm | Scope lens. end max ø |
|---|---|---|---|
| **1.** *Quickmount for Sako TRG* | | | |
| 1" | Low | 30,5 | 58 |
| 1" | Medium | 35,5 | 68 |
| 1" | High | 40,5 | 78 |
| 30 mm | Low | 32,5 | 62 |
| 30 mm | Medium | 36,5 | 70 |
| 30 mm | High | 40,5 | 78 |
| **2.** *Steel base mount for Sako 75.* *Extended version also available.* | | | |
| 1" | Low | 30,5 | 55...63 |
| 1" | Medium | 35,5 | 65...73 |
| 1" | High | 40,5 | 75...83 |
| 30 mm | Low | 32,5 | 59...67 |
| 30 mm | Medium | 36,5 | 67...75 |
| 30 mm | High | 40,5 | 75...83 |
| **3.** *Stainless base mount for Sako 75* | | | |
| 1" | Low | 30,5 | 55...63 |
| 1" | Medium | 35,5 | 65...73 |
| 30 mm | Low | 32,5 | 59...67 |
| 30 mm | Medium | 36,5 | 67...75 |
| **4.** *Steel ring mount for Sako 75* | | | |
| 1" | Low | 27 | 48...56 |
| 30 mm | Low | 29 | 52...60 |
| Special aluminum scope mount for 11 mm rail for Sako Finnfire | | | |
| 1" | Low | 27 | 48...56 |

Standard rings without inner Optilock fastening ring.

Indicated maximum outer diameter of objective end shows values both for heavy barrel (smaller) and standard barrel.

# SCHMIDT & BENDER RIFLE SCOPES

### L.E.R. 2.5-10X56 VARIABLE POWER SCOPE $1390.00

*Also available:* 1.25-4X20 VARIABLE POWER SCOPE . . . **$995.00**
**1.5-6X42** VARIABLE POWER SCOPE . . . . . . . . . . . . **1125.00**
**3-12X42** VARIABLE POWER SCOPE. . . . . . . . . . . **1290.00**
**3-12X50** VARIABLE POWER SCOPE. . . . . . . . . . . **1360.00**
**4-16X50** VARIABLE POWER SCOPE. . . . . . . . . . . **1525.00**
*Note:* All variable power scopes have glass reticles and are available in steel and aluminum

*Also available:*
**4X36** FIXED POWER SCOPE
1" Steel Tube w/o Mounting Rail . . . . . . . . . . . . **$760.00**
**6X42** FIXED POWER SCOPE
Steel Tube w/o Mounting Rail . . . . . . . . . . . . . . **835.00**
**8X56** FIXED POWER SCOPE
Steel Tube w/o Mounting Rail . . . . . . . . . . . . . . **960.00**
**10X42** FIXED POWER SCOPE
Steel Tube w/o Mounting Rail . . . . . . . . . . . . . . **955.00**

## ILLUMINATED SCOPES

This 1.25-4x is designed for use on magnum rifles and for quick shots at dangerous game. Long eye relief, and a wide field of view (31.5 yards at 200 yards) speed your aim. The new Flash Dot reticle shows up bright against the target at the center of the crosswire.

*Magnification:* 1.25-4X
*Objective lens diameter:* 12.7-20mm
*Field of view at 100m:* 32m-10m; at 100 yards: 96'-16'
*Objective housing diameter:* 30mm
*Scope tube diameter:* 30mm
*Twilight factor:* 3,7-8,9  *Lenses:* hard multi-coating
*Click value 1 click @100 meters:* 15mm; @100 yards: .540"
*Price:* . . . . . . . . . . . . . . . . . . . . . . . . . . . **$1480.00**
*Also available:*
ILLUMINATED RETICLES
1.5-6x42 . . . . . . . . . . . . . . . . . . . . . . . . . . . **1525.00**
3-12x50 . . . . . . . . . . . . . . . . . . . . . . . . . . . **1640.00**
2.5-10x56 . . . . . . . . . . . . . . . . . . . . . . . . . . **1725.00**

## VARMINT

Designed for long-range target shooters and varmint hunters, Schmidt & Bender 4-16X50 "Varmint" riflescope features a precise parallax adjustment located in a third turret on the left side of the scope, making setting adjustments quick and convenient. The fine crosshairs of Reticle No. 6 and 8 cover only 1.5mm at 100 meters (.053" at 100 yards) throughout the entire magnification range.

*Magnification:* 4-16X
*Objective lens diameter:* 50mm
*Field of view at 100m:* 7.5-2.5m; at 100 yards: 22.5'-7.5'
*Objective housing diameter:* 57mm
*Scope tube diameter:* 30mm
*Twilight factor:* 14-28
*Lenses:* Hard multi-coating
*Click value 1 click @100 meters:* 10mm; @100 yards: .360"
*Price:* . . . . . . . . . . . . . . . . . . . . . . . . . . . **$1,595.00**

## POLICE/MARKSMAN RIFLESCOPES
### (shown next page)

This line of riflescopes was designed specifically to meet the needs of the precision sharpshooter. It includes fixed-power scopes in 6X42 and 10X42 magnifications and variable-power scopes in 1.5-6X42, 3-12X42 and 3-12X50 configurations. The 3-12X50 is available in two models: Standard (for shooting to 500 yards) and a military version (MIL) designed for ranges up to 1000 yards. Each scope is equipped with two elevation adjustment rings: a neutral ring with 1/4" 100-yard clicks, which can be matched to any caliber and bullet weight, and a second ring calibrated for a 308 (7.62 NATO) 168-grain bullet.

### POLICE/MARKSMAN

|  |  | 30mm | Alum. |
|---|---|---|---|
| 10x42 PMII | P3 | 1085.00 | 813.75 |
|  |  | 34mm | Alum. |
| 3-12x50 PMII | P1-P3 | 1555.00 | 1166.25 |
| 3-12x50/Parallax | P1-P3 | 1785.00 | 1338.75 |
| 3-12x50/Lighted | P3L | 1905.00 | 1428.75 |
| 4-16x50/Parallax | P3 | 1870.00 | 1402.50 |

# SCHMIDT & BENDER

## POLICE/MARKSMAN II

**PM II**

## SPECIFICATIONS

| | 10 x 42 | 3-12 x 50 | 3-12 x 50 W/PARALLAX ADJ. | 3-12 x 50 ILLLUMINATED | 4-16 x 50 W/PARALLAX ADJ. |
|---|---|---|---|---|---|
| Magnification | 10x | 3-12x | 3-12x | 3-12x | 4-16x |
| Field of View | 4m | 11.1-4.2m | 11.1-4.2m | 11.1-4.2m | 7.5-2.5m |
| (100m/100yd) | 12' | 33.3-12.6' | 33.3-12.6' | 33.3-12.6' | 22.5-7.5' |
| Objective | | | | | |
| Diameter | 42mm | 50mm | 50mm | 50mm | 5mm |
| Exit Pupil | 4.2mm | 14.3-4.3mm | 14.3-4.3mm | 14.3-4.3mm | 12.5-3.1mm |
| (mm/inches) | .165" | .563-.169" | .563-.169" | .563-.169" | .492"-.122" |
| Twilight Factor | 20.5 | 11.4-24.5 | 11.4-24.5 | 11.4-24.5 | 14-28 |
| Eye Relief | 95mm | 995mm | 95mm | 95mm | 95mm |
| (mm/inches) | 3.74" | 3.74" | 3.74" | 3.74" | 3.74" |
| Middle Tube | | | | | |
| Diameter | 30mm | 34mm | 34mm | 34mm | 34mm |
| Weight | 520g | 7600g | 810g | 780g | 880g |
| (gram/lb., oz.) | 1 lb. 2 oz. | 1 lb. 2.5 oz. | 1 lb. 12.5 oz. | 1 lb. 11.5 oz. | 1 lb. 15 oz. |
| Adj. Range @ | *270 cm/97" | 200 cm/72" | 200 cm/72" | 200 cm/72" | 185 cm/67" |
| (100m/100 yd) | **250 cm/990" | 180 cm/64.8" | 180 cm/64.8" | 180 cm/64.8" | 170 cm/61.2" |
| | ***130 cm/46.8" | 130 cm/46.8" | 130 cm/46.8" | 130 cm/46.8" | 130 cm/46.8" |

*Using the very ends of the elevation adjustment will reduce the windage adjustment range   **Sighting-in adjustment range without restriction of windage
***With adjustment knob locked in place

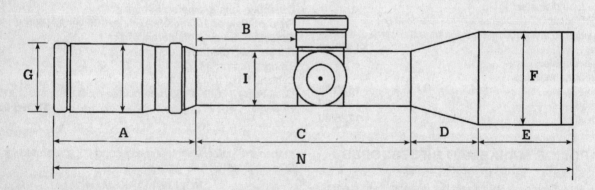

## DIMENSIONS

| Model | A | B | C | D | E | F | G | I | N |
|---|---|---|---|---|---|---|---|---|---|
| 10x42 | 98mm | 56mm | 139mm | 55mm | 54mm | 50mm | 43mm | 30mm | 346mm |
| | 3.858" | 2,204" | 5.472" | 2.165" | 2.126" | 1.969" | 1.693" | | 13.622" |
| 3-12x50 | 101.3mm | 68.3mm | 145.4mm | 43.5mm | 64.8mm | 57mm | 43mm | 34mm | 355mm |
| | 3.988" | 2.689" | 6.076" | 1.713" | 3.354" | 2.244" | 1.693" | | 13.976" |
| 4-16x50 | 101.3mm | 68.3mm | 145.4mm | 85.2mm | 75.5mm | 57mm | 43mm | 34mm | 405.7mm |
| | 3.988" | 2.689" | 6.076" | 1.713" | 3.354" | 2.244" | 1.693" | | 15.972" |

# SCHMIDT & BENDER

## SCOPES FOR LONG RANGE SHOOTING

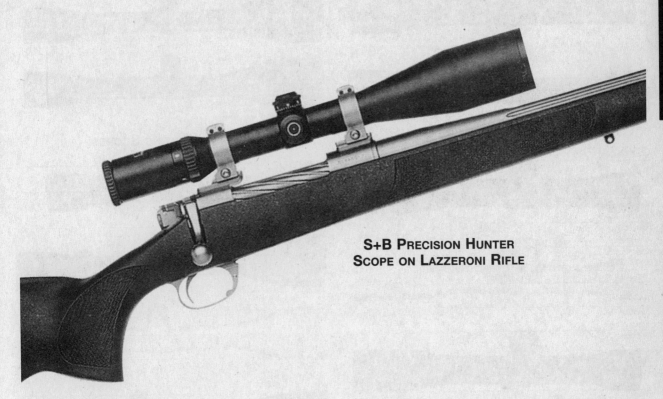

**S+B PRECISION HUNTER
SCOPE ON LAZZERONI RIFLE**

## PRECISION HUNTER

Very accurate rifles, high-speed cartridges and modern bullets make it possible to shoot very accurately at long distances...with the right scope. Your scope must let you see the target clearly. It must help determine the distance, bullet drop, and wind drift, and it must do it quickly and precisely.

PRECISION HUNTER scopes combine the optical quality of S&B hunting scopes, the most appropriate magnification ranges, and a sophisticated mil-dot reticle (developed by the U.S. Marine Corps) with a bullet drop compensator to give you the ability and confidence to place an accurate shot at up to 500 yards. Three different models are available:

### 4-16 X 50 PRECISION HUNTER SCOPE WITH PARALLAX ADJUSTMENT

Set on 4 power, the mil-dot reticle with fine crosshairs and four posts allows quick target acquisition.

Turned up to 16 power, the mil-dots become visible and can be used for range, trajectory and windage calculations. The top-mounted bullet drop compensator has 5mm (1/5") clicks, permitting quick adjustments up to 500 yards.

The windage adjustment also has 5mm (1/5") clicks, allowing for precise sighting in.

The standard elevation adjustment knob has graduations and numbers that allow you to create a meaningful distance chart for your preferred caliber. A blank elevation knob can be special-ordered with markings you can specify after sighting in your rifle.

A parallax adjustment is conveniently located in a third turret on the left side. This allows you to easily make necessary adjustments with the rifle shouldered, ready to shoot.
*Price:* . . . . . . . . . . . . . . . . . . . . . . . . . . . . . . . . **$1,555.00**

### 3-12 X 50 PRECISION HUNTER

Identical to the 4-16 x 50 with mil-dot reticle but 1cm (2/5") clicks and no parallax adjustment. It is factory-adjusted to be parallax free at 200 meters.
*Price:* . . . . . . . . . . . . . . . . . . . . . . . . . . . . . . . . **$1,285.00**

### 2.5-10 X 56 PRECISION HUNTER

Identical to the 3-12 x 50, but with 1 cm (2/5") clicks for windage and elevation adjustment and with our Reticle No. 9, which makes it suitable for dangerous game.
*Price:* . . . . . . . . . . . . . . . . . . . . . . . . . . . . . . . . **$1,325.00**

# SIGHTRON SCOPES

## SIGHTRON SHOTGUN SCOPES

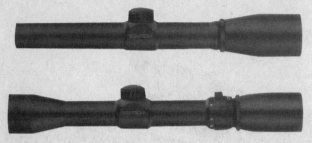

## SIGHTRON PISTOL SCOPES

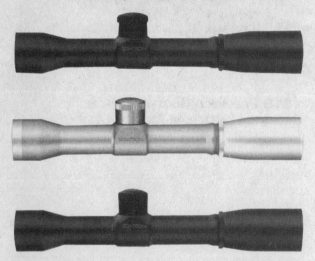

## SIGHTRON SERIES III 10x42 WITH SIDE-MOUNTED ("SADDLE") PARALLAX ADJUSTMENT

Sightron's scopeline offers nearly 40 models in fixed and variable power at modest prices. The SII series features 1-inch alloy tubes; the SIII 10 x 42 and 3.5-10x44 have 30 mm magnesium tubes, multicoated lenses, aspherical eyepiece glass and "saddle" mounted parallax adjustments. Most target and competition scopes feature 1/8-minute clicks. Sightron offers stainless finish and a broad choice of reticles including the mil dot.

*Prices:* SIII 10x42 mil dot . . . . . . . . . . . . . . . . . . . . **$596.00**
SIII 3.5-10x44 mil dot . . . . . . . . . . . . . . . . . . . . . . . **696.00**
SII shotgun 2.5-7x32 . . . . . . . . . . . . . . . . . . . . . . . **200.00**
SII shotgun 2.5x20 . . . . . . . . . . . . . . . . . . . . . . . . . **147.00**
SII pistol 1x28 . . . . . . . . . . . . . . . . . . . . . . . . . . . . **161.00**
SII pistol 2x28 . . . . . . . . . . . . . . . . . . . . . . . . . . . . **161.00**
*SII hunting scopes:*
3-9x42 . . . . . . . . . . . . . . . . . . . . . . . . . . . . . . . . . . **247.00**
1.5-6x42 . . . . . . . . . . . . . . . . . . . . . . . . . . . . . . . . . **260.00**

## SIGHTRON BENCHREST SCOPES

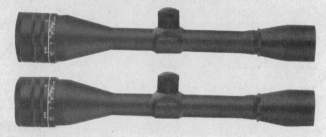

## SIGHTRON HUNTING SCOPES

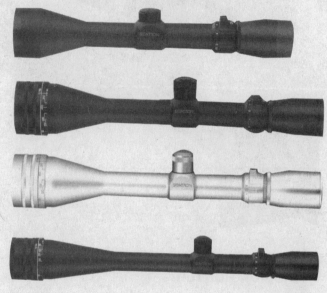

2.5-8x42 . . . . . . . . . . . . . . . . . . . . . . . . . . . . . . . . **234.00**
3-12x42 . . . . . . . . . . . . . . . . . . . . . . . . . . . . . . . . . **262.00**
3.5-10x42 . . . . . . . . . . . . . . . . . . . . . . . . . . . . . . . **273.00**
3.5-10x50 . . . . . . . . . . . . . . . . . . . . . . . . . . . . . . . **318.00**
4.5-14x42 . . . . . . . . . . . . . . . . . . . . . . . . . . . . . . . **341.00**
4.5-14x50 . . . . . . . . . . . . . . . . . . . . . . . . . . . . . . . **341.00**
6.5-25x50 . . . . . . . . . . . . . . . . . . . . . . . . . . . . . . . **422.00**
*SII target scopes:*
4-16x42 . . . . . . . . . . . . . . . . . . . . . . . . . . . . . . . . . **342.00**
6-24x42 . . . . . . . . . . . . . . . . . . . . . . . . . . . . . . . . . **354.00**
10-40x42 . . . . . . . . . . . . . . . . . . . . . . . . . . . . . . . . **400.00**
*SII competition scopes:*
3-9x42 mil dot . . . . . . . . . . . . . . . . . . . . . . . . . . . . **278.00**
3-12x42 mil dot . . . . . . . . . . . . . . . . . . . . . . . . . . . **300.00**
4-16x42 mil dot . . . . . . . . . . . . . . . . . . . . . . . . . . . **403.00**
6-24x42 mil dot . . . . . . . . . . . . . . . . . . . . . . . . . . . **428.00**
24x42 AO . . . . . . . . . . . . . . . . . . . . . . . . . . . . . . . **296.00**
36x42 AO . . . . . . . . . . . . . . . . . . . . . . . . . . . . . . . **378.00**
6x42 AO . . . . . . . . . . . . . . . . . . . . . . . . . . . . . . . . **291.00**
*SII compact scopes:*
4x32 . . . . . . . . . . . . . . . . . . . . . . . . . . . . . . . . . . . **154.00**
2.5-10x32 . . . . . . . . . . . . . . . . . . . . . . . . . . . . . . . **234.00**

# SIGHTRON SCOPES

## EXACTRACK

Conventional scopes have a curve surface against a flat surface. This contact is only complete at zero adjustment. As the adjustments press the erector tube in any direction, the contact becomes imperfect causing the reticle to drift from the optical center. Also, in many cases since the point of contact is less than what is required to hold the erector tube in position, point of impact can shift. Sightron has developed a new erector tube with an integral ring. ExacTrack will keep constant and perfect point-of-impact, at or off zero. This constant pressure point will insure the accuracy of all Sightron scopes under heavy recoil and severe use afield.

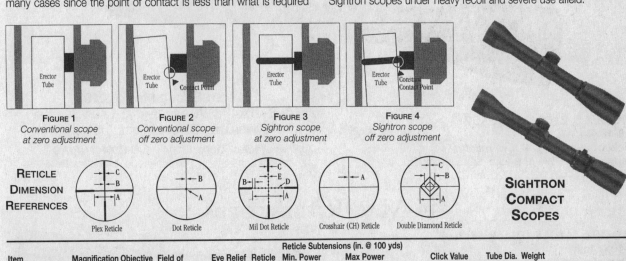

**FIGURE 1**
Conventional scope
at zero adjustment

**FIGURE 2**
Conventional scope
off zero adjustment

**FIGURE 3**
Sightron scope
at zero adjustment

**FIGURE 4**
Sightron scope
off zero adjustment

**RETICLE DIMENSION REFERENCES**

Plex Reticle    Dot Reticle    Mil Dot Reticle    Crosshair (CH) Reticle    Double Diamond Reticle

**SIGHTRON COMPACT SCOPES**

| Item Number | Magnification | Objective Dia. (mm) | Field of View (ft @ 100 yds.) | Eye Relief (in.) | Reticle Type | Reticle Subtensions (in. @ 100 yds) | | Click Value (in. @ 100 yds) | Tube Dia. (in.) | Weight (oz.) | Finish | A |
|---|---|---|---|---|---|---|---|---|---|---|---|---|
| | | | | | | Min. Power A/B/C/D/E | Max Power A/B/C/D/E | | | | | |
| **SIII SERIES RIFLE SCOPES** | | | | | | | | | | | | |
| **30 mm Side Saddle Rifle Scopes** | | | | | | | | | | | | |
| SIII10X42MD | 10X | 42 | 9.2 | 3.5 | Mil-Dot | 36/3.6/1.15/.8/.23 | | 1/4 MOA | 1.1875 | 23.60 | Satin Black | 13.56 |
| SIII3.510X44MD | 3.5-10X | 44 | 28-9.2 | 3.5 | Mil-Dot | 102.6/10.26/3.25/2.2/.69 | 36/3.6/1.15/.8/.23 | 1/4 MOA | 1.1875 | 24.60 | Satin Black | 13.56 |
| **SII SERIES RIFLE SCOPES** | | | | | | | | | | | | |
| **Variable Power Rifle Scopes** | | | | | | | | | | | | |
| SII.56X42 | 1.5-6X | 42 | 50-15 | 4.0-3.8 | Plex | 79.0/1.33/5.32 | 19.8/.33/1.32 | 1/4 MOA | 1.0 | 14.00 | Satin Black | 11.69 |
| SII2.58X42 | 2.5-8X | 42 | 36-12 | 3.6-4.2 | Plex | 48.0/.80/3.20 | 15.0/.25/1.0 | 1/4 MOA | 1.0 | 12.82 | Satin Black | 11.89 |
| SII39X42 | 3-9X | 42 | 34-12 | 3.6-4.2 | Plex | 39.9/.66/2.66 | 13.2/.22/.88 | 1/4 MOA | 1.0 | 13.22 | Satin Black | 12.00 |
| SII39X42ST | 3-9X | 42 | 34-12 | 3.6-4.2 | Plex | 39.9/.66/2.66 | 13.2/.22/.88 | 1/4 MOA | 1.0 | 13.22 | Stainless | 12.00 |
| SII39X42D | 3-9X | 42 | 34-12 | 3.6-4.2 | Dot | 4/.66 | 1.3/.22 | 1/4 MOA | 1.0 | 13.22 | Satin Black | 12.00 |
| SII312X42 | 3-12X | 42 | 32-9 | 3.6-4.2 | Plex | 39.9/.66/2.66 | 9.9/.16/.66 | 1/4 MOA | 1.0 | 12.99 | Satin Black | 11.89 |
| SII3.510X50 | 3.5-10X | 50 | 30-10 | 4 | Plex | 34.2/.57/2.28 | 12.0/.20/.80 | 1/4 MOA | 1.0 | 14.77 | Satin Black | 11.89 |
| SII4.514X50 | 4.5-14X | 50 | 23-8 | 3.8 | Plex | 26.4/.44/1.76 | 8.4/.14/.56 | 1/4 MOA | 1.0 | 15.45 | Satin Black | 11.89 |
| SII6.525X50 | 6.5-25X | 50 | 15-4.2 | 4 | Plex | 18.5/.3/1.2 | 4.8/0.1/.3 | 1/4 MOA | 1.0 | 19.30 | Satin Black | 14.70 |
| **Variable Power Target Scopes** | | | | | | | | | | | | |
| SII416X42 | 4-16X | 42 | 26-7 | 3.6 | Plex | 30/.50/2.0 | 7.5/.125/.50 | 1/8 MOA | 1.0 | 16.00 | Satin Black | 13.62 |
| SII416X2ST | 4-16X | 42 | 26-7 | 3.6 | Plex | 30/.50/2.0 | 7.5/.125/.50 | 1/8 MOA | 1.0 | 16.00 | Stainless | 13.62 |
| SII416X42D | 4-16X | 42 | 26-7 | 3.6 | Dot | 1.7/.10 | .425/.025 | 1/8 MOA | 1.0 | 16.00 | Satin Black | 13.62 |
| SII416X42DST | 4-16X | 42 | 26-7 | 3.6 | Dot | 1.7/.10 | .425/.025 | 1/8 MOA | 1.0 | 16.00 | Stainless | 13.62 |
| SII624X42 | 6-24X | 42 | 15.7-4.4 | 3.6 | Plex | 19.8/.33/1.32 | 4.8/.08/.32 | 1/8 MOA | 1.0 | 18.70 | Satin Black | 14.60 |
| SII624X42ST | 6-24X | 42 | 15.7-4.4 | 3.6 | Plex | 19.8/.33/1.32 | 4.8/.08/.32 | 1/8 MOA | 1.0 | 18.70 | Stainless | 14.60 |
| SII624X42D | 6-24X | 42 | 15.7-4.4 | 3.6 | Dot | 1.12/.066 | .27/.016 | 1/8 MOA | 1.0 | 18.70 | Satin Black | 14.60 |
| SII624X42DST | 6-24X | 42 | 15.7-4.4 | 3.6 | Dot | 1.12/.066 | .27/.016 | 1/8 MOA | 1.0 | 18.70 | Stainless | 14.60 |
| SII1040X42 | 10-40X | 42 | 8.9-4.0 | 3.6 | Dot | .50/.066 | 0.12/.016 | 1/8 MOA | 1.0 | 19.00 | Satin Black | 16.06 |
| **Competition/Tactical Scopes** | | | | | | | | | | | | |
| SII39X42MD | 3-9X | 42 | 34-14 | 3.6-4.2 | Mil-Dot | 150/15/10/4/1 | 50/5/3.3/1/3/.3 | 1/4 MOA | 1.0 | 13.22 | Satin Black | 12.00 |
| SII312X42MD | 3-12X | 42 | 32-9 | 3.6-4.2 | Mil-Dot | 144/14/7.7/3.1/.7 | 36/3.6/1.2/.79/.1 | 1/4 MOA | 1.0 | 12.99 | Satin Black | 11.89 |
| SII416X42MD | 4-16X | 42 | 26-7 | 3.6 | Mil-Dot | 144/14/4.7/3.1/.6 | 36/3.6/1.2/.79/.1 | 1/8 MOA | 1.0 | 16.00 | Satin Black | 13.62 |
| SII416X42MDST | 4-16X | 42 | 26-7 | 3.6 | Mil-Dot | 144/14/4.7/3.1/.6 | 36/3.6/1.2/.79/.1 | 1/8 MOA | 1.0 | 16.00 | Stainless | 13.62 |
| SII624X42MD | 6-24X | 42 | 15.7-4.4 | 3.6 | Mil-Dot | 144/14/4.7/3.1/.4 | 36/3.6/1.2/.79/.1 | 1/8 MOA | 1.0 | 18.70 | Satin Black | 14.60 |
| SII624X42MDST | 6-24X | 42 | 15.7-4.4 | 3.6 | Mil-Dot | 144/14/4.7/3.1/.4 | 36/3.6/1.2/.79/.1 | 1/8 MOA | 1.0 | 18.70 | Stainless | 14.60 |
| SII24X42 | 24X | 42 | 4.1 | 4.33 | Dot | .27/.016 | | 1/8 MOA | 1.0 | 15.87 | Satin Black | 13.30 |
| SII36X42BRD | 36X | 42 | 3.65 | 3.92 | Dot | .125/.020 | | 1/8 MOA | 1.0 | 18.70 | Satin Black | 13.30 |
| SII6X42HBR | 6X | 42 | 20 | 4.00 | CH | .33 | | 1/8 MOA | 1.0 | 16.00 | Satin Black | 12.91 |
| SII6X42HBRD | 6X | 42 | 20 | 4.00 | Dot | .375/.070 | | 1/8 MOA | 1.0 | 16.00 | Satin Black | 12.91 |
| **Compact Rifle Scopes** | | | | | | | | | | | | |
| SII4X32 | 4X | 32 | 25 | 4.52 | Plex | 30/.50/2.0 | | 1/4 MOA | 1.0 | 9.34 | Satin Black | 9.69 |
| SII2.510X32 | 2.5-10X | 32 | 25 | 4.0 | Plex | 48.0/24/.80 | 12.0/.20/.80 | 1/4 MOA | 1.0 | 10.93 | Satin Black | 10.90 |
| **Shotgun Scopes** | | | | | | | | | | | | |
| SII2.5X20SG | 2.5X | 20 | 41 | 4.33 | Plex | 48.0/.80/3.20 | | 1/4 MOA | 1.0 | 8.46 | Satin Black | 10.28 |
| SII2.57X32 | 2.5-7X | 32 | 26-7 | 4.33 | DD | 48/24/.60 | 17/8.5/.26 | 1/4 MOA | 1.0 | 8.46 | Satin Black | 10.90 |
| **Pistol Scopes** | | | | | | | | | | | | |
| SII1X28P | 1X | 28 | 30 | 9-24 | Plex | 120.0/2.0/8.0 | | 1/8 MOA | 1.0 | 8.46 | Satin Black | 9.49 |
| SII1X28PST | 1X | 28 | 30 | 9-24 | Plex | 120.0/2.0/8.0 | | 1/8 MOA | 1.0 | 8.46 | Satin Black | 9.49 |
| SII2X28P | 2X | 28 | 16-10 | 9-24 | Plex | 60.0/1.0/4.0 | | 1/8 MOA | 1.0 | 8.28 | Satin Black | 9.49 |

# SIMMONS SCOPES

## AETEC

**MODEL 2101**

**MODELS 2100/2101/2102**
2.8-10X44 WA
*Field of view:* 44'-14'  *Eye relief:* 5"
*Length:* 11.9"  *Weight:* 15.5 oz.  *Reticle:* Truplex
*Price:* . . . . . . . . . . . . . . . . . . . . . . . . . $234.99

**AETEC SCOPE MODEL 2101**
2.8-10x44 WA ASPHERICAL LENS SYSTEM
w/SUNSHADE, BLACK MATTE (not shown)

*Also available:*  MODEL 2104 – 3.8-12X44 WA/AO
Aspherical Lens System w/sunshade, black matte
*Price:* . . . . . . . . . . . . . . . . . . . . . . . . . $259.99

## 44 MAG RIFLESCOPES

**MODEL M1044 (Black Matte)**
3-10X44mm
*Field of view:* 34'-10.5'  *Eye relief:* 3"
*Length:* 12.75"  *Weight:* 15.5 oz.
*Price:* . . . . . . . . . . . . . . . . . . . . . . . . . $179.99

**MODEL M1050DM**
**44 DIAMOND MAG (Black Matte)**
**RANGE-CALCULATING SMART RETICLE**
**(Black Matte)**
3.8-12X44mm
*Field of view:* 26'-9'  *Eye relief:* 3"
*Length:* 13.08"  *Weight:* 16.75 oz.
*Price:* . . . . . . . . . . . . . . . . . . . . . . . . . $269.99

**MODEL M1045 (Black Matte)**
4-12X44mm
*Field of view:* 29.5'-9.5'  *Eye relief:* 3"
*Length:* 13.2"  *Weight:* 18.25 oz.
*Price:* . . . . . . . . . . . . . . . . . . . . . . . . . $278.99

**MODEL M1050DM**

**MODEL M1047 (Black Matte)**
6.5-20X44mm
*Field of view:* 14'-5'
*Eye relief:* 2.6"-3.4"
*Length:* 12.8"
*Weight:* 19.5 oz.
*Price:* . . . . . . . . . . . . . . . . . . . . . . . . . $224.99
*Also available:*
MODEL M1048
6.5-20X44 Target Turrets  Black Matte (¹/₈" MOA) . **$259.99**
Sunshade for M1047/M1048 . . . . . . . . . . . . . . **10.45**

## PROHUNTER RIFLESCOPES

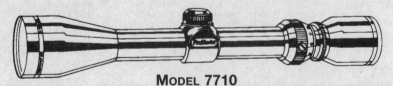

**MODEL 7710**

**MODEL 7710**
3-9X40mm Wide Angle Riflescope
*Field of view:* 36'-13'
*Eye relief:* 3"  *Length:* 12.6"
*Weight:* 13.5 oz.  *Features:* Truplex reticle; silver matte finish
*Price:* . . . . . . . . . . . . . . . . . . . . . . . . . $139.99

(Same in black matte or black polish, Models 7711 and 7712)
*Also available:*
MODEL 7700 2-7X32 Black Matte . . . . . . . . . . . . **$124.99**
MODEL 7716 4-12X40 Black Matte AO . . . . . . . . . **159.99**
MODEL 7721 6-18X40 AO Black Matte . . . . . . . . . **179.99**
MODEL 7740 6X40 Black Matte . . . . . . . . . . . . . . **120.70**

# SIMMONS SCOPES

## WHITETAIL CLASSIC SERIES

### MODEL WTC11

### MODEL WTC12

**WHITETAIL CLASSIC SCOPES**

**MODEL WTC11 (Black Granite)**
1.5-5X20mm
*Field of view:* 75'-23' *Eye relief:* 3.4"
*Length:* 9.3" *Weight:* 9.7 oz.
*Price:* . . . . . . . . . . . . . . . . . . . . . . . . . . . $184.99

**MODEL WTC12**
2.5-8X36mm
*Field of view:* 45'-14' *Eye relief:* 3.2"
*Length:* 11.3 *Weight:* 13 oz.
*Price:* . . . . . . . . . . . . . . . . . . . . . . . . . . . $199.99

**MODEL WTC13 (Black Granite)**
3.5-10X40mm
*Field of view:* 30'-10.5' *Eye relief:* 3.2"
*Length:* 12.4" *Weight:* 13.5 oz.
*Price:* . . . . . . . . . . . . . . . . . . . . . . . . . . . $209.99

**MODEL WTC15**
3.5-10X50 Black Granite
*Field of view:* 29.5-11.5' *Eye relief:* 3.2"
*Length:* 12.75" *Weight:* 13.5 oz.
*Price:* WTC15 . . . . . . . . . . . . . . . . . . . . . $289.99

**MODEL WTC 45 (Black Granite)**
4.5-14X40 AO
*Field of view:* 22.5'-8.6' *Eye relief:* 3.2"
*Length:* 13.2" *Weight:* 14 oz.
*Price:* . . . . . . . . . . . . . . . . . . . . . . . . . . . $259.99

*Also Available:* Simmons Pro 50 Riflescopes with 50mm objectives
2.5-10x . . . . . . . . . . . . . . . . . . . . . . . . . . **179.99**
4-12x . . . . . . . . . . . . . . . . . . . . . . . . . . . **219.99**
6-18x . . . . . . . . . . . . . . . . . . . . . . . . . . . **239.99**

## PROHUNTER PISTOL SCOPES

**MODEL 7738 (4X)**

**MODEL 7732 (2X)**

**MODEL #7732/7733 (Silver Matte)**
**SPECIFICATIONS**
*Magnification:* 2X *Field Of View:* 22'
*Eye Relief:* 9-17" *Length:* 8.75"
*Weight:* 7 oz. *Reticle:* Truplex
*Finish:* Black matte
*Price:* . . . . . . . . . . . . . . . . . . . . . . . . . . . $139.99

**MODEL #7738/7739 (Silver Matte)**
**SPECIFICATIONS**
*Magnification:* 4X *Field Of View:* 15'
*Eye Relief:* 11.8-17.6" *Length:* 9"
*Weight:* 8 oz. *Reticle:* Truplex
*Finish:* Black matte
*Price:* . . . . . . . . . . . . . . . . . . . . . . . . . . . $149.99

# SIMMONS SCOPES

## 1022T RIMFIRE TARGET SCOPE

*Magnification:* 3-9X32mm WA/AO
*Finish:* Black matte
*Features:* Adjustable for windage and elevation; adjustable objective lens, target knobs
*Price:* ...................................... $166.99
*Also available:*
**1022** 4X32 black matte w/22 rings ........... $69.99
**1031** 4X28 22 Mag Mini black matte w/22 rings ... **79.99**
**1032** 4X28 22 Mag Mini silver matte w/22 rings ... **79.99**
**1033** 4X32 silver matte w/22 rings ............ **74.99**
**1037** 3-9X32 silver matte w/22 rings. .......... **85.99**
**1039** 3-9X32 black matte w/22 rings ........... **84.99**

**1022T RIMFIRE TARGET SCOPE**

## BLACK POWDER SCOPES

**MODEL BP2732M**

### MODEL BP2732M
*Magnification:* 2-7X32  *Finish:* Black matte
*Field of view:* 57.7'-16.6' 100 yards  *Eye relief:* 3"
*Reticle:* Truplex  *Length:* 11.6"  *Weight:* 12.4 oz.
*Price:* ...................................... $135.99
*Also available:*
**MODELS BP400M/400S**
4X20 Black Matte or Silver Matte, Long Body

*Field of view:* 28'  *Eye relief:* 5.0"
*Length:* 10.25"  *Weight:* 8.7 oz.  *Reticle:* Truplex
*Price:* ...................................... $49.99
### MODELS BPO420M/420S
4X20 Octagon Body
*Field of view:* 19.5'  *Eye relief:* 4"
*Length:* 7.5"  *Weight:* 8.3 oz.  *Reticle:* Truplex
*Price:* ...................................... $114.99

## SHOTGUN SCOPES

**MODEL 7790D**

### MODELS 21004/7790D
*Magnification:* 4X32
*Finish:* Black matte
*Field of view:* 16' (Model 21004); 17' (Model 7790D)
*Eye relief:* 5.5"
*Reticle:* Truplex (Model 21004); ProDiamond (Model 7790D)
*Length:* 8.5" (8.8" Model 21004)
*Weight:* 8.75 oz. (9.1 oz. Model 7790D)

*Prices:*
**MODEL 21004** ......................... $84.99
**MODEL 7790D** ......................... 114.99
*Also available:*
**MODEL 21005** 2.5X20 Black matte (Truplex reticle) .... 59.99
**MODEL 7789D** 2X32 Black matte
(ProDiamond reticle) ...................... 99.99
**MODEL 7791D** 1.5-5X20 WA Black matte
(ProDiamond reticle) ...................... 138.99

# SIMMONS SCOPES

## 8-POINT

SIMMONS offers a scope to fit almost every firearm and budget. The new 8 Point series is aimed at the entry level or budget-minded shooter who needs a reliable scope that will do the job at an affordable price. The 8 Point family includes seven scopes in popular configurations: 3-9x32mm, 3-9x40mm, 3-9x50mm, 4x32mm, 4-12x40mm AO, and 4x32 mm shotgun.

All versions are offered in black matte finish, and the 3-9x40mm is also available in silver. Fully coated lenses enhance light transmission for low-light viewing and reduce reflections. Simmons' popular Truplex reticle is standard. Windage and elevation are adjusted in 1/4-MOA increments. The new 8 Point scopes are shockproof, waterproof, and fogproof.

**SIMMONS 8 POINT
3-9x40 BLACK**

### 8-POINT SCOPE
### 4-12X40MM AO

*Magnification:* 4-12X
*Field of View:* 29 - 10 ft. at 100 yards
*Eye Relief:* 3 inches at 4X and 2 7/8 inches at 12X
*Length:* 13.5 inches
*Weight:* 15.75 oz.
*Reticle:* Duplex
*Finish:* Black Matte
*Price:* . . . . . . . . . . . . . . . . . . . . . . . . . . . . . . . $129.99

### 8-POINT SCOPE
### 4X32MM

*Magnification:* 4X
*Field of View:* 28.75 ft. at 100 yards
*Eye Relief:* 3 inches
*Length:* 11.625 inches
*Weight:* 14.25 oz.
*Reticle:* Duplex
*Finish:* Black Matte
*Price:* . . . . . . . . . . . . . . . . . . . . . . . . . . . . . . . $44.99

### 8-POINT SCOPE
### 3-9X32 MM

*Magnification:* 3-9X
*Field of View:* 37.5 - 13 ft. at 100 yards
*Eye Relief:* 3 inches at 3X and 2 7/8 inches at 9X
*Length:* 11.875 inches
*Weight:* 11.5 oz.
*Reticle:* Duplex
*Finish:* Black Matte
*Price:* . . . . . . . . . . . . . . . . . . . . . . . . . . . . . . . $60.99

### 8-POINT SCOPE
### 3-9X40MM

*Magnification:* 3-9X
*Field of View:* 37 - 13 ft. at 100 yards
*Eye Relief:* 3 inches at 3X and 2 7/8 inches at 9X
*Length:* 12.25 inches
*Weight:* 12.25 oz.
*Reticle:* Duplex
*Finish:* Black Matte or Silver
*Price:* Black Matte . . . . . . . . . . . . . . . . . . . . . . . . $84.99
Silver . . . . . . . . . . . . . . . . . . . . . . . . . . . . . . . . 94.99

### 8-POINT SCOPE
### 3-9X50MM

*Magnification:* 3-9X
*Field of View:* 32 - 11.75 ft. at 100 yards
*Eye Relief::* 3 inches at 3X and 2 7/8 inches at 9X
*Length:* 13 inches
*Weight:* 15.25 oz.
*Reticle:* Duplex
*Finish:* Black Matte
*Price:* . . . . . . . . . . . . . . . . . . . . . . . . . . . . . . . $97.99

# SIMMONS SCOPES

## WHITETAIL EXPEDITION

Simmons introduced aspherical lenses to shooters with the AETEC series of riflescopes. Now, Simmons offers aspherical lenses in a new Whitetail Expedition series. Because aspherical lenses eliminate minor aberrations found in regular spherical lens systems, these scopes produce a sharp, crisp view all the way to the edges of the lens. Field of view is 30% greater than that of other scopes of comparable magnification and objective lens size. All lens surfaces of the new Whitetail Expedition scopes, inside and out, are fully-multicoated for maximum edge-to-edge brightness and reflection reduction. The scopes have a Truplex reticle, the most versatile and popular in the marketplace, and are shockproof, waterproof, and fogproof. Configurations available in the Whitetail Expedition series are: 1.5-6x32mm WA, 3-9x42mm WA, 4-12x42mm WA, and 6-18x42mm WA. The two higher-range scopes have adjustable objective lenses for precision shooting at any range. Adjustments for windage and elevation are 1/4-MOA increments.

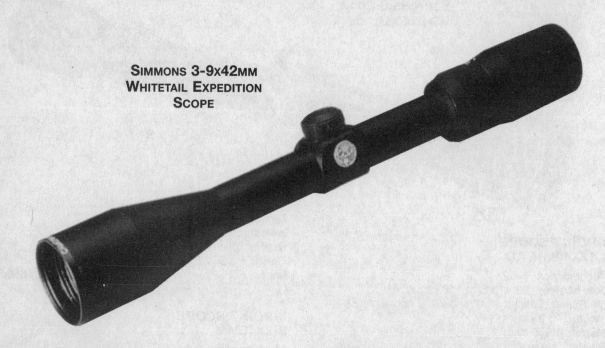

**SIMMONS 3-9X42MM WHITETAIL EXPEDITION SCOPE**

### WHITETAIL EXPEDITION 1.5-6X32MM

*Magnification:* 1.5-6X
*Field of View:* 72 - 19 ft. at 100 yards
*Eye Relief:* 3 inches
*Length:* 11.16 inches
*Weight:* 15 oz.
*Reticle:* Duplex
*Finish:* Black Matte
*Price:* . . . . . . . . . . . . . . . . . . . . . . . . . . . . . $289.99

### WHITETAIL EXPEDITION 3-9X42MM

*Magnification:* 3-9X
*Field of View:* 40 - 13.5 ft. at 100 yards
*Eye Relief:* 3 inches
*Length:* 13.2 inches
*Weight:* 17.5 oz.
*Reticle:* Duplex
*Finish:* Black Matte
*Price:* . . . . . . . . . . . . . . . . . . . . . . . . . . . . . $309.99

### WHITETAIL EXPEDITION 4-12X42MM

*Magnification:* 4-12X
*Field of View:* 29 - 9.6 ft. at 100 yards
*Eye Relief:* 3 inches
*Length:* 13.46 inches
*Weight:* 21.25 oz.
*Reticle:* Duplex
*Finish:* Black Matte
*Price:* . . . . . . . . . . . . . . . . . . . . . . . . . . . . . $334.99

### WHITETAIL EXPEDITION 6-18X42MM

*Magnification:* 6-18X
*Field of View:* 18.3 - 6.5 ft. at 100 yards
*Eye Relief:* 3 inches
*Length:* 15.35 inches
*Weight:* 22.5 oz.
*Reticle:* Duplex
*Finish:* Black Matte
*Price:* . . . . . . . . . . . . . . . . . . . . . . . . . . . . . $364.99

# SWAROVSKI SCOPES

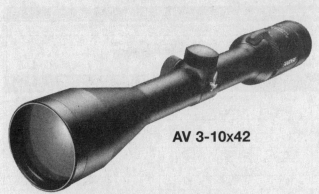

**AV 3-10x42**

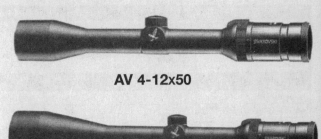

**AV 4-12x50**

**AV 3-9x36**

## SWAROVSKI AV-SERIES LIGHTWEIGHT 1-INCH SCOPES

Developed for American hunters, the AV scopes feature constant-size reticles, lightweight alloy tubes and satin finish. Totally waterproof even with caps removed, these scopes have fully multi-coated lenses and the quality that has made Swarovski famous.

**Prices:** AV 3-10 x 42 . . . . . . . . . . . . . . . . . . . . $798.00
AV 4-12 x 50 . . . . . . . . . . . . . . . . . . . . . . . . 821.00
AV 3-9 x 36 . . . . . . . . . . . . . . . . . . . . . . . . . 754.00

### AV RETICLES AVAILABLE:

*4*       *4A*       *Plex*

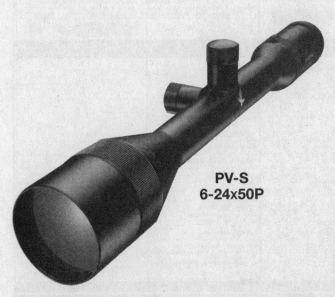

**PV-S 6-24x50P**

*Specially designed for competition shooting: rectangular reticle adjustment area for extended elevation setting (1 click = 4.8 mm at 100 m/.18" @ 100 yds. approx. 1/6")*

*Parallax correction for ultra-precision, even over long distances.*

## HABICHT PV-S MODEL

For sporting big shots: Swarovski PV-S 6-24x50 P. Specially designed for competition shooting with parallax correction, sun shield, target turrets, reticle adjustment with extended elevation adjustment range and reticle in the 2nd image plane. Ultra-precise at the all-important moment. It has, of course, all the other benefits of the P-series.

**Price:** PV-S 6-24 x 50 P . . . . . . . . . . . . . . . . $1,665.00

### PV-S RETICLES AVAILABLE:

 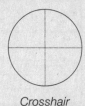 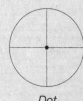

*Plex*       *Crosshair*       *Dot*

# SWAROVSKI RIFLESCOPES

## RIFLE SCOPES

Functional temperature: –4 to +131° F • Storage temperature: –22 to +158° F • Submersion tightness: 13 ft, filled with nitrogen
Parallax-free at 100 m/110 yds (PV 6-24 x 50 P and PV 4-16 x 50 P: ∞ – 50 m/55 yds)

| | PF 6 x 42 | PF/PF-N 8 x 50 | PF/PF-N 8 x 56 | PV/PV-1 1.25-4 x 24 | PV 1.5-6 x 42 | PV/PV-N 2.5-10 x 42 | PV/PV-N 2.5-10 x 56 | PV/PV-N 3-12 x 50 | PV 4-16 x 50 P | PV 6-24 x 50 P |
|---|---|---|---|---|---|---|---|---|---|---|
| Magnification | 6x | 8x | 8x | 1.25-4x | 1.5-6x | 2.5-10x | 2.5-10x | 3-12x | 4-16x | 6-24x |
| Objective lens diameter (mm) (in) | 42 1.65 | 50 1.97 | 56 2.20 | 17-24 0.67-0.94 | 20-42 0.79-1.65 | 33-42 1.3-1.65 | 33-56 1.3-2.20 | 39-50 1.54-1.97 | 50 1.97 | 50 1.97 |
| Exit pupil, diameter (mm) (in) | 7 0.28 | 6.25 0.25 | 7 0.28 | 12.5-6 0.49-0.24 | 13.1-7 0.52-0.28 | 13.1-4.2 0.52-0.17 | 13.1-5.6 0.52-0.22 | 13.1-4.2 0.52-0.17 | 12.5-3.1 0.49-0.12 | 8.3-2.1 0.33-0.08 |
| Eye relief (mm) (in) | 80 3.15 | 80 3.15 | 80 3.15 | 80 3.15 | 80 3.15 | 80 3.15 | 80 3.15 | 80 3.15 | 80 3.15 | 80 3.15 |
| Field of view, real (m/100 m) (ft/100 yds) | 7 21 | 5.2 15.6 | 5.2 15.6 | 32.8-10.4 98.4-31.2 | 21.8-7 65.4-21 | 13.2-4.2 39.6-12.6 | 13.2-4.1 39.6-12.3 | 11-3.5 33-10.5 | 9.1-2.6 27.3-7.8 | 6.2-1.8 18.6-5.4 |
| Field of view, real (degree) | 4 | 3 | 3 | 18.6-6 | 12.4-4 | 7.5-2.4 | 7.5-2.4 | 6.3-2 | 5.2-1.5 | 3.5-1 |
| Field of view, apparent (degree) | 23.2 | 23.2 | 23.2 | 23.2 | 23.2 | 23.2 | 23.2 | 23.2 | 23.2 | 23.2 |
| Diopter compensation (dpt) | +2, –3 | +2, –3 | +2, –3 | +2, –3 | +2, –3 | +2, –3 | +2, –3 | +2, –3 | +2, –3 | +2, –3 |
| Transmission (%) | 94 | 94/92 | 93/91 | 93/91 | 93 | 94/92 | 93/91 | 94/92 | 90 | 90 |
| Twilight factor (DIN 58388) | 16 | 20 | 21 | 4-10 | 4-16 | 7-21 | 7-24 | 9-25 | 14-28 | 17-35 |
| Impact point correction per click (mm/100 m) (in/100 yds) | 10 0.36 | 10 0.36 | 10 0.36 | 15 0.54 | 10 0.36 | 10 0.36 | 10 0.36 | 10 0.36 | 5 0.18 | 5 0.18 |
| Max. elevation/windage adjustment range (m/100 m) (ft/100 yds) | 1.3 3.9 | 1.1 3.3 | 1.3 3.9 | 3.3 9.9 | 2.2 6.6 | 1.3 3.9 | 1.3 3.9 | 1.1 3.3 | H: 1.8/S: 1 E: 5.4/W: 3 | H: 1.2/S: 0.7 E: 3.6/W: 2.1 |
| Length, approx. (mm) (in) | 326 12.83 | 354 13.94 | 337 13.27 | 270 10.63 | 330 12.99 | 336 13.23 | 346 13.62 | 364 14.33 | 361 14.21 | 392 15.43 |
| Weight, approx. (g) (oz) — S | 490 17.3 | – | – | 460 16.2 | – | – | – | – | 635 22.4 | – |
| Weight, approx. (g) (oz) — L | 340 12.0 | 420 14.8 | 450 15.9 | 360 12.7 | 460 16.2 | 430 15.2 | 510 18.0 | 480 16.9 | 630 22.2 | 670 23.6 |
| Weight, approx. (g) (oz) — LS | 380 13.4 | 450 15.9 | 480 16.9 | 390 13.8 | 495 17.5 | 465 16.4 | 540 19.0 | 520 18.3 | | |

S = Steel • L = light alloy • LS = light alloy with rail

## RIFLE SCOPES

Functional temperature: –4 to +131° F • Storage temperature: –22 to +158° F
Submersion tightness: 13 ft, filled with nitrogen • Parallax-free at 100 m/110 yds (PV-S: ∞ – 50 m)

Functional temperature: +14° F/122° F • Storage temperature: –13° F/158° F
Submersion tightness: 13 ft, filled with nitrogen • Laser: Class 1 Laser acc. to FDA 21 CFR, resp. Class 3A Laser acc. to EN 60825-1 (1994)
Power source: 4 batteries, Type AAA • Service life: min. 1,500 measurements
Measuring time: about 1 second • Parallax-free at 150 m / 164 yds

| | PV-S 6-24 x 50 P | AV 3-9 x 36 | AV 3-10 x 42 | AV 4-12 x 50 | | LRS 3-12 x 50 |
|---|---|---|---|---|---|---|
| Magnification | 6-24x | 3-9x | 3.3-10x | 4-12x | Magnification | 3-12x |
| Objective lens diameter (mm) (in) | 50 1.97 | 36 1.42 | 42 1.65 | 50 1.97 | Objective lens diameter (mm) (in) | 50 1.97 |
| Exit pupil, diameter (mm) (in) | 8.3-2.1 0.33-0.08 | 12-4 0.47-0.16 | 12.6-4.2 0.5-0.17 | 12.5-4.2 0.49-0.17 | Exit pupil, diameter (mm) (in) | 13.1-4.2 0.52-0.17 |
| Eye relief (mm) (in) | 80 3.15 | 90 3.5 | 90 3.5 | 90 3.5 | Eye relief (mm) (in) | 80 3.15 |
| Field of view, real (m/100 m) (ft/100 yds) | 6.2-1.8 18.6-5.4 | 13-4.5 39-13.5 | 11-3.9 33-11.7 | 9.7-3.3 29.1-9.9 | Field of view, real (m/100 m) (ft/100 yds) | 11-3.5 33-10.5 |
| Field of view, real (degree) | 3.5-1 | 7.4-2.6 | 6.3-2.2 | 5.5-1.9 | Field of view, real (degree) | 6.3-2 |
| Field of view, apparent (degree) | 23.2 | 22.7 | 22.7 | 22.7 | Field of view, apparent (degree) | 23.2 |
| Diopter compensation (dpt) | +2. –3 | ±2.5 | ±2.5 | ±2.5 | Diopter compensation (dpt) | +2, –3 |
| Transmission (%) | 90 | 94 | 94 | 94 | Transmission (%) | 70 |
| Twilight factor (DIN 58388) | 17-35 | 9-18 | 9-21 | 11-25 | Twilight factor (DIN 58388) | 9-25 |
| Impact point correction per click (mm/100 m) (in/100 yds) | 4.8 (1/6 MOA) 0.17 | 7 0.25 | 7 0.25 | 7 0.25 | Impact point correction per click (mm/100 m) (in/100 yds) | 10 0.36 |
| Max. elevation/windage adjustment range (m/100 m) (ft/100 yds) | H: 1.2/S: 0.7 E: 3.6/W: 2.1 | 1.6 4.8 | 1.4 4.2 | 1.2 3.6 | Max. elevation/windage adjustment range (m/100 m) (ft/100 yds) | 1.1 3.3 |
| Length, approx. (mm) (in) | 392 15.43 | 301 11.85 | 316 12.44 | 343 13.5 | Length, approx. (mm) (in) | 394 15.51 |
| Weight, approx. (g) (oz) — S | – | – | – | – | Measuring range (m) (yds) | 50-600 55-660 |
| Weight, approx. (g) (oz) — L | 695 24.5 | 330 11.6 | 360 12.7 | 395 13.9 | Accuracy and measurement resolution (m) (yds) | 2 2.2 |
| Weight, approx. (g) (oz) — LS | – | – | 385 13.6 | 430 15.2 | Weight LS (g) (oz) | 1150 40.6 |

S = Steel • L = light alloy • LS = light alloy with rail

## ILLUMINATION DEVICE FOR RIFLE SCOPES

| | BE 1 for low light reticle | BE 2 for day-time reticle |
|---|---|---|
| Height, approx. (mm) / (in) | 30 / 1.18 | 26 / 1 |
| Diameter (mm) / (in) | 27 / 1.06 | 27 / 1.06 |
| Weight, approx. (g) / (oz) | 30 / 1.1 | 25 / 0.9 |
| Power source | 3 V, CR 1620 / CR 1616 | 3V, CR 2032 |
| Battery service life, approx. (h) | 70 | 30 |

Submersion tightness: 13 ft (when mounted) • Functional temperature: -4 to +131°F • Storage temperature: -22 to +158°F

# SWAROVSKI & KAHLES RIFLESCOPES

## 2.5-10X42

Swarovski's 6-24X500mm "PH" riflescope was developed for long-range target, big-game and varmint shooting. Its waterproof parallax adjustment system should be popular with whitetail "Bean Field Shooters" and long-range varmint hunters looking for a choice of higher powers in a premium rifle scope and still deliver accuracy. The new scope will also appeal to many bench rest shooters who compete in certain classes where power and adjustment are limited. A non-magnifying, fine plex reticle and an all-new fine crosshair reticle with 1/8" MOA dot are available in the 6-24X50mm scope. Reticle adjustment clicks are 1/6" (minute) by external, waterproof target knobs. The internal optical system features a patented coil spring suspension system for dependablle accuracy and positive reticle adjustment. The objective bell, 30mm middle tube, turret housing and ocular bell are machined from one solid bar of aluminum.

**Price:** . . . . . . . . . . . . . . . . . . . . . . . . . . . . . . . . . . **$1,665.50**

### PRICES PH SERIES RIFLESCOPES

| | |
|---|---|
| PF 6x42 (4A, 7A) . . . . . . . . . . . . . . . . . . . . . . . . | **$954.00** |
| PF 8x50 (4A, 7A) . . . . . . . . . . . . . . . . . . . . . . . . | **987.00** |
| w/illum reticle (4N, PLEXN) . . . . . . . . . . . . . | **1,343.33** |
| PF 8x56 (4A, 7A) . . . . . . . . . . . . . . . . . . . . . . . . | **1,032.00** |
| w/illum reticle (4N, PLEXN) . . . . . . . . . . . . . | **1,388.88** |
| PH 1.25-4x24 (4A) . . . . . . . . . . . . . . . . . . . . . . | **1,065.00** |
| PH 1.5-6x42 (4A, 7A) . . . . . . . . . . . . . . . . . . . . | **1,187.00** |
| PH 2.5-10x42 (4A, 7A, PLEX) . . . . . . . . . . . . | **1,354.00** |
| illum reticle . . . . . . . . . . . . . . . . . . . . . . . . | **1,654.00** |
| PH 2.5-10x56 (4A, 7A) . . . . . . . . . . . . . . . . . . | **1,398.89** |

| | |
|---|---|
| w/illum reticle (4N, PLEXN) . . . . . . . . . . . . . | **1,765.55** |
| PH 3-12x50 (4A, 7A) . . . . . . . . . . . . . . . . . . . . | **1,387.00** |
| TDS reticle . . . . . . . . . . . . . . . . . . . . . . . . | **1,498.00** |
| w/illum reticle (4N, PLEXN) . . . . . . . . . . . . . | **1,698.88** |
| PH 6-24x50 (aluminum only) with low turret . . . . | **1,587.00** |
| Kahles 3-9x42 . . . . . . . . . . . . . . . . . . . . . . . . . | **549.00** |
| Swarovski 3-9x36 AV . . . . . . . . . . . . . . . . . . . . | **680.00** |
| 4-16x50 (4A, PLEX) . . . . . . . . . . . . . . . . . . . . | **1,443.00** |
| #24 Battue reticle additional in 1.25-4x24 and 1.5-642 | |

## LRS 3-12x50

### HOW THE LASER DISTANCE METER WORKS

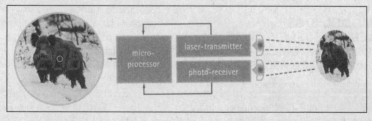

*The laser sends out a signal which is then reflected back by the targeted object and picked up by the receiver. The chip calculates the distance from the time lapse between the outgoing and incoming signals.*

### SWAROVSKI RANGEFINDING RIFLE SCOPE

The only one of its kind worldwide: Swarovski LRS 3-12 x 50. The first rifle scope with integrated rangefinder. Excellent in unfamiliar terrain, tricky light conditions and when stalking. Makes precise target range identification fast, easy: exact distance display in field of view, very easy-to-read LED display and very reliable solid-state electronics. Lightweight but very rugged thanks to light alloy housing with scratchproof surface.

**Price:** . . . . . . . . . . . . . . . . . . . . . . . . . . . . . . . . . . **$3,000.00**

# SWIFT RIFLE AND PISTOL SCOPES

Swift Instruments, Inc., a prominent name in the optics industry since 1926, has four new scopes in its line: 3 rifle scopes that offer faster focusing with the Swift Speed Focus feature and one new shock resistant pistol scope. All four are waterproof, shock tested and have multi-coated lenses for a bright image from dawn to dusk without glare.

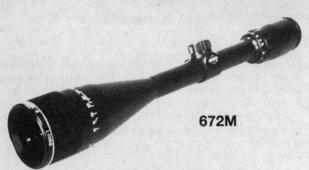

**672M**

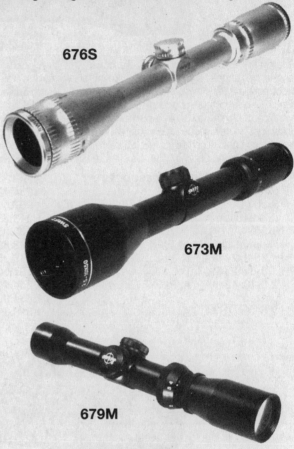

**676S**

**673M**

**679M**

## MODEL 672M
### SWIFT PREMIER RIFLE SCOPE
6-18X, 50MM - WA - MULTI-COATED - WATERPROOF - SPEED FOCUS

A great scope for varmint, silhouette and target shooters. The Speed Focus feature presents optimum focusing ability at any power setting. Multi-coated lenses with an adjustable objective to correct parallax. New longer tube body allows more eye relief adjustment in long action firearms. Black matte finish.
*Price:* . . . . . . . . . . . . . . . . . . . . . . . . . . . . . . . . . . $255.00

## MODEL 627M
### SWIFT PREMIER RIFLE SCOPE
FEATURING A 30MM TUBE FOR A BRIGHTER IMAGE AT DAWN OR DUSK 2.5-10X, 50 - WIDE ANGLE - WATERPROOF - MULTI-COATED - SPEED FOCUS

This scope with a 30mm tube and a 50mm objective is brighter than other scopes under poor light condition. It has an extremely wide field. The objective adjustment allows accurate shooting from close up to distant ranges. Elevation and windage adjustments, full saddle hard anodized 30mm tube.
*Price:* . . . . . . . . . . . . . . . . . . . . . . . . . . . . . . . . . . $290.00

## MODEL 676S
### SWIFT PREMIER RIFLE SCOPE
4-12X, 40 - WA - WATERPROOF - MULTI-COATED - SPEED FOCUS

With a parallax adjustment from 10 yards to infinity this scope is highly adaptable and excellent for use as a varmint scope or on gas powered air rifles. Elevation and windage adjustments are mounted full saddle on the hard anodized 1-inch tube. Speed Focus adjustment brings you on target easily. The objectives are multi-coated; Quadraplex reticle is standard. Available in regular (676), matte (676M), and silver finish (676S).
*Price:* . . . . . . . . . . . . . . . . . . . . . . . . . . . . . $174.00
Gloss . . . . . . . . . . . . . . . . . . . . . . . . . . . . . . . . . 170.00
Matte . . . . . . . . . . . . . . . . . . . . . . . . . . . . . . . . . 172.00

## MODEL 679M
### SWIFT PISTOL SCOPE
1.25-4X, 28MM - 8.2 OZ.

An extremely versatile full saddle scope with excellent eye relief of 23 inches at 1.25x, 15 inches at 4x. This ruggedly made scope is shock resistant and waterproof. It has 7 magenta coated lens elements and weighs only 8.2 ounces. Matte finished.
*Price:* . . . . . . . . . . . . . . . . . . . . . . . . . . . . . . . . . . $212.00

*Swift offers a broad range of scopes, including:*

| SHOTGUN | THE PREMIER LINE FEATURES |
|---|---|
| 1x20 | 4x32 |
| 4x32 | 4x40 |
| 1.5-4.5x21 | 6x40 |
| 3-9x40 | 2-7x40 |
| 3-9x50 | 3-9x32 |
| 2.5-10x50 | 3.9x40 |
| 6-18x44 | 3.5-10x44 |
| 6-18x50 | 4-12x50 |

# TASCO SCOPES

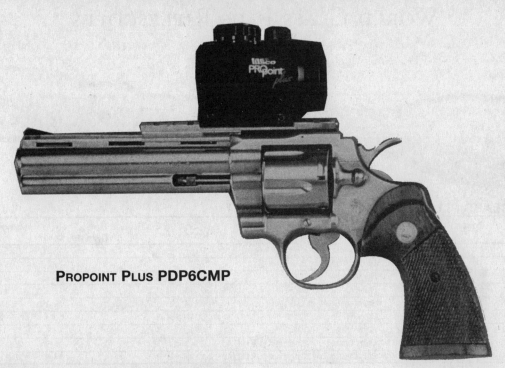

PROPOINT PLUS **PDP6CMP**

## PROPOINT® MULTI-PURPOSE SCOPES

Tasco's ProPoint is a true 1X-30mm scope with electronic red dot reticle that features unlimited eye relief, enabling shooters to shoot with both eyes open. It is available with a 3X booster and also has application for rifle, shotgun, bow and black powder. The compact version (PDP2) houses a lithium battery pack, making it 1.25 inches narrower than previous models and lighter as well (5.5 oz.). A mercury battery converter is provided for those who prefer standard batteries. Tasco's 3X booster with crosshair reticle weights 6.1 oz. and is 5.5 inches long.

## PROPOINT SCOPES

| Model | Power | Objective Diameter | Finish | Reticle | Field of View @ 100 Yds. | Eye Relief | Tube Diam. | Scope Length | Scope Weight | Prices |
|---|---|---|---|---|---|---|---|---|---|---|
| PDP2 | 1X | 25mm | Black Matte | 5 M.O.A. Dot | 40' | Unlimited | 30mm | 5" | 5.5 oz. | $267.37 |
| PDP2ST | 1X | 25mm | Stainless | 5 M.O.A. Dot | 40' | Unlimited | 30mm | 5" | 5.5 oz. | 267.37 |
| PDP2BD | 1x | 25mm | Black Matte | 10 M.O.A. Dot | 40' | Unlimited | 30mm | 5" | 5.5 oz. | 267.37 |
| PDP2BDST | 1X | 25mm | Stainless | 10 M.O.A. Dot | 40' | Unlimited | 30mm | 5" | 5.5 oz. | 267.37 |
| PDP3 | 1X | 25mm | Black Matte | 5 M.O.A. Dot | 52' | Unlimited | 30mm | 5" | 5.5 oz. | 320.85 |
| PDP3ST | 1X | 25mm | Stainless | 10 M.O.A. Dot | 52' | Unlimited | 30mm | 5" | 5.5 oz. | 320.85 |
| PDP3BD | 1X | 25mm | Black Matte | 10 M.O.A. Dot | 52' | Unlimited | 30mm | 5" | 5.5 oz. | 320.85 |
| PDPBDST | 1X | 25mm | Stainless | 10 M.O.A. Dot | 52' | Unlimited | 30mm | 5" | 5.5 oz. | 320.85 |
| PDP3CMP | 1X | 30mm | Black Matte | 10 M.O.A. Dot | 68' | Unlimited | 33mm | 4.75" | 5.4 oz. | 373.47 |
| PDP5CMP | 1X | 45mm | Black Matte | 4,8,12,16 M.O.A. Dot | 82' | Unlimited | 47mm | 4" | 8 oz. | 427.80 |
| PDP6CMP | 1X | 30mm | Black Matte | 10 M.O.A. Dot | 72' | Unlimited | 38mm | 3" | 5.8 oz. | 409.97 |
| PDP5VR | 1X | 28mm | Black Matte | | 14.9' | Unlimited | 30mm | | | 669.70 |

## PISTOL SCOPES

| Model | Power | Objective Diameter | Finish | Reticle | Field of View @ 100 Yds. | Eye Relief | Tube Diam. | Scope Length | Scope Weight | Prices |
|---|---|---|---|---|---|---|---|---|---|---|
| P2X20 | 2X | 20mm | Black Gloss | 30/30 | 21' | 10"-23" | 1" | 8" | 6.5 oz. | 126.47 |
| P2X20ST | 2X | 20mm | Stainless | 30/30 | 21' | 10"-23" | 1" | 8" | 6.5 oz. | 126.47 |
| P1.254X28 | 1.25X-4X | 28mm | Black Gloss | 30/30 | 23'-9' | 15"-23" | 1" | 9.25" | 8.2 oz. | 194.38 |
| P1.254X28ST | 1.25X-4X | 28mm | Stainless | 30/30 | 23'-9' | 15"-23" | 1" | 9.25" | 8.2 oz. | 194.38 |

# TASCO SCOPES

## WORLD CLASS PLUS RIFLESCOPES

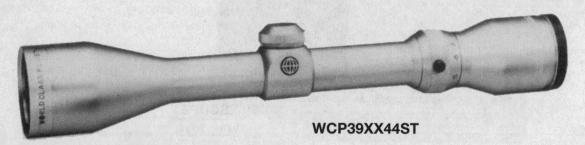

**WCP39XX44ST**

## WORLD CLASS PLUS RIFLESCOPES

| MODEL | POWER | OBJECTIVE DIAMETER | FINISH | RETICLE | F.O.V. @ 100 YD.S | EYE RELIEF | TUBE DIAMETER | LENGTH | WEIGHT | PRICES |
|-------|-------|-----|--------|---------|------|------|------|------|------|------|
| WCP4X44 | 4X | 44mm | Black Gloss | 30/30 | 32' | 3.25" | 1" | 12.75" | 13.5 oz. | $237.70 |
| DWCP4X44 | 4X | 44mm | Black Matte | 30/30 | 32' | 3.25" | 1" | 12.75" | 13.5 oz. | 237.70 |
| WCP39X44 | 3X-9X | 44mm | Black Gloss | 30/30 | 39'-14' | 3.5" | 1" | 12.75" | 15.8 oz. | 305.57 |
| DWCP39X44 | 3X-9X | 44mm | Black Matte | 30/30 | 39'-14' | 3.5" | 1" | 12.75" | 15.8 oz. | 305.57 |
| WCP39X44ST | 3X-9X | 44mm | Stainless Steel | 30/30 | 39'-14' | 3.5" | 1" | 12.75" | 15.8 oz. | 305.57 |
| WCP3.510X50 | 3.5X-10X | 50mm | Black Gloss | 30/30 | 30'-10.5' | 3.75" | 1" | 13" | 17.1 oz. | 322.54 |
| DWCP3.510X50 | 3.5X-10X | 50mm | Black Matte | 30/30 | 30'-10.5' | 3.75" | 1" | 13" | 17.1 oz. | 322.54 |
| DWCP832X50 | 8X-32X | 50mm | Black Matte | Crosshair* (1/8 M.O.A.) | 13'-4' | 3" | 1" | 14.5" | 25.1 oz. | 560.00 |
| DWCP1040X50 | 10X-40X | 50mm | Black Matte | Crosshair* (1/8 M.O.A.) | 11'-2.5' | 3" | 1" | 14.5" | 25.3 oz. | 611.00 |

## TACTICAL SCOPES

| MODEL | POWER | OBJECTIVE DIAMETER | FINISH | RETICLE | F.O.V. @ 100 YD.S | EYE RELIEF | TUBE DIAMETER | LENGTH | WEIGHT | PRICES |
|-------|-------|-----|--------|---------|------|------|------|------|------|------|
| CU840X56M | 8X-40X | 56mm | Black Matte | Mil Dot | 11.5'-2.6' | 3" | 30mm | 16" | 31.5 oz. | 1324.13 |
| SS10X42M | 10X | 42mm | Black Matte | Super Sniper | 13' | 4" | 30mm | 14.25" | 26 oz. | 933.68 |

*With 1/8 M.O.A.

**OPTIMA 2000 SIGHT**

## OPTIMA 2000

What makes this newest ProPoint so revolutionary is that, unlike previous ProPoints, it does not have a tube design. It's smaller (only 1 1/2") and lighter (only 1/2 oz.) than any other sighting device. It's also extremely durable and rugged. After thousands of test rounds it held its point of aim and its one-piece, dovetailed-style slide mount remained immovable. Its red dot was always on, with no time lost turning it on. While used primarily on pistols, the Optima 2000 can be mounted on shotguns for skeet or trap shooting or for duck hunting. It also works well on rifles for close-cover hunting. Optima 2000 is available with a bright, in-focus 3.5 or 7 M.O.A. dot on the same plane as iron sights for fast target acquisition.
**Price:** . . . . . . . . . . . . . . . . . . . . . . . . . . . . . . . $475.33

# TASCO RIFLESCOPES

**MODEL 1.75X-5X**

## WORLD CLASS™ WIDE-ANGLE® RIFLESCOPES

**Features:**
- 25% larger field of view
- Fully coated for maximum light transmission
- 1/4-minute clicks
- Waterproof, shockproof, fogproof
- Free haze filter lens caps
- TASCO's unique World Class Lifetime Warranty

## WORLD CLASS, WIDE-ANGLE VARIABLE ZOOM RIFLESCOPES

| Model No. | Power | Objective Diameter | Finish | Reticle | F.O.V. @100 Yds. | Eye Relief | Tube Diameter | Length | Weight | Price |
|---|---|---|---|---|---|---|---|---|---|---|
| **RIFLESCOPES** | | | | | | | | | | |
| WA1.755X20 | 1.75X-5X | 20mm | Black Gloss | 30/30 | 72'-24' | 3" | 1" | 10.5" | 10 oz. | **160.42** |
| WA27X32 | 2X-7X | 32mm | Black Gloss | 30/30 | 56'-17' | 3.25" | 1" | 11.5" | 12 oz. | **160.42** |
| R-DWC39X40* | 3X-9X | 40mm | Black Matte | 30/30 | 41'-15' | 3" | 1" | 12.75" | 13 oz. | **169.76** |
| R-WA39X40* | 3X-9X | 40mm | Black Gloss | 30/30 | 41'-15' | 3" | 1" | 12.75" | 13 oz. | **169.76** |
| R-WA39X40TV* | 3X-9X | 40mm | Black Gloss | 30/30 TV | 41'-15' | 3" | 1" | 12.75" | 13 oz. | **169.76** |
| WA39X40ST | 3X-9X | 40mm | Stainless | 30/30 | 41'-15' | 3" | 1" | 12.75" | 13 oz. | **169.76** |
| **RIFLESCOPE & BINOCULAR COMBO: R-DWC39X50** | | | | | | | | | | |
| WC28X32 | 2-8x32 | Compact | Black | 30/30 | 56-16 | 3" | 1" | 11" | 11 oz. | **169.76** |
| WC4X32 | 4x32 | Compact | Black | 30/30 | 27 | 3 | 1" | 10" | 9 oz. | **145.99** |

**MAG-IV 4X-16X50mm**

## MAG-IV-50™ RIFLESCOPES

Tasco's MAG-IV™ riflescopes now feature large 50mm objective lenses and are especially designed for dawn and dusk use. The 4X-16X50mm, 5X20X50mm and 5X 20X50mm with bullet drop compensation have Super-Con® multi-layered lens coating, fully coated optics, and black matte finish. Tasco's MAG-IV scopes feature windage and elevation adjustments with 1/4-minute clickstops and an Opti-Centered® 30/30 range-finding reticle.

**Prices:**
MODEL W416X50 . . . . . . . . . . . . . . . . . . . . . . . $127.80
MODEL W520X50 . . . . . . . . . . . . . . . . . . . . . 144.50
MODEL W520X50 BDC . . . . . . . . . . . . . . . . . 155.60
**Also available:**
MAG-IV RIFLESCOPES 3X-12X40mm,
  4X-16X40mm, 6X-24X40mm . . . . . . . . . . . $254.65

## PRONGHORN

| Model No. | Power | Objective Diameter | Finish | Reticle | F.O.V. @100 Yds. | Eye Relief | Tube Diameter | Length | Weight | Price |
|---|---|---|---|---|---|---|---|---|---|---|
| PH4X32 | 4X | 32mm | Black Gloss | 30/30 | 32' | 3" | 1" | 12" | 12.5 oz. | **61.11** |
| PH39X32 | 3X-9X | 32mm | Black Gloss | 30/30 | 39'-13' | 3" | 1" | 12" | 11 oz. | **83.18** |
| PH39X40 | 3X-9X | 40mm | Black Gloss | 30/30 | 39'-13' | 3" | 1" | 13" | 12.1 oz. | **110.34** |

### AIRGUN

| | | | | | | | | | | |
|---|---|---|---|---|---|---|---|---|---|---|
| AG4X32N | 4X | 32mm | Black Matte | 30/30 | 30' | 3" | 1" | 12.25" | 13.5 oz. | **151.09** |

### RIMFIRE

| | | | | | | | | | | |
|---|---|---|---|---|---|---|---|---|---|---|
| RF4X15* | 4X | 15mm | Black Gloss | Crosshair | 22.5' | 2.5" | 3/4" | 11" | 4 oz. | **16.13** |
| RF4X20WA* | 4X | 20mm | Black Matte | 30/30 | 23' | 2.5" | 3/4" | 10.5" | 3.8 oz. | **23.77** |
| RF4X32DS | 4X | 32mm | Black Matte/St. | 30/30 | 27' | 3.3" | 1" | 12.25" | 12.1 oz. | **74.69** |
| RF37X20* | 3X-7X | 20mm | Black Gloss | 30/30TV | 24'-11' | 2.5" | 3/4" | 11.5" | 5.7 oz. | **40.74** |
| RF39X32DS | 3X-9X | 32mm | Black Matte/St. | 30/30 | 35.5'-11.5' | 2.8"-2.8" | 1" | 12.75" | 11.3 oz. | **101.34** |

*Includes rings

# TRIJICON RIFLE SCOPES

## FIBER-OPTIC

**TRIJICON COMPACT ACOG**

Solid forged-aluminum housing, allowing ACOG to survive tremendous punishment and maintain its accuracy.

M-16 BASE MODEL

Internally adjustable, with far greater strength than other military riflescopes that use an external adjustment mechanism.

Glow-in-the-dark tritium illuminates the aiming triangle, dot or crosshairs when there is little or no ambient light, for more effective, low-light shooting.

Flourescent fiber light-gathering system causes the reticle to glow brightly during the day so it can be clearly seen and less brightly in low-light conditions, for balanced target contrast.

SPECIAL RING MODEL

Windage and elevation adjustments are easy to change with a small screwdriver, cartridge case or coin.

**AccuPoint Scopes**

Compact design, based on a 12mm roof prism assembly.

Trijicon, Inc. manufactures tritium-enhanced iron sights and optical sights. New for 2000 is the AccuPoint 1.25-4x24 dual-illuminated riflescope, specifically designed for close-range safari hunting. As with the original AccuPoint 3-9x40, it's dual-illuminated (by tritium and an advanced fiber-optic light collector) triangle aiming point is highly visible on dark animals, and does not disappear, as do traditional cross hairs. The new model's lower magnification and wide field of view are ideal for taking fast moving animals in thick cover. The AccuPoint's freedom from failure-prone batteries offers an additional margin of security. The 1.25-4x model also meets the European demand for riflescopes in this magnification range. Like the AccuPoint 3-9x, the 1.25-4x allows hunters to take a trophy that would be impossible using an ordinary scope that lacks AccuPoint's exclusive features. Using the two-eye-open aiming method for wide peripheral vision, in conjunction with AccuPoint's brightly illuminated aiming point (without batteries), the AccuPoint provides instant target acquisition. Both the original AccuPoint 3-9x40 riflescope and the new AccuPoint 1.25-4x24 are available with a red reticle, as well as the original amber reticle. On both models, shooters can manually vary brightness by turning a shutter, covering the daylight fiber-optic light collector. The tritium illu-

minates the aiming point even in total darkness. When sufficient light is present, the fiber-optic light collector automatically balances aiming point brightness to ambient light levels. In appearance, AccuPoint resembles conventional hunting scopes, except for the clear, high-impact, polycarbonate cover that protects the coiled, fiber-optic light collector. It features an aircraft-quality aluminum body with a non-reflective matte black finish.

## SPECIFICATIONS

| Description Power/ Objective Lens | Magnification x | Eye Relief (in) | Exit Pupil (mm) | Field of View (deg) | Length (in) | Weight BAC w/ M16/ AR15 Base (oz) | Weight BAC w/ Special Ring Base (oz) | Field of View 100 Yards (ft) |
|---|---|---|---|---|---|---|---|---|
| 1.5 x 16 | 1.5 | 2.4 | 10.7 | 8.3 | 5.34 | 5.31 | 5.02 | 43.8 |
| 1.5 x 24 | 1.5 | 3.6 | 16 | 5.5 | 5.76 | 5.92 | 5.63 | 28.9 |
| 2 x 20 | 2 | 2.1 | 10 | 6.3 | 5.30 | 5.82 | 5.54 | 33.1 |
| 3 x 24 | 3 | 1.4 | 8 | 5.5 | 5.00 | 5.89 | 5.60 | 28.9 |

**Prices:**
ACOG: 1.5x24, 2x20, 3x24 . . . . . . . . . . . . . . . . $695.00
AccuPoint 1.25-4x24 . . . . . . . . . . . . . . . . . . . . . . . 599.00
3-9x40 . . . . . . . . . . . . . . . . . . . . . . . . . . . . . . . . . 699.00

# WEAVER SCOPES

## T-SERIES TARGET/VARMINT T-36

**T-SERIES TARGET/VARMINT SCOPES** - These fixed-power scopes feature Weaver's patented Micro-Trac adjustment system utilizing a dual-spring, four-bearing contact design that allows independent movement of windage and elevation. Optics are fully multi-coated, delivering premium image clarity in virtually all light conditions. Adjustable objective lens allows for zero parallax from 50' to infinity. Choice of fine cross hair or dot reticles. Scopes come with sunshade, extra pair of oversize benchrest adjustment knobs, and screw-in metal lens caps.

**Model:** T-36 **Magnification/Objective:** 36X40mm **Field Of View:** 3.0' **Eye Relief:** 3.0" **Length:** 15.1" **Weight:** 16.7 oz. **Reticle:** 1/8 MOA Dot, Fine Crosshair **Finish:** Matte black or silver
**Price:** . . . . . . . . . . . . . . . . . . . . . . . . . . . . . . **$794.99**
    T-6 6x40 Satin Black. . . . . . . . . . . . . . . . . . . . 424.99

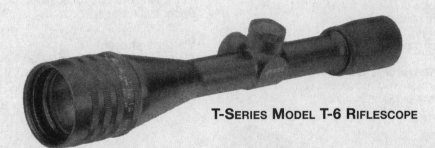

## T-SERIES MODEL T-6 RIFLESCOPE

Weaver's T-6 competition 6x scope is only 12.7 inches long and weighs less than 15 ounces. All optical surfaces are fully multi-coated for maximum clarity and light transmission. The T-6 features Weaver's Micro-Trac precision adjustments in 1/8-minute clicks to ensure parallel tracking. The protected target-style turrets are a low-profile configuration combining ease of adjustment with weight reduction. A 40mm adjustable objective permits parallax correction from 50 feet to infinity without shifting the point of impact. A special AO lock ring eliminates bell vibration or shift. The T-6 comes with screw-in metal lens caps and features a competition matte black finish.
**Reticles:** dot, Fine Crosshair
**Price:** . . . . . . . . . . . . . . . . . . . . . . . . . . . . . . **$424.95**

### WEAVER TACTICAL SCOPES (not shown)

These new tactical scopes have a first-plane reticle, meaning the crosshair measurement maintains the same relativity to the size of the target at any power. The range-calculating reticle of the Tactical scope is etched into the glass in front of the adjustment housing.

At the center of the reticle is a small diamond that covers one inch outside. Marks beyond the diamond on the crosspieces can be used to bracket a target and determine range. Tactical scopes have 1/8-minute-of-angle windage and elevation adjustments with target-style knobs. The knobs also offer a "guaranteed zero" feature that allows the shooter to move the reticle for a specific shooting need, then return the scope to zero without sighting in again. An adjustable objective lens is also included on the 4.5-14x44mm scope for precise parallax-free adjustments.

All air-to-glass lens surfaces are fully multi-coated, and the scopes are waterproof to 10,000 feet and to 120 degrees with 100% humidity. Weaver's Tactical scopes are offered in black matte finish.
**Price:** . . . . . . . . . . . . . . . . . . . . . . . . . . . . . . **$769.99**

## SPECIFICATIONS

| Magnification X Obj. Diam. (mm) | Exit Pupil (mm) | FOV (Ft. @ 100 Yds.) | Eye Relief (In.) | Overall Length (In.) | Weight (Oz.) | Reticle |
|---|---|---|---|---|---|---|
| 3-9x40 | 13.3-4.4 | 33-14.5 | 4.17-3.02 | 12.5 | 17.0 | Diamond |
| 4.5-14x44 | 10-3 | 22-9.4 | 4.1-2.8 | 15.2 | 20.6 | Diamond |

# WEAVER SCOPES

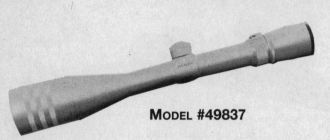

**MODEL #49837**

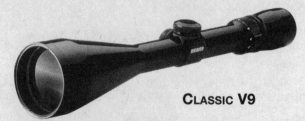

**CLASSIC V9**

**V16 RIFLESCOPES** - The V16 is popular for a variety of shooting applications, from close shots that require a wide field of view to long-range varmint or benchrest shooting. Adjustable objective allows a parallax-free view from 30 feet to infinity. Features one-piece tube for strength and moisture resistance and multicoated lenses for clear, crisp images. Two finishes and three reticle options.
*Magnification/Objective:* 4-16X42mm *Field Of View:* 26.8'-6.8' *Eye Relief:* 3.1" *Length:* 13.9" *Weight:* 16.5 oz. *Reticle:* Choice of Dual-X, 1/4 MOA Dot, or Fine Crosshair *Finish:* Matte black
*Price:* . . . . . . . . . . . . . . . . . . . . . . . . . . . . . **$434.99**
V24 6-24x42 (not shown) black matte. . . . . . . . . 509.99

**OTHER V-SERIES RIFLESCOPES** (not shown)- With broad magnification ranges, these versatile scopes come in a choice of finishes, with dual X-reticle.

**V10 (not shown)**
*Magnification/Objective:* 2-10X38mm *Field Of View:* 38.5-9.5 *Eye Relief:* 3.5 *Length:* 12.2" *Weight:* 11.2 oz. *Reticle:* Dual-X *Finish:* Matte black, silver
*Price:* Matte black . . . . . . . . . . . . . . . . . . . . . . **$269.99**
Silver. . . . . . . . . . . . . . . . . . . . . . . . . . . . . . . 265.99
In gloss black . . . . . . . . . . . . . . . . . . . . . . . . 259.99
**V9**
*Magnification/Objective:* 3.9x38
*Field Of View:* 34-11' *Eye Relief:* 3.5" *Length:* 12" *Weight:* 11 oz. *Finish:* Matte black, gloss
*Price:* Matte black . . . . . . . . . . . . . . . . . . . . . . **$249.99**
Gloss . . . . . . . . . . . . . . . . . . . . . . . . . . . . . . . 299.99
**V3 (not shown)**
*Magnification/Objective:* 1-3x20
*Field Of View:* 100x34 *Eye Relief:* 3.5" *Length:* 9"
*Weight:* 9 oz. *Finish:* Matte black
*Price:* Matte black . . . . . . . . . . . . . . . . . . . . . . **$299.99**

**CLASSIC HANDGUN 1.5-4x20**

**RIMFIRE 2-7x**

**RIMFIRE 4X MATTE SCOPE**

## WEAVER CLASSIC HANDGUN SCOPES
Fixed-power scopes include 2x28 and 4x28 scopes in gloss black or silver. Variables in 1.5-4x20 and 2.5-8x28 come with a gloss black finish. The 2.5-8x28 is also available in black matte. One-piece tubes, fully multi-coated lenses and generous eye relief (4-29") make these scopes top performers on hunting handguns.
**Prices:**
2x28 . . . . . . . . . . . . . . . . . . . **$212.99 (224.99 in silver)**
4x28 . . . . . . . . . . . . . . . . . . . . . . . . . . . . . . . 234.99
1.5-4x20 . . . . . . . . . . . . . . . . . . . . . . . . . . . . 289.99
2.5-8x28 . . . . . . . . . . . . . . . . . . . . . . . . . . . . 299.99

## RIMFIRE SCOPE 2.5-7X
Lenses are multi-coated for bright, clear low-light performance and the one-piece tube design is shockproof and waterproof.
**Prices:**
49622 2.5-7x Rimfire Matte . . . . . . . . . . . . . . . **$184.99**
49623 2.5-7x Rimfire Silver. . . . . . . . . . . . . . . . 189.99
## RIMFIRE SCOPE 4X
Fixed 4x scope is ideal for a variety of shooting applications. It's durable, light-weight and waterproof.
**Prices:**
49620 4x Rimfire Matte . . . . . . . . . . . . . . . . . . . **$159.99**

# WEAVER SCOPES

### GRAND SLAM SCOPE
### 3-10x40MM

## NEW WEAVER GRAND SLAM SCOPES

For 2000 Weaver has announced a new top-level scope line. Among the advanced features of the Grand Slam series are a "sure-grip" power ring and AO adjustment that let you easily adjust the variable scopes, even while wearing heavy gloves, and an offset parallax indicator so you can remain in shooting position while adjusting the scope. Grand Slam scopes feature camera-quality, fully multi-coated lenses that ensure sharp, bright viewing. For quick focusing, the eyepiece has a fast-focus adjustment ring. Simply rotate the ring until the reticle becomes sharp.

Grand Slam scopes' solid, one-piece construction makes them not only rugged and reliable, but resistant to moisture and humidity. Configurations include: 4.75x40mm, a fixed-power scope with sufficient magnification for longer shots, yet a wide field of view for finding running game close in; 1.5-5x32mm, the ideal scope for short-range rifles and fast target acquisition in brushy country; 3.5-10x40mm, the traditional choice of big-game hunters for short- or long-range shooting; 3.5-10x50mm, which provides the brightest view in low-light situations; 4.5-14x40mm AO, possibly the most versatile Grand Slam scope, with a low range suitable for stand hunting and high enough magnification for target shooting or varmint hunting; and 6-20x40mm AO, two target/varminter models.

Windage and elevation knobs have target-type finger adjustments so 1/4-MOA adjustments can be made by gripping the rim of the knob between the thumb and index finger. The Grand Slam scopes are also equipped with Micro-Trac, Weaver's patented four-point adjustment system.

All Grand Slam scopes are offered with a plex reticle (except the 6-20x model, which is offered with a choice of Weaver's Varminter reticle or fine crosshairs with a dot). The new scopes have a non-glare black matte finish with stylish cosmetics, featuring the new green and gold oval Weaver logo medallion on the scope saddle and green ring inside the objective lens hood.

*Price:* 6-20x40 AO . . . . . . . . . . . . . . . . . . . . . . . **$499.99**
4.5-14x40 AO . . . . . . . . . . . . . . . . . . . . . . . . . . . . 499.99
3.5-10x50 . . . . . . . . . . . . . . . . . . . . . . . . . . . . . . . 459.99
3-10x40 . . . . . . . . . . . . . . . . . . . . . . . . . . . . . . . . 379.99
1.5-5x32 . . . . . . . . . . . . . . . . . . . . . . . . . . . . . . . . 429.99
4.75x40 . . . . . . . . . . . . . . . . . . . . . . . . . . . . . . . . 359.99

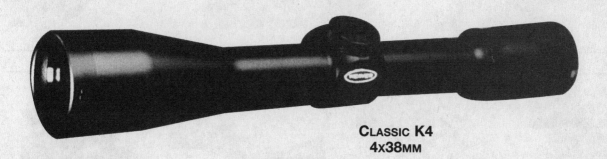

### CLASSIC K4
### 4x38MM

## WEAVER CLASSIC K SERIES

The K2.5, K4 and K6 have a long history in America's game fields. New logos distinguish these versatile hunting scopes at a glance. Reasonably priced and great values, K scopes–including the target model, KT-15–have one-piece tubes and bright optics.

*Prices:*
KT-15 (gloss) . . . . . . . . . . . . . . . . . . . . . . . . . . . . **$374.99**
K6 (black matte or gloss) . . . . . . . . . . . . . . . . . . . . 194.99
K4 (black matte or gloss) . . . . . . . . . . . . . . . . . . . . 194.99
K2.5 (gloss) . . . . . . . . . . . . . . . . . . . . . . . . . . . . . . 179.99

# WILLIAMS

## FP Series

Internal micrometer adjustments have positive internal locks. The FP is strong, rugged, dependable. The alloy used to manufacture this sight has a tensile strength of 85,000 pounds. Yet, the FP is light and compact, weighing only 1-1/2 ounces.

For big game hunting, the FP will outsell all other makes and models of receiver sights put together.

Many rifles are now being drilled and tapped at the factory for installation of the FP.

Target knobs are available on all models of the FP receiver sight if desired.

*Prices:*

| | |
|---|---|
| For most models | $61.95 |
| Target knobs | 73.40 |
| Mini 14 w/sub-base | 71.20 |

**FP-GR-TK**
on Remingto 581

**FP-Knight-TK**
**Silver** on MK-85

**FP-AG-TK**
on Beeman
Air Rifle

**FP-94 SE** shown
on Winchester
94 Side Eject

**FP Mini-14-TK**
**With Sub-Base**

---

### FP Receiver Sight Options

**Standard**

**Target Knobs (TK)**

**Shotgun/Big**
**Game Aperture**

**Blade**

# WILLIAMS

## Open Sights

### WGOS SERIES

- Made from high tensile strength Aluminum. Will not rust.
- All parts milled - no stampings.
- Streamlined and lightweight with tough anodized finish.
- Dovetailed windage and elevation - Easy to adjust, positive locks.
- Interchangeable blades available in four heights and four styles.

**Price:** . . . . . . . . . . . . . . . . . . . . . . . . . . . $16.85-22.50

Blades are sold separately, except "U" blades are available installed on WGOS octagon T/C and CVA.

**Price:** . . . . . . . . . . . . . . . . . . . . . . . . . . . . . $6.50

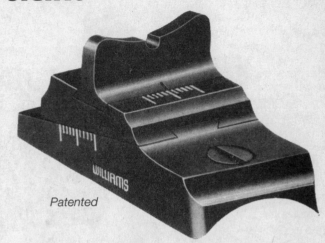

*Patented*

**"SQ"**

**"U"**

**"V"**

**"B"**

## Receiver Sights

### WGRS SERIES

- Compact Low Profile
- Lightweight, Strong, Rustproof
- Positive Windage and Elevation Locks

In most cases these sights utilize dovetail or existing screws on top of receiver for installation. They are made from an aluminum alloy that is stronger than many steels. Light. Rustproof. Williams quality throughout.

**Price:** most models . . . . . . . . . . . . . . . . . . . . . . $31.80

*WGRS-KN on MK-85 Knight Rifle*

### OPEN SIGHT BLADES FOR THE GUIDE RECEIVER SIGHT

The WGRS receiver sight can be converted to an open sight by installing a 1/4" WGOS blade in place of the aperture holder.

*WGRS-CVA on CVA Apolllo*

### "GHOST RING"

Shotgun aperture available For WGRS receiver sights. Sold separately.

# WILLIAMS

## 5D SERIES

### 5D SERIES
- *For Big Game Rifles, 22's, Shotguns*
- *Positive Windage and Elevation Locks*
- *Lightweight, Strong, Accurate*
- *Williams Quality Throughout - Rustproof*

Available for most of the more popular rifles and shotguns - the inexpensive, quality-made 5D sight. These sights have the same strength, lightweight, and neat appearance, but without the micrometer adjustments. Designed for rugged hunting use, the 5D sights are dependable and accurate. Positive locks. Clear unobstructed vision. No knobs or side plates to blot out shooter's field of vision. Wherever possible, the manufacturers' mounting screw holes in the receivers of the guns have been utilized for easy installation. The upper staff of the Williams 5D sight is readily detachable. It is only necessary to loosen one screw so that the upper staff slides easily in the close-fitting dovetail. The angular bushing locks this upper staff in a positive manner. A set screw is provided as a stop screw so that the sight will return to absolute zero upon detaching and reattaching. The material used in the manufacture of the Williams 5D sight is one of the highest grade alloys obtainable. Laboratory tests show that the material used has a tensile strength approximately 25% greater than mild steels.

***Price:*** Most 5D models. . . . . . . . . . . . . . . . . . . . . **$32.50**

## TARGET FP SERIES

HIGH

ANSCHUTZ

LOW

### TARGET - FP (HIGH)
Adjustable From 1.250" to 1.750" Above Centerline of Bore.
***Price:*** . . . . . . . . . . . . . . . . . **$77.15**

### TARGET FP-ANSCHUTZ
Designed to fit many of the Anschutz Lightweight .22 Cal. Target and Sporter Models. No Drilling and Tapping required.
***Price:*** . . . . . . . . . . . . . . . . . **$73.90**

### TARGET - FP (LOW)
Adjustable From .750" to 1.250" Above Centerline of Bore.
***Price:*** . . . . . . . . . . . . . . . . . **$77.15**

# ZEISS RIFLESCOPES

## THE "Z" SERIES

### DIAVARI-C 3-9X36
NEW LIGHTER VERSION OF THE GERMAN-MADE SCOPE NOW BUILT IN THE U.S.A.

**1.5-6x42 ZM/Z STAINLESS**

## ZM/Z SERIES RIFLESCOPE SPECIFICATIONS

| Model | DIATAL-ZM/Z 6X42T | DIAVARI-ZM/Z 1.5-6x42 T | DIAVARI-ZM/Z 3-12x56 T | DIATAL-ZM/Z 8x56 T | DIAVARI-ZM/Z 2.5-10x48 T | DIAVARI-ZM/Z 1.25-4x24 | DIAVARI-C 3-9x36 |
|---|---|---|---|---|---|---|---|
| Magnification | 6X | 1.5 X 6X | 3X 12X | 8X | 2.5X-10X | 1.25-4X | 3X 9X |
| Effective obj. diam. | 42mm/1.7" | 19.5/0.8" 42/1.7" | 38/1.5" 56/2.2" | 56mm/2.2" | 33/1.30" 48/1.89" | NA | 30.0/1.2" 36.0/1.4" |
| Diameter of exit pupil | 7mm | 13mm 7mm | 12.7mm 4.7mm | 7mm | 13.2mm 4.8mm | 12.6mm 6.3mm | 10.0 4.0mm |
| Twilight factor | 15.9 | 4.2 15.9 | 8.5 25.9 | 21.2 | 7.1 21.9 | 3.54 9.6 | 8.5 18.0 |
| Field of view at 100 m/ ft. at 100 yds. | 6.7m/20.1' | 18/54.0' 6.5/19.5' | 9.2/27.6' 3.3/9.9' | 5m/15.0' | 11.0/33.0 3.9/11.7 | 32 10 | 12.0/36.0 4.3/12.9 |
| Approx. eye relief | 8cm/3.2" | 8cm/3.2" | 8cm/3.2" | 8cm/3.2" | 8cm/3.2" | 8cm/3.2" | 3.5" |
| Click-stop adjustment 1 click - (cm at 200 m)/ (inch at 100 yds) | 1cm/0.36" | 1cm/0.36" | 1cm/0.36" | 1cm/0.36" | 1cm/0.36" | 1cm/0.36" | 107/0.25" |
| Max adj. (elv./wind.) at 100m (cm) at 100 yds. | 187 | 190 | 95 | 138 | 110/39.6 | 300 | 135/49 |
| Center tube dia. | 25.4mm/1" | 30mm/1.18" | 30mm/1.18" | 25.4mm/1" | 30mm/1.18" | 30mm/1.18" | 25.4/1.0" |
| Objective bell dia. | 48mm/1.9" | 48mm/1.9" | 62mm/2.44" | 62mm/2.44" | 54mm/2.13" | NA | 44.0/1.7 |
| Ocular bell dia. | 40mm/1.57" | 40mm/1.57" | 40mm/1.57" | 40mm/1.57" | 40mm/1.57" | NA | 42.5/1.8 |
| Length | 324mm/12.8" | 320mm/12.6" | 388mm/15.3" | 369mm/14.5" | 370mm/14.57" | 290mm/11.46" | |
| Approx. weight: ZM | 350g/15.3 oz. | 586g/20.7 oz. | 765g/27.0 oz. | 550g/19.4 oz. | 715g/25.2 oz. | 490g/17.3 oz. | NA |
|       Z | 400g/14.1 oz. | 562g/19.8 | 731g/25.8 oz. | 520g/18.3 oz. | 680g/24 oz. | NA | 430g/15.2 oz. |
| **PRICES:** | | | | | | | |
| Black Matte | $749.00 | $899.00 | $1,099.00 | $799.00 | $1,029.00 | $749.00 | $599.00 |
| Stainless | | 939.00 | 1,149.00 | | 1,069.00 | | 615.00 |
| Illum. Reticle | | | 1,499.00 | | 1,449.00 | | |

# ZEISS RIFLESCOPES

## DIAVARI C 3-9x36 MC

Introduced in 1981, the Diavari C 3-9x 36 quickly gained the respect and admiration of the North American hunter. In 1997, Zeiss moved production of this favorite scope to the USA to provide hunters with a more affordable alternative. If you are in the market for performance - on a budget, the Diavari C 3-9 x 36 MC is the logical choice. The new MC coating boasts a minimum of 90% light transmission and superb image brillance. And when compared to other scopes in its price range, the Diavari C 3-9 x 36 MC offers extraordinary value.

| | | | |
|---|---|---|---|
| POWER | 3-9x | EYE RELIEF (inch) | 3.5 |
| EFFECTIVE OBJECTIVE DIAMETER (mm) | 30-36 | CENTER TUBE DIAMETER (inch) | 1 |
| EXIT PUPIL DIAMETER (mm) | 10-4 | OBJECTIVE BELL DIAMETER (inch) | 1.7 |
| TWILIGHT FACTOR | 8.5-18 | LENGTH (inch) | 11.2 |
| FIELD OF VIEW AT 100 YARDS (feet) | 36-12.9 | WEIGHT (ounces) | 15.2 |
| MINIMUM SQUARE | | PARALLAX FREE (yards) | 100 |
| ADJUSTMENT RANGE | | Price: . . . . . . . . . . . . . . . . . . . . . . . . . . . .$599.00 | |
| AT 100 YARDS (inch) | 48.6 | Stainless or silver . . . . . . . . . . . . . . . . . . . . . . . .615.00 | |

## ZEISS HAS THE RIGHT RETICLE FOR YOU

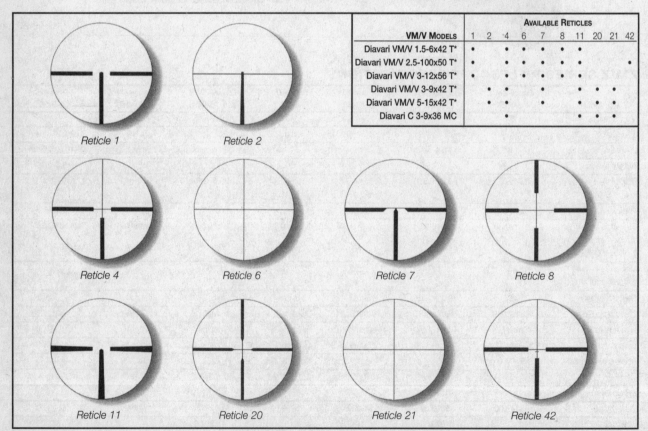

| | AVAILABLE RETICLES | | | | | | | | | |
|---|---|---|---|---|---|---|---|---|---|---|
| VM/V MODELS | 1 | 2 | 4 | 6 | 7 | 8 | 11 | 20 | 21 | 42 |
| Diavari VM/V 1.5-6x42 T* | • | | • | • | • | • | • | | | |
| Diavari VM/V 2.5-100x50 T* | • | | • | • | | • | • | | | • |
| Diavari VM/V 3-12x56 T* | • | | • | | • | • | • | | | |
| Diavari VM/V 3-9x42 T* | | • | • | | | • | | • | • | • |
| Diavari VM/V 5-15x42 T* | | • | • | | • | | | • | • | • |
| Diavari C 3-9x36 MC | | | • | | | | | • | • | • |

Reticle 1

Reticle 2

Reticle 4

Reticle 6

Reticle 7

Reticle 8

Reticle 11

Reticle 20

Reticle 21

Reticle 42

*If you already own a Zeiss riflescope, Zeiss may be abe to change the reticle for you. For more information contact your local Zeiss representative.*

# ZEISS RIFLESCOPES

## DIAVARI VM/V 3-9x42 T*

Over the years, the 3-9x power range has proven its staying power. Still the favorite power range of North American hunters, the new Diavari VM/V 3-9 x 42 T* will be the overwhelming choice of the traditionalist. The 42 mm objective, coupled with the newly developed optical system and famous Zeiss T* coating, will extend your hunting day. Whether your quarry is elk, Dall sheep or Boone and Crockett white-tail, the VM/V Diavari 3-9 x 42T* offers top quality and the right magnification.

| | | | |
|---|---|---|---|
| POWER | 3-9x | EYE RELIEF (inch) | 3.74 |
| EFFECTIVE OBJECTIVE DIAMETER (mm) | 30-42 | CENTER TUBE DIAMETER (inch) | 1 |
| EXIT PUPIL DIAMETER (mm) | 10-4.7 | OBJECTIVE BELL DIAMETER (inch) | 1.89 |
| TWILIGHT FACTOR | 8.5-18.4 | LENGTH (inch) | 13.3 |
| FIELD OF VIEW AT 100 YARDS (feet) | 39.6-13.2 | WEIGHT (ounces) | 14.8-14 |
| MINIMUM SQUARE ADJUSTMENT RANGE | | PARALLAX FREE (yards) | 109.4 |
| AT 100 YARDS (inch) | 49.7 | Price: . . . . . . . . . . . . . . . . . . . . . . . . . . . . . .$1,249.95 |

## DIAVARI VM/V 5-15x42 T*

If you enjoy testing your long range shooting skills, you are going to love this new scope. Precise windage and elevation adjustments make the new Diavari VM/V 5 - 15 x 42 T* the perfect companion for your favorite target or varmint rifle. Designed for years of trouble free service, its rugged adjustment system gives you fast, accurate and repeatable adjustments. By aligning the optical and mechanical axes, Zeiss ensures you have the full range of adjustment.

| | | | |
|---|---|---|---|
| POWER | 5-15x | EYE RELIEF (inch) | 3.74 |
| EFFECTIVE OBJECTIVE DIAMETER (mm) | 42-42 | CENTER TUBE DIAMETER (inch) | 1 |
| EXIT PUPIL DIAMETER (mm) | 8.4-2.8 | OBJECTIVE BELL DIAMETER (inch) | 1.89 |
| TWILIGHT FACTOR | 14.1-25.1 | LENGTH (inch) | 13.3 |
| FIELD OF VIEW AT 100 YARDS (feet) | 23.7-7.8 | WEIGHT (ounces) | 14.9-14 |
| MINIMUM SQUARE ADJUSTMENT RANGE | | PARALLAX FREE (yards) | 109.4 |
| AT 100 YARDS (inch) | 30 | Price: . . . . . . . . . . . . . . . . . . . . . . . . . . . . .$1,499.95 |

# ZEISS RIFLESCOPES

## DIAVARI VM/V 3-12x56 T*

In the quiet haze of dawn or the fleeting light of sunset, a riflesope is put to the ultimate test. Under these conditions, the Diavari VM/V 3-12x56 T* establishes its reputation for unrivaled performance. The patented Zeiss T* anti-reflection coating is designed to transmit the optimum percentage of light throughout the spectral range to take full advantage of your eye's sensitivity. Weighing in at a mere 13.5 ounces, the VM/V 3-12x56 T* won't slow you down. 30mm tube.

| | | | |
|---|---|---|---|
| POWER | 3-12x | EYE RELIEF (inch) | 3.54 |
| EFFECTIVE OBJECTIVE DIAMETER (mm) | 44.0-56 | CENTER TUBE DIAMETER (inch) | 1.18 |
| EXIT PUPIL DIAMETER (mm) | 14.7-4.7 | OBJECTIVE BELL DIAMETER (inch) | 2.44 |
| TWILIGHT FACTOR | 8.5-25.9 | LENGTH (inch) | 13.54 |
| FIELD OF VIEW AT 100 YARDS (feet) | 37.5-10.4 | WEIGHT (ounces) | 17.8/16.8 |
| MINIMUM SQUARE | | PARALLAX FREE (yards) | 109.4 |
| ADJUSTMENT RANGE | | Price: . . . . . . . . . . . . . . . . . . . . . . . . . . . . . . .$1,599.95 | |
| AT 100 YARDS (inch) | 36.7 | w/illuminated reticle . . . . . . . . . . . . . . . . . . . . .2,049.95 | |

## ZEISS—PREMIUM SPORTS OPTICS

**1.1-4 x 24 T***

### DIAVARI 1.1-4 X 24 T* VM/V
• Compact riflescope with 108 ft. field of view at 1.1 power
• Extremely lightweight - ideal for safari rifles
• With illuminated varipoint reticle for fast target acquisition clearly visible also in critical lighting conditions
• Especially designed for running shots and hunting in heavy brush
• Available with bullet drop compensator
• Eye relief: 3.74 in.
*Price:*. . . . . . . . . . . . . . . . . . . . . . . . . . . . . . . $1,799.95

**1.5-6 x 42 T***

### DIAVARI 1.5-6 X 42 T* VM/V
• Excellent choice for white-tail or moose hunter
• Compact and easy to handle
• Lightest scope of its class
• 72 ft. field of view - largest field of view in premium class
• Easy-grip adjustment knob
• Available with bullet drop compensator
• Eye relief: 3.54 in.
*Price:*. . . . . . . . . . . . . . . . . . . . . . . . . . . . . . . $1,349.95

**2.5-10 x 50 T***

### DIAVARI 2.5-10 X 50 T* VM/V
• High powered riflescope with superior twilight performance
• Light, compact with a wide field of view
• Available with an illuminated reticle
• Easy-grip adjustment knob
• Excellent choice for world-wide all-round hunting
• Available with bullet drop compensator
• Eye relief: 3.54 in.
*Price:*. . . . . . . . . . . . . . . . . . . . . . . . . . . . . . . $1,549.95
w/illuminated reticle . . . . . . . . . . . . . . . . . . . . 1,999.95

**Ammunition**

*For addresses and phone/fax numbers of manufacturers and distributors included in this section, please turn to **DIRECTORY OF MANUFACTURERS AND SUPPLIERS** on page 564.*

# BLACK HILLS AMMUNITION

Black Hills, aptly named for its South Dakota base of operations, offers an expanding line of factory-new and remanufactured ammunition, for handguns and rifles. The Cowboy Action Line includes loads for the .357 Magnum, .38-40, .44-40, .45 Colt, .32-20, .44 Colt, .44 Spt., .45 Schofield, .38 Spl, .38 Long Colt, .44 Russian, .45-70. Modern handgun ammunition, from .380 Auto to .44

Magnum, features a variety of bullet types. Black Hills rifle cartridges include the popular .223, .308 and .300 Win. Mag, and the potent long-range tactical round, the .338 Lapua. There's also specialty ammo, with frangible or moly-coated bullets. Black Hills sells the Norma Diamond ammunition, including such hard-to-find numbers as the 6 Norma BR and 6.5-284.

# FEDERAL AMMUNITION

*Federal's 2000 line-up includes ammunition and components for big game and wildfowl hunters and personal defense. Some examples:*

### PREMIUM BARNES EXPANDER SABOT SLUG
*The expansive hollow point of the Barnes Expander delivers expansion 150% greater than conventional sabot slugs and groups 2.5" or better at 100 yards.*

### PREMIUM SABOT SLUG
*In a rifled barrel, Premium Sabot Slugs are capable of 2.5" groups at 100 yards.*

### PREMIUM RIFLED SLUG
*Federal Premium Rifled Slugs feature helix ribbing and the unique Hydra-Shok hollow point.*

### PREMIUM SLUGS

Federal's Premium Slug line includes three highly accurate, highly effective slugs: rifled slug for smoothbores, copper-plated sabot slug for rifled barrels or rifled choke tubes and the Barnes Expander Sabot Slug for fully rifled barrels. The rifled slug delivers 2" groups at 50 yards, while both sabot styles consistently group as tight as 2.5" at 100 yards.

### NEW FEDERAL DEEP-SHOK BULLET PREMIUM WOODLEIGH WELDCORE CENTERFIRE RIFLE (NOT SHOWN)

Federal has expanded its big game ammo line with a new softpoint bullet designed for deep penetration. The Deep-Shok is more affordable than many of its competitors and comes in six popular loadings. The Woodleigh Weldcore, a bonded-core bullet with a special heavy jacket for extra penetration power, is still available in .416 and .458 loads.

### PREMIUM PERSONAL DEFENSE PISTOL

This jacketed hollow point load comes in clear plastic packaging that offers protection against moisture and rough treatment. New for 2000 is a hunting load for the .454 Casull, featuring a 300-grain Trophy Bonded bullet. Federal now offers non-toxic ammo for three handgun cartridges.

### PREMIUM TUNGSTEN-IRON TURKEY SHOTSHELL

This turkey load has the pellet energy of lead, a velocity of 1300 feet per second, and good penetration. Tight patterns and excellent penetration assure success of this load among turkey hunters. Tungsten-Polymer loads offer the same deadly performance to waterfowlers. New Gold Medal Spreader loads for target shooters and combination steel-tungsten iron loads for waterfowlers round out the 2000 shotshell line.

# FEDERAL CENTERFIRE RIFLE AMMUNITION

## PREMIUM LOAD BULLET SELECTION

### PREMIUM CENTERFIRE RIFLE

Combining the world's best brand-name bullet designs with our advanced delivery systems, Federal Premium performs better than handloads, right out of the box.

### TROPHY BONDED BEAR CLAW®

*Excellent for small to heavy game.*
Only Federal offers this famous Jack Carter design in a factory load. The jacket and core are 100% fusion bonded. Superb accuracy, 95% weight retention, deep penetration and reliable expansion from 25 yards to extreme ranges.

### TROPHY BONDED SLEDGEHAMMER®

*Excellent for large and dangerous game.*
Also a Jack Carter design, this bonded bronze solid delivers maximum stopping power. The flat nose minimizes deflection for a straight, deep wound cavity.

### BARNES XLC COATED-X BULLET™

*Superb stopping power for small to large game.*
New for 1999-2000, this hard-hitting design features a 100% copper bullet, four petal expansion and hollow cavity 1/3 the bullet length for deep penetration and 100% weight retention. Heat cured dry film lubricant prevents copper fouling, reduces bore friction and won't rub off on hands.

### WOODLEIGH® WELDCORE

*Smaller calibers are excellent for medium to large game. Larger calibers are favored for very large or dangerous game.*
Safari hunters have long respected this bonded Australian bullet for its superb accuracy and excellent stopping power. Its special heavy jacket provides 80-85% weight retention.

### NOSLER® PARTITION®

*A proven favorite for medium to large game.*
The tapered H-shaped brass jacket of the Nosler Partition allows the front half of the bullet to mushroom on impact while the rear core remains intact, providing additional penetration and stopping power.

### SIERRA GAMEKING® BOAT-TAIL

*Long-range choice for varmints to big game.*
The tapered design of the Sierra GameKing Boat-Tail provides extremely flat trajectories while offering higher retained velocity and downrange energy for excellent stopping power. Reduced wind drift makes it a good choice for long-range shots.

### NOSLER BALLISTIC TIP®

*Especially for long-range shots at varmints, predators and small to medium game.*
Proven fast, flat-shooting, wind-defying performance. Color-coded polycarbonate tip provides easy identification, prevents deformation in the magazine and drives back on impact for explosive expansion and immediate energy transfer.

Round for round, Federal Premium Centerfire Rifle is the best cartridge available. We start with the world's most technologically advanced bullets, Federal's are match with world-class brass, precision powders and legendary primers. The result is a cartridge that outperforms handloads.

# FIOCCHI AMMUNITION

Known for its shotshells and .22 rimfire ammunition, Fiocchi also markets centerfire pistol and rifle cartridges. This Italian firm has been in business since 1876. The line is too extensive to show in its entirety here.

Fiocchi Target Loads offer you many choices to suit the shell to your game. Standard 1-1/8 ounce loads for everything from registered trap and skeet to sporting clays. One ounce loads that deliver superior performance with less recoil than a comparable 1-1/8 ounce load. Also, a 7/8 ounce training load for new or recoil sensitive shooters. Other target loads include hot, 1 ounce loads for long or hard targets and 1 and 1-1/8 ounce spreaders for close, fast targets. Fiocchi lilac hulls are fully reloadable. Contact the factory or any reloading supply shop.

| Stock # | | Shell Gauge | Dram. Length | Muzzle Equiv. | Shot Velocity | Oz. | Shot Sizes | Rds./Box | Shot Type |
|---|---|---|---|---|---|---|---|---|---|
| **STEEL (WATERFOWL LOADS)** | | | | | | | | | |
| 1235ST | Speed Steel | 12 | 3 1/2" | Max. | 1460 | 1 3/8 | T BBB BB 1 | 25 | Treated Steel |
| 1235SH | Heavy Steel | 12 | 3 1/2" | Max. | 1300 | 1 9/16 | T BBB BB 1 | 25 | Treated Steel |
| 123ST | Speed Steel | 12 | 3" | Max. | 1475 | 1 1/8 | BBB BB 1 2 3 4 | 25 | Treated Steel |
| 123S | Steel | 12 | 3" | Max. | 1320 | 1 1/4 | T BBB BB 1 2 3 4 | 25 | Treated Steel |
| 123SH | Heavy Steel | 12 | 3" | Max. | 1350 | 1 3/8 | BB 1 2 3 4 | 25 | Treated Steel |
| 12S78 | Training Load | 12 | 2 3/4" | Max. | 1440 | 7/8 | 7 | 25 | Treated Steel |
| 12S1OZ | Upland Steel | 12 | 2 3/4" | Max. | 1400 | 1 | 4 6 7 | 25 | Treated Steel |
| 12S118 | Steel | 12 | 2 3/4" | Max. | 1375 | 1 1/8 | BB 1 2 3 4 6 2 5 | | Treated Steel |
| 12S114 | Heavy Steel | 12 | 2 3/4" | Max. | 1275 | 1 1/4 | BB 1 2 3 4 | 25 | Treated Steel |
| 20S | Upland Steel | 20 | 2 3/4" | Max. | 1470 | 3/4 | 3 4 6 7 | 25 | Treated Steel |
| 203ST | Speed Steel | 20 | 3" | Max. | 1500 | 7/8 | 2 3 4 | 25 | Treated Steel |
| **FIELD LOADS (UPLAND GAME LOADS)** | | | | | | | | | |
| 12HF | Heavy Field | 12 | 2 3/4" | 3 1/4 | 1225 | 1 1/4 | 6 7-1/2 / 8 9 | 25 | Lead |
| 12FLD | Field Load | 12 | 2 3/4" | 3 1/4 | 1255 | 1 1/8 | 6 7-1/2 8 9 | 25 | Lead |
| 16FLD | Field Load | 16 | 2 3/4" | 2 3/4 | 1185 | 1 1/8 | 6 7-1/2 8 | 25 | Lead |
| 20FLD | Field Load | 20 | 2 3/4" | 2 1/2 | 1165 | 1 | 6 7-1/2 8 9 | 25 | Lead |
| **DOVE LOADS** | | | | | | | | | |
| 12MS3 | Multi Sport | 12 | 2 3/4" | 3 | 1250 | 1 | 7-1/2 8 9 | 25 | Lead |
| 12GT1 | Game & Target | 12 | 2 3/4" | 3 1/4 | 1290 | 1 | 6 7-1/2 8 9 | 25 | Lead |
| 12GT118 | Game & Target | 12 | 2 3/4" | 3 | 1200 | 1 1/8 | 7-1/2 8 | 25 | Lead |
| 16GT | Game & Target | 16 | 2 3/4" | 2 1/2 | 1165 | 1 | 6 7-1/2 8 9 | 25 | Lead |
| 20GT | Game & Target | 20 | 2 3/4" | 2 1/2 | 1210 | 7/8 | 6 7-1/2 8 9 | 25 | Lead |
| 28GT | Game & Target | 28 | 2 3/4" | 2 | 1200 | 3/4 | 8 9 | 25 | Lead |
| 410GT | Game & Target | 410 | 2 1/2" | Max | 1200 | 1/2 | 8 9 | 25 | Lead |
| **TARGET LOADS** | | | | | | | | | |
| 12TL | Target Light | 12 | 2 3/4" | 2 3/4 | 1150 | 1 | 7-1/2 8 8-1/2 9 | 25 | Hi-Antimony Lead |
| 12TH | Target Heavy | 12 | 2 3/4" | 3 | 1200 | 1 | 7-1/2 8 8-1/2 | 25 | Hi-Antimony Lead |
| 12TX | Little Rino | 12 | 2 3/4" | HDCP | 1250 | 1 | 7-1/2 8 8-1/2 | 25 | Hi-Antimony Lead |
| 12CRSR | Crusher | 12 | 2 3/4" | Max | 1300 | 1 | 7-1/2 8 8-1/2 9 | 25 | Hi-Antimony Lead |
| 12LITE | Lite | 12 | 2 3/4" | 2 7/8 | 1165 | 1 1/8 | 7-1/2 8 9 | 25 | Hi-Antimony Lead |
| 12VIPL | VIP Light | 12 | 2 3/4" | 2 3/4 | 1150 | 1 1/8 | 7-1/2 8 9 | 25 | Hi-Antimony Lead |
| 12VIPH | VIP Heavy | 12 | 2 3/4" | 3 | 1200 | 1 1/8 | 7-1/2 8 9 | 25 | Hi-Antimony Lead |
| 12WRNO | White Rino | 12 | 2 3/4" | HDCP | 1250 | 1 1/8 | 7-1/2 8 8-1/2 9 | 25 | Hi-Antimony Lead |
| 12780Z | Training Load | 12 | 2 3/4" | 3 | 1200 | 7/8 | 7-1/2 8 | 25 | Hi-Antimony Lead |
| 12IN24 | International | 12 | 2 3/4" | Max | 1350 | 24 grams | 7-1/2 8 8-1/2 | 25 | Hi-Antimony Lead |
| **SUB-GAUGE** | | | | | | | | | |
| 20VIP | VIP | 20 | 2 3/4" | 2 1/2 | 1200 | 7/8 | 7-1/2 8 9 | 25 | Hi-Antimony Lead |
| 28GT | Game & Target | 28 | 2 3/4" | 2 | 1200 | 3/4 | 8 9 | 25 | Lead |
| 410GT | Game & Target | 410 | 2 1/2" | Max | 1200 | 1/2 | 8 9 | 25 | Lead |

# FIOCCHI AMMUNITION

## SHOTSHELL APPLICATION GUIDE

| Game | Lead Shot Size | Steel Shot Size | Recommended Loads |
|---|---|---|---|
| Geese | NA | T-BBB-BB-1 | Heavy Steel, Speed Steel |
| Ducks | NA | BB-1-2-3-4-6 | Heavy Steel, Speed Steel, Upland Steel |
| Pheasant | 4-5-6 | 3-4-5-6 | Golden Pheasant, HV, Speed Steel, Upland Steel, HVN |
| Turkey | 4-5-6 | 4-5 | Turkey Tunder, HV, HVN |
| Grouse/Partridge | 5-6-7 1/2-8 | 4-6-7 | Field Loads, Upland Steel, HV, HVN, HFN |
| Quail | 7 1/2-8-9 | 7 | Field Loads, HV, Upland Steel, HVN, HFN |
| Dove/Pigeon | 6-7 1/2-8-9 | 6-7 | Field Loads, GT, Dove, HV, HFN, HVN |
| Rabbit/Squirrel | 4-5-6-7 1/2 | 6-7 | Field Loads, HV, GT, Upland Steel, HFN, HVN |
| Deer/Boar | 00-Slug | NA | 12HV00BK, 12 Gauge Slug, 20 Gauge Slug |
| Trap | 7 1/2-8-8 1/2 | 6-7 | TL, TH, TX, VIP, LITE, WRNO, MS, TRAPH, TRAPL |
| Skeet | 8-8 1/2-9 | 7 | TL, TH, TX, VIP, LITE, WRNO, MS |
| Sporting Clays | 7 1/2-8-8 1/2-9 | 7 | TL, TH, TX, TIP, LITE, WRNO, MS |
| Steel Target | | | Upland Steel, Training Load |

## SHOT PELLET SIZES

| Size # | 9 | 8-1/2 | 8 | 7-1/2 | 6 | 5 | 4 | 3 | 2 | 1 | BB | BBB | T | #4 | 00 |
|---|---|---|---|---|---|---|---|---|---|---|---|---|---|---|---|
| Dia.In. | .08 | .085 | .09 | .095 | .11 | .12 | .13 | .14 | .15 | .16 | .18 | .19 | .20 | .24 | .33 |
| Dia.MM | 2.03 | 2.16 | 2.29 | 2.41 | 279 | 3.05 | 3.30 | 3.56 | 3.81 | 4.06 | 4.57 | 4.83 | 5.08 | 6.10 | 8.38 |

## NUMBER OF LEAD PELLETS IN VARIOUS LOADS

| Lead Pellets | 9 | 8-1/2 | 8 | 7-1/2 | 6 | 5 | 4 |
|---|---|---|---|---|---|---|---|
| 1 oz. | 585 | 480 | 409 | 345 | 232 | 172 | 136 |
| 1 1/8 oz. 658 | 540 | 460 | 388 | 251 | 194 | 153 | |
| 1 1/4 oz. 731 | 600 | 511 | 431 | 276 | 215 | 170 | |
| 1 3/8 oz. 804 | 660 | 562 | 474 | 307 | 237 | 187 | |
| 1 3/4 oz. - | - | - | - | 395 | 304 | 239 | |

## NUMBER OF STEEL PELLETS IN VARIOUS LOADS

| Steel Pellets | 7 | 6 | 4 | 3 | 2 | 1 | BB | BBB | T |
|---|---|---|---|---|---|---|---|---|---|
| 3/4 oz. | 315 | 237 | 143 | 115 | - | - | - | - | - |
| 7/8 oz. | 365 | - | 167 | 134 | 109 | - | - | - | - |
| 1 oz. | 420 | 316 | 191 | - | - | - | - | - | - |
| 1 1/8 oz. - | | 355 | 215 | 172 | 140 | 115 | 81 | 68 | |
| 1 1/4 oz. - | | - | 239 | 191 | 151 | 128 | 90 | - | - |
| 1 3/8 oz. - | | - | 262 | 210 | 171 | 141 | 99 | 84 | 73 |
| 1 9/16 oz. - | | - | - | - | 161 | 113 | 95 | 83 | |

**Note:** *When comparing steel shot to lead shot, increase shot size by two to get similar downrange results (i.e. Lead #4 to Steel #2).
Check your shotgun and choke manufacturer for steel shot compatibility.*

# FIOCCHI SPECIALTY SHOTSHELLS

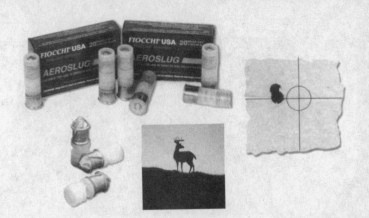

## SLUGS

Fiocchi's Slugs in both 12 and 20 gauge feature a lead slug with attached wad profiled to provide in-flight stability and increased on-target accuracy.

Three shot group measures .450 inches. Group fired at 50 yds. from a bench rest with a Mossberg 500 Crown Grade 24" fully rifled barrel and 4 power scope.

| STOCK # | GAUGE | SHELL LENGTH | DRAM. EQUIV. | MUZZLE VELOCITY | PELLET CT. | SHOT SIZES | RDS. BOX | SHOT TYPE |
|---|---|---|---|---|---|---|---|---|
| **BUCKSHOT** | | | | | | | | |
| 12HV4BKBuckshot | 12 | 2 3/4" | Max | 1325 | 27 pell. | 4 Buck | 10 | Hi-Antimony Nickel Plated |
| 12HV00BK Buckshot | 12 | 2 3/4" | Max | 1300 | 9 pell. | 00 Buck | 10 | Hi-Antimonay Nickel Plated |
| 12LE00BK Reduced Recoil* | 12 | 2 3/4" | Max | 1150 | 9 pell. | 00 Buck | 10 | Hi-Antimony Nickel Plated |

| STOCK # | GAUGE | SHELL LENGTH | MM | DRAM. EQUIV. | MUZZLE VELOCITY | SHOT OZ. | SHOT SIZES | RDS. BOX | SHOT TYPE |
|---|---|---|---|---|---|---|---|---|---|
| **SLUGS** | | | | | | | | | |
| 12TS1 Trophy Slug | 12 | 2 3/4" | 70 | Max | 1560 | 1 | Rifled Slug | 5 | Lead w/attached Wad |
| 20TS78 Trophy Slug | 20 | 2/34" | 70 | Max | 1650 | 7/8 | Rifled Slug | 5 | Lead w/attached Wad |

| STOCK # | GAUGE | SHELL LENGTH | DRAM. EQUIV. | MUZZLE VELOCITY | SHOT OZ. | SHOT SIZES | RDS. BOX | SHOT TYPE |
|---|---|---|---|---|---|---|---|---|
| **NICKEL PLATED HUNTING LOADS** | | | | | | | | |
| 12HFN Live Bird Pigeon | 12 | 2 3/4" | 3 1/4 | 1225 | 1 1/4 | 7-1/2 8 | 25 | Nickel Plated Lead |
| 12HVN High Velocity Nickel | 12 | 2 3/4" | 3 3/4 | 1330 | 1 1/4 | 4 5 6 7-1/2 8 9 | 25 | Nickel Plated Lead |
| 12GP Golden Pheasant | 12 | 2 3/4" | Max | 1250 | 1 3/8 | 4 5 6 | 25 | Nickel Plated Lead |
| 203GP Golden Pheasant 20 | 20 | 3" | Max | 1200 | 1 1/4 | 4 5 6 | 25 | Nickel Plated Lead |
| 12TT Turkey Thunder | 12 | 2 3/4" | Max | 1250 | 1 3/8 | 4 5 6 | 10 | Nickel Plated Lead |
| 123TT Turkey Thunder | 12 | 3 | Max | 1150 | 1 3/4 | 4 5 6 | 10 | Nickel Plated Lead |
| **FITASC** | | | | | | | | |
| 12HFN Live Bird Pigeon/FITASC | 12 | 2 3/4" | 3 1/4 | 1225 | 1 1/4 | 7-1/2 8 | 25 | Nickel Plated Lead |
| **INTERCEPTOR SPREADER** | | | | | | | | |
| 12CPTR Interceptor | 12 | 2 3/4" | Max | 1300 | 1 | 7-1/2 8 8-1/2 9 | 25 | Lead |
| **SPORTING CLAYS POWER SPREADERS** | | | | | | | | |
| 12SSCH Power Spreader | 12 | 2 3/4" | 3 | 1200 | 1 1/8 | 7-1/2 8 8-1/2 9 | 25 | Lead |
| 12SSCX Power Spreader | 12 | 2 3/4" | Max | 1250 | 1 1/8 | 8 8-1/2 9 | 25 | Lead |
| **STEEL TARGET LOAD** | | | | | | | | |
| 12S78 Steel Target Load | 12 | 2 3/4" | Max | 1440 | 7/8 | 7 | 25 | Steel |
| 12S1OZ Steel Target Load | 12 | 2 3/4" | Max | 1400 | 1 | 6 7 | 25 | Steel |
| 20S34 Steel Target Load | 20 | 2 3/4" | Max | 1500 | 7/8 | 6 7 | 25 | Steel |
| **ULTRA LOW RECOIL LOADS** | | | | | | | | |
| 1278OZ Trainer | 12 | 2 3/4" | Lite | 120 | 7/8 | 7-1/2 8 | 25 | Hi-Antimony Lead |

# HORNADY AMMUNITION

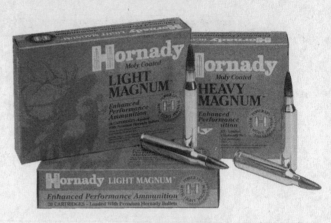

Hornady's moly-coated **LIGHT MAGNUM** ammo achieves more energy, flatter trajectory and velocities up to 200 feet per second faster than standard ammo. That same performance is now available in .280 Remington and 7mm Remington Magnum. With Light Magnum and Heavy Magnum, greater velocity is achieved from standard cartridges with no additional heat and pressure. The addition of molybdenum disulfide to these bullets cuts friction and eliminates copper fouling in the bore—more rounds can be fired without stopping to clean the rifle.

Hornady's **SST (SUPER SHOCK TIPPED)** bullets feature a premium polymer tip which, along with its profile, combine to improve the SST's ballistic coefficient. The result: greater velocity and better accuracy. Upon impact, the tip is pushed backward into the lead core to initiate immediate expansion. The specially designed jacket grips and controls the expanding core, allowing the bullet to reach its optimum mass and momentum.

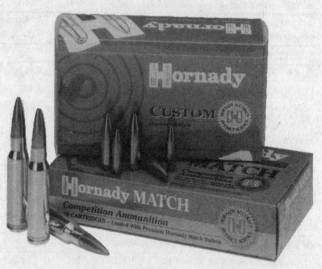

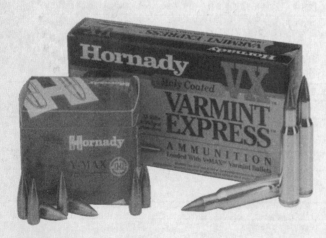

Hornady's **VARMINT EXPRESS** ammunition now features moly-coated V-MAX bullets, which offer faster speeds in most calibers. Other features include high quality brass cases, hand-inspection, individually selected primers and powders.

The effectiveness of Hornady's factory-loaded rifle match ammunition is assured by hand-selection and matching for premium uniformity. Cases, powder and primer are all loaded so as to guarantee superb ignition and pinpoint accuracy. These match cartridges are loaded with either Hornady **A-MAX** or **BTHP** match bullets, are now available with high-performance moly-coating that reduces barrel wear and increases speed.

# HORNADY

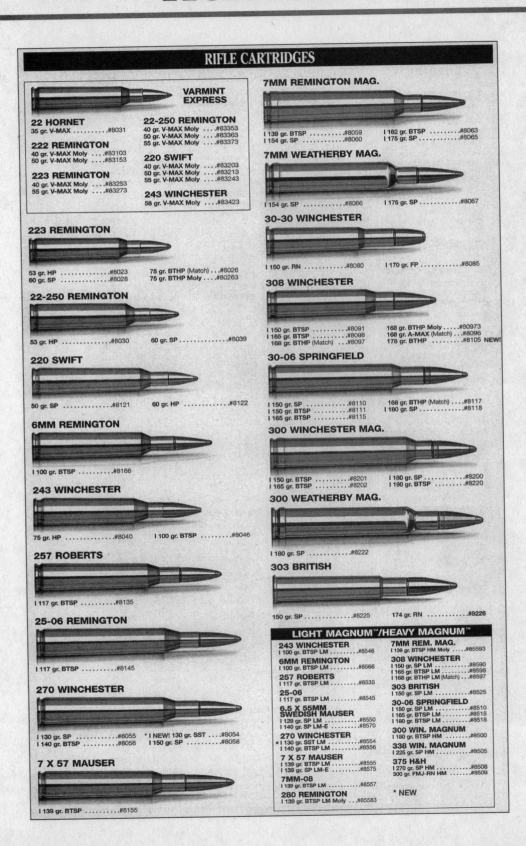

## RIFLE CARTRIDGES

### VARMINT EXPRESS

**22 HORNET**
35 gr. V-MAX .........#8031

**222 REMINGTON**
40 gr. V-MAX Moly ....#83103
50 gr. V-MAX Moly ....#83153

**223 REMINGTON**
40 gr. V-MAX Moly ....#83253
55 gr. V-MAX Moly ....#83273

**22-250 REMINGTON**
40 gr. V-MAX Moly ....#83353
50 gr. V-MAX Moly ....#83363
55 gr. V-MAX Moly ....#83373

**220 SWIFT**
40 gr. V-MAX Moly ....#83203
50 gr. V-MAX Moly ....#83213
55 gr. V-MAX Moly ....#83243

**243 WINCHESTER**
58 gr. V-MAX Moly ....#83423

### 223 REMINGTON
53 gr. HP .............#8023
60 gr. SP .............#8028
75 gr. BTHP (Match) ...#8026
75 gr. BTHP Moly ....#80263

### 22-250 REMINGTON
53 gr. HP .............#8030
60 gr. SP .............#8039

### 220 SWIFT
50 gr. SP .............#8121
60 gr. HP .............#8122

### 6MM REMINGTON
100 gr. BTSP .........#8166

### 243 WINCHESTER
75 gr. HP .............#8040
100 gr. BTSP .........#8046

### 257 ROBERTS
117 gr. BTSP .........#8135

### 25-06 REMINGTON
117 gr. BTSP .........#8145

### 270 WINCHESTER
130 gr. SP .........#8055
140 gr. BTSP .......#8056
* NEW! 130 gr. SST ..#8054
150 gr. SP .........#8058

### 7 X 57 MAUSER
139 gr. BTSP .........#8155

### 7MM REMINGTON MAG.
139 gr. BTSP .........#8059
154 gr. SP ...........#8060
162 gr. BTSP .........#8063
175 gr. SP ...........#8065

### 7MM WEATHERBY MAG.
154 gr. SP ...........#8066
175 gr. SP ...........#8067

### 30-30 WINCHESTER
150 gr. RN ...........#8080
170 gr. FP ...........#8085

### 308 WINCHESTER
150 gr. BTSP .........#8091
165 gr. BTSP .........#8098
168 gr. BTHP (Match) ..#8097
168 gr. BTHP Moly .....#80973
168 gr. A-MAX (Match) ..#8096
178 gr. BTHP .........#8105 NEW!

### 30-06 SPRINGFIELD
150 gr. SP ...........#8110
150 gr. BTSP .........#8111
165 gr. BTSP .........#8115
168 gr. BTHP (Match) ....#8117
180 gr. SP ...........#8118

### 300 WINCHESTER MAG.
150 gr. BTSP .........#8201
165 gr. BTSP .........#8202
180 gr. SP ...........#8200
190 gr. BTSP .........#8220

### 300 WEATHERBY MAG.
180 gr. SP ...........#8222

### 303 BRITISH
150 gr. SP ...........#8225
174 gr. RN ...........#8226

### LIGHT MAGNUM™/HEAVY MAGNUM™

**243 WINCHESTER**
100 gr. BTSP LM .......#8546

**6MM REMINGTON**
100 gr. BTSP LM .......#8566

**257 ROBERTS**
117 gr. BTSP LM .......#8535

**25-06**
117 gr. BTSP LM .......#8545

**6.5 X 55MM SWEDISH MAUSER**
129 gr. SP LM .......#8550
140 gr. SP LM-E .....#8570

**270 WINCHESTER**
* 130 gr. SST LM .....#8554
140 gr. BTSP LM .....#8556

**7 X 57 MAUSER**
139 gr. BTSP LM .....#8555
139 gr. SP LM-E .....#8575

**7MM-08**
139 gr. BTSP LM .....#8557

**280 REMINGTON**
139 gr. BTSP LM Moly ...#85583

**7MM REM. MAG.**
139 gr. BTSP HM Moly ....#85593

**308 WINCHESTER**
150 gr. SP LM .......#8590
165 gr. BTSP LM .....#8598
168 gr. BTHP LM (Match) ..#8597

**303 BRITISH**
150 gr. SP LM .......#8525

**30-06 SPRINGFIELD**
150 gr. SP LM .......#8510
165 gr. BTSP LM .....#8515
180 gr. BTSP LM .....#8518

**300 WIN. MAGNUM**
180 gr. BTSP HM .....#8500

**338 WIN. MAGNUM**
225 gr. SP HM .......#8505

**375 H&H**
270 gr. SP HM .......#8508
300 gr. FMJ-RN HM .....#8509

* NEW

# HORNADY

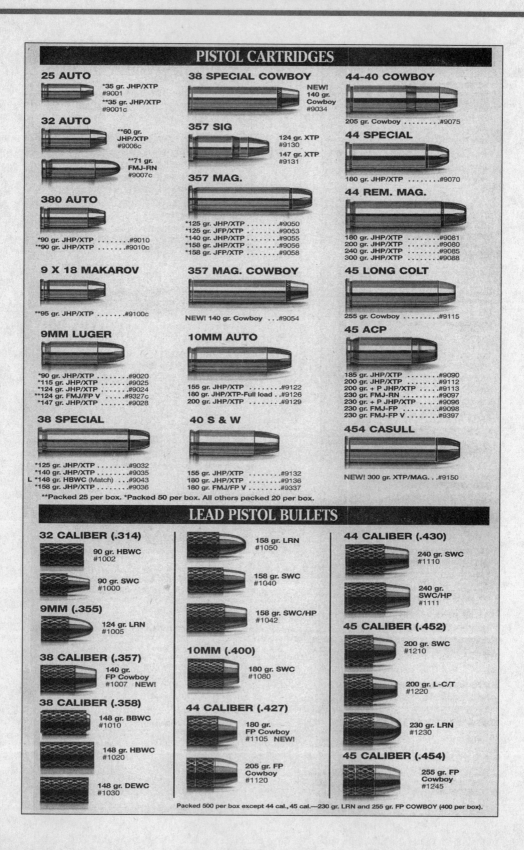

## PISTOL CARTRIDGES

### 25 AUTO
*35 gr. JHP/XTP
#9001
**35 gr. JHP/XTP
#9001c

### 32 AUTO
**60 gr.
JHP/XTP
#9006c

**71 gr.
FMJ-RN
#9007c

### 380 AUTO
*90 gr. JHP/XTP . . . . . . .#9010
**90 gr. JHP/XTP . . . . . . .#9010c

### 9 X 18 MAKAROV
**95 gr. JHP/XTP . . . . . . .#9100c

### 9MM LUGER
*90 gr. JHP/XTP . . . . . . . .#9020
*115 gr. JHP/XTP . . . . . . .#9025
*124 gr. JHP/XTP . . . . . . .#9024
*124 gr. FMJ/FP V . . . . . .#9327c
*147 gr. JHP/XTP . . . . . . .#9028

### 38 SPECIAL
*125 gr. JHP/XTP . . . . . . .#9032
*140 gr. JHP/XTP . . . . . . .#9035
L *148 gr. HBWC (Match) . . .#9043
*158 gr. JHP/XTP . . . . . . .#9036

### 38 SPECIAL COWBOY
NEW!
140 gr.
Cowboy
#9034

### 357 SIG
124 gr. XTP
#9130
147 gr. XTP
#9131

### 357 MAG.
*125 gr. JHP/XTP . . . . . . .#9050
*125 gr. JFP/XTP . . . . . . .#9053
*140 gr. JHP/XTP . . . . . . .#9055
*158 gr. JHP/XTP . . . . . . .#9056
*158 gr. JFP/XTP . . . . . . .#9058

### 357 MAG. COWBOY
NEW! 140 gr. Cowboy . . .#9054

### 10MM AUTO
155 gr. JHP/XTP . . . . . . .#9122
180 gr. JHP/XTP-Full load . .#9126
200 gr. JHP/XTP . . . . . . .#9129

### 40 S & W
155 gr. JHP/XTP . . . . . . .#9132
180 gr. JHP/XTP . . . . . . .#9136
180 gr. FMJ/FP V . . . . . . .#9337

### 44-40 COWBOY
205 gr. Cowboy . . . . . . . .#9075

### 44 SPECIAL
180 gr. JHP/XTP . . . . . . .#9070

### 44 REM. MAG.
180 gr. JHP/XTP . . . . . . .#9081
200 gr. JHP/XTP . . . . . . .#9080
240 gr. JHP/XTP . . . . . . .#9085
300 gr. JHP/XTP . . . . . . .#9088

### 45 LONG COLT
255 gr. Cowboy . . . . . . . .#9115

### 45 ACP
185 gr. JHP/XTP . . . . . . .#9090
200 gr. JHP/XTP . . . . . . .#9112
200 gr. + P JHP/XTP . . . . .#9113
230 gr. FMJ-RN . . . . . . . .#9097
230 gr. + P JHP/XTP . . . . .#9096
230 gr. FMJ-FP . . . . . . . .#9098
230 gr. FMJ-FP V . . . . . . .#9397

### 454 CASULL
NEW! 300 gr. XTP/MAG. . .#9150

**Packed 25 per box. *Packed 50 per box. All others packed 20 per box.

## LEAD PISTOL BULLETS

### 32 CALIBER (.314)
90 gr. HBWC
#1002

90 gr. SWC
#1000

### 9MM (.355)
124 gr. LRN
#1005

### 38 CALIBER (.357)
140 gr.
FP Cowboy
#1007 NEW!

### 38 CALIBER (.358)
148 gr. BBWC
#1010

148 gr. HBWC
#1020

148 gr. DEWC
#1030

158 gr. LRN
#1050

158 gr. SWC
#1040

158 gr. SWC/HP
#1042

### 10MM (.400)
180 gr. SWC
#1080

### 44 CALIBER (.427)
180 gr.
FP Cowboy
#1105 NEW!

205 gr. FP
Cowboy
#1120

### 44 CALIBER (.430)
240 gr. SWC
#1110

240 gr.
SWC/HP
#1111

### 45 CALIBER (.452)
200 gr. SWC
#1210

200 gr. L-C/T
#1220

230 gr. LRN
#1230

### 45 CALIBER (.454)
255 gr. FP
Cowboy
#1245

Packed 500 per box except 44 cal., 45 cal.—230 gr. LRN and 255 gr. FP COWBOY (400 per box).

# KYNOCH

## NITRO-EXPRESS-SPORTING AMMUNITION

**FOR SPORTING RIFLES**

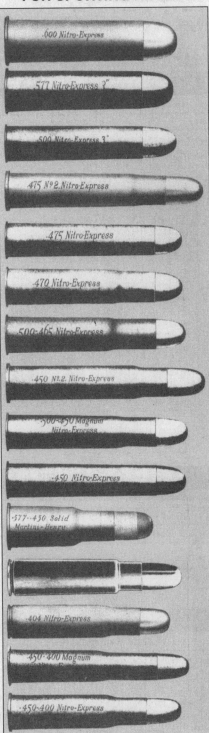

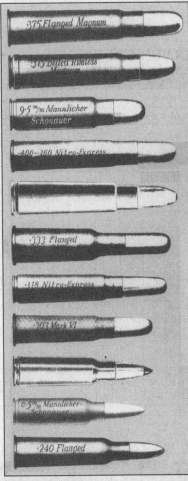

**.600 NE**
900 gr Solid or SN

**.577 NE 3"**
750 gr Solid or SN

**.500 NE 3"**
570 gr Solid or SN

**.475 No. 2 NE**
480 gr Solid or SN
for Jeffery Rifles:
500 gr Solid or SN

**.475 NE**
480 gr Solid or SN

**.470 NE**
500 gr Solid or SN

**.500/.465 NE**
480 gr Solid or SN

**.450 No. 2 NE**
480 gr Solid or SN

**.500/.450**
Magnum NE
480 gr Solid or SN

**.450 NE**
480 gr Solid or SN

**.577/.450 MH**
480 gr Solid Lead

**.416 Rigby**
410 gr Solid or SN

**.404 Rimless NE**
400 gr Solid or SN

**.450/.400**
Magnum NE
400 gr Solid or SN

**.450/.440 NE**
400 gr Solid or SN

**.375 Flanged Magnum**
300, 270 or 235 gr
Solid or SN

**.375 Belted Magnum**
300, 270 or 235 gr
Solid or SN

**9.5 mm Mannlicher**
Schonauer 270 gr Solid or SN

**.400/.360 NE for Purdey**
Rifles: 300 gr for Westley
Richards: 314 gr. Solid or SN

**.350 Rigby Magnum 225 gr**
or 250 gr, Solid or SN

**.333 Jeffrey Flanged NE**
300 gr Solid or SN

**.318 Rimless NE**
250 gr Solid or SN
180 gr SN

**.303 British**
215 gr Solid or SN

**.275 Rigby Rimless**
140 gr SN

**6.5 m/m Mannlicher**
Schonauer
160 gr SN

**.240 H&H Flanged**
100 gr SN

**AMMUNITION**

### FOR SPORTING PISTOLS

**.445 Webley & Scott**
Self-Loading Pistol
224 gr Solid

**.455 Revolver**
(Service MkII)
265 gr Solid Lead

### ADDITIONAL PROPRIETARY CALIBRES AVAILABLE:

**.700 NE**
1000 gr Solid

**.500 Jeffery**
535 gr Solid
or SN

**.450 Rigby**
Rimless
Magnum
480 gr Solid
or SN

**.400 - 3"**
Purdey
230 gr SN

**.505 Gibbs**
Magnum
525 gr Solid
or SN

**.425 Westley**
Richards
Magnum
410 gr Solid
or SN

**.300 H&H**
Flanged
Magnum
220 gr Solid
or SN

# MAGTECH AMMUNITION

Magtech Ammunition Co. imports and distributes high-quality rifle and pistol cartridges manufactured by CBC - Companhia Brasileira de Cartuchos. This firm, in business since 1926, has a modern factory in Sao Paulo, Brazil. Before 1976 it was owned and managed by Remington Arms and ICI - the UK's Imperial Chemical Company.

## MAGTECH REVOLVER CARTRIGES

| Symbol | Caliber | Bullet | | | Velocity | | | | | | Energy | | | | | | Mid-Range Trajectory | | | | Test Barrel Length | |
|---|---|---|---|---|---|---|---|---|---|---|---|---|---|---|---|---|---|---|---|---|---|---|
| | | Style | Weight | | Muzzle | | 50m | 50 yd | 100m | 100 yd | Muzzle | | 50m | 50 yd | 100m | 100 yd | 50m | 50 yd | 100 m | 100 yd | | |
| | | | g | gr | m/s | fps | m/s | fps | m/s | fps | J | ft/lbs | J | ft/lbs | J | ft lbs | cm | inch | cm | inch | cm | inch |
| 32SWA | .32 S&W | LRN | 5.50 | 85 | 207 | 680 | 195 | 645 | 187 | 610 | 118 | 87 | 105 | 78 | 96 | 70 | 7.6 | 2.5 | 36.8 | 10.5 | 7.6 | 3 |
| 32SWLA | .32 S&W Long | LRN | 6.35 | 98 | 215 | 705 | 202 | 670 | 192 | 635 | 147 | 108 | 130 | 98 | 117 | 88 | 7.0 | 2.3 | 32.0 | 10.5 | 10.2-V | 4-V |
| 32SWLB | .32 S&W Long | LWC | 6.35 | 98 | 208 | 682 | 174 | 579 | 145 | 491 | 137 | 102 | 96 | 73 | 67 | 52 | 7.0 | 2.3 | 38.5 | 12.6 | 10.2-V | 4-V |
| 32SWLC | .32 S&W Long | SJHP | 6.35 | 98 | 250 | 820 | 226 | 744 | 214 | 709 | 198 | 145 | 163 | 120 | 147 | 109 | 5.5 | 1.9 | 105.4 | 33.9 | 10.2-V | 4-V |
| 38SWA | .38 S&W | LRN | 9.45 | 146 | 209 | 686 | 199 | 655 | 190 | 267 | 207 | 152 | 188 | 139 | 170 | 127 | 6.9 | 2.3 | 134.8 | 43.6 | 10.2-V | 4-V |
| 38A | .38 SPL | LRN | 10.24 | 158 | 230 | 755 | 218 | 728 | 209 | 693 | 271 | 200 | 243 | 183 | 224 | 168 | 6.2 | 2.0 | 24.9 | 8.3 | 10.2-V | 4-V |
| 38B | .38 SPL | LWC | 9.59 | 148 | 216 | 710 | 190 | 634 | 170 | 566 | 224 | 166 | 173 | 132 | 139 | 105 | 7.4 | 2.4 | 33.7 | 10.8 | 10.2-V | 4-V |
| 38C | .38 SPL | SJSP | 10.24 | 158 | 246 | 807 | 237 | 779 | 228 | 753 | 310 | 230 | 287 | 213 | 266 | 199 | 4.0 | 1.3 | 20.4 | 6.7 | 10.2-V | 4-V |
| 38D | .38 SPL+P | SJSP | 8.10 | 125 | 286 | 938 | 270 | 891 | 257 | 851 | 331 | 245 | 295 | 220 | 267 | 200 | 4.0 | 1.3 | 16.5 | 5.1 | 10.2-V | 4-V |
| 38E | .38 SPL | SJHP | 10.24 | 158 | 246 | 807 | 237 | 779 | 228 | 753 | 310 | 230 | 287 | 213 | 266 | 199 | 4.0 | 1.3 | 20.4 | 6.7 | 10.2-V | 4-V |
| 38F | .38 SPL+P | SJHP | 8.10 | 125 | 286 | 938 | 270 | 891 | 257 | 851 | 331 | 245 | 295 | 220 | 267 | 200 | 4.0 | 1.3 | 16.5 | 5.4 | 10.2-V | 4-V |
| 38G | .38 SPL-Short | LRN | 8.10 | 125 | 209 | 686 | 199 | 649 | 189 | 628 | 177 | 130 | 160 | 120 | 145 | 109 | 6.2 | 2.0 | 29.6 | 9.7 | 10.2-V | 4-V |
| 38H | .38 SPL+P | SJHP | 10.24 | 158 | 270 | 890 | 235 | 774 | 226 | 746 | 376 | 278 | 283 | 210 | 261 | 196 | 4.3 | 1.4 | 20.2 | 30.4 | 10.2-V | 4-V |
| 38J | .38 SPL | LSWC | 10.24 | 158 | 230 | 755 | 217 | 721 | 207 | 689 | 271 | 200 | 243 | 182 | 224 | 167 | 6.1 | 2.0 | 25.6 | 8.4 | 10.2-V | 4-V |
| 357A | .357 MAG | SJSP | 10.24 | 158 | 376 | 1235 | 333 | 1104 | 305 | 1015 | 724 | 535 | 568 | 428 | 476 | 361 | 2.4 | 0.8 | 10.7 | 3.5 | 10.2-V | 4-V |
| 357B | .357 MAG | SJHP | 10.24 | 158 | 376 | 1235 | 333 | 1104 | 305 | 1015 | 724 | 535 | 568 | 428 | 476 | 361 | 2.4 | 0.8 | 10.7 | 3.5 | 10.2-V | 4-V |
| 357C | .357 MAG | LSWC | 10.24 | 158 | 376 | 1235 | 333 | 1104 | 305 | 1015 | 724 | 535 | 568 | 428 | 476 | 361 | 2.4 | 0.8 | 10.7 | 3.5 | 10.2-V | 4-V |
| 357D | .357 MAG | FMC-Flat | 10.24 | 158 | 376 | 1235 | 340 | 1125 | 314 | 1045 | 724 | 535 | 592 | 444 | 507 | 383 | 2.4 | 0.8 | 8.7 | 2.7 | 10.2-V | 4-V |
| 357E | .357 MAG | SJSP | 10.24 | 158 | 376 | 1235 | 333 | 1104 | 305 | 1015 | 724 | 535 | 868 | 428 | 476 | 361 | 2.4 | 0.5 | 10.7 | 3.6 | 10.2-V | 4-V |
| 44A | .44 REM MAG | SJSP | 15.55 | 240 | 360 | 1180 | 326 | 1081 | 304 | 1010 | 1010 | 741 | 828 | 632 | 720 | 623 | 2.8 | 0.9 | 11.4 | 3.7 | 10.2-V | 4-V |
| 44A | .44-40 WIN | LFLAT | 12.96 | 200 | 363 | 1190 | 335 | 1106 | 314 | 1041 | 854 | 630 | 727 | 543 | 639 | 481 | 9.8 | 3.1 | 48.2 | 15.5 | 61 | 24 |

V=VENTED TEST BARREL

## MAGTECH RIFLE CARTRIGES

| Symbol | Caliber | Bullet | | | Velocity | | | | | | Energy | | | | | | Mid-Range Trajectory | | | | Test Barrel Length | |
|---|---|---|---|---|---|---|---|---|---|---|---|---|---|---|---|---|---|---|---|---|---|---|
| | | Style | Weight | | Muzzle | | 50m | 50 yd | 100m | 100 yd | Muzzle | | 50m | 50 yd | 100m | 100 yd | 50m | 50 yd | 100 m | 100 yd | | |
| | | | g | gr | m/s | fps | m/s | fps | m/s | fps | J | ft/lbs | J | ft/lbs | J | ft lbs | cm | inch | cm | inch | cm | inch |
| 30A | 30 Carbine | FMC | 7.13 | 110 | 607 | 1990 | 549 | 1817 | 495 | 1654 | 1313 | 967 | 1075 | 806 | 875 | 668 | 2.2 | 0.6 | 18.4 | 5.7 | 50.8 | 20 |

## MAGTECH COWBOY ACTION CARTRIGES

| Symbol | Caliber | Bullet | | | Velocity | | | | | | Energy | | | | | | Mid-Range Trajectory | | | | Test Barrel Length | |
|---|---|---|---|---|---|---|---|---|---|---|---|---|---|---|---|---|---|---|---|---|---|---|
| | | Style | Weight | | Muzzle | | 50m | 50 yd | 100m | 100 yd | Muzzle | | 50m | 50 yd | 100m | 100 yd | 50m | 50 yd | 100 m | 100 yd | | |
| | | | g | gr | m/s | fps | m/s | fps | m/s | fps | J | ft/lbs | J | ft/lbs | J | ft lbs | cm | inch | cm | inch | cm | inch |
| 4440B | .44-40 WIN | LFN | 14.58 | 225 | 221 | 725 | 214 | 703 | 206 | 681 | 356 | 281 | 333 | 247 | 311 | 232 | 6.5 | 2.1 | 26.9 | 8.8 | 10.2 | 4 |
| 44B | .44 SPL | LFN | 15.55 | 240 | 229 | 750 | 220 | 722 | 211 | 696 | 408 | 300 | 376 | 278 | 347 | 258 | 6.1 | 2.0 | 25.4 | 8.3 | 10.2 | 4 |
| 45D | .45 Colt | LFN | 16.20 | 250 | 229 | 750 | 221 | 726 | 213 | 702 | 425 | 312 | 395 | 293 | 367 | 274 | 6.0 | 2.0 | 25.2 | 8.2 | 10.2 | 4 |
| 38L | .38 SPL | LFN | 10.24 | 158 | 244* | 800* | 236 | 776 | 228 | 753 | 305 | 225 | 285 | 211 | 267 | 199 | 5.3 | 1.8 | 22.0 | 7.2 | 10.2-V | 4-V |

*Velocity obtained from 10.2 cm (4") vented test barrel.  Abbreviation: LFN LEAD FLAT NOSE

# MAGTECH AMMUNITION

## MAGTECH GOLD™ CARTRIDGES

| Symbol | Caliber | Bullet Style | Weight g | Weight gr | Velocity Muzzle m/s | Muzzle fps | 50m m/s | 50 yd fps | 100m m/s | 100 yd fps | Energy Muzzle J | Muzzle ft/lbs | 50m J | 50 yd ft/lbs | 100m J | 100 yd ft lbs | Mid-Range Traj. 50m cm | 50 yd inch | 100 m cm | 100 yd inch | Test Barrel cm | inch |
|---|---|---|---|---|---|---|---|---|---|---|---|---|---|---|---|---|---|---|---|---|---|---|
| 380C | .380 Auto+P | JHP | 5.5 | 85 | 330 | 1,082 | 303 | 999 | 282 | 936 | 300 | 221 | 252 | 188 | 219 | 166 | 3.1 | 1.0 | 13.3 | 4.3 | 9.5 | 3-3/4 |
| 40E | .40 S&W | JHP | 10.0 | 155 | 367 | 1,025 | 338 | 1,118 | 317 | 1,052 | 677 | 500 | 596 | 430 | 523 | 381 | 2.5 | 0.8 | 10.9 | 3.5 | 12.7 | 5 |
| 45E | .45 Auto+P | JHP | 12.0 | 185 | 350 | 1,148 | 323 | 1,066 | 303 | 1,005 | 735 | 540 | 626 | 467 | 551 | 415 | 2.7 | 0.9 | 11.8 | 3.8 | 12.7 | 5 |
| 38M | .38 SPL+P | JHP | 8.10 | 125 | 310* | 1,017* | 295 | 971 | 282 | 931 | 389 | 287 | 352 | 262 | 322 | 241 | 3.4 | 1.1 | 14.3 | 4.6 | 10.2 | 4 |
| 9M | 9mm Luger+P | JHP | 7.45 | 115 | 380 | 1,246 | 344 | 1,137 | 318 | 1,056 | 538 | 397 | 441 | 330 | 377 | 285 | 2.4 | 0.8 | 10.5 | 3.4 | 10.2 | 4 |

*Velocity obtained from 10.2 cm (4") vented test barrel.   Abbreviation: JHP JACKETED HOLLOW POINT

## MAGTECH PISTOL CARTRIDGES

| Symbol | Caliber | Bullet Style | Weight g | Weight gr | Velocity Muzzle m/s | Muzzle fps | 50m m/s | 50 yd fps | 100m m/s | 100 yd fps | Energy Muzzle J | Muzzle ft/lbs | 50m J | 50 yd ft/lbs | 100m J | 100 yd ft lbs | Mid-Range Traj. 50m cm | 50 yd inch | 100 m cm | 100 yd inch | Test Barrel cm | inch |
|---|---|---|---|---|---|---|---|---|---|---|---|---|---|---|---|---|---|---|---|---|---|---|
| 25A | .25 Auto | FMC | 3.24 | 50 | 232 | 760 | 214 | 707 | 199 | 659 | 87 | 64 | 74 | 56 | 64 | 48 | 6.1 | 2.0 | 26.2 | 8.7 | 5.1 | 2 |
| •25A | .25 Auto | JHP | 2.27 | 35 | 274 | 930 | 250 | 827 | 229 | 764 | 85 | 63 | 71 | 53 | 60 | 45 | 17.8 | 5.6 | 51.6 | 29.0 | 5.1 | 2 |
| 32A | .32 Auto | FMC | 4.60 | 71 | 276 | 905 | 259 | 855 | 245 | 810 | 175 | 129 | 154 | 115 | 138 | 103 | 4.3 | 1.4 | 18.5 | 5.8 | 10.2 | 4 |
| 32B | .32 Auto | JHP | 4.60 | 71 | 276 | 905 | 259 | 855 | 245 | 810 | 175 | 129 | 154 | 115 | 138 | 103 | 4.3 | 1.4 | 18.5 | 5.8 | 9.5 | 3-3/4 |
| 380A | .380 Auto | FMC | 6.15 | 95 | 290 | 951 | 261 | 861 | 236 | 781 | 259 | 190 | 209 | 156 | 171 | 128 | 4.3 | 1.4 | 18.0 | 5.9 | 9.5 | 3-3/4" |
| 380B | .380 Auto | JHP | 6.15 | 95 | 290 | 951 | 261 | 861 | 236 | 781 | 259 | 190 | 209 | 156 | 171 | 128 | 4.3 | 1.4 | 18.0 | 5.9 | 9.5 | 3-3/4" |
| 9A | 9mm Luger | FMC | 7.45 | 115 | 346 | 1135 | 310 | 1027 | 290 | 961 | 446 | 330 | 358 | 270 | 313 | 235 | 2.7 | 0.9 | 12.2 | 4.0 | 10.2 | 4 |
| 9B | 9mm Luger | FMC | 8.03 | 124 | 338 | 1109 | 308 | 1030 | 290 | 971 | 459 | 339 | 381 | 292 | 338 | 259 | 3.1 | 1.0 | 12.5 | 4.1 | 10.2 | 4 |
| 9C | 9mm Luger | JHP | 7.45 | 115 | 352 | 1155 | 316 | 1047 | 293 | 971 | 462 | 340 | 372 | 280 | 320 | 240 | 2.7 | 0.9 | 12.2 | 3.9 | 10.2 | 4 |
| 9D | 9mm Luger | JSP Flat | 6.15 | 95 | 410 | 1345 | 356 | 1185 | 317 | 1055 | 517 | 380 | 390 | 295 | 309 | 235 | 2.4 | 0.8 | 12.4 | 3.4 | 10.2 | 4 |
| 9E | 9mm Luger | LRN | 8.03 | 124 | 334 | 1109 | 308 | 1030 | 290 | 971 | 459 | 339 | 381 | 292 | 338 | 259 | 3.1 | 1.0 | 12.5 | 4.1 | 10.2 | 4 |
| 9F | 9mm Luger | JSP Flat* | 6.15 | 95 | 410 | 1345 | 356 | 1185 | 317 | 1085 | 817 | 380 | 390 | 295 | 309 | 238 | 2.4 | 0.8 | 10.4 | 3.4 | 10.2 | 4 |
| 9G | 9mm Luger (sub-sonic) | FMC Flat | 9.52 | 147 | 302 | 990 | 286 | 945 | 274 | 907 | 434 | 320 | 389 | 292 | 357 | 268 | 3.7 | 1.2 | 14.6 | 4.8 | 10.2 | 4 |
| 9H | 9mm Luger+P+ | JHP | 7.45 | 115 | 380 | 1246 | 347 | 1145 | 322 | 1069 | 538 | 397 | 448 | 335 | 387 | 292 | 1.0 | 0.3 | 8.8 | 2.9 | 10.2 | 4 |
| 40A | .40 S&W | JHP | 11.66 | 180 | 302 | 990 | 282 | 933 | 268 | 886 | 532 | 390 | 464 | 348 | 419 | 314 | 3.7 | 1.2 | 14.6 | 5.0 | 10.2 | 4 |
| 40B | .40 S&W | FMC | 11.66 | 180 | 302 | 990 | 282 | 933 | 268 | 886 | 532 | 390 | 464 | 348 | 419 | 314 | 3.7 | 1.2 | 14.6 | 5.0 | 10.2 | 4 |
| 40C | .40 S&W | LSWC | 10.37 | 160 | 355 | 1165 | 325 | 1076 | 297 | 984 | 653 | 484 | 548 | 411 | 457 | 343 | 2.7 | 0.9 | 11.9 | 3.9 | 10.2 | 4 |
| 40D | .40 S&W | JHP | 10.05 | 155 | 367 | 1205 | 330 | 1018 | 307 | 1096 | 677 | 500 | 547 | 414 | 474 | 357 | 4.9 | 1.6 | 20.7 | 6.8 | 12.7 | 5 |
| 45A | .45 Auto | FMC | 14.90 | 230 | 255 | 837 | 242 | 800 | 232 | 767 | 484 | 356 | 436 | 326 |  | 300 | 4.9 | 1.6 | 20.7 | 6.8 | 12.7 | 5 |
| 45B | .45 Auto | FMC-SWC | 14.90 | 230 | 238 | 780 | 218 | 720 | 199 | 660 | 422 | 310 | 354 | 265 | 295 | 222 | 5.5 | 1.8 | 23.8 | 7.8 | 12.7 | 5 |
| 45C | .45 Auto | LSWC | 12.96 | 200 | 290 | 950 | 277 | 910 | 265 | 874 | 545 | 401 | 496 | 368 | 455 | 339 | 2.4 | 0.8 | 11.0 | 4.8 | 12.7 | 5 |

• Bullet without grooves   * Available early 2000

## MAGTECH CLEAN RANGE CARTRIDGES

| Symbol | Caliber | Bullet Style | Weight g | Weight gr | Velocity Muzzle m/s | Muzzle fps | 50m m/s | 50 yd fps | 100m m/s | 100 yd fps | Energy Muzzle J | Muzzle ft/lbs | 50m J | 50 yd ft/lbs | 100m J | 100 yd ft lbs | Mid-Range Traj. 50m cm | 50 yd inch | 100 m cm | 100 yd inch | Test Barrel cm | inch |
|---|---|---|---|---|---|---|---|---|---|---|---|---|---|---|---|---|---|---|---|---|---|---|
| 9J | 9mm Luger | TMJ | 8.03 | 124 | 338 | 1109 | 308 | 1030 | 290 | 971 | 459 | 339 | 381 | 292 | 338 | 259 | 3.1 | 1.0 | 12.5 | 4.1 | 10.2 | 4 |
| 9K | 9mm Luger | JSP Flat | 6.15 | 95 | 410 | 1345 | 356 | 1185 | 317 | 1055 | 517 | 380 | 390 | 295 | 309 | 235 | 2.4 | 0.8 | 10.4 | 3.4 | 10.2 | 4 |
| 38K | .38 SPL | TMJ | 10.24 | 158 | 230 | 755 | 218 | 723 | 209 | 693 | 271 | 200 | 243 | 183 | 224 | 168 | 6.2 | 2.0 | 24.9 | 8.3 | 10.2 | 4V |

Magtech ammunition is manufactured according to SAAMI and CIP technical specifications and carefully tested in fully equipped Ballistics Laboratories in order to meet prescribed values for primer sensitivity, bullet velocities, maximum, mean and port pressures, accuracy, etc.  Safety, accuracy and quality are always the prime concern at Magtech.

# PMC

PMC (Precision Made Cartridges) is the same firm as Eldorado Cartridge Company — a name that may be phased out. The company may not claim the volume of business that accrues to Winchester, Remington or Federal, but it is a fast-growing enterprise whose product line continues to expand. At this writing the firm offers more than 50 handgun loads, from .25 Auto to .44 Magnum, including five specifically for Cowboy Action shooting. The centerfire rifle stable includes cowboy action loads in .30-30 and .45-70, plus a wide variety of hunting and match ammunition from .222 Remington to .375 H&H Magnum. The selection of .22 rimfire rounds features hunting, plinking and match loads.

PMC offers a broad choice of bullet styles. In pistol ammo, there's the quick-opening Starfire hollowpoint, a traditional jacketed hollowpoint, a jacketed softpoint and a full-metal-jacket (hardball) bullet — plus lead wadcutter, semi-wadcutter and round-nose options. Rifle bullets include the Barnes X-Bullet, .30-30 Starfire hollowpoint, Sierra boat-tail hollowpoint, Sierra boat-tail softpoint, pointed softpoint, softpoint, flat-nose softpoint and full metal jacket.

PMC also manufactures shotshells, from light dove and quail and target loads to heavy steel-shot loads for geese.

One more thing that PMC has: A rural Nevada plant that offers test-firing opportunities right out the back door.

PMC has entered the popular Cowboy Action game with an assortment of low-recoil ammunition that speeds recovery for a second shot. The Lite Clay Target shotshell works at this game as well as at hand-thrown clay targets. The firm offers Cowboy Action pistol and rifle rounds in .38 Special, .357 Magnum, .44 Special, .44-40 Winchester, .45 Colt, .30-30 and .45-70 Government.

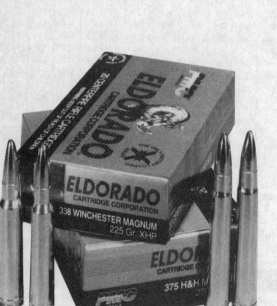

PMC rifle cartridges include hunting loads for heavy-hitters like the .338 Winchester and .375 H&H magnums as well as for varmint rounds like the .222 and .223. There are match loads for cartridges commonly used in competition. Bullet choices for big game hunters include a wide variety of softpoint and hollowpoint designs — for example, the Barnes X-Bullet and Sierra boat-tails.

PMC handgun ammunition is loaded for target, hunting and personal defense. The firm's own Starfire bullet dumps energy right away with quick, violent expansion. It is available in nine pistol cartridges, from .380 Auto to .44 magnum. Target rounds include a new 180-grain FMJ .40 S&W. There's also a low-cost practice load for the .357 SIG; it features a 124-grain FMJ bullet.

# PMC

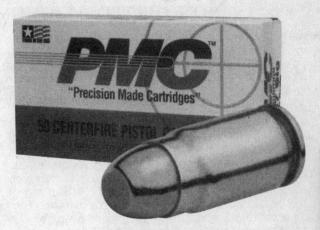

## NEW FOR 2000
### STARFIRE 357 SIG FHP

PMC has added the increasingly popular 357 SIG handgun cartridge to its high performance line of Starfire hollow point ammunition. The broad expansion of the Starfire bullet coupled with a velocity of 1350 feet per second provides excellent stopping power in a semi-automatic handgun.

## 357 SIG,
### 124 GRAIN FMC

PMC also offers the 357 SIG in an economical Bronze Line FMJ round that duplicates the bullet weight and velocity of the Starfire cartridge. This means shooters can switch from practice to duty or defensive ammunition with minimal adjustment for recoil or point of aim.

## NEW 303 BRITISH CARTRIDGES

For fans of the long-popular 303 British cartridge, PMC has added two new versions to its Bronze Line for 2000. Priced to fit any shooting budget, PMC Bronze Line ammunition allows shooters the luxury of extra practice.

### 174-GRAIN FULL METAL JACKET FOR PRACTICE
### 180-GRAIN SOFT POINT FOR BIG GAME HUNTING

The bullet weight and velocity of this new cartridge are identical to PMC's Silver Line 303 Match load, allowing competitive shooters to practice with lower cost ammunition that provides the same ballistic performance.

## 303 BRITISH,
### 180 GR. SOFT POINT

This cartridge is an excellent economical choice for deer- or elk-size big game.

### NEW 7X64 BRENNEKE

Another veteran European rifle cartridge with a long history of successful use by big game hunters. For 2000, PMC has added a Bronze Line version featuring a 170 grain Soft Point hunting bullet with a velocity of 2428 feet per second.

# REMINGTON AMMUNITION

## REMINGTON® INTRODUCES ANOTHER NON-BELTED MAGNUM—THE .338 ULTRA MAG

### PREMIER® ULTRA MAG CENTERFIRE RIFLE AMMUNITION

Remingtons powerful, flat-shooting big game cartridge, the .300 Remington Ultra Mag delivers one of the highest levels of velocity and energy ever offered in a commercially-produced, non-belted magnum. Now the .338 Ultra Mag becomes the second of a new series of high-power, non-belted Magnums planned by Remington to become the ulltimate flat-shooting long-range performers of the 21st Century.

The .338 Remington Ultra Mag is based on an original but slightly modified .404 Jeffery case. Necking down the case mouth to 33 caliber produces a 30-degree shoulder angle that permits positive headspacing on the shoulder alone. Use of the .404 Jeffery case also provides two other significant advantages. One is its generous case capacity, allowing a greater volume of slow-burning, magnum-compatible powders that deliver exceptional performance at normal pressures. By comparison, it has 12 percent more case capacity than the .340 Weatherby Magnum. The other advantage of the Remington Ultra Mag cartridges is their relatively straight-line, slightly tapered, beltless body, that creates easier, more reliable feeding and a more uniform chamber fit for improved accuracy.

The new 338 will be loaded with a 225-grain Swift A-Frame bullet at a muzzle velocity of 2860 fps from a 26-inch barrel. Use of the tough, deep penetrating, but reliably expanding Nosler® Partition® extends effective performance of this powerful round over an extremely wide spread of ranges. This new Magnum is a remarkable range-shrinker. Sighting in a .338 Remington Ultra Mag just 2 inches high at 100 yards will deliver the bullet less than 5 inches low at 300 yards.

The .338 Remington Ultra Mag will be chambered in Model 700™ bolt action rifles, with 26-inch barrels to derive maximum ballistic performance from the exceptional case capacity of the new Magnum cartridge.

Shooters who bought 300 Ultra Mag rifles have 2 new loads this year: a 180-grain Swift Scirocco at 3250 fps and a 200-grain Nosler Partition at 3025.

| 2700 fps | 2245 fps | 1730 fps | 1440 fps |
|---|---|---|---|

Swift Scirocco Bonded bullets expand reliably over a wide range of terminal velocities.

.30-06 Premier Scirocco, 180-gr. Swift Scirocco Bonded, 5 shots, 88", 100 yds.

### SWIFT SCIROCCO

The Scirocco cut-away shows how the unique combined design features make the new Premier Scirocco line the most versatile and reliable big-game ammunition ever offered. The expansion-generating polymer tip and the boat tail base combine to defy air resistance at one end, and reduce drag at the other. The progressively thickening, heavy-based, pure copper jacket is bonded to the lead core to preserve bullet integrity and retain over 75% of its weight at all velocities. Finally, the bullet's precise concentricity and secant ogive nose profile produce accuracy you would be proud of in match competition.

For 2000, Premier Scirocco Bonded is being introduced in .330 Ultra Mag and .30-06 Springfield loading, with a 180-gr bullet. Additional calibers from .243 to .338 will follow as the Premier Sciorocco family grows.

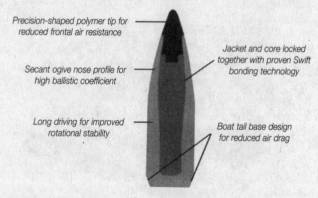

Precision-shaped polymer tip for reduced frontal air resistance

Secant ogive nose profile for high ballistic coefficient

Long driving for improved rotational stability

Jacket and core locked together with proven Swift bonding technology

Boat tail base design for reduced air drag

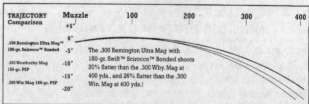

| TRAJECTORY Comparison | Muzzle | 100 | 200 | 300 | 400 |
|---|---|---|---|---|---|

The .300 Remington Ultra Mag with 180-gr. Swift™ Scirocco™ Bonded shoots 20% flatter than the .300 Wby. Mag at 400 yds., and 26% flatter than the .300 Win. Mag at 400 yds.!

#### PREMIER SCIROCCO BONDED (NEW FOR 2000)

| Caliber | Bullet Wt. (grs.) | Bullet Type |
|---|---|---|
| .30-06 Springfield | 180 | Swift Scirocco Bonded |
| .300 Remington Ultra Mag | 180 | Swift Scirocco Bonded |

| VELOCITY (ft./sec.)/ENERGY (ft.-lbs.) | Muzzle | 100 yds | 200 yds | 300 yds | 400 yds | 500 yds |
|---|---|---|---|---|---|---|
| .300 Remington Ultra Mag 180-gr. Scirocco Bonded | 3300/4352 | 3096/3831 | 29902/3365 | 2715/2947 | 2537/2572 | 2365/2235 |
| .300 Weatherby Mag 180-gr. PSP | 3120/3890 | 2866/3282 | 2626/2756 | 2398/2299 | 2182/1903 | 1977/1562 |
| .300 Win Mag 180-gr. PSP | 2960/3501 | 2745/3011 | 2540/2578 | 2344/2196 | 2157/1859 | 1978/1584 |

# REMINGTON AMMUNITION

## ETRONX AMMUNITION

To complement its new EtronX rifles, Remington has developed a new line of EtronX centerfire ammunition. New EtronX ammunition includes three highly accurate, flat-shooting centerfire loadings: the Premier Varmint .22-250 Remington, .220 Swift with 50-grain V-Max polymer-tip bullets, and Premier Ballistic Tip .243 Win. with a 90-grain Nosler Ballistic Tip bullet. The design and construction of these cartridges is identical to standard centerfire ammunition with one significant exception. They utilize new electrically ignited EtronX primers, which contain a patented electrically conductive primer mix specially formulated to ignite reliably and evenly from the electrical pulse.

Because the EtronX primer is carefully calibrated to duplicate the performance of the standard primer, cartridges can be loaded with the same amount and type of powder as they would for a mechanical firing system, with virtually no change in pressure levels or velocities.

Premier Varmint and Premier Ballistic Tip cartridges, combined with the near-zero lock time of the Model 700 EtronX rifle, promise even tighter accuracy performance than previously obtainable from over-the-counter rifles and ammunition. And for those who reload their centerfire ammunition, EtronX primers will also be available as components. They have identical ignition characteristics and external dimensions as standard large-rifle percussion primers. Shooters will be able to reload EtronX ammunition by following the same published loading data they have been using for cartridges of the same caliber and bullet weight.

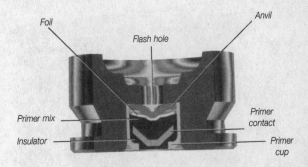

*Head of EtronX cartridge showing electrically responsive primer*

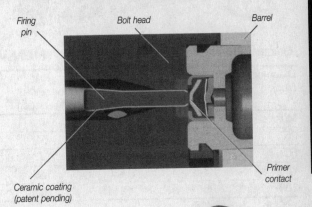

## IMPROVED COPPER SOLID™ SABOT SLUGS

### REMINGTON® IMPROVES DESIGN AND PERFORMANCE 12-GAUGE COPPER SOLID™ SABOT SLUGS

Already accurate and effective, Remington's 12-gauge Copper Solid™ slug has been designed to provide more reliable and uniform expansion and even higher weight retention. The hollow point cavity is now formed by six, separate petals in an inwardly-curved, spiral design. Upon impact, these petals mushroom open quickly to twice the diameter of the 58-caliber slug body. However, they remain intact, with no separation for deep, reliable penetration. Groups from rifled barrels stay within 3 inches at 100 yards.

These improved 12-gauge Copper Solid™ sabot slugs weigh one ounce. They are loaded in 12-gauge, 2 3/4-inch shells at a muzzle velocity of 1450 feet per second, and in three-inch shells, at 1550 feet per second.

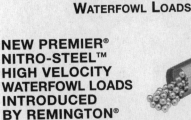

## NITRO-STEEL™ HIGH VELOCITY MAGNUM WATERFOWL LOADS

### NEW PREMIER® NITRO-STEEL™ HIGH VELOCITY WATERFOWL LOADS INTRODUCED BY REMINGTON®

Remington's line of Premier® Nitro-Steel™ High Velocity waterfowl loads is specifically designed to retain greater long-range energy with larger-size steel pellets. Because steel is lighter and has only about two-thirds the specific density of lead, larger pellets are required for comparable effectiveness. However, the larger steel pellets have greater wind resistance than smaller lead pelllets and slow down faster in flight. Remington Premier Nitro Steel HV loads have the muzzle velocity to counteract this. They deliver more energy for larger birds and reduce the required forward allowance for longer shots.

These new Premier® High Velocity steel loads will be produced in five specifications: a 12-gauge, 3-inch Magnum with 1 1/8 ounces of BB, 2 or 4 shot at 1500 feet per second; a 12-gauge 3 1/2-inch Magnum with 1 3/8 ounces of BB shot at 1450 feet per second; and a 10-gauge, 3 1/2-inch Magnum load with 1 3/8 ounces of BB shot, also at a muzzle velocity of 1450 feet per second.

# ROTTWEIL BRENNEKE CARTRIDGES

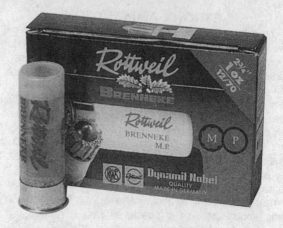

## ORIGINAL BRENNEKE® GOLDEN SLUG 12 GA 3" MAGNUM

| DISTANCE (YDS) | VELOCITY (FT/SEC) | ENERGY 1-3/8 OZ. (FT/LBS) | TIME OF FLIGHT (MILLISEC.) |
|---|---|---|---|
| Muzzle | 1476 | 2913 | 0 |
| 25 | 1286 | 2209 | 54 |
| 50 | 1138 | 1730 | 117 |
| 75 | 1036 | 1436 | 186 |
| 100 | 965 | 1244 | 261 |

## BRENNEKE MP 12 GA 2-3/4"

| DISTANCE (YDS) | VELOCITY (FT/SEC) | ENERGY 1-3/8 OZ. (FT/LBS) |
|---|---|---|
| Muzzle | 1510 | 2215 |
| 25 | 1300 | 1640 |
| 50 | 1135 | 1250 |
| 75 | 1036 | 1025 |
| 100 | 950 | 890 |

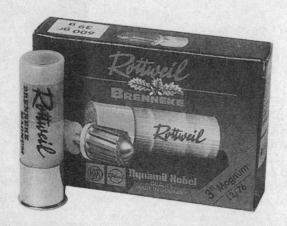

## ORIGINAL BRENNEKE® 12 & 20 GA., 410 BORE 3" MAGNUM

| DISTANCE (YDS) | VELOCITY (FT/SEC) 12 GA | ENERGY (FT/LBS) 1-3/8 OZ. | ENERGY (FT/LBS) 1 OZ. | ENERGY (FT/LBS) 1/4 OZ. | TIME OF FLIGHT (MILLISEC.) |
|---|---|---|---|---|---|
| Muzzle | 1502 | 3017 | 2117 | 780 | 0 |
| 25 | 1300 | 2261 | 1591 | 502 | 54 |
| 50 | 1144 | 1749 | 1239 | 342 | 115 |
| 75 | 1037 | 1438 | 1026 | 259 | 184 |
| 100 | 936 | 1240 | 888 | 213 | 259 |

## ORIGINAL BRENNEKE SLUG 12, 16, & 20 GA MAGNUM, 2-3/4"

| DISTANCE (YDS) | VELOCITY (FT/SEC) 12 GA | ENERGY (FT/LBS) 12 GA | ENERGY (FT/LBS) 16 GA | ENERGY (FT/LBS) 20 GA | TIME OF FLIGHT (MILLISEC.) |
|---|---|---|---|---|---|
| Muzzle | 1590 | 2745 | 2320 | 2080 | 0 |
| 25 | 1365 | 2025 | 1710 | 1530 | 51 |
| 50 | 1190 | 1540 | 13000 | 1165 | 110 |
| 75 | 1060 | 1220 | 1030 | 925 | 176 |
| 100 | 975 | 1035 | 875 | 780 | 250 |

# RWS Centerfire Cartridges

## Bullets And Ballistics For Norma

### VULKAN

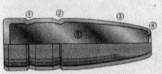

Vulkan bullets are strengthened by the folded jacket at the front. The folds protect the tip from deformation. The bullet penetrates before expansion starts. Subsequently, mushrooming to double the original diameter follows rapidly. *1. Reinforced rear jacket with lead core lock. 2. Crimping groove for secure seating in the case. 3. Thin forward jacket with internal notches. 4. Jacket folded into the lead core. 5. Antimony hardened lead core.*

### SOFT POINT

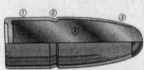

Soft Point bullets have optimum ballistic shape. They offer good penetration and mushroom well even on smaller game. The Soft Point is an excellent all-around bullet particularly suitable for small and medium game. *1. Reinforced rear jacket. 2. Crimping groove for secure seating in the case. 3. Thin forward jacket. 4. Antimony hardened lead core.*

The design of the DK bullet is the result of Dynamit Nobel's extensive ballistics research. Special laboratory tests, in conjunction with extensive practical field trials, support this. Manufactured at considerable expense, DK bullets barely splinter, mushroom in a controlled manner, have a residue body of over 50 percent, and will always produce an exit hole. A true twin core that separates to perform two separate functions upon impact, penetration and a high degree of impact force, combine to give the DK a clear advantage over more conventional bullets.

The DK is tailored exactly to the hunting conditions that hunters are faced with: medium shot distance, small to large game, and close game-reserve boundaries. The range of top-quality rifle cartridges with the traditional RWS symbol has been expanded, thanks to the new DK Bullet!

The RWS cone point bullet was designed and developed after exhaustive studies dealing with various bullet shapes and their ballistic behavior; in the laboratory as well as in the field.

A carefully engineered matching of casing and core material and an aerodynamically favorable bullet shape have been paired to produce a controlled mushrooming of the bullet and a largely uniform yield of energy in the body of the game. Mushrooming, caused by the formation of vanes, amounts to almost twice caliber size.

The rear groove, which joins the lead core and casing, controls mushrooming and preserves effective residual body to give it killing power.

Due to external shape, the RWS cone point bullet is largely insensitive to small obstacles, such as brush, in the path of its trajectory.

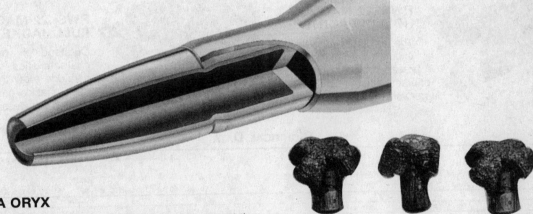

### NORMA ORYX

This is a completely new type of bullet, designed to meet the ever increasing need of hunters. The jacket and core are bonded together through a chemical process. This ensures a very high residue weight, even in hard targets. Despite the solid construction, mushrooming starts early. The Oryx bullet delivers excellent deep energy transfer and is suitable for big and medium sized game.

- *Bonded bullet-lead core soldered into copper jacket*
- *Good penetration*
- *Exceptional expansion, combined with bonding, results in deep wound channel and minimal meat damage*
- *Very high weight retention*

# RWS RIMFIRE CARTRIDGES

### GECO .22 L.R. RIFLE

Combining quality and cost effectiveness this rimfire ammunition is made in the RWS Nuremberg factory to exacting standards. Perfect for informal target shooting and entry level competition.

### GECO .22 L.R. PISTOL

The same quality and affordability as the rifle version but with a reduced velocity. For the pistol shooter looking for muzzle control.

### RWS .22 L.R. RIFLE MATCH

Perfect for the club level target competitor. Accurate and affordable.

### RWS .22 L.R. TARGET RIFLE

An ideal training and field cartridge, the .22 Long Rifle Target also excels in informal competitions. The target .22 provides the casual shooter with accuracy at an economical price.

### RWS .22 L.R. SUBSONIC HOLLOW POINT

Subsonic ammunition is a favorite ammunition of shooters whose shooting range is limited to where the noise of a conventional cartridge would be a problem.

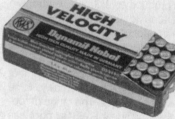

### RWS .22 L.R. HV HOLLOW POINT

A higher velocity hollow point offers the shooter greater shocking power in game, suitable for both small game and vermin.

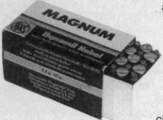

### RWS .22 MAGNUM HOLLOW POINT

The soft point allows good expansion on impact while preserving the penetration characteristics necessary for larger vermin and game.

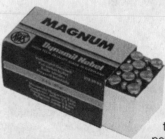

### RWS .22 MAGNUM FULL JACKET

Outstanding penetration characteristics of this cartridge allow the shooter to easily tackle game where penetration is necessary.

## TECHNICAL DATA

| Cartridges | Bullet Style | Bullet Weight (Grains) | Max. Chamber Pressure (psi) | Velocity (ft./sec.) Muzzle | 50y | 100y | Energy (ft./lbs.) Muzzle | 50y | 100y | Open Sight At | 25 yds | 50 yds | 75 yds | 100 yds | Scope Sighted In At | 25 yds | 50 yds | 75 yds | 100 yds |
|---|---|---|---|---|---|---|---|---|---|---|---|---|---|---|---|---|---|---|---|
| .22 L.R. R 50 | Lead | 40 | 25.600 | 1.070 | 970 | 890 | 100 | 80 | 70 | -- | -- | -- | -- | -- | -- | -- | -- | -- | -- |
| .22 Short R 25 | Lead | 28 | 18.500 | 560 | 490 | --- | 20 | 15 | -- | -- | -- | -- | -- | -- | -- | -- | -- | -- | -- |
| .22 L.R. Geco Rifle | Lead | 40 | 25.600 | 1.080 | 990 | 900 | 100 | 8/5 | 70 | -- | -- | -- | -- | -- | -- | -- | -- | -- | -- |
| .22 L.R. Rifle Match | Lead | 40 | 25.600 | 1.035 | 945 | 860 | 95 | 80 | 65 | 50 yds. | +0.6 | | -3.1 | -8.7 | 50 yds | +0.1 | | -2.5 | -7.5 |
| .22 L.R. Target Rifle | Lead | 40 | 25.600 | 1.080 | 990 | 900 | 100 | 80 | 70 | 50 yds. | +0.7 | | -3.2 | -9.0 | 50 yds | +0.1 | | -2.6 | -7.8 |
| .22 L.R. Subsonic | Hollow Point | 40 | 25.600 | 1.000 | 915 | 835 | 90 | 75 | 60 | 50 yds. | +0.8 | | -3.1 | -8.7 | 50 yds | +0.1 | | -2.5 | -7.5 |
| .22 L.R. HV Hollow point | Lead coppered | 40 | 25.600 | 1.310 | 1.120 | 990 | 150 | 110 | 85 | | | | -3.4 | -4.7 | 50 yds | +0.2 | | +2.8 | -8.5 |
| .22 Magnum | Soft Point | 40 | 25.600 | 2.020 | 1.710 | 1.430 | 360 | 260 | 180 | 100 yds. | +0.6 | +1.3 | +1.1 | 0 | 100 yds | -0.3 | +0.7 | +0.8 | 0 |
| .22 Magnum | Full Jacket | 40 | 25.600 | 2.020 | 1.710 | 1.430 | 360 | 260 | 180 | 100 yds. | +0.6 | +1.3 | +1.1 | 0 | 100 yds | -0.3 | +0.7 | +0.8 | 0 |

# WINCHESTER AMMUNITION

### WINCHESTER ADDS TO SUPREME POWER-POINT PLUS LINE

In 1999 Winchester introduced a new bullet in the Supreme Rifle line of ammunition. The bullet is called the Power-Point Plus and utilizes the proven Winchester Power-Point rifle bullet design.

To improve this bullet's performance for the Supreme line, Winchester Moly-coated the bullet and increased the velocities approximately 100 fps across the line. What may be the ultimate deer load is very affordably priced, and sales in 1999 were outstanding.

In 2000, two more loads are being added to the Supreme Power-Point Plus line. A new caliber will be available in the 7 mm-08 Rem with a 140 grain bullet, and a 150 gr. bullet has been added to the 270 Win caliber. A 130 gr. bullet is already offered in the 270 Win.

The 7mm-08 load has a muzzle velocity of 2875 fps and a muzzle energy of 2570 ft-lbs. This caliber has become very popular among white-tail deer hunters and the Power-Point Plus load should prove to be a very effective load.

The 270 Winchester 150 gr. load has a muzzle velocity of 2950 fps and delivers muzzle energy of 2900 ft-lbs. The 150 gr. offering will be the choice of those who want a little more punch or whose rifle favors a heavier bullet.

### NEW VALUE PRICED PERFORMANCE VARMINT LOADS FROM WINCHESTER

The popularity of varmint hunting continues to grow and Winchester Ammunitiion has introduced two value-priced loads to meet the need of high volume shooters. Both of the new USA brand 223 Rem and 22-250 Rem loads will use a new 45 gr. jacketed hollow point bullet developed by Winchester.

The new bullet was designed with the serious varmint hunter in mind. Features of the bullet include a sleek ogive for long range performance. The thin, uniform jacket wall and soft lead core will provide excellent accuracy. A pierced lead core and hollow point design creates consistent rapid fragmentation upon impact, thus reducing penetration for varmint applications and minimizing the ricochet potential on ranges.

Both loads are very high velocity with the 223 round having a muzzle velocity of 3600 fps and the 22-250 round having a muzzle velocity of 4000 fps.

The USA brand loads will be value packed 40 rounds to the carton in two 20 round trays. Cartons will stack like 20 round boxes and can easily be found on any dealer's shelf that carries Winchester Ammunition. End flaps on the box will have the word "varmint" printed in bold letters.

### WINCHESTER EXPANDS CANISTER POWDER LINE

Winchester Ammunition has added a new Extruded Rifle Powder to their canister line of powder. Designed for high velocity and magnum rifle cartridges, this new powder from Winchester will be an excellent choice for cartridges from the 25-06 Remington through the 300 Win Magnum, including the new 7mm STW Magnum category.

Extruded powders have a strong reputation for top performance in magnum and other high velocity rifles. The powder comes in either 1 or 8 pound bottles and is very competitively priced. Symbol number for the 1 pound bottle is WXR1BP and for the 8 pound bottle WXR8BP.

# WINCHESTER AMMUNITION

### RELOADING BRASS SHELLCASE AND BULLET COMPONENTS – NOW AVAILABLE FROM WINCHESTER

To meet the consumer demand for high quality Winchester components at a value price, Winchester Ammunition has introduced new convenient consumer packaging. Now Winchester bullets and unprimed handgun and rifle shellcases are available in resealable plastic bags.

All rifle and pistol bullets and handgun unprimed shell cases will be packed 100 to the bag. Rifle shellcases for the smaller calibers will also be packed 100 to the bag while the larger rifle shellcases will be packed 50 to the bag. All packaging will feature attractive Winchester graphics and carry all product packaging.

### WINCHESTER REINTRODUCES 1 OUNCE 20 GAUGE AA TARGET LOAD

Winchester Ammunition has decided to bring back a high performance 1 ounce target load for 20 gauge shooters. The 2 3/4 inch AA round will be available in shot sizes 7 1/2 and 8.

Like all Winchester AA loads the 1 ounce 20 gauge round uses high antimony shot and the famous AA one-piece plastic wad for consistent pattern performance. Clean burning Ball Powder propellant delivers the load with a muzzle velocity of 1165 fps.

The 1 ounce AA 20 gauge load will be popular with shooters for all types of clay target shooting. This load will be especially popular among sporting clays shooters who like the challenge of using a 20 gauge gun. The symbol number of the new load is AAH20 and they will be available wherever Winchester Ammunition is sold.

### MAXIMUM PERFORMANCE FROM THE NEW WINCHESTER SUPREME PARTITION GOLD SHOTGUN SLUG

Winchester Ammunition continues to improve the performance of shotgun slugs with the introduction of a brand new design called the Winchester Supreme Partition Gold. The combination of a new slug design, new powder, and a new concept in shotshell sabot technology takes the performance of this load to levels once thought unachievable in a shotgun.

Winchester started the development of this load by designing a new 50 caliber Partition Gold slug specifically adapted to shotgun use. Like other partition products, the new slug uses a center partition to separate the front and rear lead cores of the slug. The 385 gr. slug is designed to expand over a wide range of velocities increasing its effective range. The expanded slug produces an impressive mushroom yet provides deep penetration for ultimate performance.

The Partition Gold slug is nestled in a unique shotshell sabot designed by Winchester. Using advanced technology and experience gained through sabot products developed for military use, Winchester has produced a totally new concept for shotgun slug use. Using a sabot, which incorporated a patented area multiplier or reinforcing metal disc, Winchester has improved accuracy, stability and increased velocity. The sabot design has allowed Winchester to increase the velocities of this load to 1900 fps at the muzzle without negatively affecting accuracy or slug integrity. The real benefit in terms of performance is a very flat trajectory for sabot slugs that help the shooter hit his target consistently at various and unknown ranges. When the new slug is zeroed at 100 yards, it is only .7 inches high at 50 yards and 4 inches low at 150 yards. This is remarkably flat trajectory.

The new slug delivers 3086 ft-lbs. of muzzle energy. At 150 yards it's still packing 1825 ft-lbs. more than some slugs have at the muzzle.

# WINCHESTER AMMUNITION

## SuperClean NT™ (NON-TOXIC) Pistol Ammo

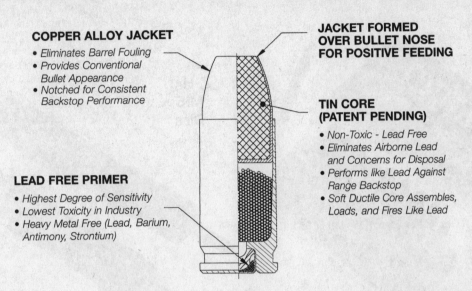

**COPPER ALLOY JACKET**
- Eliminates Barrel Fouling
- Provides Conventional Bullet Appearance
- Notched for Consistent Backstop Performance

**JACKET FORMED OVER BULLET NOSE FOR POSITIVE FEEDING**

**TIN CORE (PATENT PENDING)**
- Non-Toxic - Lead Free
- Eliminates Airborne Lead and Concerns for Disposal
- Performs like Lead Against Range Backstop
- Soft Ductile Core Assembles, Loads, and Fires Like Lead

**LEAD FREE PRIMER**
- Highest Degree of Sensitivity
- Lowest Toxicity in Industry
- Heavy Metal Free (Lead, Barium, Antimony, Strontium)

## Supreme® Fail Safe®

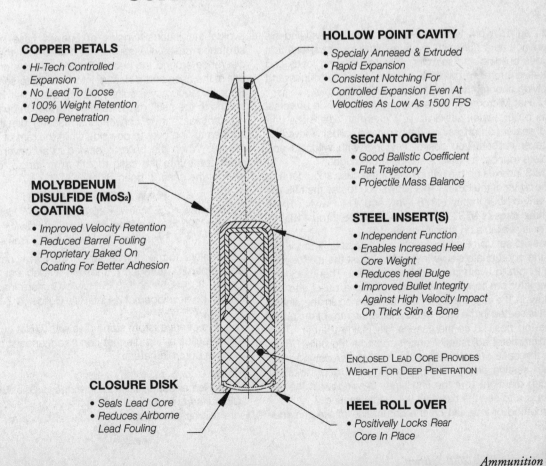

**COPPER PETALS**
- Hi-Tech Controlled Expansion
- No Lead To Loose
- 100% Weight Retention
- Deep Penetration

**HOLLOW POINT CAVITY**
- Specialy Anneaed & Extruded
- Rapid Expansion
- Consistent Notching For Controlled Expansion Even At Velocities As Low As 1500 FPS

**SECANT OGIVE**
- Good Ballistic Coefficient
- Flat Trajectory
- Projectile Mass Balance

**MOLYBDENUM DISULFIDE (MoS₂) COATING**
- Improved Velocity Retention
- Reduced Barrel Fouling
- Proprietary Baked On Coating For Better Adhesion

**STEEL INSERT(S)**
- Independent Function
- Enables Increased Heel Core Weight
- Reduces heel Bulge
- Improved Bullet Integrity Against High Velocity Impact On Thick Skin & Bone

ENCLOSED LEAD CORE PROVIDES WEIGHT FOR DEEP PENETRATION

**CLOSURE DISK**
- Seals Lead Core
- Reduces Airborne Lead Fouling

**HEEL ROLL OVER**
- Positivelly Locks Rear Core In Place

# Z-HAT

## CUSTOM DIES AND AMMUNITION

**Z-HAT
MIS
DIES**

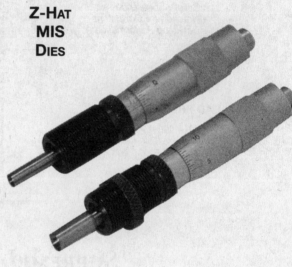

Fred Zeglin's work with Hawk wildcat cartridges, and his experience as a gunsmith, have resulted in a business that includes building and servicing rifles, developing loads and marketing premium-quality brass for Hawk cartridges and supplying shooters with match-grade loading dies.

The Z-Hat Micrometer Inline Seating (MIS) die is a universal in line bullet seater, similar to a "Vickerman" die. The universal seater comprises one die body and caliber sleeves for whatever calibers you desire. It works with wildcats and obsolete rounds, as well as standard cartridges.

The MIS indexes on the datum line of the case shoulder and on the ogive of the bullet. This allows you to use the MIS die with any caliber through .378 Wby. and 411 Hawk. There are three sizes of MIS 22 thru 7mm, and 308 throu 416. 17 caliber is available on special order.

It's easy to set up. First you gently run a case up into the die with the appropriate sleeve installed. Adjust the die for your case length to avoid crushing the shoulder. Then back the micrometer out to maximum length. Drop a bullet into the window in the die; the bullet will be retained in the sleeve until it is seated in the case neck. Raise the ram of the press to the top position so the case is fully inside the die. Turn the micrometer adjustment until it contacts the bullet. Then back the case out and adjust the micrometer down to the correct seating depth. Once you know the depth desired you can dial right to it the first time. A window in the die allows you to see the bullet as you begin seating.

The method of indexing on the datum line of the shoulder avoids the inconsistencies of uneven case mouths and stretched cases. A step is machined into the sleeve for clearance around the neck. The sleeve rests on the shoulder of the case and slides up into the MIS to seat the bullet. Superior accuracy results because the bullet is held concentric to the neck of the case all the way through the seating process. In a conventional seating die the bullet is allowed to flop over to one side while the ram of the press is raised. When the bullet is seated in a conventional die it often starts into the case mouth at an angle, causing the neck of the case to bend slightly.

### HAWK CARTRIDGES:

*240 Hawk • 257 Hawk • 264 Hawk • 270 Hawk • 284 Hawk • 300 Hawk • 8mm Hawk • 338 Hawk • 358 Hawk • 9.3 Hawk • 375 Hawk • 411 Hawk*

Z-Hat offers formed brass for all 12 Hawk cartridges, at $29.95 per 20. Loaded rounds are available at $69.95 per box, in .338, .358 and .375 Hawk. Custom loads for your rifle can be developed at Z-Hat (Rifle.Builder @ Z-Hat.com or phone 307-577-7443).

Fred also offers custom sizing dies with Z-Hat custom rifles, and he builds a ring die that can size standard bullets to fit obsolete bore diameters.

### *Prices:*
In-Line Seater set up for one cartridge . . . . . . . . **$99.00**
Caliber inserts . . . . . . . . . . . . . . . . . . . . . . . . . . **16.00**
Extra micrometer heads . . . . . . . . . . . . . . . . . . . **58.00**

# CENTERFIRE PISTOL & REVOLVER BALLISTICS

## Ballistics

*Roland Clark – The Sinkbox, 1925*

# FEDERAL HANDGUN BALLISTICS

Federal offers what may be the industry's most comprehensive lineup of handgun ammunition. A wide assortment of bullet profiles and weights, in a broad range of calibers, assures that there is a Classic load for every situation, from self-defense to hunting to target shooting.

## CLASSIC BULLET STYLES

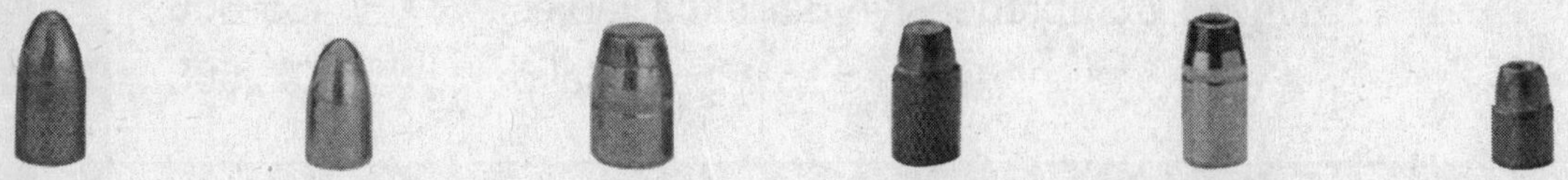

| Lead Round Nose | Full Metal Jacket | Hi-Shok Jacketed Soft Point | Lead Semi-Wadcutter | Hi-Shok Jacketed Hollow Point | Semi-Wadcutter Hollow Point |

## CLASSIC® AUTOMATIC PISTOL

| Usage | Federal Load No. | Caliber | Bullet Wgt. In Grains | Bullet Wgt. In Grams | Bullet Style* | Factory Primer No. | Muzzle | 25Yds | 50Yds | 75Yds | 100Yds | Muzzle | 25Yds | 50 Yds | 75Yds | 100Yds | 25Yds | 50Yds | 75Yds | 100Yds | Test Barrel Length Inches |
|---|---|---|---|---|---|---|---|---|---|---|---|---|---|---|---|---|---|---|---|---|---|
| | | | | | | | **Velocity In Feet Per Second (To Nearest 10 FPS)** | | | | | **Energy In Foot-Pounds (To Nearest 5 Foot-Pounds)** | | | | | **Mid-Range Trajectory** | | | | |
| 5,6 | C25AP | 25 Auto (6.35mm Browning) | 50 | 3.24 | Full Metal Jacket | 200 | 760 | 750 | 730 | 720 | 700 | 65 | 60 | 60 | 55 | 55 | 0.5 | 1.9 | 4.5 | 8.1 | 2 |
| 5,6 | C32AP | 32 Auto (7.65mm Browning) | 71 | 4.60 | Full Metal Jacket | 100 | 910 | 880 | 860 | 830 | 810 | 130 | 120 | 115 | 110 | 105 | 0.3 | 1.4 | 3.2 | 5.8 | 4 |
| 5,6 | C380AP | 380 Auto (9x17mm Short) | 95 | 6.15 | Full Metal Jacket | 100 | 960 | 910 | 870 | 830 | 790 | 190 | 175 | 160 | 145 | 130 | 0.3 | 1.3 | 3.1 | 5.8 | 3¾ |
| 6 | C380BP | 380 Auto (9x17mm Short) | 90 | 5.83 | Hi-Shok JHP | 100 | 1000 | 940 | 880 | 840 | 800 | 200 | 175 | 160 | 140 | 130 | 0.3 | 1.2 | 2.9 | 5.5 | 3¾ |
| 6 | C9MKB | 9mm Makarov (9x18 Makarov) | 90 | 5.83 | Hi-Shok JHP | 100 | 990 | 950 | 910 | 880 | 850 | 195 | 180 | 165 | 155 | 145 | 0.3 | 1.2 | 2.9 | 5.3 | 3¾ |
| 5,6 | C9AP | 9mm Luger (9x19mm Parabellum) | 124 | 8.03 | Full Metal Jacket | 100 | 1120 | 1070 | 1030 | 990 | 960 | 345 | 315 | 290 | 270 | 255 | 0.2 | 0.9 | 2.2 | 4.1 | 4 |
| 6 | C9BP | 9mm Luger (9x19mm Parabellum) | 115 | 7.45 | Hi-Shok JHP | 100 | 1160 | 1100 | 1060 | 1020 | 990 | 345 | 310 | 285 | 270 | 250 | 0.2 | 0.9 | 2.1 | 3.8 | 4 |
| 6 | C9MS | 9mm Luger (9x19mm Parabellum) | 147 | 9.52 | Hi-Shok JHP | 100 | 980 | 950 | 930 | 900 | 880 | 310 | 295 | 285 | 265 | 255 | 0.3 | 1.2 | 2.8 | 5.1 | 4 |
| 6 | C357S2 | 357 Sig | 125 | 8.10 | Full Metal Jacket | 100 | 1350 | 1270 | 1190 | 1130 | 1080 | 510 | 445 | 395 | 355 | 325 | 0.2 | 0.7 | 1.6 | 3.1 | 4 |
| 6 | C40SWA | 40 S&W | 180 | 11.66 | Hi-Shok JHP | 100 | 990 | 960 | 930 | 910 | 890 | 390 | 365 | 345 | 330 | 315 | 0.3 | 1.2 | 2.8 | 5.0 | 4 |
| 6 | C40SWB | 40 S&W | 155 | 10.04 | Hi-Shok JHP | 100 | 1140 | 1080 | 1030 | 990 | 950 | 445 | 400 | 365 | 335 | 315 | 0.2 | 0.9 | 2.2 | 4.1 | 4 |
| 6 | C10C | 10mm Auto | 180 | 11.66 | Hi-Shok JHP | 150 | 1030 | 1000 | 970 | 950 | 920 | 425 | 400 | 375 | 355 | 340 | 0.3 | 1.1 | 2.5 | 4.7 | 5 |
| 6 | C10E | 10mm Auto | 155 | 10.04 | Hi-Shok JHP | 150 | 1330 | 1230 | 1140 | 1080 | 1030 | 605 | 515 | 450 | 400 | 360 | 0.2 | 0.7 | 1.8 | 3.3 | 5 |
| 6 | C45A | 45 Auto | 230 | 14.90 | Full Metal Jacket | 150 | 850 | 830 | 810 | 790 | 770 | 370 | 350 | 335 | 320 | 305 | 0.4 | 1.6 | 3.6 | 6.6 | 5 |
| 6 | C45C | 45 Auto | 185 | 11.99 | Hi-Shok JHP | 150 | 950 | 920 | 900 | 880 | 860 | 370 | 350 | 335 | 315 | 300 | 0.3 | 1.3 | 2.9 | 5.3 | 5 |
| 6 | C45D | 45 Auto | 230 | 14.90 | Hi-Shok JHP | 150 | 850 | 830 | 810 | 790 | 770 | 370 | 350 | 335 | 320 | 300 | 0.4 | 1.6 | 3.7 | 6.7 | 5 |

*JHP = Jacketed Hollow Point

## CLASSIC® REVOLVER

| Usage | Federal Load No. | Caliber | Bullet Wgt. In Grains | Bullet Wgt. In Grams | Bullet Style* | Factory Primer No. | Muzzle | 25Yds | 50Yds | 75Yds | 100Yds | Muzzle | 25Yds | 50 Yds | 75Yds | 100Yds | 25Yds | 50Yds | 75Yds | 100Yds | Test Barrel Length Inches |
|---|---|---|---|---|---|---|---|---|---|---|---|---|---|---|---|---|---|---|---|---|---|
| | | | | | | | **Velocity In Feet Per Second (To Nearest 10 FPS)** | | | | | **Energy In Foot-Pounds (To Nearest 5 Foot-Pounds)** | | | | | **Mid-Range Trajectory** | | | | |
| 5 | C32LA | 32 S&W Long | 98 | 6.35 | Lead Wadcutter | 100 | 780 | 700 | 630 | 560 | 500 | 130 | 105 | 85 | 70 | 55 | 0.5 | 2.2 | 5.6 | 11.1 | 4 |
| 5 | C32LB | 32 S&W Long | 98 | 6.35 | Lead Round Nose | 100 | 710 | 690 | 670 | 650 | 640 | 115 | 105 | 100 | 95 | 90 | 0.6 | 2.3 | 5.3 | 9.6 | 4 |
| 6 | C32HRA | 32 H&R Magnum | 95 | 6.15 | Lead Semi-Wadcutter | 100 | 1030 | 1000 | 940 | 930 | 900 | 225 | 210 | 195 | 185 | 170 | 0.3 | 1.1 | 2.5 | 4.7 | 4½ |
| 6 | C32HRB | 32 H&R Magnum | 85 | 5.50 | Hi-Shok JHP | 100 | 1100 | 1050 | 1020 | 970 | 930 | 230 | 210 | 195 | 175 | 165 | 0.2 | 1.0 | 2.3 | 4.3 | 4½ |
| 5 | C38B | 38 Special | 158 | 10.23 | Lead Round Nose | 100 | 760 | 740 | 720 | 710 | 690 | 200 | 190 | 185 | 175 | 170 | 0.5 | 2.0 | 4.6 | 8.3 | 4-V |
| 5,6 | C38C | 38 Special | 158 | 10.23 | Lead Semi-Wadcutter | 100 | 760 | 740 | 720 | 710 | 690 | 200 | 190 | 185 | 175 | 170 | 0.5 | 2.0 | 4.6 | 8.3 | 4-V |
| 1,6 | C38E | 38 Special (High-Velocity+P) | 125 | 8.10 | Hi-Shok JHP | 100 | 950 | 920 | 900 | 880 | 860 | 250 | 235 | 225 | 215 | 205 | 0.3 | 1.3 | 2.9 | 5.4 | 4-V |
| 1,6 | C38F | 38 Special (High-Velocity+P) | 110 | 7.13 | Hi-Shok JHP | 100 | 1000 | 960 | 930 | 900 | 870 | 240 | 225 | 210 | 195 | 185 | 0.3 | 1.2 | 2.7 | 5.0 | 4-V |
| 1,6 | C38G | 38 Special (High-Velocity+P) | 158 | 10.23 | Semi-Wadcutter HP | 100 | 890 | 870 | 860 | 840 | 820 | 280 | 265 | 260 | 245 | 235 | 0.3 | 1.4 | 3.3 | 5.9 | 4-V |
| 5,6 | C38H | 38 Special (High-Velocity+P) | 158 | 10.23 | Lead Semi-Wadcutter | 100 | 890 | 870 | 860 | 840 | 820 | 270 | 265 | 260 | 245 | 235 | 0.3 | 1.4 | 3.3 | 5.9 | 4-V |
| 1,6 | C38J | 38 Special (High-Velocity+P) | 125 | 8.10 | Hi-Shok JSP | 100 | 950 | 920 | 900 | 880 | 860 | 250 | 235 | 225 | 215 | 205 | 0.3 | 1.3 | 2.9 | 5.4 | 4-V |
| 2,6 | C357A | 357 Magnum | 158 | 10.23 | Hi-Shok JSP | 100 | 1240 | 1160 | 1100 | 1060 | 1020 | 535 | 475 | 430 | 395 | 365 | 0.2 | 0.8 | 1.9 | 3.5 | 4-V |
| 1,6 | C357B | 357 Magnum | 125 | 8.10 | Hi-Shok JHP | 100 | 1450 | 1350 | 1240 | 1160 | 1100 | 580 | 495 | 430 | 370 | 335 | 0.1 | 0.6 | 1.5 | 2.8 | 4-V |
| 5 | C357C | 357 Magnum | 158 | 10.23 | Lead Semi-Wadcutter | 100 | 1240 | 1160 | 1100 | 1060 | 1020 | 535 | 475 | 430 | 395 | 365 | 0.2 | 0.8 | 1.9 | 3.5 | 4-V |
| 1,6 | C357D | 357 Magnum | 110 | 7.13 | Hi-Shok JHP | 100 | 1300 | 1180 | 1090 | 1040 | 990 | 410 | 340 | 290 | 260 | 235 | 0.2 | 0.8 | 1.9 | 3.5 | 4-V |
| 2,6 | C357E | 357 Magnum | 158 | 10.23 | Hi-Shok JHP | 100 | 1240 | 1160 | 1100 | 1060 | 1020 | 535 | 475 | 430 | 395 | 365 | 0.2 | 0.8 | 1.9 | 3.5 | 4-V |
| 2 | C357G | 357 Magnum | 180 | 11.66 | Hi-Shok JHP | 100 | 1090 | 1030 | 980 | 930 | 890 | 475 | 425 | 385 | 350 | 320 | 0.2 | 1.0 | 2.4 | 4.5 | 4-V |
| 2,6 | C357H | 357 Magnum | 140 | 9.07 | Hi-Shok JHP | 100 | 1360 | 1270 | 1200 | 1130 | 1080 | 575 | 500 | 445 | 395 | 360 | 0.2 | 0.7 | 1.6 | 3.0 | 4-V |
| 1,6 | C41A | 41 Rem. Magnum | 210 | 13.60 | Hi-Shok JHP | 150 | 1300 | 1210 | 1130 | 1070 | 1030 | 790 | 680 | 595 | 540 | 495 | 0.2 | 0.7 | 1.8 | 3.3 | 4-V |
| 1,6 | C44SA | 44 S&W Special | 200 | 12.96 | Semi-Wadcutter HP | 150 | 900 | 860 | 830 | 800 | 770 | 360 | 330 | 305 | 285 | 260 | 0.3 | 1.4 | 3.4 | 6.3 | 6½-V |
| 2,6 | C44A | 44 Rem. Magnum | 240 | 15.55 | Hi-Shok JHP | 150 | 1180 | 1130 | 1080 | 1050 | 1010 | 740 | 675 | 625 | 580 | 550 | 0.2 | 0.9 | 2.0 | 3.7 | 6½-V |
| 1,2 | C44B | 44 Rem. Magnum | 180 | 11.66 | Hi-Shok JHP | 150 | 1610 | 1480 | 1370 | 1270 | 1180 | 1035 | 875 | 750 | 640 | 555 | 0.1 | 0.5 | 1.2 | 2.3 | 6½-V |
| 1,6 | C45LCA | 45 Colt | 225 | 14.58 | Semi-Wadcutter HP | 150 | 900 | 880 | 860 | 840 | 820 | 405 | 385 | 370 | 355 | 340 | 0.3 | 1.4 | 3.2 | 5.8 | 5½ |

+P ammunition is loaded to a higher pressure. Use only in firearms recommended by the gun manufacturer. "V" indicates vented barrel to simulate service conditions.
**JHP = Jacketed Hollow Point  HP = Hollow Point  JSP = Jacketed Soft Point
Usage Key: 1 = Varmints, predators, small game  2 = Medium game  3 = Large, heavy game  4 = Dangerous game  5 = Target shooting, training, practice  6 = Self Defense

# REMINGTON HANDGUN BALLISTICS

**P & R**

### Golden Saber™ = GS    Core-Lokt® Hunting = RH    Disintegrator™ Frangible = LF

| Caliber | Order No. | Primer No. | Weight (grs.) | Bullet Style | Velocity (ft./sec.) Muzzle | 50 yds. | 100 yds. | Energy (ft.-lbs.) Muzzle | 50 yds. | 100 yds. | Mid-range Trajectory 50 yds. | 100. yds. | B.L. |
|---|---|---|---|---|---|---|---|---|---|---|---|---|---|
| .25 (6.35mm) Auto. Pistol | R25AP | 1½ | 50 | Metal Case | 760 | 707 | 659 | 64 | 56 | 48 | 2.0" | 8.7" | 2" |
| .32 S&W | R32SW | 1½ | 88 | Lead | 680 | 645 | 610 | 90 | 81 | 73 | 2.5" | 10.5" | 3" |
| .32 S&W Long | R32SWL | 1½ | 98 | Lead | 705 | 670 | 635 | 115 | 98 | 88 | 2.3" | 10.5" | 4" |
| .32 (7.65mm) Auto. Pistol | R32AP | 1½ | 71 | Metal Case | 905 | 855 | 810 | 129 | 115 | 97 | 1.4" | 5.8" | 4" |
| .357 Mag. (Vented Barrel Ballistics) | R357M7 | 5½ | 110 | Semi-Jacketed Hollow Point | 1295 | 1094 | 975 | 410 | 292 | 232 | 0.8" | 3.5" | 4" |
| | R357M1 | 5½ | 125 | Semi-Jacketed Hollow Point | 1450 | 1240 | 1090 | 583 | 427 | 330 | 0.6" | 2.8" | 4" |
| | GS357MA | 5½ | 125 | Brass-Jacketed Hollow Point | 1220 | 1095 | 1009 | 413 | 333 | 283 | 0.8" | 3.5" | 4" |
| | RH357MA | 5½ | 165 | JHP Core-Lokt® | 1290 | 1189 | 1108 | 610 | 518 | 450 | 0.7" | 3.1" | 8³/₈" |
| | R357M2 | 5½ | 158 | Semi-Jacketed Hollow Point | 1235 | 1104 | 1015 | 535 | 428 | 361 | 0.8" | 3.5" | 4" |
| | R357M3 | 5½ | 158 | Soft Point | 1235 | 1104 | 1015 | 535 | 428 | 361 | 0.8" | 3.5" | 4" |
| | R357M5 | 5½ | 158 | Semi-Wadcutter | 1235 | 1104 | 1015 | 535 | 428 | 361 | 0.8" | 3.5" | 4" |
| | R357M10 | 5½ | 180 | Semi-Jacketed Hollow Point | 1145 | 1053 | 985 | 524 | 443 | 388 | 0.9" | 3.9" | 8³/₈" |
| 9mm Luger Auto. Pistol | R9MM1 | 1½ | 115 | Jacketed Hollow Point | 1155 | 1047 | 971 | 341 | 280 | 241 | 0.9" | 3.9" | 4" |
| | R9MM10 | 1½ | 124 | Jacketed Hollow Point | 1120 | 1028 | 960 | 346 | 291 | 254 | 1.0" | 4.1" | 4" |
| | R9MM2 | 1½ | 124 | Metal Case | 1110 | 1030 | 971 | 339 | 292 | 259 | 1.0" | 4.1" | 4" |
| | R9MM3 | 1½ | 115 | Metal Case | 1135 | 1041 | 973 | 329 | 277 | 242 | 0.9" | 4.0" | 4" |
| | R9MM6 | 1½ | 115 | Jacketed Hollow Point (+P)✝ | 1250 | 1113 | 1019 | 399 | 316 | 265 | 0.8" | 3.5" | 4" |
| | R9MM8 | 1½ | 147 | Jacketed Hollow Point (Subsonic) | 990 | 941 | 900 | 320 | 289 | 264 | 1.1" | 4.9" | 4" |
| | R9MM9 | 1½ | 147 | Metal Case (Match) | 990 | 941 | 900 | 320 | 289 | 264 | 1.1" | 4.9" | 4" |
| | LF9MMA | 1½ | 101 | Disintegrator™ Plated Frangible | 1220 | 1092 | 1004 | 334 | 267 | 226 | 0.9" | 3.6" | 4" |
| | GS9MMB | 1½ | 124 | Brass-Jacketed Hollow Point | 1125 | 1031 | 963 | 349 | 293 | 255 | 1.0" | 4.0" | 4" |
| | GS9MMC | 1½ | 147 | Brass-Jacketed Hollow Point | 990 | 941 | 900 | 320 | 289 | 264 | 1.1" | 4.9" | 4" |
| | GS9MMD | 1½ | 124 | Brass-Jacketed Hollow Point (+P)✝ | 1180 | 1089 | 1021 | 384 | 327 | 287 | 0.8" | 3.8" | 4" |
| .380 Auto. Pistol | R380AP | 1½ | 95 | Metal Case | 955 | 865 | 785 | 190 | 160 | 130 | 1.4" | 5.9" | 4" |
| | R380A1 | 1½ | 88 | Jacketed Hollow Point | 990 | 920 | 868 | 191 | 165 | 146 | 1.2" | 5.1" | 4" |
| | GS380B | 1½ | 102 | Brass-Jacketed Hollow Point | 940 | 901 | 866 | 200 | 184 | 170 | 1.2" | 5.1" | 4" |
| .38 S&W | R38SW | 1½ | 146 | Lead | 685 | 650 | 620 | 150 | 135 | 125 | 2.4" | 10.0" | 4" |
| .38 Special (Vented Barrel Ballistics) | R38S10 | 1½ | 110 | Semi-Jacketed Hollow Point (+P)✝ | 995 | 926 | 871 | 242 | 210 | 185 | 1.2" | 5.1" | 4" |
| | R38S16 | 1½ | 110 | Semi-Jacketed Hollow Point | 950 | 890 | 840 | 220 | 194 | 172 | 1.4" | 5.4" | 4" |
| | R38S2 | 1½ | 125 | Semi-Jacketed Hollow Point (+P)✝ | 945 | 898 | 858 | 248 | 224 | 204 | 1.3" | 5.4" | 4" |
| | GS38SB | 1½ | 125 | Brass-Jacketed Hollow Point (+P)✝ | 975 | 929 | 885 | 264 | 238 | 218 | 1.0" | 5.2" | 4" |
| | R38S3 | 1½ | 148 | Targetmaster® Lead WC Match | 710 | 634 | 566 | 166 | 132 | 105 | 2.4" | 10.8" | 4" |
| | R38S5 | 1½ | 158 | Lead (Round Nose) | 755 | 723 | 692 | 200 | 183 | 168 | 2.0" | 8.3" | 4" |
| | R38S14 | 1½ | 158 | Semi-Wadcutter (+P)✝ | 890 | 855 | 823 | 278 | 257 | 238 | 1.4" | 6.0" | 4" |
| | R38S6 | 1½ | 158 | Semi-Wadcutter | 755 | 723 | 692 | 200 | 183 | 168 | 2.0" | 8.3" | 4" |
| | R38S12 | 1½ | 158 | Lead Hollow Point (+P)✝ | 890 | 855 | 823 | 278 | 257 | 238 | 1.4" | 6.0" | 4" |
| .38 Short Colt | R38SC | 1½ | 125 | Lead | 730 | 685 | 645 | 150 | 130 | 115 | 2.2" | 9.4" | 6" |
| .357 Sig. | R357S1 | 5½ | 125 | Jacketed Hollow Point | 1350 | 1157 | 1032 | 506 | 372 | 296 | 0.7" | 3.2" | 4" |
| .40 S&W | R40SW1 | 5½ | 155 | Jacketed Hollow Point | 1205 | 1095 | 1017 | 499 | 413 | 356 | 0.8" | 3.6" | 4" |
| | R40SW2 | 5½ | 180 | Jacketed Hollow Point | 1015 | 960 | 914 | 412 | 368 | 334 | 1.3" | 4.5" | 4" |
| | LF40SWA | 5½ | 141 | Disintegrator™ Plated Frangible | 1135 | 1056 | 996 | 403 | 349 | 311 | 0.9" | 3.9" | 4" |
| | GS40SWA | 5½ | 165 | Brass-Jacketed Hollow Point | 1150 | 1040 | 964 | 485 | 396 | 340 | 1.0" | 4.0" | 4" |
| | GS40SWB | 5½ | 180 | Brass-Jacketed Hollow Point | 1015 | 960 | 914 | 412 | 368 | 334 | 1.3" | 4.5" | 4" |
| .41 Rem. Mag. (Vented BBL Ballistics) | R41MG1 | 2½ | 210 | Soft Point | 1300 | 1162 | 1062 | 788 | 630 | 526 | 0.7" | 3.2" | 4" |
| .44 Rem. Mag. (Vented BBL Ballistics) | R44MG5 | 2½ | 180 | Semi-Jacketed Hollow Point | 1610 | 1365 | 1175 | 1036 | 745 | 551 | 0.5" | 2.3" | 4" |
| | R44MG2 | 2½ | 240 | Soft Point | 1180 | 1081 | 1010 | 741 | 623 | 543 | 0.9" | 3.7" | 4" |
| | R44MG3 | 2½ | 240 | Semi-Jacketed Hollow Point | 1180 | 1081 | 1010 | 741 | 623 | 543 | 0.9" | 3.7" | 4" |
| | RH44MGA | 2½ | 275 | JHP Core-Lokt® | 1235 | 1142 | 1070 | 931 | 797 | 699 | 0.8" | 3.3" | 6¹/₂" |
| .44 S&W Special | R44SW | 2½ | 246 | Lead | 755 | 725 | 695 | 310 | 285 | 265 | 2.0" | 8.3" | 6" |
| .45 Colt | R45C | 2½ | 250 | Lead | 860 | 820 | 780 | 410 | 375 | 340 | 1.6" | 6.6" | 5" |
| | R45C1 | 2½ | 225 | Semi-Wadcutter (Keith) | 960 | 890 | 832 | 460 | 395 | 346 | 1.3" | 5.5" | 5" |
| | R45AP2 | 2½ | 185 | Jacketed Hollow Point | 1000 | 939 | 889 | 411 | 362 | 324 | 1.1" | 4.9" | 5" |
| | R45AP4 | 2½ | 230 | Metal Case | 835 | 800 | 767 | 356 | 326 | 300 | 1.6" | 6.8" | 5" |
| | R45AP7 | 2½ | 230 | Jacketed Hollow Point (Subsonic) | 835 | 800 | 767 | 356 | 326 | 300 | 1.6" | 6.8" | 5" |
| | LF45AP4 | 2½ | 175 | Disintegrator™ Plated Frangible | 1020 | 923 | 851 | 404 | 331 | 281 | 1.2" | 5.1" | 5" |
| | GS45APA | 2½ | 185 | Brass-Jacketed Hollow Point | 1015 | 951 | 899 | 423 | 372 | 332 | 1.1" | 4.5" | 5" |
| | GS45APB | 2½ | 230 | Brass-Jacketed Hollow Point | 875 | 833 | 795 | 391 | 355 | 323 | 1.5" | 6.1" | 5" |
| | GS45APC | 2½ | 185 | Brass-Jacketed Hollow Point (+P)✝ | 1140 | 1042 | 971 | 534 | 446 | 388 | 1.0" | 4.0" | 5" |

✝Ammunition with (+P) on the case headstamp is loaded to higher pressure. Use only in firearms designated for this cartridge and so recommended by the gun manufacturer.

**BALLISTICS**

# WINCHESTER HANDGUN BALLISTICS

## SUPREME

| Cartridge | Symbol | Bullet Wt. Grs. | Type | User Guide | Velocity (FPS) Muzzle | 50 Yds. | 100 Yds. | Energy (Ft.Lbs.) Muzzle | 50 Yds. | 100 Yds. | Mid Range Traj. (In.) 50 Yds. | 100 Yds. | Barrel Length In. |
|---|---|---|---|---|---|---|---|---|---|---|---|---|---|
| 380 Automatic SXT | S380 | 95 | SXT | PP | 955 | 889 | 835 | 192 | 167 | 147 | 1.3 | 5.5 | 3-3/4 |
| 38 Special + P # SXT | S38SP | 130 | SXT | PP | 925 | 887 | 852 | 247 | 227 | 210 | 1.3 | 5.5 | 4V |
| 9mm Luger SXT | S9 | 147 | SXT | PP | 990 | 947 | 909 | 320 | 293 | 270 | 1.2 | 4.8 | 4 |
| 40 Smith & Wesson SXT | S401 | 165 | SXT | PP | 1130 | 1041 | 977 | 468 | 397 | 349 | 0.9 | 4.0 | 4 |
| 40 Smith & Wesson SXT | S40 | 180 | SXT | PP | 1010 | 954 | 909 | 408 | 364 | 330 | 1.1 | 4.8 | 4 |
| 45 Automatic SXT | S45 | 230 | SXT | PP | 880 | 846 | 816 | 396 | 366 | 340 | 1.5 | 6.1 | 5 |
| 357 Magnum | S357P | 180 | PartitionGold | H | 1180 | 1088 | 1020 | 557 | 473 | 416 | 0.8 | 3.6 | 8V |
| 44 Magnum | S44MP | 250 | PartitionGold | H | 1230 | 1132 | 1057 | 840 | 711 | 620 | 0.8 | 2.9 | 6.5V |
| 45 Winchester Magnum # | SPG45WM | 260 | PartitionGold | H | 1200 | 1105 | 1033 | 832 | 705 | 617 | 0.8 | 3.5 | 5 |
| 454 Casull # | SPG454 | 260 | PartitionGold | H | 1800 | 1605 | 1427 | 1871 | 1485 | 1176 | 0.4 | 1.7 | 7.5V |

## SUPER X

| Cartridge | Symbol | Bullet Wt. Grs. | Type | User Guide | Velocity (FPS) Muzzle | 50 Yds. | 100 Yds. | Energy (Ft.Lbs.) Muzzle | 50 Yds. | 100 Yds. | Mid Range Traj. (In.) 50 Yds. | 100 Yds. | Barrel Length In. |
|---|---|---|---|---|---|---|---|---|---|---|---|---|---|
| 25 Automatic | X25AXP | 45 | Expanding Point** | PP | 815 | 729 | 655 | 66 | 53 | 42 | 1.8 | 7.7 | 2 |
| 30 Luger (7.65 mm) | X30LP | 93 | Full Metal Jacket | T | 1220 | 1110 | 1040 | 305 | 255 | 225 | 0.9 | 3.5 | 4-1/2 |
| 30 Carbine # | X30M1 | 110 | Hollow Soft Point | H | 1790 | 1601 | 1430 | 783 | 626 | 500 | 0.4 | 1.7 | 10 |
| 32 Smith & Wesson | 32BL2P | Blk.Pwd. | Blank | | | | | | | | | | |
| 32 Smith & Wesson | X32SWP | 85 | Lead-Round Nose | T | 680 | 645 | 610 | 90 | 81 | 73 | 2.5 | 10.5 | 3 |
| 32 Smith & Wesson Long | X32SWLP | 98 | Lead-Round Nose | T | 705 | 670 | 635 | 115 | 98 | 88 | 2.3 | 10.5 | 4 |
| 32 Short Colt | X32SCP | 80 | Lead-Round Nose | T | 745 | 665 | 590 | 100 | 79 | 62 | 2.2 | 9.9 | 4 |
| 32 Automatic | X32ASHP | 60 | Silvertip Hollow Point | PP | 970 | 895 | 835 | 125 | 107 | 93 | 1.3 | 5.4 | 4 |
| 38 Smith & Wesson | X38SWP | 145 | Lead-Round Nose | T | 685 | 650 | 620 | 150 | 135 | 125 | 2.4 | 10.0 | 4 |
| 380 Automatic | X380ASHP | 85 | Silvertip Hollow Point | PP | 1000 | 921 | 860 | 189 | 160 | 140 | 1.2 | 5.1 | 3-3/4 |
| 38 Special | 38SBLP | Smokeless | Blank | | | | | | | | | | |
| 38 Special | X38S9HP | 110 | Silvertip Hollow Point | PP | 945 | 894 | 850 | 218 | 195 | 176 | 1.3 | 5.4 | 4V |
| 38 Special Super Match | X38SMRP | 148 | Lead-Wad Cutter | T | 710 | 634 | 566 | 166 | 132 | 105 | 2.4 | 10.8 | 4V |
| 38 Special | X38S1P | 158 | Lead-Round Nose | T | 755 | 723 | 693 | 200 | 183 | 168 | 2.0 | 8.3 | 4V |
| 38 Special | X38WCPSV | 158 | Lead-Semi Wad Cutter | T | 755 | 721 | 689 | 200 | 182 | 167 | 2.0 | 8.4 | 4V |
| 38 Special + P # | X38S7PH | 125 | Jacketed Hollow Point | PP | 945 | 898 | 858 | 248 | 224 | 204 | 1.3 | 5.4 | 4V |
| 38 Special + P # | X38S8HP | 125 | Silvertip Hollow Point | PP | 945 | 898 | 858 | 248 | 224 | 204 | 1.3 | 5.4 | 4V |
| 38 Special + P | X38SPD | 158 | Lead-Semi Wad Cutter Hollow Point | PP | 890 | 855 | 823 | 278 | 257 | 238 | 1.4 | 6.0 | 4V |
| 9mm Luger | X9MMSHP | 115 | Silvertip Hollow Point | PP | 1225 | 1095 | 1007 | 383 | 306 | 259 | 0.8 | 3.6 | 4 |
| 9mm Luger | X9MMST147 | 147 | Silvertip Hollow Point | PP | 1010 | 962 | 921 | 333 | 302 | 277 | 1.1 | 4.7 | 4 |
| 38 Super Automatic +P* | X38ASHP | 125 | Silvertip Hollow Point | T/PP | 1240 | 1130 | 1050 | 427 | 354 | 306 | 0.8 | 3.4 | 5 |
| 9 x 23 Winchester | X923W | 125 | Silvertip Hollow Point | T/PP | 1450 | 1249 | 1103 | 583 | 433 | 338 | 0.6 | 2.8 | 5 |
| 357 Magnum # | X357SHP | 145 | Silvertip Hollow Point | PP | 1290 | 1155 | 1060 | 535 | 428 | 361 | 0.8 | 3.5 | 4V |
| 357 Magnum # | X3574P | 158 | Jacketed Hollow Point | H/PP | 1235 | 1104 | 1015 | 535 | 428 | 361 | 0.8 | 3.5 | 4V |
| 357 Magnum # | X3575P | 158 | Jacketed Soft Point | H/PP | 1235 | 1104 | 1015 | 535 | 428 | 361 | 0.8 | 3.5 | 4V |
| 40 Smith & Wesson | X40SWSTHP | 155 | Silvertip Hollow Point | PP | 1205 | 1096 | 1018 | 500 | 414 | 357 | 0.8 | 3.6 | 4 |
| 10 mm Automatic | X10MMSTHP | 175 | Silvertip Hollow Point | PP | 1290 | 1141 | 1037 | 649 | 506 | 418 | 0.7 | 3.3 | 5-1/2 |
| 41 Remington Magnum # | X41MSTHP2 | 175 | Silvertip Hollow Point | H/PP | 1250 | 1120 | 1029 | 607 | 488 | 412 | 0.8 | 3.4 | 4V |
| 44 Smith & Wesson Special # | X44STHPS2 | 200 | Silvertip Hollow Point | PP | 900 | 860 | 822 | 360 | 328 | 300 | 1.4 | 5.9 | 6-1/2 |
| 44 Smith & Wesson Special | X44SP | 246 | Lead-Round Nose | T | 755 | 725 | 695 | 310 | 285 | 265 | 2.0 | 8.3 | 6-1/2 |
| 44 Remington Magnum # | X44MS | 210 | Silvertip Hollow Point | H/PP | 1250 | 1106 | 1010 | 729 | 570 | 475 | 0.8 | 3.5 | 4V |
| 44 Remington Magnum # | X44MHSP2 | 240 | Hollow Soft Point | H | 1180 | 1081 | 1010 | 741 | 623 | 543 | 0.9 | 3.7 | 4V |
| 45 Automatic | X45ASHP2 | 185 | Silvertip Hollow Point | PP | 1000 | 938 | 888 | 411 | 362 | 324 | 1.2 | 4.9 | 5 |
| 45 Automatic Subsonic | XSUB45A | 230 | Jacketed Hollow Point | PP | 880 | 842 | 808 | 396 | 363 | 334 | 1.5 | 6.1 | 5 |
| 45 Colt # | X45CSHP2 | 225 | Silvertip Hollow Point | PP | 920 | 877 | 839 | 423 | 384 | 352 | 1.4 | 5.6 | 5-1/2 |
| 45 Colt | X45CP2 | 255 | Lead-Round Nose | T | 860 | 820 | 780 | 420 | 380 | 345 | 1.5 | 6.1 | 5-1/2 |
| 45 Winchester Magnum # | X45WMA | 260 | Jacketed Hollow Point | H | 1200 | 1099 | 1026 | 831 | 698 | 607 | 0.8 | 3.6 | 5 |
| 454 Casull # | X454C3 | 250 | Jacketed Hollow Point | H | 1300 | 1151 | 1047 | 938 | 735 | 608 | 0.7 | 3.2 | 7.5V |
| 454 Casull # | X454C22 | 300 | Jacketed Flat Point | H | 1625 | 1451 | 1308 | 1759 | 1413 | 1141 | 0.5 | 2.0 | 7.5V |

## SUPER CLEAN NT (TIN)

| Cartridge | Symbol | Bullet Wt. Grs. | Type | User Guide | Velocity (FPS) Muzzle | 50 Yds. | 100 Yds. | Energy (Ft.Lbs.) Muzzle | 50 Yds. | 100 Yds. | Mid Range Traj. (In.) 50 Yds. | 100 Yds. | Barrel Length In. |
|---|---|---|---|---|---|---|---|---|---|---|---|---|---|
| 38 Special | SC38NT | 110 | Jacketed Soft Point | T | 975 | 906 | 849 | 222 | 191 | 168 | 0.2 | 3.7 | 4V |
| 9 mm Luger | SC9NT | 105 | Jacketed Soft Point | T | 1200 | 1074 | 989 | 336 | 269 | 228 | 0.8 | 3.7 | 4 |
| 357 Magnum | SC357NT | 110 | Jacketed Soft Point | T | 1275 | 1105 | 998 | 397 | 298 | 243 | 0.8 | 3.5 | 4V |
| 357 SIG | SC357SNT | 105 | Jacketed Soft Point | T | 1370 | 1179 | 1050 | 438 | 324 | 257 | 0.7 | 3.1 | 4 |
| 40 Smith & Wesson | SC40NT | 140 | Jacketed Soft Point | T | 1155 | 1039 | 960 | 415 | 336 | 286 | 1.2 | 5.3 | 4 |
| 45 Automatic | SC45NT | 170 | Jacketed Soft Point | T | 1050 | 982 | 928 | 416 | 364 | 325 | 0.9 | 0.4 | 4 |

## WinClean CENTERFIRE HANDGUN AMMUNITION

| Cartridge | Symbol | Bullet Wt. Grs. | Type | User Guide | Velocity (FPS) Muzzle | 50 Yds. | 100 Yds. | Energy (Ft.Lbs.) Muzzle | 50 Yds. | 100 Yds. | Mid Range Traj. (In.) 50 Yds. | 100 Yds. | Barrel Length In. |
|---|---|---|---|---|---|---|---|---|---|---|---|---|---|
| 380 Automatic | WC3801 | 95 gr. | Brass Enclosed Base | T | | TBA | | | | | | | |
| 38 Special WinClean | WC381 | 125 gr. | Jacketed Soft Point | T | 775 | 742 | | 167 | 153 | | | | |
| 9mm Luger WinClean | WC91 | 115 gr. | Brass Enclosed Base | T | 1190 | 1088 | | 362 | 302 | | | | |
| 357 Magnum | WC3571 | 125 gr | Jacketed Soft Point | T | | TBA | | | | | | | |
| 40 Smith & Wesson WinClean | WC401 | 165 gr. | Brass Enclosed Base | T | 1130 | 1054 | | 468 | 407 | | | | |
| 40 Smith & Wesson WinClean | WC402 | 180 gr. | Brass Enclosed Base | T | 990 | 943 | | 392 | 286 | | | | |
| 45 Automatic WinClean | WC451 | 185 gr. | Brass Enclosed Base | T | 910 | 835 | | 340 | 286 | | | | |
| 45 Automatic WinClean | WC452 | 230 gr. | Brass Enclosed Base | T | 835 | 802 | | 356 | 329 | | | | |

## COWBOY LOADS

| Cartridge | Symbol | Bullet Wt. Grs. | Type | User Guide | Velocity (FPS) Muzzle | 50 Yds. | 100 Yds. | Energy (Ft.Lbs.) Muzzle | 50 Yds. | 100 Yds. | Mid Range Traj. (In.) 50 Yds. | 100 Yds. | Barrel Length In. |
|---|---|---|---|---|---|---|---|---|---|---|---|---|---|
| 38 Special | CB38SP | 158 | Lead | T | 800 | 761 | 725 | 225 | 203 | 185 | 1.8 | 7.5 | 4 |
| 44-40 Winchester | CB4440W | 225 | Lead | T | 750 | 723 | 695 | 281 | 261 | 242 | 2.0 | 8.3 | 4 |
| 44 Special | CB44SP | 240 | Lead | T | 750 | 719 | 690 | 300 | 275 | 253 | 2.0 | 8.4 | 4 |
| 45 Colt | CB45C | 250 | Lead | T | 750 | 720 | 692 | 312 | 288 | 266 | 2.0 | 8.4 | 5 |

*T*-training  **PP**-Personal Protection  *H*-Hunting

# CENTERFIRE RIFLE BALLISTICS

## COMPREHENSIVE BALLISTICS TABLES FOR CURRENTLY MANUFACTURED SPORTING RIFLE CARTRIDGES

No more collecting catalogs and peering at microscopic print to find out what ammunition is offered for a cartridge, and how it performs relative to other factory loads! Shooter's Bible has assembled the data for you, in easy-to-read tables, by cartridge. Of course, this section will be updated every year to bring you the latest information.

**NOTES:** Data is taken from manufacturers' charts; your chronograph readings may vary. Listings are current as of February the year Shooter's Bible appears (not the cover year). Listings are not intended as recommendations. For example, the data for the .44 Magnum at 400 yards shows its effective range is much shorter. The lack of data for a 285-grain .375 H&H bullet beyond 300 yards does not mean the bullet has no authority farther out. Besides ammunition, the rifle, sights, conditions and shooter ability all must be considered when contemplating a long shot. Accuracy and bullet energy both matter when big game is in the offing. Barrel length affects velocity, and at various rates depending on the load. As a rule, figure 50 fps per inch of barrel, plus or minus, if your barrel is longer or shorter than 22 inches. Bullets are given by make, weight (in grains) and type.

**MOST TYPE ABBREVIATIONS ARE SELF-EXPLANATORY: BT**=Boat-Tail, **FMJ**=Full Metal Jacket, **HP**=Hollow Point, **SP**=Soft Point, except in Hornady listings, where SP is the firm's Spire Point. **TNT** and **TXP** are trademarked designations of Speer and Norma. **XLC** identifies a coated Barnes X bullet. **HE** indicates a Federal High Energy load, similar to the Hornady **LM** (Light Magnum) and **HM** (Heavy Magnum) cartridges. **Arc** (trajectory) is based on a zero range published by the manufacturer, from 100 to 300 yards. If a zero does not fall in a yardage column, it lies halfway between at 150 yards, for example, if the bullet's strike is at 100 yards and at 200.

| CARTRIDGE BULLET | RANGE, YARDS: | 0 | 100 | 200 | 300 | 400 |
|---|---|---|---|---|---|---|
| **.17 Remington** | | | | | | |
| Rem. 25 HP Power-Lokt | velocity, fps: | 4040 | 3284 | 2644 | 2086 | 1606 |
| | energy, ft-lb: | 906 | 599 | 388 | 242 | 143 |
| | arc, inches: | | +1.8 | 0 | -3.3 | -16.6 |
| **.218 Bee** | | | | | | |
| Win. 46 Hollow Point | velocity, fps: | 2760 | 2102 | 1550 | 1155 | 961 |
| | energy, ft-lb: | 778 | 451 | 245 | 136 | 94 |
| | arc, inches: | | 0 | -7.2 | -29.4 | |
| **.22 Hornet** | | | | | | |
| Hornady 35 V-Max | velocity, fps: | 3100 | 2278 | 1601 | 1135 | 929 |
| | energy, ft-lb: | 747 | 403 | 199 | 100 | 67 |
| | arc, inches: | | +2.8 | 0 | -16.9 | -60.4 |
| Rem. 45 Pointed Soft Point | velocity, fps: | 2690 | 2042 | 1502 | 1128 | 948 |
| | energy, ft-lb: | 723 | 417 | 225 | 127 | 90 |
| | arc, inches: | | 0 | -7.1 | -30.0 | |
| Rem. 45 Hollow Point | velocity, fps: | 2690 | 2042 | 1502 | 1128 | 948 |
| | energy, ft-lb: | 723 | 417 | 225 | 127 | 90 |
| | arc, inches: | | 0 | -7.1 | -30.0 | |
| Win. 34 Jacketed HP | velocity, fps: | 3050 | 2132 | 1415 | 1017 | 852 |
| | energy, ft-lb: | 700 | 343 | 151 | 78 | 55 |
| | arc, inches: | | 0 | -6.6 | -29.9 | |
| Win. 45 Soft Point | velocity, fps: | 2690 | 2042 | 1502 | 1128 | 948 |
| | energy, ft-lb: | 723 | 417 | 225 | 127 | 90 |
| | arc, inches: | | 0 | -7.7 | -31.3 | |
| Win. 46 Hollow Point | velocity, fps: | 2690 | 2042 | 1502 | 1128 | 948 |
| | energy, ft-lb: | 739 | 426 | 230 | 130 | 92 |
| | arc, inches: | | 0 | -7.7 | -31.3 | |
| **.222 Remington** | | | | | | |
| Federal 50 Hi-Shok | velocity, fps: | 3140 | 2600 | 2120 | 1700 | 1350 |
| | energy, ft-lb: | 1095 | 750 | 500 | 320 | 200 |
| | arc, inches: | | +1.9 | 0 | -9.7 | -31.6 |

| CARTRIDGE BULLET | RANGE, YARDS: | 0 | 100 | 200 | 300 | 400 |
|---|---|---|---|---|---|---|
| Federal 55 FMJ boat-tail | velocity, fps: | 3020 | 2740 | 2480 | 2230 | 1990 |
| | energy, ft-lb: | 1115 | 915 | 750 | 610 | 484 |
| | arc, inches: | | +1.6 | 0 | -7.3 | -21.5 |
| Hornady 40 V-Max | velocity, fps: | 3600 | 3117 | 2673 | 2269 | 1911 |
| | energy, ft-lb: | 1151 | 863 | 634 | 457 | 324 |
| | arc, inches: | | +1.1 | 0 | -6.1 | -18.9 |
| Hornady 50 V-Max | velocity, fps: | 3140 | 2729 | 2352 | 2008 | 1710 |
| | energy, ft-lb: | 1094 | 827 | 614 | 448 | 325 |
| | arc, inches: | | +1.7 | 0 | -7.9 | -24.4 |
| Norma 50 Soft Point | velocity, fps: | 3199 | 2667 | 2193 | 1771 | |
| | energy, ft-lb: | 1136 | 790 | 534 | 348 | |
| | arc, inches: | | +1.7 | 0 | -9.1 | |
| Norma 50 FMJ | velocity, fps: | 2789 | 2326 | 1910 | 1547 | |
| | energy, ft-lb: | 864 | 601 | 405 | 266 | |
| | arc, inches: | | +2.5 | 0 | -12.2 | |
| Norma 62 Soft Point | velocity, fps: | 2887 | 2457 | 2067 | 1716 | |
| | energy, ft-lb: | 1148 | 831 | 588 | 405 | |
| | arc, inches: | | +2.1 | 0 | -10.4 | |
| PMC 50 Pointed Soft Point | velocity, fps: | 3044 | 2727 | 2354 | 2012 | 1651 |
| | energy, ft-lb: | 1131 | 908 | 677 | 494 | 333 |
| | arc, inches: | | +1.6 | 0 | -7.9 | -24.5 |
| Rem. 50 Pointed Soft Point | velocity, fps: | 3140 | 2602 | 2123 | 1700 | 1350 |
| | energy, ft-lb: | 1094 | 752 | 500 | 321 | 202 |
| | arc, inches: | | +1.9 | 0 | -9.7 | -31.7 |
| Rem. 50 HP Power-Lokt | velocity, fps: | 3140 | 2635 | 2182 | 1777 | 1432 |
| | energy, ft-lb: | 1094 | 771 | 529 | 351 | 228 |
| | arc, inches: | | +1.8 | 0 | -9.2 | -29.6 |
| Rem. 50 V-Max boat-tail | velocity, fps: | 3140 | 2744 | 2380 | 2045 | 1740 |
| | energy, ft-lb: | 1094 | 836 | 629 | 464 | 336 |
| | arc, inches: | | +1.6 | 0 | -7.8 | -23.9 |
| Win. 40 Ballistic Silvertip | velocity, fps: | 3370 | 2915 | 2503 | 2127 | 1786 |
| | energy, ft-lb: | 1009 | 755 | 556 | 402 | 283 |
| | arc, inches: | | +1.3 | 0 | -6.9 | -21.5 |
| Win. 50 Pointed Soft Point | velocity, fps: | 3140 | 2602 | 2123 | 1700 | 1350 |
| | energy, ft-lb: | 1094 | 752 | 500 | 321 | 202 |
| | arc, inches: | | +2.2 | 0 | -10.0 | -32.3 |

# .223 Remington

| Cartridge Bullet | | 0 | 100 | 200 | 300 | 400 |
|---|---|---|---|---|---|---|
| Federal 50 Jacketed HP | velocity, fps: | 3400 | 2910 | 2460 | 2060 | 1700 |
| | energy, ft-lb: | 1285 | 940 | 675 | 470 | 320 |
| | arc, inches: | | +1.3 | 0 | -7.1 | -22.7 |
| Federal 50 Speer TNT HP | velocity, fps: | 3300 | 2860 | 2450 | 2080 | 1750 |
| | energy, ft-lb: | 1210 | 905 | 670 | 480 | 340 |
| | arc, inches: | | +1.4 | 0 | -7.3 | -22.6 |
| Federal 52 Sierra MatchKing BTHP | velocity, fps: | 3300 | 2860 | 2460 | 2090 | 1760 |
| | energy, ft-lb: | 1255 | 945 | 700 | 505 | 360 |
| | arc, inches: | | +1.4 | 0 | -7.2 | -22.4 |
| Federal 55 Hi-Shok | velocity, fps: | 3240 | 2750 | 2300 | 1910 | 1550 |
| | energy, ft-lb: | 1280 | 920 | 650 | 445 | 295 |
| | arc, inches: | | +1.6 | 0 | -8.2 | -26.1 |
| Federal 55 FMJ boat-tail | velocity, fps: | 3240 | 2950 | 2670 | 2410 | 2170 |
| | energy, ft-lb: | 1280 | 1060 | 875 | 710 | 575 |
| | arc, inches: | | +1.3 | 0 | -6.1 | -18.3 |
| Federal 55 Sierra GameKing BTHP | velocity, fps: | 3240 | 2770 | 2340 | 1950 | 1610 |
| | energy, ft-lb: | 1280 | 935 | 670 | 465 | 315 |
| | arc, inches: | | +1.5 | 0 | -8.0 | -25.3 |
| Federal 55 Trophy Bonded | velocity, fps: | 3100 | 2630 | 2210 | 1830 | 1500 |
| | energy, ft-lb: | 1175 | 845 | 595 | 410 | 275 |
| | arc, inches: | | +1.8 | 0 | -8.9 | -28.7 |
| Federal 55 Nosler Bal. Tip | velocity, fps: | 3240 | 2870 | 2530 | 2220 | 1920 |
| | energy, ft-lb: | 1280 | 1005 | 780 | 600 | 450 |
| | arc, inches: | | +1.4 | 0 | -6.8 | -20.8 |
| Federal 55 Sierra BlitzKing | velocity, fps: | 3240 | 2870 | 2520 | 2200 | 1910 |
| | energy, ft-lb: | 1280 | 1005 | 775 | 590 | 445 |
| | arc, inches: | | +1.4 | 0 | -6.9 | -20.9 |
| Federal 62 FMJ | velocity, fps: | 3020 | 2650 | 2310 | 2000 | 1710 |
| | energy, ft-lb: | 1225 | 970 | 735 | 550 | 405 |
| | arc, inches: | | +1.7 | 0 | -8.4 | -25.5 |
| Federal 69 Sierra MatchKing BTHP | velocity, fps: | 3000 | 2720 | 2460 | 2210 | 1980 |
| | energy, ft-lb: | 1380 | 1135 | 925 | 750 | 600 |
| | arc, inches: | | +1.6 | 0 | -7.4 | -21.9 |
| Hornady 40 V-Max | velocity, fps: | 3800 | 3305 | 2845 | 2424 | 2044 |
| | energy, ft-lb: | 1282 | 970 | 719 | 522 | 371 |
| | arc, inches: | | +0.8 | 0 | -5.3 | -16.6 |
| Hornady 53 Hollow Point | velocity, fps: | 3330 | 2882 | 2477 | 2106 | 1710 |
| | energy, ft-lb: | 1305 | 978 | 722 | 522 | 369 |
| | arc, inches: | | +1.7 | 0 | -7.4 | -22.7 |
| Hornady 55 V-Max | velocity, fps: | 3240 | 2859 | 2507 | 2181 | 1891 |
| | energy, ft-lb: | 1282 | 998 | 767 | 581 | 437 |
| | arc, inches: | | +1.4 | 0 | -7.1 | -21.4 |
| Hornady 55 Urban Tactical | velocity, fps: | 2970 | 2626 | 2307 | 2011 | 1739 |
| | energy, ft-lb: | 1077 | 842 | 650 | 494 | 369 |
| | arc, inches: | | +1.5 | 0 | -8.1 | -24.9 |
| Hornady 60 Soft Point | velocity, fps: | 3150 | 2782 | 2442 | 2127 | 1837 |
| | energy, ft-lb: | 1322 | 1031 | 795 | 603 | 450 |
| | arc, inches: | | +1.6 | 0 | -7.5 | -22.5 |
| Hornady 60 Urban Tactical | velocity, fps: | 2950 | 2619 | 2312 | 2025 | 1762 |
| | energy, ft-lb: | 1160 | 914 | 712 | 546 | 413 |
| | arc, inches: | | +1.6 | 0 | -8.1 | -24.7 |
| Hornady 75 BTHP Match | velocity, fps: | 2790 | 2554 | 2330 | 2119 | 1926 |
| | energy, ft-lb: | 1296 | 1086 | 904 | 747 | 617 |
| | arc, inches: | | +2.4 | 0 | -8.8 | -25.1 |
| Hornady 75 BTHP Tactical | velocity, fps: | 2630 | 2409 | 2199 | 2000 | 1814 |
| | energy, ft-lb: | 1152 | 966 | 805 | 666 | 548 |
| | arc, inches: | | -2.0 | 0 | -9.2 | -25.9 |
| PMC 55 HP boat-tail | velocity, fps: | 3240 | 2717 | 2250 | 1832 | 1473 |
| | energy, ft-lb: | 1282 | 901 | 618 | 410 | 265 |
| | arc, inches: | | +1.6 | 0 | -8.6 | -27.7 |
| PMC 55 FMJ boat-tail | velocity, fps: | 3195 | 2882 | 2525 | 2169 | 1843 |
| | energy, ft-lb: | 1246 | 1014 | 779 | 574 | 415 |
| | arc, inches: | | +1.4 | 0 | -6.8 | -21.1 |
| PMC 55 Pointed Soft Point | velocity, fps: | 3112 | 2767 | 2421 | 2100 | 1806 |
| | energy, ft-lb: | 1182 | 935 | 715 | 539 | 398 |
| | arc, inches: | | +1.5 | 0 | -7.5 | -22.9 |
| PMC 64 Pointed Soft Point | velocity, fps: | 2775 | 2511 | 2261 | 2026 | 1806 |
| | energy, ft-lb: | 1094 | 896 | 726 | 583 | 464 |
| | arc, inches: | | +2.0 | 0 | -8.8 | -26.1 |
| Rem. 50 V-Max, boat-tail | velocity, fps: | 3300 | 2889 | 2514 | 2168 | 1851 |
| | energy, ft-lb: | 1209 | 927 | 701 | 522 | 380 |
| | arc, inches: | | +1.4 | 0 | -6.9 | -21.2 |
| Rem. 55 Pointed Soft Point | velocity, fps: | 3240 | 2747 | 2304 | 1905 | 1554 |
| | energy, ft-lb: | 1282 | 921 | 648 | 443 | 295 |
| | arc, inches: | | +1.6 | 0 | -8.2 | -26.2 |
| Rem. 55 HP Power-Lokt | velocity, fps: | 3240 | 2773 | 2352 | 1969 | 1627 |
| | energy, ft-lb: | 1282 | 939 | 675 | 473 | 323 |
| | arc, inches: | | +1.5 | 0 | -7.9 | -24.8 |
| Rem. 55 Metal Case | velocity, fps: | 3240 | 2759 | 2326 | 1933 | 1587 |
| | energy, ft-lb: | 1282 | 929 | 660 | 456 | 307 |
| | arc, inches: | | +1.6 | 0 | -8.1 | -25.5 |
| Rem. 62 HP Match | velocity, fps: | 3025 | 2572 | 2162 | 1792 | 1471 |
| | energy, ft-lb: | 1260 | 911 | 643 | 442 | 298 |
| | arc, inches: | | +1.9 | 0 | -9.4 | -29.9 |
| Win. 40 Ballistic Silvertip | velocity, fps: | 3700 | 3166 | 2693 | 2265 | 1879 |
| | energy, ft-lb: | 1216 | 891 | 644 | 456 | 314 |
| | arc, inches: | | +1.0 | 0 | -5.8 | -18.4 |
| Win. 50 Ballistic Silvertip | velocity, fps: | 3410 | 2982 | 2593 | 2235 | 1907 |
| | energy, ft-lb: | 1291 | 987 | 746 | 555 | 404 |
| | arc, inches: | | +1.2 | 0 | -6.4 | -19.8 |
| Win. 53 Hollow Point | velocity, fps: | 3330 | 2882 | 2477 | 2106 | 1770 |
| | energy, ft-lb: | 1305 | 978 | 722 | 522 | 369 |
| | arc, inches: | | +1.7 | 0 | -7.4 | -22.7 |
| Win. 55 Pointed Soft Point | velocity, fps: | 3240 | 2747 | 2304 | 1905 | 155 |
| | energy, ft-lb: | 1282 | 921 | 648 | 443 | 295 |
| | arc, inches: | | +1.9 | 0 | -8.5 | -26.7 |
| Win. 55 Super Clean NT | velocity, fps: | 3150 | 2520 | 1970 | 1505 | 1165 |
| | energy, ft-lb: | 1212 | 776 | 474 | 277 | 166 |
| | arc, inches: | | +2.8 | 0 | -11.9 | -38.9 |
| Win. 64 Power-Point | velocity, fps: | 3020 | 2656 | 2320 | 2009 | 1724 |
| | energy, ft-lb: | 1296 | 1003 | 765 | 574 | 423 |
| | arc, inches: | | +1.7 | 0 | -8.2 | -25.1 |
| Win. 64 Power-Point Plus | velocity, fps: | 3090 | 2684 | 2312 | 1971 | 1664 |
| | energy, ft-lb: | 1357 | 1024 | 760 | 552 | 393 |
| | arc, inches: | | +1.7 | 0 | -8.2 | -25.4 |

# .5.6 x 52 R

| Cartridge Bullet | | 0 | 100 | 200 | 300 | 400 |
|---|---|---|---|---|---|---|
| Norma 71 Soft Point | velocity, fps: | 2789 | 2446 | 2128 | 1835 | |
| | energy, ft-lb: | 1227 | 944 | 714 | 531 | |
| | arc, inches: | | +2.1 | 0 | -9.9 | |

# .22 PPC

| Cartridge Bullet | | 0 | 100 | 200 | 300 | 400 |
|---|---|---|---|---|---|---|
| A-Square 52 Berger | velocity, fps: | 3300 | 2952 | 2629 | 2329 | 2049 |
| | energy, ft-lb: | 1257 | 1006 | 798 | 626 | 485 |
| | arc, inches: | | +1.3 | 0 | -6.3 | -19.1 |

# .225 Winchester

| Cartridge Bullet | | 0 | 100 | 200 | 300 | 400 |
|---|---|---|---|---|---|---|
| Win. 55 Pointed Soft Point | velocity, fps: | 3570 | 3066 | 2616 | 2208 | 1838 |
| | energy, ft-lb: | 1556 | 1148 | 836 | 595 | 412 |
| | arc, inches: | | +2.4 | +2.0 | -3.5 | -16.3 |

# .224 Weatherby Mag.

| Cartridge Bullet | | 0 | 100 | 200 | 300 | 400 |
|---|---|---|---|---|---|---|
| Wby. 55 Pointed Expanding | velocity, fps: | 3650 | 3192 | 2780 | 2403 | 2056 |
| | energy, ft-lb: | 1627 | 1244 | 944 | 705 | 516 |
| | arc, inches: | | +2.8 | +3.7 | 0 | -9.8 |

# .22-250 Remington

| Cartridge Bullet | | 0 | 100 | 200 | 300 | 400 |
|---|---|---|---|---|---|---|
| Federal 40 Sierra Varminter | velocity, fps: | 4000 | 3320 | 2720 | 2200 | 1740 |
| | energy, ft-lb: | 1420 | 980 | 660 | 430 | 265 |
| | arc, inches: | | +0.8 | 0 | -5.6 | -18.4 |
| Federal 55 Hi-Shok | velocity, fps: | 3680 | 3140 | 2660 | 2220 | 1830 |
| | energy, ft-lb: | 1655 | 1200 | 860 | 605 | 410 |
| | arc, inches: | | +1.0 | 0 | -6.0 | -19.1 |
| Federal 55 Sierra BlitzKing | velocity, fps: | 3680 | 3270 | 2890 | 2540 | 2220 |
| | energy, ft-lb: | 1655 | 1300 | 1020 | 790 | 605 |
| | arc, inches: | | +0.9 | 0 | -5.1 | -15.6 |

| CARTRIDGE BULLET | RANGE, YARDS: | 0 | 100 | 200 | 300 | 400 |
|---|---|---|---|---|---|---|
| Federal 55 Sierra GameKing BTHP | velocity, fps: | 3680 | 3280 | 2920 | 2590 | 2280 |
| | energy, ft-lb: | 1655 | 1315 | 1040 | 815 | 630 |
| | arc, inches: | | +0.9 | 0 | -5.0 | -15.1 |
| Federal 55 Trophy Bonded | velocity, fps: | 3600 | 3080 | 2610 | 2190 | 1810 |
| | energy, ft-lb: | 1585 | 1155 | 835 | 590 | 400 |
| | arc, inches: | | +1.1 | 0 | -6.2 | -19.8 |
| Hornady 40 V-Max | velocity, fps: | 4150 | 3631 | 3147 | 2699 | 2293 |
| | energy, ft-lb: | 1529 | 1171 | 879 | 647 | 467 |
| | arc, inches: | | +0.5 | 0 | -4.2 | -13.3 |
| Hornady 50 V-Max | velocity, fps: | 3800 | 3349 | 2925 | 2535 | 2178 |
| | energy, ft-lb: | 1603 | 1245 | 950 | 713 | 527 |
| | arc, inches: | | +0.8 | 0 | -5.0 | -15.6 |
| Hornady 53 Hollow Point | velocity, fps: | 3680 | 3185 | 2743 | 2341 | 1974 |
| | energy, ft-lb: | 1594 | 1194 | 886 | 645 | 459 |
| | arc, inches: | | +1.0 | 0 | -5.7 | -17.8 |
| Hornady 55 V-Max | velocity, fps: | 3680 | 3265 | 2876 | 2517 | 2183 |
| | energy, ft-lb: | 1654 | 1302 | 1010 | 772 | 582 |
| | arc, inches: | | +0.9 | 0 | -5.3 | -16.1 |
| Hornady 60 Soft Point | velocity, fps: | 3600 | 3195 | 2826 | 2485 | 2169 |
| | energy, ft-lb: | 1727 | 1360 | 1064 | 823 | 627 |
| | arc, inches: | | +1.0 | 0 | -5.4 | -16.3 |
| Norma 53 Soft Point | velocity, fps: | 3707 | 3234 | 2809 | 1716 | |
| | energy, ft-lb: | 1618 | 1231 | 928 | 690 | |
| | arc, inches: | | +0.9 | 0 | -5.3 | |
| PMC 55 HP boat-tail | velocity, fps: | 3680 | 3104 | 2596 | 2141 | 1737 |
| | energy, ft-lb: | 1654 | 1176 | 823 | 560 | 368 |
| | arc, inches: | | +1.1 | 0 | -6.3 | -20.2 |
| PMC 55 Pointed Soft Point | velocity, fps: | 3586 | 3203 | 2852 | 2505 | 2178 |
| | energy, ft-lb: | 1570 | 1253 | 993 | 766 | 579 |
| | arc, inches: | | +1.0 | 0 | -5.2 | -16.0 |
| Rem. 50 V-Max boat-tail (also in EtronX) | velocity, fps: | 3725 | 3272 | 2864 | 2491 | 2147 |
| | energy, ft-lb: | 1540 | 1188 | 910 | 689 | 512 |
| | arc, inches: | | +1.7 | +1.6 | -2.8 | -12.8 |
| Rem. 55 Pointed Soft Point | velocity, fps: | 3680 | 3137 | 2656 | 2222 | 1832 |
| | energy, ft-lb: | 1654 | 1201 | 861 | 603 | 410 |
| | arc, inches: | | +1.9 | +1.8 | -3.3 | -15.5 |
| Rem. 55 HP Power-Lokt | velocity, fps: | 3680 | 3209 | 2785 | 2400 | 2046 |
| | energy, ft-lb: | 1654 | 1257 | 947 | 703 | 511 |
| | arc, inches: | | +1.8 | +1.7 | -3.0 | -13.7 |
| Win. 40 Ballistic Silvertip | velocity, fps: | 4150 | 3591 | 3099 | 2658 | 2257 |
| | energy, ft-lb: | 1530 | 1146 | 853 | 628 | 453 |
| | arc, inches: | | +0.6 | 0 | -4.2 | -13.4 |
| Win. 50 Ballistic Silvertip | velocity, fps: | 3810 | 3341 | 2919 | 2536 | 2182 |
| | energy, ft-lb: | 1611 | 1239 | 946 | 714 | 529 |
| | arc, inches: | | +0.8 | 0 | -4.9 | -15.2 |
| Win. 55 Pointed Soft Point | velocity, fps: | 3680 | 3137 | 2656 | 2222 | 1832 |
| | energy, ft-lb: | 1654 | 1201 | 861 | 603 | 410 |
| | arc, inches: | | +2.3 | +1.9 | -3.4 | -15.9 |

## .220 Swift

| CARTRIDGE BULLET | RANGE, YARDS: | 0 | 100 | 200 | 300 | 400 |
|---|---|---|---|---|---|---|
| Federal 52 Sierra MatchKing BTHP | velocity, fps: | 3830 | 3370 | 2960 | 2600 | 2230 |
| | energy, ft-lb: | 1690 | 1310 | 1010 | 770 | 575 |
| | arc, inches: | | +0.8 | 0 | -4.8 | -14.9 |
| Federal 55 Sierra BlitzKing | velocity, fps: | 3800 | 3370 | 2990 | 2630 | 2310 |
| | energy, ft-lb: | 1765 | 1390 | 1090 | 850 | 650 |
| | arc, inches: | | +0.8 | 0 | -4.7 | -14.4 |
| Federal 55 Trophy Bonded | velocity, fps: | 3700 | 3170 | 2690 | 2270 | 1880 |
| | energy, ft-lb: | 1670 | 1225 | 885 | 625 | 430 |
| | arc, inches: | | +1.0 | 0 | -5.8 | -18.5 |
| Hornady 40 V-Max | velocity, fps: | 4200 | 3678 | 3190 | 2739 | 2329 |
| | energy, ft-lb: | 1566 | 1201 | 904 | 666 | 482 |
| | arc, inches: | | +0.5 | 0 | -4.0 | -12.9 |
| Hornady 50 V-Max | velocity, fps: | 3850 | 3396 | 2970 | 2576 | 2215 |
| | energy, ft-lb: | 1645 | 1280 | 979 | 736 | 545 |
| | arc, inches: | | +0.7 | 0 | -4.8 | -15.1 |
| Hornady 50 SP | velocity, fps: | 3850 | 3327 | 2862 | 2442 | 2060 |
| | energy, ft-lb: | 1645 | 1228 | 909 | 662 | 471 |
| | arc, inches: | | +0.8 | 0 | -5.1 | -16.1 |

| CARTRIDGE BULLET | RANGE, YARDS: | 0 | 100 | 200 | 300 | 400 |
|---|---|---|---|---|---|---|
| Hornady 55 V-Max | velocity, fps: | 3680 | 3265 | 2876 | 2517 | 2183 |
| | energy, ft-lb: | 1654 | 1302 | 1010 | 772 | 582 |
| | arc, inches: | | +0.9 | 0 | -5.3 | -16.1 |
| Hornady 60 Hollow Point | velocity, fps: | 3600 | 3199 | 2824 | 2475 | 2156 |
| | energy, ft-lb: | 1727 | 1364 | 1063 | 816 | 619 |
| | arc, inches: | | +1.0 | 0 | -5.4 | -16.3 |
| Norma 50 Soft Point | velocity, fps: | 4019 | 3380 | 2826 | 2335 | |
| | energy, ft-lb: | 1794 | 1268 | 887 | 605 | |
| | arc, inches: | | +0.7 | 0 | -5.1 | |
| Rem. 50 Pointed Soft Point | velocity, fps: | 3780 | 3158 | 2617 | 2135 | 1710 |
| | energy, ft-lb: | 1586 | 1107 | 760 | 506 | 325 |
| | arc, inches: | | +0.3 | -1.4 | -8.2 | |
| Rem. 50 V-Max boat-tail (also in EtronX) | velocity, fps: | 3780 | 3321 | 2908 | 2532 | 2185 |
| | energy, ft-lb: | 1586 | 1224 | 939 | 711 | 530 |
| | arc, inches: | | +0.8 | 0 | -5.0 | -15.4 |
| Win. 40 Ballistic Silvertip | velocity, fps: | 4050 | 3518 | 3048 | 2624 | 2238 |
| | energy, ft-lb: | 1457 | 1099 | 825 | 611 | 445 |
| | arc, inches: | | +0.7 | 0 | -4.4 | -13.9 |
| Win. 50 Pointed Soft Point | velocity, fps: | 3870 | 3310 | 2816 | 2373 | 1972 |
| | energy, ft-lb: | 1663 | 1226 | 881 | 625 | 432 |
| | arc, inches: | | +0.8 | 0 | -5.2 | -16.7 |

## 6mm PPC

| CARTRIDGE BULLET | RANGE, YARDS: | 0 | 100 | 200 | 300 | 400 |
|---|---|---|---|---|---|---|
| A-Square 68 Berger | velocity, fps: | 3100 | 2751 | 2428 | 2128 | 1850 |
| | energy, ft-lb: | 1451 | 1143 | 890 | 684 | 516 |
| | arc, inches: | | +1.5 | 0 | -7.5 | -22.6 |

## .243 Winchester

| CARTRIDGE BULLET | RANGE, YARDS: | 0 | 100 | 200 | 300 | 400 |
|---|---|---|---|---|---|---|
| Federal 70 Nosler Bal. Tip | velocity, fps: | 3400 | 3070 | 2760 | 2470 | 2200 |
| | energy, ft-lb: | 1795 | 1465 | 1185 | 950 | 755 |
| | arc, inches: | | +1.1 | 0 | -5.7 | -17.1 |
| Federal 70 Speer TNT HP | velocity, fps: | 3400 | 3040 | 2700 | 2390 | 2100 |
| | energy, ft-lb: | 1795 | 1435 | 1135 | 890 | 685 |
| | arc, inches: | | +1.1 | 0 | -5.9 | -18.0 |
| Federal 80 Sierra Pro-Hunter | velocity, fps: | 3350 | 2960 | 2590 | 2260 | 1950 |
| | energy, ft-lb: | 1995 | 1550 | 1195 | 905 | 675 |
| | arc, inches: | | +1.3 | 0 | -6.4 | -19.7 |
| Federal 85 Sierra GameKing BTHP | velocity, fps: | 3320 | 3070 | 2830 | 2600 | 2380 |
| | energy, ft-lb: | 2080 | 1770 | 1510 | 1280 | 1070 |
| | arc, inches: | | +1.1 | 0 | -5.5 | -16.1 |
| Federal 90 Trophy Bonded | velocity, fps: | 3100 | 2850 | 2610 | 2380 | 2160 |
| | energy, ft-lb: | 1920 | 1620 | 1360 | 1130 | 935 |
| | arc, inches: | | +1.4 | 0 | -6.1 | -19.2 |
| Federal 100 Hi-Shok | velocity, fps: | 2960 | 2700 | 2450 | 2220 | 1990 |
| | energy, ft-lb: | 1945 | 1615 | 1330 | 1090 | 880 |
| | arc, inches: | | +1.6 | 0 | -7.5 | -22.0 |
| Federal 100 Sierra GameKing BTSP | velocity, fps: | 2960 | 2760 | 2570 | 2380 | 2210 |
| | energy, ft-lb: | 1950 | 1690 | 1460 | 1260 | 1080 |
| | arc, inches: | | +1.5 | 0 | -6.8 | -19.8 |
| Federal 100 Nosler Partition | velocity, fps: | 2960 | 2730 | 2510 | 2300 | 2100 |
| | energy, ft-lb: | 1945 | 1650 | 1395 | 1170 | 975 |
| | arc, inches: | | +1.6 | 0 | -7.1 | -20.9 |
| Hornady 58 V-Max | velocity, fps: | 3750 | 3319 | 2913 | 2539 | 2195 |
| | energy, ft-lb: | 1811 | 1418 | 1093 | 830 | 620 |
| | arc, inches: | | +1.2 | 0 | -5.5 | -16.4 |
| Hornady 75 Hollow Point | velocity, fps: | 3400 | 2970 | 2578 | 2219 | 1890 |
| | energy, ft-lb: | 1926 | 1469 | 1107 | 820 | 595 |
| | arc, inches: | | +1.2 | 0 | -6.5 | -20.3 |
| Hornady 100 BTSP | velocity, fps: | 2960 | 2728 | 2508 | 2299 | 2099 |
| | energy, ft-lb: | 1945 | 1653 | 1397 | 1174 | 979 |
| | arc, inches: | | +1.6 | 0 | -7.2 | -21.0 |
| Hornady 100 BTSP LM | velocity, fps: | 3100 | 2839 | 2592 | 2358 | 2138 |
| | energy, ft-lb: | 2133 | 1790 | 1491 | 1235 | 1014 |
| | arc, inches: | | +1.5 | 0 | -6.8 | -19.8 |
| Norma 100 FMJ | velocity, fps: | 3018 | 2747 | 2493 | 2252 | |
| | energy, ft-lb: | 2023 | 1677 | 1380 | 1126 | |
| | arc, inches: | | +1.5 | 0 | -7.1 | |
| Norma 100 Soft Point | velocity, fps: | 3018 | 2748 | 2493 | 2252 | |
| | energy, ft-lb: | 2023 | 1677 | 1380 | 1126 | |
| | arc, inches: | | +1.5 | 0 | -7.1 | |

| Cartridge / Bullet | Range, Yards: | 0 | 100 | 200 | 300 | 400 |
|---|---|---|---|---|---|---|
| PMC 80 Pointed Soft Point | velocity, fps | 2940 | 2684 | 2444 | 2215 | 1999 |
| | energy, ft-lb | 1535 | 1280 | 1060 | 871 | 709 |
| | arc, inches: | | +1.7 | 0 | -7.5 | -22.1 |
| PMC 85 HP boat-tail | velocity, fps | 3275 | 2922 | 2596 | 2292 | 2009 |
| | energy, ft-lb | 2024 | 1611 | 1272 | 991 | 761 |
| | arc, inches: | | +1.3 | 0 | -6.5 | -19.7 |
| PMC 100 Pointed Soft Point | velocity, fps | 2743 | 2507 | 2283 | 2070 | 1869 |
| | energy, ft-lb | 1670 | 1395 | 1157 | 951 | 776 |
| | arc, inches: | | +2.0 | 0 | -8.7 | -25.5 |
| PMC 100 SP boat-tail | velocity, fps | 2960 | 2742 | 2534 | 2335 | 2144 |
| | energy, ft-lb | 1945 | 1669 | 1425 | 1210 | 1021 |
| | arc, inches: | | +1.6 | 0 | -7.0 | -20.5 |
| Rem. 75 V-Max boat-tail | velocity, fps | 3375 | 3065 | 2775 | 2504 | 2248 |
| | energy, ft-lb | 1897 | 1564 | 1282 | 1044 | 842 |
| | arc, inches: | | +2.0 | +1.8 | -3.0 | -13.3 |
| Rem. 80 Pointed Soft Point | velocity, fps | 3350 | 2955 | 2593 | 2259 | 1951 |
| | energy, ft-lb | 1993 | 1551 | 1194 | 906 | 676 |
| | arc, inches: | | +2.2 | +2.0 | -3.5 | -15.8 |
| Rem. 80 HP Power-Lokt | velocity, fps | 3350 | 2955 | 2593 | 2259 | 1951 |
| | energy, ft-lb | 1993 | 1551 | 1194 | 906 | 676 |
| | arc, inches: | | +2.2 | +2.0 | -3.5 | -15.8 |
| Rem. 90 Nosler Bal. Tip (also in EtronX) | velocity, fps | 3120 | 2871 | 2635 | 2411 | 2199 |
| | energy, ft-lb | 1946 | 1647 | 1388 | 1162 | 966 |
| | arc, inches: | | +1.4 | 0 | -6.4 | -18.8 |
| Rem. 100 PSP Core-Lokt | velocity, fps | 2960 | 2697 | 2449 | 2215 | 1993 |
| | energy, ft-lb | 1945 | 1615 | 1332 | 1089 | 882 |
| | arc, inches: | | +1.6 | 0 | -7.5 | -22.1 |
| Rem. 100 PSP boat-tail | velocity, fps | 2960 | 2720 | 2492 | 2275 | 2069 |
| | energy, ft-lb | 1945 | 1642 | 1378 | 1149 | 950 |
| | arc, inches: | | +2.8 | +2.3 | -3.8 | -16.6 |
| Speer 100 Grand Slam | velocity, fps | 2950 | 2684 | 2434 | 2197 | |
| | energy, ft-lb | 1932 | 1600 | 1315 | 1072 | |
| | arc, inches: | | +1.7 | 0 | -7.6 | -22.4 |
| Win. 55 Ballistic Silvertip | velocity, fps | 4025 | 3597 | 3209 | 2853 | 2525 |
| | energy, ft-lb | 1978 | 1579 | 1257 | 994 | 779 |
| | arc, inches: | | +0.6 | 0 | -4.0 | -12.2 |
| Win. 80 Pointed Soft Point | velocity, fps | 3350 | 2955 | 2593 | 2259 | 1951 |
| | energy, ft-lb | 1993 | 1551 | 1194 | 906 | 676 |
| | arc, inches: | | +2.6 | +2.1 | -3.6 | -16.2 |
| Win. 95 Ballistic Silvertip | velocity, fps | 3100 | 2854 | 2626 | 2410 | 2203 |
| | energy, ft-lb | 2021 | 1719 | 1455 | 1225 | 1024 |
| | arc, inches: | | +1.4 | 0 | -6.4 | -18.9 |
| Win. 100 Power-Point | velocity, fps | 2960 | 2697 | 2449 | 2215 | 1993 |
| | energy, ft-lb | 1945 | 1615 | 1332 | 1089 | 882 |
| | arc, inches: | | +1.9 | 0 | -7.8 | -22.6 |
| Win. 100 Power-Point Plus | velocity, fps | 3090 | 2818 | 2562 | 2321 | 2092 |
| | energy, ft-lb | 2121 | 1764 | 1458 | 1196 | 972 |
| | arc, inches: | | +1.4 | 0 | -6.7 | -20.0 |

## 6mm Remington

| Cartridge / Bullet | Range, Yards: | 0 | 100 | 200 | 300 | 400 |
|---|---|---|---|---|---|---|
| Federal 80 Sierra Pro-Hunter | velocity, fps | 3470 | 3060 | 2690 | 2350 | 2040 |
| | energy, ft-lb | 2140 | 1665 | 1290 | 980 | 735 |
| | arc, inches: | | +1.1 | 0 | -5.9 | -18.2 |
| Federal 100 Hi-Shok | velocity, fps | 3100 | 2830 | 2570 | 2330 | 2100 |
| | energy, ft-lb | 2135 | 1775 | 1470 | 1205 | 985 |
| | arc, inches: | | +1.4 | 0 | -6.7 | -19.8 |
| Federal 100 Nosler Partition | velocity, fps | 3100 | 2860 | 2640 | 2420 | 2220 |
| | energy, ft-lb | 2135 | 1820 | 1545 | 1300 | 1090 |
| | arc, inches: | | +1.4 | 0 | -6.3 | -18.7 |
| Hornady 100 SP boat-tail | velocity, fps | 3100 | 2861 | 2634 | 2419 | 2231 |
| | energy, ft-lb | 2134 | 1818 | 1541 | 1300 | 1088 |
| | arc, inches: | | +1.3 | 0 | -6.5 | -18.9 |
| Hornady 100 SPBT LM | velocity, fps | 3250 | 2997 | 2756 | 2528 | 2311 |
| | energy, ft-lb | 2345 | 1995 | 1687 | 1418 | 1186 |
| | arc, inches: | | +1.6 | 0 | -6.3 | -18.2 |
| Rem. 75 V-Max boat-tail | velocity, fps | 3400 | 3088 | 2797 | 2524 | 2267 |
| | energy, ft-lb | 1925 | 1587 | 1303 | 1061 | 856 |
| | arc, inches: | | +1.9 | +1.7 | -3.0 | -13.1 |
| Rem. 100 PSP Core-Lokt | velocity, fps | 3100 | 2829 | 2573 | 2332 | 2104 |
| | energy, ft-lb | 2133 | 1777 | 1470 | 1207 | 983 |
| | arc, inches: | | +1.4 | 0 | -6.7 | -19.8 |
| Rem. 100 PSP boat-tail | velocity, fps | 3100 | 2852 | 2617 | 2394 | 2183 |
| | energy, ft-lb | 2134 | 1806 | 1521 | 1273 | 1058 |
| | arc, inches: | | +1.4 | 0 | -6.5 | -19.1 |
| Win. 100 Power-Point | velocity, fps | 3100 | 2829 | 2573 | 2332 | 2104 |
| | energy, ft-lb | 2133 | 1777 | 1470 | 1207 | 983 |
| | arc, inches: | | +1.7 | 0 | -7.0 | -20.4 |

## .240 Weatherby Mag.

| Cartridge / Bullet | Range, Yards: | 0 | 100 | 200 | 300 | 400 |
|---|---|---|---|---|---|---|
| Wby. 87 Pointed Expanding | velocity, fps | 3523 | 3199 | 2898 | 2617 | 2352 |
| | energy, ft-lb | 2397 | 1977 | 1622 | 1323 | 1069 |
| | arc, inches: | | +2.7 | +3.4 | 0 | -8.4 |
| Wby. 90 Barnes-X | velocity, fps | 3500 | 3222 | 2962 | 2717 | 2484 |
| | energy, ft-lb | 2448 | 2075 | 1753 | 1475 | 1233 |
| | arc, inches: | | +2.6 | +3.3 | 0 | -8.0 |
| Wby. 95 Nosler Bal. Tip | velocity, fps | 3420 | 3146 | 2888 | 2645 | 2414 |
| | energy, ft-lb | 2467 | 2087 | 1759 | 1475 | 1229 |
| | arc, inches: | | +2.7 | +3.5 | 0 | -8.4 |
| Wby. 100 Pointed Expanding | velocity, fps | 3406 | 3134 | 2878 | 2637 | 2408 |
| | energy, ft-lb | 2576 | 2180 | 1839 | 1544 | 1287 |
| | arc, inches: | | +2.8 | +3.5 | 0 | -8.4 |
| Wby. 100 Partition | velocity, fps | 3406 | 3136 | 2882 | 2642 | 2415 |
| | energy, ft-lb | 2576 | 2183 | 1844 | 1550 | 1294 |
| | arc, inches: | | +2.8 | +3.5 | 0 | -8.4 |

## .25-20 Winchester

| Cartridge / Bullet | Range, Yards: | 0 | 100 | 200 | 300 | 400 |
|---|---|---|---|---|---|---|
| Rem. 86 Soft Point | velocity, fps | 1460 | 1194 | 1030 | 931 | 858 |
| | energy, ft-lb | 407 | 272 | 203 | 165 | 141 |
| | arc, inches: | | 0 | -22.9 | -78.9 | -173.0 |
| Win. 86 Soft Point | velocity, fps | 1460 | 1194 | 1030 | 931 | 858 |
| | energy, ft-lb | 407 | 272 | 203 | 165 | 141 |
| | arc, inches: | | 0 | -23.5 | -79.6 | -175.9 |

## .25-35 Winchester

| Cartridge / Bullet | Range, Yards: | 0 | 100 | 200 | 300 | 400 |
|---|---|---|---|---|---|---|
| Win. 117 Soft Point | velocity, fps | 2230 | 1866 | 1545 | 1282 | 1097 |
| | energy, ft-lb | 1292 | 904 | 620 | 427 | 313 |
| | arc, inches: | | +2.1 | -5.1 | -27.0 | -70.1 |

## .250 Savage

| Cartridge / Bullet | Range, Yards: | 0 | 100 | 200 | 300 | 400 |
|---|---|---|---|---|---|---|
| Rem. 100 Pointed SP | velocity, fps | 2820 | 2504 | 2210 | 1936 | 1684 |
| | energy, ft-lb | 1765 | 1392 | 1084 | 832 | 630 |
| | arc, inches: | | +2.0 | 0 | -9.2 | -27.7 |
| Win. 100 Silvertip | velocity, fps | 2820 | 2467 | 2140 | 1839 | 1569 |
| | energy, ft-lb | 1765 | 1351 | 1017 | 751 | 547 |
| | arc, inches: | | +2.4 | 0 | -10.1 | -30.5 |

## .257 Roberts

| Cartridge / Bullet | Range, Yards: | 0 | 100 | 200 | 300 | 400 |
|---|---|---|---|---|---|---|
| Federal 120 Nosler Partition | velocity, fps | 2780 | 2560 | 2360 | 2160 | 1970 |
| | energy, ft-lb | 2060 | 1750 | 1480 | 1240 | 1030 |
| | arc, inches: | | +1.9 | 0 | -8.2 | -24.0 |
| Hornady 117 SP boat-tail | velocity, fps | 2780 | 2550 | 2331 | 2122 | 1925 |
| | energy, ft-lb | 2007 | 1689 | 1411 | 1170 | 963 |
| | arc, inches: | | +1.9 | 0 | -8.3 | -24.4 |
| Hornady 117 SP boat-tail LM | velocity, fps | 2940 | 2694 | 2460 | 2240 | 2031 |
| | energy, ft-lb | 2245 | 1885 | 1572 | 1303 | 1071 |
| | arc, inches: | | +1.7 | 0 | -7.6 | -21.8 |
| Rem. 117 SP Core-Lokt | velocity, fps | 2650 | 2291 | 1961 | 1663 | 1404 |
| | energy, ft-lb | 1824 | 1363 | 999 | 718 | 512 |
| | arc, inches: | | +2.6 | 0 | -11.7 | -36.1 |
| Win. 117 Power-Point | velocity, fps | 2780 | 2411 | 2071 | 1761 | 1488 |
| | energy, ft-lb | 2009 | 1511 | 1115 | 806 | 576 |
| | arc, inches: | | +2.6 | 0 | -10.8 | -33.0 |

## .25-06 Remington

| Cartridge Bullet | | 0 | 100 | 200 | 300 | 400 |
|---|---|---|---|---|---|---|
| Federal 90 Sierra Varminter | velocity, fps: | 3440 | 3040 | 2680 | 2340 | 2030 |
| | energy, ft-lb: | 2365 | 1850 | 1435 | 1100 | 825 |
| | arc, inches: | | +1.1 | 0 | -6.0 | -18.3 |
| Federal 100 Barnes XLC | velocity, fps: | 3210 | 2970 | 2750 | 2540 | 2330 |
| | energy, ft-lb: | 2290 | 1965 | 1680 | 1430 | 1205 |
| | arc, inches: | | +1.2 | 0 | -5.8 | -17.0 |
| Federal 100 Nosler Bal. Tip | velocity, fps: | 3210 | 2960 | 2720 | 2490 | 2280 |
| | energy, ft-lb: | 2290 | 1940 | 1640 | 1380 | 1150 |
| | arc, inches: | | +1.2 | 0 | -6.0 | -17.5 |
| Federal 115 Nosler Partition | velocity, fps: | 2990 | 2750 | 2520 | 2300 | 2100 |
| | energy, ft-lb: | 2285 | 1930 | 1620 | 1350 | 1120 |
| | arc, inches: | | +1.6 | 0 | -7.0 | -20.8 |
| Federal 115 Trophy Bonded | velocity, fps: | 2990 | 2740 | 2500 | 2270 | 2050 |
| | energy, ft-lb: | 2285 | 1910 | 1590 | 1310 | 1075 |
| | arc, inches: | | +1.6 | 0 | -7.2 | -21.1 |
| Federal 117 Sierra Pro Hunt. | velocity, fps: | 2990 | 2730 | 2480 | 2250 | 2030 |
| | energy, ft-lb: | 2320 | 1985 | 1645 | 1350 | 1100 |
| | arc, inches: | | +1.6 | 0 | -7.2 | -21.4 |
| Federal 117 Sierra GameKing BTSP | velocity, fps: | 2990 | 2770 | 2570 | 2370 | 2190 |
| | energy, ft-lb: | 2320 | 2000 | 1715 | 1465 | 1240 |
| | arc, inches: | | +1.5 | 0 | -6.8 | -19.9 |
| Hornady 117 SP boat-tail | velocity, fps: | 2990 | 2749 | 2520 | 2302 | 2096 |
| | energy, ft-lb: | 2322 | 1962 | 1649 | 1377 | 1141 |
| | arc, inches: | | +1.6 | 0 | -7.0 | -20.7 |
| Hornady 117 SP boat-tail LM | velocity, fps: | 3110 | 2855 | 2613 | 2384 | 2168 |
| | energy, ft-lb: | 2512 | 2117 | 1774 | 1476 | 1220 |
| | arc, inches: | | +1.8 | 0 | -7.1 | -20.3 |
| Rem. 100 PSP Core-Lokt | velocity, fps: | 3230 | 2893 | 2580 | 2287 | 2014 |
| | energy, ft-lb: | 2316 | 1858 | 1478 | 1161 | 901 |
| | arc, inches: | | +1.3 | 0 | -6.6 | -19.8 |
| Rem. 120 PSP Core-Lokt | velocity, fps: | 2990 | 2730 | 2484 | 2252 | 2032 |
| | energy, ft-lb: | 2382 | 1985 | 1644 | 1351 | 1100 |
| | arc, inches: | | +1.6 | 0 | -7.2 | -21.4 |
| Speer 120 Grand Slam | velocity, fps: | 3130 | 2835 | 2558 | 2298 | |
| | energy, ft-lb: | 2610 | 2141 | 1743 | 1407 | |
| | arc, inches: | | +1.4 | 0 | -6.8 | -20.1 |
| Win. 90 Pos. Exp. Point | velocity, fps: | 3440 | 3043 | 2680 | 2344 | 2034 |
| | energy, ft-lb: | 2364 | 1850 | 1435 | 1098 | 827 |
| | arc, inches: | | +2.4 | +2.0 | -3.4 | -15.0 |
| Win. 115 Ballistic Silvertip | velocity, fps: | 3060 | 2825 | 2603 | 2390 | 2188 |
| | energy, ft-lb: | 2391 | 2038 | 1729 | 1459 | 1223 |
| | arc, inches: | | +1.4 | 0 | -6.6 | -19.2 |

## .257 Weatherby Mag.

| Cartridge Bullet | | 0 | 100 | 200 | 300 | 400 |
|---|---|---|---|---|---|---|
| Federal 115 Nosler Partition | velocity, fps: | 3150 | 2900 | 2660 | 2440 | 2220 |
| | energy, ft-lb: | 2535 | 2145 | 1810 | 1515 | 1260 |
| | arc, inches: | | +1.3 | 0 | -6.2 | -18.4 |
| Federal 115 Trophy Bonded | velocity, fps: | 3150 | 2890 | 2640 | 2400 | 2180 |
| | energy, ft-lb: | 2535 | 2125 | 1775 | 1470 | 1210 |
| | arc, inches: | | +1.4 | 0 | -6.3 | -18.8 |
| Wby. 87 Pointed Expanding | velocity, fps: | 3825 | 3472 | 3147 | 2845 | 2563 |
| | energy, ft-lb: | 2826 | 2328 | 1913 | 1563 | 1269 |
| | arc, inches: | | +2.1 | +2.8 | 0 | -7.1 |
| Wby. 100 Pointed Expanding | velocity, fps: | 3602 | 3298 | 3016 | 2750 | 2500 |
| | energy, ft-lb: | 2881 | 2416 | 2019 | 1680 | 1388 |
| | arc, inches: | | +2.4 | +3.1 | 0 | -7.7 |
| Wby. 115 Nosler Bal. Tip | velocity, fps: | 3400 | 3170 | 2952 | 2745 | 2547 |
| | energy, ft-lb: | 2952 | 2566 | 2226 | 1924 | 1656 |
| | arc, inches: | | +3.0 | +3.5 | 0 | -7.9 |
| Wby. 115 Barnes X | velocity, fps: | 3400 | 3158 | 2929 | 2711 | 2504 |
| | energy, ft-lb: | 2952 | 2546 | 2190 | 1877 | 1601 |
| | arc, inches: | | +2.7 | +3.4 | 0 | -8.1 |
| Wby. 117 RN Expanding | velocity, fps: | 3402 | 2984 | 2595 | 2240 | 1921 |
| | energy, ft-lb: | 3007 | 2320 | 1742 | 1302 | 956 |
| | arc, inches: | | +3.4 | +4.31 | 0 | -11.1 |
| Wby. 120 Nosler Partition | velocity, fps: | 3305 | 3046 | 2801 | 2570 | 2350 |
| | energy, ft-lb: | 2910 | 2472 | 2091 | 1760 | 1471 |
| | arc, inches: | | +3.0 | +3.7 | 0 | -8.9 |

## 6.53 (.257) Scramjet

| Cartridge Bullet | | 0 | 100 | 200 | 300 | 400 |
|---|---|---|---|---|---|---|
| Lazzeroni 85 Nosler Bal. Tip | velocity, fps: | 3960 | 3652 | 3365 | 3096 | 2844 |
| | energy, ft-lb: | 2961 | 2517 | 2137 | 1810 | 1526 |
| | arc, inches: | | +1.7 | +2.4 | 0 | -6.0 |
| Lazzeroni 100 Nosler Part. | velocity, fps: | 3740 | 3465 | 3208 | 2965 | 2735 |
| | energy, ft-lb: | 3106 | 2667 | 2285 | 1953 | 1661 |
| | arc, inches: | | +2.1 | +2.7 | 0 | -6.7 |

## 6.5x50 Japanese

| Cartridge Bullet | | 0 | 100 | 200 | 300 | 400 |
|---|---|---|---|---|---|---|
| Norma 156 Alaska | velocity, fps: | 2067 | 1832 | 1615 | 1423 | |
| | energy, ft-lb: | 1480 | 1162 | 904 | 701 | |
| | arc, inches: | | +4.4 | 0 | -17.8 | |

## 6.5x52 Carcano

| Cartridge Bullet | | 0 | 100 | 200 | 300 | 400 |
|---|---|---|---|---|---|---|
| Norma 156 Alaska | velocity, fps: | 2428 | 2169 | 1926 | 1702 | |
| | energy, ft-lb: | 2043 | 1630 | 1286 | 1004 | |
| | arc, inches: | | +2.9 | 0 | -12.3 | |

## 6.5x55 Swedish

| Cartridge Bullet | | 0 | 100 | 200 | 300 | 400 |
|---|---|---|---|---|---|---|
| Federal 140 Hi-Shok | velocity, fps: | 2600 | 2400 | 2220 | 2040 | 1860 |
| | energy, ft-lb: | 2100 | 1795 | 1525 | 1285 | 1080 |
| | arc, inches: | | +2.3 | 0 | -9.4 | -27.2 |
| Federal 140 Trophy Bonded | velocity, fps: | 2550 | 2350 | 2160 | 1980 | 1810 |
| | energy, ft-lb: | 2020 | 1720 | 1450 | 1220 | 1015 |
| | arc, inches: | | +2.4 | 0 | -9.8 | -28.4 |
| Federal 140 Sierra MatchKg. BTHP | velocity, fps: | 2630 | 2460 | 2300 | 2140 | 2000 |
| | energy, ft-lb: | 2140 | 1880 | 1640 | 1430 | 1235 |
| | arc, inches: | | +16.4 | +28.8 | +33.9 | +31.8 |
| Hornady 129 SP LM | velocity, fps: | 2770 | 2561 | 2361 | 2171 | 1994 |
| | energy, ft-lb: | 2197 | 1878 | 1597 | 1350 | 1138 |
| | arc, inches: | | +2.0 | 0 | -8.2 | -23.2 |
| Hornady140 SP LM | velocity, fps: | 2740 | 2541 | 2351 | 2169 | 1999 |
| | energy, ft-lb: | 2333 | 2006 | 1717 | 1463 | 1242 |
| | arc, inches: | | +2.4 | 0 | -8.7 | -24.0 |
| Norma 139 Vulkan | velocity, fps: | 2854 | 2569 | 2302 | 2051 | |
| | energy, ft-lb: | 2515 | 2038 | 1636 | 1298 | |
| | arc, inches: | | +1.8 | 0 | -8.4 | |
| Norma 140 Nosler Partition | velocity, fps: | 2789 | 2592 | 2403 | 2223 | |
| | energy, ft-lb: | 2419 | 2089 | 1796 | 1536 | |
| | arc, inches: | | +1.8 | 0 | -7.8 | |
| Norma 156 TXP Swift A-Fr. | velocity, fps: | 2526 | 2276 | 2040 | 1818 | |
| | energy, ft-lb: | 2196 | 1782 | 1432 | 1138 | |
| | arc, inches: | | +2.6 | 0 | -10.9 | |
| Norma 156 Alaska | velocity, fps: | 2559 | 2245 | 1953 | 1687 | |
| | energy, ft-lb: | 2269 | 1746 | 1322 | 986 | |
| | arc, inches: | | +2.7 | 0 | -11.9 | |
| Norma 156 Vulkan | velocity, fps: | 2644 | 2395 | 2159 | 1937 | |
| | energy, ft-lb: | 2422 | 1987 | 1616 | 1301 | |
| | arc, inches: | | +2.2 | 0 | -9.7 | |
| Norma 156 Oryx | velocity, fps: | 2559 | 2308 | 2070 | 1848 | |
| | energy, ft-lb: | 2269 | 1845 | 1485 | 1183 | |
| | arc, inches: | | +2.5 | 0 | -10.6 | |
| PMC 139 Pointed Soft Point | velocity, fps: | 2850 | 2560 | 2290 | 2030 | 1790 |
| | energy, ft-lb: | 2515 | 2025 | 1615 | 1270 | 985 |
| | arc, inches: | | +2.2 | 0 | -8.9 | -26.3 |
| PMC 140 HP boat-tail | velocity, fps: | 2560 | 2398 | 2243 | 2093 | 1949 |
| | energy, ft-lb: | 2037 | 1788 | 1563 | 1361 | 1181 |
| | arc, inches: | | +2.3 | 0 | -9.2 | -26.4 |
| PMC 140 SP boat-tail | velocity, fps: | 2560 | 2386 | 2218 | 2057 | 1903 |
| | energy, ft-lb: | 2037 | 1769 | 1529 | 1315 | 1126 |
| | arc, inches: | | +2.3 | 0 | -9.4 | -27.1 |
| PMC 144 FMJ | velocity, fps: | 2650 | 2370 | 2110 | 1870 | 1650 |
| | energy, ft-lb: | 2425 | 1950 | 1550 | 1215 | 945 |
| | arc, inches: | | +2.7 | 0 | -10.5 | -30.9 |
| Rem. 140 PSP Core-Lokt | velocity, fps: | 2550 | 2353 | 2164 | 1984 | 1814 |
| | energy, ft-lb: | 2021 | 1720 | 1456 | 1224 | 1023 |
| | arc, inches: | | +2.4 | 0 | -9.8 | -27.0 |

| CARTRIDGE BULLET | RANGE, YARDS: | 0 | 100 | 200 | 300 | 400 |
|---|---|---|---|---|---|---|
| Speer 140 Grand Slam | velocity, fps | 2550 | 2318 | 2099 | 1892 | |
| | energy, ft-lb | 2021 | 1670 | 1369 | 1112 | |
| | arc, inches | | +2.5 | 0 | -10.4 | -30.6 |
| Win. 140 Soft Point | velocity, fps | 2550 | 2359 | 2176 | 2002 | 1836 |
| | energy, ft-lb | 2022 | 1731 | 1473 | 1246 | 1048 |
| | arc, inches | | +2.4 | 0 | -9.7 | -28.1 |

## .260 Remington

| CARTRIDGE BULLET | RANGE, YARDS: | 0 | 100 | 200 | 300 | 400 |
|---|---|---|---|---|---|---|
| Federal 140 Sierra GameKing BTSP | velocity, fps | 2750 | 2570 | 2390 | 2220 | 2060 |
| | energy, ft-lb | 2350 | 2045 | 1775 | 1535 | 1315 |
| | arc, inches | | +1.9 | 0 | -8.0 | -23.1 |
| Federal 140 Trophy Bonded | velocity, fps | 2750 | 2540 | 2340 | 2150 | 1970 |
| | energy, ft-lb | 2350 | 2010 | 1705 | 1440 | 1210 |
| | arc, inches | | +1.9 | 0 | -8.4 | -24.1 |
| Rem. 120 Nosler Bal. Tip | velocity, fps | 2890 | 2688 | 2494 | 2309 | 2131 |
| | energy, ft-lb | 2226 | 1924 | 1657 | 1420 | 1210 |
| | arc, inches | | +1.7 | 0 | -7.3 | -21.1 |
| Rem. 125 Nosler Partition | velocity, fps | 2875 | 2669 | 2473 | 2285 | 2105 |
| | energy, ft-lb | 2294 | 1977 | 1697 | 1449 | 1230 |
| | arc, inches | | +1.71 | 0 | -7.4 | -21.4 |
| Rem. 140 PSP Core-Lokt | velocity, fps | 2750 | 2544 | 2347 | 2158 | 1979 |
| | energy, ft-lb | 2351 | 2011 | 1712 | 1448 | 1217 |
| | arc, inches | | +1.9 | 0 | -8.3 | -24.0 |
| Speer 140 Grand Slam | velocity, fps | 2750 | 2518 | 2297 | 2087 | |
| | energy, ft-lb | 2351 | 1970 | 1640 | 1354 | |
| | arc, inches | | +2.3 | 0 | -8.9 | -25.8 |

## .264 Winchester Mag.

| CARTRIDGE BULLET | RANGE, YARDS: | 0 | 100 | 200 | 300 | 400 |
|---|---|---|---|---|---|---|
| Rem. 140 PSP Core-Lokt | velocity, fps | 3030 | 2782 | 2548 | 2326 | 2114 |
| | energy, ft-lb | 2854 | 2406 | 2018 | 1682 | 1389 |
| | arc, inches | | +1.5 | 0 | -6.9 | -20.2 |
| Win. 140 Power-Point | velocity, fps | 3030 | 2782 | 2548 | 2326 | 2114 |
| | energy, ft-lb | 2854 | 2406 | 2018 | 1682 | 1389 |
| | arc, inches | | +1.8 | 0 | -7.2 | -20.8 |

## .270 Winchester

| CARTRIDGE BULLET | RANGE, YARDS: | 0 | 100 | 200 | 300 | 400 |
|---|---|---|---|---|---|---|
| Federal 130 Hi-Shok | velocity, fps | 3060 | 2800 | 2560 | 2330 | 2110 |
| | energy, ft-lb | 2700 | 2265 | 1890 | 1565 | 1285 |
| | arc, inches | | +1.5 | 0 | -6.8 | -20.0 |
| Federal 130 Sierra Pro-Hunt. | velocity, fps | 3060 | 2830 | 2600 | 2390 | 2190 |
| | energy, ft-lb | 2705 | 2305 | 1960 | 1655 | 1390 |
| | arc, inches | | +1.4 | 0 | -6.4 | -19.0 |
| Federal 130 Sierra GameKing | velocity, fps | 3060 | 2830 | 2620 | 2410 | 2220 |
| | energy, ft-lb | 2700 | 2320 | 1980 | 1680 | 1420 |
| | arc, inches | | +1.4 | 0 | -6.5 | -19.0 |
| Federal 130 Nosler Bal. Tip | velocity, fps | 3060 | 2840 | 2630 | 2430 | 2230 |
| | energy, ft-lb | 2700 | 2325 | 1990 | 1700 | 1440 |
| | arc, inches | | +1.4 | 0 | -6.5 | -18.8 |
| Federal 130 Barnes XLC | velocity, fps | 3060 | 2840 | 2620 | 2420 | 2220 |
| | energy, ft-lb | 2705 | 2320 | 1985 | 1690 | 1425 |
| | arc, inches | | +1.4 | 0 | -6.4 | -18.9 |
| Federal 130 Trophy Bonded | velocity, fps | 3060 | 2810 | 2570 | 2340 | 2130 |
| | energy, ft-lb | 2705 | 2275 | 1905 | 1585 | 1310 |
| | arc, inches | | +1.5 | 0 | -6.7 | -19.8 |
| Federal 140 Trophy Bonded | velocity, fps | 2940 | 2700 | 2480 | 2260 | 2060 |
| | energy, ft-lb | 2685 | 2270 | 1905 | 1590 | 1315 |
| | arc, inches | | +1.6 | 0 | -7.3 | -21.5 |
| Federal 140 Tr. Bonded HE | velocity, fps | 3100 | 2860 | 2620 | 2400 | 2200 |
| | energy, ft-lb | 2990 | 2535 | 2140 | 1795 | 1500 |
| | arc, inches | | +1.4 | 0 | -6.4 | -18.9 |
| Federal 150 Hi-Shok RN | velocity, fps | 2850 | 2500 | 2180 | 1890 | 1620 |
| | energy, ft-lb | 2705 | 2085 | 1585 | 1185 | 870 |
| | arc, inches | | +2.0 | 0 | -9.4 | -28.6 |
| Federal 150 Sierra GameKing | velocity, fps | 2850 | 2660 | 2480 | 2300 | 2130 |
| | energy, ft-lb | 2705 | 2355 | 2040 | 1760 | 1510 |
| | arc, inches | | +1.7 | 0 | -7.4 | -21.4 |
| Federal 150 Sierra GameKing HE | velocity, fps | 3000 | 2800 | 2620 | 2430 | 2260 |
| | energy, ft-lb | 2995 | 2615 | 2275 | 1975 | 1700 |
| | arc, inches | | +1.5 | 0 | -6.5 | -18.9 |

| CARTRIDGE BULLET | RANGE, YARDS: | 0 | 100 | 200 | 300 | 400 |
|---|---|---|---|---|---|---|
| Federal 150 Nosler Partition | velocity, fps | 2850 | 2590 | 2340 | 2100 | 1880 |
| | energy, ft-lb | 2705 | 2225 | 1815 | 1470 | 1175 |
| | arc, inches | | +1.9 | 0 | -8.3 | -24.4 |
| Hornady 130 SP | velocity, fps | 3060 | 2800 | 2560 | 2330 | 2110 |
| | energy, ft-lb | 2700 | 2265 | 1890 | 1565 | 1285 |
| | arc, inches | | +1.8 | 0 | -7.1 | -20.6 |
| Hornady 130 SST LM | velocity, fps | 3215 | 2998 | 2790 | 2590 | 2400 |
| | energy, ft-lb | 2983 | 2594 | 2246 | 1936 | 1662 |
| | arc, inches | | +1.2 | 0 | -5.8 | -17.0 |
| Hornady 140 SP boat-tail | velocity, fps | 2940 | 2747 | 2562 | 2385 | 2214 |
| | energy, ft-lb | 2688 | 2346 | 2041 | 1769 | 1524 |
| | arc, inches | | +1.6 | 0 | -7.0 | -20.2 |
| Hornady 140 SP boat-tail LM | velocity, fps | 3100 | 2894 | 2697 | 2508 | 2327 |
| | energy, ft-lb | 2987 | 2604 | 2261 | 1955 | 1684 |
| | arc, inches | | +1.4 | 0 | 6.3 | -18.3 |
| Hornady 150 SP | velocity, fps | 2800 | 2684 | 2478 | 2284 | 2100 |
| | energy, ft-lb | 2802 | 2400 | 2046 | 1737 | 1469 |
| | arc, inches | | +1.7 | 0 | -7.4 | -21.6 |
| Norma 130 SP | velocity, fps | 3140 | 2862 | 2601 | 2354 | |
| | energy, ft-lb | 2847 | 2365 | 1953 | 1600 | |
| | arc, inches | 0 | +1.3 | | -6.5 | |
| Norma 150 SP | velocity, fps | 2799 | 2555 | 2323 | 2104 | |
| | energy, ft-lb | 2610 | 2175 | 1798 | 1475 | |
| | arc, inches | 0 | +1.9 | 0 | -8.3 | |
| PMC 130 Barnes X | velocity, fps | 2910 | 2717 | 2533 | 2356 | 2186 |
| | energy, ft-lb | 2444 | 2131 | 1852 | 1602 | 1379 |
| | arc, inches | | +1.6 | 0 | -7.1 | -20.4 |
| PMC 130 SP boat-tail | velocity, fps | 3050 | 2830 | 2620 | 2421 | 2229 |
| | energy, ft-lb | 2685 | 2312 | 1982 | 1691 | 1435 |
| | arc, inches | | +1.5 | 0 | -6.5 | -19.0 |
| PMC 130 Pointed Soft Point | velocity, fps | 2816 | 2593 | 2381 | 2179 | 1987 |
| | energy, ft-lb | 2288 | 1941 | 1636 | 1370 | 1139 |
| | arc, inches | | +1.8 | 0 | -8.0 | -23.2 |
| PMC 150 Barnes X | velocity, fps | 2700 | 2541 | 2387 | 2238 | 2095 |
| | energy, ft-lb | 2428 | 2150 | 1897 | 1668 | 1461 |
| | arc, inches | | +2.0 | 0 | -8.1 | -23.1 |
| PMC 150 SP boat-tail | velocity, fps | 2850 | 2660 | 2477 | 2302 | 2134 |
| | energy, ft-lb | 2705 | 2355 | 2043 | 1765 | 1516 |
| | arc, inches | | +1.7 | 0 | -7.4 | -21.4 |
| PMC 150 Pointed Soft Point | velocity, fps | 2547 | 2368 | 2197 | 2032 | 1875 |
| | energy, ft-lb | 2160 | 1868 | 1607 | 1375 | 1171 |
| | arc, inches | | +2.4 | 0 | -9.5 | -27.5 |
| Rem. 100 Pointed Soft Point | velocity, fps | 3320 | 2924 | 2561 | 2225 | 1916 |
| | energy, ft-lb | 2448 | 1898 | 1456 | 1099 | 815 |
| | arc, inches | | +2.3 | +2.0 | -3.6 | -16.2 |
| Rem. 130 PSP Core-Lokt | velocity, fps | 3060 | 2776 | 2510 | 2259 | 2022 |
| | energy, ft-lb | 2702 | 2225 | 1818 | 1472 | 1180 |
| | arc, inches | | +1.5 | 0 | -7.0 | -20.9 |
| Rem. 130 Bronze Point | velocity, fps | 3060 | 2802 | 2559 | 2329 | 2110 |
| | energy, ft-lb | 2702 | 2267 | 1890 | 1565 | 1285 |
| | arc, inches | | +1.5 | 0 | -6.8 | -20.0 |
| Rem. 140 Swift A-Frame | velocity, fps | 2925 | 2652 | 2394 | 2152 | 1923 |
| | energy, ft-lb | 2659 | 2186 | 1782 | 1439 | 1150 |
| | arc, inches | | +1.7 | 0 | -7.8 | -23.2 |
| Rem. 140 PSP boat-tail | velocity, fps | 2960 | 2749 | 2548 | 2355 | 2171 |
| | energy, ft-lb | 2723 | 2349 | 2018 | 1724 | 1465 |
| | arc, inches | | +1.6 | 0 | -6.9 | -20.1 |
| Rem. 140 Nosler Bal. Tip | velocity, fps | 2960 | 2754 | 2557 | 2366 | 2187 |
| | energy, ft-lb | 2724 | 2358 | 2032 | 1743 | 1487 |
| | arc, inches | | +1.6 | 0 | -6.9 | -20.0 |
| Rem. 150 SP Core-Lokt | velocity, fps | 2850 | 2504 | 2183 | 1886 | 1618 |
| | energy, ft-lb | 2705 | 2087 | 1587 | 1185 | 872 |
| | arc, inches | | +2.0 | 0 | -9.4 | -28.6 |
| Rem. 150 Nosler Partition | velocity, fps | 2850 | 2652 | 2463 | 2282 | 2108 |
| | energy, ft-lb | 2705 | 2343 | 2021 | 1734 | 1480 |
| | arc, inches | | +1.7 | 0 | -7.5 | -21.6 |
| Speer 130 Grand Slam | velocity, fps | 3050 | 2774 | 2514 | 2269 | |
| | energy, ft-lb | 2685 | 2221 | 1824 | 1485 | |
| | arc, inches | | +1.5 | 0 | -7.0 | -20.9 |

| Cartridge Bullet | Range, Yards: | 0 | 100 | 200 | 300 | 400 |
|---|---|---|---|---|---|---|
| Speer 150 Grand Slam | velocity, fps: | 2830 | 2594 | 2369 | 2156 | |
| | energy, ft-lb: | 2667 | 2240 | 1869 | 1548 | |
| | arc, inches: | | +1.8 | 0 | -8.1 | -23.6 |
| Win. 130 Power-Point | velocity, fps: | 3060 | 2802 | 2559 | 2329 | 2110 |
| | energy, ft-lb: | 2702 | 2267 | 1890 | 1565 | 1285 |
| | arc, inches: | | +1.8 | 0 | -7.1 | -20.6 |
| Win. 130 Power-Point Plus | velocity, fps: | 3150 | 2881 | 2628 | 2388 | 2161 |
| | energy, ft-lb: | 2865 | 2396 | 1993 | 1646 | 1348 |
| | arc, inches: | | +1.3 | 0 | -6.4 | -18.9 |
| Win. 130 Silvertip | velocity, fps: | 3060 | 2776 | 2510 | 2259 | 2022 |
| | energy, ft-lb: | 2702 | 2225 | 1818 | 1472 | 1180 |
| | arc, inches: | | +1.8 | 0 | -7.4 | -21.6 |
| Win. 130 Ballistic Silvertip | velocity, fps: | 3050 | 2828 | 2618 | 2416 | 2224 |
| | energy, ft-lb: | 2685 | 2309 | 1978 | 1685 | 1428 |
| | arc, inches: | | +1.4 | 0 | -6.5 | -18.9 |
| Win. 140 Fail Safe | velocity, fps: | 2920 | 2671 | 2435 | 2211 | 1999 |
| | energy, ft-lb: | 2651 | 2218 | 1843 | 1519 | 1242 |
| | arc, inches: | | +1.7 | 0 | -7.6 | -22.3 |
| Win. 150 Power-Point | velocity, fps: | 2850 | 2585 | 2336 | 2100 | 1879 |
| | energy, ft-lb: | 2705 | 2226 | 1817 | 1468 | 1175 |
| | arc, inches: | | +2.2 | 0 | -8.6 | -25.0 |
| Win. 150 Power-Point Plus | velocity, fps: | 2950 | 2679 | 2425 | 2184 | 1957 |
| | energy, ft-lb: | 2900 | 2391 | 1959 | 1589 | 1276 |
| | arc, inches: | | +1.7 | 0 | -7.6 | -22.6 |
| Win. 150 Partition Gold | velocity, fps: | 2930 | 2693 | 2468 | 2254 | 2051 |
| | energy, ft-lb: | 2860 | 2416 | 2030 | 1693 | 1402 |
| | arc, inches: | | +1.7 | 0 | -7.4 | -21.6 |

## .270 Weatherby Mag.

| Cartridge Bullet | Range, Yards: | 0 | 100 | 200 | 300 | 400 |
|---|---|---|---|---|---|---|
| Federal 130 Nosler Partition | velocity, fps: | 3200 | 2960 | 2740 | 2520 | 2320 |
| | energy, ft-lb: | 2955 | 2530 | 2160 | 1835 | 1550 |
| | arc, inches: | | +1.2 | 0 | -5.9 | -17.3 |
| Federal 130 Sierra GameKing BTSP | velocity, fps: | 3200 | 2980 | 2780 | 2580 | 2400 |
| | energy, ft-lb: | 2955 | 2570 | 2230 | 1925 | 1655 |
| | arc, inches: | | +1.2 | 0 | -5.7 | -16.6 |
| Federal 140 Trophy Bonded | velocity, fps: | 3100 | 2840 | 2600 | 2370 | 2150 |
| | energy, ft-lb: | 2990 | 2510 | 2100 | 1745 | 144 |
| | arc, inches: | | +1.4 | 0 | -6.6 | -19.3 |
| Wby. 100 Pointed Expanding | velocity, fps: | 3760 | 3396 | 3061 | 2751 | 2462 |
| | energy, ft-lb: | 3139 | 2560 | 2081 | 1681 | 1346 |
| | arc, inches: | | +2.3 | +3.0 | 0 | -7.6 |
| Wby. 130 Pointed Expanding | velocity, fps: | 3375 | 3123 | 2885 | 2659 | 2444 |
| | energy, ft-lb: | 3288 | 2815 | 2402 | 2041 | 1724 |
| | arc, inches: | | +2.8 | +3.5 | 0 | -8.4 |
| Wby. 130 Nosler Partition | velocity, fps: | 3375 | 3127 | 2892 | 2670 | 2458 |
| | energy, ft-lb: | 3288 | 2822 | 2415 | 2058 | 1744 |
| | arc, inches: | | +2.8 | +3.5 | 0 | -8.3 |
| Wby. 140 Nosler Bal. Tip | velocity, fps: | 3300 | 3077 | 2865 | 2663 | 2470 |
| | energy, ft-lb: | 3385 | 2943 | 2551 | 2204 | 1896 |
| | arc, inches: | | +2.9 | +3.6 | 0 | -8.4 |
| Wby. 140 Barnes X | velocity, fps: | 3250 | 3032 | 2825 | 2628 | 2438 |
| | energy, ft-lb: | 3283 | 2858 | 2481 | 2146 | 1848 |
| | arc, inches: | | +3.0 | +3.7 | 0 | -8.7 |
| Wby. 150 Pointed Expanding | velocity, fps: | 3245 | 3028 | 2821 | 2623 | 2434 |
| | energy, ft-lb: | 3507 | 3053 | 2650 | 2292 | 1973 |
| | arc, inches: | | +3.0 | +3.7 | 0 | -8.7 |
| Wby. 150 Nosler Partition | velocity, fps: | 3245 | 3029 | 2823 | 2627 | 2439 |
| | energy, ft-lb: | 3507 | 3055 | 2655 | 2298 | 1981 |
| | arc, inches: | | +3.0 | +3.7 | 0 | -8. |

## 7-30 Waters

| Cartridge Bullet | Range, Yards: | 0 | 100 | 200 | 300 | 400 |
|---|---|---|---|---|---|---|
| Federal 120 Sierra GameKing BTSP | velocity, fps: | 2700 | 2300 | 1930 | 1600 | 1330 |
| | energy, ft-lb: | 1940 | 1405 | 990 | 685 | 470 |
| | arc, inches: | | +2.6 | 0 | -12.0 | -37.6 |

## 7mm Mauser (7x57)

| Cartridge Bullet | Range, Yards: | 0 | 100 | 200 | 300 | 400 |
|---|---|---|---|---|---|---|
| Federal 140 Sierra Pro-Hunt. | velocity, fps: | 2660 | 2450 | 2260 | 2070 | 1890 |
| | energy, ft-lb: | 2200 | 1865 | 1585 | 1330 | 1110 |
| | arc, inches: | | +2.1 | 0 | -9.0 | -26.1 |
| Federal 140 Nosler Partition | velocity, fps: | 2660 | 2450 | 2260 | 2070 | 1890 |
| | energy, ft-lb: | 2200 | 1865 | 1585 | 1330 | 1110 |
| | arc, inches: | | +2.1 | 0 | -9.0 | -26.1 |
| Federal 175 Hi-Shok RN | velocity, fps: | 2440 | 2140 | 1860 | 1600 | 1380 |
| | energy, ft-lb: | 2315 | 1775 | 1340 | 1000 | 740 |
| | arc, inches: | | +3.1 | 0 | -13.3 | -40.1 |
| Hornady 139 SP boat-tail | velocity, fps: | 2700 | 2504 | 2316 | 2137 | 1965 |
| | energy, ft-lb: | 2251 | 1936 | 1656 | 1410 | 1192 |
| | arc, inches: | | +2.0 | 0 | -8.5 | -24.9 |
| Hornady 139 SP boat-tail LM | velocity, fps: | 2830 | 2620 | 2450 | 2250 | 2070 |
| | energy, ft-lb: | 2475 | 2135 | 1835 | 1565 | 1330 |
| | arc, inches: | | +1.8 | 0 | -7.6 | -22.1 |
| Hornady 139 SP LM | velocity, fps: | 2950 | 2736 | 2532 | 2337 | 2152 |
| | energy, ft-lb: | 2686 | 2310 | 1978 | 1686 | 1429 |
| | arc, inches: | | +2.0 | 0 | -7.6 | -21.5 |
| Norma 150 Soft Point | velocity, fps: | 2690 | 2479 | 2278 | 2087 | |
| | energy, ft-lb: | 2411 | 2048 | 1729 | 1450 | |
| | arc, inches: | | +2.0 | 0 | -8.8 | |
| PMC 140 Pointed Soft Point | velocity, fps: | 2660 | 2450 | 2260 | 2070 | 1890 |
| | energy, ft-lb: | 2200 | 1865 | 1585 | 1330 | 1110 |
| | arc, inches: | | +2.4 | 0 | -9.6 | -27.3 |
| PMC 175 Soft Point | velocity, fps: | 2440 | 2140 | 1860 | 1600 | 1380 |
| | energy, ft-lb: | 2315 | 1775 | 1340 | 1000 | 740 |
| | arc, inches: | | +1.5 | -3.6 | -18.6 | -46.8 |
| Rem. 140 PSP Core-Lokt | velocity, fps: | 2660 | 2435 | 2221 | 2018 | 1827 |
| | energy, ft-lb: | 2199 | 1843 | 1533 | 1266 | 1037 |
| | arc, inches: | | +2.2 | 0 | -9.2 | -27.4 |
| Win. 145 Power-Point | velocity, fps: | 2660 | 2413 | 2180 | 1959 | 1754 |
| | energy, ft-lb: | 2279 | 1875 | 1530 | 1236 | 990 |
| | arc, inches: | | +1.1 | -2.8 | -14.1 | -34.4 |

## 7x57 R

| Cartridge Bullet | Range, Yards: | 0 | 100 | 200 | 300 | 400 |
|---|---|---|---|---|---|---|
| Norma 150 FMJ | velocity, fps: | 2690 | 2489 | 2296 | 2112 | |
| | energy, ft-lb: | 2411 | 2063 | 1756 | 1486 | |
| | arc, inches: | | +2.0 | 0 | -8.6 | |
| Norma 154 Soft Point | velocity, fps: | 2625 | 2417 | 2219 | 2030 | |
| | energy, ft-lb: | 2357 | 1999 | 1684 | 1410 | |
| | arc, inches: | | +2.2 | 0 | -9.3 | |

## 7mm-08 Remington

| Cartridge Bullet | Range, Yards: | 0 | 100 | 200 | 300 | 400 |
|---|---|---|---|---|---|---|
| Federal 140 Nosler Partition | velocity, fps: | 2800 | 2590 | 2390 | 2200 | 2020 |
| | energy, ft-lb: | 2435 | 2085 | 1775 | 1500 | 1265 |
| | arc, inches: | | +1.8 | 0 | -8.0 | -23.1 |
| Federal 140 Nosler Bal. Tip | velocity, fps: | 2800 | 2610 | 2430 | 2260 | 2100 |
| | energy, ft-lb: | 2440 | 2135 | 1840 | 1590 | 1360 |
| | arc, inches: | | +1.8 | 0 | -7.7 | -22.3 |
| Federal 140 Tr. Bonded HE | velocity, fps: | 2950 | 2660 | 2390 | 2140 | 1900 |
| | energy, ft-lb: | 2705 | 2205 | 1780 | 1420 | 1120 |
| | arc, inches: | | +1.7 | 0 | -7.9 | -23.2 |
| Federal 150 Sierra Pro-Hunt. | velocity, fps: | 2650 | 2440 | 2230 | 2040 | 1860 |
| | energy, ft-lb: | 2340 | 1980 | 1660 | 1390 | 1150 |
| | arc, inches: | | +2.2 | 0 | -9.2 | -26.7 |
| Hornady 139 SP boat-tail LM | velocity, fps: | 3000 | 2790 | 2590 | 2399 | 2216 |
| | energy, ft-lb: | 2777 | 2403 | 2071 | 1776 | 1515 |
| | arc, inches: | | +1.5 | 0 | -6.7 | -19.4 |
| Rem. 120 Hollow Point | velocity, fps: | 3000 | 2725 | 2467 | 2223 | 1992 |
| | energy, ft-lb: | 2398 | 1979 | 1621 | 1316 | 1058 |
| | arc, inches: | | +1.6 | 0 | -7.3 | -21.7 |
| Rem. 140 PSP Core-Lokt | velocity, fps: | 2860 | 2625 | 2402 | 2189 | 1988 |
| | energy, ft-lb: | 2542 | 2142 | 1793 | 1490 | 1228 |
| | arc, inches: | | +1.8 | 0 | -7.8 | -22.9 |
| Rem. 140 PSP boat-tail | velocity, fps: | 2860 | 2656 | 2460 | 2273 | 2094 |
| | energy, ft-lb: | 2542 | 2192 | 1881 | 1606 | 1363 |
| | arc, inches: | | +1.7 | 0 | -7.5 | -21.7 |
| Rem. 140 Nosler Bal. Tip | velocity, fps: | 2860 | 2670 | 2488 | 2313 | 2145 |
| | energy, ft-lb: | 2543 | 2217 | 1925 | 1663 | 1431 |
| | arc, inches: | | +1.7 | 0 | -7.3 | -21.2 |
| Speer 145 Grand Slam | velocity, fps: | 2845 | 2567 | 2305 | 2059 | |
| | energy, ft-lb: | 2606 | 2121 | 1711 | 1365 | |
| | arc, inches: | | +1.9 | 0 | -8.4 | -25.5 |

**BALLISTICS**

| CARTRIDGE BULLET | RANGE, YARDS: | 0 | 100 | 200 | 300 | 400 |
|---|---|---|---|---|---|---|
| Win. 140 Power-Point | velocity, fps: | 2800 | 2523 | 2268 | 2027 | 1802 |
| | energy, ft-lb: | 2429 | 1980 | 1599 | 1277 | 1010 |
| | arc, inches: | | +2.0 | 0 | -8.8 | -26.0 |
| Win. 140 Power-Point Plus | velocity, fps: | 2875 | 2597 | 2336 | 2090 | 1859 |
| | energy, ft-lb: | 2570 | 1997 | 1697 | 1358 | 1075 |
| | arc, inches: | | +2.0 | 0 | -8.8 | 26.0 |
| Win. 140 Fail Safe | velocity, fps: | 2760 | 2506 | 2271 | 2048 | 1839 |
| | energy, ft-lb: | 2360 | 1953 | 1603 | 1304 | 1051 |
| | arc, inches: | | +2.0 | 0 | -8.8 | -25.9 |
| Win. 140 Ballistic Silvertip | velocity, fps: | 2770 | 2572 | 2382 | 2200 | 2026 |
| | energy, ft-lb: | 2386 | 2056 | 1764 | 1504 | 1276 |
| | arc, inches: | | +1.9 | 0 | -8.0 | -23.8 |

## 7x64 Brenneke

| CARTRIDGE BULLET | RANGE, YARDS: | 0 | 100 | 200 | 300 | 400 |
|---|---|---|---|---|---|---|
| Federal 160 Nosler Partition | velocity, fps: | 2650 | 2480 | 2310 | 2150 | 2000 |
| | energy, ft-lb: | 2495 | 2180 | 1895 | 1640 | 1415 |
| | arc, inches: | | +2.1 | 0 | -8.7 | -24.9 |
| Norma 154 Soft Point | velocity, fps: | 2821 | 2605 | 2399 | 2203 | |
| | energy, ft-lb: | 2722 | 2321 | 1969 | 1660 | |
| | arc, inches: | | +1.8 | 0 | -7.8 | |
| Norma 170 Vulkan | velocity, fps: | 2756 | 2501 | 2259 | 2031 | |
| | energy, ft-lb: | 2868 | 2361 | 1927 | 1558 | |
| | arc, inches: | | +2.0 | 0 | -8.8 | |
| Norma 170 Oryx | velocity, fps: | 2756 | 2481 | 2222 | 1979 | |
| | energy, ft-lb: | 2868 | 2324 | 1864 | 1478 | |
| | arc, inches: | | +2.1 | 0 | -9.2 | |
| Norma 170 Plastic Point | velocity, fps: | 2756 | 2519 | 2294 | 2081 | |
| | energy, ft-lb: | 2868 | 2396 | 1987 | 1635 | |
| | arc, inches: | | +2.0 | 0 | -8.6 | |
| Rem. 175 PSP Core-Lokt | velocity, fps: | 2650 | 2445 | 2248 | 2061 | 1883 |
| | energy, ft-lb: | 2728 | 2322 | 1964 | 1650 | 1378 |
| | arc, inches: | | +2.2 | 0 | -9.1 | -26.4 |
| Speer 160 Grand Slam | velocity, fps: | 2600 | 2376 | 2164 | 1962 | |
| | energy, ft-lb: | 2401 | 2006 | 1663 | 1368 | |
| | arc, inches: | | +2.3 | 0 | -9.8 | -28.6 |
| Speer 175 Grand Slam | velocity, fps: | 2650 | 2461 | 2280 | 2106 | |
| | energy, ft-lb: | 2728 | 2353 | 2019 | 1723 | |
| | arc, inches: | | +2.4 | 0 | -9.2 | -26.2 |

## 7x65 R

| CARTRIDGE BULLET | RANGE, YARDS: | 0 | 100 | 200 | 300 | 400 |
|---|---|---|---|---|---|---|
| Norma 170 Plastic Point | velocity, fps: | 2625 | 2390 | 2167 | 1956 | |
| | energy, ft-lb: | 2602 | 2157 | 1773 | 1445 | |
| | arc, inches: | | +2.3 | 0 | -9.7 | |
| Norma 170 Vulkan | velocity, fps: | 2657 | 2392 | 2143 | 1909 | |
| | energy, ft-lb: | 2666 | 2161 | 1734 | 1377 | |
| | arc, inches: | | +2.3 | 0 | -9.9 | |
| Norma 170 Oryx | velocity, fps: | 2657 | 2378 | 2115 | 1871 | |
| | energy, ft-lb: | 2666 | 2135 | 1690 | 1321 | |
| | arc, inches: | | +2.3 | 0 | -10.1 | |

## .284 Winchester

| CARTRIDGE BULLET | RANGE, YARDS: | 0 | 100 | 200 | 300 | 400 |
|---|---|---|---|---|---|---|
| Win. 150 Power-Point | velocity, fps: | 2860 | 2595 | 2344 | 2108 | 1886 |
| | energy, ft-lb: | 2724 | 2243 | 1830 | 1480 | 1185 |
| | arc, inches: | | +2.1 | 0 | -8.5 | -24.8 |

## .280 Remington

| CARTRIDGE BULLET | RANGE, YARDS: | 0 | 100 | 200 | 300 | 400 |
|---|---|---|---|---|---|---|
| Federal 140 Sierra Pro-Hunt. | velocity, fps: | 2990 | 2740 | 2500 | 2270 | 2060 |
| | energy, ft-lb: | 2770 | 2325 | 1940 | 1605 | 1320 |
| | arc, inches: | | +1.6 | 0 | -7.0 | -20.8 |
| Federal 140 Trophy Bonded | velocity, fps: | 2990 | 2630 | 2310 | 2040 | 1730 |
| | energy, ft-lb: | 2770 | 2155 | 1655 | 1250 | 925 |
| | arc, inches: | | +1.6 | 0 | -8.4 | -25.4 |
| Federal 140 Tr. Bonded HE | velocity, fps: | 3150 | 2850 | 2570 | 2300 | 2050 |
| | energy, ft-lb: | 3085 | 2520 | 2050 | 1650 | 1310 |
| | arc, inches: | | +1.4 | 0 | -6.7 | -20.0 |
| Federal 150 Hi-Shok | velocity, fps: | 2890 | 2670 | 2460 | 2260 | 2060 |
| | energy, ft-lb: | 2780 | 2370 | 2015 | 1695 | 1420 |
| | arc, inches: | | +1.7 | 0 | -7.5 | -21.8 |

| CARTRIDGE BULLET | RANGE, YARDS: | 0 | 100 | 200 | 300 | 400 |
|---|---|---|---|---|---|---|
| Federal 150 Nosler Partition | velocity, fps: | 2890 | 2690 | 2490 | 2310 | 2130 |
| | energy, ft-lb: | 2780 | 2405 | 2070 | 1770 | 1510 |
| | arc, inches: | | +1.7 | 0 | -7.2 | -21.1 |
| Federal 160 Trophy Bonded | velocity, fps: | 2800 | 2570 | 2350 | 2140 | 1940 |
| | energy, ft-lb: | 2785 | 2345 | 1960 | 1625 | 1340 |
| | arc, inches: | | +1.9 | 0 | -8.3 | -24.0 |
| Hornady 139 SPBT LMmoly | velocity, fps: | 3110 | 2888 | 2675 | 2473 | 2280 |
| | energy, ft-lb: | 2985 | 2573 | 2209 | 1887 | 1604 |
| | arc, inches: | | +1.4 | 0 | -6.5 | -18.6 |
| Norma 170 Vulkan | velocity, fps: | 2592 | 2346 | 2113 | 1894 | |
| | energy, ft-lb: | 2537 | 2078 | 1686 | 1354 | |
| | arc, inches: | | +2.4 | 0 | -10.2 | |
| Norma 170 Oryx | velocity, fps: | 2690 | 2416 | 2159 | 1918 | |
| | energy, ft-lb: | 2732 | 2204 | 1760 | 1389 | |
| | arc, inches: | | +2.2 | 0 | -9.7 | |
| Norma 170 Plastic Point | velocity, fps: | 2707 | 2468 | 2241 | 2026 | |
| | energy, ft-lb: | 2767 | 2299 | 1896 | 1550 | |
| | arc, inches: | | +2.1 | 0 | -9.1 | |
| Rem. 140 PSP Core-Lokt | velocity, fps: | 3000 | 2758 | 2528 | 2309 | 2102 |
| | energy, ft-lb: | 2797 | 2363 | 1986 | 1657 | 1373 |
| | arc, inches: | | +1.5 | 0 | -7.0 | -20.5 |
| Rem. 140 PSP boat-tail | velocity, fps: | 2860 | 2656 | 2460 | 2273 | 2094 |
| | energy, ft-lb: | 2542 | 2192 | 1881 | 1606 | 1363 |
| | arc, inches: | | +1.7 | 0 | -7.5 | -21.7 |
| Rem. 140 Nosler Bal. Tip | velocity, fps: | 3000 | 2804 | 2616 | 2436 | 2263 |
| | energy, ft-lb: | 2799 | 2445 | 2128 | 1848 | 1593 |
| | arc, inches: | | +1.5 | 0 | -6.8 | -19.0 |
| Rem. 150 PSP Core-Lokt | velocity, fps: | 2890 | 2624 | 2373 | 2135 | 1912 |
| | energy, ft-lb: | 2781 | 2293 | 1875 | 1518 | 1217 |
| | arc, inches: | | +1.8 | 0 | -8.0 | -23.6 |
| Rem. 165 SP Core-Lokt | velocity, fps: | 2820 | 2510 | 2220 | 1950 | 1701 |
| | energy, ft-lb: | 2913 | 2308 | 1805 | 1393 | 1060 |
| | arc, inches: | | +2.0 | 0 | -9.1 | -27.4 |
| Speer 145 Grand Slam | velocity, fps: | 2900 | 2619 | 2354 | 2105 | |
| | energy, ft-lb: | 2707 | 2207 | 1784 | 1426 | |
| | arc, inches: | | +2.1 | 0 | -8.4 | -24.7 |
| Speer 160 Grand Slam | velocity, fps: | 2890 | 2652 | 2425 | 2210 | |
| | energy, ft-lb: | 2967 | 2497 | 2089 | 1735 | |
| | arc, inches: | | +1.7 | 0 | -7.7 | -22.4 |
| Win. 140 Fail Safe | velocity, fps: | 3050 | 2756 | 2480 | 2221 | 1977 |
| | energy, ft-lb: | 2893 | 2362 | 1913 | 1533 | 1216 |
| | arc, inches: | | +1.5 | 0 | -7.2 | -21.5 |
| Win. 140 Ballistic Silvertip | velocity, fps: | 3040 | 2842 | 2653 | 2471 | 2297 |
| | energy, ft-lb: | 2872 | 2511 | 2187 | 1898 | 1640 |
| | arc, inches: | | +1.4 | 0 | -6.3 | -18.4 |

## 7mm Remington Mag.

| CARTRIDGE BULLET | RANGE, YARDS: | 0 | 100 | 200 | 300 | 400 |
|---|---|---|---|---|---|---|
| A-Square 175 Monolithic Solid | velocity, fps: | 2860 | 2557 | 2273 | 2008 | 1771 |
| | energy, ft-lb: | 3178 | 2540 | 2008 | 1567 | 1219 |
| | arc, inches: | | +1.92 | 0 | -8.7 | -25.9 |
| Federal 140 Nosler Partition | velocity, fps: | 3150 | 2930 | 2710 | 2510 | 2320 |
| | energy, ft-lb: | 3085 | 2660 | 2290 | 1960 | 1670 |
| | arc, inches: | | +1.3 | 0 | -6.0 | -17.5 |
| Federal 140 Trophy Bonded | velocity, fps: | 3150 | 2910 | 2680 | 2460 | 2250 |
| | energy, ft-lb: | 3085 | 2630 | 2230 | 1880 | 1575 |
| | arc, inches: | | +1.3 | 0 | -6.1 | -18.1 |
| Federal 150 Hi-Shok | velocity, fps: | 3110 | 2830 | 2570 | 2320 | 2090 |
| | energy, ft-lb: | 3220 | 2670 | 2200 | 1790 | 1450 |
| | arc, inches: | | +1.4 | 0 | -6.7 | -19.9 |
| Federal 150 Sierra GameKing BTSP | velocity, fps: | 3110 | 2920 | 2750 | 2580 | 2410 |
| | energy, ft-lb: | 3220 | 2850 | 2510 | 2210 | 1930 |
| | arc, inches: | | +1.3 | 0 | -5.9 | -17.0 |
| Federal 150 Nosler Bal. Tip | velocity, fps: | 3110 | 2910 | 2720 | 2540 | 2370 |
| | energy, ft-lb: | 3220 | 2825 | 2470 | 2150 | 1865 |
| | arc, inches: | | +1.3 | 0 | -6.0 | -17.4 |
| Federal 160 Sierra Pro-Hunt. | velocity, fps: | 2940 | 2730 | 2520 | 2320 | 2140 |
| | energy, ft-lb: | 3070 | 2640 | 2260 | 1920 | 1620 |
| | arc, inches: | | +1.6 | 0 | -7.1 | -20.6 |

| CARTRIDGE BULLET | RANGE, YARDS: | 0 | 100 | 200 | 300 | 400 |
|---|---|---|---|---|---|---|
| Federal 160 Nosler Partition | velocity, fps: | 2950 | 2770 | 2590 | 2420 | 2250 |
| | energy, ft-lb: | 3090 | 2715 | 2375 | 2075 | 1800 |
| | arc, inches: | | +1.5 | 0 | -6.7 | -19.4 |
| Federal 160 Trophy Bonded | velocity, fps: | 2940 | 2660 | 2390 | 2140 | 1900 |
| | energy, ft-lb: | 3070 | 2505 | 2025 | 1620 | 1280 |
| | arc, inches: | | +1.7 | 0 | -7.9 | -23.3 |
| Federal 165 Sierra GameKing BTSP | velocity, fps: | 2950 | 2800 | 2650 | 2510 | 2370 |
| | energy, ft-lb: | 3190 | 2865 | 2570 | 2300 | 2050 |
| | arc, inches: | | +1.5 | 0 | -6.4 | -18.4 |
| Federal 175 Hi-Shok | velocity, fps: | 2860 | 2650 | 2440 | 2240 | 2060 |
| | energy, ft-lb: | 3180 | 2720 | 2310 | 1960 | 1640 |
| | arc, inches: | | +1.7 | 0 | -7.6 | -22.1 |
| Federal 175 Trophy Bonded | velocity, fps: | 2860 | 2600 | 2350 | 2120 | 1900 |
| | energy, ft-lb: | 3180 | 2625 | 2150 | 1745 | 1400 |
| | arc, inches: | | +1.8 | 0 | -8.2 | -24.0 |
| Hornady 139 SPBT | velocity, fps: | 3150 | 2933 | 2727 | 2530 | 2341 |
| | energy, ft-lb: | 3063 | 2656 | 2296 | 1976 | 1692 |
| | arc, inches: | | +1.2 | 0 | -6.1 | -17.7 |
| Hornady 139 SPBT HMmoly | velocity, fps: | 3250 | 3041 | 2822 | 2613 | 2413 |
| | energy, ft-lb: | 3300 | 2854 | 2458 | 2106 | 1797 |
| | arc, inches: | | +1.1 | 0 | -5.7 | -16.6 |
| Hornady 154 Soft Point | velocity, fps: | 3035 | 2814 | 2604 | 2404 | 2212 |
| | energy, ft-lb: | 3151 | 2708 | 2319 | 1977 | 1674 |
| | arc, inches: | | +1.3 | 0 | -6.7 | -19.3 |
| Hornady 162 SP boat-tail | velocity, fps: | 2940 | 2757 | 2582 | 2413 | 2251 |
| | energy, ft-lb: | 3110 | 2735 | 2399 | 2095 | 1823 |
| | arc, inches: | | +1.6 | 0 | -6.7 | -19.7 |
| Hornady 175 SP | velocity, fps: | 2860 | 2650 | 2440 | 2240 | 2060 |
| | energy, ft-lb: | 3180 | 2720 | 2310 | 1960 | 1640 |
| | arc, inches: | | +2.0 | 0 | -7.9 | -22.7 |
| Norma 170 Vulkan | velocity, fps: | 3018 | 2747 | 2493 | 2252 | |
| | energy, ft-lb: | 3439 | 2850 | 2346 | 1914 | |
| | arc, inches: | | +1.5 | 0 | -2.8 | |
| Norma 170 Oryx | velocity, fps: | 2887 | 2601 | 2333 | 2080 | |
| | energy, ft-lb: | 3147 | 2555 | 2055 | 1634 | |
| | arc, inches: | | +1.8 | 0 | -8.2 | |
| Norma 170 Plastic Point | velocity, fps: | 3018 | 2762 | 2519 | 2290 | |
| | energy, ft-lb: | 3439 | 2880 | 2394 | 1980 | |
| | arc, inches: | | +1.5 | 0 | -7.0 | |
| PMC 140 Barnes X | velocity, fps: | 3000 | 2808 | 2624 | 2448 | 2279 |
| | energy, ft-lb: | 2797 | 2451 | 2141 | 1863 | 1614 |
| | arc, inches: | | +1.5 | 0 | -6.6 | 18.9 |
| PMC 140 Pointed Soft Point | velocity, fps: | 3099 | 2878 | 2668 | 2469 | 2279 |
| | energy, ft-lb: | 2984 | 2574 | 2212 | 1895 | 1614 |
| | arc, inches: | | +1.4 | 0 | -6.2 | -18.1 |
| PMC 140 SP boat-tail | velocity, fps: | 3125 | 2891 | 2669 | 2457 | 2255 |
| | energy, ft-lb: | 3035 | 2597 | 2213 | 1877 | 1580 |
| | arc, inches: | | +1.4 | 0 | -6.3 | -18.4 |
| PMC 160 Barnes X | velocity, fps: | 2800 | 2639 | 2484 | 2334 | 2189 |
| | energy, ft-lb: | 2785 | 2474 | 2192 | 1935 | 1703 |
| | arc, inches: | | +1.8 | 0 | -7.4 | -21.2 |
| PMC 160 Pointed Soft Point | velocity, fps: | 2914 | 2748 | 2586 | 2428 | 2276 |
| | energy, ft-lb: | 3016 | 2682 | 2375 | 2095 | 1840 |
| | arc, inches: | | +1.6 | 0 | -6.7 | -19.4 |
| PMC 160 SP boat-tail | velocity, fps: | 2900 | 2696 | 2501 | 2314 | 2135 |
| | energy, ft-lb: | 2987 | 2582 | 2222 | 1903 | 1620 |
| | arc, inches: | | +1.7 | 0 | -7.2 | -21.0 |
| PMC 175 Pointed Soft Point | velocity, fps: | 2860 | 2645 | 2442 | 2244 | 2957 |
| | energy, ft-lb: | 3178 | 2718 | 2313 | 1956 | 1644 |
| | arc, inches: | | +2.0 | 0 | -7.9 | -22.7 |
| Rem. 140 PSP Core-Lokt | velocity, fps: | 3175 | 2923 | 2684 | 2458 | 2243 |
| | energy, ft-lb: | 3133 | 2655 | 2240 | 1878 | 1564 |
| | arc, inches: | | +2.2 | +1.9 | -3.2 | -14.2 |
| Rem. 140 PSP boat-tail | velocity, fps: | 3175 | 2956 | 2747 | 2547 | 2356 |
| | energy, ft-lb: | 3133 | 2715 | 2345 | 2017 | 1726 |
| | arc, inches: | | +2.2 | +1.6 | -3.1 | -13.4 |
| Rem. 150 PSP Core-Lokt | velocity, fps: | 3110 | 2830 | 2568 | 2320 | 2085 |
| | energy, ft-lb: | 3221 | 2667 | 2196 | 1792 | 1448 |
| | arc, inches: | | +1.3 | 0 | -6.6 | -20.2 |
| Rem. 150 Nosler Bal. Tip | velocity, fps: | 3110 | 2912 | 2723 | 2542 | 2367 |
| | energy, ft-lb: | 3222 | 2825 | 2470 | 2152 | 1867 |
| | arc, inches: | | +1.2 | 0 | -5.9 | -17.3 |
| Rem. 160 Swift A-Frame | velocity, fps: | 2900 | 2659 | 2430 | 2212 | 2006 |
| | energy, ft-lb: | 2987 | 2511 | 2097 | 1739 | 1430 |
| | arc, inches: | | +1.7 | 0 | -7.6 | -22.4 |
| Rem. 160 Nosler Partition | velocity, fps: | 2950 | 2752 | 2563 | 2381 | 2207 |
| | energy, ft-lb: | 3091 | 2690 | 2333 | 2014 | 1730 |
| | arc, inches: | | +0.6 | -1.9 | -9.6 | -23.6 |
| Rem. 175 PSP Core-Lokt | velocity, fps: | 2860 | 2645 | 2440 | 2244 | 2057 |
| | energy, ft-lb: | 3178 | 2718 | 2313 | 1956 | 1644 |
| | arc, inches: | | +1.7 | 0 | -7.6 | -22.1 |
| Speer 145 Grand Slam | velocity, fps: | 3140 | 2843 | 2565 | 2304 | |
| | energy, ft-lb: | 3174 | 2602 | 2118 | 1708 | |
| | arc, inches: | | +1.4 | 0 | -6.7 | |
| Speer 175 Grand Slam | velocity, fps: | 2850 | 2653 | 2463 | 2282 | |
| | energy, ft-lb: | 3156 | 2734 | 2358 | 2023 | |
| | arc, inches: | | +1.7 | 0 | -7.5 | -21.7 |
| Win. 140 Fail Safe | velocity, fps: | 3150 | 2861 | 2589 | 2333 | 2092 |
| | energy, ft-lb: | 3085 | 2544 | 2085 | 1693 | 1361 |
| | arc, inches: | | +1.4 | 0 | -6.6 | -19.5 |
| Win. 140 Ballistic Silvertip | velocity, fps: | 3100 | 2889 | 2687 | 2494 | 2310 |
| | energy, ft-lb: | 2988 | 2595 | 2245 | 1934 | 1659 |
| | arc, inches: | | +1.3 | 0 | -6.2 | -17.9 |
| Win. 150 Power-Point | velocity, fps: | 3090 | 2812 | 2551 | 2304 | 2071 |
| | energy, ft-lb: | 3181 | 2634 | 2167 | 1768 | 1429 |
| | arc, inches: | | +1.5 | 0 | -6.8 | -20.2 |
| Win. 150 Power-Point Plus | velocity, fps: | 3130 | 2849 | 2586 | 2337 | 2102 |
| | energy, ft-lb: | 3264 | 2705 | 2227 | 1819 | 1472 |
| | arc, inches: | | +1.4 | 0 | -6.6 | -19.6 |
| Win. 150 Ballistic Silvertip | velocity, fps: | 3100 | 2903 | 2714 | 2533 | 2359 |
| | energy, ft-lb: | 3200 | 2806 | 2453 | 2136 | 1853 |
| | arc, inches: | | +1.3 | 0 | -6.0 | -17.5 |
| Win. 160 Partition Gold | velocity, fps: | 2950 | 2743 | 2546 | 2357 | 2176 |
| | energy, ft-lb: | 3093 | 2674 | 2303 | 1974 | 1682 |
| | arc, inches: | | +1.6 | 0 | -6.9 | -20.1 |
| Win. 160 Fail Safe | velocity, fps: | 2920 | 2678 | 2449 | 2331 | 2025 |
| | energy, ft-lb: | 3030 | 2549 | 2131 | 1769 | 1457 |
| | arc, inches: | | +1.7 | 0 | -7.5 | -22.0 |
| Win. 175 Power-Point | velocity, fps: | 2860 | 2645 | 2440 | 2244 | 2057 |
| | energy, ft-lb: | 3178 | 2718 | 2313 | 1956 | 1644 |
| | arc, inches: | | +2.0 | 0 | -7.9 | -22.7 |

## 7mm Weatherby Mag.

| CARTRIDGE BULLET | RANGE, YARDS: | 0 | 100 | 200 | 300 | 400 |
|---|---|---|---|---|---|---|
| Federal 160 Nosler Partition | velocity, fps: | 3050 | 2850 | 2650 | 2470 | 2290 |
| | energy, ft-lb: | 3305 | 2880 | 2505 | 2165 | 1865 |
| | arc, inches: | | +1.4 | 0 | -6.3 | -18.4 |
| Federal 160 Sierra GameKing BTSP | velocity, fps: | 3050 | 2880 | 2710 | 2560 | 2400 |
| | energy, ft-lb: | 3305 | 2945 | 2615 | 2320 | 2050 |
| | arc, inches: | | +1.4 | 0 | -6.1 | -17.4 |
| Federal 160 Trophy Bonded | velocity, fps: | 3050 | 2730 | 2420 | 2140 | 1880 |
| | energy, ft-lb: | 3305 | 2640 | 2085 | 1630 | 1255 |
| | arc, inches: | | +1.6 | 0 | -7.6 | -22.7 |
| Hornady 154 Soft Point | velocity, fps: | 3200 | 2971 | 2753 | 2546 | 2348 |
| | energy, ft-lb: | 3501 | 3017 | 2592 | 2216 | 1885 |
| | arc, inches: | | +1.2 | 0 | -5.8 | -17.0 |
| Hornady 175 Soft Point | velocity, fps: | 2910 | 2709 | 2516 | 2331 | 2154 |
| | energy, ft-lb: | 3290 | 2850 | 2459 | 2111 | 1803 |
| | arc, inches: | | +1.6 | 0 | -7.1 | -20.6 |
| Wby. 139 Pointed Expanding | velocity, fps: | 3340 | 3079 | 2834 | 2601 | 2380 |
| | energy, ft-lb: | 3443 | 2926 | 2478 | 2088 | 1748 |
| | arc, inches: | | +2.9 | +3.6 | 0 | -8.7 |
| Wby. 140 Nosler Partition | velocity, fps: | 3303 | 3069 | 2847 | 2636 | 2434 |
| | energy, ft-lb: | 3391 | 2927 | 2519 | 2159 | 1841 |
| | arc, inches: | | +2.9 | +3.6 | 0 | -8.5 |
| Wby. 150 Nosler Bal. Tip | velocity, fps: | 3300 | 3093 | 2896 | 2708 | 2527 |
| | energy, ft-lb: | 3627 | 3187 | 2793 | 2442 | 2127 |
| | arc, inches: | | +2.8 | +3.5 | 0 | -8.2 |

| Cartridge Bullet | Range, Yards: | 0 | 100 | 200 | 300 | 400 |
|---|---|---|---|---|---|---|
| Wby. 150 Barnes X | velociy, fps: | 3100 | 2901 | 2710 | 2527 | 2352 |
| | energy, ft-lb: | 3200 | 2802 | 2446 | 2127 | 1842 |
| | arc, inches: | | +3.3 | +4.0 | 0 | -9.4 |
| Wby. 154 Pointed Expanding | velociy, fps: | 3260 | 3028 | 2807 | 2597 | 2397 |
| | energy, ft-lb: | 3634 | 3134 | 2694 | 2307 | 1964 |
| | arc, inches: | | +3.0 | +3.7 | 0 | -8.8 |
| Wby. 160 Nosler Partition | velocity, fps: | 3200 | 2991 | 2791 | 2600 | 2417 |
| | energy, ft-lb: | 3638 | 3177 | 2767 | 2401 | 2075 |
| | arc, inches: | | +3.1 | +3.8 | 0 | -8.9 |
| Wby. 175 Pointed Expanding | velocity, fps: | 3070 | 2861 | 2662 | 2471 | 2288 |
| | energy, ft-lb: | 3662 | 3181 | 2753 | 2373 | 2034 |
| | arc, inches: | | +3.5 | +4.2 | 0 | -9.9 |

## 7mm Dakota

| Cartridge Bullet | Range, Yards: | 0 | 100 | 200 | 300 | 400 |
|---|---|---|---|---|---|---|
| Dakota 140 Barnes X | velocity, fps: | 3500 | 3253 | 3019 | 2798 | 2587 |
| | energy, ft-lb: | 3807 | 3288 | 2833 | 2433 | 2081 |
| | arc, inches: | | +2.0 | +2.1 | -1.5 | -9.6 |
| Dakota 160 Barnes X | velocity, fps: | 3200 | 3001 | 2811 | 2630 | 2455 |
| | energy, ft-lb: | 3637 | 3200 | 2808 | 2456 | 2140 |
| | arc, inches: | | +2.1 | +1.9 | -2.8 | -12.5 |

## 7mm STW

| Cartridge Bullet | Range, Yards: | 0 | 100 | 200 | 300 | 400 |
|---|---|---|---|---|---|---|
| A-Square 140 Nos. Bal. Tip | velocity, fps: | 3450 | 3254 | 3067 | 2888 | 2715 |
| | energy, ft-lb: | 3700 | 3291 | 2924 | 2592 | 2292 |
| | arc, inches: | | +2.2 | +3.0 | 0 | -7.3 |
| A-Square 160 Nosler Part. | velocity, fps: | 3250 | 3071 | 2900 | 2735 | 2576 |
| | energy, ft-lb: | 3752 | 3351 | 2987 | 2657 | 2357 |
| | arc, inches: | | +2.8 | +3.5 | 0 | -8.2 |
| A-Square 160 SP boat-tail | velocity, fps: | 3250 | 3087 | 2930 | 2778 | 2631 |
| | energy, ft-lb: | 3752 | 3385 | 3049 | 2741 | 2460 |
| | arc, inches: | | +2.8 | +3.4 | 0 | -8.0 |
| Federal 140 Trophy Bonded | velocity, fps: | 3330 | 3080 | 2850 | 2630 | 2420 |
| | energy, ft-lb: | 3435 | 2950 | 2520 | 2145 | 1815 |
| | arc, inches: | | +1.1 | 0 | -5.4 | -15.8 |
| Federal 150 Trophy Bonded | velocity, fps: | 3250 | 3010 | 2770 | 2560 | 2350 |
| | energy, ft-lb: | 3520 | 3010 | 2565 | 2175 | 1830 |
| | arc, inches: | | +1.2 | 0 | -5.7 | -16.7 |
| Federal 160 Sierra GameKing BTSP | velocity, fps: | 3200 | 3020 | 2850 | 2670 | 2530 |
| | energy, ft-lb: | 3640 | 3245 | 2890 | 2570 | 2275 |
| | arc, inches: | | +1.1 | 0 | -5.5 | -15.7 |
| Rem. 140 PSP Core-Lokt | velocity, fps: | 3325 | 3064 | 2818 | 2585 | 2364 |
| | energy, ft-lb: | 3436 | 2918 | 2468 | 2077 | 1737 |
| | arc, inches: | | +2.0 | +1.7 | -2.9 | -12.8 |
| Rem. 140 Swift A-Frame | velocity, fps: | 3325 | 3020 | 2735 | 2467 | 2215 |
| | energy, ft-lb: | 3436 | 2834 | 2324 | 1892 | 1525 |
| | arc, inches: | | +2.1 | +1.8 | -3.1 | -13.8 |
| Speer 145 Grand Slam | velocity, fps: | 3300 | 2992 | 2075 | 2435 | |
| | energy, ft-lb: | 3506 | 2882 | 2355 | 1909 | |
| | arc, inches: | | +1.2 | 0 | -6.0 | -17.8 |
| Win. 140 Ballistic Silvertip | velocity, fps: | 3320 | 3100 | 2890 | 2690 | 2499 |
| | energy, ft-lb: | 3427 | 2982 | 2597 | 2250 | 1941 |
| | arc, inches: | | +1.1 | 0 | -5.2 | -15.2 |
| Win. 150 Power-Point | velocity, fps: | 3250 | 2957 | 2683 | 2424 | 2181 |
| | energy, ft-lb: | 3519 | 2913 | 2398 | 1958 | 1584 |
| | arc, inches: | | +1.2 | 0 | -6.1 | -18.1 |
| Win. 160 Fail Safe | velocity, fps: | 3150 | 2894 | 2652 | 2422 | 2204 |
| | energy, ft-lb: | 3526 | 2976 | 2499 | 2085 | 1727 |
| | arc, inches: | | +1.3 | 0 | -6.3 | -18.5 |

## 7.21 (.284) Firehawk

| Cartridge Bullet | Range, Yards: | 0 | 100 | 200 | 300 | 400 |
|---|---|---|---|---|---|---|
| Lazzeroni 140 Nosler Part. | velocity, fps: | 3580 | 3349 | 3130 | 2923 | 2724 |
| | energy, ft-lb: | 3985 | 3488 | 3048 | 2656 | 2308 |
| | arc, inches: | | +2.2 | +2.9 | 0 | -7.0 |
| Lazzeroni 160 Swift A-Fr. | velocity, fps: | 3385 | 3167 | 2961 | 2763 | 2574 |
| | energy, ft-lb: | 4072 | 3565 | 3115 | 2713 | 2354 |
| | arc, inches: | | +2.6 | +3.3 | 0 | -7.8 |

## 7.5x55 Swiss

| Cartridge Bullet | Range, Yards: | 0 | 100 | 200 | 300 | 400 |
|---|---|---|---|---|---|---|
| Norma 180 Soft Point | velocity, fps: | 2651 | 2432 | 2223 | 2025 | |
| | energy, ft-lb: | 2810 | 2364 | 1976 | 1639 | |
| | arc, inches: | | +2.2 | 0 | -9.3 | |

## 7.62x39 Russian

| Cartridge Bullet | Range, Yards: | 0 | 100 | 200 | 300 | 400 |
|---|---|---|---|---|---|---|
| Federal 123 Hi-Shok | velocity, fps: | 2300 | 2030 | 1780 | 1550 | 1350 |
| | energy, ft-lb: | 1445 | 1125 | 860 | 655 | 500 |
| | arc, inches: | | 0 | -7.0 | -25.1 | |
| Federal 124 FMJ | velocity, fps: | 2300 | 2030 | 1780 | 1560 | 1360 |
| | energy, ft-lb: | 1455 | 1135 | 875 | 670 | 510 |
| | arc, inches: | | +3.5 | 0 | -14.6 | -43.5 |
| Norma 150 Soft Point | velocity, fps: | 2953 | 2622 | 2314 | 2028 | |
| | energy, ft-lb: | 2905 | 2291 | 1784 | 1370 | |
| | arc, inches: | | +1.8 | 0 | -8.3 | |
| Norma 180 Soft Point | velocity, fps: | 2575 | 2360 | 2154 | 1960 | |
| | energy, ft-lb: | 2651 | 2226 | 1856 | 1536 | |
| | arc, inches: | | +2.4 | 0 | -9.9 | |
| PMC 123 FMJ | velocity, fps: | 2350 | 2072 | 1817 | 1583 | 1368 |
| | energy, ft-lb: | 1495 | 1162 | 894 | 678 | 507 |
| | arc, inches: | | 0 | -5.0 | -26.4 | -67.8 |
| PMC 125 Pointed Soft Point | velocity, fps: | 2320 | 2046 | 1794 | 1563 | 1350 |
| | energy, ft-lb: | 1493 | 1161 | 893 | 678 | 505 |
| | arc, inches: | | 0 | -5.2 | -27.5 | -70.6 |
| Rem. 125 Pointed Soft Point | velocity, fps: | 2365 | 2062 | 1783 | 1533 | 1320 |
| | energy, ft-lb: | 1552 | 1180 | 882 | 652 | 483 |
| | arc, inches: | | 0 | -6.7 | -24.5 | |
| Win. 123 Soft Point | velocity, fps: | 2365 | 2033 | 1731 | 1465 | 1248 |
| | energy, ft-lb: | 1527 | 1129 | 818 | 586 | 425 |
| | arc, inches: | | +3.8 | 0 | -15.4 | -46.3 |

## .30 Carbine

| Cartridge Bullet | Range, Yards: | 0 | 100 | 200 | 300 | 400 |
|---|---|---|---|---|---|---|
| Federal 110 Hi-Shok RN | velocity, fps: | 1990 | 1570 | 1240 | 1040 | 920 |
| | energy, ft-lb: | 965 | 600 | 375 | 260 | 210 |
| | arc, inches: | | 0 | -12.8 | -46.9 | |
| Federal 110 FMJ | velocity, fps: | 1990 | 1570 | 1240 | 1040 | 920 |
| | energy, ft-lb: | 965 | 600 | 375 | 260 | 210 |
| | arc, inches: | | 0 | -12.8 | -46.9 | |
| PMC 110 FMJ | velocity, fps: | 1927 | 1548 | 1248 | | |
| | energy, ft-lb: | 906 | 585 | 380 | | |
| | arc, inches: | | 0 | -14.2 | | |
| Rem. 110 Soft Point | velocity, fps: | 1990 | 1567 | 1236 | 1035 | 923 |
| | energy, ft-lb: | 967 | 600 | 373 | 262 | 208 |
| | arc, inches: | | 0 | -12.9 | -48.6 | |
| Win. 110 Hollow Soft Point | velocity, fps: | 1990 | 1567 | 1236 | 1035 | 923 |
| | energy, ft-lb: | 967 | 600 | 373 | 262 | 208 |
| | arc, inches: | | 0 | -13.5 | -49.9 | |

## .30-30 Winchester

| Cartridge Bullet | Range, Yards: | 0 | 100 | 200 | 300 | 400 |
|---|---|---|---|---|---|---|
| Federal 125 Hi-Shok HP | velocity, fps: | 2570 | 2090 | 1660 | 1320 | 1080 |
| | energy, ft-lb: | 1830 | 1210 | 770 | 480 | 320 |
| | arc, inches: | | +3.3 | 0 | -16.0 | -50.9 |
| Federal 150 Hi-Shok FN | velocity, fps: | 2390 | 2020 | 1680 | 1400 | 1180 |
| | energy, ft-lb: | 1900 | 1355 | 945 | 650 | 460 |
| | arc, inches: | | +3.6 | 0 | -15.9 | -49.1 |
| Federal 170 Hi-Shok RN | velocity, fps: | 2200 | 1900 | 1620 | 1380 | 1190 |
| | energy, ft-lb: | 1830 | 1355 | 990 | 720 | 535 |
| | arc, inches: | | +4.1 | 0 | -17.4 | -52.4 |
| Federal 170 Sierra Pro-Hunt. | velocity, fps: | 2200 | 1820 | 1500 | 1240 | 1060 |
| | energy, ft-lb: | 1830 | 1255 | 845 | 575 | 425 |
| | arc, inches: | | +4.5 | 0 | -20.0 | -63.5 |
| Federal 170 Nosler Partition | velocity, fps: | 2200 | 1900 | 1620 | 1380 | 1190 |
| | energy, ft-lb: | 1830 | 1355 | 990 | 720 | 535 |
| | arc, inches: | | +4.1 | 0 | -17.4 | -52.4 |
| Hornady 150 Round Nose | velocity, fps: | 2390 | 1973 | 1605 | 1303 | 1095 |
| | energy, ft-lb: | 1902 | 1296 | 858 | 565 | 399 |
| | arc, inches: | | 0 | -8.2 | -30.0 | |

| CARTRIDGE BULLET | | 0 | 100 | 200 | 300 | 400 |
|---|---|---|---|---|---|---|
| **Hornady 170 Flat Point** | velocity, fps: | 2200 | 1895 | 1619 | 1381 | 1191 |
| | energy, ft-lb: | 1827 | 1355 | 989 | 720 | 535 |
| | arc, inches: | | | 0 | -8.9 | -31.1 |
| **Norma 150 Soft Point** | velocity, fps: | 2329 | 2008 | 1716 | 1459 | |
| | energy, ft-lb: | 1807 | 1344 | 981 | 709 | |
| | arc, inches: | | +3.6 | 0 | -15.5 | |
| **PMC 150 Starfire HP** | velocity, fps: | 2100 | 1769 | 1478 | | |
| | energy, ft-lb: | 1469 | 1042 | 728 | | |
| | arc, inches: | | | 0 | -10.8 | |
| **PMC 150 Flat Nose** | velocity, fps: | 2159 | 1819 | 1554 | | |
| | energy, ft-lb: | 1552 | 1102 | 804 | | |
| | arc, inches: | | | 0 | -9.0 | |
| **PMC 170 Flat Nose** | velocity, fps: | 1965 | 1680 | 1480 | | |
| | energy, ft-lb: | 1457 | 1065 | 827 | | |
| | arc, inches: | | | 0 | -10.7 | |
| **Rem. 55 PSP (sabot) "Accelerator"** | velocity, fps: | 3400 | 2693 | 2085 | 1570 | 1187 |
| | energy, ft-lb: | 1412 | 886 | 521 | 301 | 172 |
| | arc, inches: | | +1.7 | 0 | -9.9 | -34.3 |
| **Rem. 150 SP Core-Lokt** | velocity, fps: | 2390 | 1973 | 1605 | 1303 | 1095 |
| | energy, ft-lb: | 1902 | 1296 | 858 | 565 | 399 |
| | arc, inches: | | | 0 | -7.6 | -28.8 |
| **Rem. 170 SP Core-Lokt** | velocity, fps: | 2200 | 1895 | 1619 | 1381 | 1191 |
| | energy, ft-lb: | 1827 | 1355 | 989 | 720 | 535 |
| | arc, inches: | | | 0 | -8.3 | -29.9 |
| **Rem. 170 HP Core-Lokt** | velocity, fps: | 2200 | 1895 | 1619 | 1381 | 1191 |
| | energy, ft-lb: | 1827 | 1355 | 989 | 720 | 535 |
| | arc, inches: | | | 0 | -8.3 | -29.9 |
| **Speer 150 Flat Nose** | velocity, fps: | 2370 | 2067 | 1788 | 1538 | |
| | energy, ft-lb: | 1870 | 1423 | 1065 | 788 | |
| | arc, inches: | | +3.3 | 0 | -14.4 | -43.7 |
| **Win. 150 Hollow Point** | velocity, fps: | 2390 | 2018 | 1684 | 1398 | 1177 |
| | energy, ft-lb: | 1902 | 1356 | 944 | 651 | 461 |
| | arc, inches: | | | 0 | -7.7 | -27.9 |
| **Win. 150 Power-Point** | velocity, fps: | 2390 | 2018 | 1684 | 1398 | 1177 |
| | energy, ft-lb: | 1902 | 1356 | 944 | 651 | 461 |
| | arc, inches: | | | 0 | -7.7 | -27.9 |
| **Win. 150 Silvertip** | velocity, fps: | 2390 | 2018 | 1684 | 1398 | 1177 |
| | energy, ft-lb: | 1902 | 1356 | 944 | 651 | 461 |
| | arc, inches: | | | 0 | -7.7 | -27.9 |
| **Win. 150 Power-Point Plus** | velocity, fps: | 2480 | 2095 | 1747 | 1446 | 1209 |
| | energy, ft-lb: | 2049 | 1462 | 1017 | 697 | 487 |
| | arc, inches: | | | 0 | -6.5 | -24.5 |
| **Win. 170 Power-Point** | velocity, fps: | 2200 | 1895 | 1619 | 1381 | 1191 |
| | energy, ft-lb: | 1827 | 1355 | 989 | 720 | 535 |
| | arc, inches: | | | 0 | -8.9 | -31.1 |
| **Win. 170 Silvertip** | velocity, fps: | 2200 | 1895 | 1619 | 1381 | 1191 |
| | energy, ft-lb: | 1827 | 1355 | 989 | 720 | 535 |
| | arc, inches: | | | 0 | -8.9 | -31.1 |

## .300 Savage

| CARTRIDGE BULLET | | 0 | 100 | 200 | 300 | 400 |
|---|---|---|---|---|---|---|
| **Federal 150 Hi-Shok** | velocity, fps: | 2630 | 2350 | 2100 | 1850 | 1630 |
| | energy, ft-lb: | 2305 | 1845 | 1460 | 1145 | 885 |
| | arc, inches: | | +2.4 | 0 | -10.4 | -30.9 |
| **Federal 180 Hi-Shok** | velocity, fps: | 2350 | 2140 | 1940 | 1750 | 1570 |
| | energy, ft-lb: | 2205 | 1825 | 1495 | 1215 | 985 |
| | arc, inches: | | +3.1 | 0 | -12.4 | -36.1 |
| **Rem. 150 PSP Core-Lokt** | velocity, fps: | 2630 | 2354 | 2095 | 1853 | 1631 |
| | energy, ft-lb: | 2303 | 1845 | 1462 | 1143 | 806 |
| | arc, inches: | | +2.4 | 0 | -10.4 | -30.9 |
| **Rem. 180 SP Core-Lokt** | velocity, fps: | 2350 | 2025 | 1728 | 1467 | 1252 |
| | energy, ft-lb: | 2207 | 1639 | 1193 | 860 | 626 |
| | arc, inches: | | | 0 | -7.1 | -25.9 |
| **Win. 150 Power-Point** | velocity, fps: | 2630 | 2311 | 2015 | 1743 | 1500 |
| | energy, ft-lb: | 2303 | 1779 | 1352 | 1012 | 749 |
| | arc, inches: | | +2.8 | 0 | -11.5 | -34.4 |

## .307 Winchester

| CARTRIDGE BULLET | | 0 | 100 | 200 | 300 | 400 |
|---|---|---|---|---|---|---|
| **Win. 180 Power-Point** | velocity, fps: | 2510 | 2179 | 1874 | 1599 | 1362 |
| | energy, ft-lb: | 2519 | 1898 | 1404 | 1022 | 742 |
| | arc, inches: | | +1.5 | -3.6 | -18.6 | -47.1 |

## .30-40 Krag

| CARTRIDGE BULLET | | 0 | 100 | 200 | 300 | 400 |
|---|---|---|---|---|---|---|
| **Rem. 180 PSP Core-Lokt** | velocity, fps: | 2430 | 2213 | 2007 | 1813 | 1632 |
| | energy, ft-lb: | 2360 | 1957 | 1610 | 1314 | 1064 |
| | arc, inches: | | | 0 | -5.6 | -18.6 |
| **Win. 180 Power-Point** | velocity, fps: | 2430 | 2099 | 1795 | 1525 | 1298 |
| | energy, ft-lb: | 2360 | 1761 | 1288 | 929 | 673 |
| | arc, inches: | | | 0 | -7.1 | -25.0 |

## .308 Winchester

| CARTRIDGE BULLET | | 0 | 100 | 200 | 300 | 400 |
|---|---|---|---|---|---|---|
| **Federal 150 Hi-Shok** | velocity, fps: | 2820 | 2530 | 2260 | 2010 | 1770 |
| | energy, ft-lb: | 2650 | 2140 | 1705 | 1345 | 1050 |
| | arc, inches: | | +2.0 | 0 | -8.8 | -26.3 |
| **Federal 150 Nosler Bal. Tip.** | velocity, fps: | 2820 | 2610 | 2410 | 2220 | 2040 |
| | energy, ft-lb: | 2650 | 2270 | 1935 | 1640 | 1380 |
| | arc, inches: | | +1.8 | 0 | -7.8 | -22.7 |
| **Federal 150 FMJ boat-tail** | velocity, fps: | 2820 | 2620 | 2430 | 2250 | 2070 |
| | energy, ft-lb: | 2650 | 2285 | 1965 | 1680 | 1430 |
| | arc, inches: | | +1.8 | 0 | -7.7 | -22.4 |
| **Federal 150 Barnes XLC** | velocity, fps: | 2820 | 2610 | 2400 | 2210 | 2030 |
| | energy, ft-lb: | 2650 | 2265 | 1925 | 1630 | 1370 |
| | arc, inches: | | +1.8 | 0 | -7.8 | -22.9 |
| **Federal 155 Sierra MatchKg. BTHP** | velocity, fps: | 2950 | 2740 | 2540 | 2350 | 2170 |
| | energy, ft-lb: | 2995 | 2585 | 2225 | 1905 | 1620 |
| | arc, inches: | | +13.2 | +23.3 | +28.1 | +26.5 |
| **Federal 165 Sierra GameKing BTSP** | velocity, fps: | 2700 | 2520 | 2330 | 2160 | 1990 |
| | energy, ft-lb: | 2670 | 2310 | 1990 | 1700 | 1450 |
| | arc, inches: | | +2.0 | 0 | -8.4 | -24.3 |
| **Federal 165 Trophy Bonded** | velocity, fps: | 2700 | 2440 | 2200 | 1970 | 1760 |
| | energy, ft-lb: | 2670 | 2185 | 1775 | 1425 | 1135 |
| | arc, inches: | | +2.2 | 0 | -9.4 | -27.7 |
| **Federal 165 Tr. Bonded HE** | velocity, fps: | 2870 | 2600 | 2350 | 2120 | 1890 |
| | energy, ft-lb: | 3020 | 2485 | 2030 | 1640 | 1310 |
| | arc, inches: | | +1.8 | 0 | -8.2 | -24.0 |
| **Federal 168 Sierra MatchKg. BTHP** | velocity, fps: | 2600 | 2410 | 2230 | 2060 | 1890 |
| | energy, ft-lb: | 2520 | 2170 | 1855 | 1580 | 1340 |
| | arc, inches: | | +17.7 | +31.0 | +37.2 | +35.4 |
| **Federal 180 Hi-Shok** | velocity, fps: | 2620 | 2390 | 2180 | 1970 | 1780 |
| | energy, ft-lb: | 2745 | 2290 | 1895 | 1555 | 1270 |
| | arc, inches: | | +2.3 | 0 | -9.7 | -28.3 |
| **Federal 180 Sierra Pro-Hunt.** | velocity, fps: | 2620 | 2410 | 2200 | 2010 | 1820 |
| | energy, ft-lb: | 2745 | 2315 | 1940 | 1610 | 1330 |
| | arc, inches: | | +2.3 | 0 | -9.3 | -27.1 |
| **Federal 180 Nosler Partition** | velocity, fps: | 2620 | 2430 | 2240 | 2060 | 1890 |
| | energy, ft-lb: | 2745 | 2355 | 2005 | 1700 | 1430 |
| | arc, inches: | | +2.2 | 0 | -9.2 | -26.5 |
| **Federal 180 Nosler Part. HE** | velocity, fps: | 2740 | 2550 | 2370 | 2200 | 2030 |
| | energy, ft-lb: | 3000 | 2600 | 2245 | 1925 | 1645 |
| | arc, inches: | | +1.9 | 0 | -8.2 | -23.5 |
| **Hornady 110 Urban Tactical** | velocity, fps: | 3170 | 2825 | 2504 | 2206 | 1937 |
| | energy, ft-lb: | 2454 | 1950 | 1532 | 1189 | 916 |
| | arc, inches: | | +1.5 | 0 | -7.2 | -21.2 |
| **Hornady 150 SP boat-tail** | velocity, fps: | 2820 | 2560 | 2315 | 2084 | 1866 |
| | energy, ft-lb: | 2648 | 2183 | 1785 | 1447 | 1160 |
| | arc, inches: | | +2.0 | 0 | -8.5 | -25.2 |
| **Hornady 150 SP LM** | velocity, fps: | 2980 | 2703 | 2442 | 2195 | 1964 |
| | energy, ft-lb: | 2959 | 2433 | 1986 | 1606 | 1285 |
| | arc, inches: | | +1.6 | 0 | -7.5 | -22.2 |
| **Hornady 155 A-Max** | velocity, fps: | 2815 | 2610 | 2415 | 2229 | 2051 |
| | energy, ft-lb: | 2727 | 2345 | 2007 | 1709 | 1448 |
| | arc, inches: | | +1.9 | 0 | -7.9 | -22.6 |
| **Hornady 165 SP boat-tail** | velocity, fps: | 2700 | 2496 | 2301 | 2115 | 1937 |
| | energy, ft-lb: | 2670 | 2283 | 1940 | 1639 | 1375 |
| | arc, inches: | | +2.0 | 0 | -8.7 | -25.2 |

**BALLISTICS**

| Cartridge Bullet | Range, Yards: | 0 | 100 | 200 | 300 | 400 |
|---|---|---|---|---|---|---|
| Hornady 165 SPBT LM | velocity, fps: | 2870 | 2658 | 2456 | 2283 | 2078 |
| | energy, ft-lb: | 3019 | 2589 | 2211 | 1877 | 1583 |
| | arc, inches: | | +1.7 | 0 | -7.5 | -21.8 |
| Hornady 168 BTHP Match | velocity, fps: | 2700 | 2524 | 2354 | 2191 | 2035 |
| | energy, ft-lb: | 2720 | 2377 | 2068 | 1791 | 1545 |
| | arc, inches: | | +2.0 | 0 | -8.4 | -23.9 |
| Hornady 168 BTHP Match LM | velocity, fps: | 2640 | 2630 | 2429 | 2238 | 2056 |
| | energy, ft-lb: | 3008 | 2579 | 2201 | 1868 | 1577 |
| | arc, inches: | | +1.8 | 0 | -7.8 | -22.4 |
| Hornady 168 A-Max Match | velocity, fps: | 2620 | 2446 | 2280 | 2120 | 1972 |
| | energy, ft-lb: | 2560 | 2232 | 1939 | 1677 | 1450 |
| | arc, inches: | | +2.6 | 0 | -9.2 | -25.6 |
| Hornady 168 A-Max | velocity, fps: | 2700 | 2491 | 2292 | 2102 | 1921 |
| | energy, ft-lb: | 2719 | 2315 | 1959 | 1648 | 1377 |
| | arc, inches: | | +2.4 | 0 | -9.0 | -25.9 |
| Hornady 178 A-Max | velocity, fps: | 2965 | 2778 | 2598 | 2425 | 2259 |
| | energy, ft-lb: | 3474 | 3049 | 2666 | 2323 | 2017 |
| | arc, inches: | | +1.6 | 0 | -6.9 | -19.8 |
| Hornady 180 A-Max Match | velocity, fps: | 2550 | 2397 | 2249 | 2106 | 1974 |
| | energy, ft-lb: | 2598 | 2295 | 2021 | 1773 | 1557 |
| | arc, inches: | | +2.7 | 0 | -9.5 | -26.2 |
| Norma 150 Soft Point | velocity, fps: | 2861 | 2537 | 2235 | 1954 | |
| | energy, ft-lb: | 2727 | 2144 | 1664 | 1272 | |
| | arc, inches: | | +2.0 | 0 | -9.0 | |
| Norma 165 TXP Swift A-Fr. | velocity, fps: | 2700 | 2459 | 2231 | 2015 | |
| | energy, ft-lb: | 2672 | 2216 | 1824 | 1488 | |
| | arc, inches: | | +2.1 | 0 | -9.1 | |
| Norma 180 Plastic Point | velocity, fps: | 2612 | 2365 | 2131 | 1911 | |
| | energy, ft-lb: | 2728 | 2235 | 1815 | 1460 | |
| | arc, inches: | | +2.4 | 0 | -10.1 | |
| Norma 180 Nosler Partition | velocity, fps: | 2612 | 2414 | 2225 | 2044 | |
| | energy, ft-lb: | 2728 | 2330 | 1979 | 1670 | |
| | arc, inches: | | +2.2 | 0 | -9.3 | |
| Norma 180 Alaska | velocity, fps: | 2612 | 2269 | 1953 | 1667 | |
| | energy, ft-lb: | 2728 | 2059 | 1526 | 1111 | |
| | arc, inches: | | +2.7 | 0 | -11.9 | |
| Norma 180 Vulkan | velocity, fps: | 2612 | 2325 | 2056 | 1806 | |
| | energy, ft-lb: | 2728 | 2161 | 1690 | 1304 | |
| | arc, inches: | | +2.5 | 0 | -10.8 | |
| Norma 180 Oryx | velocity, fps: | 2612 | 2305 | 2019 | 1755 | |
| | energy, ft-lb: | 2728 | 2124 | 1629 | 1232 | |
| | arc, inches: | | +2.5 | 0 | -11.1 | |
| Norma 200 Vulkan | velocity, fps: | 2461 | 2215 | 1983 | 1767 | |
| | energy, ft-lb: | 2690 | 2179 | 1747 | 1387 | |
| | arc, inches: | | +2.8 | 0 | -11.7 | |
| PMC 147 FMJ boat-tail | velocity, fps: | 2751 | 2473 | 2257 | 2052 | 1859 |
| | energy, ft-lb: | 2428 | 2037 | 1697 | 1403 | 1150 |
| | arc, inches: | | +2.3 | 0 | -9.3 | -27.3 |
| PMC 150 Barnes X | velocity, fps: | 2700 | 2504 | 2316 | 2135 | 1964 |
| | energy, ft-lb: | 2428 | 2087 | 1786 | 1518 | 1284 |
| | arc, inches: | | +2.0 | 0 | -8.6 | -24.7 |
| PMC 150 Pointed Soft Point | velocity, fps: | 2643 | 2417 | 2203 | 1999 | 1807 |
| | energy, ft-lb: | 2326 | 1946 | 1615 | 1331 | 1088 |
| | arc, inches: | | +2.2 | 0 | -9.4 | -27.5 |
| PMC 150 SP boat-tail | velocity, fps: | 2820 | 2581 | 2354 | 2139 | 1935 |
| | energy, ft-lb: | 2648 | 2218 | 1846 | 1523 | 1247 |
| | arc, inches: | | +1.9 | 0 | -8.2 | -24.0 |
| PMC 165 Barnes X | velocity, fps: | 2600 | 2425 | 2256 | 2095 | 1940 |
| | energy, ft-lb: | 2476 | 2154 | 1865 | 1608 | 1379 |
| | arc, inches: | | +2.2 | 0 | -9.0 | -26.0 |
| PMC 168 HP boat-tail | velocity, fps: | 2650 | 2460 | 2278 | 2103 | 1936 |
| | energy, ft-lb: | 2619 | 2257 | 1935 | 1649 | 1399 |
| | arc, inches: | | +2.1 | 0 | -8.8 | -25.6 |
| PMC 180 Pointed Soft Point | velocity, fps: | 2410 | 2223 | 2044 | 1874 | 1714 |
| | energy, ft-lb: | 2320 | 1975 | 1670 | 1404 | 1174 |
| | arc, inches: | | +2.8 | 0 | -11.1 | -32.0 |
| PMC 180 SP boat-tail | velocity, fps: | 2620 | 2446 | 2278 | 2117 | 1962 |
| | energy, ft-lb: | 2743 | 2391 | 2074 | 1790 | 1538 |
| | arc, inches: | | +2.2 | 0 | -8.9 | -25.4 |

| Cartridge Bullet | Range, Yards: | 0 | 100 | 200 | 300 | 400 |
|---|---|---|---|---|---|---|
| Rem. 150 PSP Core-Lokt | velocity, fps: | 2820 | 2533 | 2263 | 2009 | 1774 |
| | energy, ft-lb: | 2648 | 2137 | 1705 | 1344 | 1048 |
| | arc, inches: | | +2.0 | 0 | -8.8 | -26.2 |
| Rem. 165 PSP boat-tail | velocity, fps: | 2700 | 2497 | 2303 | 2117 | 1941 |
| | energy, ft-lb: | 2670 | 2284 | 1942 | 1642 | 1379 |
| | arc, inches: | | +2.0 | 0 | -8.6 | -25.0 |
| Rem. 165 Nosler Bal. Tip | velocity, fps: | 2700 | 2613 | 2333 | 2161 | 1996 |
| | energy, ft-lb: | 2672 | 2314 | 1995 | 1711 | 1460 |
| | arc, inches: | | +2.0 | 0 | -8.4 | -24.3 |
| Rem. 168 HPBT Match | velocity, fps: | 2680 | 2493 | 2314 | 2143 | 1979 |
| | energy, ft-lb: | 2678 | 2318 | 1998 | 1713 | 1460 |
| | arc, inches: | | +2.1 | 0 | -8.6 | -24.7 |
| Rem. 180 SP Core-Lokt | velocity, fps: | 2620 | 2274 | 1955 | 1666 | 1414 |
| | energy, ft-lb: | 2743 | 2066 | 1527 | 1109 | 799 |
| | arc, inches: | | +2.6 | 0 | -11.8 | -36.3 |
| Rem. 180 PSP Core-Lokt | velocity, fps: | 2620 | 2393 | 2178 | 1974 | 1782 |
| | energy, ft-lb: | 2743 | 2288 | 1896 | 1557 | 1269 |
| | arc, inches: | | +2.3 | 0 | -9.7 | -28.3 |
| Rem. 180 Nosler Partition | velocity, fps: | 2620 | 2436 | 2259 | 2089 | 1927 |
| | energy, ft-lb: | 2743 | 2371 | 2039 | 1774 | 1485 |
| | arc, inches: | | +2.2 | 0 | -9.0 | -26.0 |
| Speer 150 Grand Slam | velocity, fps: | 2900 | 2599 | 2317 | 2053 | |
| | energy, ft-lb: | 2800 | 2249 | 1788 | 1404 | |
| | arc, inches: | | +2.1 | 0 | -8.6 | -24.8 |
| Speer 165 Grand Slam | velocity, fps: | 2700 | 2475 | 2261 | 2057 | |
| | energy, ft-lb: | 2670 | 2243 | 1872 | 1550 | |
| | arc, inches: | | +2.1 | 0 | -8.9 | -25.9 |
| Speer 180 Grand Slam | velocity, fps: | 2620 | 2420 | 2229 | 2046 | |
| | energy, ft-lb: | 2743 | 2340 | 1985 | 1674 | |
| | arc, inches: | | +2.2 | 0 | -9.2 | -26.6 |
| Win. 150 Power-Point | velocity, fps: | 2820 | 2488 | 2179 | 1893 | 1633 |
| | energy, ft-lb: | 2648 | 2061 | 1581 | 1193 | 888 |
| | arc, inches: | | +2.4 | 0 | -9.8 | -29.3 |
| Win. 150 Power-Point Plus | velocity, fps: | 2900 | 2558 | 2241 | 1946 | 1678 |
| | energy, ft-lb: | 2802 | 2180 | 1672 | 1262 | 938 |
| | arc, inches: | | +1.9 | 0 | -8.9 | -27.0 |
| Win. 150 Partition Gold | velocity, fps: | 2900 | 2645 | 2405 | 2177 | 1962 |
| | energy, ft-lb: | 2802 | 2332 | 1927 | 1579 | 1282 |
| | arc, inches: | | +1.7 | 0 | -7.8 | -22.9 |
| Win. 150 Ballistic Silvertip | velocity, fps: | 2810 | 2601 | 2401 | 2211 | 2028 |
| | energy, ft-lb: | 2629 | 2253 | 1920 | 1627 | 1370 |
| | arc, inches: | | +1.8 | 0 | -7.8 | -22.8 |
| Win. 150 Fail Safe | velocity, fps: | 2820 | 2533 | 2263 | 2010 | 1775 |
| | energy, ft-lb: | 2649 | 2137 | 1706 | 1346 | 1049 |
| | arc, inches: | | +2.0 | 0 | -8.8 | -26.2 |
| xWin. 168 Ballistic Silvertip | velocity, fps: | 2670 | 2484 | 2306 | 2134 | 1971 |
| | energy, ft-lb: | 2659 | 2301 | 1983 | 1699 | 1449 |
| | arc, inches: | | +2.1 | 0 | -8.6 | -24.8 |
| Win. 168 HP boat-tail Match | velocity, fps: | 2680 | 2485 | 2297 | 2118 | 1948 |
| | energy, ft-lb: | 2680 | 2303 | 1970 | 1674 | 1415 |
| | arc, inches: | | +2.1 | 0 | -8.7 | -25.1 |
| Win. 180 Power-Point | velocity, fps: | 2620 | 2274 | 1955 | 1666 | 1414 |
| | energy, ft-lb: | 2743 | 2066 | 1527 | 1109 | 799 |
| | arc, inches: | | +2.9 | 0 | -12.1 | -36.9 |
| Win. 180 Silvertip | velocity, fps: | 2620 | 2393 | 2178 | 1974 | 1782 |
| | energy, ft-lb: | 2743 | 2288 | 1896 | 1557 | 1269 |
| | arc, inches: | | +2.6 | 0 | -9.9 | -28.9 |

## .30-06 Springfield

| Cartridge Bullet | Range, Yards: | 0 | 100 | 200 | 300 | 400 |
|---|---|---|---|---|---|---|
| A-Square 180 M & D-T | velocity, fps: | 2700 | 2365 | 2054 | 1769 | 1524 |
| | energy, ft-lb: | 2913 | 2235 | 1687 | 1251 | 928 |
| | arc, inches: | | +2.4 | 0 | -10.6 | -32.4 |
| A-Square 220 Monolithic Solid | velocity, fps: | 2380 | 2108 | 1854 | 1623 | 1424 |
| | energy, ft-lb: | 2767 | 2171 | 1679 | 1287 | 990 |
| | arc, inches: | | +3.1 | 0 | -13.6 | -39.9 |
| Federal 125 Sierra Pro-Hunt. | velocity, fps: | 3140 | 2780 | 2450 | 2140 | 1850 |
| | energy, ft-lb: | 2735 | 2145 | 1660 | 1270 | 955 |
| | arc, inches: | | +1.5 | 0 | -7.3 | -22.3 |
| Federal 150 Hi-Shok | velocity, fps: | 2910 | 2620 | 2340 | 2080 | 1840 |
| | energy, ft-lb: | 2820 | 2280 | 1825 | 1445 | 1130 |
| | arc, inches: | | +1.8 | 0 | -8.2 | -24.4 |

| CARTRIDGE BULLET | RANGE, YARDS: | 0 | 100 | 200 | 300 | 400 |
|---|---|---|---|---|---|---|
| Federal 150 Sierra Pro-Hunt. | velocity, fps: | 2910 | 2640 | 2380 | 2130 | 1900 |
| | energy, ft-lb: | 2820 | 2315 | 1880 | 1515 | 1205 |
| | arc, inches: | | +1.7 | 0 | -7.9 | -23.3 |
| Federal 150 Sierra GameKing BTSP | velocity, fps: | 2910 | 2690 | 2480 | 2270 | 2070 |
| | energy, ft-lb: | 2820 | 2420 | 2040 | 1710 | 1430 |
| | arc, inches: | | +1.7 | 0 | -7.4 | -21.5 |
| Federal 150 Nosler Bal. Tip | velocity, fps: | 2910 | 2700 | 2490 | 2300 | 2110 |
| | energy, ft-lb: | 2820 | 2420 | 2070 | 1760 | 1485 |
| | arc, inches: | | +1.6 | 0 | -7.3 | -21.1 |
| Federal 150 FMJ boat-tail | velocity, fps: | 2910 | 2710 | 2510 | 2320 | 2150 |
| | energy, ft-lb: | 2820 | 2440 | 2100 | 1800 | 1535 |
| | arc, inches: | | +1.6 | 0 | -7.1 | -20.8 |
| Federal 165 Sierra Pro-Hunt. | velocity, fps: | 2800 | 2560 | 2340 | 2130 | 1920 |
| | energy, ft-lb: | 2875 | 2410 | 2005 | 1655 | 1360 |
| | arc, inches: | | +1.9 | 0 | -8.3 | -24.3 |
| Federal 165 Sierra GameKing BTSP | velocity, fps: | 2800 | 2610 | 2420 | 2240 | 2070 |
| | energy, ft-lb: | 2870 | 2490 | 2150 | 1840 | 1580 |
| | arc, inches: | | +1.8 | 0 | -7.8 | -22.4 |
| Federal 165 Sierra GameKing HE | velocity, fps: | 3140 | 2900 | 2670 | 2450 | 2240 |
| | energy, ft-lb: | 3610 | 3075 | 2610 | 2200 | 1845 |
| | arc, inches: | | +1.5 | 0 | -6.9 | -20.4 |
| Federal 165 Nosler Bal. Tip | velocity, fps: | 2800 | 2610 | 2430 | 2250 | 2080 |
| | energy, ft-lb: | 2870 | 2495 | 2155 | 1855 | 1585 |
| | arc, inches: | | +1.8 | 0 | -7.7 | -22.2 |
| Federal 165 Trophy Bonded | velocity, fps: | 2800 | 2540 | 2290 | 2050 | 1830 |
| | energy, ft-lb: | 2870 | 2360 | 1915 | 1545 | 1230 |
| | arc, inches: | | +2.0 | 0 | -8.7 | -25.4 |
| Federal 165 Tr. Bonded HE | velocity, fps: | 3140 | 2860 | 2590 | 2340 | 2100 |
| | energy, ft-lb: | 3610 | 2990 | 2460 | 2010 | 1625 |
| | arc, inches: | | +1.6 | 0 | -7.4 | -21.9 |
| Federal 168 Sierra MatchKg. BTHP | velocity, fps: | 2700 | 2510 | 2320 | 2150 | 1980 |
| | energy, ft-lb: | 2720 | 2350 | 2010 | 1720 | 1460 |
| | arc, inches: | | +16.2 | +28.4 | +34.1 | +32.3 |
| Federal 180 Hi-Shok | velocity, fps: | 2700 | 2470 | 2250 | 2040 | 1850 |
| | energy, ft-lb: | 2915 | 2435 | 2025 | 1665 | 1360 |
| | arc, inches: | | +2.1 | 0 | -9.0 | -26.4 |
| Federal 180 Sierra Pro-Hunt. RN | velocity, fps: | 2700 | 2350 | 2020 | 1730 | 1470 |
| | energy, ft-lb: | 2915 | 2200 | 1630 | 1190 | 860 |
| | arc, inches: | | +2.4 | 0 | -11.0 | -33.6 |
| Federal 180 Nosler Partition | velocity, fps: | 2700 | 2500 | 2320 | 2140 | 1970 |
| | energy, ft-lb: | 2915 | 2510 | 2150 | 1830 | 1550 |
| | arc, inches: | | +2.0 | 0 | -8.6 | -24.6 |
| Federal 180 Nosler Part. HE | velocity, fps: | 2880 | 2690 | 2500 | 2320 | 2150 |
| | energy, ft-lb: | 3315 | 2880 | 2495 | 2150 | 1845 |
| | arc, inches: | | +1.7 | 0 | -7.2 | -21.0 |
| Federal 180 Sierra GameKing BTSP | velocity, fps: | 2700 | 2540 | 2380 | 2220 | 2080 |
| | energy, ft-lb: | 2915 | 2570 | 2260 | 1975 | 1720 |
| | arc, inches: | | +1.9 | 0 | -8.1 | -23.1 |
| Federal 180 Barnes XLC | velocity, fps: | 2700 | 2530 | 2360 | 2200 | 2040 |
| | energy, ft-lb: | 2915 | 2550 | 2220 | 1930 | 1670 |
| | arc, inches: | | +2.0 | 0 | -8.3 | -23.8 |
| Federal 180 Trophy Bonded | velocity, fps: | 2700 | 2460 | 2220 | 2000 | 1800 |
| | energy, ft-lb: | 2915 | 2410 | 1975 | 1605 | 1290 |
| | arc, inches: | | +2.2 | 0 | -9.2 | -27.0 |
| Federal 180 Tr. Bonded HE | velocity, fps: | 2880 | 2630 | 2380 | 2160 | 1940 |
| | energy, ft-lb: | 3315 | 2755 | 2270 | 1855 | 1505 |
| | arc, inches: | | +1.8 | 0 | -8.0 | -23.3 |
| Federal 220 Sierra Pro-Hunt. RN | velocity, fps: | 2410 | 2130 | 1870 | 1630 | 1420 |
| | energy, ft-lb: | 2835 | 2215 | 1705 | 1300 | 985 |
| | arc, inches: | | +3.1 | 0 | -13.1 | -39.3 |
| Hornady 150 SP | velocity, fps: | 2910 | 2617 | 2342 | 2083 | 1843 |
| | energy, ft-lb: | 2820 | 2281 | 1827 | 1445 | 1131 |
| | arc, inches: | | +2.1 | 0 | -8.5 | -25.0 |
| Hornady 150 SP LM | velocity, fps: | 3100 | 2815 | 2548 | 2295 | 2058 |
| | energy, ft-lb: | 3200 | 2639 | 2161 | 1755 | 1410 |
| | arc, inches: | | +1.4 | 0 | -6.8 | -20.3 |
| Hornady 150 SP boat-tail | velocity, fps: | 2910 | 2683 | 2467 | 2262 | 2066 |
| | energy, ft-lb: | 2820 | 2397 | 2027 | 1706 | 1421 |
| | arc, inches: | | +2.0 | 0 | -7.7 | -22.2 |

| CARTRIDGE BULLET | RANGE, YARDS: | 0 | 100 | 200 | 300 | 400 |
|---|---|---|---|---|---|---|
| Hornady 165 SP boat-tail | velocity, fps: | 2800 | 2591 | 2392 | 2202 | 2020 |
| | energy, ft-lb: | 2873 | 2460 | 2097 | 1777 | 1495 |
| | arc, inches: | | +1.8 | 0 | -8.0 | -23.3 |
| Hornady 165 SPBT LM | velocity, fps: | 3015 | 2790 | 2575 | 2370 | 2176 |
| | energy, ft-lb: | 3330 | 2850 | 2428 | 2058 | 1734 |
| | arc, inches: | | +1.6 | 0 | -7.0 | -20.1 |
| Hornady 168 HPBT Match | velocity, fps: | 2790 | 2620 | 2447 | 2280 | 2120 |
| | energy, ft-lb: | 2925 | 2561 | 2234 | 1940 | 1677 |
| | arc, inches: | | +1.7 | 0 | -7.7 | -22.2 |
| Hornady 180 SP | velocity, fps: | 2700 | 2469 | 2258 | 2042 | 1846 |
| | energy, ft-lb: | 2913 | 2436 | 2023 | 1666 | 1362 |
| | arc, inches: | | +2.4 | 0 | -9.3 | -27.0 |
| Hornady 180 SPBT LM | velocity, fps: | 2880 | 2676 | 2480 | 2293 | 2114 |
| | energy, ft-lb: | 3316 | 2862 | 2459 | 2102 | 1786 |
| | arc, inches: | | +1.7 | 0 | -7.3 | -21.3 |
| Norma 150 Soft Point | velocity, fps: | 2972 | 2640 | 2331 | 2043 | |
| | energy, ft-lb: | 2943 | 2321 | 1810 | 1390 | |
| | arc, inches: | | +1.8 | 0 | -8.2 | |
| Norma 180 Alaska | velocity, fps: | 2700 | 2351 | 2028 | 1734 | |
| | energy, ft-lb: | 2914 | 2209 | 1645 | 1202 | |
| | arc, inches: | | +2.4 | 0 | -11.0 | |
| Norma 180 Nosler Partition | velocity, fps: | 2700 | 2494 | 2297 | 2108 | |
| | energy, ft-lb: | 2914 | 2486 | 2108 | 1777 | |
| | arc, inches: | | +2.1 | 0 | -8.7 | |
| Norma 180 Plastic Point | velocity, fps: | 2700 | 2455 | 2222 | 2003 | |
| | energy, ft-lb: | 2914 | 2409 | 1974 | 1603 | |
| | arc, inches: | | +2.1 | 0 | -9.2 | |
| Norma 180 Vulkan | velocity, fps: | 2700 | 2416 | 2150 | 1901 | |
| | energy, ft-lb: | 2914 | 2334 | 1848 | 1445 | |
| | arc, inches: | | +2.2 | 0 | -9.8 | |
| Norma 180 Oryx | velocity, fps: | 2700 | 2387 | 2095 | 1825 | |
| | energy, ft-lb: | 2914 | 2278 | 1755 | 1332 | |
| | arc, inches: | | +2.3 | 0 | -10.2 | |
| Norma 180 TXP Swift A-Fr. | velocity, fps: | 2700 | 2479 | 2268 | 2067 | |
| | energy, ft-lb: | 2914 | 2456 | 2056 | 1708 | |
| | arc, inches: | | +2.0 | 0 | -8.8 | |
| Norma 200 Vulkan | velocity, fps: | 2641 | 2385 | 2143 | 1916 | |
| | energy, ft-lb: | 3098 | 2527 | 2040 | 1631 | |
| | arc, inches: | | +2.3 | 0 | -9.9 | |
| Norma 200 Oryx | velocity, fps: | 2625 | 2362 | 2115 | 1883 | |
| | energy, ft-lb: | 3061 | 2479 | 1987 | 1575 | |
| | arc, inches: | | +2.3 | 0 | -10.1 | |
| PMC 150 X-Bullet | velocity, fps: | 2750 | 2552 | 2361 | 2179 | 2005 |
| | energy, ft-lb: | 2518 | 2168 | 1857 | 1582 | 1339 |
| | arc, inches: | | +2.0 | 0 | -8.2 | -23.7 |
| PMC 150 Pointed Soft Point | velocity, fps: | 2773 | 2542 | 2322 | 2113 | 1916 |
| | energy, ft-lb: | 2560 | 2152 | 1796 | 1487 | 1222 |
| | arc, inches: | | +1.9 | 0 | -8.4 | -24.6 |
| PMC 150 SP boat-tail | velocity, fps: | 2900 | 2657 | 2427 | 2208 | 2000 |
| | energy, ft-lb: | 2801 | 2351 | 1961 | 1623 | 1332 |
| | arc, inches: | | +1.7 | 0 | -7.7 | -22.5 |
| PMC 150 FMJ | velocity, fps: | 2773 | 2542 | 2322 | 2113 | 1916 |
| | energy, ft-lb: | 2560 | 2152 | 1796 | 1487 | 1222 |
| | arc, inches: | | +1.9 | 0 | -8.4 | -24.6 |
| PMC 165 Barnes X | velocity, fps: | 2750 | 2569 | 2395 | 2228 | 2067 |
| | energy, ft-lb: | 2770 | 2418 | 2101 | 1818 | 1565 |
| | arc, inches: | | +1.9 | 0 | -8.0 | -23.0 |
| PMC 180 Barnes X | velocity, fps: | 2650 | 2487 | 2331 | 2179 | 2034 |
| | energy, ft-lb: | 2806 | 2472 | 2171 | 1898 | 1652 |
| | arc, inches: | | +2.1 | 0 | -8.5 | -24.3 |
| PMC 180 Pointed Soft Point | velocity, fps: | 2550 | 2357 | 2172 | 1996 | 1829 |
| | energy, ft-lb: | 2598 | 2220 | 1886 | 1592 | 1336 |
| | arc, inches: | | +2.4 | 0 | -9.7 | -28.2 |
| PMC 180 SP boat-tail | velocity, fps: | 2700 | 2523 | 2352 | 2188 | 2030 |
| | energy, ft-lb: | 2913 | 2543 | 2210 | 1913 | 1646 |
| | arc, inches: | | +2.0 | 0 | -8.3 | -23.9 |
| Rem. 55 PSP (sabot) "Accelerator" | velocity, fps: | 4080 | 3484 | 2964 | 2499 | 2080 |
| | energy, ft-lb: | 2033 | 1482 | 1073 | 763 | 528 |
| | arc, inches: | | +1.4 | +1.4 | -2.6 | -12.2 |

| Cartridge / Bullet | Range, Yards: | 0 | 100 | 200 | 300 | 400 |
|---|---|---|---|---|---|---|
| Rem. 125 Pointed Soft Point | velocity, fps: | 3140 | 2780 | 2447 | 2138 | 1853 |
| | energy, ft-lb: | 2736 | 2145 | 1662 | 1269 | 953 |
| | arc, inches: | | +1.5 | 0 | –7.4 | -22.4 |
| Rem. 150 PSP Core-Lokt | velocity, fps: | 2910 | 2617 | 2342 | 2083 | 1843 |
| | energy, ft-lb: | 2820 | 2281 | 1827 | 1445 | 1131 |
| | arc, inches: | | +1.8 | 0 | -8.2 | -24.4 |
| Rem. 150 Bronze Point | velocity, fps: | 2910 | 2656 | 2416 | 2189 | 1974 |
| | energy, ft-lb: | 2820 | 2349 | 1944 | 1596 | 1298 |
| | arc, inches: | | +1.7 | 0 | -7.7 | -22.7 |
| Rem. 150 Nosler Bal. Tip | velocity, fps: | 2910 | 2696 | 2492 | 2298 | 2112 |
| | energy, ft-lb: | 2821 | 2422 | 2070 | 1769 | 1485 |
| | arc, inches: | | +1.6 | 0 | -7.3 | -21.1 |
| Rem. 165 PSP Core-Lokt | velocity, fps: | 2800 | 2534 | 2283 | 2047 | 1825 |
| | energy, ft-lb: | 2872 | 2352 | 1909 | 1534 | 1220 |
| | arc, inches: | | +2.0 | 0 | -8.7 | -25.9 |
| Rem. 165 PSP boat-tail | velocity, fps: | 2800 | 2592 | 2394 | 2204 | 2023 |
| | energy, ft-lb: | 2872 | 2462 | 2100 | 1780 | 1500 |
| | arc, inches: | | +1.8 | 0 | -7.9 | -23.0 |
| Rem. 165 Nosler Bal. Tip | velocity, fps: | 2800 | 2609 | 2426 | 2249 | 2080 |
| | energy, ft-lb: | 2873 | 2494 | 2155 | 1854 | 1588 |
| | arc, inches: | | +1.8 | 0 | -7.7 | -22.3 |
| Rem. 180 SP Core-Lokt | velocity, fps: | 2700 | 2348 | 2023 | 1727 | 1466 |
| | energy, ft-lb: | 2913 | 2203 | 1635 | 1192 | 859 |
| | arc, inches: | | +2.4 | 0 | -11.0 | -33.8 |
| Rem. 180 PSP Core-Lokt | velocity, fps: | 2700 | 2469 | 2250 | 2042 | 1846 |
| | energy, ft-lb: | 2913 | 2436 | 2023 | 1666 | 1362 |
| | arc, inches: | | +2.1 | 0 | -9.0 | -26.3 |
| Rem. 180 Bronze Point | velocity, fps: | 2700 | 2485 | 2280 | 2084 | 1899 |
| | energy, ft-lb: | 2913 | 2468 | 2077 | 1736 | 1441 |
| | arc, inches: | | +2.1 | 0 | -8.8 | -25.5 |
| Rem. 180 Swift A-Frame | velocity, fps: | 2700 | 2465 | 2243 | 2032 | 1833 |
| | energy, ft-lb: | 2913 | 2429 | 2010 | 1650 | 1343 |
| | arc, inches: | | +2.1 | 0 | -9.1 | -26.6 |
| Rem. 180 Nosler Partition | velocity, fps: | 2700 | 2512 | 2332 | 2160 | 1995 |
| | energy, ft-lb: | 2913 | 2522 | 2174 | 1864 | 1590 |
| | arc, inches: | | +2.0 | 0 | -8.4 | -24.3 |
| Rem. 220 SP Core-Lokt | velocity, fps: | 2410 | 2130 | 1870 | 1632 | 1422 |
| | energy, ft-lb: | 2837 | 2216 | 1708 | 1301 | 988 |
| | arc, inches, s: | 0 | | -6.2 | | -22.4 |
| Speer 150 Grand Slam | velocity, fps: | 2975 | 2669 | 2383 | 2114 | |
| | energy, ft-lb: | 2947 | 2372 | 1891 | 1489 | |
| | arc, inches: | | +2.0 | 0 | -8.1 | -24.1 |
| Speer 165 Grand Slam | velocity, fps: | 2790 | 2560 | 2342 | 2134 | |
| | energy, ft-lb: | 2851 | 2401 | 2009 | 1669 | |
| | arc, inches: | | +1.9 | 0 | -8.3 | -24.1 |
| Speer 180 Grand Slam | velocity, fps: | 2690 | 2487 | 2293 | 2108 | |
| | energy, ft-lb: | 2892 | 2472 | 2101 | 1775 | |
| | arc, inches: | | +2.1 | 0 | -8.8 | -25.1 |
| Win. 125 Pointed Soft Point | velocity, fps: | 3140 | 2780 | 2447 | 2138 | 1853 |
| | energy, ft-lb: | 2736 | 2145 | 1662 | 1269 | 953 |
| | arc, inches: | | +1.8 | 0 | -7.7 | -23.0 |
| Win. 150 Power-Point | velocity, fps: | 2920 | 2580 | 2265 | 1972 | 1704 |
| | energy, ft-lb: | 2839 | 2217 | 1708 | 1295 | 967 |
| | arc, inches: | | +2.2 | 0 | -9.0 | -27.0 |
| Win. 150 Power-Point Plus | velocity, fps: | 3050 | 2685 | 2352 | 2043 | 1760 |
| | energy, ft-lb: | 3089 | 2402 | 1843 | 1391 | 1032 |
| | arc, inches: | | +1.7 | 0 | -8.0 | -24.3 |
| Win. 150 Silvertip | velocity, fps: | 2910 | 2617 | 2342 | 2083 | 1843 |
| | energy, ft-lb: | 2820 | 2281 | 1827 | 1445 | 1131 |
| | arc, inches: | | +2.1 | 0 | -8.5 | -25.0 |
| Win. 150 Partition Gold | velocity, fps: | 2960 | 2705 | 2464 | 2235 | 2019 |
| | energy, ft-lb: | 2919 | 2437 | 2022 | 1664 | 1358 |
| | arc, inches: | | +1.6 | 0 | -7.4 | -21.7 |
| Win. 150 Ballistic Silvertip | velocity, fps: | 2900 | 2687 | 2483 | 2289 | 2103 |
| | energy, ft-lb: | 2801 | 2404 | 2054 | 1745 | 1473 |
| | arc, inches: | | +1.7 | 0 | -7.3 | -21.2 |
| Win. 150 Fail Safe | velocity, fps: | 2920 | 2625 | 2349 | 2089 | 1848 |
| | energy, ft-lb: | 2841 | 2296 | 1838 | 1455 | 1137 |
| | arc, inches: | | +1.8 | 0 | -8.1 | -24.3 |

| Cartridge / Bullet | Range, Yards: | 0 | 100 | 200 | 300 | 400 |
|---|---|---|---|---|---|---|
| Win. 165 Pointed Soft Point | velocity, fps: | 2800 | 2573 | 2357 | 2151 | 1956 |
| | energy, ft-lb: | 2873 | 2426 | 2036 | 1696 | 1402 |
| | arc, inches: | | +2.2 | 0 | -8.4 | -24.4 |
| Win. 165 Fail Safe | velocity, fps: | 2800 | 2540 | 2295 | 2063 | 1846 |
| | energy, ft-lb: | 2873 | 2365 | 1930 | 1560 | 1249 |
| | arc, inches: | | +2.0 | 0 | -8.6 | -25.3 |
| Win. 168 Ballistic Silvertip | velocity, fps: | 2790 | 2599 | 2416 | 2240 | 2072 |
| | energy, ft-lb: | 2903 | 2520 | 2177 | 1872 | 1601 |
| | arc, inches: | | +1.8 | 0 | -7.8 | -22.5 |
| Win. 180 Power-Point | velocity, fps: | 2700 | 2348 | 2023 | 1727 | 1466 |
| | energy, ft-lb: | 2913 | 2203 | 1635 | 1192 | 859 |
| | arc, inches: | | +2.7 | 0 | -11.3 | -34.4 |
| Win. 180 Power-Point Plus | velocity, fps: | 2770 | 2563 | 2366 | 2177 | 1997 |
| | energy, ft-lb: | 3068 | 2627 | 2237 | 1894 | 1594 |
| | arc, inches: | | +1.9 | 0 | -8.1 | -23.6 |
| Win. 180 Silvertip | velocity, fps: | 2700 | 2469 | 2250 | 2042 | 1846 |
| | energy, ft-lb: | 2913 | 2436 | 2023 | 1666 | 1362 |
| | arc, inches: | | +2.4 | 0 | -9.3 | -27.0 |
| Win. 180 Partition Gold | velocity, fps: | 2790 | 2581 | 2382 | 2192 | 2010 |
| | energy, ft-lb: | 3112 | 2664 | 2269 | 1920 | 1615 |
| | arc, inches: | | +1.9 | 0 | -8.0 | -23.2 |
| Win. 180 Fail Safe | velocity, fps: | 2700 | 2486 | 2283 | 2089 | 1904 |
| | energy, ft-lb: | 2914 | 2472 | 2083 | 1744 | 1450 |
| | arc, inches: | | +2.1 | 0 | -8.7 | -25.5 |

## .300 H&H Mag.

| Cartridge / Bullet | Range, Yards: | 0 | 100 | 200 | 300 | 400 |
|---|---|---|---|---|---|---|
| Federal 180 Nosler Partition | velocity, fps: | 2880 | 2620 | 2380 | 2150 | 1930 |
| | energy, ft-lb: | 3315 | 2750 | 2260 | 1840 | 1480 |
| | arc, inches: | | +1.8 | 0 | -8.0 | -23.4 |
| Win. 180 Fail Safe | velocity, fps: | 2880 | 2628 | 2390 | 2165 | 1952 |
| | energy, ft-lb: | 3316 | 2762 | 2284 | 1873 | 1523 |
| | arc, inches: | | +1.8 | 0 | -7.9 | -23.2 |

## .308 Norma Mag.

| Cartridge / Bullet | Range, Yards: | 0 | 100 | 200 | 300 | 400 |
|---|---|---|---|---|---|---|
| Norma 200 Vulkan | velocity, fps: | 2903 | 2624 | 2361 | 2114 | |
| | energy, ft-lb: | 3744 | 3058 | 2476 | 1985 | |
| | arc, inches: | 0 | +1.8 | 0 | -8.0 | |

## .300 Winchester Mag.

| Cartridge / Bullet | Range, Yards: | 0 | 100 | 200 | 300 | 400 |
|---|---|---|---|---|---|---|
| A-Square 180 Dead Tough | velocity, fps: | 3120 | 2756 | 2420 | 2108 | 1820 |
| | energy, ft-lb: | 3890 | 3035 | 2340 | 1776 | 1324 |
| | arc, inches: | | +1.6 | 0 | -7.6 | -22.9 |
| Federal 150 Sierra Pro Hunt. | velocity, fps: | 3280 | 3030 | 2800 | 2570 | 2360 |
| | energy, ft-lb: | 3570 | 3055 | 2600 | 2205 | 1860 |
| | arc, inches: | | +1.1 | 0 | -5.6 | -16.4 |
| Federal 150 Trophy Bonded | velocity, fps: | 3280 | 2980 | 2700 | 2430 | 2190 |
| | energy, ft-lb: | 3570 | 2450 | 2420 | 1970 | 1590 |
| | arc, inches: | | +1.2 | 0 | -6.0 | -17.9 |
| Federal 180 Sierra Pro Hunt. | velocity, fps: | 2960 | 2750 | 2540 | 2340 | 2160 |
| | energy, ft-lb: | 3500 | 3010 | 2580 | 2195 | 1860 |
| | arc, inches: | | +1.6 | 0 | -7.0 | -20.3 |
| Federal 180 Barnes XLC | velocity, fps: | 2960 | 2780 | 2600 | 2430 | 2260 |
| | energy, ft-lb: | 3500 | 3080 | 2700 | 2355 | 2050 |
| | arc, inches: | | +1.5 | 0 | -6.6 | -19.2 |
| Federal 180 Trophy Bonded | velocity, fps: | 2960 | 2700 | 2460 | 2220 | 2000 |
| | energy, ft-lb: | 3500 | 2915 | 2410 | 1975 | 1605 |
| | arc, inches: | | +1.6 | 0 | -7.4 | -21.9 |
| Federal 180 Tr. Bonded HE | velocity, fps: | 3100 | 2830 | 2580 | 2340 | 2110 |
| | energy, ft-lb: | 3840 | 3205 | 2660 | 2190 | 1790 |
| | arc, inches: | | +1.4 | 0 | -6.6 | -19.7 |
| Federal 180 Nosler Partition | velocity, fps: | 2960 | 2700 | 2450 | 2210 | 1990 |
| | energy, ft-lb: | 3500 | 2905 | 2395 | 1955 | 1585 |
| | arc, inches: | | +1.6 | 0 | -7.5 | -22.1 |
| Federal 190 Sierra MatchKg. BTHP | velocity, fps: | 2900 | 2730 | 2560 | 2400 | 2240 |
| | energy, ft-lb: | 3550 | 3135 | 2760 | 2420 | 2115 |
| | arc, inches: | | +12.9 | +22.5 | +26.9 | +25.1 |
| Federal 200 Sierra GameKing BTSP | velocity, fps: | 2830 | 2680 | 2530 | 2380 | 2240 |
| | energy, ft-lb: | 3560 | 3180 | 2830 | 2520 | 2230 |
| | arc, inches: | | +1.7 | 0 | -7.1 | -20.4 |

| CARTRIDGE BULLET | RANGE, YARDS: | 0 | 100 | 200 | 300 | 400 |
|---|---|---|---|---|---|---|
| Federal 200 Nosler Part. HE | velocity, fps: | 2930 | 2740 | 2550 | 2370 | 2200 |
| | energy, ft-lb: | 3810 | 3325 | 2885 | 2495 | 2145 |
| | arc, inches: | | +1.6 | 0 | -6.9 | -20.1 |
| Federal 200 Trophy Bonded | velocity, fps: | 2800 | 2570 | 2350 | 2150 | 1950 |
| | energy, ft-lb: | 3480 | 2935 | 2460 | 2050 | 1690 |
| | arc, inches: | | +1.9 | 0 | -8.2 | -23.9 |
| Hornady 150 SP boat-tail | velocity, fps: | 3275 | 2988 | 2718 | 2464 | 2224 |
| | energy, ft-lb: | 3573 | 2974 | 2461 | 2023 | 1648 |
| | arc, inches: | | +1.2 | 0 | -6.0 | -17.8 |
| Hornady 165 SP boat-tail | velocity, fps: | 3100 | 2877 | 2665 | 2462 | 2269 |
| | energy, ft-lb: | 3522 | 3033 | 2603 | 2221 | 1887 |
| | arc, inches: | | +1.3 | 0 | -6.5 | -18.5 |
| Hornady 180 SP boat-tail | velocity, fps: | 2960 | 2745 | 2540 | 2344 | 2157 |
| | energy, ft-lb: | 3501 | 3011 | 2578 | 2196 | 1859 |
| | arc, inches: | | +1.9 | 0 | -7.3 | -20.9 |
| Hornady 180 SPBT HM | velocity, fps: | 3100 | 2879 | 2668 | 2467 | 2275 |
| | energy, ft-lb: | 3840 | 3313 | 2845 | 2431 | 2068 |
| | arc, inches: | | +1.4 | 0 | -6.4 | -18.7 |
| Hornady 190 SP boat-tail | velocity, fps: | 2900 | 2711 | 2529 | 2355 | 2187 |
| | energy, ft-lb: | 3549 | 3101 | 2699 | 2340 | 2018 |
| | arc, inches: | | +1.6 | 0 | -7.1 | -20.4 |
| Norma 180 Soft Point | velocity, fps: | 3018 | 2780 | 2555 | 2341 | |
| | energy, ft-lb: | 3641 | 3091 | 2610 | 2190 | |
| | arc, inches: | | +1.5 | 0 | -7.0 | |
| Norma 180 Plastic Point | velocity, fps: | 3018 | 2755 | 2506 | 2271 | |
| | energy, ft-lb: | 3641 | 3034 | 2512 | 2062 | |
| | arc, inches: | | +1.6 | 0 | -7.1 | |
| Norma 180 TXP Swift A-Fr. | velocity, fps: | 2920 | 2688 | 2467 | 2256 | |
| | energy, ft-lb: | 3409 | 2888 | 2432 | 2035 | |
| | arc, inches: | | +1.7 | 0 | -7.4 | |
| Norma 200 Vulkan | velocity, fps: | 2887 | 2609 | 2347 | 2100 | |
| | energy, ft-lb: | 3702 | 3023 | 2447 | 1960 | |
| | arc, inches: | | +1.8 | 0 | -8.2 | |
| Norma 200 Oryx | velocity, fps: | 3018 | 2755 | 2506 | 2271 | |
| | energy, ft-lb: | 4046 | 3371 | 2791 | 2292 | |
| | arc, inches: | | +1.5 | 0 | -7.0 | |
| PMC 150 Barnes X | velocity, fps: | 3135 | 2918 | 2712 | 2515 | 2327 |
| | energy, ft-lb: | 3273 | 2836 | 2449 | 2107 | 1803 |
| | arc, inches: | | +1.3 | 0 | -6.1 | -17.7 |
| PMC 150 Pointed Soft Point | velocity, fps: | 3150 | 2902 | 2665 | 2438 | 2222 |
| | energy, ft-lb: | 3304 | 2804 | 2364 | 1979 | 1644 |
| | arc, inches: | | +1.3 | 0 | -6.2 | -18.3 |
| PMC 150 SP boat-tail | velocity, fps: | 3250 | 2987 | 2739 | 2504 | 2281 |
| | energy, ft-lb: | 3517 | 2970 | 2498 | 2088 | 1733 |
| | arc, inches: | | +1.2 | 0 | -6.0 | -17.4 |
| PMC 180 Barnes X | velocity, fps: | 2910 | 2738 | 2572 | 2412 | 2258 |
| | energy, ft-lb: | 3384 | 2995 | 2644 | 2325 | 2037 |
| | arc, inches: | | +1.6 | 0 | -6.9 | -19.8 |
| PMC 180 PSP | velocity, fps: | 2853 | 2643 | 2446 | 2258 | 2077 |
| | energy, ft-lb: | 3252 | 2792 | 2391 | 2037 | 1724 |
| | arc, inches: | | +1.7 | 0 | -7.5 | -21.9 |
| PMC 180 SP boat-tail | velocity, fps: | 2900 | 2714 | 2536 | 2365 | 2200 |
| | energy, ft-lb: | 3361 | 2944 | 2571 | 2235 | 1935 |
| | arc, inches: | | +1.6 | 0 | -7.1 | -20.3 |
| Rem. 150 PSP Core-Lokt | velocity, fps: | 3290 | 2951 | 2636 | 2342 | 2068 |
| | energy, ft-lb: | 3605 | 2900 | 2314 | 1827 | 1859 |
| | arc, inches: | | +1.6 | 0 | -7.0 | -20.2 |
| Rem. 180 PSP Core-Lokt | velocity, fps: | 2960 | 2745 | 2540 | 2344 | 2157 |
| | energy, ft-lb: | 3501 | 3011 | 2578 | 2196 | 1424 |
| | arc, inches: | | +2.2 | +1.9 | -3.4 | -15.0 |
| Rem. 180 Nosler Partition | velocity, fps: | 2960 | 2725 | 2503 | 2291 | 2089 |
| | energy, ft-lb: | 3501 | 2968 | 2503 | 2087 | 1744 |
| | arc, inches: | | +1.6 | 0 | -7.2 | -20.9 |
| Rem. 180 Nosler Bal. Tip | velocity, fps: | 2960 | 2774 | 2595 | 2424 | 2259 |
| | energy, ft-lb: | 3501 | 3075 | 2692 | 2348 | 2039 |
| | arc, inches: | | +1.5 | 0 | -6.7 | -19.3 |
| Rem. 190 PSP boat-tail | velocity, fps: | 2885 | 2691 | 2506 | 2327 | 2156 |
| | energy, ft-lb: | 3511 | 3055 | 2648 | 2285 | 1961 |
| | arc, inches: | | +1.6 | 0 | -7.2 | -20.8 |

| CARTRIDGE BULLET | RANGE, YARDS: | 0 | 100 | 200 | 300 | 400 |
|---|---|---|---|---|---|---|
| Rem. 200 Swift A-Frame | velocity, fps: | 2825 | 2595 | 2376 | 2167 | 1970 |
| | energy, ft-lb: | 3544 | 2989 | 2506 | 2086 | 1722 |
| | arc, inches: | | +1.8 | 0 | -8.0 | -23.5 |
| Speeer 180 Grand Slam | velocity, fps: | 2950 | 2735 | 2530 | 2334 | |
| | energy, ft-lb: | 3478 | 2989 | 2558 | 2176 | |
| | arc, inches: | | +1.6 | 0 | -7.0 | -20.5 |
| Speer 200 Grand Slam | velocity, fps: | 2800 | 2597 | 2404 | 2218 | |
| | energy, ft-lb: | 3481 | 2996 | 2565 | 2185 | |
| | arc, inches: | | +1.8 | 0 | -7.9 | -22.9 |
| Win. 150 Power-Point | velocity, fps: | 3290 | 2951 | 2636 | 2342 | 2068 |
| | energy, ft-lb: | 3605 | 2900 | 2314 | 1827 | 1424 |
| | arc, inches: | | +2.6 | +2.1 | -3.5 | -15.4 |
| Win. 150 Fail Safe | velocity, fps: | 3260 | 2943 | 2647 | 2370 | 2110 |
| | energy, ft-lb: | 3539 | 2884 | 2334 | 1871 | 1483 |
| | arc, inches: | | +1.3 | 0 | -6.2 | -18.7 |
| Win. 165 Fail Safe | velocity, fps: | 3120 | 2807 | 2515 | 2242 | 1985 |
| | energy, ft-lb: | 3567 | 2888 | 2319 | 1842 | 1445 |
| | arc, inches: | | +1.5 | 0 | -7.0 | -20.0 |
| Win. 180 Power-Point | velocity, fps: | 2960 | 2745 | 2540 | 2344 | 2157 |
| | energy, ft-lb: | 3501 | 3011 | 2578 | 2196 | 1859 |
| | arc, inches: | | +1.9 | 0 | -7.3 | -20.9 |
| Win. 180 Power-Point Plus | velocity, fps: | 3070 | 2846 | 2633 | 2430 | 2236 |
| | energy, ft-lb: | 3768 | 3239 | 2772 | 2361 | 1999 |
| | arc, inches: | | +1.4 | 0 | -6.4 | -18.7 |
| Win. 180 Ballistic Silvertip | velocity, fps: | 2950 | 2764 | 2586 | 2415 | 2250 |
| | energy, ft-lb: | 3478 | 3054 | 2673 | 2331 | 2023 |
| | arc, inches: | | +1.5 | 0 | -6.7 | -19.4 |
| Win. 180 Fail Safe | velocity, fps: | 2960 | 2732 | 2514 | 2307 | 2110 |
| | energy, ft-lb: | 3503 | 2983 | 2528 | 2129 | 1780 |
| | arc, inches: | | +1.6 | 0 | -7.1 | -20.7 |
| Win. 180 Partition Gold | velocity, fps: | 3070 | 2859 | 2657 | 2464 | 2280 |
| | energy, ft-lb: | 3768 | 3267 | 2823 | 2428 | 2078 |
| | arc, inches: | | +1.4 | 0 | -6.3 | -18.3 |

## .300 Weatherby Mag.

| CARTRIDGE BULLET | RANGE, YARDS: | 0 | 100 | 200 | 300 | 400 |
|---|---|---|---|---|---|---|
| A-Square 180 Dead Tough | velocity, fps: | 3180 | 2811 | 2471 | 2155 | 1863 |
| | energy, ft-lb: | 4041 | 3158 | 2440 | 1856 | 1387 |
| | arc, inches: | | +1.5 | 0 | -7.2 | -21.8 |
| A-Square 220 Monolythic Solid | velocity, fps: | 2700 | 2407 | 2133 | 1877 | 1653 |
| | energy, ft-lb: | 3561 | 2830 | 2223 | 1721 | 1334 |
| | arc, inches: | | +2.3 | 0 | -9.8 | -29.7 |
| Federal 180 Sierra GameKing BTSP | velocity, fps: | 3190 | 3010 | 2830 | 2660 | 2490 |
| | energy, ft-lb: | 4065 | 3610 | 3195 | 2820 | 2480 |
| | arc, inches: | | +1.2 | 0 | -5.6 | -16.0 |
| Federal 180 Trophy Bonded | velocity, fps: | 3190 | 2950 | 2720 | 2500 | 2290 |
| | energy, ft-lb: | 4065 | 3475 | 2955 | 2500 | 2105 |
| | arc, inches: | | +1.3 | 0 | -5.9 | -17.5 |
| Federal 180 Tr. Bonded HE | velocity, fps: | 3330 | 3080 | 2850 | 2750 | 2410 |
| | energy, ft-lb: | 4430 | 3795 | 3235 | 2750 | 2320 |
| | arc, inches: | | +1.1 | 0 | -5.4 | -15.8 |
| Federal 180 Nosler Partition | velocity, fps: | 3190 | 2980 | 2780 | 2590 | 2400 |
| | energy, ft-lb: | 4055 | 3540 | 3080 | 2670 | 2305 |
| | arc, inches: | | +1.2 | 0 | -5.7 | -16.7 |
| Federal 180 Nosler Part. HE | velocity, fps: | 3330 | 3110 | 2810 | 2710 | 2520 |
| | energy, ft-lb: | 4430 | 3875 | 3375 | 2935 | 2540 |
| | arc, inches: | | +1.0 | 0 | -5.2 | -15.1 |
| Federal 200 Trophy Bonded | velocity, fps: | 2900 | 2670 | 2440 | 2230 | 2030 |
| | energy, ft-lb: | 3735 | 3150 | 2645 | 2200 | 1820 |
| | arc, inches: | | +1.7 | 0 | -7.6 | -22.2 |
| Hornady 180 SP | velocity, fps: | 3120 | 2891 | 2673 | 2466 | 2268 |
| | energy, ft-lb: | 3890 | 3340 | 2856 | 2430 | 2055 |
| | arc, inches: | | +1.3 | 0 | -6.2 | -18.1 |
| Rem. 180 PSP Core-Lokt | velocity, fps: | 3120 | 2866 | 2627 | 2400 | 2184 |
| | energy, ft-lb: | 3890 | 3284 | 2758 | 2301 | 1905 |
| | arc, inches: | | +2.4 | +2.0 | -3.4 | -14.9 |
| Rem. 190 PSP boat-tail | velocity, fps: | 3030 | 2830 | 2638 | 2455 | 2279 |
| | energy, ft-lb: | 3873 | 3378 | 2936 | 2542 | 2190 |
| | arc, inches: | | +1.4 | 0 | -6.4 | -18.6 |

| CARTRIDGE BULLET | RANGE, YARDS: | 0 | 100 | 200 | 300 | 400 |
|---|---|---|---|---|---|---|
| Rem. 200 Swift A-Frame | velocity, fps: | 2925 | 2690 | 2467 | 2254 | 2052 |
| | energy, ft-lb: | 3799 | 3213 | 2701 | 2256 | 1870 |
| | arc, inches: | | +2.8 | +2.3 | -3.9 | -17.0 |
| Speer 180 Grand Slam | velocity, fps: | 3185 | 2948 | 2722 | 2508 | |
| | energy, ft-lb: | 4054 | 3472 | 2962 | 2514 | |
| | arc, inches: | | +1.3 | 0 | -5.9 | -17.4 |
| Wby. 150 Pointed Expanding | velocity, fps: | 3540 | 3225 | 2932 | 2657 | 2399 |
| | energy, ft-lb: | 4173 | 3462 | 2862 | 2351 | 1916 |
| | arc, inches: | | +2.6 | +3.3 | 0 | -8.2 |
| Wby. 150 Nosler Partition | velocity, fps: | 3540 | 3263 | 3004 | 2759 | 2528 |
| | energy, ft-lb: | 4173 | 3547 | 3005 | 2536 | 2128 |
| | arc, inches: | | +2.5 | +3.2 | 0 | -7.7 |
| Wby. 165 Pointed Expanding | velocity, fps: | 3390 | 3123 | 2872 | 2634 | 2409 |
| | energy, ft-lb: | 4210 | 3573 | 3021 | 2542 | 2126 |
| | arc, inches: | | +2.8 | +3.5 | 0 | -8.5 |
| Wby. 165 Nosler Bal. Tip | velocity, fps: | 3350 | 3133 | 2927 | 2730 | 2542 |
| | energy, ft-lb: | 4111 | 3596 | 3138 | 2730 | 2367 |
| | arc, inches: | | +2.7 | +3.4 | 0 | -8.1 |
| Wby. 180 Pointed Expanding | velocity, fps: | 3240 | 3004 | 2781 | 2569 | 2366 |
| | energy, ft-lb: | 4195 | 3607 | 3091 | 2637 | 2237 |
| | arc, inches: | | +3.1 | +3.8 | 0 | -9.0 |
| Wby. 180 Barnes X | velocity, fps: | 3190 | 2995 | 2809 | 2631 | 2459 |
| | energy, ft-lb: | 4067 | 3586 | 3154 | 2766 | 2417 |
| | arc, inches: | | +3.1 | +3.8 | 0 | -8.7 |
| Wby. 180 Nosler Partition | velocity, fps: | 3240 | 3028 | 2826 | 2634 | 2449 |
| | energy, ft-lb: | 4195 | 3665 | 3193 | 2772 | 2396 |
| | arc, inches: | | +3.0 | +3.7 | 0 | -8.6 |
| Wby. 200 Nosler Partition | velocity, fps: | 3060 | 2860 | 2668 | 2485 | 2308 |
| | energy, ft-lb: | 4158 | 3631 | 3161 | 2741 | 2366 |
| | arc, inches: | | +3.5 | +4.2 | 0 | -9.8 |
| Wby. 220 RN Expanding | velocity, fps: | 2845 | 2543 | 2260 | 1996 | 1751 |
| | energy, ft-lb: | 3954 | 3158 | 2495 | 1946 | 1497 |
| | arc, inches: | | +4.9 | +5.9 | 0 | -14.6 |

## .300 Dakota

| | | | | | | |
|---|---|---|---|---|---|---|
| Dakota 165 Barnes X | velocity, fps: | 3200 | 2979 | 2769 | 2569 | 2377 |
| | energy, ft-lb: | 3751 | 3251 | 2809 | 2417 | 2070 |
| | arc, inches: | | +2.1 | +1.8 | -3.0 | -13.2 |
| Dakota 200 Barnes X | velocity, fps: | 3000 | 2824 | 2656 | 2493 | 2336 |
| | energy, ft-lb: | 3996 | 3542 | 3131 | 2760 | 2423 |
| | arc, inches: | | +2.2 | +1.5 | -4.0 | -15.2 |

## .300 Pegasus

| | | | | | | |
|---|---|---|---|---|---|---|
| A-Square 180 SP boat-tail | velocity, fps: | 3500 | 3319 | 3145 | 2978 | 2817 |
| | energy, ft-lb: | 4896 | 4401 | 3953 | 3544 | 3172 |
| | arc, inches: | | +2.3 | +2.9 | 0 | -6.8 |
| A-Square 180 Nosler Part. | velocity, fps: | 3500 | 3295 | 3100 | 2913 | 2734 |
| | energy, ft-lb: | 4896 | 4339 | 3840 | 3392 | 2988 |
| | arc, inches: | | +2.3 | +3.0 | 0 | -7.1 |
| A-Square 180 Dead Tough | velocity, fps: | 3500 | 3103 | 2740 | 2405 | 2095 |
| | energy, ft-lb: | 4896 | 3848 | 3001 | 2312 | 1753 |
| | arc, inches: | | +1.1 | 0 | -5.7 | -17.5 |

## .300 Remington Ultra Mag

| | | | | | | |
|---|---|---|---|---|---|---|
| Federal 180 Trophy Bonded | velocity, fps: | 3250 | 3000 | 2770 | 2550 | 2340 |
| | Energy, ft-lb: | 4220 | 3605 | 3065 | 2590 | 2180 |
| | Arc, inches: | | +1.2 | 0 | -5.7 | -16.8 |
| Rem. 180 Nosler Partition | velocity, fps: | 3250 | 3037 | 2834 | 2640 | 2454 |
| | energy, ft-lb: | 4221 | 3686 | 3201 | 2786 | 2407 |
| | arc, inches: | | +2.4 | +1.8 | -3.0 | -12.7 |
| Rem. 180 Swift Scirocco | velocity, fps: | 3250 | 3048 | 2856 | 2672 | 2495 |
| | energy, ft-lb: | 4221 | 3714 | 3260 | 2853 | 2487 |
| | arc, inches: | | +2.0 | +1.7 | -2.8 | -12.3 |
| Rem. 200 Nosler Partition | velocity, fps: | 3025 | 2826 | 2636 | 2454 | 2279 |
| | energy, ft-lb: | 4063 | 3547 | 3086 | 2673 | 2308 |
| | arc, inches: | | +2.4 | +2.0 | -3.4 | -14.6 |

| CARTRIDGE BULLET | RANGE, YARDS: | 0 | 100 | 200 | 300 | 400 |
|---|---|---|---|---|---|---|

## .30-378 Weatherby Mag.

| | | | | | | |
|---|---|---|---|---|---|---|
| Wby. 165 Nosler Bal. Tip | velocity, fps: | 3500 | 3275 | 3062 | 2859 | 2665 |
| | energy, ft-lb: | 4488 | 3930 | 3435 | 2995 | 2603 |
| | arc, inches: | | +2.4 | +3.0 | 0 | -7.4 |
| Wby. 180 Barnes X | velocity, fps: | 3450 | 3243 | 3046 | 2858 | 2678 |
| | energy, ft-lb: | 4757 | 4204 | 3709 | 3264 | 2865 |
| | arc, inches: | | +2.4 | +3.1 | 0 | -7.4 |
| Wby. 200 Nosler Partition | velocity, fps: | 3160 | 2955 | 2759 | 2572 | 2392 |
| | energy, ft-lb: | 4434 | 3877 | 3381 | 2938 | 2541 |
| | arc, inches: | | +3.2 | +3.9 | 0 | -9.1 |

## 7.82 (.308) Warbird

| | | | | | | |
|---|---|---|---|---|---|---|
| Lazzeroni 150 Nosler Part. | velocity, fps: | 3680 | 3432 | 3197 | 2975 | 2764 |
| | energy, ft-lb: | 4512 | 3923 | 3406 | 2949 | 2546 |
| | arc, inches: | | +2.1 | +2.7 | 0 | -6.6 |
| Lazzeroni 180 Nosler Part. | velocity, fps: | 3425 | 3220 | 3026 | 2839 | 2661 |
| | energy, ft-lb: | 4689 | 4147 | 3661 | 3224 | 2831 |
| | arc, inches: | | +2.5 | +3.2 | 0 | -7.5 |
| Lazzeroni 200 Swift A-Fr. | velocity, fps: | 3290 | 3105 | 2928 | 2758 | 2594 |
| | energy, ft-lb: | 4808 | 4283 | 3808 | 3378 | 2988 |
| | arc, inches: | | +2.7 | +3.4 | 0 | -7.9 |

## 7.65x53 Argentine

| | | | | | | |
|---|---|---|---|---|---|---|
| Norma 180 Soft Point | velocity, fps: | 2592 | 2386 | 2189 | 2002 | |
| | energy, ft-lb: | 2686 | 2276 | 1916 | 1602 | |
| | arc, inches: | | +2.3 | 0 | -9.6 | |

## .303 British

| | | | | | | |
|---|---|---|---|---|---|---|
| Federal 150 Hi-Shok | velocity, fps: | 2690 | 2440 | 2210 | 1980 | 1780 |
| | energy, ft-lb: | 2400 | 1980 | 1620 | 1310 | 1055 |
| | arc, inches: | | +2.2 | 0 | -9.4 | -27.6 |
| Federal 180 Sierra Pro-Hunt. | velocity, fps: | 2460 | 2230 | 2020 | 1820 | 1630 |
| | energy, ft-lb: | 2420 | 1995 | 1625 | 1315 | 1060 |
| | arc, inches: | | +2.8 | 0 | -11.3 | -33.2 |
| Federal 180 Tr. Bonded HE | velocity, fps: | 2590 | 2350 | 2120 | 1900 | 1700 |
| | energy, ft-lb: | 2680 | 2205 | 1795 | 1445 | 1160 |
| | arc, inches: | | +2.4 | 0 | -10.0 | -30.0 |
| Hornady 150 Soft Point | velocity, fps: | 2685 | 2441 | 2210 | 1992 | 1787 |
| | energy, ft-lb: | 2401 | 1984 | 1627 | 1321 | 1064 |
| | arc, inches: | | +2.2 | 0 | -9.3 | -27.4 |
| Hornady 150 SP LM | velocity, fps: | 2830 | 2570 | 2325 | 2094 | 1884 |
| | energy, ft-lb: | 2667 | 2199 | 1800 | 1461 | 1184 |
| | arc, inches: | | +2.0 | 0 | -8.4 | -24.6 |
| Norma 150 Soft Point | velocity, fps: | 2723 | 2438 | 2170 | 1920 | |
| | energy, ft-lb: | 2470 | 1980 | 1569 | 1228 | |
| | arc, inches: | | +2.2 | 0 | -9.6 | |
| PMC 180 SP boat-tail | velocity, fps: | 2450 | 2276 | 2110 | 1951 | 1799 |
| | energy, ft-lb: | 2399 | 2071 | 1779 | 1521 | 1294 |
| | arc, inches: | | +2.6 | 0 | -10.4 | -30.1 |
| Rem. 180 SP Core-Lokt | velocity, fps: | 2460 | 2124 | 1817 | 1542 | 1311 |
| | energy, ft-lb: | 2418 | 1803 | 1319 | 950 | 687 |
| | arc, inches, s: | | 0 | -5.8 | -23.3 | |
| Win. 180 Power-Point | velocity, fps: | 2460 | 2233 | 2018 | 1816 | 1629 |
| | energy, ft-lb: | 2418 | 1993 | 1627 | 1318 | 1060 |
| | arc, inches, s: | | 0 | -6.1 | -20.8 | |

## 7.7x58 Japanese Arisaka

| | | | | | | |
|---|---|---|---|---|---|---|
| Norma 180 Soft Point | velocity, fps: | 2493 | 2291 | 2099 | 1916 | |
| | energy, ft-lb: | 2485 | 2099 | 1761 | 1468 | |
| | arc, inches: | | +2.6 | 0 | -10.5 | |

## .32-20 Winchester

| | | | | | | |
|---|---|---|---|---|---|---|
| Rem. 100 Lead | velocity, fps: | 1210 | 1021 | 913 | 834 | 769 |
| | energy, ft-lb: | 325 | 231 | 185 | 154 | 131 |
| | arc, inches: | | 0 | -31.6 | -104.7 | |
| Win. 100 Lead | velocity, fps: | 1210 | 1021 | 913 | 834 | 769 |
| | energy, ft-lb: | 325 | 231 | 185 | 154 | 131 |
| | arc, inches: | | 0 | -32.3 | -106.3 | |

| CARTRIDGE Bullet | RANGE, YARDS: | 0 | 100 | 200 | 300 | 400 |
|---|---|---|---|---|---|---|

## .32 Winchester Special

| Cartridge Bullet | | 0 | 100 | 200 | 300 | 400 |
|---|---|---|---|---|---|---|
| Federal 170 Hi-Shok | velocity, fps | 2250 | 1920 | 1630 | 1370 | 1180 |
| | energy, ft-lb | 1910 | 1395 | 1000 | 710 | 520 |
| | arc, inches | | 0 | -8.0 | -29.2 | |
| Rem. 170 SP Core-Lokt | velocity, fps | 2250 | 1921 | 1626 | 1372 | 1175 |
| | energy, ft-lb | 1911 | 1393 | 998 | 710 | 521 |
| | arc, inches | | 0 | -8.0 | -29.3 | |
| Win. 170 Power-Point | velocity, fps | 2250 | 1870 | 1537 | 1267 | 1082 |
| | energy, ft-lb | 1911 | 1320 | 892 | 606 | 442 |
| | arc, inches | | 0 | -9.2 | -33.2 | |

## 8mm Mauser (8x57)

| Cartridge Bullet | | 0 | 100 | 200 | 300 | 400 |
|---|---|---|---|---|---|---|
| Federal 170 Hi-Shok | velocity, fps | 2360 | 1970 | 1620 | 1330 | 1120 |
| | energy, ft-lb | 2100 | 1465 | 995 | 670 | 475 |
| | arc, inches | | 0 | -7.6 | -28.5 | |
| Norma 196 Alaska | velocity, fps | 2395 | 2112 | 1850 | 1611 | |
| | Energy, ft-lb | 2714 | 2190 | 1754 | 1399 | |
| | Arc, inches | | 0 | -6.3 | -22.9 | |
| Norma 196 Soft Point (JS) | velocity, fps | 2526 | 2244 | 1981 | 1737 | |
| | energy, ft-lb | 2778 | 2192 | 1708 | 1314 | |
| | arc, inches | | +2.7 | 0 | -11.6 | |
| Norma 196 Vulkan (JS) | velocity, fps | 2526 | 2276 | 2041 | 1821 | |
| | energy, ft-lb | 2778 | 2256 | 1813 | 1443 | |
| | arc, inches | | +2.6 | 0 | -11.0 | |
| PMC 170 Pointed Soft Point | velocity, fps | 2360 | 1969 | 1622 | 1333 | 1123 |
| | energy, ft-lb | 2102 | 1463 | 993 | 671 | 476 |
| | arc, inches | | +1.8 | -4.5 | -24.3 | -63.8 |
| Rem. 170 SP Core-Lokt | velocity, fps | 2360 | 1969 | 1622 | 1333 | 1123 |
| | energy, ft-lb | 2102 | 1463 | 993 | 671 | 476 |
| | arc, inches | | 0 | -7.6 | -28.6 | |
| Win. 170 Power-Point | velocity, fps | 2360 | 1969 | 1622 | 1333 | 1123 |
| | energy, ft-lb | 2102 | 1463 | 993 | 671 | 476 |
| | arc, inches | | 0 | -8.2 | -29.8 | |

## 8mm Remington Mag.

| Cartridge Bullet | | 0 | 100 | 200 | 300 | 400 |
|---|---|---|---|---|---|---|
| A-Square 220 Monolithic Solid | velocity, fps | 2800 | 2501 | 2221 | 1959 | 1718 |
| | energy, ft-lb | 3829 | 3055 | 2409 | 1875 | 1442 |
| | arc, inches | | +2.1 | 0 | -9.1 | -27.6 |
| Rem. 200 Swift A-Frame | velocity, fps | 2900 | 2623 | 2361 | 2115 | 1885 |
| | energy, ft-lb | 3734 | 3054 | 2476 | 1987 | 1577 |
| | arc, inches | | +1.8 | 0 | -8.0 | -23.9 |

## .338-06

| Cartridge Bullet | | 0 | 100 | 200 | 300 | 400 |
|---|---|---|---|---|---|---|
| A-Square 200 Nos. Bal. Tip | velocity, fps | 2750 | 2553 | 2364 | 2184 | 2011 |
| | energy, ft-lb | 3358 | 2894 | 2482 | 2118 | 1796 |
| | arc, inches | | +1.9 | 0 | -8.2 | -23.6 |
| A-Square 250 SP boat-tail | velocity, fps | 2500 | 2374 | 2252 | 2134 | 2019 |
| | energy, ft-lb | 3496 | 3129 | 2816 | 2528 | 2263 |
| | arc, inches | | +2.4 | 0 | -9.3 | -26.0 |
| A-Square 250 Dead Tough | velocity, fps | 2500 | 2222 | 1963 | 1724 | 1507 |
| | energy, ft-lb | 3496 | 2742 | 2139 | 1649 | 1261 |
| | arc, inches | | +2.8 | 0 | -11.9 | -35.5 |

## .338 Winchester Mag.

| Cartridge Bullet | | 0 | 100 | 200 | 300 | 400 |
|---|---|---|---|---|---|---|
| A-Square 250 SP boat-tail | velocity, fps | 2700 | 2568 | 2439 | 2314 | 2193 |
| | energy, ft-lb | 4046 | 3659 | 3302 | 2972 | 2669 |
| | arc, inches | | +4.4 | +5.2 | 0 | -11.7 |
| A-Square 250 Triad | velocity, fps | 2700 | 2407 | 2133 | 1877 | 1653 |
| | energy, ft-lb | 4046 | 3216 | 2526 | 1956 | 1516 |
| | arc, inches | | +2.3 | 0 | -9.8 | -29.8 |
| Federal 210 Nosler Partition | velocity, fps | 2830 | 2600 | 2390 | 2180 | 1980 |
| | energy, ft-lb | 3735 | 3160 | 2655 | 2215 | 1835 |
| | arc, inches | | +1.8 | 0 | -8.0 | -23.3 |
| Federal 225 Sierra Pro-Hunt. | velocity, fps | 2780 | 2570 | 2360 | 2170 | 1980 |
| | energy, ft-lb | 3860 | 3290 | 2780 | 2340 | 1960 |
| | arc, inches | | +1.9 | 0 | -8.2 | -23.7 |
| Federal 225 Trophy Bonded | velocity, fps | 2800 | 2560 | 2330 | 2110 | 1900 |
| | energy, ft-lb | 3915 | 3265 | 2700 | 2220 | 1800 |
| | arc, inches | | +1.9 | 0 | -8.4 | -24.5 |

| Cartridge Bullet | | 0 | 100 | 200 | 300 | 400 |
|---|---|---|---|---|---|---|
| Federal 225 Tr. Bonded HE | velocity, fps | 2940 | 2690 | 2450 | 2230 | 2010 |
| | energy, ft-lb | 4320 | 3610 | 3000 | 2475 | 2025 |
| | arc, inches | | +1.7 | 0 | -7.5 | -22.0 |
| Federal 250 Nosler Partition | velocity, fps | 2660 | 2470 | 2300 | 2120 | 1960 |
| | energy, ft-lb | 3925 | 3395 | 2925 | 2505 | 2130 |
| | arc, inches | | +2.1 | 0 | -8.8 | -25.1 |
| Federal 250 Nosler Part HE | velocity, fps | 2800 | 2610 | 2420 | 2250 | 2080 |
| | energy, ft-lb | 4350 | 3775 | 3260 | 2805 | 2395 |
| | arc, inches | | +1.8 | 0 | -7.8 | -22.5 |
| Hornady 225 Soft Point HM | velocity, fps | 2920 | 2678 | 2449 | 2232 | 2027 |
| | energy, ft-lb | 4259 | 3583 | 2996 | 2489 | 2053 |
| | arc, inches | | +1.8 | 0 | -7.6 | -22.0 |
| Norma 250 Nosler Partition | velocity, fps | 2657 | 2470 | 2290 | 2118 | |
| | energy, ft-lb | 3920 | 3387 | 2912 | 2490 | |
| | arc, inches | | +2.1 | 0 | -8.7 | |
| PMC 225 Barnes X | velocity, fps | 2780 | 2619 | 2464 | 2313 | 2168 |
| | energy, ft-lb | 3860 | 3426 | 3032 | 2673 | 2348 |
| | arc, inches | | +1.8 | 0 | -7.6 | -21.6 |
| Rem. 200 Nosler Bal. Tip | velocity, fps | 2950 | 2724 | 2509 | 2303 | 2108 |
| | energy, ft-lb | 3866 | 3295 | 2795 | 2357 | 1973 |
| | arc, inches | | +1.6 | 0 | -7.1 | -20.8 |
| Rem. 210 Nosler Partition | velocity, fps | 2830 | 2602 | 2385 | 2179 | 1983 |
| | energy, ft-lb | 3734 | 3157 | 2653 | 2214 | 1834 |
| | arc, inches | | +1.8 | 0 | -7.9 | -23.2 |
| Rem. 225 PSP Core-Lokt | velocity, fps | 2780 | 2572 | 2374 | 2184 | 2003 |
| | energy, ft-lb | 3860 | 3305 | 2815 | 2383 | 2004 |
| | arc, inches | | +1.9 | 0 | -8.1 | -23.4 |
| Rem. 225 Swift A-Frame | velocity, fps | 2785 | 2517 | 2266 | 2029 | 1808 |
| | energy, ft-lb | 3871 | 3165 | 2565 | 2057 | 1633 |
| | arc, inches | | +2.0 | 0 | -8.8 | -25.2 |
| Rem. 250 PSP Core-Lokt | velocity, fps | 2660 | 2456 | 2261 | 2075 | 1898 |
| | energy, ft-lb | 3927 | 3348 | 2837 | 2389 | 1999 |
| | arc, inches | | +2.1 | 0 | -8.9 | -26.0 |
| Speer 250 Grand Slam | velocity, fps | 2645 | 2442 | 2247 | 2062 | |
| | energy, ft-lb | 3883 | 3309 | 2803 | 2360 | |
| | arc, inches | | +2.2 | 0 | -9.1 | -26.2 |
| Win. 200 Power-Point | velocity, fps | 2960 | 2658 | 2375 | 2110 | 1862 |
| | energy, ft-lb | 3890 | 3137 | 2505 | 1977 | 1539 |
| | arc, inches | | +2.0 | 0 | -8.2 | -24.3 |
| Win. 200 Ballistic Silvertip | velocity, fps | 2950 | 2724 | 2509 | 2303 | 2108 |
| | energy, ft-lb | 3864 | 3294 | 2794 | 2355 | 1972 |
| | arc, inches | | +1.6 | 0 | -7.1 | -20.8 |
| Win. 230 Fail Safe | velocity, fps | 2780 | 2573 | 2375 | 2186 | 2005 |
| | energy, ft-lb | 3948 | 3382 | 2881 | 2441 | 2054 |
| | arc, inches | | +1.9 | 0 | -8.1 | -23.4 |
| Win. 250 Partition Gold | velocity, fps | 2650 | 2467 | 2291 | 2122 | 1960 |
| | energy, ft-lb | 3899 | 3378 | 2914 | 2520 | 2134 |
| | arc, inches | | +2.1 | 0 | -8.7 | -25.2 |

## .340 Weatherby Mag.

| Cartridge Bullet | | 0 | 100 | 200 | 300 | 400 |
|---|---|---|---|---|---|---|
| A-Square 250 SP boat-tail | velocity, fps | 2820 | 2684 | 2552 | 2424 | 2299 |
| | energy, ft-lb | 4414 | 3999 | 3615 | 3261 | 2935 |
| | arc, inches | | +4.0 | +4.6 | 0 | -10.6 |
| A-Square 250 Triad | velocity, fps | 2820 | 2520 | 2238 | 1976 | 1741 |
| | energy, ft-lb | 4414 | 3524 | 2781 | 2166 | 1683 |
| | arc, inches | | +2.0 | 0 | -9.0 | -26.8 |
| Federal 225 Trophy Bonded | velocity, fps | 3100 | 2840 | 2600 | 2370 | 2150 |
| | energy, ft-lb | 4800 | 4035 | 3375 | 2800 | 2310 |
| | arc, inches | | +1.4 | 0 | -6.5 | -19.4 |
| Wby. 200 Pointed Expanding | velocity, fps | 3221 | 2946 | 2688 | 2444 | 2213 |
| | energy, ft-lb | 4607 | 3854 | 3208 | 2652 | 2174 |
| | arc, inches | | +3.3 | +4.0 | 0 | -9.9 |
| Wby. 200 Nosler Bal. Tip | velocity, fps | 3221 | 2980 | 2753 | 2536 | 2329 |
| | energy, ft-lb | 4607 | 3944 | 3364 | 2856 | 2409 |
| | arc, inches | | +3.1 | +3.9 | 0 | -9.2 |
| Wby. 210 Nosler Partition | velocity, fps | 3211 | 2963 | 2728 | 2505 | 2293 |
| | energy, ft-lb | 4807 | 4093 | 3470 | 2927 | 2452 |
| | arc, inches | | +3.2 | +3.9 | 0 | -9.5 |

| CARTRIDGE BULLET | RANGE, YARDS: | 0 | 100 | 200 | 300 | 400 |
|---|---|---|---|---|---|---|
| Wby. 225 Pointed Expanding | velocity, fps: | 3066 | 2824 | 2595 | 2377 | 2170 |
| | energy, ft-lb: | 4696 | 3984 | 3364 | 2822 | 2352 |
| | arc, inches: | | +3.6 | +4.4 | 0 | -10.7 |
| Wby. 225 Barnes X | velocity, fps: | 3001 | 2804 | 2615 | 2434 | 2260 |
| | energy, ft-lb: | 4499 | 3927 | 3416 | 2959 | 2551 |
| | arc, inches: | | +3.6 | +4.3 | 0 | -10.3 |
| Wby. 250 Pointed Expanding | velocity, fps: | 2963 | 2745 | 2537 | 2338 | 2149 |
| | energy, ft-lb: | 4873 | 4182 | 3572 | 3035 | 2563 |
| | arc, inches: | | +3.9 | +4.6 | 0 | -11.1 |
| Wby. 250 Nosler Partition | velocity, fps: | 2941 | 2743 | 2553 | 2371 | 2197 |
| | energy, ft-lb: | 4801 | 4176 | 3618 | 3120 | 2678 |
| | arc, inches: | | +3.9 | +4.6 | 0 | -10.9 |

## .330 Dakota

| | | 0 | 100 | 200 | 300 | 400 |
|---|---|---|---|---|---|---|
| Dakota 200 Barnes X | velocity, fps: | 3200 | 2971 | 2754 | 2548 | 2350 |
| | energy, ft-lb: | 4547 | 3920 | 3369 | 2882 | 2452 |
| | arc, inches: | | +2.1 | +1.8 | -3.1 | -13.4 |
| Dakota 250 Barnes X | velocity, fps: | 2900 | 2719 | 2545 | 2378 | 2217 |
| | energy, ft-lb: | 4668 | 4103 | 3595 | 3138 | 2727 |
| | arc, inches: | | +2.3 | +1.3 | -5.0 | -17.5 |

## .338 Remington Ultra Mag

| | | 0 | 100 | 200 | 300 | 400 |
|---|---|---|---|---|---|---|
| Remington 250 Swift A-Fr. | velocity, fps: | 2860 | 2645 | 2440 | 2244 | 2057 |
| | energy, ft-lb: | 4540 | 3882 | 3303 | 2794 | 2347 |
| | arc, inches: | | +1.7 | 0 | -7.6 | -22.1 |

## .338-378 Weatherby Mag.

| | | 0 | 100 | 200 | 300 | 400 |
|---|---|---|---|---|---|---|
| Wby. 200 Nosler Bal. Tip | velocity, fps: | 3350 | 3102 | 2868 | 2646 | 2434 |
| | energy, ft-lb: | 4983 | 4273 | 3652 | 3109 | 2631 |
| | arc, inches: | 0 | +2.8 | +3.5 | 0 | -8.4 |
| Wby. 225 Barnes X | velocity, fps: | 3180 | 2974 | 2778 | 2591 | 2410 |
| | energy, ft-lb: | 5052 | 4420 | 3856 | 3353 | 2902 |
| | arc, inches: | 0 | +3.1 | +3.8 | 0 | -8.9 |
| Wby. 250 Nosler Partition | velocity, fps: | 3060 | 2856 | 2662 | 2475 | 2297 |
| | energy, ft-lb: | 5197 | 4528 | 3933 | 3401 | 2927 |
| | arc, inches: | 0 | +3.5 | +4.2 | 0 | -9.8 |

## 8.59 (.338) Titan

| | | 0 | 100 | 200 | 300 | 400 |
|---|---|---|---|---|---|---|
| Lazzeroni 200 Nos. Bal. Tip | velocity, fps: | 3430 | 3211 | 3002 | 2803 | 2613 |
| | energy, ft-lb: | 5226 | 4579 | 4004 | 3491 | 3033 |
| | arc, inches: | | +2.5 | +3.2 | 0 | -7.6 |
| Lazzeroni 225 Nos. Partition | velocity, fps: | 3235 | 3031 | 2836 | 2650 | 2471 |
| | energy, ft-lb: | 5229 | 4591 | 4021 | 3510 | 3052 |
| | arc, inches: | | +3.0 | +3.6 | 0 | -8.6 |
| Lazzeroni 250 Swift A-Fr. | velocity, fps: | 3100 | 2908 | 2725 | 2549 | 2379 |
| | energy, ft-lb: | 5336 | 4697 | 4123 | 3607 | 3143 |
| | arc, inches: | | +3.3 | +4.0 | 0 | -9.3 |

## .338 A-Square

| | | 0 | 100 | 200 | 300 | 400 |
|---|---|---|---|---|---|---|
| A-Square 200 Nos. Bal. Tip | velocity, fps: | 3500 | 3266 | 3045 | 2835 | 2634 |
| | energy, ft-lb: | 5440 | 4737 | 4117 | 3568 | 3081 |
| | arc, inches: | | +2.4 | +3.1 | 0 | -7.5 |
| A-Square 250 SP boat-tail | velocity, fps: | 3120 | 2974 | 2834 | 2697 | 2565 |
| | energy, ft-lb: | 5403 | 4911 | 4457 | 4038 | 3652 |
| | arc, inches: | | +3.1 | +3.7 | 0 | -8.5 |
| A-Square 250 Triad | velocity, fps: | 3120 | 2799 | 2500 | 2220 | 1958 |
| | energy, ft-lb: | 5403 | 4348 | 3469 | 2736 | 2128 |
| | arc, inches: | | +1.5 | 0 | -7.1 | -20.4 |

## .338 Excaliber

| | | 0 | 100 | 200 | 300 | 400 |
|---|---|---|---|---|---|---|
| A-Square 200 Nos. Bal. Tip | velocity, fps: | 3600 | 3361 | 3134 | 2920 | 2715 |
| | energy, ft-lb: | 5755 | 5015 | 4363 | 3785 | 3274 |
| | arc, inches: | | +2.2 | +2.9 | 0 | -6.7 |
| A-Square 250 SP boat-tail | velocity, fps: | 3250 | 3101 | 2958 | 2684 | 2553 |
| | energy, ft-lb: | 5863 | 5339 | 4855 | 4410 | 3998 |
| | arc, inches: | | +2.7 | +3.4 | 0 | -7.8 |
| A-Square 250 Triad | velocity, fps: | 3250 | 2922 | 2618 | 2333 | 2066 |
| | energy, ft-lb: | 5863 | 4740 | 3804 | 3021 | 2370 |
| | arc, inches: | | +1.3 | 0 | -6.4 | -19.2 |

## .348 Winchester

| | | 0 | 100 | 200 | 300 | 400 |
|---|---|---|---|---|---|---|
| Win. 200 Silvertip | velocity, fps: | 2520 | 2215 | 1931 | 1672 | 1443 |
| | energy, ft-lb: | 2820 | 2178 | 1656 | 1241 | 925 |
| | arc, inches: | | 0 | -6.2 | -21.9 | |

## .357 Magnum

| | | 0 | 100 | 200 | 300 | 400 |
|---|---|---|---|---|---|---|
| Federal 180 Hi-Shok HP Hollow Point | velocity, fps: | 1550 | 1160 | 980 | 860 | 770 |
| | energy, ft-lb: | 960 | 535 | 385 | 295 | 235 |
| | arc, inches: | | 0 | -22.8 | -77.9 | -173.8 |
| Win. 158 Jacketed SP | velocity, fps: | 1830 | 1427 | 1138 | 980 | 883 |
| | energy, ft-lb: | 1175 | 715 | 454 | 337 | 274 |
| | arc, inches: | | 0 | -16.2 | -57.0 | -128.3 |

## .35 Remington

| | | 0 | 100 | 200 | 300 | 400 |
|---|---|---|---|---|---|---|
| Federal 200 Hi-Shok | velocity, fps: | 2080 | 1700 | 1380 | 1140 | 1000 |
| | energy, ft-lb: | 1920 | 1280 | 840 | 575 | 445 |
| | arc, inches: | | 0 | -10.7 | -39.3 | |
| Rem. 150 PSP Core-Lokt | velocity, fps: | 2300 | 1874 | 1506 | 1218 | 1039 |
| | energy, ft-lb: | 1762 | 1169 | 755 | 494 | 359 |
| | arc, inches: | | 0 | -8.6 | -32.6 | |
| Rem. 200 SP Core-Lokt | velocity, fps: | 2080 | 1698 | 1376 | 1140 | 1001 |
| | energy, ft-lb: | 1921 | 1280 | 841 | 577 | 445 |
| | arc, inches: | | 0 | -10.7 | -40.1 | |
| Win. 200 Power-Point | velocity, fps: | 2020 | 1646 | 1335 | 1114 | 985 |
| | energy, ft-lb: | 1812 | 1203 | 791 | 551 | 431 |
| | arc, inches: | | 0 | -12.1 | -43.9 | |

## .356 Winchester

| | | 0 | 100 | 200 | 300 | 400 |
|---|---|---|---|---|---|---|
| Win. 200 Power-Point | velocity, fps: | 2460 | 2114 | 1797 | 1517 | 1284 |
| | energy, ft-lb: | 2688 | 1985 | 1434 | 1022 | 732 |
| | arc, inches: | | +1.6 | -3.8 | -20.1 | -51.2 |

## .358 Winchester

| | | 0 | 100 | 200 | 300 | 400 |
|---|---|---|---|---|---|---|
| Win. 200 Silvertip | velocity, fps: | 2490 | 2171 | 1876 | 1610 | 1379 |
| | energy, ft-lb: | 2753 | 2093 | 1563 | 1151 | 844 |
| | arc, inches: | | +1.5 | -3.6 | -18.6 | -47.2 |

## .35 Whelen

| | | 0 | 100 | 200 | 300 | 400 |
|---|---|---|---|---|---|---|
| Federal 225 Trophy Bonded | velocity, fps: | 2600 | 2400 | 2200 | 2020 | 1840 |
| | energy, ft-lb: | 3375 | 2865 | 2520 | 2030 | 1690 |
| | arc, inches: | | +2.3 | 0 | -9.4 | -27.3 |
| Rem. 200 Pointed Soft Point | velocity, fps: | 2675 | 2378 | 2100 | 1842 | 1606 |
| | energy, ft-lb: | 3177 | 2510 | 1958 | 1506 | 1145 |
| | arc, inches: | | +2.3 | 0 | -10.3 | -30.8 |
| Rem. 250 Pointed Soft Point | velocity, fps: | 2400 | 2197 | 2005 | 1823 | 1652 |
| | energy, ft-lb: | 3197 | 2680 | 2230 | 1844 | 1515 |
| | arc, inches: | | +1.3 | -3.2 | -16.6 | -40.0 |

## .358 Norma Mag.

| | | 0 | 100 | 200 | 300 | 400 |
|---|---|---|---|---|---|---|
| A-Square 275 Triad | velocity, fps: | 2700 | 2394 | 2108 | 1842 | 1653 |
| | energy, ft-lb: | 4451 | 3498 | 2713 | 2072 | 1668 |
| | arc, inches: | | +2.3 | 0 | -10.1 | -29.8 |
| Norma 250 Woodleigh | velocity, fps: | 2799 | 2442 | 2112 | 1810 | |
| | energy, ft-lb: | 4350 | 3312 | 2478 | 1819 | |
| | arc, inches: | | +2.2 | 0 | -10.0 | |

## .358 STA

| | | 0 | 100 | 200 | 300 | 400 |
|---|---|---|---|---|---|---|
| A-Square 275 Triad | velocity, fps: | 2850 | 2562 | 2292 | 2039 | 1764 |
| | energy, ft-lb: | 4959 | 4009 | 3208 | 2539 | 1899 |
| | arc, inches: | | +1.9 | 0 | -8.6 | -26.1 |

## 9.3x57

| | | 0 | 100 | 200 | 300 | 400 |
|---|---|---|---|---|---|---|
| Norma 232 Vulkan | velocity, fps: | 2329 | 2031 | 1757 | 1512 | |
| | energy, ft-lb: | 2795 | 2126 | 1591 | 1178 | |
| | arc, inches: | | +3.5 | 0 | -14.9 | |
| Norma 286 Alaska | velocity, fps: | 2067 | 1857 | 1662 | 1484 | |
| | energy, ft-lb: | 2714 | 2190 | 1754 | 1399 | |
| | arc, inches: | | +4.3 | 0 | -17.0 | |

## 9.3x62

| Cartridge / Bullet | | 0 | 100 | 200 | 300 | 400 |
|---|---|---|---|---|---|---|
| A-Square 286 Triad | velocity, fps: | 2360 | 2089 | 1844 | 1623 | 1369 |
| | energy, ft-lb: | 3538 | 2771 | 2157 | 1670 | 1189 |
| | arc, inches: | | +3.0 | 0 | -13.1 | -42.2 |
| Norma 232 Vulkan | velocity, fps: | 2625 | 2327 | 2049 | 1792 | |
| | energy, ft-lb: | 3551 | 2791 | 2164 | 1655 | |
| | arc, inches: | | +2.5 | 0 | -10.8 | |
| Norma 232 Oryx | velocity, fps: | 2625 | 2294 | 1988 | 1708 | |
| | energy, ft-lb: | 3535 | 2700 | 2028 | 1497 | |
| | arc, inches: | | +2.5 | 0 | -11.4 | |
| Norma 286 Plastic Point | velocity, fps: | 2362 | 2141 | 1931 | 1736 | |
| | energy, ft-lb: | 3544 | 2911 | 2370 | 1914 | |
| | arc, inches: | | +3.1 | 0 | -12.4 | |
| Norma 286 Alaska | velocity, fps: | 2362 | 2135 | 1920 | 1720 | |
| | energy, ft-lb: | 3544 | 2894 | 2342 | 1879 | |
| | arc, inches: | | +3.1 | 0 | -12.5 | |

## 9.3x64

| Cartridge / Bullet | | 0 | 100 | 200 | 300 | 400 |
|---|---|---|---|---|---|---|
| A-Square 286 Triad | velocity, fps: | 2700 | 2391 | 2103 | 1835 | 1602 |
| | energy, ft-lb: | 4629 | 3630 | 2808 | 2139 | 1631 |
| | arc, inches: | | +2.3 | 0 | -10.1 | -30.8 |

## 9.3x74 R

| Cartridge / Bullet | | 0 | 100 | 200 | 300 | 400 |
|---|---|---|---|---|---|---|
| A-Square 286 Triad | velocity, fps: | 2360 | 2089 | 1844 | 1623 | |
| | energy, ft-lb: | 3538 | 2771 | 2157 | 1670 | |
| | arc, inches: | | +3.6 | 0 | -14.0 | |
| Norma 232 Vulkan | velocity, fps: | 2625 | 2327 | 2049 | 1792 | |
| | energy, ft-lb: | 3551 | 2791 | 2164 | 1655 | |
| | arc, inches: | | +2.5 | 0 | -10.8 | |
| Norma 232 Oryx | velocity, fps: | 2526 | 2191 | 1883 | 1605 | |
| | energy, ft-lb: | 3274 | 2463 | 1819 | 1322 | |
| | arc, inches: | | +2.9 | 0 | -12.8 | |
| Norma 286 Alaska | velocity, fps: | 2362 | 2135 | 1920 | 1720 | |
| | energy, ft-lb: | 3544 | 2894 | 2342 | 1879 | |
| | arc, inches: | | +3.1 | 0 | -12.5 | |
| Norma 286 Plastic Point | velocity, fps: | 2362 | 2135 | 1920 | 1720 | |
| | energy, ft-lb: | 3544 | 2894 | 2342 | 1879 | |
| | arc, inches: | | +3.1 | 0 | -12.5 | |

## .375 Winchester

| Cartridge / Bullet | | 0 | 100 | 200 | 300 | 400 |
|---|---|---|---|---|---|---|
| Win. 200 Power-Point | velocity, fps: | 2200 | 1841 | 1526 | 1268 | 1089 |
| | energy, ft-lb: | 2150 | 1506 | 1034 | 714 | |
| | arc, inches: | | 0 | -9.5 | -33.8 | |

## .375 H&H Magnum

| Cartridge / Bullet | | 0 | 100 | 200 | 300 | 400 |
|---|---|---|---|---|---|---|
| A-Square 300 SP boat-tail | velocity, fps: | 2550 | 2415 | 2284 | 2157 | 2034 |
| | energy, ft-lb: | 4331 | 3884 | 3474 | 3098 | 2755 |
| | arc, inches: | | +5.2 | +6.0 | 0 | -13.3 |
| A-Square 300 Triad | velocity, fps: | 2550 | 2251 | 1973 | 1717 | 1496 |
| | energy, ft-lb: | 4331 | 3375 | 2592 | 1964 | 1491 |
| | arc, inches: | | +2.7 | 0 | -11.7 | -35.1 |
| Federal 250 Trophy Bonded | velocity, fps: | 2670 | 2360 | 2080 | 1820 | 1580 |
| | energy, ft-lb: | 3955 | 3100 | 2400 | 1830 | 1380 |
| | arc, inches: | | +2.4 | 0 | -10.4 | -31.7 |
| Federal 270 Hi-Shok | velocity, fps: | 2690 | 2420 | 2170 | 1920 | 1700 |
| | energy, ft-lb: | 4340 | 3510 | 2810 | 2220 | 1740 |
| | arc, inches: | | +2.4 | 0 | -10.9 | -33.3 |
| Federal 300 Hi-Shok | velocity, fps: | 2530 | 2270 | 2020 | 1790 | 1580 |
| | energy, ft-lb: | 4265 | 3425 | 2720 | 2135 | 1665 |
| | arc, inches: | | +2.6 | 0 | -11.2 | -33.3 |
| Federal 300 Nosler Partition | velocity, fps: | 2530 | 2320 | 2120 | 1930 | 1750 |
| | energy, ft-lb: | 4265 | 3585 | 2995 | 2475 | 2040 |
| | arc, inches: | | +2.5 | 0 | -10.3 | -29.9 |
| Federal 300 Trophy Bonded | velocity, fps: | 2530 | 2280 | 2040 | 1810 | 1610 |
| | energy, ft-lb: | 4265 | 3450 | 2765 | 2190 | 1725 |
| | arc, inches: | | +2.6 | 0 | -10.9 | -32.8 |
| Federal 300 Tr. Bonded HE | velocity, fps: | 2700 | 2440 | 2190 | 1960 | 1740 |
| | energy, ft-lb: | 4855 | 3960 | 3195 | 2550 | 2020 |
| | arc, inches: | | +2.2 | 0 | -9.4 | -28.0 |
| Federal 300 Trophy Bonded Sledgehammer Solid | velocity, fps: | 2530 | 2160 | 1820 | 1520 | 1280 |
| | energy, ft-lb: | 4265 | 3105 | 2210 | 1550 | 1090 |
| | arc, inches, s: | | 0 | -6.0 | -22.7 | -54.6 |
| Hornady 270 SP HM | velocity, fps: | 2870 | 2620 | 2385 | 2162 | 1957 |
| | energy, ft-lb: | 4937 | 4116 | 3408 | 2802 | 2296 |
| | arc, inches: | | +2.2 | 0 | -8.4 | -23.9 |
| Hornady 300 FMJ RN HM | velocity, fps: | 2705 | 2376 | 2072 | 1804 | 1560 |
| | energy, ft-lb: | 4873 | 3760 | 2861 | 2167 | 1621 |
| | arc, inches: | | +2.7 | 0 | -10.8 | -32.1 |
| Norma 300 Soft Point | velocity, fps: | 2549 | 2211 | 1900 | 1619 | |
| | energy, ft-lb: | 4329 | 3258 | 2406 | 1747 | |
| | arc, inches: | | +2.8 | 0 | -12.6 | |
| Norma 300 TXP Swift A-Fr. | velocity, fps: | 2559 | 2296 | 2049 | 1818 | |
| | energy, ft-lb: | 4363 | 3513 | 2798 | 2203 | |
| | arc, inches: | | +2.6 | 0 | -10.9 | |
| PMC 270 Barnes X | velocity, fps: | 2690 | 2528 | 2372 | 2221 | 2076 |
| | energy, ft-lb: | 4337 | 3831 | 3371 | 2957 | 2582 |
| | arc, inches: | | +2.0 | 0 | -8.2 | -23.4 |
| PMC 300 Barnes X | velocity, fps: | 2530 | 2389 | 2252 | 2120 | 1993 |
| | energy, ft-lb: | 4263 | 3801 | 3378 | 2994 | 2644 |
| | arc, inches: | | +2.3 | 0 | -9.2 | -26.1 |
| Rem. 270 Soft Point | velocity, fps: | 2690 | 2420 | 2166 | 1928 | 1707 |
| | energy, ft-lb: | 4337 | 3510 | 2812 | 2228 | 1747 |
| | arc, inches: | | +2.2 | 0 | -9.7 | -28.7 |
| Rem. 300 Swift A-Frame | velocity, fps: | 2530 | 2245 | 1979 | 1733 | 1512 |
| | energy, ft-lb: | 4262 | 3357 | 2608 | 2001 | 1523 |
| | arc, inches: | | +2.7 | 0 | -11.7 | -35.0 |
| Speer 285 Grand Slam | velocity, fps: | 2610 | 2365 | 2134 | 1916 | |
| | energy, ft-lb: | 4310 | 3540 | 2883 | 2323 | |
| | arc, inches: | | +2.4 | 0 | -9.9 | |
| Speer 300 African GS Tungsten Solid | velocity, fps: | 2609 | 2277 | 1970 | 1690 | |
| | energy, ft-lb: | 4534 | 3453 | 2585 | 1903 | |
| | arc, inches: | | +2.6 | 0 | -11.7 | -35.6 |
| Win. 270 Fail Safe | velocity, fps: | 2670 | 2447 | 2234 | 2033 | 1842 |
| | energy, ft-lb: | 4275 | 3590 | 2994 | 2478 | 2035 |
| | arc, inches: | | +2.2 | 0 | -9.1 | -28.7 |
| Win. 300 Fail Safe | velocity, fps: | 2530 | 2336 | 2151 | 1974 | 1806 |
| | energy, ft-lb: | 4265 | 3636 | 3082 | 2596 | 2173 |
| | arc, inches: | | +2.4 | 0 | -10.0 | -26.9 |

## .375 Dakota

| Cartridge / Bullet | | 0 | 100 | 200 | 300 | 400 |
|---|---|---|---|---|---|---|
| Dakota 270 Barnes X | velocity, fps: | 2800 | 2617 | 2441 | 2272 | 2109 |
| | energy, ft-lb: | 4699 | 4104 | 3571 | 3093 | 2666 |
| | arc, inches: | | +2.3 | +1.0 | -6.1 | -19.9 |
| Dakota 300 Barnes X | velocity, fps: | 2600 | 2316 | 2051 | 1804 | 1579 |
| | energy, ft-lb: | 4502 | 3573 | 2800 | 2167 | 1661 |
| | arc, inches: | | +2.4 | -0.1 | -11.0 | -32.7 |

## .375 Weatherby

| Cartridge / Bullet | | 0 | 100 | 200 | 300 | 400 |
|---|---|---|---|---|---|---|
| A-Square 300 SP boat-tail | velocity, fps: | 2700 | 2560 | 2425 | 2293 | 2166 |
| | energy, ft-lb: | 4856 | 4366 | 3916 | 3503 | 3125 |
| | arc, inches: | | +4.5 | +5.2 | 0 | -11.9 |
| A-Square 300 Triad | velocity, fps: | 2700 | 2391 | 2103 | 1835 | 1602 |
| | energy, ft-lb: | 4856 | 3808 | 2946 | 2243 | 1710 |
| | arc, inches: | | +2.3 | 0 | -10.1 | -30.8 |

## .375 JRS

| Cartridge / Bullet | | 0 | 100 | 200 | 300 | 400 |
|---|---|---|---|---|---|---|
| A-Square 300 SP boat-tail | velocity, fps: | 2700 | 2560 | 2425 | 2293 | 2166 |
| | energy, ft-lb: | 4856 | 4366 | 3916 | 3503 | 3125 |
| | arc, inches: | | +4.5 | +5.2 | 0 | -11.9 |
| A-Square 300 Triad | velocity, fps: | 2700 | 2391 | 2103 | 1835 | 1602 |
| | energy, ft-lb: | 4856 | 3808 | 2946 | 2243 | 1710 |
| | arc, inches: | | +2.3 | 0 | -10.1 | -30.8 |

## .375 A-Square

| Cartridge / Bullet | | 0 | 100 | 200 | 300 | 400 |
|---|---|---|---|---|---|---|
| A-Square 300 SP boat-tail | velocity, fps: | 2920 | 2773 | 2631 | 2494 | 2360 |
| | energy, ft-lb: | 5679 | 5123 | 4611 | 4142 | 3710 |
| | arc, inches: | | +3.7 | +4.4 | 0 | -9.8 |
| A-Square 300 Triad | velocity, fps: | 2920 | 2596 | 2294 | 2012 | 1762 |
| | energy, ft-lb: | 5679 | 4488 | 3505 | 2698 | 2068 |
| | arc, inches: | | +1.8 | 0 | -8.5 | -25.5 |

BALLISTICS

## .378 Weatherby

| Cartridge Bullet | | 0 | 100 | 200 | 300 | 400 |
|---|---|---|---|---|---|---|
| A-Square 300 SP boat-tail | velocity, fps: | 2900 | 2754 | 2612 | 2475 | 2342 |
| | energy, ft-lb: | 5602 | 5051 | 4546 | 4081 | 3655 |
| | arc, inches: | | +3.8 | +4.4 | 0 | -10.0 |
| A-Square 300 Triad | velocity, fps: | 2900 | 2577 | 2276 | 1997 | 1747 |
| | energy, ft-lb: | 5602 | 4424 | 3452 | 2656 | 2034 |
| | arc, inches: | | +1.9 | 0 | -8.7 | -25.9 |
| Wby. 270 Pointed Expanding | velocity, fps: | 3180 | 2921 | 2677 | 2445 | 2225 |
| | energy, ft-lb: | 6062 | 5115 | 4295 | 3583 | 2968 |
| | arc, inches: | | +1.3 | 0 | -6.1 | -18.1 |
| Wby. 270 Barnes X | velocity, fps: | 3150 | 2954 | 2767 | 2587 | 2415 |
| | energy, ft-lb: | 5948 | 5232 | 4589 | 4013 | 3495 |
| | arc, inches: | | +1.2 | 0 | -5.8 | -16.7 |
| Wby. 300 RN Expanding | velocity, fps: | 2925 | 2558 | 2220 | 1908 | 1627 |
| | energy, ft-lb: | 5699 | 4360 | 3283 | 2424 | 1764 |
| | arc, inches: | | +1.9 | 0 | -9.0 | -27.8 |
| Wby. 300 FMJ | velocity, fps: | 2925 | 2591 | 2280 | 1991 | 1725 |
| | energy, ft-lb: | 5699 | 4470 | 3461 | 2640 | 1983 |
| | arc, inches: | | +1.8 | 0 | -8.6 | -26.1 |

## .38-40 Winchester

| Cartridge Bullet | | 0 | 100 | 200 | 300 | 400 |
|---|---|---|---|---|---|---|
| Win. 180 Soft Point | velocity, fps: | 1160 | 999 | 901 | 827 | |
| | energy, ft-lb: | 538 | 399 | 324 | 273 | |
| | arc, inches: | | 0 | -23.4 | -75.2 | |

## .38-55 Winchester

| Cartridge Bullet | | 0 | 100 | 200 | 300 | 400 |
|---|---|---|---|---|---|---|
| Win. 255 Soft Point | velocity, fps: | 1320 | 1190 | 1091 | 1018 | |
| | energy, ft-lb: | 987 | 802 | 674 | 587 | |
| | arc, inches: | | 0 | -33.9 | -110.6 | |

## .450/.400 (3")

| Cartridge Bullet | | 0 | 100 | 200 | 300 | 400 |
|---|---|---|---|---|---|---|
| A-Square 400 Triad | velocity, fps: | 2150 | 1910 | 1690 | 1490 | |
| | energy, ft-lb: | 4105 | 3241 | 2537 | 1972 | |
| | arc, inches: | | +4.4 | 0 | -16.5 | |

## .450/.400 (3 1/4")

| Cartridge Bullet | | 0 | 100 | 200 | 300 | 400 |
|---|---|---|---|---|---|---|
| A-Square 400 Triad | velocity, fps: | 2150 | 1910 | 1690 | 1490 | |
| | energy, ft-lb: | 4105 | 3241 | 2537 | 1972 | |
| | arc, inches: | | +4.4 | 0 | -16.5 | |

## .404 Jeffery

| Cartridge Bullet | | 0 | 100 | 200 | 300 | 400 |
|---|---|---|---|---|---|---|
| A-Square 400 Triad | velocity, fps: | 2150 | 1901 | 1674 | 1468 | 1299 |
| | energy, ft-lb: | 4105 | 3211 | 2489 | 1915 | 1499 |
| | arc, inches: | | +4.1 | 0 | -16.4 | -49.1 |

## .416 Taylor

| Cartridge Bullet | | 0 | 100 | 200 | 300 | 400 |
|---|---|---|---|---|---|---|
| A-Square 400 Triad | velocity, fps: | 2350 | 2093 | 1853 | 1634 | 1443 |
| | energy, ft-lb: | 4905 | 3892 | 3049 | 2371 | 1849 |
| | arc, inches: | | +3.2 | 0 | -13.6 | -39.8 |

## .416 Hoffman

| Cartridge Bullet | | 0 | 100 | 200 | 300 | 400 |
|---|---|---|---|---|---|---|
| A-Square 400 Triad | velocity, fps: | 2380 | 2122 | 1879 | 1658 | 1464 |
| | energy, ft-lb: | 5031 | 3998 | 3136 | 2440 | 1903 |
| | arc, inches: | | +3.1 | 0 | -13.1 | -38.7 |

## .416 Remington Magnum

| Cartridge Bullet | | 0 | 100 | 200 | 300 | 400 |
|---|---|---|---|---|---|---|
| A-Square 400 Triad | velocity, fps: | 2380 | 2122 | 1879 | 1658 | 1464 |
| | energy, ft-lb: | 5031 | 3998 | 3136 | 2440 | 1903 |
| | arc, inches: | | +3.1 | 0 | -13.2 | -38.7 |
| Federal 400 Trophy Bonded Sledgehammer Solid | velocity, fps: | 2400 | 2150 | 1920 | 1700 | 1500 |
| | energy, ft-lb: | 5115 | 4110 | 3260 | 2565 | 2005 |
| | arc, inches: | | 0 | -6.0 | -21.6 | -49.2 |
| Federal 400 Trophy Bonded | velocity, fps: | 2400 | 2180 | 1970 | 1770 | 1590 |
| | energy, ft-lb: | 5115 | 4215 | 3440 | 2785 | 2245 |
| | arc, inches: | | 0 | -5.8 | -20.6 | -46.9 |
| Rem. 400 Swift A-Frame | velocity, fps: | 2400 | 2175 | 1962 | 1763 | 1579 |
| | energy, ft-lb: | 5115 | 4201 | 3419 | 2760 | 2214 |
| | arc, inches: | | 0 | -5.9 | -20.8 | |

## .416 Rigby

| Cartridge Bullet | | 0 | 100 | 200 | 300 | 400 |
|---|---|---|---|---|---|---|
| A-Square 400 Triad | velocity, fps: | 2400 | 2140 | 1897 | 1673 | 1478 |
| | energy, ft-lb: | 5115 | 4069 | 3194 | 2487 | 1940 |
| | arc, inches: | | +3.0 | 0 | -12.9 | -38.0 |
| Federal 400 Trophy Bonded | velocity, fps: | 2370 | 2150 | 1940 | 1750 | 1570 |
| | energy, ft-lb: | 4990 | 4110 | 3350 | 2715 | 2190 |
| | arc, inches: | | 0 | -6.0 | -21.3 | -48.1 |
| Federal 400 Trophy Bonded Sledgehammer Solid | velocity, fps: | 2370 | 2120 | 1890 | 1660 | 1460 |
| | energy, ft-lb: | 4990 | 3975 | 3130 | 2440 | 1895 |
| | arc, inches: | | 0 | -6.3 | -22.5 | -51.5 |
| Federal 410 Woodleigh Weldcore | velocity, fps: | 2370 | 2110 | 1870 | 1640 | 1440 |
| | energy, ft-lb: | 5115 | 4050 | 3165 | 2455 | 1895 |
| | arc, inches: | | 0 | -7.4 | -24.8 | -55.0 |
| Federal 410 Solid | velocity, fps: | 2370 | 2110 | 2870 | 1640 | 1440 |
| | energy, ft-lb: | 5115 | 4050 | 3165 | 2455 | 1895 |
| | arc, inches: | | 0 | -7.4 | -24.8 | -55.0 |
| Norma 400 TXP Swift A-Fr. | velocity, fps: | 2350 | 2127 | 1917 | 1721 | |
| | energy, ft-lb: | 4906 | 4021 | 3266 | 2632 | |
| | arc, inches: | | +3.1 | 0 | -12.5 | |

## .416 Rimmed

| Cartridge Bullet | | 0 | 100 | 200 | 300 | 400 |
|---|---|---|---|---|---|---|
| A-Square 400 Triad | velocity, fps: | 2400 | 2140 | 1897 | 1673 | |
| | energy, ft-lb: | 5115 | 4069 | 3194 | 2487 | |
| | arc, inches: | | +3.3 | 0 | -13.2 | |

## .416 Dakota

| Cartridge Bullet | | 0 | 100 | 200 | 300 | 400 |
|---|---|---|---|---|---|---|
| Dakota 400 Barnes X | velocity, fps: | 2450 | 2294 | 2143 | 1998 | 1859 |
| | energy, ft-lb: | 5330 | 4671 | 4077 | 3544 | 3068 |
| | arc, inches: | | +2.5 | -0.2 | -10.5 | -29.4 |

## .416 Weatherby

| Cartridge Bullet | | 0 | 100 | 200 | 300 | 400 |
|---|---|---|---|---|---|---|
| A-Square 400 Triad | velocity, fps: | 2600 | 2328 | 2073 | 1834 | 1624 |
| | energy, ft-lb: | 6004 | 4813 | 3816 | 2986 | 2343 |
| | arc, inches: | | +2.5 | 0 | -10.5 | -31.6 |
| Wby. 350 Barnes X | velocity, fps: | 2850 | 2673 | 2503 | 2340 | 2182 |
| | energy, ft-lb: | 6312 | 5553 | 4870 | 4253 | 3700 |
| | arc, inches: | | +1.7 | 0 | -7.2 | -20.9 |
| Wby. 400 Swift A-Fr. | velocity, fps: | 2650 | 2426 | 2213 | 2011 | 1820 |
| | energy, ft-lb: | 6237 | 5227 | 4350 | 3592 | 2941 |
| | arc, inches: | | +2.2 | 0 | -9.3 | -27.1 |
| Wby. 400 RN Expanding | velocity, fps: | 2700 | 2417 | 2152 | 1903 | 1676 |
| | energy, ft-lb: | 6474 | 5189 | 4113 | 3216 | 2493 |
| | arc, inches: | | +2.3 | 0 | -9.7 | -29.3 |
| Wby. 400 Monolithic Solid | velocity, fps: | 2700 | 2411 | 2140 | 1887 | 1656 |
| | energy, ft-lb: | 6474 | 5162 | 4068 | 3161 | 2435 |
| | arc, inches: | | +2.3 | 0 | -9.8 | -29.7 |

## 10.57 (.416) Meteor

| Cartridge Bullet | | 0 | 100 | 200 | 300 | 400 |
|---|---|---|---|---|---|---|
| Lazzeroni 400 Swift A-Fr. | velocity, fps: | 2730 | 2532 | 2342 | 2161 | 1987 |
| | energy, ft-lb: | 6621 | 5695 | 4874 | 4147 | 3508 |
| | arc, inches: | | +1.9 | 0 | -8.3 | -24.0 |

## .425 Express

| Cartridge Bullet | | 0 | 100 | 200 | 300 | 400 |
|---|---|---|---|---|---|---|
| A-Square 400 Triad | velocity, fps: | 2400 | 2136 | 1888 | 1662 | 1465 |
| | energy, ft-lb: | 5115 | 4052 | 3167 | 2454 | 1906 |
| | arc, inches: | | +3.0 | 0 | -13.1 | -38.3 |

## .44-40 Winchester

| Cartridge Bullet | | 0 | 100 | 200 | 300 | 400 |
|---|---|---|---|---|---|---|
| Rem. 200 Soft Point | velocity, fps: | 1190 | 1006 | 900 | 822 | 756 |
| | energy, ft-lb: | 629 | 449 | 360 | 300 | 254 |
| | arc, inches: | | 0 | -33.1 | -108.7 | -235.2 |
| Win. 200 Soft Point | velocity, fps: | 1190 | 1006 | 900 | 822 | 756 |
| | energy, ft-lb: | 629 | 449 | 360 | 300 | 254 |
| | arc, inches: | | 0 | -33.3 | -109.5 | -237.4 |

## .44 Remington Magnum

| Cartridge Bullet | | 0 | 100 | 200 | 300 | 400 |
|---|---|---|---|---|---|---|
| Federal 240 Hi-Shok HP | velocity, fps: | 1760 | 1380 | 1090 | 950 | 860 |
| | energy, ft-lb: | 1650 | 1015 | 640 | 485 | 395 |
| | arc, inches: | | 0 | -17.4 | -60.7 | -136.0 |

| Cartridge Bullet | Range, Yards: | 0 | 100 | 200 | 300 | 400 |
|---|---|---|---|---|---|---|
| Rem. 210 Semi-Jacketed HP | velocity, fps: | 1920 | 1477 | 1155 | 982 | 880 |
| | energy, ft-lb: | 1719 | 1017 | 622 | 450 | 361 |
| | arc, inches: | | 0 | -14.7 | -55.5 | -131.3 |
| Rem. 240 Soft Point | velocity, fps: | 1760 | 1380 | 1114 | 970 | 878 |
| | energy, ft-lb: | 1650 | 1015 | 661 | 501 | 411 |
| | arc, inches: | | 0 | -17.0 | -61.4 | -143.0 |
| Rem. 240 Semi-Jacketed Hollow Point | velocity, fps: | 1760 | 1380 | 1114 | 970 | 878 |
| | energy, ft-lb: | 1650 | 1015 | 661 | 501 | 411 |
| | arc, inches: | | 0 | -17.0 | -61.4 | -143.0 |
| Rem. 275 JHP Core-Lokt | velocity, fps: | 1580 | 1293 | 1093 | 976 | 896 |
| | energy, ft-lb: | 1524 | 1020 | 730 | 582 | 490 |
| | arc, inches: | | 0 | -19.4 | -67.5 | -210.8 |
| Win. 210 Silvertip HP | velocity, fps: | 1580 | 1198 | 993 | 879 | 795 |
| | energy, ft-lb: | 1164 | 670 | 460 | 361 | 295 |
| | arc, inches: | | 0 | -22.4 | -76.1 | -168.0 |
| Win. 240 Hollow Soft Point | velocity, fps: | 1760 | 1362 | 1094 | 953 | 861 |
| | energy, ft-lb: | 1650 | 988 | 638 | 484 | 395 |
| | arc, inches: | | 0 | -18.1 | -65.1 | -150.3 |

## .444 Marlin

| Cartridge Bullet | Range, Yards: | 0 | 100 | 200 | 300 | 400 |
|---|---|---|---|---|---|---|
| Rem. 240 Soft Point | velocity, fps: | 2350 | 1815 | 1377 | 1087 | 941 |
| | energy, ft-lb: | 2942 | 1755 | 1010 | 630 | 472 |
| | arc, inches: | | +2.2 | -5.4 | -31.4 | -86.7 |

## .45-70 Government

| Cartridge Bullet | Range, Yards: | 0 | 100 | 200 | 300 | 400 |
|---|---|---|---|---|---|---|
| Federal 300 Sierra Pro-Hunt. HP FN | velocity, fps: | 1880 | 1650 | 1430 | 1240 | 1110 |
| | energy, ft-lb: | 2355 | 1815 | 1355 | 1015 | 810 |
| | arc, inches: | | 0 | -11.5 | -39.7 | -89.1 |
| Rem. 300 Jacketed HP | velocity, fps: | 1810 | 1497 | 1244 | 1073 | 969 |
| | energy, ft-lb: | 2182 | 1492 | 1031 | 767 | 625 |
| | arc, inches: | | 0 | -13.8 | -50.1 | -115.7 |
| Rem. 405 Soft Point | velocity, fps: | 1330 | 1168 | 1055 | 977 | 918 |
| | energy, ft-lb: | 1590 | 1227 | 1001 | 858 | 758 |
| | arc, inches: | | 0 | -24.0 | -78.6 | -169.4 |
| Win. 300 Jacketed HP | velocity, fps: | 1880 | 1650 | 1425 | 1235 | 1105 |
| | energy, ft-lb: | 2355 | 1815 | 1355 | 1015 | 810 |
| | arc, inches: | | 0 | -12.8 | -44.3 | -95.5 |
| Win. 300 Partition Gold | velocity, fps: | 1880 | 1558 | 1292 | 1103 | 988 |
| | energy, ft-lb: | 2355 | 1616 | 1112 | 811 | 651 |
| | arc, inches: | | 0 | -12.9 | -46.0 | -104.9 |

## .450 Nitro Express (3 1/4")

| Cartridge Bullet | Range, Yards: | 0 | 100 | 200 | 300 | 400 |
|---|---|---|---|---|---|---|
| A-Square 465 Triad | velocity, fps: | 2190 | 1970 | 1765 | 1577 | |
| | energy, ft-lb: | 4952 | 4009 | 3216 | 2567 | |
| | arc, inches: | | +4.3 | 0 | -15.4 | |

## .450 #2

| Cartridge Bullet | Range, Yards: | 0 | 100 | 200 | 300 | 400 |
|---|---|---|---|---|---|---|
| A-Square 465 Triad | velocity, fps: | 2190 | 1970 | 1765 | 1577 | |
| | energy, ft-lb: | 4952 | 4009 | 3216 | 2567 | |
| | arc, inches: | | +4.3 | 0 | -15.4 | |

## .458 Winchester Mag.

| Cartridge Bullet | Range, Yards: | 0 | 100 | 200 | 300 | 400 |
|---|---|---|---|---|---|---|
| A-Square 465 Triad | velocity, fps: | 2220 | 1999 | 1791 | 1601 | 1433 |
| | energy, ft-lb: | 5088 | 4127 | 3312 | 2646 | 2121 |
| | arc, inches: | | +3.6 | 0 | -14.7 | -42.5 |
| Federal 350 Soft Point | velocity, fps: | 2470 | 1990 | 1570 | 1250 | 1060 |
| | energy, ft-lb: | 4740 | 3065 | 1915 | 1205 | 870 |
| | arc, inches: | | 0 | -7.5 | -29.1 | -71.1 |
| Federal 400 Trophy Bonded | velocity, fps: | 2380 | 2170 | 1960 | 1770 | 1590 |
| | energy, ft-lb: | 5030 | 4165 | 3415 | 2785 | 2255 |
| | arc, inches: | | 0 | -5.9 | -20.9 | -47.1 |
| Federal 500 Solid | velocity, fps: | 2090 | 1870 | 1670 | 1480 | 1320 |
| | energy, ft-lb: | 4850 | 3880 | 3085 | 2440 | 1945 |
| | arc, inches: | | 0 | -8.5 | -29.5 | -66.2 |
| Federal 500 Trophy Bonded | velocity, fps: | 2090 | 1870 | 1660 | 1480 | 1310 |
| | energy, ft-lb: | 4850 | 3870 | 3065 | 2420 | 1915 |
| | arc, inches: | | 0 | -8.5 | -29.7 | -66.8 |
| Federal 500 Trophy Bonded Sledgehammer Solid | velocity, fps: | 2090 | 1860 | 1650 | 1460 | 1300 |
| | energy, ft-lb: | 4850 | 3845 | 3025 | 2365 | 1865 |
| | arc, inches: | | 0 | -8.6 | -30.0 | -67.8 |

| Cartridge Bullet | Range, Yards: | 0 | 100 | 200 | 300 | 400 |
|---|---|---|---|---|---|---|
| Federal 510 Soft Point | velocity, fps: | 2090 | 1820 | 1570 | 1360 | 1190 |
| | energy, ft-lb: | 4945 | 3730 | 2790 | 2080 | 1605 |
| | arc, inches: | | 0 | -9.1 | -32.3 | -73.9 |
| Hornady 500 FMJ-RN HM | velocity, fps: | 2260 | 1984 | 1735 | 1512 | |
| | energy, ft-lb: | 5670 | 4368 | 3341 | 2538 | |
| | arc, inches: | | 0 | -7.4 | -26.4 | |
| Norma 500 TXP Swift A-Fr. | velocity, fps: | 2116 | 1903 | 1705 | 1524 | |
| | energy, ft-lb: | 4972 | 4023 | 3228 | 2578 | |
| | arc, inches: | | +4.1 | 0 | -16.1 | |
| Rem. 450 Swift A-Frame PSP | velocity, fps: | 2150 | 1901 | 1671 | 1465 | 1289 |
| | energy, ft-lb: | 4618 | 3609 | 2789 | 2144 | 1659 |
| | arc, inches: | | 0 | -8.2 | -28.9 | |
| Speer 500 African GS Tungsten Solid | velocity, fps: | 2120 | 1845 | 1596 | 1379 | |
| | energy, ft-lb: | 4989 | 3780 | 2828 | 2111 | |
| | arc, inches: | | 0 | -8.8 | -31.3 | |
| Speer African Grand Slam | velocity, fps: | 2120 | 1853 | 1609 | 1396 | |
| | energy, ft-lb: | 4989 | 3810 | 2875 | 2163 | |
| | arc, inches: | | 0 | -8.7 | -30.8 | |
| Win. 510 Soft Point | velocity, fps: | 2040 | 1770 | 1527 | 1319 | 1157 |
| | energy, ft-lb: | 4712 | 3547 | 2640 | 1970 | 1516 |
| | arc, inches: | | 0 | -10.3 | -35.6 | |

## .458 Lott

| Cartridge Bullet | Range, Yards: | 0 | 100 | 200 | 300 | 400 |
|---|---|---|---|---|---|---|
| A-Square 465 Triad | velocity, fps: | 2380 | 2150 | 1932 | 1730 | 1551 |
| | energy, ft-lb: | 5848 | 4773 | 3855 | 3091 | 2485 |
| | arc, inches: | | +3.0 | 0 | -12.5 | -36.4 |

## .450 Ackley

| Cartridge Bullet | Range, Yards: | 0 | 100 | 200 | 300 | 400 |
|---|---|---|---|---|---|---|
| A-Square 465 Triad | velocity, fps: | 2400 | 2169 | 1950 | 1747 | 1567 |
| | energy, ft-lb: | 5947 | 4857 | 3927 | 3150 | 2534 |
| | arc, inches: | | +2.9 | 0 | -12.2 | -35.8 |

## .460 Short A-Square

| Cartridge Bullet | Range, Yards: | 0 | 100 | 200 | 300 | 400 |
|---|---|---|---|---|---|---|
| A-Square 500 Triad | velocity, fps: | 2420 | 2198 | 1987 | 1789 | 1613 |
| | energy, ft-lb: | 6501 | 5362 | 4385 | 3553 | 2890 |
| | arc, inches: | | +2.9 | 0 | -11.6 | -34.2 |

## .450 Dakota

| Cartridge Bullet | Range, Yards: | 0 | 100 | 200 | 300 | 400 |
|---|---|---|---|---|---|---|
| Dakota 500 Barnes Solid | velocity, fps: | 2450 | 2235 | 2030 | 1838 | 1658 |
| | energy, ft-lb: | 6663 | 5544 | 4576 | 3748 | 3051 |
| | arc, inches: | | +2.5 | -0.6 | -12.0 | -33.8 |

## .460 Weatherby Magnum

| Cartridge Bullet | Range, Yards: | 0 | 100 | 200 | 300 | 400 |
|---|---|---|---|---|---|---|
| A-Square 500 Triad | velocity, fps: | 2580 | 2349 | 2131 | 1923 | 1737 |
| | energy, ft-lb: | 7389 | 6126 | 5040 | 4107 | 3351 |
| | arc, inches: | | +2.4 | 0 | -10.0 | -29.4 |
| Wby. 450 Barnes X | velocity, fps: | 2700 | 2518 | 2343 | 2175 | 2013 |
| | energy, ft-lb: | 7284 | 6333 | 5482 | 4725 | 4050 |
| | arc, inches: | | +2.0 | 0 | -8.4 | -24.1 |
| Wby. 500 RN Expanding | velocity, fps: | 2600 | 2301 | 2022 | 1764 | 1533 |
| | energy, ft-lb: | 7504 | 5877 | 4539 | 3456 | 2608 |
| | arc, inches: | | +2.6 | 0 | -11.1 | -33.5 |
| Wby. 500 FMJ | velocity, fps: | 2600 | 2309 | 2037 | 1784 | 1557 |
| | energy, ft-lb: | 7504 | 5917 | 4605 | 3534 | 2690 |
| | arc, inches: | | +2.5 | 0 | -10.9 | -33.0 |

## .500/.465

| Cartridge Bullet | Range, Yards: | 0 | 100 | 200 | 300 | 400 |
|---|---|---|---|---|---|---|
| A-Square 480 Triad | velocity, fps: | 2150 | 1928 | 1722 | 1533 | |
| | energy, ft-lb: | 4926 | 3960 | 3160 | 2505 | |
| | arc, inches: | | +4.3 | 0 | -16.0 | |

## .470 Nitro Express

| Cartridge Bullet | Range, Yards: | 0 | 100 | 200 | 300 | 400 |
|---|---|---|---|---|---|---|
| A-Square 500 Triad | velocity, fps: | 2150 | 1912 | 1693 | 1494 | |
| | energy, ft-lb: | 5132 | 4058 | 3182 | 2478 | |
| | arc, inches: | | +4.4 | 0 | -16.5 | |
| Federal 500 Woodleigh Weldcore | velocity, fps: | 2150 | 1890 | 1650 | 1440 | 1270 |
| | energy, ft-lb: | 5130 | 3965 | 3040 | 2310 | 1790 |
| | arc, inches: | | 0 | -9.3 | -31.3 | -69.7 |

| Cartridge / Bullet | Range, Yards: | 0 | 100 | 200 | 300 | 400 |
|---|---|---|---|---|---|---|
| Federal 500 Woodleigh Weldcore Solid | velocity, fps: | 2150 | 1890 | 1650 | 1440 | 1270 |
| | energy, ft-lb: | 5130 | 3965 | 3040 | 2310 | 1790 |
| | arc, inches: | | 0 | -9.3 | -31.3 | -69.7 |
| Federal 500 Trophy Bonded | velocity, fps: | 2150 | 1940 | 1740 | 1560 | 1400 |
| | energy, ft-lb: | 5130 | 4170 | 3360 | 2695 | 2160 |
| | arc, inches: | | 0 | -7.8 | -27.1 | -60.8 |
| Federal 500 Trophy Bonded Sledgehammer Solid | velocity, fps: | 2150 | 1940 | 1740 | 1560 | 1400 |
| | energy, ft-lb: | 5130 | 4170 | 3360 | 2695 | 2160 |
| | arc, inches: | | 0 | -7.8 | -27.1 | -60.8 |

## .470 Capstick

| Bullet | Range, Yards: | 0 | 100 | 200 | 300 | 400 |
|---|---|---|---|---|---|---|
| A-Square 500 Triad | velocity, fps: | 2400 | 2172 | 1958 | 1761 | 1553 |
| | energy, ft-lb: | 6394 | 5236 | 4255 | 3445 | 2678 |
| | arc, inches: | | +2.9 | 0 | -11.9 | -36.1 |

## .475 #2

| Bullet | Range, Yards: | 0 | 100 | 200 | 300 | 400 |
|---|---|---|---|---|---|---|
| A-Square 480 Triad | velocity, fps: | 2200 | 1964 | 1744 | 1544 | |
| | energy, ft-lb: | 5158 | 4109 | 3240 | 2539 | |
| | arc, inches: | | +4.1 | 0 | -15.6 | |

## .475 #2 Jeffery

| Bullet | Range, Yards: | 0 | 100 | 200 | 300 | 400 |
|---|---|---|---|---|---|---|
| A-Square 500 Triad | velocity, fps: | 2200 | 1966 | 1748 | 1550 | |
| | energy, ft-lb: | 5373 | 4291 | 3392 | 2666 | |
| | arc, inches: | | +4.1 | 0 | -15.6 | |

## .495 A-Square

| Bullet | Range, Yards: | 0 | 100 | 200 | 300 | 400 |
|---|---|---|---|---|---|---|
| A-Square 570 Triad | velocity, fps: | 2350 | 2117 | 1896 | 1693 | 1513 |
| | energy, ft-lb: | 6989 | 5671 | 4552 | 3629 | 2899 |
| | arc, inches: | | +3.1 | 0 | -13.0 | -37.8 |

## .500 Nitro Express (3")

| Bullet | Range, Yards: | 0 | 100 | 200 | 300 | 400 |
|---|---|---|---|---|---|---|
| A-Square 570 Triad | velocity, fps: | 2150 | 1928 | 1722 | 1533 | |
| | energy, ft-lb: | 5850 | 4703 | 3752 | 2975 | |
| | arc, inches: | | +4.3 | 0 | -16.1 | |

## .500 A-Square

| Bullet | Range, Yards: | 0 | 100 | 200 | 300 | 400 |
|---|---|---|---|---|---|---|
| A-Square 600 Triad | velocity, fps: | 2470 | 2235 | 2013 | 1804 | 1620 |
| | energy, ft-lb: | 8127 | 6654 | 5397 | 4336 | 3495 |
| | arc, inches: | | +2.7 | 0 | -11.3 | -33.5 |

## .505 Gibbs

| Bullet | Range, Yards: | 0 | 100 | 200 | 300 | 400 |
|---|---|---|---|---|---|---|
| A-Square 525 Triad | velocity, fps: | 2300 | 2063 | 1840 | 1637 | |
| | energy, ft-lb: | 6166 | 4962 | 3948 | 3122 | |
| | arc, inches: | | +3.6 | 0 | -14.2 | |

## .577 Nitro Express

| Bullet | Range, Yards: | 0 | 100 | 200 | 300 | 400 |
|---|---|---|---|---|---|---|
| A-Square 750 Triad | velocity, fps: | 2050 | 1811 | 1595 | 1401 | |
| | energy, ft-lb: | 6998 | 5463 | 4234 | 3267 | |
| | arc, inches: | | +4.9 | 0 | -18.5 | |

## .577 Tyrannosaur

| Bullet | Range, Yards: | 0 | 100 | 200 | 300 | 400 |
|---|---|---|---|---|---|---|
| A-Square 750 Triad | velocity, fps: | 2460 | 2197 | 1950 | 1723 | 1516 |
| | energy, ft-lb: | 10077 | 8039 | 6335 | 4941 | 3825 |
| | arc, inches: | | +2.8 | 0 | -12.1 | -36.0 |

## .600 Nitro Express

| Bullet | Range, Yards: | 0 | 100 | 200 | 300 | 400 |
|---|---|---|---|---|---|---|
| A-Square 900 Triad | velocity, fps: | 1950 | 1680 | 1452 | 1336 | |
| | energy, ft-lb: | 7596 | 5634 | 4212 | 3564 | |
| | arc, inches: | | +5.6 | 0 | -20.7 | |

## .700 Nitro Express

| Bullet | Range, Yards: | 0 | 100 | 200 | 300 | 400 |
|---|---|---|---|---|---|---|
| A-Square 1000 Monolithic Solid | velocity, fps: | 1900 | 1669 | 1461 | 1288 | |
| | energy, ft-lb: | 8015 | 6188 | 4740 | 3685 | |
| | arc, inches: | | +5.8 | 0 | -22.2 | |

Hornady's **SST (SUPER SHOCK TIPPED)** bullets feature a premium polymer tip which, along with its profile, combine to improve the SST's ballistic coefficient.

Hornady's moly-coated **LIGHT MAGNUM** ammo achieves more energy, flatter trajectory and velocities up to 200 feet per second faster than standard ammo.

Hornady's **VARMINT EXPRESS** ammunition now features moly-coated V-MAX bullets, which offer faster speeds in most calibers.

Hornady **A-MAX** or **BTHP** match bullets, are now available with high-performance moly-coating that reduces barrel wear and increases speed.

# SAKO RIFLE BALLISTICS

| CALIBER | BULLET GRS | WEIGHT/TYPE TYPE | VELOCITY IN FEET PER SECOND | | | | | |
|---------|-----------|------------------|--------|------|------|------|------|------|
| | | | MUZZLE | 100Y | 200Y | 300Y | 400Y | 500Y |
| 22 Hornet | 45 | SPEEDHEAD FMJ | 2300 | 1724 | 1291 | 1069 | 944 | 861 |
| | 45 | SOFT POINT RN | 2300 | 1724 | 1291 | 1069 | 944 | 861 |
| | 42 | HOLLOW PIONT | 2700 | 2193 | 1764 | 1419 | 1161 | 1011 |
| 22 PPC USA | 52 | HPBT MATCH | 3400 | 2990 | 2613 | 2255 | 1920 | 1616 |
| 222 Remington | 50 | SPEEDHEAD FMJ | 3200 | 2663 | 2182 | 1776 | 1447 | 1192 |
| 222 | 50 | SOFT POINT P | 3200 | 2663 | 2182 | 1776 | 1447 | 1192 |
| | 55 | SOFT POINT P | 3280 | 2800 | 2372 | 1978 | 1637 | 1350 |
| | 52 | HPBT MATCH | 3035 | 2613 | 2235 | 1894 | 1589 | 1333 |
| 222 Remington | 50 | SPEEDHEAD FJM | 3230 | 2690 | 2207 | 1798 | 1466 | 1207 |
| | 50 | SOFT POINT P | 3230 | 2690 | 2207 | 1798 | 1466 | 1207 |
| | 55 | SOFT POINT P | 3330 | 2848 | 2414 | 2016 | 1671 | 1378 |
| 223 Remington | 50 | SPEEDHEAD FJM | 3230 | 2690 | 2207 | 1798 | 1466 | 1207 |
| | 50 | SOFT POINT P | 3230 | 2690 | 2207 | 1798 | 1466 | 1207 |
| | 55 | SOFT POINT P | 3330 | 2848 | 2414 | 2016 | 1671 | 1378 |
| 22-250 Remington | 50 | SPEEDHEAD FMJ | 3770 | 3168 | 2639 | 2168 | 1751 | 1396 |
| | 50 | SOFT POINT P | 3770 | 3168 | 2639 | 2168 | 1751 | 1396 |
| | 55 | SOFT POINT P | 3660 | 3146 | 2681 | 2255 | 1871 | 1533 |
| 6PPC USA | 70 | HPBT MATCH | 3200 | 2740 | 2407 | 2090 | 1793 | 1527 |
| 243 Winchester | 90 | SPEEDHEAD FJM | 2855 | 2587 | 2340 | 2110 | 1895 | 1693 |
| | 90 | SOFT POINT P | 3130 | 2850 | 2587 | 2343 | 2114 | 1898 |
| 6.5X55 Swedish | 100 | SPEEDHEAD FJM | 2625 | 2270 | 1946 | 1651 | 1397 | 1196 |
| | 139 | HPBT MATCH | 2790 | 2648 | 2512 | 2381 | 2252 | 2129 |
| | 156 | SOFT POINT RN | 2625 | 23843 | 2156 | 1941 | 1740 | 1554 |
| 270 Wlinchester | 130 | SPEEDHEAD FMJ | 2820 | 2506 | 2212 | 1938 | 1687 | 1463 |
| | 156 | HAMMERHEAD | 2755 | 2470 | 2208 | 1967 | 1743 | 1538 |
| 7x33 Sako | 78 | SPEEDHEAD FJM | 2430 | 1920 | 1500 | 1190 | 1013 | 906 |
| | 78 | SOFT POINT SP | 2430 | 1920 | 1500 | 1190 | 1013 | 906 |
| 7mm Mauser(7x57) | 78 | SPEEDHEAD FJM | 2950 | 2324 | 783 | 1362 | 1090 | 950 |
| | 170 | SOFT POINT SP | 2495 | 2283 | 2086 | 1901 | 1728 | 1567 |
| 7x64 | 120 | SOFT POINT P | 3100 | 2816 | 2545 | 2296 | 2069 | 1856 |
| | 170 | HAMMERHEAD | 2790 | 2563 | 2351 | 2154 | 1967 | 1791 |
| 7x65R | 170 | HAMMERHEAD | 2625 | 2409 | 2208 | 2019 | 1839 | 1670 |
| 7mm Remington Mag | 170 | HAMMERHEAD | 2970 | 2734 | 2512 | 2303 | 2108 | 1924 |
| 7.62x39 Russian | 123 | SPEEDHEAD FMJ | 2345 | 2096 | 1863 | 1651 | 1466 | 1305 |
| | 123 | SPEEDHEAD FMJ | 2345 | 2096 | 1863 | 1651 | 1466 | 1305 |
| | 123 | SOFT POINT P | 2345 | 2096 | 1863 | 1651 | 1466 | 1305 |
| 30-30 Winchester | 93 | SPEEDHEAD FMJ | 2970 | 2354 | 1818 | 1400 | 1126 | 976 |
| | 150 | SOFT POINT FP | 2310 | 1982 | 1681 | 1439 | 1240 | 1096 |
| 308 Winchester | 93 | SPEEDHEAD FMJ | 2970 | 2354 | 1818 | 1400 | 1126 | 976 |
| | 123 | SPEEDHEAD FMJ | 2920 | 2622 | 2347 | 2097 | 1868 | 1654 |
| | 123 | SOFT POINT P | 3035 | 2734 | 2455 | 2194 | 1958 | 1738 |
| | 156 | S-HAMMERHEAD | 2790 | 2563 | 2353 | 2158 | 1973 | 1800 |
| | 180 | HAMEMRHEAD | 2610 | 2382 | 2169 | 1971 | 1786 | 1612 |
| | 180 | S-HAMMERHEAD | 2610 | 2400 | 2204 | 2017 | 1839 | 1672 |
| | 200 | HAMMERHEAD | 2445 | 2210 | 1990 | 1782 | 1588 | 1415 |
| | 123 | RANGE | 2950 | 2652 | 2378 | 2126 | 1895 | 1679 |
| | 102 | SUPER RANGE | 3120 | 2712 | 2342 | 2003 | 1695 | 1428 |
| | 168 | HPBT MATCH | 2690 | 2500 | 2321 | 2159 | 2004 | 1857 |
| | 190 | HPBT MATCH | 2525 | 2372 | 2224 | 2080 | 1940 | 1806 |
| 7.62x53R | 93 | SPEEDHEAD FMJ | 2970 | 2354 | 1818 | 1400 | 1126 | 976 |
| | 123 | SPEEDHEAD FMJ | 2920 | 2622 | 2347 | 2097 | 1868 | 1654 |
| | 156 | S-HAMMERHEAD | 2790 | 2563 | 2353 | 2158 | 1973 | 1800 |
| | 180 | S-HAMMERHEAD | 2610 | 2400 | 2204 | 2017 | 1839 | 1672 |
| | 200 | HAMMERHEAD | 2445 | 2210 | 1990 | 1782 | 1588 | 1415 |
| | 123 | RANGE | 2950 | 2652 | 2378 | 2126 | 1895 | 1679 |
| 30-06 Springfield | 123 | SPEEDHEAD FMJ | 2920 | 2622 | 2347 | 2097 | 1868 | 1654 |
| | 123 | SOFT POINT P | 3120 | 2800 | 2510 | 2250 | 2010 | 1786 |
| | 156 | S-HAMMERHEAD | 2900 | 2670 | 2454 | 2255 | 2070 | 1893 |
| | 180 | HAMMERHEAD | 2700 | 2465 | 2242 | 2042 | 1857 | 1682 |
| | 180 | S-HAMMERHEAD | 2700 | 2500 | 2295 | 2100 | 1920 | 1750 |
| | 220 | HAMMERHEAD | 2410 | 2200 | 2000 | 1826 | 1664 | 1517 |
| | 123 | RANGE | 2950 | 2652 | 2378 | 2126 | 1895 | 1679 |
| 300 Winchester Mag | 156 | S-HAMMERHEAD | 3150 | 2905 | 2673 | 2453 | 2243 | 2044 |
| | 180 | HAMMERHEAD | 2950 | 2700 | 2467 | 2243 | 2031 | 1833 |
| | 180 | S-HAMMERHEAD | 2950 | 2730 | 2517 | 2314 | 2121 | 1938 |
| | 168 | HPBT MATCH | 3020 | 2816 | 2622 | 2438 | 2260 | 2090 |
| 8.2x57JRS | 200 | HAMMERHEAD | 2395 | 2093 | 1815 | 1563 | 1347 | 1176 |
| 338 Winchester Mag | 250 | HAMMERHEAD | 2676 | 2413 | 2169 | 1946 | 1742 | 1554 |
| 9.3x53R Finnish | 256 | SOFT POINT RN | 2330 | 2000 | 1695 | 1439 | 1236 | 1091 |
| 9.3x62 | 250 | POWERHEAD BARNES | 2360 | 2170 | 1988 | 1815 | 1652 | 1503 |
| 375 H&H Mag | 270 | POWERHEAD BARNES | 2720 | 2535 | 2354 | 2181 | 2015 | 1857 |

SPEEDHEAD=FMJ-Full Metal Jacket • HAMMERHEAD=Soft Point Bonded Core • HPBT=Hollow Point Boat Tail, Precision • SP P=Soft Point Pointed • HP = Hollow Point, Varmint, Precision • RANGE=Full Metal Jacket

*(Continued on following page)*

BALLISTICS

# SAKO RIFLE BALLISTICS

| | ENERGY IN FOOT-POUNDS | | | | | | TRAJECTORY INCHES/YARDS | | | | | | BOX |
| --- | --- | --- | --- | --- | --- | --- | --- | --- | --- | --- | --- | --- | --- |
| | MUZZLE | 100Y | 200Y | 300Y | 400Y | 500Y | MUZZLE | 100Y | 200Y | 300Y | 400Y | 500Y | PCS |
| 22 Hornet | 524 | 295 | 165 | 114 | 89 | 74 | -1.5 | 0 | -14.3 | -47.1 | -108.9 | -203.5 | 20 |
| | 524 | 295 | 165 | 114 | 89 | 74 | -1.5 | 0 | -14.3 | -47.1 | -108.9 | -203.5 | 20 |
| | 652 | 428 | 277 | 179 | 120 | 91 | -1.5 | 0 | -6.6 | -24.5 | -60.1 | -120.9 | 20 |
| 22 PPC USA | 1342 | 1040 | 795 | 592 | 429 | 304 | -1.5 | 1.2 | 0 | -6.0 | -19.1 | -41.8 | 20 |
| 222 Remington | 1135 | 786 | 528 | 350 | 232 | 158 | -1.5 | 1.2 | 0 | -10.3 | -31.1 | -67.3 | 20 |
| 222 | 1135 | 786 | 528 | 350 | 232 | 158 | -1.5 | 1.7 | 0 | -10.3 | -31.1 | -67.3 | 20 |
| | 1312 | 958 | 686 | 477 | 326 | 222 | -1.5 | 1.4 | 0 | -8.0 | -24.8 | -54.5 | 20 |
| | 1072 | 795 | 581 | 417 | 294 | 207 | -1.5 | 1.8 | 0 | -9.0 | -27.9 | -60.7 | 20 |
| 222 Remington | 1159 | 803 | 540 | 359 | 238 | 161 | -1.5 | 1.6 | 0 | -10.0 | -30.3 | -67.0 | 20 |
| | 1159 | 803 | 540 | 359 | 238 | 161 | -1.5 | 1.6 | 0 | -10.0 | -30.3 | -67.0 | 20 |
| | 1352 | 989 | 710 | 495 | 340 | 231 | -1.5 | 1.4 | 0 | -7.7 | -23.8 | -51.9 | 20 |
| 223 Remington | 1159 | 803 | 540 | 359 | 238 | 161 | -1.5 | 1.6 | 0 | -10.0 | -30.3 | -67.0 | 20 |
| | 1159 | 803 | 540 | 359 | 238 | 161 | -1.5 | 1.6 | 0 | -10.0 | -30.3 | -67.0 | 20 |
| | 1352 | 989 | 710 | 495 | 340 | 231 | -1.5 | 1.4 | 0 | -7.7 | -23.8 | -51.9 | 20 |
| 22-250 Remington | 1579 | 1113 | 773 | 522 | 340 | 216 | -1.5 | 1.0 | 0 | -6.0 | -19.5 | -44.0 | 20 |
| | 1579 | 1113 | 7773 | 522 | 340 | 216 | -1.5 | 1.0 | 0 | -6.0 | -19.5 | -44.0 | 20 |
| | 1631 | 1206 | 876 | 620 | 426 | 286 | -1.5 | 1.0 | 0 | -5.9 | -18.7 | -41.3 | 20 |
| 6PPC USA | 1481 | 1156 | 892 | 673 | 495 | 359 | -1.5 | 1.5 | 0 | -7.2 | -22.8 | -49.2 | 20 |
| 243 Winchester | 1618 | 1329 | 1087 | 884 | 713 | 569 | -1.5 | 1.9 | 0 | -8.2 | -24.3 | -49.9 | 20 |
| | 1949 | 1612 | 1329 | 1090 | 887 | 715 | -1.5 | 1.5 | 0 | -6.5 | -19.5 | -40.2 | 20 |
| 6.5X55 Swedish | 1533 | 1147 | 842 | 606 | 434 | 319 | -1.5 | 2.6 | 0 | -11.9 | -36.0 | -76.8 | 20 |
| | 2396 | 2161 | 1945 | 1746 | 1563 | 1396 | -1.5 | 1.7 | 0 | -7.2 | -20.5 | -40.7 | 20 |
| | 2382 | 1966 | 1607 | 1303 | 1047 | 835 | -1.5 | 2.3 | 0 | -9.8 | -28.9 | -59.7 | 20 |
| 270 Wlinchester | 2290 | 1805 | 1407 | 1080 | 818 | 616 | -1.5 | 2.0 | 0 | -9.2 | -27.5 | -58.3 | 20 |
| | 2625 | 2111 | 1685 | 1338 | 1051 | 818 | -1.5 | 2.2 | 0 | -9.3 | -27.6 | -57.5 | 20 |
| 7x33 Sako | 1029 | 643 | 392 | 247 | 179 | 143 | -1.5 | 0 | -8.5 | -31.0 | -78.8 | -158.0 | 50 |
| | 1029 | 643 | 392 | 247 | 179 | 243 | -1.5 | 0 | -8.5 | -31.0 | -78.8 | -158.0 | 50 |
| 7mm Mauser(7x57) | 1522 | 943 | 555 | 324 | 208 | 158 | -1.5 | 2.6 | 0 | -14.9 | -50.4 | -112.2 | 20 |
| | 2324 | 1962 | 1638 | 1361 | 1125 | 925 | -1.5 | 2.6 | 0 | -10.8 | -31.1 | -63.3 | 20 |
| 7x64 | 2567 | 2117 | 1730 | 1408 | 1143 | 920 | -1.5 | 1.4 | 0 | -7.3 | -20.9 | -42.6 | 20 |
| | 2929 | 2473 | 2081 | 1747 | 1458 | 1208 | -1.5 | 1.9 | 0 | -8.2 | -23.9 | -48.6 | 20 |
| 7x65R | 2594 | 2186 | 1836 | 1535 | 1274 | 1050 | -1.5 | 2.3 | 0 | -9.4 | -27.4 | -55.6 | 20 |
| 7mm Remington Mag | 3320 | 2814 | 2376 | 1996 | 1674 | 1394 | -1.5 | 1.6 | 0 | -7.2 | -21.0 | -42.5 | 20 |
| 7.62x39 Russian | 1507 | 1203 | 951 | 747 | 589 | 466 | -1.5 | 0 | -6.5 | -23.6 | -53.2 | -98.5 | 30 |
| | 1507 | 1203 | 951 | 747 | 589 | 466 | -1.5 | 0 | -6.5 | -23.6 | -53.2 | -98.5 | 250 |
| | 1507 | 1203 | 951 | 747 | 589 | 466 | -1.5 | 0 | -6.5 | -23.6 | -53.2 | -98.5 | 30 |
| 30-30 Winchester | 1811 | 1138 | 679 | 403 | 260 | 196 | -1.5 | 0 | -4.9 | -21.8 | -57.7 | -117.3 | 20 |
| | 1777 | 1304 | 938 | 688 | 510 | 400 | -1.5 | 0 | -8.1 | -28.3 | -65.6 | -125.6 | 20 |
| 308 Winchester | 1811 | 1138 | 679 | 403 | 260 | 196 | -1.5 | 0 | -4.9 | -21.8 | -56.7 | -117.3 | 20 |
| | 2335 | 1883 | 1509 | 1205 | 955 | 749 | -1.5 | 1.8 | 0 | -8.4 | -24.5 | -50.7 | 20 |
| | 2523 | 2047 | 1650 | 1318 | 1050 | 827 | -1.5 | 1.6 | 0 | -7.6 | -22.4 | -46.2 | 20 |
| | 2689 | 2271 | 1914 | 1610 | 1346 | 1120 | -1.5 | 2.0 | 0 | -8.2 | -23.9 | -48.9 | 20 |
| | 2725 | 2273 | 1885 | 1556 | 1277 | 1041 | -1.5 | 2.4 | 0 | -9.9 | -28.6 | -58.1 | 20 |
| | 2725 | 2310 | 1946 | 1629 | 1355 | 1119 | -1.5 | 2.3 | 0 | -9.5 | -27.5 | -55.8 | 20 |
| | 2660 | 2172 | 1762 | 1414 | 1122 | 891 | -1.5 | 2.8 | 0 | -11.3 | -33.7 | -70.1 | 20 |
| | 2388 | 1927 | 1549 | 1238 | 983 | 772 | -1.5 | 1.8 | 0 | -8.0 | -23.7 | -49.0 | 50 |
| | 2195 | 1662 | 1240 | 907 | 649 | 461 | -1.5 | 1.6 | 0 | -8.0 | -24.7 | -53.7 | 50 |
| | 2701 | 2328 | 2010 | 1739 | 1499 | 1286 | -1.5 | 2.3 | 0 | -8.5 | -24.5 | -49.1 | 20 |
| | 2688 | 2369 | 2082 | 1822 | 1585 | 1373 | -1.5 | 2.4 | 0 | -9.0 | -26.3 | -52.9 | 20 |
| 7.62x53R | 1811 | 1138 | 679 | 403 | 260 | 196 | -1.5 | 0 | -4.9 | -21.8 | -56.7 | -117.3 | 20 |
| | 2335 | 1883 | 1509 | 1205 | 955 | 749 | -1.5 | 1.8 | 0 | -8.4 | -24.5 | -50.7 | 20 |
| | 2689 | 2271 | 1914 | 1610 | 1346 | 1120 | -1.5 | 2.0 | 0 | -8.2 | -23.9 | -48.9 | 20 |
| | 2725 | 2310 | 1946 | 1629 | 1355 | 1119 | -1.5 | 2.3 | 0 | -9.5 | -27.5 | -55.8 | 20 |
| | 2660 | 2172 | 1762 | 1414 | 1122 | 891 | -1.5 | 2.8 | 0 | -11.3 | -33.7 | -70.1 | 20 |
| | 2388 | 1927 | 1549 | 1238 | 983 | 772 | -1.5 | 1.8 | 0 | -8.0 | -23.7 | -49.0 | 50 |
| 30-06 Springfield | 2335 | 1883 | 1509 | 1205 | 955 | 749 | -1.5 | 1.8 | 0 | -8.4 | -24.5 | -50.7 | 20 |
| | 2661 | 2148 | 1726 | 1385 | 1106 | 873 | -1.5 | 1.6 | 0 | -7.3 | -21.3 | -43.9 | 20 |
| | 2915 | 2466 | 2083 | 1759 | 1481 | 1240 | -1.5 | 1.8 | 0 | -7.8 | -22.2 | -44.7 | 20 |
| | 2935 | 2433 | 2013 | 1670 | 1381 | 1133 | -1.5 | 2.3 | 0 | -9.4 | -27.0 | -54.5 | 20 |
| | 2935 | 2495 | 2105 | 1768 | 1475 | 1223 | -1.5 | 2.1 | 0 | -8.7 | -25.3 | -51.3 | 20 |
| | 2847 | 2369 | 1963 | 1632 | 1356 | 1126 | -1.5 | 3.3 | 0 | -12.4 | -34.7 | -69.6 | 20 |
| | 2388 | 1927 | 1549 | 1238 | 983 | 772 | -1.5 | 1.8 | 0 | -8.0 | -23.7 | -49.0 | 50 |
| 300 Winchester Mag | 3430 | 2918 | 2470 | 2080 | 1740 | 1445 | -1.5 | 1.3 | 0 | -6.1 | -18.1 | -37.0 | 20 |
| | 3493 | 2926 | 2438 | 2015 | 1653 | 1345 | -1.5 | 1.6 | 0 | -7.4 | -21.7 | -44.4 | 20 |
| | 3493 | 2983 | 2537 | 2144 | 1801 | 1504 | -1.5 | 1.6 | 0 | -7.1 | -20.7 | -42.0 | 20 |
| | 3400 | 2959 | 2566 | 2217 | 1905 | 1630 | -1.5 | 1.5 | 0 | -6.5 | -18.8 | -38.0 | 20 |
| 8.2x57JRS | 2553 | 1949 | 1465 | 1087 | 807 | 616 | -1.5 | 3.3 | 0 | -13.9 | -42.0 | -89.7 | 20 |
| 338 Winchester Mag | 3966 | 3229 | 2608 | 21012 | 1683 | 1339 | -1.5 | 2.3 | 0 | -10.0 | -29.1 | -59.7 | 20 |
| 9.3x53R Finnish | 3010 | 2211 | 1593 | 1148 | 847 | 660 | -1.5 | 3.6 | 0 | -16.9 | -50.3 | -107.0 | 20 |
| 9.3x62 | 3095 | 2612 | 2192 | 1828 | 1514 | 1253 | -1.5 | 3.0 | 0 | -11.8 | -34.2 | -69.4 | 10 |
| 375 H&H Mag | 4440 | 3848 | 3319 | 2848 | 2432 | 2066 | -1.5 | 1.9 | 0 | -8.3 | -23.8 | -48.0 | 10 |

S-HAMMERHEAD=SUPER HAMMERHEAD=Hollow Point Bonded Core • SP SP = Soft Point Semi Pointed • SP FP = Soft Point Flat Point • POWERHEAD BARNES = Hollow Piont Solid Copper • SUPER RANGE = HPBT, Varmint, Precision • SP RN = Soft Point Round Nose

# Reloading

*Roland Clark – Open Water, 1928*

*For addresses and phone/fax numbers of manufacturers and distributors included in this section, please turn to **DIRECTORY OF MANUFACTURERS AND SUPPLIERS** on page 564.*

# BARNES BULLETS

In 1989 Barnes introduced the **X-Bullet**. It has since supplanted the company's lead-core softpoints (still made) as a premier big game bullet. Now the **X-Bullet** is also available for handguns, muzzleloaders and shotguns, and for rifles with a special blue dry-film lubricant–the **XLC**. The **XLC** promises higher velocities at modest pressures.

**308 Cal. 180 GR. XBT**
recovered from a Moose
98% Wgt. Retention.

## X-Bullets
### PISTOL

| | Dia. | Bullet Weight | Desr. | Sect. Dens. | Ballist. Coeff. | Cat. # |
|---|---|---|---|---|---|---|
| 44 | .429" | 200 GR | "X" PB | .155 | .172 | 42920 |
| | .429" | 225 GR | "X" PB | .175 | .195 | 42922 |
| 45 | 451" | 250 GR | "X" PB | .176 | 188 | 45123 |
| 50 | .500" | 275 GR | "X" PB | .157 | .183 | 50025 |

## Expander MZ
### MUZZLELOADER

| | Dia. | Bullet Weight | Desr. | Sect. Dens. | Ballist. Coeff. | Cat. # |
|---|---|---|---|---|---|---|
| 50 Cal | .451" | 250 GR | MZ | .176 | .189 | 45125 |
| | .451" | 300 GR | MZ | .211 | .207 | 45130 |
| 54 Cal | .500" | 275 GR | MZ | .157 | .184 | 50027 |
| | .500" | 325 GR | MZ | .186 | .204 | 50032 |

## Expander SGS
### SHOTGUN

| Dia. | Bullet Weight | Desr. | Sect. Dens. | Ballist. Coeff. | Cat. # |
|---|---|---|---|---|---|
| .575" | 438 GR | SGS | .189 | .214 | 57500 |

## COATED X-BULLETS
# RIFLE

| | Dia. | Bullet Weight | Desr. | Sect. Dens. | Ballist. Coeff. | Cat. # |
|---|---|---|---|---|---|---|
| NEW 22 | .224" | 45 GR | "XLC" BT | .128 | .203 | 22452 |
| | .224" | 50 GR | "XLC" S | .142 | .220 | 22454 |
| | .224" | 53 GR | "XLC" S | .151 | .231 | 22455 |
| 6mm | .243" | 85 GR | "XLC" BT | .206 | .401 | 24352 |
| 25 | .257" | 100 GR | "XLC" BT | .216 | .420 | 25754 |
| 6.5 | .264" | 140 GR | "XLC" S | .287 | .522 | 26453 |
| 270 | .277" | 130 GR | "XLC" BT | .242 | .466 | 27754 |
| 7mm | .284" | 140 GR | "XLC" BT | .248 | .477 | 28455 |
| | .284" | 160 GR | "XLC" S | .283 | .508 | 28458 |
| 30 | .308" | 150 GR | "XLC" S | .226 | .428 | 30854 |
| | .308" | 165 GR | "XLC" BT | .247 | .505 | 30857 |
| NEW | .308" | 180 GR | "XLC" S | .271 | .511 | 30858 |
| NEW | .308" | 180 GR | "XLC" BT | .271 | .552 | 30859 |
| NEW 338 | .338" | 185 GR | "XLC" BT | .231 | .437 | 33854 |
| | .338" | 225 GR | "XLC" S | .281 | .482 | 33855 |
| NEW 375 | .375" | 235 GR | "XLC" S | .239 | .400 | 37553 |
| NEW | .375" | 270 GR | "XLC" S | .275 | .503 | 37557 |
| NEW 416 | .416" | 400 GR | "XLC" S | .330 | .546 | 41658 |
| NEW 470 | .474" | 500 GR | "XLC" S | .326 | .318 | 47550 |
| NEW 500 | .509" | 570 GR | "XLC" S | .335 | .316 | 50957 |

# BARNES BULLETS

## X-BULLETS RIFLE

| Dia. | Bullet Weight | Desr. | Sect. Dens. | Ballist. Coeff. | Cat. # |
|------|---------------|-------|-------------|-----------------|--------|
| .224" | 50 GR | "X" S | .142 | .220 | 22450 |
| .224" | 53 GR | "X" S | .151 | .231 | 22453 |
| .243" | 85 GR | "X" BT | .206 | .401 | 24310 |
| .243" | 90 GR | "X" S | .218 | .382 | 24315 |
| .243" | 95 GR | "X" S | .230 | .398 | 24320 |
| .257" | 90 GR | "X" BT | .195 | .343 | 25710 |
| .257" | 100 GR | "X" S | .216 | .401 | 25715 |
| .257" | 100 GR | "X" BT | .216 | .420 | 25717 |
| .257" | 115 GR | "X" S | .249 | .429 | 25722 |
| .264" | 100 GR | "X" S | .205 | .381 | 26400 |
| .264" | 120 GR | "X" S | .246 | .441 | 26402 |
| .264" | 130 GR | "X" S | .266 | .479 | 26403 |
| .264" | 140 GR | "X" S | .287 | .522 | 26405 |
| .277" | 120 GR | "X" S | .223 | .406 | 27712 |
| .277" | 120 GR | "X" BT | .223 | .423 | 27713 |
| .277" | 130 GR | "X" S | .242 | .428 | 27715 |
| .277" | 130 GR | "X" BT | .242 | .466 | 27717 |
| .277" | 140 GR | "X" S | .261 | .462 | 27725 |
| .277" | 140 GR | "X" BT | .261 | .497 | 27727 |
| .277" | 150 GR | "X" S | .279 | .491 | 27735 |
| .284" | 100 GR | "X" S | .177 | .335 | 28405 |
| .284" | 120 GR | "X" S | .213 | .371 | 28415 |
| .284" | 120 GR | "X" BT | .213 | .411 | 28417 |
| .284" | 130 GR | "X" BT | .230 | .444 | 28420 |
| .284" | 140 GR | "X" S | .248 | .436 | 28425 |
| .284" | 140 GR | "X" BT | .248 | .477 | 28426 |
| .284" | 150 GR | "X" S | .266 | .488 | 28427 |
| .284" | 150 GR | "X" BT | .266 | .529 | 28428 |
| .284" | 160 GR | "X" S | .283 | .508 | 28435 |
| .284" | 175 GR | "X" S | .310 | .530 | 28445 |
| .308" | 110 GR | "X" S | .166 | .322 | 30800 |
| .308" | 130 GR | "X" BT | .196 | .374 | 30808 |
| .308" | 140 GR | "X" BT | .211 | .398 | 30810 |
| .308" | 150 GR | "X" S | .226 | .386 | 30815 |
| .308" | 150 GR | "X" BT | .226 | .428 | 30817 |
| .308" | 165 GR | "X" S | .247 | .456 | 30825 |
| .308" | 165 GR | "X" BT | .247 | .505 | 30827 |
| .308" | 180 GR | "X" S | .271 | .511 | 30835 |
| .308" | 180 GR | "X" BT | .271 | .552 | 30840 |
| .308" | 200 GR | "X" S | .301 | .550 | 30845 |
| .308" | 150 GR | "X" FN | .226 | .269 | 30819 |
| .308" | 165 GR | "X" FN | .247 | .302 | 30829 |
| .323" | 180 GR | "X" S | .246 | .382 | 32305 |
| .323" | 200 GR | "X" S | .274 | .429 | 32310 |
| .323" | 220 GR | "X" S | .301 | .462 | 32315 |
| .338" | 160 GR | "X" S | .200 | .337 | 33878 |
| .338" | 175 GR | "X" S | .218 | .392 | 33880 |

# BARNES BULLETS

## X-BULLETS RIFLE

| Día. | Bullet Weight | Desr. | Sect. Dens. | Ballist. Coeff. | Cat. # |
|------|---------------|-------|-------------|-----------------|--------|
| .358" | 250 GR | "X" S | .279 | .458 | 35835 |
| .366" | 250 GR | "X" S | .267 | .428 | 36605 |
| .366" | 286 GR | "X" S | .305 | .468 | 36615 |
| .375" | 210 GR | "X" S | .213 | .341 | 37575 |
| .375" | 250 GR | "X" S | .254 | .450 | 37582 |
| .375" | 270 GR | "X" S | .275 | .503 | 37585 |
| .375" | 300 GR | "X" S | .305 | .555 | 37590 |
| .411" | 300 GR | "X" S | .254 | .401 | 41180 |
| .411" | 325 GR | "X" S | .275 | .478 | 41182 |
| .411" | 350 GR | "X" S | .296 | .536 | 41185 |
| .411" | 400 GR | "X" S | .338 | .562 | 41190 |
| .416" | 300 GR | "X" S | .247 | .394 | 41680 |
| .416" | 325 GR | "X" S | .268 | .467 | 41682 |
| .416" | 350 GR | "X" S | .289 | .521 | 41685 |
| .416" | 400 GR | "X" S | .330 | .546 | 41690 |
| .423" | 350 GR | "X" S | .279 | .481 | 42382 |

## X-BULLETS RIFLE

| Dia. | Bullet Weight | Desr. | Sect. Dens. | Ballist. Coeff. | Cat. # |
|------|---------------|-------|-------------|-----------------|--------|
| .458" | 300 GR | "X" S | .204 | .340 | 45802 |
| .458" | 350 GR | "X" S | .283 | .402 | 45805 |
| .458" | 400 GR | "X" S | .272 | .457 | 45815 |
| .458" | 500 GR | "X" S | .341 | .526 | 45822 |
| .458" | 250 GR | "X" FN | .170 | .172 | 45831 |
| .458" | 300 GR | "X" FN | .206 | .204 | 45832 |
| .338" | 185 GR | "X" BT | .231 | .437 | 33881 |
| .338" | 200 GR | "X" S | .250 | .440 | 33882 |
| .338" | 210 GR | "X" BT | .263 | .471 | 33883 |
| .338" | 225 GR | "X" S | .281 | .482 | 33885 |
| .338" | 250 GR | "X" S | .313 | .521 | 33890 |
| .348" | 200 GR | "X" FN | .234 | .291 | 34800 |
| .348" | 220GR | "X" FN | .260 | .315 | 34802 |
| .358" | 180 GR | "X" S | .201 | .298 | 35810 |
| .358" | 200 GR | "X" S | .223 | .346 | 35815 |
| .358" | 225 GR | "X" S | .250 | .405 | 35825 |

# BARNES BULLETS

## SOLIDS RIFLE

| Dia. | Bullet Weight | Desr. | Sect. Dens. | Ballist. Coeff. | Cat. # |
|------|--------------|-------|-------------|-----------------|--------|
| .224" | 45 GR | Solid | .128 | .212 | 22401 |
| .224" | 50 GR | Solid | .142 | .235 | 22402 |
| .243" | 75 GR | Solid | .181 | .330 | 24301 |
| .243" | 85 GR | Solid | .206 | .353 | 24302 |
| .257" | 75 GR | Solid | .162 | .297 | 25718 |
| .257" | 90 GR | Solid | .195 | .324 | 25720 |
| .264" | 100 GR | Solid | .205 | .395 | 26410 |
| .264" | 120 GR | Solid | .246 | .453 | 26411 |
| .264" | 130 GR | Solid | .266 | .461 | 26412 |
| .277" | 100 GR | Solid | .186 | .370 | 27700 |
| .277" | 120 GR | Solid | .223 | .418 | 27702 |
| .277" | 130 GR | Solid | .242 | .448 | 27720 |
| .277" | 150 GR | Solid | .279 | .307 | 27722 |
| .284" | 100 GR | Solid | .177 | .343 | 28401 |
| .284" | 120 GR | Solid | .213 | .399 | 28403 |
| .284" | 140 GR | Solid | .248 | .448 | 28431 |
| .284" | 160 GR | Solid | .283 | .522 | 28432 |
| .284" | 175 GR | Solid | .310 | .321 | 28433 |
| .308" | 110 GR | Solid | .166 | .337 | 30811 |
| .308" | 125 GR | Solid | .188 | .372 | 30812 |
| .308" | 165 GR | Solid | .248 | .481 | 30822 |
| .308" | 220 GR | Solid | .331 | .305 | 30842 |
| .323" | 220 GR | Solid | .301 | .294 | 32332 |
| .338" | 200 GR | Solid | .250 | .465 | 33818 |
| .338" | 210 GR | Solid | .263 | .480 | 33820 |

## SOLIDS RIFLE

| Dia. | Bullet Weight | Desr. | Sect. Dens. | Ballist. Coeff. | Cat. # |
|------|--------------|-------|-------------|-----------------|--------|
| .338" | 225 GR | Solid | .281 | .506 | 33821 |
| .338" | 250 GR | Solid | .313 | .326 | 33825 |
| .358" | 250 GR | Solid | .285 | .313 | 35822 |
| .366" | 286 GR | Solid | .305 | .342 | 36612 |
| .375" | 235 GR | Solid | .239 | .442 | 37503 |
| .375" | 250 GR | Solid | .313 | .551 | 37505 |
| .375" | 270 GR | Solid | .275 | .284 | 37512 |
| .375" | 300 GR | Solid | .305 | .307 | 37525 |
| .411" | 350 GR | Solid | .296 | .374 | 41128 |
| .411" | 400 GR | Solid | .338 | .406 | 41160 |
| .416" | 350 GR | Solid | .289 | .364 | 41628 |
| .416" | 400 GR | Solid | .330 | .388 | 41660 |
| .423" | 350 GR | Solid | .279 | .347 | 42308 |
| .423" | 400 GR | Solid | .319 | .361 | 42330 |
| .435" | 410 GR | Solid | .310 | .390 | 43520 |
| .458" | 400 GR | Solid | .272 | .321 | 45825 |
| .458" | 450 GR | Solid | .306 | .362 | 45840 |
| .458" | 500 GR | Solid | .341 | .394 | 45855 |

RELOADING

# BARNES BULLETS

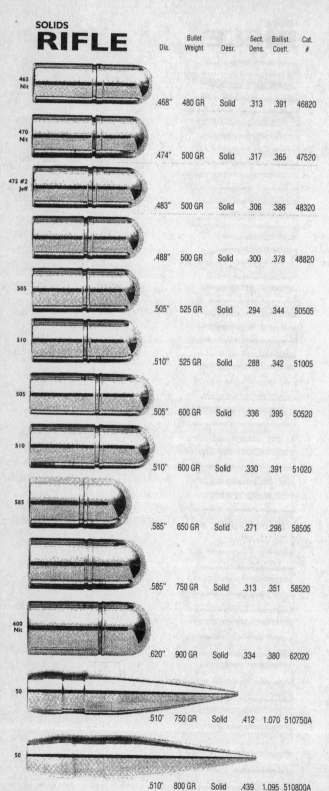

**SOLIDS**
## RIFLE

| | Dia. | Bullet Weight | Desr. | Sect. Dens. | Ballist. Coeff. | Cat. # |
|---|------|--------|-------|------|---------|--------|
| 465 Nit | .468" | 480 GR | Solid | .313 | .391 | 46820 |
| 470 Nit | .474" | 500 GR | Solid | .317 | .365 | 47520 |
| 475 #2 Jeff | .483" | 500 GR | Solid | .306 | .386 | 48320 |
| | .488" | 500 GR | Solid | .300 | .378 | 48820 |
| 505 | .505" | 525 GR | Solid | .294 | .344 | 50505 |
| 510 | .510" | 525 GR | Solid | .288 | .342 | 51005 |
| 505 | .505" | 600 GR | Solid | .336 | .395 | 50520 |
| 510 | .510" | 600 GR | Solid | .330 | .391 | 51020 |
| 585 | .585" | 650 GR | Solid | .271 | .296 | 58505 |
| | .585" | 750 GR | Solid | .313 | .351 | 58520 |
| 600 Nit | .620" | 900 GR | Solid | .334 | .380 | 62020 |
| 50 | .510" | 750 GR | Solid | .412 | 1.070 | 510750A |
| 50 | .510" | 800 GR | Solid | .439 | 1.095 | 510800A |

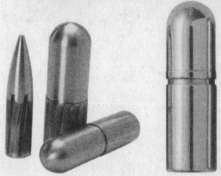

## BARNES SOLIDS-UNBEATABLE STOPPING POWER FOR HUNTING DANGEROUS GAME

Barnes Round Nose Solids, made of copper/zinc alloy, do not disintegrate or deflect when striking heavy bone. Rather, they plow on through to the vitals. Designed for stopping large, dangerous game, Barnes Solids are also availble in Spitzer shape in some calibers for hunting fur bearing animals. They do minimal damage to valuable pelts.

## BARNES ORIGINALS-THE PREFERRED BULLET OF DISCRIMINATING HUNTERS FOR MORE THAN 65 YEARS

In 1932 this bullet started it all. Designed by Fred Barnes for his own use on big game, it quickly gained favor in circles of serious hunters. That demand started Barnes Bullets. Made by pressure forming a thick copper jacket around a pure lead core, the Original typically expands to more than 200 percent of its original diameter and retains 70-90 percent of its original bullet weight.

# BARNES BULLETS

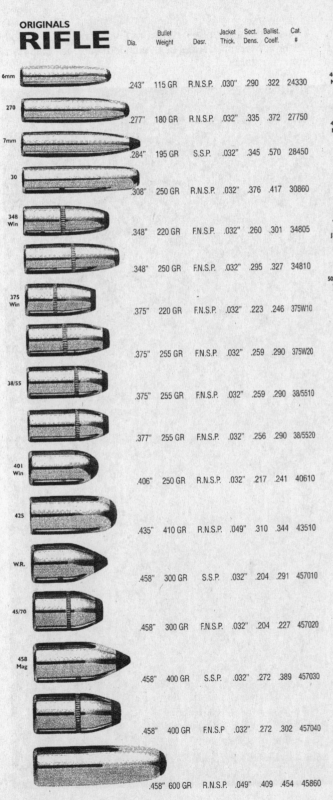

## ORIGINALS RIFLE

| Dia. | Bullet Weight | Desr. | Jacket Thick. | Sect. Dens. | Ballist. Coeff. | Cat. # |
|------|------|------|------|------|------|------|
| .243" | 115 GR | R.N.S.P. | .030" | .290 | .322 | 24330 |
| .277" | 180 GR | R.N.S.P. | .032" | .335 | .372 | 27750 |
| .284" | 195 GR | S.S.P. | .032" | .345 | .570 | 28450 |
| .308" | 250 GR | R.N.S.P. | .032" | .376 | .417 | 30860 |
| .348" | 220 GR | F.N.S.P. | .032" | .260 | .301 | 34805 |
| .348" | 250 GR | F.N.S.P. | .032" | .295 | .327 | 34810 |
| .375" | 220 GR | F.N.S.P. | .032" | .223 | .246 | 375W10 |
| .375" | 255 GR | F.N.S.P. | .032" | .259 | .290 | 375W20 |
| .375" | 255 GR | F.N.S.P. | .032" | .259 | .290 | 38/5510 |
| .377" | 255 GR | F.N.S.P. | .032" | .256 | .290 | 38/5520 |
| .406" | 250 GR | R.N.S.P. | .032" | .217 | .241 | 40610 |
| .435" | 410 GR | R.N.S.P. | .049" | .310 | .344 | 43510 |
| .458" | 300 GR | S.S.P. | .032" | .204 | .291 | 457010 |
| .458" | 300 GR | F.N.S.P. | .032" | .204 | .227 | 457020 |
| .458" | 400 GR | S.S.P. | .032" | .272 | .389 | 457030 |
| .458" | 400 GR | F.N.S.P | .032" | .272 | .302 | 457040 |
| .458" | 600 GR | R.N.S.P. | .049" | .409 | .454 | 45860 |

Row labels (left): 6mm, 270, 7mm, 30, 348 Win, 375 Win, 38/55, 401 Win, 425, W.R., 45/70, 458 Mag

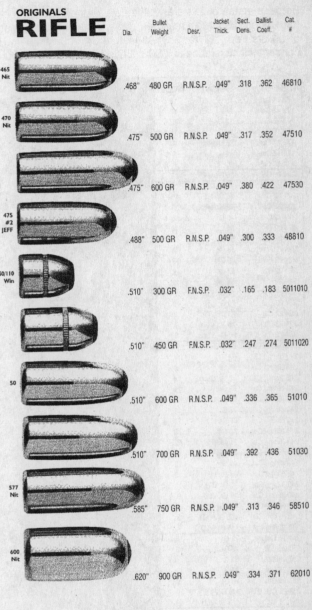

## ORIGINALS RIFLE

| Dia. | Bullet Weight | Desr. | Jacket Thick. | Sect. Dens. | Ballist. Coeff. | Cat. # |
|------|------|------|------|------|------|------|
| .468" | 480 GR | R.N.S.P. | .049" | .318 | .362 | 46810 |
| .475" | 500 GR | R.N.S.P. | .049" | .317 | .352 | 47510 |
| .475" | 600 GR | R.N.S.P. | .049" | .380 | .422 | 47530 |
| .488" | 500 GR | R.N.S.P. | .049" | .300 | .333 | 48810 |
| .510" | 300 GR | F.N.S.P. | .032" | .165 | .183 | 5011010 |
| .510" | 450 GR | F.N.S.P. | .032" | .247 | .274 | 5011020 |
| .510" | 600 GR | R.N.S.P. | .049" | .336 | .365 | 51010 |
| .510" | 700 GR | R.N.S.P. | .049" | .392 | .436 | 51030 |
| .585" | 750 GR | R.N.S.P. | .049" | .313 | .346 | 58510 |
| .620" | 900 GR | R.N.S.P. | .049" | .334 | .371 | 62010 |

Row labels (right): 465 Nit, 470 Nit, 475, 475 #2 JEFF, 50/110 Win, 50, 577 Nit, 600 Nit

# BERGER BULLETS

Berger's match bullets are well-known for their superior performance in benchrest matches. Now Berger offers a variety of bullets from .17 to .30. All feature J4 jackets with wall concentricity tolerance of .0003. Lead cores are 99.9% pure and swaged in dies to within .0001 of round. Berger's line includes several profiles: Low Drag, Very Low Drag, Length Tolerant, Maximum-expansion, standard flat-base and standard boat-tail.

| ITEM | WEIGHT | TWIST |
|------|--------|-------|
| .172 17 Cal. | 15 Gr. MEF | 12 |
| .172 17 Cal. | 18 Gr. MEF | 12 |
| .172 17 Cal. | 20 Gr. | 12 |
| .172 17 Cal. | 22 Gr. | 11 |
| .172 17 Cal. | 25 Gr. | 10 |
| .172 17 Cal. | 30 Gr. | 9 |
| .172 17 Cal. | 37 Gr. VLD | 6 |
| .204 20 Cal. | 36 Gr. MEF | 12 |
| .224 22 Cal. | 30 Gr MEF | 15 |
| .224 22 Cal. | 35 Gr. MEF | 15 |
| .224 22 Cal. | 40 Gr. MEF | 15 |
| .224 22 Cal. | 45 Gr. | 15 |
| .224 22 Cal. | 50 Gr. | 14 |
| .224 22 Cal. | 52 Gr. | 14 |
| .224 22 Cal. | 55 Gr. | 14 |
| .224 22 Cal. | 60 Gr. | 12 |
| .224 22 Cal. | 62 Gr. | 12 |
| .224 22 Cal. | 64 Gr. | 12 |
| .224 22 Cal. | 70 Gr. VLD | 9 |
| .224 22 Cal. | 70 Gr. LTB | 10 |
| .224 22 Cal. | 73 Gr. LTB | 9 |
| .224 22 Cal. | 75 Gr. VLD | 9 |
| .224 22 Cal. | 80 Gr. VLD | 8 |
| .243 (6mm) Cal. | 60 Gr. | 14 |
| .243 (6mm) Cal. | 62 Gr | 14 |
| .243 (6mm) Cal. | 65 Gr | 13 |
| .243 (6mm) Cal. | 65 Gr. Short | 14 |
| .243 (6mm) Cal. | 65 Gr. BT | 13 |
| .243 (6mm) Cal. | 66 Gr. LD | 13 |
| .243 (6mm) Cal. | 68 Gr. | 13 |
| .243 (6mm) Cal. | 69 Gr. LD | 12 |
| .243 (6mm) Cal. | 70 Gr. | 13 |
| .243 (6mm) Cal. | 71 Gr. BT | 12 |
| .243 (6mm) Cal. | 74 Gr. | 13 |
| .243 (6mm) Cal. | 80 Gr. | 12 |
| .243 (6mm) Cal. | 88 Gr. LD | 10 |
| .243 (6mm) Cal. | 90 Gr. BT | 10 |
| .243 (6mm) Cal. | 95 Gr. VLD | 9 |
| .243 (6mm) Cal. | 105 Gr. LTB | 9 |
| .243 (6mm) Cal. | 105 Gr. VLD | 8 |
| .243 (6mm) Cal. | 115 Gr. VLD | 7 |
| .257 25 Cal. | 72 Gr. | 15 |
| .257 25 Cal. | 78 Gr. | 13 |
| .257 25 Cal. | 82 Gr. | 14 |
| .257 25 Cal. | 87 Gr. | 13 |
| .257 25 Cal. | 95 Gr. | 12 |
| .257 25 Cal. | 110 Gr. | 12 |
| .257 25 Cal. | 115 Gr. VLD | 10 |
| .264 (6.5mm) Cal. | 140 Gr. VLD | 9 |
| .284 (7mm) Cal. | 168 Gr. VLD | 10 |
| .284 (7mm) Cal. | 180 Gr. VLD | 9 |
| .308 30 Cal. | 110 Gr. | 19 |
| .308 30 Cal. | 125 Gr. | 19 |
| .308 30 Cal. | 135 Gr. | 16 |
| .308 30 Cal. | 150 Gr. | 15 |
| .308 30 Cal. | 155 Gr. LTB | 14 |
| .308 30 Cal. | 155 Gr. VLD | 14 |
| .308 30 Cal. | 168 Gr. LTB | 13 |
| .308 30 Cal. | 168 Gr. VLD | 13 |
| .308 30 Cal. | 175 Gr. VLD | 13 |
| .308 30 Cal. | 185 Gr. VLD | 12 |
| .308 30 Cal. | 190 Gr. VLD | 12 |
| .308 30 Cal. | 210 Gr. VLD | 11 |

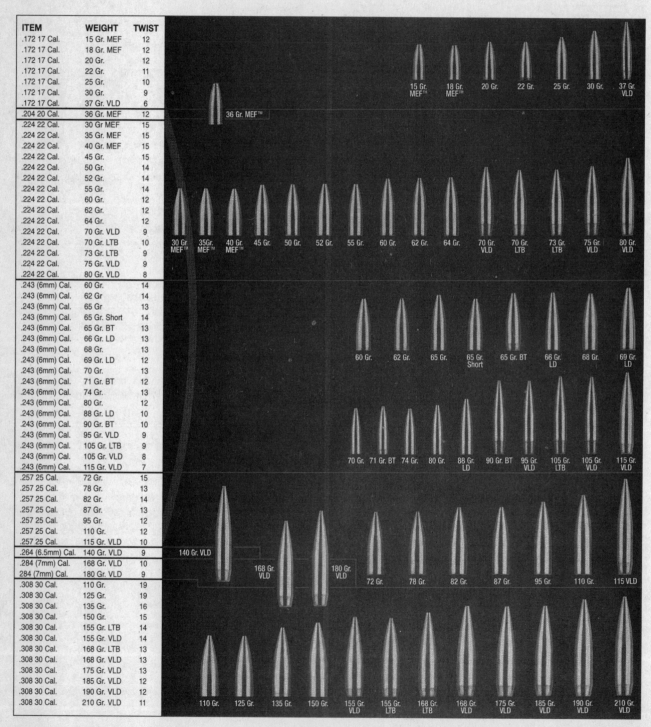

# FEDERAL RIFLE BULLETS

## CLASSIC CENTERFIRE RIFLE

Federal Classic Rifle ammunition is still the choice of many serious hunters who know what it takes to succeed in the field. Whether you choose the Sierra Pro-Hunter®, the most widely reloaded bullet in America, or Federal's renowned Hi-Shok® bullet, you'll get dependable, consistent performance with deadly accuracy and double-caliber expansion.

**Soft Point**

**Soft Point Round Nose**

**Soft Point Flat Nose**

**Hollow Point**

**Full Metal Jacket Boat-Tail**

### SOFT POINT
*Excellent for small game and thin-skinned medium game.*
The aerodynamic tip provides flat shooting, and the exposed soft point expands rapidly, even at reduced velocities found at longer ranges.

### SOFT POINT ROUND NOSE
*A traditional choice for deer and bear in the brush.*
A large exposed tip, extra weight, and specially tapered jacket provide controlled expansion, good weight retention, and deep penetration.

### SOFT POINT FLAT NOSE
*A good choice for light to medium game, even in brush.*
Especially designed for rifles with tubular magazines, the flat nose prevents accidental discharge. It also expands reliably and offers deep penetration.

### HOLLOW POINT
*A great mid-distance load for medium game.*
Available in 30-30 Win., 357 Mag., 44 Rem. Mag., and 45-70 Govt., the hollow-point provides hard-hitting accuracy and dramatic expansion.

### FULL METAL JACKET BOAT-TAIL
*Excellent for fur-bearing animals and target shooting.*
The jacket prevents point deformation for smooth, reliable feeding in semi-automatics. The non-expanding bullet leaves a small exit hole for minimal pelt damage.

## CLASSIC HANDGUN

Federal offers breadth of selection and quality that are second to none. The lineup includes wadcutters for clean target marking, hollow-point loads favored by law enforcement officials and soft points that are the choice of countless handgun hunters. All are available in a wide variety of calibers to ensure the perfect load for specific needs.

**Lead Round Nose**
*An accurate, economical training round.*

**Full Metal Jacket**
*A good choice for recreational shooting.*

**Hi-Shok Jacketed Soft Point**
*Good for small to medium-sized game.*

**Lead Semi-Wadcutter**
*Good for target shooting and personal defense.*

**Hi-Shok Jacketed Hollow Point**
*Excellent for personall defense.*

**Semi-Wadcutter Hollow Point**
*For small game and personal defense.*

RELOADING

# HORNADY RIFLE BULLETS

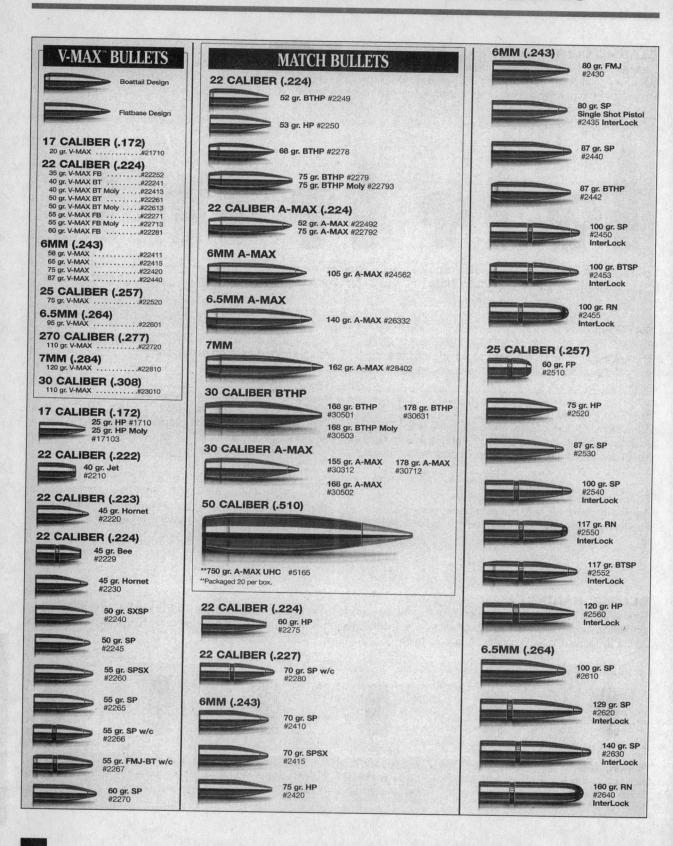

## V-MAX™ BULLETS

Boattail Design

Flatbase Design

**17 CALIBER (.172)**
20 gr. V-MAX . . . . . . . . . . . #21710

**22 CALIBER (.224)**
35 gr. V-MAX FB . . . . . . . . #22252
40 gr. V-MAX BT . . . . . . . . #22241
40 gr. V-MAX BT Moly . . . . #22413
50 gr. V-MAX BT . . . . . . . . #22261
50 gr. V-MAX BT Moly . . . . #22613
55 gr. V-MAX FB . . . . . . . . #22271
55 gr. V-MAX FB Moly . . . . #22713
60 gr. V-MAX FB . . . . . . . . #22281

**6MM (.243)**
58 gr. V-MAX . . . . . . . . . . #22411
65 gr. V-MAX . . . . . . . . . . #22415
75 gr. V-MAX . . . . . . . . . . #22420
87 gr. V-MAX . . . . . . . . . . #22440

**25 CALIBER (.257)**
75 gr. V-MAX . . . . . . . . . . #22520

**6.5MM (.264)**
95 gr. V-MAX . . . . . . . . . . #22601

**270 CALIBER (.277)**
110 gr. V-MAX . . . . . . . . . . #22720

**7MM (.284)**
120 gr. V-MAX . . . . . . . . . . #22810

**30 CALIBER (.308)**
110 gr. V-MAX . . . . . . . . . . #23010

**17 CALIBER (.172)**
25 gr. HP #1710
25 gr. HP Moly
#17103

**22 CALIBER (.222)**
40 gr. Jet
#2210

**22 CALIBER (.223)**
45 gr. Hornet
#2220

**22 CALIBER (.224)**
45 gr. Bee
#2229

45 gr. Hornet
#2230

50 gr. SXSP
#2240

50 gr. SP
#2245

55 gr. SPSX
#2260

55 gr. SP
#2265

55 gr. SP w/c
#2266

55 gr. FMJ-BT w/c
#2267

60 gr. SP
#2270

## MATCH BULLETS

**22 CALIBER (.224)**
52 gr. BTHP #2249

53 gr. HP #2250

68 gr. BTHP #2278

75 gr. BTHP #2279
75 gr. BTHP Moly #22793

**22 CALIBER A-MAX (.224)**
52 gr. A-MAX #22492
75 gr. A-MAX #22792

**6MM A-MAX**
105 gr. A-MAX #24562

**6.5MM A-MAX**
140 gr. A-MAX #26332

**7MM**
162 gr. A-MAX #28402

**30 CALIBER BTHP**
168 gr. BTHP #30501       178 gr. BTHP #30631
168 gr. BTHP Moly #30503

**30 CALIBER A-MAX**
155 gr. A-MAX #30312      178 gr. A-MAX #30712
168 gr. A-MAX #30502

**50 CALIBER (.510)**

**750 gr. A-MAX UHC #5165
**Packaged 20 per box.

**22 CALIBER (.224)**
60 gr. HP
#2275

**22 CALIBER (.227)**
70 gr. SP w/c
#2280

**6MM (.243)**
70 gr. SP
#2410

70 gr. SPSX
#2415

75 gr. HP
#2420

## 6MM (.243)

80 gr. FMJ
#2430

80 gr. SP
Single Shot Pistol
#2435 InterLock

87 gr. SP
#2440

87 gr. BTHP
#2442

100 gr. SP
#2450
InterLock

100 gr. BTSP
#2453
InterLock

100 gr. RN
#2455
InterLock

## 25 CALIBER (.257)

60 gr. FP
#2510

75 gr. HP
#2520

87 gr. SP
#2530

100 gr. SP
#2540
InterLock

117 gr. RN
#2550
InterLock

117 gr. BTSP
#2552
InterLock

120 gr. HP
#2560
InterLock

## 6.5MM (.264)

100 gr. SP
#2610

129 gr. SP
#2620
InterLock

140 gr. SP
#2630
InterLock

160 gr. RN
#2640
InterLock

# HORNADY RIFLE BULLETS

## MATCH BULLETS
### (Continued)

### 270 CALIBER (.277)

100 gr. SP
#2710

110 gr. HP
#2720

130 gr. SP
#2730
InterLock

130 gr. BT SST
#27302

140 gr. BTSP
#2735
InterLock

150 gr. SP
#2740
InterLock

150 gr. RN
#2745
InterLock

### 7MM (.284)

100 gr. HP
#2800

120 gr. SP
#2810

120 gr. SP
Single Shot Pistol
#2811 InterLock

120 gr. SSBB
Tipped NEW!
#22811

120 gr. HP
#2815

139 gr. SP
#2820
InterLock

139 gr. FP
#2822
InterLock

139 gr. BTSP
#2825
InterLock

154 gr. SP
#2830
InterLock

154 gr. RN
#2835
InterLock

162 gr. BTSP
#2845
InterLock

175 gr. SP
#2850
InterLock

175 gr. RN
#2855
InterLock

### 30 CALIBER (.308)

100 gr. SJ
#3005

110 gr. SP
#3010

110 gr. RN
#3015

110 gr. FMJ
#3017

130 gr. SP
#3020

130 gr. SP
Single Shot Pistol
#3021
InterLock

150 gr. SP
#3031
InterLock

150 gr. BTSP
#3033
InterLock

150 gr. RN (30-30)
#3035
InterLock

150 gr. FMJ-BT
#3037

165 gr. SP
#3040
InterLock

165 gr. BTSP
#3045
InterLock

170 gr. FP (30-30)
#3060
InterLock

180 gr. SP
#3070
InterLock

180 gr. BTSP
#3072
InterLock

180 gr. RN
#3075
InterLock

190 gr. BTSP
#3085
InterLock

220 gr. RN
#3090
InterLock

### 7.62 X 39 (.310)

123 gr. SP
#3140

123 gr. FMJ
#3147

### 303 CAL. AND 7.7 JAP (.312)

150 gr. SP
#3120
InterLock

174 gr. RN
#3130
InterLock

174 gr. FMJ-BT
#3131

### 32 SPECIAL (.321)

170 gr. FP
#3210
InterLock

### 8MM (.323)

125 gr. SP
#3230

150 gr. SP
#3232
InterLock

170 gr. RN
#3235
InterLock

220 gr. SP
#3238
InterLock

### 338 CALIBER (.338)

200 gr. SP
#3310
InterLock

200 gr. FP
(33 Win)
#3315
InterLock

225 gr. SP
#3320
InterLock

250 gr. RN
#3330
InterLock

250 gr. SP
#3335
InterLock

### 348 CALIBER (.348)

200 gr. FP
#3410
InterLock

### 35 CALIBER (.358)

180 gr. SP
Single Shot Pistol
#3505
InterLock

200 gr. SP
#3510
InterLock

200 gr. RN
#3515
InterLock

250 gr. SP
#3520
InterLock

250 gr. RN
#3525
InterLock

**RELOADING**

# HORNADY BULLETS

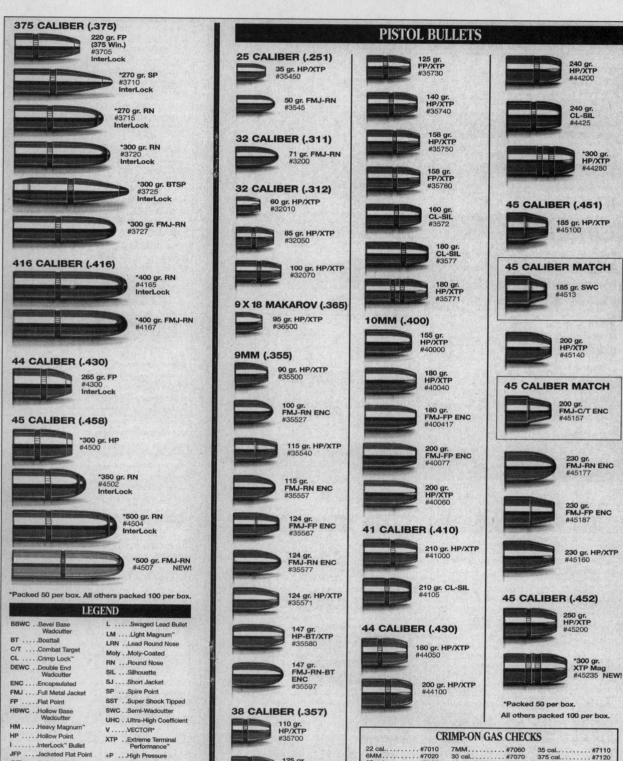

## 375 CALIBER (.375)

- 220 gr. FP (375 Win.) #3705 InterLock
- *270 gr. SP #3710 InterLock
- *270 gr. RN #3715 InterLock
- *300 gr. RN #3720 InterLock
- *300 gr. BTSP #3725 InterLock
- *300 gr. FMJ-RN #3727

## 416 CALIBER (.416)

- *400 gr. RN #4165 InterLock
- *400 gr. FMJ-RN #4167

## 44 CALIBER (.430)

- 265 gr. FP #4300 InterLock

## 45 CALIBER (.458)

- *300 gr. HP #4500
- *350 gr. RN #4502 InterLock
- *500 gr. RN #4504 InterLock
- *500 gr. FMJ-RN #4507 NEW!

*Packed 50 per box. All others packed 100 per box.

### LEGEND

| | |
|---|---|
| BBWC . . Bevel Base Wadcutter | L . . . . . Swaged Lead Bullet |
| BT . . . . . Boattail | LM . . . Light Magnum™ |
| C/T . . . . Combat Target | LRN . . . Lead Round Nose |
| CL . . . . . Crimp Lock™ | Moly . . Moly-Coated |
| DEWC . . Double End Wadcutter | RN . . . . Round Nose |
| | SIL . . . Silhouette |
| ENC . . . . Encapsulated | SJ . . . . Short Jacket |
| FMJ . . . . Full Metal Jacket | SP . . . . Spire Point |
| FP . . . . . Flat Point | SST . . . Super Shock Tipped |
| HBWC . . Hollow Base Wadcutter | SWC . . . Semi-Wadcutter |
| | UHC . . . Ultra-High Coefficient |
| HM . . . . . Heavy Magnum™ | V . . . . . VECTOR® |
| HP . . . . . Hollow Point | XTP . . . Extreme Terminal Performance™ |
| I . . . . . . . InterLock™ Bullet | +P . . . . High Pressure |
| JFP . . . Jacketed Flat Point | -E . . . . . EuroSpec (Exceeds SAMMI Standards) |
| JHP . . . Jacketed Hollow Point | |

## PISTOL BULLETS

### 25 CALIBER (.251)

- 35 gr. HP/XTP #35450
- 50 gr. FMJ-RN #3545

### 32 CALIBER (.311)

- 71 gr. FMJ-RN #3200

### 32 CALIBER (.312)

- 60 gr. HP/XTP #32010
- 85 gr. HP/XTP #32050
- 100 gr. HP/XTP #32070

### 9 X 18 MAKAROV (.365)

- 95 gr. HP/XTP #36500

### 9MM (.355)

- 90 gr. HP/XTP #35500
- 100 gr. FMJ-RN ENC #35527
- 115 gr. HP/XTP #35540
- 115 gr. FMJ-RN ENC #35557
- 124 gr. FMJ-FP ENC #35567
- 124 gr. FMJ-RN ENC #35577
- 124 gr. HP/XTP #35571
- 147 gr. HP-BT/XTP #35580
- 147 gr. FMJ-RN-BT ENC #35597

### 38 CALIBER (.357)

- 110 gr. HP/XTP #35700
- 125 gr. HP/XTP #35710

- 125 gr. FP/XTP #35730
- 140 gr. HP/XTP #35740
- 158 gr. HP/XTP #35750
- 158 gr. FP/XTP #35780
- 160 gr. CL-SIL #3572
- 180 gr. CL-SIL #3577
- 180 gr. HP/XTP #35771

### 10MM (.400)

- 155 gr. HP/XTP #40000
- 180 gr. HP/XTP #40040
- 180 gr. FMJ-FP ENC #400417
- 200 gr. FMJ-FP ENC #40077
- 200 gr. HP/XTP #40060

### 41 CALIBER (.410)

- 210 gr. HP/XTP #41000
- 210 gr. CL-SIL #4105

### 44 CALIBER (.430)

- 180 gr. HP/XTP #44050
- 200 gr. HP/XTP #44100

- 240 gr. HP/XTP #44200
- 240 gr. CL-SIL #4425
- *300 gr. HP/XTP #44280

### 45 CALIBER (.451)

- 185 gr. HP/XTP #45100

### 45 CALIBER MATCH

- 185 gr. SWC #4513
- 200 gr. HP/XTP #45140

### 45 CALIBER MATCH

- 200 gr. FMJ-C/T ENC #45157
- 230 gr. FMJ-RN ENC #45177
- 230 gr. FMJ-FP ENC #45187
- 230 gr. HP/XTP #45160

### 45 CALIBER (.452)

- 250 gr. HP/XTP #45200
- *300 gr. XTP Mag #45235 NEW!

*Packed 50 per box.
All others packed 100 per box.

### CRIMP-ON GAS CHECKS

| | | | | | |
|---|---|---|---|---|---|
| 22 cal. | #7010 | 7MM | #7060 | 35 cal. | #7110 |
| 6MM | #7020 | 30 cal. | #7070 | 375 cal. | #7120 |
| 25 cal. | #7030 | 32 cal. (8MM) | #7080 | 416 cal. | #7125 |
| 6.5MM | #7040 | 338 cal. | #7090 | 44 cal. | #7130 |
| 270 cal. | #7050 | 348 cal. | #7100 | 45 cal. | #7140 |

# NOSLER BULLETS

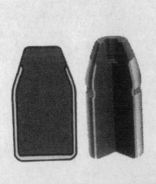

## NOSLER J4 COMPETITION

Nosler has blended the renowned accuracy of J4 bullet jacket with its own ultra-precise lead alloy cores to create a new performance standard for the popular .30 caliber match bullets.

## Bullets for Pistols

| Cal. Dia. | BULLET WEIGHT AND STYLE | SECT. DENS. | BAL. COEF. | PART# |
|---|---|---|---|---|
| 30 .308" | *New* 155 GR. HPBT 250 QUANTITY BULK PACK | .233 | .450 | 53155 53169 |
| | 168 GR. HPBT 250 QUANTITY BULK PACK | .253 | .462 | 53164 53168 |
| 9mm .355" | 115 GR. HOLLOW POINT 250 QUANTITY BULK PACK | .130 | .110 | 43009 44848 |
| 38 .357" | 115 GR. HOLLOW POINT PRACTICAL PISTOL™ 250 QUANTITY BULK PACK | .129 | .110 | 44835 |
| | 135 GR. PRACTICAL PISTOL™ 250 QUANTITY BULK PACK | .151 | .149 | 44836 |
| 10mm .400" | 135 GR. HOLLOW POINT 250 QUANTITY BULK PACK | .121 | .093 | 44838 44852 |
| | 150 GR. HOLLOW POINT | .134 | .106 | 44849 |
| 45 .451" | 185 GR. HOLLOW POINT 250 QUANTITY BULK PACK | .130 | .142 | 42062 44847 |
| | 230 GR. FULL METAL JACKET | .162 | .183 | 42064 |

## Bullets for Revolvers

| Cal. Dia. | BULLET WEIGHT AND STYLE | SECT. DENS. | BAL. COEF. | PART# |
|---|---|---|---|---|
| 38 .357" | 125 GR. HOLLOW POINT 250 QUANTITY BULK PACK | .140 | .143 | 42055 44840 |
| | 158 GR. HOLLOW POINT 250 QUANTITY BULK PACK | .177 | .182 | 42057 44841 |
| | 180 GR. SILHOUETTE 250 QUANTITY BULK PACK | .202 | .210 | 44851 |
| 41 .410" | 210 GR. HOLLOW POINT | .178 | .170 | 43012 |
| 44 .429" | 200 GR. HOLLOW POINT 250 QUANTITY BULK PACK | .155 | .151 | 42060 44846 |
| | 240 GR. HOLLOW POINT 250 QUANTITY BULK PACK | .186 | .173 | 42061 44842 |
| | 240 GR. SOFT POINT | .186 | .177 | 42068 |
| | 300 GR. HOLLOW POINT | .233 | .206 | 42069 |
| 45 Colt .451" | 250 GR. HOLLOW POINT | .176 | .177 | 43013 |

## Partition-HG™

| | | |
|---|---|---|
| 50 cal/250 GR. JHP | .429" | 50429 |
| 50 cal/260 GR. JHP | .451" | 50260 |
| 54 cal/260 GR. JHP | .451" | 54260 |
| 50 cal/300 GR. JPP | .451" | 50280 *New* |
| 54 cal/300 GR. JPP | .451" | 54280 *New* |

## S.H.O.T.S.™

| | | |
|---|---|---|
| 50 cal/250 grain JHP | .451" | 50250 |
| 50 cal/300 grain JHP | .429" | 50300 |
| 54 cal/250 grain JHP | .451" | 54250 |

*High volume shooters can now get Nosler's specially designed plastic muzzleloading sabots in 50-count Bulk Packs:*

| | | |
|---|---|---|
| 50 cal. sabots for .429" bullets | 50095 | *New* |
| 50 cal. sabots for .451" bullets | 50096 | *New* |
| 54 cal. sabots for .451" bullets | 50097 | *New* |

# NOSLER BULLETS

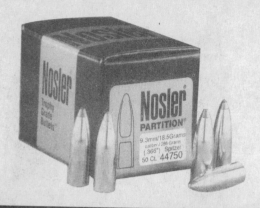

## NOSLER PARTITION® BULLETS

The Nosler Partition® bullet earned its reputation among professional guides and serious hunters for one reason: it doesn't fail. The patented Partition® design offers a dual core that is unequallled in mushrooming, weight retention and hydrostatic shock.

| Cal. Dia. | BULLET WEIGHT AND STYLE | SECT. DENS. | BAL. COEF. | PART# |
|---|---|---|---|---|
| 22 / .224" | 60 GR. SPITZER New | .171 | .228 | 16316 |
| 6mm / .243" | 85 GR. SPITZER | .206 | .315 | 16314 |
| | 95 GR. SPITZER | .230 | .365 | 16315 |
| | 100 GR. SPITZER | .242 | .384 | 35642 |
| 25 / .257" | 100 GR. SPITZER | .216 | .377 | 16317 |
| | 115 GR. SPITZER | .249 | .389 | 16318 |
| | 120 GR. SPITZER | .260 | .391 | 35643 |
| 6.5mm / .264" | 100 GR. SPITZER | .205 | .326 | 16319 |
| | 125 GR. SPITZER | .256 | .449 | 16320 |
| | 140 GR. SPITZER | .287 | .490 | 16321 |
| 270 / .277" | 130 GR. SPITZER | .242 | .416 | 16322 |
| | 150 GR. SPITZER | .279 | .465 | 16323 |
| | 160 GR. SEMI SPITZER | .298 | .434 | 16324 |
| 7mm / .284" | 140 GR. SPITZER | .248 | .434 | 16325 |
| | 150 GR. SPITZER | .266 | .456 | 16326 |
| | 160 GR. SPITZER | .283 | .475 | 16327 |
| | 175 GR. SPITZER | .310 | .519 | 35645 |
| 30 / .308" | 150 GR. SPITZER | .226 | .387 | 16329 |
| | 165 GR. SPITZER | .248 | .410 | 16330 |
| | 170 GR. ROUND NOSE | .256 | .252 | 16333 |
| | 180 GR. PROTECTED POINT | .271 | .361 | 25396 |

| Cal. Dia. | BULLET WEIGHT AND STYLE | SECT. DENS. | BAL. COEF. | PART# |
|---|---|---|---|---|
| | 180 GR. SPITZER | .271 | .474 | 16331 |
| | 200 GR. SPITZER | .301 | .481 | 35626 |
| | 220 GR. SEMI SPITZER | .331 | .351 | 16332 |
| 8mm / .323" | 200 GR. SPITZER | .274 | .426 | 35277 |
| 338 / .338" | 210 GR. SPITZER | .263 | .400 | 16337 |
| | 225 GR. SPITZER | .281 | .454 | 16336 |
| | 250 GR. SPITZER | .313 | .473 | 35644 |
| 35 / .358" | 225 GR. SPITZER | .251 | .430 | 44800 |
| | 250 GR. SPITZER | .279 | .446 | 44801 |
| 9.3mm / .366" | 286 GR. SPITZER (18.5 GRAM) | .307 | .482 | 44750 |
| 375 / .375" | 260 GR. SPITZER | .264 | .314 | 44850 |
| | 300 GR. SPITZER | .305 | .398 | 44845 |
| 416 / .416" | 400 GR. SPITZER | .330 | .390 | 45200 New |
| 45-70 / .458" | 300 GR. PROTECTED POINT | .204 | .199 | 45325 New |
| 38 / .357" (PARTITION-HG™) | 180 GR. HOLLOW POINT | .202 | .201 | 35180 |
| 44 / .429" (PARTITION-HG™) | 250 GR. HOLLOW POINT | .194 | .200 | 44250 |
| 45 / .451" (PARTITION-HG™) | 260 GR. HOLLOW POINT | .182 | .174 | 45260 |
| | 300 GR. PROTECTED POINT | .211 | .199 | 45350 New |

# NOSLER BULLETS

## NOSLER BALLISTIC TIP® HUNTING BULLETS

Nosler has replaced the familiar lead point of the Spitzer with a tough polycarbonate tip. The purpose of this new Ballistic Tip® is to resist deforming in the magazine and feed ramp of many rifles. The Solid Base® design produces controlled expansion for excellent mushrooming and exceptional accuracy.

### Varmint Bullets

| Cal. Dia. | BULLET WEIGHT AND STYLE | | SECT. DENS. | BAL. COEF. | PART# |
|---|---|---|---|---|---|
| 22 .224" | 40 GR. SPITZER (ORANGE TIP) 250 CT. VARMINT PAK™ | | .114 | .221 | 39510 39555 |
| | 45 GR. HORNET (SOFT LEAD TIP) | | .128 | .144 | 35487 |
| | 50 GR. SPITZER (ORANGE TIP) New– 250 CT. VARMINT PAK™ | | .142 | .238 | 39522 39557 |
| | 55 GR. SPITZER (ORANGE TIP) 250 CT. VARMINT PAK™ | | .157 | .267 | 39526 39560 |
| 6mm .243" | 55 GR. SPITZER (PURPLE TIP) New– 250 CT. VARMINT PAK™ | | .133 | .276 | 24055 39565 |
| | 70 GR. SPITZER (PURPLE TIP) New– 250 CT. VARMINT PAK™ | | .169 | .310 | 39532 39570 |
| | 80 GR. SPITZER (PURPLE TIP) | New | .194 | .339 | 24080 |
| 25 .257" | 85 GR. SPITZER (BLUE TIP) | | .183 | .331 | 43004 |

### Hunting Bullets

| Cal. Dia. | BULLET WEIGHT AND STYLE | | SECT. DENS. | BAL. COEF. | PART# |
|---|---|---|---|---|---|
| 6mm .243" | 90 GR. SPITZER (PURPLE TIP) | New | .218 | .365 | 24090 |
| | 95 GR. SPITZER (PURPLE TIP) | | .230 | .379 | 24095 |
| 25 .257" | 100 GR. SPITZER (BLUE TIP) | | .216 | .393 | 25100 |
| | 115 GR. SPITZER (BLUE TIP) | | .249 | .453 | 25115 |
| 6.5mm .264" | 100 GR. SPITZER (BROWN TIP) | | .205 | .350 | 26100 |
| | 120 GR. SPITZER (BROWN TIP) | | .246 | .458 | 26120 |

| Cal. Dia. | BULLET WEIGHT AND STYLE | SECT. DENS. | BAL. COEF. | PART# |
|---|---|---|---|---|
| 270 .277" | 130 GR. SPITZER (YELLOW TIP) | .242 | .433 | 27130 |
| | 140 GR. SPITZER (YELLOW TIP) | .261 | .456 | 27140 |
| | 150 GR. SPITZER (YELLOW TIP) | .279 | .496 | 27150 |
| 7mm .284" | 120 GR. FLAT POINT (SOFT LEAD TIP) | .213 | .195 | 28121 |
| | 120 GR. SPITZER (RED TIP) | .213 | .417 | 28120 |
| | 140 GR. SPITZER (RED TIP) | .248 | .485 | 28140 |
| | 150 GR. SPITZER (RED TIP) | .266 | .493 | 28150 |
| 30 .308" | 125 GR. SPITZER (GREEN TIP) | .188 | .366 | 30125 |
| | 150 GR. SPITZER (GREEN TIP) | .226 | .435 | 30150 |
| | 165 GR. SPITZER (GREEN TIP) | .248 | .475 | 30165 |
| | 180 GR. SPITZER (GREEN TIP) | .271 | .507 | 30180 |
| 8mm .323" | 180 GR. SPITZER (GUNMETAL TIP) New | .247 | .394 | 32180 |
| 338 .338" | 180 GR. SPITZER (MAROON TIP) | .225 | .372 | 33180 |
| | 200 GR. SPITZER (MAROON TIP) | .250 | .414 | 33200 |
| 35 .358" | 225 GR. WHELEN (BUCKSKIN TIP) | .251 | .421 | 35225 |
| 9.3mm .366" | 250 GR. SPITZER (OLIVE TIP) New Available Mid-year | .267 | .494 | 36250 |

# NOSLER BULLETS

## BALLISTIC SILVER TIP

| Cal. | Dia. | Bullet Weight | Sect. Dens. | Bal. Coef. | Part # | Cal. | Dia. | Bullet Weight | Sect. Dens. | Bal. Coef. | Part # |
|------|------|---------------|-------------|------------|--------|------|------|---------------|-------------|------------|--------|
| 22 | .224" | 40 grain | .114 | .221 | 51005 | 270 | .277" | 130 grain | .242 | .433 | 51075 |
| 22 | .224" | 50 grain | .142 | .238 | 51010 | 7mm | .284" | 140 grain | .248 | .485 | 51105 |
| 22 | .224" | 55 grain | .157 | .267 | 51031 | 7mm | .284" | 150 grain | .266 | .493 | 51110 |
| 6mm | .243" | 55 grain | .133 | .276 | 51030 | 30 | .308" | 150 grain | .226 | .435 | 51150 |
| 6mm | .243" | 95 grain | .230 | .379 | 51040 | 30 | .308" | 168 grain | .253 | .490 | 51160 |
| 25 | .257" | 85 grain | .183 | .331 | 51045 | 30 | .308" | 180 grain | .271 | .507 | 51170 |
| 25 | .257" | 115 grain | .249 | .453 | 51050 | 338 | .338" | 200 grain | .250 | .414 | 51200 |

## FAIL SAFE

| Cal. | Dia. | Bullet Weight | Sect. Dens. | Bal. Coef. | Part # |
|------|------|---------------|-------------|------------|--------|
| 270 | .277" | 140 grain | .261 | .322 | 53140 |
| 7mm | .284" | 140 grain | .248 | .323 | 53150 |
| 7mm | .284" | 160 grain | .283 | .382 | 53160 |
| 30 | .308" | 150 grain | .226 | .308 | 53170 |
| 30 | .308" | 165 grain | .248 | .314 | 53175 |
| 30 | .308" | 180 grain | .271 | .391 | 53180 |
| 338 | .338" | 230 grain | .288 | .436 | 53230 |
| 375 | .375" | 270 grain | .274 | .393 | 53350 |
| 375 | .375" | 300 grain | .305 | .441 | 53360 |

*Ballistic Silvertip, Fail Safe and Partition Gold bullets are made by Nosler for loading in Winchester ammunition in a project known as Combined Technology.*

## PARTITION GOLD

| Cal. | Dia. | Bullet Weight | Sect. Dens. | Bal. Coef. | Part # |
|------|------|---------------|-------------|------------|--------|
| 270 | .277" | 150 grain | .279 | .465 | 52100 |
| 7mm | .284" | 160 grain | .283 | .475 | 52150 |
| 30 | .308" | 150 grain | .226 | .387 | 52200 |
| 30 | .308" | 180 grain | .271 | .474 | 52230 |
| 338 | .338" | 250 grain | .313 | .473 | 52280 |

## PARTITION GOLD MOLY-FREE

| Cal. | Dia. | Bullet Weight | Sect. Dens. | Bal. Coef. | Part # |
|------|------|---------------|-------------|------------|--------|
| New! 270 | .277" | 150 grain | .279 | .465 | 52101 |
| New! 7mm | .284" | 160 grain | .283 | .475 | 52151 |
| New! 30 | .308" | 150 grain | .226 | .387 | 52201 |
| New! 30 | .308" | 180 grain | .271 | .474 | 52231 |
| New! 338 | .338" | 250 grain | .313 | .473 | 52281 |

# SIERRA BULLETS

## RIFLE BULLETS

### .22 Caliber Hornet (.223/5.66MM Diameter)

40 gr. Hornet
Varminter #1100

45 gr. Hornet
Varminter #1110

### .22 Caliber Hornet (.224/5.69MM Diameter)

40 gr. Hornet
Varminter #1200

45 gr. Hornet
Varminter #1210

### .22 Caliber (.224/5.69MM Diameter)

40 gr. HP
Varminter #1385

40 gr.
BlitzKing #1440

45 gr. SMP
Varminter #1300

45 gr. SPT
Varminter #1310

50 gr. SMP
Varminter #1320

50 gr. SPT
Varminter #1330

50 gr. Blitz
Varminter #1340

50 gr.
BlitzKing #1450

52 gr. HPBT
MatchKing #1410

53 gr. HP
MatchKing #1400

55 gr. Blitz
Varminter #1345

55 gr. SMP
Varminter #1350

55 gr. FMJBT
GameKing #1355

55 gr. SPT
Varminter #1360

55 gr. SBT
GameKing #1365

55 gr. HPBT
GameKing #1390

55 gr.
BlitzKing #1455

60 gr. HP
Varminter #1375

63 gr. SMP
Varminter #1370

69 gr. HPBT
MatchKing #1380
*7"-10" TWST BBLS*

### 6MM .243 Caliber (.243/6.17MM Diameter)

55 gr.
BlitzKing #1502

60 gr. HP
Varminter #1500

70 gr. HPBT
MatchKing #1505

70 gr.
BlitzKing #1507

75 gr. HP
Varminter #1510

80 gr. Blitz
Varminter #1515

85 gr. SPT
Varminter #1520

85 gr. HPBT
GameKing #1530

90 gr. FMJBT
GameKing #1535

100 gr. SPT
Pro-Hunter #1540

100 gr. SMP
Pro-Hunter #1550

100 gr. SBT
GameKing #1560

107 gr. HPBT
MatchKing #1570
*7"-8" TWST BBLS*

### .25 Caliber (.257/6.53MM Diameter)

75 gr. HP
Varminter #1600

87 gr. SPT
Varminter #1610

90 gr. HPBT
GameKing #1615

100 gr. SPT
Pro-Hunter #1620

100 gr. SBT
GameKing #1625

100 gr. HPBT
MatchKing #1628

117 gr. SBT
GameKing #1630

117 gr. SPT
Pro-Hunter #1640

120 gr. HPBT
GameKing #1650

### 6.5MM .264 Caliber (.264/6.71MM Diameter)

85 gr. HP
Varminter #1700

100 gr. HP
Varminter #1710

107 gr. HPBT
MatchKing #1715

### 6.5MM .264 Caliber (cont.)
(.264/6.71MM Diameter)

120 gr. SPT
Pro-Hunter #1720

120 gr. HPBT
MatchKing #1725

140 gr. SBT
GameKing #1730

140 gr. HPBT
MatchKing #1740

142 gr. HPBT
MatchKing #1742

160 gr. SMP
Pro-Hunter #1750

### .270 Caliber (.277/7.04MM Diameter)

90 gr. HP
Varminter #1800

110 gr. SPT
Pro-Hunter #1810

130 gr. SBT
GameKing #1820

130 gr. SPT
Pro-Hunter #1830

135 gr. HPBT
MatchKing #1833

140 gr. HPBT
GameKing #1835

140 gr. SBT
GameKing #1845

150 gr. SBT
GameKing #1840

150 gr. RN
Pro-Hunter #1850

### 7MM .284 Caliber (.284/7.21MM Diameter)

100 gr. HP
Varminter #1895

120 gr. SPT
Pro-Hunter #1900

130 gr. HPBT
MatchKing #1903

140 gr. SBT
GameKing #1905

140 gr. SPT
Pro-Hunter #1910

150 gr. SBT
GameKing #1913

150 gr. HPBT
MatchKing #1915

160 gr. SBT
GameKing #1920

160 gr. HPBT
GameKing #1925

168 gr. HPBT
MatchKing #1930

# SIERRA BULLETS

## RIFLE BULLETS

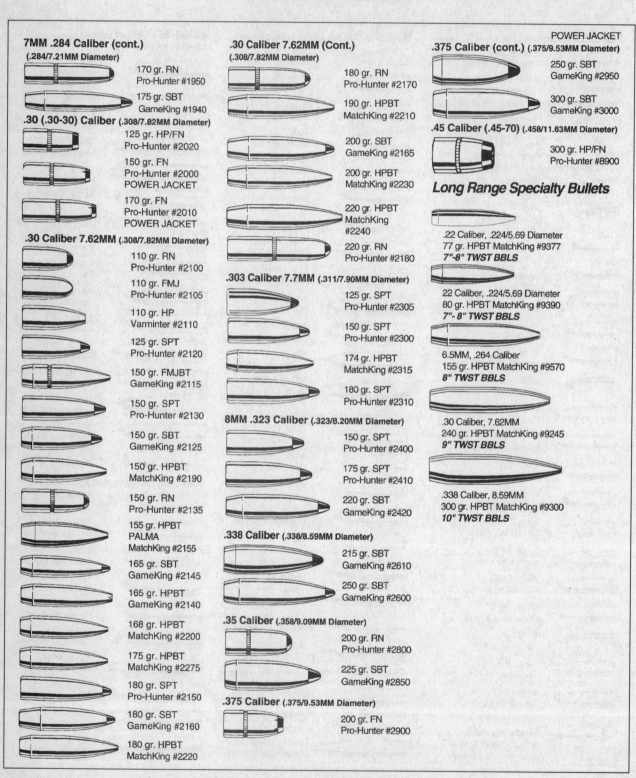

**7MM .284 Caliber (cont.)**
(.284/7.21MM Diameter)

170 gr. RN
Pro-Hunter #1950

175 gr. SBT
GameKing #1940

**.30 (.30-30) Caliber** (.308/7.82MM Diameter)

125 gr. HP/FN
Pro-Hunter #2020

150 gr. FN
Pro-Hunter #2000
POWER JACKET

170 gr. FN
Pro-Hunter #2010
POWER JACKET

**.30 Caliber 7.62MM** (.308/7.82MM Diameter)

110 gr. RN
Pro-Hunter #2100

110 gr. FMJ
Pro-Hunter #2105

110 gr. HP
Varminter #2110

125 gr. SPT
Pro-Hunter #2120

150 gr. FMJBT
GameKing #2115

150 gr. SPT
Pro-Hunter #2130

150 gr. SBT
GameKing #2125

150 gr. HPBT
MatchKing #2190

150 gr. RN
Pro-Hunter #2135

155 gr. HPBT
PALMA
MatchKing #2155

165 gr. SBT
GameKing #2145

165 gr. HPBT
GameKing #2140

168 gr. HPBT
MatchKing #2200

175 gr. HPBT
MatchKing #2275

180 gr. SPT
Pro-Hunter #2150

180 gr. SBT
GameKing #2160

180 gr. HPBT
MatchKing #2220

**.30 Caliber 7.62MM (Cont.)**
(.308/7.82MM Diameter)

180 gr. RN
Pro-Hunter #2170

190 gr. HPBT
MatchKing #2210

200 gr. SBT
GameKing #2165

200 gr. HPBT
MatchKing #2230

220 gr. HPBT
MatchKing
#2240

220 gr. RN
Pro-Hunter #2180

**.303 Caliber 7.7MM** (.311/7.90MM Diameter)

125 gr. SPT
Pro-Hunter #2305

150 gr. SPT
Pro-Hunter #2300

174 gr. HPBT
MatchKing #2315

180 gr. SPT
Pro-Hunter #2310

**8MM .323 Caliber** (.323/8.20MM Diameter)

150 gr. SPT
Pro-Hunter #2400

175 gr. SPT
Pro-Hunter #2410

220 gr. SBT
GameKing #2420

**.338 Caliber** (.338/8.59MM Diameter)

215 gr. SBT
GameKing #2610

250 gr. SBT
GameKing #2600

**.35 Caliber** (.358/9.09MM Diameter)

200 gr. RN
Pro-Hunter #2800

225 gr. SBT
GameKing #2850

**.375 Caliber** (.375/9.53MM Diameter)

200 gr. FN
Pro-Hunter #2900

POWER JACKET

**.375 Caliber (cont.)** (.375/9.53MM Diameter)

250 gr. SBT
GameKing #2950

300 gr. SBT
GameKing #3000

**.45 Caliber (.45-70)** (.458/11.63MM Diameter)

300 gr. HP/FN
Pro-Hunter #8900

### Long Range Specialty Bullets

.22 Caliber, .224/5.69 Diameter
77 gr. HPBT MatchKing #9377
*7"-8" TWST BBLS*

22 Caliber, .224/5.69 Diameter
80 gr. HPBT MatchKing #9390
*7"- 8" TWST BBLS*

6.5MM, .264 Caliber
155 gr. HPBT MatchKing #9570
*8" TWST BBLS*

.30 Caliber, 7.62MM
240 gr. HPBT MatchKing #9245
*9" TWST BBLS*

.338 Caliber, 8.59MM
300 gr. HPBT MatchKing #9300
*10" TWST BBLS*

# SIERRA BULLETS

## HANDGUN

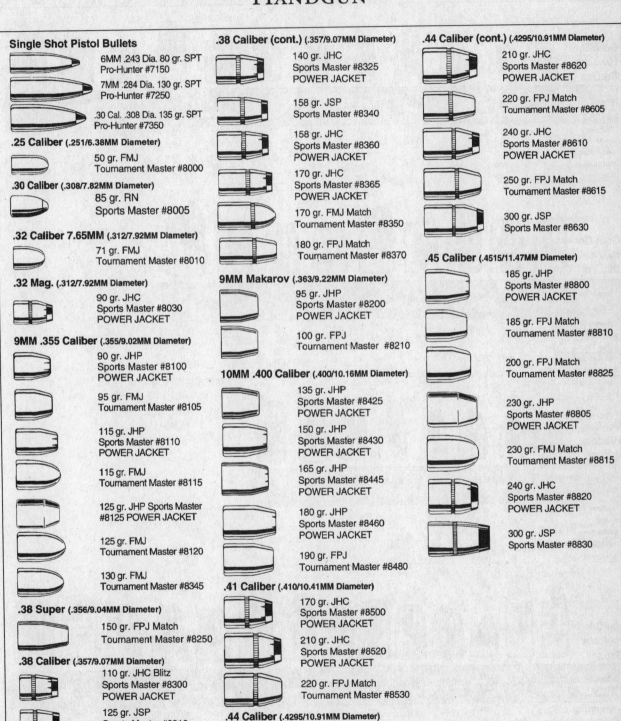

**Single Shot Pistol Bullets**

6MM .243 Dia. 80 gr. SPT
Pro-Hunter #7150

7MM .284 Dia. 130 gr. SPT
Pro-Hunter #7250

.30 Cal. .308 Dia. 135 gr. SPT
Pro-Hunter #7350

**.25 Caliber** (.251/6.38MM Diameter)

50 gr. FMJ
Tournament Master #8000

**.30 Caliber** (.308/7.82MM Diameter)

85 gr. RN
Sports Master #8005

**.32 Caliber 7.65MM** (.312/7.92MM Diameter)

71 gr. FMJ
Tournament Master #8010

**.32 Mag.** (.312/7.92MM Diameter)

90 gr. JHC
Sports Master #8030
POWER JACKET

**9MM .355 Caliber** (.355/9.02MM Diameter)

90 gr. JHP
Sports Master #8100
POWER JACKET

95 gr. FMJ
Tournament Master #8105

115 gr. JHP
Sports Master #8110
POWER JACKET

115 gr. FMJ
Tournament Master #8115

125 gr. JHP Sports Master
#8125 POWER JACKET

125 gr. FMJ
Tournament Master #8120

130 gr. FMJ
Tournament Master #8345

**.38 Super** (.356/9.04MM Diameter)

150 gr. FPJ Match
Tournament Master #8250

**.38 Caliber** (.357/9.07MM Diameter)

110 gr. JHC Blitz
Sports Master #8300
POWER JACKET

125 gr. JSP
Sports Master #8310

125 gr. JHC
Sports Master #8320
POWER JACKET

**.38 Caliber (cont.)** (.357/9.07MM Diameter)

140 gr. JHC
Sports Master #8325
POWER JACKET

158 gr. JSP
Sports Master #8340

158 gr. JHC
Sports Master #8360
POWER JACKET

170 gr. JHC
Sports Master #8365
POWER JACKET

170 gr. FMJ Match
Tournament Master #8350

180 gr. FPJ Match
Tournament Master #8370

**9MM Makarov** (.363/9.22MM Diameter)

95 gr. JHP
Sports Master #8200
POWER JACKET

100 gr. FPJ
Tournament Master #8210

**10MM .400 Caliber** (.400/10.16MM Diameter)

135 gr. JHP
Sports Master #8425
POWER JACKET

150 gr. JHP
Sports Master #8430
POWER JACKET

165 gr. JHP
Sports Master #8445
POWER JACKET

180 gr. JHP
Sports Master #8460
POWER JACKET

190 gr. FPJ
Tournament Master #8480

**.41 Caliber** (.410/10.41MM Diameter)

170 gr. JHC
Sports Master #8500
POWER JACKET

210 gr. JHC
Sports Master #8520
POWER JACKET

220 gr. FPJ Match
Tournament Master #8530

**.44 Caliber** (.4295/10.91MM Diameter)

180 gr. JHC
Sports Master #8600
POWER JACKET

**.44 Caliber (cont.)** (.4295/10.91MM Diameter)

210 gr. JHC
Sports Master #8620
POWER JACKET

220 gr. FPJ Match
Tournament Master #8605

240 gr. JHC
Sports Master #8610
POWER JACKET

250 gr. FPJ Match
Tournament Master #8615

300 gr. JSP
Sports Master #8630

**.45 Caliber** (.4515/11.47MM Diameter)

185 gr. JHP
Sports Master #8800
POWER JACKET

185 gr. FPJ Match
Tournament Master #8810

200 gr. FPJ Match
Tournament Master #8825

230 gr. JHP
Sports Master #8805
POWER JACKET

230 gr. FMJ Match
Tournament Master #8815

240 gr. JHC
Sports Master #8820
POWER JACKET

300 gr. JSP
Sports Master #8830

# SPEER HANDGUN/RIFLE BULLETS

## GOLD DOT HANDGUN BULLETS

| Caliber & Type | 25 Auto Gold Dot HP | 32 Auto Gold Dot HP | 380 Auto Gold Dot HP | 9mm Gold Dot HP | 9mm Gold Dot HP | 9mm Gold Dot HP | 357 SIG 38 Super Gold Dot HP | 38/357 Gold Dot HP | 38/357 Gold Dot HP | 9x18mm Makarov Gold Dot HP | 40/10mm Gold Dot HP | 40/10mm Gold Dot HP |
|---|---|---|---|---|---|---|---|---|---|---|---|---|
| Diameter | .251" | .312" | .355" | .355" | .355" | .355" | .355" | .357" | .357" | .364" | .400" | .400" |
| Weight (grs.) | 35 | 60 | 90 | 115 | 124 | 147 | 125 | 125 | 158 | 90 | 155 | 165 |
| Ballist. Coef. | 0.091 | 0.118 | 0.101 | 0.125 | 0.134 | 0.164 | 0.141 | 0.140 | 0.168 | 0.107 | 0.123 | 0.138 |
| Part Number | 3985 | 3986 | 3992 | 3994 | 3998 | 4002 | 4360 | 4012 | 4215 | 3999 | 4400 | 4397 |
| Box Count | 100 | 100 | 100 | 100 | 100 | 100 | 100 | 100 | 100 | 100 | 100 | 100 |

## GOLD DOT HANDGUN BULLETS

| Caliber & Type | 40/10mm Gold Dot HP | 44 Special Gold Dot HP | 44 Mag Gold Dot HP | 44 Mag Gold Dot SP | 44 Mag Gold Dot SP | 45 Gold Dot HP | 45 Gold Dot HP | 45 Gold Dot HP | 475 Linebaugh Gold Dot SP |
|---|---|---|---|---|---|---|---|---|---|
| Diameter | .400" | .429" | .429" | .429" | .429" | .451" | .451" | .451" | .475" |
| Weight (grs.) | 180 | 200 | 240 | 240 | 270 | 185 | 200 | 230 | 400 |
| Ballist. Coef. | 0.143 | 0.145 | 0.175 | 0.175 | 0.193 | 0.109 | 0.138 | 0.143 | 0.178 |
| Part Number | 4406 | 4427 | 4455 | 4456 | 4461 | 4470 | 4478 | 4483 | 3976 |
| Box Count | 100 | 100 | 100 | 100 | 50 | 100 | 100 | 100 | 50 |

## UNI-COR HANDGUN BULLETS

| Caliber & Type | 25 Auto TMJ | 380 Auto TMJ | 9mm TMJ | 9mm SP | 9mm TMJ | 357 SIG 38 Super TMJ | 38/357 TMJ | 38/357 TMJ |
|---|---|---|---|---|---|---|---|---|
| Diameter | .251" | .355" | .355" | .355" | .355" | .355" | .357" | .357" |
| Weight | 50 | 95 | 115 | 124 | 147 | 125 | 125 | 158 |
| Ballist. Coef. | 0.110 | 0.131 | 0.177 | 0.115 | 0.208 | 0.147 | 0.146 | 0.173 |
| Part Number | 3982 | 4001 | 3995 | 3997 | 4006 | 4362 | 4015 | 4207 |
| Box Count | 100 | 100 | 100 | 100 | 100 | 100 | 100 | 100 |

## UNI-COR HANDGUN BULLETS

| Caliber & Type | 357 Mag Sil. Match TMJ | 357 Mag Sil. Match TMJ | 9x18mm Makarov TMJ | 40/10mm TMJ | 40/10mm TMJ | 40/10mm TMJ | 10mm TMJ | 44 Mag Sil. Match TMJ | 44 Mag SP | 45 Match TMJ | 45 Match TMJ | 45 Auto TMJ | 45 Colt 454 Casull SP | 50 Action Express HP |
|---|---|---|---|---|---|---|---|---|---|---|---|---|---|---|
| Diameter | .357" | .357" | .364" | .400" | .400" | .400" | .400" | .429" | .429" | .451" | .451" | .451" | .451" | .500" |
| Weight | 180 | 200 | 95 | 155 | 165 | 180 | 200 | 240 | 300 | 185 | 200 | 230 | 300 | 325 |
| Ballist. Coef. | 0.230 | 0.236 | 0.127 | 0.125 | 0.135 | 0.143 | 0.208 | 0.206 | 0.213 | 0.090 | 0.128 | 0.153 | 0.199 | 0.149 |
| Part Number | 4229 | 4231 | 4375 | 4399 | 4410 | 4402 | 4403 | 4459 | 4463 | 4473 | 4475 | 4480 | 4485 | 4495 |
| Box Count | 100 | 100 | 100 | 100 | 100 | 100 | 100 | 100 | 50 | 100 | 100 | 100 | 50 | 50 |

# SPEER HANDGUN/RIFLE BULLETS

**JACKETED HANDGUN BULLETS**

| Caliber & Type | 32 JHP | 32 JHP | 9mm JHP | 38/357 JHP | 38/357 JSP | 38/357 JHP | 38/357 JHP | 38/357 JHP-SWC | 38/357 JHP |
|---|---|---|---|---|---|---|---|---|---|
| Diameter | .312" | .312" | .355" | .357" | .357" | .357" | .357" | .357" | .357" |
| Weight | 85 | 100 | 115 | 110 | 125 | 125 | 140 | 146 | 158 |
| Ballist. Coef. | 0.121 | 0.167 | 0.118 | 0.122 | 0.140 | 0.135 | 0.152 | 0.159 | 0.158 |
| Part Number | 3987 | 3981 | 3996 | 4007 | 4011 | 4013 | 4203 | 4205 | 4211 |
| Box Count | 100 | 100 | 100 | 100 | 100 | 100 | 100 | 100 | 100 |

**JACKETED HANDGUN BULLETS**

| Caliber & Type | 38/357 JSP | 41 Mag JHP-SWC | 41 Mag JSP-SWC | 44 Mag JHP | 44 Mag JHP-SWC | 44 Mag JSP-SWC | 44 Mag JHP | 44 Mag JSP | 45 JHP | 45 JHP | 45 JHP |
|---|---|---|---|---|---|---|---|---|---|---|---|
| Diameter | .357" | .410" | .410" | .429" | .429" | .429" | .429" | .429" | .451" | .451" | .451" |
| Weight | 158 | 200 | 220 | 200 | 225 | 240 | 240 | 240 | 200 | 225 | 260 |
| Ballist. Coef. | 0.158 | 0.113 | 0.137 | 0.122 | 0.146 | 0.157 | 0.165 | 0.164 | 0.138 | 0.169 | 0.183 |
| Part Number | 4217 | 4405 | 4417 | 4425 | 4435 | 4447 | 4453 | 4457 | 4477 | 4479 | 4481 |
| Box Count | 100 | 100 | 100 | 100 | 100 | 100 | 100 | 100 | 100 | 100 | 100 |

## LEAD HANDGUN BULLETS

Want to shoot more for less money? Speer lead handgun bullets give you an economical alternative to jacketed bullets. Swaged, not cast, construction means you get the same quality–box after box. No worries about voids or slag that can cause flyers with cast bullets. Each Speer lead handgun bullet is coated with a clean lubricant to reduce fouling. Available in a variety of styles in calibers from 32 to 45.

**LEAD HANDGUN BULLETS**

| Caliber & Type | 32 HB-WC | 9mm RN | 38 BB-WC | 38 DE-WC | 38 HB-WC | 38 SWC | 38 HP-SWC | 38 RN | 44 SWC | 45 SWC | 45 RN | 45 SWC |
|---|---|---|---|---|---|---|---|---|---|---|---|---|
| Diameter | .314" | .356" | .358" | .358" | .358" | .358" | .358" | .358" | .430" | .452" | .452" | .452" |
| Weight (grs.) | 98 | 125 | 148 | 148 | 148 | 158 | 158 | 158 | 240 | 200 | 230 | 250 |
| Part Number | -- | 4601 | 4605 | -- | 4617 | 4623 | 4627 | 4647 | 4660 | 4677 | 4690 | 4683 |
| Bulk Part No. | 4600 | 4602 | 4606 | 4611 | 4618 | 4624 | 4628 | 4648 | 4661 | 4678 | 4691 | 4684 |

# SPEER RIFLE BULLETS

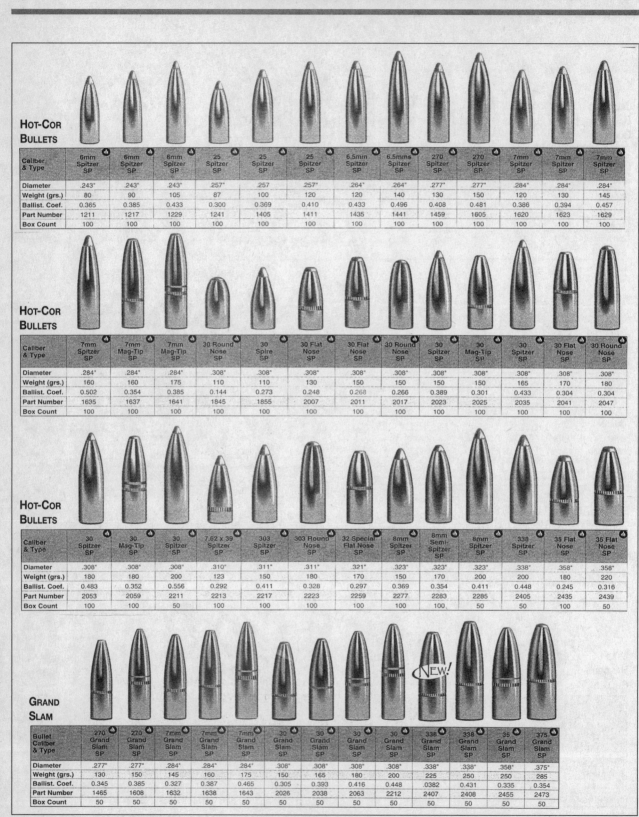

## HOT-COR BULLETS

| Caliber & Type | 6mm Spitzer SP | 6mm Spitzer SP | 6mm Spitzer SP | 25 Spitzer SP | 25 Spitzer SP | 25 Spitzer SP | 6.5mm Spitzer SP | 6.5mms Spitzer SP | 270 Spitzer SP | 270 Spitzer SP | 7mm Spitzer SP | 7mm Spitzer SP | 7mm Spitzer SP |
|---|---|---|---|---|---|---|---|---|---|---|---|---|---|
| Diameter | .243" | .243" | .243" | .257" | .257 | .257" | .264" | .264" | .277" | .277" | .284" | .284" | .284" |
| Weight (grs.) | 80 | 90 | 105 | 87 | 100 | 120 | 120 | 140 | 130 | 150 | 120 | 130 | 145 |
| Ballist. Coef. | 0.365 | 0.385 | 0.433 | 0.300 | 0.369 | 0.410 | 0.433 | 0.496 | 0.408 | 0.481 | 0.386 | 0.394 | 0.457 |
| Part Number | 1211 | 1217 | 1229 | 1241 | 1405 | 1411 | 1435 | 1441 | 1459 | 1605 | 1620 | 1623 | 1629 |
| Box Count | 100 | 100 | 100 | 100 | 100 | 100 | 100 | 100 | 100 | 100 | 100 | 100 | 100 |

## HOT-COR BULLETS

| Caliber & Type | 7mm Spitzer SP | 7mm Mag-Tip SP | 7mm Mag-Tip SP | 30 Round Nose SP | 30 Spire SP | 30 Flat Nose SP | 30 Flat Nose SP | 30 Round Nose SP | 30 Spitzer SP | 30 Mag-Tip SP | 30 Spitzer SP | 30 Flat Nose SP | 30 Round Nose SP |
|---|---|---|---|---|---|---|---|---|---|---|---|---|---|
| Diameter | .284" | .284" | .284" | .308" | .308" | .308" | .308" | .308" | .308" | .308" | .308" | .308" | .308" |
| Weight (grs.) | 160 | 160 | 175 | 110 | 110 | 130 | 150 | 150 | 150 | 150 | 165 | 170 | 180 |
| Ballist. Coef. | 0.502 | 0.354 | 0.385 | 0.144 | 0.273 | 0.248 | 0.268 | 0.266 | 0.389 | 0.301 | 0.433 | 0.304 | 0.304 |
| Part Number | 1635 | 1637 | 1641 | 1845 | 1855 | 2007 | 2011 | 2017 | 2023 | 2025 | 2035 | 2041 | 2047 |
| Box Count | 100 | 100 | 100 | 100 | 100 | 100 | 100 | 100 | 100 | 100 | 100 | 100 | 100 |

## HOT-COR BULLETS

| Caliber & Type | 30 Spitzer SP | 30 Mag-Tip SP | 30 Spitzer SP | 7.62 x 39 Spitzer SP | 303 Spitzer SP | 303 Round Nose SP | 32 Special Flat Nose SP | 8mm Spitzer SP | 8mm Semi Spitzer SP | 8mm Spitzer SP | 338 Spitzer SP | 35 Flat Nose SP | 35 Flat Nose SP |
|---|---|---|---|---|---|---|---|---|---|---|---|---|---|
| Diameter | .308" | .308" | .308" | .310" | .311" | .311" | .321" | .323" | .323" | .323" | .338" | .358" | .358" |
| Weight (grs.) | 180 | 180 | 200 | 123 | 150 | 180 | 170 | 150 | 170 | 200 | 200 | 180 | 220 |
| Ballist. Coef. | 0.483 | 0.352 | 0.556 | 0.292 | 0.411 | 0.328 | 0.297 | 0.369 | 0.354 | 0.411 | 0.448 | 0.245 | 0.316 |
| Part Number | 2053 | 2059 | 2211 | 2213 | 2217 | 2223 | 2259 | 2277 | 2283 | 2285 | 2405 | 2435 | 2439 |
| Box Count | 100 | 100 | 50 | 100 | 100 | 100 | 100 | 100 | 100 | 50 | 50 | 100 | 50 |

## GRAND SLAM

| Bullet Caliber & Type | 270 Grand Slam SP | 270 Grand Slam SP | 7mm Grand Slam SP | 7mm Grand Slam SP | 7mm Grand Slam SP | 30 Grand Slam SP | 30 Grand Slam SP | 30 Grand Slam SP | 30 Grand Slam SP | 338 Grand Slam SP | 338 Grand Slam SP | 35 Grand Slam SP | 375 Grand Slam SP |
|---|---|---|---|---|---|---|---|---|---|---|---|---|---|
| Diameter | .277" | .277" | .284" | .284" | .284" | .308" | .308" | .308" | .308" | .338" | .338" | .358" | .375" |
| Weight (grs.) | 130 | 150 | 145 | 160 | 175 | 150 | 165 | 180 | 200 | 225 | 250 | 250 | 285 |
| Ballist. Coef. | 0.345 | 0.385 | 0.327 | 0.387 | 0.465 | 0.305 | 0.393 | 0.416 | 0.448 | 0.382 | 0.431 | 0.335 | 0.354 |
| Part Number | 1465 | 1608 | 1632 | 1638 | 1643 | 2026 | 2038 | 2063 | 2212 | 2407 | 2408 | 2455 | 2473 |
| Box Count | 50 | 50 | 50 | 50 | 50 | 50 | 50 | 50 | 50 | 50 | 50 | 50 | 50 |

# SPEER RIFLE BULLETS

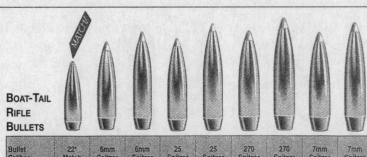

## BOAT-TAIL RIFLE BULLETS

| Bullet Caliber & Type | 22* Match HPBT | 6mm Spitzer SPBT | 6mm Spitzer SPBT | 25 Spitzer SPBT | 25 Spitzer SPBT | 270 Spitzer SPBT | 270 Spitzer SPBT | 7mm Spitzer SPBT | 7mm Spitzer SPBT |
|---|---|---|---|---|---|---|---|---|---|
| Diameter | .224" | .243" | .243" | .257" | .257" | .277" | .277" | .284" | .284" |
| Weight (grs.) | 52 | 85 | 100 | 100 | 120 | 130 | 150 | 130 | 145 |
| Ballist. Coef. | 0.253 | 0.404 | 0.430 | 0.393 | 0.435 | 0.449 | 0.496 | 0.411 | 0.502 |
| Part Number | 1036 | 1213 | 1220 | 1408 | 1410 | 1458 | 1604 | 1624 | 1628 |
| Box Count | 100 | 100 | 100 | 100 | 100 | 100 | 100 | 100 | 100 |

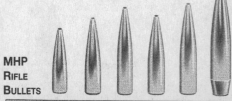

## MHP RIFLE BULLETS

| Caliber & Type | 22 MHP HP | 6mm MHP HP | 25 MHP HP | 270 MHP HP | 7mm MHP HP | 30 MHP Match HPBT |
|---|---|---|---|---|---|---|
| Diameter | .224" | .243" | .257" | .277" | .284" | .308" |
| Weight | 50 | 70 | 87 | 90 | 110 | 168 |
| Ballist. Coef. | 0.234 | 0.296 | 0.325 | 0.289 | 0.355 | 0.504 |
| Part Number | 1031 | 1207 | 1247 | 1457 | 1615 | 2039 |
| Box Count | 100 | 100 | 100 | 100 | 100 | 100 |

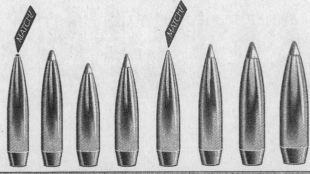

## BOAT-TAIL RIFLE BULLETS

| Bullet Caliber & Type | 7mm* Match HPBT | 7mm Spitzer SPBT | 30 Spitzer SPBT | 30 Spitzer SPBT | 30* Match HPBT | 30 Spitzer SPBT | 338 Spitzer SPBT | 375 Spitzer SPBT |
|---|---|---|---|---|---|---|---|---|
| Diameter | .284" | .284" | .308" | .308" | .308" | .308" | .338" | .375" |
| Weight (grs.) | 145 | 160 | 150 | 165 | 168 | 180 | 225 | 270 |
| Ballist. Coef. | 0.465 | 0.556 | 0.423 | 0.477 | 0.480 | 0.540 | 0.484 | 0.429 |
| Part Number | 1631 | 1634 | 2022 | 2034 | 2040 | 2052 | 2406 | 2472 |
| Box Count | 100 | 100 | 100 | 100 | 100 | 100 | 50 | 50 |

*Match bullets are not recommended for use on game animals.

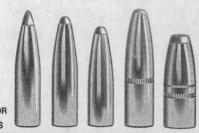

## HOT-COR BULLETS

| Caliber & Type | 35 Spitzer SP | 9.3mm Semi-Spitzer SP | 375 Semi-Spitzer SP | 416 Mag-Tip SP | 45 Flat Nose SP ‡ |
|---|---|---|---|---|---|
| Diameter | .358" | .366" | .375" | .416" | .458" |
| Weight (grs.) | 250 | 270 | 235 | 350 | 350 |
| Ballist. Coef. | 0.446 | 0.361 | 0.317 | 0.332 | 0.232 |
| Part Number | 2453 | 2459 | 2471 | 2477 | 2478 |
| Box Count | 50 | 50 | 50 | 50 | 50 |

‡ Not recommended for lever-action rifles.

## RIFLE BULLETS

| Caliber & Type | 218 Bee Flat Nose SP | 22 FMJ BT | 22 FMJ BT ‡ | 25-20 Win Flat Nose SP | 7-30 Waters Flat Nose SP | 30 Carbine FMJ | 30 FMJ BT | 32-20 Win HP |
|---|---|---|---|---|---|---|---|---|
| Diameter | .224" | .224" | .224" | .257" | .284" | .308" | .308" | .312" |
| Weight | 46 | 55 | 62 | 75 | 130 | 110 | 150 | 100 |
| Ballist. Coef. | 0.094 | 0.269 | 0.307 | 0.133 | 0.257 | 0.179 | 0.425 | 0.167 |
| Part Number | 1024 | 1044 | 1050 | 1237 | 1625 | 1846 | 2018 | 3981 |
| Box Count | 100 | 100 | 100 | 100 | 100 | 100 | 100 | 100 |

‡ Recommended for twist rates of 1 in 10" or faster.

## GRAND SLAM

| Bullet Caliber & Type | 6mm GS SP | 25 GS SP | 6.5mm GS SP |
|---|---|---|---|
| Diameter | .243" | .257" | .264" |
| Weight (grs.) | 100 | 120 | 140 |
| Ballist. Coef. | 0.351 | 0.328 | 0.385 |
| Part Number | 1222 | 1415 | 1444 |
| Box Count | 50 | 50 | 50 |

# SPEER RIFLE BULLETS

## African Grand Slam

| Bullet Caliber & Type | 375 AGS SP | 375 AGS Tungsten Solid | 416 AGS SP | 416 AGS Tungsten Solid | 45 AGS SP | 45 AGS Tungsten Solid |
|---|---|---|---|---|---|---|
| Diameter | .375" | .375" | .416" | .416" | .458" | .458" |
| Weight (grs.) | 300 | 300 | 400 | 400 | 500 | 500 |
| Ballist. Coef. | 0.323 | 0.258 | 0.318 | 0.262 | 0.285 | 0.277 |
| Part Number | 2470 | 2474 | 2475 | 2476 | 2485 | 2486 |
| Box Count | 25 | 25 | 25 | 25 | 25 | 25 |

## Rifle Bullets

| Caliber & Type | 22 Spire SP | 22 Spitzer SP | 22 Spitzer SP | 22 HP | 22 Spitzer SP | 22 Spitzer SP w/cann. | 22 Semi-Spitzer SP | 6mm HP |
|---|---|---|---|---|---|---|---|---|
| Diameter | .224" | .224" | .224" | .224" | .224" | .224" | .224" | .243" |
| Weight | 40 | 45 | 50 | 52 | 55 | 55 | 70 | 75 |
| Ballist. Coef. | 0.144 | 0.167 | 0.231 | 0.225 | 0.255 | 0.241 | 0.214 | 0.234 |
| Part Number | 1017 | 1023 | 1029 | 1035 | 1047 | 1049 | 1053 | 1205 |
| Box Count | 100 | 100 | 100 | 100 | 100 | 100 | 100 | 100 |

## Rifle Bullets

| Caliber & Type | 25 HP | 270 HP | 7mm HP | 30 Plinker RN SP | 30 HP | 30 HP | 45 Flat Nose SP |
|---|---|---|---|---|---|---|---|
| Diameter | .257" | .277" | .284" | .308" | .308" | .308" | .458" |
| Weight | 100 | 100 | 115 | 100 | 110 | 130 | 400 |
| Ballist. Coef. | 0.255 | 0.225 | 0.257 | 0.124 | 0.136 | 0.263 | 0.214 |
| Part Number | 1407 | 1447 | 1617 | 1805 | 1835 | 2005 | 2479 |
| Box Count | 100 | 100 | 100 | 100 | 100 | 100 | 50 |

## TNT Rifle Bullets

| Caliber & Type | 22 TNT HP | 6mm TNT HP | 25 TNT HP | 6.5mm TNT HP | 270 TNT HP | 7mm TNT HP | 30 TNT HP |
|---|---|---|---|---|---|---|---|
| Diameter | .224" | .243" | .257" | .264" | .277" | .284" | .308" |
| Weight | 50 | 70 | 87 | 90 | 90 | 110 | 125 |
| Ballist. Coef. | 0.223 | 0.282 | 0.310 | 0.281 | 0.275 | 0.338 | 0.326 |
| Part Number | 1030 | 1206 | 1246 | 1445 | 1446 | 1616 | 1986 |
| Box Count | 100 | 100 | 100 | 100 | 100 | 100 | 100 |

# SWIFT

*Swift Scirocco® Polymer-Tipped Bullet Combines Accuracy, Reliable Expansion and Integrity On Virtually All Game At All Velocities*

**SWIFT SCIROCCO™ BONDED**
*30 cal. (.308") 180-gr.
Polymer Tip/Boat Tail Spitzer*

*Tapered jacket and proprietary bonding process produce controlled mushrooming with high weight retention. Ideally suited to fast, flat-shooting calibers.*

The Swift Bullet Company has designed what it believes is the most versatile and broadly effective hunting bullet ever developed.

The **Scirocco** design starts with its tough, pointed, polymer tip that reduces air resistance, prevents tip deformation, and blends symetrically into the curved radius of its secant ogive nose section. A moderate 15-degree boat tail base reduces drag and eases seating. The thick base prevents bullet deformation during launch. **Scirocco's** shape creates two other significant advantages. One is an extremely high ballistic coefficient. The other, derived from the secant ogive nose, is a comparatively long bearing surface for a sharply pointed bullet, a feature that improves rotational stability.

**SWIFT SCIROCCO™ BONDED**
*30 cal. (.308") 180-gr.
Polymer Tip/Boat Tail Spitzer*

Inside, the **Scirocco** has a bonded-core construction with a pure lead core encased in a tapered, progressively thickening jacket of pure copper. Pure copper was selected because it is more malleable and less brittle than less expensive gilding metal. Both jacket and core are bonded together by Swift's proprietary bonding process so that the bullet expands without break-up as if the two parts were the same metal. In tests, the new bullet mushroomed effectively at velocities as low as 1440 fps, yet stayed together at velocities in excess of 3,000 fps, with over 70 percent weight retention.

*The SWIFT A-FRAME, noted for deep penetration in tough game, is loaded in Remington Premier ammuni-*

Swift's A-Frame bullet, with its mid-section wall of copper, is still earning praise for its deep-driving dependability in tough game. Less aerodynamic than the Scirocco, it produces a broad mushroom while carrying almost all its weight through muscle and bone. Available in a wide range of weights and diameters, it is also a bonded-core bullet.

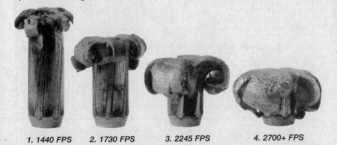

1. 1440 FPS    2. 1730 FPS    3. 2245 FPS    4. 2700+ FPS

*Swift Scirocco™ Expands dependably over a wide range of velocities, and maintains high jacket/core integrity.*

# SWIFT

## A-FRAME RIFLE BULLET SPECIFICATIONS

| Cal. | A-Frame™ Bullet | Dia. | Wt. (gr.) | Profile | Sect. Den. | Ball. Coef. |
|------|-----------------|------|-----------|---------|-----------|-------------|
| .25 | | .257" | 100 | AF/SS | .216 | .318 |
| | | .257" | 120 | AF/SS | .260 | .382 |
| 6.5 mm | | .264" | 120 | AF/SS | .246 | .344 |
| | | .264" | 140 | AF/SS | .287 | .401 |
| .270 | | .277" | 130 | AF/SS | .242 | .323 |
| | | .277" | 140 | AF/SS | .261 | .414 |
| | | .277" | 150 | AF/SS | .279 | .444 |
| 7mm | | .284" | 140 | AF/SS | .248 | .335 |
| | | .284" | 160 | AF/SS | .283 | .450 |
| | | .284" | 175 | AF/SS | .310 | .493 |
| .30 | | .308" | 150 | AF/FN | .226 | .218 |
| | | .308" | 165 | AF/SS | .249 | .367 |
| | | .308" | 180 | AF/SS | .271 | .400 |
| | | .308" | 200 | AF/SS | .301 | .444 |
| 8mm | | .323" | 200 | AF/SS | .274 | .357 |
| | | .323" | 220 | AF/SS | .301 | .393 |
| .338 | | .338" | 225 | AF/SS | .281 | .384 |
| | | .338" | 250 | AF/SS | .313 | .427 |
| | | .338" | 275 | AF/SS | .344 | .469 |
| .35 | | .358" | 225 | AF/SS | .251 | .312 |
| | | .358" | 250 | AF/SS | .279 | .347 |
| | | .358" | 280 | AF/SS | .312 | .388 |

| Cal. | A-Frame™ Bullet | Dia. | Wt. (gr.) | Profile | Sect. Den. | Ball. Coef. |
|------|-----------------|------|-----------|---------|-----------|-------------|
| 9.3 mm | | .366" | 250 | AF/SS | .267 | .285 |
| | | .366" | 300 | AF/SS | .320 | .342 |
| .375 | | .375" | 250 | AF/SS | .254 | .271 |
| | | .375" | 300 | AF/SS | .305 | .325 |
| .411 | | .411" | 350 | AF/SS | .296 | .328 |
| | | .411" | 400 | AF/SS | .338 | .375 |
| .416 | | .416" | 350 | AF/SS | .289 | .321 |
| | | .416" | 400 | AF/SS | .330 | .367 |
| .458 | | .458" | 400 | AF/FN | .272 | .258 |
| | | .458" | 450 | AF/SS | .307 | .325 |
| | | .458" | 500 | AF/SS | .341 | .361 |
| .470 | | .475" | 500 | AF/RN | .329 | .364 |

### HANDGUN BULLET SPECIFICATIONS

| Cal. | | Dia. | Wt. (gr.) | Profile | Sect. Den. | Ball. Coef. |
|------|---|------|-----------|---------|-----------|-------------|
| .44 | | .430" | 240 | AF/HP | .185 | .119 |
| | | .430" | 280 | AF/HP | .216 | .139 |
| | | .430" | 300 | AF/HP | .232 | .147 |
| .45 | | .452" | 300 | AF/HP | .210 | .135 |

AF/SS = A-Frame Semi-Spitzer • AF/FN = A-Frame Flat Nose • AF/RN = A-Frame Round Nose • AF/HP = A-Frame Hollow Point

# WOODLEIGH PREMIUM BULLETS

### WELDCORE SOFT NOSE

Woodleigh Weldcore Soft Nose bullets are made from 90/100 gilding metal (90% copper: 10% zinc) 1.6 mm thick. Maximum retained weight is obtained by fusing the pure lead to the gilding metal jacket, hence the name "Weldcore."

### FULL METAL JACKET

Made from gilding metal-clad steel 2mm thick, jackets on fmj bullets are heavy at the nose for extra impact resistance. The jacket then tapers towards the base to assist rifling engraving.

| Calibre Diameter | Bullet | Type | Wt. Gr. | SD | BC | Cat. No. |
|---|---|---|---|---|---|---|
| 270 Win .277" | | PP | 130 | .241 | .409 | 72 |
| | | PP | 150 | .278 | .463 | 73 |
| 7mm .284" | | PP | 140 | .247 | .436 | 74 |
| | | PP | 160 | .282 | .486 | 75 |
| | | PP | 175 | .312 | .530 | 76 |
| 275 H&H .287" | | PP | 160 | .275 | .474 | 77 |
| | | PP | 175 | .301 | .518 | 78 |
| 308 Cal. .308" | | PP | 165 | .250 | .320 | 65A |
| | | PP | 180 | .273 | .376 | 65B |
| | | RN | 220 | .331 | .367 | 65C |
| | | FMJ | 220 | .331 | .359 | 65 |
| 300 .308 Win Mag | | PP | 180 | .273 | .435 | 65D |
| 303 British .312 | | SN | 215 | .316 | .359 | 68 |
| 8mm .323" | | SN | 196 | .268 | .370 | 64B |
| | | SN | 220 | .302 | .363 | 64C |
| | | SN | 250 | .343 | .389 | 64D |
| 318 Westley Richards .330" | | SN | 250 | .328 | .420 | 63 |
| | | FMJ | 250 | .328 | .364 | 64 |
| 333 Jeffery .333" | | SN | 250 | .322 | .400 | 60 |
| | | SN | 300 | .386 | .428 | 61 |
| | | FMJ | 300 | .386 | .419 | 62 |

| Calibre Diameter | Bullet | Type | Wt. Gr. | SD | BC | Cat. No. |
|---|---|---|---|---|---|---|
| 338 Mag .338" | | PP | 225 | .281 | .425 | 56A |
| | | SN | 250 | .313 | .332 | 56 |
| | | PP | 250 | .313 | .470 | 56B |
| | | FMJ | 250 | .313 | .326 | 57 |
| | | SN | 300 | .375 | .416 | 58 |
| | | FMJ | 300 | .375 | .398 | 59 |
| 358 Cal. .358" | | SN | 225 | .250 | .277 | 51 |
| | | FMJ | 225 | .250 | .298 | 52 |
| | | SN | 250 | .285 | .365 | 53 |
| | | SN | 310 | .346 | .400 | 54 |
| | | FMJ | 310 | .346 | 378 | 55 |
| 9.3mm .366" | | SN | 250 | .267 | .296 | 47A |
| | | SN | 286 | .305 | .331 | 47 |
| | | FMJ | 286 | .305 | .324 | 48 |
| 360 No.2 .366" | | SN | 320 | .341 | .378 | 49 |
| | | FMJ | 320 | .341 | .362 | 50 |
| 375 Mag. .375" | | PP | 235 | .239 | .331 | 42A |
| | | RN | 270 | .275 | .305 | 42 |
| | | SP | 270 | .275 | .380 | 43 |
| | | PP | 270 | .275 | .352 | 43A |
| | | RN | 300 | .305 | .340 | 44 |
| | | SP | 300 | .305 | .425 | 45 |
| | | PP | 300 | .305 | .420 | 45A |
| | | FMJ | 300 | .305 | .307 | 46 |
| 405 Win .411" | | SN | 300 | .254 | .194 | 71 |
| 450/400 Nitro .411" or .408" | | SN | 400 | .338 | .384 | 40 |
| | | FMJ | 400 | .338 | .433 | 41 |
| 416 Rigby .416" | | SN | 410 | .338 | .375 | 37 |
| | | FMJ | 410 | .338 | .341 | 38 |
| | | PP | 340 | .281 | .425 | 39 |
| 10.75 x68mm .423" | | SN | 347 | .277 | .355 | 36 |
| | | FMJ | 347 | .277 | .307 | 36A |
| 404 Jeffery .423" | | SN | 400 | .319 | .354 | 33 |
| | | FMJ | 400 | .319 | .358 | 34 |
| | | SN | 350 | .279 | .357 | 35 |
| 425 Westley Richards .435" | | SN | 410 | .310 | .344 | 31 |
| | | FMJ | 410 | .310 | .336 | 32 |
| 11.2x72 Schuler .440" | | SN | 401 | .296 | .411 | 67 |
| 45/70 .458" | | FN | 405 | | | 30B |

# WOODLEIGH PREMIUM BULLETS

| Calibre Diameter | Type | Wt. Gr. | SD | BC | Cat. No. |
|---|---|---|---|---|---|
| 458 Mag. .458" | SN | 500 | .341 | .430 | 26 |
| | SN | 550 | .375 | .480 | 27 |
| | FMJ | 500 | .341 | .405 | 28 |
| | FMJ | 550 | .375 | .426 | 29 |
| | PP | 400 | .272 | .420 | 30 |
| | RN | 350 | .238 | .305 | 30A |
| 450 Nitro .458" | SN | 480 | .327 | .419 | 24 |
| | FMJ | 480 | .327 | .410 | 25 |
| 465 Nitro .468" | SN | 480 | .318 | .410 | 22 |
| | FMJ | 480 | .318 | .407 | 23 |
| 470 Nitro .474" | SN | 500 | .318 | .411 | 20 |
| | FMJ | 500 | .318 | .410 | 21 |
| 475 Nitro .476" | SN | 480 | .227 | .307 | 69 |
| | FMJ | 480 | .227 | .257 | 70 |
| 476 Westley Richards .476" | SN | 520 | .328 | .420 | 18 |
| | FMJ | 520 | .328 | .455 | 19 |
| 475 No.2 .483" | SN | 480 | .294 | .334 | 15 |
| | FMJ | 480 | .294 | .326 | 16 |

| Calibre Diameter | Type | Wt. Gr. | SD | BC | Cat. No. |
|---|---|---|---|---|---|
| 475 No.2 Jeffery .488" | SN | 500 | .300 | .420 | 13 |
| | FMJ | 500 | .300 | .416 | 14 |
| 500 Nitro .510" | SN | 570 | .313 | .474 | 6 |
| | FMJ | 570 | .313 | .434 | 7 |
| 500 BP .510" | SN | 440 | .242 | .336 | 8 |
| 500 Jeffery .510" | SN | 535 | .304 | .460 | 9 |
| | FMJ | 535 | .304 | .422 | 10 |
| 505 Gibbs .505" | SN | 525 | .294 | .445 | 11 |
| | FMJ | 525 | .294 | .408 | 12 |
| 577 BP .585" | SN | 650 | .271 | .320 | 5 |
| 577 Nitro .585" | SN | 750 | .313 | .346 | 3 |
| | FMJ | 750 | .313 | .351 | 4 |
| 600 Nitro .620" | SN | 900 | .334 | .371 | 1 |
| | FMJ | 900 | .334 | .334 | 2 |
| 700 Nitro .700" | SN | 1000 | .292 | .340 | A |
| | FMJ | 1000 | .292 | .340 | B |

# ALLIANT SMOKELESS POWDERS

# ALLIANT RIFLE, SHOTGUN AND PISTOL POWDERS

| POWDER | RELATIVE QUICKNESS | PRINCIPAL PURPOSE | SECONDARY USES |
|---|---|---|---|
| BULLSEYE® | 100% | Handgun Loads | 12 ga. Light Target Loads |
| RED DOT® | 94.1% | Light & Standard 12 & 16 ga. Target Loads | Handgun Loads |
| AMERICAN SELECT® | 81.0% | 12 ga. Target Loads | Cowboy Action Handgun Loads |
| GREEN DOT® | 77.9% | Handicap Trap Loads | 20 & 28 ga. Target Loads |
| UNIQUE® | 61.6% | All-around Shotshell Powder, 12, 16 & 20 ga. | Handgun Loads |
| POWER PISTOL® | 58.6% | High Performance 9mm, .40 S&W & 10mm | Moderate Pistol Cartridges |
| HERCO® | 56.1% | Heavy Shotshell Loads 10, 12 16, 20 & 28 ga. | Heavy Handgun Loads |
| BLUE DOT® | 37.8% | Magnum Shotshell Loads 10, 12, 16, 20 & 28 ga. | Magnum Handgun Loads |
| STEEL™ | 34.0% | Non-Toxic Hunting Shotshell | 2 oz. Turkey Loads |
| 2400® | 27.00% | Magnum Handgun Loads | .22 Hornet & 218 Bee |
| RELOADER® 7 | 19.4% | Light Rifle | 45-70 Gov't |
| RELOADER® 15 | 13.7% | Medium Rifle | Silhouette Rifle |
| RELOADER® 19 | 11.3% | Standard Rifle | Light Magnum Rifle |
| RELOADER® 22 | 11.1% | Magnum Rifle | Heavy Bullet Stand Rifle |
| RELOADER® 25 | 10.5% | Heavy Magnum Rifle | Magnum Rifle |

# HODGDON SMOKELESS POWDER

**PYRODEX PELLETS**
Both rifle and pistol pellets eliminate powder measures, speeds shooting for black powder enthusiasts.

**EXTREME H4198**
H4198 was developed especially for small and medium capacity cartridges.

**EXTREME H322**
This powder fills the gap between H4198 and BL-C9(2). Performs best in small to medium capacity cases.

**Extreme Benchmark**
A fine choice for small rifle cases like the .223 Rem and PPC competition rounds. Appropriate also for the 300-30 and 7x57.

**SPHERICAL BL-C2**
Best performance is in the 222, .308 other cases smaller than 30/06.

**SPHERICAL H335®**
Similar to BL-C(2), H335 is popular for its performance in medium capacity cases, especially in 222 and 308 Winchester.

**EXTREME VARGET**
Features small extruded grain powder for uniform metering, plus higher velocities/normal pressures in such calibers as .223, 22-250, 306, 30-06, 375 H&H

**EXTREME H4895®**
4895 gives desirable performance in almost all cases from 222 Rem. to 458 Win. Reduced loads, to as low as 3/5 maximum, still give target accuracy.

**SPHERICAL H380®**
This number fills a gap between 4320 and 4350. It is excellent in 22/250, 220 Swift, the 6mm's, 257 and 30/06.

**SPHERICAL H414®**
In many popular medium to medium-large calibers, pressure velocity relationship is better.

**EXTREME H4350**
This powder gives superb accuracy at optimum velocity for many large capacity metallic rifle cartridges.

**EXTREME H4831®**
Outstanding performance with medium and heavy bullets in the 6mm's, 25/06, 270 and Magnum calibers. Also available with shortened grains (H4831SC) for easy metering.

**EXTREME H1000 EXTRUDED POWDER**
Fills the gap between H4831 and H870. Works especially well in overbore capacity cartridges (1,000-yard shooters take note).

**EXTREME H50 BMG**
Designed for the 50 Browning Machine Gun cartridge. Highly insensitive to extreme temperature changes.

**CLAYS**
Tailored for use in 12 ga., 7/8, 1-oz. and 1 1/8-oz. loads. Also performs well in many handgun applications, including .38 Special, .40 S&W and 45 ACP. Perfect for 1 1/8 and 1 oz. loads.

**Universal Clays**
Loads nearly all of the straight-wall pistol cartridges as well as 12 ga. 1.25 oz. thru 28 ga. 3/4 oz. target loads.

**International Clays**
Ideal for 12 and 20 ga. autoloaders who want reduced recoil.

**Titewad**
This 12 ga. flattened spherical shotgun powder is ideal for 7/8, 1 and 1 1/8 oz. loads, with minimum recoil and mild muzzle report.

**HS-6 AND HS-7**
HS-6 and HS-7 for Magnum field loads are unsurpassed, since they do not pack in the measure. They deliver uniform charges and are dense to allow sufficient wad column for best patterns.

**Longshot**
A new spherical powder for heavy shotgun loads.

**HP38**
A fast pistol powder for most pistol loading. Especially recommended for mid-range 38 specials.

**Titegroup**
Excellent for most straight-walled pistol cartridges, incl. 38 Spec., 44 Spec., 45 ACP. Low charge weights, clean burning; position insensitive and flawless ignition.

**H110**
A spherical powder made especially for the 30 M1 carbine. H110 also does very well in 357, 44 spec., 44 Mag. or .410 ga. shotshell. Magnum primers are recommended for consistent ignition.

**H4227**
An extruded powder similar to H110, it is the fastest burning in Hodgdon's line. Recommended for the 22 Hornet and some specialized loading in the 45-70 caliber. Also excellent in magnum pistol and .410 shotgun.

**LIL' GUN**
This powder was developed specifically for the .410 shotgun but works very well in rifle cartridges like the .22 Hornet and in the .44 magnum.

# RAMSHOT POWDERS

WESTERN POWDERS, INC. recently introduced a line of nine spherical powders for shooters. They are all double-base propellants, meaning they contain nitrocellulose and nitroglycerine. While some spherical or ball powders are known for leaving plenty of residue in barrels, Ramshots people say these new fuels burn very clean. They meter easily, as do all ball powders. Plastic cannisters are designed for spill-proof use and include basic loading data on the labels. More extensive loading information is being prepared.

**RAMSHOT COMPETITION** is for the clay target shooter. A fast-burning powder comparable to 700-X or Red Dot it performs well in a variety of 12-gauge target loads, offering low recoil, consistent pressures and clean combustion.

**RAMSHOT TRUE BLUE** was designed for small to medium-size handgun cartridges. Similar to Winchester 231 and Hodgdon HP-38, it has enough bulk to nearly fill most cases, thereby better positioning the powder for ignition.

**RAMSHOT ZIP**, a fast-burning target powder for cartridges like the .38 Special and .45 ACP, gives competitors uniform velocities.

**RAMSHOT SILHOUETTE** is ideal for the 9mm handgun cartridge, from light to heavy loads. It also works well in the .40 Smith & Wesson and combat loads for the .45 Auto.

**RAMSHOT ENFORCER** a match for high-performance handgun hulls like the .40 Smith & Wesson. It is designed for full-power loading and high velocities.

**Ramshot X-Terminator**, a fast-burning rifle powder, excels in small-caliber, medium-capacity cartridges. It has the versatility to serve in both target and high-performance varmint loads.

**RAMSHOT TAC** was formulated for tactical rifle cartridges, specifically the .223 and .308. It has produced exceptional accuracy with a variety of bullets and charge weights.

**RAMSHOT BIG GAME** is a versatile propellant for cartridges as diverse as the .30-06 and the .338 Winchester, and for light-bullet loads in small-bore magnums.

**RAMSHOT BIG BOY** is the slowest powder of the Western line, and does its best work in cartridges with lots of case volume and small to medium bullet diameter. It is the powder of choice in 7mm and .30 Magnums.

# DILLON PRECISION RELOADERS

Dillon Precision is a leader in the shotgun shooting sports market with its SL 900 progressive shotshell reloader. Based on Dillon's proven XL 650 O-frame design, it incorporates the same powerful compound linkage. The automatic case insert system, fed by an electric case collator, ranks high among the new features of this reloader. Adjustable shot and powder bars come as standard equipment. Both the powder and shot bars are case-activated, so no powder or shot can spill when no shell is at that station. Should the operator forget to insert a wad during the reloading process, the SL 900 will not dispense shot into the powder-charged hull. Both powder and shot systems are based on Dillon's adjustable powder bar design, which is accurate to within a few tenths of a grain. These systems also eliminate the need for fixed-volume bushings. Simply adjust the measures to dispense the exact charges required.

The Dillon SL 900 is the first progressive shotshell loader on which it is practical to change gauges. An interchangeable tool-head makes it quick and easy to change from one gauge to another. The SL 900 also has an extra large, remote shot hopper that holds an entire 25-pound bag of shot, making it easy to fill with a funnel. The unique shot reservoir/dispenser helps ensure that a consistent volume of shot is delivered to each shell.

For shotgunners who shoot and load for multiple gauges or different kinds of shooting, the SL 900's interchangeable toolhead feature makes quick work of changing from one gauge to another. It uses a collet-type sizing die that re-forms the base of the shotshell to factory specifications—a feature that ensure reliable feeding in all shotguns. The heat-treated steel crimp die forms and folds the hull before the final taper crimp die radiuses and blends the end of the hull and locks the crimp into place.

## MODEL RL550B PROGRESSIVE LOADER

- Accomodates over 120 calibers
- Interchangeable toolhead assembly
- Auto/Powder priming systemsa
- Uses standard 7/8" by 14 dies
- Loading rate: 500-600 rounds per hour

*Price:* . . . . . . . . . . . . . . . . . . . . . . . . . . . . . . . .$325.95

## MODEL SL900
## $819.95

# DILLON PRECISION RELOADERS

### MODEL SQUARE DEAL B

- Automatic Indexing
- Auto Powder/Priming Systems
- Available in 14 handgun calibers
- Loading rate: 400-500 rounds per hour
- Loading dies standard
- Factory adjusted, ready-to-use

**Price:** $252.95

### MODEL RL 1050

- Automatic indexing
- Auto powder/priming systems
- Automatic casefeeder
- Commercial grade machine
- Swages military primer pockets
- Loading rate: 1000-1200 rounds per hour
- Weighs 54 lbs.
- Eight station

**Price:** $1,199.95

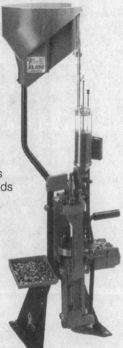

### MODEL XL 650

- New primer system design (uses rotary indexing plate)
- Automatic indexing
- Uses standard 7/8" x 14 dies
- Loading rate: 800-1000 rounds per hour
- Five station interchangeable toolhead

**Price:** $443.95

### MODEL AT-500

- Loads over 40 calibers
- Uses standard 7/8" by 14 dies
- Upgradeable to Model RL 550B
- Interchangeable toolhead
- Switch from one caliber to another in 30 seconds
- Universal shellplate

**Price:** $193.95

# FORSTER RELOADING

## CO-AX® BENCH REST® RIFLE DIES

Bench Rest Rifle Dies are glass hard and polished mirror smooth with special attention given to headspace, tapers and diameters. Sizing die has an elevated expander button to ensure better alignment of case and neck.

| | |
|---|---|
| BENCH REST® DIE SET | $69.98 |
| WEATHERBY BENCH REST DIE SET | .69.98 |
| ULTRA BENCH REST DIE SET | .92.98 |
| FULL LENGTH SIZER | .32.98 |
| BENCH REST SEATING DIE | .39.98 |

**PRIMER SEATER**

**CO-AX® CARTRIDGE INSPECTOR**

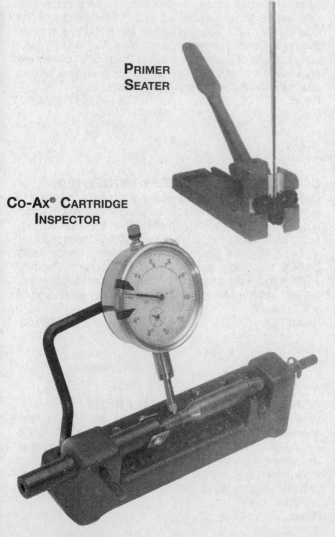

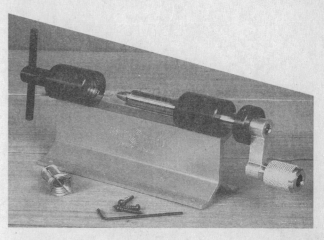

## HAND CASE TRIMMER

Shell holder is a Brown & Sharpe-type collet. Case and cartridge conditioning accessories include inside neck reamer, outside neck turner, deburring tool, hollow pointer and primer pocket cleaners. The case trimmer trims all cases, ranging from 17 to 458 Winchester caliber.
*Price:* .................................$59.00

## PRIMER SEATER
### With "E-Z-Just" Shellholder

The Bonanza Primer Seater is designed so that primers are seated Co-Axially (primer in line with primer pocket). Mechanical leverage allows primers to be seated fully without crushing. With the addition of one extra set of Disc Shell Holders and one extra Primer Unit, all modern cases, rim or rimless, from 222 up to 458 Magnum, can be primed. Shell holders are easily adjusted to any case by rotating to contact rim or cannelure of the case.

| | |
|---|---|
| PRIMER SEATER | $69.00 |
| PRIMER POCKET CLEANER | .6.98 |

## "CLASSIC 50" CASE TRIMMER (not shown)

Handles more than 100 different big bore calibers–500 Nitro Express, 416 Rigby, 50 Sharps, 475 H&H, etc. *Also available:* .50 BMG Case Trimmer, designed specifically for reloading needs of .50 Cal. BMG Shooters.

| | |
|---|---|
| *Price:* "CLASSIC 50" CASE TRIMMER | $84.00 |
| .50 BMG CASE TRIMMER | .89.00 |

## CO-AX® CASE AND CARTRIDGE INSPECTOR

*One tool to perform three vital measurements.* Accurate performance from your ammunition is absolutely dependent on uniformity of both the bullet and the case. Achieving that uniformity is not possible without an accurate, reliable measuring device.

Forster's exclusive Co-Ax® Case & Cartridge Inspector provides you with the ability to ensure uniformity by measuring three critical dimensions: • Neck wall thickness • Case neck concentricity • Bullet runout.

Measurements are in increments of one-thousandth of an inch so accuracy is superb.

The Inspector is unique because it checks both the bullet and case alignment in relation to the centerline (axis) of the entire cartridge or case.

# FORSTER RELOADING

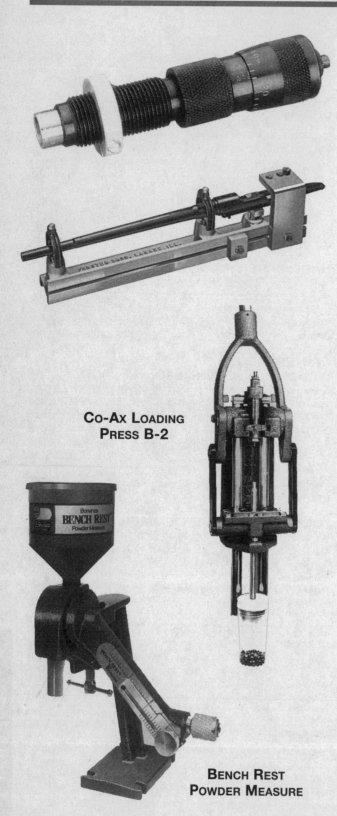

**CO-AX LOADING PRESS B-2**

**BENCH REST POWDER MEASURE**

## ULTRA BULLET SEATER DIE
Forster's new Ultra Die is available in 56 calibers, more than any other brand of micrometer-style seater. Adjustment is identical to that of a precision micrometer—the head is graduated to .001" increments with .025" bullet movement per revolution. The cartridge case, bullet and seating stem are completely supported and perfectly aligned in a close-fitting chamber before and during the bullet seating operation.
*Price:* . . . . . . . . . . . . . . . . . . . . . . . . . . . . . . . . .**$62.98**

## UNIVERSAL SIGHT MOUNTING FIXTURE
This product fills the exacting requirements needed for drilling and tapping holes for the mounting of scopes, receiver sights, shotgun beads, etc. The fixture handles any single-barrel gun—bolt-action, lever-action or pump-action—as long as the barrel can be laid into the "V" blocks of the fixture. Rifles with tube magazines are drilled in the same manner by removing the magazine tube. The fixture's main body is made of aluminum casting. The two "V" blocks are adjustable for height and are made of hardened steel ground accurately on the "V" as well as the shaft.
*Price:* . . . . . . . . . . . . . . . . . . . . . . . . . . . . . . . .**$368.00**

## CO-AX® LOADING PRESS MODEL B-2
Designed to make reloading easier and more accurate, this press offers the following features: Snap-in and snap-out die change • Positive spent primer catcher • Automatic self-acting shell holder • Floating guide rods • Working room for right- or left-hand operators • Top priming device seats primers to factory specifications • Uses any standard 7/8"X14 dies • No torque on the head • Perfect alignment of die and case • Three times the mechanical advantage of a "C" press
*Price:* . . . . . . . . . . . . . . . . . . . . . . . . . . . . . . . .**$298.00**

## BENCH REST POWDER MEASURE
When operated uniformly, this measure will throw uniform charges from 2 1/2 grains Bullseye to 95 grains #4320. No extra drums are needed. Powder is metered from the charge arm, allowing a flow of powder without extremes in variation while minimizing powder shearing. Powder flows through its own built-in baffle so that powder enters the charge arm uniformly.
*Price:* . . . . . . . . . . . . . . . . . . . . . . . . . . . . . . . .**$109.98**

# HORNADY

## LOCK-N-LOAD CLASSIC PRESS

Lock-N-Load is available on Hornady's single stage and progressive reloader models. This bushing system locks the die into the press like a rifle bolt. Instead of threading dies in and out of the press, you simply lock and unlock them with a slight twist. Dies are held firmly in a die bushing that stays with the die and retains the die setting. The Lock-N-Load Classic Press features an easy-grip handle, an O-style frame made of high-strength alloy, and a positive priming system that feeds, aligns and seats the primer smoothly and automatically.

*Prices:*
LOCK-N-LOAD CLASSIC PRESS KIT . . . . . . . . . . . . .$259.95

## LOCK-N-LOAD AUTO PROGRESSIVE PRESS

The Lock-N-Load Automatic Progressive reloading press featuring the Lock-N-Load bushing system offers the flexibility to add a roll or taper crimp die. Dies and powder measure are inserted into Lock-N-Load die bushings, which lock securely into the press. The bushings remain with the die and powder measure and can be removed in seconds. They also fit on other presses. Other features include: deluxe powder measure, automatic indexing, off-set handle, power-pac linkage, case ejector.

LOCK-N-LOAD AUTO PROGRESSIVE PRESS (includes five die bushings, shellplate, primer catcher, Positive Priming System, powder drop, Deluxe Powder Measure, automatic primer feed) . . . . . . . . . . . . . . . .$367.65

## MODEL 366 AUTO SHOTSHELL RELOADER

The 366 Auto features full-length resizing with each stroke, automatic primer feed, swing-out wad guide, three-state crimping featuring Taper-Loc for factory tapered crimp, automatic advance to the next station and automatic ejection. The turntable holds 8 shells for 8 operations with each stroke. Automatic charge bar loads shot and powder, dies and crimp starters for 6 point, 8 point and paper crimps.

MODEL 366 AUTO SHOTSHELL RELOADER:
12, 20, 28 gauge or .410 bore . . . . . . . . . . . . .$434.95

## CUSTOM GRADE RELOADING DIES

Features an Elliptical Expander that minimizes friction and reduces case neck stretch, plus the need for a tapered expander for "necking up" to the next larger caliber. Other recent design changes include a hardened steel decap pin that will not break, bend or crack even when depriming stubborn military cases. A bullet seater alignment sleeve guides the bullet and case neck into the die for in-line benchrest alignment. All New Dimension Reloading Dies include: collar and collar lock to center expander precisely; one-piece expander spindle with tapered bottom for easy cartridge insertion; wrench flats on die body, Sure-Loc™ lock rings and collar lock for easy tightening; and built-in crimper.

NEW DIMENSION CUSTOM GRADE RELOADING DIES:
SERIES I TWO-DIE RIFLE SET . . . . . . . . . . . . . . . .$28.97
SERIES II THREE-DIE RIFLE SET . . . . . . . . . . . . . . .30.60
SERIES II THREE-DIE PISTOL SET (w/Titanium Nitride) . . . . . . 40.49
50 CALIBER BMG DIES (TWO-DIE SET) . . . . . . . . . .243.00

LOCK-N-LOAD CLASSIC RELOADING PRESS

LOCK-N-LOAD

MODEL 366

# LYMAN RELOADING TOOLS

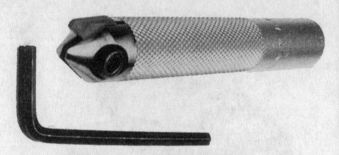

## MODEL 1200 CLASSIC TURBO TUMBLER

Features a redesigned base and drive system, plus a stronger suspension system and built-in exciters for better tumbling action and faster cleaning

| | |
|---|---|
| MODEL 1200 CLASSIC | $79.95 |
| MODEL 1200 AUTO-FLO | 99.95 |
| *Also available:* | |
| MODEL 600 | 69.95 |
| MODEL 2200 | 116.50 |
| MODEL 2200 AUTO-FLO | 125.00 |
| MODEL 3200 | 164.95 |
| MODEL 3200 AUTO-FLO | 184.95 |

## "INSIDE/OUTSIDE" DEBURRING TOOL

This tool features an adjustable cutting blade that adapts easily to the mouth of any rifle or pistol case from 22 caliber to 45 caliber with a simple hex wrench adjustment. Inside deburring is completed by a conical internal section with slotted cutting edges, thus providing uniform inside and outside deburring in one simple operation. The deburring tool is mounted on an anodized aluminum handle that is machine-knurled for a sure grip.

DEBURRING TOOL ..........................$13.50

## TUBBY TUMBLER

This case tumbler features a clear plastic "see thru" lid that fits on the outside of the vibrating tub. The Tubby has a polishing action that cleans more than 100 pistol cases in less than two hours. The built-in handle allows easy dumping of cases and media. An adjustable tab also allows the user to change the tumbling speed for standard or fast action.

TUBBY TUMBLER .........................$54.95

## MASTER CASTING KIT

Designed especially to meet the needs of blackpowder shooters, this kit features Lyman's combination round ball and maxi ball mould blocks. It also contains a combination double cavity mould, mould handle, mini-mag furnace, lead dipper, bullet lube, a user's manual and a cast bullet guide. Kits are available in 45, 50 and 54 caliber.

MASTER CASTING KIT .....................$158.00

# LYMAN RELOADING TOOLS

## FOR RIFLE OR PISTOL CARTRIDGES

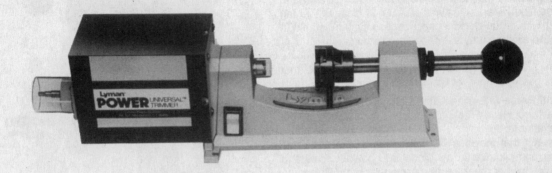

### POWER CASE TRIMMER

The new Lyman Power Trimmer is powered by a fan-cooled electric motor designed to withstand the severe demands of case trimming. The unit, which features the Universal™ Chuckhead, allows cases to be positioned for trimming or removed with fingertip ease. The Power Trimmer package includes Nine-Pilot Multi-Pack. In addition to two cutter heads, a pair of wire end brushes for cleaning primer pockets are included. Other features include safety guards, on-off rocker switch, heavy cast base with receptacles for nine pilots, and bolt holes for mounting on a work bench. Available for 110 V or 220 V systems.

*Prices:* 110 V Model . . . . . . . . . . . . . . . . . . . . . .$189.95
220 V Model . . . . . . . . . . . . . . . . . . . . . . . . . .189.95

### ACCULINE OUTSIDE NECK TURNER
### (not shown)

To obtain perfectly concentric case necks, Lyman's Outside Neck Turner assures reloaders of uniform neck wall thickness and outside neck diameter. The unit fits Lyman's Universal Trimmer and AccuTrimmer. In use, each case is run over a mandrel, which centers the case for the turning operation. The cutter is carefully adjusted to remove a minimum amount of brass. Rate of feed is adjustable and a mechanical stop controls length of cut. Mandrels are available for calibers from .17 to .375; cutter blade can be adjusted for any diameter from .195" to .405".

**OUTSIDE NECK TURNER** w/extra blade, 6 mandrels . .$28.95
**INDIVIDUAL MANDRELS** . . . . . . . . . . . . . . . . . . . . . . . .4.00

### CRUSHER II PRO KIT

Includes press, loading block, case lube kit, primer tray, Model 500 Pro scale, powder funnel and *Lyman Reloading Handbook.*
**STARTER KIT** . . . . . . . . . . . . . . . . . . . . . . . . . . . .$154.95

### LYMAN CRUSHER II RELOADING PRESS

The only press for rifle or pistol cartridges that offers the advantage of powerful compound leverage combined with a true Magnum press opening. A unique handle design transfers power easily where you want it to the center of the ram. A 4 1/2-inch press opening accommodates even the largest cartridges.

**CRUSH II PRESS**
With Priming Arm and Catcher . . . . . . . . . . . . . .$112.50

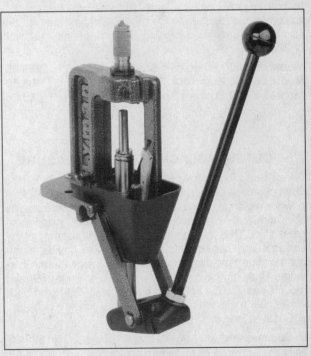

**CRUSHER II**

# LYMAN RELOADING TOOLS

## T-MAG II TURRET RELOADING PRESS

With the T-Mag II you can mount up to six different reloading dies on one turret. This means you can have all your dies set up, precisely mounted, locked in and ready to reload at all times. The T-Mag works with all 7/8 x 14 dies. The T-Mag II turret with its quick-disconnect release system is held in rock-solid alignment by a 3/4-inch steel stud.

Also featured is Lyman's Crusher II compound leverage system. It has a longer handle with a ball-type knob that mounts easily for right- or left-handed operation.

**T-Mag II Press** w/Priming Arm & Catcher . . . . .**$154.95**
Extra Turret Head . . . . . . . . . . . . . . . . . . . . . .**36.00**
*Also available:*
**Expert Kit** that includes T-MAG II Press, Universal Case Trimmer and pilot Multi-Pak, Model 500 powder scale and Model 50 powder measure, plus accessories and Reloading Manual. Available in calibers 9mm Luger, 38/357, 44 Mag., 45 ACP and 30-06 . . . . . . . . . . . . . . . . . . . . . .**$384.95**

## ELECTRONIC SCALE MODEL LE-1000

Accurate to 1/10 grain, Lyman's new LE: 1000 measures up to 1000 grains of powder and easily converts to the gram mode for metric measurements. The push-button automatic calibration feature eliminates the need for calibrating with a screwdriver. The scale works off a single 9V battery or AC power adapter (included with each scale). Its compact design allows the LE-1000 to be carried to the field easily. A sculpted carrying case is optional. 110 Volt or 220 Volt.

**Model LE-1000 Electronic Scale** . . . . . . . . . . .**$259.95**
**Model LE-300 Electronic Scale** . . . . . . . . . . . . .**166.50**
**Model LE-500 Electric Scale** . . . . . . . . . . . . . . .**183.25**

**Model LE-500 Electronic Scale**

## 55 CLASSIC BLACK POWDER MEASURE

Lyman's new 55 Classic Powder Measure is ideal for the Cowboy Action Competition or the growing number of black powder cartridge shooters. The large, one pound capacity aluminum reservoir, along with brass powder meter eliminates static. The new internal powder baffel assures highly accurate and consistent charges. The 24" powder compacting drop tube allows the maximum charge in each cartridge. Drop tube works on calibers .38 through .50, and mounts easily to the bottom of the measure. Clamp on back allows easy mounting of the measure at a convenient height, when using long drop tubes.

**55 Classic Powder Measure** (std model-no tubes) . . . . .**$99.95**
**55 Classic Powder Measure** (with drop tubes) . . . . . .**116.60**
**Powder Drop Tubes Only** . . . . . . . . . . . . . . . . . .**20.95**

**Electronic Digital Micrometer $94.95**

**Black Powder Measure**

# LYMAN RELOADING TOOLS

## UNIVERSAL TRIMMER
## WITH NINE PILOT MULTI-PACK

This trimmer with patented chuckhead accepts all metallic rifle or pistol cases, regardless of rim thickness. To change calibers, simply change the case head pilot. Other features include coarse and fine cutter adjustments, an oil-impregnated bronze bearing, and a rugged cast base to assure precision alignment and years of service. Optional carbide cutter available. Trimmer Stop Ring includes 20 indicators as reference marks.

REPLACEMENT CARBIDE CUTTER . . . . . . . . . . . . . . .$42.00
TRIMMER MULTI-PACK (incl. 9 pilots: 22, 24, 27,
   28/7mm, 30, 9mm, 35, 44 and 4A . . . . . . . . . .64.95
NINE PILOT MULTI-PACK . . . . . . . . . . . . . . . . . . . . .10.75
POWER PACK TRIMMER . . . . . . . . . . . . . . . . . . . . .74.95
UNIVERSAL TRIMMER POWER ADAPTER . . . . . . . . . . .16.50

## DRILL PRESS CASE TRIMMER

Intended for competitive shooters, varmint hunters, and other sportsmen who use large amounts of reloaded ammunition, this new drill press case trimmer consists of the Universal™ Chuckhead, a cutter shaft adapted for use in a drill press, and two quick-change cutter heads. Its two major advantages are speed and accuracy. An experienced operator can trim several hundred cases in an hour, and each will be trimmed to a precise length.

DRILL PRESS CASE TRIMMER . . . . . . . . . . . . . . . . .$46.50

## UNIVERSAL TRIMMER POWER ADAPTER

## ACCU-TRIMMER

Lyman's Accu Trimmer can be used for all rifle and pistol cases from 22 to 458 Winchester Magnum. Standard shell-holders are used to position the case, and the trimmer incorporates standard Lyman cutter heads and pilots. Mounting options include bolting to a bench, C-clamp or vise.

ACCU TRIMMER w/9-pilot multi-pak . . . . . . . . . . . .$43.00

## ELECTRONIC DIGITAL CALIPER
## (not shown)

Lyman's 6" electronic caliper gives a direct digital readout for both inches and millimeters and can perform both inside and outside depth measurements. Its zeroing function allows the user to select zeroing dimensions and sort parts or cases by their plus or minus variation. The caliper works on a single, standard 1.5 volt silver oxide battery and comes with a fitted wooden storage case.

ELECTRONIC CALIPER . . . . . . . . . . . . . . . . . . . . . . . .
$94.95

RELOADING

# LYMAN RELOADING TOOLS

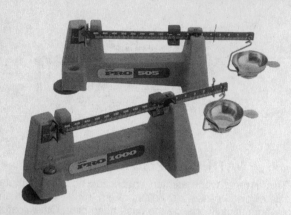

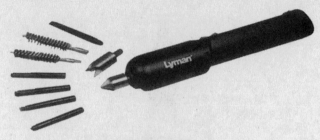

## PRO 1000 & 505 RELOADING SCALES

Features include improved platform system; hi-tech base design of high-impact styrene; extra-large, smooth leveling wheel; dual agate bearings; larger damper for fast zeroing; built-in counter weight compartment; easy-to-read beam

PRO 1000 SCALE . . . . . . . . . . . . . . . . . . . . . . . . . . $57.95
PRO 500 SCALE . . . . . . . . . . . . . . . . . . . . . . . . . . . .42.95

**PREMIUM 4-DIE SET WITH TAPER CRIMP AND POWDER CHARGE EXPANDING DIE**

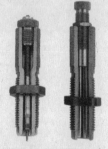

**PISTOL DIES FEATURE ONE PIECE HARDENED STEEL DECAPPING ROD**

## RIFLE DIE SETS

Lyman precision rifle dies are manufactured on state of the art computer controlled equipment insuring that each die is chambered perfectly, and has a super smooth finish. Each sizing die for bottle-necked rifle cartridges is then carefully vented. This vent hole is precisely placed to prevent air traps that can damage cartridge cases. Each sizing die is polished, then heat treated for toughness. It receives a final hand polish for extra smoothness. Fine adjustment threads on the bullet seating stem allow for precision adjustments of bullet seating depth. Lyman dies fit all popular presses using industry standard 7/8 x 14 threads, including RCBS, Lee, Hornady, Dillon, Redding and others.

## POWER DEBURRING KIT

Features a high torque, rechargeable power driver plus a complete set of accessories, including inside and outside deburr tools, large and small reamers and cleaners and case neck brushes. No threading or chucking required. Set also includes battery recharger and standard flat and phillips driver bits.

POWER DEBURRING KIT . . . . . . . . . . . . . . . . . . . . . $54.95

## RIFLE 2-DIE SETS

Set consists of a full length resizing die with decapping stem and neck expanding button and a bullet seating die for loading jacketed bullets in bottlenecked rifle cases. For those who load cast bullets, use a neck expanding die, available separately.

*Price:* . . . . . . . . . . . . . . . . . . . . . . . . . . . . . . . . . . $28.00

## RIFLE 3-DIE SETS

Straight wall rifle cases require these three die sets consisting of a full length resizing die with decapping stem, a two step neck expanding (M) die and a bullet seating die. These sets are ideal for loading cast bullets due to the inclusion of the neck expanding die.

*Price:* . . . . . . . . . . . . . . . . . . . . . . . . . . . . . . . . . . $37.50

## PREMIUM CARBIDE 4-DIE SETS FOR PISTOLS

Lyman 4-Die Sets feature a separate taper crimp die and powder charge/expanding die. The powder charge/expand die has a special hollow 2-step neck expanding plug which allows powder to flow through the die from a powder measure directly into the case. The powder charge/expanding die has a standard 7/8 x 14 thread and will accept Lyman's 55 Powder Measure, or most other powder measures.

*Price:* . . . . . . . . . . . . . . . . . . . . . . . . . . . . . . . . . . $54.00

## 3-DIE CARBIDE PISTOL DIE SETS

Lyman originated the Tungsten Carbide (T-C) sizing die and the addition of extra seating screws for pistol die sets and the two step neck expanding die. Multi-Deluxe Die sets offer these features; a one-piece hardened steel decapping rod and extra seating screws for all popular bullet nose shapes; all-steel construction.

*Price:* . . . . . . . . . . . . . . . . . . . . . . . . . . . . . . . . . . $40.95

## STANDARD PISTOL DIE SETS

These 3-die pistol sets are designed for bottleneck pistol cases. The full length sizing die is precision machined from solid steel. 3-Die sets also feature Lyman's two step neck expanding die.

*Price:* . . . . . . . . . . . . . . . . . . . . . . . . . . . . . . . . . . $29.95

# MEC Shotshell Reloaders

### MODEL 600 JR. MARK V

This single-stage reloader features a cam-action crimp die to ensure that each shell returns to its original condition. MEC's 600 Jr. Mark 5 can load 6 to 8 boxes per hour and can be updated with the 285 CA primer feed. Press is adjustable for 3" shells. Die sets are available in 10, 12, 16, 20, 28 and .410 gauges at: . . . . . . . . . . . . . . . . . . . . . . . . . .$59.38
MODEL 600 . . . . . . . . . . . . . . . . . . . . . . . . . .$102.13

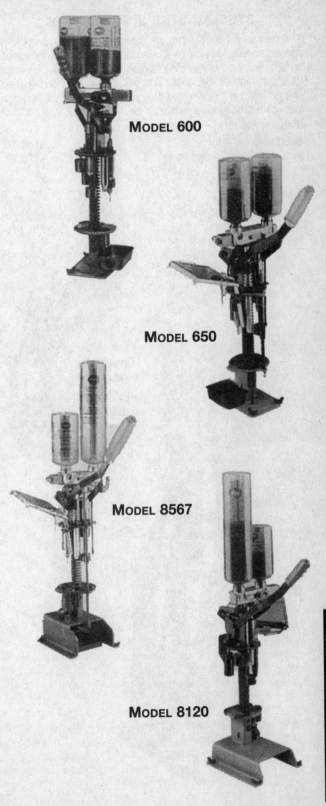

MODEL 600

MODEL 650

### MODEL 650

This reloader works on 6 shells at once. A reloaded shell is completed with every stroke. The MEC 650 does not resize except as a separate operation. Automatic Primer feed is standard. Simply fill it with a full box of primers and it will do the rest. Reloader has 3 crimping stations: the first one starts the crimp, the second closes the crimp, and the third places a taper on the shell. Available in 12, 16, 20 and 28 gauge and .410 bore. No die sets are available.
*Price:* . . . . . . . . . . . . . . . . . . . . . . . . . . . . . .$200.85

### MODEL 8567 GRABBER

This reloader features 12 different operations at all 6 stations, producing finished shells with each stroke of the handle. It includes a fully automatic primer feed and Auto-Cycle charging, plus MEC's exclusive 3-stage crimp. The "Power Ring" resizer ensures consistent, accurately sized shells without interrupting the reloading sequence. Simply put in the wads and shell casings, then remove the loaded shells with each pull of the handle. Optional kits to load 3" shells and steel shot make this reloader tops in its field. Resizes high and low base shells. Available in 12, 16, 20, 28 gauge and .410 bore. No die sets are available.
*Price:* . . . . . . . . . . . . . . . . . . . . . . . . . . . . .$288.13

MODEL 8567

MODEL 8120

### MODEL 8120 SIZEMASTER

Sizemaster's "Power Ring" collet resizer returns each base to factory specifications. This generation resizing station handles brass or steel heads, both high and low base. An 8-fingered collet squeezes the base back to original dimensions, then opens up to release the shell easily. The E-Z Prime auto primer feed is standard equipment (not offered in .410 bore). Press is adjustable for 3" shells and is available in 10, 12, 16, 20, 28 gauge and .410 bore. Die sets are available at: $88.67 ($104.06 in 10 ga.)
MODEL 8120 . . . . . . . . . . . . . . . . . . . . . . . . . .$153.90

RELOADING

# MEC RELOADING

## STEELMASTER SINGLE STATE

The only shotshell reloader equipped to load steel shotshells as well as lead ones. Every base is resized to factory specs by a precision "power ring" collet. Handles brass or steel heads in high or low base. The E-Z prime auto primer feed dispenses primers automatically and is standard equipment. Separate presses are available for 12 gauge 2 3/4", 3", 12 gauge 3 1/2" and 10 gauge.

STEELMASTER . . . . . . . . . . . . . . . . . . . . . . . . . .$160.16
In 12 ga. 3 1/2" only . . . . . . . . . . . . . . . . . . . . . . .176.27

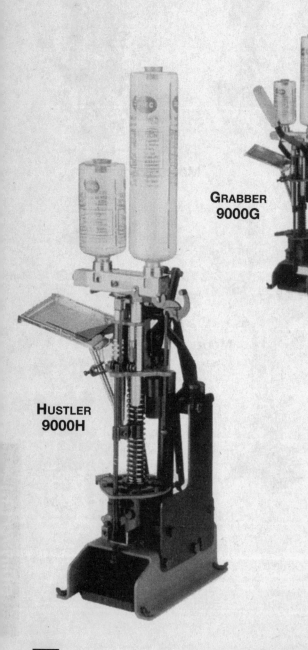

**GRABBER 9000G**

**HUSTLER 9000H**

## E-Z PRIME "S" AND "V" AUTOMATIC PRIMER FEEDS

From carton to shell with security, these primer feeds provide safe, convenient primer positioning and increase rate of production. Reduce bench clutter, allowing more free area for wads and shells.

- Primers transfer directly from carton to reloader, tubes and tube fillers
- Positive mechanical feed (not dependent upon agitation of press)
- Visible supply
- Automatic. Eliminate hand motion
- Less susceptible to damage
- Adapt to all domestic and most foreign primers with adjustment of the cover
- May be purchased separately to replace tube-type primer feed or to update your present reloader

**E-Z PRIME "S"** (for Super 600, 650) or
**E-Z PRIME "V"** (for 600 Jr. Mark V & VersaMEC) . . .$39.71

## MEC 9000 SERIES SHOTSHELL RELOADER

MEC's 9000 Series features automatic indexing and finished shell ejection for quicker and easier reloading. The factory set speed provides uniform movement through every reloading stage. Dropping the primer into the reprime station no longer requires operator "feel." The reloader requires only a minimal adjustment from low to high brass domestic shells, any one of which can be removed for inspection from any station. Can be set up for automatic or manual indexing. Available in 12, 16, 20 and 28 gauge and .410 bore. No die sets are available.

MEC 9000H . . . . . . . . . . . . . . . . . . . . . . . . . . . .$845.18
MEC 9000G SERIES . . . . . . . . . . . . . . . . . . . . . . . .349.84

# MIDWAY

## LOADING AND RANGE ACCESSORIES

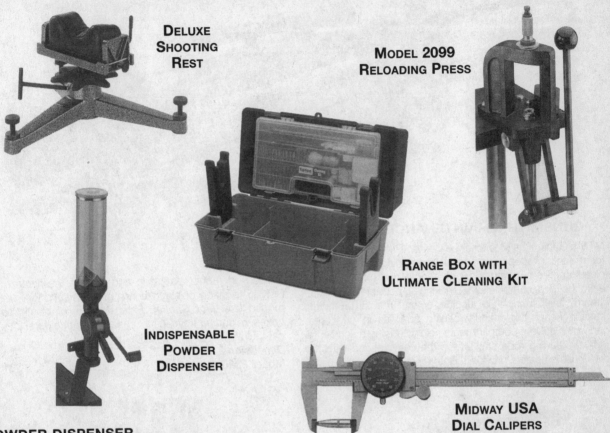

**DELUXE SHOOTING REST**

**MODEL 2099 RELOADING PRESS**

**RANGE BOX WITH ULTIMATE CLEANING KIT**

**INDISPENSABLE POWDER DISPENSER**

**MIDWAY USA DIAL CALIPERS**

## POWDER DISPENSER

Precision metering and quick-change caliber-specific drop tubes are hallmarks of this powder dispenser. Shelf bracket is included with both rifle and pistol versions. A master kit is also available, with the dispenser, bench mount and shelf mount brackets, a powder funnel and clear drop tube. The dispenser is equipped for loading both rifle and pistol cases.
*Price:* . . . . . . . . . . . . . . . . . . . . . . . . . . . . . . . . . . . .$90.00
 Master Kit . . . . . . . . . . . . . . . . . . . . . . . . . . . .125.00

## STAINLESS STEEL DIAL CALIPERS

Accuracy at the range starts with accuracy at the loading bench. This useful tool is a must for serious handloaders.
*Price:* . . . . . . . . . . . . . . . . . . . . . . . . . . . . . . . . . .$24.00

## RELOADING PRESS

The Midway USA Model 2099 reloading press incorporates state-of-the-industry advances in tool design and metallurgy. The 2099 is manufactured to the strictest tolerances and has the strength to handle tough tasks like case forming. Its huge clearance enables you to load cartridges as big as the 3 3/4-inch Sharps, plus British Express cartridges.
*Price:* . . . . . . . . . . . . . . . . . . . . . . . . . . . . . . . . . .$100.00

## RANGE BOX

Once in a while an accessory comes along that makes so much sense you wonder why someone didn't come up with it earlier. The Midway range box is essentially a portable shop, which you can use to hold your firearms for repair or cleaning. It's many compartments hold tools and cleaning supplies. A complete cleaning kit comes with each box. The cradle can be used as an impromptu shooting rest.
*Price*
 rifle . . . . . . . . . . . . . . . . . . . . . . . . . . . . . . . . . . .$125.00
 shotgun . . . . . . . . . . . . . . . . . . . . . . . . . . . . . . . .97.00

## DELUXE SHOOTING REST

The Gibraltar Deluxe Shooting Rest is among the finest on the market, with a wide, heavy-duty base to ensure stability and adjustable feet to give you exactly the right angle of support. The cradle is adjustable for height. Made of steel and aluminum for years of dependable performance, the Gibraltar Rest weighs 5.5 pounds.
*Price:* . . . . . . . . . . . . . . . . . . . . . . . . . . . . . . . . . .$100.00

# MTM RELOADING

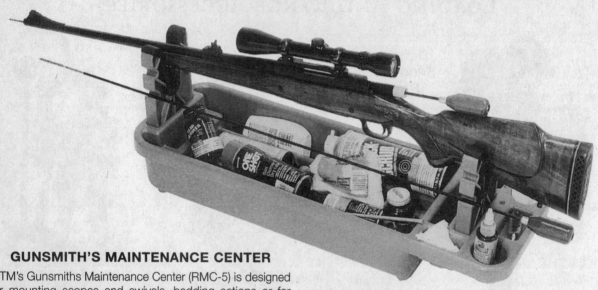

## GUNSMITH'S MAINTENANCE CENTER

MTM's Gunsmiths Maintenance Center (RMC-5) is designed for mounting scopes and swivels, bedding actions or for cleaning rifles and shotguns. Multi-positional forks allow for eight holding combinations, making it possible to service firearm level, upright or upside down. The large middle section keeps tools and cleaning supplies in one area. Individual solvent compartments help to eliminate accidental spills. Cleaning rods stay where they are needed with the two built-in holders provided. Both forks (covered with a soft molded-on rubber pad) grip and protect the firearm. The RMC-5 is made of engineering- grade plastic for years of rugged use. ***Not Shown:*** Extensive line of plastic ammo boxes, reloading trays, pistol cases, target holders, clay target throwers, arrow and tackle boxes.

***Dimensions:*** 29.5" X 9.5"

**MODEL RMC-5** . . . . . . . . . . . . . . . . . . . . . . . . . .$31.63

## PISTOL REST MODEL PR-30

MTM's new PR-30 Pistol Rest will accommodate any size handgun, from a Derringer to a 14" Contender. A locking front support leg adjusts up or down, allowing 20 different positions. Rubber padding molded to the tough polypropylene fork protects firearms from scratches. Fork clips into the base when not in use for compact storage.

***Dimensions:*** 6" x 11" x 2.5

**PISTOL REST MODEL PR-30** . . . . . . . . . . . . . . .$15.77

## CARD-GARD WITH WILD CAMO

The CASE-GARD SF-100 holds 100 shotshells in two removable trays. Designed primarily for hunters, this dust and moisture resistant carrier features a heavy-duty latch, fold-down handle, integral hinge and textured finish.

***Price:***

**SF-100** 12 or 20 ga.

    **WILD CAMO SHOTSHELL BOX** . . . . . . . . . . . . . . .$15.81

# RCBS Reloading Tools

## ROCK CHUCKER PRESS

With its easy operation, outstanding strength and versatility, a Rock Chucker press is ideal for beginner and pro alike. It can also be upgraded to a progressive press with an optional Piggyback II conversion unit.

- Heavy-duty cast iron for easy case-resizing
- 1" ram held in place by 12.5 sq. in. of rambearing surface
- Toggle blocks of ductile iron
- Compound leverage system
- Pins ground from hardened steel
- 1 1/4" - 12 thread for shotshell die kits and Piggyback II
- 7/8" - 14 thread for all standard reloading dies and accessories
- Milled slot and set screws accept optional RCBS automatic primer feed

*Price:* . . . . . . . . . . . . . . . . . . . . . . . . . . . . . . .$137.95

## ROCK CHUCKER MASTER RELOADING KIT

For reloaders who want the best equipment, the Rock Chucker Master Reloading Kit includes all the tools and accessories needed. Included are the following: • Rock Chucker Press • RCBS 505 Reloading Scale • Speer TrimPro Manual #12 • Uniflow Powder Measure • RCBS Rotary Case Trimmer-2 • deburring tool • case loading block • Primer Tray-2 • Automatic Primer Feed Combo • powder funnel • case lube pad • case neck brushes • fold-up hex key set • Trim Pro Manual Case Trimmer Kit

*Price:* . . . . . . . . . . . . . . . . . . . . . . . . . . . . .$382.95

## .50 BMG PACK

Shooters of the .50 BMG need not look for hard-to-find items individually with the new .50 BMG Pack from RCBS®. The Pack includes the press, dies, and accessory items needed, all in one box. The shooter saves money over buying the parts separately. The press is the powerful Ammo Master® Single Stage rigged for 1.5-inch dies. It has a massive 1.5-inch solid steel ram and plenty of height for the big .50. The kit also has a set of RCBS .50 BMG, 1.5-inch reloading dies, including both full-length sizer and seater. Other items are a shell holder, ram priming unit, and a trim die.

*Price:* . . . . . . . . . . . . . . .$531.95

**ROCK CHUCKER**

**RELOADER SPECIAL-5**

**AMMOMASTER SINGLE STAGE**

## RELOADER SPECIAL-5

The Reloader Special press features a comfortable ball handle and a primer arm so that cases can be primed and resized at the same time.

- Compound leverage system
- Solid aluminum black "O" frame offset for unobstructed access
- Corrosion-resistant baked-powder finish
- Can be upgraded to progressive reloading with an optional Piggyback II conversion unit
- 1 1/4" - 12 thread for shotshell die kits and Piggyback II
- 7/8" - 14 thread for all standard reloading dies and accessories

*Price:* . . . . . . . . . . . . . . . . . . . . . . . . . . . . . . . .$109.95

## AMMOMASTER RELOADING SYSTEM

The AmmoMaster offers the handloader the freedom to configure a press to his particular needs and preferences. It covers the complete spectrum of reloading, from single stage through fully automatic progressive reloading, from .25 Auto to .50 caliber. The AmmoMaster Auto has all the features of a five-station press.

**SINGLE STAGE** . . . . . . . . . . . . . . . . . . . . . . . . . . .$200.95

# RCBS RELOADING TOOLS

## APS BENCH-MOUNTED PRIMING TOOL

The APS Bench-Mounted Priming Tool was created for reloaders who prefer a separate, specialized tool dedicated to priming only. The handle of the bench-mounted tool is designed to provide hours of comfortable loading. Handle position can be adjusted for bench height.
**Price:** . . . . . . . . . . . . . . . . . . . . . . . . . . . . . . . .$89.95

**APS BENCH-MOUNTED PRIMING TOOL**

## APS PRIMER STRIP LOADER

For those who keep a supply of CCI primers in conventional packaging, the APS primer strip loader allows quick filling of empty strips. Each push of the handle seats 25 primers.
**Price:** . . . . . . . . . . . . . . . . . . . . . . . . . . . . . . . .$24.95

## POW'R PULL BULLET PULLER (not shown)

The RCBS Pow'r Pull bullet puller features a three-jaw chuck that grips the case rim—just rap it on any solid surface like a hammer, and powder and bullet drop into the main chamber for re-use. A soft cushion protects bullets from damage. Works with most centerfire cartridges from .22 to .45 (not for use with rimfire cartridges).
**Price:** . . . . . . . . . . . . . . . . . . . . . . . . . . . . . . . .$26.95

## APS PRESS-MOUNTED PRIMING TOOL

This APS press-mounted priming tool provides the same features as the bench-mounted tool except it attaches to any single-stage press that accepts standard 7/8" x 14 dies.
**Price:** . . . . . . . . . . . . . . . . . . . . . . . . . . . . . . . .$57.95

## RELOADING SCALE MODEL 5-0-5

This 511-grain capacity scale has a three-poise system with widely spaced, deep beam notches to keep them in place. Two smaller poises on right side adjust from 0.1 to 10 grains, larger one on left side adjusts in full 10-grain steps. The first scale to use magnetic dampening to eliminate beam oscillation, the 5-0-5 also has a sturdy die-cast base with large leveling legs for stability. Self-aligning agate bearings support the hardened steel beam pivots for a guaranteed sensitivity to 0.1 grains.
**Price:** . . . . . . . . . . . . . . . . . . . . . . . . . . . . . . . .$78.95

## TRIM PRO™ CASE TRIMMER

Cartridge cases are trimmed quickly and easily with a few turns of the RCBS Trim Pro case trimmer. The lever-type handle is more accurate to use than draw collet systems. A flat plate shell holder keeps cases locked in place and aligned. A micrometer fine adjustment bushing offers trimming accuracy to within .001". Made of die-cast metal with hardened cutting blades. The power model is like having a personal lathe, delivering plenty of torque. Positive locking handle and in-line power switch make it simple and safe.
**Price:** Power 110 Vac Kit . . . . . . . . . . . . . . . . . .$216.95
Manual . . . . . . . . . . . . . . . . . . . . . . . . . . . . . . .$70.95
*Also available:*
**TRIM PRO CASE TRIMMER STAND** . . . . . . . . . . . . . . .$15.95
**CASE HOLDER ACCESSORY** . . . . . . . . . . . . . . . . . . .36.95

# RCBS Reloading Tools

## POWDER PRO™ DIGITAL SCALE

The RCBS Powder Pro Digital Scale has a 1500-grain capacity. Powder, bullets, even cases with accuracy up to 0.1 grain can be weighed. Includes infra-red data port for transferring information to the Powdermaster Electronic Powder Dispenser and electronic powder trickler. *Price:* . . . . . . . . . . . . . . . . . . . .$221.95

## POWDERMASTER ELECTRONIC POWDER DISPENSER

Works in combination with the RCBS Powder Pro Digital Scale and with all types of smokeless powder. Can be used as a power trickler as well as a powder dispenser. Accurate to one-tenth of a grain.
*Price:* . . . . . . . . . . . . . . . .$235.95

## RC-130 MECHANICAL SCALE

The new RC130 features a 130 grain capacity and maintenance-free movement, plus a magnetic dampening system for fast readings. A 3-poise design incorporates easy adjustments with a beam that is graduated in increments of 10 grains and one grain. A micrometer poise measures in 0.1 grain increments with acuracy to ±0.1 grain.
*Price:* . . . . . . . . . . . . . . . . . . . . . . . . . . . . . .$35.95

## POWDER CHECKER (not shown)

Operates on a free-moving rod for simple, mechanical operation with nothing to break. Standard 7/8x14 die body can be used in any progressive loader.
*Price:* . . . . . . . . . . . . . . . . . . . . . . . . . . . . . .$25.95

## ELECTRONIC POWDER TRICKLER (not shown)

Works with Powder Pro scale and Uniflow Powder Measure to ensure charge weights +/- .01 grain.
*Price:* . . . . . . . . . . . . . . . . . . . . . . . . . . . . . .$205.95

## RELOADING SCALE MODEL 10-10
### Up to 1010 Grain Capacity

Normal capacity is 510 grains, which can be increased, without loss of sensitivity, by attaching the included extra weight.
   Features include micrometer poise for quick, precise weighing, special approach-to-weight indicator, easy-to-read graduation, magnetic dampener, agate bearings, anti-tip pan, and dustproof lid snaps on to cover scale for storage. Sensitivity is guaranteed to 0.1 grains.
*Price:* . . . . . . . . . . . . . . . . . . . . . . . . . . . . . .$125.95

## PARTNER ELECTRONIC POWDER SCALE

Accurate for +/- one-tenth of a grain up to 350 grains and +/- two-tenths from 350 to 750 grains. Large LCD display is angled for easy reading over a wide range of positions. Powered by 9-volt battery.
*Price:* . . . . . . . . . . . . . . . . . . . . . . . . . . . . . . .
$157.95

# RCBS RELOADING TOOLS

### RCBS TURRET PRESS

Handloaders who want to speed up the loading process without giving up the level of control offered by a single-stage press can boost their output fourfold with the new RCBS Turret Press. With pre-set dies in the six-station turret head, the Turret Press can increase production from 50 to 200 rounds per hour with a simple manual operation.

The frame, links, and toggle block of the new press are constructed of strong, reliable, cast iron. The handle offers compound leverage for full-length sizing of any caliber from .25 ACP to .460 Weatherby Magnum. Priming is accomplished with a reliable tube feed priming system.

Six stations allow the handloader to customize his set-up with the options of using a lube die in station one and seating and crimping bullets in separate operations. The quick-change turret head makes caliber changes fast and easy. Dies can be left in the turret head to eliminate set-up and tear-down time. This press accepts all standard 7/8 - 14 dies and shell holders and comes with the RCBS no-questions-asked lifetime warranty.

### RCBS PRO 2000 PROGRESSIVE PRESS

Constructed of strong and reliable cast iron, the Pro 2000 features five reloading stations. It can be set up with a lube die in station one, sizing dies in station two and three, a Powder Checker or Lock Out Die in station four and seating die in station five. Bullet seating and crimping can also be done in separate operations in station four and five.

### THE PRO 2000

The Die Plate removes and installs in seconds. The Powder Measure remains on the press when changing calibers without the need to disconnect or remove it as with other progressive presses. Primer plug changeover is quick and easy, as is changing the Shell Plate with the removal of one bolt.

Automated powder dispensing is perfected with the Pro 2000. The case-actuated powder measure assures repeatability of dispensing powder and eliminates spillage caused from dropping a powder charge when no case is in the powder charge station. A Micrometer Adjustment Screw allows you to precisely return to previously recorded powder charges. The Powder Measure easily adjusts to various case lengths and works perfectly with all powders. It is easily removed for cleaning and/or removing excess powder. All dies are standard 7/8-14, including the Expander Die.

The new press incorporates RCBS's exclusive APS Priming System, the safest, most reliable and convenient priming system on the market. Using preloaded plastic priming strips, it completely eliminates handling of primers and loading tube priming. An alternate tube primer is available as an optional purchase. A primer seating depth adjustment screw allows for precise setting of primer seating, and spent primers of 100% are contained in a clear, easy-to-empty catcher.

Compound leverage in the press allows effortless full-length sizing in any caliber, from .32 Auto to the huge .460 Weatherby Magnum. Manual indexing eliminates a complicated automatic advancing mechanism and gives the user total control and "feel" when cases are indexed.

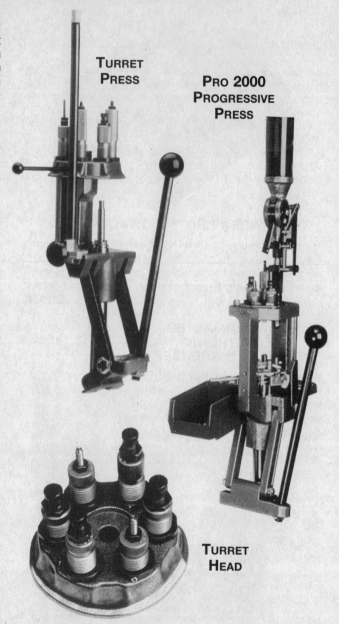

TURRET PRESS

PRO 2000 PROGRESSIVE PRESS

TURRET HEAD

Other features of the Pro 2000 include a Shell Plate Holder machined to remove extraneous powder from the Shell Plate and provide smooth, positive indexing; a larger working window for greater visibility and easy access to all stations; a Universal Case Retention System for simple, one-step removal and installation/insertion of cases at any station with no screws to loosen or buttons to remove; and the inclusion of a bullet tray, empty case box, and loaded cartridge box.

Like other RCBS equipment, the new press is covered by the RCBS Lifetime Warranty. If it ever breaks or doesn't work, RCBS will repair or replace it free, with no time limit, no questions asked.

*Price:* RCBS PRO 2000 PROGRESSIVE PRESS . . . . . . . . $448.95

# REDDING RELOADING TOOLS

### MODEL 721 "THE BOSS" PRESS

This "O" type reloading press features a rigid cast iron frame whose 36° offset provides the best visibility and access of comparable presses. Its "Smart" primer arm moves in and out of position automatically with ram travel. The priming arm is positioned at the bottom of ram travel for lowest leverage and best feel. Model 721 accepts all standard 7/8-14 threaded dies and universal shell holders.

MODEL 721 "THE BOSS" . . . . . . . . . . . . . . . . . . . $135.00
  With Shellholder and 10A Dies . . . . . . . . . . . . .172.00
*Also available:*
BOSS PRO-PAK DELUXE RELOADING KIT. Includes Boss Reloading Press, #2 Powder and Bullet Scale, Powder Trickler, Reloading Dies . . . . . . . . . . . . . . . . . . . . $354.00
  w/o dies and shellholder . . . . . . . . . . . . . . . . . .309.00

### ULTRAMAG MODEL 7000

Unlike other reloading presses that connect the linkage to the lower half of the press, the Ultramag's compound leverage system is connected at the top of the press frame. This allows the reloader to develop tons of pressure without the usual concern about press frame deflection. Huge frame opening will handle 50 x 3 1/4-inch Sharps with ease.

NO. 700 PRESS, complete . . . . . . . . . . . . . . . . . .$298.50
NO. 700K KIT, includes shell holder and
  one set of dies . . . . . . . . . . . . . . . . . . . . . . . . . .336.00

### METALLIC TURRET RELOADING PRESS MODEL 25000

Extremely rugged, ideal for production reloading. No need to move shell, just rotate turret head to positive alignment. Ram accepts any standard snap-in shell holder. Includes primer arm for seating both small and large primers.

NO. 25 PRESS, complete . . . . . . . . . . . . . . . . . . .$298.50
NO. 25K KIT, includes press, shell holder, and one
  set of dies . . . . . . . . . . . . . . . . . . . . . . . . . . . . . .336.00

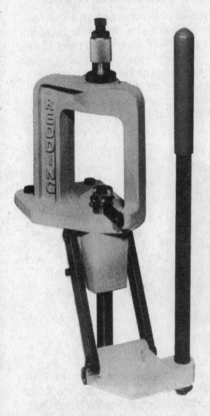

**MODEL 721**

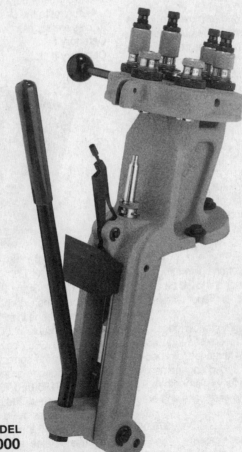

**MODEL 25000**

**MODEL 7000**

# REDDING RELOADING DIES

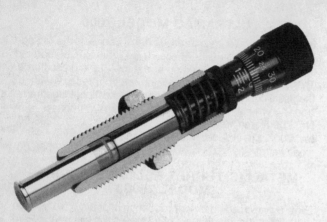

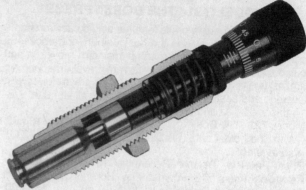

## NEW! COMPETITION BULLET SEATING DIE FOR HANDGUN & STRAIGHT-WALL RIFLE CARTRIDGES

### ADVANCED BULLET ALIGNMENT

Positive alignment between the bullet and cartridge case prior to bullet seating is essential to fine accuracy. Here is how this die works:

The precision fitting seating stem is allowed to move well down into the chamber of the die to accomplish early bullet contact. The spring loading of the seating stem provides the positive alignment bias between its tapered nose and the bullet ogive. Thus spring loading and bullet alignment are maintained as the bullet and cartridge case move upward until the actual seating of the bullet begins.

Redding's new Advanced Bullet Alignment feature assures the straightest possible bullet alignment for handgun and straight-wall rifle cartridges.

### MICROMETER ADJUSTMENT

The micrometer adjustment simplifies setting and recording bullet seating depth. By recording the micrometer setting of reloads can return to that same overall length by simply "dialing it in." The micrometer is calibrated in .001" increments, is infinitely adjustable and has a "zero" set feature that allows setting desired load to zero if desired.

### SEPARATE CRIMP

Competition shooters generally prefer bullet crimping as a separate operation from bullet seating. A superior crimp will be accomplished by using a Redding "Profile Crimp" or "Taper Crimp" die.

### PROGRESSIVE PRESS COMPATIBLE

The new Competition Seating Die for straight-wall cartridges has been made compatible with all popular progressive reloading presses. The industry standard 7/8 x 14 threaded die bodies have been slightly extended to allow full thread engagement of the lock ring. An oversize bell-mouth chamfer with smooth radius has been added to the bottom of the die to ease case and bullet entry in progressive presses.

*Price:* . . . . . . . . . . . . . . . . . . . . . . . . . . . . . . . . .$75.00
Competition bullet seating dies for bottleneck cases
   Category I . . . . . . . . . . . . . . . . . . . . . . . . . . . . . . . .99.00
   Category II . . . . . . . . . . . . . . . . . . . . . . . . . . . . . . .120.00

## COMPETITION BUSHING STYLE - NECK SIZING DIE

This die allows you to fit the neck of your case perfectly in the chamber. As in the Competition Seating Die, the cartridge case is completely supported and aligned with the sizing bushing and remains supported in the tightly chambered, sliding sleeve as it moves upward while the resizing bushing self-centers on the case neck. The micrometer adjustment of the bushing position delivers precise control to the desired amount of neck length to be sized. *All dies are supplied without bushings.*

**Category I** . . . . . . . . . . . . . . . . . . . . . . . . . . . . . .$99.00
**Category II** . . . . . . . . . . . . . . . . . . . . . . . . . . . . . .120.00

## NECK SIZING BUSHINGS

Redding Neck Sizing Bushings are available in two styles. Both share the same external dimensions (1/2" O.D. x 3/8" long) and freely interchange in all Redding Bushing style Neck Sizing Dies. They are available in .001" size increments throughout the range of .185" thru .365", covering all calibers from .17 to .338.

By selecting the correct bushing, the right amount of neck tension is provided to properly hold the bullet.

**Part No. 73185 thru 73365** . . . . . . . . . . . . . . . . . . . .$12.50
*Heat treated steel.* The sizing diameters are hand-polished with a surface hardness of Rc 60-62 to reduce sizing effort.

**Part No. 76185 thru 76365** . . . . . . . . . . . . . . . . . . . .19.50
Heat treated steel as above but with the addition of a *Titanium Nitride* surface treatment to further increase the effective surface hardness and reduce sizing friction.

# REDDING RELOADING TOOLS

## MASTER POWDER MEASURE MODEL 3

Universal- or pistol-metering chambers interchange in seconds. Measures charges 100 grains. Unit is fitted with lock ring for fast dump with large "clear" plastic reservoir. "See-thru" drop tube accepts all calibers from 22 to 600. Precision-fitted rotating drum is critically honed to prevent powder escape. Knife-edged powder chamber shears coarse-grained powders with ease, ensuring accurate charges.

| | |
|---|---|
| MODEL MASTER POWDER MEASURE (specify Universal- or Pistol-Metering chamber) | $124.80 |
| 3K KIT, includes both Chambers | 150.00 |
| BENCH STAND | 28.50 |
| MATCH GRADE 3BR measure | 156.00 |
| 3BR KIT, with both Chambers | 196.50 |
| PISTOL METERING chamber (0-10 grains) | 34.50 |
| or (BR) | 46.80 |

## MASTER CASE TRIMMER MODEL 1400

This unit features a universal collet that accepts all rifle and pistol cases. The frame is cast iron with storage holes in the base for extra pilots. Coarse and fine adjustments are provided for case length.

- Six pilots (22, 6mm, 25, 270, 7mm and 30 cal.)
- Universal collet
- Two neck cleaning brushes (22 thru 30 cal.)
- Two primer pocket cleaners (large and small)

| | |
|---|---|
| No. 1400 MASTER CASE TRIMMER COMPLETE | $93.00 |
| No. 1500 PILOTS | 3.90 |

## COMPETITION MODEL BR-30 POWDER MEASURE (not shown)

This powder measure features a drum and micrometer that limit the overall charging range from a low of 10 grains to a maximum of approx. 50 grains. The diameter of Model 3BR's metering cavity has been reduced, and the metering plunger has a unique hemispherical shape, creating a powder cavity that resembles the bottom of a test tube. The result: irregular powder setting is alleviated and charge-to-charge uniformity is enhanced.

COMPETITION MODEL BR-30 POWDER MEASURE . . .$187.50

## STANDARD POWDER AND BULLET SCALE MODEL RS-1

For the beginner or veteran reloader. Only two counterpoises need to be moved to obtain the full capacity range of 1/10 grain to 380 grains.

MODEL NO. RS-1 . . . . . . . . . . . . . . . . . . . . . . . . .$52.50

*Also available:*

MASTER POWDER & BULLET SCALE. Same as standard model, but includes a magnetic dampened beam swing for extra fast readings. 505-grain capacity . . . . . . . . . . . . .$79.50

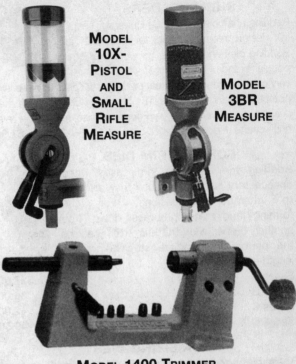

MODEL 10X-PISTOL AND SMALL RIFLE MEASURE

MODEL 3BR MEASURE

MODEL 1400 TRIMMER

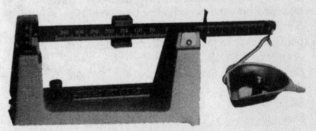

MODEL RS-1 SCALE

## COMPETITION MODEL 10X-PISTOL AND SMALL RIFLE POWDER MEASURE

This powder measure uses all of the special features of Competition Model BR-30 combined with new drum and metering unit designed to provide the most uniform metering of small charge weights. To achieve the best metering possible at the targeted charge weight of approximately 10 grains, the diameter of the metering cavity is reduced and the metering plunger is given a unique hemispherical shape. Charge range: 1 to 25 grains.

To provide increased versatility, the 10X-Pistol Powder Measure has a drum assembly that can be easily changed from right to left-handed operation. In addition to offering left-handed reloaders increased ease of operation, this feature adapts the 10X-Pistol Powder Measure to progressive reloading presses.

No. 03400 COMPETITION MODEL 10X-PISTOL POWDER MEASURE . . . . . . . . . . . . . . . . . . . . . . .$187.50

**RELOADING**

# REDDING RELOADING ACCESSORIES

### SHELLHOLDERS

Redding shellholders are of a Universal "snap-in" design recommended for use with all Redding dies and presses, as well as all other popular brands. They are precision machined to very close tolerances and heat treated to fit cases and eliminate potential resizing problems. The outside knurling makes them easier to handle and change. For proper size, refer to die reference charts. *Price:* ......................$7.95

### FORM & TRIM DIES

Redding trim dies file trim cases without unnecessary resizing because they are made to chamber dimensions. For case forming and necking brass down from another caliber, Redding trim dies can be the perfect intermediate step before full length resizing.

Series A ........................$27.00
Series B ...........................36.00
Series C ...........................42.00
Series D ...........................49.50

### NECK SIZING DIES

These dies size only the necks of bottleneck cases to prolong brass life and improve accuracy. These dies size only the neck and not the shoulder or body, fired cases should not be interchanged between rifles of the same caliber. Available individually or in Deluxe Die Sets.

Series A ........................$31.50
Series B ...........................42.00
Series C ...........................51.00
Series D ...........................58.50

### CARBIDE SIZE BUTTON KITS

Make inside neck sizing smoother and easier without lubrication. Now die sets can be upgraded with a carbide size button kit. Available for bottleneck cartridges 22 thru 338 cal. The carbide size button is free floating on the decap rod allowing it to self-center in the case neck. Kits contain: carbide size button, retainer and spare decapping pin. These kits also fit all Type-S dies.

Kit No. 48223 ......................22 cal.
Kit No. 48242 .........................6MM
Kit No. 48256 ......................25 cal.
Kit No. 48263 .......................6.5MM
Kit No. 49276 .....................270 cal.
Kit No. 49283 .........................7MM
Kit No. 49307 ......................30 cal.
Kit No. 49337 .....................338 cal.
*Price:* ............................$22.50

### PISTOL TRIM DIES

Redding trim dies for pistol calibers allow trimming cases without excessive resizing. Pistol trim dies require extended shellholders.

Series A ........................$27.00
Series B ...........................36.00
Series C ...........................42.00
Series D ...........................49.50

### PROFILE CRIMP DIES

For handgun cartridges which do not headspace on the case mouth. These dies were designed for those who want the best possible crimp. Profile crimp dies provide a tighter, more uniform roll type crimp, and require the bullet to be seated to the correct depth in a previous operation.

Series A ........................$24.90
Series B ...........................30.00
Series C ...........................34.50
Series D ...........................39.00

### TAPERED SIZE BUTTONS

These long tapered expander (size buttons) are made for expanding the necks of bottleneck cartridges up to the desired size.

No. 42242T ...............6mm (.17 to 6mm)
No. 42256T ...........25 cal. (.22 to 25 cal.)
No. 42263T ...........6.5mm (.22 to 6.5mm)
No. 41276T ...........270 cal. (.22 to .270)
No. 41283T ...............7mm (.22 to 7mm)
No. 41307T ...........30 cal (6mm to 30 cal.)
No. 41322T ...........8mm (25 ca. to 8mm)
No. 41337T ...........338 cal. (6.5 to .338)
No. 41356T ...........35 cal. (7mm to 35 cal.)
No. 41373T ...........375 cal. (30 cal. to .375 cal.)
Tapered size button only ..............$12.90
Decapping rod assembly with tapered size button, specify caliber ..................18.00

### EXTENDED SHELL HOLDERS

Extended shellholders are required when trimming short cases under 1½" O.A.L. They are machined to the same tolerances as standard shellholders except they're longer.
*Price:* ...........................$12.90

### TAPER AND CRIMP DIES

Designed for handgun cartridges which headspace on the case mouth where conventional roll crimping is undesirable. Also available for some revolver cartridges, for those who prefer the uniformity of a taper crimp. Now available in the following *rifle* calibers: 223 Rem.. 7.62MM x 39, 30-30, 308 Win, 30-06, 300 Win Mag

Series A ........................$24.90
Series B ...........................30.00
Series C ...........................34.50
Series D ...........................39.00

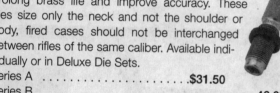

*Roland Clark – Top O'The Morning, 1931*

**Reference**

# Directory Of Manufacturers And Suppliers

The following manufacturers, suppliers and distributors of firearms, reloading equipment, sights, scopes, ammo and accessories all appear with their products in the Specifications and/or "Manufacturers' Showcase" sections of this edition of SHOOTER'S BIBLE.

**ACCURATE ARMS CO., INC.**
5891 Hwy, 230W
McEwen, Tennessee 37101
Tel: 931-729-4207 Fax: 931-729-4211
Web site: www.accuratepowder.com

**AIMPOINT** (sights, scopes, mounts)
420 West Main St.
Geneseo, Illinois 61254
Tel: 309-944-1702 Fax: 309-944-3676
Web site: www.springfield-armory.com

**ALLIANT POWDER** (gunpowder)
Route 114, P.O. Box 6 Bldg. 229
Radford, Virginia 24141-0096
Tel: 540-639-7806 Fax: 540-639-8496

**AMERICAN ARMS** (handguns; Franchi
shotguns;
2604 N.E. Industrial Dr. #290
N. Kansas City, Missouri 64117
Tel: 816-474-3161 Fax: 816-474-1225
Web site: www.americanarms.com

**AMERICAN DERRINGER CORP.** (handguns)
127 North Lacy Drive
Waco, Texas 76705
Tel: 817-799-9111 Fax: 817-799-7935
Web site: www.amderringer.com

**AMERICAN FRONTIER FIREARMS**
(black-powder arms)
P.O. Box 744
Aguanga, California 92536
Tel: 909-763-2209 Fax: 909-763-0014

**AMERICAN HUNTING RIFLES, INC.**
P.O. Box 300
Hamilton MT 59840

**AMERICAN SECURITY PRODUCTS**
(AMSEC) (safes)
11925 Pacific Avenue
Fontana, CA 92337
Tel: 800-423-1881 Fax: 909-681-9056

**AMT/GALENA INDUSTRIES**
(AMT handguns, rifles)
3551 Mayer Ave.
Sturgis, SD 57785
Tel: 605-423-4105

**A.G. ANSCHUTZ GmbH**
Postfach 1128
D-89001 Ulm, Germany
Tel: 731-40120 Fax: 731-4012700
E-mail: JGA-Info@anschuetz-sport.com

**ARMES DE CHASSE** (AyA shotguns;
Francotte rifles, shotguns)
P.O. Box 86
Hertford, North Carolina 27944
Tel: 919-426-2245 Fax: 919-426-1557

**ARMSCOR** (handguns, rifles, shotguns)
Available through K.B.I., Inc.

**ARMSPORT, INC.** (Bernardelli handguns,
shotguns)
P.O. Box 523066
Miami, Florida 33152-3066
Tel: 305-635-7850 Fax: 305-633-2877

**ARNOLD ARMS CO. INC.** (rifles)
P.O. Box 1011
Arlington, Washington 98223
Tel: 800-371-1011 Fax: 360-435-7304
Web site: www.arnoldarms.com

**A-SQUARE COMPANY INC.** (rifles)
Liberty Centre II, Suite 220
1230 S. Hurstbourne Parkway
Louisville, KY 40222
Web site: www.a-square.net

**ASHLEY OUTDOORS**
2401 Ludelle St.
Fort Worth, TX 76105
Tel: 888-744-4880 Fax: 800-734-7939
Web site: www.ashleyoutdoors.com
*(see also p. 94 in Manufacturers' Showcase)*

**AUSTIN & HALLECK** (blackpowder rifles)
1099 Welt
Weston, Missouri 64098
Tel: 816-386-2176 Fax: 816-386-2177

**AUTO-ORDNANCE CORP.** (handguns, rifles)
Williams Lane
West Hurley, New York 12491
Tel: 914-679-7225 Fax: 914-679-2698

**BARNES BULLETS**
P.O. Box 215
American Fork UT 84003
Tel: 800-574-9200 Fax: 8001-756-2465
Web site: www.barnesbullets.com

**BAUSCH & LOMB/BUSHNELL** (scopes)
Sports Optics
9200 Cody
Overland Park, Kansas 66214
Tel: 913-752-3400 Fax: 913-752-3550
Web site: www.bushnell.com

**BENELLI USA CORP.**
17601 Indian Head Hwy.
Accokeek, MD 20607-2501
Tel: 301-283-6981 Fax: 301-283-6988
Web site: www.benelliusa.com

**BERETTA U.S.A. CORP.** (handguns, rifles,
shotguns)
17601 Beretta Drive
Accokeek, Maryland 20607
Tel: 301-283-2191 Fax: 301-283-0435
Web site: www.berettausa.com

**BERGER BULLETS, LTD.**
5342 West Camelback, Suite 200
Glendale, AZ 85301
Tel: 602-842-4001 Fax: 602-934-9083
Web site: www.bergerbullets.com

**BERNARDELLI** (handguns, shotguns)
Available through Armsport

**BERSA** (handguns)
Available through Eagle Imports Inc.

**ROGER BIESEN**
W 5021 Rosewood
Spokane, WA 92008
Tel: 509-328-9340

**BLACK HILLS AMMUNITION**
P.O. Box 3090
Rapid City, SD 57709
Tel: 605-348-5150 Fax: 605-348-9827

**BLASER USA, INC.** (rifles)
Available through Sigarms

**BLUE BOOK PUBLICATIONS, INC.** (books)
8009 34th Ave. South, Suite 175
Minneapolis, Minnesota 55425
Tel: 612-854-5229 Fax: 612-853-1486
*(See p. 95 in Manufacturers' Showcase)*

**BLOUNT, INC.** (RCBS reloading equipment;
Speer bullets; Weaver scopes)
P.O. Box 856
Lewiston, Idaho 83501
Tel: 208-746-2351 Fax: 208-799-3904

**BONANZA** (reloading tools)
See Forster Products

**BOND ARMS INC.** (handguns)
P.O. Box 1296
Granbury, Texas 76048
Tel: 817-573-4445 Fax: 817-573-5636
*(see p. 96 in Manufacturers' Showcase)*

**KENT BOWERLY (CUSTOM GUNS)**
710 Golden Pheasant Dr.
Redmond, OR 97756
Tel: 541-923-3501

**BRENNEKE OF AMERICA LTD.**
81 Eades Drive
Irvine, California 40336-9463
Tel: 606-723-1045 Fax: 606-723-3253

**BRNO** (rifles)
Available through Euro-Imports
Web site: www.zbrojouka.com

**BROWN PRECISION, INC.** (custom rifles)
7786 Molinos Avenue; P.O. Box 270 W.
Los Molinos, California 96055
Tel: 530-384-2506 Fax: 530-384-1638

**BROWNING** (handguns, rifles, shotguns,
  blackpowder guns)
One Browning Place
Morgan, Utah 84050-9326
Tel: 801-876-2711 Fax: 801-876-3331
Web site: www.browning.com

**BSA OPTICS, INC.**
3911 SW 47th Ave., Ste 914
Ft. Lauderdale, FL 33314
Tel: 954-581-2144 Fax: 954-581-3165
E-mail: bsaoptic@bellsouth.net

**BURRIS COMPANY, INC.** (scopes)
331 East Eighth Street, P.O. Box 1747
Greeley, Colorado 80631
Tel: 970-356-1670 Fax: 970-356-8702
Web site: www.burrisoptics.com

**CABELA'S INC.** (blackpowder arms)
812 13th Ave.
Sidney, Nebraska 69160
Tel: 308-254-5505 Fax: 308-254-6669

**CHEYENNE PIONEER PRODUCTS**
P.O. Box 28425
Kansas City, MO 664188
Tel: 816-413-9196 Fax: 816-455-2859
Web site: www.cartridgesboxes.com
*(see p. 93 in Manufacturers' Showcase)*

**CHRISTENSEN ARMS** (rifles)
192 E. 100 N.
Fayette, Utah 84630
Tel: 801-528-7199
Web site: www.christensenarms.com

**CIMARRON FIREARMS CO.**
105 Winding Oaks Rd.
Fredericksburg, TX 78624
Tel: 830-997-9090 Fax: 830-997-0802
Web site: www.cimarron-firearm.com

**JIM COFFIN (CUSTOM GUNS)**
1224 NW Fernwood Circle
Corvallis, OR 97330-2909
Tel: 541-754-7662 Fax: 541-754-0255

**COLT BLACKPOWDER ARMS CO.**
  (blackpowder arms)
110 8th Street
Brooklyn, New York 11215
Tel: 718-499-4678 Fax: 718-768-8052

**COLT'S MANUFACTURING CO., INC.**
  (handguns, rifles)
P.O. Box 1868
Hartford, Connecticut 06144-1868
Tel: 800-962-COLT  Fax: 860-244-1442
Web site: www.colt.com

**CONNECTICUT SHOTGUN MFG. CO.**
  (A. H. Fox shotguns)
35 Woodland Street, P.O. Box 1692
New Britain, Connecticut 06051-1692
Tel: 860-225-6581 Fax: 860-832-8707

**COOPER FIREARMS** (rifles)
P.O. Box 114
Stevensville, Montana 59870
Tel: 406-777-5534
Web site: www.cooperfirearms.com

**COR-BON BULLET COMPANY**
1311 Industry Road
Sturgis, South Dakota 57885
Tel: 800-626-7266 Fax: 800-923-2666

**CUMBERLAND MOUNTAIN ARMS**
  (blackpowder rifles)
1045 Dinah Shore Blvd., P.O. Box 710
Winchester, Tennessee 37398
Tel: 931-967-8414 Fax: 931-967-9199

**CVA** (blackpowder arms)
5988 Peachtree Corners East
Norcross, Georgia 30071
Tel: 800-320-8767 Fax: 770-242-8546
Web site: www.cva.com

**CZ-USA**
P.O. Box 171073
Kansas City, KKS 66117-0073
Tel: 913-321-1811 Fax: 913-321-2251
Web site: www.cz-usa.com

**DAEWOO PRECISION** (handguns)
Available through Kimber of America

**DAKOTA** (handguns)
Available through E.M.F. Co., Inc.

**DAKOTA ARMS, INC.** (rifles, shotguns)
HC 55, Box 326
Sturgis, South Dakota 57785
Tel: 605-347-4686 Fax: 605-347-4459
Web site: www.dakotaarms.com

**CHARLES DALY** (shotguns)
Available through K.B.I., Inc.

**DAVIS INDUSTRIES** (handguns)
15150 Sierra Bonita Ln.
Chino, California 91710
Tel: 909-597-4726 Fax: 909-393-9771
Web site: www.davisindguns.com

**DESERT EAGLE** (handguns)
Available through Magnum Research Inc.

**DESERT MOUNTAIN MFG.** (rifle rests)
P.O. Box 130184
Coram, Montana 59913
Tel: 800-477-0762 Fax: 406-387-5361
Web site: www.bench-master.com
*(see p. 90 in Manufacturers' Showcase)*

**DGS, INC.**
Dale A. Storey (custom guns)
1117 E. 12th St.
Casper, WY 82601
Tel: 307-237-2414

**DILLON PRECISION PRODUCTS**
  (reloading equipment)
8009 East Dillon's Way
Scottsdale, Arizona 85260-1809
Tel: 800-223-4570 Fax: 602-998-2786
Web site: www.dillonprecision.com

**DIXIE GUN WORKS** (blackpowder guns)
P.O. Box 684, Highway 51 S.
Union City, Tennessee 38281
Tel: 901-885-0561 Fax: 901-885-0440

**DOCTER OPTIC**
B.C. Outdoors
P.O. Box 61497
Boulder City, NV 89006
Tel: 702-294-3056

**DOWNSIZER CORPORATION** (handguns)
P.O. Box 710316
Santee, California 92072-0316
Tel: 619-448-5510 Fax: 619-448-5780

**DYNAMIT NOBEL/RWS** (Rottweil shotguns)
81 Ruckman Road
Closter, New Jersey 07624
Tel: 201-767-1995 Fax: 201-767-1589

**EAGLE IMPORTS, INC.** (Bersa handguns)
1750 Brielle Avenue, Unit B1
Wanamassa, New Jersey 07712
Tel: 732-493-0333 Fax: 732-493-0301

**D'ARCY ECHOLS**
98 West 300 South, P.O. Box 421
Millville, UT 84326
Tel: 435-755-6842

**ELECTRONIC SHOOTERS PROTECTION**
11997 West 85th Place
Arvada, CO 80005
Tel: 303-456-8964 Fax: 303-456-7179
Web site: www.ESPAmerica.com
*(see p. 91 in Manufacturers' Showcase)*

**E.M.F. COMPANY, INC.** (Dakota handguns;
  Uberti handguns, blackpowder arms)
1900 East Warner Avenue 1-D
Santa Ana, California 92705
Tel: 714-261-6611 Fax: 714-756-0133
Web site: www.emf-company.com

**ENTRÉPRISE ARMS** (handguns)
15861 Business Center Drive
Irwindale, California 91706-2062
Tel: 626-962-8712 Fax: 626-962-4692
Web site: www.entreprise.com

**EUROARMS OF AMERICA INC.**
  (blackpowder guns)
P.O. Box 3277
Winchester, Virginia 22604
Tel: 540-662-1863

**EURO-IMPORTS** (Brno rifles)
614 Millar Avenue
El Cajon, California 92020
Tel: 619-442-7005 Fax: 619-442-7005

**EUROPEAN AMERICAN ARMORY CORP.**
  (E.A.A. handguns, rifles)
P.O. Box 1299
Sharpes, Florida 32959
Tel: 800-536-4442 Tel: 321-639-4842
Fax: 321-639-7006
Web site: www.eaacorp.com

**FEDERAL CARTRIDGE CO.** (ammunition)
900 Ehlen Drive
Anoka, Minnesota 55303-7503
Tel: 612-323-3740 Fax: 612-323-2506
Web site: www.federalcartridge.com

**FEG** (handguns)
Available through Interarms and K.B.I., Inc.

**FIOCCHI U.S.A**
5030 Fremont Rd.
Ozark, MO 65721
Tel: 417-725-4118 Fax: 417-725-1039
Web site: www.fiocchiusa.com

**FIREARMOUR LLC** (gunlocks)
2115 Buffalo Heights
Garden City, KS 67846
Tel: 888-486-5625 Fax: 316-276-2456

**FLINTLOCKS, ETC.** (Pedersoli replica rifles)
160 Rossiter Road, P.O. Box 181
Richmond, Massachusetts 01254
Tel: 413-698-3822 Fax: 413-698-3866
E-mail: flintetc@vgernet.net

**FORREST INC.**
P.O. Box 326
Lakeside, California 92040
Tel: 619-561-5800 Fax: 1-888-GUNCLIP
E-mail: SFORR10675@AOL.COM
*(see also p. 96 in Manufacturers' Showcase)*

**FORSTER PRODUCTS** (reloading)
310 East Lanark Avenue
Lanark, Illinois 61046
Tel: 815-493-6360 Fax: 815-493-2371
Web site: www.forsterproducts.com

**A. H. FOX** (shotguns)
Available thru Connecticut Shotgun Mfg. Co.

**FRANCHI** (shotguns)
Available through American Arms

**FRANCOTTE** (rifles)
Available through Armes de Chasse

**FREEDOM ARMS** (handguns)
One Freedom Lane, P.O. Box 150
Freedom, Wyoming 83120-0150
Tel: 307-883-2468 Fax: 307-883-2005
Web site: www.freedomarms.com

**GARY REEDER CUSTOM GUNS**
2710 N. Steves Blvd., Suite 22
Flagstaff, Arizona 86004
Tel: 520-526-3313 Fax: 520-527-0840
Web site: www.reedercustomguns.com
*(see p. 94 & 95 in Manufacturers' Showcase)*

**GLASER SAFETY SLUG, INC.**
(ammunition, gun accessories)
P.O. Box 8223
Foster City, California 94404
Tel: 800-221-3489 Fax: 510-785-6685
*(See p. 93 in Manufacturers' Showcase)*

**GLOCK, INC.** (handguns)
P.O. Box 369, Suite 190
Smyrna, Georgia 30081
Tel: 770-432-1202 Fax: 770-433-8719

**GONIC ARMS** (blackpowder rifles)
134 Flagg Road
Gonic, New Hampshire 03839
603-332-8456 Fax: 603-332-8457
Web site: www.gonic.com

**GRIZZLY INDUSTRIAL, INC.**
3 Locations: Bellingham, WA •
Williamsport, PA • Springfield, MO
Tel: 1-800-523-4777 Fax: 1-800-438-5901
Web site: www.grizzly.com
*(see p. 90, 91, 92, 93, 94 in Manufacturers' Showcase)*

**GSI (GUN SOUTH INC.)** (Mauser rifles;
Merkel shotguns; Steyr-Mannlicher rifles)
7661 Commerce Lane, P.O. Box 129
Trussville, Alabama 35173
Tel: 205-655-8299 Fax: 205-655-7078
Web site: www.gsifirearms.com

**H&R 1871 INC.** (see Harrington &
Richardson or New England Firearms)

**H-S PRECISION**
1301 Turbine Drive
Rapid City, SD 57703
Tel: 605-341-3006 Fax: 605-342-8964
Web site: www.hsprecision.com

**HÄMMERLI U.S.A.** (handguns)
19296 Oak Grove Circle
Groveland, California 95321
Tel: 209-962-5311 Fax: 209-962-5931

**HARRINGTON & RICHARDSON**
(handguns, rifles, shotguns)
60 Industrial Rowe
Gardner, Massachusetts 01440
Tel: 978-632-9393 Fax: 978-632-2300
*(see p. 90, 92, 93, 94 in Manufacturers' Showcase)*

**HARRIS ENGINEERING INC.** (bipods)
Barlow, Kentucky 42024
Tel: 502-334-3633 Fax: 502-334-3000
*(see p. 91 in Manufacturers' Showcase)*

**HECKLER & KOCH** (handguns, rifles; Benelli
and Fabarms shotguns)
21480 Pacific Boulevard
Sterling, Virginia 20166
Tel: 703-450-1900 Fax: 703-450-8160

**HENRY REPEATING ARMS CO.** (rifles)
110 8th Street
Brooklyn, New York 11215
Tel: 718-499-5600 Fax: 718-768-8056
Web site: www.henryrepeating.com

**DARWIN HENSLEY**
63133 E. Barlow Trail Rd.
Brightwood, OR 97011
Tel: 503-622-5411

**HERITAGE MANUFACTURING** (handguns)
4600 NW 135 St.
Opa Locka, Florida 33054
Tel: 305-685-5966 Fax: 305-687-6721
Web site: www.heritagemfg.com

**HI-POINT FIREARMS** (handguns)
MKS Supply, Inc.
5990 Philadelphia Drive
Dayton, Ohio 45415
Tel/Fax: 937-275-4991
Web site: www.hi-pointfirearms.com

**HIGH STANDARD MFG CO.** (handguns)
10606 Hempstead Highway #116
Houston, Texas 77092
Tel: 713-462-4200 Fax: 713-686-9699
Web site: www.highstandard.com

**HODGDON POWDER CO., INC.** (gunpowder)
6231 Robinson, P.O. Box 2932
Shawnee Mission, Kansas 66201
Tel: 913- 362-9455 Fax: 913-362-1307
Web site: www.hodgdon.com

**PATRICK HOLEHAN**
5758 E. 34th St.
Tucson, AZ 85711
Tel: 520-745-0622
E-mail: plholehan@juno.com

**HORNADY MANUFACTURING COMPANY**
(ammunition, reloading)
P.O. Box 1848
Grand Island, Nebraska 68802-1848
Tel: 308-382-1390 Fax: 308-382-5761
Web site: www.hornady.com

**HOWA** (rifles)
Available through Interarms

**STEVEN DODD HUGHES**
P.O. Box 545
Livingston, MT 59047
Tel: 406-222-9377

**ICC/KKAIR INTERNATIONAL**
P.O. Box 9912
Spokane, Washington 99209
Tel: 800-262-3322 Fax: 509-326-5436
*(see p. 95 in Manufacturers' Showcase)*

**IGA SHOTGUNS**
Available through Stoeger Industries

**INTERARMS** (FEG handguns; Howa rifles;
Rossi handguns, rifles; Walther handguns)
10 Prince Street, Alexandria, Virginia 22314
Tel: 703-548-1400 Fax: 703-549-7826
Web site: www.interarms.com

**ISRAEL ARMS INT'L. INC.** (handguns)
5709 Hartsdale
Houston, Texas 77036
Tel: 713-789-0745 Fax: 713-789-7513

**ITHACA GUN CO.** (shotguns)
891 Route 34-B
Kings Ferry, New York 13081
Tel: 315-364-7171 Fax: 315-364-5134
Web site: www.ithacagun.com

**JARRETT RIFLES INC.** (custom rifles)
383 Brown Road
Jackson, South Carolina 29831
Tel: 803-471-3616 Fax: 803-471-9246
Web site: www.jarrettrifles.com

**JOHANNSEN** (Express Rifle)
Reimer Johannsen Inc.
438 Willow Brook Rd.
Plainfield, N.H. 03781
Tel: 603-469-3450 Fax: 603-469-3471

**KAHLES (SCOPES)**
2 Slater Rd.
Cranston, RI 02920
Fax: 401-734-5888

**KAHR ARMS** (handguns)
P.O. Box 220
Blauvelt, New York 10913
Tel: 914-353-5996 Fax: 914-353-7833
Web site: www.kahr.com

**K.B.I., INC.** (Armscor rifles, handguns, shotguns; Charles Daly shotguns; FEG handguns)
P.O. Box 6625
Harrisburg, Pennsylvania 17112-0625
Tel: 717-540-8518 Fax: 717-540-8567
Web site: www.kbi-inc.com

**KIMBER MANUFACTURING, INC.**
(handguns, rifles)
2590 Hwy. 35, Suite B
Kalispell, MT 59901
Tel: 406-758-2222 Fax: 406-758-2223

**KOWA OPTIMED, INC.** (scopes)
20001 South Vermont Avenue
Torrance, California 90502
Tel: 310-327-1913 Fax: 310-327-4177

**KRIEGHOFF INTERNATIONAL INC.**
(rifles, shotguns)
337A Route 611, P.O. Box 549
Ottsville, Pennsylvania 18942
Tel: 610-847-5173 Fax: 610-847-8691

**KYNOCH AMMUNITION**
Kynamco Limited
The Old Railway Station
Mildenhall, IP28 7DT England
Tel: +44 (0) 1638 711999
Fax: +44 (0) 1638 515251

**L.A.R. MANUFACTURING, INC.** (Grizzly rifles)
4133 West Farm Road
West Jordan, Utah 84088-4997
Tel: 801-280-3505 Fax: 801-280-1972

**LASERAIM TECHNOLOGIES INC.**
(sights)
721 Main St., P.O. Box 3548
Little Rock, Arkansas 72203-3548
Tel: 501-375-2227 Fax: 501-372-1445

**LAZZERONI ARMS CO.** (rifles)
P.O. Box 26696
Tucson, Arizona 85726-6696
Tel: 520-577-7500 Fax: 520-624-4250
Web site: www.lazzeroni.com
*(see p. 92 in Manufacturers' Showcase)*

**LEUPOLD & STEVENS, INC.**
(scopes, mounts)
14400 N.W. Greenbriar Parkway,
P.O. Box 688
Beaverton, Oregon 97075
Tel: 503-646-9171 Fax: 503-526-1475
Web site: www.leupstv.com

**LEICA CAMERA INC.** (rifle scopes)
156 Ludlow Avenue
Northvale, New Jersey 07647
Tel: 800-222-0118 Fax: 201-767-8666

**LLAMA** (handguns)
Available through SGS Importers Int'l

**LONE STAR RIFLE CO., INC.**
11231 Rose Road
Conroe TX 77303
Tel: 409-856-3363
Web site: www.lonstarrifle.com

**LYMAN PRODUCTS CORP.** (rifles, blackpowder guns, reloading tools)
475 Smith Street
Middletown, Connecticut 06457
Tel: 860-632-2020 Fax: 860-632-1699
Web site: www.lymanproducts.com

**MAGNUM RESEARCH INC.** (Desert Eagle handguns; CZ handguns; Brno rifles)
7110 University Avenue N.E.
Minneapolis, Minnesota 55432
Tel: 612-574-1868 Fax: 612-574-0109

**MAGTECH AMMUNITION CO., INC.**
5030 Paradise Rd, Suite A104
Las Vegas, NV 89119
Tel: 702-736-2043 Fax: 702-736-2140
E-mail: jpetrille@magtechammo.com

**MARKESBERY MUZZLELOADERS, INC.**
(black-powder guns)
7785 Foundation Drive, Suite 6
Florence, Kentucky 41042
Tel: 606-342-5553- Fax: 606-342-2380
Web site: www.markesbery.com

**MARLIN FIREARMS COMPANY** (rifles, shotguns, blackpowder)
100 Kenna Drive, P.O. Box 248
North Haven, Connecticut 06473
Tel: 203-239-5621 Fax: 203-234-7991
Web site: www.marlinfirearms.com

**MAROCCHI** (Conquista shotguns)
Available through Precision Sales Int'l.

**MAUSER** (rifles)
Available through GSI (Gun South Inc.)

**MAVERICK OF MOSSBERG** (shotguns)
Available through O. F. Mossberg

**MEC INC.** (reloading tools)
c/o Mayville Engineering Co.
715 South Street
Mayville, Wisconsin 53050
Tel: 920-387-4500 Fax: 920-387-5802
Web site: www.mayri.com

**MERKEL** (shotguns)
Available through GSI (Gun South Inc.)
Web site: www.gsifirearms.com

**MIDWAY USA**
5875 West Van Horn Tavern Rd.
Columbia, MO 65203
Tel: 573-445-6363 Fax: 800-992-8312
Web site: midwayusa.com

**DAVID MILLER** (custom rifles)
3131 E. Greenlee Rd.
Tucson, AZ 85716

**M.O.A. CORP.** (handguns)
2451 Old Camden Pike
Eaton, Ohio 45302
Tel: 937-456-3669 Fax: 937-456-9331

**MODERN MUZZLELOADING INC.**
(Knight rifles)
P.O. Box 130, 21852 Hwy. J46
Centerville, Iowa 52544
Tel: 515-856-2626 Fax: 515-856-2628
Web site: www.knightrifles.com

**WILLIAM L. MOORE & CO.** (Garbi, Rizinni, and Piotti shotguns)
8340 E. Raintree Dr., Suite B-7
Scottsdale, AZ 85260

**O. F. MOSSBERG & SONS, INC.** (shotguns)
7 Grasso Avenue; P.O. Box 497
North Haven, Connecticut 06473
Tel: 203-230-5300 Fax: 203-230-5420
Web site: www.mossberg.com

**MTM CASE-GUARD** (reloading tools)
P.O. Box 13117, Dayton, Ohio 45413
Tel: 937-890-7461 Fax: 937-890-1747
Web site: www.mtmcase-gard.com
*(See p. 92 in Manufacturers' Showcase)*

**MUZZLELOADING TECHNOLOGIES INC.**
(black-powder guns)
25 E. Hwy. 40, Suite 330-12
Roosevelt, Utah 84066
Tel: 435-722-5996 Fax: 435-722-5909

**NAVY ARMS COMPANY, INC.** (handguns, rifles, blackpowder guns)
689 Bergen Boulevard
Ridgefield, New Jersey 07657
Tel: 201-945-2500 Fax: 201-945-6859
Web site: www.navyarms.com

**NEW ENGLAND ARMS** (Rizzini shotguns)
Lawrence Lane, P.O. Box 278
Kittery Point, Maine 03905
Tel: 207-439-0593 Fax: 207-439-6726

**NEW ENGLAND CUSTOM GUN SERVICE, LTD.**
(Schmidt & Bender Scopes)
438 Willow Brook Road
Plainfield, NH 03781
Tel: 603-469-3450

**NEW ENGLAND FIREARMS CO., INC.**
(handguns, rifles, shotguns)
60 Industrial Rowe
Gardner, Massachusetts 01440
Tel: 978-632-9393 Fax: 978-632-2300

**NIKON INC.** (scopes)
1300 Walt Whitman Road
Melville, New York 11747-3064
Tel: 516-547-4200 Fax: 516-547-0309
Web site: www.nikonusa.com

**NORTH AMERICAN ARMS** (handguns)
2150 South 950 East
Provo, Utah 84606-6285
Tel: 801-374-9990 Fax: 801-374-9998
Web site: www.naaminis.com

**NOSLER BULLETS, INC.** (bullets)
P.O. Box 671
Bend, Oregon 97709
Tel: 541-382-3921 Fax: 541-388-4667
Web site: www.nosler.com

**OLIN/WINCHESTER** (ammunition, primers, cases)
427 No. Shamrock St.
East Alton, Illinois 62024
Tel: 618-258-2936 Fax: 618-258-3609

**PARA-ORDNANCE** (handguns)
980 Tapscott Road
Scarborough, Ontario, Canada M1X 1E7
Tel: 416-297-7855 Fax: 416-297-1289

**PARKER REPRODUCTIONS** (shotguns)
Reagent Chemical & Research
124 River Road
Middlesex, New Jersey 08846
Tel: 908-469-0100 Fax: 908-469-9692

**PEDERSOLI, DAVIDE** (replica rifles)
Available through Flintlocks Etc.
Web site: www.davide-pedersoli.com

**PENTAX** (scopes)
P.O. Box 6509 (80155)
35 Inverness Drive East
Englewood, Colorado 80112
Tel: 303-728-0261 Fax: 303-790-1131
Web site: www.pentax.com

**PERAZZI U.S.A.** (shotguns)
1207 S. Shamrock Ave.
Monrovia, California 91016
Tel: 626-303-0068 Fax: 626-303-2081

**PIOTTI** (shotguns)
Available through W. L. Moore & Co.

**PMC CARTRIDGES**
Eldorado Cartridge Corp.
P.O. Box 62508
Boulder City, NV 89005
Tel: 702-294-0025 Fax: 702-294-0121
Web site: www.pmcammo.com

**POWER CUSTOM INC.** (gun accessories)
29739 Highway, J. Dept. SB
Gravois Mills, MO 65037
Tel: 573-372-5864 Fax: 573-372-5799
*(see p. 95 in Manufacturers' Showcase)*

**PRAIRIE GUN WORKS** (rifles)
1-761 Marion St.
Winnipeg, Manitoba, Canada R2J 0K6
Tel: 204-231-2976 Fax: 204-231-8566
Web site: www.prairiegunworks.com

**PRECISION SALES INTERNATIONAL**
(Marocchi shotguns)
P.O. Box 1776
Westfield, Massachusetts 01086
Tel: 413-562-5055 Fax: 413-562-5056
Web site: www.precision-sales.com

**PRECISION SMALL ARMS** (handguns)
155 Carleton Rd.
Charlottesville, Virginia 22902
Tel: 804-293-6124 Fax: 804-295-0780

**JAMES PURDEY & SONS**
844 Madison Ave.
New York, NY 10021
Tel: 212-639-1500 Fax: 212-452-9675

**QUARTON USA LTD. CO.** (laser sights)
7042 Alamo Downs Parkway, Suite 370
San Antonio, Texas 78238-4518
Tel: 800-520-8435 Fax: 210-520-8433

**RAMSHOT PROPELLANT**
Western Powders
P.O. Box 158
Miles City, MT 59301
Tel: 406-232-0422 Fax: 406-232-0430
Web site: www.westernpowders.com

**RCBS, INC.** (reloading tools)
Available through Blount, Inc.

**REDDING RELOADING EQUIPMENT**
(reloading tools)
1089 Starr Road
Cortland, New York 13045
Tel: 607-753-3331 Fax: 607-756-8445
Web site: www.redding-reloading.com

**GARY REEDER CUSTOM GUNS**
Tel: 520-526-3313
Web site: www.reedercustomguns.com
*(see p. 94 & 95 in Manufacturers' Showcase)*

**ROTTWEIL COMPETITION** (Paragon shotguns)
1330 Glassel, Suite M
Orange, California 92667
Tel: 714-538-3109

**REMINGTON ARMS COMPANY, INC.**
(rifles, shotguns, blackpowder, ammunition)
870 Remington Drive, P.O. Box 700
Madison, North Carolina 27025-0700
Tel: 800-243-9700 Fax: 910-548-7814

**RIFLES, INC.** (rifles)
873 West 5400 North
Cedar City, Utah 84720
Tel: 435-586-5995 Fax: 435-586-5996

**RIZZINI** (shotguns)
Available through New England Arms
Web site: www.rizzini.it

**ROSSI** (handguns, rifles)
Available through Interarms

**ROTTWEIL** (shotguns)
Available through Paragon Competition

**RUGER** (handguns, rifles, shotguns, blackpowder guns). See Sturm, Ruger & Company, Inc.

**SAFARI ARMS** (handguns)
c/o Olympic Arms, Inc.
620-626 Old Pacific Highway Southeast
Olympia, Washington 98513
Tel: 360-459-7940 Fax: 360-491-3447
Web site: www.olyarms.com

**SAKO** (rifles, actions, scope mounts, ammo)
Available through Stoeger Industries

**SAUER** (rifles)
c/o Paul Company, Inc.
27385 Pressonville Road
Wellsville, Kansas 66092
Tel: 913-883-4444 Fax: 913-883-2525

**SAVAGE ARMS** (rifles, shotguns)
100 Springdale Road
Westfield, Massachusetts 01085
Tel: 413-568-7001 Fax: 413-562-7764
Web site: www.savagearms.com

**SCHMIDT AND BENDER INC.** (scopes)
Schmidt & Bender U.S.A.
P.O. Box 134
Meriden, New Hampshire 03770
Tel: 800-468-3450 Fax: 603-469-3471
Web site: www.schmidt-bender.de

**ANTHONY SCHUELKE (CUSTOM GUNS)**
1606 N. Baxter Ave.
Glencoe, MN 55336
Tel: 320-864-3905

**SGS IMPORTERS INTERNATIONAL INC.**
(Llama handguns)
1750 Brielle Avenue, Unit B1
Wanamassa, New Jersey 07712
Tel: 732-493-0333 Fax: 732-493-0301

**SIERRA BULLETS** (bullets)
P.O. Box 818
1400 West Henry St.
Sedalia, Missouri 65301
Tel: 660-827-6300 Fax: 660-827-4999
Web site: www.sierrabullets.com

**SIGARMS INC.** (Sig-Sauer shotguns and handguns, Blaser rifles)
Corporate Park
Exeter, New Hampshire 03833
Tel: 603-772-2302 Fax: 603-772-1481
Web site: www.sigarms.com

**SIGHTRON, INC.**
1672B Highway 96
Franklin, NC 27525
Tel: 919-528-8783 Fax: 919-528-0995

**GENE SIMILLION**
220 S. Wisconsin
Gunnison, CO 81230
Tel: 970-641-1126

**SIMMONS OUTDOOR CORP.** (scopes)
2120 Killarney Way
Tallahassee, Florida 32308-3402
Tel: 904-878-5100 Fax: 904-893-5472

**SISK RIFLES**
Charlie Sisk
16607 Port O'Call
Crosby, TX 77532
Tel: 281-328-5458

**SKB SHOTGUNS** (shotguns)
Omaha, Nebraska 68137-1253
Tel: 800-752-2767 Fax: 402-330-8029
Web site: www.skbshotguns.com

**SMITH & WESSON** (handguns)
2100 Roosevelt Avenue, P.O. Box 2208
Springfield, Massachusetts 01102-2208
Tel: 800-331-0852 Tel: 413-747-3299
Fax: 413-747-3677
Web site: www.smith-wesson.com

**SPEER** (bullets)
Available through Blount, Inc.

**SPORTSLINE** (stands, rests, totes & seats)
16607 Blanco Rd., Suite 100
San Antonio, TX 78232
Tel: 210-492-8405

**SPRINGFIELD INC.** (handguns, rifles,
  Aimpoint scopes and sights)
420 West Main Street
Geneseo, Illinois 61254
Tel: 309-944-5631 Fax: 309-944-3676
Web site: www.springfield-armory.com

**STEYR-MANNLICHER** (rifles)
Available through GSI (Gun South Inc.)
Web site: www.gsifirearms.com

**STOEGER INDUSTRIES** (IGA shotguns;
  Sako ammo, bullets, actions, mounts, rifles;
  Tikka rifles, Luger shotguns)
5 Mansard Court
Wayne, New Jersey 07470
Tel: 800-631-0722 Tel: 973-872-9500
Fax: 973-872-2230
*(see p. 96 in Manufacturers' Showcase)*

**STURM, RUGER AND COMPANY, INC.**
  (Ruger handguns, rifles, shotguns,
  blackpowder revolver)
Lacey Place
Southport, Connecticut 06490
Tel: 203-259-4537 Fax: 203-259-2167
Web site: www.ruger-firearms.com

**SWAROVSKI OPTIK NORTH AMERICA**
(scopes)
2 Slater Rd.
Cranston, Rhode Island 02920
Tel: 401-734-1800 Fax: 401-734-5888

**SWIFT BULLET CO.** (bullets)
201 Main St.
P.O. Box 27
Quinter, Kansas 67752
Tel: 785-754-3959 Fax: 785-754-2359

**SWIFT INSTRUMENTS, INC.**
  (scopes, mounts)
952 Dorchester Avenue
Boston, Massachusetts 02125
Tel: 800-446-1116 Fax: 617-436-3232
Web site: www.swift-optics.com

**SZECSEI & FUCHS**
450 Charles St.
Windsor, Ontario
N8X 371 Canada
Tel: 001 519 966 1234

**TASCO** (scopes, mounts)
Box 269000
Pembroke Pines, FL 33026
Tel: 954-252-3600 Fax: 954-252-3705
Web site: www.tascosales.com

**TAURUS INT'L, INC.** (handguns)
16175 N.W. 49th Avenue
Miami, Florida 33014-6314
Tel: 305-624-1115 Fax: 305-623-7506
Web site: www.taurususa.com

**TAYLOR'S & CO. INC.** (rifles, carbines)
304 Lenoir Drive
Winchester, Virginia 22603
Tel: 540-722-2017 Fax: 540-722-2018
Web site: www.taylorsfirearms.com

**THOMPSON/CENTER ARMS** (handguns,
  rifles, reloading, blackpowder arms)
Farmington Road, P.O. Box 5002
Rochester, New Hampshire 03866
Tel: 603-332-2333 Fax: 603-332-5133
Web site: www.tcarms.com

**THOMPSON & CAMPBELL**
Cromarty - The Black Isle
Ross-Shire IV11 8YB Scotland
Tel: +44 (0) 1381 600 536
Fax: +44 (0) 1381 600 767

**TIKKA** (rifles, shotguns)
Available through Stoeger Industries

**TRADITIONS, INC.** (blackpowder arms)
P.O. Box 776
Old Saybrook, Connecticut 06475-0776
Tel: 860-388-4656 Fax: 860-388-4657
Web site: www.traditionsmuzzle.com

**TRIUS PRODUCTS, INC.** (traps, targets)
221 South Miami Avenue, P.O. Box 25
Cleves, Ohio 45002
Tel: 513-941-5682 Fax: 513-941-7970
*(see p. 91 in Manufacturers' Showcase)*

**UBERTI USA, INC.** (handguns, rifles,
  blackpowder guns). See also American
  Arms, EMF, Navy Arms
362 Limerock Rd., P.O. Box 509
Lakeville, Connecticut 06039
Tel: 860-435-8068

**ULTRA LIGHT ARMS COMPANY** (rifles)
214 Price Street, P.O. Box 1270
Granville, West Virginia 26534
Tel: 304-599-5687 Fax: 304-599-5687

**U.S. REPEATING ARMS CO.** (Winchester
  rifles, shotguns)
One Browning Place
Morgan, Utah 84050-9326
Tel: 801-876-3440 Fax: 801-876-3737

**VERSATILE RACK CO.**
5761 Anderson Street
Vernon, CA 90058
Tel: 323-588-0137 Fax: 323-588-5067

**VIVITAR CORPORATION** (optics)
P.O. Box 2559
Newbury Park, CA 91319-8559
Tel: 805-498-7008 Fax: 805-498-5086

**WALTHER** (handguns)
Available through Interarms

**WEATHERBY, INC.** (rifles, shotguns,
  handguns, ammunition)
3100 El Camino Real
Atascadero, California 93422
Tel: 805-466-1767 Fax: 805-466-2527
Web site: www.weatherby.com

**WEAVER** (scopes, mount rings)
Available through Blount, Inc.

**WICHITA ARMS** (handguns)
P.O. Box 11371, 923 E. Gilbert
Wichita, Kansas 67211
Tel: 316-265-0661

**WILDEY F.A. INC.** (handguns)
Angevine Rd.
Warren, Connecticut 06754
Tel: 860-355-9000 Fax: 860-354-7759
Web site: www.wildeyguns.com

**WILLIAMS GUN SIGHT CO.**
7389 Lapeer Road
P.O. Box 329
Davison, Michigan 48423
Tel: 810-653-2131 Fax: 810-658-2140
Web site: www.williamsgunsight.com

**WINCHESTER** (ammunition, primers, cases)
Available through Olin/Winchester
Web site: www.winchester.com

**WINCHESTER** (rifles, shotguns)
Available through U.S. Repeating Arms Co.
Web site: www.winchester-guns.com

**WOODLEIGH BULLETS**
P.O. Box 15
Murrabit, Victoria
Australia
Handled in U.S. by:
**HUNTINGTON DIE SPECIALTIES**
601 OroDam Blvd.
P.O. Box 991
Oroville, CA 95965
Tel: 916-534-1210 Fax: 916-534-1212

**ZEISS OPTICAL, INC.** (scopes)
1015 Commerce Street
Petersburg, Virginia 23803
Tel: 800-338-2984 Fax: 804-733-4024
Web site: www.zeiss.com

**Z-HAT CUSTOM DIES**
4010A S. Poplar, Suite 72
Casper, WY 82601
Tel: 307-577-7443
Web site: www.z-hat.com
E-mail: RifleBuilder@z-hat.com

# GUNFINDER

*To help you find the model of your choice, the following index includes every firearm found in the SHOOTER'S BIBLE 2001, listed by type of gun.*

## REVOLVERS

# RIFLES

## Centerfire Bolt Action

## Centerfire Lever Action

| Models 336M | 224 |
| Model 444P & 1895G | 224 |
| Model 1894 P | 224 |
| Model 1895SS | 226 |

**WINCHESTER**

| Model 94 Big-Bore Walnut | 291 |
| Model 94 Standard Walnut | 290 |
| Model 94 Legacy | 291 |
| Model 94 Trail's End | 291 |
| Model 94 Ranger | 291 |
| Model 94 Walnut Trapper Carbine | 290 |
| Model 94 Pack | 291 |
| Model 94 Timber Carbine | 290 |

### CENTERFIRE SEMIAUTOMATIC & SLIDEACTION

**AUTO-ORDNANCE**

| Thompson Model M1 Carbine | 185 |
| Thompson Model 1927 A1 Deluxe, Lightweight and Commando | 185 |

**BROWNING**

| BAR Mark II Safari & Lightweight | 193 |
| Model BPR Pump | 193 |

**COLT**

| Match Target, Lightweight | 199 |

**HECKLER & KOCH**

| .45 ACP Autoloading Carbine | 208 |
| .223 Autoloading | 208 |

**MARLIN**

| Model 922M | 221 |

**REMINGTON**

| Models 7400 & 7600 | 242 |
| Model 700 Etronx | 242 |

**RUGER**

| Model PC9 Auto | 246 |
| Mini-14/5 Carbine, 14/5R Ranch | 247 |
| Model Mini-Thirty, Mini-14 | 247 |

**SPRINGFIELD**

| M1A Standard | 270 |
| M1 A-A1 Scout | 270 |

### CENTERFIRE SINGLE SHOT

**BROWNING**

| Model 1885 Low & High Wall | 190 |
| Model BPR Pump | 193 |

**DAKOTA ARMS**

| Dakota 10 Single Shot | 204 |

**HARRINGTON & RICHARDSON**

| Ultra Single Shot Rifles | 207 |

**L.A.R.**

| Grizzly Big Boar Competitor | 217 |

**LONE STAR**

| Silhouette | 219 |
| Sporting | 219 |
| Cowboy Action | 219 |

**MOSSBERG**

| Model SSI-One Single Shot Rifle/Shotgun | 227 |

**NEW ENGLAND FIREARMS**

| Synthetic Handi-Rifle | 232 |
| Super Light Youth Handi-Rifle | 232 |

**RUGER**

| No. 1A Light & 1S Medium Sporters | 249 |
| No. 1B Standard/1V Special Varminter | 249 |
| No. 1H Tropical | 249 |
| No. 1RSI International | 249 |

**THOMPSON/CENTER**

| Contender Carbines | 277 |
| Encore | 277 |

### RIMFIRE BOLT ACTION & SINGLE SHOT

**ANSCHUTZ**

| Model 2013 Supermatch | 177 |
| Model 1907 | 178 |
| Model 1808 "Running Target" | 179 |
| Model 54, 18 MSR Silhouette | 179 |
| Model 1827 "Fortner" | 179 |
| Model 1903 | 180 |
| Model 1451 | 180 |
| Model 1451R Sport Target | 180 |
| Model 2013 Benchrest | 180 |

**EUROPEAN AMERICAN ARMORY**

| HW660 Weihrauch Target | 206 |

**JARRETT**

| Rimfire Rifle | 213 |

**KBI/CHARLES DALY**

| Model CDGA Empire and Field Grades | 215 |
| Model M-12Y Youth | 215 |

**KIMBER**

| Model 82C Series | 216 |

**MARLIN**

| Model 81TS | 222 |
| Model 15YN "Little Buckaroo" | 223 |
| Models 25MN & 25N | 222 |
| Models 883 Magnum, 883SS | 222 |
| Model 922 Magnum | 221 |
| Model 2000L Target | 227 |

**REMINGTON**

| Models 40-XR | 243 |
| Models 541-T | 243 |

**RUGER**

| 77/22 Rimfire Series | 250 |

**SAKO**

| Finnfire (Scout, Hunter, Varmint) | 255, 258 |

**SAVAGE**

| Mark I-G Single Shot | 268 |
| Model 93G Magnum, 93F Magnum, FVSS | 267 |
| Model 900TR | 269 |
| Mark II-FV Heavy Barrel, Mark II-FSS | |
| Mark II-LV | 268 |

**WINCHESTER**

| Model 52B | 294 |
| Model 1895.405 | 294 |

### RIMFIRE LEVER ACTION

**BROWNING**

| Model BL-22 | 189 |

**HENRY REPEATING ARMS**

| Henry Rifle | 209 |
| U.S. Survival | 209 |
| Golden Boy | 209 |

**MARLIN**

| Golden 39AS | 223 |
| 1897 Cowboy | 223 |

**WINCHESTER**

| Model 9422 Traditional | 292 |
| Model 9422, Legacy, Trapper | 292 |

### RIMFIRE SEMIAUTOMATIC & SLIDE ACTION

**BROWNING**

| 22 Semiauto Grades I & VI | 189 |

**BROWN PRECISION**

| Custom Team Challenger | 194 |

**HENRY**

| Pump Action .22 | 209 |

**KBI/CHARLES DALY**

| Model CDGA Empire Grade | 215 |
| Model M-20P Standard | 215 |

**MARLIN**

| Models 60, 60SS | 221 |
| Models 7000 | 221 |
| Model 70PSS "Papoose" | 221 |

**REMINGTON**

| Model 597 Series | 244 |
| Model 552 BDL Speedmaster | 243 |
| Model 572 BDL Fieldmaster | 243 |

**RUGER**

| Model 10/22 Series | 246, 248 |

**SAVAGE**

| Model 64 Series (FV, F, G) | 269 |

**SPRINGFIELD**

| Model M-6 Scout Combo | 270 |

**THOMPSON/CENTER**

| Model T/C 22LR Classic | 277 |

### DOUBLE RIFLES, ACTIONS & DRILLINGS

**BERETTA**

| Express Rifles (5506, 455) | 186 |
| Silver/Gold Sable II Over/Under | 187 |

**FRANCOTTE**

| Boxlocks/Sidelocks/Mountain | 207 |